Lecture Notes in Computer Science

Lecture Notes in Artificial Intelligence 16132

Founding Editor

Jörg Siekmann

Series Editors

Randy Goebel, *University of Alberta, Edmonton, Canada*
Wolfgang Wahlster, *DFKI, Berlin, Germany*
Zhi-Hua Zhou, *Nanjing University, Nanjing, China*

The series Lecture Notes in Artificial Intelligence (LNAI) was established in 1988 as a topical subseries of LNCS devoted to artificial intelligence.

The series publishes state-of-the-art research results at a high level. As with the LNCS mother series, the mission of the series is to serve the international R & D community by providing an invaluable service, mainly focused on the publication of conference and workshop proceedings and postproceedings.

Mariacarla Staffa · John-John Cabibihan ·
Bruno Siciliano · Shuzhi Sam Ge ·
Leon Bodenhagen · Adriana Tapus · Silvia Rossi ·
Filippo Cavallo · Laura Fiorini ·
Marco Matarese · Hongsheng He
Editors

Social Robotics + AI

17th International Conference, ICSR+AI 2025
Naples, Italy, September 10–12, 2025
Proceedings, Part II

Editors
Mariacarla Staffa
University of Naples Parthenope
Naples, Italy

Bruno Siciliano
University of Naples Federico II
Naples, Italy

Leon Bodenhagen
University of Southern Denmark
Odense, Denmark

Silvia Rossi
University of Naples Federico II
Naples, Napoli, Italy

Laura Fiorini
University of Florence
Florence, Italy

Hongsheng He
The University of Alabama
Tuscaloosa, AL, USA

John-John Cabibihan
Qatar University
Doha, Qatar

Shuzhi Sam Ge
National University of Singapore
Queenstown, Singapore

Adriana Tapus
ENSTA
Palaiseau, France

Filippo Cavallo
University of Florence
Florence, Italy

Marco Matarese
Italian Institute of Technology
Genoa, Italy

ISSN 0302-9743 ISSN 1611-3349 (electronic)
Lecture Notes in Artificial Intelligence
ISBN 978-981-95-2381-8 ISBN 978-981-95-2382-5 (eBook)
https://doi.org/10.1007/978-981-95-2382-5

LNCS Sublibrary: SL7 – Artificial Intelligence

© The Editor(s) (if applicable) and The Author(s), under exclusive license to Springer Nature Singapore Pte Ltd. 2026

This work is subject to copyright. All rights are solely and exclusively licensed by the Publisher, whether the whole or part of the material is concerned, specifically the rights of translation, reprinting, reuse of illustrations, recitation, broadcasting, reproduction on microfilms or in any other physical way, and transmission or information storage and retrieval, electronic adaptation, computer software, or by similar or dissimilar methodology now known or hereafter developed.
The use of general descriptive names, registered names, trademarks, service marks, etc. in this publication does not imply, even in the absence of a specific statement, that such names are exempt from the relevant protective laws and regulations and therefore free for general use.
The publisher, the authors and the editors are safe to assume that the advice and information in this book are believed to be true and accurate at the date of publication. Neither the publisher nor the authors or the editors give a warranty, expressed or implied, with respect to the material contained herein or for any errors or omissions that may have been made. The publisher remains neutral with regard to jurisdictional claims in published maps and institutional affiliations.

This Springer imprint is published by the registered company Springer Nature Singapore Pte Ltd.
The registered company address is: 152 Beach Road, #21-01/04 Gateway East, Singapore 189721, Singapore

If disposing of this product, please recycle the paper.

Preface

The 17th International Conference on Social Robotics (ICSR)+AI 2025 took place in Naples, Italy as an in-person event from September 10–12, 2025. ICSR+AI 2025 was hosted by the University of Naples Parthenope with the support of Global Robotics, Arts, and Science Synergies (GRASS).

These three LNCS volumes comprise the peer-reviewed proceedings of the conference. From a total of 276 submitted manuscripts that were single-blindly reviewed by an international team of program committee, associate editors, and reviewers, 117 regular papers and 57 short papers were selected for inclusion in the proceedings and presented during the technical sessions.

The theme of this year's conference was "Emotivation at the Core: Empowering Social Robots to Inspire and Connect". The conference featured 3 keynote speeches, 15 regular sessions, 5 Special Sessions, 2 poster sessions, 11 workshops, and 3 robot competitions. The first plenary speech was delivered by Dr. Daniela Rus, who is the Andrew (1956) and Erna Viterbi Professor of Electrical Engineering and Computer Science and Director of the Computer Science and Artificial Intelligence Laboratory (CSAIL) at Massachusetts Institute of Technology. The second plenary speech was delivered by Dr. Jérôme Monceaux, who is a co-founder of Aldebaran Robotics. The third plenary speech was delivered by Dr. Anouk Wipprecht, who is a pioneering Dutch fashion designer and innovator at the forefront of the FashionTech movement.

The conference brought together researchers and practitioners working on the interaction between humans and intelligent robots and on the integration of social robots into our society, including innovative ideas and concepts, new discoveries and improvements, novel applications based on the latest fundamental advances in the core technologies that form the backbone of social robotics, as well as distinguished studies and projects pertaining to social robotics and its interaction with and impact on our society.

We extend our sincere gratitude to all members of the organizing committee and the volunteers for their dedication, which made the conference a resounding success. We are also deeply indebted to the program committee, associate editors, and reviewers for their rigorous review of the papers. Finally, we are immensely grateful for the continued support from the authors, participants, and sponsors, without whom ICSR+AI 2025 would not have been possible.

September 2025

Mariacarla Staffa
John-John Cabibihan
Bruno Siciliano
Shuzhi Sam Ge
Leon Bodenhagen
Adriana Tapus
Silvia Rossi
Filippo Cavallo
Laura Fiorini
Marco Matarese
Hongsheng He

Organization

Honorary Chair

Bruno Siciliano — University of Naples Federico II, Italy

General Chair

Mariacarla Staffa — University of Naples Parthenope, Italy

General Co-chair

John-John Cabibihan — Qatar University, Qatar

Steering Committee Chair

Shuzhi Sam Ge — National University of Singapore, Singapore

Program Chairs

Leon Bodenhagen — University of Southern Denmark, Denmark
Adriana Tapus — ENSTA Paris, France
Silvia Rossi — University of Naples Federico II, Italy
Filippo Cavallo — University of Florence, Italy

Special Session Committee

Alessandra Sciutti — Italian Institute of Technology, Italy
Luisa Damiano — IULM University, Italy
Kerstin Sophie Haring — University of Denver, USA

Workshop Committee

Maryam Alimardani   Vrije Universiteit Amsterdam, Netherlands
Patrick Holthaus   University of Hertfordshire, UK
Alberto Pirni   Scuola Superiore Sant'Anna di Pisa, Italy

Short Papers Committee

Alessandra Sorrentino   University of Florence, Italy
Jauwairia Nasir   Universität Augsburg, Germany
Alessandro Umbrico   CNR, Italy

Young Leader Committee

Lorenzo D'Errico   University of Naples Federico II, Italy
Francesco Vigni   University of Naples Federico II, Italy
Tamara Siegmann   University of Applied Sciences and Arts
                                                Northwestern Switzerland
Nihan Karatas   Nagoya University, Japan

Award Committee

Antonio Sgorbissa   University of Genoa, Italy
Abderrahmane Kheddar   LIRMM Montpellier, France and CNRS-AIST,
                                               Japan
Vali Lalioti   University of the Arts London, UK

Art and Robotics Committee

Hooman Samani   University of the Arts London, UK
Vali Lalioti   University of the Arts London, UK

Women in Robotics Committee

Hatice Gunes	University of Cambridge, UK
Micol Spitale	Politecnico di Milano, Italy
Samira Rasouli	University of Waterloo, Canada
Natalia Calvo	Uppsala University, Sweden

Publication Committee

Hongsheng He	The University of Alabama, USA
Marco Matarese	Italian Institute of Technology, Italy
Laura Fiorini	University of Florence, Italy

Social Media Chair

Francesca Cocchella   Italian Institute of Technology, Italy

Press Office Chair

Daniela Passariello   University of Naples Federico II, Italy

Publicity Committee

Oliver Bendel	FHNW University of Applied Sciences and Arts Northwestern Switzerland
Antonio Andriella	Artificial Intelligence Research Institute (IIIA), Spain
Minsu Jang	Electronics and Telecommunications Research Institute, South Korea
Oskar Palinko	University of Southern Denmark, Denmark

Competition Chairs

Amit Kumar Pandey	Rovial Space, France
Alessandra Rossi	University of Naples Federico II, Italy
Luca Iocchi	Sapienza University of Rome, Italy

Local Arrangement Chairs

Diana di Luccio   University of Naples Parthenope, Italy

Sustainability Chairs

Elvira Buonocore   University of Naples Parthenope, Italy
Franziska Kirstein   University of Southern Denmark, Denmark

Standing Committee

Oussama Khatib   Stanford University, USA
Maja Mataric   University of Southern California, USA
Haizhou Li   Chinese University of Hong Kong, China
Jong Hwan Kim   Korea Advanced Institute of Science and Technology, South Korea
Paolo Dario   Scuola Superiore Sant'Anna, Italy
Abderrahmane Kheddar   LIRMM Montpellier, France and CNRS-AIST, Japan
Tianmiao Wang   Beihang University, China

Associate Editors

Alessandra Rossi   University of Naples Federico II, Italy
Alessandra Sciutti   Italian Institute of Technology, Italy
Alessandra Sorrentino   University of Florence, Italy
Alessandro Umbrico   Centro Nazionale delle Ricerche, Italy
Antonio Andriella   Artificial Intelligence Research Institute (IIIA), Spain
Antonio Fleres   IULM University, Italy
Bipin Indurkhya   Jagiellonian University, Poland
Britta Wrede   University of Bielefeld, Germany
Cristina Gena   University of Turin, Italy
Eleonora Zedda   Centro Nazionale delle Ricerche, Italy
Ester Fuoco   IULM University/ISPF CNR, Italy
Filippo Cavallo   University of Florence, Italy
Francesca Cordella   University Campus Biomedico, Italy
Giacinto Barresi   University of the West of England, UK

Giulia Perugia	Eindhoven University of Technology, The Netherlands
Giuliana Vitiello	University of Salerno, Italy
Gökçe Nur Yılmaz	Ankara University, Turkey
Grazia D'Onofrio	IRCSS Ospedale Casa Sollievo della Sofferenza, Italy
Hongsheng He	University of Alabama, USA
Igor Farkaš	Comenius University Bratislava, Slovenia
Ilaria Alfieri	IULM University, Italy
Jauwairia Nasir	Universität Augsburg, Germany
John-John Cabibihan	Qatar University, Qatar
Kutluk Arikan	Ankara University, Turkey
Laura Fiorini	University of Florence, Italy
Lorenzo D'Errico	University of Naples Federico II, Italy
Luisa Damiano	IULM University, Italy
Marco Matarese	Italian Institute of Technology, Italy
Mariacarla Staffa	University of Naples Parthenope, Italy
Nele Russwinkel	University of Lübeck, Germany
Olive Bendel	University of Applied Sciences and Arts Northwestern Switzerland, Switzerland
Omar Eldardeer	Italian Institute of Technology, Italy
Oskar Palinko	University of Southern Denmark, Denmark
Patrick Holthaus	University of Hertfordshire, UK
Piotr Mirowski	Google DeepMind, UK
Rebecca Mannocci	IULM University, Italy
Thomas Sievers	University of Lübeck, Germany
Yue Hu	University of Waterloo, Canada

Contents

Emotion and Affective Interaction

Visualizing the Past: Emotional and Cognitive Impacts of AI-Generated Images in Human-Robot Interaction 3
   Ilaria Amaro, Domenico Rossi, Attilio Della Greca, Fabiola De Marco, Alessia Auriemma Citarella, Luigi Di Biasi, Cesare Tucci, and Genoveffa Tortora

When Robots Care: Elderly Reactions to Emotionally Intelligent Android 16
   Sonabayim Huseynzade, Rainer Wieching, Toshimi Ogawa, Yoshio Matsumoto, Volker Wulf, and Yasuyuki Taki

A Multimodal Emotion Recognition Approach for Socially Assistive Robots 30
   Christian Tamantini, Martina Fabrizi, Loredana Zollo, and Francesca Cordella

Empathy in Child-Robot Interaction: The Role of Narrative Framing, Age, Gender, and Baseline Empathy 42
   Marine Bruttin, Luca M. Leisten, and Emily S. Cross

Driven by Personality? Human Perceptions of Intraverted and Extraverted Robots in Car Driving Scenarios 58
   Jasmin Bernotat, Doreen Jirak, Laura Triglia, Francesco Rea, and Alessandra Sciutti

Applications in Real-World Case Studies

EBO Robot in Elderly Care: Interaction Styles and Multimodal Engagement Through Serious Games in Care Centers 79
   Antonio Blanco, Alicia Condón, Zoraida Clavijo, Trinidad Rodríguez, and Pedro Núñez

Participatory Design for Human-Robot Interaction with Syrian Refugees and Asylum Seekers 92
   Shaul Ashkenazi, Rawan Srour-Zreik, Gabriel Skantze, Jane Stuart-Smith, and Mary Ellen Foster

Using the Pepper Robot to Support Sign Language Communication 106
   Giulia Botta, Marco Botta, Cristina Gena, Alessandro Mazzei,
   Massimo Donini, and Alberto Lillo

Evaluating the Role of Robot Form and Intelligence in the Ultimatum Game . . . 120
   Triniti Armstrong, Christopher A. Sanchez, and Naomi T. Fitter

Designing User Experiences with Social Robots: A Field Study
on Acceptance in Public Libraries 130
   Artur Lisetschko, Nadine Jansen, and Ayşegül Doğangün

LLMs and Conversational/Verbal Interaction

Connecting Through Shared Memories. Episodic Memory for Social
Robots Using Offline LLMs 149
   Sofía Álvarez-Arias, Marcos Maroto-Gómez, Arecia Segura-Bencomo,
   Juan Rodríguez-Huelves, and María Malfaz

Intuitive Control of a Social Robot Using Natural Language with a Large
Language Model and Error Correction Capabilities 166
   Federico Biagi, Paolo Alberto Gasparini, Maria Grazia Modena,
   and Luigi Biagiotti

Storytelling and Self-other Integration with Robots: Creation
and Validation of Storytelling Stimuli that Induce Social Identification
with the QT Robot 181
   Francesca Ciardo, Francesca Foini, and Micol Spitale

Personalized Socially Assistive Robots with End-to-End Speech-Language
Models for Well-Being Support 192
   Mengxue Fu, Zhonghao Shi, Minyu Huang, Siqi Liu, Mina Kian,
   Yirui Song, and Maja J. Matarić

Towards Improving Turn-Taking in Social Robots Using Visual-Only
Voice Activity Detection in Multimodal Dialogue Systems 207
   Antonio Cano, Guillermo Perez, Luis Merino, and Randy Gomez

Motion Control, Prosthetics and Functional Robotics

HaptiCam: Skin-Drag Haptic Feedback for Real-Time Communication
of Camera Settings 225
   Michael Ha and Timothy Merritt

Optimizing Prosthetic Wrist Movement: A Model Predictive Control
Approach 239
   Francesco Schetter, Shifa Sulaiman, Shoby George, Paolino De Risi,
   and Fanny Ficuciello

Vision Based Hybrid IK Task Planning with Feedforward Neural Network
for Collaborative Plant-Robot Interaction in Precision Farming 253
   V. P. Tharun and Abhra Roy Chowdhury

Slosh-Aware Trajectory Control in a Reconfigurable Staircase Service
Robot 268
   Veerajagadheswar Prabakaran, Abdullah Aamir Hayat,
   Manivannan Kalimuthu, Madan Mohan Rayguru,
   and Mohan Rajesh Elara

A Mixed Reality User-Friendly Interface for Robot Teleoperation 283
   Mariia Chemerys, Matvei Novoselov, Sofia Diniz Melo Santos,
   Riccardo Aliotta, Francesco Cufino, and Fabio Ruggiero

Context Awareness and Explainability

Classification of User Satisfaction in HRI with Social Signals in the Wild 299
   Michael Schiffmann, Sabina Jeschke, and Anja Richert

Bayesian Goal Inference Engine for Intent Prediction in Human-Robot
Interaction 314
   Martina Pelosi, Nikolas Helling, Andrea Maria Zanchettin,
   and Paolo Rocco

Pluri-perspectivism in Human-Robot Co-creativity with Older Adults 327
   Marianne Bossema, Rob Saunders, Aske Plaat, and Somaya Ben Allouch

Exploring Avoidance Strategies Between Humans and Robots in Social
Navigation 342
   Meriam Moujahid, Christian Dondrup, Daniel Hernandez Garcia,
   and Marta Romeo

Improving Human-Swarm Interaction Through Speech Control
and Peer-to-Peer Micro-agent Communication 356
   Giovanni De Gasperis, Daniele Di Ottavio, and Sante Dino Facchini

Ethics, Trust and Social Acceptability

Ethical and Societal Challenges Facing Social and Educational Robots - Insights from the KASPAR Experience 375
Gabriella Lakatos, Vignesh Velmurugan, Catherine Menon, Luke Jai Wood, Ben Robins, and Farshid Amirabdollahian

Bayesian Proximal Policy Optimization with Adaptive Learning and Episodic Memory for Social Robot Navigation 387
Diego Resende Faria

Automatic Assessment of Speaking Proficiency for Language Practice Robots 400
Eva Verhelst, Pieter Lecompte, Ruben Janssens, Vanessa De Wilde, and Tony Belpaeme

Evaluating Social Impact of Pedipulation with Quadrupedal Robot 413
Marco Tabita, Carmine T. Recchiuto, Enrico Simetti, and Antonio Sgorbissa

Improving Engagement in Robot Lecture Through Personality Expressed by Teacher Robot 428
So Sasaki and Akihiro Kashihara

Trust, Autonomy, and Cognitive Models

Dynamic Trust Modeling in Robot Teleoperation Using a Bayesian Approach 443
Juan José García Cárdenas and Adriana Tapus

Effects of Perceived Robot Autonomy and Personal Differences on Trust in Human-Robot Interactions 459
Ali Fallahi, Patrick Holthaus, Farshid Amirabdollahian, and Gabriella Lakatos

Multimodal Assessment of Human Trust and Cognitive Load in Legged Robot Interaction 473
Juan José García Cárdenas, Changda Tian, Panos Trahanias, and Adriana Tapus

Interactive Robotic-Assisted Cognitive Training for Run-Time Personalization: a Preliminary Study 488
Riccardo De Benedictis, Claudia Di Napoli, Gabriella Cortellessa, Francesca Fracasso, and Annamaria Galluccio

Playing Smart: The Role of Embodiment and Strategy in Multi-agent
Competitive Card Game 500
    Laura Triglia, Francesco Rea, Pablo Barros, and Alessandra Sciutti

Short Papers Session 2

A Social Robot Conductor for Public Buses: Promoting Safety
and Reducing Driver Burden 519
    Nihan Karatas, Linjing Jiang, Yuki Yoshihara, Tetsuya Hirota,
    Ryugo Fujita, and Takahiro Tanaka

Evaluation of Conversation Continuity Through Social Experiments Using
LLM for Daily Text Chats with Virtual Robots 525
    Masayuki Kanbara and Taishi Sawabe

The Interaction Blueprint: A Human-Centred Design Tool for Cognitive
Human–Robot Interaction 531
    Nagore Osa, Ganix Lasa, Maitane Mazmela, Ainhoa Apraiz,
    and Oscar Escallada

Acceptability and Expectations of Social Robots in Speech and Language
Therapy - A Survey 538
    Melanie Jouaiti, Elisabetta Casagrande, and Negin Azizi

SRWToolkit: An Open Source Wizard of Oz Toolkit to Create Social
Robotic Avatars 547
    Atikkhan Faridkhan Nilgar, Kristof Van Laerhoven, and Ayub Kinoti

On the Influence of Social Robots During Ethical-Decision Making:
A Preliminary Study 554
    Marco Matarese, Vittorio Guerrieri, Rabiya Kahya, Francesco Rea,
    and Alessandra Sciutti

Towards Reconfigurability of Plan-Based Controllers Through
Metacognition 560
    Alessandro Umbrico, Sebastian Stock, Martin Atzmueller,
    Amedeo Cesta, Elisa Foderaro, Joachim Hertzberg,
    Oscar Lima, Juan Carlos Saborío, Marc Vinci, Nicola Pedrocchi,
    and Andrea Orlandini

Towards Perception Through Planning and Epistemic Models of Actions 568
    Gloria Beraldo, Angelo Oddi, Riccardo Rasconi, Andrea Orlandini,
    and Alessandro Umbrico

HAMI: A Robotic Assistant for Active Hand Rehabilitation 575
    Alexander Martinez, Sebastian Caballa, and Dante A. Elias

Towards Emotion-Aware and Context-Sensitive Decision-Making
in Social Robotics: Insights from MUSIC4D and MHARA 581
    *Valeria Seidita, Alessandro Giambanco, Antonio Pio Sciacchitano,
and Antonio Chella*

RoboPudica: Enhancing Awareness in Human - Plant Interaction
via Biomimetic Interface 587
    Hao Liu, Hooman Samani, and Saina Akhond

TactiCall: ML-Powered Haptic Wristband for Alerting Hearing-Impaired
Users 593
    Haofei Niu, Saina Akhond, and Hooman Samani

Towards a Sustainable Role for Social Robots: A Conceptual Framework 599
    Ilaria Alfieri

Affective Evaluation of Rehabilitation Tasks Demonstrated by a Service
Robot in Joint and Operational Spaces 607
    *Francesco Scotto di Luzio, Christian Tamantini, Clemente Lauretti,
Federica Candeloro, and Loredana Zollo*

Designing AI Robots for the SLD Community: The Role of the Dual
Pyramid Framework in Human-Centered Development 613
    *Alireza Mortezapour, Mafalda Ingenito, Francesca Perillo,
Amirreza Mortezapour, and Giuliana Vitiello*

A Personal Social Robot to Support Physical Activity for Seniors at Home 624
    *Berardina De Carolis, Davide Lofrese, Giuseppe Palestra,
Aurora Toma, and Cristina Gena*

Influence of Robot Role on Japanese Learners' English Communication
Learning 630
    Ami Hakiri and Akihiro Kashihara

Toward Human and Context-Aware Behavior Generation 636
    Carmine Grimaldi and Silvia Rossi

A Social Robot Supporting Artistic Activities with Older Adults: A Pilot
Study 642
    *Sara Carrasco-Martínez, Marcos Maroto-Gómez,
Fernando Alonso-Martín, Álvaro Castro-González,
and Miguel Ángel Salichs*

Toward Human-Robot Co-learning in Manufacturing 650
  Emilia Pietras, Raquel Salcedo-Gil, Guglielmo Borzone,
  Sonja Rispens, and Leon Bodenhagen

Grounding Natural Language Mission Requests in Robotic Skill
Specifications via Large Language Models 658
  Mario Barbato, Marco Grazioso, Azzurra Mancini, Valentina Russo,
  and Martina Di Bratto

The Cobra Effect in Trust Repair: Unintended Consequences of Rebuilding
Trust in Human-Robot Collaboration 664
  Russell Perkins, Boris Berkovich, and Paul Robinette

ARIS: A Socially Assistive Robot with Emotional Monitoring and Haptic
Feedback for Prosthetic Hand Adaptation and Hand Rehabilitation 671
  Alexandra Espinoza, Sebastian Caballa, and Dante A. Elias

Role-Adaptive Communication Framework with Large Language Models
for Multi-robot Systems 677
  Junhu Song, Minwoo Lee, Joey Back, Peter Cheong, and Ho Seok Ahn

Affected by Soft Robots: Insights into Social Relations with Soft Robots 684
  Pat Treusch and Jonas Jørgensen

Human Motion Mimicking and Motion Translation for Different Social
Robots 692
  Finn Tracey, Bruce MacDonald, and Ho Seok Ahn

Multimodal Prediction of Valence and Arousal from Speech
for Emotion-Aware Interaction Systems 698
  Safal Dhungana, Maria Pinto-Bernal, and Tony Belpaeme

Adaptive Defense Against Socio-emotional Exploitation in Social Robots:
A Review of Physiologically-Informed Approaches 706
  Danilo Greco and Lorenzo D'Errico

Exploring Students' Perceptions of an Educational Robot: The Influence
of Voice and Video Modalities 722
  Maria Sarno, Marialucia Cuciniello, Terry Amorese,
  Gennaro Cordasco, Vasco D'Agnese, and Anna Esposito

Author Index 722

Emotion and Affective Interaction

Visualizing the Past: Emotional and Cognitive Impacts of AI-Generated Images in Human-Robot Interaction

Ilaria Amaro[✉], Domenico Rossi, Attilio Della Greca, Fabiola De Marco, Alessia Auriemma Citarella, Luigi Di Biasi, Cesare Tucci, and Genoveffa Tortora

University of Salerno, Salerno, Italy
{iamaro,dorossi,adellagreca,fdemarco,aauriemmacitarella,
ldibiasi,ctucci,tortora}@unisa.it
https://caislab.di.unisa.it/

Abstract. This study explores the cognitive and emotional impact of AI-generated images in a human-robot interaction context aimed at stimulating autobiographical memory. An integrated system combining the Pepper robot with a generative model for real-time visualization of user-narrated memories was developed. A preliminary evaluation conducted on 15 participants highlighted a significant reduction in negative emotionality in users after interacting with the system ($p = .01$). Although the approach is promising for therapeutic applications, the results obtained suggest the need to improve the alignment between facial emotion recognition and self-reported affectivity, highlighting the importance of multimodal assessment tools.

Keywords: Human-Robot Interaction · Mental Health · Autobiographical memory · Cognitive stimulation · Generative Artificial Intelligence · Emotion Recognition

1 Introduction

Autobiographical memory can be considered a subcategory of episodic memory, which allows the conscious recall of personal experiences and events in time and space [40]. This type of memory plays a crucial role in the structuring and maintenance of individual identity, as it is responsible for three main functions [6,35]: (a) an intrapersonal function, since it contributes to maintaining the coherence and continuity of individual identity, (b) a social function, since it facilitates the creation of interpersonal bonds and the sharing of experiences and (c) a directive function, since an individual's problem-solving abilities are conditioned by the memory of past experiences.

Scientific literature has highlighted a correlation between impairments of autobiographical memory and various neurodegenerative diseases. However, the deterioration profile of autobiographical memory varies depending on the neuropsychopathological framework of reference.

For example, in Alzheimer's disease, the deterioration of autobiographical memories would seem to follow Ribot's law, according to which older memories are better preserved than recent ones [20,25,29], while in the temporal variant of frontotemporal dementia - known as semantic dementia - a greater tendency to the loss of remote memories has been observed [21,42].

Several studies in the literature have also shown the existence of associations between the level of specificity of autobiographical memories and psychopathologies such as depression [14,26,43] and post-traumatic stress disorder [11,24]. Furthermore, it seems that nonspecific autobiographical memories significantly predict poor social problem-solving skills, hopelessness, and dysfunctional thoughts about the future [1,48].

In light of the evidence showing a relationship between the specificity of autobiographical memory and various psychopathologies, some authors have hypothesized that an improvement in autobiographical memory may lead to a symptomatic improvement of some conditions such as depression [36,41]. Recognizing the existence of a link between autobiographical memory and mood disorders has made possible the development of rehabilitative interventions such as reminiscence therapy (RT), an approach widely used in the clinical field to improve the psychological well-being of older adults affected by various forms of dementia, in particular Alzheimer's dementia [47]. RT focuses on two main objectives: (i) the stimulation of autobiographical memory and (ii) the improvement of the patient's emotions and mood [33].

In particular, to improve the well-being of people with dementia, RT uses the sharing of life stories and the recovery of significant events [46] by exploiting language (written or spoken) or integrating tangible elements such as photographs, videos, and music that have a symbolic value for the patient [12].

However, in many cases, elderly patients do not have visual material related to past periods, such as childhood or adolescence, and the absence of visual support can reduce the effectiveness of the therapy. To fill this gap, several works in the literature have proposed strategies to improve traditional RT by introducing tools such as digital books, mobile applications, and computer-assisted programs [23,27], highlighting the effectiveness of the combination of RT and technological tools.

Although RT interventions supported by digital technologies have been developed, such as the InspireD Reminiscence [39] and Memory Tracks [13] applications, these solutions are mainly based on two-dimensional visual stimuli and auditory input, neglecting fundamental non-verbal communication modalities such as eye contact, facial expressions, and body language. In order to fill these gaps and promote a more realistic and immersive interaction, in recent years, there has been an increasing use of social robots as complementary tools within traditional interventions for mental health. These systems are potentially more effective in promoting communicative interaction and spontaneous retrieval of autobiographical memories [50]. Furthermore, the application of social robots in RT contexts represents a promising alternative to address the care burden on caregivers of patients with AD, thanks to the possibility of administering interventions systematically, repeatedly, and fatigue-free.

Starting from these theoretical premises, the present study introduces a robotic system designed to stimulate and evaluate autobiographical memory through a multimodal human-robot interaction. The system integrates two main components: the social robot Pepper, which provides a physically embodied interaction, and an image generation module via Generative Artificial Intelligence (GAI) [3], which allows real-time visualization of memories narrated by users, thus offering visual support to facilitate memory recall. The system was designed to perform two main functions: (a) a rehabilitative function, aimed at stimulating autobiographical recall and emotional processing through the presentation of personalized visual stimuli, and (b) an evaluative function, which aims to monitor the emotional impact of the images generated during the interaction. To assess the emotional impact of the images, both objective and subjective measurements were used: an emotion recognition module, integrated into the system, detects in real time the user's affective state during the interaction, while subjective assessments of the emotional experience were collected through the Self-Assessment Manikin (SAM) [7] scale, filled in by the user at the end of viewing each image.

The following sections of this paper will present a preliminary study conducted on healthy subjects, aimed at exploring the acceptability of the system and its emotional impact, with particular attention to the effect of the generated images, the emotional intensity aroused, and the connection between image and evoked memory. The main objective of this preliminary study is to investigate the potential of integrating this approach within existing therapeutic protocols, such as RT, to optimize the cognitive and emotional effects of existing therapies.

This work is an evolution of a previous study that introduced the Retromind framework [45], designed for image generation using the Pepper robot. In this phase, the Retromind system was extended with the integration of an emotion recognition module, which allowed the evaluation of the emotional impact of the generated images through a case study.

The article is divided into the following sections: (1) Introduction, (2) Related works, (3) Methodology, (4) Results, (5) Discussion and (6) Conclusions.

2 Related Works

In recent years, there has been an increase in demand for mental health care, and scientific research has shown that the use of social robots could represent a valid alternative to respond to this health emergency [32].

Socially assistive robots (SAR) are a class of robots designed to assist users through non-physical but socially guided interactions, exploiting speech, facial expressions, and gestures [31]. Unlike traditional rehabilitation robotics, which focuses on physical assistance, SAR systems provide motivational, cognitive, emotional, and therapeutic support to encourage learning, development, or recovery of cognitive functions. These robotic systems are generally intended for vulnerable populations, such as stroke patients, the elderly [4], or people with atypical development [16], to improve the quality of life of users through personalized and non-invasive, safe, and effective involvement [28].

In recent years, there has been an increasing use of SARs in the field of mental health and one of the main objectives that guides the design and planning of these systems is still, to this day, that of establishing a significant robot-user relationship, essential for achieving therapeutic objectives. Scientific evidence in the literature has shown positive effects of the use of social robots both on the cognitive stimulation of patients with dementia and on the well-being of their caregivers. An example is given by a recent work by Bevilacqua [5] and colleagues who showed how a combined intervention between traditional cognitive stimulation and interaction with the social robot Paro can lead to an improvement in the quality of life in patients with dementia, with secondary positive effects on cognitive functions, mood and behavior. The authors of the work also observed a good acceptance of the technology by patients and caregivers and a reduction in the general care burden. Another work involved and analyzed the use of the humanoid robot Pepper in the reproduction of personalized music for people with dementia to evaluate its impact on emotional well-being and its effectiveness in terms of cognitive stimulation. The study's results showed that 71.4% of participants started recalling autobiographical memories and 42.9% reported increased emotional comfort during the interaction with the robot. Despite some critical issues identified by the authors related to limitations in voice recognition, difficulty concentrating, or inadequate volume, the intervention proved promising in promoting positive emotional expressions and activating patients' episodic memory while highlighting the need for technological improvements for the effective use of the system in healthcare settings [15].

In addition to the directly observable results obtained through cognitive and emotional stimulation, the use of robotic systems in mental health has numerous advantages. For example, talking to a robot about sensitive topics can reduce the perception of judgment, stigma, or fear of "wasting someone's time" [38]. For people with social anxiety, robotic assistants can help reduce anticipatory anxiety and improve treatment adherence, for example, by simulating social situations in a safe environment [37].

Despite their use with different types of users in the healthcare sector, scientific literature has mainly focused on interventions for people with dementia [10]. In geriatric care, social robots are effective in alleviating depressive symptoms, reducing loneliness, and improving overall quality of life [9]. However, the design of effective robotic systems still presents numerous challenges.

First, the effective use of such technologies requires technical skills that may exceed those possessed by therapists and patients, such as the need to reprogram robots to adapt to changes in therapeutic goals or individual specificities [17]. Furthermore, although simplified user interfaces are being developed to increase the accessibility [2,19] of SARs, most of these systems are still experimental. They are not ready for widespread clinical application [30]. Further limitations concern the ability of these systems to dynamically adapt to the interaction with the user, maintain a high level of involvement, and ensure operational robustness adequate to real-world contexts of use. Furthermore, it is necessary to consider the challenges related to the initial resistance of users to integrating such technologies into therapeutic pathways, a phenomenon already observed with medical robotics [34].

3 Methodology

This preliminary study investigates the impact of autobiographical image generation in robot-mediated interactions. Specifically, it assesses the effectiveness of a robotic system in stimulating autobiographical memory by examining users' perceived coherence between generated images and their narrated memories, as well as their level of emotional engagement during the interaction.

The study was approved by the Ethics Committee of the Department of Computer Science, University of Salerno.

3.1 Functional Architecture of the System

The proposed system is structured as an automated pipeline, developed in Python, enabling multimodal interaction with the `Pepper` robot[1] to acquire, process, and store audio-visual data during an autobiographical interview.

Communication with Pepper occurs via the `qi` library[2], which allows access to the robot's internal audio recording and image acquisition services. During the interaction, audio is recorded using the `ALAudioRecorder` service, securely transferred to the local system via SSH, and transcribed into text using the OpenAI Whisper model. In parallel, an image of the user's face is acquired through the integrated camera and analyzed using the FER (Facial Expression Recognition) library[3] to automatically identify facial emotions. The transcribed text is used as a semantic prompt for automatically generating a coherent visual image using the DALL E model, and the resulting file is downloaded and stored locally. All the data produced - transcription, detected emotions, and generated images - are aggregated in a structured log file. The entire process is managed by a main script that synchronizes the execution of the components in asynchronous mode, ensuring operational efficiency and temporal coherence between the different phases of the interaction.

3.2 Participants

The study involved fifteen volunteers (age 20–35; M = 24.6), all undergraduates or graduates of the University of Salerno. Participants provided informed consent after being informed about the research objectives and the possibility of withdrawing at any time. Data were collected and processed anonymously, in compliance with current regulations on protecting personal data.

---

[1] http://doc.aldebaran.com/2-5/home_pepper.html.
[2] http://doc.aldebaran.com/2-5/dev/libqi/api/python/index.html.
[3] https://pypi.org/project/fer/.

3.3 Experimental Procedure

The experimental procedure was structured in three distinct phases: (1) pre-test, (2) experimental session, and (3) post-test. The interaction between the participants and the robotic system was conducted in a controlled environment, with the humanoid robot Pepper as the main interlocutor.

The robot was designed to (a) conduct the interaction, (b) collect narrative data, (c) detect the emotions expressed by the participants, and (d) generate visual images consistent with the narrated autobiographical memories (Fig. 1).

1. **Pre-test phase**: In this phase, the initial affective state of the participants was assessed by administering two standardized questionnaires: the Self-Assessment Manikin (SAM) [7] and the short-form of Positive and Negative Affect Schedule (PANAS) [44]. The SAM allowed to measure the basic emotional state through three main dimensions: valence (positive or negative affectivity), activation (level of emotional arousal) and dominance (perception of control over the emotion). The PANAS, instead, was used for a subjective assessment of the emotional state of the participants before the beginning of the experiment.
2. **Experimental session**: During the central phase of the experiment, participants were asked four autobiographical questions, each related to a specific period of their life: childhood, adolescence, adulthood, or recent events. Participants were asked to tell a personal memory related to each question, with the aim of stimulating the narration of significant experiences. During the narration, the Pepper robot analyzed the emotions expressed through facial expressions and automatically transcribed the content.

    In addition, a visual image was generated that reflected the described memory. At the end of the narration and the viewing of the image, participants completed the SAM and a questionnaire based on a Likert scale (see Table 1).
3. **Post-test phase**: In this phase, the PANAS evaluation tool was used to verify any variations in the global affective state compared to the pre-test phase.

    The entire experimental protocol was developed with the aim of minimizing confounding variables while ensuring respect for the participant's subjective experience.

4 Results

4.1 Effects of Generated Images: Emotional Responses and Affective Changes

To evaluate the effect of the images generated by Pepper starting from the autobiographical memories narrated by the users, the emotional responses of the participants, measured by the SAM, and the affective dimensions detected by the PANAS were analyzed.

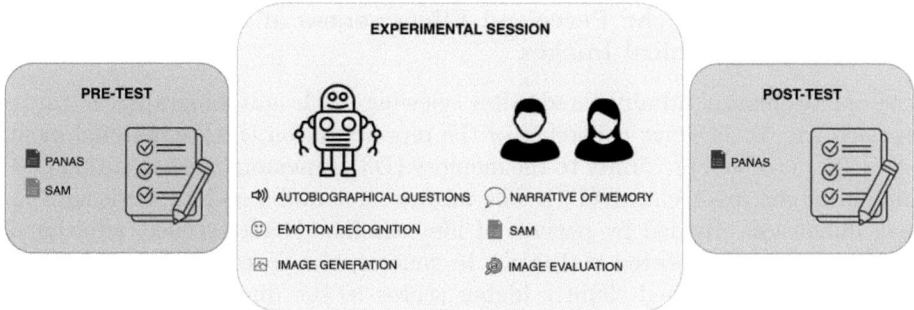

Fig. 1. Experimental flow

Table 1. Participants rated their agreement (from 1 = not at all to 5 = very much) with each statement.

Item label	Item description
D1	The image faithfully represents the memory I told.
D2	Looking at the image helped me emotionally relive the memory.
D3	The image made me feel closer to the memory.
D4	The image somehow changed my perception of the memory.
D5	I felt emotionally involved looking at the image.

As regards the SAM scores, a within-subject analysis was conducted using the Friedman test to compare the three emotional dimensions (valence, arousal and dominance) in relation to the temporal phase of the evoked memory (childhood, adolescence, adulthood, recent memories). The results of the analysis did not highlight statistically significant differences between the different periods of lifes (valence: $p = 0.778$; arousal: $p = 0.228$; dominance: $p = 0.334$), suggesting that the emotional response of the participants remained relatively stable, regardless of the life phase narrated and represented by the images.

In parallel, the PANAS allowed us to evaluate the pre-post intervention changes in the affective dimensions. A preliminary normality check using the Shapiro-Wilk test confirmed the normal distribution of the difference scores (both for positive and negative affectivity), thus justifying the use of a paired samples t-test for statistical comparison. The calculated delta and p-values showed a slight but non-significant reduction in positive affectivity (ΔPos = -0.20; p = 0.104), suggesting that the participants' positive emotional state remained stable and did not undergo statistically significant changes. On the contrary, negative affectivity decreased significantly (ΔNeg = 0.42; p = 0.01), indicating that the experience had a positive impact in reducing the negative emotional states perceived by the participants.

4.2 Evaluation of the Perceived Effectiveness of the Generated Autobiographical Images

The questionnaire administered after viewing each autobiographical image assessed five dimensions: coherence of the representation (D1), emotional memory (D2), perceived proximity to the memory (D3), mnemonic restructuring (D4) and emotional involvement (D5). The mean scores and standard deviations for each dimension, divided by periods of life (childhood, adolescence, adulthood, recent event), are reported in Table 2. In general, images related to adolescence and adulthood obtained slightly higher scores in the dimensions of perceived proximity (D3: M = 2.87 for both phases) and emotional involvement (D5: M = 2.80), suggesting a tendency towards a greater subjective resonance compared to those of childhood or recent events. However, these differences did not reach statistical significance. Repeated measures analysis of variance (ANOVA) conducted on the aggregated total score (sum of D1–D5 dimensions) did not reveal significant effects between the four periods of lifes, $F(3, 42) = 0.481$, $p = .6973$. Univariate ANOVAs conducted on each dimension also confirmed the absence of significant differences (e.g., D1: $p = .8176$; D5: $p = .8497$). Similarly, a multivariate analysis of variance (MANOVA) did not reveal an overall effect of the periods of life on the response profile. Psychometrically, the questionnaire showed excellent internal consistency, with Cronbach's α values ranging from .86 to .94 across the different periods of lifes, indicating high measurement reliability (see Table 3).

4.3 FER–SAM Correspondence Analysis

Out of a total of 60 images presented to participants, 49 produced valid data, defined as instances in which the FER successfully detected a codable emotion. Within these valid cases, 16 instances exhibited a correspondence between the valence automatically detected by the FER system and the self-reported valence via the SAM questionnaire. This correspondence resulted in an overall accuracy rate of 32.65%. The observed low concordance between the automatically detected emotions and those self-reported by participants may be attributable to several factors, including the quality and intensity of the facial expressions exhibited, the nature of the autobiographical experiences evoked, and potential interference from contextual variables such as the experimental setting.

5 Discussion

The present study investigated the cognitive and emotional impact of the integration of AI-generated images in a human-robot interaction mediated by the Pepper robot to evaluate the effectiveness of this approach in promoting memory retrieval and affective regulation. The results obtained, which combine subjective (SAM, PANAS), automated (FER) and qualitative (perceived efficacy questionnaire) measures, show a spectrum of the possible effects of the combination of GAI and robotic systems in stimulating autobiographical memory.

Table 2. Means and standard deviations for each dimension of the questionnaire and for each life stage

Periods of life	D1		D2		D3		D4		D5	
	M	SD	M	SD	M	SD	M	SD	M	SD
Childhood	2.53	1.41	2.93	1.49	2.73	1.39	1.53	0.74	2.93	1.33
Adolescence	2.47	1.25	2.67	1.59	2.87	1.64	1.73	1.28	2.80	1.37
Adulthood	2.87	1.41	3.00	1.56	2.87	1.55	1.67	0.82	2.80	1.47
Recent event	2.60	1.30	2.33	1.29	2.27	1.16	1.40	0.91	2.53	1.25

Table 3. Reliability coefficients (Cronbach's alpha) by phase

Phase	Cronbach's α
Childhood	0.86
Adolescence	0.94
Adulthood	0.90
Recent event	0.87

The analysis of the users' emotional responses, assessed by SAM, showed substantial stability in the valence, activation and dominance scores, regardless of the life period evoked (childhood, adolescence, adulthood, recent events) and represented graphically. The absence of significant variations suggests that the chronological characteristics of memories are not determining for the affective impact; presumably subjective factors such as the personal meaning attributed to the content of the memory assume greater relevance rather than the time of encoding. This finding is consistent with evidence on the fundamental role of autobiographical memory in shaping individual identity and affectivity, as discussed by Holland et al. [22].

In parallel, the pre-post comparison with the PANAS scale revealed a significant reduction in negative affectivity (ΔNeg = 0.42; p = .01), while positive affectivity did not undergo significant variations (ΔPos = −0.20; p = .104). These data indicate that the interaction with the proposed system had a regulatory effect on negative emotions, probably through a narrative re-elaboration process facilitated by the visual component. The lack of variation in the levels of positive affectivity could instead reflect the reflective and introspective nature of the autobiographical task, more oriented to the reduction of emotional stress rather than the elicitation of positive emotions.

Overall, the results obtained from the analysis of the dimensions of the PANAS support the hypothesis that the activation of personal memories mediated by images can promote functional emotional regulation [8]. As regards the perceived effectiveness of the generated images, the mean scores obtained by the participants on the five items of the questionnaire indicate a slight tendency towards higher values for memories related to adolescence and adulthood. In particular, this emerged in the dimensions of perceived proximity to the memory (D3) and emotional involvement (D5). Although these differences did not reach statistical significance, the results suggest that the system was generally well received and perceived as effective in facilitating emotional recollection, regardless of the life phase to which the evoked autobiographical memory was associated. Confirming the quality of these measurements, the internal reliability coefficients (Cronbach's α between 0.86 and 0.94) indicate a high consistency between the items of the questionnaire, guaranteeing the solidity of the instrument used for the evaluation. Finally, the values related to the concordance emerged between the quantitative (FER) and self-reported (SAM) assessments (32.65%), indicating a discrepancy between automatic emotional recognition and subjective perception of affective states. This data confirms what has already been highlighted in the literature regarding the limits of facial recognition systems in ecologically complex and non-standardized contexts [49], and highlights the opportunity to integrate multimodal approaches for a more accurate detection of emotional responses [18]. These results, together with the small sample size and the absence of a clinical population, constitute some of the main limitations of this study.

For this reason, among the objectives of future work there is to expand the experimentation to diversified samples including real therapeutic contexts and improve the adaptivity of the generation and recognition models in order to optimize the personalization of the interaction and the ecological validity of the intervention.

6 Conclusion

The results of this preliminary study suggest that the use of AI-generated images during robot-mediated autobiographical recall can effectively support emotional regulation and enhance the user's connection to personal memories. Although no significant differences were found for different life periods, the integration of generative AI with the social robot Pepper showed a significant reduction in negative emotional states, suggesting its potential use in therapeutic settings. Participants in this preliminary study perceived the system as emotionally engaging and coherent, although discrepancies between automatic emotion recognition and subjective reports highlight current technological limitations. These insights pave the way for future research involving clinical populations and advanced adaptive models, aiming to optimize personalization, ecological validity, and therapeutic impact in memory-based mental health interventions.

Acknowledgements. The work was supported by "RESTART - Robot Enhanced Social abilities based on Theory of mind for Acceptance of Robot in assistive Treatments" (CUP: I53D23003780001), funded by the MIUR with D.D. no.861 under the PNRR and by Next Generation EU.

References

1. Arie, M., Apter, A., Orbach, I., Yefet, Y., Zalzman, G.: Autobiographical memory, interpersonal problem solving, and suicidal behavior in adolescent inpatients. Compr. Psychiatry **49**(1), 22–29 (2008)
2. Atherton, J.A., Goodrich, M.A.: Supporting clinicians in robot-assisted therapy for autism spectrum disorder: creating and editing robot animations with full-body motion tracking. In: Human-Robot Interaction: Perspectives and Contributions to Robotics from the Human Sciences Workshop at Robotics Science and Systems. Los Angeles, CA, USA (2011)
3. Banh, L., Strobel, G.: Generative artificial intelligence. Electron. Mark. **33**(1), 63 (2023)
4. Bemelmans, R., Gelderblom, G.J., Jonker, P., De Witte, L.: Socially assistive robots in elderly care: a systematic review into effects and effectiveness. J. Am. Med. Dir. Assoc. **13**(2), 114–120 (2012)
5. Bevilacqua, R., et al.: Social robotics to support older people with dementia: a study protocol with Paro seal robot in an Italian alzheimer's day center. Front. Public Health **11**, 1141460 (2023)
6. Bluck, S., Alea, N.: Exploring the functions of autobiographical memory: why do i remember the autumn? (2002)
7. Bradley, M.M., Lang, P.J.: Measuring emotion: the self-assessment manikin and the semantic differential. J. Behav. Ther. Exp. Psychiatry **25**(1), 49–59 (1994)
8. Burnside, I., Baldwin, R., O'Shea, E.: Reminiscence therapy for older adults with depressive symptoms: a systematic review and meta-analysis. Aging Mental Health **25**(5), 824–836 (2021)
9. Chen, S.C., Moyle, W., Jones, C., Petsky, H.: A social robot intervention on depression, loneliness, and quality of life for Taiwanese older adults in long-term care. Int. Psychogeriatr. **32**(8), 981–991 (2020)
10. Chu, M.T., Khosla, R., Khaksar, S.M.S., Nguyen, K.: Service innovation through social robot engagement to improve dementia care quality. Assist. Technol. **29**(1), 8–18 (2017)
11. Crane, C., Heron, J., Gunnell, D., Lewis, G., Evans, J., Williams, J.M.G.: Childhood traumatic events and adolescent overgeneral autobiographical memory: findings in a UK cohort. J. Behav. Ther. Exp. Psychiatry **45**(3), 330–338 (2014)
12. Cuevas, P.E.G., Davidson, P.M., Mejilla, J.L., Rodney, T.W.: Reminiscence therapy for older adults with alzheimer's disease: a literature review. Int. J. Ment. Health Nurs. **29**(3), 364–371 (2020)
13. Cunningham, S., et al.: Assessing wellbeing in people living with dementia using reminiscence music with a mobile app (memory tracks): a mixed methods cohort study. J. Healthcare Eng. **2019**(1), 8924273 (2019)
14. Dalgleish, T., et al.: Reduced specificity of autobiographical memory and depression: the role of executive control. J. Exp. Psychol. Gen. **136**(1), 23 (2007)
15. De Kok, R., Rothweiler, J., Scholten, L., van Zoest, M., Boumans, R., Neerincx, M.: Combining social robotics and music as a non-medical treatment for people with dementia. In: 2018 27th IEEE International Symposium on Robot and Human Interactive Communication (RO-MAN), pp. 465–467. IEEE (2018)
16. Feil-Seifer, D., Matarić, M.J.: Toward socially assistive robotics for augmenting interventions for children with autism spectrum disorders. In: Experimental Robotics: The Eleventh International Symposium, pp. 201–210. Springer (2009). https://doi.org/10.1007/978-3-642-00196-3_24

17. Giullian, N., Ricks, D., Atherton, A., Colton, M., Goodrich, M., Brinton, B.: Detailed requirements for robots in autism therapy. In: 2010 IEEE International Conference on Systems, Man and Cybernetics, pp. 2595–2602. IEEE (2010)
18. Gonzalez, E., Martinez, H., Kopp, S.: Multimodal affect recognition: current trends and future directions in human-centered AI. ACM Trans. Multimed. Comput. Commun. Appl. **18**(4), 1–28 (2022)
19. Gorostiza, J.F., Salichs, M.A.: End-user programming of a social robot by dialog. Robot. Auton. Syst. **59**(12), 1102–1114 (2011)
20. Greene, J.D., Hodges, J.R., Baddeley, A.D.: Autobiographical memory and executive function in early dementia of alzheimer type. Neuropsychologia **33**(12), 1647–1670 (1995)
21. Hodges, J.R., Graham, K.S.: Episodic memory: insights from semantic dementia. Philos. Trans. R. Soc. London Ser. B Biol. Sci. **356**(1413), 1423–1434 (2001)
22. Holland, A.C., Kensinger, E.A.: Autobiographical memory and emotional regulation: the role of valence and vividness in memory recall. Cogn. Emot. **34**(7), 1365–1377 (2020)
23. Imtiaz, D., Khan, A., Seelye, A.: A mobile multimedia reminiscence therapy application to reduce behavioral and psychological symptoms in persons with alzheimer's. J. Healthcare Eng. **2018**(1), 1536316 (2018)
24. Kleim, B., Ehlers, A.: Reduced autobiographical memory specificity predicts depression and posttraumatic stress disorder after recent trauma. J. Consult. Clin. Psychol. **76**(2), 231 (2008)
25. Kopelman, M.D.: The "new" and the "old": components of the anterograde and retrograde memory loss in korsakoff and alzheimer patients (1992)
26. Kuyken, W., Howell, R., Dalgleish, T.: Overgeneral autobiographical memory in depressed adolescents with, versus without, a reported history of trauma. J. Abnorm. Psychol. **115**(3), 387 (2006)
27. Lancioni, G.E., et al.: A computer-aided program for helping patients with moderate alzheimer's disease engage in verbal reminiscence. Res. Dev. Disabil. **35**(11), 3026–3033 (2014)
28. Law, M., et al.: Developing assistive robots for people with mild cognitive impairment and mild dementia: a qualitative study with older adults and experts in aged care. BMJ Open **9**(9), e031937 (2019)
29. Leplow, B., Dierks, C., Herrmann, P., Pieper, N., Annecke, R., Ulm, G.: Remote memory in parkinson's disease and senile dementia. Neuropsychologia **35**(4), 547–557 (1997)
30. Lin, P., Abney, K., Bekey, G.: Robot ethics: mapping the issues for a mechanized world. Artif. Intell. **175**(5–6), 942–949 (2011)
31. Matarić, M.J., Scassellati, B.: Socially assistive robotics. Springer Handbook of Robotics, pp. 1973–1994 (2016). https://doi.org/10.1007/978-3-319-32552-1_73
32. Moitra, M., et al.: Global mental health: where we are and where we are going. Curr. Psychiatry Rep. **25**(7), 301–311 (2023)
33. Okumura, Y., Tanimukai, S., Asada, T.: Effects of short-term reminiscence therapy on elderly with dementia: a comparison with everyday conversation approaches. Psychogeriatrics **8**(3), 124–133 (2008)
34. Orr, G.: Diffusion of innovations, by everett rogers **21**, 2005 (2003)
35. Pillemer, D.: Directive functions of autobiographical memory: the guiding power of the specific episode. Memory **11**(2), 193–202 (2003)
36. Raes, F., Williams, J.M.G., Hermans, D.: Reducing cognitive vulnerability to depression: a preliminary investigation of memory specificity training (MEST) in

inpatients with depressive symptomatology. J. Behav. Ther. Exp. Psychiatry **40**(1), 24–38 (2009)
37. Rasouli, S., Gupta, G., Nilsen, E., Dautenhahn, K.: Potential applications of social robots in robot-assisted interventions for social anxiety. Int. J. Soc. Robot. **14**(5), 1–32 (2022)
38. Robinson, N.L., Kavanagh, D.J.: A social robot to deliver a psychotherapeutic treatment: qualitative responses by participants in a randomized controlled trial and future design recommendations. Int. J. Hum. Comput. Stud. **155**, 102700 (2021)
39. Ryan, A.A., et al.: 'There is still so much inside': the impact of personalised reminiscence, facilitated by a tablet device, on people living with mild to moderate dementia and their family carers. Dementia **19**(4), 1131–1150 (2020)
40. Schacter, D.L.: The seven sins of memory: perspectives from functional neuroimaging. In: Memory, Consciousness and the Brain, pp. 119–137. Psychology Press (2013)
41. Selva, J.P.S., et al.: Life review therapy using autobiographical retrieval practice for older adults with clinical depression. Psicothema **24**(2), 224–229 (2012)
42. Snowden, J.S., Griffiths, H.L., Neary, D.: Semantic-episodic memory interactions in semantic dementia: implications for retrograde memory function. Cogn. Neuropsychol. **13**(8), 1101–1139 (1996)
43. Spinhoven, P., Bockting, C.L., Schene, A.H., Koeter, M.W., Wekking, E.M., Williams, J.M.G.: Autobiographical memory in the euthymic phase of recurrent depression. J. Abnorm. Psychol. **115**(3), 590 (2006)
44. Thompson, E.R.: Development and validation of an internationally reliable short-form of the positive and negative affect schedule (PANAS). J. Cross Cult. Psychol. **38**(2), 227–242 (2007)
45. Tucci, C., Amaro, I., Della Greca, A., Tortora, G.: Retromind and the image of memories: a preliminary study of a support tool for reminiscence therapy. In: International Conference on Human-Computer Interaction, pp. 456–468. Springer (2024). https://doi.org/10.1007/978-3-031-60615-1_31
46. Wang, J.J.: Group reminiscence therapy for cognitive and affective function of demented elderly in Taiwan. Int. J. Geriatr. Psychiatry J. Psychiatry Late Life Allied Sci. **22**(12), 1235–1240 (2007)
47. Webster, J.D.: Construction and validation of the reminiscence functions scale. J. Gerontol. **48**(5), P256–P262 (1993)
48. Williams, J.M.G., Barnhofer, T., Crane, C., Beck, A.: Problem solving deteriorates following mood challenge in formerly depressed patients with a history of suicidal ideation. J. Abnorm. Psychol. **114**(3), 421 (2005)
49. Yang, W., Zhao, X., Wang, L.: Facial emotion recognition in the wild: a review of datasets, methods, and challenges. IEEE Trans. Affect. Comput. **14**(2), 780–798 (2023)
50. Yuan, F., Klavon, E., Liu, Z., Lopez, R.P., Zhao, X.: A systematic review of robotic rehabilitation for cognitive training. Front. Robot. AI **8**, 605715 (2021)

When Robots Care: Elderly Reactions to Emotionally Intelligent Android

Sonabayim Huseynzade[1](✉)[iD], Rainer Wieching[2][iD], Toshimi Ogawa[3][iD], Yoshio Matsumoto[4][iD], Volker Wulf[2][iD], and Yasuyuki Taki[3][iD]

[1] Technical University Dortmund, August-Schmidt-Straße 4, 44227 Dortmund, Germany
sonabayim.huseynzade@tu-dortmund.de
[2] Siegen University, Adolf-Reichwein-Straße 2a, 57076 Siegen, Germany
[3] Tohoku University, 2 Chome-1-1 Katahira, Aoba Ward, Sendai, Miyagi 980-8577, Japan
[4] Tokyo University of Science, 6-3-1 Niijuku, Katsushika, Tokyo 125-8585, Japan

Abstract. The rapid growth of the older adult population calls for conversational robots that foster social participation and community inclusion. We report a pilot study at Tohoku University in which eight adults (65–78 years old) each held a 20-minute semi-structured dialogue with *Android*, a hyper-realistic android equipped with Japanese BERT emotion recognition and GPT-3.5-based response generation. Sentiment logs and post-interaction interviews showed that participants generally felt at ease, described the robot as a "good listener," and remained engaged throughout the exchange; only occasional affective mismatches disrupted rapport. These preliminary results suggest that real-time affect adaptation can support empathic HRI, yet also expose the need for tighter timing and context control. Our mixed-methods findings lay the groundwork for designing emotionally responsive humanoids that enrich eldercare settings.

Keywords: Social Robots · Human-Robot Interaction · Large Language Models

1 Introduction

By 2050, one in six people globally will be over 65 [1]. In Japan, 29.3% of the population was aged 65 or older in 2024, and this is projected to rise to one-third within two decades [2]. This demographic shift will intensify challenges related to healthcare, autonomy, and social well-being. Loneliness exacerbates these pressures, as social isolation is linked to depression, cognitive decline, and increased mortality [23]. The COVID-19 pandemic further amplified these effects [5].

Socially assistive robots (SARs) offer a scalable response. Humanoid platforms like Pepper [3] and Nadine [4] provide companionship, but rely on scripted dialogue with limited emotional nuance [6]. This motivates the integration of generative models capable of affect aware, unscripted interaction. Advances in large language models such as GPT-3.5 [7, 8] now enable robots to detect user emotion and generate linguistically and emotionally aligned responses.

Despite growing interest in affect-adaptive robots, little is known about how older adults respond when a hyper-realistic android combines real-time emotion recognition with large-language model (LLM) dialogue. To address this gap, we conducted an exploratory pilot study at Tohoku University (2023), where eight older adults engaged in semi-structured conversations with Android a life-sized android with nuanced facial expressions, gaze, and GPT-3.5 driven speech. Our research asks: *How do older adults subjectively perceive and respond to humanoid robots capable of displaying and interpreting affective expressions during social interaction?* Beyond surface impressions, we examine constructs such as empathy, trust, and agency attribution. This pilot offers a proof of concept for integrating GPT-based dialogue with synchronized facial affect in an android embodiment. While limited in scale, the findings reveal both meaningful engagement and recurrent empathic breakdowns, offering early design cues for emotionally responsive eldercare robots.

2 Related Work

Research on conversational robots for older adults spans socially assistive robotics (SAR), affective computing, and large language model (LLM) dialogue systems. Early SAR studies showed that humanoid robots like Pepper and NAO can reduce loneliness and improve mood, even with scripted dialogue. For instance, older adults exhibited more positive affect over time during cognitive training sessions with Pepper, though its fixed prompts limited emotional adaptability [9]. The Ryan robot, equipped with basic multimodal affect recognition, was preferred in its "empathic" mode, which mirrored users' emotional tone through gestures and expressions [10]. Yet dialogue in such systems remained template-based and rigid. These studies underscore a core limitation: while some robots detect or display affect, few dynamically adapt their conversational content to users' emotional cues.

The emergence of GPT class models has renewed interest in open domain human–robot dialogue. One study integrated fine-tuned GPT-3.5 into the QT robot for wellness chats; while users found it comforting, the absence of affect recognition led to generic responses [12]. Another paired GPT-3.5 with Furhat in free form conversations with 34 older adults; users appreciated the dialogue flexibility, but latency, repetition, and hallucinations undermined reliability [11]. These advances in fluency reveal a key gap: LLM driven robots can speak naturally but remain largely insensitive to user emotion.

Hyper-realistic androids offer unique potential for affective HRI through expressive embodiment. Android has been validated for rendering facial Action Units [13], and older adults have responded positively to its presence, despite noting limited expressivity and scripted dialogue [14]. Yet no study has evaluated a lifelike android that detects user emotion in real time and modulates LLM dialogue particularly in eldercare, where emotional nuance is essential.

Current LLM-based robots typically decouple sentiment detection from dialogue generation and avoid emotionally complex topics like grief or loneliness. As a result, how trust, empathy, and sustained engagement develop in elder–robot interaction remains poorly understood. This study addresses that gap by demonstrating a closed-loop, sentiment-adaptive system that synchronizes verbal and non-verbal responses to user emotion. It offers new insight into emotional alignment, user comfort, and the design of emotionally intelligent eldercare robots.

2.1 Humanoid Robot: AL-G109ST-F

Humanoid robots occupy a distinct niche in socially assistive technology due to their lifelike appearance and expressive capabilities [13]. This study employed *AL-G109ST-F*, a life-sized female android developed by A-Lab Co. Ltd. Known for its realistic skin texture, dynamic facial expressions, and eye-gaze behavior, androids has been widely studied in healthcare and affective HRI [15,16]. It features 18 pneumatic actuators across the face, neck, torso, and arms, enabling expressive behaviors such as head tilts, eye contact, and basic gestures. Facial expressions are generated via silicone-based facial action units (e.g., AU12 smile, AU15 sadness), while a vision system and microphones support proximity- and speech-based feedback. Although it lacks locomotion, androids are well suited for seated interactions in controlled environments. For this study, it was deployed in a lab setting simulating informal social conversation. Android has previously been used in hospital reception trials and emotional interaction studies, where its human-like expressiveness was found to support comfort and engagement among older adults, though responses vary with the realism and timing of affective cues [18]. Ethical concerns have also been raised regarding transparency and user expectations in emotionally sensitive settings [17].

Figure 1 shows the four affective expressions displayed during interaction.

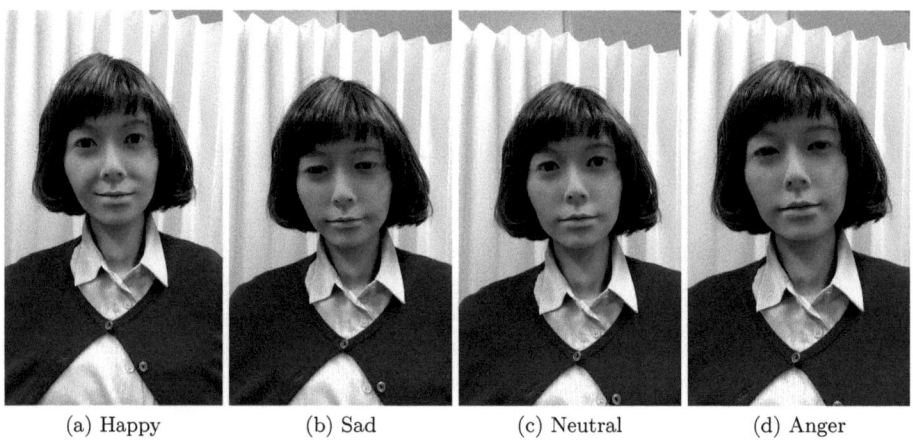

(a) Happy   (b) Sad   (c) Neutral   (d) Anger

Fig. 1. Facial expressions of the humanoid robot used in the study.

2.2 System Architecture

All system components: ASR(Automatic Speech Recognition), emotion detection, LLM-based response generation, and motion control ran on an external control unit connected to Android via a socket-based API. The architecture integrated four layers: hardware, perception and language modules, UDP-based messaging, and an end-to-end data pipeline enabling real-time, affect-adaptive dialogue (Fig. 2). Spoken input was transcribed into Japanese using Google Speech-to-Text [25], then analyzed for emotional valence using a fine-tuned Japanese BERT model [26]. The resulting emotion label and dialogue history informed GPT-3.5 Turbo [28], which generated emotionally aligned replies. Verbal responses were paired with gesture commands and transmitted to Android for synchronized speech and movement.

The architecture described above corresponds directly to the components shown in Fig. 2 and serves as the operational backbone for our user facing interactions.

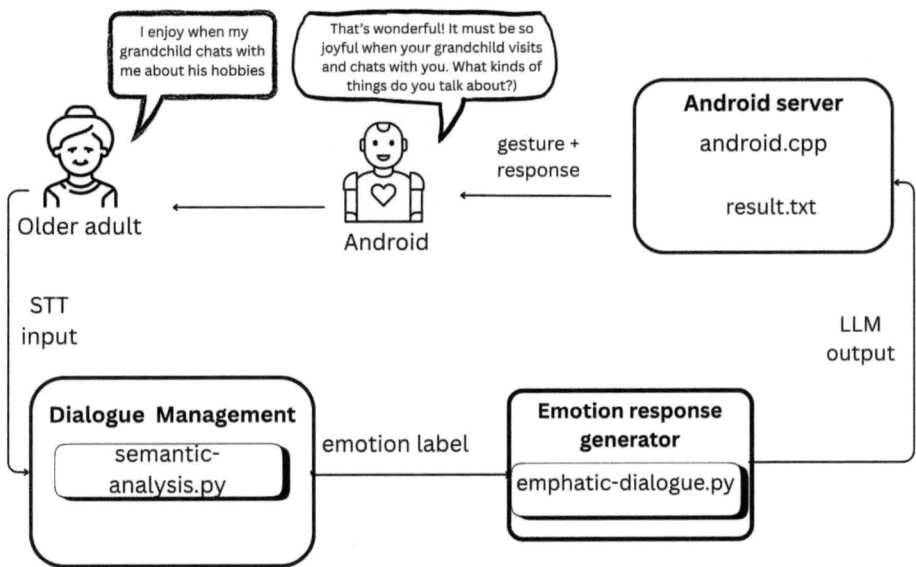

Fig. 2. System workflow showing modular components, data flow, and a sample user-robot interaction.

This closed-loop system enabled real-time, sentiment-adaptive interaction, laying the foundation for the mixed-methods analysis detailed in the following section.

3 Participants and Methodology

The study was conducted at Tohoku University's Smart-Aging Research Center in Sendai and approved by the university's Ethics Committee (Approval ID: 2023-HR-014). All procedures followed national and institutional guidelines on human experimentation and data protection. Eligible participants were aged 65 or older, open to conversing with a robot, and able to engage independently in a 20-minute session. Stable chronic conditions (e.g., controlled hypertension) were permitted. Of nine individuals attending the orientation, eight (5 female, 3 male; aged 64–75, $M = 71.4$) completed the study. All had normal or corrected vision and hearing, no prior experience with Android, and required no mobility support.

Table 1 summarizes their demographics.

The study was designed to investigate how emotional responsiveness in humanoid robots influences the interaction experience of older adults. Participants were introduced to an android robot programmed to conduct a semi-structured conversation. Interaction was fully autonomous; participants could speak on any topic. An A5 sheet was provided with optional ice-breaker questions in Japanese, including prompts such as "Have you read any books recently?" and "What has been the happiest event in your life?"[1] Participants were free to ignore the sheet and pursue their own narratives. They were encouraged to speak freely to allow themes to emerge naturally and assess their comfort during a first encounter. They were only asked to speak clearly and keep turns under two minutes for processing. The robot, using facial expressions and GPT-3.5-based dialogue, responded in real time. A post-interaction interview assessed emotional understanding, comfort, and perceived usefulness. These responses were systematically prepared for subsequent analysis, as detailed in the following subsection.

Table 1. Participant demographics.

ID	Gender	Age	Living condition
B	Female	74	with family
C	Male	72	alone
D	Female	72	with family
E	Male	64	with family
F	Female	71	alone
G	Male	75	with family
H	Female	75	alone
I	Female	68	with family

---

[1] The full list of original Japanese prompts is available in the project's GitHub repository.

Data Analysis

Corpus and Sentiment Annotation. ASR transcripts were manually corrected and segmented into 279 user and 336 robot utterances; only cleaned text was retained (Ethics ID: 2023-HR-014). User utterances were labeled using a Japanese **GoEmotions** model (34 labels, macro-$F_1 = 0.71$), with top-1 labels grouped into *positive, negative,* or *neutral* classes as needed. These annotations informed the corpus distribution (Fig. 3), sentiment flow (Fig. 4), and alignment analysis (Fig. 5). Post-interaction interviews were human translated; dialogues used DeepL (Feb 2025). A bilingual rater evaluated 10% of DeepL outputs ($n = 30$) for adequacy (M = 4.6 ± 0.3) and fluency (M = 4.7 ± 0.2). VADER sentiment scores were computed on the English interviews).

Analytical Procedures. Statistical analyses evaluated corpus wide emotion distribution using a χ^2 goodness-of-fit test against a uniform baseline, with Cramer's V as the effect size. Inter-participant variation was assessed by computing z-normalized emotion means and applying the non-parametric Friedman test, with Kendall's W indicating concordance. To examine temporal sentiment dynamics, a first-order Markov transition matrix was constructed, and shifts from negative to positive sentiment were tested against persistence rates using an exact binomial test. Affective alignment between user and robot was analyzed via a confusion matrix comparing expressed and displayed emotions turn by turn, with metrics including accuracy, macro-averaged F_1, and Cohen's κ, all reported with 1,000 sample bootstrap confidence intervals.

A reflexive thematic analysis was conducted on all non-neutral user utterances and the full set of post-interaction interviews [24]. From 167 coded excerpts, inter-coder reliability reached $\kappa = 0.79$, and six higher-order themes were identified, including *shared joy, processing of loss,* and *misalignment repair.* Quantitative and qualitative findings were integrated using a joint display approach to highlight convergence and complementarity. One notable link was a negative correlation between in session expressions of *sadness* and post-interaction sentiment polarity ($\rho = -0.64$, $p = .09$), mirroring the rebound dynamics observed in sentiment transitions. Data processing used the GoEmotions classifier and standard visualization tools; all transcripts and analysis scripts will be released on GitHub, the full data set is available to qualified researchers upon request and Ethics Committee approval.

4 Results

This section addresses our central research question: *How do older adults subjectively perceive and respond to a humanoid robot capable of displaying and interpreting affective expressions during social interaction?* The study produced two complementary data sources: (1) *naturalistic dialogue transcripts* from interactions with Android, and (2) *semi-structured interviews* conducted afterward. We adopt a mixed-methods approach, combining quantitative affective metrics with qualitative narrative analysis to examine how participants navigated emotional engagement both when the robot's affective responses resonated and when they fell short.

Participants responded with a blend of openness, warmth, and critical awareness. While positive tone predominated, moments of grief, philosophical reflection, and subtle resistance also surfaced, revealing how emotional credibility was variously accepted, interpreted, or challenged across both live interaction and reflective commentary.

Quantitative Analysis of Affective Interaction Patterns

Corpus-Level Footprint. To provide a high level view of affective expression, we aggregated emotion labels across all user utterances (Fig. 3). From 279 utterances, 41% carried non-neutral emotion, with a clear skew toward prosocial states such as *curiosity*, *love*, and *admiration*. A χ^2 goodness of fit test confirmed the non-uniform distribution ($\chi^2(12) = 620.09$, $p < 10^{-120}$, Cramer's $V = 0.40$). Strongly negative emotions were rare, suggesting participants generally perceived the robot as a safe, agreeable partner.

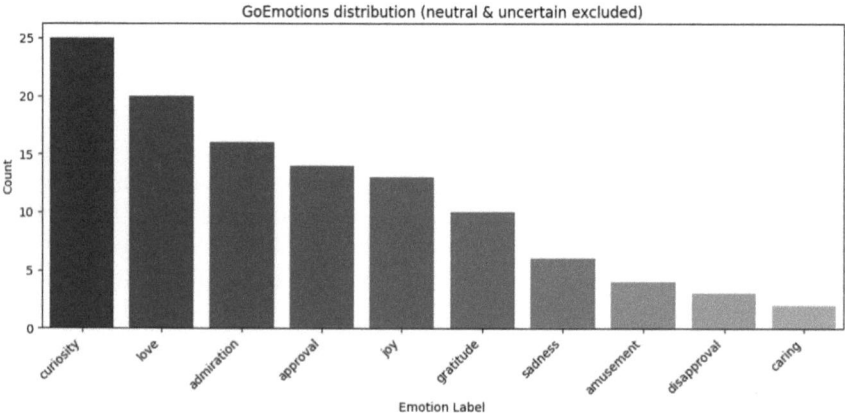

Fig. 3. Affective label distribution after removing *neutral* and *uncertain*. Prosocial categories dominate, strong negatives are rare.

The prevalence of *joy* and *approval* reflects moments of lighthearted rapport and familial warmth. One participant, amused by her grandson's reaction to borrowed socks. These affiliative emotions were common in family themed exchanges, supported by the robot's affirming tone. In contrast, instances of *curiosity* and *sadness* marked deeper disclosures. Although emotion recognition relied solely on textual input, the prominence of affiliative and introspective emotions suggests the robot enabled diverse affective expression.

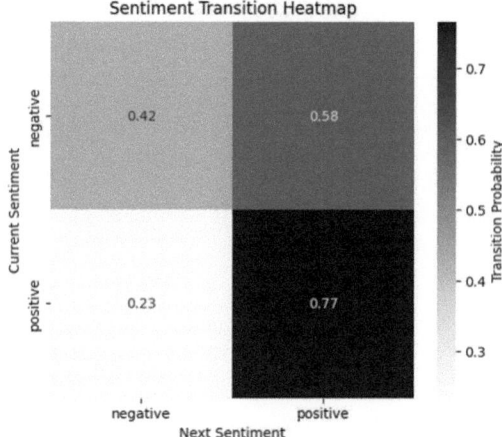

Fig. 4. Sentiment transition probabilities between consecutive utterances.

Temporal Sentiment Flow. To examine emotional dynamics, we grouped labels into positive and negative categories and calculated first-order transition probabilities (Fig. 4). Positive affect showed strong continuity, with 77% of utterances followed by another positive one. Negative affect more often shifted to positive (58%) than persisted (42%), a statistically significant trend ($p < .01$). This pattern suggests older adults entered with a prosocial stance and actively restored positive tone after brief lapses, viewing the robot as an emotionally credible partner.

Robot-Human Affective Alignment. To assess the alignment between the robot's emotional responses and user affect, we compared the robot's selected emotion at each turn with the label assigned to the preceding user utterance (Fig. 5). Overall alignment accuracy was 61.7%, with a macro averaged F_1 score of 0.43 and Cohen's $\kappa = 0.35$, indicating fair agreement per Landis and Koch. Alignment varied by emotion category. The robot best matched user expressions of *joy* (79%) and *neutrality* (56%), but performed poorly on *sadness*, with only 33% agreement. This asymmetry suggests stronger sensitivity to positive or neutral cues, and reduced consistency in responding to negative emotions.

These results show that while the robot's affective responses exceeded chance performance, gaps in emotional attunement remained. Participants often managed these mismatches through adaptive strategies such as humor, polite deflection, or topic shifts (cf. Sect. 5). Despite occasional misalignment, many still perceived the robot as emotionally responsive. To better understand how users interpreted and navigated these interactions, we turn next to the qualitative findings.

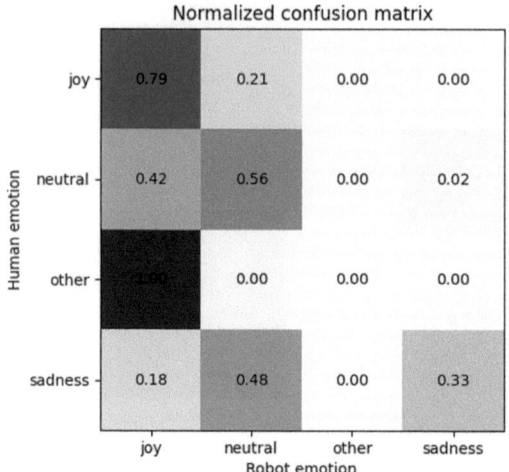

Fig. 5. Normalized confusion matrix comparing user emotion labels (y-axis) with the robot's displayed emotions (x-axis). The model achieved an overall alignment accuracy of 61.7%.

Qualitative Insights

The quantitative panorama in Figs. 3, 4 and 5 shows that affiliative emotions dominated the corpus and that users generally steered interaction back to positivity after minor lapses. A close reading of 167 quotation level codes[2] reveals *how* participants accomplished this and where the boundaries of emotional copresence were felt.

Emotional Comfort and Relational Warmth. Across all eight sessions, Android's steady eye gaze and nodding gestures created what participants later described as a *"relaxed atmosphere."* Several noted a surprising sense of comfort and quickly normalized the idea of confiding in a machine. P003 shared a personal routine:

"I started swimming after turning 60, it's been about five years now. I'm still not very good at the crawl, but after I finish and get into the bath, I feel calm."

This seemingly mundane utterance maps onto the *curiosity* and *love* peaks in Fig. 3, supporting the quantitative trend toward positive, self-regulatory talk.

Reminiscence and Processing of Loss. When sadness surfaced, the robot sometimes matched the tone effectively. P001, reflecting on bereavement, shared:

---

[2] All Japanese originals are archived in an online appendix; only English translations appear in the main text to conserve space.

> "Since my mother passed away, the only time I feel calm is when I'm at the mahjong table."

Here, Android sustained a five-turn grief narrative, demonstrating alignment with *sadness*. In contrast, P002's account of losing her husband received only a neutral response:

> "Twelve years ago, I lost my husband to lung cancer... That was definitely the hardest time."

These mixed outcomes align with the system's low agreement rate for *sadness* (33%) and reveal limits in nuanced affective responsiveness.

Shared Joy and Relational Identity. Grand-parenting stories offered opportunities for joy and relational pride. P004 recalled story about her grand-kid:

> "He said he needed new tabi socks, so I offered him mine from my kimono days. He said, 'No way!'"

The robot's enthusiastic reply sustained the affective tone, reflecting the high *joy* and *gratitude* scores observed for P004 in Fig. 5.

Misalignment and Emotional Incongruence. Although most exchanges were fluid, occasional mismatches occurred. In one case, the robot gave an irrelevant response, prompting blunt correction. Out of 336 turns, only 7 contained clear errors. For instance, speech recognition misinterpreted P006's hobby "詰碁" (Go puzzles) as a dessert recipe. She replied:

> "That's tasty, but I meant the board game."

Rather than expressing frustration, she redirected the conversation a pattern reflected in 58% of negative turns shifting to positive sentiment. The low incidence of anger or disapproval (Fig. 3) suggests participants often responded to limitations with humor, or topic changes. These findings underscore that beyond emotional tone, contextual relevance is crucial; without it, the robot's affect may feel hollow, diminishing user engagement.

Post-interaction Reflections and Sentiment Trends
Sentiment analysis of the eight post-interaction interviews ($N = 4,716$ words) revealed predominantly positive polarity (M = 0.57, SD = 0.12). Most participants described the encounter as enjoyable and emotionally engaging. As one noted, "It was fun ... I really enjoyed it. If I had to rank it, I'd put it at the top" (P8, compound = 0.72). Others expressed nuanced views, recognizing the robot's limitations: "She responds better to pleasant stories. When I mentioned my husband's death she said nothing ... Maybe she doesn't like sad things?" (P2, compound = 0.65). Despite these gaps, participants generally perceived the robot as friendly and emotionally supportive.

Quantitatively, expressed *sadness* during dialogue (Fig. 5) correlated negatively with interview polarity ($\rho = -.64$, $p = .09$). Yet participants who disclosed loss (e.g., P2, P8) still reported positive impressions echoing the rebound trend in Fig. 4. These self-reports support our central claim: *older adults experienced Android as a supportive partner, despite and sometimes because of its limited affective range.* Their curiosity about the robot's "personality" further underscores the potential for emotionally responsive robots in eldercare contexts.

5 Discussion

Key Findings Relative to Research Question. We examined how older adults perceive and emotionally respond to a humanoid robot that both *displays* and *interprets* affect. Three key patterns emerged. First, participants showed **rapid social acceptance**, with all eight describing the robot as "friendly" or "easy to talk to" within minutes. Second, conversations prompted **deep self-disclosure**, as six participants voluntarily shared emotionally significant life events, including bereavement and family pride. Third, moments of **fragile empathy** arose when negative emotions were unacknowledged, leading some to describe the robot as "too cheerful" or "mechanical." These findings echo prior work showing that non-verbal cues like gaze and timing can evoke perceived empathy, even without true emotional understanding [20].

Breakdowns occurred briefly when (a) valence switched mid-turn or (b) the user's utterance exceeded 30 s, exhausting the GPT context window. Such surface-level affect can *backfire* if the response tone lags the user's mood [19,21]. While static affective strategies can provide short term comfort, sustained interaction requires contextual sensitivity, particularly in domains such as elder care, where emotional nuance is paramount.

Design Implications. We propose three design recommendations for improving affect adaptive dialogue with older adults. First, systems should implement an **adaptive prompt width** strategy minimizing conversational history during neutral exchanges, and dynamically expanding it when deeper or emotionally significant topics arise. Second, **prosodic alignment** is essential: facial expressions should be synchronized with speech synthesis that reflects the appropriate emotional tone. Participants were generally tolerant of minor lexical inaccuracies but reacted negatively to mismatched vocal prosody. Third, we suggest **memory scaffolding** that retains user specific facts such as names or hobbies, yet surfaces them selectively and contextually to avoid perceptions of over personalization or intrusiveness.

This study, while offering useful insights, has several limitations. First, the small sample size (8 participants) and the qualitative nature of many findings mean that results should be interpreted as exploratory. A larger study would be needed to generalize these findings to the broader elderly population. Additionally, all participants were from a single region and shared similar socio-cultural backgrounds; cultural factors can shape how people perceive and respond to robots. What is warmly accepted in one context may be viewed differently elsewhere, underscoring the need for cross-cultural research. Another limitation is the single condition study design. We did not compare the emotionally intelligent robot to a non emotive control. Thus, we cannot isolate the specific impact of affect adaptivity in this pilot. Future studies should include such a baseline to quantify the benefits of emotional responsiveness.

In addition, future research should explore the use of personalized memory systems. Participants frequently referenced personal histories, family relationships, and daily routines topics that could serve as anchors for continuity over time. Even lightweight memory (e.g.:remembering previous topics or names) may enhance feelings of connection and support relational identity construction. However, memory must be carefully calibrated to avoid privacy concerns and ethical dilemmas around anthropomorphism and emotional dependency [17].

6 Conclusions

Themes of reminiscence, philosophical reflection, and identity construction emerged naturally during interaction, suggesting that older adults are willing to share rich, emotionally charged content even with artificial agents. This presents a dual challenge: while such disclosures offer opportunities for deep affective engagement, the robot's inability to respond meaningfully in these moments can undermine perceived authenticity. Prior work highlights the need for "empathic attunement" in conversational agents [22]; our findings reinforce that timing, tone, and responsiveness are critical during emotionally sensitive exchanges.

This pilot offers the first empirical look at older adults interacting with a hyper-realistic android guided by a closed-loop LLM pipeline. While participants engaged openly, they also quickly detected empathic lapses highlighting that *credible* empathy requires not only linguistic fluency, but well-timed prosody and cultural sensitivity. By identifying where breakdowns occur, this study offers a concrete testbed for advancing emotionally intelligent eldercare robots.

In summary, this study reveals both the potential and the limitations of current affective robotics. While participants responded positively to the emotional cues of Android, the gaps in contextual responsiveness and semantic depth illustrate the road still ahead. Building emotionally credible robots requires not just better AI but better insight into the emotional lives they are meant to support.

Acknowledgments. This work was supported by the European Union's Horizon 2020 program (Grant No. 101016453, e-VITA) and Japan's Ministry of Internal Affairs and Communication (Grant No. JPJ000595). We thank the e-VITA consortium and Tohoku University's Smart-Aging Research Center for their support. The content reflects the authors' views; the EU and MIC are not responsible for any use of the information herein.

References

1. About the human rights of older persons, UN (2023). https://www.ohchr.org/en/special-procedures/ie-older-persons/about-human-rights-older-persons
2. Annual Report on the Ageing Society 2024 (Cabinet Office of Japan). https://www8.cao.go.jp/kourei/english/annualreport/2024/pdf/2024.pdf
3. Pandey, A.K., Gelin, R.: A mass-produced sociable humanoid robot: pepper: the first machine of its kind. IEEE Robot. Autom. Mag. **25**(3), 40–48 (2018). https://doi.org/10.1109/MRA.2018.2833157
4. Thalmann, N.M., Mishra, N., Tulsulkar, G.: Nadine the social robot: three case studies in everyday life. In: Li, H., et al. (eds.) ICSR 2021. LNCS (LNAI), vol. 13086, pp. 107–116. Springer, Cham (2021). https://doi.org/10.1007/978-3-030-90525-5_10
5. Jeffers, A., et al.: Impact of social isolation during the COVID-19 pandemic on mental health, substance use, and homelessness: qualitative interviews with behavioral health providers. Int. J. Environ. Res. Public Health **19**(19), 121 (2022). https://doi.org/10.3390/ijerph191912120
6. Rietz, F., Sutherland, A., Bensch, S., Wermter, S., Hellström, T.: WoZ4U: an open-source wizard-of-oz interface for easy, efficient and robust HRI experiments. Front. Robot. AI **8**, 668057 (2021). https://doi.org/10.3389/frobt.2021.668057
7. Mishra, C., Verdonschot, R., Hagoort, P., Skantze, G.: Real-time emotion generation in human-robot dialogue using large language models. Front. Robot. AI **10**, 1271610 (2023). https://doi.org/10.3389/frobt.2023.1271610
8. Zhang, C., Chen, J., Li, J., Peng, Y., Mao, Z.: Large language models for human–robot interaction: a review. Biomimetic Intell. Robot. **3**, 100131 (2023). https://doi.org/10.1016/j.birob.2023.100131
9. Castellano, G., De Carolis, B., Macchiarulo, N., Pino, O.: Detecting emotions during cognitive stimulation training with the pepper robot. In: Palli, G., Melchiorri, C., Meattini, R. (eds.) Human-Friendly Robotics 2021. Springer Proceedings in Advanced Robotics, vol. 23. Springer, Cham (2022). https://doi.org/10.1007/978-3-030-96359-0_5
10. Abdollahi, H., Mahoor, M.H., Zandie, R., Siewierski, J., Qualls, S.H.: Artificial emotional intelligence in socially assistive robots for older adults: a pilot study. IEEE Trans. Affect. Comput. **14**(3), 2020–2032 (2022). https://doi.org/10.1109/TAFFC.2022.3143803
11. Irfan, B., Kuoppamäki, S., Hosseini, A., et al.: Between reality and delusion: challenges of applying large language models to companion robots for open-domain dialogues with older adults. Auton. Robots **49**, 9 (2025). https://doi.org/10.1007/s10514-025-10190-y
12. Khoo, W., et al.: Spill the tea: when robot conversation agents support well-being for older adults. In: ACM/IEEE International Conference on Human-Robot Interaction (HRI 2023 Companion). ACM, New York (2023)
13. Sato, W., Namba, S., Yang, D., Nishida, S., Ishi, C., Minato, T.: An android for emotional interaction: spatiotemporal validation of its facial expressions. Front. Psychol. **12**, 800657 (2022). https://doi.org/10.3389/fpsyg.2021.800657
14. Carros, F., et al.: Not that uncanny after all? an ethnographic study on android robots perception of older adults in Germany and Japan. In: Cavallo, F., et al. (eds.) Social Robotics. ICSR 2022, Lecture Notes in Computer Science, vol. 13818. Springer, Cham (2022). https://doi.org/10.1007/978-3-031-24670-8_51

15. Kumazaki, H., et al.: How the realism of robot is needed for individuals with autism spectrum disorders in an interview setting. Front. Psychiatry **10**, 486 (2019). https://doi.org/10.3389/fpsyt.2019.00486
16. Yoshikawa, M., Matsumoto, Y., Sumitani, M., Ishiguro, H.: Development of an android robot for psychological support in medical and welfare fields. In: 2011 IEEE International Conference on Robotics and Biomimetics, ROBIO 2011, pp. 600–605. IEEE, Phuket, Thailand (2011). https://doi.org/10.1109/ROBIO.2011.6181654
17. Friedman, C.: Ethical concerns with replacing human relations with humanoid robots: an ubuntu perspective. AI Ethics **3**, 527–538 (2023). https://doi.org/10.1007/s43681-022-00186-0
18. Ahmed, E., Buruk, O., Hamari, J.: Human–robot companionship: current trends and future agenda. Int. J. Soc. Robot. **16**, 1809–1860 (2024). https://doi.org/10.1007/s12369-024-01160-y
19. Mhlanga, D.: artificial intelligence in elderly care: navigating ethical and responsible AI adoption for seniors. In: Working paper, No. 4675564. Available at SSRN (2023). https://doi.org/10.2139/ssrn.4675564, https://ssrn.com/abstract=4675564
20. Urakami, J., Seaborn, K.: Nonverbal cues in human–robot interaction: a communication studies perspective. ACM Trans. Hum.-Robot Interact. **12**, 1–21 (2023). https://doi.org/10.1145/3570169
21. Dai, N., et al.: AI-assisted flexible electronics in humanoid robot heads for natural and authentic facial expressions. Innovation (Camb) **6**, 100752 (2025). https://doi.org/10.1016/j.xinn.2024.100752
22. Jolibois, S.C., Ito, A., Nose, T.: The development of an emotional embodied conversational agent and the evaluation of the effect of response delay on user impression. Appl. Sci. **15**, 4256 (2025). https://doi.org/10.3390/app15084256
23. Yang, Y., Wang, C., Xiang, X., An, R.: AI applications to reduce loneliness among older adults: a systematic review of effectiveness and technologies. Healthcare (Basel) **13**, 446 (2025). https://doi.org/10.3390/healthcare13050446
24. Braun, V., Clarke, V.: Using thematic analysis in psychology. Qual. Res. Psychol. **3**(2), 77–101 (2006). https://doi.org/10.1191/1478088706qp063oa
25. Google Cloud: Speech-to-text API documentation. https://cloud.google.com/speech-to-text. Accessed 12 Jan 2025
26. Kawahara, Y., Komachi, M.: Pre-training Japanese BERT on a corpus of web and books. In: Calzolari, N. et al. (eds.) Proceedings of LREC 2020, ELRA, Marseille (2020)
27. Hutto, C.J., Gilbert, E.: VADER: a parsimonious rule-based model for sentiment analysis of social media text. In: Proceedings of ICWSM 2014, pp. 216–225. AAAI Press, Palo Alto (2014)
28. OpenAI: GPT-3.5 model card and technical report (2023). https://platform.openai.com/docs/model-index-for-researchers. Accessed 12 Jan 2025

A Multimodal Emotion Recognition Approach for Socially Assistive Robots

Christian Tamantini[1,2](✉), Martina Fabrizi[1], Loredana Zollo[1], and Francesca Cordella[1]

[1] Department of Engineering, Research Unit of Advanced Robotics and Human-Centred Technologies, Università Campus Bio-Medico di Roma, Rome 00128, Italy
[2] Institute of Cognitive Sciences and Technologies, National Research Council of Italy, Rome 00196, Italy
christian.tamantini@cnr.it

Abstract. Social assistive robots need emotion recognition to enable adaptive and user-centered interactions. Traditional facial expression recognition is often unreliable, especially in real-world settings. Moreover, most literature studies face the classification of binary conditions considering the Russell affective state model. This study proposes a multimodal emotion recognition system, integrating physiological monitoring with kinematic analysis from RGB-D skeletal tracking to capture both autonomic and postural markers of emotion to estimate the seven basic emotions of Ekman's model.

Results show that Random Forest achieves the highest accuracy ($71.30 \pm 3.47\%$) when using Multimodal features to classify the seven basic emotions, significantly outperforming physiological and kinematic data alone. The findings confirm that body movements and autonomic responses provide complementary information, enhancing emotion classification. This approach offers a robust alternative to methods that rely on a single modality, improving the feasibility of real-time emotion recognition in social robotics.

Keywords: Emotion Recognition · Affective Computing · Social Robotics

1 Introduction

The use of social robots for assisting elderly individuals and people with disabilities at home is rapidly expanding [10, 21]. These systems have demonstrated a positive impact on reducing loneliness by providing continuous engagement and entertainment [3].

A key factor in enhancing human-robot interaction at home is the capability of the robot to recognize and respond to emotions [16, 20]. Identifying emotional states during daily activities provides insights into psychological well-being and stress levels. Incorporating emotion recognition allows robots to adapt interactions based on user mood, making their behavior more engaging and natural [19]. This capability is particularly valuable in long-term monitoring, where emotional trends may indicate psychological or behavioural changes [1,13].

Scientific models have been proposed to classify emotions, such as Ekman's and Russell's models. Ekman's model defines six universal emotions: joy, sadness, anger, fear, surprise, and disgust, often accompanied by a neutral emotional state [22], while Russell's circumplex model organizes emotions along the valence-arousal dimensions [4]. These models serve as the foundation for developing emotion recognition systems.

Emotion recognition has been widely explored, with various stimuli and sensing modalities employed for classification. Facial expression recognition (FER) is a dominant approach, achieving high accuracy in controlled settings [2]. However, FER presents significant challenges in home environments, where natural interactions introduce occlusions, variable lighting, and diverse head poses, affecting accuracy and requiring large, diverse datasets for robustness [7].

To address these limitations, researchers have explored physiological signals from wearable sensors for emotion recognition. Electrocardiogram (ECG) and galvanic skin response (GSR) have effectively captured heart activity and skin conductance variations, which are key indicators of emotional arousal. Studies report high classification accuracy in binary valence and arousal classification tasks (up to 92%) using ECG [9,18], while GSR has been successful in detecting emotional intensity but struggles with differentiating emotions of similar arousal [5,11]. Despite their effectiveness, physiological signal-based methods lack movement analysis, which could enhance emotion recognition accuracy and generalizability in human-robot interactions.

Recently, movement analysis has gained attention as an alternative, exploiting body posture and movement patterns to infer affective states. Research has established strong links between kinematics and emotions, with posture and upper-body gestures playing a significant role. RGB-D-based skeletal tracking, particularly with Kinect sensors, was introduced for emotion classification. The particularity of these studies lies in the fact that participants are asked to physically interpret the target emotions, and an attempt is made to use postural information to identify the affective state. Kinematic features were extracted from the kinematic reconstruction obtained from the vision systems, achieving accuracies of 61.3% and 63% when the system was asked to discriminate six basic emotions into [14] and [17], respectively. By reducing the number of emotions to be recognised to five, kinematic features were introduced in [8] to identify the emotion played by actors with an accuracy of up to 93%. While reducing the number of classes may increase the performance of the presented classification system, it limits the pool of emotions that can occur during an interaction scenario with robotic systems. It is therefore of interest to investigate how the integration of physiological information obtained through wearable systems can help to complement the information available from vision systems to increase the recognition performance of a subject's emotional state.

This study investigates integrating physiological monitoring and movement analysis to enhance emotion recognition in social robotics. Unlike previous studies that rely solely on wearable biosensors or kinematic tracking, we combine wearable physiological sensors with an RGB-D camera-based skeleton tracking system to capture both autonomic responses and expressive body movements. Through a structured experimental study, we evaluate the effectiveness of different machine learning models in classifying seven basic emotions and analyzing the contribution of physiological and movement-based features. By systematically comparing different feature sets, we aim to determine an optimal multimodal configuration, improving emotion recognition robustness for future integration in socially interactive robots intended to work in real-world settings.

2 Materials and Methods

2.1 Multimodal Monitoring

Human motion and physiological signals provide complementary insights into emotional states. Body posture and movement patterns convey expressive cues, while cardiorespiratory activity and skin conductance reflect autonomic responses. RGB-D skeleton tracking allows for non-intrusive motion analysis, capturing joint displacements and posture dynamics. Meanwhile, heart rate (HR), respiratory rate (RR), and GSR provide involuntary indicators of arousal and affective states. By integrating kinematic and physiological monitoring, the proposed approach aims to enhance emotion recognition accuracy, leveraging both external behavioral expressions and internal physiological responses for multimodal affective computing in social robotics.

2.2 Feature Extraction

To enable multimodal emotion recognition, physiological and kinematic features were extracted from the recorded signals. Physiological data, acquired through wearable sensors, included features derived from HR, RR, and GSR. For HR and RR, we computed mean, standard deviation, minimum, maximum, and mean difference to capture both baseline values and short-term variations. GSR features were split into tonic and phasic components, namely the skin conductance level (SCL) and the skin conductance response (SCR), respectively, with additional measures such as the number of peaks, peak amplitude, peak variability, and signal power to reflect autonomic arousal responses.

Kinematic features were extracted from skeleton tracking data obtained via RGB-D imaging, focusing on upper-body motion. We computed the mean, standard deviation, minimum, maximum, and range of five key joint angles to describe postural adjustments and expressive movements. Additionally, movement dynamics were quantified using mean angular derivatives, while postural symmetry, mean joint distances and body volume were included to assess variations in body stance.

These multimodal features were used to train and evaluate classification models, allowing for a comprehensive representation of both autonomic and postural correlates of emotional states.

2.3 Supervised Model for Emotion Recognition

Emotion recognition is formulated as a supervised classification problem, where multimodal features extracted from physiological signals and movement data are used to predict the user's emotional state. Given that emotions are inherently complex and influenced by multiple factors, the classification task requires models that can effectively capture nonlinear relationships and high-dimensional patterns in multimodal data.

In this study, the system is designed to classify seven basic emotions, drawing from Ekman's model of universal emotions. Joy is typically associated with increased body movement, open postures, and heightened physiological arousal, whereas sadness is characterized by reduced movement amplitude, contracted postures, and decreased autonomic activation. Anger is often expressed through tense posture, abrupt movements, and elevated heart rate, while fear manifests through defensive body positioning, increased heart rate, and rapid breathing. Surprise is linked to sudden posture adjustments and momentary physiological activation, whereas disgust is displayed through aversive gestures and moderate changes in physiological signals. Lastly, neutral represents a baseline state with no pronounced emotional expressions or significant physiological variations.

To classify these emotions, a comparative analysis of multiple machine learning classifiers with distinct characteristics was carried out in this study. More in detail, the supervised classifiers implemented in this work were the following:

- Support Vector Machine (SVM) with a radial basis function kernel is employed due to its robustness in high-dimensional spaces and ability to capture complex decision boundaries. SVM is well-suited for emotion classification, as it can handle nonlinear separability, which is often observed in physiological and kinematic features [6].
- K-Nearest Neighbors (KNN) is used as a distance-based classifier, leveraging the similarity between feature vectors to assign emotional labels. KNN is simple and effective, particularly in settings where local patterns in the feature space are meaningful for classification [4].
- Random Forest (RF), an ensemble learning method, is chosen for its high interpretability and ability to model interactions between features. RF is particularly effective in handling heterogeneous data sources, such as physiological and kinematic features, making it a strong candidate for multimodal emotion classification [15].

2.4 Experimental Validation

The experimental setup used in this study, shown in Fig. 1, is the multimodal monitoring system composed of an RGB-D camera and wearable physiological sensors. To capture body movement and posture, we employed the Kinect v2 sensor, positioned in front of the participant to record the upper body movements in a standing position. The RGB-D camera embedded in the device provides both color and depth data, enabling real-time 3D skeleton tracking. The system estimates joint positions and movement kinematics at a sampling frequency 30 Hz with a depth resolution of 640 × 480 pixels.

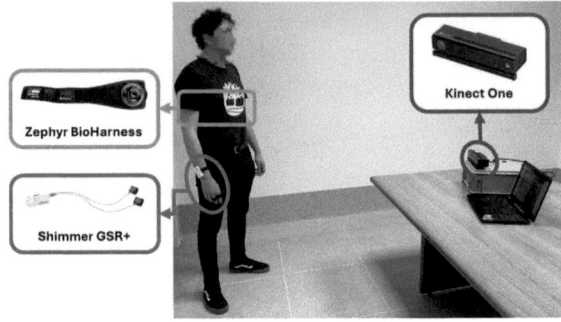

Fig. 1. Experimental Setup used to collect the multimodal data.

Two wearable physiological sensors were used to measure autonomic responses related to emotional states:

- Zephyr BioHarness 3.0 was employed for cardiorespiratory monitoring. This chest-worn device provides HR, heart rate variability (HRV), and RR. The sampling frequency 250 Hz for HR 100 Hz for RR. The device features an elastic band with embedded sensors to ensure secure and comfortable wearability during movement.
- Shimmer GSR+ was used to record GSR. The system consists of two electrodes placed on the index and middle fingers and a data acquisition unit worn on the wrist. It operates at a frequency of 52.1 Hz, measuring skin conductance variations associated with emotional arousal.

Motion and physiological signals were acquired along with their timestamps using dedicated software, and subsequently aligned during post-processing.

A total of eight healthy participants (three females, five males, mean age 25.75 ± 3.10 years) were recruited for the study. Before starting the experiment, each participant provided basic demographic information and was introduced to the seven target emotions. Example images depicting these emotions were presented to ensure a consistent reference for expression.

The experimental session consisted of the following steps:

1. Baseline Recording: Participants were instructed to assume a neutral standing posture for 20 s, serving as a baseline reference.

2. Emotion Elicitation: Participants were asked to perform each of the seven emotions through upper body movements and posture, based on their own interpretation rather than predefined stereotypes. While this does not reflect spontaneous emotional responses, it provides a controlled yet individualized proxy.
3. Repetition and Randomization: The baseline and emotion expression trials were repeated three times, with the order of emotions randomized in each session to prevent adaptation effects.

Each recording session lasted approximately 20 min per participant, ensuring a balanced dataset across subjects and emotions. Figure 2 shows a representative participant interpreting the seven emotions analyzed in this work along with the skeleton reconstruction obtained from the RGB-D camera.

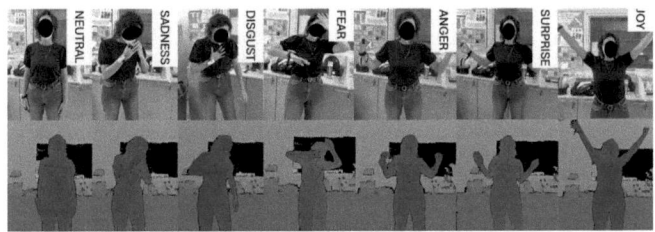

Fig. 2. Illustration of the emotion expression protocol used in the study. The top row displays a participant performing seven basic emotions: Neutral, Sadness, Disgust, Fear, Anger, Surprise, and Joy. The bottom row shows the corresponding depth images acquired with the RGB-D camera, along with the reconstructed skeletal model used for kinematic feature extraction.

Model Validation. In order to evaluate the efficacy of the proposed multimodal emotion recognition system, a supervised classification approach was employed, and the models were validated using 10-fold Stratified K-Fold cross-validation. The selection of this method was driven by the necessity to ensure the maintenance of the distribution of emotional classes across all training and testing folds, thus preventing biases that could arise from class imbalance. The Stratified K-Fold approach is particularly well-suited to emotion recognition tasks, as it provides a reliable estimate of model performance while ensuring that each emotion category is adequately represented in both the training and testing phases.

We evaluated the model using different feature sets corresponding to the available physiological and kinematic data. The classification models were trained and tested on features extracted from BioHarness, GSR, Kinect-based movement data, and a combination of all modalities. This ablation study allowed us to investigate how different sources of information contribute to emotion classification accuracy and whether the fusion of physiological and kinematic features enhances overall performance.

To analyze the classification capabilities of different approaches, we compared the three aforementioned machine learning models: SVM with a radial basis function kernel, KNN, and RF. Each classifier was trained on normalized feature sets, ensuring comparability across physiological and movement-based features. Model performance was assessed by computing classification accuracy across different validation folds, providing insights into the effectiveness of each feature combination and classification algorithm.

Performance Indicators. To evaluate the performance of the emotion recognition models, standard classification metrics were computed to provide a comprehensive assessment of the system accuracy and reliability. Given the nature of the task, which involves the classification of multiple emotional states, we relied on accuracy, precision, recall, F1-score, and confusion matrices as key indicators of model effectiveness.

Accuracy was used as the primary measure to quantify the overall correctness of predictions across all emotional classes. It is defined as the proportion of samples that have been correctly classified over the total number of predictions made by the model. This provides a general measure of the performance of the model. Furthermore, we computed precision, recall, and F1 scores for each emotion category. Precision measures the proportion of correctly predicted instances of a given class relative to the total instances predicted as that class, indicating how specific the model is in assigning labels. Recall, also known as sensitivity, evaluates how well the model identifies all instances of a given emotion by computing the proportion of correctly classified samples within that class. The F1-score offers a balanced measure that considers both precision and recall, providing a more reliable metric when class distribution is not perfectly uniform.

Furthermore, the confusion matrix was analyzed, providing detailed insights into model errors by displaying the number of correct and misclassified predictions for each emotion. This analysis enabled the identification of frequent errors in classification, including emotions that are often confused with one another, and provided insights into the potential limitations of the system.

Statistical Analysis. Statistical analysis was conducted to determine whether significant differences exist among the implemented classification models and to evaluate the impact of feature ablation on system performance. To make a comparison between multiple classifiers, the Wilcoxon signed-rank test was used, as this is a non-parametric alternative that does not assume that the data are normally distributed. This test will assess whether performance differences between models are statistically significant. The Bonferroni correction was applied to adjust the significance threshold and control the risk of Type I errors. Furthermore, the Wilcoxon signed-rank test for paired samples was performed to analyze the impact of feature ablation. This will involve comparing the system accuracy before and after the removal of specific modalities. The significance level was set at alpha = 0.05, with Bonferroni adjustment applied based on the number of comparisons. This statistical evaluation will provide insights into which classifiers perform significantly better and whether the exclusion of physiological or kinematic features has a measurable impact on the system accuracy, guiding the identification of the most effective multimodal emotion recognition approach.

3 Results and Discussion

Figure 3 presents the comparison of classification models that have been trained on the multimodal feature set, which integrates physiological and kinematic data. The findings demonstrate that RF consistently exhibits superior performance in comparison to SVM and KNN, as indicated by various evaluation metrics, including accuracy, precision, recall, and F1-score. The statistical analysis confirms that RF significantly surpasses the other models, highlighting its ability to effectively manage high-dimensional, heterogeneous data. The superior performance of RF is likely due to its ability to capture complex, nonlinear relationships and assign importance to the most relevant features, which is particularly advantageous when dealing with multimodal affective data. In light of these findings, RF was selected as the primary classifier for further analysis of the impact of different feature sets.

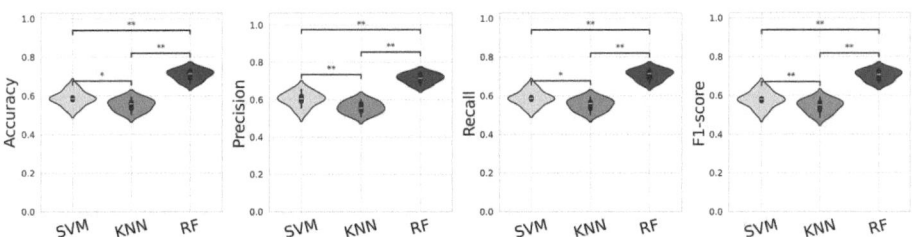

Fig. 3. Performance comparison of the three classification models using the Multimodal feature set across validation folds. A Wilcoxon signed-rank test was used to compare model performances, with p-values adjusted using Bonferroni. Asterisks indicate significance levels as follows: * $(1 \cdot 10^{-2} < p \leq 5 \cdot 10^{-2})$, ** $(1 \cdot 10^{-3} < p \leq 1 \cdot 10^{-2})$.

The results of the ablation analysis are presented in Fig. 4. This analysis investigates the contribution of each feature set to emotion classification performance using RF. The findings suggest that the integration of physiological and kinematic data in the Multimodal feature set results in significantly higher classification accuracy (71.30 ± 3.47) compared to unimodal feature sets with p-values of $9.9 \cdot 10^{-4}$ and $1.9 \cdot 10^{-3}$ when comparing Multimodal with Physio and Kinematic feature sets, respectively. Among the unimodal configurations, kinematic features demonstrate not statistically significant but still marginally superior performance (63.13 ± 3.38) compared to physiological features (61.01 ± 4.12), with a p-value of $5.9 \cdot 10^{-1}$, thereby reinforcing the notion that body posture and movement encompass crucial affective cues. However, physiological signals remain valuable as they provide autonomic responses that are not captured through motion analysis. The BioHarness and GSR feature sets, when used in isolation, yield the lowest accuracy (42.37 ± 3.75 and 39.76 ± 2.36, respectively), suggesting that a single physiological sensor alone is not sufficient for robust emotion recognition. Statistical analysis confirms significant differences between the multimodal approach and all unimodal conditions, emphasizing the necessity of integrating both physiological and kinematic information for optimal classification performance.

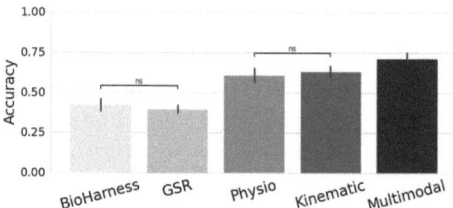

Fig. 4. Comparison of classification accuracy across different feature sets using the Random Forest classifier. The bars represent mean accuracy with standard deviation, while statistical significance is determined using the Wilcoxon signed-rank test with Bonferroni correction. The results highlight that Physio and Kinematic feature sets significantly outperform unimodal BioHarness and GSR, while the Multimodal feature set achieves the highest accuracy.

Figure 5 presents the confusion matrices obtained during the RF validation process using Physiological, Kinematic, and Multimodal feature sets. The physiological model performs well in recognizing fear and sadness, likely due to their strong association with heart rate and respiratory variations. However, it is observed to encounter difficulties in differentiating between Surprise and Anger, which are characterized by distinct body movements. The Kinematic model demonstrates a particular aptitude for the classification of Joy, Anger, and Surprise, which are typically conveyed through expressive postural and gestural changes. The Multimodal model demonstrates the highest level of overall accuracy, achieving a substantial reduction in misclassifications across all emotions. This finding corroborates the hypothesis that the amalgamation of physiological and kinematic data furnishes a more comprehensive depiction of emotional states, thereby facilitating the development of a more reliable and accurate emotion recognition system.

In summary, these results demonstrate that RF is the most effective classifier for multimodal emotion recognition and that the integration of physiological and kinematic data significantly improves classification accuracy. The previously mentioned works from the literature exhibit slightly lower accuracies when the number of emotion classes to be recognised is all six basic emotions plus the seventh neutral one (61.3% and 63.0% in [14] and [17], respectively). Furthermore, another point to note in this study is that physiological cues turn out to be predictors of emotions even when the user is asked to interpret a certain emotion,

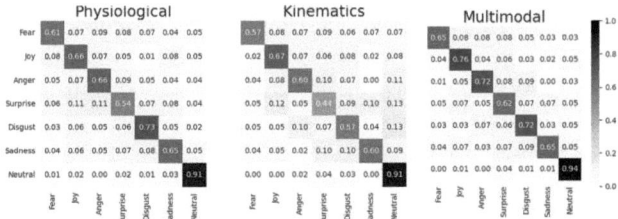

Fig. 5. Normalized confusion matrices for emotion classification using different feature sets with the Random Forest classifier. Each matrix represents the proportion of correctly and incorrectly classified samples for each emotion category. The Multimodal approach achieves the highest classification accuracy across all emotions, particularly improving the recognition of Joy, Anger, and Surprise. Neutral remains the most easily distinguishable emotion across all modalities.

not only when ad-hoc stimuli are administered [4,12]. Multimodal analysis thus allows for a holistic understanding of the subject, in structured environments such as the experimental settings in which these methodologies are trained and tested as well as in real-world scenarios, highlighting its importance in the context of social care robotics. Real-time emotion recognition can indeed enable adaptive and user-centred interactions, improving the robot ability to respond appropriately to the user's emotional state.

3.1 Limitations

While the results demonstrate the effectiveness of the proposed multimodal emotion recognition approach, several limitations must be acknowledged. First, the study involved a small sample of participants with similar age and demographic background, which limits the generalizability of the findings. Emotional expressions and physiological responses are known to be influenced by individual traits and cultural norms, potentially affecting the interpretation and consistency of emotion-related signals. Future studies should include more diverse participant groups to account for such variability and improve the robustness of the system across different populations.

Second, the experimental protocol required participants to interpret the seven basic emotions, which may not fully reflect natural emotional expressions encountered in real-world settings. In spontaneous emotional states, body language and physiological signals might manifest differently, potentially affecting the model ability to generalize beyond the controlled environment. Further research should investigate emotion recognition in real-life, unconstrained interactions, particularly in the context of social robotics applications.

4 Conclusions

This study explored a multimodal emotion recognition approach for potential applications in social robotics, integrating physiological and kinematic monitoring to classify seven basic emotions. Participants were recorded using wearable sensors (heart rate, respiratory rate, and galvanic skin response) and an RGB-D camera (for skeletal motion tracking), with extracted features used to train machine learning models.

The results showed that RF achieved the best performance, with Multimodal features yielding $71.30 \pm 3.47\%$ accuracy, significantly outperforming kinematic and physiological data alone. The ablation study confirmed that body motion and autonomic responses provide complementary information, with Fear and Sadness being better captured by physiological signals, while Joy, Anger, and Surprise benefited more from kinematic features.

Future work should prioritize the recognition of spontaneous emotions, involve larger and more diverse participant groups, and include end-users, i.e., older adults, in the validation of the technology. A further development foresees the integration of vocal features (e.g., pitch, prosody, speech rate) as additional input modalities. This multimodal approach could improve the robustness and ecological validity of emotion recognition in real-world assistive contexts.

Acknowledgments. This work was supported partly by the Italian Ministry of Research, under the complementary actions to the NRRP "Fit4MedRob - Fit for Medical Robotics" Grant (PNC0000007), (CUP: B53C22006990001) and partly by the National Institute for Insurance against Accidents at Work (INAIL) prosthetic center with the BioArmNext project (CUP: E58D19000650005).

Disclosure of Interests. The authors declare no conflicts of interest.

References

1. Beraldo, G., Tamantini, C., Umbrico, A., Orlandini, A.: Fostering behavior change through cognitive social robotics. In: International Conference on Social Robotics, pp. 279–291. Springer (2024)
2. Canal, F.Z., et al.: A survey on facial emotion recognition techniques: a state-of-the-art literature review. Inf. Sci. **582**, 593–617 (2022)
3. Cesta, A., Cortellessa, G., Orlandini, A., Tiberio, L.: Long-term evaluation of a telepresence robot for the elderly: methodology and ecological case study. Int. J. Soc. Robot. **8**, 421–441 (2016)
4. Cittadini, R., Tamantini, C., Scotto di Luzio, F., Lauretti, C., Zollo, L., Cordella, F.: Affective state estimation based on Russell's model and physiological measurements. Sci. Rep. **13**(1), 9786 (2023)
5. Dissanayake, T., Rajapaksha, Y., Ragel, R., Nawinne, I.: An ensemble learning approach for electrocardiogram sensor based human emotion recognition. Sensors **19**(20), 4495 (2019)
6. Gouizi, K., Bereksi Reguig, F., Maaoui, C.: Emotion recognition from physiological signals. J. Med. Eng. Technol. **35**(6–7), 300–307 (2011)
7. Kang, D., et al.: Beyond superficial emotion recognition: modality-adaptive emotion recognition system. Expert Syst. Appl. **235**, 121097 (2024)
8. Kaza, K., et al.: Body motion analysis for emotion recognition in serious games. In: Antona, M., Stephanidis, C. (eds.) UAHCI 2016, Part II. LNCS, vol. 9738, pp. 33–42. Springer, Cham (2016). https://doi.org/10.1007/978-3-319-40244-4_4

9. Maaoui, C., Pruski, A.: Emotion recognition through physiological signals for human-machine communication. Cutting Edge Robot. **2010**(317–332), 11 (2010)
10. Mahmoudi Asl, A., Molinari Ulate, M., Franco Martin, M., van der Roest, H.: Methodologies used to study the feasibility, usability, efficacy, and effectiveness of social robots for elderly adults: scoping review. J. Med. Internet Res. **24**(8), e37434 (2022)
11. Nasoz, F., Alvarez, K., Lisetti, C.L., Finkelstein, N.: Emotion recognition from physiological signals using wireless sensors for presence technologies. Cogn. Technol. Work **6**, 4–14 (2004)
12. Pan, B., Hirota, K., Jia, Z., Dai, Y.: A review of multimodal emotion recognition from datasets, preprocessing, features, and fusion methods. Neurocomputing **561**, 126866 (2023)
13. Park, S., Whang, M.: Empathy in human-robot interaction: designing for social robots. Int. J. Environ. Res. Public Health **19**(3), 1889 (2022)
14. Piana, S., Stagliano, A., Odone, F., Verri, A., Camurri, A.: Real-time automatic emotion recognition from body gestures. arXiv preprint arXiv:1402.5047 (2014)
15. Pinto, G., Carvalho, J.M., Barros, F., Soares, S.C., Pinho, A.J., Brás, S.: Multimodal emotion evaluation: a physiological model for cost-effective emotion classification. Sensors **20**(12), 3510 (2020)
16. Rasouli, S., Gupta, G., Nilsen, E., Dautenhahn, K.: Potential applications of social robots in robot-assisted interventions for social anxiety. Int. J. Soc. Robot. **14**(5), 1–32 (2022)
17. Sapiński, T., Kamińska, D., Pelikant, A., Anbarjafari, G.: Emotion recognition from skeletal movements. Entropy **21**(7), 646 (2019)
18. Selvaraj, J., Murugappan, M., Wan, K., Yaacob, S.: Classification of emotional states from electrocardiogram signals: a non-linear approach based on Hurst. Biomed. Eng. Online **12**, 1–18 (2013)
19. Stock-Homburg, R.: Survey of emotions in human-robot interactions: perspectives from robotic psychology on 20 years of research. Int. J. Soc. Robot. **14**(2), 389–411 (2022)
20. Tamantini, C., et al.: Integrating physical and cognitive interaction capabilities in a robot-aided rehabilitation platform. IEEE Syst. J. **17**(4), 6516–6527 (2023)
21. Tamantini, C., Umbrico, A., Orlandini, A.: Repair platform: robot-aided personalized rehabilitation. In: International Conference of the Italian Association for Artificial Intelligence, pp. 301–314. Springer (2024)
22. Wang, Y., et al.: A systematic review on affective computing: emotion models, databases, and recent advances. Inf. Fusion **83**, 19–52 (2022)

Empathy in Child-Robot Interaction: The Role of Narrative Framing, Age, Gender, and Baseline Empathy

Marine Bruttin, Luca M. Leisten(✉), and Emily S. Cross

Social Brain Sciences Lab, Department of Humanities, Social, and Political Sciences,
ETH Zurich, Zürich, Switzerland
{luca.leisten,emily.cross}@gess.ethz.ch

Abstract. The integration of social robots into educational contexts is steadily increasing, as these agents are used to foster engagement, support personalized learning, and create interactive experiences. In these contexts, empathy towards a social robot is a crucial mechanism to build trust, motivation, and social connections. Narrative framing has been shown to support the elicitation of empathy. However, little is known about how children's empathy towards robots is affected by different narrative framing and how individual factors shape this relationship. Across two preregistered experiments, we investigated 7–15-year-olds' empathy towards a social robot in focus groups (Experiment 1; $n = 19$) and the effect of narrative framing (sad vs. neutral), baseline empathy, age, and gender thereon in an experimental study (Experiment 2; $n = 73$). Experiment 1 showed that robot perception, personal experiences, and social norms affected children's empathy towards a robot. Experiment 2 showed no significant effects of narrative framing, age, or baseline empathy on children's empathy towards the robot. However, varying the narrative framing of the robot resulted in gender differences in elicited empathy, with girls showing higher empathy than boys in the neutral narrative condition. Our findings indicate that contextual and relational cues might exert a stronger influence on children's empathic responses towards robots than developmental factors or dispositional traits specific to individual children. The two experiments that compose this study offer valuable insights into how empathy might be elicited through social robots. These insights hold promise for informing how best to design robotic agents that children can connect with in meaningful and effective ways in education and learning contexts.

Keywords: Human–Robot Interaction · Child–Robot Interaction · Empathy

1 Introduction

Social robots are becoming increasingly important in educational environments, where they are used to support learning and engagement [6]. In these contexts, empathy plays a vital role to strengthen social relationships, create supportive and cooperative interactions, build trust, and increase motivation and learning outcomes [15,45,51]. Empathy involves the ability to recognize and understand others' emotions, and responding appropriately to the affective states of others – whether through direct observation or imaginative processes (for a review see [45]). Recent studies show that people can experience empathy towards social robots, perceiving them as having emotional and mental states (e.g., [45,53,54]). This tendency seems rooted in our broader capacity to form emotional connections with non-human agents, as demonstrated by [52], a capacity that is especially pronounced in children, who often attribute emotions and intentions to toys during imaginative play [46]. In Human–Robot Interaction (HRI), empathy is a key mechanism for fostering social cooperation and prosocial behavior, with robots that elicit empathy shown to be more engaging and effective, especially in interactions with children [36,37].

Narrative framing - such as presenting one's backstory in a sad, neutral or happy light - has been shown to be a particularly effective way to affect people's empathy towards humans (for a review see [43,65]), but also social robots [58]. For example, [19] found a sad narrative framing to elicit significantly more helping behaviors in adults towards a robot compared to a happy narrative. Additionally, first-person narratives—where the robot "speaks" from its own perspective—tend to foster stronger emotional bonds than third-person accounts, which can feel more distant and objective [24,40,58]. Introspective dialogue to externalize a robot's internal reasoning represent another powerful tool for influencing empathy elicitation in human-robot interaction. [2] investigated this approach by enabling robots to articulate their inner states (such as conflicting goals or emotional dilemmas) through monologues. In their study involving children aged 10–15, this narrative strategy significantly enhanced children's empathic responses, particularly along the cognitive dimension of state empathy.

Empathy may not only be affected by conversational characteristics such as narrative framing, but also by individual factors, such as children's age, gender, and baseline empathy. For instance, empathy begins to develop early in life and continues to develop through infancy, childhood, and adolescence, shaped by both biological growth and social experiences [18,29]. The period between 7 and 14 years—spanning from middle childhood to early adolescence—is particularly significant for the development of empathy, as children undergo significant brain maturation related to their empathy development ([31]; for a review see [62]). The transition to adolescence also brings increased social pressure to conform to traditional gender roles, which may lead girls to develop and express higher empathy levels than boys [21]. Empirical findings support this pattern, with longitudinal studies showing an increase in empathy among girls between 7–14, contrasted with stable low levels of boys' empathy [31]. In the context of HRI, evidence suggest that gender may also influence how individuals perceive and respond to robots. For example, males have been found to be more sensitive to distinctions between robotic and human-like movements, whereas females tend to attribute more anthropomorphic qualities to robotic movements, regardless of how mechanical or natural the movements actually are [1].

Lastly, empathy is often conceptualized as a dispositional trait, whereby individuals scoring high on empathy measures are generally expected to respond strongly to a wide range of empathy inducing situations [22]. In HRI, [16] found that individuals with high trait empathic concern were more hesitant to strike a robot, particularly when it was accompanied by an emotional backstory. [2] found that trait cognitive empathy was a significant predictor of state cognitive empathy, as measured in 10–15-year-olds' interaction with a social robot. Those results suggest that people with stronger dispositional empathy may be more likely to extend empathic responses to robots. However, this area of research remains underexplored, and further studies are needed to better understand how baseline empathy and other individual factors such as age and gender influence empathy towards robots. In addition to these individual factors, children's perception of robots plays a crucial role in empathy elicitation. Rather than viewing robots as mere tools or toys, children often see them as social, relational and interactive beings with emotions, minds, and intentions [30]. This relational framing places robots in an "in-between" category of neither fully animate nor inanimate, fostering emotional engagement and the formation of social bonds [23,27]. When children relate to robots as social beings rather than objects they engage emotional and empathic processes similar to those used in human social bonds [30,35]. Gaining insights into how children empathize with robots is essential, not only for understanding the emotional dynamics of child–robot interaction, but also for informing the design of socially responsive and emotionally intelligent robots. Such technologies should not only instruct but also foster meaningful connections and interactions with children to effectively support their long-term engagement, sustained motivation, and improved learning outcomes [9,10,39,55].

1.1 The Present Study

In this preregistered, two-experiment paper, the primary goal was to (i) investigate children's empathy towards a social robot and to (ii) identify the effect of narrative type, age, gender, and baseline empathy thereon. Experiment 1 aimed to explore children's empathy towards social robots through qualitative focus groups. Experiment 2 experimentally tested children's empathy towards a social robot, examining how a sad versus neutral narrative affects children's empathy and how individual factors such as age, gender, and baseline empathy moderate this relationship. We used the social robots Blossom [59] and Furhat [20] that allow for customization in appearance and functionality, which make them particularly well suited for research on child–robot interaction (CRI), especially in educational and affective contexts.

We aimed to answer the following research questions: (i) How do children empathize with a social robot when it appears in distress and how do they justify (not) wanting to help the robot? (ii) How does narrative framing affect children's empathy towards a robot? (iii) How do age, gender, and baseline empathy affect children's empathy towards a robot in different narrative framings?

We hypothesized, that children show more empathy towards a robot in a sad narrative condition (**H1**). This is based on [63,65], who demonstrated that stories conveyed with a compassionate or vulnerable tone tend to evoke greater empathic responses than neutral accounts. Second, we hypothesized differences in children's empathy towards a social robot based on children's age [18,29], gender [21,31], and baseline empathy [16,22] as outlined above (**H2**). As prior work focused mainly on human-human interaction, adults, or reported mixed findings, we did not specify directional hypotheses for these factors.

2 Methods and Materials

2.1 Participants

Experiment 1: Focus Groups. A total of 19 participants between 10–15 years[1] (10 female, 9 male; $M = 12.1$, $SD = 1.67$) were recruited from a rural German secondary school. Fourteen children had prior contact with robots, mainly in restaurant contexts or as toys. Children were German native speakers. Prior to participation, parents and children aged 14 and above signed a consent form. The experiment was approved by the ETH Zurich's ethics committee (24 ETHICS-361).

Experiment 2: CRI. We collected a convenience sample of 73 participants between 7–14 years (36 female, 35 male; $M = 11.44$, $SD = 1.82$) from a rural German comprehensive school. Participants were required to have basic reading skills and were native German speakers. Prior to participation, parents and children aged 14 provided written consent. The experiment was approved by the ETH Zurich's ethics committee (25 ETHICS-045).

2.2 Robots

Experiment 1: Focus Groups. We used the open-source social robot Blossom, which is constructed from soft, handcrafted materials and has a compliant mechanical structure [59]. Blossom's modular design allows for customization in both appearance and functionality. Paired with its low complexity and low price point, these features make it highly interesting for applications in education contexts. We built our own Blossom robot, with a Grey, knitted shell, a blue scarf and yellow 3D-printed ears (Fig. 1). As the focus groups were part of a bigger project reported elsewhere [34], we also brought three other Blossoms with us, including a second knitted version, a cardboard version, and a shell-less version, showcasing the 3D-printed internal structure of the robot. Due to technical difficulties, the robots remained turned off during the sessions.

---

[1] The focus groups were part of a bigger project [34], and thus included children slightly older than our targeted age group.

Experiment 2: CRI. We used the Furhat robot[2] ([20]; Fig. 1), which consists of a human-like head with interchangeable masks and a torso. Its face is highly expressive and capable of displaying natural movements, such as blinking, micro-expressions, and gestures, driven by built-in behaviors. We used a child-like face together with a female voice (Seraphina by Microsoft Text-To-Speech [41]), due to a lack of available children's voices. The Furhat robot was controlled using a Wizard-of-Oz approach, using one Python per condition ([49]; see [12] for scripts and videos showcasing the interaction).

2.3 Procedure

A comprehensive overview of both experiments can be seen in Fig. 1.

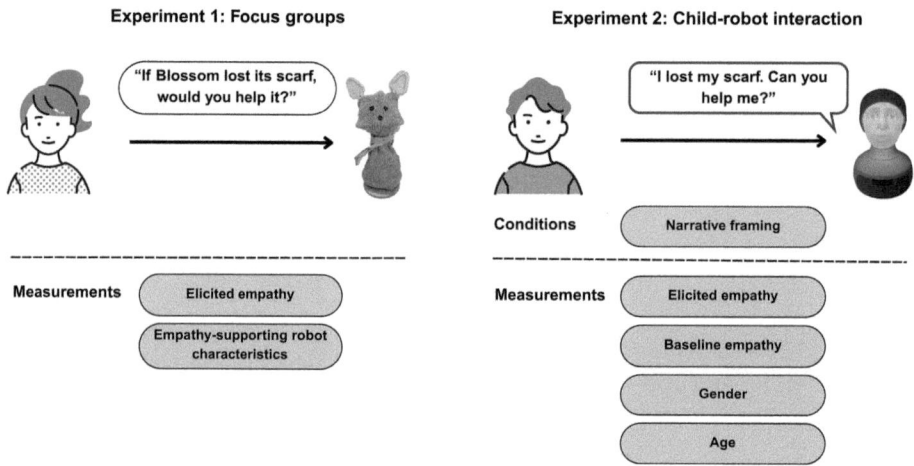

Fig. 1. Experimental design of both experiments including conditions and measurements where applicable.

Experiment 1: Focus Groups. We conducted three focus groups, split between three age groups (10–11 years, $n = 8$; 12–13 years, $n = 6$; 14–15 years, $n = 5$). Focus groups are group discussions aimed at exploring a specific topic with approximately four to six participants, with similar demographic variables [11,28]. After an introduction and four activities concerning sustainability and social equity that are discussed elsewhere [34], we presented children with an imaginary scenario: "You can see that Blossom has a small scarf. Imagine that this scarf was a gift from another robot and is very important to Blossom.

---

[2] We originally planned to conduct Experiment 1 and 2 with the Blossom robot, but due to technical issues had to opt for the Furhat robot in Experiment 2.

Now, Blossom cannot find its scarf". We then facilitated discussion around children's reasons to (not) help Blossom. The sessions were audio-recorded and lasted between 45–55 min. Transcripts can be found in our Open Science Framework (OSF) project [12].

Experiment 2: CRI. We used a between-subjects experimental design, where children were randomly assigned to one of two conditions: (1) A sad narrative condition, in which the robot told a melancholic story with emotional content or (2) a neutral narrative condition, in which the robot presented the same story in a neutral manner (see Fig. 2A for experimental procedure). The narratives were based on the scenario of Experiment 1, in which the robot looses its scarf and asks children to help find it (see Fig. 2A for excerpts. For full scenarios see [12]). Children were introduced to the task and completed the first questionnaire to measure children's baseline empathy. After completion, children were guided to the Furhat robot and started the interaction in which they assisted the robot to find its lost scarf[3]. Lastly, children filled in the second questionnaire to measure their empathy towards the robot, were debriefed, and selected a sticker as a gift. The researcher remained in a separate room and was only present to guide children to the different locations in between tasks, to keep experimenter influence minimal (see Fig. 2B for an overview of the experimental setup). The experiment took approximately 15 min.

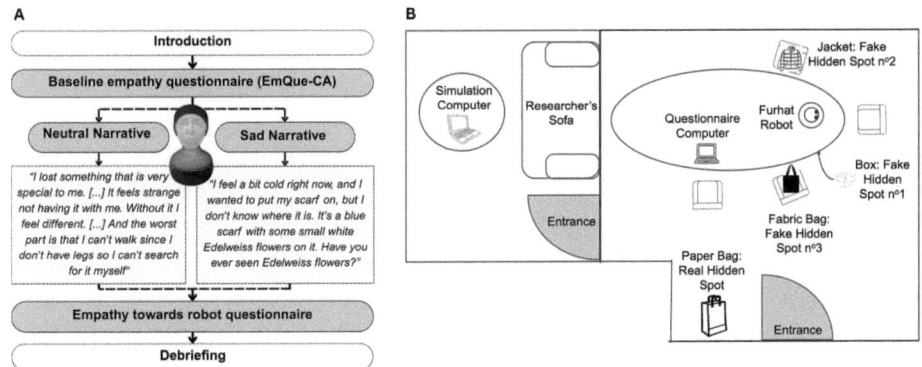

Fig. 2. Experimental Design. A) shows the experimental procedure. B) shows a schematic overview of the room setup.

2.4 Measurements

Experiment 1: Focus Groups. We asked children if they would want to help Blossom find its scarf, why (not), and what characteristics Blossom would need for them to help.

---
[3] Technical issues, such as connection drops and delayed robot responses were encountered in 36% of the sessions.

Experiment 2: CRI. We measured children's general empathic tendencies with the Empathy Questionnaire for Children and Adolescents (EmQue-CA; [44]). The EmQue-CA is a self-report questionnaire, designed to assess empathy through the three scales affective empathy, cognitive empathy, and intention to comfort. It consists of 18 statements, each answered on a 3-point scale ("not true" (0); "sometimes true" (1); "often true" (2)), resulting in a sum score ranging from 0 to 36. The EmQue-CA was validated in 8–16-year-olds with acceptable internal validity [38,44]. To ensure understanding for the younger children in our sample, we simplified and adapted the items (see [12]), added a visual answer scale (i.e., increasing circles), and automatically read them out loud. MB and LL (native German speaker) translated the questionnaire into German and reviewed the translation twice.

To assess children's empathy towards the social robot, we adapted a survey developed by [19], to investigate how affective narratives affect adults' empathy towards a robot. We adapted the original 10-items questionnaire, using emotion-understanding guidelines for children developed by [3]. The adapted questionnaire consisted of six positive (e.g. "When I saw the robot, I felt happy") and six reverse coded statements (e.g., "When I saw the robot, I did not feel anything"). The questionnaire was again translated to German by MB and LL. Responses were given on a 5-point Likert-scale ranging from −2 ("not at all") to +2 ("yes, totally"), resulting in a sum score from −24 to 24. Items were presented with the same visual answer scale as above.

2.5 Data Analysis

Experiment 1: Focus Groups. We analyzed the data using thematic analysis [8]. Thematic analysis is a method for identifying, analyzing, and interpreting patterns of meaning, so called themes, within qualitative data. The audio recordings were transcribed using Trint [61]. Codes and themes were extracted by MB and LL using MaxQDA [64] (see [12] for coded segments).

Experiment 2: CRI. Statistical analyses were performed in R [50] using RStudio [48]. To address RQ1, we examined the direct effect of narrative framing (sad vs. neutral) on children's empathy scores using a Mann-Whitney U test for non-parametric data. To address RQ2, we examined the moderating role of age, gender, and baseline empathy on children's empathic responses in both narrative conditions separately. To do so, we ran two linear regression models using the lme function of the lme4 package[4] [4].

---

[4] Additionally, we grouped participants by technically disrupted versus not disrupted sessions and visually and statistically compared their empathy scores to assess possible bias. There were no differences between groups, although the statistical findings have to be treated with caution due to low sample sizes.

3 Results and Discussion

3.1 Experiment 1: Focus Groups

A comprehensive summary of themes including exemplary quotes is presented in Fig. 3. Empathy and prosocial behaviors towards the robot were shaped by a combination of robot perception (such as the perceived anthropomorphism and sentient of the robot; **Theme 1**), personal experience (**Theme 3**), and social relationships (**Theme 2**) and context (**Theme 4**). Children who viewed the robot as a social companion referenced emotional bonds and were inclined to help, while those who saw it as a machine seemed more emotionally detached. Interestingly, children in the oldest focus group did not want to help, mainly due to the robot's lack of emotions and its robot-likeness. Children's reasoning to (not) help the robot was related to internal factors (such as empathy, anticipated guilt, or desire for reward) and external influences (like social expectations or distractions).

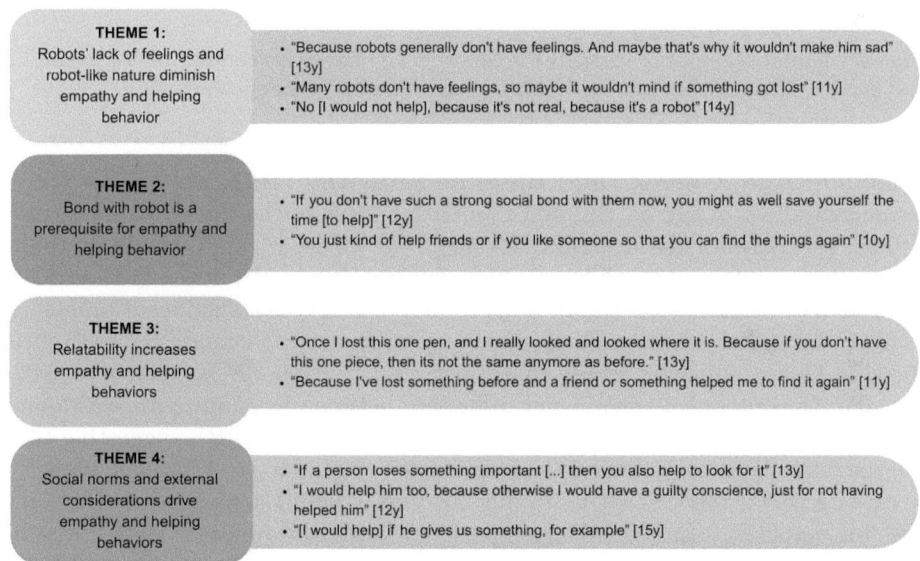

Fig. 3. Themes derived from thematic analysis with exemplary quotes.

3.2 Experiment 2: CRI

Effect of Narrative (H1). We did not find a significant difference between children's empathy towards the robot in the neutral ($M = 11.21$, $SD = 6.31$) and sad condition ($M = 11.49$, $SD = 4.60$; $U = 673$; $p = .93$; (Fig. 4A), indicating that the type of narrative did not affect children's empathy towards the robot.

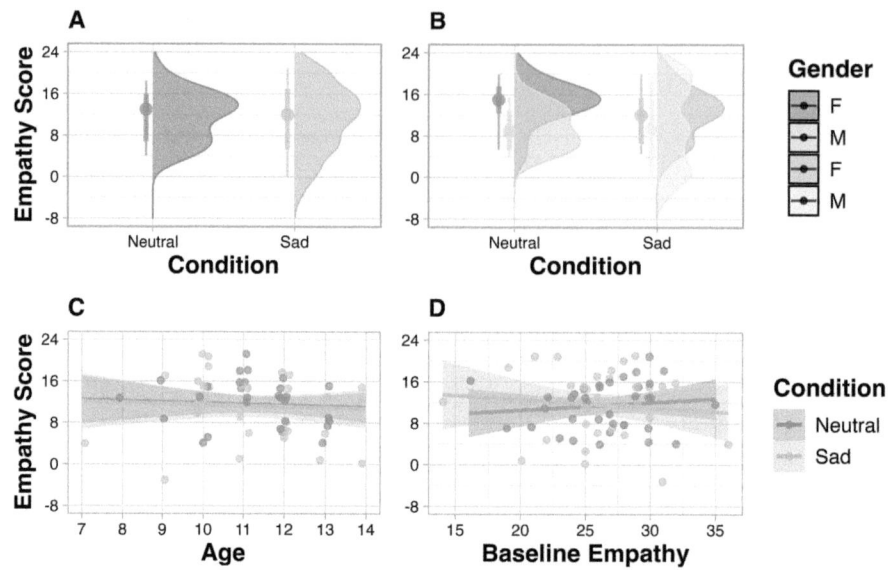

Fig. 4. Children's empathy towards the robot by (A) narrative condition, (B) narrative and gender, C) narrative and age, and D) narrative and baseline empathy.

Effects of Age, Gender, and Baseline Empathy (H2). We did not find a significant effect of age on children's empathy levels in the sad ($\beta = -0.19$, $SE = 0.55$, $p = .73$) nor the neutral ($\beta = 0.08$, $SE = 0.44$, $p = .86$) condition, indicating that children's age did not affect children's empathy towards the robot, regardless of the narrative condition (Fig. 4C). There was a significant difference in boys' and girls' empathy scores in the neutral narrative condition, with girls showing higher empathy scores than boys ($\beta = -5.08$, $SE = 1.49$, $p = .002$, Fig. 4B). In contrast, no significant difference between boys and girls was found in the sad condition ($\beta = -2.59$, $SE = 2.14$, $p = 0.23$; Fig. 4B), suggesting that the narrative type may moderate the influence of gender on children's empathy towards a social robot. Lastly, we did not find a significant effect of children's baseline empathy scores on their empathy towards the robot in neither condition (neutral: $\beta = -0.06$, $SE = 0.20$, $p = .76$; sad: $\beta = 0.12$, $SE = 0.19$, $p = .54$; Fig. 4D), indicating that children's baseline empathy did not affect their empathy towards the robot.

4 Discussion

In this two-experiments study, we sought to explore children's empathy towards a social robot and the effect of individual differences thereon. In Experiment 1, we conducted focus groups to explore children's empathic responses to a social robot using a hypothetical scenario. In Experiment 2, we experimentally tested this scenario, to assess children's empathy with a robot using different narrative types, while also examining individual factors such as age, gender, and baseline empathy. We used the social robots Blossom and Furhat, which allowed us to showcase a low complexity, cost effective, and customizable robot (Blossom), and to manipulate the narrative and affective degree of a conversation (Furhat) to investigate children's empathy.

4.1 Experiment 1: Qualitative Findings

Experiment 1 showed that children's perception of the robot affected their empathy and willingness to help. Some children viewed the robot as a non-sentient machine, while others saw it as a friend or companion. Notably, younger children seemed more likely to anthropomorphize the robot, viewing it as a social being or companion rather than a mere tool, which in turn facilitated stronger emotional connections and greater willingness to help. In contrast, older children perceived the robot as a functional tool, which limited their empathic engagement and may explain their unanimous refusal to help. Children's willingness to help was influenced by both internal factors (e.g., anticipated guilt, self-reward, empathy) and external factors (e.g., social norms, expectations of reciprocity, and practical concerns), highlighting the nuanced mechanisms behind helping behaviors and empathy.

4.2 Experiment 2: The Effect of Narrative

Against our expectations, we did not find a difference in children's empathy between narrative conditions. This finding is in contrast with previous work by [63, 65], who demonstrated that the emotional tone of a story plays a critical role in empathy elicitation in adults. This result suggests that narrative content alone may not be sufficient to elicit measurable empathetic differences in children, particularly in short interactions.

An alternative explanation could be the context of the interaction. Context plays a key role in shaping how people respond to different narratives with previous studies suggesting that emotional narratives are more effective when they match the emotional tone of the setting [19, 57]. In our experiment, both narrative conditions were delivered in the same relatively neutral setting, possibly reducing the effect of narrative framing.

The delivery of the narrative is another crucial factor. Furhat's limited facial expressions and monotone voice may have reduced the emotional salience of the sad story. Prior research (e.g., [17, 42]) suggests that verbal storytelling alone might be insufficient to elicit empathy, and that multimodal expressiveness – including intonation, facial cues, and gestures – is often necessary. Moreover, [19] emphasized the importance of the early moments of interaction for emotional engagement. In our case, the sad narrative was introduced after several neutral exchanges (i.e., the robot introducing itself), possibly weakening its impact. Future studies should explore how different environment settings, tasks, and types of expressiveness interact with storytelling to influence empathy towards robots.

4.3 Experiment 2: The Effect of Age, Gender and Baseline Empathy

Age. Against the findings of Experiment 1, we did not find an interaction between age and narrative style on children's empathy. This finding contradicts previous literature, which typically reports a gradual increase in empathy during childhood and early adolescence in human-human interaction [18,22,29]. One possible explanation is that empathy towards robots may not follow the same developmental pattern as empathy toward humans. To our knowledge, there are no studies that directly investigate how empathy towards robots develops across childhood, making it unclear whether the same age-related trends observed in human-human empathy apply to human-robot interaction.

An alternative explanation could be younger children's tendency to anthropomorphize robots, attributing human-like emotions, intentions, and social presence to them [27]. This could have led younger children to respond empathically, regardless of their cognitive maturity. In this context, empathy may be influenced more by how the child perceives the robot (i.e., as a social and emotional partner) than by their stage of emotional development [32]. At the same time, older children, while possibly more capable of empathy, may have perceived the robot as less human-like, resulting in lower empathy levels [27]. Therefore, while empathy in children might generally increase with age, the perception of robots could counterbalance this growth. Further research is needed to confirm this hypothesis.

Gender. We found that a significant difference between girls' and boys' empathy in the neutral narrative condition, with girls showing significantly higher empathy than boys. This finding is consistent with previous research, showing that girls show greater emotional sensitivity and responsiveness to others' feelings [31,56]. Interestingly, this gender difference was not observed in the sad narrative condition, where empathy scores were similar between girls and boys. A possible explanation for this finding is that the sad narrative may have enhanced boys' empathic responses, bringing them closer to those of girls and reducing the gender gap. While our experiment did not formally test the interaction between gender and narrative style, these observations suggest that gender may moderate children's emotional responses to a robot's narrative style. A replication with a larger sample size would allow for a formal investigation of this interaction.

Baseline Empathy. Lastly, we did not find a significant relationship between children's baseline empathy and their empathy towards the robot. This finding challenges the common assumption that individuals with higher baseline empathy will necessarily show stronger emotional reactions to empathy-inducing stimuli [22]. As highlighted by [47], trait empathy may guide general prosocial tendencies, but it might not always predict empathic reactions to every situation. Contextual variables—such as familiarity with the robot, perceived social presence, or narrative delivery—can also modulate empathic responses [5,7]. Thus, while baseline empathy may play a role, it might not fully account for the variability in children's empathic responses to robots.

4.4 Limitations

First, although the Furhat robot offers flexible facial expressions and speech capabilities monotonic speech, lack of emotional variation, and reduced realism in facial expressions may have reduced emotional expressiveness [60]. It would have been valuable to assess children's perceptions of Furhat's emotional sentience, as this theme emerged in the focus groups. Second, due to time constraints, we implemented a Wizard-of-Oz approach in place of an autonomous prompt response system. This, together with connection disruptions, may have reduced the naturalness and spontaneity of interactions although we did not find a systematic bias introduced by these issues. An autonomous approach could help reduce these issues in the future. Lastly, we adapted the empathy questionnaire from a scale designed for adults, which may not have appropriately captured younger children's empathic responses. Future research should address these limitations by ensuring emotionally congruent robot behaviors, developing validated, age-appropriate empathy measures, and exploring how perceived sentience affects children's empathy towards social robots.

4.5 Conclusion

To conclude, our work offers complementary qualitative and quantitative insights into how children experience and express empathy towards social robots. Our qualitative results suggest that children's perception of a robot affects their empathy towards it. Some children viewed the robot as a non-sentient machine, limiting their emotional involvement, while others saw it as a friend or companion. These perceptions, along with children's previous experiences and social norms, shaped children's empathic responses and helping behavior. Our quantitative findings indicate that contextual and relational cues may affect empathic responses more strongly than developmental factors or dispositional traits. Our results contribute to the expanding field of HRI, by deepening our understanding of the emotional and social dimensions of children's engagement with robots. Such understanding is critical for designing robots that children can connect with in meaningful and supportive way in education contexts. As robots become more integrated into children's lives, it is essential that future research continues to explore how empathy towards robots can be effectively supported and adapted to diverse user needs.

Acknowledgments. We would like to thank Dr. Ryssa Moffat for her help with data analyses. Additionally, we would like to thank the Realschule Tiengen and the Alemannenschule Wutöschingen for their collaboration.

Data Availability. All our measures, data collection procedures, and hypotheses were preregistered [13]. All data, measures, and materials can be found in our OSF project [12].

Disclosure of Interests. The authors have no competing interests to declare.

References

1. Abel, M., et al.: Gender effects in observation of robotic and humanoid actions. Front. Psychol. **11** (2020). https://doi.org/10.3389/fpsyg.2020.00797
2. Augello, A.: Unveiling the reasoning processes of robots through introspective dialogues in a storytelling system: a study on the elicited empathy. Cogn. Syst. Res. **73**, 12–20 (2022). https://doi.org/10.1016/j.cogsys.2021.11.006. https://www.sciencedirect.com/science/article/pii/S1389041721000863
3. Baron-Cohen, S., Golan, O., Wheelwright, S., Granader, Y., Hill, J.: Emotion word comprehension from 4 to 16 years old: a developmental survey. Front. Evol. Neurosci. **2** (2010). https://doi.org/10.3389/fnevo.2010.00009
4. Bates, D., Mächler, M., Bolker, B., Walker, S.: Fitting linear mixed-effects models using LME4. J. Stat. Softw. **67**(1), 1–48 (2015). https://doi.org/10.18637/jss.v067.i01. https://cran.r-project.org/package=lme4
5. Batson, C.D., Lishner, D.A., Cook, J., Sawyer, S.: Similarity and nurturance: two possible sources of empathy for strangers. Basic Appl. Soc. Psychol. **27**(1), 15–25 (2005). https://doi.org/10.1207/s15324834basp2701_3
6. Belpaeme, T., Kennedy, J., Ramachandran, A., Scassellati, B., Tanaka, F.: Social robots for education: a review. Sci. Robot. **3**(21) (2018). https://doi.org/10.1126/scirobotics.aat5954
7. Bloom, P.: Against Empathy: The Case for Rational Compassion. Random House (2017)
8. Braun, V., Clarke, V.: Using thematic analysis in psychology. Qual. Res. Psychol. **3**(2), 77–101 (2006). https://doi.org/10.1191/1478088706qp063oa
9. Breazeal, C.: Designing Sociable Robots. MIT Press (2004)
10. Breazeal, C., Dautenhahn, K., Kanda, T.: Social Robotics (2016)
11. Breen, R.L.: A practical guide to focus-group research. J. Geogr. High. Educ. **30**(3), 463–475 (2006). https://doi.org/10.1080/03098260600927575
12. Bruttin, M., Leisten, L.M.: Design and deployment of a soft social robot to investigate elicited empathy in child-robot interaction: the role of narrative framing, age, and gender. Technol. Work Cogn. (2025)
13. Bruttin, M., Leisten, L.M., Caruana, N., Cross, E.: Assessing children's empathy toward social robots in education: the impact of narrative framing, age and gender (2025). https://doi.org/10.17605/OSF.IO/HGAU2
14. Cerda, G., Aragón, E., Pérez, C., Navarro, J.I., Aguilar, M.: The open algorithm based on numbers (ABN) method: an effective instructional approach to domain-specific precursors of arithmetic development. Front. Psychol. **9** (2018). https://doi.org/10.3389/fpsyg.2018.01811
15. Cooper, B., Brna, P., Martins, A.: Effective affective in intelligent systems – building on evidence of empathy in teaching and learning. In: Paiva, A. (ed.) IWAI 1999. LNCS (LNAI), vol. 1814, pp. 21–34. Springer, Heidelberg (2000). https://doi.org/10.1007/10720296_3
16. Darling, K., Nandy, P., Breazeal, C.: Empathic concern and the effect of stories in human-robot interaction. In: 2015 24th IEEE International Symposium on Robot and Human Interactive Communication (RO-MAN), pp. 770–775. IEEE (2015)
17. De Beir, A., Cao, H.L., Gomez Esteban, P., Van de Perre, G., Vanderborght, B.: Enhancing NAO expression of emotions using pluggable eyebrows (2015). https://doi.org/10.13140/RG.2.1.4414.6648, researchGate
18. Decety, J.: The neurodevelopment of empathy in humans. Dev. Neurosci. **32**(4), 257–267 (2010). https://doi.org/10.1159/000317171

19. Frederiksen, M.R., Fischer, K., Matarić, M.: Robot vulnerability and the elicitation of user empathy. In: 2022 31st IEEE International Conference on Robot and Human Interactive Communication (RO-MAN), pp. 52–58. IEEE (2022)
20. Furhat Robotics: Furhat Robot (2024). https://furhatrobotics.com. Social robot platform. Accessed Apr 2025
21. Galambos, N.L., Berenbaum, S.A., McHale, S.M.: Gender development in adolescence. In: Lerner, R.M., Steinberg, L. (eds.) Handbook of Adolescent Psychology, pp. 305–357. Wiley (2009)
22. Gaspar, A., Esteves, F.: Empathy development from adolescence to adulthood and its consistency across targets. Front. Psychol. **13** (2022). https://doi.org/10.3389/fpsyg.2022.936053
23. Gaudiello, I., L.S., Zibetti, E.: The ontological and functional status of robots: how firm our representations are? Comput. Hum. Behav. **50(1)**, 259–273 (2015)
24. Gilani, S.N., Sheetz, K., Lucas, G., Traum, D.: What kind of stories should a virtual human swap? In: Traum, D., Swartout, W., Khooshabeh, P., Kopp, S., Scherer, S., Leuski, A. (eds.) What kind of stories should a virtual human swap? LNCS (LNAI), vol. 10011, pp. 128–140. Springer, Cham (2016). https://doi.org/10.1007/978-3-319-47665-0_12
25. Hermans, E.J., Putman, P., Van Honk, J.: Testosterone administration reduces empathetic behavior: a facial mimicry study. Psychoneuroendocrinology **31**(7), 859–866 (2006). https://doi.org/10.1016/j.psyneuen.2006.04.011
26. Kahn, P.H., et al.: The new ontological category hypothesis in human-robot interaction. In: Proceedings of the 6th International Conference on Human-Robot Interaction, pp. 159–160 (2011)
27. Kahn, P.H., Jr., et al.: "Robovie, you'll have to go into the closet now": children's social and moral relationships with a humanoid robot. Dev. Psychol. **48**(2), 303–314 (2012). https://doi.org/10.1037/a0027033
28. Kitzinger, J.: The methodology of focus groups: the importance of interaction between research participants. Sociol. Health Illn. **16**(1), 103–121 (1994). https://doi.org/10.1111/1467-9566.ep11347023
29. Knafo, A., Zahn-Waxler, C., Van Hulle, C., Robinson, J.L., Rhee, S.H.: The developmental origins of a disposition toward empathy: genetic and environmental contributions. Emotion **8**(6), 737 (2008). https://doi.org/10.1037/a0014179
30. Kory-Westlund, J.: Implications of children's social, emotional, and relational interactions with robots for human–robot empathy, pp. 256–278 (2023). https://doi.org/10.4324/9781003189978-17
31. Lam, C.B., Solmeyer, A.R., McHale, S.M.: Sibling relationships and empathy across the transition to adolescence. J. Youth Adolesc. **41**(12), 1657–1670 (2012). https://doi.org/10.1007/s10964-012-9781-8
32. Lee, K.M., Jung, Y., Kim, J., Kim, S.R.: Are physically embodied social agents better than disembodied social agents?: The effects of physical embodiment, tactile interaction, and people's loneliness in human-robot interaction. Int. J. Hum Comput Stud. **64**(10), 962–973 (2006). https://doi.org/10.1016/j.ijhcs.2006.04.003
33. Leisten, L.M., Caruana, N., Cross, E.S.: Teachers perceive distinct competency profiles in soft and hard social robots for supporting learning (2025). https://doi.org/10.31219/osf.io/zvkbp_v1
34. Leisten, L.M., Moffat, R., Caruana, N., Cross, E.S.: Social robots as a tool for probing children's understanding of social equality and sustainability (nd, in preparation)

35. Leisten, L.M., Heyselaar, E., Bosse, T., Hortensius, R.: Children's reciprocity and relationship formation with a robot across age. Technol. Mind Behav. (2024). https://doi.org/10.1037/tumb0000131
36. Leite, I., Castellano, G., Pereira, A., Martinho, C., Paiva, A.: Empathic robots for long-term interaction: evaluating social presence, engagement and perceived support in children. Int. J. Soc. Robot. **6**, 329–341 (2014). https://doi.org/10.1007/s12369-014-0233-8
37. Leite, I., Pereira, A., Mascarenhas, S., Martinho, C., Prada, R., Paiva, A.: The influence of empathy in human-robot relations. Int. J. Hum Comput Stud. **71**(3), 250–260 (2013). https://doi.org/10.1016/j.ijhcs.2012.10.004
38. Liang, Z., Mazzeschi, C., Delvecchio, E.: Empathy questionnaire for children and adolescents: Italian validation. Eur. J. Dev. Psychol. **20**(3), 567–579 (2023). https://doi.org/10.1080/17405629.2023.2196725
39. Lillo, A., Saracco, A., Siletto, E., Mattutino, C., Gena, C.: Investigating the relationship between empathy and attribution of mental states to robots. arXiv preprint arXiv:2405.01019 (2024)
40. Lukin, S.M., Walker, M.A.: Narrative variations in a virtual storyteller. In: Brinkman, W.-P., Broekens, J., Heylen, D. (eds.) Narrative variations in a virtual storyteller. LNCS (LNAI), vol. 9238, pp. 320–331. Springer, Cham (2015). https://doi.org/10.1007/978-3-319-21996-7_34
41. Microsoft Corporation: Microsoft corporation (2024). https://www.microsoft.com. Accessed Apr 2025
42. Niklaus, D.: The influence on empathy by humanoid robot NAO portraying sadness using speech and gestures. Master's thesis, Tilburg University (2022). http://arno.uvt.nl/show.cgi?fid=161976
43. Oliver, M.B., Dillard, J.P., Bae, K., Tamul, D.J.: The effect of narrative news format on empathy for stigmatized groups. J Mass. Commun. Q. **89**(2), 205–224 (2012). https://doi.org/10.1177/1077699012436662
44. Overgaauw, S., Rieffe, C., Broekhof, E., Crone, E.A., Güroglu, B.: Assessing empathy across childhood and adolescence: validation of the empathy questionnaire for children and adolescents (EMQUE-CA). Front. Psychol. **8** (2017). https://doi.org/10.3389/fpsyg.2017.00870
45. Paiva, A., Leite, I., Boukricha, H., Wachsmuth, I.: Empathy in virtual agents and robots: a survey. ACM Trans. Interact. (2017)
46. Pashevich, E.: Can communication with social robots influence how children develop empathy? Best-evidence synthesis. AI Soc. **37**(2), 579–589 (2022). https://doi.org/10.1007/s00146-021-01149-3
47. Pfattheicher, S., Nockur, L., Böhm, R., Sassenrath, C., Petersen, M.B.: The emotional path to action: empathy promotes physical distancing and wearing of face masks during the COVID-19 pandemic. Psychol. Sci. **31**(11), 1363–1373 (2020). https://doi.org/10.1177/0956797620950967
48. Posit Software, PBC: Rstudio: Integrated development environment for R (2024). https://posit.co/, formerly RStudio. Accessed Apr 2025
49. Python Software Foundation: Python programming language, version 3.x (2024). https://www.python.org. Accessed Apr 2025
50. R Core Team: R: A Language and Environment for Statistical Computing. R Foundation for Statistical Computing, Vienna, Austria (2024). https://www.r-project.org/. Accessed Apr 2025
51. Ratka, A.: Empathy and the development of affective skills. Am. J. Pharm. Educ. **82**(10) (2018)

52. Reeves, B., Nass, C.: The Media Equation: How People Treat Computers, Television, and New Media Like Real People. Cambridge University Press (1996)
53. Riddoch, K.A., Cross, E.S.: "Hit the robot on the head with this mallet"–making a case for including more open questions in HRI research. Front. Robot. AI **8** (2021). https://doi.org/10.3389/frobt.2021.603510
54. Riek, L.D., Rabinowitch, T.C., Chakrabarti, B., Robinson, P.: Empathizing with robots: fellow feeling along the anthropomorphic spectrum. In: 2009 3rd International Conference on Affective Computing and Intelligent Interaction and Workshops, pp. 1–6. IEEE (2009)
55. Rohlfing, K.J., et al.: Social/dialogical roles of social robots in supporting children's learning of language and literacy—a review and analysis of innovative roles. Front. Robot. AI **9** (2022). https://doi.org/10.3389/frobt.2022.971749
56. Rose, A.J., Rudolph, K.D.: A review of sex differences in peer relationship processes: potential trade-offs for the emotional and behavioral development of girls and boys. Psychol. Bull. **132**(1), 98–131 (2006). https://doi.org/10.1037/0033-2909.132.1.98
57. Severson, R.L., Woodard, S.R.: Imagining others' minds: the positive relation between children's role play and anthropomorphism. Front. Psychol. **9** (2018). https://doi.org/10.3389/fpsyg.2018.01811
58. Spitale, M., Okamoto, S., Gupta, M., Xi, H., Matarić, M.J.: Socially assistive robots as storytellers that elicit empathy. ACM Trans. Hum.-Robot Interact. (THRI) **11**(4), 1–29 (2022). https://doi.org/10.1145/3524534
59. Suguitan, M., Hoffman, G.: Blossom: a handcrafted open-source robot. ACM Trans. Hum.-Robot Interact. (THRI) **8**(1), 1–27 (2019). https://doi.org/10.1145/3337021
60. Thunberg, S., Arnelid, M., Ziemke, T.: Older adults' perception of the Furhat robot. In: Proceedings of the 10th International Conference on Human-Agent Interaction (HAI 2022), pp. 4–12. ACM (2022). https://doi.org/10.1145/3527188.3561924
61. Trint Ltd: Trint (2024). https://trint.com. Accessed Apr 2025
62. Uzefovsky, F., Knafo-Noam, A.: Empathy development throughout the life span. In: Social Cognition, pp. 89–115. Routledge (2016)
63. Van Laer, T., De Ruyter, K., Visconti, L.M., Wetzels, M.: The extended transportation-imagery model: a meta-analysis of the antecedents and consequences of consumers' narrative transportation. J. Consum. Res. **40**(5), 797–817 (2014). https://doi.org/10.1086/673383
64. VERBI Software: MAXQDA (2024). https://www.maxqda.com. Accessed Apr 2025
65. Zhao, H.: Emotion in interactive storytelling. In: Proceedings of the International Conference on the Foundations of Digital Games, pp. 183–189. ACM (2013)

Driven by Personality? Human Perceptions of Intraverted and Extraverted Robots in Car Driving Scenarios

Jasmin Bernotat[1](✉)[ID], Doreen Jirak[2][ID], Laura Triglia[1,3][ID], Francesco Rea[1][ID], and Alessandra Sciutti[1][ID]

[1] Italian Institute of Technology (IIT), Via Enrico Melen 83, 16152 Genoa, Italy
{jasmin.bernotat,laura.triglia,francesco.rea,alessandra.sciutti}@iit.it
[2] University of Antwerp, Paardenmarkt 94, 2000 Antwerp, Belgium
doreen.jirak@uantwerpen.be
[3] University of Genoa, Via Montallegro 1, 16145 Genoa, Italy
https://contact.iit.it/, https://www.uantwerpen.be/en,
https://dibris.unige.it/en

Abstract. The success or failure of human-robot interaction (HRI) is influenced by various human-centered factors, including personality traits. These variables shape users' perceptions, engagement, and trust in robotic systems. One key concept in this domain is the similarity hypothesis, which posits that people are more likely to respond positively to robots that exhibit traits or behaviors similar to their own. Understanding how personality alignment affects HRI outcomes is crucial for designing effective and socially compatible robotic agents. While the similarity hypothesis has found support in, e.g., assistive healthcare contexts, its applicability to driving scenarios remains underexplored. To address this research gap, we used the CARLA simulator to create a driving scenario with the humanoid iCub robot endowed with either an extraverted or intraverted personality expressed through nonverbal cues (e.g., motion, gaze) and speech characteristics (e.g., pitch, frequency). Although robot personality was successfully manipulated, participants perceived the robot as more extraverted and preferred it as a driving assistant rather than a social companion. Perceived similarity in extraversion influenced their preferences, partially supporting the similarity hypothesis. Regardless of assigned personality, the robot was seen as more machine-like than human-like. The intraverted robot elicited greater cognitive trust, suggesting confidence in its functional reliability. Participants' ability to imagine the driving scenario with a robot significantly shaped their perceptions of HRI, underscoring the role of repeated interactions in developing trust and social bonds in HRI.

Keywords: Social Robot · Similarity Hypothesis · Complementary Hypothesis · Robot Personality · Human-Robot Interaction

1 Introduction

Human-robot interaction (HRI) has emerged as a multidisciplinary field that explores the dynamic interplay between humans and robots in various contexts, including collaborations in work, healthcare, education, and social environments. Given that automotive technologies and the integration of driver assistance systems are gaining importance (see [34]), the possible introduction of robots is also evaluated in such a context. Being a novel application, several questions need to be addressed in the development of suitable robotic agents.

To illustrate, a robot's role during car driving can not be as easily defined. During car driving, on the one hand, a robot could be thought of as a social companion, which should be communicative, outgoing, and social. On the other hand, it could be expected to be a mere technical assistant, for which being focused, rational, discrete, and reserved could be desirable. As such, the robot could embody different roles that could be associated with the preference of different behavioral characteristics, which in humans are linked to different personality traits such as extraversion and intraversion [35].

The importance of extraversion in social interactions has been confirmed in the fields of psychology as well as in HRI (e.g., [2,24]). As such, extraversion was found to be one of the most crucial traits (among agreeableness, conscientiousness, openness, and emotional stability, for instance [24,38]) to make a good team player [2,24]. In human-agent interaction, highly extraverted agents were more positively perceived in terms of social presence and communication satisfaction. In addition, higher levels of an agent's extraversion resulted in perceptions of the agent as human-like [2]. Similar results were obtained in HRI research: Participants who had interacted with an extraverted (vs. intraverted) robot reported higher levels of the robot's friendliness and anthropomorphism [37]. Chen et al. [18] supposed that due to frequent and active conversations, extraverted robots would increase the emotional bonding between robots and humans, leading to perceptions of the robot as emotional and human-like. Robot extraversion resulted indeed in higher levels of trust in HRI [3,18].

Nevertheless, participants' preferences for an extraverted or an intraverted robot were found to be dependent on a specific task. An extraverted robot was preferred for a healthcare task, while an intraverted robot was preferred for a security task [50]. Explanations as to why people make this distinction might lie in the fact that health care requires more social interaction than a security task, where the extraverted robot might have been considered better fulfilling participants' needs compared to the intraverted robot. Analogously, [33] found a clear preference for an extraverted (vs. intraverted) robot performing as a barista, which requires not just serving drinks but communicating with people.

Additionally, participants' own personality traits were found to affect their preferences for a robot personality as well as their trust toward the robot. Byrne and Nelson [17] were among the first to establish a linear relationship between attitudinal similarity and interpersonal attraction, providing evidence that individuals generally evaluate interactions with like-minded others more positively than those characterized by attitudinal complementarity. In contrast, Rosenbaum [43] stated that complementary traits foster mutual understanding and comfort as they might create a balanced and synergistic relationship, a notion known as the complementary hypothesis. Both hypotheses have found their way into HRI research (e.g., [7,26,30], see also [27,42,45] for recent reviews) as the potential (mis)alignment of personalities may serve as a predictor for the interaction qualities between a human and a social robot [29]. Since then, HRI research on this topic has produced mixed results. For instance, Andriella et al. [5] reported a preference for similar attitudes in robots when engaging in a memory car game. Likewise, Andrist et al. [6] found that varying a robot's gaze behavior increased user engagement during repetitive tasks, emphasizing the importance of matching human-robot personalities for sustained interaction. However, Park et al. [37] found that while participants felt more comfortable with robots mirroring their personality, introverted participants reported less social presence with introverted robots, suggesting nuanced implications for robot design.

Analyzing this collection of previous research, it emerges that designing a robot's behavior appropriate for it to interact within a car while someone is driving poses several open questions. What should be its role, and which personality (extraverted or introverted) should it express in its behavior to be effectively appreciated by the driver? Can there be a general answer, or would this depend on the driver's personality? To address these interrogatives, we designed an online study. We showed 96 participants videos of a simulated driving scenario where the humanoid robot iCub assisted as if it were in the car and exhibited either an introverted or an extraverted behavior, and we asked a series of questions to gauge participants' preferences. The results provided insights on the factors that have to be considered when designing robots for driving scenarios.

1.1 Research Questions

In the present research, we explored what role participants would prefer for a robot in the car driving context in terms of being a *social companion* (H1a) and a *driving assistant* (H1b) and whether they preferred an *extraverted* (H2a) or *introverted* (H2b) robot. Then, tying with [31], we evaluated whether participants' preferences for an extraverted (vs. introverted) robot would depend on their own level of extraversion (H3a) and introversion (H3b). To investigate the effect of perceived similarity (vs. complementarity) [15,16] in more detail, we examined whether participants' preferences were driven by perceived similarity in terms of being social (H3c) (a characteristic of extraversion), and reserved (H3d) (a characteristic of introversion) [19–21]. Following research by [2,18,37], according to which extraverted (vs. introverted) robots were perceived as more human-like, a team player [2,24,35], and elicited higher trust [3,18], we investigated whether an extraverted robot would evoke higher perceptions of human-likeness (H4a), and affective trust (H4b) (reflecting trust in the robot's benevolence, [10,11]). Conversely, we hypothesized that an introverted (vs. extraverted) robot would evoke more perceptions of machine-likeness (H5a), and cognitive trust (H5b) (reflecting trust in the robot's functions, [10,11]). Testing the hypotheses, we controlled for the effects of participants' ability to imagine the video scenario and their perceptions of the robot's extraversion and intraversion. This was done to make sure that a potential lack of imaginability of the scenario and perceptions of the robot's extraversion (vs. intraversion) did not affect the results of the online study.

2 Methods

2.1 Experimental Procedure

To test our hypotheses, an online study with a between-subjects design (extraverted vs. intraverted robot personality type) was realized.

The study was realized online using *SoSciSurvey* [46], a tool for online studies. The online format was chosen to provide a representation of a possible futuristic implementation of robots' driving assistants, while maximizing the number of participants. Therefore, participants were recruited via *Prolific* [40], a subject pool that allows for reaching large sample sizes within a short time. Study completion was rewarded with 2.68. After giving consent to participate in the study, a short video sequence of about two minutes was presented. The video sequence displayed the CARLA driving scene on the left half of the screen and the iCub robot commenting on the scene on the right half of the screen (see Fig. 1). According to the between-subjects design, the robot either represented an extraverted or an intraverted personality type which was designed based on changes of the robot's behavior and speech style, such as the prosody and frequency based on [25] (see Sect. 2.3 for further details on the implementation of the robot's personality type).

Fig. 1. A snapshot of a video sequence displaying the iCub robot next to the CARLA driving scene.

After having watched the video sequence, participants completed a questionnaire with the measured constructs reported in Sect. 2.4. In total, participants needed about 15 min to complete the study.

2.2 CARLA Simulator

The CARLA simulator is a Python-based open source software project[1] [23] primarily developed to provide a framework for the autonomous driving (AD) research community. CARLA offers a diverse range of driving maps (towns), different traffic and weather conditions, and diverse car types to choose from. The traffic manager module allows for the control of those simulation parameters, including the NPC spawn locations, additionally populating the town scenes and thus introducing more challenges for the autonomous driving agent. For the purpose of this study, we only used the CARLA library itself without using its full functionality for the sake of simplicity in the video creation process. Specifically, we started the CARLA client with its default town but parametrized the scenario with the number of NPCs, weather conditions, and the usage of auto-pilot (yes/no). Based on these parameters, we created different scenarios and videos, from which we selected one with mild weather and traffic conditions but an informative driving environment (e.g., museum, fire truck). The latter aspect was important to provide elements in the scene that could be leveraged by the robot in its conversation with the driver, creating an occasion to exhibit its personality. An example from the video is shown in Fig. 1. For reproducibility purposes, we give the details of the CARLA set up: we installed the CARLA simulator version 09.13. Using pip3 on a Linux computer with Ubuntu 20.04 distribution and NVIDIA GTX 1060 GPU, which resulted in reasonably good rendering results. In the video generation, we used the "Audacity" software (included in Ubuntu) to eliminate the noises generated by robot motion and enhance its voice. Finally, both the CARLA and the robot videos were synchronized using the "Shotcut" software (Windows).

2.3 Implementation of the Robot's Personality: Extraversion vs. Intraversion

In the videos, the robot reacted to a variety of contextual stimuli in the driving scenario generated with CARLA, such as distinctive buildings, pedestrians crossing the road, and environmental changes. Toward the end of the scenario, the driver in the simulation committed a traffic infraction, followed by the appearance of a firefighter vehicle. The robot was programmed to respond to these events with comments and reactions.

We decided to manipulate the robot's behavior to exhibit intraverted and extraverted personality traits. Drawing on Esteban's previous study [25], we designed both verbal and non-verbal behaviors. Specifically, we tailored the robot's speech parameters such as volume, speed, and pitch, along with its facial expressions and gestures. Table 1 summarizes our implementation, adapted from Esteban's framework. For instance, the extraverted robot spoke more loudly, quickly, and with a higher pitch, used dynamic gestures, and expressed emotions like happiness or surprise, saying phrases such as "I had never noticed how beautiful the museum building is." In contrast, the intraverted version spoke more

---
[1] https://carla.org//.

softly and slowly, with a lower pitch, minimal movement, and neutral expressions, using phrases like "I saw the exhibition about Michelangelo, it was interesting." Unlike Esteban's setup with the mobile Pepper robot, our implementation did not require spatial navigation. However, the robot still reacted to its environment and contextual stimuli during the scenario—for example, commenting on a particular building, noticing a pedestrian crossing the street, or responding to a traffic violation committed by the driver. These adaptations ensured that personality traits were consistently conveyed across multiple behavioral channels while maintaining relevance to the specific situational cues in our setup.

Table 1. The robot's extraverted and intraverted dimension

Robot Features	Extraverted	Intraverted
Speech Volume	20% higher than the default volume	20% lower than the default volume
Speech Speed	30% higher than the default speed	20% lower than the default speed
Speech Pitch	20% higher than the default pitch	20% lower than the default pitch
Facial Expression	Mostly happy, angry, or surprise	Mostly neutral, then angry
Gestures	Wide movements of the head, the arms, and the gaze	More static, little movements of the head

2.4 Questionnaire Measures

Except for some demographics, we used 7-point Likert scales to capture participants' agreement with an item's content. High scores indicated high agreement with an item's content. Items were re-coded if necessary. Summated scales were composed based on their Cronbach's alphas (α), a measure of scales' internal consistency and reliability [1, 22].

All measured constructs showed satisfying reliabilities of $\alpha \geq .70$ [22]. The following constructs were assessed in the questionnaire:

Dependent Measures

Preferred Robot Personality Type: With one self-generated Likert scale item, participants indicated to what extent they would like to use the robot they had seen in the video for car driving (1 = not at all, 7 = very much). **Perceived similarity to the robot:** With two items by [41], participants indicated to what extent they thought the robot they had seen in the video and themselves matched in terms of being 1. social and 2. reserved. **Robot machine-likeness vs. human-likeness:** Six items [8] each were used to evaluate to what extent participants perceived the robot they had just seen in the video as machine-like and as human-like. **Cognitive vs. affective Trust:** With ten items each by [10,11], we assessed participants' levels of cognitive trust towards the robot they had seen in the video, reflecting participants' trust in the robot's functions. Analogously, ten items measured participants' levels of affective trust in the robot they had just seen, reflecting participants' trust in the robot's benevolence [10,11].

Covariates

Experience with Technology, Robots, and the Driving Scenario: Using two items by [8], participants indicated the extent to which they had experience with 1. technology in general and 2. robots in particular. In addition, to get more insights into participants' level of experience with robots, they had to indicate from which context they mainly knew robots (i.e., media (movies, books), work, home, other studies, other contexts). Then, using two dichotomous items, participants were asked whether they had known the iCub robot that was shown in the video before from 1. other studies or 2. media (see [12]) and whether they had known the driving scenario that we had presented in the study before.

Imaginability of the driving scenario: Eight self-generated items were used to capture participants' ability to imagine the driving scenario with the robot as presented in the video. That means their ability to put themselves into the driving scenario, to imagine the presented scenario to be real, and to imagine a robot being intraverted vs. extraverted.

Demographics: Participants' demographics were assessed (i.e., age, gender, native language, nationality, educational level, professional status).

In addition, we measured participants' positive vs. negative attitudes toward robots [12,36] and motivation to respond in a socially desirable way [47,48] to control for these effects. Likewise, participants were given the opportunity to freely write down additional roles of robots during car driving. However, due to limited space and scope in a conference paper, we focus on answering the main hypotheses.

Manipulation Check

Robot Extraversion vs. Intraversion: Analogous to the assessment of their own level of extraversion vs. intraversion, participants were asked to indicate the extent to which they perceived the robot they had just been presented in the video as 1. social and 2. as reserved [41]. This was done to ensure that the manipulation of robot personality type had worked. **Video quality:** Finally, to make sure that participants could watch the video properly, they had to indicate whether they could watch the video properly with image and audio (see [12]).

2.5 Participant Sample

$N = 96$ individuals participated in the study. $n = 25$ participants had to be excluded from statistical analyses due to issues with watching the video properly with image and audio ($n = 9$) or not reporting whether they could watch the video properly ($n = 16$). All of the remaining $n = 71$ participants reported being able to watch the video properly. Notably, all of them correctly identified the robot's language as Italian and reported that they could fairly well understand the robot's comments. Participants showed discrete response patterns, indicating that they completed the study seriously and thoughtfully. The sample was well balanced in terms of experimental conditions (extraverted robot condition: $n = 35$, intraverted robot condition: $n = 36$) and consisted as follows: **gender:** male: $n = 38$, female: $n = 31$, non-binary: $n = 2$; **age:** $M_{age} = 31.45$, $SD_{age} = 8.67$, age range = 19 to 53 years; **nationality:** Italian nationality: $n = 65$, other nationality: $n = 6$ (i.e., French, Portuguese, Romanian, Turkish, Ukrainian). Overall, participants reported a good command of technology use in general: $M = 5.75$, $SD = 1.12$ but fairly less experience with robots in particular: $M = 2.92$, $SD = 1.37$. Most participants reported to know robots mainly from the media (e.g., movies, books): $n = 66$, followed by the work context: $n = 21$, other studies: $n = 18$, home: $n = 17$, and other contexts: $n = 3$ (e.g., lectures, university, one participant indicated to have no experience with robots at all). Participants had no prior experience with the CARLA driving simulation and the iCub robot.

3 Results

3.1 Preferred Robot Role

To assess what role would participants prefer for a robot in the car driving context in terms of being a H1a) social companion and H1b) driving assistant, a mixed models Multivariate Analysis of Covariance (MANCOVA) was performed. Participants' preferences for a robot's role were tested within participants with robot personality (extraverted vs. intraverted) as a between-subjects factor. The effects of participants' ability to imagine the driving scenario and to perceive the robot's personality as presented in the video were considered as covariates. Following the principle of parsimony [49], covariates that did not statistically significantly contribute to the final statistical model were removed step-wise. The final statistical model was reached in two steps: The main effect of preferred robot role was statistically significant, $F(1,68) = 14.45$, $p < .001$, $\eta p^2 = .175$. The main effect of robot personality, $F(1,68) = 2.33$, $p = .132$, $\eta p^2 = .033$, and the interaction effect between participants' preferred robot role and robot personality were not statistically significant, $F(1,68) = 0.61$, $p = .437$, $\eta p^2 = .009$. That means that, independent of whether participants saw an extraverted vs. intraverted robot in the video, they preferred a robot being a driving assistant rather than a social companion (see also Fig. 2). In addition, participants' ability to imagine the driving scenario with the robot as displayed in the video statistically significantly affected their preferences for a robot's role during car driving, $F(1,68) = 18.49$, $p < .001$, $\eta p^2 = .214$. Pearson correlations revealed that, the more participants could imagine the driving scene with the robot, the more they preferred a robot being a social companion during car driving, $r(69) = .44$, $p < .001$ (see Sect. 3.4 for mean scores on participants' ability to imagine the presented scenario with the robot).

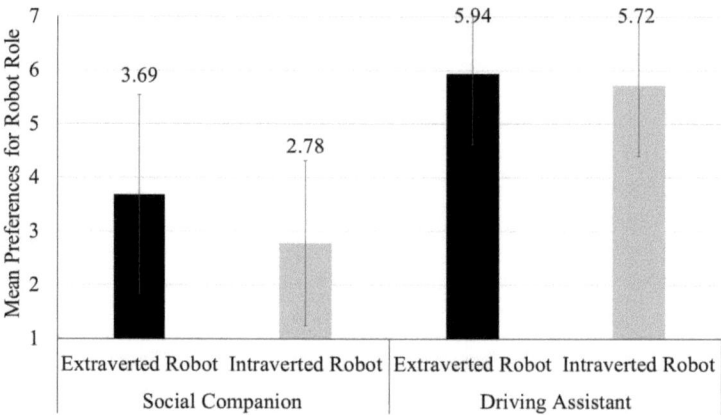

Fig. 2. Participants' mean scores on preferred robot role as a social companion vs. driving assistant by robot personality type (bars) and standard deviations (lines).

3.2 Preferred Robot Personality

To test whether participants' preferred an extraverted vs. intraverted robot personality (H2a and H2b) depending of their own level of extraversion vs. intraversion (H3a and H3b), and the similarity they perceived to the robot in terms of being outgoing vs. reserved as characteristics of extraversion vs. intraversion (H4a and H4b), one single Univariate Analysis of Covariance (ANCOVA) was performed. Testing Hypotheses H2 and H3 in one single analysis was done to avoid α error inflation [14]. Participants' preferences to use a robot for car driving (H2a and H2b) were investigated by robot personality (extraverted vs. intraverted) as a between-subjects factor. Participants' own levels of extraversion and intraversion (H3a and H3b), and their perceived similarity with the robot in being outgoing and reserved (H3c and H3d) were considered as covariates. In addition, we controlled for the effects of participants' ability to imagine the driving scenario and their perceptions of the robot as being extraverted vs. intraverted. Following the principle of parsimony [49], the final statistical model was reached in three steps: The main effect of robot personality was not statistically significant, $F(1,67) = 0.64$, $p < .426$, $\eta p^2 = .009$. That is, no robot personality type was preferred over the other, which also becomes obvious when displaying mean preferences per robot personality (see Fig. 3). However, in line with H2a, the main effect of participants' perceived similarity with the robot in being outgoing was statistically significant, $F(1,67) = 4.15$, $p = .046$, $\eta p^2 = .058$. The same accounted for the main effect of participants' ability to imagine the driving scenario with the robot, $F(1,67) = 8.25$, $p = .005$, $\eta p^2 = .110$. In line with H3c, participants reported more preferences to use a robot for car driving, the more similarity with the robot in being outgoing they perceived, $r(69) = .26$, $p = .031$. Likewise, the more participants could imagine the presented driving scenario with the robot, the higher their preferences for robot use during car driving, $r(69) = .34$, $p = .004$. The effects of the remaining covariates, of participants' own level of extraversion (H3a), intraversion (H3b), their perceived similarity with the robot in being reserved (H3d), and of participants' ability to perceive the robot's extraversion and intraversion were not statistically significant ($ps > .05$). Overall, participants reported to be rather intraverted $M = 5.20$, $SD = 1.52$, than extraverted, $M = 4.20$, $SD = 1.69$, and reported relatively low levels of similarity to the robot in being outgoing, $M = 3.21$, $SD = 1.79$, and reserved, $M = 2.79$, $Sd = 1.57$.

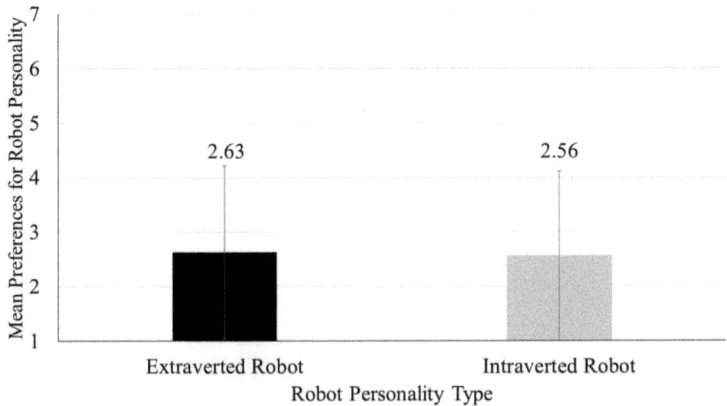

Fig. 3. Participants' mean preferences for the extraverted vs. intraverted robot personality type (bars) and standard deviations (lines).

3.3 Perceptions of Robot Human-Likeness vs. Machine-Likeness and Cognitive vs. Affective Trust

To test Hypotheses 4a to 5b, a Multivariate Analysis of Covariance (MANCOVA) was performed with participants' perceptions of robot human-likeness (H4a), machine-likeness (H5a), affective trust (H4b), and cognitive trust (H5b) as a function of robot personality. Participants' ability to imagine the driving scenario and their perceptions of robot personality were considered as covariates. The main effect of robot personality on cognitive trust was statistically significant, $F(1,67) = 8.98$, $p = .004$, $\eta p^2 = .118$. That is, in line with H5b, the intraverted (vs. extraverted) robot evoked higher levels of cognitive trust (see Fig. 5). The main effects of robot personality on robot human-likeness, machine-likeness, and affective trust were not statistically significant ($ps > .05$). That is, Hypotheses H4a, H4b, and H5a were not supported. Both robots evoked equal levels of human-likeness and machine-likeness and evoked equal levels of affective trust (see Fig. 4 and Fig. 5). Displaying mean scores shows that both robot personality types were rather perceived as machine-like than as human-like (see Fig. 4). In addition, the main effect of participants' perceptions of robot intraversion on their attributions of affective trust was statistically significant, $F(1,67) = 6.23$,

$p = .015$, $\eta p^2 = .085$. Pearson correlations revealed that the more participants perceived the robot as intraverted, the higher their levels of affective trust, $r(69) = .28$, $p = .019$. Moreover, participants' ability to imagine the driving scenario had statistically significant effects on their indications of robot human-likeness, $F(1,67) = 9.78$, $p = .003$, $\eta p^2 = .127$, robot machine-likeness, $F(1,67) = 9.52$, $p = .003$, $\eta p^2 = .124$, affective trust, $F(1,67) = 35.39$, $p < .001$, $\eta p^2 = .346$, and cognitive trust, $F(1,67) = 26.36$, $p < .001$, $\eta p^2 = .282$. Pearson correlations showed that the more participants were able to imagine the driving scenario, the higher their levels of robot human-likeness, $r(69) = .33$, $p = .004$, robot machine-likeness, $r(69) = .33$, $p = .004$, affective trust, $r(69) = .58$, $p < .001$, and cognitive trust, $r(69) = .46$, $p < .001$.

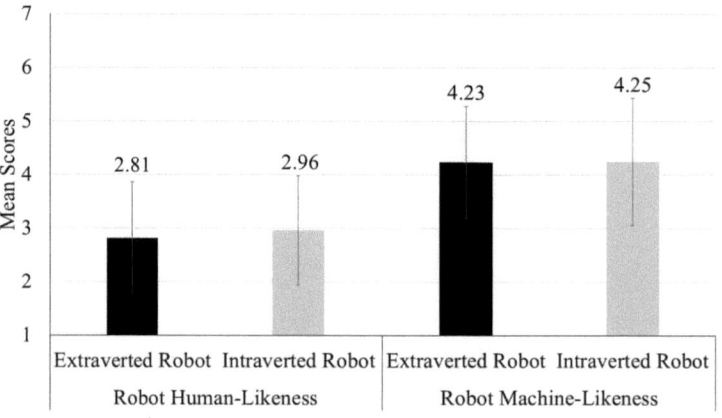

Fig. 4. Participants' mean scores on robot human- vs. machine-likeness by robot personality type (bars) and standard deviations (lines).

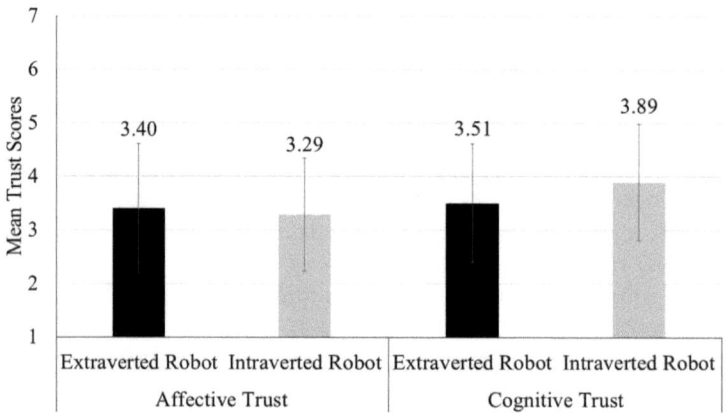

Fig. 5. Participants' mean scores on cognitive vs. affective trust by robot personality type (bars) and standard deviations (lines).

3.4 Manipulation Check

In order to check to what extent participants perceived both robot personality types as extraverted vs. intraverted according to their respective behavior, a mixed models MANCOVA was performed with participants' perceptions of the robot's extraversion vs. intraversion by the robot's designed personality as a between-subjects factor. In addition, participants' ability to imagine the displayed driving scenario with the robot was considered a covariate. The main effect of perceived robot personality was statistically significant, $F(1,69) = 16.73$, $p < .001$, $\eta p^2 = .195$, while the main effect of designed robot personality was not statistically significant, $F(1,69) = 0.75$, $p = .388$, $\eta p^2 = .011$. The interaction effect between perceived and designed robot personality was not statistically significant, $F(1,69) = 4.18$, $p = .045$, $\eta p^2 = .057$. The main effect of participants' ability to imagine the driving scenario with the robot was not statistically significant ($p > .05$). It was thus removed from the final statistical model. These results indicate that our experimental manipulation of robot personality had worked. Though independent of whether participants saw an extraverted or intraverted robot in the video, they perceived the robot as still more extraverted than intraverted. This effect was more apparent when the extraverted robot was presented than when the intraverted robot was displayed (see Fig. 6).

Participants' ability to imagine the driving scenario with a robot as presented in the video was fairly good: $M = 4.31$, $SD = 0.95$, when the extraverted robot was displayed and, $M = 3.81$, $SD = 0.97$, when the intraverted robot was displayed. An independent t-test revealed that participants' ability to imagine the driving scenario statistically significantly differed by robot personality type, $t(69) = 2.20$, $p = .031$. That is, participants could better imagine the driving scenario with the robot when an extraverted (vs. intraverted) robot was displayed.

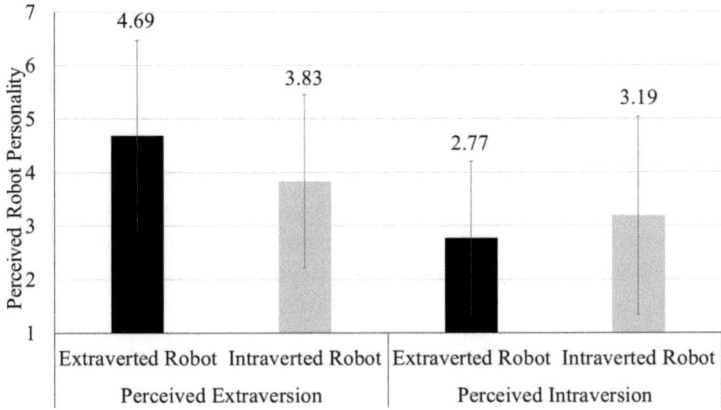

Fig. 6. Participants' mean perceptions of robot personality (extraverted vs. intraverted) by designed robot personality type (bars) and standard deviations (lines).

4 Discussion

Robot assistance is foreseen to gain more and more importance in a variety of contexts, one of which is intelligent driving assistance [39]. Since robotic agents are not yet common during car driving, there is still some ambivalence about their potential role. On the one hand, people might envision the robot during car driving as a social companion. On the other hand, people might prefer a robot to be a driving assistant with a focus on its functions rather than its social skills. Moreover, it is yet unknown which kind of robot personality (i.e., extraverted vs. intraverted) would be preferred by the driver in such a context and whether such preference would depend on it matching (or not) the participant's own personality [15]. Therefore, we conducted an online study where we displayed the video of a driving scenario in a CARLA simulation [23] paired with the iCub robot as if it were in the car with the driver (see Fig. 1). The iCub commented on the elements and events in the (simulated) street with a behavior designed to express an extraverted or an intraverted personality in a between-subjects design.

The responses provided after watching the videos revealed that participants clearly preferred a robot to be a driving assistant rather than a social companion during car driving. This finding was independent of the robot's designed personality. However, participants' ability to imagine the driving scenario with a robot determined their preferences for the robot's role: the better participants could imagine a robot during car driving, the more they preferred a robot to be a social companion. This suggests that participants were motivated to consider a robot as a social companion, but maybe this vision conflicted with the stereotypical image of robots as technically sophisticated agents, which is still prevalent in the media [44] and in people's minds [8]. Indeed, our participants had reported mainly knowing robots just from the media (see Sect. 2.5). The video showing a robot in a car driving scenario may have helped the more imaginative participants to overcome the stereotype, especially when the robot was extraverted and commented on the traffic in an informal, chatty manner. This chatty behavior of the extraverted robot might have made the scenario easier to imagine, which might explain participants' tendency to perceive the robot as extraverted rather than as intraverted, regardless of its designed personality.

Exploring participants' preferences for an extraverted or intraverted robot in more detail, no preference for either robot personality was found. However, participants' perceived similarity with the robot in being outgoing determined their preferences for either robot personality, partially supporting the similarity hypothesis [15]. In other words, the more participants perceived the robot to be similar to them in being outgoing, the higher their overall preferences to use a robot during car driving, although effect sizes were relatively small. Moreover, participants' ability to imagine the driving scenario with the robot affected their overall preferences for HRI during car driving, with moderate to large effect sizes. Conversely, participants' own levels of extraversion and intraversion and feelings of similarity to the robot in being reserved did not affect their overall preferences. Remarkably, participants' perceptions of a similarity to the robot in being outgoing and reserved were relatively low. These indications may explain why participants' own personality traits and perceptions of similarity with the robot in being reserved did not turn out statistically significant. [28] defined "unique humanness" a variety of traits (i.e., humble, thorough, organized, broadminded, and polite) that would be unique to humans. According to [32], participants' beliefs about unique humanness to be lacking in robots resulted in a reduced tendency to anthropomorphize and thus to accept and to socially bond with social robots. Given participants' little prior experience with robots—and perhaps also due to prevalent hesitations toward them [8,9]—participants may have struggled to imagine robots being similar to themselves in terms of personality traits—traits that are primarily prevalent in, and to some extent unique to, humans.

In terms of trust and perception of the robot, according to our hypothesis, the intraverted robot elicited more cognitive trust than the extraverted, indicating higher trust in the robot's functions. However, both robot personality types evoked similar levels of affective trust in the robot's benevolence. Likewise, in line with prior research [10,11], both robot personality types were perceived as equally human-like and machine-like, while there was a tendency to generally perceive both robot personality types as machine-like rather than as human-like. Remarkably, participants' ability to imagine the driving scenario with the robot affected their evaluations of the robot's human-likeness, machine-likeness, and cognitive and affective trust: the better participants could imagine, the higher the scores on all measured constructs.

The crucial effect of the scenario's imaginability was probably due to the study being conducted online. The online format allowed us to reach large sample sizes of participants. In addition, tying on research by [13], it could be considered an initial step of HRI research that allows us to gain first insights into participants' preferences for a robot's role and personality on which later development processes in HRI could be built. Future research will need to include a real interactive human-robot driving scenario in which participants do not merely imagine but rather directly experience human-robot interaction. The present findings are useful as a base to select the most appropriate robot behavior and personality to be tested in such an HRI test.

Despite the online format, participants' ability to imagine the presented scenario with the robot was fairly good. As a result, we could gain insight into which role would be preferable for a robot to have in driving scenarios, with a clear indication toward the choice of robots as driving assistants rather than social companions. Moreover, it emerged how, in such a context and role, it is not the robot's personality per se that matters for the participants, but rather its similarity (at least in terms of being outgoing) with the participants' own personality. Also, the robot's personality influenced the degree of cognitive trust toward it. These indications could represent useful guidelines in the development of robots in the emergent domain of intelligent driving assistance.

However, these judgments could change if robots were to become actually more pervasive in our environment, allowing more and more people to have a direct experience of their actual abilities and competences. Indeed, as with interpersonal relationships, realizing the full benefits of HRI requires time and repeated collaborations [4,28], which are essential for the development of trust and social bonds. Therefore, before thinking about how to program a robot in a way to evoke perceptions of human-likeness, personality or the like, the most important thing for developers and researchers in HRI is to enable frequent collaborations between humans and robots in various (secure) settings. This way, people's ability to imagine HRI and to be ready to benefit from it can be enhanced.

References

1. Adeniran, A.O.: Application of Likert Scale's type and Cronbach's alpha analysis in an airport perception study. Scholar J. Appl. Sci. Res. **2**(4), 1–5 (2019)
2. Ahmad, R., Siemon, D., Robra-Bissantz, S.: Communicating with machines: conversational agents with personality and the role of extraversion. In: Proceedings of the 54th Hawaii International Conference on System Sciences (HICSS), pp. 1170–1179. Hawaii International Conference on System Sciences (2021). https://doi.org/10.24251/HICSS.2021.142. https://hdl.handle.net/10125/71109
3. Alarcon, G.M., Capiola, A., Pfahler, M.D.: The role of human personality on trust in human-robot interaction. In: Trust in Human-Robot Interaction, pp. 159–178. Elsevier (2021)
4. Allport, G.W.: The Nature of Prejudice. Addison-Wesley, Reading, MA (1954)
5. Andriella, A., et al.: Do I have a personality? Endowing care robots with context-dependent personality traits. Int. J. Soc. Robot. **13**, 2081–2102 (2021)
6. Andrist, S., Mutlu, B., Tapus, A.: Look like me: matching robot personality via gaze to increase motivation. In: Proceedings of the 33rd Annual ACM Conference on Human Factors in Computing Systems, pp. 3603–3612 (2015)
7. Arora, A.S., Fleming, M., Arora, A., Taras, V., Xu, J.: Finding "h" in HRI: examining human personality traits, robotic anthropomorphism, and robot likeability in human-robot interaction. Int. J. Intell. Inf. Technol. (IJIIT) **17**(1), 1–20 (2021)
8. Bernotat, J.: Keep an eye on stereotypes–the impact of gender stereotypes (toward humans and robots) on language processing. Ph.D. dissertation, Bielefeld University (2021)
9. Bernotat, J., Eyssel, F.: Can (t) wait to have a robot at home?-Japanese and German users' attitudes toward service robots in smart homes. In: 2018 27th IEEE International Symposium on Robot and Human Interactive Communication (RO-MAN), pp. 15–22. IEEE (2018)
10. Bernotat, J., Eyssel, F., Sachse, J.: Shape it–the influence of robot body shape on gender perception in robots. In: Social Robotics: 9th International Conference, ICSR 2017, Tsukuba, Japan, November 22–24, 2017, Proceedings, vol. 9, pp. 75–84. Springer (2017)
11. Bernotat, J., Eyssel, F., Sachse, J.: The (FE) male robot: how robot body shape impacts first impressions and trust towards robots. Int. J. Soc. Robot. **13**(3), 477–489 (2021)
12. Bernotat, J., Landolfi, L., Pasquali, D., Nardelli, A., Rea, F.: Remember me-user-centered implementation of working memory architectures on an industrial robot. Front. Rob. AI **10**, 1257690 (2023)

13. Bernotat, J., et al.: Welcome to the future – how Naïve users intuitively address an intelligent robotics apartment. In: Agah, A., Cabibihan, J.-J., Howard, A.M., Salichs, M.A., He, H. (eds.) ICSR 2016. LNCS (LNAI), vol. 9979, pp. 982–992. Springer, Cham (2016). https://doi.org/10.1007/978-3-319-47437-3_96
14. Bhandari, P.: Type I & type II errors | differences, examples, visualizations, 22 June 2023. https://www.scribbr.com/statistics/type-i-and-type-ii-errors/. Accessed 3 Sept 2024
15. Byrne, D.: The Attraction Paradigm. Academic Press, New York (1971). Includes a Discussion of Complementarity
16. Byrne, D., Clore, G.L., Smeaton, G.: The attraction hypothesis: do similar attitudes affect anything? (1986)
17. Byrne, D., Nelson, D.: Attraction as a linear function of proportion of positive reinforcements. J. Pers. Soc. Psychol. **1**(6), 659 (1965)
18. Chen, N., Liu, X., Hu, X.: Effects of robots' character and information disclosure on human-robot trust and the mediating role of social presence. Int. J. Soc. Robot. **16**(4), 811–825 (2024)
19. Costa Jr. P.T., McCrae, R.R.: The NEO Personality Inventory Manual. Psychological Assessment Resources, Odessa, FL (1985)
20. Costa, P.T., McCrae, R.R.: NEO PI-R Professional Manual. Psychological Assessment Resources, Odessa, FL (1992)
21. Costa Jr. P.T., McCrae, R.R.: Four ways five factors are basic. Personality Individ. Differ. **13**(6), 653–665 (1992)
22. Cronbach, L.J.: Coefficient alpha and the internal structure of tests. Psychometrika **16**, 297–334 (1951). https://doi.org/10.1007/BF02310555
23. Dosovitskiy, A., Ros, G., Codevilla, F., Lopez, A., Koltun, V.: CARLA: an open urban driving simulator. In: Proceedings of the 1st Annual Conference on Robot Learning (CoRL), pp. 1–16. PMLR (2017). http://proceedings.mlr.press/v78/dosovitskiy17a/dosovitskiy17a.pdf
24. Driskell, J.E., Goodwin, G.F., Salas, E., O'Shea, P.G.: What makes a good team player? Personality and team effectiveness. Group Dyn. Theory Res. Pract. **10**(4), 249 (2006)
25. Esteban, P.G., et al.: Should I be introvert or extrovert? A pairwise robot comparison assessing the perception of personality-based social robot behaviors. Int. J. Soc. Rob., 1–11 (2022)
26. Esterwood, C., Essenmacher, K., Yang, H., Zeng, F., Robert, L.P.: Birds of a feather flock together: but do humans and robots? A meta-analysis of human and robot personality matching. In: 2021 30th IEEE International Conference on Robot & Human Interactive Communication (RO-MAN), pp. 343–348. IEEE (2021)
27. Esterwood, C., Essenmacher, K., Yang, H., Zeng, F., Robert, L.P.: A meta-analysis of human personality and robot acceptance in human-robot interaction. In: Proceedings of the 2021 CHI Conference on Human Factors in Computing Systems, pp. 1–18 (2021)
28. Haslam, N., Bain, P., Douge, L., Lee, M., Bastian, B.: More human than you: attributing humanness to self and others. J. Pers. Soc. Psychol. **89**(6), 937 (2005)
29. Hinz, N.A., Ciardo, F., Wykowska, A.: Individual differences in attitude toward robots predict behavior in human-robot interaction. In: Salichs, M.A., et al. (eds.) Social Robotics, pp. 64–73. Springer International Publishing, Cham (2019)
30. Jaffar, A., Ali, S., Iqbal, K.F., Ayaz, Y., Sajid, M., Asgher, U.: Personality prediction in human-robot-interaction (HRI). In: Industrial Cognitive Ergonomics and Engineering Psychology, vol. 35, p. 53 (2022)

31. Joosse, M., Lohse, M., Perez, J.G., Evers, V.: What you do is who you are: the role of task context in perceived social robot personality. In: 2013 IEEE International Conference on Robotics and Automation, pp. 2134–2139. IEEE (2013)
32. Li, S., Xu, L., Yu, F., Peng, K.: Does trait loneliness predict rejection of social robots? The role of reduced attributions of unique humanness (exploring the effect of trait loneliness on anthropomorphism and acceptance of social robots). In: Proceedings of the 2020 ACM/IEEE International Conference on Human-Robot Interaction, HRI 2020, pp. 271–280. Association for Computing Machinery, New York, NY, USA (2020). https://doi.org/10.1145/3319502.3374777
33. Lim, M.Y., et al.: We are all individuals: the role of robot personality and human traits in trustworthy interaction. In: 2022 31st IEEE International Conference on Robot and Human Interactive Communication (RO-MAN), pp. 538–545. IEEE (2022)
34. Mathes, J.: Auf dem weg zur vision zero – kein automobil ohne fahrerassistenz [on the way to vision zero – no automobile without driver assistance]. ATZ Automobiltechnische Zeitschrift **125**, 32–35 (2023). https://doi.org/10.1007/s35148-023-1616-2
35. McCrae, R.R., John, O.P.: An introduction to the five-factor model and its applications. J. Pers. **60**(2), 175–215 (1992)
36. Nomura, T., Suzuki, T., Kanda, T., Kato, K.: Measurement of negative attitudes toward robots. Interact. Studies. Soc. Behav. Commun. Biol. Artifi. Syst. **7**(3), 437–454 (2006)
37. Park, E., Jin, D., Del Pobil, A.P.: The law of attraction in human-robot interaction. Int. J. Adv. Rob. Syst. **9**(2), 35 (2012)
38. Peeters, M.A., Van Tuijl, H.F., Rutte, C.G., Reymen, I.M.: Personality and team performance: a meta-analysis. Eur. J. Pers. Published Eur. Asso. Pers. Psychol. **20**(5), 377–396 (2006)
39. Pisarov, J.: Autonomous driving. IPSI J. IPSI BgD Trans. Adv. Res. (TAR) **17**(2), 19–27 (2021)
40. Prolific: Prolific (2024). https://www.prolific.com. Version used, May 2024
41. Rammstedt, B., John, O.P.: Kurzversion des big five inventory (BFI-K). Diagnostica **51**(4), 195–206 (2005)
42. Robert Jr. L.P., et al.: A review of personality in human–robot interactions. Found. Trends® Inf. Syst. **4**(2), 107–212 (2020)
43. Rosenbaum, M.E.: The repulsion hypothesis: on the nondevelopment of relationships. J. Pers. Soc. Psychol. **51**(6), 1156 (1986)
44. Sandoval, E.B., Mubin, O., Obaid, M.: Human robot interaction and fiction: a contradiction. In: Beetz, M., Johnston, B., Williams, M.-A. (eds.) ICSR 2014. LNCS (LNAI), vol. 8755, pp. 54–63. Springer, Cham (2014). https://doi.org/10.1007/978-3-319-11973-1_6
45. Santamaria, T., Nathan-Roberts, D.: Personality measurement and design in human-robot interaction: a systematic and critical review. In: Proceedings of the Human Factors and Ergonomics Society Annual Meeting, vol. 61, pp. 853–857. SAGE Publications Sage CA, Los Angeles, CA (2017)
46. SoSciSurvey: Platform for online surveys (SoSci Survey GmbH, Munich, Germany). https://www.soscisurvey.de/
47. Stöber, J.: Die soziale-erwünschtheits-skala-17 (ses-17): entwicklung und erste befunde zu reliabilität und validität [the social desirability scale-17 (SDS-17): development and first findings on reliability and validity]. Diagnostica **45**(4), 173–177 (1999)

48. Stöber, J.: The social desirability scale-17 (SDS-17): convergent validity, discriminant validity, and relationship with age. Eur. J. Psychol. Assess. **17**(3), 222 (2001)
49. Tabachnick, B.G., Fidell, L.S.: Experimental designs using ANOVA. Thomson/Brooks/Cole, Belmont, CA (2007)
50. Tay, B., Jung, Y., Park, T.: When stereotypes meet robots: the double-edge sword of robot gender and personality in human-robot interaction. Comput. Hum. Behav. **38**, 75–84 (2014)

Applications in Real-World Case Studies

EBO Robot in Elderly Care: Interaction Styles and Multimodal Engagement Through Serious Games in Care Centers

Antonio Blanco, Alicia Condón, Zoraida Clavijo, Trinidad Rodríguez, and Pedro Núñez[✉]

RoboLab - Robotics and Artificial Vision Lab, Universidad de Extremadura, Cáceres, Spain
pnuntru@unex.es

Abstract. This paper presents preliminary findings from a six-week study evaluating the interaction between older adults and the EBO social robot across an elderly care center in Cáceres, Spain. The research examined how different robot configurations and interaction modalities influence engagement, satisfaction, and performance among 18 older adults with mild to moderate cognitive impairment (MMSE $\geq$ 21). Following a structured protocol approved by the UEX Bioethics and Biosafety Commission, participants engaged in twice-weekly sessions combining conversational interactions (3–5 min) and serious games, including Storytelling, Pasapalabra (word quiz game), and Simon Says (10–15 min). The study implemented a cross-over design alternating between two distinct robotic platform and interaction modes: Mode 1 (positive reinforcement, emotive expression, proximal positioning) and Mode 2 (neutral language, limited emotional expression, distant positioning). Preliminary results reveal that performance in cognitive games improved progressively across the intervention period, with 15% higher success rates observed in Mode 1 compared to Mode 2 interactions. Notably, both participants and professionals demonstrated clear preferences for emotive interaction styles over neutral approaches. These findings contribute valuable insights for designing and implementing social robots in gerontological settings, highlighting the importance of emotionally expressive interaction protocols when working with older adult populations.

Keywords: social robots · multi-modal interaction · cognitive stimulation

The aging population presents substantial challenges for healthcare systems worldwide, with projections indicating that by 2050, one in six people globally will be over the age of 65 [1]. This demographic shift has accelerated research into assistive technologies, with social robotics emerging as a promising field to enhance care delivery while addressing caregiver shortages. Social robots offer opportunities for continuous engagement, cognitive stimulation, and social interaction for older adults, particularly those in residential care settings where social isolation and cognitive decline are prevalent concerns [2,3].

Recent studies have demonstrated the potential benefits of human-robot interaction (HRI) in elderly care, including reduced feelings of loneliness [4], improved mood [5], and enhanced cognitive function through regular engagement with robotic platforms [6]. However, significant questions remain regarding optimal design parameters, interaction modes, and activity protocols that maximize both user acceptance and therapeutic efficacy. Determining which robotic features and interaction styles most effectively engage older adults with varying degrees of cognitive impairment is particularly challenging, an area where empirical evidence remains limited [7].

The EBO robot platform represents an emerging technology designed explicitly for interaction with older adults in assistive care environments [8]. EBO's current version combines conversational capabilities with serious games designed to stimulate cognitive functions while providing entertainment value. Two versions of the robot (EBO v1 and EBO v2) have been developed with incrementally enhanced capabilities, offering an opportunity to evaluate how different technological configurations affect user experience and engagement. Of particular interest is how emotionally expressive behaviors and interaction styles influence acceptance and performance among the target population.

This paper presents the methodology and preliminary findings from a study conducted in an elderly care center in Extremadura, Spain. The research follows a structured protocol approved by the Bioethics and Biosafety Commission of the University of Extremadura (89_2024_CERT), to examine how different versions of the EBO robot and varying interaction styles influence engagement, satisfaction, and performance among older adults with diverse cognitive profiles (Mini-Mental State Examination, MMSE, ≥ 21). By employing a cross-over design with multiple assessment time points, including initial, intermediate, and follow-up evaluations, the study aims to provide robust data on both immediate and sustained effects of robot-assisted interventions. Each interaction consisted of a 16–20 minute individual session twice weekly, including personalized conversational interactions (3–5 minutes) and participation in serious games (10–15 minutes) such as Storytelling, Simon Says, and Pasapalabra (word quiz game)[1] The games were version-specific: EBO v1 sessions utilized Storytelling, Conversation, and Pasapalabra, whereas EBO v2 sessions included Storytelling, Conversation, and Simon Says. Notably, except for Simon Says (fully autonomous), the therapist manually entered participant responses for Storytelling and Pasapalabra, following a *Wizard of Oz* approach. Audio from the sessions was recorded to facilitate subsequent phenomenological descriptive analyses.

Quantitative user performance metrics were integrated with qualitative assessments from participants and professional caregivers, gathered through specifically designed questionnaires assessing satisfaction, acceptability (USEQ scale), and clinical applicability. Additionally, two distinct robot interaction modes were systematically alternated weekly: Mode 1 (positive reinforcement, emotive expressions, proximal positioning) and Mode 2 (neutral language, lim-

---

[1] Readers can view a video demonstration of the EBO robot interacting during serious game sessions at: https://youtu.be/W8egkrkm050.

ited emotional expression, distant positioning). This allowed the exploration of how emotional expressiveness and positioning influenced user engagement and performance.

The findings from this research contribute to the growing evidence base for social robotics in eldercare and hold implications for the design of future robot-assisted therapies. By identifying specific robot configurations and interaction protocols that maximize engagement and therapeutic potential for older adults, this work addresses a critical gap in the literature regarding implementing social robots in real-world care settings. The insights gained may inform both technological development and clinical practice, potentially enhancing quality of life for older adults while supporting the work of professional caregivers.

1 Related Works

Social robots have been increasingly explored as tools for supporting elderly care, particularly for those with varying degrees of cognitive impairment. Sommerlad et al. [9] conducted a systematic review of 66 studies examining robot-based interventions for older adults, finding promising evidence for improvements in quality of life, reduced depression, and enhanced social engagement. Similarly, Pu et al. [3] performed a meta-analysis of randomized controlled trials involving social robots, reporting moderate positive effects on agitation, anxiety, and loneliness. These findings align with Cruz-Sandoval et al. [10], who identified key design requirements for robots aimed at older adults, emphasizing personalized interactions, appropriate emotional expression, and age-appropriate communication styles. Particularly relevant to cognitive stimulation, a review by Góngora Alonso et al. [11] identified 17 platforms used specifically for cognitive rehabilitation in dementia care, highlighting a growing trend toward integrating serious games and cognitive exercises within robot-mediated interventions.

The emotional expressiveness of social robots has emerged as a critical factor in user acceptance and engagement. Henschel et al. [12] identified emotional responsiveness as a key predictor of continued interaction in long-term care facilities. Tschida et al. [17] extended this by conducting a Wizard-of-Oz study in an independent living facility, where older adults appreciated robots capable of recalling personal details and showing expressive verbal and nonverbal behavior. Similarly, Zedda et al. [18] found that older users preferred cognitive training with robots exhibiting distinct personality traits, suggesting that social presence and affective expressivity enhance engagement in cognitively demanding tasks. These studies suggest that carefully designed emotional expressions and personalized styles may enhance both immediate engagement and long-term acceptance.

Implementing serious games within robotic platforms represents another active area. While earlier work such as Tapus et al. [14] focused on younger populations, recent studies address older users in clinical contexts. Cavallaro et al. [19] evaluated the Furhat robot for administering cognitive assessments in a healthcare setting, reporting high usability and acceptance. This reflects a growing movement toward validating socially assistive technologies in real-world environments. The present study builds upon this literature while addressing critical gaps. First, while previous work explored either robot design or interaction protocols [18] separately, our study jointly examines hardware configurations (EBO v1 vs. EBO v2) and interaction styles (emotive vs. neutral) within the same population. Second, we implement a crossover design with multiple assessment timepoints in a care facility. Third, our research incorporates participant performance metrics and caregiver assessments, offering a more comprehensive evaluation of clinical applicability. Finally, the study was conducted in a real-world environment over an extended period, enhancing ecological validity and providing insights into practical implementation challenges. These methodological advances contribute valuable data to inform both technological development and clinical application of social robots in cognitive rehabilitation.

2 Methodology

2.1 Participants

Participants included 18 residents from an elderly care center in Cáceres, Extremadura, Spain. Eligible participants were adults aged 65 or older with mild to moderate cognitive impairment (72% female, 28% male), determined by a Mini-Mental State Examination score equal to or greater than 21. Individuals with severe cognitive impairment or significant language impairments preventing effective verbal communication with the robot were excluded. All participants voluntarily consented to participate, and ethical approval was granted by the Bioethics and Biosafety Commission of the University of Extremadura.

2.2 Robot Description: EBO v1 and EBO v2

The robotic system utilized in this study comprises two versions of the EBO platform, EBO v1 and EBO v2 (see Fig. 1). Both robots share a compact, user-friendly design tailored explicitly for elderly interaction. They are characterized by their small size, ease of use, and expressive digital face, designed to foster emotional connection and reduce apprehension towards technology.

EBO v1 features conversational interaction capabilities and implements two serious games: Storytelling and Pasapalabra. Both games involve active therapist participation (therapist-in-the-loop) using a *Wizard of Oz* method, where the therapist manually inputs participants' responses during gameplay. EBO v2 builds upon EBO v1 by integrating an additional serious game, Simon Says, which operates autonomously. Simon Says is a color-sequencing cognitive game designed to challenge and engage participants through adjustable difficulty levels, adapting dynamically to the user's responses. Additionally, EBO v2 includes upgraded hardware allowing improved real-time interactions and responsiveness. Both versions leverage modular hardware architecture with affordable components, facilitating scalable implementation in care settings (Table 1).

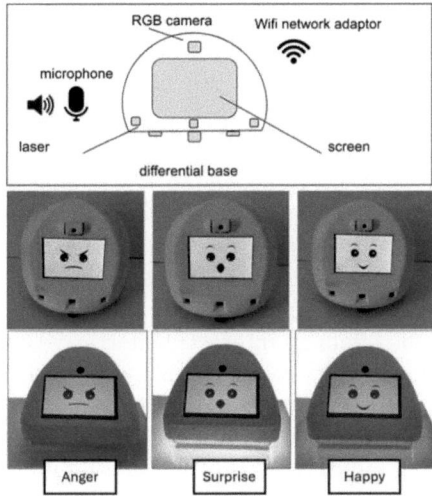

Fig. 1. Hardware overview and emotional expression of the EBO social robot. Top: schematic representation of main components including sensors, actuators, and network connectivity. Middle row: EBO v1 displaying emotional expressions (anger, surprise, and happiness) on its screen. Bottom row: EBO v2 showing the same emotions, enhanced with synchronized LED lighting to reinforce affective display

The software architecture of EBO allows seamless integration of the COR-TEX cognitive architecture, enabling adaptive and personalized user interactions [16].

Table 1. Comparison between EBOv1 and EBOv2

Aspect	EBOv1	EBOv2
Controller	Raspberry Pi 3	Jetson Xavier NX
Sensors	4 individual LiDAR sensors, individual microphone	10 individual LiDAR sensors, omnidirectional microphone
Movement	Differential base	Differential base
Camera	Mobile camera	Fixed wide-angle camera
Human-Robot Interaction	Movement, sound, 3-inch screen	Movement, sound, 7-inch screen, LED lights
Programming Interface	Robocomp, LearnBlock	Robocomp, LearnBlock

2.3 Detailed Description of Serious Games

The interaction experiences provided by the EBO platforms are divided into two main categories: conversational interactions, aimed at promoting verbal expression, memory recall, and emotional engagement; and serious games, focused on cognitive stimulation through structured game-based tasks.

2.3.1 Conversational Interactions

- Conversation Game: The user engages in a dialogue with the robot in this game. The robot dynamically adapts the conversation to focus on personally relevant topics, such as the user's hobbies or family members. The primary aim is to encourage verbal expression and promote emotional engagement through personalized interaction.
- Storytelling This game offers an interactive narrative experience, where EBO guides the user through a story related to accomplishing a daily living activity. The robot narrates the story and presents the user with binary choices at key decision points. The session concludes once the user completes the activity's objective. This format supports executive functioning, decision-making, and narrative thinking.

2.3.2 Serious Games

- Pasapalabra (word quiz game) Inspired by the well-known television game, Pasapalabra targets vocabulary retrieval, sustained attention, processing speed, and semantic memory. The game consists of a series of word-definition associations arranged alphabetically. Question sets are thematically organized and aligned with topics commonly used in cognitive therapy for older adults.
- Simon Says This cognitive challenge is based on sequences of colored lights paired with audio cues. The user must memorize and accurately replicate each sequence, which increases in length with each round. Difficulty is adjustable and adapts to user performance, promoting working memory, inhibition control, and attentional flexibility.

2.4 Session Control and Data Management with CORTEX

Game execution and data management within the EBO platform are coordinated through a modular architecture built on CORTEX, a distributed agent-based cognitive framework [16]. CORTEX agents ensure consistent execution, centralized data handling, and future scalability of the platform across settings and user profiles.

- Session Coordination Agent: This central agent represents the session workflow upon receiving therapist-provided configuration parameters—such as the user's name, cognitive profile, selected game, difficulty level, and game-specific variables. It initiates the appropriate Game Agent, transmits the relevant settings, and logs session metadata. The Session Coordination Agent ensures that each session is properly structured according to the therapeutic plan and maintains synchronization between the EBO robot and the backend system.

- **Game-Specific Agents:** Each serious game in the platform is managed by an individual CORTEX agent. These agents handle their corresponding games' logic and control flow during execution. Once initiated, a Game Agent takes over interaction management, monitors user input (manually entered by the therapist in most cases), and stores key performance metrics and session outcomes. These results are persisted in a structured database, allowing therapists to later review session history, track progress over time, and adjust future interventions accordingly.

This architecture supports modular extensibility: new games can be added by implementing a corresponding Game Agent without altering the platform's core logic. Separating coordination, execution, and data storage improves maintainability and facilitates therapist-guided personalization and long-term monitoring (Fig. 2).

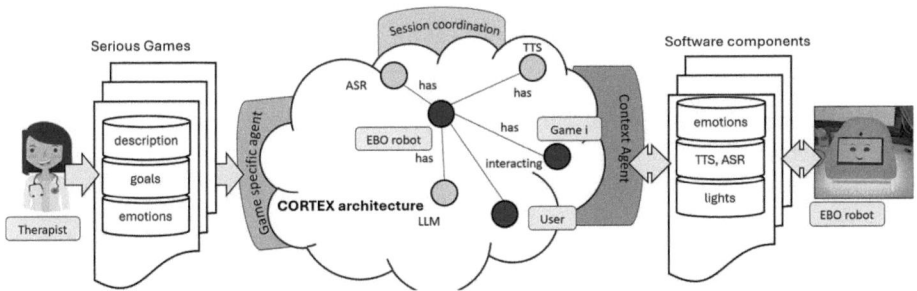

Fig. 2. System architecture for serious game interaction using the EBO robot. Therapists configure game sessions by defining descriptions, goals, and associated emotions. The CORTEX architecture orchestrates session coordination, speech recognition (ASR), text-to-speech (TTS), and large language model (LLM) components. A context-aware agent manages the integration of game-specific logic and user interaction. Software components on the EBO robot control emotional expressions, lighting, and speech interfaces to deliver adaptive, engaging sessions.

2.5 Experimental Design

The study employed a cross-over design conducted across six weeks, alternating weekly between two distinct interaction modes:

- **Mode 1:** Positive reinforcement, expressive emotions, proximal positioning.
- **Mode 2:** Neutral interaction, limited emotional expression, distant positioning.

Each mode reflects a specific social interaction style to modulate user experience and engagement. Mode 1 reflects an affirmative and emotionally supportive interaction style aimed at fostering user motivation and rapport. It employs a combination of verbal encouragement (e.g., "Well done!", "That's okay, try again"), a warm and enthusiastic tone of voice, and expressive visual cues such as animated facial expressions and synchronized LED lighting. The LEDs were color-coded to represent basic emotions (e.g., happiness, sadness, fear, etc.), enhancing the affective display. These cues were dynamically triggered based on user performance and emotional engagement.

In contrast, Mode 2 employs a more restrained and neutral style. Neutral interaction consists of generic, unsentimental verbal responses (e.g., "correct" or "incorrect"), without affective modulation. Limited emotional expression is reflected in a consistently serious facial demeanor, with no changes in tone or lighting throughout the interaction. Finally, distant positioning is implemented by placing the robot farther from the user and at an indirect angle, avoiding direct gaze or alignment, reducing the interaction's perceived immediacy and emotional salience.

Each robot was alternately configured with both interaction modes, resulting in four distinct experimental conditions:

- **Condition A:** EBO v1 in Mode 1
- **Condition B:** EBO v1 in Mode 2
- **Condition C:** EBO v2 in Mode 1
- **Condition D:** EBO v2 in Mode 2

Each participant engaged in two weekly sessions, each lasting 16–20 min, involving conversational interactions (3–5 min) and serious game participation (10–15 min). The structured alternation and combination of different robot embodiments with varying interaction styles allowed for a comprehensive evaluation of technological and behavioral influences on participant engagement, satisfaction, and cognitive performance.

2.6 Procedure

Researchers individually conducted sessions with support from facility professionals, including occupational therapists and psychologists. The therapist manually entered participant-specific data (name, cognitive impairment level, hobbies, and family members) into the robot interface for the conversation game. Once initiated, the therapist manually relayed participant responses to the robot, enabling controlled and personalized conversational interaction. In Storytelling, the therapist entered participant information and selected the specific game scenario focused on an activity of daily living. After initiating the session, the therapist manually provided participant responses to the robot, following the same procedure described for the Conversation game. For Pasapalabra, the therapist inputted the participant's name and selected a predefined set of questions for the session. During gameplay, a menu displaying the correct answers allowed the therapist to manually indicate whether the participant's response was incorrect, skipped, or if the question needed to be repeated in case the participant did not hear it. In contrast, for Simon Says, the therapist configured the participant's name, number of rounds, allowed attempts, and difficulty level before game initiation; subsequently, the game operated autonomously without further therapist intervention. Sessions were audio-recorded for subsequent qualitative phenomenological analysis, maintaining strict adherence to ethical guidelines for data privacy and participant anonymity (Fig. 3).

(a) EBO interacting with an older adult during a supervised session involving touchscreen support and therapist assistance (Simon Says).

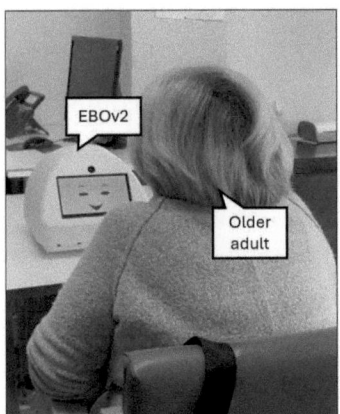

(b) EBO facilitating an autonomous session with an older adult (Pasapalabra).

Fig. 3. Examples of HRI during study sessions with older adults.

2.7 Outcome Measures

Primary outcomes included user satisfaction, acceptability, cognitive and game performance. Specific scales utilized were MMSE, Barthel Index, Yessevag scale, NARS, USEQ, and custom-designed satisfaction questionnaires. Additionally, professional caregiver feedback regarding clinical applicability and robot acceptability was collected through structured qualitative assessments.

3 Results and Discussion

3.1 User Satisfaction and Acceptability

Preliminary findings from participant satisfaction surveys indicate statistically significant differences in satisfaction ratings between robot versions, with EBO v2 receiving higher overall ratings ($p < 0.05$). Users consistently preferred interaction Mode 1, highlighting the importance of emotional expressiveness and positive reinforcement. Overall user satisfaction was rated at 4.38/5, while conversational pleasantness received a high rating of 4.46/5. Users strongly recommended interacting with EBO, averaging 4.68/5. The ease of conversation and the robot's voice and appearance were also highly rated, with averages of 4.47/5 and 4.56/5, respectively.

Participants indicated that the robot's emotions were relatively easy to interpret (3.94/5), although they found emotional expressions moderately motivating (3.94/5) and generally beneficial for enhancing the interaction experience (4.00/5).

3.2 Cognitive and Performance Outcomes

Performance data revealed progressive improvement in cognitive game tasks across the intervention period. Notably, interactions under Mode 1 showed approximately 15% higher success rates compared to Mode 2, based on descriptive measures such as the percentage of correct responses, total rounds completed, and session-level performance trends. These findings suggest a beneficial impact of emotionally expressive and engaging interaction protocols on cognitive performance and sustained user involvement. Participants reported the robot's language to be clear and comprehensible (4.26/5), comfortable (4.30/5), and helpful in task resolution (4.10/5).

3.3 Professional Caregivers Feedback

Qualitative assessments from professional caregivers indicated high acceptance of the EBO platform (average rating 4.2/5). Caregivers underscored specific strengths, such as improved user engagement, clear therapeutic applications in cognitive stimulation, and the robot's adaptability. Professionals confirmed distinct differences between EBO versions, noting a preference for EBO v2 due to its advanced autonomous functionalities and interactive responsiveness.

3.4 Detailed Statistical Analysis

Table 2 presents detailed statistical results, including means, standard deviations, and 95% confidence intervals for key user satisfaction and interaction variables measured in the study. Overall, satisfaction and acceptance metrics showed consistently high scores, indicating positive user experiences and perceived effectiveness of the robot's interaction capabilities. Emotional expressiveness and conversational clarity were notably important to participants.

Table 2. Detailed statistical results of user satisfaction and interaction variables.

Metric	Mean	Std. Dev.	95% CI Lower	95% CI Upper
General Satisfaction	4.38	0.59	4.24	4.52
Conversational Pleasantness	4.46	0.69	4.30	4.62
Conversation Comprehension	4.26	0.65	4.11	4.42
Recommendation to Others	4.68	0.53	4.56	4.80
Ease of Conversation	4.47	0.71	4.31	4.64
Emotions Easy to Interpret	3.94	0.84	3.75	4.14
Emotions Enhanced Motivation	3.94	0.94	3.72	4.17
Emotional Expression Improved Experience	4.00	0.93	3.78	4.22
Clear Language	4.26	0.80	4.07	4.45
Comfortable Language	4.30	0.83	4.10	4.49
Language Facilitated Tasks	4.10	0.86	3.90	4.30
Appropriate Interaction Distance	3.65	1.16	3.38	3.93
Orientation Favored Communication	3.77	1.35	3.45	4.10
Defined and Coherent Personality	4.33	0.61	4.19	4.48
Attractive and Pleasant Personality	4.25	0.71	4.08	4.42

Our findings align with prior research indicating that emotionally expressive robots can foster higher engagement and satisfaction among older adults with mild cognitive impairment compared to neutral approaches [10,13]. The 15% increase in task success rates under Mode 1 is consistent with the positive reinforcement strategies that other studies have shown to be effective in enhancing cognitive performance [3,12]. Moreover, the multi-site nature of our trial addresses a gap often noted in single-site experiments, adding ecological validity to the results and supporting the feasibility of implementing EBO robots in diverse gerontological settings.

4 Conclusions

The findings of this study highlight the effectiveness of social robotic interventions, specifically using the EBO platforms, in engaging elderly adults and supporting cognitive stimulation through personalized, adaptive interactions. Emotionally expressive interaction styles (Mode 1) significantly improved user satisfaction, engagement, and cognitive performance compared to neutral interaction modes.

These outcomes underscore the critical importance of tailoring interventions to each user and evaluating their impact over extended periods. Future research should focus on integrating AI-driven adaptive game algorithms that continuously adjust challenge levels, content, and feedback based on individual performance and preferences. Additionally, future work will incorporate inferential statistical analyses (e.g., ANOVA or effect size estimation) to rigorously test for statistically significant differences across experimental conditions. Long-term studies are essential to determine whether personalized and dynamically evolving interventions can sustain improvements in cognitive and emotional outcomes for older adults, thus ensuring that robotic therapies remain effective and relevant in real-world elderly care settings.

Acknowledgments. This work has been partially funded by the FEDER Project 0124_EUROAGE_MAS_4_E (POCTEP Program 2021–2027).

References

1. World Health Organization. Ageing and health. World Health Organization (2021). https://www.who.int/news-room/fact-sheets/detail/ageing-and-health. Accessed 20 Mar 2025
2. Abdi, J., Al-Hindawi, A., Ng, T., Vizcaychipi, M.P.: Scoping review on the use of socially assistive robot technology in elderly care. BMJ Open **8**(2), e018815 (2018). https://doi.org/10.1136/bmjopen-2017-018815
3. Pu, L., Moyle, W., Jones, C., Todorovic, M.: The effectiveness of social robots for older adults: a systematic review and meta-analysis of randomized controlled studies. Gerontologist **59**(1), e37–e51 (2019). https://doi.org/10.1093/geront/gny046
4. Robinson, H., MacDonald, B., Kerse, N., Broadbent, E.: The psychosocial effects of a companion robot: a randomized controlled trial. J. Am. Med. Dir. Assoc. **14**(9), 661–667 (2013). https://doi.org/10.1016/j.jamda.2013.02.007
5. Moyle, W., et al.: Use of a robotic seal as a therapeutic tool to improve dementia symptoms: a cluster-randomized controlled trial. J. Am. Med. Dir. Assoc. **18**(9), 766–773 (2017). https://doi.org/10.1016/j.jamda.2017.03.018
6. Soler, A.V., et al.: Social robots in advanced dementia. Front. Aging Neurosci. **7**, 133 (2015). https://doi.org/10.3389/fnagi.2015.00133
7. Vandemeulebroucke, T., de Casterlé, B.D., Gastmans, C.: The use of care robots in aged care: a systematic review of argument-based ethics literature. Arch. Gerontol. Geriatr. **74**, 15–25 (2018). https://doi.org/10.1016/j.archger.2017.08.014
8. Blanco, A., Pérez, G., Condón, A., Rodríguez, T., Núñez, P.: AI-enhanced social robots for older adults care: evaluating the efficacy of ChatGPT-powered storytelling in the EBO platform. In: 2024 33rd IEEE International Conference on Robot and Human Interactive Communication (RO-MAN), Pasadena, CA, USA, pp. 2109-2116 (2024). https://doi.org/10.1109/RO-MAN60168.2024.10731292

9. Yu, C., Sommerlad, A., Sakure, L., Livingston, G.: Socially assistive robots for people with dementia: systematic review and meta-analysis of feasibility, acceptability and the effect on cognition, neuropsychiatric symptoms and quality of life. Ageing Res. Rev. **78**, 101633 (2022). https://doi.org/10.1016/j.arr.2022.101633
10. Cruz-Sandoval, D., Favela, J., Sandoval, E.B.: Strategies to facilitate the acceptance of a social robot by people with dementia. In: Proceedings of ACM/IEEE International Conference on Human-Robot Interaction (HRI), Cambridge, UK, pp. 197–205 (2018). https://doi.org/10.1145/3173386.3177081
11. Alonso, S.G., et al.: Social robots for people with aging and dementia: a systematic review of literature. Telemed. e-Health **25**(7), 533–540 (2019). https://doi.org/10.1089/tmj.2018.0051
12. Henschel, A., Laban, G., Cross, E.S.: What makes a robot social? A review of social robots from science fiction to a home or hospital near you. Curr. Rob. Rep. **2**(1), 9–19 (2021). https://doi.org/10.1007/s43154-020-00035-0
13. Chu, M.T., Khosla, R., Khaksar, S.M.S., Nguyen, K.: Service innovation through social robot engagement to improve dementia care quality. Assist. Technol. **29**(1), 8–18 (2017). https://doi.org/10.1080/10400435.2016.1171807
14. Tapus, A., et al.: Children with autism social engagement in interaction with Nao, an imitative robot: a series of single case experiments. Interact. Stud. **13**(3), 315–347 (2012). https://doi.org/10.1075/is.13.3.01tap
15. Huang, X., Ali, N.M., Sahrani, S.: Evolution and future of serious game technology for older adults. Information **15**, 385 (2024). https://doi.org/10.3390/info15070385
16. Bustos, P., Manso, L.J., Bandera, A.J., Bandera, J.P., García-Varea, I., Martíínez-Gómez, J.: The cortex cognitive robotics architecture: Use cases. Cogn. Syst. Res. **55**, 107–123 (2019). https://doi.org/10.1016/j.cogsys.2019.01.003
17. Tschida, C., Smith, J., Johnson, E.: A wizard-of-oz study of social robot conversational support for independent older adults. In: Proceedings of the 2025 ACM Conference on Human Factors in Computing Systems (CHI) (2025). https://doi.org/10.1145/3434074.3447179.
18. Zedda, E., Manca, M., Paternò, F., Santoro, C.: Older adults' user experience with introvert and extravert humanoid robot personalities. Univ. Access Inf. Soc. **24**(1), 357–373 (2023). https://doi.org/10.1007/s10209-023-01054-2
19. Cavallaro, A., Rossi, M., Bianchi, L.: Clinical deployment of a social robot for neuropsychological assessment in older adults. IEEE Trans. Technol. Soc. 123–134 (2024). https://doi.org/10.1109/TTS.2024.3521341.

Participatory Design for Human-Robot Interaction with Syrian Refugees and Asylum Seekers

Shaul Ashkenazi[1]( ), Rawan Srour-Zreik[1], Gabriel Skantze[2], Jane Stuart-Smith[3], and Mary Ellen Foster[1]

[1] School of Computing Science, University of Glasgow, Glasgow, UK
shaul.ashkenazi@glasgow.ac.uk
[2] Division of Speech, Music and Hearing, KTH Royal Institute of Technology, Stockholm, Sweden
[3] School of Critical Studies, University of Glasgow, Glasgow, UK

Abstract. The Syrian refugee crisis is among the largest globally. We are developing a social robot tailored to the needs of displaced Syrians hosted in Scotland. As part of a mixed-methods study to understand the needs of this population and the possible use cases of the robot, we conducted two focus groups with Syrian refugees and asylum seekers residing in Glasgow. Using thematic analysis, we identified these participants' unmet needs and existing gaps in access to services. Participants observed an Arabic-speaking social robot, and together we explored its potential as a solution to help navigate bureaucratic processes and access services. The participants expressed curiosity and enthusiasm about the robot. As they shared experiences of homelessness and displacement, they also highlighted bureaucracy and the English language as key barriers to accessing services. This study identifies key design requirements for developing a multilingual support robot for refugees and asylum seekers.

Keywords: Human-robot interaction · Field studies · Focus groups · Refugees · Asylum seekers · Migrants · Arabic

1 Introduction

Millions of people worldwide flee their countries for reasons including wars, climate change and hostile environments. One of the largest refugee crises is in the Syrian Arab Republic, where over 6 million Syrians have been displaced from their homeland [37]. According to the UK Home Office, Scotland has received around 16% of the 20,319 Syrian refugees placed in the UK under the Vulnerable Persons Resettlement Scheme [26]. In addition, the Scottish Refugee Council (SRC) reports that approximately 650 Syrians in Scotland currently have pending asylum applications [29]. Refugees and asylum seekers such as these require a gradual integration in their new host country, including support with access to resources and services [13].

We are developing a social robot designed to meet the needs of displaced Syrians hosted in Scotland. As part of the design process, we have collaborated with a Scottish charity supporting refugees. Through the charity, we recruited 9 Syrian refugees and asylum seekers currently residing in Glasgow. We carried out two focus groups where the participants were invited to share their perspectives in Levantine Arabic, their native language, with the goal of co-designing a social robot that addresses their specific needs and enhances their well-being.

2 Related Work

Refugees and asylum seekers have diverse experiences in their host countries, including homelessness [25]. Those who find themselves displaced and applying for asylum often encounter what has been described as *"being kept in a perpetual limbo"* [12] and they may face prolonged detention and expulsion [5]. The newly arrived are often not fluent in the spoken host language, and rely on cultural mediators such as integration advisors [33]. A further shared experience is navigating bureaucratic processes, requiring significant time and energy for appointments and paperwork. [19].

At the national level, non-government organizations such as Refugee Action and Migrant Help play a central role in supporting and caring for refugees and asylum seekers across the UK [7]. In Scotland, these efforts are complemented by the *New Scots Refugee Integration Strategy*, a collaborative effort by the Scottish Government, COSLA (the Convention of Scottish Local Authorities), and the Scottish Refugee Council (SRC), aimed at supporting refugees and asylum seekers in Scotland. The term "New Scots" was chosen as it *"conveys a helpful message of inclusion to all who need safety in Scotland for as long as they need it"* [28]. The SRC provides refugees with a welcome package translated into five languages, including Arabic, containing essential information about emergency services, benefits, healthcare, finance, and more [27]. However, due to significant mental strain and distress caused by displacement, many refugees were unable to focus on the package contents, despite its informative nature [15].

To better understand the experiences of refugees and asylum seekers, researchers have conducted focus groups and interviews, often with the assistance of translators. For instance, focus groups with refugees from conflict-affected regions, such as Somalia and Ethiopia, identified key barriers to discussing mental health, including factors such as a history of political repression, fear, lack of knowledge, and shame [30]. Other studies, conducted in Germany and Turkey have further examined the challenges Syrian refugees face in accessing services. Participants reported being unable to book appointments over the phone due to limited host language proficiency [11], or being unaware of available services in their own language [21]. In Scotland, interviews with Syrian refugee families highlighted socio-cultural differences as major barriers to accessing services [15]. A year-long design research project conducted in informal Syrian refugee settlements in Lebanon emphasized the crucial role of NGOs in building trust between researchers and participants [34].

Fig. 1. Syrian women observing the robot system in action

Participatory design of a social robot has become a common practice, working with different user groups, such as senior adults [23], children [2], blind people [6], and many more. Only a few studies have been conducted with migrants, and even fewer with refugees. For example, in one study, researchers interviewed teachers at an international primary school in Switzerland, and proposed the use of social robots in classrooms to support the inclusion of migrant-background children [36]. Another study engaged three Middle Eastern refugees and four professionals in a co-design process. The project focused on developing an egg-shaped robot prototype aimed at supporting refugee integration in Portugal [31].

Research in the field of migrants and HCI is extensive, as demonstrated by a survey of 282 research publications published between 2010 and 2019 [24]. The authors noted that HCI research on migration remains exploratory, given its limited technological focus and number of intervention studies. Recent studies have focused on designing chatbot assistants (e.g., [16,38]). However, such online solutions may distance migrants from the aid agencies and there is a potential risk of misinformation, in case the data is out-of-date [14]. To bridge this gap, we present the design process of what we believe to be the first social robot co-designed with refugees and asylum seekers to address their bureaucratic needs. The robot is envisioned to work alongside human support staff, with up-to-date, organization-specific data to ensure relevant and effective assistance. This work lays the groundwork for its future development.

3 Materials and Methods

Our overall goal is to develop a social robot that is able to support Syrian refugees and asylum seekers with access to services and support. As part of the

Table 1. Participant detailed characteristics

ID	Age	Gender	Civil Status	Education	Residence Status	Living Situation
1	35	Male	Single	Middle School	Refugee	Alone
2	36	Male	Single	University	Refugee	Alone
3	39	Male	Single	University	Refugee	Alone
4	31	Male	Single	University	Refugee	Alone
5	43	Male	Married	Primary School	Refugee	Alone
6	48	Male	Married	University	Refugee	With family
7	34	Female	Married	University	Asylum Seeker	With family
8	41	Female	Married	University	Asylum Seeker	With family
9	37	Female	Married	Middle School	Asylum Seeker	With family

design process, we carried out focus group studies in the refugees' own language to assess the needs of this group, as well as their overall attitudes toward robots.

Prior research on second-language interaction and access to services has found that clients prefer communicating in their native language, as it allows them to express emotions, articulate problems, and reflect on situations more thoroughly (e.g., [17,35]). Based on these findings, we had the following research questions for this study:

RQ1 What services do Syrian refugees and asylum seekers need access to, and how do they currently access these services?

RQ2 Do Syrian refugees and asylum seekers prefer accessing services in their native language, even if provided by a robot? Additionally, does the robot's appearance, including gender and religious attire, influence their preference?

RQ3 Will Syrian refugees and asylum seekers have a more positive view of using a robot after observing it in action?

3.1 Participants

The focus groups involved a total of nine Syrian refugees and asylum seekers currently living in Glasgow, UK (Table 1). We collaborated with *Central and Western Integration Network* (CWIN), a Scottish charity supporting refugees, asylum seekers and migrant workers throughout Glasgow (www.cwin.org.uk), where the first author has been volunteering with the drop-in service since April 2023. In the last year, 152 individuals from Syria have come to CWIN to participate in their activities and to seek support (30% women). Participants were recruited through the charity's different WhatsApp groups and through posts on Facebook.

3.2 Focus Groups

Two focus groups were conducted in Levantine Arabic by the second author, a native speaker: this is notable, as previous studies have shown that using interpreters can interrupt the flow of conversation and cause distractions [32], while a shared language between researcher and participants fosters trust [24]. The first group took place in December 2024 with six men, and the second in March 2025 with three women (Fig. 1). Each session lasted two hours and was held at a multicultural center in Glasgow, where the CWIN charity is based.

3.3 Robot System

As part of each focus group, participants were shown the multilingual student support robot system described in [4]. At a hardware level, the robot incorporates the Furhat robot [1] and a Kindle Fire tablet, along with a microphone (Fig. 2). An interaction with the system will start by clicking on the tablet, and choosing between English or Modern Standard Arabic. The interaction will start in that language, using a language-specific synthetic voice from Amazon Polly [3]. Each session ends with a QR code that the user can scan, which will lead to further information in the language chosen at the beginning of the interaction.

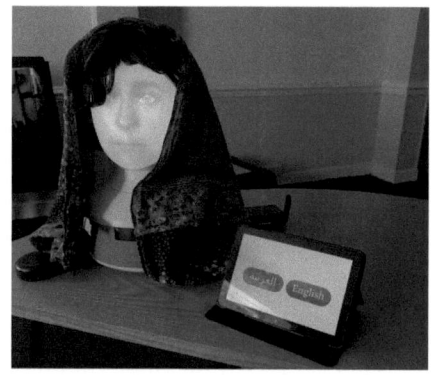

Fig. 2. The robot system.

3.4 Data Analysis

Thematic Analysis The Arabic recordings of the two focus groups were transcribed using Whisper [20], then divided into speakers in the Speaker Diarization process using Pyannote.Audio [9]. The diarized transcripts were then translated into English using DeepL Pro, a secured online translator [10]. The transcripts and the English translations were verified by the second author. Following the six steps outlined by Braun and Clark [8], we then generated codes and themes.

NARS Questionnaire Analysis The Negative Attitude toward Robot Scale (NARS) [18] is commonly used to explore populations' acceptability of robots. It is classified into 3 subscales:

S1: *Negative Attitude toward Situations of Interaction with Robots.*
S2: *Negative Attitude toward the Social Influence of Robots.*
S3: *Negative Attitude toward Emotions in Interaction with Robots.*

We translated the NARS questionnaire into Arabic for use in the study (see Fig. 4 in Appendix). Participants completed it before and after observing the robot system in action, and their responses were compared to explore trends in their attitudes. Each statement was evaluated on a 7-likert scale (1 = Strongly

Disagree, 7 = Strongly Agree). Scores for positively worded statements were reversed (e.g., 1 = 7, 2 = 6). For each participant, we calculated three average scores, one for each subscale, for both the *before* and *after* phases. This resulted in 27 data points per phase.

3.5 Procedure

Participants in each focus group were welcomed to a designated room, where they were told that they will be asked about access to services and their views about robots and AI. They then filled in the NARS questionnaire, containing 14 statements concerning the negative attitude toward robots. They were asked about the difficulties they had when they arrived in the UK, and a discussion started. Afterwards, they were shown the robot system, with two interactions concerning local tax exemption, first in Arabic, and then in English, to showcase the system's multilingual capabilities. The robot's appearance was modified by first dressing it with a wig and a hijab (see Fig. 2), and then switched to a bearded face with a hat. They were asked about using the robot to assist them and about its appearance. After the system introduction, they filled the NARS questionnaire again. All participants were compensated for their participation with a £20 shopping voucher.

4 Qualitative Results

We report four themes: 1) *Experiences of Refugees and Asylum Seekers* with subthemes: a) Housing Insecurity b) Being Displaced; 2) *Barriers to Services* with subthemes: a) Language b) Bureaucracy and Knowledge Gaps; 3) *Existing Support Systems*; 4) *Exploring Potential Support Solutions* with subthemes: a) Interaction b) Robot Appearance. The first three themes were identified in the transcript of the discussions prior to the robot demonstration, while the fourth theme primarily occurred in the discussion afterward.

4.1 Experiences of Refugees and Asylum Seekers

Housing insecurity is a common challenge faced by refugees and asylum seekers. Participants described times without housing or work—and even when they were housed, it was often temporary, as one stated *"God willing, you will be in the hotel. We stayed for about a month. Then we got a temporary house"* (Woman, 41). The feeling of helplessness and lack of agency was emphasized in the words of another participant, *"this is one of the first difficulties, the most difficult one, which means you spend a week or two without a home and without a job"* (Man, 31).

Participants discussed reasons for leaving Syria and looking for a new host country, *"because of the war and destruction, people were displaced, it wasn't an economic reason, it was a political reason, people were afraid for themselves and their lives"* (Man, 43). A major concern is the long wait for asylum decisions, during which they may face detention and have to rely on lawyers to speak with authorities. They fled Syria for a better future, yet remain at the mercy of others: "*it depends on the official officer who investigates and takes the case, and based on the evidence you give him, he decides whether you deserve asylum or not*" (Man, 36).

4.2 Barriers to Services

Two key barriers to accessing services were identified: language and bureaucratic knowledge gaps. The language barrier was especially pronounced when participants had to use the phone to book appointments, a situation that leads to frustration or being dependent on one's community and friends. "*I'd have to get a friend who speaks English and they only accept reservations from a private number, so I have to call a friend to book me a GP appointment*" (Man, 35) or "*as for the GP, it's difficult to call at exactly 8:30am, and you can't go in person – they don't answer the phone, you can only book for the same day, and there's no interpreter*" (Man, 43). Fluency in English is either required or highly favorable for university study or employment. While ESOL (English for Speakers of Other Languages) courses are available for free, they often have long waiting lists, and individuals may wait up to a year before they can begin. "*there are young people here who say that they had to wait, for example, 6 months or 8 months until they were accepted*" (Man, 39).

The lack of reliable information sources is a major barrier, especially when dealing with bureaucracy. Participants encountered many difficulties when trying to access basic services such as registering in a clinic without a home address. "*When you apply for asylum, they're supposed to understand your situation – that you're new to the country and don't know your way around... The problem is, when you try to register with a GP, you need a proof of address. But when we first arrived, we didn't have one... It took a long time before we could finally register*" (Man, 35). They had to rely on their wit and knowledge in order to find their way around: "*there was no one to help us, no one to inform us. No organization or official body shared this information with us – we had to find out on our own, and only managed because we were educated*" (Woman, 34).

4.3 Existing Support Systems

Participants acknowledged the importance of local NGOs and charities operating in Glasgow. They often text or email them in order to receive support. "*If I have an application form that I don't understand, I can send it (to the SRC) on WhatsApp or if I want, for example, Travel Documentation, if I don't know how to make the application, they will help me*" (Woman, 41). On the other hand, there are many organizations which help, but each is responsible for a different aspect, so it can be difficult to know where to go and for what purpose: "*when you try to call, they either say it's full, say no, or don't answer–because you don't speak English. So you have to go to an organization for help, but then they refer you to another one, or give you appointments weeks in advance, or* add more steps. There's no single organization that provides everything, so the information really needs to be centralized" (Man, 31). The participants expressed interest in having a single platform having all the information in one place. Specifically, regarding ESOL course enrollment, they suggested having a list of nearby colleges offering such courses, "if all the information is there – the names of the colleges, the levels, the registration times, things like that. So it can be useful for refugees" (Man, 43). They also emphasized the need for support with registering at a doctor's clinic.

4.4 Exploring Potential Support Solutions

This theme was identified during the conversations that took place after the participants observed the robot and the support interactions in Arabic and English. While participants understood that the focus was on an Arabic-speaking robot, they emphasized the importance of making it multilingual to support other refugee groups: "the robot provides services to Syrian refugees who speak Arabic, it should also provide services to the Kurdish brothers who speak Kurdish" (Man, 45). Participants added that they would like it to be polite and empathetic, and discussed the positive aspects of using a robot: "it can be embarrassing if you talk to a person, but if you talk to a robot... there's a comfort level" (Woman, 43).

The participants were amused by the robot's appearance, but they did not display a preference to a gender or an attire. "it's important that it gives me the result I want in the end... Sometimes, you feel that some people trust a man more when he's the one speaking – like the information feels more accurate and convincing. But others who, on the contrary, feel more comfortable if it's a woman" (Woman, 37). Participants emphasized the importance of having services such as ESOL course registration and access to official information available in a single location. In addition, they suggested that the robot could assess students' English proficiency: "The robot can determine the level of the student and start working with him or guide him forward" (Man, 48). More generally, participants felt that any solution complementing existing services would be valuable, as one noted, "this is a very positive step that will make it easier for refugees and asylum seekers to access services very quickly." (Man, 35).

5 Quantitative Results

Figure 3 shows the overall NARS scores of participants before and after they observed the robot system. Participants' attitudes toward interaction with robots were generally positive, with average scores of 2.85 before and 2.8 after the observation. Their attitudes toward the social influence of robots were neutral, with average scores of 4.16 before and 4.36 after the observation. Lastly, their attitudes toward emotions in interaction with robots were neutral before the observation, average score of 4.33, and it was a bit more positive afterward with an average score of 3.44.

To control for multiple comparisons, we applied the Bonferroni correction, adjusting the significance threshold for all tests to $\alpha = 0.0167$. Paired t-tests did not find significant differences in any of the subscales (S1: $t(8) = 0.15, p = .88, d = .06$; S2: $t(8) = -0.35, p = .73, d = -.16$; S3: $t(8) = 2.07, p = .073, d = .91$). Thus, with this very small data sample, we were unable to find quantitative evidence to address RQ3.

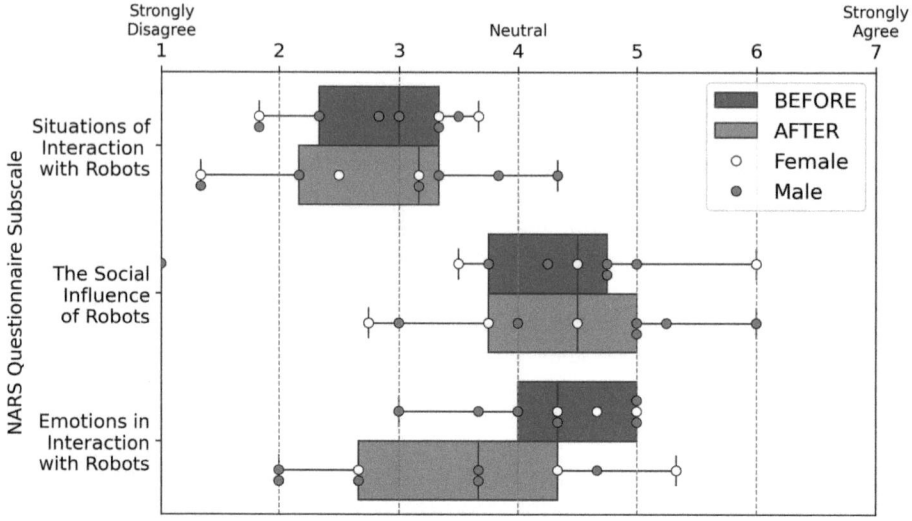

Fig. 3. Negative Attitude Toward Robots (n=9) [1=positive; 7=negative]

6 Discussion

In the discussions prior to showing the robot to the participants, three primary themes were identified: 1) *Experiences of Refugees and Asylum Seekers*; 2) *Barriers to Services*; 3) *Existing Support Systems*. Discussion on all of these themes addressed RQ1 regarding the services that Syrian refugees access and the way that they currently access them. The results also agree with previous research carried out in different host countries on the needs and challenges faced by refugees and asylum seekers (e.g., [21,30]), which is relevant to this group in Scotland. In the fourth theme identified after the robot demonstration, *Exploring Potential Support Solutions*, participants addressed RQ2 and were positive about using the robot as a complement to existing services delivered in their native language. Finally, participants' overall attitudes toward the robot ranged from neutral to positive, with no significant differences between before and after the demonstration, likely due to the small data sample used, and no evidence was found to address RQ3.

The experiences participants shared concerning housing insecurity and being displaced were also observed in previous work (e.g., [5,12,25]). The major barriers to accessing services identified were language and bureaucratic knowledge gaps. Participants expressed a strong preference for communicating in their native language, Arabic, due to the difficulties posed by having to rely on others. This observation aligns with existing literature and has been reported among refugees in Turkey, Germany and Scotland (e.g., [11,21,33]). Concerning bureaucracy, our data is also similar to previous findings (e.g., [19]). In the third theme, participants recognized the value and limitations of support from local charities, in relation to their own personal challenges. Similar claims were made in previous studies (e.g., [7,15,34]). These discussions revealed the services most important to them, particularly ESOL registration and access to healthcare, thereby addressing RQ1. They also emphasized the need for a reliable source of official information, ideally a unified platform.

Discussions continued after the participants observed the robot and examples for support interactions in Arabic and English. Participants explored potential support solutions, and indicated they would willingly use a robot, regardless of its gender or religious appearance (RQ2).

While a previous study using the NARS questionnaire reported fairly positive attitudes toward humanoid robots among Arabs who were not displaced [22], this study found similarly neutral to positive attitudes among Syrian refugees. This suggests that positive perceptions of humanoid robots may persist even in the context of displacement (Fig. 3). Having observed the robot in an interaction with the second author, both in Arabic and English, did not change their attitude significantly (RQ3).

7 Conclusions and Future Work

This study engaged refugees and asylum seekers in the first co-design process of a social robot aimed at addressing their bureaucratic needs. In a qualitative thematic analysis, we found that participants in our focus groups reported similar challenges that have been found in previous studies. When introduced to the idea of a social robot as a complement to existing support systems, participants were willing and enthusiastic about the robot addressing their needs, which was especially encouraging.

Based on our findings, we are currently developing a social robot speaking Modern Standard Arabic, Sorani Kurdish and Persian, in addition to English, with the goal of accommodating refugees and asylum seekers from Syria as well as the other regions that are registered at the CWIN charity. This robot will mainly provide information about healthcare services and other organizations operating in the city for its pilot version, and based on the feedback from the participants we will also explore support for other common and challenging tasks such as ESOL course registration.

Acknowledgments. The authors would like to thank the Syrian participants for taking part in the focus groups and the CWIN charity for their help. This work was supported by the *UKRI Centre for Doctoral Training in Socially Intelligent Artificial Agents*, Grant Number EP/S02266X/1.

Conflict of Interest. Author GS was employed by Furhat Robotics AB. The authors have no competing interests to declare that are relevant to the content of this article.

Appendix

أوافق بشدة Strongly Agree	أوافق Agree	أوافق إلى حد ما Somewhat Agree	لا أوافق ولا أعارض Neutral	أعارض إلى حد ما Somewhat Disagree	أعارض Disagree	أعارض بشدة Strongly Disagree	
							1. سأشعر بعدم الارتياح إذا امتلكت الروبوتات مشاعر بالفعل. (I would feel uneasy if robots really had emotions.)
							2. قد يحدث شيء سيئ إذا تطورت الروبوتات إلى كائنات حية. (Something bad might happen if robots developed into living beings.)
							3. سأشعر بالراحة عند التحدث مع الروبوتات. (I would feel relaxed talking with robots.)
							4. سأشعر بعدم الارتياح إذا أعطيت وظيفة تتطلب مني استخدام الروبوتات. (I would feel uneasy if I was given a job where I had to use robots.)
							5. إذا امتلكت الروبوتات مشاعر، سأتمكن من تكوين صداقات معها. (If robots had emotions, I would be able to make friends with them.)
							6. أشعر بالراحة عندما أكون مع روبوتات لديها مشاعر. (I feel comforted being with robots that have emotions.)
							7. كلمة "روبوت" لا تعني لي شيئًا. (The word "robot" means nothing to me.)
							8. سأشعر بالتوتر أثناء تشغيل روبوت أمام أشخاص آخرين. (I would feel nervous operating a robot in front of other people.)
							9. سأكره فكرة أن الروبوتات أو الذكاء الاصطناعي يقومون بإصدار أحكام حول الأشياء. (I would hate the idea that robots or artificial intelligences were making judgments about things.)
							10. سأشعر بالتوتر الشديد بمجرد الوقوف أمام روبوت. (I would feel very nervous just standing in front of a robot.)
							11. أشعر أنه إذا اعتمدت كثيرًا على الروبوتات، قد يحدث شيء سيئ. (I feel that if I depend on robots too much, something bad might happen.)
							12. سأشعر بالارتياب (الخوف الشديد) عند التحدث مع روبوت. (I would feel paranoid talking with a robot.)
							13. أشعر بالقلق من أن تكون الروبوتات تأثيرًا سيئًا على الأطفال. (I am concerned that robots would be a bad influence on children.)
							14. أشعر أن المجتمع في المستقبل سيكون تحت سيطرة الروبوتات. (I feel that in the future society will be dominated by robots.)

Fig. 4. NARS Questionnaire in Arabic

References

1. Al Moubayed, S., Beskow, J., Skantze, G., Granström, B.: FURHAT: a back-projected human-like robot head for multiparty human-machine interaction. In: Esposito, A., Esposito, A.M., Vinciarelli, A., Hoffmann, R., Müller, V.C. (eds.) Cognitive Behavioural Systems. LNCS, vol. 7403, pp. 114–130. Springer, Heidelberg (2012). https://doi.org/10.1007/978-3-642-34584-5_9
2. Alves-Oliveira, P., Arriaga, P., Paiva, A., Hoffman, G.: Children as robot designers. In: Proceedings of the 2021 ACM/IEEE International Conference on Human-Robot Interaction, pp. 399–408 (2021)
3. Amazon: Text to voice, text to speech software - amazon POLLY - AWS. https://aws.amazon.com/polly
4. Ashkenazi, S., Skantze, G., Stuart-Smith, J., Foster, M.E.: Goes to the heart: Speaking the user's native language. In: Companion of the 2024 ACM/IEEE International Conference on Human-Robot Interaction, pp. 214–218 (2024). https://doi.org/10.1145/3610978.3640633
5. Atak, I., Crépeau, F.: Asylum in the twenty-first century: trends and challenges. Routledge handbook of immigration and refugee studies, pp. 358–370 (2022)
6. Azenkot, S., Feng, C., Cakmak, M.: Enabling building service robots to guide blind people a participatory design approach. In: 2016 11th ACM/IEEE International Conference on Human-Robot Interaction (HRI), pp. 3–10. IEEE (2016)
7. Ballentyne, S., Drury, J.: Boundaries beyond borders: the impact of institutional discourse on the identities of asylum seekers. Curr. Res. Ecol. Soc. Psychol. **5**, 100130 (2023)
8. Braun, V., Clarke, V.: Using thematic analysis in psychology. Qual. Res. Psychol. **3**(2), 77–101 (2006)
9. Bredin, H.: pyannote.audio 2.1 speaker diarization pipeline: principle, benchmark, and recipe. In: Proceedings of the INTERSPEECH 2023 (2023)
10. DeepL GmbH: Deepl translator. https://www.deepl.com/translator
11. Doğan, N., Dikeç, G., Uygun, E.: Syrian refugees' experiences with mental health services in Turkey: i felt lonely because i wasn't able to speak to anyone. Perspect. Psychiatr. Care **55**(4), 673–680 (2019)
12. Isaacs, A., Burns, N., Macdonald, S., O'Donnell, C.A.: I don't think there's anything i can do which can keep me healthy: how the UK immigration and asylum system shapes the health & wellbeing of refugees and asylum seekers in Scotland. Crit. Public Health **32**(3), 422–432 (2022)
13. Lloyd, A., Anne Kennan, M., Thompson, K.M., Qayyum, A.: Connecting with new information landscapes: information literacy practices of refugees. J. Documentation **69**(1), 121–144 (2013)
14. Madianou, M.: Nonhuman humanitarianism: when 'AI for good' can be harmful. Inf. Commun. Soc. **24**(6), 850–868 (2021)
15. Martzoukou, K., Burnett, S.: Exploring the everyday life information needs and the socio-cultural adaptation barriers of Syrian refugees in Scotland. J. Documentation **74**(5), 1104–1132 (2018)
16. Meditskos, G., et al.: Towards semantically conscious, conversation-based chatbot services for migrants. In: Maglogiannis, I., Iliadis, L., Macintyre, J., Avlonitis, M., Papaleonidas, A. (eds.) IFIP International Conference on Artificial Intelligence Applications and Innovations, pp. 139–148. Springer, Cham (2024). https://doi.org/10.1007/978-3-031-63219-8_11

17. de Moissac, D., et al.: Chapter 8 issues and challenges in providing services in the minority language: the experience of bilingual professionals in the health and social service network, pp. 187–208. University of Ottawa Press, Ottawa (2017). https://doi.org/10.1515/9780776625645-011
18. Nomura, T., Suzuki, T., Kanda, T., Kato, K.: Measurement of negative attitudes toward robots. Int. Stud. Soc. Behav. Commun. Biol. Artif. Syst. **7**(3), 437–454 (2006)
19. Pearlman, W.: Culture or bureaucracy? Challenges in Syrian refugees' initial settlement in Germany. Middle East Law Gov. **9**(3), 313–327 (2017)
20. Radford, A., Kim, J.W., Xu, T., Brockman, G., McLeavey, C., Sutskever, I.: Robust speech recognition via large-scale weak supervision (2022). https://doi.org/10.48550/ARXIV.2212.04356, https://arxiv.org/abs/2212.04356
21. Renner, A., et al.: Syrian refugees in Germany: perspectives on mental health and coping strategies. J. Psychosom. Res. **129**, 109906 (2020)
22. Riek, L.D., et al.: IBN SINA steps out: exploring Arabic attitudes toward humanoid robots. In: Proceedings of the 2nd International Symposium on New Frontiers in Human–Robot Interaction, AISB, Leicester, vol. 1, p. 8 (2010)
23. Rogers, W.A., Kadylak, T., Bayles, M.A.: Maximizing the benefits of participatory design for human-robot interaction research with older adults. Hum. Factors **64**(3), 441–450 (2022)
24. Sabie, D., Ekmekcioglu, C., Ahmed, S.I.: A decade of international migration research in HCI: overview, challenges, ethics, impact, and future directions. ACM Trans. Comput. Hum. Interact. (TOCHI) **29**(4), 1–35 (2022)
25. Samari, D., Groot, S.: Potentially exploring homelessness among refugees: a systematic review and meta-analysis. J. Soc. Distress Homelessness **32**(1), 135–150 (2023)
26. Scottish Government: New scots refugee integration strategy 2018 to 2022: evaluation. https://www.gov.scot/publications/evaluation-new-scots-refugee-integration-strategy-2018-2022/pages/4 (2023). Accessed 27 Apr 2025
27. Scottish Refugee Council: Welcome pack for new scots. https://scottishrefugeecouncil.org.uk/welcome-pack-for-new-scots (2021). Accessed 27 Apr 2025
28. Scottish Refugee Council: New Scots refugee integration strategy: delivery plan 2024 to 2026. https://www.gov.scot/publications/new-scots-refugee-integration-strategy-delivery-plan-2024-2026 (2024). Accessed 27 Apr 2025
29. Scottish Refugee Council: Syrian refugees tell FM: our children's futures are here in Scotland. https://scottishrefugeecouncil.org.uk/syrian-refugees-tell-fm-our-childrens-futures-are-here-in-scotland (2024). Accessed 27 Apr 2025
30. Shannon, P.J., Wieling, E., Simmelink-McCleary, J., Becher, E.: Beyond stigma: barriers to discussing mental health in refugee populations. J. Loss Trauma **20**(3), 281–296 (2015)
31. Simão, H., Avelino, J., Duarte, N., Figueiredo, R.: GeeBot: a robotic platform for refugee integration. In: Companion of the 2018 ACM/IEEE International Conference on Human-Robot Interaction, pp. 365–366 (2018)
32. Smith, H.J., Chen, J., Liu, X.: Language and RIGOUR in qualitative research: problems and principles in analyzing data collected in mandarin. BMC Med. Res. Methodol. **8**, 1–8 (2008)
33. Strang, A.B., Baillot, H., Mignard, E.: I want to participate. Transition experiences of new refugees in Glasgow. J. Ethnic Migrat. Stud. **44**(2), 197–214 (2018)

34. Talhouk, R., et al.: Involving Syrian refugees in design research: lessons learnt from the field. In: Proceedings of the 2019 on Designing Interactive Systems Conference, pp. 1583–1594 (2019)
35. Timony, P., Gauthier, A., Wenghofer, E., Hien, A.: The impact of linguistic concordance and the active offer of French language services on patient satisfaction. Divers. Res. Health J. **5**(1) (2022)
36. Tozadore, D.C., Guneysu Ozgur, A., Kuoppamäki, S.: Teacher's perception on social robots to promote the integration of children with migration background. In: Proceedings of the 11th International Conference on Human-Agent Interaction, pp. 392–394 (2023)
37. UNHCR: Syria situation. https://reporting.unhcr.org/operational/situations/syria-situation (2025). Accessed 27 Apr 2025
38. Wanner, L., et al.: Towards a versatile intelligent conversational agent as personal assistant for migrants. In: Dignum, F., Corchado, J.M., De La Prieta, F. (eds.) PAAMS 2021. LNCS (LNAI), vol. 12946, pp. 316–327. Springer, Cham (2021). https://doi.org/10.1007/978-3-030-85739-4_26

Using the Pepper Robot to Support Sign Language Communication

Giulia Botta[1], Marco Botta[2], Cristina Gena[2(✉)], Alessandro Mazzei[2], Massimo Donini[2], and Alberto Lillo[1,2]

[1] Politecnico di Torino, Torino, Italy
[2] Dipartimento di Informatica, Università di Torino, Torino, Italy
cristina.gena@unito.it

Abstract. Social robots are increasingly experimented in public and assistive settings, but their accessibility for Deaf users remains quite underexplored. Italian Sign Language (LIS) is a fully-fledged natural language that relies on complex manual and non-manual components. Enabling robots to communicate using LIS could foster more inclusive human-robot interaction, especially in social environments such as hospitals, airports, or educational settings. This study investigates whether a commercial social robot, Pepper, can produce intelligible LIS signs and short signed LIS sentences. With the help of a Deaf student and his interpreter, an expert in LIS, we co-designed and implemented 52 LIS signs on Pepper using either manual animation techniques or a MATLAB-based inverse kinematics solver. We conducted a exploratory user study involving 12 participants proficient in LIS, both Deaf and hearing. Participants completed a questionnaire featuring 15 single-choice video-based sign recognition tasks and 2 open-ended questions on short signed sentences. Results shows that the majority of isolated signs were recognized correctly, although full sentence recognition was significantly lower due to Pepper's limited articulation and temporal constraints. Our findings demonstrate that even commercially available social robots like Pepper can perform a subset of LIS signs intelligibly, offering some opportunities for a more inclusive interaction design. Future developments should address multi-modal enhancements (e.g., screen-based support or expressive avatars) and involve Deaf users in participatory design to refine robot expressivity and usability.

Keywords: Social Robots · Italian Sign Language · Human-Robot Interaction

1 Introduction

Over the past decades, the field of robotics has experienced rapid growth, with robots initially deployed in industrial contexts, for example, as robotic arms in assembly lines or as autonomous vehicles in warehouses [30]. These systems, designed to assist with repetitive or physically demanding tasks, are typically characterized as autonomous or automated machines with high practical utility. However, their interaction with humans has traditionally been limited and functionally driven, differing substantially from human-to-human communication.

Social robots [8,12,15] are designed to engage with humans on a social level. They convey communicative intent both verbally and non-verbally, recognize and express emotions, and support users, including those with impairments, in everyday social interactions. As social robots become more capable and accessible, they are expected to emerge as one of the most disruptive technologies of the near future. The increasing availability of commercial social robots, such as Pepper, makes it plausible to envision their widespread adoption in homes and public settings alike [20,31].

Currently, most social robots interact using speech synthesis and visual displays. However, their integration into inclusive environments raises some question about accessibility. In particular, individuals who are Deaf[1] or hard of hearing continue to face significant communication barriers, as robots or avatars capable of signing remain relatively rare, and text transcription offers only a partial solution. Addressing this gap is a crucial step toward ensuring equitable access to human robot interaction.

In this study, we explore whether, and to what extent, a commercial social robot like *Pepper* can produce *Italian Sign Language* (Lingua Italiana dei Segni, LIS) to support a more accessible interaction. Given Pepper's physical limitations, such as the inability to move its fingers independently, our goal is not to implement the full LIS lexicon but to assess which signs can be feasibly reproduced and to evaluate their intelligibility for LIS users. We aim to address the following research question (**RQ1**): *What are the technical and communicative limits of using a commercial social robot such as Pepper to express LIS for a more accessible Deaf-robot interaction?*. To achieve this goal, with the help of a Deaf student and his tutor, an expert in LIS, we co-designed and implemented a set of LIS signs on Pepper using both manual animation techniques and a semi-automated method based on inverse kinematics. We then conducted a user study with 12 participants proficient in LIS, participants to assess recognition of individual signs and short signed sentences. This exploratory investigation seeks to contribute to the broader discussion on inclusive robotics and the potential for sign language as a modality in human-robot communication.

The remainder of the paper is structured as follows. Section 2 introduces key concepts related to sign languages and reviews related work. Section 3 describes our implementation of LIS signs on the Pepper robot. Section 4 presents the experimental evaluation and results. Finally, Sect. 5 offers conclusions and directions for future work.

2 Background and Related Works

We begin by briefly introducing the main features of sign languages, followed by a review of relevant work related to our project.

---

[1] We follow the common convention of capitalizing *Deaf* to denote native signers.

2.1 Sign Languages

Sign languages are fully natural languages in every respect [9]. They do not have a strict correspondence with specific spoken languages but are governed by grammars that share many lexical and syntactic mechanisms with spoken languages.

Unlike vocal languages, sign languages rely on multiple *articulators*, including hands, facial expressions, and body movements, rather than vocal sound. Signs differ from the spontaneous gestures people use while speaking, as they serve a distinct morpho-syntactic-semantic linguistic function. Each sign language is typically associated with a specific community, often national but sometimes regional. Since sign languages develop independently within each community, the same concept may be expressed using different signs across languages, and conversely, the same sign may convey different meanings [26, 28].

Until recently, sign languages were not officially recognized as full-fledged languages. However, in the past few decades, awareness and recognition of the Deaf community and its languages have grown, accompanied by initiatives to support their use and study. For instance, in 1987, the first official description of LIS was published, and more recently, a comprehensive work has further defined its structure and grammar [6].

In this paper, we focus specifically on LIS and its vocabulary. LIS signs are characterized by several parameters, including location, hand shape, movement, orientation, facial expressions, mouth movements, gaze, and posture. LIS also follows grammatical rules for the formation of complex nouns and verbs and typically adopts a Subject-Object-Verb (SOV) word order for declarative sentences [6].

We are aware of the morpho-syntactic role played by the collocation in the space of the signs and its importance for the correctness and the naturalness of a signed sentence. Similarly, we know the mobility limitations of the Pepper's arms and fingers. Our intention is to provide a preliminary study that shed light on the current possibilities and limitations of a widespread social robot in producing comprehensible signs. We believe that this kind of study can guide and encourage towards the design and the realization of more accessible social robots.

2.2 Related Works

Research on the use of social robots for sign language communication began in 2012, with a study that used the NAO H25 robot to teach sign language to Deaf children [16]. The researchers focused on Turkish Sign Language (TSL), comparing the robot's signing to that of a human teacher. The evaluation revealed limitations in the robot's structure and mobility. In subsequent work, the same group used a modified version of the Robovie R3 robot, which could move each finger independently. R3 outperformed NAO in the authors' evaluation of sign production, as its independently articulated fingers allowed for a closer approximation of human hand movements.

In 2019, a study on Persian Sign Language (PSL) introduced a custom-built robot called RASA (Robot Assistant for Social Aims) [25]. The robot featured a human-like face and two hands with independently movable fingers, and was programmed with 70 signs selected to represent diverse PSL configurations. Although the robot executed the signs quite well, participants noted that the lack of facial expressions and mouth movements negatively affected sign clarity and expressiveness.

Another 2019 study focused on teaching sign language to autistic children [2]. Researchers customized the InMoov robot and programmed it with nine signs. The study found that autistic children were engaged by the robot and showed a willingness to imitate its movements, suggesting potential for learning.

Even in 2019, researchers developed a system to convert natural language into Spanish Sign Language (LSE), using the assistive robot TEO [13].

Several recent works have addressed sign language production using virtual avatars focusing on multi-articulator control and linguistic expressiveness. SignAvatar [17] introduces a transformer-based framework capable of generating accurate word-level signs in 3D, capturing realistic hand, face, and body motions. SignAvatars [1] provides the largest dataset of full-body sign language motion, enabling end-to-end training for both generation and recognition tasks. SGNify [4] reconstructs expressive 3D avatars from monocular video using linguistic priors, improving articulation accuracy, particularly in facial expressions and hand configurations. While these systems primarily target American Sign Language (ASL) or British Sign Language (BSL), their multimodal architectures are language independent and can be adapted to LIS.

Many recent studies have focused on multimodal sign language production, aiming to generate coherent and expressive signing sequences by integrating different input sources such as spoken language, textual transcriptions, or gloss annotations[2]. MS2SL [32] investigates how continuous sign language sequences can be generated from either speech or text, emphasizing the alignment between modalities. The approach is evaluated on PHOENIX14T and How2Sign: PHOENIX14T is a benchmark dataset for German Sign Language (DGS) containing parallel sequences of spoken German, gloss annotations and signing videos, while How2Sign includes full-body signing aligned with English instructional videos, offering rich multimodal data. Neural Sign Actors [5] aims to produce realistic full-body signing animations from textual input, focusing on accurate timing and coordination across articulators (hands, face, torso). Mixed SIGNals [10] explores how sign language movements can be composed from reusable motion segments, enhancing the fluidity and expressiveness of the generated signs. A complementary line of research has explored inclusion in cultural settings by developing the GAMGame, a web app designed for the d/Deaf community, which uses affective-driven storytelling and emotion-based recommendations to foster diverse and empathic interpretations of museum content,

---

[2] Gloss annotations are a common convention used to represent sign language utterances in written form by mapping individual signs to approximate equivalents in a spoken language, typically using capitalized words (e.g., HOUSE, GO, I). [11]

integrating user-generated stories with AI-based reasoning systems for cultural sensemaking [18].

Finally, a few research projects specifically studied automatic translation and/or generation of LIS. The ATLAS-LIS4ALL projectc concerned the production from an avatar of LIS sentence regarding weather-forecast and rail-station messages respectively [3,22,24]. More recently, a deep learning system for automatic recognition of LIS signs in the news domain has been proposed [21].

3 Methodology

The approach adopted in this study was grounded in a participatory and iterative design process, involving members of the Deaf community from the early stages of development. Initially, a preliminary selection of LIS signs was implemented on Pepper through consultation of the *Radutzky* LIS dictionary *"Dizionario bilingue elementare della lingua dei segni italiana"* [27]. However, recognizing the limitations of a top-down design approach, we subsequently involved a Deaf student from the Department of Computer Science and his LIS interpreter in the project. After presenting the project objectives, along with the capabilities and constraints of the Pepper robot, we collaboratively selected a subset of signs and short sentences considered compatible with Pepper's physical affordances (e.g., lack of independent finger movement, limited wrist rotation, restricted hand-to-body contact, etc.). Each proposed sign was implemented on the robot and demonstrated to the student and his tutor, then iteratively redesigned with their input until they were satisfied. Their feedback informed multiple cycles of refinement and re-implementation. This co-design phase lasted approximately two months.

The initial implementations were created manually using the Pepper SDK's Animation Editor. In a second phase, a semi-automated pipeline was developed to facilitate sign generation, based on a MATLAB inverse kinematics solver and a Python-based exporter to generate Pepper-compatible animation files. This hybrid methodology ensured both linguistic validity and technical scalability. These approaches will be described in the following.

3.1 Apparatus and Material

Pepper[3] is one of the most used social robotics platform [19]. It features a human-like head, a built-in touchscreen tablet on its chest, a wheeled base that mimics human legs, and two arms ending in hands with five fingers each. However, the fingers are not independently controllable, they can only open and close simultaneously. This physical limitation makes it impossible to reproduce sign language configurations that require differentiated finger positioning. Consequently, our work focused on signs that can be performed using hand configurations in which all fingers are either open or closed.

---

[3] https://us.softbankrobotics.com/pepper/.

Another distinctive feature of Pepper, the chest-mounted tablet, can facilitate interaction in many applications. However, in the context of sign language, it may pose a constraint: the tablet interferes with arm movements, making it difficult or impossible to perform signs that require gestures in close proximity to the torso.

Despite these limitations, we successfully co-designed and implemented a total of 52 LIS signs[4] The selected signs span several semantic categories, including school-related terms, common actions and nouns, and work-related vocabulary. These signs were primarily created using the Animation Editor, a tool included in the Android Studio plugin Pepper SDK. This tool enables the definition of keyframe animations by specifying joint configurations at individual timesteps, allowing the creation of time-based movement sequences that the robot can execute.

After generating the individual signs, we addressed a more complex challenge: the composition of short sentences. We co-designed and implemented four simple sentences, adhering to the grammatical structure of LIS, which typically follows a Subject-Object-Verb (SOV) word order, as opposed to the Subject-Verb-Object (SVO) order of standard Italian. Each sentence consists of a subject (first person, Pepper), a verb representing an action (e.g., "to eat", "to go"), and an object (or complement).

The following Figs. 1a,1b, 2a, 2b illustrate a selection of example signs implemented on the robot:

"Amare" (To Love). This sign is performed with both arms, which execute the

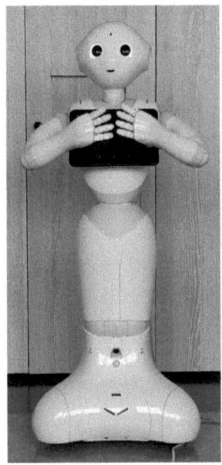
(a) Starting position

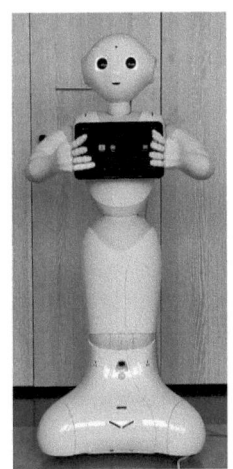
(b) Ending position

Fig. 1. Starting and ending positions for the Italian word amare (to love) in LIS.

---

[4] Videos of the signs are available at the following URL: https://github.com/CodeCruncher63/ISCR2025.

same movement. The sign consists of a single motion that is repeated twice. The movement begins as shown in Fig. 1a and ends as in Fig. 1b.

"Andare" (To Go). This sign is performed with both arms, which move differently: the left arm remains stationary while the right arm performs a single movement without repetition. The gesture starts as shown in Fig. 2a and ends as shown in Fig. 2b.

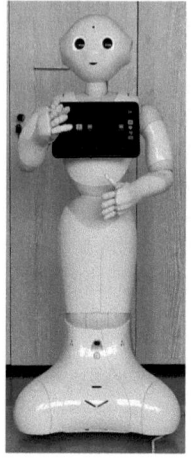 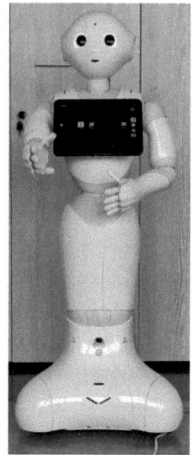

(a) Starting position   (b) Ending position

Fig. 2. Starting and ending positions for the Italian word andare (to go) in LIS.

3.2 Automating the Creation of LIS Signs on Pepper

To streamline the implementation of sign language animations for the Pepper robot, we developed a toolchain that automates the conversion of 3D hand trajectories into joint values and animation files. The system comprises two main components: a MATLAB function that calculates the inverse kinematics for the right arm using a numerical solver, and a Python script that serves as a wrapper, managing user input and generating the final animation file.

We chose to use a numeric solver since inverting the kinematics equations by hand was too complex. Furthermore, the inverted equations that can be found online [29] were obtained by making some simplifications of the inverted kinematics equations that can not be applied in this study.

The MATLAB function receives 5 parameters: the 3D coordinates to be reached, its orientation, and hand configuration (open, closed, or neutral), a flag to mirror the joint values on the left arm and the weights to be used. Then it checks the correctness of the parameters and uses the *inverseKinematics* system object, from the Robotics System Toolbox, to create a numeric solver which computes the joint values. The robot's kinematic model used in the system object was derived from a customized *Unified Robot Description Format* (URDF file) that contains a description of the robot anatomic model; in particular, we considered only the torso and the right arm model description.

The Python script handles data preprocessing and user-defined parameters such as movement timing, solver weights, and the mirroring option. It invokes the MATLAB function passing all the needed inputs and receives as output the joint values. Then it writes the values in the Animation Editor-compatible .qianim XML format, which can be loaded into the Animation Editor (see Fig. 3) and can be used to move the robot in the same way as a file hand-made in this editor.

```
<?xml version="1.0" encoding="UTF-8"?>
<Animation xmlns:editor="http://www.ald.softbankrobotics.com/animation/editor" typeVersion="2.0" editor:fps="25">
    <ActuatorCurve fps="25" actuator="LShoulderPitch" mute="false" unit="degree">
        <Key value="90.5273514" frame="0">
            <Tangent side="right" abscissaParam="10" ordinateParam="0" editor:interpType="bezier_auto"/>
        </Key>
        <Key value="90.5273514" frame="30">
            <Tangent side="left" abscissaParam="-10" ordinateParam="0" editor:interpType="bezier_auto"/>
            <Tangent side="right" abscissaParam="6.66666667" ordinateParam="0" editor:interpType="bezier_auto"/>
        </Key>
        <Key value="90.5273514" frame="50">
            <Tangent side="left" abscissaParam="-6.66666667" ordinateParam="0" editor:interpType="bezier_auto"/>
            <Tangent side="right" abscissaParam="6.66666667" ordinateParam="0" editor:interpType="bezier_auto"/>
        </Key>
        <Key value="90.5273514" frame="80">
            <Tangent side="left" abscissaParam="-6.66666667" ordinateParam="0" editor:interpType="bezier_auto"/>
        </Key>
    </ActuatorCurve>
    ...
```

Fig. 3. A fragment of a qianim-XML example

This approach successfully automated the generation of 38 out of the 52 manually implemented signs (73%). Ten signs could not be reproduced due to asymmetric or body-involving movements, and four others failed due to kinematic infeasibility or solver instability. Nonetheless, the method proved advantageous for generating smooth, circular movements and significantly reduced the manual workload. On average, the manual creation of a sign required approximately 45–60 min, while the automated method reduced this to under 10 min per sign, including coordinate setup and execution.

The main difference between the automated signs and the manually crafted ones, was in the elbow movement: the manually developed signs had the elbow staying still while the arm was moving around it; on the contrary, in the automated signs, the joint values found by the IK solver also involved the elbow moving together with the arm. Anyway, this difference in movement had no impact on the recognition ability of the Deaf student and his sign language interpreter. These results, namely 38 out of the 52, confirm the feasibility of automated sign generation for a substantial subset of LIS signs on Pepper and pave the way for further improvements through solver refinement or data-driven methods.

4 Exploratory Evaluation

To assess the intelligibility and clarity of the signs produced by the Pepper robot, we designed an on line evaluation based on a questionnaire targeting sign language users. The aim was to determine whether the robot's gestures, both individual signs and short sentences, could be correctly interpreted by human observers.

The questionnaire consisted of two parts:

- **Single-choice closed questions:** 15 questions, each showing a video of Pepper performing a single sign. Participants were asked to select the correct sign from four options: three plausible alternatives, one of which was correct, and one "None of the above" option;
- **Open-ended questions:** 2 questions in which Pepper performed a short sentence composed of multiple signs. Participants were asked to write the meaning of each sentence in natural language. Note that in this experiment, for sake of simplicity, we are neglecting the "spatial accord" among signs of a sentence, a feature that in most sign languages is used to assign (or confirm) the syntactic roles (e.g. *patient*) to the participants [23]. We believe that this simplification so not impact the findings of this exploratory experiment.

4.1 Participants

The questionnaire was completed by 12 participants, 4 of whom were LIS interpreters, while the remaining were Deaf individuals who use Italian Sign Language (LIS) on a daily basis. Gender was not collected in order to preserve participant anonymity and focus the analysis solely on sign recognition performance, which was not expected to vary significantly by gender. Participants were between 18 and 60 years old and came from various regions of Italy. Regional differences in LIS usage may have influenced recognition in some cases, although the signs implemented aimed to reflect the most commonly used versions of the signs. Participants were simply instructed to respond sincerely based on their interpretation of the robot's gestures.

4.2 Results

Single-Choice Questions. The 15 presented signs were chosen among the implemented signs with the help of the LIS interpreter and the Deaf student. The idea was that signs performed with one and two hands were well represented among the chosen signs. Moreover, their intrinsic and grammatical meaning was taken into account and we picked signs belonging to these different categories.

Table 1 summarizes the recognition rates and key observations for each tested sign.

To evaluate whether the recognition of each sign was significantly above chance level (25%), we performed one-tailed binomial tests. The results are summarized in Table 1. Several signs, including *Dimenticare*, *Finire/Fatto*, *Shampoo*, and *Università*, showed statistically significant recognition rates ($p < 0.0001$). Other signs, such as *Doccia* and *Che/Come?*, also yielded recognition rates significantly above chance. Conversely, signs like *Insegnare* and *Libro* did not reach significance, likely due to articulation constraints.

Table 1. Recognition accuracy, binomial test results, and qualitative notes for each sign.

Sign	Recognition Rate (%)	Correct (out of 12)	Binomial p-value	Notes
Acqua (Water)	50.0	6	0.1035	Often confused with "Apple" (25%); intelligibility confirmed.
Antipatico (Unpleasant)	58.3	7	0.0436	Some false recognition (17%).
Capriccioso (Capricious)	58.3	7	0.0436	Some false recognition (17%).
Che/Come? (What/How?)	83.3	10	<0.0001	High recognition confirms validity.
Chiedere (To ask)	41.7	5	0.2267	Mixed responses; confusion with "Insegnare".
Dimenticare (To forget)	100.0	12	<0.0001	Iconic and well-executed.
Doccia (Shower)	66.7	8	0.0041	Some confusion with "Idea".
Finire/Fatto (Done)	100.0	12	<0.0001	Fully recognized.
Idea	91.7	11	<0.0001	Widely recognized.
Insegnare (To teach)	33.3	4	0.4110	Low recognition, high confusion.
Libro (Book)	50.0	6	0.1035	Recognition affected by Pepper's movement limitations.
Profumo (Perfume)	0.0	0	1.0000	All selected "Good" due to gesture similarity.
Shampoo	100.0	12	<0.0001	Fully recognized.
Spaventarsi (To get scared)	58.3	7	0.0436	None of the above answer, 50% selected it correctly.
Università (University)	100.0	12	<0.0001	Fully recognized.

Open-Ended Questions. Performance in the open-ended section was notably lower than in the single-choice section, suggesting greater difficulty in interpreting full signed sentences:

- **Sentence 1:** *"Ho mangiato una mela"* (I ate an apple), composed of *mela* (apple) - *mangiare* (to eat) - *fatto* (done).
  Most participants interpreted the sequence as *"Ho bevuto e mangiato"* (I drank and ate), likely due to the confusion between the signs for "apple" and "water". Only one participant correctly interpreted the full sentence. All other 11 participants attempted a response and correctly recognized at least 2 signs out of 3.
- **Sentence 2:** *"Vado a casa a studiare"* (I go home to study), composed of *casa* (home) - *studiare* (to study) - *andare* (to go).
  This sentence had a low recognition rate. One participant gave a correct response; one provided a nearly correct interpretation. The 11 remaining participants either misunderstood the sentence or declared it unintelligible. The sign for *casa* was likely a limiting factor due to Pepper's restricted movement range.

To analyze more in depth the open-ended responses, we applied an inductive thematic coding approach [7]. Three main categories emerged: (i) lexical confusion due to similar handshape/movement (e.g., mela vs. acqua), (ii) sentence structure misinterpretation, and (iii) partial recognition with correct identification of individual signs but incorrect sequencing. For example, one participant interpreted the sentence 'mela - mangiare - fatto' as 'ho bevuto e mangiato,' reflecting confusion between 'apple' and 'water,' likely due to hand orientation limits. This suggests that iconic similarity can hinder clarity when physical constraints distort precise configurations.

5 Discussion and Conclusions

The evaluation results confirm that Pepper is capable of performing a substantial number of LIS signs with a good level of intelligibility. Recognition accuracy was notably higher for individual signs than for complete sentences, likely due to the added complexity of temporal sequencing and the cognitive load involved in integrating multiple gestures into a coherent semantic unit. Performance varied significantly across signs, some signs were occasionally misinterpreted, often due to Pepper's physical constraints.

To answer research question RQ1, the study identified several technical and communicative limitations that constrain the use of a commercial social robot such as Pepper for expressing LIS in accessible Deaf-robot interaction.

From a technical standpoint, the most prominent limitation is Pepper's inability to move fingers independently, which excludes a wide range of handshapes fundamental to LIS. Additionally, constrained wrist and elbow mobility, along with the presence of the chest-mounted tablet, interferes with gesture execution, particularly for signs that require close-body movements or fine spatial articulation. These constraints directly impact the robot's ability to faithfully reproduce the complexity of LIS signs.

From a communicative perspective, while many isolated signs were recognized correctly by LIS users, especially those with iconic or simplified motion–sentence-level comprehension proved significantly more challenging. This highlights Pepper's limited capacity to convey temporal and syntactic structure, which is essential for interpreting full utterances in sign language. Furthermore, some signs were misinterpreted due to articulation ambiguity, while other signs were unexpectedly recognized, suggesting a nuanced relationship between physical execution and human perception of signs.

While Pepper demonstrates the potential to perform a limited yet meaningful subset of LIS signs, its current embodiment imposes notable constraints on expressivity and intelligibility. These findings underscore the importance of integrating multimodal channels (e.g., visual display, expressive avatars) and maintaining a participatory design process to enhance accessibility in future human-robot interaction systems.

As limitation, we acknowledge that the evaluation was conducted with a relatively small sample of 12 participants. While this number is within acceptable bounds for exploratory user studies in HRI, it does limit the statistical power and generalizability of the findings. However, it is important to note that recruiting Deaf participants for this type of research presents some challenge. Despite our efforts to collaborate with local communities and institutions, we encountered a degree of hesitation and resistance from potential participants. These barriers may reflect broader issues of trust. As such, we consider the current sample size not only as a methodological limitation, but also as a reflection of the practical and ethical complexity of engaging marginalized groups in HRI research.

Future work should aim to foster longer-term collaborations with Deaf organizations and educators, build trust through participatory approaches, and develop more inclusive research environments to support broader recruitment and sustained engagement.

Although this study focused on physical sign reproduction, future work may explore multimodal augmentation. The project LIS4ALL has showed the advantages of multimodality in LIS translation. The main idea was to augment a virtual agent with "blended written forms", which are a sort of road signs, for communicate the names of less-known rail stations [14,22]. In the case of Pepper, multimodality could consist in the coordination of arms and images/videos. For instance, integrating Pepper's tablet to display a LIS avatar (or subtitles) could enhance intelligibility for complex signs. However, such integration requires careful synchronization and user validation, particularly in real-time contexts. We consider this a promising yet technically demanding direction for future participatory co-design efforts.

Beyond experimental contexts, future applications of this technology could include interactive environments such as museums, public information points, or healthcare facilities, where Deaf users may come into contact with service robots. In these scenarios, even a partial command of LIS, supported by multimodal output, could play a key role in reducing communication barriers and fostering more inclusive interactions. Advancing in this direction will require ongoing collaboration with the Deaf community, user-centered design processes, and testing in real-world conditions to evaluate long-term usability and acceptance.

Acknowledgments. We are particularly grateful to Flavio and his LIS interpreter Simonetta for the considerable help in choosing which signs to implement, generate them and discard the ones that Pepper was not performing correctly.

References

1. Axel, A.A., Doosti, B., Daelman, N., et al.: SignAvatars: a large-scale 3D dataset for holistic sign language production and understanding (2023). https://arxiv.org/abs/2310.20436, to appear in ECCV 2024. Preprint on arXiv:2310.20436
2. Axelsson, M., Racca, M., Weir, D., Kyrki, V.: A participatory design process of a robotic tutor of assistive sign language for children with autism. In: 2019 28th IEEE International Conference on Robot and Human Interactive Communication (RO-MAN). IEEE (2019)
3. Winkler, M.H., Plischke, H., Jensch, W. (2015). Subjective Ratings of Biological Effective Light in Seminar Rooms and How to Handle Small Sample Sizes of Ordinal Data. In: Antona, M., Stephanidis, C. (eds.) UAHCI 2015. LNCS, vol. 9176. Springer, Cham (2015). https://doi.org/10.1007/978-3-319-20681-3
4. Biswas, S., Kulkarni, A., et al.: SGNIFY: linguistically-aware expressive 3d avatar generation from sign language videos. In: Proceedings of the IEEE/CVF Conference on Computer Vision and Pattern Recognition (CVPR) (2023). https://arxiv.org/abs/2304.10482

5. Bolkart, T., Johnson, B.D., Habermann, M., et al.: Neural sign actors: a diffusion model for 3D sign language production from text (2023). https://arxiv.org/abs/2312.02702, arXiv preprint arXiv:2312.02702
6. Branchini, C., Mantovan, L. (eds.): Grammatica della lingua dei segni italiana (LIS). Ca' Foscari, Venezia (2022)
7. Braun, V., Clarke, V.: Using thematic analysis in psychology. Qual. Res. Psychol. **3**(2), 77–101 (2006). https://doi.org/10.1191/1478088706qp063oa
8. Breazeal, C., Dautenhahn, K., Kanda, T.: Social Robotics. In: Siciliano, B., Khatib, O. (eds.) Springer Handbook of Robotics, pp. 1935–1972. Springer, Cham (2016). https://doi.org/10.1007/978-3-319-32552-1_72
9. Brentari, D. (ed.): Sign Languages. Cambridge University Press, Cambridge (2010)
10. Camgoz, N.C., Koller, O., Hadfield, S., Bowden, R.: Mixed signals: sign language production via a mixture of motion primitives (2021). https://arxiv.org/abs/2107.11317, arXiv preprint arXiv:2107.11317
11. Cormier, K., Crasborn, O.A., Bank, R.: Digging into signs: emerging annotation standards for sign language corpora. In: Efthimiou, E., et al. (eds.) Proceedings of the 7th Workshop on the Representation and Processing of Sign Languages: Corpus Mining, pp. 35–40. ELRA, Portorož, Slovenia (2016)
12. Fong, T., Nourbakhsh, I., Dautenhahn, K.: A survey of socially interactive robots. Robot. Auton. Syst. **42**(3–4), 143–166 (2003)
13. Gago, J.J., Vasco, V., Łukawski, B., Pattacini, U., Tikhanoff, V., Victores, J.G., Balaguer, C.: Sequence-to-sequence natural language to humanoid robot sign language (2019). https://doi.org/10.48550/arXiv.1907.04198, preprint
14. Geraci, C., Mazzei, A.: Last train to "Rebaudengo Fossano": the case of some names in avatar translation. In: Crasborn, O., Efthimiou, E., Fotinea, S.E., Hanke, T., Hochgesang, J.A., Kristoffersen, J., Mesch, J. (eds.) Proceedings of the LREC2014 6th Workshop on the Representation and Processing of Sign Languages: Beyond the Manual Channel, pp. 63–66. European Language Resources Association (ELRA), Reykjavik, Iceland (2014). https://www.sign-lang.uni-hamburg.de/lrec/pub/14017.pdf
15. Kanda, T., Ishiguro, H.: Human-Robot Interaction in Social Robotics. CRC Press (2017)
16. Kose, H., Yorganci, R., Algan, E.H., Syrdal, D.S.: Evaluation of the robot assisted sign language tutoring using video-based studies. Int. J. Soc. Robot. **4**(3), 273–283 (2012)
17. Li, X., Meng, Y., Wang, X., et al.: SignAvatar: a holistic 3D sign language production framework with a new benchmark (2024). https://arxiv.org/abs/2405.07974, arXiv preprint arXiv:2405.07974
18. Lieto, A., et al.: A sensemaking system for grouping and suggesting stories from multiple affective viewpoints in museums. Hum. Comput. Interact. **39**(1–2), 109–143 (2024)
19. Liu, B., Tetteroo, D., Markopoulos, P.: A systematic review of experimental work on persuasive social robots. Int. J. Soc. Robot. **14**, 1–40 (2022). https://doi.org/10.1007/s12369-022-00870-5
20. Macis, D., Perilli, S., Gena, C.: Employing socially assistive robots in elderly care. In: Adjunct proceedings of the 30th ACM Conference on User Modeling, Adaptation and Personalization, pp. 130–138 (2022)
21. Marchisio, M., Mazzei, A., Sammaruga, D.: Introducing deep learning with data augmentation and corpus construction for LIS. In: CLiC-it 2023 (2023)

22. Mazza, I., Geraci, C., Mazzei, A., Vernero, F.: Poster: an exploratory analysis to elicit requirements for avatar-based interfaces aimed at the deaf community. In: CHItaly 2023, pp. 40:1–40:4 (2023)
23. Mazzei, A.: Sign language generation with expert systems and CCG. In: Proceedings of the Seventh International Natural Language Generation Conference, pp. 105–109. INLG 2012, Association for Computational Linguistics, USA (2012)
24. Mazzei, A., Lesmo, L., Battaglino, C., Vendrame, M., Bucciarelli, M.: Deep natural language processing for Italian sign language translation. In: AI*IA 2013, pp. 193–204 (2013)
25. Meghdari, A., Alemi, M., Zakipour, M., Kashanian, S.A.: Design and realization of a sign language educational humanoid robot. J. Intell. Robot. Syst. **95**(1), 3–17 (2019)
26. Padden, C.: Sign Language Geography. Deaf Around the world: The Impact of Language, pp. 19–37 (2010)
27. Radutzky, E., Torossi, C.: Dizionario bilingue elementare della lingua italiana dei segni: oltre 2.500 significati. Kappa, Roma (1992). con il contributo del Mason Perkins Deafness Fund e dell'Associazione Nazionale Logopedisti
28. Sandler, W., Lillo-Martin, D.C.: Sign Language and Linguistic Universals. Cambridge University Press (2006)
29. Stoeva, D., Frijns, H.A., Gelautz, M., Schürer, O.: Analytical solution of pepper's inverse kinematics for a pose matching imitation system. In: 2021 30th IEEE International Conference on Robot & Human Interactive Communication (RO-MAN), pp. 167–174. IEEE (2021)
30. Sutikno, T.: An overview of emerging trends in robotics and automation. IAES Int. J. Robot. Autom. (IJRA) **12**(4), 405–411 (2023)
31. Thunberg, S., Ziemke, T.: Are people ready for social robots in public spaces? In: Companion of the 2020 ACM/IEEE International Conference on Human-Robot Interaction, pp. 482–484 (2020)
32. Xu, Z., Chen, M., Ren, X., et al.: MS2SL: multimodal spoken data-driven continuous sign language production via sequential diffusion (2024). https://arxiv.org/abs/2407.12842, arXiv preprint arXiv:2407.12842

Evaluating the Role of Robot Form and Intelligence in the Ultimatum Game

Triniti Armstrong[✉], Christopher A. Sanchez, and Naomi T. Fitter

Oregon State University (OSU), Corvallis 97331, OR, USA
{armsttri,christopher.sanchez,naomi.fitter}@oregonstate.edu

Abstract. As interactions between humans and robots become increasingly common, robots are being entrusted with greater autonomy in decision-making, particularly in resource allocation-related tasks. Building on past work from our research group, we aimed to better understand the impact of robot form and intelligence on participants' responses in decision-making tasks related to resource allocation. To achieve this goal, we conducted an online study in which participants played the Ultimatum Game with a random number generator, a series of humans, and three different embodied robots (i.e., table-like, single-armed, and dual-armed), each with two different purported intelligence levels (i.e., non-AI-enabled and AI-enabled). We found that participants tend to treat AI-enabled robots more like humans when receiving unfair Ultimatum Game offers from these systems. Taken together, the results of this work can help to explain human decision making around everyday robots, providing helpful insights for those who wish to design better and more successful robotic systems.

1 Introduction

Interactions between humans and robots are becoming increasingly more typical as robots are being entrusted with greater autonomy in decision-making, particularly when it comes to resource allocation or management. For example, a robot in customer service may need to decide how much time is acceptable to spend helping one customer while others are waiting for help. Delivery robots decide on ways to use and share common spaces such as roads and sidewalks with human counterparts. Robots in warehouse settings make choices about what items to deliver to which human picker, and at which time. How fair would we expect the human customers and passers-by to find the robots decisions in these cases?

In our own previous work [10], building on a decade or so of research on human-robot interaction in the Ultimatum game (e.g., [11,12]), we aimed to address this important question. We investigated how people respond to unfairness in decision-making scenarios involving "unintelligent" computer opponents, human opponents, and artificially intelligent opponents with and without a robot embodiment. The Ultimatum Game, a social decision-making activity that involves repeated decisions to accept/reject proposed splits of a pot of money that are fair/unfair, was used to examine how perceptions of fairness influenced decision making against these various opponents. The results of the study suggested that although participants were more reluctant to accept unfair bids from intelligent opponents (i.e., humans or AI-enabled systems), the embodiment of an intelligent agent had no effect on participants' responses to the Ultimatum Game. This latter finding was interesting as it stands in direct contrast to some previous work on embodiment and social decision making with robots. For example, in [16], the authors found that participants rejected unfair offers from computers more, while treating robots similarly to humans arguably because they appeared more 'human-like.' Furthermore, [8] found that requiring participants to speak to the robot, as well as the robot having a physically embodied appearance, resulted in participants also treating the robot more like a human while playing the Ultimatum Game. Thus, given these inconsistent results, it seems worthwhile to explore further whether and how a robot's physical embodiment can be manipulated to make a difference in playing the Ultimatum Game, consistent with or in addition to the findings of apparent intelligence.

In this paper, we aimed to build on previous research by examining how a range of embodiment types (the exploratory factor) and intelligence (a replication of past work) influence fairness judgments when playing the Ultimatum Game. To investigate this topic, we conducted an online study in which participants played the Ultimatum Game with a random number generator (i.e., unintelligent and non-embodied computer), human opponents, and three different types of robot embodiments (each of which was described as "unintelligent" or "intelligent"). These factors, as well as the other study methods and analysis tactics, are discussed in more detail in Sect. 2. Section 3 outlines the results of the study. In Sect. 4, we discuss the results and their broader implications. Overall, the key contributions of this work include offering new insights on how much ranging robot embodiment impacts Ultimatum Game decisions, as well as a replication of past findings on the influence of apparently intelligent computerized systems on the perception of fairness.

2 Methods

We conducted a study to investigate the effects that robots' embodied form (i.e., a table-like robot, a single-armed robot, and a dual-armed robot) and professed intelligence (i.e., non-AI-enabled and AI-enabled) had on responses to the Ultimatum Game. This study was approved under Oregon State Institutional Review Board protocol #IRB-2019-0172.

2.1 Study Design

In this study, participants played multiple rounds of the Ultimatum Game against different opponents (within factor). All participants played a round against a random number generator (RNG; Fig. 1), human opponents (Fig. 2), and then each of the three embodied robot types (Fig. 3). However, the professed

Fig. 1. The opponent image shown to participants for the random number generator trials.

Fig. 2. Example opponent images shown to participants for the human trials.

intelligence of the embodied robot types was varied between groups; participants either played against non-AI-enabled robots or AI-enabled robots. The RNG and human opponents were identical across groups.

The five types of overall opponents faced within-subjects in the Ultimatum Game trials are detailed below:

- ***RNG:*** Participants were told that the current offer came from a random number generator that randomly selected values between $1 and $9. This condition helps us compare direction to past work on human-computer interaction in the Ultimatum Game [4,7].
- ***Human:*** Participants were presented with a picture of a human opponent that had previously played the game, and were told that this individual made the current offer.
- ***Table-Like Robot:*** Participants were presented with a picture and video of a table-like robot and were told that this robot made the current offer. The robot media was edited from footage of the Labrador Retriever robot, a commercial robotic table.
- ***Single-Armed Robot:*** Participants were presented with a picture and video of a single-armed robot and were told that this robot made the current offer. The robot media was edited from footage of the Hello Robot Stretch robot, a commercial mobile manipulator robot.
- ***Dual-Armed Robot:*** Participants were presented with a picture and video of a dual-armed robot and were told that this robot made the current offer.

The robot media was edited from footage of the PAL Robotics TIAGo robot, a commercial dual-armed mobile manipulator robot.

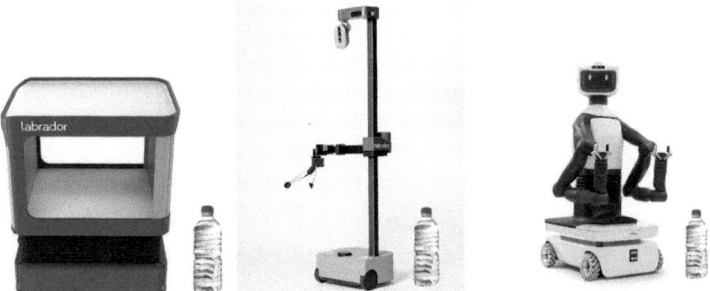

Fig. 3. The opponent images shown to participants for the robot trials. From left to right: Table-Like Robot, Single-Armed Robot, Dual-Armed Robot.

Importantly, the three robots were presented as having one of two levels of intelligence: non-AI-enabled or AI-enabled. Robots were described as follows:

- **Non-AI-Enabled:** The participants were informed that the robot proposer was "BASIC" and the picture and video of the robot were accompanied with a brief description of the robot's simple programming, which did not involve modern AI. The specific prompt provided for the basic table-like robot was as follows: "For this round, you will be playing against a BASIC TABLE ROBOT that has had simple software installed that will enable it to play the Ultimatum Game."
- **AI-Enabled:** The participants were informed that the robot proposer was "AI-ENABLED" and the picture and video of the robot were accompanied with a brief definition of the artificial intelligence that the robot possessed. The specific prompt provided for the AI-enabled table-like robot was as follows: "For this round, you will be playing against an AI-ENABLED TABLE ROBOT equipped with modern artificial intelligence. One common definition of artificial intelligence is as follows: technology that allows computers and machines to mimic the problem solving and decision-making capabilities of the human mind."

2.2 Measures

The number of accepted and rejected offers were tracked for each opponent. We collected the demographic information of age, gender, ethnicity, and major. Participants' existing views of robots (using the standard Negative Attitudes towards Robots Scale (NARS) [13]) were collected as well, using a 7-pt Likert scale from "Strongly Disagree" to "Strongly Agree."

2.3 Participants

A total of $N = 106$ participants took part in this online study to receive course credit in an introductory psychology course at Oregon State University. Four participants did not fully complete the study, so their data was removed from final analysis. The remaining 102 participants were aged 18 to 55 ($M = 24.3$, $SD = 7.98$). 67.7% of the participants were female, while 28.4% were male, and 3.9% reported another gender identity. Demographic breakdowns were as follows: 64.7% White, 9.8% Asian, 9.8% Latino, 2.0% Black, and 13.7% two or more races/ethnicities.

The breakdown of most participants' majors was as follows: 51.9% Psychology, 12.7% Biology, 9.8% BioHealth Science, 3.9% Computer Science, 3.9% Kinesiology, 2.0% Exploratory Studies, 2.0% Human Development and Family Sciences, 2.0% Creative Writing, 2.0% Public Health, and 2.0% Horticulture. The remaining 7.8% of the majors were split evenly among Nutrition, Secondary Education, Liberal Studies, Pre-Graphic Design, Business Management, Science and Health, Economics, and Zoology.

For the NARS questions, the responses to each standard scale were as follows: interaction ($M = 3.62 \pm 1.69$), social ($M = 4.81 \pm 1.66$), and emotional ($M = 3.50 \pm 1.68$). (Each scale reflects a level of worry about the respective aspect of robotics, with 7 as the highest possible rating.)

2.4 Procedure

Participants played five rounds of the Ultimatum Game. Each round involved playing a different opponent type mentioned above (i.e., RNG, human, and three robot rounds). Each round, regardless of opponent, consisted of 20 trials. For each trial, participants received a numeric offer, which was accompanied by the image of the opponent. Further, prior to the start of each robot round, to ensure that participants understood their robot counterparts, participants saw a short video of the robot moving in a room (i.e., not playing the Ultimatum game), and also read a brief description about its purported intelligence.

In each trial, the proposer (i.e., RNG, human, or robot) would offer a split of a $10 pot. Participants played as the responder, and had the option to either accept or reject the proposed offer. Standard rules of the Ultimatum Game state that if the participant accepts the offer, the pot is split as described, but if the participant rejects the offer, then neither player receives any monies. Although getting some money is (in reality) better than getting no money from these opponents, people still demonstrate a mix of offer acceptance and rejection based on how fair the offer seems [3,5,6,14]. Trials were split into two overall fairness groups: *neutral* and *unfair*. In neutral trials, the proposer offered an even $5 split to the participant. There were six neutral trials. In the remaining 14 trials, the proposer gave unfair offers to participants; these offers were further split into subgroups of slightly unfair offers and very unfair offers. In six trials, the proposer gave slightly unfair bids of $3 or $4, but in the remaining eight trials, the proposer gave very unfair offers of $1 or $2. Participants always played the RNG first, and then the human participants. The order of embodied robot opponents was randomized across the remaining 3 blocks.

After participants played the final opponent, they then completed the NARS and demographic questions.

2.5 Hypotheses

We sought to assess the following hypotheses in this work:

H1: The robot proposers will be treated more similarly to the human proposers when compared to the RNG proposer.
H2: The AI-enabled proposers will be treated more similarly to the human proposers when compared to the non-AI-enabled proposers.
H3: The more human-like the robot form, the less likely opponents will be to accept unfair bids from the system.

H1 and **H2** originate from our previous work, which found that embodied robots were treated more similarly to humans when compared to computers, specifically when endowed with intelligence [10]. The final hypothesis (**H3**) was an exploratory expectation aimed explicitly at testing whether previous findings showing an influence of embodiment (e.g., [16]) might hold true for different levels or types of embodiment.

2.6 Analysis

The analyses in this paper focus on the accepted neutral and unfair offers during the Ultimatum Game, as well as the collected NARS data. The offer acceptance data was evaluated using mixed-measures analysis of variance (ANOVA) tests with an $\alpha = 0.05$ significance level. For the ANOVA, the within-subjects factor was the five proposer types (RNG, human, table-like robot, single-armed robot, and dual-armed robot), and the between-subjects factor was the purported intelligence of the robots. Assumptions of normality were assessed using the Shapiro-Wilk test, which did produce a significant value on this test. However, due to the large sample size ($N = 102$), the ANOVA was considered robust to these violations [2]. When testing for sphericity, Mauchly's test also indicated a violation; the Greenhouse-Geisser correction was applied to affected analyses. In case of significant effects, we used Tukey's test to identify any pairwise differences. Effect size for significant analyses was estimated using η^2. All statistical analyses were conducted using Jamovi [15].

3 Results

Neutral Offers. For neutral offers, nearly all of the offers were accepted by participants, regardless of proposer or intelligence, as illustrated in Fig. 4. A mixed-measures ANOVA showed no significant effects of proposer type ($p = 0.974$) or intelligence ($p = 0.074$) on the proportion of neutral offers accepted. Additionally, there was no interaction between proposer type and intelligence on neutral offers ($p = 0.463$).

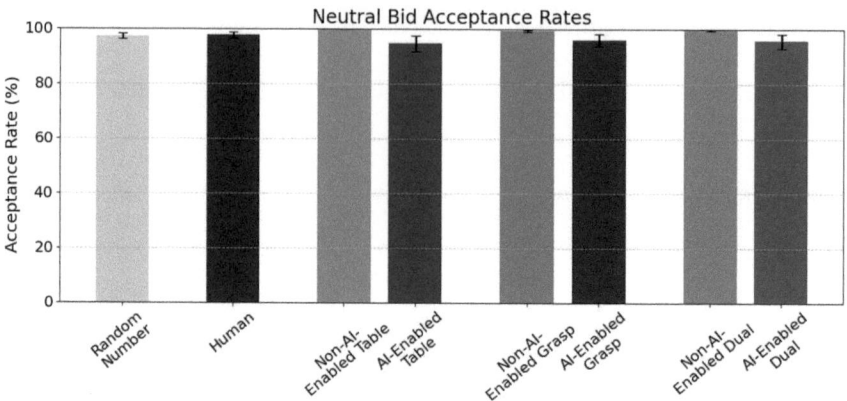

Fig. 4. Mean and standard error of the percent of neutral trial offers accepted for each opponent type.

Slightly Unfair Offers. When presented with slightly unfair offers, participants tended to accept more offers from the RNG and non-AI-enabled robots than from the human proposers and AI-enabled robots, as shown in Fig. 5. A mixed-measures ANOVA test on slightly unfair offers showed there was no significant main effect of proposer type ($p = 0.074$). However, there was a significant effect found for intelligence ($F(1, 100) = 8.62$, $p = 0.004$, $\eta^2 = 0.061$), such that slightly unfair offers were accepted at a lower rate for intelligent opponents, compared to unintelligent opponents.

There was also a significant interaction effect between proposer type and intelligence ($F(2.69, 268.92) = 3.05$, $p = 0.034$, $\eta^2 = 0.007$). Pairwise comparisons showed that for both the table-like and single-armed robots, the AI-enabled version of the robot had fewer accepted offers. A similar pattern presented itself for the non-AI-enabled single-armed robot vs. the AI-enabled dual-armed robot, as well as for the non-AI-enabled table-like robot vs. any other AI-enabled robot. Participants were also more likely to take offers from the non-AI-enabled single-armed robot compared to the human proposer.

Very Unfair Offers. Similarly to the slightly unfair offer results, when participants received a very unfair offer, they tended to accept more offers from the RNG and non-AI-enabled robots than from the human proposers and AI-enabled robots. These results appear in Fig. 6. The mixed-measures ANOVA test for the unfair offers showed significant effects for both proposer type ($F(2.55, 255.11) = 4.622$, $p = 0.006$, $\eta^2 = 0.012$) and intelligence ($F(1, 100) = 5.27$, $p = 0.024$, $\eta^2 = 0.037$). For proposer type, pairwise comparisons showed that significantly more offers were accepted for the RNG compared to the human proposer or the single-armed robot. For intelligence, fewer offers were accepted for AI-enabled robots. There was no significant interaction between proposer type and intelligence ($p = 0.780$).

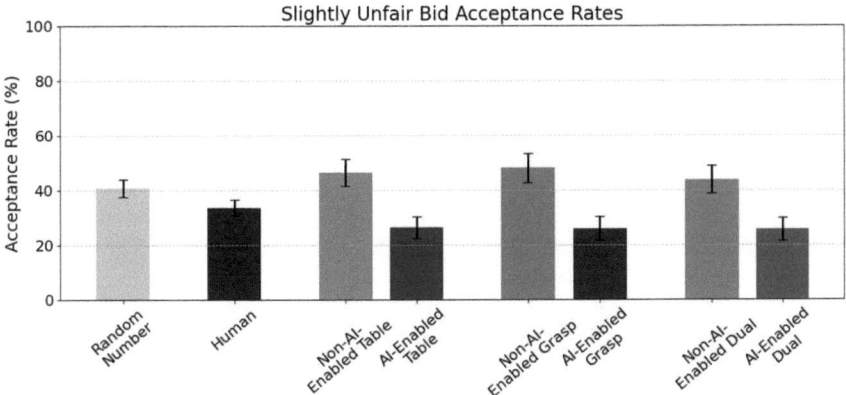

Fig. 5. Mean and standard error of the percent of slightly unfair trial offers accepted for each opponent type.

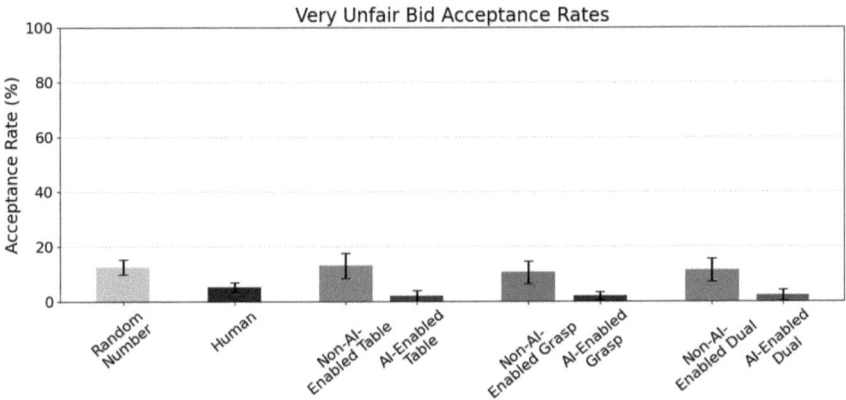

Fig. 6. Mean and standard error of the percent of very unfair offers accepted for each opponent type.

4 Discussion

In this work, we conducted an online study to understand the impact of how the perceived intelligence and the embodied form of a robot might affect how participants respond in a decision-making task. The results suggest that for neutral offers, neither intelligence nor form had any significant impact on participants' acceptance rate. These results were in line with expectations from past research with humans that found a majority of neutral offers are often accepted [10]. When assessing **H1**, it seems that robot proposers were treated similarly to the human proposer, at least in some cases. Relevant to **H2**, the factor that seems to underlie this similar treatment has to do with the intelligence of the robot. For both slightly and very unfair offers, the AI-enabled robots were treated more similarly to humans by participants when compared to the non-AI-enabled robots, supporting **H2** and providing a partial confirmation of **H1**. For **H3**, there was no clear evidence from the data that supported that the form of the robot affected participants' responses at all. As is visible in Fig. 5 and Fig. 6, the pattern of offer acceptance was not different across the different embodied conditions for either slightly or very unfair offers.

This work provides meaningful insights on impacts relevant to the concepts of robot embodiment, human-robot teaming (HRT), and resource allocation. It seems to suggest that again physical embodiment has very little effect on offer acceptance, consistent with our past work [10], but inconsistent with the work of others [16]. Thus, researchers should likely focus on the perceived intelligence of systems in HRT contexts before considering embodied form, particularly in environments where fairness and resource distribution are key (i.e., customer service, healthcare, or collaborative tasks). However, the digital presentation of robot embodiment onscreen (rather than in-person) in the current study may be a constraining factor, as past research has shown that participants react differently to physically present robots vs. robots being presented on a screen [1, 9]. Thus, running future studies in the presence of a physical robot might clarify the current lack of embodiment results. Further, it might be worth investigating a larger range of embodiment, and examining whether even more humanoid or abstract robotic forms may influence participants' responses in the Ultimatum Game.

In conclusion, the work considers the impact of intelligence and form of a robot on responses to unfair behavior in a decision-making task. We found that participants tend to treat AI-enabled robots more like humans when receiving unfair offers, but variations in the embodiment of these robots did not additionally affect this behavior. This work can help researchers design more effective interactions in human-robot collaboration, specifically when more (or less) anthropomorphic treatment of robots is required.

Acknowledgments. We thank the Oregon State SHARE Lab for support in editing this manuscript.

References

1. Bainbridge, W.A., Hart, J., Kim, E.S., Scassellati, B.: The effect of presence on human-robot interaction. In: Proc. of the IEEE International Symposium on Robot and Human Interactive Communication (RO-MAN), pp. 701–706 (2008)
2. Blanca-Mena, M.J., Arnau, J., García-Castro, F.J., Alarcón-Postigo, R., Bono Cabré, R., et al.: Non-normal data in repeated measures anova: impact on type I error and power (2022)
3. Bolton, G., Zwick, R.: Anonymity versus punishment in ultimatum bargaining. Games Econom. Behav. **10**(1), 95–121 (1995)
4. Claudy, M.C., Aquino, K., Graso, M.: Artificial intelligence can't be charmed: the effects of impartiality on laypeople's algorithmic preferences. Front. Psychol. **13**, 898027 (2022)

5. Guth, W., Schmittberger, R., Schwarze, B.: An experimental analysis of ultimatum bargaining. J. Econ. Behav. Organization **3**(4), 367–388 (1982)
6. Henrich, J., Boyd, R., Bowles, S., Camerer, C., Fehr, E., Gintis, H., McElreath, R.: In search of homo economicus: behavioral experiments in 15 small-scale societies. Am. Econ. Rev. **91**(2), 73–78 (2001)
7. Moretti, L., Di Pellegrino, G.: Disgust selectively modulates reciprocal fairness in economic interactions. Emotion **10**(2), 169 (2010)
8. Nishio, S., Ogawa, K., Kanakogi, Y., Itakura, S., Ishiguro, H.: Do robot appearance and speech affect people's attitude? Evaluation through the ultimatum game. Geminoid Studies: Science and Technologies for Humanlike Teleoperated Androids, pp. 263–277 (2018)
9. Powers, A., Kiesler, S., Fussell, S., Torrey, C.: Comparing a computer agent with a humanoid robot. In: Proc. of the ACM/IEEE International Conference on Human-Robot Interaction, pp. 145–152 (2007)
10. Sanchez, C.A., Hildenbrand, L., Fitter, N.: We see them as we are: how humans react to perceived unfair behavior by artificial intelligence in a social decision-making task. Comput. Hum. Behav. Artif. Hum. **4**, 100154 (2025)
11. Sandoval, E.B., Brandstatter, J., Yalcin, U., Bartneck, C.: Robot likeability and reciprocity in human robot interaction: using ultimatum game to determinate reciprocal likeable robot strategies. Int. J. Soc. Robot. **13**(4), 851–862 (2021)
12. Sandoval, E.B., Brandstetter, J., Obaid, M., Bartneck, C.: Reciprocity in human-robot interaction: a quantitative approach through the prisoner's dilemma and the ultimatum game. Int. J. Soc. Robot. **8**, 303–317 (2016)
13. Syrdal, D.S., Dautenhahn, K., Koay, K.L., Walters, M.L.: The negative attitudes towards robots scale and reactions to robot behaviour in a live human-robot interaction study. Adaptive and Emergent Behaviour and Complex Systems (2009)
14. Thaler, R.H.: Anomalies: the ultimatum game. J. Econ. Perspectives **2**(4), 195–206 (1988)
15. The jamovi project: jamovi (2022). https://www.jamovi.org, Computer Software
16. Torta, E., van Dijk, E., Ruijten, P.A., Cuijpers, R.H.: The ultimatum game as measurement tool for anthropomorphism in human–robot interaction. In: Social Robotics: 5th International Conference, ICSR 2013, Bristol, UK, October 27-29, 2013, Proceedings 5, pp. 209–217. Springer (2013)

Designing User Experiences with Social Robots: A Field Study on Acceptance in Public Libraries

Artur Lisetschko[(✉)](https://orcid.org/), Nadine Jansen, and Aysegül Dogangün

Institute of Computer Science, Ruhr West University of Applied Sciences,
Lützowstraße 5, 46236 Bottrop, Germany
{artur.lisetschko,nadine.jansen,ayseguel.doganguen}@hs-ruhrwest.de

Abstract. Social robots are becoming increasingly integrated into public spaces such as libraries, offering opportunities to enhance services and foster meaningful interactions. Designing a positive user experience (UX) that addresses factors like well-being, comfort, and perceived control is critical to their acceptance. This study presents a Wizard-of-Oz (WoZ) field experiment (N = 64) conducted in two public libraries, exploring key UX dimensions, including pragmatic and hedonic qualities, attractiveness, perceived control and privacy concerns. Findings indicate that pragmatic and hedonic qualities significantly influence the intention to use social robots in libraries, while perceived attractiveness plays a minor role. Moreover, high perceived control positively correlates with a favorable UX, even when privacy concerns are present. These insights inform specific design implications to improve the usability and application of social robots in public spaces. By addressing user needs and fostering trust, this research contributes to the successful integration of social robots into everyday environments, supporting their role in creating more engaging public spaces.

Keywords: Social Robot · Human-Robot Interaction · Public Library · User Experience · Field Study · Usability

1 Introduction

Public libraries are a popular application domain for studying how social robots can enhance public spaces [1,2]. These robots, designed to interact with humans and operate in social environments [3], are expected to be treated as human [4]. Leveraging social interaction capabilities, they can offer more engaging and delightful experiences for people compared to non-embodied technologies (e.g., digital kiosk) [5–8]. As versatile service agents they can take on tasks, such as disseminating information, navigation, social interaction or offering recommendations [9] and are studied in different public spaces, such as hotels [10], museums [11], and retail [12].

Still, the lack of social acceptance of robots by naive users is a key issue preventing them from being extensively deployed in public to this day [13]. Ensuring a positive user experience (UX) with social robots that considers user's well-being (e.g., privacy concerns) and comfort (e.g. control perception) [14,15] is suggested to facilitate acceptance of robots [16] and improve the willingness of people to share space with them [13]. For instance, consider that robots might threaten data privacy in libraries. Operations of autonomous robots will depend on continuous processing of information gathered by sensors potentially opening the door for constant monitoring and collection of increasingly sensitive user data [17,18]. Users lacking transparency about what information the robot collects, by which modes and for what purpose can lead to privacy concerns [19] and induce negative attitudes and distrust jeopardizing robot acceptance [20]. Consequently, when the robot covertly adapts its behavior based on personalized information unbeknownst to the user a loss of control may occur. Due to this, the user will neither be able to understand nor predict the robot's behavior and no longer be able to effectively influence the course and outcome of the interaction [21]. This may hinder successful interaction and infringe on the user's decision autonomy [22]. In turn, perceived user control is suggested as an important pragmatic facet of engaging user experiences [23] in terms of dependability. In the context of explainable artificial intelligence (XAI) control perceptions were shown to result from having developed representative mental models about the system's inner workings [24], making its behavior explainable [25] and to relate positively to user satisfaction and overall trust in the system [26,27].

This paper explores the results of a Wizard of Oz (WoZ) field study conducted in public libraries, studying the user experience (UX) with a humanoid social robot, and its relationship with user privacy concerns, control perceptions and acceptance in the context of presenting book recommendation. Present study aims to enrich our understanding of social robot acceptance in the wild by deriving following research question and hypotheses from related work.

RQ1: How does UX with a social robot relate to library visitors' usage intention?

H1: When using social robots in public libraries, the contributions of perceived hedonic and pragmatic qualities and attractiveness are statistically significant in the prediction of library visitors' usage intention.

RQ2: How do user privacy concerns and control perception relate to the attractiveness of a social robot?

H2: When using social robots in public libraries, the contributions of user privacy concerns and control perception are statistically significant in the prediction of library visitors' perceived attractiveness of a social robot.

2 Related Work

2.1 User Experience and Acceptance of Robots

While human-robot interaction (HRI) as a research discipline started to acknowledge the relevance of UX over the last years [16], a unified understanding is still missing. Generally understood as the study of users' thoughts and feelings when interacting with robots [28], stemming from the intricate interplay of user, robot, and context characteristics, it is deemed essential for designing acceptable and transparent robots [29]. Hence, there is an abundance of work on UX in HRI studying peoples emotional and social reactions to robots [30].

A widely applied model used to study UX being adopted by present research is the one proposed by Hassenzahl et al. [31]. It assumes UX to be determined by the user's perception of pragmatic and hedonic qualities when interacting with an artifact. Pragmatic qualities relate to the usability component and hedonic qualities result from the fulfillment of psychological and emotional needs. The perception of both qualities is reflected in attractiveness and expressed in summary evaluations of the artifact leading to its adoption or rejection [32]. Indeed, research suggests that pragmatic (e.g., usefulness) and hedonic (e.g., enjoyment) qualities significantly influence acceptance of social robots [16,30,33,34]. This view overlaps with the Technology Acceptance Model (TAM) [35] postulating that the perception of usefulness and ease of use of a system are primary predictors of an individual's attitude toward system usage and determine whether an intention to use is formed and actual system usage occurs [36]. TAM is based on theories of reasoned action [37] and planned behavior [38] which distinguish between beliefs, attitudes, and intentions postulating that beliefs govern attitudes and attitudes govern intentions [36]. For instance, perceived behavioral control is a key belief from theory of planned behavior, also included in TAM (e.g., [39]). While originally acknowledged to be mainly concerned with technology acceptance in utilitarian settings, TAM was extended to consider intrinsic motivators, such as perceived enjoyment, linking it closer to UX [40]. TAM describes intention to use as a direct determinant of actual usage defining use of technology as expression of acceptance. TAM was adapted and expanded to measure the acceptance of social service robots [41] by using behavioral indicators, such as intention to use a robot [42,43].

Combining these perspectives, Golchinfar et al. [44] conducted a WoZ field study at a shopping mall's service point investigating how the UX with Pepper in handling open customer requests affects the intention to use social robots in retail. The authors found only hedonic qualities to significantly predict users' intention to use social robots in retail, suggesting that customers are reluctant to acknowledge pragmatic qualities of social robots, concluding that UX evaluation in HRI may require additional predictors. The present study sought to test if the findings of the authors [44] were replicable in a library setting.

2.2 Social Robots in Libraries

Leveraging anthropomorphism in social robot design is argued to be crucial for user acceptance [45], inspiring the design of humanoid forms for robots as it is assumed that people interact with both living and non-living entities by using human social cues [46–48]. As social robots can serve multiple functions (e.g., Pepper [49]), human users may accept them in the role of librarians [47]. They generally assume simple information tasks, such as reception of new customers (e.g., [53]), instruction in library services (e.g., registration, lending) or navigation support [2], but remain assistants due to their lack of autonomous emotional, communicative and intellectual abilities [52]. Impact wise social robots were found acting as community builders that engage, entertain, connect, and empower people, improving the public image of libraries [50]. They can promote learning, for example, Shen & Lin [51] combined the social robot Nao [49] with a digital picture book to present short stories for children. Stories were verbally and gestural presented. Results demonstrated that children wanted to listen to the robot again and to borrow a copy of the recited story. Muben et al. [54] conducted an observational field study with Pepper providing guidance in a university library to explore first impressions of students. Finding more than half of the initial emotional responses to be negative, with sporadic positive remarks focusing on Pepper's technological novelty, they conclude that autonomous robots in public may intimidate naive users.

In terms of robot recommender systems, embodied humanoid robots were found to influence consumer decisions more compared to another human [55] and reach a trend for higher acceptance rates in movie recommendations compared to a mobile app [56]. While social robots were demonstrated as engaging storytellers, they were not yet studied as recommendation agents in a library setting, a role traditionally reserved for librarians. As findings about the reception of social robots in public libraries are mixed, current study sought to investigate the UX with a humanoid social robot in public libraries acting in the role of a librarian in terms of recommending books and the reading of excerpts, as determinant of user acceptance.

2.3 Social Robots and Privacy Considerations

Chung et al. [57] studied the influence of spatial contexts and verbal anthropomorphism on UX, including privacy concerns, with the non-humanoid robot 'Jibo' introducing participants into book lending. Results show higher anthropomorphism facilitated positive UX in terms of likability but did not significantly affect users' privacy concerns. Only context significantly influenced privacy concern with participants feeling greater concerns when interacting in a public lobby of a university library with many passersby as compared to an enclosed lab environment. The authors demonstrate that spatial context is an important factor to consider in HRI for privacy concerns.

Effects of system embodiment and transparency about data processing in context of a face identification application on users' privacy considerations and UX were studied [19,58]. Comparing the enrollment procedure on an humanoid robot with a digital kiosk, users significantly disclosed more information to the robot as compared to the kiosk when transparency was given [58]. However, this effect was not significant when comparing systems in non-transparent conditions. While transparency exerted a significant positive effect on UX for both systems it did not significantly affect users' privacy considerations within the same system. Additionally, the transparent kiosk elicited significantly more privacy concerns in users compared to the transparent robot giving the same information. Results suggest that the pairing of system embodiment and transparency may potentially alter users' risk perception regarding the disclosure of personal information and privacy concerns.

With research highlighting privacy concerns and control perception as important to users' well-being and comfort [14,15], present study was interested in exploring the extent to which an anthropomorphic robot may elicit privacy concerns, as the natural mode of interaction may facilitate control perceptions reducing the risk perception to disclose personal information.

3 Method

3.1 Study Setup

The field study was conducted in two public libraries, from January 15–20 2024 in library 1, and from March 4–9 2024 in library 2. The libraries involved in this study were chosen under consideration of comparable services structures and user demographics. Displays and posters were placed at the study area informing visitors that a scientific study is being conducted. Softbank's social robot "Pepper" was used in present study as this model has been examined in many real-world scenarios (e.g., [59,60]) and user perceptions of anthropomorphic appearing systems were of interested. Pepper was selected for its advanced humanoid design, featuring a tablet interface, expressive gestures, and the ability to interact through speech and visualizations. This makes it ideal for libraries, where both verbal and non-verbal communication are crucial. Pepper has two arms, one head with a humanoid face, rolls for locomotion, and a integrated tablet display on its chest. During the study period, Pepper was placed in an enclosed reading cubicle located on the third floor where the interaction with participants occurred. This was decided as the study was designed for single user interaction and to ensure that the library's operations remained unaffected.

WoZ was employed to enhance Pepper's conversation skills. In collaboration with local staff, librarians remotely controlled Pepper's responses from an adjacent cubicle on the same floor using a custom-developed user interface. The wizard remotely controlled Pepper's responses from an adjacent cubicle on the same floor using a custom-developed user interface. Through external cameras and microphones in the cubicle, participants were tracked. See Wizard were trained in prior and supervised by one researcher during the study to verify that the robot's responses complied with the interaction scenario, creating a consistent interaction experience across all participants. Before interaction, participants were not told that a human operator was controlling the robot.

3.2 Procedure

The study procedure was reviewed and approved by the local Ethics Commission. Arriving at the study area, participants were given an overview of the tasks to complete with the robot. They were informed about the purpose and duration of trials, that participation was voluntarily and could be withdrawn at any time without incurring any disadvantages and ensured that data collection is anonymized. Participants gave written consent and received an individual 'ID card' featuring a QR code to initiate the trial with.

Before interaction, participants were asked to choose between a librarian or Pepper for phase one. Then, participants were guided to the interaction cubicle and scanned their ID card. Depending on their choice, participants first passed the recommendation phase with either Pepper or a librarian to create a wish list from recommended books. However, all participants interacted for the reading phase with Pepper reading text samples. First, participants were greeted by Pepper or a librarian and told that they could request book recommendations based on genre categories (crime, thriller, science fiction, fantasy, romance, family, historical novel, classic, universal literature). Choosing a genre, participants were randomly presented with a respective book title out of a curated list by reading aloud the cover text and naming the author and publication year. Here, participants had multiple choices. They were asked if they wanted additional information about the title or if it should be added to their wish list. The interlocutor would then handle any upcoming inquiries and add titles to the wish list of participants as desired. If participants had no interest in the item, they could hear another recommendation from the same genre or switch genres. When participants did not wish for any more recommendations, the reading phase started. If participants interacted with a librarian before, the librarian would ask the participant to interact with Pepper and listen to it reading text samples out of chosen books. Otherwise, Pepper announced the reading phase. Pepper asked participants if there was any title on their list, they wanted samples from. After hearing each sample, participants could request additional samples from the same book, request samples from a different book on their list or end the interaction here. On termination, Pepper bid goodbye to participants concluding the interaction. Afterwards, participants filled out the survey. After the trial, participants were thanked, debriefed and dismissed. Procedure completion time for participants ranged between 15 to 30 min.

3.3 Recruitment and Participants

Participants were recruited in both libraries during data collection and calls for participation on social media, library websites, and on-site posters informing that "testing of a social robot was taking place". Inclusion criteria for participation were being of legal age and having sufficient verbal language skills. Data were collected from 65 participants across both libraries, with gender and age distribution shown in Table 1 ($M = 47.73$, $SD = 20.89$). Over 81.5% of participants visited the library regularly, from several times a year to weekly (see Table 1). Most participants ($n = 48$) had no prior experience with robots, indicating that robots were yet unfamiliar technology for them. Despite this, the majority of participants ($n = 54$) decided to interact from the start with the robot, while 11 chose a human librarian instead to request book recommendations from. However, due to incomplete reporting one data set was excluded from further analyses, leaving 64 data sets for hypothesis testing.

Table 1. Participants' Characteristics, Experiences with Robots, and Library Usage Frequency. $N = 65$

Age Group	n (%)	Gender	n (%)	Robot Experience	n (%)	Library Usage	n (%)
18–24	14 (21.5%)	Female	27 (42.2%)	Yes	13 (20.0%)	Daily	3 (4.6%)
25–34	9 (13.8%)	Male	37 (57.8%)	No	48 (73.8%)	Several times a week	12 (18.5%)
35–44	7 (10.8%)	no answer	1 (1.5%)	I don't remember	4 (6.2%)	Several times a month	27 (41.5%)
45–54	5 (7.7%)					Several times a year	14 (21.5%)
55–64	9 (13.8%)					Once a year	1 (1.5%)
65 or over	21 (32.3%)					Less than once a year	8 (12.3%)
no answer	1 (1.5%)						

3.4 Measures

To answer the research questions, quantitative data were collected via survey including questionnaires to assess usability, UX, perceived user control and privacy concerns. Selected measures were based on prior studies and modified to reflect the interaction with Pepper. Brief measures were necessary, as library visitors primarily focus on their tasks and have limited time for lengthy questionnaires. For questionnaires using the Likert response format (usability, control perception, privacy concerns), participants answers were collected on a 7-point scale anchored by "Strongly Disagree" (1) and "Fully Agree" (7).

The *Usability Metric for User Experience* (UMUX) [61] is a short four-item Likert scale and was used for participants' assessment of the robot's perceived usability. To achieve parity with the System Usability Score (SUS) metric, UMUX scores were transformed by following calculation rule: odd-numbered items are scored [score - 1] and even-numbered items [7 - score]. The sum of the scores of the items is then divided by 24 and multiplied by 100. (Cronbach's α = .63).

A short version of the *User Experience Questionnaire* (UEQ-S) developed by [32] was used to assess participants' UX with Pepper. Following the authors suggestions to retain the original theoretical model of the UEQ, a slightly extended short version was used. This version reduces the number of items from 26 in the original to 14 items and preserves interpretability of the UEQ at the scale level allowing still for consideration of the individual dimensions and facets of UX. This version measures the hedonic dimension with 4 items split into the subscales stimulation and novelty, the pragmatic dimension with 6 items covering the subscales efficiency, perspicuity and dependability with 2 items each, and attractiveness with 4 items. The UEQ-S uses semantically differential items, each consisting of a pair of terms with opposite meanings presented as anchors on a 7-point scale. Answers are rated on a scale from -3 (full agreement with the negative term) to +3 (full agreement with the positive term). For instance a score of 7 for unpleasant – pleasant would indicate that the experience with Pepper was perceived as pleasant. (Cronbach's α values for hedonic quality = .80; pragmatic quality = .76; attractiveness = .88). The order of positive and negative terms as well as item order was randomized.

For assessing *user control perception*, as the "users' perceptions on their capability, resources, and skills for naturally performing the behavior and usage of a particular service or system" [62], the scale of [63] was adapted. Previously, this scale proofed useful for studying the acceptance of smart home applications. (Cronbach's $\alpha = .81$).

To measure *privacy concerns*, the scale of [64] from research on privacy concerns in using virtual assistants was adapted and used. (Cronbach's $\alpha = .90$).

To measure library visitors *intention to use* the robot, participants were asked to rate the likelihood of using the robot again on their next visit on a 10-point Likert like scale. *"How likely are you to use the robot again the next time you visit the library?"*.

3.5 Data Analysis

IBM SPSS Statistics version 26.0 was used for data analysis. The significance level for all statistical tests was $p = .05$. Effect sizes are reported according to Cohen (1988) [65] with Pearson's r correlation coefficient r (r = .10, low; r = .30, moderate; r = .50, strong) to explore relationships between measures and Cohen's d (d = .20, small; d = .50, medium; d = .80, large). If a variable is ordinal scaled Spearman's ρ is calculated instead of Pearson's r for assessing correlations. H1 was tested by means of ordinal logistic regression as intention to use was ordinal scaled, while all predictors (hedonic quality, pragmatic quality, and attractiveness) followed metric scaling. H2 was tested by means of multiple linear regression with privacy concerns and control perception entered as predictor variables and the UX dimension of attractiveness as criteria variable.

4 Results

Table 2. Descriptive Statistics of UEQ-S scores per scale. $n = 64$

UEQ-S Scales	M(SD)
Attractiveness	1.21(.15)
Hedonic Qualities	.89(.14)
Stimulation	.91(.15)
Novelty	.87(.16)
Pragmatic Qualities	1.17(.12)
Efficiency	.94(.14)
Perspicuity	1.45(.17)
Dependability	1.11(.13)

Table 3. Descriptive Statistics for UMUX, Perceived Control, Privacy Concerns and Intention to Use. $n = 64$

Instrument	M(SD)
UMUX	66.93(2.47)
Perceived Control	4.71(.19)
Privacy Concerns	3.67(.21)
Intention to Use	5.77(.43)

4.1 Regression Analyses

To test H1 an ordinal regression was conducted to assess the contribution of hedonic qualities, pragmatic qualities, and attractiveness in the prediction of participants' intention to use a social robot. Among predictor variables no multicollinearity was observed (all r < .7). Chi-square test indicated significant improvement in fit of the final model over the null model ($\chi^2(3) = 60.16$, $p < .001$). Assumption of proportional odds was satisfied as indicated by the test of parallel lines ($\chi^2(24) = 8.74$, $p = .998$). The model is capable of explaining between 22% (McFadden $R^2 = .22$) and 62% (Nagelkerke $R^2 = .62$) of the variance in participants' intention to use a social robot. Hedonic ($B = 1.17$, $p < .001$) and pragmatic qualities ($B = .82$, $p = .037$) were found to be significant predictors of intention to use, while attractiveness failed to contribute significantly ($B = .43$, $p = .227$). For every unit increase on hedonic or pragmatic qualities, there is a predicted increase of 1.17 or .82 respectively in the log odds of participants being in a higher level of the intention to use variable. This indicates that a participant reporting higher perception of hedonic or pragmatic qualities was also more likely to indicate greater intention to use the robot on their next visit. Odds ratios indicate that the odds of being in a higher category on intention to use increases by a factor of 3.22 or 2.26 respectively for every one unit increase on hedonic or pragmatic qualities.

Multiple linear regression analysis was conducted to test H2 and assess the predictive value of privacy concerns and control perception on attractiveness using the forced entry method with all predictors included in the model. Two data sets were identified as residual outliers and removed for analysis. Data showed no signs of multicollinearity (tolerance < .10) and homoscedasticity was satisfied. Residuals were normally distributed and independent according to the Durbin-Watson statistic of 2.19 [66]. The resulting model was significant ($F(2, 59) = 7.69$, $p < .001$) explaining 20.7% ($R^2 = .207$) of variance in attractiveness. Perceived control contributed significantly to the prediction of attractiveness ($\beta = .46$, $T(59) = 3.90$, $p < .001$), while privacy concerns did not ($\beta = .01$, $T(59) = .11$, $p = .914$). With an increase of one point in perceived control, an increase of .31 units in attractiveness can be expected. Means and standard deviations of employed instruments are shown in Table 2 and 3.

5 Discussion

5.1 Interpretation of Findings

Findings suggest overall that participants enjoyed Pepper's book presentation, assessed its functionality as acceptable and expressed a tendency to interact anew. Complementing prior research (e.g., [67]), UX was identified as relevant factor for intention to use social robots in public spaces in terms of library environments. However, the perception of hedonic qualities being rated lower than attractiveness and pragmatic qualities suggests that participants assess Pepper to be more acceptable on a functional than on a social level and that attributing high hedonic qualities are not necessary for reporting a net positive experience. Participants rating intention to use slightly above average, indicates an ambivalent attitude acceptance towards the robot or that the interaction was perceived neither particularly positively nor negatively. Intention to use the robot seems to rather dependent on situational circumstances paired with the perceived scope of its services, especially when hedonic qualities are found to be lacking.

Analysis only partially confirmed H1 indicating that hedonic and pragmatic qualities positively correlate with and significantly predict participants' intention to use robots, while attractiveness did not. This hints at a preference for hedonic and pragmatic qualities over attractiveness when interacting with library robots. These results differ compared to findings of Golchinfar et al. [44], who report only hedonic qualities as significant predictor of intention to use social robots in retail. Participants presumably acknowledged Pepper's pragmatic qualities in the present study more as it provided library specific services. While the authors' model explained only up to 23.2% of variance of intention to use [44], present model data managed to explain up to 62% of variance, confirming it as a viable mean to approximate usage intentions for a social library robot (**H1**). Regression results complement studies highlighting greater importance to hedonic qualities of UX in HRI compared to pragmatic qualities [68,69] and demonstrate how UX constructs relate to TAM constructs [36]. Similarly, van Schaik and Ling [40] studied the synthesis of both models finding perceived enjoyment as strong predictor of behavioral intention.

Participants felt on average in control of the robot but were unsure if using the robot posed a privacy risk. For H2, results showed only perceived control to significantly predict ratings of attractiveness, but not privacy concerns. This suggests that control perception positively correlates with reporting a positive interaction experience and the latter being independent from privacy concerns. This contrasts with work finding privacy concerns impacting user acceptance of Pepper as information medium in the business context [70]. Participants may have had no significant privacy concerns because of a high control perception suggesting that no loss of control occurred. High control perception may have been due to the rather simple and natural interaction design with Pepper and absence of any inscrutable personalization features, facilitating the acquisition of a representative mental model [71] making Pepper's behavior explainable [25] and its output appear trustworthy [72]. Despite interacting with an anthropomorphic robot in an enclosed space, privacy concerns of participants were average. This may be as neither what information the robot collects nor for what purposes was transparent to participants [19]. This highlights the additional need for more transparency regarding the handling of user data to reduce privacy concerns (e.g., [73]), improve user trust [74], enhance willingness to provide personal information [75] and improve UX [19].

5.2 Limitations

Consideration must be given to the social robot chosen, as its appearance and affordances, including possible range of motion can significantly impact user expectations and the subsequent experience [76]. Here, the UX with Pepper was exclusively studied and not compared with other social robot models (e.g., NAO). The asymmetrical study design did not allow for an in-depth comparison between library visitors' interaction experience with a social robot and visitors' experience with a human librarian. The interaction was stationary and the environment enclosed, which may have circumvented external confounding factors (e.g., ambient noise) natural to library environments limiting its ecological validity. Pepper's behavior was limited to scripted recommendations and reading tasks, which may not fully capture the diverse social interactions envisioned for public library services. Present findings are based on self-assessment data gathered post interaction, and may be subject to biased responses as participants assess their experience retrospectively promoting the possibility of drawing inadequate conclusions (e.g., [77]).

6 Conclusion and Outlook of Future Research

We conducted a field study with the Pepper robot for the presentation of book recommendations in public libraries to explore user acceptance surveying for various acceptance indicators. The results demonstrate a relationship between UX and TAM theory. UX can be a factor to explain intention to use social robots in public environments with both hedonic and pragmatic qualities contributing positively to usage intentions. Assessing the interaction with a robot as attractive may not be enough to explain usage behavior, as a more functional than social acceptance of a robot might still yield a positive UX. Findings emphasize that functionality and usability should not be neglected compared to relevant psychological needs to achieve high user acceptance in a broad range of users. Consideration of additional UX factors [67,78] in HRI could further improve model accuracy. Results showed perceived control to significantly contribute to a positive interaction experience independently from privacy concerns. Future research might explore further if and how a high control perception alleviates privacy concerns of users as suggested given that privacy concerns might impact user acceptance of social robots. HRI is still in need of more accessible methods and instruments that facilitate the collection of data in situ. Moreover, with the overall experience of social robots contingent on the interaction of user expectations, the robot itself, and contextual factors [79], designing and evaluating for a suitable robot personality and behavior considering its application context, will be crucial for developing robots that provide tangible benefits and appear acceptable in real-world scenarios [80]. In case of libraries for instance, more symmetrical balanced study in the future comparing the interaction experience of library visitors with a social robot with that between visitor and human librarian, could be helpful to generate deeper insights for moving towards this ambitious goal.

Acknowledgments. The presented work was supported by the RuhrBots (www.ruhrbots.de) competence center (16SV8693) funded by the Federal Ministry of Research, Technology and Space Germany.

Disclosure of Interests. The authors have no competing interests to declare that are relevant to the content of this article.

References

1. Behan, J., O'Keeffe, D.T.: The development of an autonomous service robot. Implementation: "Lucas"–The library assistant robot. Intell. Serv. Robot. **1**(1), 73–89 (2008)
2. Harada, T.: Robotics and artificial intelligence technology in Japanese libraries. Information Technology Satellite Meeting "Robots in libraries: challenge or opportunity? (2019)
3. Breazeal, C., Takanishi, A., Kobayashi, T.: Social Robots that Interact with People. In: Bruno, S., Oussama, K. (eds.) Springer Handbook of Robotics, pp. 1349–1369. Springer, Heidelberg (2008). https://doi.org/10.1007/978-3-540-30301-5_59
4. Reeves, B., Nass C. I.:The Media Equation. How People Treat Computers, Television, and New Media Like Real People and Places. Cambridge University Press (1996)
5. Dumouchel, P., Damiano, L., DeBevoise, M.: Living with Robots. Harvard University Press (2017)
6. Takayuki, K., Takayuki, H., Daniel, E., Hiroshi, I.: Interactive robots as social partners and peer tutors for children: a field trial. Hum.-Comput. Interact. **19**(1–2), 61–84 (2004). https://doi.org/10.1080/07370024.2004.9667340
7. Ludewig, Y.: Untersuchung des Einflusses sozio-emotionaler Faktoren auf die soziale Akzeptanz und Nutzungsintention bei Lotsenrobotern. University of Technology Ilmenau (2016)
8. Ulhøi, J.P., Nørskov, S.: The emergence of social robots: Adding physicality and agency to technology. J. Eng. Tech. Manage. **65**, 101703 (2022). https://doi.org/10.1016/j.jengtecman.2022.101703
9. Hansen, S. T., Hansen, K. D.: What's a robot doing in the Citizen Service Centre? In: Cindy, B., Ana, P., Elizabeth, B., David, F.-S., Daniel, S. (eds.): Companion of the 2021 ACM/IEEE International Conference on Human-Robot Interaction, New York, pp. 677–679. ACM (2021)
10. Pan, Y., Okada, H., Uchiyama, T., Suzuki, K.: On the reaction to robot's speech in a hotel public space. Int. J. Soc. Robot. **7**(5), 911–920 (2015). https://doi.org/10.1007/s12369-015-0320-0
11. Faber, F., Bennewitz, M.E., Clemens, G., Attila, G., Christoph, J., et al.: The humanoid museum tour guide Robotinho. In: RO-MAN 2009 - The 18th IEEE International Symposium on Robot and Human Interactive Communication, pp. 891–896. IEEE (2009)
12. Okafuji, Y., Song, S., Baba, J., Yoshikawa, Y., Ishiguro, H.: Influence of collaborative customer service by service robots and clerks in bakery stores. Front. Robot. AI **10**, 1125308. https://doi.org/10.3389/frobt.2023.1125308
13. Tiddi, I., Bastianelli, E., Daga, E., d'Aquin, M., Motta, E.: Robot-city interaction: mapping the research landscape—a survey of the interactions between robots and modern cities. Int. J. Soc. Robot. **12**(2), 299–324 (2020)

14. Frennert, S., Aminoff, H., Östlund, B.: Technological frames and care robots in eldercare. Int. J. Soc. Robot. **13**(2), 311–325 (2021). https://doi.org/10.1007/s12369-020-00641-0
15. Lamers, M.H., Verbeek, F.J.: Human-Robot Personal Relationships. Springer, Heidelberg (2011). https://doi.org/10.1007/978-3-642-19385-9
16. Shourmasti, E.S., Colomo-Palacios, R., Holone, H., Demi, S.: User experience in social robots. Sensors **21**(15), 5052 (2021). https://doi.org/10.3390/s21155052
17. Calo, R.: Robots and privacy. In: Patrick, L., Bekey, G., Abney, K. (eds.) Robot Ethics: The Ethical and Social Implications of Robotics, pp. 187–202. MIT Press, Cambridge (2010)
18. Lutz, C., Schöttler, M., Hoffmann, C.P.: The privacy implications of social robots: scoping review and expert interviews. Mob. Media Commun. **7**(3), 412–434 (2019). https://doi.org/10.1177/2050157919843961
19. Vitale, J., et al.: Be more transparent and users will like you. In: Proceedings of the 2018 ACM/IEEE International Conference on Human-Robot Interaction, New York, pp. 379–387. ACM (2018)
20. Xiao, L., Kumar, V.: Robotics for customer service: a useful complement or an ultimate substitute? J. Serv. Res. **24**(1), 9–29. https://doi.org/10.1177/1094670519878881
21. Sharkey, A., Sharkey, N.: Granny and the robots: ethical issues in robot care for the elderly. Ethics Inf. Technol. **14**(1), 27–40 (2012). https://doi.org/10.1007/s10676-010-9234-6
22. Turkle, S.: In good company? In: Wilks, Y. (ed.) Close Engagements with Artificial Companions, pp. 3–10. John Benjamins Publishing Company (Natural Language Processing), Amsterdam (2010)
23. O'Brien, H.L., Toms, E.G.: What is user engagement? A conceptual framework for defining user engagement with technology. J. Am. Soc. Inform. Sci. Technol. **59**(6), 938–955 (2008). https://doi.org/10.1002/asi.20801
24. Norman, D.: Some observations on mental models. In: Gentner, D., Stevens, A.L. (eds.) Mental Models, pp. 7–14. Lawrence Erlbaum Associates, Inc (Cognitive Science), New Jersey (1983)
25. Chan, M.: Mental Models. Nielsen Norman Group (2024). Accessible under https://www.nngroup.com/articles/mental-models/
26. Lyons, J.B., et al.: Shaping trust through transparent design: theoretical and experimental guidelines. In: Savage-Knepshield, P., Chen, J. (eds.) Advances in Human Factors in Robots and Unmanned Systems. AISC, pp. 127–136. Springer, Cham (2017). https://doi.org/10.1007/978-3-319-41959-6_11
27. Eiband, M., Schneider, H., Bilandzic, M., Fazekas-Con, J., Haug, M., Hussmann, H.: Bringing transparency design into practice. In: 23rd International Conference on Intelligent User Interfaces, New York, pp. 211–223. ACM (2018). https://doi.org/10.1145/3172944.3172961
28. Tonkin, M., Vitale, J., Herse, S., Williams, M.-A., Judge, W.,; Wang, X.: Design methodology for the UX of HRI. In: Proceedings of the 2018 ACM/IEEE International Conference on Human-Robot Interaction, New York, pp. 407–415. ACM (2018)
29. Babel, F., Kraus, J., Baumann, M.: Findings from a qualitative field study with an autonomous robot in public: exploration of user reactions and conflicts. Int. J. Soc. Robot. **14**(7), 1625–1655 (2022)
30. Alenljung, B., Lindblom, J., Andreasson, R., Ziemke, T.: User experience in social human-robot interaction. Int. J. Ambient Comput. Intell. (IJACI) **8**(2), 12–31 (2017)

31. Hassenzahl, M., Diefenbach, S., Göritz, A.: Needs, affect, and interactive products - Facets of user experience. Interact. Comput. **22**(5), 353–362 (2010). https://doi.org/10.1016/j.intcom.2010.04.002
32. Alberola, C., Walter, G., Brau, H.: Creation of a short version of the user experience questionnaire UEQ. i-com **17**(1), 57–64 (2018). https://doi.org/10.1515/icom-2017-0032
33. Beheshtian, N., Kaipainen, K., Kähkönen, K., Ahtinen, A.: Color game. In: Markku Turunen (Hg.): Proceedings of the 23rd International Conference on Academic Mindtrek. AcademicMindtrek '20: Academic Mindtrek 2020. Tampere Finland, 29 01 2020 30 01 2020, New York, NY, USA, pp. 10–19. ACM (2020)
34. de Graaf, M.M.A.; Ben Allouch, S.; van Dijk, J.A.G.M.: Long-term evaluation of a social robot in real homes. IS **17**(3), 461–490 (2016). https://doi.org/10.1075/is.17.3.08deg
35. Davis, F.D.: Perceived usefulness, perceived ease of use, and user acceptance of information technology. MIS Q. **13**(3), 319–40 (1989)
36. Hornbæk, K., Hertzum, M.: Technology acceptance and user experience. ACM Trans. Comput.-Hum. Interact. **24**(5), 1–30 (2017). https://doi.org/10.1145/3127358
37. Fishbein, M., Ajzen, I.: Belief, Attitude, Intention and Behavior. An Introduction to Theory and Research (Addison-Wesley Series in Social Psychology). Addison-Wesley, Reading (1975)
38. Ajzen, I.: The theory of planned behavior. Organ. Behav. Hum. Decis. Process. **50**(2), 179–211 (1991). https://doi.org/10.1016/0749-5978(91)90020-T
39. Koufaris, M.: Applying the technology acceptance model and flow theory to online consumer behavior. Inf. Syst. Res. **13**(2), 205–223 (2002). https://doi.org/10.1287/isre.13.2.205.83
40. van Schaik, P., Ling, J.: An integrated model of interaction experience for information retrieval in a Web-based encyclopaedia. Interact. Comput. **23**(1), 18–32 (2011). https://doi.org/10.1016/j.intcom.2010.07.002
41. Heerink, M., Kröse, B., Evers, V., Wielinga, B.: Assessing acceptance of assistive social agent technology by older adults: the almere model. Int. J. Soc. Robot. **2**(4), 361–375 (2010)
42. Iwamura, Y., Shiomi, M., Kanda, T., Ishiguro, H., Hagita, N.: Do elderly people prefer a conversational humanoid as a shopping assistant partner in supermarkets? In: Billard, A., Kahn, P., Adams, J.A., Trafton, G. (eds.): Proceedings of the 6th International Conference on Human-Robot Interaction. HRI'11: International Conference on Human-Robot Interaction. Lausanne Switzerland, 06-03-2011–09-03-2011. New York, NY, USA, pp. 449–456. ACM (2011)
43. Naneva, S., Sarda Gou, M., Webb, T.L., Prescott, T.J.: A systematic review of attitudes, anxiety, acceptance, and trust towards social robots. Int. J. Soc. Robot. **12**(6), 1179–1201 (2020). https://doi.org/10.1007/s12369-020-00659-4
44. Golchinfar, D., Vaziri, D.D., Stevens, G., Schreiber, D.: Let's go to the mall: investigating the role of user experience in customers' intention to use social robots in a shopping mall. In: Designing Interactive Systems Conference (DIS '22), pp. 377–386 (2022)
45. Duffy, B.R.: Anthropomorphism and the social robot. Robot. Auton. Syst. **42**(3–4), 177–190 (2003)
46. Bar-Cohen, Y., Breazeal, C.:Biologically Inspired Intelligent Robots: SPIE PRESS (2003)

47. Kang, D., Hwang, H., Kwak, S.S.: Collabot: a robotic system that assists library users through collaboration between robots. In: Proceedings of the 2024 ACM/IEEE International Conference on Human-Robot Interaction (HRI '24), pp. 352–360 (2024)
48. Tella, A.: Robots are coming to the libraries: are librarians ready to accommodate them? LHTN **37**(8), 13–17 (2020). https://doi.org/10.1108/LHTN-05-2020-0047
49. SoftBank Robotics, For better business just add Pepper (2024)
50. Nguyen, L.: An investigation of humanoid robots and their implications for Australian public libraries: research report. Australian Library and Information Association (2019)
51. Shen, W.-W., Lin, J.-M.: Robot assisted reading: a preliminary study on the robotic storytelling service to children in the library. In: Wu, T.-T., Huang, Y.-M., Shadieva, R., Lin, L., Starčič, A.I. (eds.) ICITL 2018. LNCS, vol. 11003, pp. 528–535. Springer, Cham (2018). https://doi.org/10.1007/978-3-319-99737-7_56
52. Schmiederer, S.: Der Einsatz humanoider Roboter in Bibliotheken. Humboldt-University Berlin (2021)
53. Wang, Z.: How do library staff view librarian robotics? Librarian staff's ignored humanistic views on the impact and threat of robotics adoption. In: IFLA 2019 KM Satellite Conference (2019)
54. Mubin, O., Kharub, I., Khan, A.: Pepper in the library "students' first impressions". In: Extended Abstracts of the 2020 CHI Conference on Human Factors in Computing Systems, pp. 1–9 (2020)
55. Ogawa, K., Bartneck, C., Sakamoto, D., Kanda, T., Ono, T., Ishiguro, H.: Can an android persuade you? In: RO-MAN 2009 - The 18th IEEE International Symposium on Robot and Human Interactive Communication, pp. 516–521. IEEE (2009). https://doi.org/10.1109/ROMAN.2009.5326352
56. Staffa, M., Rossi, S.: Recommender interfaces: the more human-like, the more humans like. In: Agah, A., Cabibihan, J.-J., Howard, A.M., Salichs, M.A., He, H. (eds.) ICSR 2016. LNCS (LNAI), vol. 9979, pp. 200–210. Springer, Cham (2016). https://doi.org/10.1007/978-3-319-47437-3_20
57. Chung, H., Lee, S., Jun, S.: How to make robots' optimal anthropomorphism level: manipulating social cues and spatial context for an improved user experience. In: 2022 17th ACM/IEEE International Conference on Human-Robot Interaction (HRI), pp. 731–736. IEEE (2022)
58. Tonkin, M., et al.: Embodiment, privacy and social robots: may i remember you? In: Kheddar, A., Yoshida, E., Ge, S.S., Suzuki, K., Cabibihan, J.-J., Eyssel, F., He, H. (eds.) Social Robotics. LNCS, vol. 10652, pp. 506–515. Springer, Cham (2017). https://doi.org/10.1007/978-3-319-70022-9_50
59. Aaltonen, I., Arvola, A., Heikkilä, P., Lammi, H.: Hello pepper, may i tickle you? In: Mutlu, B., Tscheligi, M., Weiss, A., Young, J.E. (eds.): Proceedings of the Companion of the 2017 ACM/IEEE International Conference on Human-Robot Interaction. HRI '17: ACM/IEEE International Conference on Human-Robot Interaction. Vienna Austria, 06 03 2017 09 03 2017, New York, NY, USA, pp. 53–54. ACM (2017)
60. Heikkilä, P., et al.: Should a robot guide like a human? A qualitative four-phase study of a shopping mall robot. In: Salichs, M.A., et al. (eds.) ICSR 2019. LNCS (LNAI), vol. 11876, pp. 548–557. Springer, Cham (2019). https://doi.org/10.1007/978-3-030-35888-4_51
61. Finstad, K.: The usability metric for user experience. Interact. Comput. **22**(5), 323–327 (2010). https://doi.org/10.1016/j.intcom.2010.04.004

62. Lu, Y., Zhou, T., Wang, B.: Exploring Chinese users' acceptance of instant messaging using the theory of planned behavior, the technology acceptance model, and the flow theory. Comput. Hum. Behav. **25**(1), 29–39 (2009). https://doi.org/10.1016/j.chb.2008.06.002
63. Park, E., Kim, S., Kim, Y., Kwon, S.J.: Smart home services as the next mainstream of the ICT industry: determinants of the adoption of smart home services. Univ. Access Inf. Soc. **17**(1), 175–190 (2018). https://doi.org/10.1007/s10209-017-0533-0
64. Ha, Q.-A., Chen, J.V., Uy, H.U., Capistrano, E.P.: Exploring the privacy concerns in using intelligent virtual assistants under perspectives of information sensitivity and anthropomorphism. Int. J. Hum.-Comput. Interact. **37**(6), 512–527 (2021). https://doi.org/10.1080/10447318.2020.1834728
65. Cohen, J.: Statistical Power Analysis for the Behavioral Sciences, 2nd edn. Erlbaum, Hillsdale (1988)
66. Field, A.: Discovering statistics Using IBM SPSS Statistics. And Sex and Drugs and Rock 'n' Roll. 4th edn. Sage, London (2013)
67. Kaipainen, K., Ahtinen, A., Hiltunen, A.: Nice surprise, more present than a machine. In: Proceedings of the 22nd International Academic Mindtrek Conference, New York, pp. 163–171. ACM (2018)
68. De Graaf, M.M., Allouch, S.B.: Exploring influencing variables for the acceptance of social robots. Robot. Auton. Syst. **61**(12), 1476–1486 (2013)
69. Barnett, W., Foos, A., Gruber, T., Keeling, D., Keeling, K., Nasr, L.: Consumer perceptions of interactive service robots: a value-dominant logic perspective. In: The 23rd IEEE International Symposium on Robot and Human Interactive Communication, pp. 1134–1139. IEEE (2014)
70. Schmidbauer, C., Umele, M., Zigart, T., Weiss, A., Schlund, S.: On the Intention to Use the Pepper Robot as Communication Channel in a Business Context. In: Obaid, M., Mubin, O., Nagai, Y., Osawa, H., Abdelrahman, Y., Fjeld, M. (eds.) Proceedings of the 8th International Conference on Human-Agent Interaction, New York, pp. 204–211. ACM (2020)
71. Tullio, J., Dey, A. K., Chalecki, J., Fogarty, J.: How it works. In: Rosson, M. B., Gilmore, D. (eds.) Proceedings of the SIGCHI Conference on Human Factors in Computing Systems, New York, pp. 31–40. ACM (2007)
72. Schaffer, J., Giridhar, P., Jones, D., Höllerer, T., Abdelzaher, T., O'Donovan, J.: Getting the message? In: Brdiczka, O., Chau, P., Carenini, G., Pan, S., Kristensson, P. O. (eds.) Proceedings of the 20th International Conference on Intelligent User Interfaces, New York, pp. 345–356. ACM (2015)
73. Culnan, M.J., Milberg, S.: The second exchange: managing customer information in marketing relationships. Soc. Sci. Res. Netw. (1998). https://doi.org/10.2139/ssrn.2621796
74. Hinde, S.: Privacy and security — the drivers for growth of E-Commerce. Comput. Secur. **17**(6), 475–478 (1998). https://doi.org/10.1016/S0167-4048(98)80069-2
75. Wu, K.-W., Huang, S.Y., Yen, D.C., Popova, I.: The effect of online privacy policy on consumer privacy concern and trust. Comput. Hum. Behav. **28**(3), 889–897 (2012). https://doi.org/10.1016/j.chb.2011.12.008
76. Hoffman, G., Ju, W.: Designing robots with movement in mind. J. Hum.-Robot Interact. **3**(1), 91–122 (2014). https://doi.org/10.5898/JHRI.3.1.Hoffman
77. Anzalone, S.M., Boucenna, S., Ivaldi, S., Chetouani, M.: Evaluating the engagement with social robots. Int. J. Soc. Robot. **7**(4), 465–478 (2015)

78. Hassenzahl, M., Eckoldt, K., Diefenbach, S., Laschke, M., Lenz, E., Kim, J.: Designing moments of meaning and pleasure. Experience design and happiness. Int. J. Des. **7**, 21–31 (2013)
79. Young, J.E., et al.: Evaluating human-robot interaction. Int. J. Soc. Robot. **3**(1), 53–67 (2011). https://doi.org/10.1007/s12369-010-0081-8
80. Dautenhahn, K.: Socially intelligent robots: dimensions of human-robot interaction. Philos. Trans. R. Soc. Lond. B Biol. Sci. **362**(1480), 679–704 (2007). https://doi.org/10.1098/rstb.2006.2004

LLMs and Conversational/Verbal Interaction

Connecting Through Shared Memories. Episodic Memory for Social Robots Using Offline LLMs

Sofía Álvarez-Arias[✉], Marcos Maroto-Gómez, Arecia Segura-Bencomo, Juan Rodríguez-Huelves, and María Malfaz

Systems Engineering and Automation, Universidad Carlos III de Madrid, Avenida de la Universidad, 30, 28911 Leganés, Madrid, Spain
sofalvar@pa.u3cm.es

Abstract. The recent rise of Large Language Models enables novel possibilities within social robotics. Human-robot interaction and verbal communication, in particular, stand to benefit significantly from how these models generate and interpret language. Recent experiments with our social robot revealed that users expect the robot to answer general knowledge questions and recall previous activities and conversations, creating bonds and engaging interactions. This paper introduces an Episodic Memory System for social robots based on offline Large Language Models designed to store and recall past experiences. The system records relevant episodes to answer user queries about previous activities and conversations and proactively suggests personalised activities based on those the user has previously enjoyed or completed. The goal is to define personalised interactions to promote human-robot bonding and engagement as humans do. We evaluated four open-source language models, comparing them in terms of success rate to answer questions about past episodes, computational requirements, and response time. We selected these models considering the robot's hardware limitations and computational needs. We found the well-known Meta LLaMA 3 Large Language Model the best option, providing accurate responses in reasonable response times. We then integrated the model into the Mini social robot to show the system's performance in a human-robot interaction case study.

Keywords: Social Robotics · Episodic Memory · Human-Robot Interaction · Offline LLMs · User Personalisation · Adaptation

1 Introduction

Social Assistive Robots provide social support using multimodal interaction strategies such as speech, facial expressions, and motion [18]. The recent rise of Large Language Models (LLMs) to generate text from natural language processing enables new possibilities to improve Human-Robot Interaction (*HRI*)

[28]. LLMs offer new strategies by generating coherent text and responses to user queries given prior information about interaction episodes [14]. Conversations between humans typically benefit from sharing experiences and remembering past events, so including such personalisation in robots might enhance how users perceive the robot and their bonding [14].

The RoboticsLab research group develops social robots like Mini, devoted to assist older adults in their daily lives. The findings of our previous experiments [15,16] with Mini revealed that one of the features people expected from Mini is not only to answer general questions but to recall past interaction experiences such as their best activities and answer questions about what happened in them such as when the activity occurred. Users suggested that this function would enhance Mini's ability to create meaningful conversations about shared experiences, as humans do. Therefore, this paper presents the design and integration of an *Episodic Memory System* for the Mini social robot [21] to generate proactive and personalised interaction using real-life experiences (called episodes) between the robot and its users to promote human-robot bonding and engaging conversations. The system combines perception (vision and audio) and interaction data (for example, if the user liked the activity or the time it was executed) to store meaningful experiences in the robot's memory that are later used in two different ways. First, proactively generate personalised activities and conversations for the user based on the user preferences obtained in previous interactions (for example, suggesting playing a game the user completed before). Second, answer user questions about specific episodes that occurred in the past (for example, talking about when or where a particular activity occurred and its result).

The *Episodic Memory System* developed in this work employs GPT4All [2], an ecosystem desgined to run LLMs on everyday desktops without GPU. Specifically, we utilise its Python API to integrate it into the robot's software architecture to produce appropriate responses to users' questions and generate personalised activities using the episodes in the memory. The system exchanges information with a Decision-Making System *DMS*, which decides when to create an episode and when to produce a proactive activity and requests the memory of the information requested by the user. Since it is intractable to store all episodes, the system stores them when it is relevant and an intense stimulus (e.g., receiving a hit) occurs or randomly with a low probability. The perception system obtains perception (vision and audio) and interaction data to shape the episode content, which is stored as structured data.

We compared four offline open-source light LLM models (*Meta LLaMa 3, Nous Hermes 2, German Mistral,* and *MPT 7b Chat*) to obtain the best performance (*success rate, response time,* and *computation usage*) since our Mini robot has hardware constraints in data storage, internet connectivity, and computational resources. Then, we show the *Episodic Memory System* working in a case study where the Mini robot chats and performs activities with a user. The following sections contextualise this research and describe the Mini robot and the *Episodic Memory System*, focusing on episode generation and its use in human-robot interaction. Finally, the manuscript presents the results and conclusions of this study.

2 Background

This section introduces the core concepts of this study and provides similar research in robotics with an impact on the methods applied in this work.

2.1 Episodic Memory

Episodic memory is a long-term memory primarily processed by the brain's medial temporal lobe where past experiences are stored and recalled [23]. This kind of memory recalls past events along with contextual information about the *what*, *where*, and *when*. It is a human-like faculty since no animal can perceive subjective time or a sense of self [8,23].

Episodic memory is becoming a topic of interest in robotics to increase robot functions, as some research works explore [11,19,20,26]. Recent research highlights its potential for human-robot interaction and robot navigation. Wu et al. [25] used episodic memory in navigation and path-planning applications. They created a cognitive map based on events and environmental perception to navigate recalling previously visited locations safely. Behbahani et al. [6] used episodic memory for industrial robots to learn sequences of actions. Taking the example of an apprentice in a new job, the instructor shows the procedure once, and the apprentice has to memorise it to replicate it. In this case, a robotic arm uses a vision system to learn to grasp items and place them in empty trays.

Episodic memory has gained attention in HRI in the last few years. Bärmann et al. [5] proposed a way to encode events that the robot perceives. Then, when the user asks the robot for a specific event, it can access this data and recall the event to answer. The *Episodic Memory Encoder* stores the event's data in four stages. First, the robot saves the time when it happens. Second, it collects symbolic information, which refers to the semantic data, like the robot's task and status. Third, subsymbolic information keeps numeric data, such as object position or human pose data. Finally, the robot stashes a pre-encoded latent vector to save an image frame. In a later article, Bärmann et al. [4] introduced a system to store this information in the long term to answer user queries about past events. They structure the memory in a history tree. This tree has five levels: raw experience, scene graph, events, goals, and summaries. This method allows searching for the correct answer in a more manageable way when the robot needs to recall something.

2.2 Natural Language Generation in Social Robotics

Social robots with verbal communication reduce their naturalness if they cannot answer user questions, recall past events, and use this information during the interaction [1]. Large Language Models (LLMs) appeared to facilitate verbal interaction and might mitigate this effect by providing coherent speech answering to user queries [7,22]. Recently, Bärmann et al. [5] explored LLMs to give the robot speech abilities and to understand natural language. The robot could understand the questions and provide an answer based on its history using LLMs. In their latest article, Bärmann et al. [4] mentioned that the advantage of using LLMs is that there is no need to train the model, and it can manage different situations based on the prompt.

Prompts give the robot context to the LLM. Choosing the right one can be challenging. Kim et al. [14] reviewed the challenges of integrating LLMs on intelligent robots and advised how to choose the appropriate prompt for basic situations. According to these authors, the problems of using LLMs are generating unexpected responses, the uncertainty of the contexts, and the unstandardised ways to write prompts. Kim et al. also divide language generation into two types based on the dependence on a task. The model focuses on executing the function if the robot's goal is essential. Meanwhile, if it is task-independent, the natural language production is centred on the HRI with social and emotional objectives. Zeng et al. [27] reviewed robots with LLMs and their applications. They compare the most popular models (GPT-3.5, GPT-4, BERT, T5, and LLaMA) and the benefits of using LLMs, such as more intelligent, capable, and efficient robots. Finally, Ichikura et al. [12] propose an automatic diary generation system on joint human-robot interaction experiences using Google's DialogFlow. The authors save shared experiences in structured data to create a conversation history that the robot can access to create meaningful conversations. User impressions highlight high comfort and robot performance during the experiments.

These investigations focus on the user taking the initiative in the interaction. Once the user asks a question, the robot answers after accessing its episodic memory using LLMs. Our study combines episodic memory with speech generation to endow our Mini robot with proactivity to generate personalised activities and conversations based on previous events. This might engage users in the interaction since the robot talks and remembers about past situations, creating bonds with the user.

3 Mini Social Robot

Mini [21] is a desktop robot developed at the RoboticsLab at the University Carlos III of Madrid. It aims to assist older adults in improving their quality of life by providing support and entertainment by conducting activities such as cognitive stimulation exercises.

Mini has a cute, user-friendly appearance designed in response to user feedback. It has a variety of components that provide perception, actuation, and multimodal interaction. It contains an Intel NUC i7 8GB RAM 512GB storage computer that runs the software architecture and manages all sensors and actuators. The robot includes a 3D camera, a microphone, and touch sensors in the belly and shoulders to perceive its environment. Regarding its actuation

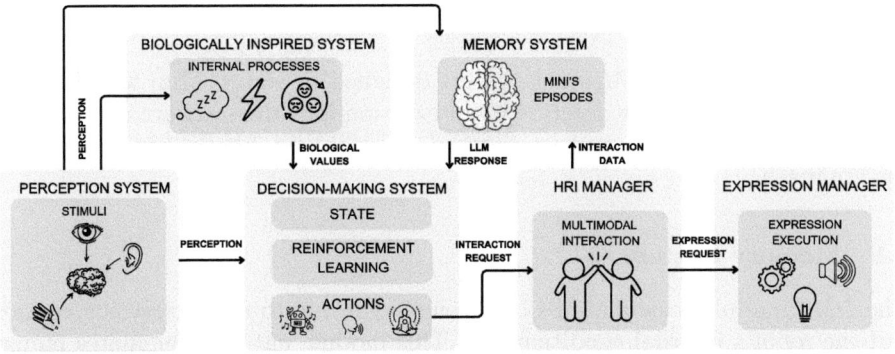

Fig. 1. Representation of the general architecture of the Mini social robot.

capabilities, Mini has LED lights in the mouth, cheeks, and heart, which provide visual feedback by indicating different affective states. Besides, Mini moves the hip, arms, neck, and head to show lively expressions.

A modular software architecture for autonomous human-robot interaction controls the hardware. Figure 1 shows the software architecture that provides a personalised interactive experience for each user. One of the main modules included for a proactive personalisation of the interaction is the *Perception Manager*. It is responsible for acquiring information from the environment, enabling real-time interaction. It allows the robot to perceive the user's actions and adapt the robot's behaviour according to perceived stimuli. The Biologically Inspired System simulates human-like processes to endow Mini with lively and natural behaviour. These processes emulate human functions such as sleep, energy, and entertainment, naturally regulating the robot's behaviour by eliciting the execution of actions.

The *DMS* selects appropriate actions based on perceived stimuli, memory episodes, and internal processes. Action selection depends on the robot's state, which represents the robot's internal and external condition. A Reinforcement Learning system analyses previous interactions and the robot state, optimising Mini's action selection over time to maximise robot and user well-being. The *HRI Manager* is closely bonded to the previous modules. This module ensures that the user can correctly use the robot, implementing multimodal interaction based on speech, touch, and vision receiving requests from the *DMS*. Finally, the *Expression Manager* controls the execution of different expressions modulating the actuators. These expressions aim to correctly communicate the robot's actions and intentions, facilitating understanding with the user.

The *Memory System*, the main contribution of this work, integrates the robot's episodic memory. This module receives perception information from the *Perception Manager* and interaction data from the *HRI Manager* to exchange data with the *DMS* to personalise the activities and conversations proposed to the user and generate appropriate answers to user questions about past experiences, as described in the following section.

4 Episodic Memory in Mini

This section details the *Memory System* designed to endow Mini with episodic memory using LLMs. We describe its integration into the software architecture, how it generates episodes and retrieves information and, finally, how we evaluate the approach.

4.1 Memory System

The *DMS* module selects Mini's behaviour according to the interaction context and the robot's internal condition [17]. This module naturally emulates human decision-making, receiving information from a Biologically Inspired System and the *Perception Manager*. Mini selects actions and personalises the interaction in two ways: using a high-level controller to choose actions that regulate its internal state and adapt its behaviour to the user characteristics and a recommender system to propose their favourite activities to each user. These mechanisms enable autonomous and personalised interaction, but the robot cannot remember the details of its past user experiences and personalise interaction accordingly. Therefore, we develop a *Memory System* integrated into the Mini architecture to aid interaction personalisation, increasing the naturalness of human-robot interaction, bonding, and engagement.

The *Memory System* is based on GPT4All Python API [2], an open-source ecosystem to run LLMs in machines with low computational resources without GPU. Figure 2 shows the integration of the *Memory System* into Mini's software architecture. Communication mechanisms between modules are represented using continuous lines, while dashed lines represent memory information. Episodes are in YAML files storing interaction and perception data answering the *what*, *when*, and *where* questions. The *Perception Manager* perceives the environment's information using different detectors, such as the users' presence and identification using face recognition and emotion. The *Memory System* saves interaction data from the *HRI Manager*, such as the activity performed, its date and time, and the event's location.

The *Memory System* uses a chat session that loads all the episodes stored in YAML files as structured data (number of episodes is limited to 20). This session is created every time the robot is started since, in the Mini robot, the initialisation requires around 20 seconds to load the episode history. In addition to the set of episodes, the session initialisation receives a prompt in Spanish. We selected the model's prompts following the prompt engineering guidelines presented in [13] for HRI. The prompt states the agent's *role*, *task*, *context*, and *response format*. The initial prompt given to the LLM is the following:

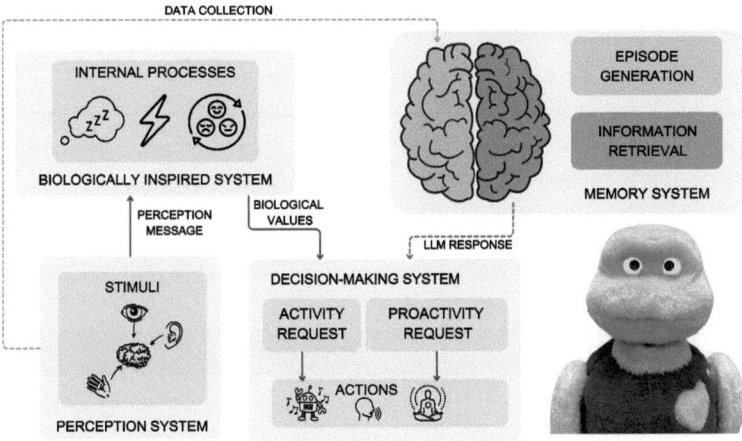

Fig. 2. Representation of the Memory System integration into Mini's social robot architecture with the communication sources, memory information flow, and differentiated memory phases.

> **Agent initial prompt**
>
> You are Mini, an assistive social robot. Answer me concisely in the first person, only in Spanish. I want you to store the episodes I provide as your memories. You answer the user's requests about these episodes. This answer is a single sentence with less than ten words.

The system produces text responses in two situations: when a user requests some information from the robot and when the robot proactively suggests the user the execution of previously liked activities. In the first case, the user requests information using a tablet menu that activates an automatic speech recognition system based on Vosk[1], an open-source engine that translates speech to text. The user question is the prompt passed to the chat session that stores interaction history, and the generated text response is sent to the *HRI Manager* so the robot can say the response. In this particular case, there are as many prompts as questions the user makes. These prompts are recorded in real-time through the interaction as a conversation history.

In the second case, the robot's proactivity occurs with some likelihood every time the robot decides on a new activity. The LLM seeks in its memory those episodes that contain activities that the user liked in the past to personalise the interaction. The *DMS* requests a new activity for the LLM model using the following prompt:

---

[1] https://alphacephei.com/vosk/.

> **Agent proactivity prompt for general use**
>
> Can you propose an activity of interest to the user?

The robot also proposes activities that the user did not complete correctly in the recent past, especially if these activities are important for the user and were scheduled by a therapist. Mini works closely with these health specialists to assist them in cognitive stimulation therapies for older adults in healthcare centres. In these exceptional cases, the prompt used to request an activity is the following:

> **Agent proactivity prompt for therapy use**
>
> Kindly suggest a therapy activity to the user for which they have not achieved the highest score in the last two weeks.

All prompts, except the initial one (because it opens the chat session), have the same parameters to generate the response:

- **Max tokens:** It sets the limit of tokens supported by the response. In our case, this maximum is 30 tokens to produce quick and short answers. Fast responses lead to smooth interaction.
- **Top p:** This parameter adjusts the kernel sampling between 0 and 1. The closer the value is to 1, the more creative the responses become. We choose a default value of 0.4 to give more rigid responses that adhere to the input information.
- **Temperature:** It determines the creativity of the model. The lower the value, the more conservative the answers are. As we need it to fit the information in the episodes, we have set the value to 0.

4.2 Episode Generation

Episode generation constitutes an essential phase in the *Episodic Memory System*. This phase is responsible for collecting and classifying the information received from the *Perception Manager* to store episodes of the HRI experiences. The information stored for each episode is as follows:

- **Date and time:** The system stores the date and time when the user and the robot started and finished the interaction. This information is used to provide temporal context.
- **User:** Mini can identify the user who participated in the episode using computer vision algorithms and its camera. If it is the first time a user and Mini meet, the robot asks for the user's name and generates a unique profile with user pictures.
- **User's emotion:** Mini detects the user's emotions using its camera. The system recognises happiness, sadness, anger, and calm. The system saves the list of emotions experienced during the episode.

- **Localisation:** The robot stores the event location using the information in the user's profile. When a new user interacts with the robot, Mini asks for and stores where the robot is. This location can be a room or office, among others.
- **Activity:** The system saves the activity the robot and the user performed during the episode.
- **Events:** The *Memory System* saves remarkable events that occurred while the robot performed an activity, such as hits, caresses, or correct and wrong answers to questions(for example, during the quiz game, the user caresses Mini when it congratulates him on successfully ended the game.)

The human brain usually stores remarkable episodes in its memory, those that are associated with intense stimuli and emotions [3,9]. We can find some domains in human memories that the *Memory System* saves. Just as the human brain does not store all events performed by humans [24] and due to limitations in the LLM, such as the increase in processing time with context volume, Mini's memory keeps only some of the interactions with each user. The system uses two methods to determine which episode is saved and which is not. The system saves random episodes with a 1/10% probability to create a repertoire of episodes that can be used to personalise the interaction. Besides, if the robot perceives intense or relevant stimuli such as receiving a caress or hit from the user or a significantly good (e.g. completing an activity excellent or the user indicates they loved the activity) or bad interaction. In these cases, the episode is always saved since it is considered relevant. An example of a bad interaction is when a therapist recommends an activity, and the user does not complete it or does it wrong. In these situations, an episode is generated to repeat the activity in the future. All data stored in each episode is recorded by the Mini's Perception System.

4.3 Evaluation

Due to Mini's limited computational resources to run large models, we needed to determine which open-source model produces the best results during the human-robot interaction. For this reason, we selected four state-of-the-art open-source LLM models (*Meta LLaMa 3 8B Instruct, Nous Hermes 2 Mistral DPO, EM German Mistral, MPT 7b Chat*) that require only 8GB of memory RAM to be executed in CPU, fitting the limitations of our Mini robot. Table 1 shows the models characteristics [10]. We discarded other models that, in preliminary tests, provided very inaccurate results, required more memory RAM than the available Mini, and produced significantly high response times (above 10 seconds) since

Table 1. Characteristics for each model tested to integrate the Memory System.

Model	Meta Llama 3	Nous Hermes 2	German Mistral	MPT 7b Chat
Characteristics	Fast responses, chat-based model and trained by Meta, Meta Llama 3 Community license	Fast responses, chat-based model, trained by Mistral AI, licensed for commercial use	Fast responses, chat-based, trained by Mosaic ML, cannot be used commercially	Fast responses, chat-based model, trained by Ellamind, licensed for commercial use

Table 2. Episodes used to test the environment.

ID	User	Date/Time	Emotion	Duration	Location	Event	Text
0	Marcos	20/09/2024 10:00	Happy	15 min	Office	Quiz game	Marcos played a quiz game against Mini and won
1	Sara	09/04/2024 08:35	Stress	20 min	Office	Braintraining	Sara did not answer correctly to the game questions
2	Sofía	15/10/2024 14:45	Sad	15 s	Lab	Memory game	Mini and Sofía did not complete a game and Sofía hit Mini

long response times affect the robot's naturalness. To discern which of the four models works better in Mini, we conducted an experiment. In this experiment, a user asks the same questions about three episodes (see Table 2) generated in previous experiences. These episodes include all the fields stated in Sect. 4.2 but with different content (date and time, location, users involved, and activities performed).

The questions to evaluate the models included information about the content stored in the three episodes. The model received seven questions (questions one to seven) three times, changing the target episode by modifying explicit data stored in each episode (totalling 21 questions). This was made to analyse wether the system correctly relates the question with the chat history. Therefore, if necessary, some questions modified their formulation to match the information stored in each episode (for example, if asking about the month when the episode occurred, we explicitly asked for the month name). Besides, we included four additional questions (questions eight and nine formulated twice) to test the model's capability to understand and relate the information of all episodes and the conversation history as a whole. These questions help determine if they can identify the same data in different episodes and provide specific details for each. For example, two episodes stored in Table 2 share the location, so questions eight and nine intended to analyse whether the model can find meaningful information simultaneously in more than one episode. The questions presented to each model were:

1. Where were you in September/April/October?
2. With whom?
3. What activity did you play?
4. What day did you play?
5. At what time?
6. For how long did you play?
7. Did anything relevant happen?
8. How many times did you play in the lab/office?
9. With whom and when did you play?

The evaluation and comparison of the four models consisted of measuring the average *response time* to generate the text response, the average *CPU consumption*, and the average *success rate* in answering the questions.

- **Response time:** Average time to generate a response since the model receives the prompt in seconds.

Table 3. Response time, CPU usage, and success rate results for the 25 questions in Sect. 4.3.

Model	Response time (s)	CPU usage (%)	Success rate (%)									
			1	2	3	4	5	6	7	8	9	Average
Meta LLaMA 3	3.65	87.61	100	100	100	100	100	100	100	100	100	100
Nous Hermes 2	3.89	98.31	66.67	66.67	66.67	100	100	33.33	66.67	100	0	68
German Mistral	3.93	97.73	100	0	66.67	100	100	33.33	66.67	50	0	60
MPT 7b Chat	7.58	99.44	0	0	33.33	0	0	0	0	0	0	4

- **CPU usage:** Percentage of CPU usage considering that the model has been limited to use only 4 cores from the 16 cores available. We limited the number of cores because other critical processes are running in the robot.
- **Success rate:** Percentage of questions correctly answered by the model from the total asked. Since the model generates text, we checked the adequacy of the response to the question.

We calculate the success rate by taking the LLM response and evaluating whether it contains the information asked in the episode we referred to. If it included the information, we considered the information correct. To be deemed appropriate, we also ensured the answer was in the first person since Mini is responding with a single sentence and less than ten words to avoid long delays in the generation.

5 Results

We evaluate and show the *Memory System* operation in two stages. First, we compare the offline models in terms of *success rate, CPU consumption*, and *response time* to different questions about memory episodes to determine which one works better in Mini's architecture. Second, we describe (and show with a video) a case study showing a user interacting naturally with Mini in a conversation where the robot exhibits its memory capabilities. For this second phase, we integrated the best model in the robot.

5.1 Models Comparison

Table 3 shows the results comparing the four models. Regarding the *response time*, the model that provides the faster responses is *Meta LLaMA 3* with an average of 3.65 seconds. In contrast, the *MPT 7b Chat* model takes an average of 7.58 seconds to generate a response. This makes sense as Meta Llama fits the initial prompt better, providing more concise responses that take less time to develop. On the other hand, *MPT 7b Chat* does not fit the prompt and gives very long responses that need more time to generate. Nous Hermes 2 and German Mistral provide reasonable response times, slightly above Meta LLaMA, but offer direct, short answers without adding context to the response.

The *CPU consumption* shows that *Meta LLaMA 3* is the least demanding model, using, on average, 87.61% of the reserved four cores. The rest of the models require almost all 4 cores to generate a response. This represents a difference of around 10% between *Meta LLaMA 3* and the others, affecting the *response time*. Due to the hardware limitations of our robot, this is a crucial aspect to consider.

Finally, the *success rate* analyses all questions detailed in Sect. 4.3. We considered incorrect answers if the content of the answer is not within the episode data if the length is above 10 words, and if the context is wrong (for example, adding information not in the chat history). The *success rate* shows that the *Meta LLaMA 3* model correctly answers all questions about all episodes. *Nous Hermes* model does not get it right in some cases, performing worse on questions involving temporal interpretation such as activity duration or relating activities in more than one episode. *German Mistral* stands out for its inefficiency in recognising the user and remembering where the activities occurred. This model also fails to interpret the episode duration correctly. Finally, the *MPT 7b Chat* model provides incorrect answers for almost every question.

Questions from one to seven were asked three times, with each question adapted to match the content of one of the three episodes. Questions eight and nine were asked twice to assess whether the model could establish connections between different episodes. A detailed analysis of the *success rate* for each question revealed that the *Nous Hermes 2* model achieved an accuracy of 66.67% for questions 1, 2 and 3. For question 6, it got it right in 1 of 3 instances, representing a *success rate* of 33.33%; all the failed answers lacked content in the episodes. In the seventh question of the third memory, it made a mistake, as it did not behave like Mini, providing an answer that did not meet the requirements of the initial prompt. Although the answer's content was correct for question 9, it did not meet the length requested in the initial prompt, constituting another failure.

The *German Mistral* model showed poor performance in question 2, where user data is required. Regarding question 3, the model failed once by providing the wrong content by giving as an answer the event of the memory 0 when asked for episode 1. For question 6, the model failed 2 questions out of 3. It produced invented answers for the first and third episodes that did not correspond to any actual episode. For question 7, the model failed to find the relevant event in the third recall due to several factors. First, the model did not respond using less than 10 words; second, it did not build the sentence coherently nor treat the memory as its own. Additionally, in question 8, the model failed to count the number of times it played in the lab. Finally, in question 9, the model could not provide the correct location, providing inaccurate and excessively lengthy responses.

The *MPT 7b Chat* model failed to answer question 1 for all episodes. The answer was correct, but the model included unrequested information, providing a very long response. In question 2, it failed two of the three questions using content from an episode other than the one specified. This fact indicates that the model does not correctly identify the episode. Moreover, the 3 answers exceeded

10 words. In question 3, the model failed by exceeding the length restriction and the content of the answers, adding information not present in the episodes. The model failed all the temporally related questions. For question 4, the answer exceeded the requested length and failed to address the question. The time and duration fields were not distinguishable. In question 7, it did not understand the question, and in question 8, it could not find the localisation field, creating a long answer. Finally, in question 9, although the model correctly identified the relevant information, it produced an excessively long response.

The previous results show *Meta LLaMa 3* as the best model for our application. First, it produces appropriate response times to maintain a real-time conversation without affecting the robot's naturalness. Second, it produced correct answers for all questions, overcoming the results provided by the other models. Finally, it is the model with the lowest *CPU consumption*, another critical aspect of our robot.

In all model tests, all episodes stored in the robot are loaded. We observed that if you did not clean the chat session history after about 10 questions the answers started to be inconsistent with what the user had been asked. This limitation prompted us to clear that chat session every 10 questions. This causes the context to reload at each clean-up increasing the waiting time which in turn increases with the number of episodes. Therefore, we limited the number of saved episodes to 20 per user, which are the most recent episodes. In the normal use of the Memory System, the robot only interacts with one user in each interaction, so the Decision-Making System ensures that it only accesses the information of that specific user. For this work, and for the sole purpose of testing the models' ability to access and interpret the information stored in the robot, all the information is loaded into the robot. The Memory System aims to personalise the way the robot treats the user, so it is important that the robot can access the user's information.

5.2 Case Study

The case study illustrates two scenarios where the *Memory System* applies. These scenarios are available in a video on the following website[2]. Figure 3 shows three situations presented in the case study. First, we show the user asking the robot about past episodes and the robot responding to these queries. Second, we show the robot proposing an activity not completed the day before, changing the user's mind. The first scenario shows Mini responding to user queries about past experiences stored in its memory. The questions involve different episodes to demonstrate Mini's good memory capabilities. This answer mode starts when the user requests Mini to answer some questions by voice (using the touch screen is also possible by pressing the option *Ask me*). Once the mode becomes active, the robot asks the user what she wants to ask. The user asks the robot where it was in September. The robot finds it in its memory and responds it is in the office. Following, the user asks with whom, and Mini answers that it was with

---

[2] Link to video: https://youtu.be/susNM-9n4mw?si=u3GVrX1_ez-PLook.

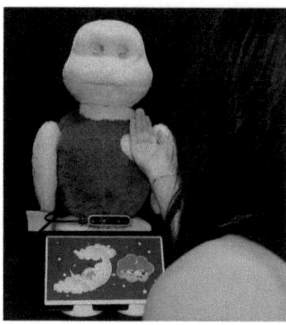  

(a) The user wakes up Mini to start a new interaction.
(b) Mini presents the available menu to the user to let the user decide.
(c) Mini is ready to answer the user's requests.

Fig. 3. Different views of the robot interacting with the user.

Marcos. Then, the user changes the target episode, asking when it played with Sara. The robot correctly answers on the 9th of April, and the user continues the conversation, asking how long they played. The robot answers for 20 minutes, and the conversation continues.

The user then asks which game it played with Sofia. This information is in another episode. The robot answers and plays the Guess the Monument game. The user asks the robot if something relevant happens, and Mini remembers that Sofía hit the robot. Finally, the user asks for information in more than one episode simultaneously with the question of how many times the robot has played in the office. Mini answers were played twice in the office. To conclude, the user asked with whom and when they played in the office; Mini answered that they played with Marcos on the $20th$ of September and Sara on the $9th$ of April.

The second example shows how Mini personalises the activities the user completes based on previous information stored in its memory. At the beginning, Mini is sleeping. Then, the user wakes the robot to start a new activity together. The user requests to play a quiz game, one of the activities included in the robot's repertoire. However, the robot finds in its previous episodes that an important activity was not completed the day before, a maths game. Mini suggests the user complete the maths game instead of the quiz game, showing a question to let the user decide. The user responds by voice (touching the touch screen is also allowed) to accept the robot proposal, and the activity starts.

6 Limitations

The use of LLMs in HRI is gaining attention due to their potential to generate coherent text and improve conversation. However, known limitations might reduce their application to real-time scenarios like social robotics. One of the most critical limitations of this work is related to the robot hardware and internet connectivity. Mini requires light open-source models that can run offline since their computational capabilities are limited and are dedicated to running other software simultaneously. Besides, since it is a social robot intended to assist older people, internet connectivity is not assured in all environments. Different models with internet connectivity might produce better results. Still, we wanted to use open-source light offline models to ensure the robot can operate in all scenarios.

As presented in the results section, the *Meta LLaMa 3* model provides the best *response time*, *CPU consumption*, and *success rate*. However, short answers (less than 10 words) require around 4 seconds. This makes verbal communication slightly slower than human verbal communication but still fits our time requirements. However, generating longer answers increases response times, affecting real-time conversations. Besides, we noticed that extremely long chat histories affect the model's capacity to find information and generate appropriate answers, so we had to restore the history buffer to the last 10 interactions and the number of episodes to 20 to strengthen the text generation process. In case a new episode is stored exceeding 20, the oldest one is deleted.

7 Conclusions

This paper presents a *Memory System* for social robots based on open-source light and offline LLMs. We compared different models, finding that *Meta LLaMa 3* provides accurate outcomes to generate responses to user queries and proactivity. It suggests users with their favourite activities using episodes experienced in past interactions. We demonstrate the system's performance in a case study by showing a user interacting with Mini. In this scenario, the robot answers the user's general information and custom questions about past experiences. It proactively suggests the execution of other successful activities in past interactions.

8 Future Work

LLMs are gaining attention due to their potential, especially in robotics and related fields. The future work of this research will be oriented in three directions. First, the episodes should be extended with new information to improve the robot responses and dialogues about such episodes. Second, episodes can promote a more diverse interaction by, for example, generating imaginary situations that engage the robot in the interaction. Finally, and most importantly, test the users' perception of the robot when including the *Memory System* and its effects on HRI.

Acknowledgements. These results have been funded by *Evaluación del comportamiento del robot social Mini en residencias de mayores* with grant number 2024/00742/001 in the programme *Ayudas para la Actividad Investigadora de los Jóvenes Doctores, Programa Propio de Investigación* awarded by Universidad Carlos III de Madrid; Robots sociales para mitigar la soledad y el aislamiento en mayores (SOROLI), PID2021-123941OA-I00 and Robots sociales para reducir la brecha digital de las personas mayores (SoRoGap), TED2021-132079B-I00, both funded by Agencia Estatal de Investigación (AEI), Spanish Ministerio de Ciencia e Innovación. Mejora del nivel de madurez tecnológica del robot Mini (MeNiR) funded by MCIN/AEI/10 13039/501100011033 and the European Union NextGenerationEU/PRTR. Portable Social Robot with High Level of Engagement (PoSoRo) PID2022-140345OB-I00 funded by MCIN/AEI/10.13039/501100011033 and ERDF A way of making Europe.

References

1. Addlesee, A., et al.: A multi-party conversational social robot using llms. In: Companion of the 2024 ACM/IEEE International Conference on Human-Robot Interaction, pp. 1273–1275 (2024)
2. Anand, Y., et al.: Gpt4all: an ecosystem of open source compressed language models. arXiv preprint arXiv:2311.04931 (2023)
3. Atucha, E., et al.: Noradrenergic activation of the basolateral amygdala maintains hippocampus-dependent accuracy of remote memory. Proc. Natl. Acad. Sci. **114**(34), 9176–9181 (2017)
4. Bärmann, L., et al.: Episodic memory verbalization using hierarchical representations of life-long robot experience. arXiv preprint arXiv:2409.17702 (2024)
5. Bärmann, L., Peller-Konrad, F., Constantin, S., Asfour, T., Waibel, A.: Deep episodic memory for verbalization of robot experience. IEEE Rob. Autom. Lett. **6**(3), 5808–5815 (2021)
6. Behbahani, S., Chhatpar, S., Zahrai, S., Duggal, V., Sukhwani, M.: Episodic memory model for learning robotic manipulation tasks. arXiv preprint arXiv:2104.10218 (2021)
7. Bertacchini, F., Demarco, F., Scuro, C., Pantano, P., Bilotta, E.: A social robot connected with chatgpt to improve cognitive functioning in asd subjects. Front. Psychol. **14**, 1232177 (2023)
8. Bevandi?, J., et al.: Episodic memory development: bridging animal and human research. Neuron **112**(7), 1060–1080 (2024)
9. Braun, E.K., Wimmer, G.E., Shohamy, D.: Retroactive and graded prioritization of memory by reward. Nat. Commun. **9**(1), 4886 (2018)
10. Gpt4all desktop model explorer (2025). https://docs.gpt4all.io/gpt4all_desktop/models.html. Accessed 20 June 2025
11. Huang, W., Chella, A., Cangelosi, A.: A cognitive robotics implementation of global workspace theory for episodic memory interaction with consciousness. IEEE Trans. Cogn. Dev. Syst. **16**(1), 266–283 (2024). https://doi.org/10.1109/TCDS.2023.3266103
12. Ichikura, A., Kawaharazuka, K., Obinata, Y., Shinjo, K., Okada, K., Inaba, M.: Automatic diary generation system including information on joint experiences between humans and robots. In: International Conference on Intelligent Autonomous Systems, pp. 399–412. Springer, Heidelberg (2023). https://doi.org/10.1007/978-3-031-44981-9_33
13. Karakaya, K.: Human-AI interaction with large language models in complex information tasks: prompt engineering strategies. Asian J. Dist. Educ. (2025)
14. Kim, Y., Kim, D., Choi, J., Park, J., Oh, N., Park, D.: A survey on integration of large language models with intelligent robots. Intell. Serv. Rob. **17**(5), 1091–1107 (2024)

15. Maroto-Gómez, M., Huisa-Rojas, A., Castro-González, Á., Malfaz, M., Salichs, M.Á.: Personalizing multi-modal human-robot interaction using adaptive robot behavior. In: International Conference on Social Robotics, pp. 382–393. Springer, Heidelberg (2023). https://doi.org/10.1007/978-981-99-8718-4_33
16. Maroto-Gómez, M., Malfaz, M., Castillo, J.C., Castro-González, Á., Salichs, M.Á.: Personalizing activity selection in assistive social robots from explicit and implicit user feedback. Int. J. Social Rob. 1–19 (2024)
17. Maroto-Gómez, M., Malfaz, M., Castro-González, Á., Salichs, M.Á.: Deep reinforcement learning for the biologically inspired social behaviour of autonomous robots acting in dynamic environments. IEEE Access (2024)
18. Matarić, M.J., Scassellati, B.: Socially assistive robotics. In: Springer Handbook of Robotics, pp. 1973–1994 (2016)
19. Park, G.M., Yoo, Y.H., Kim, D.H., Kim, J.H.: Deep art neural model for biologically inspired episodic memory and its application to task performance of robots. IEEE Trans. Cybern. **48**(6), 1786–1799 (2018). https://doi.org/10.1109/TCYB.2017.2715338
20. Prescott, T.J., Dominey, P.F.: Synthesizing the temporal self: robotic models of episodic and autobiographical memory. Phil. Trans. B **379**(1913), 20230415 (2024)
21. Salichs, M.A., et al.: Mini: a new social robot for the elderly. Int. J. Social Rob. **12**, 1231–1249 (2020)
22. Sobrín-Hidalgo, D., González-Santamarta, M.A., Guerrero-Higueras, Á.M., Rodríguez-Lera, F.J., Matellán-Olivera, V.: Explaining autonomy: enhancing human-robot interaction through explanation generation with large language models. arXiv preprint arXiv:2402.04206 (2024)
23. Tulving, E.: Episodic memory: from mind to brain. Ann. Rev. Psychol. **53**(1), 1–25 (2002)
24. Wixted, J.T., et al.: Coding of episodic memory in the human hippocampus. Proc. Natl. Acad. Sci. **115**(5), 1093–1098 (2018)
25. Wu, J., Xu, H., Wu, C., Yu, S., Sun, R., Sun, L.: Robotic path planning based on episodic memory fusion. In: 36th Youth Academic Annual Conference of Chinese Association of Automation (YAC), pp. 523–528 (2021)
26. Yang, C.Y., Gamborino, E., Fu, L.C., Chang, Y.L.: A brain-inspired self-organizing episodic memory model for a memory assistance robot. IEEE Trans. Cogn. Dev. Syst. **14**(2), 617–628 (2022). https://doi.org/10.1109/TCDS.2021.3061659
27. Zeng, F., Gan, W., Wang, Y., Liu, N., Yu, P.S.: Large language models for robotics: a survey. arXiv preprint arXiv:2311.07226 (2023)
28. Zhang, B., Soh, H.: Large language models as zero-shot human models for human-robot interaction. In: 2023 IEEE/RSJ International Conference on Intelligent Robots and Systems (IROS), pp. 7961–7968. IEEE (2023)

Intuitive Control of a Social Robot Using Natural Language with a Large Language Model and Error Correction Capabilities

Federico Biagi[1](✉), Paolo Alberto Gasparini[2], Maria Grazia Modena[3], and Luigi Biagiotti[1]

[1] Department of Engineering "Enzo Ferrari", University of Modena and Reggio Emilia, Modena, Italy
{federico.biagi,luigi.biagiotti}@unimore.it
[2] CHIMOMO Dept. c/o Policlinico di Modena, Modena, Italy
225849@studenti.unimore.it
[3] CHIMOMO Dept. and PASCIA Center, University of Modena and Reggio Emilia, Modena, Italy
mariagrazia.modena@unimore.it

Abstract. In this paper, a novel framework for interacting with the social robot NAO using natural language commands is proposed. The motivation for this work arises from the needs of operators at the PASCIA Center (Heart Failure Care Program, Childhood Heart Diseases, and Those at Risk), a specialized department at the Polyclinic of Modena focused on childhood heart diseases. They aim to use the NAO robot during cardiology visits with young patients affected by autism spectrum disorders. To overcome the barrier that prevents unskilled operators from independently controlling the robot, a new interface has been developed. By leveraging the capabilities of Large Language Models, particularly ChatGPT, operators' requests expressed in natural language can be transformed into concrete actions executed by the robot. Additionally, a mechanism has been implemented to assist doctors in adjusting and correcting ChatGPT's responses based on a feedback loop. The results have been evaluated using accuracy metrics to compare successful and failed tasks performed by the robot. The findings demonstrate the framework's efficiency and usability.

Keywords: Robotics · LLM · NAO Robot · Social Robotics

1 Introduction

In the last 15 years, robotics advancements have enabled the development and diffusion of social and human-like robots, establishing novel forms of interaction between users and machines. Social robots are artificial systems capable of fulfilling social roles in environments with both human and non-human agents [22] and are now applied in healthcare, education, and entertainment scenarios. In healthcare scenarios, they offer cognitive support through social interaction [9], improving patient care and easing patient burden. At the Polyclinic of Modena, the PASCIA Center established a specialized unit for treating cardiological issues in children with Autism Spectrum Disorder (ASD), incorporating the NAO robot during examinations. This approach is supported by studies confirming NAO's effectiveness in hospital and autism therapy settings [3, 19, 23, 24]. Figure 1 illustrates scenes from clinical use at PASCIA.

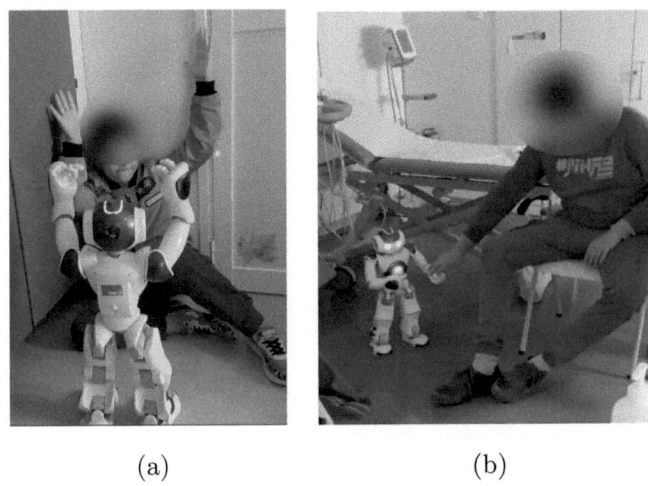

Fig. 1. NAO Robot interacting with children with special needs during hospital examinations at PASCIA Center.

1.1 Barriers to Social Robot Usage

A major barrier to the deployment of social and assistive robots in real-world and healthcare contexts is the lack of user expertise [2, 33]. Operators often lack skills in programming, troubleshooting, and maintenance. Additionally, control interfaces are frequently unintuitive. Luo et al. [15] highlighted these challenges in a study with 36 participants from Chinese retirement homes. With minimal instruction, participants interacted with a social robot and reported usability barriers. Similarly, Barakova et al. [7] identified a gap between research and practical adoption. Despite promising results, real-world use remains limited due to high platform costs, inadequate user needs recognition, poor personalization, and lack of user-friendly interfaces for non-experts. These challenges also apply to NAO robots. While NAO includes predefined dialogues and actions, tailoring its behavior requires technical knowledge. At PASCIA, doctors need to autonomously command interactions such as dances, dialogues, and movements of the robot in real time to respond to patients' needs. Aldebaran provides

Choregraphe, a graphical IDE for NAO robot programming. Although it simplifies code writing via drag-and-drop blocks, PASCIA staff found it cumbersome and confusing. Its rigid structure limits adaptability, making it impractical for dynamic clinical settings. Moreover, precise limb control is essential for engaging ASD patients during visits. To overcome these issues, research has explored alternative control methods, including Kinect-based motion tracking [4–6] and brain–computer interfaces [11]. ERM Robotique also introduced a more accessible programming tool, "AskNAO Blocky," which uses puzzle-like blocks to simplify customization. This paper proposes a different solution: controlling NAO using a Large Language Model (LLM). Prompt and source code for this project are publicly available for research and informative purposes at NaoLLMControl.

2 Related Work

The use of Large Language Models (LLMs) in robotics is not new [31]. Several studies have leveraged ChatGPT to enhance dialogue capabilities in social robots. For instance, Bertacchini et al. [8] integrated ChatGPT with Aldebaran's Pepper robot to enable real time interaction, showing promising results with children with neurodevelopmental disorders. Similarly, Hireche et al. [12] developed a ChatGPT-powered News Reporter assistant using Pepper. In contrast, our focus is on full control of the NAO robot via ChatGPT's natural language capabilities. The core idea is to issue human language commands as prompts to the LLM, which returns code instructions interpreted by the robot to complete the task, regardless of how the prompt is phrased. This requires the LLM to have prior knowledge of the robot's functions and control methods. A key inspiration comes from Microsoft's study [27], which defined design principles for prompt engineering to give ChatGPT contextual information over robot interactions. Jin et al. [14] extended this by implementing a multi-agent GPT framework with distinct roles: a decision bot, a corrector bot, and an evaluation bot to ensure accurate task completion. Wake et al. [28] explored ChatGPT for planning object manipulation, combining language instructions with environmental data to improve spatial awareness. Our novel contribution is the integration of ChatGPT with the NAO robot to create an interactive framework that allows doctors to control and program robot behavior in real time during patients treatments. This system includes a correction mechanism that enables the robot to refine its execution like a junior assistant learning through practice.

3 Materials and Methods

The protagonist of this research work is undoubtedly the NAO Robot, a humanoid-programmable robot developed by the French company Aldebaran. It was first presented in 2006 and, in time, many versions have been released. NAO has a total of 25 degrees of freedom (DoFs), with 11 DoFs in its lower limbs and another 14 DoFs in its upper parts. This configuration provides the robot with great mobility and allows it to mimic human motion [25].

NAO is controlled by a Linux-based operating system called NAOqi. The main features of the robot include audio reproduction, extremely natural movements, speech recognition, and face recognition. In order to access the robot's functionalities from a lower programming level (and thus in a more flexible way [17]), Aldebaran provides a Software Development Kit for Python.

3.1 Speech Recognition

The internal Speech Recognition module of the robot lacked accuracy in understanding Italian language, thus making the task of recording the user voice difficult. Please note that one of the main goals of the project is to use the user's native language (in our case, Italian) to command the robot. To solve the issue, we decided to delegate the Speech Recognition task to the OpenAI Whisper [20] services, which serves as a speech-to-text artificial intelligence module.

3.2 Large Language Model and ChatGPT

Advancements in Natural Language Processing and AI model architectures have led to the emergence of Large Language Models (LLMs) [21,32]. LLMs exhibit impressive capabilities in understanding and generating human language, and are at the core of widely used chatbots like ChatGPT (OpenAI, 2023), Google Gemini [10], Meta's LLaMA [26], and Mistral [13]. In robotics and generative AI, LLMs are gaining increasing interest in solving complex challenges such as speech-to-speech reasoning [16]. A Large Language Model predicts the next token in a sequence, capturing both semantic and positional meaning [18]. A Multimodal Large Language Model (MLLM) extends this ability to multimodal inputs, including text and images [30]. In this paper, we use LLMs to bridge the expertise gap in controlling the NAO Robot, addressing limitations associated with Choregraphe by enabling robot control via speech and Python programming. Specifically, we use ChatGPT (GPT-4) for task planning and code generation [1,29], though our framework is compatible with any LLM supporting chat completion. Using the Python OpenAI API, we send natural language prompts such as "give me a high five!" or "give me your hand and walk with me", and receive executable Python-like code that the NAO Robot can interpret to perform the task.

This method eliminates the need for Choregraphe, simplifying robot programming for medical staff at the PASCIA Center and enabling real-time, speech-based interaction with the NAO Robot.

3.3 NAO Robot Control via ChatGPT and Whisper

The pipeline that enables interaction between the user and the NAO robot is schematically shown in Fig. 2. It consists of four macro-actions that are triggered by a user request and executed in sequence.

① In the first step of the scheme, NAO Robot records the phrase of the user as soon as a trigger word is heard by the robot. Subsequently, the audio is retrieved via File Transfer Protocol and is transferred to the laptop.

170 F. Biagi et al.

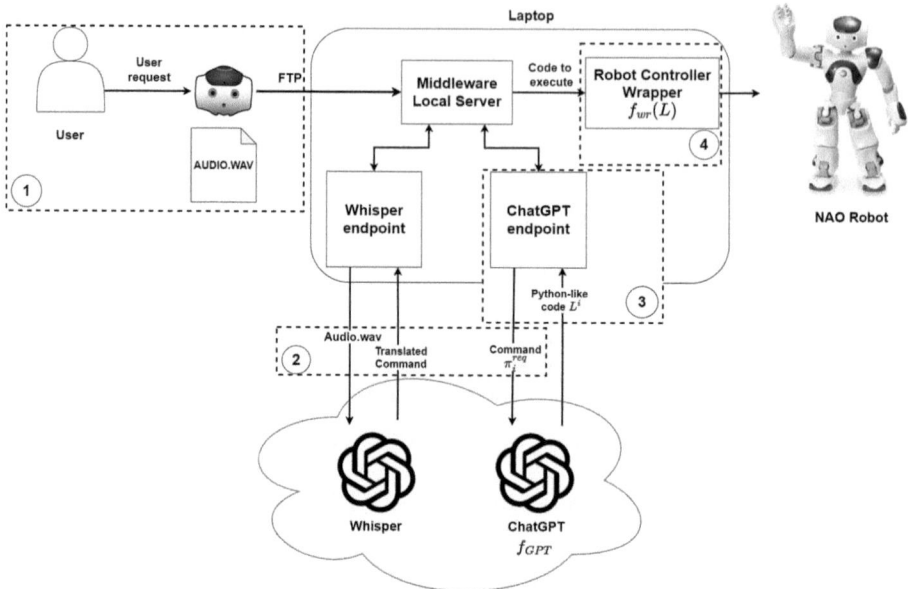

Fig. 2. Main workflow of the interaction between user, ChatGPT service f_{GPT}, and NAO Robot.

② The Python OpenAI bindings grant access to Whisper and GPT online services through HTTP requests embedded in Python methods. The audio request is thus sent to the Whisper Speech To Text service to retrieve the user's translated request in text format. The request π^{req}, as it will be explained in Sect. 3.3 is a command that the user tells the robot so that it can act to solve a task.

Afterwards, the request is sent to ChatGPT service to produce a response based on the prompt provided by the user. The format required to send a request to the ChatGPT service is defined as:

```
completion = self.client.chat.completions.create(
    model=self.gpt_model,
    messages= self.chat_history,
    temperature = 0
)
```

The *model* parameter is used to specify the version of the GPT model, the *messages* parameter is used to insert the request ChatGPT should respond (the meaning of the chat history parameter will be later explained in the discussion), the *temperature* parameter defines the randomness of the model in picking the next word during text creation. If the *temperature* parameter is set to 0, the responses get very predictable and consistent: facts, accuracy and repetitive answers are important. If the *temperature* is set to 1, the model picks more creative and unpredictable words for its responses. As the Python OpenAI bindings are only supported on Python 3+ version and the NAOqi Robot Controller methods only work on Python 2.7, the instantiation of a Local Middleware Server was necessary for the correct exchange of information. The whole software infrastructure has been installed on Windows operative system, but the framework is not Windows dependent and it could be installed also in other operative systems that support Python language.

③ From a logical point of view ChatGPT provides an output containing a list of Python methods which should make the robot move and act in order to solve the task:
$$f_{GPT}(\pi_i^{req}) \rightarrow L^i$$
$$L^i = [\lambda_1^i(\alpha), ..., \lambda_n^i(\alpha)]$$
where ChatGPT service can be seen as a function f_{GPT} that maps a generic request π_i^{req} (formalized in Sect. 3.3) into a set of Python-like commands to satisfy the user. L^i is the list of Python-like commands λ_k, $k = 1, \ldots, n$ referring to the solution of the i-th request. n is the total number of commands produced by ChatGPT to solve the task in the i-th request. Each Python-like method produced by ChatGPT accepts a list of parameters which is dependent on the specific Python-like method produced by ChatGPT, the Python-like methods and their parameters are defined in the *Output Format Explanation* of the Instruction Prompt which will be later explained in Sect. 3.3. The decision regarding which values to assign to each parameter is delegated to ChatGPT, based on the instructions and rules defined in the Instruction Prompt.

The NAO Controller retrieves the code produced by ChatGPT via HTTP method, querying the dedicated Local Middleware Server endpoint.

④ The Python-like code provided by ChatGPT is then processed by a Python script wrapper f_{wr} on the user's laptop to map the Python commands in accurate NAOqi Python commands (Sect. 3.3). As a result, the robot performs a series of actions to satisfy the user's request. This enhances the robot's adaptability to different scenarios without the need to program everything in advance.

Teaching ChatGPT. In this subsection, we describe how ChatGPT is instructed to generate code for planning robot tasks. Our approach adapts the method proposed in [27] for the NAO Robot, incorporating additional features.

A key component is the Instruction Prompt, denoted by the Greek letter Pi (π), which is a text file parsed at startup to teach ChatGPT how to behave. It consists of three main sections:

- *Context Explanation*: defines ChatGPT's role in the conversation.
- *Output Format Explanation*: outlines the Python-like commands used to control the robot, with notes on axes and parameters. This section is extendable.
- *List of Examples*: provides sample prompts and expected responses to guide behavior.

With this structure, ChatGPT gains sufficient understanding to translate natural language requests into executable robot commands.

The prompt is loaded into memory as a dictionary and sent to ChatGPT using the *system* role, forming the set π^I. The roles with which the programmer submits a message define how the GPT model perceives that message:

- *user*: process the message taking into account what the user has provided.
- *system*: process the message as an instruction to learn something about the context and what the chatbot represents to the user.
- *assistant*: it can be used to tell ChatGPT what was the response to the previous request, so that the model keeps track of the whole conversation.

The Instruction Prompt is embedded at the start of every session, transparently to the user. It is also included in the Chat History, ensuring continuity and memory throughout the interaction.

Flow of Interaction with ChatGPT. The Chat History is fed to ChatGPT after each user interaction to mantain the flow of the conversation. The Chat History at timestep i can be formalized as the Set π_i^{ch}. After each user request, which is a robot command, the ChatGPT response is sent to the model with the *assistant* role to remember the response for future requests. ChatGPT's response are the Python-like methods L_i to satisfy the task, and thus, L_i is appended to the Chat History under 'assistant' role.

The first message is the GPT Startup Prompt with *system* role, which is required for the correct initialization of ChatGPT. Then, we have two feedings per request (except for the first request in the conversation) as we provide ChatGPT not only the current user's request but also the response to the previous request for the sake of maintaining the context of the conversation.

Formally the π_i^{ch} at timestep i before the user formulates its i-th request is defined as follows:

$$\pi_i^{ch} = [\pi^I, \pi_1^c, L^1, \pi_2^c, L^2, \ldots, \pi_{i-1}^c, L^{i-1}]$$

where the Chat History concatenates the Instruction Prompt π^I and the whole conversation up to the *(i-1)*-th element. As the user provides his new command π_i^c, it gets appendend to the Chat History and sent to GPT Service f_{GPT} creating the Request:

$$\pi_i^{req} = [\pi_i^{ch}, \pi_i^c]$$

The diagram in Fig. 3 shows the sequence of steps of a typical conversation with ChatGPT.

Code Execution. The next step involves the extraction of the Python code and the mapping of the code ChatGPT produced into NAOqi Python commands. In fact, each line of code thought to the ChatGPT model has been simplified with respect to the NAOqi Python SDK method invocations to control the robot. This is done for the sake of easing the learning task for ChatGPT. To map each Python ChatGPT command in a concrete robot action we defined a wrapper

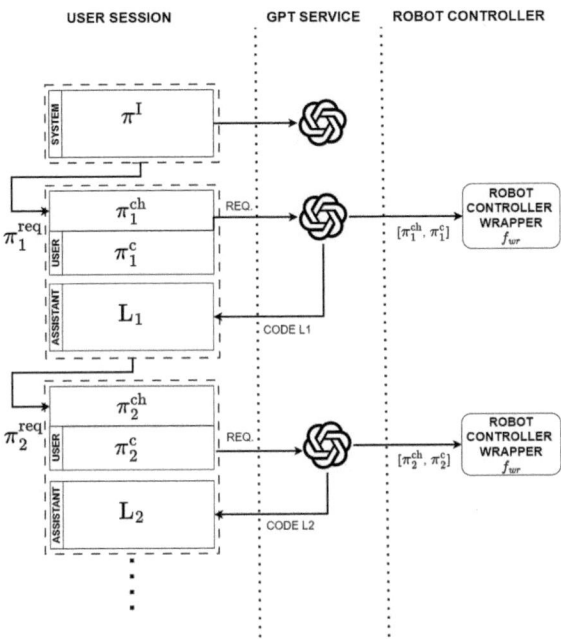

Fig. 3. Flow Diagram portraying the sequences of prompts and steps that take part in a typical interaction with the NAO Robot through ChatGPT. The left side of the figure portrays the User Session, consisting of the Chat History which is progressively updated with the user requests and ChatGPT answers.

class f_{wr} that hides the complexity of these methods. The procedure can be formalized as:

$$f_{wr}(L^i) \rightarrow \Sigma^i = [f_{wr}(\lambda_1^i), \ldots, f_{wr}(\lambda_n^i)]$$
$$f_{wr}(\lambda_j^i) = [\sigma_1^i, \ldots, \sigma_{m_j}^i]$$

where f_{wr} is the wrapper class represented as a function that maps GPT commands L^i into NAOqi commands. To each command λ_j^i corresponds a list of m_j Python methods interpretable by the NAOqi robot controller. The choice of which parameter values to assign to each Python-like method is delegated to ChatGPT. The parameters are simplified with respect to the NAOqi Python methods parameters. The code execution can be defined in a hierarchy as a portrayed in Fig. 4. The time required for the NAO Robot to reach a joint configuration through interpolation is fixed. The execution of the code is delegated to the Robot Controller Script as illustrated on the right side of Fig. 3. Each command is executed sequentially and no command can be parallelized.

Chat History and Token Limit Issues. To maintain context in a conversation, each request to ChatGPT must include the entire chat history. While

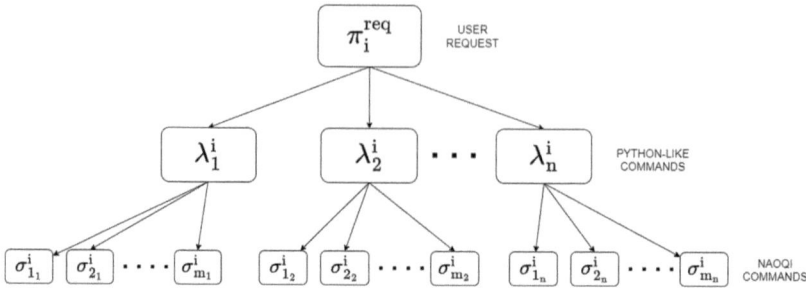

Fig. 4. Code execution hierarchy.

necessary, this can introduce processing overhead and risks exceeding token limits, especially in long interaction sessions.

ChatGPT has a maximum token limit for each prompt. While not a concern for brief interactions, intensive usage can cause the model to forget critical information (such as context information) compromising its ability to issue commands for the NAO Robot. As chat history grows, so does the likelihood of hitting the token limit.

To address this problem, we implemented a truncation strategy that shortens the chat history once the token count reaches the limit. Token estimation is handled using the *tiktoken* library with the *o200k_base* encoding. Assuming ChatGPT has generated the response to the i-th request, we denote the updated history as π_{i+1}^{ch}. To preserve context, we retain the first two prompts (Instruction Prompt and GPT initialization) and the most recent two user-NAO interactions. Thus, before sending the next request π_{i+1}^{c}, the history is truncated accordingly to maintain model performance and prevent context loss.

$$\pi_i^{tch} = [\pi^I, \pi_{i-k}^c, L^{i-k}, \pi_{i-k+1}^c, L^{i-k+1} \ldots, \pi_i^c, L^i]$$

where in our application $k = 2$.

Moreover, adding examples to the Instruction Prompt (as it will be discussed in Sect. 3.4) increases the Chat History size with each correction. A large Instruction Prompt may exceed the token limit even at the start of the conversation.

To mitigate this, we implemented a strategy to delete older examples, retaining only the two most recent ones once the token count approaches the limit.

Although effective, this truncation strategy does not consider the semantic value of chat history. Future work may explore methods to prioritize context on semantic meaning.

3.4 Error Correction

The user has the ability to correct the ChatGPT output, according to his satisfaction with the action performed by the robot. Keeping track of the whole conversation enables ChatGPT to adjust its output based on the details provided by the user. Unfortunately, ChatGPT only learns from mistakes as long

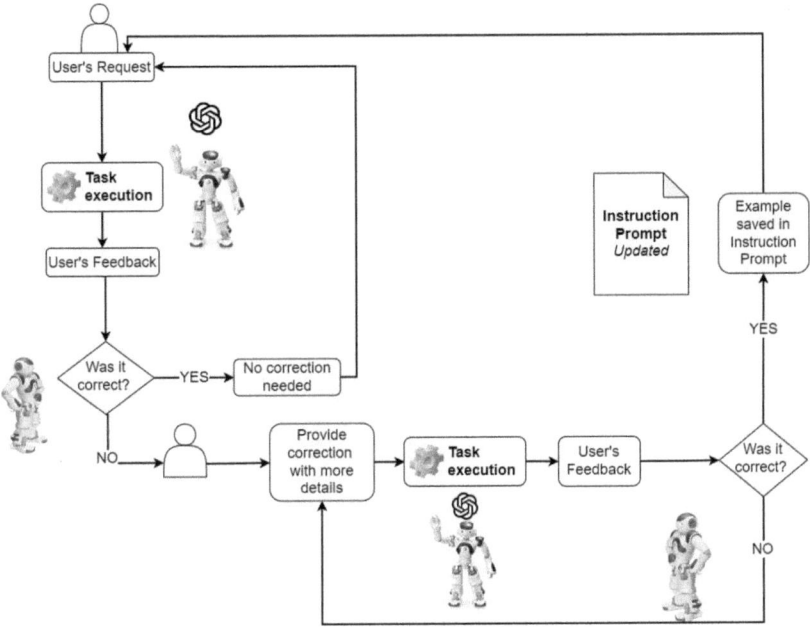

Fig. 5. Detailed Flow Diagram of the Error Correction algorithm.

as the conversation is active. As soon as the program stops and the robot shuts down, ChatGPT loses all the corrections learned during the user's session. To solve the issue we created a Training Session where the uses gives a feedback to the robot.

After each action, NAO robot explicitly asks the user if it performed good or bad. If the user is satisfied, everything went according to the plan. If the user is dissatisfied, the NAO Robot requests a correction based on its previous action. The user must then provide a more detailed verbal request in natural language, along with hints on how to improve the robot's actions. After the subsequent attempt, if the user expresses satisfaction, the sequence of steps for completing the task is saved and added to the list of examples provided in the initial setup prompt, following the user's original natural language request:

$$\pi^I = [\pi^I, \pi^c_{err}, L^i]$$

where the Instruction Prompt π^I is updated by concatenating it with the initial user request π^c_{err} that caused an error in the robot's task completion along with the correctly evaluated response code L^i at timestep i. Here, we refer to timestep i as the timestep in which the correction is considered successful. Appending this information to the end of the Instruction Prompt adds the correct example to the "List of Examples" section. The graphical representation of this process is portrayed in the flow diagram in Fig. 5. Thanks to this method, ChatGPT will be prompted in future requests with the example it once failed and, if requested, it will know how to correctly perform it.

4 Performance Evaluation

In order to evaluate the proposed control architecture, a group of 10 people was involved in the experiments. The subjects, 2 females and 8 males, were aged between 25 and 72 years old and had different professional backgrounds, with some working in the medical field and others in the engineering field.

The subjects had no experience with NAO Robots. The experiments were conducted in an office room. The participants received basic training on how to interact with the robot, along with information about its mechanical limitations.

The objective was to test the robustness of the software architecture in meeting user requests in order to determine if a synergy between ChatGPT and NAO Robot is feasible.

A score was taken into account to evaluate the performance of the pipeline with requests assigned to different difficulty levels. To compute the Difficulty Score (DS) we defined the following formula taking inspiration from the evaluation metrics defined by Jin et al. [14]:

$$\text{DS} = 0.5 * n_a + 0.3 * n_j + 0.2 * t \qquad (1)$$

where parameter n_a is the number of attempts required for the successful completion of the task when the correction mechanism is activated, parameter n_j is the number of joints involved in the task execution (speech and walking tasks count as 1 joint complexity, as they require just one method invocation to be executed via the robot controller), and parameter t is the time in seconds required for the code production. The contribution of each parameter has been weighed according to an estimation of the different influence on the score. The n_a value is the most significant indicator and thus weighed more. Conversely, t is the least

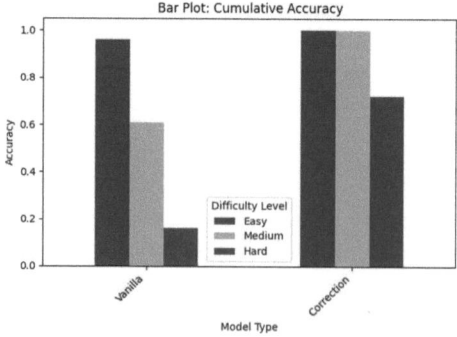

Fig. 6. Bar Plot graphically portraying the Error Correction algorithm robustness against different difficulty levels (Easy, Medium, Hard), with respect to the faulty Vanilla version.

reliable parameter, as the completion time may be affected by external conditions such as connection problems, high latency, and OpenAI server request load. The n_j is weighed more than t but less than n_a because the number of joints is highly dependent on how ChatGPT translates the user's request into robot actions.

Based on the numerical value of parameter DS, the difficulty level was ranked as:

$$\begin{cases} \text{Easy,} & \text{if } 0.0 \leq \text{DS} < 2.0 \\ \text{Medium,} & \text{if } 2.0 \leq \text{DS} < 4.0 \\ \text{Hard,} & \text{if } \text{DS} \geq 4.0. \end{cases}$$

The more the task requires complex movements, the more the difficulty score increases. This means that ChatGPT is forced to repeat the action multiple times in order to satisfy the user, to reason on multiple joint configurations and to waste time reasoning on the task completion. Generally, tasks that involve NAO Robot's movements are more difficult than tasks that just require speech.

With the Error Correction algorithm involved, the task is considered impossible to complete and thus failed when the number of attempts in completing the task is equal to 7.

The Error Correction algorithm helped in bridging the gaps of the vanilla approach, ensuring a robust response in both difficult and easy requests, as illustrated in the bar plot in Fig. 6.

5 Conclusion

In conclusion, the project achieved several goals. First, the PASCIA medical team successfully controlled the NAO Robot without encountering difficulties. Secondly, this research proved the potential of Large Language Models applied to NAO Robots. The infrastructure was proven robust across diverse user backgrounds, and the ability to save corrections and tune ChatGPT based on user feedback ensures adaptability.

Finally, the work showed that Artificial Intelligence can make robotics more accessible, narrowing the gap between expert and non-expert users.

Despite these promising results, improvements are needed. A key issue involved the lack of a "time" concept in ChatGPT, which affected time control in the robot's joints interpolation. This was addressed by arbitrarily setting timestep values, but future solutions should address the issue.

A second aspect that will be subject to further research is enabling the system to autonomously evaluate task success, possibly by integrating continuous feedback to let ChatGPT self-correct.

Lastly, the current framework is limited to NAO Robots remotely controlled using the NAOqi SDK for Python. Adapting it to other robots would require updating the wrappers that map ChatGPT outputs to robot-specific commands.

Acknowledgement. This work has been supported by the University of Modena and Reggio Emilia under the FAR (Fondo di Ateneo per la Ricerca – Linea Fomo) project titled *ROBIN3: a ROBotic INTelligent, INTuitive, and INTeractive platform for NAO-Mediated Autistic Healthcare*.

Data Availability Statement. The code and data repository for this article can be found in the following Github repository https://github.com/federicobiagi/NaoLLMControl.

References

1. Abdullah, M., Madain, A., Jararweh, Y.: Chatgpt: fundamentals, applications and social impacts (2022). https://doi.org/10.1109/SNAMS58071.2022.10062688
2. Aguiar Noury, G., Walmsley, A., Jones, R.B., Gaudl, S.E.: The barriers of the assistive robotics market what inhibits health innovation? Sensors **21**(9), 3111 (2021). https://doi.org/10.3390/s21093111
3. Amirova, A., Rakhymbayeva, N., Yadollahi, E., Sandygulova, A., Johal, W.: 10 years of human-nao interaction research: a scoping review. Front. Rob. AI **8** (2021). https://doi.org/10.3389/frobt.2021.744526. https://www.frontiersin.org/articles/10.3389/frobt.2021.744526
4. Assad-Uz-Zaman, M., Islam, M.R., Rahman, M.H., Wang, Y.C., McGonigle, E.: Kinect controlled nao robot for telerehabilitation. J. Intell. Syst. **30**(1), 224–239 (2020). https://doi.org/10.1515/jisys-2019-0126
5. Avalos, J., Cortez, S., Vasquez, K., Murray, V., Ramos, O.E.: Telepresence using the kinect sensor and the nao robot (2016). https://doi.org/10.1109/LASCAS.2016.7451070
6. Balmik, A., Jha, M., Nandy, A.: Nao robot teleoperation with human motion recognition. Arab. J. Sci. Eng. **47**(2), 1137–1146 (2021). https://doi.org/10.1007/s13369-021-06051-2
7. Barakova, E., Väänänen, K., Kaipainen, K., Markopoulos, P.: Benefits, challenges and research recommendations for social robots in education and learning: a meta-review, pp. 2555–2561 (2023). https://doi.org/10.1109/RO-MAN57019.2023.10309345
8. Bertacchini, F., Demarco, F., Scuro, C., Pantano, P., Bilotta, E.: A social robot connected with chatgpt to improve cognitive functioning in asd subjects. Front. Psychol. **14** (2023). https://doi.org/10.3389/fpsyg.2023.1232177. https://www.frontiersin.org/journals/psychology/articles/10.3389/fpsyg.2023.1232177
9. Cifuentes, C.A., Pinto, M.J., Céspedes, N., Múnera, M.: Social robots in therapy and care. Curr. Rob. Rep. **1**(3), 59–74 (2020). https://doi.org/10.1007/s43154-020-00009-2
10. Gemini Team: Gemini: A family of highly capable multimodal models (2023). https://doi.org/10.48550/arXiv.2312.11805
11. Guo, Y., Wang, M., Zheng, T., Li, Y., Wang, P., Qin, X.: Nao robot limb control method based on motor imagery EEG (2020). https://doi.org/10.1109/IS3C50286.2020.00141
12. Hireche, A., Belkacem, A.N., Jamil, S., Chen, C.: Newsgpt: chatgpt integration for robot-reporter (2023). https://doi.org/10.48550/arXiv.2311.06640

13. Jiang, A.Q., et al.: Mistral 7b (2023). https://doi.org/10.48550/arXiv.2310.06825
14. Jin, Y., et al.: Robotgpt: robot manipulation learning from chatgpt (2023). https://doi.org/10.48550/arXiv.2312.01421
15. Luo, C., Yang, C., Yuan, R., Liu, Q., Li, P., He, Y.: Barriers and facilitators to technology acceptance of socially assistive robots in older adults - a qualitative study based on the capability, opportunity, and motivation behavior model (comb) and stakeholder perspectives. Geriatric Nurs. **58**, 162–170 (2024). https://doi.org/10.1016/j.gerinurse.2024.05.025
16. Mandi, Z., Jain, S., Song, S.: Roco: dialectic multi-robot collaboration with large language models (2023). https://doi.org/10.48550/arXiv.2307.04738
17. Miskam, M.A., Shamsuddin, S., Yussof, H., Omar, A.R., Muda, M.Z.: Programming platform for nao robot in cognitive interaction applications (2014). https://doi.org/10.1109/ROMA.2014.7295877
18. Naveed, H., et al.: A comprehensive overview of large language models (2023). https://doi.org/10.48550/arXiv.2307.06435
19. Puglisi, A., et al.: Social humanoid robots for children with autism spectrum disorders: a review of modalities, indications, and pitfalls. Children **9**(7), 953 (2022). https://doi.org/10.3390/children9070953
20. Radford, A., Kim, J.W., Xu, T., Brockman, G., McLeavey, C., Sutskever, I.: Robust speech recognition via large-scale weak supervision (2022). https://doi.org/10.48550/arXiv.2212.04356
21. Radford, A., Wu, J., Child, R., Luan, D., Amodei, D., Sutskever, I., et al.: Language models are unsupervised multitask learners. OpenAI Blog **1**(8), 9 (2019)
22. Ragno, L., Borboni, A., Vannetti, F., Amici, C., Cusano, N.: Application of social robots in healthcare: review on characteristics, requirements, technical solutions. Sensors **23**(15), 6820 (2023). https://doi.org/10.3390/s23156820
23. Rossi, S., et al.: Using the social robot nao for emotional support to children at a pediatric emergency department: randomized clinical trial. J. Med. Internet Res. **24**(1), e29656 (2022). https://doi.org/10.2196/29656
24. Sannicandro, K., De Santis, A., Bellini, C., Minerva, T.: A scoping review on the relationship between robotics in educational contexts and e-health. Front. Educ. **7** (2022). https://doi.org/10.3389/feduc.2022.955572
25. Shamsuddin, S., et al.: Humanoid robot nao: review of control and motion exploration, pp. 511–516 (2011). https://doi.org/10.1109/ICCSCE.2011.6190579
26. Touvron, H., et al.: Llama: open and efficient foundation language models (2023). https://doi.org/10.48550/arXiv.2302.13971
27. Vemprala, S., Bonatti, R., Bucker, A., Kapoor, A.: Chatgpt for robotics: design principles and model abilities. Technical Report. MSR-TR-2023-8, Microsoft (2023). https://www.microsoft.com/en-us/research/publication/chatgpt-for-robotics-design-principles-and-model-abilities/
28. Wake, N., Kanehira, A., Sasabuchi, K., Takamatsu, J., Ikeuchi, K.: Chatgpt empowered long-step robot control in various environments: a case application. IEEE Access **11**, 95060–95078 (2023). https://doi.org/10.1109/ACCESS.2023.3310935
29. Yan, D., Gao, Z., Liu, Z.: A closer look at different difficulty levels code generation abilities of chatgpt (2023). https://doi.org/10.1109/ASE56229.2023.00096
30. Yin, S., Fu, C., Zhao, S., Li, K., Sun, X., Xu, T., Chen, E.: A survey on multimodal large language models. IEEE Trans. Pattern Anal. Mach. Intell. (2023). https://doi.org/10.48550/arXiv.2306.13549

31. Zhang, C., Chen, J., Li, J., Peng, Y., Mao, Z.: Large language models for human robot interaction: a review. Biomimetic Intell. Rob. **3**(4), 100131 (2023). https://doi.org/10.1016/j.birob.2023.100131
32. Zhao, W.X., et al.: A survey of large language models (2023). https://doi.org/10.48550/arXiv.2303.18223
33. Zheng, X., Fu, S., Liu, G.: Understanding barriers to service robot usage: a qualitative study in hotels. In: Wuhan International Conference on E-Business (2021). https://api.semanticscholar.org/CorpusID:249618016

Storytelling and Self-other Integration with Robots: Creation and Validation of Storytelling Stimuli that Induce Social Identification with the QT Robot

Francesca Ciardo[1(✉)], Francesca Foini[1], and Micol Spitale[2]

[1] Department of Psychology, University of Milan-Bicocca, Milan, Italy
francesca.ciardo@unimib.it
[2] Department of Electronics, Information and Bioengineering, Politecnico di Milano, Milan, Italy

Abstract. In recent years, socially assistive robots (SARs) have gained an important role in areas such as healthcare, education, and rehabilitation, thanks to their ability to support humans without the need for physical interaction. However, for SARs to be effective, it is essential to understand the mechanisms that facilitate their acceptance and the establishment of an empathetic bond with users. Among the strategies to strengthen empathy towards robots, storytelling has proven to be a powerful tool capable of evoking emotions and fostering engagement.

The present study aims to (i) validate and select emotional stories that can be used for eliciting empathy toward robots; (ii) identify which elements of storytelling contribute to promoting integration and social identification with a robot.

To this end, we created a series of emotional narratives (Valence: positive, negative, neutral), which were narrated by the humanoid robot QTrobot. Participants were asked to evaluate: (i) the emotional valence; (ii) the level of arousal elicited by each story; and (iii) the degree to which they identified with the robot, as an implicit measure of empathy. The results showed that participants confirmed the pre-established classification of the stories, and those associated with higher arousal, regardless of their valence, triggered higher social identification with the robot. In conclusion, the present work confirms and extends the literature on the importance of using emotionally engaging narratives to improve human-robot interaction and foster empathy toward SARs.

Keywords: Human-Robot Interaction · Storytelling · Social Identification · Empathy Elicitation

1 Introduction

The narration of stories, or *Storytelling*, is a form of oral communication that allows for the creation of human connections, the transmission of humanity's historical and cultural and the development of emotional, empathic, and social skills.

Storytelling has proven to be a valuable tool for increasing empathy in humans towards robots, particularly in the case of Socially Assistive Robots (SARs) (Costa et al., 2016; Gena et al., 2023). Elements such as the quality of the narrative, the robot's emotional expressiveness, and the perception of the robot's vulnerability play a crucial role in determining the effectiveness of storytelling in eliciting empathy (Frederiksen et al., 2022). A robot, as an embodied artificial agent, narrating emotionally charged stories, captures more attention and evokes stronger emotions in the listener compared to a disembodied virtual conversational agent (Costa et al., 2016).

In a recent study by Mathur, Spitale, Xi, Li, & Matarić (2021), participants listened to a robot narrating stories and then completed questionnaires to measure their empathy level. The results showed that the robot's storytelling was effective in eliciting empathic responses, highlighting that even technologically mediated interactions can promote human empathy (Mathur et al., 2021). Gomez and colleagues (2021) used Haru, a table-top experimental robot for multimodal communication, which utilized both verbal and non-verbal channels for interactions and was able to promote empathy in individuals through engaging storytelling. Haru could communicate through physical movements, sounds, and lights; it was capable of tilting forward or backwards, rotating its base to follow the user's gaze, and moving its eyes to simulate behaviors such as interest or doubt (Gomez et al., 2018). The robot told stories by combining voice, facial expressions, and body movements, actively interacting with the user, responding to and adapting to their reactions, to maintain a high level of attention (Gomez et al., 2021). Haru was able to generate empathy in the participants, and this effect was observed not only when the robot itself narrated the story, but also when it acted as a facilitator, synchronizing its gestures with a pre-recorded human narration (Gomez et al., 2021).

Frederiksen, Fischer, & Matarić (2022) investigated the effect of different narrative strategies on listeners. In this study, the robot told various types of stories: a light and humorous one, a sad and melancholic one, and a neutral one, while showing a progressive reduction in its functionalities during a task (Frederiksen et al., 2022). A sad narrative significantly increased participants' willingness to help the robot and their empathy toward it, suggesting that negative emotional narratives can enhance empathy toward robots (Frederiksen et al., 2022). The fact that sad narratives increased empathy and willingness to help the robot is interesting because it shows the potential of stories to stimulate emotional and behavioral responses that reflect a deep human connection, even towards artificial entities. This result further supports the idea that storytelling is not just a communication tool, but also a powerful engagement strategy capable of influencing the interaction between humans and robots, strengthening the emotional bond between the two (Frederiksen et al., 2022).

In this context, the use of emotionally charged narratives could represent a key strategy to improve the effectiveness of SARs, both in assistive and educational contexts, where building an empathetic relationship with the user is crucial to facilitate interaction and active engagement. Spitale, Okamoto, Gupta, Xi & Matarić (2022) demonstrated that the narrator's voice affects the effectiveness of storytelling: stories in which the robot was both the narrator and the protagonist elicited more empathy in listeners compared to stories told in the third person.

The reviewed evidence highlights how the use of storytelling by a robot has the potential to foster empathy in the user, due to its ability to engage the user in an immersive and personal way, especially if the narrative is in a first-person perspective (Spitale et al., 2022). This is particularly true when it comes to robots with a strong social presence, embodied and capable of expressing emotions through verbal and non-verbal behavior (Matarić & Scassellati, 2016). However, a fundamental question remains open: how does the attribution of empathy towards a robot vary depending on the emotional valence of the story? That is, can listeners feel empathy towards a robot always, or only based on the valence (positive or negative) of the told story? Answering this question would allow for a better understanding of whether empathy towards a robot is triggered by the valence of the content of a story or if it is the result of emotionally charged stories inducing a general state of activation in the listener.

1.1 Aim

The present study aimed to (i) validate and select emotional stories that can be used for eliciting empathy toward robots; and (ii) identify which elements of storytelling contribute to promoting self-other integration and social identification with a robot. To this end, we created and validated emotionally charged stories that can be used to address the question of whether humans feel empathy towards a robot only based on the valence (positive or negative) of the story it tells. Using an artificial intelligence system (ChatGPT), we generated a series of emotionally charged narratives (valence: positive, negative, neutral) with prompting strategies that could be narrated in the first person by a humanoid robot (QT robot). For each story, we evaluated: (i) the emotional valence attributed by the listener to the story narrated by the robot; (ii) the level of emotional activation state (arousal) induced in the listener; (iii) the degree of empathy, measured as the level of identification of the listener with the robot, induced by the emotional context generated by the storytelling.

The first goal of this study was, therefore, to validate the emotional valence of the stories created with ChatGPT and identify the stories that are appropriately recognized based on the expected emotional valence and that are capable of inducing the highest level of activation (arousal). We expected a higher level of emotional engagement (arousal) for stories with positive and negative valence, compared to neutral ones (Megalakaki et al., 2019). Regarding the degree of implicit empathy induced by the emotional context generated by the storytelling, we hypothesized that if the tendency to identify with the robot is due to the content of the story, then participants should report comparable values of self-other identification across different emotional contexts, as none of the stories narrated by the robot can be linked to an individual experience. On the other hand, if the empathy felt towards a robot in a storytelling context is elicited by the narrative's ability to induce a state of activation in the listener, then the degree of identification with the robot should be higher for emotionally charged contexts (Valence: positive, negative) compared to emotionally neutral contexts (Valence: neutral). Finally, if emotional activation (arousal) is sufficient to induce identification with the robot, regardless of the valence, then participants' ratings of emotional activation state (arousal) should predict the degree to which they identify with the robot. On the contrary, valence ratings should also predict how much participants perceive themselves as similar to the robot.

2 Materials and Methods

2.1 Sample

The experimental sample consisted of 15 right-handed adults (13 females, 2 males), ranging from 19 to 27 years (M = 21.8, SD = 2.8 years). The participants were recruited through the Sona System. Before starting the study, the participants stated that they had normal or adequately corrected vision, no motor and/or auditory deficits, no psychiatric and/or neurological disorders, and no diagnoses of social or attention disorders. Additionally, they stated that they did not use drugs or substances that alter brain activity. All participants read and signed the informed consent before the start of the experiment. The study was approved by the Committee for Research Evaluation (CRIP) Department of Psychology at the University of Milano-Bicocca, which operates under the supervision of the Ethics Committee of Athenaeum (Prot.RM-2024-861). The study was conducted in compliance with the ethical principles of the "Declaration of Helsinki" and of the Convention on Human Rights and Biomedicine (Oviedo Convention).

2.2 Materials and Methods

The Narrative Stories
In order to create stories that could be told by the robot, we followed the steps outlined below to construct the stimuli.

We used the dialogue system designed to understand and generate written text, based on an advanced machine-learning model called GPT (Generative Pre-trained Transformer) (An, Ding, & Lin, 2023). We asked ChatGPT to create stories lasting about 3 min, narrated in the first-person perspective by a robot. The English version of ChatGPT is more extensive and detailed compared to the Italian version, as English is the predominant language in the global digital landscape (W3Techs - extensive and reliable web technology surveys, n.d.) and is also the primary language used in technological research and the training of language models (Brown et al., 2020). For these reasons, the request was made using a prompt written in English: see https://osf.io/k4w5h/. Each story had to be characterized by a specific emotional valence: positive, neutral, or negative. In total, 6 stories were generated for each type of valence, for a total of 18 stories. We tried to diversify the stories as much as possible, considering the context, characters, and themes addressed, especially for the neutral-valence stories, which tended to be very similar. Subsequently, the obtained stories (see https://osf.io/k4w5h/ for the original version of the stories) were translated into Italian, also using ChatGPT.

From Text to Speech
To simulate the robot's voice, the stories were transformed from written text into synthesized spoken text using the Amazon Polly APIs, a cloud service by Amazon Web Services (AWS) that transforms written text into natural, realistic speech. For the experimental stories, we chose the male voice "Giorgio". The system also supports the use of Speech Synthesis Markup Language (SSML) for greater customization. This feature was used to create forced pauses, correct syllabication, and make the speech flow more smoothly. Specifically, compared to the default settings, which had very short pauses

at commas and periods, we set the pause duration to 0.5 s for commas and 1 s for periods: < break time = '0.5s' / > and <break time = '1s' / >. However, we noticed several issues with the speech: prosody was incorrect, pauses were almost nonexistent, and some words were mispronounced. Additionally, the intonation was either absent or inadequate, making the narration monotone and lacking expression. Models that learn how to synthesize speech in the Italian language have less data available, which is why Italian models are less accurate than English models, which have more data resources (Languages in Amazon Polly - Amazon Polly, n.d.). These shortcomings reduced the effectiveness of the communication, highlighting the need for further optimizations in the syntax of the stories to ensure a more realistic and engaging delivery. For this reason, we carefully revised each paragraph of the stories, focusing on the insertion of commas and pauses at specific points to modulate the voice's intonation in the spoken text. The goal was to best replicate the rhythm and tone of human speech in Italian. This involved adding commas and pauses even in unusual positions to create a more natural and engaging effect. Among these changes were the introduction of a pause after every comma and period, lasting 0.25 and 0.6 s, respectively, and the addition of a comma before the conjunction "e" (and). Intonation and rhythm problems were mitigated by avoiding overly long sentences and replacing words that were mispronounced (e.g., "suppliche" [supplications]) with synonyms (e.g., "preghiere" [prayers]). This process was applied to each story, listening to them in full to ensure the result was smooth (the complete version of all the stories is included in https://osf.io/k4w5h/.

Implementation of Speech on the Robot

The audio files produced were then implemented on the QT robot, using the HARMONI framework. The speech was synchronized with the movements of the robot's eyes and mouth, making the interaction more natural and engaging. HARMONI (Human And Robot Modular OpeN Interaction) is an open-source tool designed for the development and management of social interactions between humans and robots (Spitale et al., 2021). The framework includes advanced tools for voice recognition and synthesis, such as the Speech-To-Text modules, which convert human speech into text, and Text-To-Speech, which transform text into synthetic speech using services like Amazon Polly (Spitale et al., 2021). Finally, a last revision of the stories was carried out, as some of them greatly exceeded the three-minute limit. Some of these were modified and shortened to meet the set time constraint.

Creation of Video Stimuli

After the final revision of the stories, we recorded videos of the robot while narrating each story. Since the audio recordings had various background noises and the robot's voice sounded overly metallic, Adobe Premiere Pro, was used to improve the sound quality and optimize the background. Using noise reduction and reverb reduction functions, background noises such as voices from the hallway and the hum of the computer were minimized. The design and optimization options allowed the robot's voice to sound less metallic and clearer. To keep the video focused on the robot, a black mask was applied around the robot. The final version of video are available here https://osf.io/k4w5h/ (in Italian).

2.3 Procedure

Participants were asked to watch videos of the QT robot narrating the created stories.

Each trial began with a fixation point presented for 1 s. After that, the video was presented for its entire duration (approximately 3 min). At the end of each video, participants were asked to rate how emotionally activated they felt by the story just told, using a 7-point Likert scale (1 = not at all, 7 = completely). Subsequently, participants had to rate the valence of the story on a 7-point Likert scale (1 = negative, 5 = neutral, 7 = positive). In both cases, once participants clicked on the scale, a red triangle appeared to allow them to view their response and confirm it by pressing the spacebar. No time limit was set for the response. The participants listened to the 18 stories using headphones. Stories were presented in 3 blocks of 6, divided according to their valence (a priori valence: positive, negative, neutral); within each block, the order of the stories (stimuli) was randomized. At the end of each block, participants fulfilled the self-other integration scale (IOS scale, Woosnam, 2010) to indicate how they identify themselves with the robot, as an indirect measure of the empathy felt toward it. Again, no time limit was set for the response. After completing the IOS scale, participants could take a short self-managed break before continuing with the next block. Each experimental session lasted about 90 min and took place in a quiet room where participants were alone for the entire duration of the experiment. Participants were seated about 60 cm from a 21" screen (1280x800 pixels) connected to a laptop (4.00 GB RAM, processor: Intel® Core (TM)^2 Duo CPU 2.53GHz). Responses were collected using a mouse and a QWERTY keyboard. The experimental session was recorded with a camera positioned at the top of the screen. Participants were aware that they were being recorded and gave their consent. Stimulus presentation and data collection were controlled by Psychopy software (v2023.2.3).

3 Data Analysis

The data from one participant was excluded from the analysis due to an error in running the program.

3.1 Analysis of Valence and Validation of Stimuli

First, we examined how participants rated the stories in terms of valence in order to understand if the a priori valence we assigned, based on the instructions provided to ChatGPT, corresponded to the valence attributed by the participants. To do this, initially, the participants' ratings were converted into categories according to the scheme reported in Table 1. The frequencies of the ratings were compared using Pearson's chi-square test (x^2), both based on the a priori valence attributed and the type of stimulus. The valence ratings were standardized for each participant and analysed using a mixed linear model with the factor "a priori valence" as a fixed effect and the factor "participant" as a random effect (intercept and slope).

3.2 Analysis of Arousal

The ratings of the emotional activation state induced by the stories were standardized for each participant and analyzed using a mixed linear model with the factor "a priori valence" as a fixed effect and the factor "participant" as a random effect (intercept and slope).

3.3 Analysis of Self-Other Integration

The scores from the IOS scale were standardized for each participant and analyzed using three different mixed linear models:

- **M1:** A priori valence as a fixed effect and participant as a random effect (intercept and slope).
- **M2:** A priori valence and attributed valence rating (standardized values) and their interaction as fixed effects, with the factor participant as a random effect (intercept and slope).
- **M3:** A priori valence and arousal rating (standardized values) and their interaction as fixed effects, with the factor participant as a random effect (intercept and slope).

4 Results

4.1 Valence and Validation of Stimuli

The results of the chi-square test showed that the valence of the stories was rated consistently with the a priori assigned valence [$x^2 (4) = 138.30$, $p < 0.001$]. See Fig. 1 left panel.

Regarding the evaluation of individual stimuli, the results of the chi-square test showed that the valence of the stories was rated consistently with the a priori assigned valence [$x^2 (34) = 169.34$, $p < 0.05$]. The results showed differences in valence ratings between the experimental conditions [$F (2, 236) = 118.33$, $p < 0.001$]. Specifically, the valence ratings differed across all conditions (all p-values < 0.001). See Fig. 1, right panel.

Table 1. Conversion criteria from valence rating values to valence labels

Rating Value	Assigned Label
<=3	Negative
4	Neutral
>=3	Positive

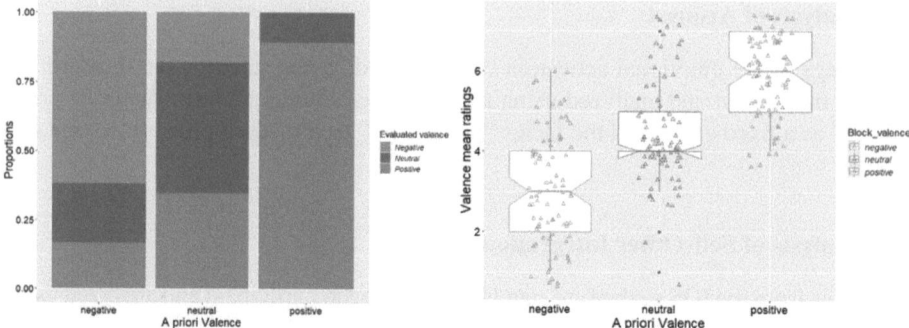

Fig. 1. Left Panel: Proportions of the valence ratings as a function of A priori assigned Valence condition. Right: panel: Average ratings of perceived valence of stories ratings as a function of A priori assigned Valence condition.

4.2 Arousal

The results showed that the arousal ratings differed between the conditions of a priori assigned valence [F (2, 236) = 50.22, p < 0.001]. Specifically, the arousal ratings for the positive and negative stimuli differed from those for the neutral stimuli (all p-values < 0.001) but did not differ from each other (p = 0.52). See Fig. 2, left panel.

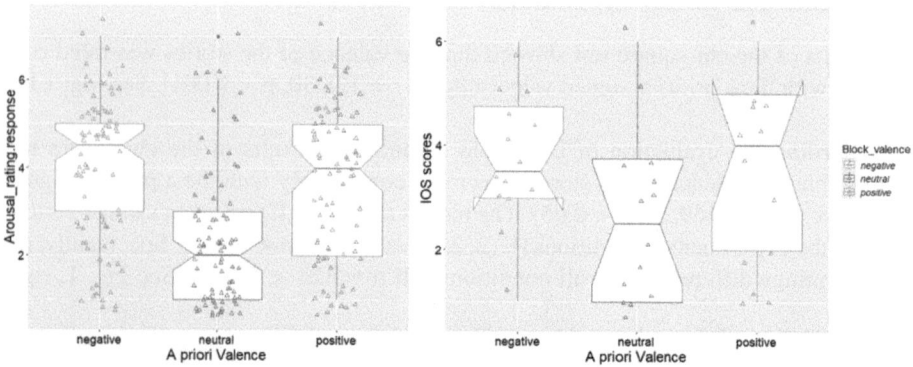

Fig. 2. Left Panel: Average ratings of arousal elicited by the stories as a function of A priori assigned Valence condition. Right: panel: Average Self-Other Integration scores a function of A priori assigned Valence condition.

4.3 Self-Other Integration

The results showed that the implicit empathy scores (IOS scale) marginally differed between the conditions of a priori assigned valence [F (2, 26) = 3.27, p = 0.054]; see Fig. 2, right panel. Specifically, IOS scores for the positive and negative stimuli differed from those for the neutral stimuli (all p-values < 0.001) but did not differ from each other (all p = 1). Finally, the IOS scores were significantly predicted by the arousal ratings [F (1, 29) = 40.46, p < 0.001], as shown in Fig. 3, left panel. The higher the participants evaluated their emotional engagement, the more they identified themselves with the robot. Valence ratings did not predict indirect IOS scores [F (1, 30) = 1.03, p = 0.32], see Fig. 3 left panel.

5 Discussion

This study aimed to validate and select emotional stories that could be used to investigate the effect of storytelling in eliciting empathy towards robots. Using an AI system (ChatGPT), we created a series of emotional narratives (A priori Valence: positive, negative, neutral) narrated in first-person narrative perspective by the QT robot. Participants were asked to evaluate for each story: (i) the emotional valence, to validate the a priori emotional content; (ii) the level of emotional engagement (arousal) perceived while listening to the story; (iii) how much they identified with the robot, as an implicit measure of empathy. Firstly, we hypothesized that higher emotional engagement (arousal) while listening to the stories would be reported by participants for stories with positive and negative valence compared to neutral ones (Megalakaki et al., 2019). Regarding the implicit empathy induced by the emotional context, we hypothesized that if the tendency to identify with the robot is due to the content of the story, then participants should report comparable values of self-other identification across different emotional contexts, as none of the stories narrated by the robot could be associated with a personal experience. On the other hand, if the empathy experienced towards a robot in a storytelling context is elicited by the narrative's ability to induce emotional engagement, then the degree of identification with the robot should be higher for emotional narrative contexts (Valence: positive, negative) compared to the neutral one (Valence: neutral). Finally, if emotional engagement (arousal) is sufficient to induce identification with the robot, then the arousal ratings should have predicted the level of identification with the robot, regardless of the valence. In contrast, if perceived valence ratings also play a role in determining how participants identify themselves with a robot, then social identification with the robot should differ as a function of the emotional context, namely IOS scores should have been predicted by perceived valence of the stories.

In general, the results confirm that participants evaluated the stories consistently with the valence that was assigned a priori (see Figs. 1, left panel); validating our stimulus generation process and confirming the emotional valence assigned a priori. Regarding the evaluation of emotional engagement induced by the stories, the results support the hypothesis that stories generated with positive and negative valence elicited emotional activation in participants compared to neutral ones. Specifically, the results showed that the emotional engagement reported by participants (arousal ratings) did not differ between positive and negative contents of the story (Fig. 2, right panel).

To assess whether the emotional context of the stories influenced the implicit empathy towards the robot, participants indicated their level of identification with the robot using the Self-Other Integration (IOS) scale. The results showed that the IOS scores mirrored the results of emotional engagement, with less identification occurring for neutral emotional contexts compared to the emotional ones (Valence: positive and negative). Interestingly, for the emotional context, no differences were reported in the level of identification with the QT robot as a function of the valence (see Fig. 2, right panel).

This result is also supported by the fact that the level of identification with the robot was predicted by the average arousal ratings. Participants who reported higher arousal levels also showed a greater degree of identification with the robot. This effect did not differ as a function of the valence of the emotional context, and it was comparable between positive, neutral, and negative contexts, as shown in Fig. 3, left panel. This result is in line with the literature, which highlights that emotional intensity plays a key role in facilitating engagement and connection with the storyteller (Paiva et al., 2017). In addition, results showed that the perceived valence attributed by participants (valence ratings) did not predict the extent to which they identified themselves with the robot (Fig. 3, right panel).

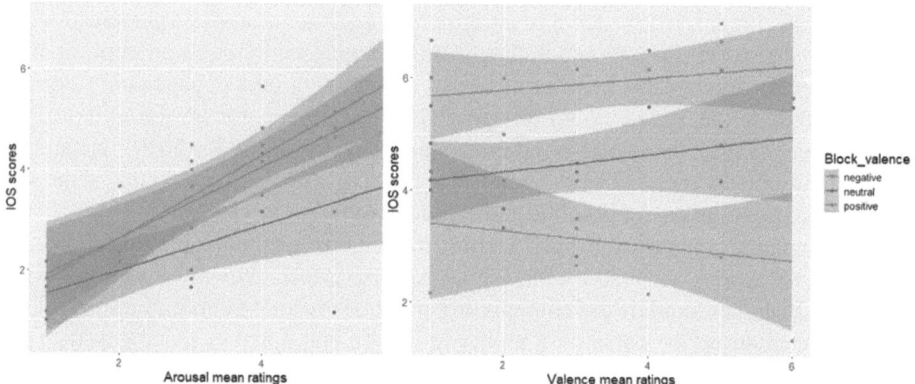

Fig. 3. Self-Other integration scores plotted as a function of arousal ratings (left panel) and valence rating (right panel).

6 Limitations and Future Studies

While this study offers valuable insights into affective storytelling via robotic narration, several limitations must be considered. First, despite our attempts to correct the prosody of the speech by adding pauses, the voice of the robot was low in naturalness and sounded synthetic, which likely compromised the emotional depth of the storytelling and may have influenced the participants' engagement and empathy. Future studies may consider validating the same stories read by a human actor. Secondly, empathy was evaluated via implicit self-report measures, which may not fully capture participants' emotional responses. Future research should incorporate multimodal emotional metrics, including both behavioral and physiological metrics, to validate self-report measures and provide a more nuanced understanding of emotional engagement. Third, we did not include a comparison with other storytelling agents (e.g., human narrator, virtual assistant). Future studies should deepen our results by evaluating both the effect of embodiment, through the presence of the robot, and human-likeness. Finally, the sample was small and mostly included females within a narrow age range, which limits generalizability. Future studies should include a larger and more diverse participant pool to enhance statistical power and external validity.

7 Conclusions

Taken together, our results suggest that when using storytelling to induce empathy toward robots, emotional engagement elicited by the narrative is sufficient to elicit social identification with it. In other words, regardless of the content of the narrative (positive, negative, or neutral), the higher the emotional engagement (arousal) evoked by the story, the higher the empathy participants may attribute to the robot.

References

Costa, S., Brunete, A., Bae, B.-C., Mavridis, N.: emotional storytelling using virtual and robotic agents. arXiv e-prints (2016). https://doi.org/10.48550/arXiv.1607.05327

Gena, C., Manini, F., Lieto, A., Lillo, A., Vernero, F.: Can empathy affect the attribution of mental states to robots? (arXiv:2309.02897). arXiv e-prints (2023). https://doi.org/10.48550/arXiv.2309.02897

Frederiksen, M.R., Fischer, K., Matarić, M.: Robot vulnerability and the elicitation of user empathy. In: 2022 31st IEEE International Conference on Robot and Human Interactive Communication (RO-MAN), pp. 52–58. IEEE (2022). https://doi.org/10.1109/RO-MAN53752.2022.9900573

Mathur, L., Spitale, M., Xi, H., Li, J., Matarić, M.J.: Modeling user empathy elicited by a robot storyteller (arXiv:2107.14345). arXiv e-prints (2021). https://doi.org/10.48550/arXiv.2107.14345

Gomez, R., et al.: Exploring affective storytelling with an embodied agent. In: 2021 30th IEEE International Conference on Robot and Human Interactive Communication (RO-MAN), pp. 1249–1255. IEEE (2021). https://doi.org/10.1109/RO-MAN50785.2021.951532390

Gomez, R., Szapiro, D., Galindo, K., Nakamura, K.: Haru: hardware design of an experimental tabletop robot assistant. In: Proceedings of 2018 ACM/IEEE International Conference on Human-Robot Interaction, pp. 233–240. ACM/IEEE (2018)

Spitale, M., Okamoto, S., Gupta, M., Xi, H., Matarić, M.J.: Socially assistive robots as storytellers that elicit empathy. ACM Trans. Hum.-Robot Interact. **11**(4), 1–29 (2022). https://doi.org/10.1145/3538409

Matarić, M.J., Scassellati, B.: Socially assistive robotics. In: Siciliano, B., Khatib, O. (eds.) Springer Handbook of Robotics, pp. 1973–1994. Springer, Cham (2016). https://doi.org/10.1007/978-3-319-32552-1_73

Megalakaki, O., Ballenghein, U., Baccino, T.: Effects of valence and emotional intensity on the comprehension and memorization of texts. Front. Psychol. **10** (2019)

Spitale, M., Birmingham, C., Swan, R.M., Matarić, M.J.: Composing HARMONI: an open-source tool for human and robot modular OpeN interaction. In: 2021 IEEE International Conference on Robotics and Automation (ICRA), pp. 3322–3329. IEEE (2021). https://doi.org/10.1109/ICRA48506.2021.9560992

An, J., Ding, W., Lin, C.: ChatGPT: tackle the growing carbon footprint of generative AI. Nature **615**(7953), 586 (2023). https://doi.org/10.1038/d41586-023-00843-2

Brown, T.B., et al.: Amodei: Language Models are Few-Shot Learners, arXiv:2005.14165 (2020). https://doi.org/10.48550/arXiv.2005.14165

Woosnam, K.M.: The inclusion of other in the self (IOS) scale. Ann. Tour. Res. **37**(3), 857–860 (2010)

Paiva, A., Leite, I., Boukricha, H., Wachsmuth, I.: Empathy in virtual agents and robots: a survey. ACM Trans. Interact. Intell. Syst. **7**(3), 1–40 (2017)

D'Arco, L., Rossi, A., Rossi, S.: Assessing emotion mitigation through robot facial expressions for human-robot interaction. In: Workshop on Advanced AI Methods and Interfaces for Human-Centered Assistive and Rehabilitation Robotics – AIxIA 2024 (2024)

Personalized Socially Assistive Robots with End-to-End Speech-Language Models for Well-Being Support

Mengxue Fu[✉], Zhonghao Shi, Minyu Huang, Siqi Liu, Mina Kian, Yirui Song, and Maja J. Matarić

Department of Computer Science, University of Southern California,
Los Angeles, CA, USA
`{mishafu,zhonghas,minyuhua,liusiqi,kian,yfsong,mataric}@usc.edu`

Abstract. Socially assistive robots (SARs) have shown great potential for supplementing well-being support. However, prior studies have found that existing dialogue pipelines for SARs remain limited in real-time latency, back-channeling, and personalized speech dialogue. Toward addressing these limitations, we propose using integrated end-to-end speech-language models (SLMs) with SARs. This work 1) evaluated the usability of an SLM-enabled SAR dialogue system through a small user study, and 2) identified remaining limitations through study user feedback to inform future improvements. We conducted a small within-participant user study with university students (N = 11) whose results showed that participants perceived an SLM-enabled SAR system as capable of providing empathetic feedback, natural turn-taking, back-channeling, and adaptive responses. We also found that participants reported the robot's nonverbal behaviors as lacking variability and synchronization with conversation, and the SLM's verbal feedback as generic and repetitive. These findings highlighted the need for real-time robot movement synchronized with conversation, improved prompting or fine-tuning to generate outputs better aligned with mental health practices, and more expressive, adaptive vocal generation.

Keywords: Socially Assistive Robots · Dialogue Systems · Speech-Language Models · Human-Robot Interaction · Well-being

1 Introduction

Well-being is a fundamental aspect of human health, encompassing emotional, psychological, and social dimensions. In recent years, concerns about well-being have grown in the United States, particularly among young adults, including college students, as mental health issues such as stress, anxiety, and depression continue to rise [9]. Despite the increasing need for well-being support, access to mental health care remains limited, particularly for individuals without adequate

Fig. 1. Experiment setup. The participant interacts with our SLM-enabled SAR system by pressing and holding the mouse to speak, then releasing it to yield the turn to the robot. See Fig. 3 for an overview of the interaction flow.

insurance coverage [15]. This disparity highlights the need for more accessible and cost-effective well-being support (Fig. 1).

A large body of prior work has shown that socially assistive robots (SARs) offer a promising approach to supplement the efforts of mental health professionals by providing accessible and interactive individualized support. Prior research in human-robot interaction (HRI) has demonstrated the effectiveness of SARs in fostering social engagement, emotional support, and positive behavior change [7,17]. However, as shown in Fig. 2, existing SAR systems largely relied on a cascaded dialogue pipeline that connects multiple machine learning (ML) models, including speech-to-text (STT), a dialogue management system, and text-to-speech (TTS) [16,19]. This pipeline introduces response latency in robot's verbal speech and non-verbal back-channeling, leading to unnatural turn-taking between the robot and the user. In addition, the pipeline approach made it difficult to personalize verbal feedback and vocal tone in speech output in response to the conversational and emotional context. These limitations contributed to lowered user-perceived levels of empathy, hindering engagement and rapport between the robot and the user, and reducing the effectiveness of SARs for well-being support [2].

To address these limitations, in this work we replace the existing cascaded dialogue approach with a unified end-to-end speech-language model (SLM). In the validation work we describe, the SLM was GPT-4o-realtime [12], which is pre-trained for real-time speech conversation, directly tokenizing audio input and synthesizing audio output without intermediate text representation. This architecture enables low response latency and context-aware speech generation [12]. Compared to SARs that rely on scripted or cascaded speech processing, which often introduces substantial latency, integration of an end-to-end SLM has the potential to support real-time, adaptive, and expressive conversations that more closely resemble natural human interactions in well-being support settings.

To the best of the authors' knowledge, this is the first attempt to integrate an end-to-end SLM into a SAR and evaluate it in a well-being support context. This context is challenging because it requires the robot to respond in real time while conveying empathy to ensure effectiveness. For evaluation, we conducted a small N=11 within-subjects study in which the robot guided each participant through a 40-minute gratitude-based exercise for well-being support, followed by a semi-structured participatory design interview. Our quantitative and qualitative results showed that participants perceived the SLM-enabled SAR system as capable of providing empathetic feedback, natural turn-taking, back-channeling, and adaptive responses. Despite these promising findings, our results also showed that the robot's nonverbal behaviors still lacked variability and synchronization with the speech output from the SLM. Additionally, although the SLM was capable of real-time conversation, its verbal feedback was perceived as generic and repetitive, limiting its ability to build the personal and emotional rapport essential for effective well-being support. These insights suggest that future work is needed to enable real-time robot movement generation synchronized with conversation, develop more sophisticated prompting frameworks and fine-tuning methods to align SLM outputs with evidence-based practices from mental health experts, and to improve SLMs to produce more expressive and adaptive vocal tones in their speech output.

The main contributions of this work are: 1) proposing the use of end-to-end speech-language models (SLMs) for socially assistive robots (SARs) and validating usability through a small user study focused on well-being support; and 2) identifying existing limitations and engaging users in co-design to inform future improvements of SLM-enabled SARs.

2 Related Work

2.1 SARs for Well-Being Support

A large body of prior work has validated the potential of socially assistive robots (SARs) to supplement the efforts of mental health professionals in providing more accessible well-being support [3]. Studies have also demonstrated the effectiveness of SARs in promoting psychological well-being and facilitating behavioral change [17]. For example, Kidd et al. [8] developed robotic coaches aimed at supporting positive behavioral change over a 4–6 week period, specifically targeting dietary habits. Their findings highlighted the potential of SARs to support sustained behavioral modifications.

Prior work has further explored the use of SARs in well-being and mindfulness interventions. For example, Jeong et al. [6] developed a well-being coach for college students using the robot Jibo and found significant improvements in participants' overall psychological well-being. Similarly, Bodala et al. [3] compared a robotic mindfulness coach to a human one, noting that while the human coach was rated higher, both interventions led to positive outcomes. Moreover, work by Spitale et al. [19] explored personalization in SAR-based well-being coaching, demonstrating that adaptive interactions over a four-week longitudinal study improved engagement and well-being outcomes. Additionally, Kian et al. [7] demonstrated that a large language model (LLM)-powered SAR delivering daily cognitive behavioral therapy (CBT)-based at-home exercises achieved significant reductions in psychological distress and short-term anxiety among university students, outperforming chatbot and worksheet baselines. Their findings validated the potential of LLM-enabled SARs to improve adherence and therapeutic outcomes in mental health interventions.

2.2 Dialogue Management Pipelines for SAR: Cascaded vs. End-to-End Speech

According to a published survey on dialogue management in HRI [14], the dialogue management systems used in HRI often followed a cascaded pipeline, as shown in Fig. 2a, consisting of the following steps: 1) the user's speech was first processed by the spoken language understanding module often using a speech-to-text (STT) model to transcribe spoken input into natural language transcription; 2) the transcription was then fed into a dialogue management module, which may be a language model (LM), to generate the robot's textual response; and 3) the textual response was then passed to the speech generation module, which often used a text-to-speech (TTS) model to produce the corresponding robot speech.

Using this cascaded pipeline, Xu et al. [21] developed the conversational capabilities of a SAR for diary studies, where each step is handled by a separate machine learning model. Similarly, prior work on dialogue systems in HRI by Scheutz et al. [16] has explored the use of this cascaded dialogue management pipeline to enable real-time human-robot interactions. Although this pipeline successfully supported conversational interaction between humans and robots, they found that the inference time introduced by each module contributed to latency and negatively affected the usability of the conversational system. Prior work on SARs for well-being by Spitale et al. [19] integrated LLM-based dialogue generation for adaptive well-being coaching, replacing rule-based, predefined dialogue trees. Their system, VITA, demonstrates the potential of multi-modal

SAR coaching; however, it also highlights similar limitations, including unnatural turn-taking caused by response latency. These issues hindered the robot's perceived empathy and its ability to establish rapport with human users.

Similar findings were discussed in the design study on SARs for well-being support by Axelsson et al. [2]. The authors found that the limitations of existing cascaded dialogue management pipelines can be summarized by the following key points [2]:

- **Response latency and unnatural turn-taking:** Awkward pauses or interruptions caused by latency disrupt the flow of conversation and make interactions feel unnatural.
- **Inadequate back-channeling:** Also due to latency, robots that do not exhibit synchronized back-channeling behaviors are perceived as inattentive, diminishing the user's sense of being heard and reducing perceived empathy.
- **Lack of personalization:** When dialogue management system relies solely on rule-based, pre-defined dialogue trees instead of a language model, the robot's responses are not adapted or personalized to the user's input or conversational context.
- **Lack of voice expressiveness:** The robot's voice lacks emotional expressiveness and is not matched with the contextual information or emotional tone of the speech.

Advances in end-to-end SLMs [1,5] trained directly on speech input and output made these models candidates for effectively eliminating the cascaded structure of traditional dialogue pipelines. This substitution enabled real-time inference and speech generation, offering great potential for more natural dialogue in HRI. To the best of our knowledge, no existing work has yet utilized end-to-end SLM for SAR, particularly in the context of well-being support. Figure 2 illustrates the differences between the existing cascaded pipeline and our proposed end-to-end SLMs.

3 Methods

3.1 Integration of End-to-End SLMs with SARs

In this work, we used a modified version of the *Blossom* robot [18], a handcrafted, open-source robot made of 3D-printed parts and wool, and capable of expressive movements [20]. We chose GPT-4o-realtime, accessed through OpenAI's real-time API [12,13], because, to the best of our knowledge, it was the only commercially available speech-language model with real-time capabilities at the time of our system setup and development, and there were no comparable proprietary or open-source alternatives. As shown in Fig. 3, *Blossom* was connected to a web application interfacing with OpenAI's GPT-4o-realtime via its API. We implemented three non-verbal robot movements–idle, speaking, and listening–that corresponded to different states of the interaction:

- **Idle State** - The robot expands and contracts slightly to simulate breathing.

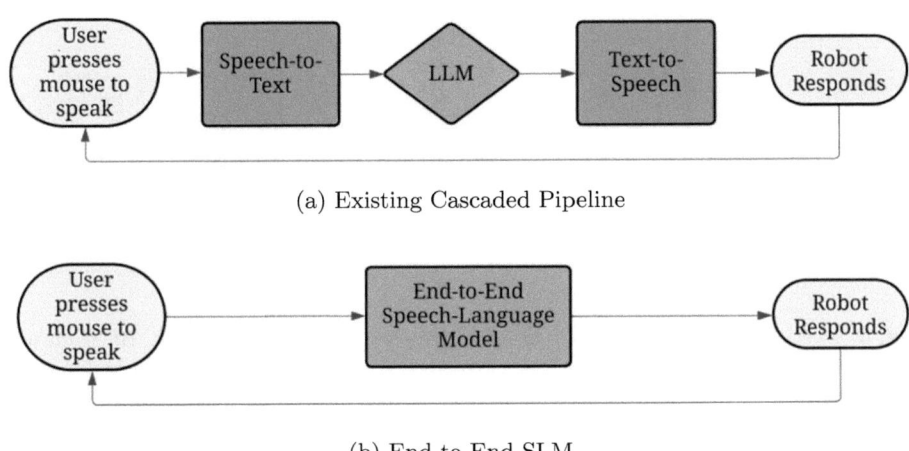

(a) Existing Cascaded Pipeline

(b) End-to-End SLM

Fig. 2. Comparison between the cascaded dialogue pipeline and an end-to-end SLM for SARs. SLM enabled real-time inference and speech generation, offering great potential for more natural dialogue in HRI.

- **Speaking State** - The robot shakes its head sideways while generating speech.
- **Listening State** - The robot nods while waiting for the participant's response, indicating active listening.

As shown in Fig. 3, movement-related modules are shown in blue, interaction components are shown in grey, the speech-language model is shown in red, and the robot control module is shown in green.

During the interaction, the *Blossom* robot transitioned between three movement states (idle, listening, and speaking; highlighted in blue) based on the context of the conversation. When no one was speaking, the robot entered the idle state and performed subtle breathing motions to indicate it was powered on and awaiting input. When the participant pressed and held the mouse to speak, the Flask server (highlighted in green) received a signal from the SLM (GPT-4o-realtime, shown in red) and the robot entered the listening state, during which it nodded to convey active listening. When the participant released the mouse, signaling the end of their turn, the robot entered the speaking state and generated speech while performing side-to-side head movements. These synchronized non-verbal behaviors aligned with turn-taking patterns and provided real-time back-channeling cues, aiming to enhance the robot's perceived attentiveness and ability to build rapport. Full documentation and code are available at: https://github.com/interaction-lab/RealTime_SAR_Well-being_Study[1].

---

[1] We developed our code based on the OpenAI real-time API beta repo: https://github.com/openai/openai-realtime-api-beta.

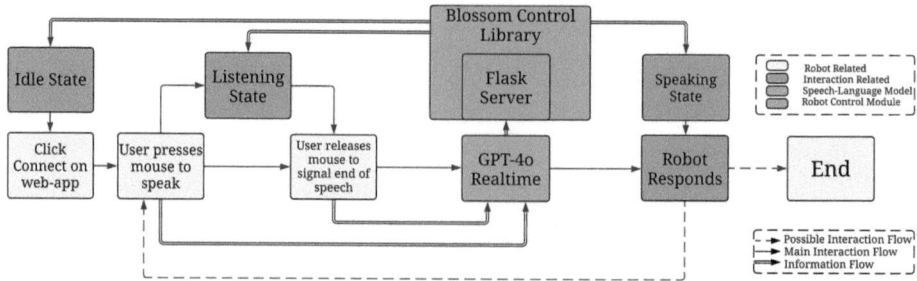

Fig. 3. Overview of the integration of an end-to-end SLM with *Blossom*. *Blossom* was connected to a SLM, GPT-4o-realtime, through the real-time API provided by OpenAI. A Python Flask server was used to enable synchronized back-channeling movements of the robot.

3.2 Research Hypotheses

The main research hypotheses of this work are as follows:

Turn-taking and Latency: Participants will perceive the robot's turn-taking as natural (**H1**).

Back-channeling: Participants will perceive that the robot's non-verbal behaviors are effectively synchronized with its conversation (**H2a**) and that the robot is actively listening (**H2b**).

Adaptive Responses: Participants will perceive the content of the robot's responses as adaptive to the flow of the conversation (**H3**).

Voice: Participants will perceive the robot's voice as appropriate for well-being support (**H4a**) and will acknowledge that it adapts to their own vocal tone and emotional expression (**H4b**).

Overall Interaction: Participants will feel comfortable sharing emotions (**H5a**) and personal experiences (**H5b**) with the robot. They will feel satisfied with the robot's responses (**H5c**), consider the robot to be empathetic (**H5d**), report feeling positive during the interaction (**H5e**), and feel that the robot helped them appreciate aspects of their lives (**H5f**).

Participant Well-being Outcomes: Interacting with the robot will improve participants' self-reported levels of gratitude (**H6a**) and life satisfaction (**H6b**).

3.3 Recruitment and Participants

The study was approved by the Institutional Review Board at the University of Southern California (USC IRB #UP-25-00176). Inclusion criteria were: being a USC undergraduate, Master's, or PhD student over 18 years of age, proficient in English, with normal or corrected hearing. Eleven students consented to and participated in the study; 7 self-identified as female and 4 as male, with ages ranging from 18 to 29, except one participant who chose not to disclose their exact age. All participants reviewed the consent information sheet prior to their study session outlining how their data would be collected and used, and consented to participate. They were compensated with a US$12 Amazon gift card for their time.

3.4 Procedure

For each session, before the interaction with the robot began, participants were asked to complete a quantitative pre-test questionnaire (detailed in Sect. 3.5), which took approximately five minutes.

Once the interaction began, participants engaged with the robot, which was prompted to guide them through sharing two things they are grateful for and two personal achievements [2]. The prompt also instructed the robot to provide positive reinforcement, remain conversational, and offer personalized responses throughout the interaction. This phase lasted approximately 15 min.

After the interaction, participants completed a quantitative post-test questionnaire (see Sect. 3.5) and then participated in a qualitative, semi-structured interview with a member of the research team to discuss their ratings and overall experience. This final portion took approximately 20 min.

3.5 Quantitative and Qualitative Measures

To quantitatively evaluate the robot's usability (**H1–H5**), we designed Likert-scale questions to assess participants' experiences with the robot, informed by usability constructs and themes identified in prior HRI research [2,14]. After the interaction with the robot, participants were asked to rate their experience on a 7-point scale (1 = strongly disagree, 7 = strongly agree) across several dimensions: naturalness of turn-taking (**H1**), synchronization of movements with conversation (**H2a**), active listening (**H2b**), adaptiveness of response content (**H3**), appropriateness of voice for well-being support (**H4a**), adaptiveness of voice tone and emotional expression (**H4b**), comfort in sharing emotions (**H5a**) and personal experiences (**H5b**), satisfaction with the robot's responses (**H5c**), perception of the robot as empathetic (**H5d**), feeling positive during the interaction (**H5e**), and feeling that the robot helped them appreciate aspects of their lives (**H5f**). These questions regarding robot's usability were included as part of the post-test questionnaire.

To quantitatively evaluate **H6**, we used Likert-scale questions validated in previous gratitude studies including: 1) Six-Item Form (GQ-6) [10]; 2) Multi-Component Gratitude Measure (MCGM) [11]; and 3) The Satisfaction With Life Scale (SWLS) [4]. All items from the GQ-6, MCGM, and SWLS used a 7-point scale (1 = strongly disagree, 7 = strongly agree). These questions regarding the participants' self-reported levels of gratitude and life satisfaction were included as part of both the pre-test and post-test questionnaire.

To qualitatively explore participants' responses to the questionnaires, we conducted a semi-structured interview following the questionnaires. We asked open-ended questions to gather qualitative feedback on potential improvements, including personalization, engagement, and design adjustments. These interviews aimed to identify both the strengths and areas for enhancement in the robot's interaction capabilities.

3.6 Data Analysis

We analyzed robot-related measures **H1–H5** using both quantitative and qualitative methods. Quantitatively, we used a two-sided one-sample Wilcoxon signed-rank test to assess whether there was a significant difference between the neutral point (4) on the Likert scale and the median of the participants' responses. Qualitatively, we incorporated insights from the post-interaction semi-structured interviews to contextualize and enrich the quantitative findings.

For participant well-being metrics **H6**, we conducted a quantitative analysis only. To evaluate significant differences between pre- and post-test scores, we used the two-sided Wilcoxon signed-rank test, a non-parametric method for paired data. This test was selected because it does not assume a normal distribution and is well-suited for evaluating changes in responses collected from the same participants.

For hypotheses that contained multiple statistical tests (i.e., **H2**, **H4**, **H5**, and **H6**), we applied the Holm-Bonferroni correction using the formula $\alpha' = \frac{\alpha}{m-n+1}$ to determine the nth test's significance within each hypothesis group independently. In all Wilcoxon signed-rank tests, p denotes the two-tailed probability of observing the result under the null hypothesis, and r denotes the effect size (with $r \geq 0.5$ considered large).

4 Results

All 11 sessions were completed without major issues. In one session, the system failed to record the participant's response in the transcript; however, the participant from that session reported that the conversation proceeded smoothly. Two participants reported a single instance of lag during their sessions, likely caused by network issues (Fig. 4).

H1 (Turn-taking Feels Natural): Participants rated turn-taking higher than the neutral midpoint (Mean = 5.45, Median = 5.00). The Wilcoxon signed-rank test revealed a statistically significant difference from the neutral midpoint of 4 ($r = 0.870$, $p = .004$).

H2 (Back-Channeling): The level of movement synchronization with conversation was rated slightly higher than the neutral midpoint (Mean = 4.82, Median = 5.00). For **H2a**, there was no statistically significant difference from 4 ($r = 0.463$, $p = .125$). Participants rated the robot's ability to actively listen higher than the neutral midpoint (Mean = 5.82, Median = 6.00). For **H2b**, the Wilcoxon test showed a statistically significant difference from 4 ($r = 0.870$, $p = .004$).

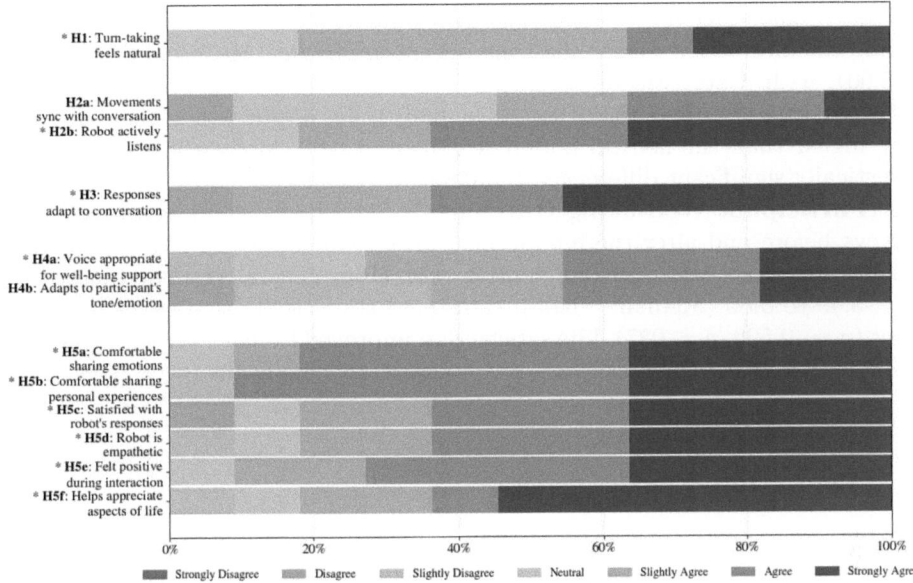

Fig. 4. Participant feedback on robot characteristics ($* = p < .05$, $** = p < .001$)

H3 (Adaptive Responses): Participants rated the adaptiveness of the robot's responses to conversation higher than the neutral midpoint (Mean = 5.82, Median = 6.00). For **H3**, there was a statistically significant difference from the midpoint ($r = 0.779$, $p = .010$).

H4 (Voice): The appropriateness of the robot's voice for well-being support was rated higher than the neutral midpoint (Mean = 5.27, Median = 5.00). For **H4a**, the difference from 4 was statistically significant ($r = 0.704$, $p = .020$). The robot's ability to adapt to the participant's tone and emotion was rated slightly higher than the neutral midpoint (Mean = 4.82, Median = 5.00). For **H4b**, the Wilcoxon test showed no statistically significant difference from 4 ($r = 0.414$, $p = .170$).

H5 (Overall Interaction): Participants rated their comfort sharing emotions with the robot higher than the neutral midpoint (Mean = 6.09, Median = 6.00). For **H5a**, the difference from neutral was statistically significant ($r = 0.934$, $p = .002$). Participants rated their comfort sharing personal experiences higher than the neutral midpoint (Mean = 6.09, Median = 6.00). For **H5b**, the test found a statistically significant difference ($r = 0.934$, $p = .002$). Satisfaction with the robot's responses was rated higher than the neutral midpoint (Mean = 5.64, Median = 6.00). For **H5c**, the difference was statistically significant ($r = 0.729$, $p = .016$). The robot's empathy was rated higher than the neutral midpoint (Mean = 5.73, Median = 6.00). For **H5d**, the Wilcoxon test indicated a statistically significant difference ($r = 0.802$, $p = .008$). Participants reported feeling more positive during the interaction compared to the neutral midpoint

(Mean = 6.00, Median = 6.00). For **H5e**, participants rated feeling positive during the interaction higher than the neutral midpoint (Mean = 6.00, Median = 6.00), with a statistically significant difference ($r = 0.934$, $p = .002$). For **H5f**, participants rated the robot as helping them appreciate aspects of their lives higher than the neutral midpoint (Mean = 6.00, Median = 7.00), with a statistically significant difference ($r = 0.802$, $p = .008$).

H6 (Participant Well-being Outcomes): Participants completed well-being surveys before and after the interaction. All measures showed statistically significant improvements post-intervention. For **H6a**, general gratitude increased from 5.49 to 5.86 (Median = 6.00), showing a statistically significant improvement ($r = -0.590$, $p = .027$). Life satisfaction improved from 4.24 to 4.86 (Median = 4.80). For **H6b**, this difference was statistically significant ($r = -0.489$, $p = .022$).

5 Discussion

This work presents a first small-scale exploration of integrating end-to-end speech-language models (SLMs) with socially assistive robots (SARs) to support well-being.

Hypothesis Testing Results. Our results show that turn-taking was rated significantly above neutral (**H1** is supported). Although participants preferred the robot's movement over static behavior, its synchronization with conversation was rated no differently than neutral (**H2a** is not supported). In contrast, participants rated the robot's active listening ability as significantly above neutral (**H2b** is supported). Participants considered the robot's responses as adaptive (**H3** is supported), though interview data suggested room for improvement in personalization. The robot's voice suitability for well-being support was rated significantly above neutral (**H4a** is supported), while its adaptation to participants' vocal tone and emotional expression was not observed (**H4b** is not supported). Participants reported high comfort in sharing emotions (**H5a** is supported) and personal experiences (**H5b** is supported), were satisfied with the robot's responses (**H5c** is supported), viewed the robot as empathetic (**H5d** is supported), reported feeling positive during the interaction (**H5e** is supported), and felt that the robot helped them appreciate aspects of their lives (**H5f** is supported). Finally, all well-being outcomes showed statistically significant improvements from pre- to post-test, including general gratitude (**H6a** is supported) and life satisfaction (**H6b** is supported).

End-to-End SLMs can Effectively Support Turn-taking in Real-time SAR Interactions. As reported in Sect. 4, for **H1**, our quantitative results show that participants perceived the robot's turn-taking as natural. These findings are further supported by our qualitative analysis of interview transcripts, where no participants reported issues with turn-taking or latency. Instead, interactions were frequently described as natural and fluid. One participant remarked, "It was as similar as if I was speaking to a person." These results suggest that integrating an end-to-end SLM in place of the cascaded dialogue pipeline may be a promising approach for enabling more effective real-time turn-taking in SARs.

Back-channeling Robot Movements are Helpful, but More Diverse and Synchronized Generation is Needed to Reduce Repetitiveness. For **H2a** and **H2b**, our results show that participants perceived the robot as actively listening during the interaction but did not feel that its movements were well-synchronized with the conversation. Our qualitative findings revealed that participants preferred movement over a static posture; however, repetitive nodding that lacked synchronization with the conversational context was often perceived as robotic. As one participant noted, "There was one part where it was nodding a lot, and then I felt it looked too much like a robot." Some participants also mentioned that motor noise during pauses was distracting. While back-channeling movements were generally seen as beneficial, repetitive or unrefined behaviors may have detracted from the overall experience. These findings suggest a need for generating more diverse robot movements synchronized with both the robot's and the user's speech.

The Content of Robot Responses Adapts to Participant Input, Albeit in a Rigid, Generic, and Predictable Structure. For **H3**, our quantitative results showed that participants perceived the robot's responses as adaptive to the conversation. However, our qualitative results revealed that while participants agreed the responses were relevant, they also described them as "too structured." One participant remarked, "I felt like it heard me, but I didn't feel understood." Suggested improvements from the participants included more selective summarization and varied phrasing. This suggests that a more sophisticated prompting framework or fine-tuning of the models may be needed to better align SLM responses with best practices from mental health experts.

The Robot's Voice is Perceived as Well-suited for Well-being Support. For **H4a**, our results found that participants perceived it as appropriate for the context of well-being support. However, some noted a mismatch between the voice and the robot's childlike appearance. Suggested improvements included voice customization and the addition of natural interjections (e.g., "hmm," "oh") to enhance authenticity. As one participant remarked, "I just wish the voice sounded more like a friend than a sort of counselor."

The Tone and Emotion of the Voice did Not Appear to Adapt Dynamically to Participants. For **H4b**, participants reported that the SLM's voice output did not adapt its tone or emotional expression to the context of the conversation. This likely reflects limitations in the underlying SLM, which still lacks the expressiveness and capability to dynamically adjust tone based on conversational cues. Participants described the robot's voice as flat and lacking emotional nuance, with one noting, "I didn't really see a big change in the tone." They suggested that more accurate mirroring of participants' mood and energy levels could enhance engagement.

Overall, Participants Found the Interaction with the Robot to be Comfortable, Emotionally Supportive, and Positively Engaging, Though Sometimes Limited in Depth. For **H5a** and **H5b**, participants reported that they felt comfortable in sharing both emotions and personal experiences with the robot. Participants shared that speaking with a robot made them feel more at ease opening up emotionally. As one participant explained, "I felt comfortable because it's not a real person—it can't judge you." Many also appreciated the robot's consistent positivity. For **H5c** and **H5d**, participants were satisfied with the robot's responses and perceived it as empathetic; however, our qualitative results suggested this perception was largely influenced by modest expectations. Participants did not anticipate human-level dialogue and were therefore more easily satisfied. For **H5e**, participants perceived the robot as positive throughout the interaction. Although the research team was initially concerned about the risk of model hallucinations or inappropriate responses, no such instances occurred during the study. In fact, several participants noted that the robot's positivity occasionally felt excessive. Finally, for **H5f**, participants agreed that the robot helped them reflect on and appreciate aspects of their lives. This outcome aligns with the goals of the well-being intervention and supports prior findings, providing preliminary evidence for the potential of integrating end-to-end SLMs into SARs.

A 15-Min Interaction Helped Improve Short-term Well-being Outcomes. As shown in Sect. 4, for **H6**, both self-reported ratings of general gratitude and life satisfaction significantly improved from pre-test to post-test. This was somewhat unexpected given the brief 15-minute interaction, and may reflect a novelty effect from the robot. Additionally, we acknowledge that expecting substantial changes in life satisfaction following a single 40-minute session is not realistic. Accordingly, these findings should be interpreted as preliminary indicators of potential for long-term impact and explored further. Nonetheless, they suggest the promise of speech-based SARs to positively support well-being. As one participant noted, "It helped me reflect and made me feel grateful."

5.1 Limitations

We acknowledge several limitations of this work. First, this study is a small-scale preliminary exploration ($N = 11$) aimed at validating the potential of end-to-end speech-language models (SLMs) to enable more effective real-time dialogue for socially assistive robots (SARs). Second, the user study followed a single-session design, with each session lasting a maximum of 15 min and no follow-up interactions. As a result, the positive outcomes observed for **H6** may have been influenced by a novelty effect. To confirm the long-term impact of SLM-enabled SARs, larger-scale, longitudinal, and ecologically valid field studies are needed. In addition, we did not include a baseline condition to directly compare end-to-end SLMs with a cascaded dialogue pipeline. Although our results show promising potential, future work should incorporate such comparisons to validate the observed improvements.

While turn-taking was rated positively, participants were required to press and hold a mouse button to speak and release it to yield their turn. This design simplified the turn-taking process but does not reflect the challenges of free-form conversational turn-taking. Future research should further investigate SLMs' capabilities in managing natural, real-time conversational flow with free-form turn-taking. Moreover, the robot was limited to fixed movements; future work should enhance non-verbal synchrony by incorporating multi-modal signal alignment and gesture-generation models. Lastly, our implementation relied solely on basic prompt engineering, without the use of a sophisticated prompting framework. Further exploration is needed to evaluate how more advanced prompting or fine-tuning techniques might enhance SLM performance in SAR contexts.

6 Conclusion

This paper presented an exploration of integrating real-time, end-to-end speech-language models (SLMs) with socially assistive robots (SARs), providing preliminary results and insights from a small-scale user study that can inform future development of SLM-enabled SARs. While our findings highlight the promising potential of SLMs to support more empathetic feedback, natural turn-taking, back-channeling, and adaptive responses in SARs, further work is needed to enable more synchronized real-time movement, align SLM outputs with best practices from mental health experts, and improve expressive, adaptive voice generation.

Acknowledgments. This work is supported in part by the National Science Foundation (IIS-1925083), departmental funding from the University of Southern California, and the Center for Undergraduate Research in Viterbi Engineering (CURVE) Fellowship at the University of Southern California.

References

1. Achiam, J., et al.: Gpt-4 technical report. arXiv preprint arXiv:2303.08774 (2023)
2. Axelsson, M., Spitale, M., Gunes, H.: Robots as mental well-being coaches: design and ethical recommendations. ACM Trans. Hum.-Robot Interact. **13**(2), 15–19 (2024)
3. Bodala, I.P., Churamani, N., Gunes, H.: Teleoperated robot coaching for mindfulness training: a longitudinal study. In: Proceedings of the 2021 30th IEEE International Conference on Robot Human Interactive Communication (RO-MAN), pp. 939–944. IEEE (2021)
4. Diener, E., Emmons, R.A., Larsen, R.J., Griffin, S.: The satisfaction with life scale. J. Pers. Assess. **49**(1), 71–75 (1985)
5. Fang, Q., Guo, S., Zhou, Y., Ma, Z., Zhang, S., Feng, Y.: Llama-omni: seamless speech interaction with large language models. arXiv preprint arXiv:2409.06666 (2024)
6. Jeong, S., et al.: A robotic positive psychology coach to improve college students' wellbeing. In: Proceedings of the RO-MAN 2020, pp. 187–194. IEEE (2020)
7. Kian, M.J., et al.: Can an llm-powered socially assistive robot effectively and safely deliver cognitive behavioral therapy? a study with university students. arXiv preprint arXiv:2402.17937 (2024). https://doi.org/10.48550/arXiv.2402.17937, https://arxiv.org/abs/2402.17937

8. Kidd, C.D., et al.: Robots at home: understanding long-term human-robot interaction. In: IEEE/RSJ IROS, pp. 3230–3235. IEEE (2008)
9. Liu, C.H., Stevens, C., Wong, S.H., Yasui, M., Chen, J.A.: The prevalence and predictors of mental health diagnoses and suicide among us college students: implications for addressing disparities in service use. Depress. Anxiety **36**(1), 8–17 (2019)
10. McCullough, M.E., Emmons, R.A., Tsang, J.A.: The grateful disposition: a conceptual and empirical topography. J. Pers. Soc. Psychol. **82**(1), 112–127 (2002)
11. Morgan, B., Gulliford, L., Kristjánsson, K.: A new approach to measuring moral virtues: the multi-component gratitude measure. Personality Individ. Differ. **107**, 179–189 (2017)
12. OpenAI: Gpt-4o realtime. https://platform.openai.com/docs/models/gpt-4o-realtime-preview, Accessed 29 Mar 2025
13. OpenAI: introducing the real-time api (2024), https://openai.com/index/introducing-the-realtime-api/, Accessed 6-Sep-2024
14. Reimann, M.M., Kunneman, F.A., Oertel, C., Hindriks, K.V.: A survey on dialogue management in human-robot interaction. ACM Trans. Hum.-Robot Interact. **13**(2), 1–22 (2024)
15. Rowan, K., McAlpine, D.D., Blewett, L.A.: Access and cost barriers to mental health care, by insurance status, 1999–2010. Health Affairs (Project Hope) **32**(10), 1723–1730 (2013). https://doi.org/10.1377/hlthaff.2013.0133
16. Scheutz, M., Cantrell, R., Schermerhorn, P.: Toward humanlike task-based dialogue processing for human-robot interaction. AI Mag. **32**(4), 77–84 (2011)
17. Scoglio, A.A., et al.: Use of social robots in mental health and wellbeing research: systematic review. JMIR **21**, e13322 (2019)
18. Shi, Z., et al.: Build your own robot friend: an open-source learning module for accessible and engaging ai education. In: Proceedings of the AAAI Conference on Artificial Intelligence, vol. 38, pp. 23137–23145 (2024)
19. Spitale, M., Axelsson, M., Gunes, H.: Vita: a multi-modal llm-based system for longitudinal, autonomous and adaptive robotic mental well-being coaching. ACM Trans. Hum.-Robot Interact. **14**(2), 1–28 (2025)
20. Suguitan, M., Hoffman, G.: Blossom: a handcrafted open-source robot. ACM Trans. Hum.-Robot Interact. **8**(1), 1–27 (2019). https://doi.org/10.1145/3310356
21. Xu, M.F., Mutlu, B.: Exploring the use of robots for diary studies. arXiv preprint arXiv:2501.04860 (2025)

Towards Improving Turn-Taking in Social Robots Using Visual-Only Voice Activity Detection in Multimodal Dialogue Systems

Antonio Cano[1,2,3](✉), Guillermo Perez[2], Luis Merino[3], and Randy Gomez[1,2,3]

[1] Honda Research Institute Wako Saitama 351-0188, Japan
r.gomez@jp.honda-ri.com
[2] 4i Intelligent Insights, Sevilla, 41092, Spain
g.perez@4i.ai
[3] Universidad Pablo de Olavide, 41013 Sevilla, Spain
aantcan@alu.upo.es, lmercab@upo.es

Abstract. Accurate active speaker detection is essential for natural verbal human-robot interaction. The available solutions have mainly focused on audio-based Voice Activity Detection (VAD), but these approaches become insufficient when audio is compromised or unavailable due to contextual factors. In such cases, the robot must infer whether someone is speaking using only video input. This paper establishes a foundation to enhance robot multimodal dialogue systems by integrating Visual Voice Activity Detection (VVAD) into the social robot Haru. Unlike prior studies that focus on detecting isolated speech segments, our method shifts toward accurately identifying speech boundaries, enabling the robot to handle turns from a visual perspective. We propose new metrics that better capture VVAD behavior in dynamic turn-taking scenarios, as well as overall speech and silence detection. Our results, which align with state-of-the-art benchmarks in isolated segments, highlight the effectiveness of VVAD in accurately identifying relevant speech instances with a simple expansion of a chunk-based algorithm to mark turns. These findings indicate the feasibility of incorporating VVAD into vision-based robotics and encourage further exploration in real-world applications to address remaining challenges in speech-based human-robot interaction, where visual detection is often the most reliable—if not the only—method for identifying speakers.

Keywords: Visual VAD · Turn-taking · Human-Robot Interaction · Social robotics · Visual Speaker Detection · Multimodal Dialogue Systems

1 Introduction

In Human-Robot Interaction (HRI), accurately identifying and localizing when a user is speaking is indispensable to achieve natural and effective verbal communication. This research is carried out as part of the Haru social robot project

[1], designed, among other applications, to interact with groups of children as a mediator in educational activities [2] (see Fig. 1). At present, Haru's conversational module relies, as a preliminary step, on the signal processing technology Voice Activity Detection (VAD) which processes the incoming audio chunks to label speech segments, distinguishing them from those with no speech activity. VAD is fundamental for ensuring that the Automatic Speech Recognition (ASR) system receives clean, precise audio input to accurately transcribe and understand the user's speech. In addition to segmenting speech, the module must filter out irrelevant parts of a conversation, such as noise or verbal fillers, and when a speaker is active to support the robot's contextual understanding. To achieve this, it is responsible for detecting, through configurable thresholds, the exact moments when a user starts and finishes speaking , following an approach commonly referred to as silence-based [3,4].

In contrast, real-world scenarios, like the one in Fig. 1, present very often challenging conditions, such as noise or background voices, under which these audio-only VAD methods lower their effectiveness.

Fig. 1. The social robot Haru interacting with children.

Without effective VAD, transcription quality can degrade, adding complexity to the robot's ability to respond appropriately. Thus, VAD not only helps with the coherence of the robot's responses but also enables it to recognize the right time to answer after the interaction, an equally important factor in maintaining natural conversations. This problem [5], which is still prevalent in current commercial solutions, translates into misunderstanding turn-taking, with the consequence of generating confusion and often frustration for users. Some examples are when a robot interrupts the conversation giving a premature answer before the user finishes speaking, or provides an incorrect response in time and content because of processing another non-relevant voice. Moreover, relying exclusively on the audio modality limits the robot's ability to interpret and distinguish between different audio sources.

To address these limitations, visual features are commonly incorporated, as they are insensitive to background noise and can assist in identifying the speaker

[6]. Although many approaches combine both audio and visual modalities, there are specific robotic scenarios that require the system to rely entirely on video. This is especially important in environments where audio data is compromised and/or unavailable, such as when the robot itself is speaking, and the audio becomes intrinsically noisy. For instance, in 'barge-in' situations where a human wants to interrupt the robot during its own speech, it must detect the user speaking and pause itself to listen.

The task of identifying silent (vocally inactive) and non-silent (vocally active) with the use of visual information is known as Visual Voice Activity Detection (VVAD) [7]. Despite its potential, VVAD is still in its early stages of development, particularly in the context of robotics.

This research makes several significant contributions to the field of VVAD in multimodal dialogue systems, specifically designed for robotics:

- **Novel VVAD Application**: introduces the application of VVAD within dialogue systems for social robotics, an area not previously explored in depth.
- **Shift to Turn-Level Detection**: This research adopts a turn-level detection approach to better capture natural dialogue dynamics, instead of a single-segment evaluation.
- **New dialogue-centric metrics proposal**: Proposes novel metrics to better assess the performance of VVAD in terms of turn-taking and overall speech and silence detection within dialogues.
- **Enhanced VVAD evaluation**: Our metrics offer a clearer interpretation of the behavior of VVADs, helping to better analyze how the system detects human conversational speech and assess its overall performance.

2 Related Work

Researchers have explored areas such as video conferencing, lip reading, speaker diarization, visual speech recognition, and attention in musical video streams, with most solutions relying on audio as the primary modality and incorporating visual input only as a supplement. In contrast, Visual Voice Activity Detection (VVAD) has recently gained attention for its potential to enhance human-robot interaction and related fields [8]; however, its application remains limited, especially in segmenting dialogue features. This gap is even more noticeable in solutions dedicated to purely robotic applications of VVAD, leaving the literature deeply scarce. For instance, [9] applied VVAD to robotic systems using a probabilistic approach to determine mouth openness, integrating audio signals for speech detection, but without addressing dialogue segmentation. [10] investigated turn-taking in robots by tracking humans and employing probabilistic models with hand-crafted features to identify active speakers, but without visually detecting speech. In the field of projection of voice activity (VA) and its robotic adaptation [4,11] adopted a Self-Supervised Learning (SSL) approach to forecast turn-taking behavior in HRI, offering an elegant mapping of VA dynamics between two interlocutors. Although these works contribute with valuable knowledge and perspective, their predicting formulation differs fundamentally from our classification-based strategy on observable silence patterns. This difference, combined with their unimodal audio-based solution, despite some recent efforts towards multimodality [12], makes direct comparison unsuitable.

Nevertheless, most existing VVAD research, though not originally designed for robotics, has techniques that can be easily adapted for such contexts. These studies primarily aim to identify active speakers using audio-visual features, with some methods depending only on visual data, and others combining both audio and visual information. In both, researchers have focused on specific facial areas relevant to speech production, such as the lips and surrounding muscles. Some researchers have opted to use the full face [13–19] and others specifically the cropped mouth region [9,20]. Other studies have expanded to include the whole body [10], employing techniques such as optical flow [21] or dynamic images [22,23] to capture motion patterns. More recently, a middle-ground strategy has emerged, using a Regions of Interest (RoI) [24–27] that isolate the lower face area increases model performance more effectively.

Currently, there exist two main methodologies for frame-level processing: *parallel inference*, which processes all frames simultaneously, and *sequential inference*, which uses a sliding window to predict activity across each sequence. Optimal video sequence length lacks an established consensus and varies considerably across solutions, but there is a trend towards using sequences over static frames, as dynamic features capture speech activity more effectively. For example, [23] used 25 frames, [13] focused on 0.4 s, [19,22] used 10 and 15 consecutive RGB frames, respectively, [16] analyzed sequences of 0.8 s and [28] extended to 4 s.

Audio-Visual Multimodality

Multimodal approaches, which mainly combine audio and visual modalities, dominate research in VVAD. For example, [20] combines a WaveNet encoder with a ResNet-based visual stream using multimodal compact bilinear pooling and LSTMs to model temporal dependencies. SPELL [15] processes egocentric video with a CNN-RNN pipeline, while Light-ASD [16] applies a GRU-based cross-modal framework optimized for efficiency. TS-TalkNet [14], a common reference in recent work, aligns audio embeddings with facial and lip movements to improve target speaker detection. MIMO-TSVAD [26] incorporates acoustic footprints and lip tracks through sequence-to-sequence learning for diarization, and LoCoNet [18] leverages spatio-temporal features through 3D CNNs and TCNs for robust speaker activity detection.

These approaches have probed the effectiveness of multimodal fusion. However, most still use audio as the dominant modality, with vision as a complementary role. As a result, they are not directly applicable in scenarios where audio is lacking, highlighting the need for vision-only solutions.

Visual Modality

Research continues to explore a single visual modality in VVAD, particularly valuable in scenarios where multimodal approaches are not feasible. For example, [27] integrates optical flow and dynamic RGB images using a ResNet50-based model to capture motion cues, showing a significant improvement in detecting speech activity with automatic labeling from audio modality that acts as supervisor. In [23], dynamic images and a MultiModal Transfer Module (MMTM) within a 3D Convolutional Neural Network (3DCNN) capture human motion for speech detection, particularly when faces are obscured. [22] combines dynamic images from RGB frames with a ResNet50 for VVAD computation. [21] introduces two deep architectures: one with facial landmarks and LSTMs, the other using optical flow with a CNN. Similarly, [19] presents EASEE, an end-to-end network that learns multimodal embeddings and aggregates spatiotemporal context using interleaved Graph Neural Network (iGNN) blocks. [28] proposes an architecture that combines a 3D-CNN and Video Temporal Convolutional Block (V-TCN) to capture lip movement dynamics.

Altogether, these studies highlight the progression of VVAD methodologies and demonstrate that visual-only approaches, when combined with appropriate image preprocessing and effective spatio-temporal architectures, can also achieve competitive performance in speech detection, making them suitable for use in robotics.

Evaluation Metrics

In this work, we refer to metrics such as accuracy, F1 score, precision, or recall as traditional evaluation metrics. Several prior studies [20–23, 25, 27, 29–34] have reported strong results using these classical approaches to evaluate VVAD at the segment level. In contrast, some researchers (e.g.: [10, 29, 32]) have explored dialogue-based approaches that provide insights into dialogue systems, but with metrics that cannot be adapted to VVAD in managing turns. As [35] hypothesize, F1 scores throughout the clip or around turn-taking events using threshold-based detection neglect the continuous and overlapping nature of real-world conversations. Instead, they propose per-frame mean average precision (mAP), which evaluates how well the model anticipates speech by averaging precision across thresholds and time steps from frame-level confidence scores.

Moving toward temporal precision, the Average Timestamp Difference (T-δ) metric [36] evaluates the temporal accuracy of word timing by measuring the deviation of predicted start and end times, using techniques such as dynamic time warping to align predicted and actual timestamps. Similarly, the Word Absolute Start Time Delta (WASTD) metric [37] quantifies the error between hypothesized and reference word start times, providing an assessment of timing accuracy in speech recognition systems. These metrics are more aligned with our objectives, as they are designed for the evaluation of spoken language systems. However, similar to the limitations observed with traditional metrics, their focus on word-level accuracy and timing can overlook important aspects of HRI and limit their ability to fully evaluate turn-level behavior. More in accordance with this work, [38] defined the Moment Detection Error (MDE) that quantifies the deviation between the predicted and actual speech onset/offset, calculated at two levels: frame level (F-MDE) and time level (T-MDE).

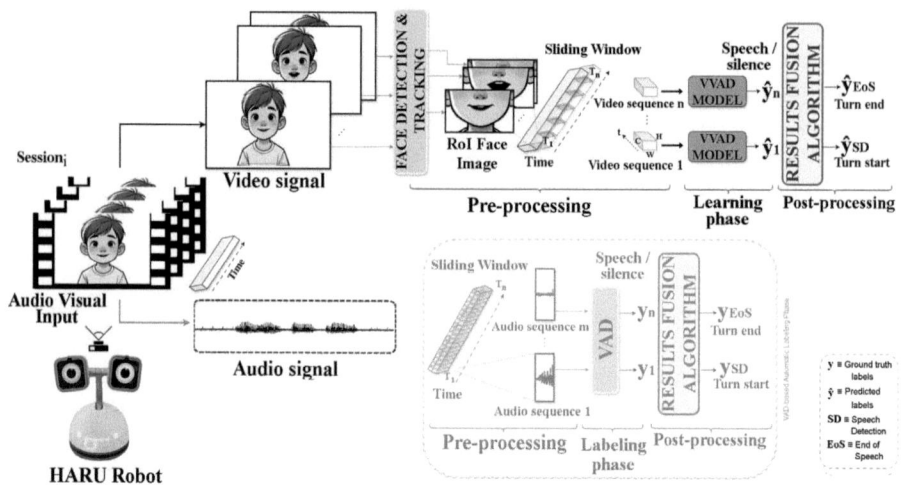

Fig. 2. Diagram of Image-based Training and Audio Label Generation: The system processes synchronized audio and video. VAD is applied to audio sequences to extract the ground truth SD and EoS, while a face tracker extract valid RoIs from video frames. These are segmented into fixed-length sequences, and VVAD predictions are computed and aggregated to determine the SD - **turn start** and EoS - **turn end**.

Accordingly, existing studies provide valuable insights and inspiration for general VVAD evaluation, but they use techniques that do not fully cover the evaluation from a turn-taking dynamic, which may undermine the effectiveness of the visual-related aspects of the robot's dialogue system.

3 Proposed Method

Our approach differs from previous solutions by shifting the focus to turn-level detection in VVAD, motivated by the requirements of social robots in speech interactions and challenges posed by an open-microphone setting. From a dialogue perspective, the objective extends beyond merely detecting speech in single chunks to ensure that the system comprehends and processes entire sentence content with minimal noise interference. By consolidating this idea, the robot can better manage turn-taking and reduce erroneous behavior. To achieve the transformation, the process first involves labeling isolated sequences, followed by an algorithm that aggregates these labels into coherent turn labels. This change also needs to be accompanied by a more accurate evaluation of the system's performance on turn-level detection instead of average accuracy over individual frames. The previous methods have lacked this focus, which justifies the need for robust VVAD metrics at the turn level to ensure a precise assessment of VVAD's behavior in dialogue systems. The following subsections explain the components of the visual-related pipeline shown in Fig. 2.

3.1 VAD-Based Automatic Labeling Phase

Figure 2 illustrates the automatic labeling procedure. First, the audio signal is segmented into m sequences. Each resulting audio sequence is then processed for speech activity using the selected VAD algorithm. Due to the differences in window size between the video and audio, the labels are synchronized with the video sequences by intersecting the audio and video labels. If more than 50% of the video chunk overlaps with "speech" VAD labels, then the sequence is labeled as "speech". Otherwise, it is labeled as "silence". Finally, the fusion result algorithm consolidates these labels to generate turn markers. Although the VAD algorithm could introduce intrinsic labeling errors, these are assumed to be minor given the clean audio conditions of the datasets.

3.2 Pre-processing Stage - RoI Extraction

The preprocessing starts by dividing the video signal into n sequences using a fixed-length windowing approach, with no overlap between the sequences. The subsequent step is face detection, and for each face, we use a facial landmark detector [39] to identify the lower face area, encompassing the nose, mouth, and chin [27] to extract the Regions of Interest (RoI). Given the natural proportions of the face, the RoI is always rectangular, but since square images are more common as input, black padding is applied to the top and bottom to preserve aspect ratio before resizing. In addition, a facial tracking algorithm [40] is used to ensure that the speaker's face remains within the frame throughout the sequence.

Due to the absence of agreement on the visual window length, this research employs a range of sizes with a selection criterion inspired by empirical observations of dialogue logical concepts related to word lengths. So, it should exceed the minimum length at which visual information becomes irrelevant to the model, while choosing an optimal maximum window size that avoids excessive noise and senseless video features. This approach balances the need for sufficient visual context with the need to prevent confusion with irrelevant silent periods mixed with positive samples.

3.3 Model Architecture

This work adopts well-proven state-of-the-art models incorporating certain adaptations to fit the VVAD task applied only in visual modality to cover a range of solutions to determine our new perspective. The implementations includes a standard Convolutional Neural Network (CNN) for handling spatial dimensions, combined with a recurrent neural network for temporal information processing, specifically integrating ResNet-18 with a Bidirectional Long Short-Term Memory (BiLSTM) layer. In addition, we have tested the system with a non-pre-trained version of the I3D network [41]. Furthermore, we develop a variant of the model proposed in [42], which closely resembles TS-TalkNet [14] and LoCoNet [18]. This model integrates a 3D Convolutional Neural Network (3DCNN) with a ResNet-like structure to extract spatial and temporal features from RoI sequences, followed by a Temporal Convolutional Network (TCN) and a Fully Connected (FC) layer to classify sequences as speech or silence.

3.4 Post-processing Stage

The results are processed using a straightforward algorithm that manages the dynamic detection of speech segments through continuous monitoring. The algorithm [43] begins by initially tracking the labels associated with speech segments, and when the number of detected speech instances reaches a certain threshold, the algorithm indicates the beginning of the speech, $\hat{y}_{SD}$ = true. Subsequently, the algorithm transitions to silence monitoring. The silence segment labels accumulate until they reach a predefined threshold, at which point the end of the speech is marked $\hat{y}_{EoS}$ = true. The algorithm's parameters are fully configurable, allowing it to adapt to different evaluation windows for audio and video data, taking into account the temporal characteristics inherent to each modality. The simplicity of this algorithm lies in its assumption that speech, once initiated, will eventually be followed by silence, making it efficient and effective in delineating the boundaries of speech activity.

4 Evaluation and Proposed Metrics

Building on the previous discussion, current literature and existing works in VVAD lack for metrics specifically designed to evaluate VVAD in speech exchange dynamics. In dialogue systems for robots, VVAD must precisely detect the beginning of someone speaking or Speech Detection (SD) as well as the end of the same person's speech, End of Speech (EoS), which correspond to the start and end of a turn. Traditional metrics used to evaluate VVAD performance for general speech tasks are insufficient to capture its effectiveness in turn-based interaction contexts, and could provide a misleading sense of good behavior by only averaging results across isolated traditional evaluations. To move beyond these limitations, we introduce two novel metrics specially designed to evaluate VVAD performance in detecting turn boundaries. They capture the effectiveness of VVAD in turn-taking and overall speech-silence detection by focusing on qualitative and quantitative evaluation of the system's ability to correctly classify SD and EoS, addressing insights that traditional metrics may overlook or miss.

Before defining these metrics, we need to set some basic key concepts. As illustrated in Fig. 3, a *False Positive* (FP) occurs when a detected label exceeds a temporal threshold defined by the fusion algorithm. A *False Negative* (FN) refers to a missing or undetected SD or EoS label, under the assumption that each turn should include both markers. The metrics do not focus on evaluating long periods of silence or *True Negatives* (TN), but center their measurement in the significant amount of knowledge of activity periods and its transitions or *True Positives* (TP).

Regarding temporal precision, the new metric is partially inspired by T-δ [36], WASTD [37] and T-MDE [38], since as them, they seek to assess the temporal alignment of predicted SD and EoS with the ground truth. It is calculated as the absolute timestamp difference across all turns, where a lower T-δ value indicates higher chronological accuracy.

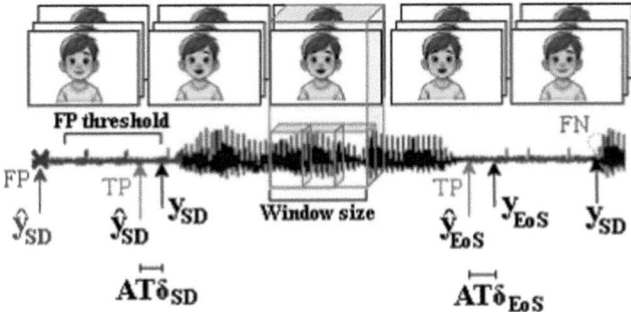

Fig. 3. Visual representation of key concepts for evaluating the effectiveness of VVAD in predicting SD and EoS.

We present the proposed metrics below as part of this paper's contributions:

- Detection Efficiency (DE): combines two critical aspects of detection performance - the Miss Rate (MR) or False Negative Rate (FNR) and False Discovery Rate (FDR) to measure the system's ability to accurately detect the initial or the end speech point of a turn. This metric provides a balanced assessment of the system's ability to accurately detect the start and end of speech while minimizing both missed detection and false alarms.

$$\mathrm{DE}_X = \begin{cases} 0, & \text{if } TP=0 \text{ and } (FP=0 \text{ or } FN>0) \\ \alpha \cdot (1 - \mathrm{MR}_X) + (1 - \alpha) \cdot (1 - \mathrm{FDR}_X), & \text{otherwise} \end{cases} \quad X \in \mathrm{SD}, \mathrm{EoS};$$

- $\alpha = 0.5$ gives equal weight to Recall and FDR.
- $\alpha > 0.5$ gives more importance to Recall. $\alpha \in [0, 1]$
- $\alpha < 0.5$ gives more importance to minimizing false discoveries.

- Average Time Delta (AT-δ): calculates the average difference between the predicted speech activation or end of speech time and the actual speech onset or offset time. This metric evaluates the temporal accuracy of the system in detecting these points.

$$\mathrm{AT} - \delta_X = \frac{1}{N} \sum_{i=1}^{N} |T_{\mathrm{pred},X_i} - T_{\mathrm{true},X_i}|, \ X \in \{\mathrm{SD}, \mathrm{EoS}\}$$

These metrics capture the balance between accurately predicting sentence boundaries, including the initiation and termination of turns, and evaluating the precision of these predictions. By reliably identifying sentence boundaries in conversational contexts, the system provides clearer insights into how turns are handled, and consequently, this approach better reflects the system's reliability of VVAD in robotics applications, ensuring a more comprehensive evaluation.

5 Experiments and Results

5.1 Datasets and Experimental Setup

Audio signals are divided into 125 ms chunks and labeled using the Silero VAD algorithm. The results are integrated into the fusion algorithm using a fixed window size, with two consecutive speech labels for SD and four for EoS, to generate the ground-truth SD and EoS for visual modality. For training, the RoIs are first extracted using 68 face alignment landmarks and then resized to $112 \times 112 \times 3$ pixels. The selected window sizes stack consecutive RoIs based on the corresponding audio labels to train the VVAD algorithm. The fusion result algorithm counts consecutive predicted labels for each sequence, specifically four, two, and one for both SD and EoS, based on the selected visual windows of 0.25, 0.5 and 0.75, respectively. We selected the following datasets because they contain clean, well-structured audiovisual data and can be used to simulate a controlled scenario where a single person is speaking to Haru, with each sentence processed as if spoken by a user in a single-speaker agent setting that mirrors the one-on-one interactions typically encountered in social robotics. These datasets have also been frequently used in previous solutions. The datasets are divided into 80% of speakers for training, 10% for validation, and 10% for testing while ensuring speaker independence:

- The TCD-TIMIT database [44] includes high-quality recordings of 62 speakers reading 6,913 phonetically rich sentences in front of a green screen.
- RAVDESS dataset [45] consists of 7,356 recordings of emotional speech and song from 24 professional actors, with equal representation of men and women.

5.2 Results

To explore the potential of our solution for main speaker detection in a single-agent interaction, we developed a set of tests to assess its feasibility, aiming to fully cover a range of state-of-the-art model architectures and window sizes, following the previously explained window criteria. Table 1 presents the experimental results from the two selected datasets, comparing three model architectures and three different window sizes, evaluated with automatically generated labels computed from the audio source. The table summarizes VVAD's performance in detecting turns, as measured by the new metrics with $\alpha = 0.5$. The best result for TCD-TIMIT was achieved with model 3DResNet + TCN using a window size of 0.75, and for RAVDESS with model 3DResNet + TCN and window size 0.5, despite the individual metrics not always being the highest scores. These results align with the performance of state-of-the-art methods while also providing the ability to interpret the outcomes over turn detection.

Table 1. Results for Different Models, Window Sizes, and Databases.

Dataset	Window Size	Model	$\frac{DE}{SD}$	$\frac{AT\delta}{SD}$	$\frac{DE}{EoS}$	$\frac{AT\delta}{EoS}$	F1	TNR	TPR	Acc
TCD-TIMIT	0.25 s	CNN + BiLSTM	0.84	0.389	0.75	0.21	0.83	0.78	0.84	0.81
		I3D	0.85	**0.21**	0.75	0.27	0.81	**0.92**	0.72	0.82
		3DResNet + TCN	**0.90**	0.32	**0.82**	**0.17**	**0.88**	0.82	**0.89**	**0.86**
	0.5 s	CNN + BiLSTM	0.85	0.21	0.77	0.21	0.87	0.90	0.84	0.86
		I3D	0.90	0.18	**0.84**	**0.19**	**0.93**	0.90	**0.93**	**0.92**
		3DResNet + TCN	**0.91**	**0.13**	0.84	0.22	0.92	**0.94**	0.88	0.91
	0.75 s	CNN + BiLSTM	0.90	0.31	0.81	0.22	0.89	0.85	0.89	0.87
		I3D	0.95	**0.29**	0.93	0.22	0.93	**0.92**	0.92	0.93
		3DResNet + TCN	**0.95**	0.31	**0.94**	**0.21**	**0.95**	0.85	**0.97**	**0.94**
RAVDESS	0.25 s	CNN + BiLSTM	0.84	0.33	0.71	0.30	0.78	0.89	0.70	**0.88**
		I3D	0.86	0.29	0.78	0.26	**0.94**	0.6	**0.90**	0.77
		3DResNet TCN	**0.92**	**0.28**	**0.86**	**0.18**	0.81	**0.90**	0.77	0.83
	0.5 s	CNN + BiLSTM	0.84	0.33	0.72	0.30	0.78	0.89	0.70	0.79
		I3	0.90	0.29	0.83	**0.20**	0.89	0.84	**0.91**	0.88
		3DResNet + TCN	**0.94**	**0.16**	**0.92**	0.20	**0.92**	**0.94**	0.90	**0.92**
	0.75 s	CNN + BiLSTM	0.87	0.35	0.79	**0.23**	0.85	0.84	0.83	0.83
		I3D	0.91	0.35	0.83	0.26	0.90	0.88	0.89	0.88
		3DResNet + TCN	**0.93**	0.35	**0.90**	0.24	**0.91**	**0.89**	**0.90**	**0.89**

6 Discussion and Future Work

Current approaches make it difficult to assess whether VVAD truly enhances human-robot communication. Traditional metrics, while useful for evaluating isolated sequences, often fail to capture the entire dynamics of the interaction. This may lead to inflated scores and an incomplete or misleading sense of system effectiveness, especially when the VVAD performs well on individual chunks but struggles with managing conversational flow. To address this, we change the focus to identifying when a user is actively speaking to the robot and when they are awaiting a response. This change, motivated by the limitations of existing metrics, also forces the evaluation to change from isolated performance to turn-taking effectiveness.

Working in the context of VVAD in social robotics, this research adopts a silence-based approach and applies similar models that have proven successful in the VVAD field. We not only achieved comparable results on selected datasets when evaluated with classical metrics, but we also gained a deeper understanding of how VVAD operates under turn-taking conditions. The results, particularly with models such as 3DResNet+TCN across both databases, demonstrate meaningful performance with a straightforward algorithm that marks the SD and EoS timestamps, achieving significant levels of accuracy. Furthermore, when analyzing the entire Table 1 it becomes clear that some models perform worse from a dialogue perspective compared to what traditional metrics suggest, showing that the new metrics successfully uncover insights overlooked by conventional methods. For instance, when setting a 0.25 s visual window size in RAVDESS. If we were to base our decision only on observing the accuracy, we might mistakenly choose CNN+BiLSTM; similarly, if we entirely rely on the F1 score, we would select I3D, over 3DResNet+TCN instead, which, as the new metrics expose, adapts better to turn-taking tasks than both algorithms. Regarding AT-δ_{SD} and AT-δ_{EoS}, as expected, it provides clarity on the temporal precision of the boundary predictions, achieving satisfactory values in some cases but reflecting the need for further research on optimal temporal windowing.

For VVAD to be successfully applied in practice, it must be tested in more natural scenarios where users behave spontaneously and challenges such as RoI occlusions and lateral positions emerge. Addressing these challenges supports the development of advanced algorithms capable of managing the unpredictability of real human-robot interactions. Considering these obstacles, the advances proposed in this work should be seen as the first steps towards the proper development of robust VVAD systems capable of detecting the active speaker in dialogue systems. The results highlight the importance of further refining perspectives and evaluation methods to adopt a turn-taking approach, where dialogue-based performance is more effectively understood. This positions VVAD as a feasible tool for understanding when someone is speaking to a robot only using visual modality, along with all the applications that this can encompass, and encourages further exploration in this promising area to fully realize its potential.

7 Conclusions

In open microphone setting, robots like Haru need to accurately identify who is speaking and the duration of the active speech. This task is usually performed using audio processing, but there are some situations in which the audio becomes unavailable or is inherently noisy, such as robot itself is speaking. This work highlights the importance of integrating vision modality, as it is unaffected by the same noise issues, and when the audio system encounters difficulties, VVAD provides a significant advantage by allowing the robot to detect the speaker's speech activity, its spatial location, and link it with the corresponding face.

However, unlike existing solutions, integrating VVAD into a conversational social robot requires moving beyond the classification of isolated segments to turn-taking solutions with an evaluation method adjusted accordingly. The current evaluation approaches, which are not focused on turns, can create a misleading impression of success by focusing solely on isolated performance rather than assessing the system's effectiveness within the full interaction. In this paper, we present this new perspective along with new evaluation metrics that overcome these limitations. The tests conducted demonstrate that the metrics ensure that VVAD is evaluated not only in its ability to visually detect speech segments, but also in how it assesses the overall dialogue flow.

This application of VVAD in social robots can expand human-robot engagement by addressing current limitations, such as preventing cross-talk or not permitting users to interrupt robots during irrelevant conversations. This work contributes an approach for applying VVAD within multimodal dialogue systems and lays the groundwork for developing and evaluating systems that enable social robots like Haru to use visual perception to better manage turn-taking and respond more effectively in complex, human-centered interactions.

Acknowledgments. This work was partially funded by the Spanish Ministry of Science and Innovation and the State Research Agency (MCIN/AEI/10.13039/5011-00011033) under the projects **TIFON** [MIG-20232039/PLEC2023-010251] (A.C., G.P.) and **PICRAH4.0** [PLEC2023-010353] (L.M.).

References

1. Gomez, R., Szapiro, D., Galindo, K., Nakamura, K.: Haru: hardware design of an experimental tabletop robot assistant, pp. 233–240, February 2018
2. Gomez, R., et al.: Design of embodied mediator haru for remote cross cultural communication. In: Proceedings of the IEEE International Conference on Robotics and Automation, pp. 5505–5511 (2024)
3. Jaiswal, R., Hines, A.: The sound of silence: How traditional and deep learning based voice activity detection influences speech quality monitoring, December 2018
4. Ekstedt, E., Skantze, G.: Voice activity projection: Self-supervised learning of turn-taking events (2022)
5. Aneja, D., McDuff, D., Czerwinski, M.: Conversational error analysis in human-agent interaction. In: Proceedings of the 20th ACM International Conference on Intelligent Virtual Agents, IVA 2020, (New York, NY, USA), ACM (2020)
6. Blauth, D.A., Minotto, V.P., Jung, C.R., Lee, B., Kalker, T.: Voice activity detection and speaker localization using audiovisual cues. Pattern Recogn. Lett. **33**(4), 373–380 (2012). Intelligent Multimedia Interactivity
7. Sodoyer, D., Rivet, B., Girin, L., Savariaux, C., Schwartz, J.-l., Jutten, C.: A study of lip movements during spontaneous dialog and its application to voice activity detection. J. Acoust. Soc. Am. **125**, 1184–96 (2009)
8. Siohan, O., de Pinho Forin Braga, O.: Best of both worlds: multi-task audio-visual automatic speech recognition and active speaker detection (2022)
9. Yoshida, T., Nakadai, K.: Audio-visual voice activity detection based on an utterance state transition model. Adv. Robot. **26**(10), 1183–1201 (2012)
10. Gebru, I.D., Ba, S., Evangelidis, G., Horaud, R.: Audio-visual speech-turn detection and tracking. In: Vincent, E., Yeredor, A., Koldovský, Z., Tichavský, P. (eds.) LVA/ICA 2015. LNCS, vol. 9237, pp. 143–151. Springer, Cham (2015). https://doi.org/10.1007/978-3-319-22482-4_17
11. Skantze, G., Irfan, B.: Applying general turn-taking models to conversational human-robot interaction. In: Proceedings of the 2025 ACM/IEEE International Conference on Human-Robot Interaction, HRI 2025, pp. 859–868. IEEE Press (2025)
12. Onishi, K., Tanaka, H., Nakamura, S.: Multimodal voice activity prediction: Turn-taking events detection in expert-novice conversation. In: Proceedings of the 11th International Conference on Human-Agent Interaction, HAI 2023, (New York, NY, USA), pp. 13–21. ACM (2023)

13. Tesema, F.B., Gu, J., Song, W., Wu, H., Zhu, S., Lin, Z.: Efficient audiovisual fusion for active speaker detection. IEEE Access **11**, 45140–45153 (2023)
14. Jiang, Y., Tao, R., Pan, Z., Li, H.: Target active speaker detection with audio-visual cues (2023)
15. Min, K.: Intel labs at ego4d challenge 2022: a better baseline for audio-visual diarization (2023)
16. Liao, J., Duan, H., Feng, K., Zhao, W., Yang, Y., Chen, L.: A light weight model for active speaker detection (2023)
17. Vasireddy, S.S.N., Zhang, C., Guo, X., Tian, Y.: Robust active speaker detection in noisy environments (2024)
18. Wang, X., Cheng, F., Bertasius, G.: Loconet: long-short context network for active speaker detection. In: Proceedings of the IEEE/CVF Conference on Computer Vision and Pattern Recognition (CVPR), pp. 18462–18472, June 2024
19. Alcazar, J.L., Cordes, M., Zhao, C., Ghanem, B.: End-to-end active speaker detection (2022)
20. Ariav, I., Cohen, I.: An end-to-end multimodal voice activity detection using wavenet encoder and residual networks. IEEE J. Sel. Top. Sig. Process. **13**(2), 265–274 (2019)
21. Guy, S., Lathuilière, S., Mesejo, P., Horaud, R.: Learning visual voice activity detection with an automatically annotated dataset (2020)
22. Shahid, M., Beyan, C., Murino, V.: S-vvad: visual voice activity detection by motion segmentation. In: 2021 IEEE Winter Conference on Applications of Computer Vision (WACV), pp. 2331–2340 (2021)
23. Yamazaki, K., Tamura, S., Gotoh, Y., Nose, M.: Visual-only voice activity detection using human motion in conference video. In: Proceedings of the 11th International Conference on Pattern Recognition Applications and Methods - Volume 1: ICPRAM, pp. 570–577, INSTICC, SciTePress (2022)
24. Wang, Z., et al.: The multimodal information based speech processing (misp) 2022 challenge: Audio-visual diarization and recognition (2023)
25. Chung, J.S., Zisserman, A.: Learning to lip read words by watching videos. Comput. Vis. Image Underst. **173**, 76–85 (2018)
26. Cheng, M., Li, M.: Multi-input multi-output target-speaker voice activity detection for unified, flexible, and robust audio-visual speaker diarization (2024)
27. Caus, D., Carbajal, G., Gerkmann, T., Frintrop, S.: See the silence: improving visual-only voice activity detection by optical flow and RGB fusion, pp. 41–51, September 2021
28. Tao, R., Qian, X., Das, R.K., Gao, X., Wang, J., Li, H.: Enhancing real-world active speaker detection with multi-modal extraction pre-training (2024)
29. Shahverdi, P., Tyshka, A., Trombly, M., Louie, W.-Y.G.: Learning turn-taking behavior from human demonstrations for social human-robot interactions. In: 2022 IEEE/RSJ International Conference on Intelligent Robots and Systems (IROS), pp. 7643–7649 (2022)
30. Sharma, R., Somandepalli, K., Narayanan, S.: Toward visual voice activity detection for unconstrained videos. In: 2019 IEEE International Conference on Image Processing (ICIP), pp. 2991–2995 (2019)
31. Patrona, F., Iosifidis, A., Tefas, A., Nikolaidis, N., Pitas, I.: Visual voice activity detection in the wild. IEEE Trans. Multimedia **18**(6), 967–977 (2016)
32. Fujie, S., Katayama, H., Sakuma, J., Kobayashi, T.: Timing generating networks: neural network based precise turn-taking timing prediction in multiparty conversation. In: Interspeech (2021)

33. Hou, Y., et al.: Attention-based cross-modal fusion for audio-visual voice activity detection in musical video streams (2021)
34. Benatan, M.: Audio-visual speech processing for multimedia localisation (2016)
35. Kim, J., et al.: Egospeak: learning when to speak for egocentric conversational agents in the wild (2025)
36. Yamasaki, H., Louradour, J., Hunter, J., Prévot, L.: Transcribing and aligning conversational speech: a hybrid pipeline applied to french conversations, pp. 1–6, December 2023
37. Jeon, W.: Timestamped embedding-matching acoustic-to-word ctc asr (2023)
38. Zhang, J., Cao, J., Sun, J.: Learning spatiotemporal lip dynamics in 3d point cloud stream for visual voice activity detection. Biomed. Signal Process. Control **87**, 105410 (2024)
39. Bulat, A., Patterson, G.G.: face-alignment (2016). Accessed 05 Oct 2023
40. Geitgey, A.: face_recognition: recognize and manipulate faces from python or from the command line. https://github.com/ageitgey/face_recognition (2017)
41. Carreira, J., Zisserman, A.: Quo vadis, action recognition? A new model and the kinetics dataset, *CoRR*, vol. arXiv:1705.07750 (2017)
42. Martinez, B., Ma, P., Petridis, S., Pantic, M.: Lipreading using temporal convolutional networks (2020)
43. Tao, F., Hansen, J.H., Busso, C.: Improving boundary estimation in audiovisual speech activity detection using bayesian information criterion. Interspeech **2016**, 2130–2134 (2016)
44. Harte, N., Gillen, E.: Tcd-timit: an audio-visual corpus of continuous speech. IEEE Trans. Multimedia **17**(5), 603–615 (2015)
45. Livingstone, S.R., Russo, F.A.: The ryerson audio-visual database of emotional speech and song (ravdess): a dynamic, multimodal set of facial and vocal expressions in north American English. PLOS ONE **13**, 1–35 (2018)

Motion Control, Prosthetics and Functional Robotics

HaptiCam: Skin-Drag Haptic Feedback for Real-Time Communication of Camera Settings

Michael Ha[1] and Timothy Merritt[2]

[1] Aarhus University, Aarhus, Denmark
[2] Aalborg University, 9220 Aalborg Ø, Denmark
merritt@cs.aau.dk

Abstract. Learning photography with digital cameras can be challenging and may take hours of exploration of the camera settings. Instructors often guide students verbally and encourage students to take many shots, evaluate, and scroll the control wheel across the range of settings until the photo looks acceptable. Verbal guidance takes time, can be confusing, and might not be appropriate in a public setting. HaptiCam provides tactile guidance in real-time through skin drag using two tactors embedded in an augmented sleeve. The student receives guidance by comparing the perceived position of the tactor mapped to their camera in relation to the tactor mapped to the instructor's camera–and adjusting their settings to match. We explored communication using voice and tactile cues with instructors, experts, and novices with initial impressions suggesting that two-tactor skin drag displays could be a viable strategy for communication when voice communication is not possible.

Keywords: haptic tactor · wearable · learning · photography

1 Introduction

The saying "a picture is worth a thousand words" emphasizes that photography is not simply about objectively capturing the world as we see it or a moment in time, but is also about capturing stories from the photographer's point of view. The expressiveness of these stories can be brought to life through various techniques of building the image, which requires a thorough understanding of how light is captured as an image and proficiency with the equipment in order to obtain the desired effect. The "exposure triangle" is a fundamental conceptual model that photographers learn as it explains the relationship between three key parameters that influence the resulting image. Often drawn as a triangular 2-dimensional space [14], the exposure triangle involves the relationships between the sensitivity of the film or digital sensor expressed as an ISO number, shutter speed as fractions of a second, and the size of the aperture expressed as F-stop values. Aspiring photographers often find it difficult to transition from the camera's automatic mode in which the exposure triangle is managed for them and the more manual or semi-manual modes that place higher demands of skill and control of the settings. Live instruction from a photography teacher can accelerate the development of the skills of the novice–usually accomplished through voice instruction and guided experimentation. However, it can be difficult to follow the thought process of the expert when the student is just beginning to understand the fundamentals. For the teacher, being vocally explicit on setting every single parameter value can be a cumbersome process. A common activity while learning photography involves taking many photos and scrolling the control wheel through the settings and constantly reflecting on the result. Recent research suggests that hand over hand training–and haptic communication tools [19] can be helpful in various learning situations. We developed *HaptiCam*, a haptic sleeve, which facilitates one-to-one non-verbal communication between the teacher and student to support the learning process of digital photography (see Fig. 1 & Concept Video[1]). This work represents an initial step toward the design of haptic communication tools for teachers and students.

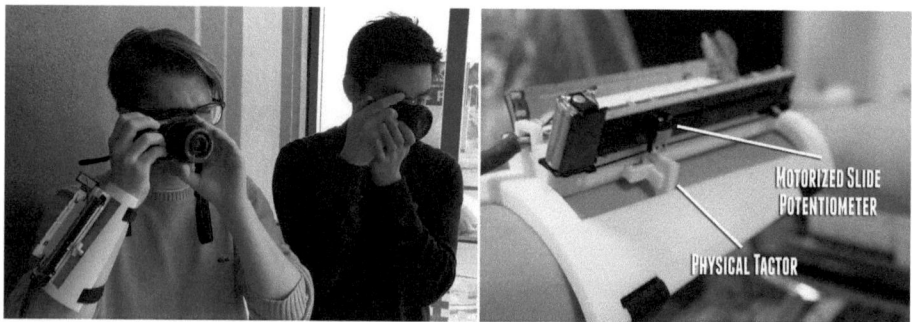

Fig. 1. HaptiCam (Left) In use by student receiving tactile cues on arm indicating settings of his and his instructor's camera through 2 skin-drag tactors. (Right) Detailed photo of HaptiCam sleeve including 3D printed frame, motorized slide potentiometer, and physical tactor.

2 Related Work

Research that informs this work can be broadly grouped into four areas, theories of assisted learning, research on tactile perception, haptic learning systems, and recent hci research focused on the physical camera.

The zone of proximal development (ZPD) concept was developed by Lev Vygotsky as "the distance between the actual developmental level as determined by independent problem solving and the level of potential development as determined through problem solving under adult guidance, or in collaboration with

---

[1] https://youtu.be/Y55UtB2S4x4.

more capable peers" [21]. In other words, Vygotsky distinguishes between what a learner can do without guidance and what he or she can do with guidance–with guidance, learners develop much faster. The skilled instructor is able to carefully monitor the student and adjusts the level of guidance given.

Studies have explored the perception of tactile stimuli over various parts of the body indicating possible challenges in term of sensitivity as well as difficulties in perceiving more than one stimulus. Researchers found that the accuracy of participants' judgments when counting up to seven simultaneous vibrotactile stimuli, decreased linearly as the number of stimuli increased [6]. The scroll wheel of a typical DSLR involves 1°C of freedom–rotation left/right which corresponds to a linear range of values. Two-point discrimination studies suggest that the sensitivity of the skin differs depending on the part of the body because the skin receptors are not uniformly distributed across the body [15,22]. Skin drag with one tactor has been shown to provide improved accuracy and performance for recognizing symbols due to the combined sensation of pulling on the skin and point pressure [13]. Research into the perception of multiple tactors for skin drag has not been well documented in the literature.

Haptic interfaces have been widely used as tools for learning and guidance. Linked-Stick is a shape-changing device that supports communication between a teacher and student by mirroring movements of one stick onto another [18]. Research also suggest that haptic interfaces can be utilized as a means to guide users with examples including CAD tools to help users navigate 3D environments with haptic forcefeedback [9] and physical navigation for pedestrians by ear-pulling, handheld or embedded belt devices [10–12,16]. Research has also suggested that haptic interfaces can be utilized to communicate geometric shapes and characters to users by dragging a physical tactor across the skin of the forearm [13]. Tactile interfaces have also been utilized in contexts where voice communication is limited. Research on communication between kiteboarding instructor and student suggests that position of the hands can be communicated effectively through embedded vibrotactile actuators [19]. Tactile interfaces have also been utilized to teach snowboard skills and body position with real-time tactile instructions [20].

There are two recent examples of research focused specifically on cameras, which are important to discuss. The rich user interface (RUI) camera is aimed at finding alternatives to the prevalent paradigm of buttons and screens [5] and instead focusing on shape coding and tangible controls with dynamic affordances to navigate and control the camera. In the Photocation learnning system, users are invited to explore and learn about the parameter settings of the camera - shutter speed, aperture and ISO [17]. These parameters are represented in tangible forms so that people can physically manipulate and explore how these parameters interact with each other. These tangible forms act as tokens, which can be inserted into the sockets of the DLSR camera mock-up. While these examples provide interesting perspectives on the redesign of cameras, we strive to develop a more general system that can be used with existing cameras and to facilitate the learning process with minimal changes to the physical equipment already in use.

3 Method

We followed a research through design approach (RtD) [23] to investigate haptic feedback to complement the communication between the novice and the photography teacher for the exploration of camera settings. We now describe the design of HaptiCam and the user evaluations conducted including quantitative and qualitative studies.

3.1 Design Process

We conducted two semi-structured interviews, one with a photography instructor with 20 years of experience, and a second with a design student with 7 years experience in photography. It was stressed by both experts that the position of the hand and grip of a camera is crucial for taking a high-quality image; any instability or movement should be minimized. We created quick & dirty prototypes of the wearable learning tool concepts and conducted bodystorming sessions to get a better understanding of how the sketched ideas would fit the body and find a place within common photography practices (see Fig. 2). Through this design activity, it became clear that the forearm was the most appropriate area of the body to deliver tactile feedback. First and foremost, the most sensitive areas of the body such as the hands and fingers, are both occupied with holding and stabilizing the camera. Furthermore, implementing wearables for the hands and fingers did not seem feasible or practical, since such wearables would restrict the user interaction with the camera. Secondly, the photographer needs to hold their arms close to the body to stabilize the camera, which made the chest and abdomen area unfit for placing wearable learning tools. Thirdly, the remaining body areas were less sensitive than the forearm. These considerations led to the HaptiCam prototype in its current form.

3.2 HaptiCam System

HaptiCam is designed to facilitate the one-to-one communication between the novice and instructor (see Fig. 3). In other words, we aim to support Zone of Proximal Development activities by tying the learner and the more competent peer closer together by offloading the parameter values from the visual to the haptic perception channel. The system is a wearable sleeve with two embedded motorized slide potentiometers. Tactors made from a small piece of firm latex rubber was mounted to the motorized slide potentiometers so that they remain in contact with the skin of the forearm. The position of one is controlled by the novice user's camera and the other controlled by the instructor's camera. The system enables the novice to compare his settings with the settings of the

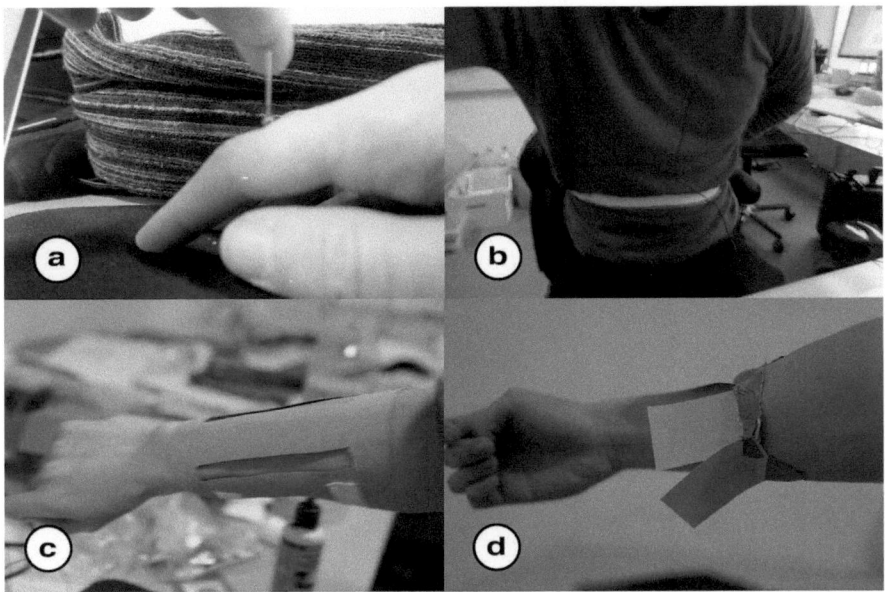

Fig. 2. Shows the bodystorming exercise with the quick & dirty prototypes of the wearable learning tools. a) skin-drag with a needle along the finger. b) a belt that loosens or tighten according to the aperture setting. c) early version of HaptiCam. d) a wearable device for the peripheral vision, it opens or closes accordingly to the aperture settings.

instructor allowing the novice to follow the thought process of the photography instructor as the instructor changes the settings while scrolling the control wheel. The device allows the photography instructor to be implicit in his or her communication and allows the instructor to focus vocal communication on other aspects of photography such as composition.

Two Sony cameras were used in HaptiCam, a Sony NEX-6 and A6000, which can be controlled with a prebuilt remote control application and interfaced with the Sony Remote Control API beta SDK. We developed a Processing sketch running on a laptop, which sends Remote Procedure Calls to the camera to read and write settings to the camera. More specifically, an API call in form of an HTTP request with a JSON object is sent to the camera. Subsequently, an HTTP response with a JSON object is sent from the camera. The response JSON object contains data about the parameter values of the camera depending on the get request. For example, a getFNumber API call will return the current aperture value or F number in a JSON object. Both the HTTP requests and responses are handled in Processing. Finally, In order to control the motorized slide potentiometer with the aperture values setting, the Processing sketch communicates to an Arduino microcontroller through serial communication.

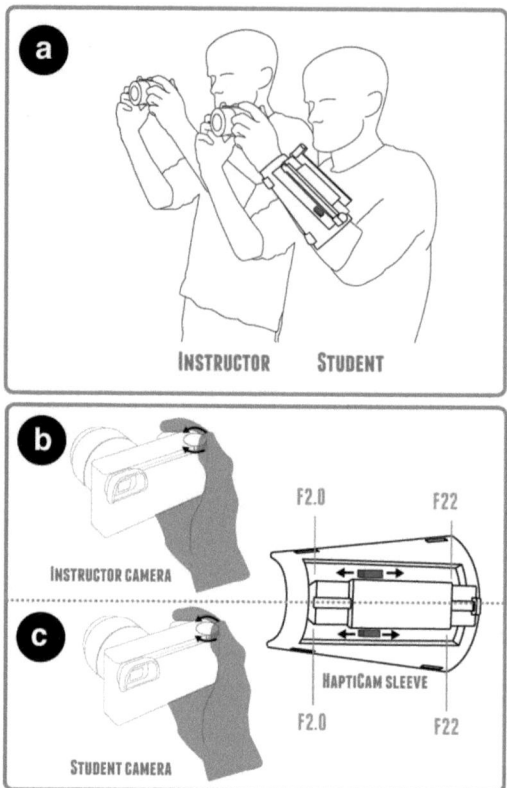

Fig. 3. (a) instructor and student scenario with student wearing the HaptiCam sleeve. (b) aperture settings manipulated on the instructor camera result in movement of the tactor on the upper channel of the HaptiCam sleeve. (c) aperture settings manipulated on the student camera result in movement of the tactor on the lower channel of the HaptiCam sleeve.

3.3 Qualitative Study - Novice and Instructor

We evaluated how haptics complements the communication between photography novice and instructor in term of setting the parameters. Four test participants were divided over two study sessions–two photography experts and two novices. Design students served as novice users and expert photographers with some teaching experience took the role of instructors.

We began with a short interview to assess the skills and knowledge level of the novice photographer. Participants were asked questions to examine their understanding of shutter speed, aperture, and ISO. Furthermore, the test participants were briefly shown how to interact with the camera. Subsequently, HaptiCam was presented as a learning tool that helps to feel the settings of the novice and instructor cameras in real-time. The test participants were encouraged to try the learning device for five minutes in order to get familiar with the haptic sensation. During the study, the test participants were asked to take pictures of their own projects. Here, the instructor is instructed to help the novice. After the study, we conducted a focus group interview with the test participants. This was on the basis that we wanted the novice and the instructor to reflect on the answers of the other. Furthermore, the test participants were asked to reflect on their experience with HaptiCam as a communication tool.

3.4 Quantitative Study

We evaluated the accuracy and the time to arrive at the target position. The users were asked to match the tactor position representing their settings with the tactor representing the settings of the instructor. The time to reach the target was measured and compared with the same series of targets given through voice requests. We recruited five people from a university between 25 to 29 years old. HaptiCam was attached on the underside of the forearm. We first vocally asked the test participants to scroll through a sequence of ten different aperture values with the haptic device turned off. For each step of the sequence, we measured the time it took for changing from one aperture to another with the only indication being the visual display on the body of the camera. Subsequently, participants were asked to scroll through an identical sequence of aperture values using the HaptiCam device. Here, we positioned the tactors to correspond to certain aperture values of the sequence. Participants were instructed to match the aperture setting through the haptic device by matching the position of the tactors.

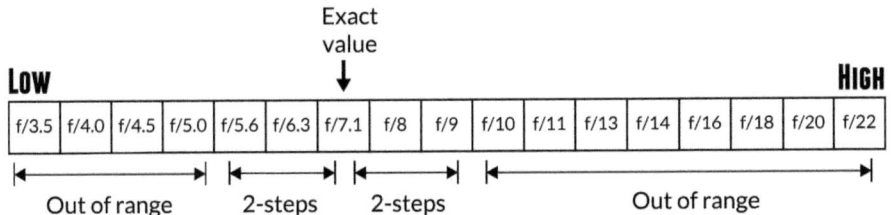

Fig. 4. Aperture steps for Sony a6000 and NEX6 cameras. In the study, the target value was considered achieved when the participant matched the target value within 2 stops.

The results suggest that using HaptiCam is slower compared to voice communication, as shown in Fig. 5. Furthermore, the average to set the aperture value is *9.77 s* for haptic and *4.48 s* for vocal. This means that it takes nearly twice the amount of time to set the aperture value through the haptic matching as shown in Fig. 5. In terms of accuracy, the test participants were able to get the wiper within range *62%* of the time and in other cases were within 2 f-stops.

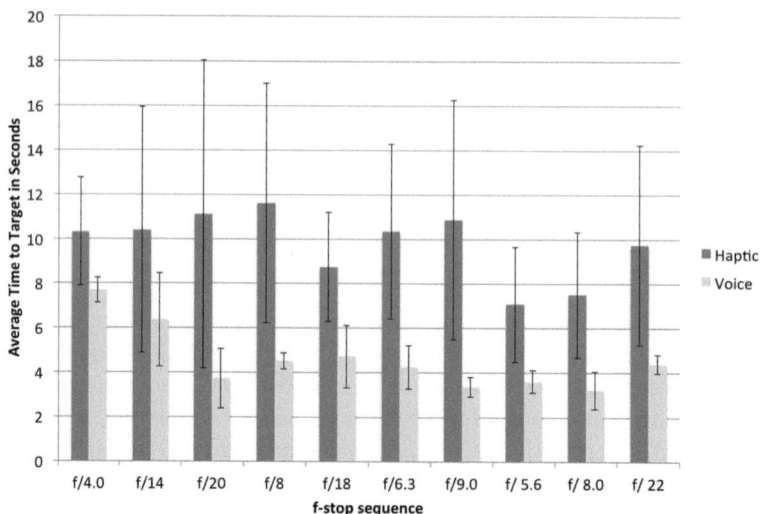

Fig. 5. Average time to reach target f-stop value using voice vs. haptic modalities.

3.5 Expert Review - Photography Instructor

The system was reviewed by two photography instructors to gain insights about how it could fit into photography teaching practice.

The instructors responded positively to the concept and appreciated the qualities of haptic communication. One elaborated that, it could be helpful for those students who are unable to visualize the parameters, noting that it is difficult to for some student to visualize that the different mechanics have an impact on the exposure value. In this case, the visualization of a closing and opening aperture and the click movements of the shutter, which are two completely different physical changes. His students found it difficult to connect with brightness/exposure of the picture. The second instructor also responded positively that the prototype seemed to fit well on the forearm, without interfering with the way one should hold the camera.

While there were some positive aspects in the prototype, there are also some issues that needed to be addressed: First and foremost, the prototype has to incorporate all four aspects, in order to be an effective learning tool. That is, it has to displays the aperture, shutter speed, ISO and exposure at the same time. According to the instructor, it will make it possible for novices to infer the causality between their action and the results of the final picture. In other words, how the shutter speed, ISO, and aperture, altogether have an impact on the final exposure value.

4 Results

In this section, we briefly present the quantitative and qualitative results from the user studies. Finally, we describe the review of the prototype with the photography teachers.

Some issues were identified during the qualitative study. The novice photographers remarked that they could not feel the slider when it was resting. In addition, it was difficult for the novice photographer to remember, where the instructor had placed his slider. In order to make it present in his tactile attention, the novice photographer asked the instructor to turn the camera dial in order to wiggle the instructor's slider. Secondly, the novice mentioned it was difficult to make an exact match between his slider and the instructor's slider. The novice elaborated that it could be due to the angle that the device sitting on the on the forearm. It other words, he thought that the angle of the device can make the position of the slider feel higher or lower than they actually are. The photographer instructor, however, pointed out that it was not important whether or not the novice could find the exact aperture value. Rather, he found it more important that the novice was in the same range and that they would learn how to explore values across the range of settings.

In measuring the learning system, the quantitative data showed that the haptic request was much slower than the vocal request. However, the data also shows that the test participants' performance gradually improved. For example, two of the average time for the haptic request in the columns f/5.6 and f/8.0 are lower than the average vocal time for f.4.0, as shown in Fig. 5. Furthermore, the test participants seemed to be improving in both short and long jumps. It would be interesting to conduct a more extensive study to understand how the performance changes over time as the participants become more proficient with HaptiCam.

During the review with the photography instructors, it was mentioned that all the parameter and the exposure values should be displayed simultaneously. Designing for learning of the relationship between elements, one cannot design for isolated elements. Rather, it seems that all the elements should be included simultaneously and designed holistically. In other words, the relationship between the elements are lost when isolating the elements. In would be interesting to take a more holistic approach to designing a photography learning system for future studies.

5 Discussion

Key findings from the evaluations raised attention to expectations in the communication between instructor and student as well as insights about resolution and sensations created by the haptic communication system.

5.1 Novice Presumptions

It was interesting to find that the instructor and novice come with different presumptions and expectations for giving and receiving guidance in general.

Whether instruction is given through voice commands or tactile cues, the novice is often hypersensitive and tries to match very precisely to the instructor. However, the instructor mentioned that precision was not important as long the novice was somewhat close to the indicated setting. This observation seems surprising as one would normally assume that a novice would not be sensitive to the fine points. When observing the extremely fine controls offered by the camera interface, it is not surprising that the novice would assume that they should aim to master this level of detail.

5.2 Resolution of the Prototype

In line with the previous discussion, it is also important to discuss the haptic resolution of the prototype. The prototype could represent a wide range of very granular aperture values, which seemed to give the impression that the novice should be precise in setting the parameter. The instructor in our study claimed that being somewhat close to the target, but not matching exactly was sufficient. Considering this, the camera settings could be presented differently, for example, instead of having a high resolution as the current system, one could utilize three vibrotactile motors on the forearm to signal low, medium, and high in only 3 positions as in previous work [19]. Furthermore, the aperture number could be suppressed early in the lessons so the student would not focus on the precise values, but after becoming proficient, the more detailed settings could be shown. Recent studies on tangible self-report devices examined accuracy of user input across various input devices including a rotary potentiometer, which is similar to the rotary knob of the digital camera [3]. Considering the additional feedback provided by HaptiCAM, it would be interesting to test whether and how such feedback could improve the input accuracy of self-report devices.

5.3 Disappearing Haptic Sensation

In the user studies, it was mentioned by test participants that the haptic sensation seemed like it disappeared when the wiper was resting on the skin, whereas it became noticeable again when moving. Previous research suggests that tactile stimulus fades rapidly and involves a fading sensory trace [7]. We first tried to address this issue by attaching a vibration motor to the tactors to ensure the users would continually sense the position. Although the wipers become slightly more noticeable when resting, they also resulted in aggressive noises and seemed to diminish the comparative effect of the two tactors. As noted in [4], additional anchor points might enrich the accuracy of tactile cues, and with HaptiCam, it seems that the two tactors provided dynamic anchor points and acceptable guidance. In future work, we plan to investigate strategies for these dynamic anchor points to improve accuracy. One simple strategy is to make the tactors wiggle slightly so that the user is more aware of their location. We are currently exploring this technique as initial indications suggest that if the amplitude of the wiggle movement is too high, it can be described as a mild tickling sensation and thus negatively impacting acceptance. Clearly, it also has to be implemented in a manner that does not interfere with the positioning movements of the wiper. We intend to explore how the wiggling of the tactor can be implemented in future work. Work on tactile communication through a shape-changing interface [1] targeted the feet with findings suggesting that haptic sensations can also be delivered with pressure and patterns of movement on the skin instead of sensations focused on discreet points [8].

5.4 Position on the Forearm

During the review with the photography instructor, his colleague suggested that the device could sit on the underside of the forearm. He elaborated that on the upper side of his forearm, he felt the wiper was sliding on top of the hairs instead of his skin. However, it also seems that the skin is more sensitive on the underside than on the upper side of the forearm. Besides the sensitivity of the skin, there are also other reasons for placing it on the underside. That is, the underside of the forearm is facing inwards when holding the camera. This means that it creates opportunities for designing a haptic device that can be visually seen in the periphery of the user's attention. In others words, the visual periphery could be considered to a larger extent in the design process.

5.5 Differences in Performance with Haptic Cues

Participants differed in their speed and accuracy of reaching the target. The standard deviation of the average time to target using HaptiCam was considerably higher than the average vocal time. We observed some of the participants overshooting the target and then overcorrecting, resulting in oscillating around the target value before settling on the target position. In future studies, we will examine how this oscillating behavior changes over time and may try additional techniques to reduce this, perhaps by combining audible cues with haptics or through a confirmation pulse when the target is achieved as discussed in [19].

In terms of differences in accuracy, HaptiCam led to fairly positive results– 78% of the haptic events resulted in participants perceiving the stimulus and then achieving the target. However, we noticed that some participants would perceive a new target event through a perceived movement of the tactor, and they would look at the HaptiCam prototype mounted on their forearms as if to confirm the haptic sensation. While this did not occur in all participants, this may suggest that visual confirmation could enhance the accuracy for some users, perhaps through visual cues in the periphery.

6 Limitations and Future Work

In this section, we examine the most salient limitations of this work including those related to technical features and the evaluations conducted.

In terms of technical limitations, the most obvious is the weight and size of the device, which results in a bulky system that is wearable, yet somewhat cumbersome. This was due to the size and weight of the actuators utilized in the prototype, which are re-purposed motorized slide potentiometers. While, we recognize that the size and weight impact the experience and acceptance of the prototype beyond the lab setting, with improvements to the design and placement of the actuators, it may be possible to reduce the size considerably.

The evaluations conducted in this paper are initial evaluations over a short time period. In the future, more long-term studies can be helpful in refining the prototype and identifying ways in which the system is appropriated by the users. It may be that the instructors will change the way they teach new photography students, and through field studies in photography classes, we may uncover new strategies to most effectively guide the users through the learning process. However, the present work has provided initial confirmation that the system is useful and desirable for instructors to some degree. Furthermore, in long-term studies, we will examine to what extent the learning process is improved and insights into how the system can be refined or used in combination with verbal cues and tasks.

For future work, we intend to conduct longitudinal studies to explore how teachers and students appropriate technology into their practices. We are also inspired to examine other contexts in which this haptic communication system could be useful including activities in which people are engaged in visually demanding activities or when voice communication is limited such as in kitesurfing, aviation, and other scenarios involving real-time coordination.

7 Conclusion

We presented a dual-skin-drag haptic system that lets instructors guide photography students through exposure-setting adjustments. Field studies with novices and experts confirmed that haptic cues can function as a shared reference—much like verbal instructions—but also revealed a critical mismatch: novices treated the cues as commands for exact settings, whereas instructors intended them as approximate guides. This suggests future designs must surface and reconcile learner assumptions to prevent reinforcing oversensitivity. Our quantitative results showed steady improvement over repeated trials under haptic feedback, underscoring the system's learning potential.

Haptic interaction is a fundamental modality for human engagement, carrying substantial informational content. While this work focuses on haptic feedback to guide photography novices, the findings have broader implications for social interaction and collaborative learning. The observed mismatch between an instructor's intent and a novice's precise interpretation, for instance, highlights that haptic communication is not merely a technical channel but a social one. This perspective suggests that understanding the role of haptic feedback can enhance performance and foster shared understanding, which is crucial for developing more effective collaborative systems between people and other social contexts including collaboration and communication in human-robot interaction [2].

References

1. Alexander, J., et al.: Grand challenges in shape-changing interface research. In: Proceedings of the 2018 CHI Conference on Human Factors in Computing Systems, CHI 2018, pp. 1–14. ACM, New York, NY, USA (2018). https://doi.org/10.1145/3173574.3173873
2. Baraka, K., Alves-Oliveira, P., Ribeiro, T.: An extended framework for characterizing social robots. In: Jost, C. (ed.) Human-Robot Interaction. SSBN, vol. 12, pp. 21–64. Springer, Cham (2020). https://doi.org/10.1007/978-3-030-42307-0_2
3. van Berkel, N., Merritt, T., Bruun, A., Skov, M.B.: Tangible self-report devices: accuracy and resolution of participant input. In: Proceedings of the Sixteenth International Conference on Tangible, Embedded, and Embodied Interaction. TEI 2022, ACM, New York, NY, USA (2022). https://doi.org/10.1145/3490149.3501309
4. Cholewiak, R., Collins, A.: Vibrotactile localization on the arm: effects of place, space, and age **65**(7), 1058–1077 (2003).https://doi.org/10.3758/bf03194834, http://dx.doi.org/10.3758/bf03194834
5. Frens, J.W.: Designing for rich interaction: integrating form, interaction, and function (2006)
6. Gallace, A., Tan, H., Spence, C.: Numerosity judgments for tactile stimuli distributed over the body surface. Perception **35** (2006)
7. Gilson, E.Q., Baddeley, A.: Tactile short-term memory. Quart. J. Exp. Psychol. **21**(2), 180–184 (1969)
8. Hansen, K.L., et al.: Feetback: providing haptic directional cues through a shape-changing floor. In: Nordic Human-Computer Interaction Conference. NordiCHI 2022, ACM, New York, NY, USA (2022). https://doi.org/10.1145/3546155.3546653, https://doi-org.zorac.aub.aau.dk/10.1145/3546155.3546653
9. Haulrik, N., Petersen, R.M., Merritt, T.: CADLens: haptic feedback for navigating in 3D environments. In: Proceedings of the 2017 ACM Conference Companion Publication on Designing Interactive Systems, DIS 2017, pp. 127–131. Companion, Association for Computing Machinery, New York, NY, USA (2017). https://doi.org/10.1145/3064857.3079132
10. Hemmert, F., Hamann, S., Löwe, M., Wohlauf, A., Zeipelt, J., Joost, G.: Take me by the hand: haptic compasses in mobile devices through shape change and weight shift. In: Proceedings of the 6th Nordic Conference on Human-Computer Interaction: Extending Boundaries, NordiCHI 2010, pp. 671–674. ACM, New York, NY, USA (2010). https://doi.org/10.1145/1868914.1869001, http://doi.acm.org/10.1145/1868914.1869001
11. Heuten, W., Henze, N., Boll, S., Pielot, M.: Tactile wayfinder: a non-visual support system for wayfinding. In: Proceedings of the 5th Nordic Conference on Human-computer Interaction: Building Bridges, NordiCHI 2008 pp. 172–181. ACM, New York, NY, USA (2008). https://doi.org/10.1145/1463160.1463179, http://doi.acm.org/10.1145/1463160.1463179
12. Imamura, Y., Arakawa, H., Kamuro, S., Minamizawa, K., Tachi, S.: Hapmap: haptic walking navigation system with support by the sense of handrail. In: ACM SIGGRAPH 2011 Emerging Technologies, SIGGRAPH 2011, pp. 6:1–6:1. ACM, New York, NY, USA (2011). https://doi.org/10.1145/2048259.2048265, http://doi.acm.org/10.1145/2048259.2048265
13. Ion, A., Wang, E.J., Baudisch, P.: Skin drag displays: dragging a physical tactor across the user's skin produces a stronger tactile stimulus than vibrotactile. In: Proceedings of the 33rd Annual ACM Conference on Human Factors in Computing

Systems, CHI 2015, pp. 2501–2504. ACM, New York, NY, USA (2015). https://doi.org/10.1145/2702123.2702459, http://doi.acm.org.ez.statsbiblioteket.dk:2048/10.1145/2702123.2702459
14. Judge, A.: Mastering aperture, shutter speed, ISO and exposure: how they interact and affect each other. CreateSpace Independent Publishing Platform, January 2013, http://www.amazon.com/exec/obidos/redirect?tag=citeulike07-20&path=ASIN/1482314452
15. Klatzky, R.L., Lederman, S.J.: Touch. In: Weiner, I.B., Healy, A.F., Proctor, R.W. (eds.) Handbook of Psychology, Experimental Psychology, vol. 4, chap. 6, pp. 147–176. Wiley, Hoboken, New Jersey (2003)
16. Kojima, Y., Hashimoto, Y., Fukushima, S., Kajimoto, H.: Pull-navi: a novel tactile navigation interface by pulling the ears. In: ACM SIGGRAPH 2009 Emerging Technologies, SIGGRAPH 2009, pp. 19:1–19:1. ACM, New York, NY, USA (2009). https://doi.org/10.1145/1597956.1597975
17. Moser, K., Kiechle, M., Ryokai, K.: Photocation: tangible learning system for dslr photography. In: CHI 2012 Extended Abstracts on Human Factors in Computing Systems, CHI EA 2012, pp. 1691–1696. ACM, New York, NY, USA (2012). https://doi.org/10.1145/2212776.2223694
18. Nakagaki, K., Inamura, C., Totaro, P., Shihipar, T., Akikyama, C., Shuang, Y., Ishii, H.: Linked-stick: conveying a physical experience using a shape-shifting stick. In: Proceedings of the 33rd Annual ACM Conference Extended Abstracts on Human Factors in Computing Systems, CHI EA 2015, pp. 1609–1614. ACM, New York, NY, USA (2015). https://doi.org/10.1145/2702613.2732712, http://doi.acm.org.ez.statsbiblioteket.dk:2048/10.1145/2702613.2732712
19. Schmidt, A., Kleemann, M., Merritt, T., Selker, T.: Tactile communication in extreme contexts: exploring the design space through kiteboarding. In: Abascal, J., Barbosa, S., Fetter, M., Gross, T., Palanque, P., Winckler, M. (eds.) INTERACT 2015. LNCS, vol. 9299, pp. 37–54. Springer, Cham (2015). https://doi.org/10.1007/978-3-319-22723-8_4
20. Spelmezan, D.: An investigation into the use of tactile instructions in snowboarding. In: Proceedings of the 14th International Conference on Human-computer Interaction with Mobile Devices and Services, MobileHCI 2012, pp. 417–426. ACM, New York, NY, USA (2012). https://doi.org/10.1145/2371574.2371639, http://doi.acm.org.ez.statsbiblioteket.dk:2048/10.1145/2371574.2371639
21. Vygotsky, L.S.: Interaction between learning and development. In: Mind in society: The development of higher psychological processes, chap. 4, pp. 79–91. Harvard University Press, Cambridge, MA (1978)
22. Weinstein, S.: Intensive and extensive aspects of tactile sensitivity as a function of body part, sex, and laterality. In: Kenshalo, D.R. (ed.) The skin senses, pp. 195–222. Thomas, Springfield, IL (1968)
23. Zimmerman, J., Forlizzi, J., Evenson, S.: Research through design as a method for interaction design research in HCI. In: Proceedings of the SIGCHI Conference on Human Factors in Computing Systems, CHI 2007, pp. 493–502. ACM, New York, NY, USA (2007). https://doi.org/10.1145/1240624.1240704, http://dx.doi.org/10.1145/1240624.1240704

Optimizing Prosthetic Wrist Movement: A Model Predictive Control Approach

Francesco Schetter[1], Shifa Sulaiman[1(✉)] , Shoby George[2], Paolino De Risi[1], and Fanny Ficuciello[1]

[1] Department of Information Technology and Electrical Engineering, Università degli Studi di Napoli Federico II, Claudio, 21, 80125 Napoli, Italy
ssajmech@gmail.com
[2] Genrobotic Innovations Pvt., Ltd., Kazhakkoottam, Kerala, India

Abstract. The integration of advanced control strategies into prosthetic hands is essential to improve their adaptability and performance. In this study, we present an implementation of a Model Predictive Control (MPC) strategy to regulate the motions of a soft continuum wrist section attached to a tendon-driven prosthetic hand with less computational effort. MPC plays a crucial role in enhancing the functionality and responsiveness of prosthetic hands. By leveraging predictive modeling, this approach enables precise movement adjustments while accounting for dynamic user interactions. This advanced control strategy allows for the anticipation of future movements and adjustments based on the current state of the prosthetic device and the user's intentions. Kinematic and dynamic modelings are performed using Euler-Bernoulli beam and Lagrange's methods respectively. Through simulation and experimental validations, we demonstrate the effectiveness of MPC in optimizing wrist articulation and user control. Our findings suggest that this technique significantly improves the prosthetic hand's dexterity, making movements more natural and intuitive. This research contributes to the field of robotics and biomedical engineering by offering a promising direction for intelligent prosthetic systems.

Keywords: Model predictive controller · Soft continuum wrist section · Prosthetic hand · Soft robotics

1 Introduction

Soft robotic prostheses [1] represent a significant breakthrough, offering individuals with limb disabilities a more comfortable and natural range of motions compared to conventional rigid prosthetics. The incorporation of soft continuum components enables intricate movements, making these devices suitable for a wide array of applications. Additionally, elastic wires integrated into these soft sections function like tendons, providing flexibility, lightweight characteristics, cost-effectiveness, and the ability to endure substantial tensile forces [2].

Model predictive control (MPC) is essential in the development of prosthetic hands as it enables a more intuitive and seamless interaction between the user and the device. By forecasting the necessary actions and adjusting the control inputs accordingly, this approach ensures that the prosthetic hand can execute complex movements with precision. This capability is particularly important for users who require fine motor skills for daily activities, as it allows for smoother transitions and greater adaptability to different scenarios.

Furthermore, the integration of MPC strategy in prosthetic hands contributes to the overall safety and reliability of these devices. By continuously monitoring the system's performance and making real-time adjustments, potential issues can be identified and addressed before they lead to malfunctions or accidents. Major contributions of this work are as follows:

- Kinematic and dynamic modelings of a soft continuum wrist using Euler-Bernoulli beam and Lagrange's method respectively.
- Development of an MPC scheme for the wrist motions.
- Simulation studies to demonstrate the advantages of the proposed controller.
- Experimental validations proving the effectiveness of the proposed controller during real-time implementations with reduced computational effort.

The implementation of MPC plays a crucial role in the domain of prosthetic hand motion management. This significance arises from its ability to optimize movements and functionalities of prosthetic devices, ensuring that they respond accurately to the user's intentions and environmental conditions. By utilizing predictive algorithms, this control method can anticipate future states and adjust the prosthetic's actions accordingly, leading to more natural and efficient hand movements. Moreover, MPC enhances the adaptability of prosthetic hands by allowing for real-time adjustments based on sensory feedback. This capability is essential for users who require precise control over their prosthetic devices, as it enables the hands to perform complex tasks with greater ease and reliability. The integration of such advanced control strategies not only improves the overall user experience but also contributes to the development of more sophisticated and responsive prosthetic technologies. In addition, the relevance of MPC extends beyond mere motion management; it also encompasses the potential for learning and improvement over time. As users interact with their prosthetic hands, the control system can gather data and refine its predictive models, leading to enhanced performance tailored to individual preferences and needs. This continuous learning process is vital for the evolution of prosthetic technology, ultimately aiming to provide users with a level of functionality that closely resembles that of a natural hand.

Spinelli *et al.* [3] proposed a modular MPC framework for soft continuum manipulators, integrating internal and external constraints. The approach successfully implemented Task-Space MPC, improving dynamic control. The method relies on Piece-wise Constant Curvature (PCC) assumptions, which may limit its applicability to highly deformable soft robots. Johnson *et al.* [4] introduced a hybrid modeling approach, combining machine learning with first-principles models to enhance MPC performance. The method improved control accuracy by 52% on average. The reliance on large datasets for training deep learning models may hinder real-time adaptability. Pal et al. [5] proposed a data-driven MPC design using Bayesian optimization for cable-actuated soft robots. Instead of modeling complex dynamics, the approach searches for an optimal low-dimensional prediction model iteratively. The method required multiple iterations to converge, which may limit real-time applications.

Yang et al. [6] introduced a distributionally robust MPC (DRMPC) scheme based on neural network modeling to achieve trajectory tracking control for robotic manipulators with state and control torque constraints. Their approach converted motion data into a linear prediction model and applies chance constraints to optimize control decisions. The reliance on statistical analysis of modeling errors may introduce computational complexity, limiting real-time applications. Huang et al. [7] developed a physics-learning hybrid modeling approach combining absolute nodal coordinate formulation (ANCF) with multilayer neural networks (MLNN) to enhance dynamic control accuracy. The method significantly reduced tracking errors and improves real-time simulation efficiency. The complexity of hybrid modeling required extensive parameter tuning, making implementation challenging for new robotic designs.

Gonzales et al. [8] introduced a multi-agent receding-horizon feedback motion planning approach using Probably Approximately Correct Nonlinear MPC (PAC-NMPC). The method enhanced formation control and obstacle avoidance in dynamic environments while accounting for model and measurement uncertainty. The computational complexity of PAC-NMPC limited scalability for large multi-robot teams. Kalibala et al. [9] developed a deep neural network (DNN)-based MPC framework for pressure-driven vine robots. Their approach significantly improves control performance and computational efficiency, reducing computation time by a factor of 11 compared to traditional nonlinear first-principles models. The data-driven nature of the model requires extensive training, which may limit adaptability to new robotic designs. Chen et al. [10] proposed Vision-Language Model Predictive Control (VLMPC), integrating vision-language models (VLMs) with MPC for robotic manipulation planning. The approach enhances environmental perception and improves trajectory generation accuracy. The computational overhead of integrating vision-language models can restrict real-time applications.

An extensive examination of the literature on soft continuum robots revealed that soft robots face multiple challenges, including inadequate kinematic and dynamic modeling methods, suboptimal control strategies, and increased computational requirements. This research introduces modeling techniques and control strategies designed to develop an MPC for a soft wrist component incorporated into a prosthetic hand, with the goal of enhancing response times and reducing computational demands. The organization of this paper is as follows: Sect. 2 provides an overview of the modeling methodologies employed. The MPC strategy is presented in Sect. 3. Section 4 highlights the results from simulations and experiments. Lastly, Sect. 5 offers a conclusion to the study.

2 Mathematical Model of a Soft Wrist Section

The proposed design for the soft wrist segment, as outlined in [11], consists of five rigid discs, five springs, and five flexible tendons attached to a prosthetic hand named 'PRISMA HAND II' [12], as shown in Fig. 1(a). The dimensions of the rigid discs incorporated in this wrist segment are presented in Fig. 1(b). Furthermore, Fig. 1(c) illustrates the bending configuration of the soft wrist segment with length l, radius r, and a bending angle of α. The rigid discs incorporate the springs and tendons, which are attached to a stable platform. By exerting precise tensions on each tendon via a motor, the intended movements of the wrist segment can be achieved. Four peripheral tendons are incorporated to enable rotational movements in four different directions. Tendons one and two are engaged for radial deviation of the wrist, while tendons four and five facilitated movements in the ulnar direction. Additionally, tendons one and four are responsible for extension motions, whereas flexion is managed by tendons two and five. The lowest disc (disc one) was secured to a stable platform, and the highest disc (disc five) was connected to the hand. Even though the wrist section is actuated using four tendons, there is also a middle tendon used as a primary backbone to provide stability during motions. Figure 2 illustrates the constructed model of the wrist section combined with a prosthetic hand. Variations in tendon tensions result in distinct bending moments on the soft wrist segment, enabling its behavior to be represented as a cantilever beam under bending stress. The placement of the end effector relative to the wrist's curvature is established based on bending beam theory, as indicated in [13].

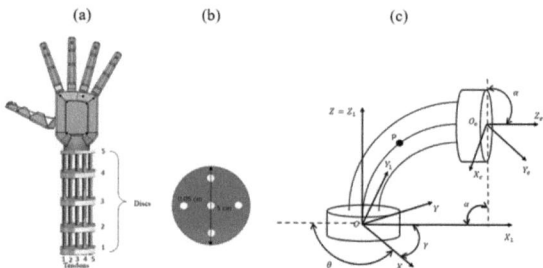

Fig. 1. Soft wrist section (a) Conceptual design of wrist section attached to hand (b) Dimension of disc (c) Bending structure of wrist section.

The transformation matrix, T of the last disc five with respect to the base disc one is expressed as follows:

$$T = \begin{bmatrix} R & P \\ 0 & 1 \end{bmatrix} \quad (1)$$

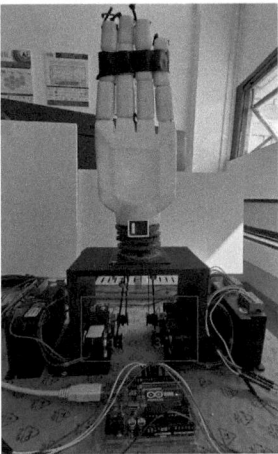

Fig. 2. Fabricated model.

where rotation matrix, R is obtained as given in Eq. (2)

$$R = Rot(Z,\gamma)Rot(Y,\alpha)Rot(Z,-\gamma) = \begin{bmatrix} c^2\gamma c\alpha + s^2\gamma & c\gamma s\gamma c\alpha - c\gamma s\gamma & c\gamma s\alpha \\ c\gamma s\gamma c\alpha - c\gamma s\gamma & s^2\gamma c\alpha + c^2\gamma & s\gamma s\alpha \\ -c\gamma s\alpha & -s\gamma c\alpha & c\alpha \end{bmatrix} \quad (2)$$

Translational matrix P is given in Eq. (3).

$$P = [x\ y\ z]^T = \left[\tfrac{l}{\alpha}(1-\cos\tfrac{s\alpha}{l})\cos\gamma\ \tfrac{l}{\alpha}(1-\cos\tfrac{s\alpha}{l})\sin\gamma\ \tfrac{l}{\alpha}\sin\tfrac{s\alpha}{l}\right] \quad (3)$$

The kinetic energy of the wrist section motions is obtained by calculating the derivative of the positions given in Eq. (3). The velocities of motion can be expressed as follows:

$$\begin{cases} \dfrac{dx}{dt} = \dfrac{1}{\alpha}[s\sin\dfrac{s\alpha}{l}\cos\gamma - \dfrac{l}{\alpha}(1-\cos\dfrac{s\alpha}{l})\cos\gamma]\dfrac{d\alpha}{dt} \\ \qquad - \dfrac{1}{\alpha}(1-\cos\dfrac{s\alpha}{l})\sin\gamma\dfrac{d\gamma}{dt} \\ \dfrac{dy}{dt} = \dfrac{1}{\alpha}[s\sin\dfrac{s\alpha}{l}\sin\gamma - \dfrac{l}{\alpha}(1-\cos\dfrac{s\alpha}{l})\sin\gamma]\dfrac{d\alpha}{dt} \\ \qquad + \dfrac{1}{\alpha}(1-\cos\dfrac{s\alpha}{l})\cos\gamma\dfrac{d\gamma}{dt} \\ \dfrac{dz}{dt} = \dfrac{1}{\alpha}(s\cos\dfrac{s\alpha}{l} - \dfrac{l}{\alpha}\sin\dfrac{s\alpha}{l})\dfrac{d\alpha}{dt} \end{cases} \quad (4)$$

The kinetic energy of the primary backbone (central tendon), E_{k1} of the soft wrist can be obtained as follows:

$$E_{k1} = \frac{1}{2}\int_0^l \left[(\tfrac{dx}{dt})^2 + (\tfrac{dy}{dt})^2 + (\tfrac{dz}{dt})^2\right]\rho A ds \quad (5)$$

where ρ and A represent density and cross-sectional area of the wrist section. Substituting Eq. (4) in Eq. (5), we obtained the kinetic energy as given in Eq. (6).

$$E_{k1} = \frac{1}{6}m_1 l^2 (\frac{d\alpha}{dt})^2 K_1 + \frac{1}{8}m_1 l^2 (\frac{d\gamma}{dt})^2 K_2 \tag{6}$$

where m_1 is the mass of the primary backbone and K_1 and K_2 are the kinetic energy equivalent factors. Kinetic energy coefficients, K_1 and K_2 are determined as given in Eqs. (7) and (8).

$$K_1 = (\alpha^3 + 6\alpha - 12\sin\alpha + 6\alpha\cos\alpha)/\alpha^5 \tag{7}$$

$$K_2 = (6\alpha 8 \sin\alpha + \sin 2\alpha)/\alpha^3 \tag{8}$$

From Eq. (7) and (8), we can express K_1 and K_2 as a function of bending angle α. The two Eqs. can be simplified using least square fit, as given in Eqs. (9) and (10):

$$K_1 = -0.00426\alpha^2 - 0.00277\alpha + 0.15085 \tag{9}$$

$$K_2 = -0.05567\alpha^3 + 0.2328\alpha^2 + 0.006216\alpha - 0.00406 \tag{10}$$

The transformation between cartesian and joint spaces can be expressed as follows:

$$\begin{cases} q_1 = r\alpha\cos(\gamma) \\ q_2 = r\alpha\cos(-\gamma + \theta) \\ q_3 = r\alpha\cos(\gamma + \theta) \end{cases} \tag{11}$$

where, $q_i, (i = 1, 2, 3)$ is the length of each driving wire and r is the distance from each secondary backbone to the primary backbone (the secondary backbone tendons are equidistant from the primary backbone), and $\theta = 2\pi/3$. The driving velocities are obtained by performing derivatives of Eq. (11), and obtained as follows:

$$\begin{cases} \frac{dq_1}{dt} = r\cos(\gamma)\frac{d\alpha}{dt} - r\alpha\sin(\gamma)\frac{d\gamma}{dt} \\ \frac{dq_2}{dt} = r\cos(-\gamma + \theta)\frac{d\alpha}{dt} + r\alpha\sin(-\gamma + \theta)\frac{d\gamma}{dt} \\ \frac{dq_3}{dt} = r\cos(\gamma + \theta)\frac{d\alpha}{dt} - r\alpha\sin(\gamma + \theta)\frac{d\gamma}{dt} \end{cases} \tag{12}$$

The secondary backbone consisted of four tendons. However, the tendons present on each side during motion are considered as a single tendon for the analysis. For example, if the tendons are rotating in ulnar deviation direction, tendons four and five are considered as a single tendon and tendons one and two are considered as two tendons itself. The total kinetic energy, E_{k2} of the secondary backbone consisted of four tendons are given in Eq. (13).

$$E_{k2} = E_{k11} + E_{k22} \tag{13}$$

where $E_{k11} = E_{k1}$ and the second component, E_{k22} arises from the driven kinetic energy as given in following Eq.:

$$E_{k22} = \frac{1}{2}m_1 \left[(\frac{dq_1}{dt})^2 + (\frac{dq_2}{dt})^2 + (\frac{dq_3}{dt})^2\right] \tag{14}$$

Substituting Eq. (12) in Eq. (14), we obtain the following Eqs. (15)–(18)

$$E_{k2} = \frac{1}{2}m_2\left[(\frac{d\alpha}{dt})^2 K_3 + \frac{d\alpha}{dt}\frac{d\gamma}{dt}K_4 + (\frac{d\gamma}{dt})^2 K_5\right] \tag{15}$$

$$K_3 = r^2\left[\cos^2(\gamma) + \cos^2(-\gamma+\theta) + \cos^2(\gamma+\theta)\right] \tag{16}$$

$$K_4 = r^2\alpha\left[-\sin(2\gamma) + \sin(2(-\gamma+\theta)) - \sin(2(\gamma+\theta))\right] \tag{17}$$

$$K_5 = r^2\alpha^2\left[\sin^2(\gamma) + \sin^2(-\gamma+\theta) + \sin^2(\gamma+\theta)\right] \tag{18}$$

where m_2 is the mass of the secondary backbone and K_3, K_4 and K_5 are kinetic energy equivalent factors. The kinetic energy of the discs can be obtained as:

$$E_{k3} = \frac{1}{2}m_3(\frac{d\alpha}{dt})^2 K_6 + \frac{1}{2}m_3(\frac{d\gamma}{dt})^2 K_7 \tag{19}$$

where, m_3 is the mass of a disk and K_6 and K_7 are kinetic energy equivalent factors. If n and h are determined, the kinetic energy equivalent factors K_6 and K_7 can be expressed as a function of bending angle α. Assuming that $n = 5$ and $h = 15\ mm$, the form of K_6 and K_7 can be simplified by using least square fit, shown as follows:

$$K_6 = (-0.00043\alpha^2 - 0.00031\alpha + 0.01435)/2 \tag{20}$$

$$K_7 = (-0.00394\alpha^3 + 0.01575\alpha^2 + 0.00131\alpha - 0.00047)/2 \tag{21}$$

For a continuum robot, the total potential energy is comprised of two components: elastic potential energy and gravitational potential energy. In this context, the gravitational potential energy can be considered negligible compared to the elastic potential energy. The elastic energy, E_p associated with the wrist section with Young's Modulus E and inertia I is given as follows:

$$E_p = \frac{2EI}{l}\alpha^2 \tag{22}$$

The Lagrange Eq. of the wrist section is expressed as follows:

$$\frac{d}{dt}\frac{\partial E_k}{\partial \dot{p}_j} - \frac{\partial E_k}{\partial p_j} + \frac{\partial E_p}{\partial p_j} = Q_j, (j=1,2) \tag{23}$$

where Q_j represents the generalized force of system, $E_k = E_{k1} + E_{k2} + E_{k3}$, $p_1 = \alpha$ and $p_2 = \gamma$. The dynamical Eq. of the wrist is obtained as follows:

$$\begin{bmatrix} M_{11} & M_{12} \\ M_{21} & M_{22} \end{bmatrix}\begin{bmatrix} \ddot{\alpha} \\ \ddot{\gamma} \end{bmatrix} + \begin{bmatrix} C_{11} & C_{12} & C_{13} \\ C_{21} & C_{22} & C_{23} \end{bmatrix}\begin{bmatrix} \dot{\alpha}^2 \\ \dot{\alpha}\dot{\gamma} \\ \dot{\gamma}^2 \end{bmatrix} + \begin{bmatrix} K_{11} & K_{12} \\ K_{21} & K_{22} \end{bmatrix}\begin{bmatrix} \alpha \\ \gamma \end{bmatrix} = \begin{bmatrix} D_{11} & D_{12} \\ D_{21} & D_{22} \end{bmatrix}\begin{bmatrix} F_1 \\ F_2 \end{bmatrix} \tag{24}$$

where M_{ij}, C_{ij}, K_{ij}, D_{ij} are moment of inertia, Coriolis, stiffness, actuation matrix elements respect to each rotation angle.

In the context of planar motion, where $\gamma = 0$, we determined the Eq. of motion as follows:

$$M(\alpha)\ddot{\alpha} + C(\alpha)\dot{\alpha}^2 + K\alpha = DF \tag{25}$$

where:

$$D = r\cos(\gamma)$$

$$K = \frac{4EI}{l}$$

$$C = -\frac{1}{6}(4m_2 l^2 \frac{\partial K_1}{\partial \alpha}) + 3m_2(\frac{\partial K_3}{\partial \alpha}) + 3m_3(\frac{\partial K_6}{\partial \alpha})$$

$$M = \frac{1}{3}(4m_2 l^2 K_1 + 3m_2 K_3 + 3m_3 K_6)$$

3 Inverse Dynamic Model Predictive Control Developed for the Soft Wrist Section

The advancement of prosthetic technology has increasingly focused on achieving natural and adaptive movement to enhance user experience and functionality. A crucial component of the method is the implementation MPC, particularly Inverse Dynamic Model Predictive Control, for managing the movements of soft wrist components in prosthetic hands. By utilizing predictive modeling, this approach enables precise, real-time adjustments to control inputs, significantly improving motion fluidity and responsiveness. Unlike traditional control methods, Inverse Dynamic MPC anticipates future states, allowing for smoother, more intuitive interactions that reduce cognitive load and enhance usability. The control strategy developed for the wrist section is shown in Fig. 3. Desired states such as bending angles (α) and rate of bending angles ($\dot{\alpha}$) are fed to the MPC block. Optimised output y and the predicted state values $\hat{\alpha}$ and $\dot{\hat{\alpha}}$ from the Model Predictive Control (MPC) are utilized to calculate the control law, $u = F$, and estimated $\hat{\tilde{M}}$ and $\hat{n}(\hat{\alpha}, \dot{\hat{\alpha}})$.

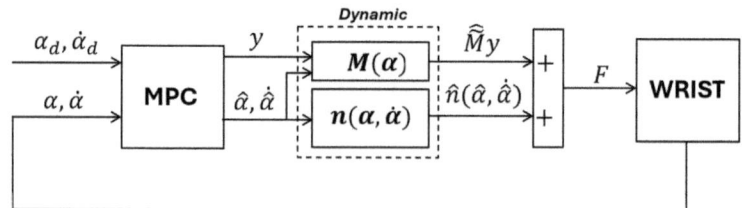

Fig. 3. Inverse Dynamic Model Predictive Control scheme.

We can rewrite dynamic equation of wrist section given in Eq. (25) as follows:

$$\tilde{M}\ddot{\alpha} + \tilde{C}(\alpha, \dot{\alpha})\dot{\alpha} + \tilde{K}\alpha = u \tag{26}$$

where $\tilde{M}(\alpha) = D^{-1}M(\alpha)$, $\tilde{C}(\alpha,\dot{\alpha}) = D^{-1}C(\alpha)\dot{\alpha}$, $\tilde{K} = D^{-1}K$. u is chosen as given in equation (27) for a feedback linearization control action.

$$u = \tilde{M}y + n(\alpha,\dot{\alpha}) \tag{27}$$

where $n(\alpha,\dot{\alpha}) = \tilde{C}(\alpha,\dot{\alpha})\dot{\alpha} + \tilde{K}\alpha$, and we can obtain optimised output, y as follows:

$$\ddot{\alpha} = y \tag{28}$$

From Eq. (28), we can compute the state space form as follows:

$$A = \begin{bmatrix} 0 & 0 \\ 1 & 0 \end{bmatrix}, B = \begin{bmatrix} 1 \\ 0 \end{bmatrix}, C = \begin{bmatrix} 1 & 0 \\ 0 & 1 \end{bmatrix}, D = 0 \tag{29}$$

The prediction and control horizons are established as $p = 10$ and $\nu = 5$. The cost function that the MPC aims to optimize is as follows:

$$J(z_k) = J_x(z_k) + J_{\Delta u}(z_k) + J_\varepsilon(z_k) \tag{30}$$

where,

$$J_x(z_k) = \sum_{j=1}^{n_x}\sum_{i=1}^{p}\left\{\frac{w_{i,j}^x}{s_j^x}[r_j(k+i|k) - x_j(k+i|k)]\right\}^2 \tag{31}$$

$$J_{\Delta u}(z_k) = \sum_{j=1}^{n_u}\sum_{i=0}^{p-1}\left\{\frac{w_{i,j}^{\Delta u}}{s_j^u}[u_j(k+i|k) - u_j(k+i-1|k)]\right\}^2 \tag{32}$$

$$J_\varepsilon(z_k) = \rho_\varepsilon \varepsilon_k 2 \tag{33}$$

where,

ε_k Slack variable at the control interval k
ρ_ε Constraint violation penalty weight
z_k QP decision variables vector
k Current control interval
p Prediction horizon
n_x Number of plant output variables
n_u Number of manipulated variables
s_j^x Scale factor for the jth plant output
s_j^u Scale factor for the jth MV
$w_{i,j}^x$ Tuning weight for the jth plant output at the ith prediction horizon step
$w_{i,j}^{\Delta u}$ Tuning weight for the jth MV movement at the ith prediction horizon step
$r_j(k+i|k)$ Reference value for the jth plant output at the ith prediction horizon step
$x(k+i|k)$ Predicted value of the jth plant output at the ith prediction horizon step

The KWIK active-set algorithm is employed to address the quadratic programming (QP) problem. The active constraints include a position constraint that limits motion to a maximum of $\pi/4$ radians and a rate of change for the manipulated variable to ensure a smoother signal. Additionally, the predicted state values $\hat{\alpha}$ and $\dot{\hat{\alpha}}$ from the Model Predictive Control (MPC) are utilized to calculate an estimated $\hat{n}(\hat{\alpha},\dot{\hat{\alpha}})$ and $\hat{\tilde{M}}$.

4 Results and Discussions

This research introduces an MPC tailored for the soft wrist of a prosthetic hand. The kinematic and dynamic modeling of the wrist are performed using Timoshenko beam theory. To evaluate the effectiveness of the proposed position controller while the soft wrist section is in motion with a payload, a series of simulations and experimental tests were conducted.

4.1 Simulation Study

The control scheme simulation is conducted using Simulink, a software platform based on MATLAB, on a PC equipped with an Intel Core Ultra 7 processor and 16 GB of RAM. The wrist segment is capable of moving along trajectories in the directions of radial deviation, ulnar deviation, flexion, and extension, as illustrated in Figs. 4 (a) - (h). The wrist segment is observed to flex from its initial position, as depicted in Fig. 4, achieving a final bending angle of 35^0 in the direction of ulnar deviation relative to disc 5, which is attached to the hand. Desired and obtained positions and velocities are shown in Fig. 5(a). Additionally, the

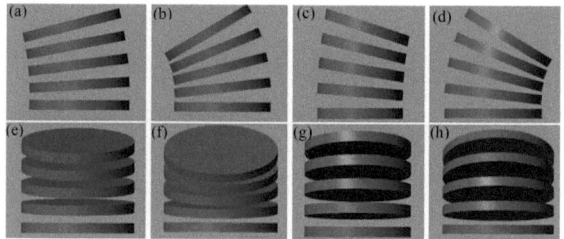

Fig. 4. Motion of wrist (a) Radial-1 (b) Radial-2 (c) Ulnar-1 (d) Ulnar-2 (e) Flexion-1 (f) Flexion-2 (g) Extension-1 (h) Extension-2.

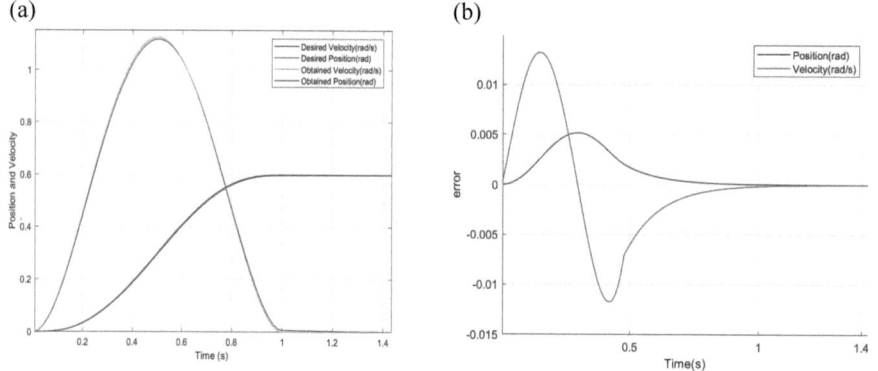

Fig. 5. (a) Comparison of response with reference signal (b) Error in motions during simulation.

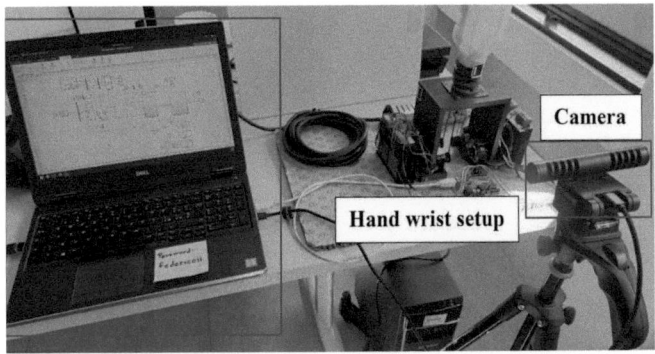

Fig. 6. Experimentation set up.

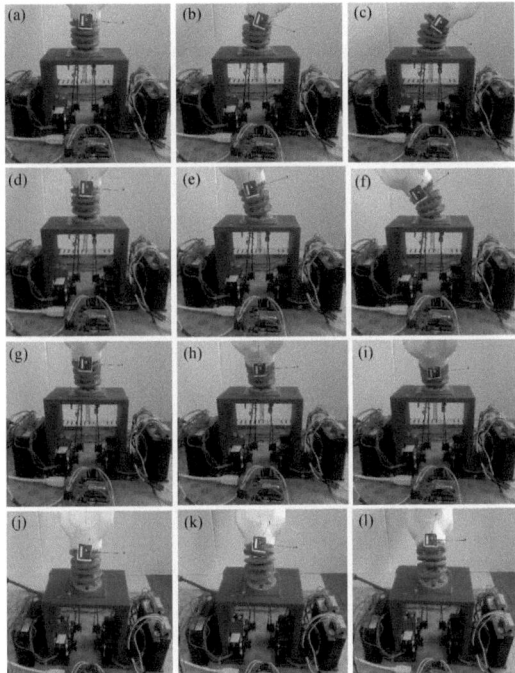

Fig. 7. Motion of the wrist section along with hand (a)-(c) Ulnar (d)-(f) Radial (g)-(i) Extension (j)-(l) Flexion.

discrepancies in positions and velocities recorded during the simulation are presented in Fig. 5(b). The values for Root Mean Square (RMSE), settling time, and steady state error are determined as 2.1×10^{-3} rad, 1.2 s, and 0.4×10^{-5} rad, respectively.

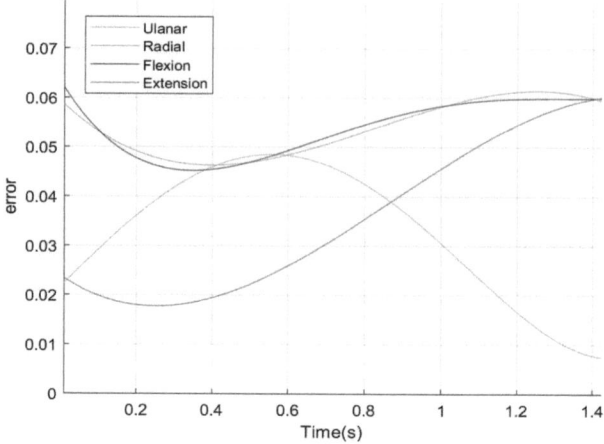

Fig. 8. Error of motions during experimentations.

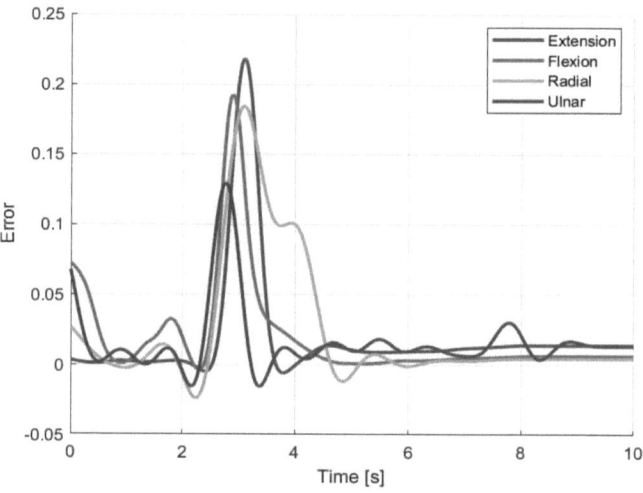

Fig. 9. Error of motions in presence of force during experimentations.

4.2 Experimental Validation

The experimental configuration for the developed wrist and hand model, along with its electronic components, is depicted in Fig. 6. An ArUco marker attached to the hand enabled the tracking of its poses during the experiments. The setup comprised four stepper motors, two motor drivers, a 3D depth camera, and an Arduino controller to facilitate real-time operations. Furthermore, ROS and MATLAB software were utilized for tracking the ArUco poses and implementing the control scheme, respectively. The hand's motion in all directions is illustrated in Fig. 7 (a) - (l), with the associated motion errors presented in Fig. 8. Throughout the experimentation, the average RMSE values for deflection, settling time, and steady-state error across all directions as recorded as: 6×10^{-2} rad, 1.35 s, and 6×10^{-2} rad, respectively. The findings clearly indicated that the error values observed during the experimental phase are significantly higher than those recorded in the simulation study, primarily due to the lower stiffness of the springs used in the wrist segment.

To evaluate the robustness of the proposed controller under external disturbances, an impulse force of 2 N was applied perpendicular to the wrist's motion at $t = 2$ s. As illustrated in Fig. 9, the tracking error increased immediately following the disturbance, reaching its peak shortly thereafter, and gradually diminished, stabilizing around $t = 5$ s for extension and flexion directions. However, radial and ulnar motions converged around 6.7 s and 8.6 s respectively.

5 Conclusion

An MPC system was developed utilizing a mathematical model derived from bending beam theory, specifically for the wrist section of a prosthetic hand. The proposed controller approach allowed the system to maintain the intended motion trajectories, effectively compensating for variations in the robot's physical properties and external environmental conditions. The integration of model improved controller efficiency by reducing computational time, while the MPC strategy contributed to a quicker response. Simulation results indicated that the proposed controller achieved a shorter settling time of less than 1.5 s, with the RMSE and steady-state errors remaining within acceptable limits. However, experimental RMSE values exceeded those from simulations, primarily due to inconsistencies in spring stiffness. Future research will focus on redesigning the wrist for greater structural integrity and enhancing controller strategies by integrating real-time sensor feedback to boost motion precision.

Acknowledgement. This work was supported by the Italian Ministry of Research under the complementary actions to the NRRP "Fit4MedRob - Fit for Medical Robotics" Grant (PNC0000007).

References

1. Jyothish, K.J., Mishra, S.: A survey on robotic prosthetics: neuroprosthetics, soft actuators, and control strategies. ACM Comput. Surv. **56**(8), 1–44 (2024). https://doi.org/10.1145/3648355
2. Gohari, M., Sulaiman, S., Schetter, F., Ficuciello, F.: A sliding mode controller design based on Timoshenko beam theory developed for a prosthetic hand wrist. In: Proceedings of the 2025 11th International Conference on Automation, Robotics, and Applications (ICARA), Italy, pp. 338–342. IEEE (2025)
3. Spinelli, F.A., Katzschmann, R.K.: A unified and modular model predictive control framework for soft continuum manipulators under internal and external constraints. In: Proceedings of the 2022 IEEE/RSJ International Conference on Intelligent Robots and Systems (IROS), Japan, pp. 9393–9400. IEEE (2022)

4. Johnson, C.C., Quackenbush, T., Sorensen, T., Wingate, D., Killpack, M.D.: Using first principles for deep learning and model-based control of soft robots. Front. Robot. AI **8**, 654398 (2021). https://doi.org/10.3389/frobt.2021.654398
5. Pal A., He T., Wei W.: Sample-efficient model predictive control design of soft robotics by bayesian optimization. arXiv preprint arXiv:2210.08780 (2022)
6. Yang, Y., Zhang, K., Chen, Z., Li, B.: Distributionally robust model predictive control for constrained robotic manipulators based on neural network modeling. Appl. Math. Mech. **45**(12), 2183–2202 (2024)
7. Huang, X., Rong, Y., Gu, G.: High-precision dynamic control of soft robots with the physics-learning hybrid modeling approach. IEEE/ASME Trans. Mechatron. (2024). https://doi.org/10.1109/TMECH.2024.3390169
8. Gonzales, M., Polevoy, A., Kobilarov, M., Moore, J.: Multi-agent feedback motion planning using probably approximately correct nonlinear model predictive control. arXiv preprint arXiv:2501.12234 (2025)
9. Kalibala, A., Nada, A.A., Ishii, H., El-Hussieny, H.: Real-time force/position control of soft growing robots: a data-driven model predictive approach. Nonlinear Eng. **14**(1), 20250099 (2025). https://doi.org/10.1515/nleng-2023-0121
10. Chen J., et al.: Vision-language model predictive control for manipulation planning and trajectory generation. arXiv preprint arXiv:2504.05225 (2025)
11. Sulaiman S., Menon, M., Schetter, F., Ficuciello, F.: Design, modelling, and experimental validation of a soft continuum wrist section developed for a prosthetic hand. In: Proceedings of the 2024 IEEE/RSJ International Conference on Intelligent Robots and Systems (IROS), pp. 11347–11354. IEEE (2024)
12. Liu, H., Ferrentino, P., Pirozzi, S., Siciliano, B., Ficuciello, F.: The PRISMA hand II: a sensorized robust hand for adaptive grasp and in-hand manipulation. In: Proceedings of the International Symposium on Robotics Research (ISRR), pp. 971–986. Springer, Cham (2019). https://doi.org/10.1007/978-3-030-95459-8_60
13. Howell, L.L.: Compliant Mechanism. McGraw-Hill, New York (2001)

Vision Based Hybrid IK Task Planning with Feedforward Neural Network for Collaborative Plant-Robot Interaction in Precision Farming

V. P. Tharun[1] and Abhra Roy Chowdhury[2(✉)]

[1] CATT Labs, University of Maryland, College Park, USA
[2] Department of Design and Manufacturing, Indian Institute of Science, Bangalore 560012, India
abhra@iisc.ac.in

Abstract. Collaborative robotic manipulators-based precision farming robots need to accurately reach a target plant and safely handle poses performing plant-centered operations like weeding and irrigation with minimal plant-robot interaction. Unwanted contacts could inhibit the potential growth of plants. In this paper, we propose a human behavior-based hybrid inverse kinematics solver reinforced with a task planning algorithm inspired from the method of making 'Flower Carpets' for the commercial greenhouses to improve the reachability, safety (of plants) and success rate of collaborative manipulation-based tasks in greenhouse environments. A unified vision-based approach with feedforward neural network is used to approximate plant related geometric features like root location, area of spread and plant bed layout to implement an end- to-end manipulation-based precision robot is discussed with implementation results. Furthermore, the system was implemented and evaluated on gazebo simulation as well as a real mobile manipulator robot that was made to operate in a greenhouse setup. The proposed Hybrid IK planner is found to have a 32.27% increase in success rate in comparison to the standard IK solver. Unwanted plant interactions per task were reduced by an average of 0.45 Contact Factor. Similarly, the execution time was also reduced by an average of 58 s.

Keywords: Neural network Hybrid IK Planner · Robotic Vision · Manipulator task-planning · Plan-Robot Interaction · Collaborative Precision Farming

1 Introduction

Greenhouses comprise of translucent glass-based infrastructures for supporting faster plant growth [1]. The ambience and controlled environment within greenhouses provides favorable growing conditions not just for the crops but even for the other unwanted plants or weeds that naturally grow along with them [2]. Safe and efficient 'Plant-Robot' interaction in precision farming-based site- specific actions are highly recommended for greenhouse-based scenarios to ensure optimal usage of resources like water and pesticides. Though widely used due to the ease and comfort of application, agrochemicals and herbicides are not the most appropriate way to handle infestations in plants. A more environmentally friendly and efficient alternative would be mechanical weeding techniques like picking, plucking, cutting, and stamping. However, it's a mundane and boring task that could pose a threat to the safety of human workers and even to the quality of crops if done wrong. Therefore, automation of collaborative agricultural operations has a prominent social and economic impact [1]. Automated and collaborative robotic weeding and irrigation systems, however, require a well-developed perception system to execute operations at a per-plant level. As far as the above precision operations are concerned the two of the most important tasks are accurate detection of plant physical features and designing of an efficient task planning algorithm to execute safe and seamless robotic manipulations within the robotic arm-based manipulations tend to be highly constrained due to the limitations in the cartesian poses that can traversed within the defined workspace of the manipulator see Fig. 1. Especially for actions like pick and discard for weeding or target and approach for irrigation, the traversable workspace within the vertical farming setups maintained in greenhouses are minimal and restricted. Often the standard Inverse Kinematics (IK) solvers fail to find an optimal solution to the given target poses causing a task failure. We have proposed a hybrid IK controller based on a feed-forward neural network that enables the end-effect of the arm to reach the end pose with certainty. The human behavior inspired flower carpet task planner reinforces the efficacy of the controller by stitching a well curated task (weeding and irrigation) execution plan. Our approach proposes (i) techniques to extract the prominent geometrical features like leaf area spread, plant root location and plant bed arrangement to enable manipulation-based precision operations prioritizing crop safety and execution time; (ii) a way to increase the success rate of manipulation tasks.

Fig. 1. Agricultural mobile manipulator performing collaborative plan-robot interaction (precision farming) in the lab greenhouse setup.

2 Related Work

Control algorithms designed for manipulators, those which are responsible for moving the arm to target poses based on the given joint angles tend to be highly complex due to the large non-linearities involved in solving the forward kinematic equations [3]. Therefore, neural network-based function approximators that can closely fit non-linear functions tend to be an efficient solution. Some of the popularly used neural network architectures for solving control problems in robotics are feed forward neural network and recurrent neural network. Solving the forward kinematics equation which is one-one mapping function between joint angles and Cartesian pose is a relatively simpler problem for neural network models. Inverse kinematics is used in occasions where the goal is to find the respective joint configurations for a given end-effector pose which makes it a difficult problem for it has dependency on the physical configuration of the robot. This in turn means it is a many-to-one function having multiple solutions. However, a neural network trained to predict inverse kinematics generates only a single solution per pose [5]. This is the same proposition which we have used to our advantage in the approach proposed in this paper, see Fig. 2.

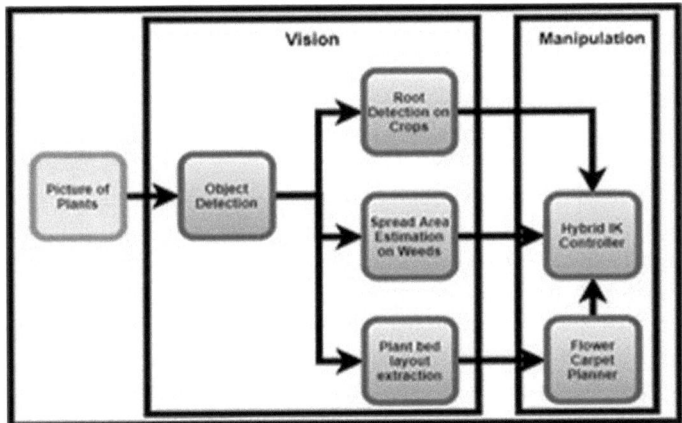

Fig. 2. Collaborative Plan-Robot Interaction System Architecture

3 Methodology

The main objective of our work is to enable agricultural mobile manipulators to effectively execute precision operations in space constrained indoor environments like commercial greenhouses. We have put forth a feed forward network-based IK solver and human behavior inspired task planners to perform agricultural operations like weeding and irrigation taking factors like accuracy, execution time, plant safety and hardware efficiency into consideration. A vision-based detection system is also implemented to aid the manipulator in making operation specific decisions. The process flow of the system can be described (see Fig. 2) as follows: (1) First, the plants under consideration are accurately localized and broadly classified into crops and weeds. The detected crops and weeds are further segregated for irrigation and weeding respectively. Prior to the start of the manipulations, physical features of the plants like area of spread for safe weeding and root location for precision irrigation of the crops are extracted. Second, based on the localized poses of the crops and weeds, the Flower Carpet planner is used to sequence the order of task execution. Finally, the end effector of the manipulator is made to traverse to saved locations of the target crops and weeds using the Hybrid IK

3.1 Manipulation

Hybrid IK Controller. The pose of each of the localized crop and weed are taken as distinct waypoints that are way-point traversing waypoint implies moving the end effector of the arm to the pose that defines each of the way- point. Such a problem fundamentally is solved using Inverse Kinematics where, given a target pose, the corresponding joint angles of the arm are calculated. However, due to the complexity involved in the geometry of robotic arms and the convoluted trigonometric equations that map the Cartesian space to the joint space [3], solving IK for any random but valid pose in the Cartesian space is challenging which often results in task disruptions. From experience it was understood that as the reachability of the target pose from the arm becomes difficult in terms of distance and orientation, the chances of the IK solver finding a solution become lesser. The Hybrid IK controller works in multiple stages. Firstly, the Euclidean distance between the end effector target poses and the current pose is calculated. If the calculated distance falls above a threshold value, a feed forward network trained on a custom dataset is used for approximating the IK solution. Again, the separation in terms of the Euclidean distance is calculated. if the separation is below the threshold, the end effector is assumed to have reached the target pose. Otherwise, the standard IK solver is used to mathematically find the joint angles corresponding to the target pose. The reason that the standard IK solver has a higher failure rate if the target pose is out of reach is why the neural network-based solver is used in the first stage to move the manipulator to a pose closer to the target. as the calculated current pose nears the target pose, the standard IK solver is used to find the solution with certainty.

Feedforward Neural Network (OMX Net). The OMX Net or the feed-forward neural network (shown in Fig. 5), part of the Hybrid IK controller is used for generating joint angles ($\theta 1$, $\theta 2$, $\theta 3$, $\theta 4$) for a given target cartesian pose (x,y,z). The dataset used for training the model comprises of 10000 samples (80%-20% split) of randomly sampled joint angles and their respective cartesian poses. The samples were such that it spanned only the workspace of interest with no duplication. The warped workspace [Fig. 4(b)] also ensures minimal singularities in comparison to the original workspace [Fig. 4(a)]. The sigmoid [Eq. 1] and linear [Eq. 2] activation functions are used for the hidden and output layers respectively.

$$y = \sigma(x) = \frac{1}{1 + (e^{-x})} \qquad (1)$$

$$y = x \qquad (2)$$

$$\begin{bmatrix} \theta_1 \\ \theta_2 \\ \theta_3 \\ \theta_4 \end{bmatrix} = W_o \cdot \sigma \left(W \; t \cdot \begin{bmatrix} x_e \\ y_e \\ z_e \end{bmatrix} + B_t \right) + \begin{bmatrix} b_{0_1} \\ b_{0_2} \\ b_{0_3} \end{bmatrix} \qquad (3)$$

Flower Carpet Task Planner. The layout task planner is inspired by the way 'Flower Carpets' are designed for the indoor greenhouse setups. In the flower carpet designing routine, initially the entire design in hand is analyzed and the underlying symmetry of the design is extracted. Further, the idea is to take advantage of the symmetrical workspace and divide the workspace into zones with a 'Store point', where resources(flowers) necessary to complete the design in each zone area, are allocated from the storehouse. This way of zone-specific resource allocation eliminates the need for shuttling between zones and the storehouse, saving time and improving work efficiency.

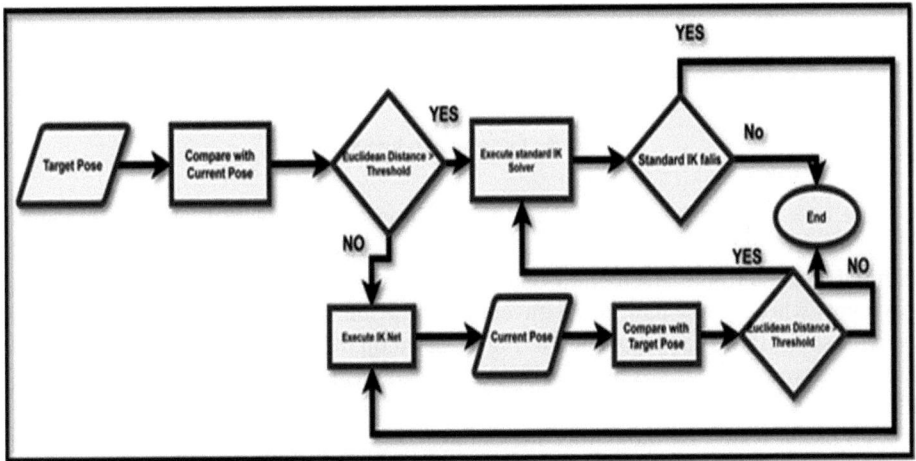

Fig. 3. Hybrid IK Controller flow chart

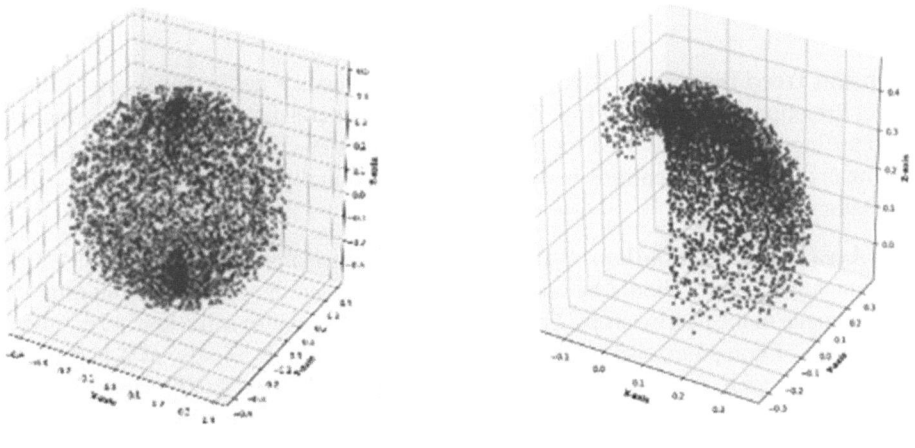

(a) Original (b) Warped workspace

Fig. 4. Workspace Warping [4][4]

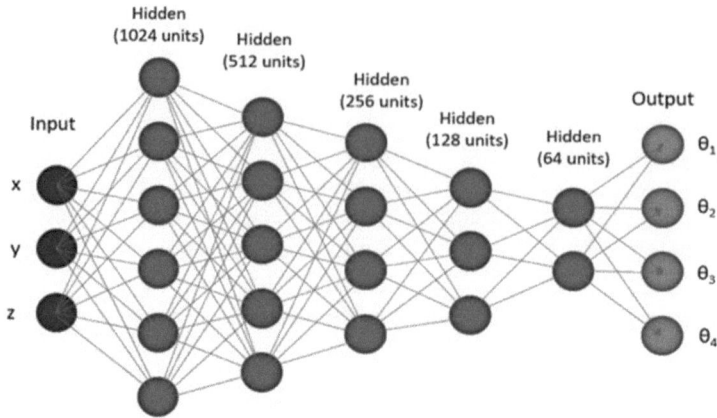

Fig. 5. OmxNet Architecture

The task planner proposed in our work follows a similar task allocation routine where the symmetry of the workspace is defined based on the detected crops and weeds within the vision frame. Each of the detected crops and weeds are considered as separate waypoints whose poses have to be traversed by the manipulator. Upon segmentation of the workspace into zones as shown in Fig. 6 based on the embedded arrangement of the plants, the waypoints based on their degree of Euclidean separation from the center are allotted to each of the segmented zones within the workspace. The geometrical center of each of the zones are the points analogous to the'Store points'. Unlike how flowers were collected from the Store points to fill in the marked design within each zone, here the store points are the intermediate'Halt points' for the manipulator while performing operations within each zone.

3.2 Vision

Crop and Weed Detection. Detection of crops and weeds is performed using YOLOR object detection algorithm see Fig. 7. A custom dataset consisting of 3000 training and 1000 testing images were used for training the object detection model for 100 epochs. All the crops and weed entities in the image were manually annotated using an online annotator.

Leaf Area Spread Estimation. Estimating the leaf spread area is important for it defines how much the gripper should be opened to carefully grasp the weeds causing minimal or no damage to the nearby crops. Our method attempts to estimate the leaf spread using a sequence of computer vision techniques as shown in Fig. 8. Firstly, as a part of the prepossessing, gray scale conversion is performed on the obtained RGB images followed by edge detection. Edge detection is performed to obtain a clearer outer boundary around the leaves. The thresholder image is made to undergo dilation operation three consecutive times. Dilation helps to eliminate artifacts in images and connect masks that incorrectly appear as separate blobs. As the last step, Connected Component Analysis is performed to obtain connected blobs like regions in the image. Further The relative leaf spread area of the plant is calculated by calculating the ratio of pixels comprising each blob to the total number of pixels in the image.

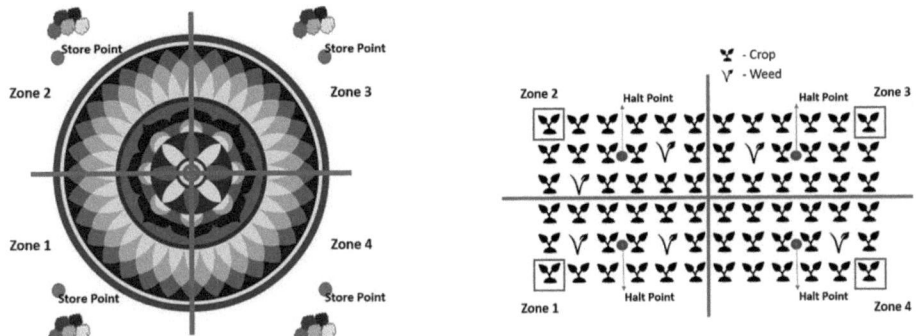

Fig. 6. Flower Carpet planner

Root Detection. Localizing the root for precision irrigation while ensuring minimal contact with the plant body itself is the objective of the root detection algorithm. The plants under consideration are assumed to have their stem center vertically aligned to the root position with a maximum error margin of 2 cm. The error margin of 2cm is acceptable for the plants are seeded with a minimum separation of 5cm for the experiment. Given that, the first step in root detection is to estimate the stem location of the plant body for which we are adapting the techniques stated in [2]. Once the stem location is pinpointed as shown in Fig. 9, the distance between the stem of the plant and the ground is calculated using the depth camera mounted on the manipulator, see Fig. 10. Upon obtaining the distance, the approximate root location is estimated using the stem position and relative distance with the ground. Finally, a contact-less or minimum contact trajectory for the manipulator is defined along the perimeter of an imaginary semi-circle passing through the stem center and estimated root position.

Fig. 7. Crop and Weed detection performed using YOLOR

Plant Bed Layout Extraction. Plant bed layout refers to the way the crops and weeds are arranged. It acts as an important piece of information for the Flower carpet planner to function. The first step is to perform a vegetation index-based segmentation. The mask used for segmentation is generated using the Excess Green Index given in Eq. (3). High frequency noises in the image are removed using a Gaussian filter. An iterative three count dilation operation is performed on the filtered image to merge the pixels those which incorrectly occur as separate regions or blobs in the image. Finally, a contour extraction with 'Simple Approximation' is performed on the image to obtain the contours of the plant species in the image. The extracted contours are used to obtain the region centroids which closely represent the position of the detected plants in the frame using which plant bed layout can be defined.

$$I_{Ex}G_{i,j} = 2xI_{G(i,j)} - I_{R(i,j)} - I_{B(i,j)} \tag{4}$$

4 Experiments and Results

4.1 Hardware Architecture

The popular open-source *Open manipulator X* arm attached to the *Nex Robotics 0X Delta* mobile robot was used for performing and evaluating the experiments. A side mount-based design as shown in the Fig was adopted to ensure proximity between the greenhouse horizontal stack arrangement and the manipulator. The RealSense depth camera attached to the arm in an 'Eye-In-Hand' fashion is responsible for capturing the images required for physical feature detection of the plant species.

4.2 Results

A simulation of the actual mobile manipulator was performed in *Gazebo* for preliminary validation of the results. Upon obtaining satisfactory results, the software written within the *ROS* framework was transferred to the real robot for testing. As discussed above, the main objective of our work is to provide a vision-based manipulation pipeline for safe and efficient precision farming in constrained greenhouse environments. All the experiments were conducted in a greenhouse setup where plants were sown in 3 horizontal stacks in three distinct layouts. Each layout had a different number of plants indicating 3 vegetation density (*i.e.,*) Low, Medium, and High. The total number of tasks that need to be completed per layout is termed as a 'routine'. All the metrics used for comparing the IK solvers and task planners are defined *w.r.t* a single routine.

Input Image   Otsu Threshold   Connected Component Analysis   Leaf area estimated from relative white pixel count

Fig. 8. Leaf area estimation pipeline

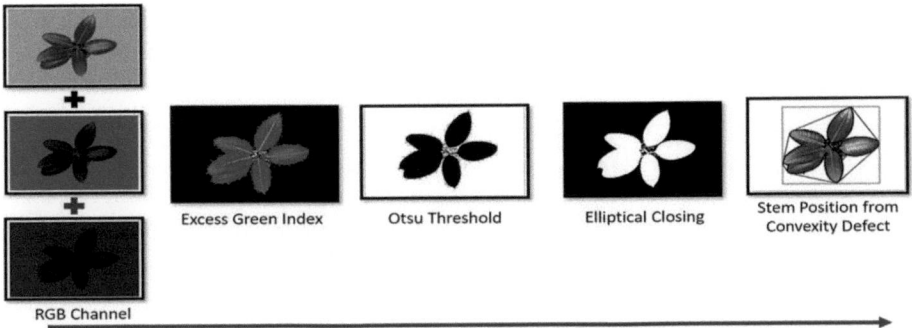

Fig. 9. Stem center detection pipeline

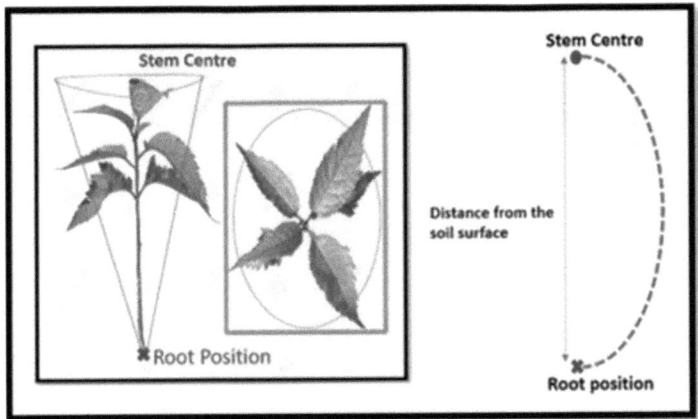

Fig. 10. Root Detection

4.3 Evaluation Metrics

Contact Factor (CF) - Contact factor defines the degree to which the manipulation is causing plant safety concerns. It is formulated as the ratio of the total number of unwanted interactions (It) and the total number of tasks (N_e) executed in a routine.

$$CF = \frac{\sum_{i=1}^{N_e}(I_{t_i})}{N_e} \qquad (5)$$

Safety Quotient (SQ) - It can be assessed as a metric to define the overall safety provided by the system. It is given as the inverse of the Contact Factor

$$CF = \frac{1}{CF} \qquad (6)$$

Success Rate (S) - Success rate accounts for the ability of the system to successfully complete a given task. It is given as the fraction of the number of successful task executions (N_e) by the total number of scheduled tasks in a routine (N).

$$Success\ Rate = \frac{N_e}{N} \qquad (7)$$

Cartesian Error (C_e) - It is defined as the error between the ground truth pose (x_{gt}, y_{gt}, z_{gt}) and the pose predicted by the OMXnet model (x, y, z) of the localized waypoints.

$$C_e = \frac{1}{N}\sqrt{\sum_{i=1}^{n}\left(x_{gt} - x_{pred_i}\right)^2 + \left(y_{gt} - y_{pred_i}\right)^2 + \left(Z_{gt} - Z_{pred_i}\right)^2} \qquad (8)$$

Execution Time (T_e) - It is defined as the total time taken to execute all the given task in a routine.

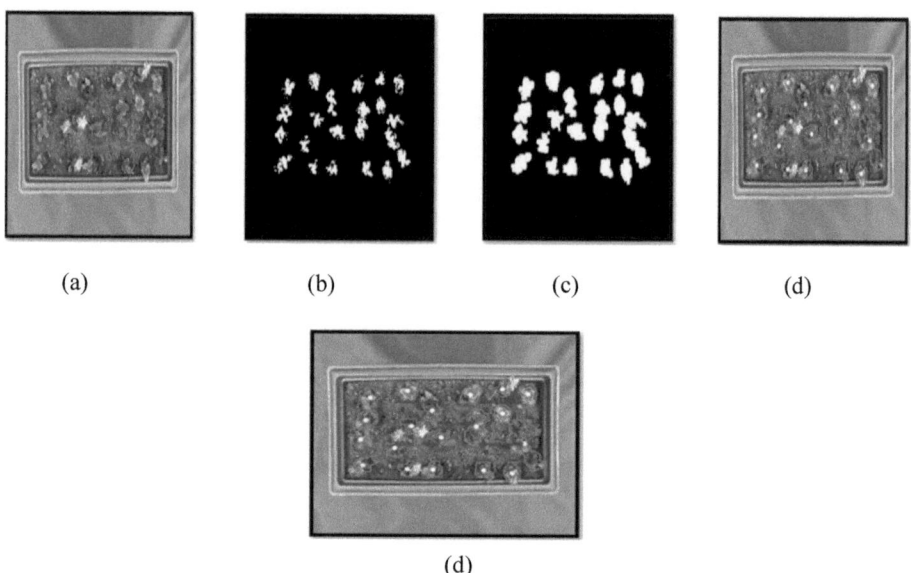

Fig. 11. Plant bed layout detection - (a) Plant bed (b) Threshold Image (c) Dilation Output (d) Contour centroids (e) Detection zone center.

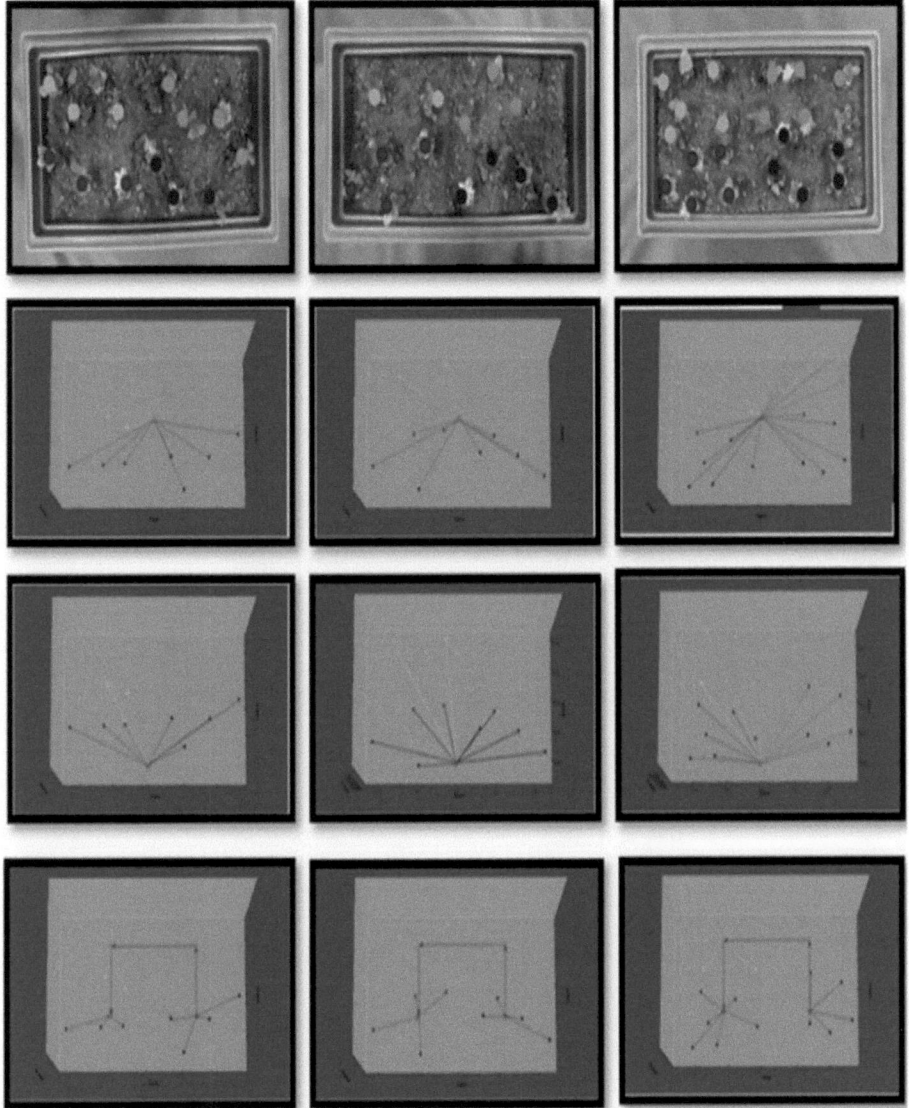

Fig. 12. Comparison of the manipulator trajectory with different task planners for low, medium, and high-density layouts

4.4 Experimental Evaluation

Figures 11 and 12 show the way-point traversing pattern followed by the manipulator for three different plant bed layouts. Each of them varies in terms of the plant density with the number of plants being 12, 14 and 22 in the layouts respectively. Each of the rows display the waypoint traversing pattern designed for the respective layouts by the three planners under consideration. Figure 13 shows the training and validation loss of Omxnet over 100 epochs. From the graphs it can be inferred that the model trained on the warped workspace seems to generalize better for its validation loss is systematically decreasing with the increase in the number of epochs similar to the training loss. The RMSE values of each of the models when trained in different workspaces is as given in Table 3. From Fig. 14, it can be inferred that the direction of error in x, y and z direction is consistent and could be solved by increasing the samples in the OmxNet model training dataset. Solution in one run, the Hybrid IK controller tries to iteratively Unlike the standard IK solver which attempts to find the IK reach the target pose by minimizing the error because of which the success rate is significantly higher at the cost of a longer execution time as can be seen in Table 2. Table 1 compares task planner algorithms based on safety quotient and execution time for the three plant bed layouts. Three task planner algorithms used basically differ from each other based on their 'Halt point'. 'Home to Pose' planner requires the manipulator to come back to its default 'Home' position at the end of each task while the 'Center to Pose' planner gets the manipulator to halt at the geometrical center of the plant bed. The 'Flower Carpet' task planner as discussed above brings the manipulator to the geometrical center of the segmented zones and seems to outperform others in terms of Execution time and Safety Quotient. The reason that the 'Halt Point' is at an intermediate pose between the center of the plant bed and the target plant itself ensures faster traversal and safer trajectories between waypoints.

Table 1. Comparison of Task Planner

Task Planner	Execution Time(s)			Safety Quotient (#)		
	Low	Medium	High	Low	Medium	High
Home2Pose	261	217	432	12	7	3.6
Center2Pose	210	169	382	inf	inf	5.5
Flower Carpet(ours)	185	148	336	inf	inf	22

Table 2. Comparison of Hybrid IK and Standard IK solvers

Solver	Success Rate (%)			Execution Time(s)		
	Low	Medium	High	Low	Medium	High
Standard IK	46.3	43.1	36.36	131	105	213
Hybrid IK (ours)	78.57	66.6	59.2	193	172	336

Table 3. Comparison of OMXnet model architecture

OMX Net	RMSE(m)	
	Original	Warped
Model 1	0.0085	0.003
Model 2(ours)	0.0079	0.0025

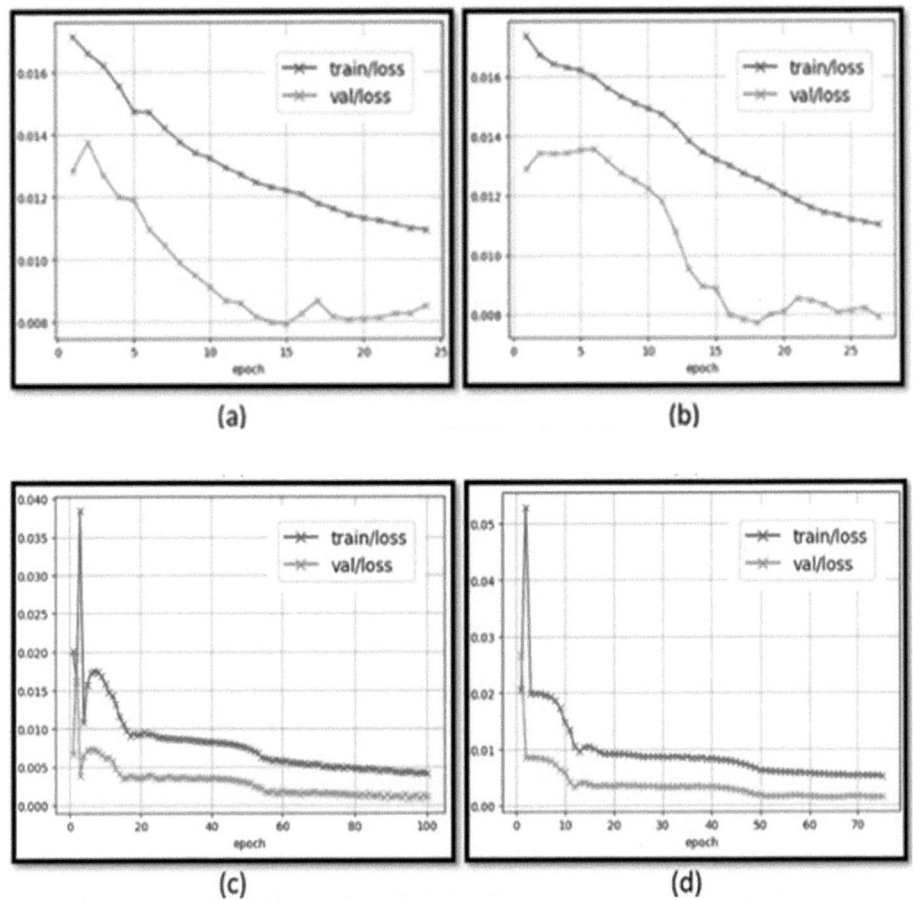

Fig. 13. Model training results of OmxNet: (a) Model 1 – Workspace -1 (b) Model 2 - Workspace 1 (c) Model 1 - Workspace 2 (d) Model 2 - Workspace 2.

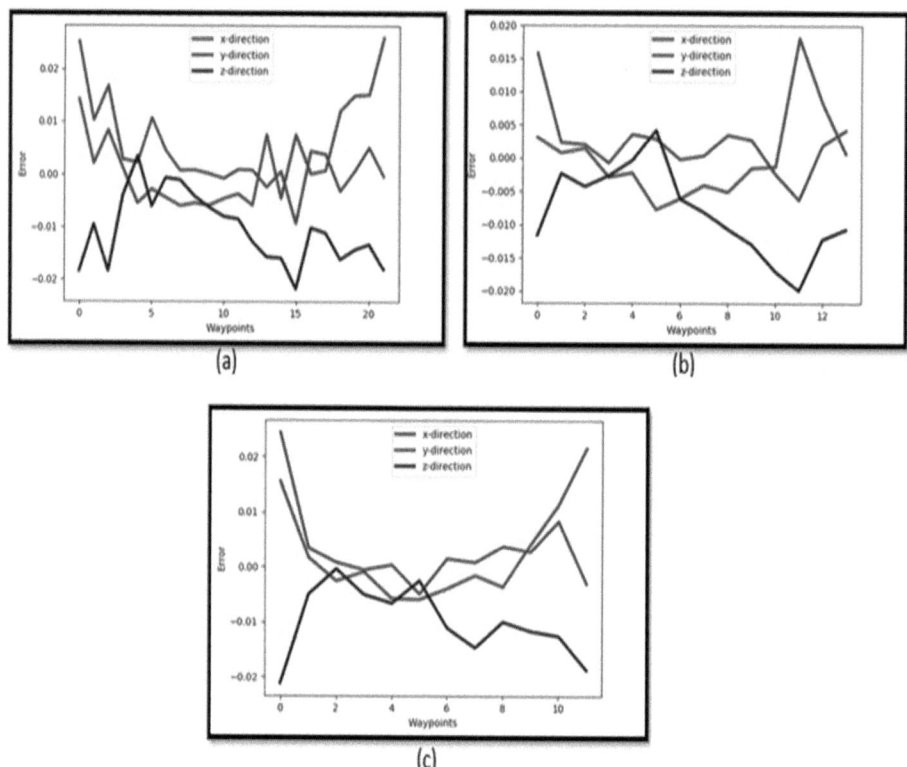

Fig. 14. Error between the actual and predicted pose for the waypoints in x, y, z directions: (a) Layout 1 (b) Layout 2 (c) Layout 3

5 Conclusions

An end-to-end pipeline for manipulation-based plant-robot interactive precision operations like weeding and irrigation was executed. Geometrical features of the plant samples were extracted for obtaining information necessary for safe and precise manipulation. A feedforward neural network *Hybrid IK* planner and controller that iteratively moves to the target pose and ensures a higher success rate of 32.27% in comparison to the standard IK solver was implemented and evaluated on plant beds of varying plant density. It was observed that the success rate was more dependent on the plant distribution rather than density. The improved model performance on the warped workspace implies that for problems having multiple solutions like that of solving the IK of the manipulator, a curated dataset that is representative of the workspace of the application in hand works better than one that considers the whole workspace of the arm. A human behavior inspired task planner algorithm showing considerable improvement in the execution time by an average 58s and crop safety was introduced and compared with few standard planners. A higher success rate was observed at the cost of a higher execution time.

References

1. Acaccia, G.M., Michelini, R.C., Molfino, R.M., Razzoli, R.P.: Mobile robots in greenhouse cultivation: inspection and treatment of plants. In: 1st International Workshop on Advances in Service Robotics, 13–15 March (2003). http://www.dimec.unige.it/pmar/pages/download/papers/Razz10.pdf
2. Langer, F., Mandtler, L., Milioto, A., Palazzolo, E., Stachniss, C.: Geometrical Stem Detection from Image Data for Precision Agriculture. 2–7 (2018). http://arxiv.org/abs/1812.05415
3. Theofanidis, M., Sayed, S.I., Cloud, J., Brady, J., Make- don, F.: Kinematic estimation with neural networks for robotic manipulators. Lecture Notes in Computer Science (Including Subseries Lecture Notes in Artificial Intelligence and Lecture Notes in Bioinformatics), vol. 11141 LNCS, pp. 795–802, November 2018. https://doi.org/10.1007/978.3.030.01424-7.77
4. Ting, H.Z., Zaman, M.H.M., Ibrahim, M.F., Moubark, A.M.: Kinematic analysis for trajectory planning of open-source 4-DoF robot arm. Int. J. Adv. Comput. Sci. Appl. **12**(6), 769–777 (2021). https://doi.org/10.14569/IJACSA.2021.0120690
5. Craig, J.J.: Introduction to Robotics: Mechanics and Control, vol. 3. Pearson/Prentice Hall, Upper Saddle River (2005)

Slosh-Aware Trajectory Control in a Reconfigurable Staircase Service Robot

Veerajagadheswar Prabakaran[1(✉)], Abdullah Aamir Hayat[2], Manivannan Kalimuthu[1], Madan Mohan Rayguru[3], and Mohan Rajesh Elara[1]

[1] Engineering Product Development, Singapore University of Technology and Design, Singapore 487372, Singapore
{prabakaran,rajeshelara}@sutd.edu.sg,
manivannan_kalimuthu@mymail.sutd.edu.sg
[2] Department of Mechanical and Aerospace Engineering, United Arab Emirates University, Abu Dhabi 15551, UAE
aamirhayat@uaeu.ac.ae
[3] University of Louisville, Louisville, KY, USA
madanmohan.rayguru@louisville.edu

Abstract. Automating staircase cleaning remains a challenging task due to the confined spatial constraints, complex motion requirements, and the added instability introduced by liquid sloshing in mobile cleaning robots. This paper presents a novel control strategy for a reconfigurable staircase service robot, sTetro-SR, which carries a cleaning liquid and must safely traverse stairs without compromising stability. The key contribution of this work is the development of an optimal output feedback controller that simultaneously achieves trajectory tracking and suppresses sloshing, modelled using simple pendulum dynamics. A decoupled state-space representation of the robot and slosh system is derived, and the control problem is formulated as a constrained dynamic optimisation problem. The proposed solution employs a Kalman filter-based Model Predictive Control (MPC) framework, ensuring that both motion and slosh dynamics remain within safe bounds. Experimental results in real-world staircase scenarios demonstrate that the proposed method significantly outperforms conventional PID control by reducing slosh-induced deviations and enabling precise trajectory tracking. This integrated approach advances the safe and efficient deployment of service robots in complex environments such as staircases.

Keywords: Slosh Suppression · Reconfigurable robots · ArModel Predictive Control (MPC) · Trajectory Tracking · Service Robot

---

Supplementary Information The online version contains supplementary material available at https://doi.org/10.1007/978-981-95-2382-5_19.

1 Introduction

In the last decade, floor cleaning robots have evolved with enhanced functionalities such as mopping and scrubbing. To meet the demand for cleaning multistorey buildings, new robotic platforms capable of staircase cleaning have emerged. A robot that autonomously climbs stairs and performs cleaning was proposed in [3], while a leapfrog-based ascending/descending system was introduced in [30]. Prior studies on the sTetro platform addressed mechanical design and autonomy [8,10,24]. Another reconfigurable robot, s-Sacrr, demonstrated area coverage across stairs and slopes [14,15,23].

Designing cleaning and maintenance (CaM) robots is often limited by fixed morphologies, constraining their operational scope [7]. Reconfigurable robots, as explored in works such as [9,20], offer flexibility but introduce new challenges in designing subsystems and transformations using principles like expand/collapse, expose/cover, and fuse/divide. These transformation strategies are shown to significantly enhance system versatility in real-world applications. Control and compliance also become essential considerations in dynamic environments, particularly when human-robot or robot-robot interactions are expected [22].

Various mobile platforms (differential drive, omnidirectional, holonomic) have led to control strategies like robust [17], adaptive [11], predictive [25], and neuro-fuzzy control [2]. With the rise of Industry 4.0, liquid-handling robots are gaining popularity, yet sloshing introduces challenges in trajectory tracking [4,12]. Slosh effects—typically modelled using pendulum or spring-damper systems [1,21]—are often integrated with robot dynamics. Feed-forward control methods are proposed in [1,12,13], while feedback-based strategies include sliding mode [21], frequency smoothing [26], LMI [27,28], and active vibration suppression [4].

Motivation: Similar control problems also arise in self-reconfigurable robots to ensure their mobility. Modelling and path tracking control designs for self-reconfigurable cleaning robots are studied in the papers [18], [6], [16] and [5], to name a few. The challenge of navigating tight spaces by developing an anti-collision static rotation local planner for robots or vehicles is addressed in [29]. However, the functionality of a cleaning robot is as important as its mobility. As the cleaning robots carry liquid detergent for fulfilling their functionality, tracking and slosh suppression have to be ensured simultaneously. For the staircase cleaning robot sTetro-SR (refer to Fig. 1), the sloshing effects may force the robot to deviate from its designated path, and this problem could be fatal if the robot comes off the stairs and topples. Even though there are several studies in the literature that focus on the dynamic modelling and trajectory tracking of the cleaning robots, none of the existing work discusses the effect of sloshing along with the mobility for vertically reconfigured robots.

Contributions: To this end, we present a motion-slosh control strategy for our indigenous staircase cleaning robot. The key contributions of this paper are: a) Derivation of a state-space model capturing both mobility and sloshing dynamics of the sTetro-SR platform; b) Development of a predictive control scheme that

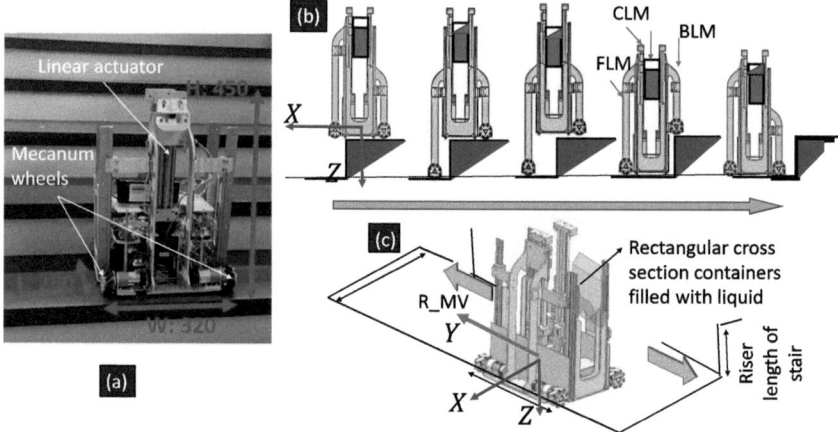

Fig. 1. (a) sTetro on the staircase (b) Gait of the robot while ascending/descending the stairs in XZ-plane (c) Movement of the holonomic base across the stairs.

minimises trajectory tracking errors and slosh-induced disturbances under state and actuator constraints; c) Experimental validation of the proposed controller on the physical robot in real-world staircase cleaning scenarios.

The next section discusses basic mechanical and electronic components of sTetro-SR. Section 3 derives the state space model for the control problem. Section 4 explains the model predictive control strategy, followed by an experiment section discussing the results from control law implementation.

2 sTetro Platform

To address the mechanical and functional adaptability to stair geometries, the design process of sTetro-SR incorporated the Transformation Design Principles—expand/collapse, expose/cover, and fuse/divide—as proposed in [9], ensuring compliance with staircase morphology through systematic subsystem reconfiguration.

The detailed design of a staircase-accessing robot which can stably translate on the stairs was reported earlier in [24]. In this paper, we refer to the staircase robot as sTetro-SR, which is equipped with a water (cleaning liquid) tank to provide the essential cleaning liquid during mopping. The modular design of the robot enables it to access the staircase along with the addition of cleaning units. A brief description of these modules, namely, mechanical design and locomotion unit, reconfiguration unit, and cleaning unit, and the system architecture is discussed for brevity.

Figure 1 shows the modular design of sTetro-SR, comprising three vertically reconfigurable modules—FLM, CLM, and BLM—connected by linear actuators for stable stair climbing. With dimensions of $280 \times 320 \times 490$ mm, the robot fits a single stair step and uses Mecanum wheels for holonomic motion, aided by passive Omniwheels for stability during transition. A cleaning liquid container (130 × 110 × 130 mm) is mounted on the CLM, increasing the robot's weight from 14.5 kg to 17 kg when filled. The added liquid mass introduces sloshing during movement, posing risks of instability and toppling, thus requiring active control.

3 Mathematical Modelling for Slosh Dynamics

In this section, we derive the mathematical model governing the sloshing and motion for the robot sTetro-SR.

3.1 Robot Motion Model

The schematic model for the sTetro-SR with all four wheels touching ground, i.e., no vertical reconfiguration is there is shown in Fig. 2. Frames $Y_I O_I X_I$ and $Y_r O_r X_r$ are the inertial and robot frames, respectively. The Mecanum wheels are identical to the passive rollers for wheels $1, 3$ are inclined at $45°$ and for wheels $2, 4$ at $-45°$ respectively. The inverse kinematic relation, i.e., mapping the robot with the wheel velocities [19] is given as:

$$\dot{\boldsymbol{\xi}}_r = \frac{r_w}{4} \begin{bmatrix} -1 & 1 & -1 & 1 \\ 1 & 1 & 1 & 1 \\ s_1 & -s_1 & -s_1 & s_1 \end{bmatrix} \dot{\boldsymbol{\phi}}_w \quad (1)$$

where the robot velocity vector $\dot{\boldsymbol{\xi}}_r \equiv [\dot{x}_r \ \dot{y}_r \ \dot{\theta}_r]^T$ and the wheel velocity vector as $\dot{\boldsymbol{\phi}}_w \equiv [\dot{\phi}_1 \ \dot{\phi}_2 \ \dot{\phi}_3 \ \dot{\phi}_4]^T$ and the constant $s_1 = 1/(a+b)$. The length and breadth

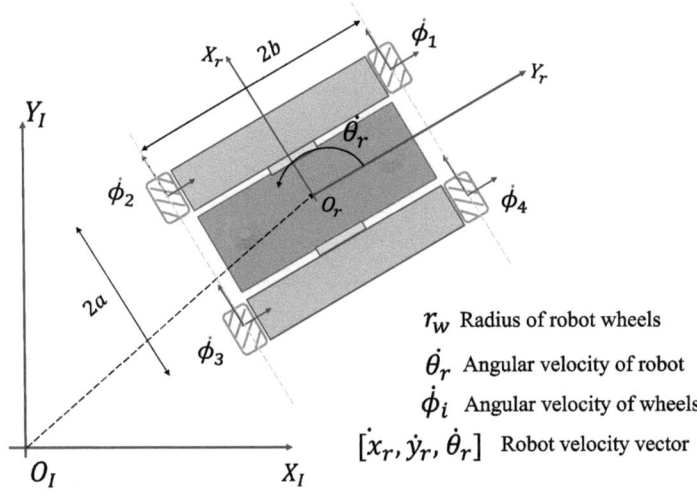

Fig. 2. Schematic of the sTetro-SR robot with two scrubbers.

based on the point of contact of the four wheels are 2a and 2b respectively. The velocity of the robot in the inertial frame is given by:

$$\dot{\xi}_I = \mathbf{R}(\theta_r)\dot{\xi}_r \tag{2}$$

where $\xi_I \equiv [\dot{x}\ \dot{y}\ \dot{\theta}]^T \equiv [[\dot{\mathbf{x}}]^T\ \dot{\theta}]$ is the robot velocity vector in the inertial frame and $\mathbf{R}(\theta_r)$ is the rotation matrix about Z-axis.

The cleaning operation on the stairs require the robot to move along straight lines. Therefore, the robot doesn't need to change orientation much, and the state evolution arising from $\dot{\theta}$ can be neglected for the stair cleaning operation. The kinematics considered for the paper can be written as:

$$\dot{\xi} = \frac{r_w}{4}\begin{bmatrix}\cos(\theta) & -\sin(\theta)\\ \sin(\theta) & \cos(\theta)\end{bmatrix}\begin{bmatrix}-1 & 1 & -1 & 1\\ 1 & 1 & 1 & 1\end{bmatrix}\dot{\phi}_w \tag{3}$$

where $\xi = [x, y]^T$. The equation (3) describes the motion of the cleaning robot, provided the dynamical effects like friction and Coriolis forces are neglected (the staircase cleaning robot has to move slowly, and these effects are minimal). However, the sloshing effects are generally activated due to the acceleration of the robot in different directions. So, the acceleration of the robot along the x and y directions are needed. Differentiating (3), we get

$$\ddot{\xi} = \frac{r_w}{4}\begin{bmatrix}\cos(\theta) & -\sin(\theta)\\ \sin(\theta) & \cos(\theta)\end{bmatrix}\begin{bmatrix}-1 & 1 & -1 & 1\\ 1 & 1 & 1 & 1\end{bmatrix}\ddot{\phi}_w$$
$$+ \frac{r_w\dot{\theta}}{4}\begin{bmatrix}\cos(\theta) & -\sin(\theta)\\ \sin(\theta) & \cos(\theta)\end{bmatrix}\begin{bmatrix}-1 & 1 & -1 & 1\\ 1 & 1 & 1 & 1\end{bmatrix}\dot{\phi}_w \tag{4}$$

As the orientation of the robot is not changing much for a straight line motion along the stairs, $\dot{\theta}$ can be neglected. The acceleration along x and y can be written as:

$$\ddot{\xi} = \frac{r_w}{4}\begin{bmatrix}\cos(\theta) & -\sin(\theta)\\ \sin(\theta) & \cos(\theta)\end{bmatrix}\begin{bmatrix}(\ddot{\phi}_2+\ddot{\phi}_4)-(\ddot{\phi}_1+\ddot{\phi}_3)\\ (\ddot{\phi}_1+\ddot{\phi}_3)+(\ddot{\phi}_2+\ddot{\phi}_4)\end{bmatrix} \tag{5}$$

The equation (5) is an overactuated model. So, to reduce the complexity the one can choose

$$\begin{aligned}(\ddot{\phi}_2+\ddot{\phi}_4)-(\ddot{\phi}_1+\ddot{\phi}_3) &= u_x\\ (\ddot{\phi}_2+\ddot{\phi}_4)+(\ddot{\phi}_1+\ddot{\phi}_3) &= u_y.\end{aligned} \tag{6}$$

The individual wheel accelerations are chosen as: $\ddot{\phi}_2 = \ddot{\phi}_4 = \frac{u_x+u_y}{4}$ and $\ddot{\phi}_2 = \ddot{\phi}_4 = \frac{u_y-u_x}{4}$. To further simplify the sloshing controller design, the acceleration along the x and y direction can be decoupled by selecting the control law as:

$$\begin{bmatrix}u_x\\ u_y\end{bmatrix} = \frac{4}{r}\begin{bmatrix}\cos(\theta) & -\sin(\theta)\\ \sin(\theta) & \cos(\theta)\end{bmatrix}^{-1}\begin{bmatrix}v_x\\ v_y\end{bmatrix} \tag{7}$$

With (7), the mathematical model for accelerations can be derived as:

$$\ddot{\xi} = \begin{bmatrix}\ddot{x}\\ \ddot{y}\end{bmatrix} = \begin{bmatrix}v_x\\ v_y\end{bmatrix} \tag{8}$$

3.2 Slosh Model

The cleaning solutions are placed in rectangular containers and fitted with the STetro-SR robot Fig. 3(a). The sloshing effects are approximated by the dynamics of a simple pendulum as shown in Fig. 3(b). The sloshing due to the acceleration of the robot in x and y direction are modelled as the swing angle of the pendulum in the respective directions.

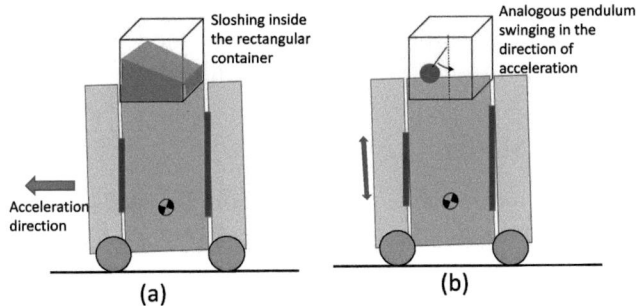

Fig. 3. Sloshing in the sTetro-SR modelled approximated using a simple pendulum during sideways movement on the stairs.

The liquid carrying container is fitted with the robot body in such a way that, relative inclination between them is zero. Adding this factor with the planar movement of the robot while cleaning and small angle approximation, the slosh dynamics due to the acceleration along the x direction can be modelled as:

$$\ddot{\alpha}_x = -\frac{g}{l}\alpha_x - \frac{c}{M_p}\dot{\alpha}_x + \frac{1}{l}v_x \quad (9)$$

where α_x is the swing angle of the pendulum along the direction of motion; l is the pendulum length; M_p is the mass of the pendulum, and c is the damping constant. The sloshing in the y-direction can be modelled similarly as:

$$\ddot{\alpha}_y = -\frac{g}{l}\alpha_y - \frac{c}{M_p}\dot{\alpha}_y + \frac{1}{l}v_y \quad (10)$$

where v_x and v_y are the control signals defined in (8), and will be designed in the next section. These equations can't be used for the controller design as the parameters of the model, like c, M_p, l are unknown. For this reason, a simple system identification technique based on impulse response is carried out. A second-order transfer function is derived from the linearised pendulum dynamics (9), for which the natural frequency (ω) and damping constant (ζ) can be evaluated to be $\omega = \sqrt{\frac{g}{l}}$, $\zeta = \frac{c}{2M_p\omega}$. The rectangular container is excited with an impulse-like force, and the sloshing motion is recorded. The Fourier transform is used on the data to find the maximum amplitude of the dominant mode, and using that, other parameters are computed by comparing it with the analytical impulse response expression. The parameters are computed as: $M_p = 2.3$, $l = 0.032$, $c = 0.00035$. The validity of the obtained parameters is also tested through unit step response comparison with the actual sloshing behaviour in the fitted container in the presence of a constant acceleration.

Although the pendulum model offers a computationally efficient abstraction of liquid motion, it simplifies the behaviour of fluid surfaces, particularly at higher fill ratios or under nonlinear interactions like wave breaking or vortex generation. In future iterations, we plan to integrate computational fluid dynamics (CFD)-derived data or employ nonlinear slosh models (e.g., multi-mode or shallow water equations) to better represent such regimes.

3.3 Motion-Slosh Model

Due to the decoupled nature of the motion model (8) and the sloshing models, the motion-slosh dynamics for the robot can be decoupled in the following form.

$$\begin{bmatrix} \dot{x}_1 \\ \dot{x}_2 \\ \dot{\alpha}_1 \\ \dot{\alpha}_2 \end{bmatrix} = \begin{bmatrix} x_2 \\ 0 \\ \alpha_2 \\ \frac{-c\alpha_2}{M_p} + \frac{-g\alpha_1}{l} \end{bmatrix} + \begin{bmatrix} 0 \\ 1 \\ 0 \\ \frac{1}{l} \end{bmatrix} v_x. \tag{11}$$

$$\begin{bmatrix} \dot{y}_1 \\ \dot{y}_2 \\ \dot{\alpha}_3 \\ \dot{\alpha}_4 \end{bmatrix} = \begin{bmatrix} y_2 \\ 0 \\ \alpha_4 \\ \frac{-c\alpha_4}{M_p} + \frac{-g\alpha_3}{l} \end{bmatrix} + \begin{bmatrix} 0 \\ 1 \\ 0 \\ \frac{1}{l} \end{bmatrix} v_y \tag{12}$$

where $x_1 = x, x_2 = \dot{x}, \alpha_1 = \alpha_x, \alpha_2 = \dot{\alpha}_x, y_1 = y, y_2 = \dot{y}, \alpha_3 = \alpha_y, \alpha_4 = \dot{\alpha}_y$.

4 Motion-Slosh Controller

This part of the paper discusses a constrained optimal feedback for simultaneous control of motion and slosh, for the state space models (11) and (12). However, the models are continuous, and a control input has to be implemented using digital processing devices (see Sect. 2). Hence, the discrete time model can be a suitable option for the controller design. The discrete time (DT) models for (11) and (12) are derived using zero order hold (ZOH) based discretization technique. The DT model for (11) can be expressed as:

$$Z_x(k+1) = A_{zx}Z(k) + B_{zx}v_x(k) + w_{sx}(k)$$
$$Y_{zx}(k) = \begin{bmatrix} x_1(k) \\ x_2(k) \end{bmatrix} = C_{zx}Z_x(k) + w_{mx}(k) \tag{13}$$

where $Z_x = [x_1, x_2, \alpha_1, \alpha_2]^T$, A_{zx}, B_{zx} are the discretized version of system matrices in (11), and w_{sx}, w_{mx} are process and measurement noise with covariance W_s, W_m respectively. A similar DT model can also be derived for (12) for controller design purpose. The discrete time model and the controller designed for this model can provide closed loop stability to the actual continuous time system as long as the sampling is high.

Control Objective: Choose two suitable control inputs $v_x(k), v_y(k)$ such that the sTetro-SR track a desired trajectory (or maintain a desired velocity) without the effects of sloshing.

In this regard, define the desired trajectory for the robot to be $Y_{zxd}(k)$ and tracking error to be $e_x(k) = Y_{zx}(k) - Y_{zxd}$. The control design goal for (13) can be reformulated as a dynamic optimisation problem as:

$$\min \sum_{k=1}^{\infty} \frac{1}{2} e(k)^T Q e(k) + v_x(k-1)^T R v_x(k-1)$$

subject to
$$Z_x(k+1) = A_{zx} Z(k) + B_{zx} v_x(k) + w_{sx}(k)$$
$$Y_{zx}(k) = C_{zx} Z_x(k) + w_{mx}(k) \tag{14}$$
$$Z_{lx} \leq Z_x(k) \leq Z_{ux}$$
$$v_{lx} \leq v_x(k) \leq v_{ux}$$

where Q, R are positive definite matrices, $Z_{lx}, v_{lx}, Z_{ux}, v_{ux}$ are lower and upper bounds for states and control input, respectively. The lower and upper bounds on the state can enforce the slosh to be constrained in a desired range.

The problem considered in (14) is a constrained dynamic optimisation problem, and an analytical solution is difficult to obtain. Model predictive control (MPC) is an efficient technique which exploits a sliding horizon strategy to solve the problem iteratively. The MPC converts the optimal problem (14) into a finite

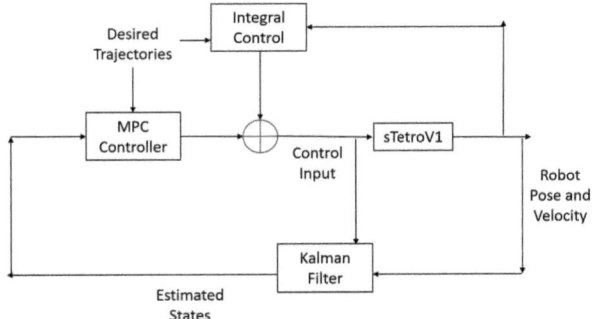

Fig. 4. Control scheme.

time optimal control problem given by

$$\min \sum_{k=1}^{N} \frac{1}{2} e(k)^T Q e(k) + v_x(k-1)^T R v_x(k-1)$$

subject to
$$Z_x(k+1) = A_{zx} Z(k) + B_{zx} v_x(k) + w_{sx}(k) \quad (15)$$
$$Y_{zx}(k) = C_{zx} Z_x(k) + w_{mx}(k)$$
$$Z_{lx} \leq Z_x(k) \leq Z_{ux}$$
$$v_{lx} \leq v_x(k) \leq v_{ux}$$

which has to be solved at every sample. The constant N represents the prediction horizon, which is tuned for a trade-off between convergence and speed. However, the MPC problem (15) involves constraints on states like slosh angle which are not measurable for feedback. So, we choose a Kalman filter to estimate the states of the system (13). As the system model (13) does not capture the uncertainties, the MPC control law computed by solving (15) may be prone to some steady-state error. An integral MPC formulation can be made to take care of the issue, but then the state estimation becomes complicated. Hence, the control input is selected as

$$v_x(k) = v_{xmpc}(k) + k_i \sum (e_x(k)) \quad (16)$$

where v_{xmpc} is the output of the MPC controller and k_i is the integral gain that can be tuned according to the need. It is important to note that MPC, being an optimal controller, assures performance of the closed loop system as specified in the cost function. The stability of the closed loop is implicit in the MPC through the delayed feedback mechanism.

5 Experiments and Results

5.1 Experimental Setup

We evaluated the proposed control law with the updated STetro platform in a real-world scenario. We chose a flat staircase that has a dimension of 1400 mm (Tread length) × 320 mm (Tread depth) × 150 mm (Riser). The Tread of the stairs was constructed with a smooth concrete finish and has metal beading embedded on the nosing. Both side of the staircase was constructed with concertina string. As mentioned in Sect. 2 (a(i)), we have placed two rectangular containers on the top layer of the CBM module, filled with red-coloured water, as shown in Fig. 5. The total weight of the water-filled container during the experiment was 3.5 kg.

To solve the constrained optimisation algorithm at each step of the Kalman filter based MPC, we utilised the open-source solver. The MPC is implemented with a prediction horizon of 20 and a sampling interval of 0.01 sec. The upper and lower bounds (v_{ux}, v_{lx}) of the control inputs are chosen to be $+1$ and -1, respectively. For evaluating the cost function (15), the matrices are chosen as $Q =$

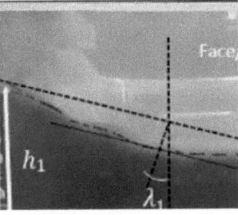

Fig. 5. Slosh measurement setup and the container with the colored liquid.

$10I$ (I is the identity matrix) and $R = 2$. For implementing the Kalman filter, the initial conditions for estimation variables are taken as zero; the Q_k matrix is considered as an identity matrix; $R_k = 1$; the initial value of the P_k matrix is taken $0.1I$. For computational simplicity the Kalman gain is calculated offline using MATLAB before implementing it with MPC in real time. The proposed control schematic (Fig. 4) is realised through a ROS-Python setup, and its output is fed to the motors.

In terms of slosh measurement, we don't need them for feedback. However, we have measured the angle of liquid deviation in two sides (λ_1, λ_2) which are directly proportional to the slosh angles α_1, α_3, so that we can present them for validating the performance of the proposed controller. We have used two USB cameras that focuses on two different directions side and the front of the liquid container. These two cameras are connected to the PC which receives the video frames and process it to extract the slosh angle. We used ROS as a software platform to extract the slosh angle and pass it back for utilisation. We created a ROS node that has the following process pipelines to get the slosh angle (1) receiving the live camera feed and separating the feed to individual frames (2) identifying the red pixels in each frame and masking it from the image (3) convert the masked frame into a gray scale image and apply Hough line detection algorithm to extract the lines (4) The max and min points of the extracted lines are used to calculate the slosh angle (5) publishing the detected angle to the Atmega controller. The same pipeline is used to detect the slosh angle in the other side of the container. Other than the slosh angle, we used ROS to execute the SLAM (gmapping) and publish the robot's pose information to the controller. All these information are recorded using ROS bag to post-process to create plots.

While the current validation was conducted exclusively on standard, straight staircases with uniform step geometry and concrete surfaces, this represents only a subset of real-world deployment conditions. To evaluate the generalizability of the proposed control strategy, future experiments will include curved staircases, uneven or staggered risers, and low-friction surfaces such as ceramic tile or polished laminate. These scenarios will better simulate the challenges encountered in residential and commercial buildings and provide more robust validation of system performance.

5.2 Results and Discussion

For evaluating the performance of the control law in a real world scenario, the sTetro-SR is tested on a straight staircase shown in Fig. 6. The figure depicts the red line as the reference line, while the yellow line shows the traced path. The control algorithm is implemented through Arduino Mega, and the required sensory information of $x_1(k), y_1(k)$ is collected from the Lidar. The desired trajectory for staircase cleaning along a straight path is chosen as $x_{1des}(t) = 0, y_{1des}(t) = 0.1T$ (T is the sample time).

The sloshing effects on the robot is presented in Fig. 7. The data for x and y, the directions (longitudinal and transversal), are plotted as plane 1 and plane 2, respectively. Further, a comparison is made between the slosh measurements from the robot when the proposed controller is active and the PID is active (without slosh control, blue colour legend). The slosh data is taken at different operational phase of the robot (1–6), to demonstrate the effect of the slosh. The phase (1–3) represents the operational phase of the robot, where it starts moving from left to right along the stairs, followed by reconfiguring through two steps (phase 2 and 3). For the starting point in every phase, the initial acceleration give rise to slosh. When the robot is operated with PID (without MPC control), almost NIL slosh suppression is noted. However, the proposed algorithm is able to suppress the slosh each time it arises. It is also interesting to note that, the starting of every phase gives rise to high control action (see Fig. 8a). As we have constrained the input to be within $[+1, -1]$, the control inputs saturate at some points. The slosh suppression can still be improved if the constraints are relaxed (or use of soft constraints) further, and the prediction horizon is increased. However, this may lead to more actuator and computational burden.

The performance of the proposed controller is tested against a conventional PID controller. The motion of the STetro-SR robot on the staircase, for different time instants, are shown in Fig. 8b. It can observed that, the PID controller performed poorly compared to the proposed MPC controller. The PID controller does not account for the side effects of the sloshing and so is not able to provide an accurate tracking performance. As the proposed controller compensates for the

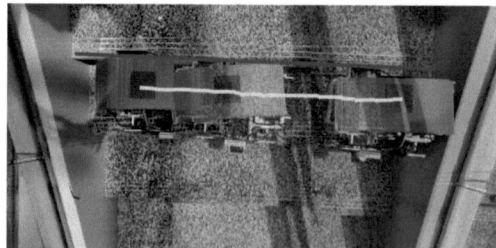

Fig. 6. The trajectory of the sTetro-SR across the staircase with the proposed control scheme implemented. The red line is the reference line, while the yellow line shows the traced path. (Color figure online)

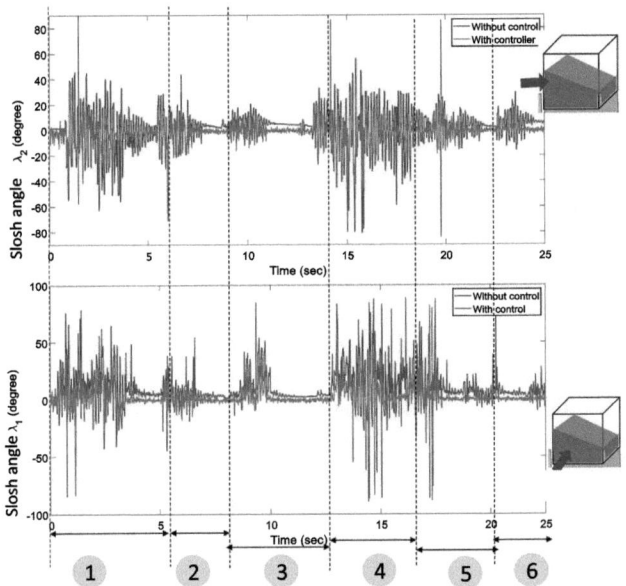

Fig. 7. Slosh across two planes while moving sideways, performing area-coverage and while descending the stairs. The slosh is captured from two sides, i.e., plane 1 and 2, and the segments are mainly ①: Moving left to right (coverage), ②: descending, ③: moving back towards riser to align, ④: moving right to left, ⑤: descending, ⑥: moving back towards riser to align, ①: Moving left to right (coverage).

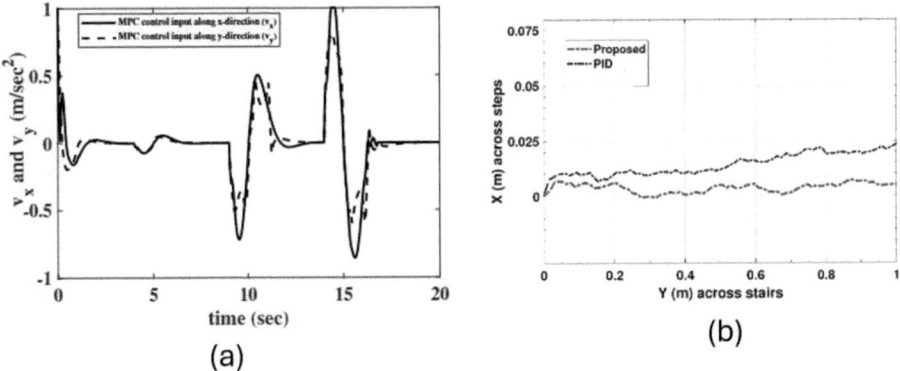

Fig. 8. MPC controller outputs.

slosh generated through the constrained dynamic optimisation, it can ensure a good tracking performance. Hence, with the proposed control scheme the sTetro-SR robot can perform safer area coverage on a staircase.

6 Conclusions

The work discusses the modelling and control aspects of motion-slosh control in a self-reconfigurable staircase cleaning robot named sTetro-SR. The state space model is derived from the kinematics equations of the robot and is decoupled to simplify the controller design. The path tracking and sloshing suppression problem is converted into a constrained dynamic optimisation problem. A Kalman filter based MPC is proposed for solving the optimisation problem without requiring full state measurements. Further, we evaluated the performance of the proposed controller on the developed platform in a real-world scenario. The experimental outcomes show that the proposed controller exhibits satisfactory performance in terms of path tracking while compensating for the disturbances created by the liquid oscillations. Future work will involve extending the testing framework to include a broader variety of staircase geometries and materials. This includes evaluating the system on spiral staircases, staggered or damaged steps, and low-friction surfaces to better simulate real-world deployment scenarios. Future extensions of the control model will also account for environments where orientation varies significantly, such as curved or irregular staircases. This includes expanding the robot's dynamic model and exploring adaptive control policies responsive to heading deviations.

Acknowledgments. This research is also supported by A*STAR under its RIE2025 IAF-PP programme, Modular Reconfigurable Mobile Robots No: M24N2a0039 and is also supported by the National Robotics Programme under its National Robotics Programme (NRP) LEO 1.0: A New Class of Bed Making Robot, No: M25N4N2028.

References

1. Biagiotti, L., Chiaravalli, D., Moriello, L., Melchiorri, C.: A plug-in feed-forward control for sloshing suppression in robotic teleoperation tasks, pp. 5855–5860. IEEE (2018)
2. Cai, Y., Zhan, Q., Xi, X.: Path tracking control of a spherical mobile robot. Mech. Mach. Theory **51**, 58–73 (2012)
3. Fan, B.: Floor climbing cleaning robot based on slide rail lifting structure. In: 2020 IEEE International Conference on Power, Intelligent Computing and Systems (ICPICS), pp. 425–428. IEEE (2020)
4. Hamaguchi, M.: Damping and transfer control system with parallel linkage mechanism-based active vibration reducer for omnidirectional wheeled robots. IEEE/ASME Trans. Mechatron. **23**(5), 2424–2435 (2018)
5. Hayat, A.A., Parween, R., Elara, M.R., Parsuraman, K., Kandasamy, P.S.: Panthera: design of a reconfigurable pavement sweeping robot. In: 2019 International Conference on Robotics and Automation (ICRA), pp. 7346–7352. IEEE (2019)
6. Hayat, A.A., Karthikeyan, P., Vega-Heredia, M., Elara, M.R.: Modeling and assessing of self-reconfigurable cleaning robot HTETRO based on energy consumption. Energies **12**(21), 4112 (2019)

7. Hayat, A.A., Yi, L., Kalimuthu, M., Elara, M.R., Wood, K.L.: Reconfigurable robotic system design with application to cleaning and maintenance. J. Mech. Des. **144**(6), 063305 (2022)
8. Ilyas, M., Yuyao, S., Mohan, R.E., Devarassu, M., Kalimuthu, M.: Design of stetro: a modular, reconfigurable, and autonomous staircase cleaning robot. J. Sensors **2018** (2018)
9. Kalimuthu, M., Hayat, A., Elara, M., Wood, K.: Transformation design principles as enablers for designing reconfigurable robots. In: International design engineering technical conferences and computers and information in engineering conference. vol. 85420, p. V006T06A008. American Society of Mechanical Engineers (2021)
10. Le, A.V., et al.: Autonomous floor and staircase cleaning framework by reconfigurable stetro robot with perception sensors. J. Intell. Robot. Syst. **101**(1), 1–19 (2021)
11. Lucet, E., Lenain, R., Grand, C.: Dynamic path tracking control of a vehicle on slippery terrain. Control. Eng. Pract. **42**, 60–73 (2015)
12. Maderna, R., Casalino, A., Zanchettin, A.M., Rocco, P.: Robotic handling of liquids with spilling avoidance: a constraint-based control approach, pp.7414–7420. IEEE (2018)
13. Moriello, L., Biagiotti, L., Melchiorri, C., Paoli, A.: Control of liquid handling robotic systems: a feed-forward approach to suppress sloshing, pp. 4286–4291. IEEE (2017)
14. Muthugala, M.V.J., Samarakoon, S.B.P., Veerajagadheswar, P., Elara, M.R.: Ensuring area coverage and safety of a reconfigurable staircase cleaning robot. IEEE Access **9**, 150049–150059 (2021)
15. Prabakaran, V., Shi, Y., Prathap, K.S., Elara, M.R., Hayat, A.A.: S-SACRR: a staircase and slope accessing reconfigurable cleaning robot and its validation. IEEE Robot. Autom. Lett. (2022)
16. Rayguru, M.M., Mohan, R.E., Parween, R., Yi, L., Le, A.V., Roy, S.: An output feedback based robust saturated controller design for pavement sweeping self-reconfigurable robot. IEEE/ASME Trans. Mechatron. **26**(3), 1236–1247 (2021)
17. Roy, S., Nandy, S., Ray, R., Shome, S.N.: Robust path tracking control of nonholonomic wheeled mobile robot: experimental validation. Int. J. Control Autom. Syst. **13**(4), 897–905 (2015). https://doi.org/10.1007/s12555-014-0178-1
18. Shi, Y., Elara, M.R., Le, A.V., Prabakaran, V., Wood, K.L.: Path tracking control of self-reconfigurable robot HTETRO with four differential drive units. IEEE Robot. Autom. Lett. **5**(3), 3998–4005 (2020)
19. Siegwart, R., Nourbakhsh, I.R., Scaramuzza, D.: Introduction to Autonomous Mobile Robots. MIT Press (2011)
20. Tan, N., Hayat, A.A., Elara, M.R., Wood, K.L.: A framework for taxonomy and evaluation of self-reconfigurable robotic systems. IEEE Access **8**, 13969–13986 (2020)
21. Thakar, P.S., Trivedi, P.K., Bandyopadhyay, B., Gandhi, P.S.: A new nonlinear control for asymptotic stabilization of a class of underactuated systems: an implementation to slosh-container problem. IEEE/ASME Trans. Mechatron. **22**(2), 1082–1092 (2016)
22. Udai, A.D., Hayat, A.A., Saha, S.K.: Parallel active/passive force control of industrial robots with joint compliance. In: 2014 IEEE/RSJ International Conference on Intelligent Robots and Systems, pp. 4511–4516. IEEE (2014)
23. Veerajagadheswar, P., Yuyao, S., Kandasamy, P., Elara, M.R., Hayat, A.A.: S-SACRR: a staircase and slope accessing reconfigurable cleaning robot and its validation. IEEE Robot. Autom. Lett. **7**(2), 4558–4565 (2022)

24. Verajagadheswa, P., Kandasamy, P.S., Elangovan, K., Elara, M.R., Bui, M.V., Le, A.V.: A novel autonomous staircase cleaning system with robust 3d-deep learning-based perception technique for area-coverage. Expert Syst. Appl. 116528 (2022)
25. Wang, D., Wei, W., Yeboah, Y., Li, Y., Gao, Y.: A robust model predictive control strategy for trajectory tracking of omni-directional mobile robots. J. Intell. Robot. Syst. **98**(2), 439–453 (2020)
26. Xing, B., Huang, J.: Control of pendulum-sloshing dynamics in suspended liquid containers. IEEE Trans. Industr. Electron. **68**(6), 5146–5154 (2020)
27. Yano, K., Higashikawa, S., Terashima, K.: Motion control of liquid container considering an inclined transfer path. Control. Eng. Pract. **10**(4), 465–472 (2002)
28. Yano, K., Terashima, K.: Sloshing suppression control of liquid transfer systems considering a 3-d transfer path. IEEE/ASME Trans. Mechatron. **10**(1), 8–16 (2005)
29. Yi, L., et al.: Anti-collision static rotation local planner for four independent steering drive self-reconfigurable robot. In: 2022 International Conference on Robotics and Automation (ICRA), pp. 5835–5841. IEEE (2022)
30. Zhang, L., Yang, Y., Gu, Y., Sun, X., Yao, X., Shuai, L.: A new compact stair-cleaning robot. J. Mech. Robot. **8**(4) (2016)

A Mixed Reality User-Friendly Interface for Robot Teleoperation

Mariia Chemerys[1], Matvei Novoselov[1], Sofia Diniz Melo Santos[1], Riccardo Aliotta[1,2], Francesco Cufino[1(✉)], and Fabio Ruggiero[1]

[1] PRISMA Lab, Department of Electrical Engineering and Information Technology, University of Naples Federico II, Via Claudio, 21, 80125 Naples, Italy
{riccardo.aliotta,francesco.cufino,fabio.ruggiero}@unina.it

[2] Department of Agricultural Sciences, University of Naples Federico II, Via Università, 100, 80055 Portici, Italy

Abstract. In this paper, we present a user-friendly mixed reality (MR) interface designed for robot teleoperation. To enable untrained users to effectively operate a robot, we developed an interactive application leveraging SwiftUI, RealityKit, and ARKit, and deployed it on an extended reality (XR) headset. Our application enables users to control a robot by moving a virtual sphere that serves as a dynamic target. Using RealityKit's support for natural hand and eye gestures, users guide the robot through easy and subtle motions, eliminating the need for controllers or exaggerated gestures. This reduces physical strain, enhances comfort, and makes teleoperation more immersive. The system has been experimentally tested and statistically validated across users with varying experience levels.

Keywords: Teleoperation · Mixed Reality · Accessible Robotics

1 Introduction

Over the years, the ability for users to directly and precisely control robotic systems—commonly referred to as *teleoperation*—has been a critical focus in robotics research with applications spanning medical, industrial, and service domains. This demand has driven the development of a wide range of control paradigms, offering safety, intuitiveness, and operational flexibility.

Traditional methods, such as teach pendant operation, allow skilled users to command robots [8], while kinesthetic teaching enables users to physically guide the robot through a demonstration that can later be replayed autonomously [4]. While these approaches enhance robot capabilities beyond basic trajectory execution, they often require expert knowledge and impose physical and cognitive load, limiting adoption by untrained users.

Recent advances led to the usage of haptic interfaces, which excel in force-sensitive tasks with tactile feedback but typically use velocity control and still require user skill [7,30,31]. To meet the growing demand for more user-friendly teleoperation applications, mixed reality (MR)-based interfaces are increasingly being developed. These interfaces enable interaction with physical objects by mixing elements of the physical and virtual worlds [27,28], providing a more immersive and intuitive mode of interaction. The integration of digital content into the physical environment boosts situational awareness by delivering context-aware information and enables even untrained users to perceive robotic behaviour and issue commands using natural, spatial gestures. By reducing the learning curve and minimizing reliance on technical knowledge, MR systems hold significant promise for widespread deployment in non-industrial settings.

In this work, we address the accessibility challenges of teleoperation by introducing a novel MR-based control framework for robotic systems. Our interface is built with SwiftUI, RealityKit, and ARKit, and deployed on an extended reality (XR) headset. It enables easy and effective robot control without requiring prior user training. Direct feedback and gesture-based commands promote a natural and low-barrier interaction model, making the system suitable for a wide range of users and applications.

1.1 Contribution

We present an MR interface for seamless robotic teleoperation, emphasizing usability and accessibility. To the best of our knowledge, this is the first teleoperation system developed using the SwiftUI, RealityKit, and ARKit technology stack and deployed on an XR headset. The interface supports gesture-based control, with interactions designed to mirror natural human motion. RealityKit, powered by ARKit, incorporates hand tracking and eye gaze [1], enabling users to issue commands through subtle gestures, such as a pinch while looking at a target. This approach eliminates the need for physical controllers or exaggerated motion, offering a more comfortable and immersive user experience [12].

An integrated calibration system ensures immediate spatial alignment between the MR environment and the real robot via a fixed marker in the robot's workspace. This removes the need for user-specific setup and facilitates quick onboarding.

The system was validated through experimental trials involving both novice and experienced users across pick-and-place tasks of varying complexity. Performance was statistically analyzed to evaluate usability and task success across experience levels. In summary, the main contributions of this work are:

- A user-friendly MR teleoperation interface developed with SwiftUI, RealityKit, and ARKit, enabling control via an XR headset without requiring prior training;
- Experimental validation through complex manipulation tasks, with statistical analysis describing user performance and subjective feedback.

2 Related Works

Teleoperation of robots, or *telerobotics*, focuses on enabling remote users to effectively control robotic systems [21]. Although not ideal for repetitive industrial tasks, it proves essential in fields like surgical robotics [9,10] and space exploration [17,24]. Research in this area has evolved to address challenges in both user interaction and long-distance communication [2,19]. To meet the growing demand for intuitive and accessible teleoperation, recent works have explored various control modalities—ranging from physically grounded haptic devices to purely visual or immersive extended reality (XR) systems.

Haptic systems aim to provide users with natural, physical interaction for robot control. In [30], the authors present *GELLO*, an affordable, intuitive teleoperation platform optimized for data collection in robot learning. Supporting bi-manual control and efficient demonstration capture, the system offers fast onboarding for novices and outperforms conventional virtual reality (VR) and 3D input devices. However, limitations in force feedback led to its exclusion.

Building upon this, [7] extends prior work [31] by enabling mobile bi-manual teleoperation. The interface moves with the user—expanding applicability to dynamic tasks such as cooking and furniture manipulation. Post-demonstration, the collected data is used for imitation learning. Usability tests with non-expert participants confirmed its accessibility and performance.

Despite their intuitive nature, haptic systems often require external hardware, which can increase cost and cognitive load [30].

Vision-based interfaces leverage cameras to interpret human gestures, eliminating the need for wearable or haptic hardware. In [18], a remote control system uses stereo vision for 6-DoF hand tracking and grasp control. Visual feedback is provided through multiple fixed and onboard cameras. A switchable shared autonomy mode enhances precision by aligning the robot to target objects.

Similarly, [22] employs a depth camera to reconstruct arm, hand, and finger motion in the DART environment [20]. A neural network interprets gestures to drive the robot, enabling dexterous control even without haptic feedback.

The work in [13] generalizes vision-based teleoperation across various robotic setups using RGB or depth input. The system translates tracked motions into commands for physical or simulated robots—and also supports multi-user collaboration, enabling shared control of multiple robots.

XR technologies enhance teleoperation by projecting contextual information into the user's visual environment [6,23,28], overcoming limited feedback of purely visual or haptic systems. In [11], a VR framework enables control of a dual-arm manipulator within virtual space. A digital twin of the robot and its environment is displayed, with camera views rendered as virtual screens. Users can operate in direct control (*Telemanip*) or goal-driven (*Approach*) modes, with previewed motion paths for verification.

To increase control fidelity, [29] introduces a hybrid interface combining a handheld VR controller and a data glove. The controller specifies end-effector goals, while the glove maps finger positions for trajectory generation. Users trigger execution manually—balancing immersion and fine control. In [27], the environment is replicated in a fully virtual robotic cell, with data from the robot used to reconstruct its current pose and the workspace. The robot is then controlled via a transparent sphere with a coordinate frame and some buttons attached.

Fig. 1. Scheme of the developed teleoperation framework.

Compared to this, our work assumes that the operator is able to see directly the robot and the workspace, and enhances the user interface.

Immersive XR environments are, however, not well suited for close-range tasks, leading to new interfaces. In [26], the authors develop an augmented reality (AR) interface tailored for industrial scenarios. Using a gamepad for control and a headset for visual overlay, the system projects essential feedback—such as target poses, joint angles, force readings, and camera streams—into the user's view. It supports both joint-space and task-space control in world and tool frames.

In [3], cues are given based on object-pose recognition. Hints on the position of the robot and gripper, on the circumference of the end effector, prediction on occlusions and on the pose of manipulated objects are projected into the AR environment. Interaction with the robot is operated by gaze and head movements.

In [25], the control is based entirely on AR input and hand gestures interpreted by the headset. The end-effector pose is controlled via gesture commands, rather than direct hand tracking, while voice commands switch modes. Control is user-initiated and intermittent, but initial calibration to align with the digital twin may cause synchronization issues.

Contrary to previous works, our framework uses both hand gestures and eye tracking to interact with the user interface, making it easier for most interactions while still remaining accessible. Moreover, an efficient calibration method is used, exploiting a physical marker that the user simply observes through the XR device—enabling fast and seamless integration into the environment. Finally, and most importantly, to the best of our knowledge, this is the first MR teleoperation framework developed with SwiftUI, RealityKit and ARKit.

3 Developed Teleoperation Framework

Our framework can be divided into two separate parts, the XR headset application and the robot interface, communicating over Local Area Network (LAN) via a socket through standard TCP/IP protocol. The headset acts as the client, sending a JSON-formatted message to the server on which a robot interface is running. A conceptual scheme of our framework is reported in Fig. 1.

3.1 MR Interface

To realize our application, we developed an app with visionOS set as the sole supported platform. The application is divided into three main components: the calibration system, the user interface, and the robot interface.

3.1.1 Calibration System

Let us consider three orthonormal frames: $O_w - x_w y_w z_w$, (the world frame, corresponding to a marker), $O_u - x_u y_u z_u$ (the user's XR headset frame), and $O_b - x_b y_b z_b$ (the robot base frame). The objective is to enable the user to define a target pose for the robot end-effector relative to the world frame. To this aim, we implemented a calibration system based on ARKit's native image tracking capabilities in visionOS. Our solution was developed using only built-in SDKs and frameworks, considering platform limitations that prevent direct access to the headset's camera feed, limiting the use of third-party recognition frameworks [16] such as YOLO, MobileNet, or FastViT. As a result, our approach relies entirely on ARKit's internal tracking mechanisms.

To enable reliable tracking, the reference image must conform to ARKit's best practices [15], including high visual detail, uniqueness, and sufficient resolution. We selected a marker satisfying these criteria and defined its physical size precisely (19.7 cm by 19.7 cm). This printed marker corresponds to the world frame with respect to which the user specifies the target commands for the robot.

Upon detection, ARKit returns a spatial anchor with a transformation matrix $T_w^u \in SE(3)$ describing the position and orientation of the marker with respect to the user XR headset frame.

This setup, exploiting the knowledge of T_w^u, allows the user to specify the desired pose in the world frame, represented as a transformation matrix $T_d^w \in SE(3)$. To execute the task, this target pose must be expressed in the robot base frame. To achieve this, we manually align the robot end effector one time with the world frame to determine the relative transformation between the base frame of the robot and the world frame, denoted $T_w^b \in SE(3)$. The target pose in the robot base frame $T_d^b \in SE(3)$ is then computed as $T_d^b = T_w^b T_d^w$.

3.1.2 User Interface

The user interface, shown in Fig. 2, consists of a visual interaction target and an attachment window. Represented as a virtual sphere, the target serves as the primary interaction point for guiding the robot's end-effector. It is selectable and manipulable via natural gestures—such as pointing, pinching, or gaze—and provides visual feedback when active.

The system interprets user input and continuously updates the position of the target. Movements made in the virtual space are reprojected into the shared coordinate system using the transformation matrix obtained during calibration. This ensures that the target's virtual position corresponds precisely to a physical position in the robot's workspace.

To support additional interaction, a spatially anchored control panel, referred to as *Attachment Window*, is displayed alongside the interaction target. Although rendered as a flat interface, it appears three-dimensional and spatially responsive in the virtual environment. Its position is dynamically linked to the target entity, allowing users to access controls without diverting attention from the task.

The Attachment Window includes the following UI elements:

1. **Position.** Visualization of position coordinates of the target sphere.

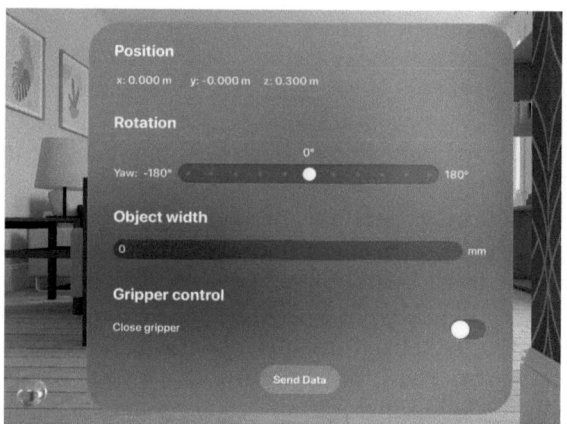

Fig. 2. User interface in a virtual environment, showing the target (blue-green sphere in bottom-left corner) and the attachment window. (Color figure online)

2. **Rotation.** End-effector orientation control along the vertical axis.
3. **Object Width.** Object width selection for gripper adjustment.
4. **Gripper Control.** Toggle to open or close the gripper.
5. **Send Data.** Start/stop control for live communication with the socket server.

This interface offers a compact and intuitive control panel for precise teleoperation in MR.

In order to integrate the virtual interface with the robot-facing code, a socket was developed, relying on standard TCP/IP protocol.

The socket client sends target position and orientation, gripper command, and object width combined in a JSON format in constant intervals of 100 ms.

3.2 Robot Interface

A custom control interface was implemented to receive commands via a TCP/IP socket. The commanded end-effector pose is expressed in the world coordinate frame—centered on the calibration marker—and then transformed into the robot's base frame. Gripper control is handled through a binary open/close signal, accompanied by a target width for object-specific adaptation.

Robot motion is governed through a Cartesian position control scheme, which interpolates between the current and target poses to produce smooth, continuous motion. The control system also supports tunable relative joint acceleration, allowing for a balance between responsiveness and fluidity—key for aligning motion behaviour with user interactions.

The control system is structured into three parallel threads:

1. Communication Thread - Listens for incoming commands from the XR headset and updates the target pose and gripper status.

Table 1. User sample description.

User profile		Value
Gender	Male	78.6%
	Female	21.4%
Prescription glasses users		57.1%
Age		26.9 ± 3.05
VR experience (1 - 5 scale)		2.43 ± 1.28
Robot experience (1 - 5 scale)		3.79 ± 1.31
iOS experience (1 - 5 scale)		2.07 ± 1.44

2. Motion Control Thread - Continuously sends commands to move the robot toward the latest received target pose, with a control loop running at a 10 ms period.
3. Gripper Control Thread - Processes gripper commands to open or close the claw to the specified width.

4 Experiments

Our framework has been experimentally evaluated through testing with a representative user sample, who performed tasks of varying complexity. The results were analyzed to assess both users' performance and their subjective experience.

4.1 User Sample

The user sample we selected for the experiments consists in 14 people with different experience with robotics systems, XR headsets and iOS platforms. This sample also includes prescription glasses users, who were asked to remove their glasses to ensure proper use of the XR headset during the experiments. A description of the user sample is provided in the Table 1. The sample was diverse in gender, prescription glasses use, age, and self-reported experience with VR, robotics, and iOS (1–5 scale). It is worth to indicate that 85.7%, 42.9%, 78.6% of participants reported medium to limited experience (≤ 3 on the 1–5 scale) in VR, robotics and iOS, respectively.

4.2 Experimental Setup

Our framework has been evaluated with the use of the following experimental setup:

- A KUKA LBR iiwa 7 robotic arm equipped with a WSG50 gripper, using the relative SmartServo-based C++ control interface;
- An XR headset;

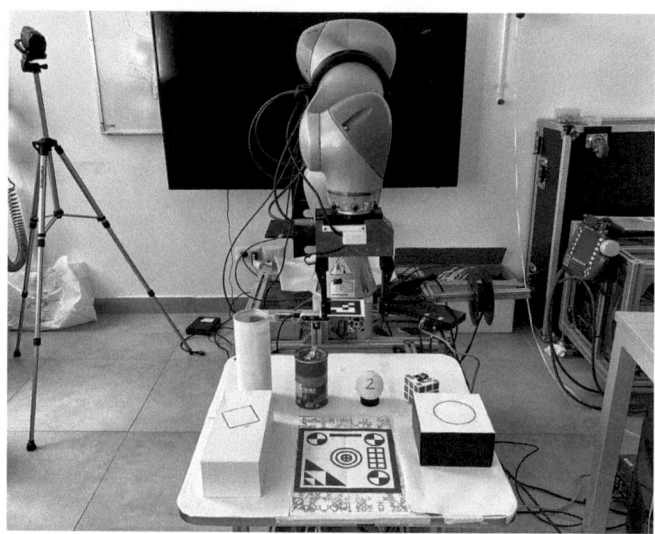

Fig. 3. Experimental Setup.

- A set of three distinct objects: a tennis ball with diameter 0.06 m, a can with diameter 0.08 m, and a Rubik's cube with side 0.056 m;
- Three target locations for object placement: a tube for the tennis ball, and two marked boxes indicating the desired pose footprints for the can and Rubik's cube;
- An OptiTrack motion capture system to accurately measure object placement errors (Fig. 3).

4.3 Tasks

To the selected user sample it was asked to complete the following tasks, in an order of their choosing:

1. **Ball task**: pick and place the tennis ball into the tube. This task is evaluated based on a binary success/failure criterion. Due to the relatively wide diameter of the tube compared to the ball, this is considered the easiest task, with minimal precision required.
2. **Can task**: pick and place the can onto its designated footprint. The objective here is precise positioning, making it a task of medium difficulty.
3. **Cube task**: pick and place the Rubik's cube onto its designated footprint with correct orientation. This is the most challenging task, as it requires both precise positioning and orientation.

The execution of these tasks of varying complexity allows for a comprehensive assessment of the system's precision, responsiveness, and usability in real-world object manipulation scenarios.

4.4 Evaluation Metrics

For each user, the success of individual tasks was recorded according to the following criteria:

- For the ball task, let us consider a binary value $s_b \in \{0, 1\}$ which denotes if the ball has been inserted into the tube ($s_b = 1$) or not ($s_b = 0$). Let us then denote the task execution time as $t_e \in \mathbb{R}$, measured in seconds. The task is considered successful if

$$s_b = 1 \wedge t_e < 120\,\text{s}. \tag{1}$$

- For the can task, we need to consider the position error, in addition to the task execution time. Let us denote by $\boldsymbol{p}_d \in \mathbb{R}^3$ the desired position and by $\boldsymbol{p} \in \mathbb{R}^3$ the reached position. Let us then define the position error $e_p \in \mathbb{R}$, expressed in meters, computed as

$$e_p = \|\boldsymbol{p}_d - \boldsymbol{p}\|_2, \tag{2}$$

with $\|\cdot\|_2$ Euclidean norm. The task is considered successful if

$$e_p < 0.02\,\text{m} \wedge t_e < 120\,\text{s}. \tag{3}$$

- For the cube task, in addition to considering the task execution time and the position error, we also have to consider the orientation error. Let us denote by $\boldsymbol{R}_d \in SO(3)$ the target rotation matrix and by $\boldsymbol{R} \in SO(3)$ the reached one. Let us then define the orientation error $e_\theta \in \mathbb{R}$, expressed in radians, computed from the angle-axis representation of the mutual orientation as

$$e_\theta = \arccos\left(\frac{\text{tr}(\boldsymbol{R}^T \boldsymbol{R}_d) - 1}{2}\right), \tag{4}$$

with $\text{tr}(\cdot)$ trace of the matrix. The task is considered successful if

$$e_p < 0.02\,\text{m} \wedge e_\theta < 0.2\,\text{rad} \wedge t_e < 120\,\text{s}. \tag{5}$$

For each user, the subjective standard measures NASA Task Load Index (TLX) and System Usability Scale (SUS) were collected, as well as a custom-designed questionnaire.

The NASA TLX is a widely adopted tool used to evaluate workload across various domains, with several variations. Specifically, the Raw NASA TLX [14] consists of six subscales—Mental Demand, Physical Demand, Temporal Demand, Performance, Effort, and Frustration—each rated from 0 to 100 in 5-point increments. The overall task load is the average of these subscale scores.

The SUS, on the other hand, is a well-established ten-item questionnaire based on a Likert scale, commonly used to assess system usability, also yielding a score from 0 to 100 [5].

The custom questionnaire evaluates user experience in terms of ease of use, with five subscales—Software, Picking, Placing, Position Control, and Orientation Control—and in terms of expected behaviour with two subscales Position Control and Orientation Control. All items are rated on a scale from 1 to 5.

Table 2. Task performance results.

Metric	Ball task	Can task	Cube task
$s\%$	92.9	78.6	64.3
t_e [s]	62.5 ± 20.2	59.8 ± 16.9	82.8 ± 17.3
e_p [10^{-3} m]	-	9.50 ± 6.10	6.70 ± 5.70
e_θ [10^{-2} rad]	-	-	8.24 ± 5.89

Table 3. Raw NASA TLX, SUS, and custom questionnaire results. Except from TLX, higher scores are index of better results.

Evaluation test		Results
TLX		31.3 ± 17.1
SUS		72.9 ± 12.3
Ease of Use (1 - 5 scale)	Software	3.71 ± 1.2
	Picking Item	3.71 ± 1.14
	Placing Item	3.64 ± 1.28
	Position Control	3.71 ± 1.2
	Orientation Control	3.07 ± 1.33
Expected Behaviour (1 - 5 scale)	Position Control	3.43 ± 1.16
	Orientation Control	3 ± 1.41

4.5 Results

Here the results of the tasks performed by the user sample are reported. The quantitative results of the performance are provided in Table 2, while the users subjective responses are collected in Table 3.

In Table 2, the parameter $s\%$ indicates the average percentage success rate, computed considering the aforementioned criterion. Position and orientation errors e_p, e_θ and execution time t_e are reported with their mean and standard deviation taking into account only the successful tasks.

As expected, the results show that the average success percentage is highest for the ball task, while it is lowest for the cube task. That is because the ball task requires less position precision, while the cube task requires both precise position and orientation. It is worth reporting that 80% of the users who failed the cube task are prescription glasses users. For users with visual impairments, it is recommended to use prescription lens inserts compatible with the headset, which were not available during testing as are specific to the user's prescription.

In terms of successful task completion, it is evident that both the error rate and execution time are well within acceptable limits. The results demonstrate that the performance of the system is reliable, with minimal errors and reasonable task completion times, indicating that the system is both efficient and effective for the intended use.

Regarding subjective user feedback, shown in Table 3, the metrics indicate low perceived workload (NASA-TLX) and high system usability (SUS). The software was found to be generally easy to use, and the users perceived both the picking and placing tasks clearly manageable. They reported a high level of satisfaction with position control, citing both ease of use and expected behaviour. However, satisfaction with orientation control was slightly lower in comparison. Some users noted that the slider interface for managing orientation (see Fig. 2) turned out to be rather sensitive. Nonetheless, overall feedback was highly positive, suggesting that the framework was easy to use and comfortable.

5 Conclusion

In this paper, we have presented our MR-based framework for robot manipulator teleoperation. The framework is based on SwiftUI, RealityKit and ARKit on the user side, relying on TCP/IP stack to communicate with the robot. The framework has been tested by 14 users with various degrees of experience with robots and XR headsets, and different metrics were used to evaluate user performance and comfort in using the framework. The results have shown the framework to be quite easy to use and responsive, while users that had to remove their prescription glasses performed, on average, worse than those without vision defects. Finally, users seem to find more ease in controlling the robot end-effector position than the orientation. Future works include refining the user interface to make the orientation control more intuitive and effective, for example, substituting the input sphere with an input cube, which can be rotated by the user. Other improvements may regard gripper close and open commands, associating them to hand gestures.

Acknowledgments. The research leading to these results has been partially supported by the ARIEL project, in the frame of the PRIN 2022 research program, grant n. 2022WS29WP, funded by the European Union Next-Generation EU; and the DARC project, in the frame of the PRIN 2022 PNRR research program, grant n. P2022MHR5C, funded by the European Union Next-Generation EU; and the MUR under program PNRR - DM 118/2023 Mis.: I.3.4 "Dottorati Transizione Digitale" - CUP: E66E23001030002, funded by the European Union Next-Generation EU. The authors are solely responsible for its content.

We thank Bruna Martins de Oliveira, Alessandra Souza da Silva and Edgar Vergara for the invaluable contribution and continued support to the project's design and development.

References

1. Altobello, M., Pereira, T.G.: Using realitykit gestures in an ar application with swiftui (2023). https://www.createwithswift.com/using-realitykit-gestures-in-an-ar-application-with-swiftui/
2. Anderson, R., Spong, M.: Bilateral control of teleoperators with time delay. IEEE Trans. Autom. Control **34**(5), 494–501 (1989). https://doi.org/10.1109/9.24201
3. Arevalo Arboleda, S., Rücker, F., Dierks, T., Gerken, J.: Assisting manipulation and grasping in robot teleoperation with augmented reality visual cues. In: Proceedings of the 2021 CHI Conference on Human Factors in Computing Systems, CHI '21. Association for Computing Machinery, New York (2021). https://doi.org/10.1145/3411764.3445398
4. Argall, B.D., Chernova, S., Veloso, M., Browning, B.: A survey of robot learning from demonstration. Robot. Auton. Syst. **57**(5), 469–483 (2009)
5. Brooke, J.: Sus: A quick and dirty usability scale. Usability Eval. Ind. **189** (11 1995)
6. De Pace, F., Manuri, F., Sanna, A., Fornaro, C.: A systematic review of augmented reality interfaces for collaborative industrial robots. Comput. Ind. Eng. **149**, 106806 (2020). https://doi.org/10.1016/j.cie.2020.106806, https://www.sciencedirect.com/science/article/pii/S0360835220305118
7. Fu, Z., Zhao, T.Z., Finn, C.: Mobile aloha: Learning bimanual mobile manipulation with low-cost whole-body teleoperation (2024). https://arxiv.org/abs/2401.02117
8. Fukui, H., Yonejima, S., Yamano, M., Dohi, M., Yamada, M., Nishiki, T.: Development of teaching pendant optimized for robot application. In: 2009 IEEE Workshop on Advanced Robotics and its Social Impacts, pp. 72–77 (2009). https://doi.org/10.1109/ARSO.2009.5587070
9. Funda, J., Taylor, R., Eldridge, B., Gomory, S., Gruben, K.: Constrained cartesian motion control for teleoperated surgical robots. IEEE Trans. Robot. Automation **12**(3), 453–465 (1996). https://doi.org/10.1109/70.499826
10. Funda, J., Taylor, R.H., Gruben, K., LaRose, D.: Optimal motion control for teleoperated surgical robots. In: Kim, W.S. (ed.) Telemanipulator Technology and Space Telerobotics, vol. 2057, pp. 211–222. International Society for Optics and Photonics, SPIE (1993). https://doi.org/10.1117/12.164902
11. Gallipoli, M., Buonocore, S., Selvaggio, M., Fontanelli, G.A., Grazioso, S., Di Gironimo, G.: A virtual reality-based dual-mode robot teleoperation architecture. Robotica **42**(6), 1935–1958 (2024). https://doi.org/10.1017/S0263574724000663
12. Gordon, W.: Apple vision pro vs. meta quest pro: Which headset wins? (2024). https://www.pcmag.com/comparisons/apple-vision-pro-vs-meta-quest-pro. Accessed 11 Apr 2025
13. Handa, A., et al.: Dexpilot: vision-based teleoperation of dexterous robotic hand-arm system. In: 2020 IEEE International Conference on Robotics and Automation (ICRA), pp. 9164–9170 (2020). https://doi.org/10.1109/ICRA40945.2020.9197124
14. Hart, S.: Nasa-task load index (nasa-tlx); 20 years later. vol. 50 (10 2006). https://doi.org/10.1177/154193120605000909
15. Inc., A.: Detecting images in an ar experience (2024). https://developer.apple.com/documentation/arkit/detecting-images-in-an-ar-experience. Accessed 11 Apr 2025
16. Inc., A.: Machine learning models (2024). https://developer.apple.com/machine-learning/models/. Accessed 11 Apr 2025
17. Jr., A.J.M., Larsen, R.L.: Nasa research in teleoperation and robotics. In: Casasent, D.P. (ed.) Robotics and Industrial Inspection, vol. 0360, pp. 22 – 31. International Society for Optics and Photonics, SPIE (1983). https://doi.org/10.1117/12.934080

18. Kofman, J., Wu, X., Luu, T., Verma, S.: Teleoperation of a robot manipulator using a vision-based human-robot interface. IEEE Trans. Industr. Electron. **52**(5), 1206–1219 (2005). https://doi.org/10.1109/TIE.2005.855696
19. Lee, D., Spong, M.: Passive bilateral teleoperation with constant time delay. IEEE Trans. Rob. **22**(2), 269–281 (2006). https://doi.org/10.1109/TRO.2005.862037
20. Lee, J., et al.: Dart: dynamic animation and robotics toolkit. J. Open Source Softw. **3**(22), 500 (2018). https://doi.org/10.21105/joss.00500
21. Niemeyer, G., Preusche, C., Stramigioli, S., Lee, D.: Telerobotics, pp. 1085–1108. Springer International Publishing, Cham (2016). https://doi.org/10.1007/978-3-319-32552-1_43
22. Qin, Y., et al.: Anyteleop: a general vision-based dexterous robot arm-hand teleoperation system (2024). https://arxiv.org/abs/2307.04577
23. Rosa-Garcia, A.d.l., Marrufo, A.I.S., Luviano-Cruz, D., Rodriguez-Ramirez, A., Garcia-Luna, F.: Bridging remote operations and augmented reality: An analysis of current trends. IEEE Access **13**, 36502–36526 (2025). https://doi.org/10.1109/ACCESS.2025.3544633
24. Ruoff, C.F.: Teleoperation and robotics in space, vol. 161. Aiaa (1994)
25. Smith, A., III, M.K.: An augmented reality interface for teleoperating robot manipulators (2025). https://arxiv.org/abs/2409.18394
26. Solanes, J.E., noz, A.M., Gracia, L., AnaMartıí, Girbés-Juan, V., Tornero, J.: Teleoperation of industrial robot manipulators based on augmented reality. Int. J. Adv. Manuf. Technol. **111**, 1077 – 1097 (2020). https://api.semanticscholar.org/CorpusID:225139528
27. Sun, D., Kiselev, A., Liao, Q., Stoyanov, T., Loutfi, A.: A new mixed-reality-based teleoperation system for telepresence and maneuverability enhancement. IEEE Trans. Hum.-Mach. Syst. **50**(1), 55–67 (2020). https://doi.org/10.1109/THMS.2019.2960676
28. Suzuki, R., Karim, A., Xia, T., Hedayati, H., Marquardt, N.: Augmented reality and robotics: a survey and taxonomy for ar-enhanced human-robot interaction and robotic interfaces. In: Proceedings of the 2022 CHI Conference on Human Factors in Computing Systems, CHI '22. Association for Computing Machinery, New York (2022). https://doi.org/10.1145/3491102.3517719
29. Wan, K., Li, C., Lo, F.S., Zheng, P.: A virtual reality-based immersive teleoperation system for remote human-robot collaborative manufacturing. Manuf. Lett. **41**, 43–50 (2024). https://doi.org/10.1016/j.mfglet.2024.09.008, https://www.sciencedirect.com/science/article/pii/S2213846324000658. 52nd SME North American Manufacturing Research Conference (NAMRC 52)
30. Wu, P., Shentu, Y., Yi, Z., Lin, X., Abbeel, P.: Gello: A general, low-cost, and intuitive teleoperation framework for robot manipulators. In: 2024 IEEE/RSJ International Conference on Intelligent Robots and Systems (IROS), pp. 12156–12163 (2024). https://doi.org/10.1109/IROS58592.2024.10801581
31. Zhao, T.Z., Kumar, V., Levine, S., Finn, C.: Learning fine-grained bimanual manipulation with low-cost hardware (2023). https://arxiv.org/abs/2304.13705

Context Awareness and Explainability

Classification of User Satisfaction in HRI with Social Signals in the Wild

Michael Schiffmann[1](✉)[🆔], Sabina Jeschke[2][🆔], and Anja Richert[1][🆔]

[1] TH Köln - University of Applied Sciences, Cologne Cobots Lab, Betzdorfer Str. 2, 50679 Cologne, Germany
{michael.schiffmann,anja.richert}@th-koeln.de
[2] KI Park e.V. & FAU - Friedrich-Alexander University of Erlangen-Nuremberg, Nuremberg, Germany

Abstract. Socially interactive agents (SIAs) are being used in various scenarios and are nearing productive deployment. Evaluating user satisfaction with SIAs' performance is a key factor in designing the interaction between the user and SIA. Currently, subjective user satisfaction is primarily assessed manually through questionnaires or indirectly via system metrics. This study examines the automatic classification of user satisfaction through analysis of social signals, aiming to enhance both manual and autonomous evaluation methods for SIAs. During a field trial at the Deutsches Museum Bonn, a Furhat Robotics head was employed as a service and information hub, collecting an "in-the-wild" dataset. This dataset comprises 46 single-user interactions, including questionnaire responses and video data. Our method focuses on automatically classifying user satisfaction based on time series classification. We use time series of social signal metrics derived from the body pose, time series of facial expressions, and physical distance. This study compares three feature engineering approaches on different machine learning models. The results confirm the method's effectiveness in reliably identifying interactions with low user satisfaction without the need for manually annotated datasets. This approach offers significant potential for enhancing SIA performance and user experience through automated feedback mechanisms.

Keywords: Social Signals · in-the-wild · Social Robots

1 Introduction

Socially interactive agents (SIA) are applied in various scenarios, such as in public spaces like a museum [6,28,32]. SIAs can be viewed from a technological and application-specific perspective: On the one hand, it is crucial by definition that they continuously adapt to users. On the other hand, operators and researchers are interested in whether SIAs deliver the desired performance in productive use. For both approaches, the automatic measurement of user satisfaction can be crucial for the evaluation and improvement of SIAs.

The integration of UX data is an essential development factor [4,26], particularly in service and information environments where the goal is to assist users. There are various ways to evaluate SIAs, for instance, indirectly through objective system metrics regarding the efficiency of the SIA's speech dialogue system, such as the number of turns or dialogue duration [7,29]. Alternatively, metrics like the number of different dialogue paths can be used to assess the complexity of potential dialogues, which, according to [7], is an indicator of efficiency and satisfaction.

Direct evaluation of subjective user satisfaction is only possible through questionnaires or interviews. An approach that captures this implicitly is necessary for the automatic collection of user satisfaction since active feedback requests interrupt the interaction, and post-interaction feedback requests risk low participation. A video-based possibility involves capturing social signals that allow insights into the user's internal state. Nonverbal social signals or cues can be used to make these inferences [20] and like [15,24,31] showed that annotated video data can be used to classify quality features like user satisfaction or user experience. Assessing the user's state is not only of interest for adaptation but also for evaluating the SIA's performance in specific applications.

In this paper, we explore how individual user satisfaction ratings can be automatically classified using social signals as a source for machine learning feature extraction, specifically body language, facial expressions, and distance, to predict user satisfaction. We use an in-the-wild dataset consisting of single user interactions and corresponding post user satisfaction ratings of each particular user. To achieve this, we utilize data collected from a field study with an autonomous SIA deployed as a service and information hub at the Deutsches Museum Bonn. Our method distinguishes itself from the state-of-the-art by using an holistic approach to capture social signals from body language, not requiring additional annotations from third parties or users. We compare three feature engineering methods to demonstrate how to classify interactions with low user satisfaction and interactions with medium to high user satisfaction ratings. Despite unpredictable conditions, realistic interaction data offer valuable insights, allowing for the study of unbiased interactions with an autonomous SIA. In the following, we first discuss the psychological background of social signals and related work. We then present the implemented system and experimental setting. In the methods section, we explain data collection, feature engineering, and the composition of the classification task before we finally present the results and discuss them in terms of the peculiarities of the "in-the-wild" approach and further research avenues arising from this work.

2 Related Work

In social interactions, individuals exchange information through verbal and nonverbal communication with their conversation partners. Social signals, including body language, gestures, and facial expressions, serve various purposes in this context and help convey one's emotional state or stance towards something (social attitude) [21]. In HRI, social signals have been effectively utilized to evaluate various psychological constructs, such as rapport [20,30], user satisfaction [24,31], user experience [15], user engagement [15], and affective assignment [13,19] within Russell's circumplex model of affect (two-dimensional model for emotions) [22]. Müller et al. [20] predicted perceived low rapport versus medium/high rapport in human-to-human group interactions using automatically derived features from social signals. They found that facial cues, including a variety of features such as indicators of happiness, synchrony indicators, the amount of mutual facing, among others were the strongest predictors of low rapport, achieving an average accuracy of 70%. Jokinen and Wilcock [15] showed in a laboratory HRI Experiment that certain aspects of user experience have a significant correlation with the user behavior and that it is possible to predict the user's experience overall and its aspects of usability, expressiveness, responsiveness, and interface from a manually annotated dataset. Wei et al. [31] studied user satisfaction (well-coordinated, awkward, unfriendly) in a Wizard-of-Oz interaction with a digital agent, assessing it through user questionnaires and self-assessments. They successfully used deep learning on multi-modal verbal and non-verbal social signals, finding that multi-modal models outperformed uni-modal ones in predicting user satisfaction. Schiffmann et al. [24] showed that user satisfaction can be predicted based on annotated valence and arousal time series features and the user satisfaction value of the respective users of human-robot interaction which was recorded in the wild. Using a generated skeleton model, McColl et al. [19] demonstrated how to predict valence and arousal levels by translating the user's body language into angles, velocities, and expansion. This approach was subsequently utilized with a rater-based method for annotating interaction data, resulting in the development of separate valence and arousal models for training and prediction. However, all these approaches share the commonality of being based on controlled laboratory studies, with training data generated through an annotation process, except in the case of [20,24].

3 System and Setting

The field trial took place from July 23, 2024, to August 15, 2024, at the Deutsches Museum Bonn (DMB). The DMB is presenting an exhibition on artificial intelligence with interactive exhibits to bring artificial intelligence closer to a broad audience. The robot "Mira", developed to answer visitor questions, was positioned near the entrance in a designated interaction area. Figure 1 illustrates and labels the experimental setup.

The Furhat robot [3] from Furhat Robotics AB is mounted on a special casing with an additional 10-inch tablet displaying the transcribed dialogue during interactions. Two wide-angle cameras are mounted on the sides of Furhat to capture the user fully, as the geometry of the housing prevents full-body capture with the integrated camera alone. Before interacting with the robotic system, museum visitors must agree to the data processing policy by pressing the privacy policy button, as informed by a poster. Video, audio data, and interaction logs

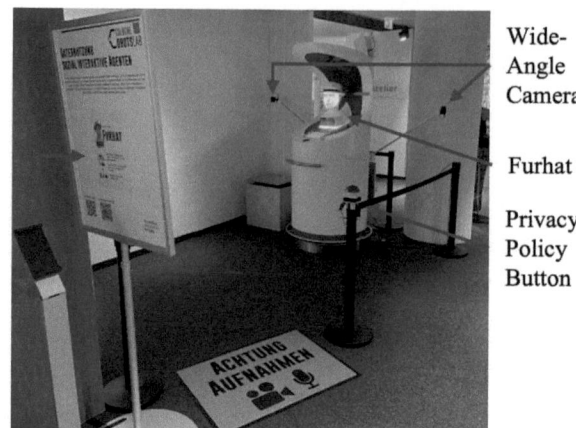

Fig. 1. Setting of the Field Test in the Museum.

were recorded for research. The Furhat robot remains in idle mode with a blue LED until consent is given. If permission isn't granted and the user is detected by the person management, the robot prompts visitors. Upon agreement, the robot initiates interaction when a user enters the area, with the LED changing to green for listening and red for processing and speaking. On a technical level, the system is divided into front-end and back-end. The front-end consists of the robot head, which runs a so-called Furhat Skill that uses the Furhat SDK for person management, speech-to-text, and text-to-speech functionalities. The back-end handles session and dialogue management and persistence of interaction data with a unique session ID. The system's conversational knowledge is either managed through intent-based natural language understanding with a Q&A database or, if that fails, generated by a locally executed LLM, Llama 3, as a fallback. The LLM receives the previous conversation history and the prompt: "This is a conversation between a visitor of the Deutsches Museum in Bonn and a robot named Mira. Mira is programmed to respond briefly and precisely, in no more than two sentences." Additionally, the back-end controls the media recordings and captures material from all cameras. The wide-angle cameras support Furhat's person management by capturing users who are too tall or short for the integrated camera or those who turn aside for too long, preventing premature interaction termination. By implementing an additional person detection with YOLO (yolov5 [14]), a double-check was realized to verify the presence of individuals in the interaction area.

4 Method

Our approach to investigate whether the user's social signals can be used to classify user satisfaction rating from time series features automatically is methodologically composed of conducting the experiment itself for data collection, data preparation and preprocessing for the respective feature engineering methods for machine learning.

4.1 Field Test Execution and Questionnaire

Museum visitors interacted freely with the robot and were informed solely through a privacy policy poster. After interacting, a researcher invited them to fill out a questionnaire. Due to the general reluctance to complete lengthy questionnaires in the field, we use a custom-designed, concise questionnaire.

The questionnaire assessed user satisfaction using five items on a 5-point Likert scale (1 = strongly disagree and 5 = strongly agree). Additionally, demographic data of the users was collected. The user is first asked for a statement on "Overall, I am satisfied with the system." which is derived from the first question of the After Scenario Questionnaire [16] and is intended to capture the individual's satisfaction according to their judgment. The second statement is "If I meet this agent again, I would talk to him again." which is supposed to assess the willingness to interact with the agent again; we expect that a satisfactory interaction will result in a desire to re-interact. The subsequent three statements target interaction dynamics and focus on the participant's perception of the conversation flow and speaker changes, as these elements are crucial for a seamless interaction. The third statement is "The agent motivated me to continue the conversation" which seeks to evaluate the persuasive ability of the agent, thereby indicating the degree to which the interaction was engaging. The fourth statement, "The alternating listening and speaking was intuitive" addresses the fluidity and naturalness of turn-taking during the interaction. Finally, "It was understandable to me when the agent was listening to me" gauges how clearly the participants could distinguish when the agent was attentive to their input. We use Cronbach's Alpha to check items' internal consistency and interrelation in this custom, not validated scale, ensuring it reliably measures user satisfaction. For the machine learning task, we combine the five items via averaging to a user satisfaction score, which is used as target label.

4.2 User Satisfaction Classification

Our approach involves the following steps: extracting a body pose, calculating various social signal metrics per camera frame, computing time series-specific features for three different feature engineering approaches, and selecting relevant features for the final training of models. We utilize two approaches for automatic feature extraction, and our own approach with handcrafted features is designed to mimic the coding used in qualitative video analyses.

Extraction of the Social Signals. In this study, we use body language, e.g., posture, facial expressions, and the user's distance to the agent. The extraction of body language is realized using MediaPipe [18]. A total of 33 body landmarks are extracted for the key nodes on the human body and are returned as normalized X, Y, Z coordinates along with a visibility value. Figure 2 shows the workflow from capturing the person to outputting the metrics. The landmarks generated from the three camera perspectives are synchronized to 30 frames per second and then fused in the combining step, where visibility and distance between the landmarks are considered, resulting in one body pose. Initially, the poses are rotated because the cameras were not aligned, yet the landmark detector assumes strict vertical and horizontal alignment of the cameras.

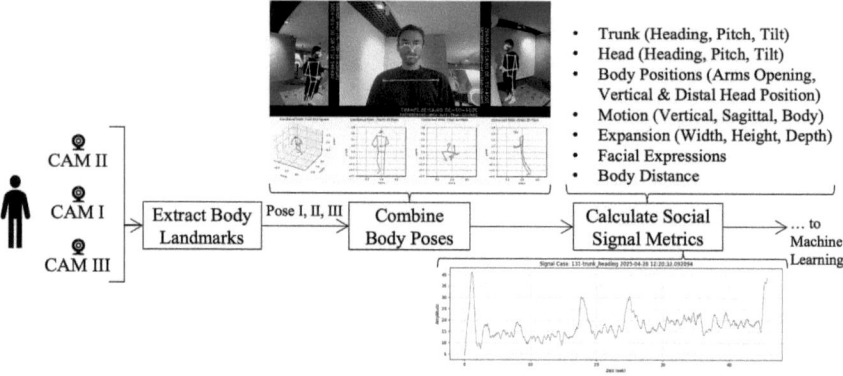

Fig. 2. Processing Flow to Extract the Body Landmarks from each Camera Frame and Combine them into one Body Posture to Calculate the Different Social Signal Metrics.

The facial expressions are extracted with py-feat [9], which uses the MediaPipe face mesh with 468 3D landmarks [18]. The output of py-feat predicts seven expressions: happiness, anger, disgust, fear, sadness, surprise, and neutral. For the distance measure, we use the approach by [1] and utilize the diameter of the user's iris to estimate the distance to the front camera since this can be assumed to have a fixed size. Body language, such as nodding, facing towards, and leaning in or out, encodes attitudes towards the SIA through posture over time. Our concept for capturing these social signals adapts the approach of McColl et al. [19] by translating a user's body posture into angle and velocity metrics such as head and torso orientation (heading, pitch, tilt), body dimensions and its velocity in three spatial directions, head position (vertical & sagittal) and arm opening —resulting in 16 time-series metrics including distance (see online Appendix [23] for more details). We use this implicit holistic approach to capture body language because we have found that users show few explicit gestures [25] such as affirmative hand gestures, nodding, head shaking or expressive facial expressions as commonly used in annotation-based research cf. [15,31]. Figure 2 shows the resulting time series for head heading (orientation to the agent) over the interaction period.

Data generation and Preprocessing. For the final dataset, only single interactions were selected where the participants were mostly alone in the interaction area. Additionally, only interactions linked to a fully completed questionnaire were chosen. The selection rules lead to a reduced data set, but this prevents the time series from containing disturbances, e.g. because another person has entered the interaction area or the person has changed, which leads to a distorted data set. We use only the main phase of the interaction because while the user is entering or leaving the interaction area, the body pose can only be combined in insufficient quality, leading to highly distorted social signals. We observed occasional body pose misclassifications during the interaction, leading to distortions and missing values, which we corrected by applying linear interpolation and smoothing techniques on the time series.

Feature Engineering Approaches. The extraction of social signals results in 23 time series to generate social signal metrics, where 16 metrics are generated from the body and seven from the face. Analyzing and generating features of these time series is challenging as they must comprehensively represent the connection between users state and user satisfaction [11]. We compare three state-of-the-art feature engineering approaches to determine their effectiveness in classifying user satisfaction.

Feature Engineering with tsfresh. The tsfresh library is an extensive Python tool for automatically extracting various features from time series data (used version 0.21.0) [10]. It enables precise analysis and classification by generating numerous relevant features and selecting suitable attributes for machine learning.

Feature Engineering with catch22. The catch22 library follows the idea to calculate 22 of the most important time series features, such as linear and nonlinear autocorrelation, successive differences, value distributions, and outliers (used version pycatch22 0.4.5) [17]. These features have been shown to capture key characteristics and patterns to facilitate effective time series classification and analysis.

Handcrafted Feature Engineering. We employ an approach mimicking interaction annotation by establishing angular ranges for each social signal metric which is crucial for interaction. For instance, for the head, we define areas that distinguish between "looking at" and "looking away" (see online Appendix [23] for more details). The social signal time series is assigned to these zones by calculating the average over a 0.5-second time window to determine the appropriate zone. Based on these assignments per time window, we compute various features per metric: average, minimum, maximum, standard deviation, the most frequently occurring zone, the distribution of individual zones, the number of zone transitions, and the longest and shortest durations within a zone. Features based on the time series' value, such as mean, minimum, maximum, and standard deviation, are also calculated for further classification. This approach uses the time series of the trunk and head, body speed, distance, and facial expressions (confidence threshold is used) for a simple and understandable assignment of zones.

Model and Training. Each of the three feature engineering methods produce a large number of features, therefore we use the "SelectKBest" method available in scikit-learn [5], which selects the best k features based on ANOVA F-value analysis. Due to the small dataset size of N = 46 instances, we simplify the classification task by dividing the dataset into two classes: the bottom 33% percentile represents the class of dissatisfied users. In contrast, the upper 66% represents moderately to highly satisfied users. The simplifications helps to prevent overfitting since models need less data per class. The classification task remains relevant, as there is a pressing need for improvement of the robot, primarily when the user is dissatisfied. In a preliminary test with the dataset, we explored artificially augmenting the data by employing SMOTE [8] and duplicating the dataset through vertical mirroring; however, we discarded these approaches due to the lack of observed benefits. The selected ten best features were standardized and used for comparison to train a diverse set of algorithms Random Forest (ensemble method), Support Vector Machine and Logistic Regression (linear models), and Naive Bayes Classifier model (probalistic model) to compare them against each other. We use the leave-one-out cross-validation method (LOOCV), since our dataset consists of 46 interactions we aim to prevent overfitting. We complemented this with a parameter search to find optimal parameters for the different models. We aim to demonstrate the feasibility of this automatic approach, which works with labeled datasets instead of manually annotated data. Therefore, the performance of the models is evaluated by analyzing accuracy and assessing the model's discriminative ability, F1 score, precision, ROC-AUC, and recall.

5 Results

The evaluation of our approach consists of a detailed description of the dataset, followed by an explanation of the results from applying the described processing chain.

Of the N = 46 participants in the experiment, 20 were women, 25 were men, and one unspecified, aged from 13 to 71. The sample consists of 5 pupils, 3 students, 23 employees, 4 civil servants, 5 self-employed individuals, 6 retirees, and 2 participants who did not specify their occupations, with the majority holding university degrees (23), followed by 10 with a high school diploma (Abitur).

The internal consistency of our user satisfaction scale, as measured by Cronbach's Alpha, is 0.78, which is considered an acceptable value and borders on being a good result according to [12]. The participants reported a user satisfaction score of 3.4 on average, with a standard deviation of 0.81, a minimum of 1.4, and a maximum of 4.8.

The Duration of an interaction was 2 min and 12 s on average, with a standard deviation of 61 s, a minimum of 35 s, and a maximum duration of 5 min and 35 s. On average, the interactions comprised seven turns, with a minimum of 2, a maximum of 16, and a standard deviation of 3 turns. The resulting machine learning dataset consists of 15 instances with low user satisfaction ratings and 31 instances with medium to high user satisfaction ratings. The accuracy results of each of the three methods are depicted in Fig. 3, and the resulting metrics are listed in Table 1.

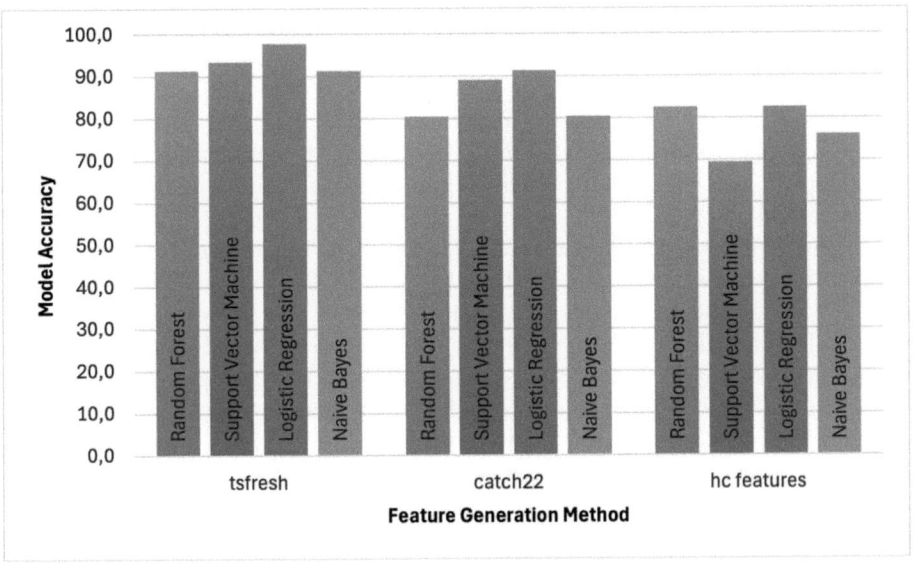

Fig. 3. Machine Learning Accuracy Results of each Model of the three Approaches.

Table 1. Macro Averages of the Metrics of the Machine Learning Training for each of the three Feature Engineering Approaches.

	Precision	Recall	F1-Score	Accuracy	ROC-AUC
tsfresh Random Forest	0,92	0,88	0,90	91,30	0,96
tsfresh Support Vector Machine	0,94	0,97	0,95	93,40	0,99
tsfresh Logistic Regression	0,97	0,98	0,98	97,80	0,99
tsfresh Naive Bayes	0,90	0,90	0,90	91,30	0,92
catch22 Random Forest	0,83	0,72	0,74	80,43	0,78
catch22 Support Vector Machine	0,82	0,82	0,83	89,13	0,93
catch22 Logistic Regression	0,92	0,88	0,90	91,30	0,96
catch22 Naive Bayes	0,78	0,77	0,77	80,43	0,83
hc features Random Forest	0,81	0,78	0,79	82,60	0,78
hc features Support Vector Machine	0,86	0,60	0,59	69,50	0,80
hc features Logistic Regression	0,82	0,77	0,79	82,60	0,84
hc features Naive Bayes	0,76	0,67	0,74	76,10	0,79

The classification results based on features computed using the tsfresh library achieved accuracies of 91.3% for Random Forest and Naive Bayes, 93.4% for Support Vector Machine, and 97.8% for Logistic Regression. Precision, Recall, F1-Score, and ROC-AUC performance metrics were generally above 0.9, except in one instance. Out of 783 features per time series the 10 most important ones selected for training (with respective significance levels), were: twice distance (p < 0.05 & p < 0.001), facial expression fear (p < 0.001), width (p < 0.001), head heading (p < 0.001), vertical motion (p < 0.001), head tilt (p < 0.001), facial expression surprise (p < 0.05), and head pitch (p < 0.05).

The top ten features result from applying a Fast Fourier Transform to the social signal time series and include coefficients from the real, imaginary, and angle components.

For the method utilizing the catch22 library, the respective models achieved classification accuracies ranging between 80,4% and 91,3% with Logistic Regression. The performance metrics were below those of the tsfresh approach. Out of 506 calculated features the ten most relevant are out of the time series of, in brackets the feature category and significance, trunk tilt (self-affine scaling, p < 0.05), head heading (extreme event timing - positive outlier timing, p < 0.05), vertical motion (nonlinear autocorrelation, p < 0.05), width (symbolic, p < 0.03), height (distribution shape, p < 0.03), depth (linear autocorrelation structure, p < 0.03), distance (nonlinear autocorrelation, p < 0.03), distance (linear autocorrelation, p < 0.03), facial expression disgust (self-affine scaling, p < 0.03) and facial expression happiness (extreme event timing - positive outlier timing, p < 0.03).

For further explanation, we refer to the catch22 feature description [2].

The models trained using handcrafted feature methods achieved classification accuracies ranging from 69.5% to 86.6% with Random Forest and Logistic Regression. The performance metrics ranged from 0.59 to 0.86 within an acceptable range, though they exhibited more variability than the other approaches. Out of 766 automatic generated features the 10 best time series features were trunk heading (Window 2 Frequency Zone 5, p < 0.03), trunk pitch (longest period Zone 2, p > 0.05), trunk pitch (shortest period Zone 2, p < 0.03), head heading (Window 1 Frequency Zone 5, p < 0.05), body speed (Count Zone Changes, p>0.05), body speed (shortest period Zone 10, p < 0.05), body speed (Window 1 Frequency Zone 8, p < 0.05), distance (Window 5 Frequency Zone3, p < 0.03), facial expression disgust (Window 1 Frequency Zone 2, p>0.05), and facial expression neutral (Count Zone Changes, p < 0.03).

For the complete feature tables we refer to the online Appendix [23].

6 Discussion

In this study, we investigated the extent to which user satisfaction in human-robot interactions can be classified based on social signals without elaborately annotating the interaction data. To achieve realistic results, we used interaction data collected in a museum through video recordings and questionnaires. Our approach includes video recording in the field, extraction of social signal metrics as time series, and feature generation using the tsfresh and catch22 libraries, as well as a hand-crafted approach

Due to the small number of $N = 46$ instances, an adapted training procedure (LOOCV) was used to minimize the risk of overfitting on the small data set, the model results need to be interpreted with this limitation. The tsfresh approach generates features with very high significance levels, based on which we achieve the best classification results in comparison. These results underline the strength of tsfresh in capturing detailed patterns in the data, as but also may indicate overfitting to some degree. With the catch22 approach, we also generate statistically significant features that allow us to classify user satisfaction with acceptable but lower performance metrics than tsfresh. One advantage of this approach is that we generate fewer features per time series, which makes processing more efficient while still achieving acceptable performance. The hand-crafted features achieve solid classification results, but fall short of the other approaches. We hypothesize that while the hand-crafted features capture the dynamics of the time series, as evidenced by the features that reflect the frequency of the classified zones, they may not be nuanced enough to enable higher classification performance.

A clear limitation of the in-the-wild condition is that the necessary selection of interactions to compile a dataset resulted in a relatively small dataset. Another limitation is the additional necessary cameras and the privacy policy button to start the conversation, which can lead to influences in the users natural behavior. Common to all approaches is that the social signals were extracted from head and torso orientation and facial expressions, and are significant in all three approaches. These features contribute to classification performance through their temporal and distributional characteristics, likely reflecting the underlying affective state associated with the resulting user satisfaction. The Fast Fourier Transform in the tsfresh approach captured statistically significant features based on the oscillatory properties of the underlying time series and reflected these in the form of coefficients. The use of catch22 additionally shows that self-affine scaling and extreme event timings indicate sudden changes in behavior or outlier events that could influence user satisfaction. The features of the hand-crafted approach complement the observations with more comprehensible features, such as the longest trunk pitch in the second zone, which corresponds to leaning forward. These observations are consistent with Tickle-Degnen and Rosenthal's [27] findings about rapport, where certain gestures indicate rapport. The observations also demonstrate the need to examine further the relationship between oscillation characteristics, e.g., the relation of frequency and amplitude of head movements, and extreme events in time series of social signals and concepts like user satisfaction, as well as higher-level psychological concepts such as rapport. This can reveal the significance of specific gestures or movement patterns, especially if recognizable patterns exist among varying groups of user satisfaction. The feature engineering methods shown do not allow any direct statement about the significance of specific gestures or similar social cues. Still, they seem to map the complex relationships of social signals to higher-order constructs such as user satisfaction.

Although we did not test the transferability directly, we hypothesize that our approach of combining social signal metrics with time series classification might also be suitable for predicting other psychological constructs such as engagement, rapport, or other quality scales, due to the highly significant features and the already known relationship between certain body language and e.g. rapport and engagement. Further research should focus on investigating the approach's generalizability, its transferability to other social interaction agents (SIA), and its practical applicability. To improve applicability, techniques should be explored that allow rapid adaptation to the specific use case and, for example, require only a small number of interactions and questionnaires, such as transfer learning models. In this study, we examined a stationary robot and were able to take pictures of the users with additional cameras while they were standing relatively still. The transferability of the approach to other agents poses a challenge, as the users' body language depends on the interaction setting. This is particularly true for mobile, humanoid robots and digital agents, as the observation angle and interaction dynamics change here, creating challenges in extracting social signal features.

7 Conclusion

The demonstrated methods pave the way for predicting user satisfaction for automatic and semi-automatic improvements by identifying the user interactions that leave users unsatisfied. Our results show that feature extraction based on social signal time series is extremely promising. In this paper, we demonstrated that it is possible to classify a user's satisfaction rating of the corresponding questionnaire using features automatically derived from time series of social signal metrics from body language, facial expressions, and distance. Based on a dataset of N = 46 in-the-wild single-user interactions recorded from the SIA's point of view, we compared three automatic feature engineering approaches, selected features based on the statistical significance, and trained different machine learning models. Our results provide insight into the trade-off between relatively tractable features and high precision in performance metrics. Despite the small data set, the approaches can provide highly relevant features for machine learning by achieving sufficient accuracies and performance metrics. The presented approach has the advantage of not relying on extensive data annotation, as existing approaches do, and instead uses the user's given user satisfaction rating after the interaction.

Acknowledgments. We thank our collaboration partner DB Systel GmbH and the Deutsches Museum Bonn, for their assistance and contributions. The Research activities were reviewed and approved by the Ethics Research Committee of TH Köln (application no. THK-2023-0004).

Disclosure of Interests. The authors acknowledge the financial support by the Federal Ministry of Education and Research of Germany in the framework FH-Kooperativ 2-2019 (project number 13FH504KX9).

References

1. MediaPipe Iris: Real-time Iris Tracking & Depth Estimation. https://research.google/blog/mediapipe-iris-real-time-iris-tracking-depth-estimation/
2. Feature Overview Table | catch22: CAnonical Time-series CHaracteristics, June 2024. https://time-series-features.gitbook.io/catch22/information-about-catch22/feature-descriptions/feature-overview-table
3. Al Moubayed, S., Beskow, J., Skantze, G., Granström, B.: Furhat: a back-projected human-like robot head for multiparty human-machine interaction. In: Esposito, A., Esposito, A.M., Vinciarelli, A., Hoffmann, R., Müller, V.C. (eds.) Cognitive Behavioural Systems, pp. 114–130. Springer, Heidelberg (2012)
4. Alenljung, B., Lindblom, J., Andreasson, R., Ziemke, T.: User Experience in Social Human-Robot Interaction. Int. J. Ambient Comput. Intell. (IJACI) 8(2), 12–31 (2017). https://doi.org/10.4018/IJACI.2017040102, https://www.igi-global.com/gateway/article/www.igi-global.com/gateway/article/179287, publisher: IGI Global
5. Buitinck, L., et al.: API design for machine learning software: experiences from the scikit-learn project. In: ECML PKDD Workshop: Languages for Data Mining and Machine Learning, pp. 108–122 (2013)
6. Cantucci, F., Falcone, R.: Autonomous critical help by a robotic assistant in the field of cultural heritage: a new challenge for evolving human-robot interaction. Multimodal Technol. Interact. 6(8), 69 (2022)
7. Cañizares, P.C., Pérez-Soler, S., Guerra, E., De Lara, J.: Automating the measurement of heterogeneous chatbot designs. In: Proceedings of the 37th ACM/SIGAPP Symposium on Applied Computing, pp. 1491–1498. ACM, Virtual Event, April 2022. https://doi.org/10.1145/3477314.3507255
8. Chawla, N.V., Bowyer, K.W., Hall, L.O., Kegelmeyer, W.P.: SMOTE: synthetic minority over-sampling technique. J. Artif. Int. Res. 16(1), 321–357 (2002)
9. Cheong, J.H., Jolly, E., Xie, T., Byrne, S., Kenney, M., Chang, L.J.: Py-Feat: Python Facial Expression Analysis Toolbox, March 2023. https://doi.org/10.48550/arXiv.2104.03509, arXiv:2104.03509 [cs]
10. Christ, M., Braun, N., Neuffer, J., Kempa-Liehr, A.W.: Time Series FeatuRe Extraction on basis of Scalable Hypothesis tests (tsfresh – A Python package). Neurocomputing 307, 72–77 (2018). https://doi.org/10.1016/j.neucom.2018.03.067, https://www.sciencedirect.com/science/article/pii/S0925231218304843
11. Fulcher, B.D.: Feature-based time-series analysis, October 2017. https://doi.org/10.48550/arXiv.1709.08055, http://arxiv.org/abs/1709.08055, arXiv:1709.08055 [cs]
12. George, D., Mallery, P.: SPSS for Windows Step by Step: A Simple Guide and Reference, 11.0 Update. Allyn and Bacon (2003), google-Books-ID: AghHAAAAMAAJ
13. Hong, A., et al.: A multimodal emotional human–robot interaction architecture for social robots engaged in bidirectional communication. IEEE Trans. Cybern. 51(12), 5954–5968 (2021). https://doi.org/10.1109/TCYB.2020.2974688, https://ieeexplore.ieee.org/document/9027136/
14. Jocher, G., et al.: Ultralytics/yolov5: V3.1 - Bug Fixes and Performance Improvements. Zenodo, October 2020. https://doi.org/10.5281/zenodo.4154370
15. Jokinen, K., Wilcock, G.: Modelling user experience in human-robot interactions. In: Böck, R., Bonin, F., Campbell, N., Poppe, R. (eds.) Multimodal Analyses enabling Artificial Agents in Human-Machine Interaction, pp. 45–56. Springer, Cham (2015). https://doi.org/10.1007/978-3-319-15557-9_5

16. Lewis, J.R.: IBM computer usability satisfaction questionnaires: Psychometric evaluation and instructions for use. Int. J. Hum.–Comput. Interact. **7**(1), 57–78 (1995). https://doi.org/10.1080/10447319509526110, publisher: Taylor & Francis _eprint: https://doi.org/10.1080/10447319509526110 _eprint: https://doi.org/10.1080/10447319509526110
17. Lubba, C.H., Sethi, S.S., Knaute, P., Schultz, S.R., Fulcher, B.D., Jones, N.S.: catch22: CAnonical Time-series CHaracteristics. Data Mining Knowl. Discovery **33**(6), 1821–1852 (2019). https://doi.org/10.1007/s10618-019-00647-x
18. Lugaresi, C., et al.: Mediapipe: a framework for perceiving and processing reality. In: Third Workshop on Computer Vision for AR/VR at IEEE Computer Vision and Pattern Recognition (CVPR) 2019 (2019)
19. McColl, D., Nejat, G.: Determining the affective body language of older adults during socially assistive HRI. In: 2014 IEEE/RSJ International Conference on Intelligent Robots and Systems. pp. 2633–2638. IEEE, Chicago, IL, USA, September 2014. https://doi.org/10.1109/IROS.2014.6942922, http://ieeexplore.ieee.org/document/6942922/
20. Müller, P., Huang, M.X., Bulling, A.: Detecting Low Rapport During Natural Interactions in Small Groups from Non-Verbal Behaviour. In: 23rd International Conference on Intelligent User Interfaces, pp. 153–164, March 2018. https://doi.org/10.1145/3172944.3172969, arXiv:1801.06055 [cs]
21. Poggi, I., Francesca, D.: Cognitive modelling of human social signals. In: Proceedings of the 2nd International Workshop on Social Signal Processing, pp. 21–26. ACM, Firenze Italy, October 2010. https://doi.org/10.1145/1878116.1878124
22. Russell, J.A.: A circumplex model of affect. J. Personality Soc. Psychol. **39**(6), 1161–1178 (1980). https://doi.org/10.1037/h0077714, https://doi.apa.org/doi/10.1037/h0077714
23. Schiffmann, M.: Additional material for the icsr2025 publication "classification of user satisfaction with social signals in-the-wild". https://github.com/lfkMichael/ICSR2025AdditionalMaterial (2025). Accessed 26 Apr 2025
24. Schiffmann, M., Chojnowsk, O., Richert, A.: Predicting user satisfaction in a public space HRI-scenario. In: 2025 20th ACM/IEEE International Conference on Human-Robot Interaction (HRI), pp. 1598–1602, March 2025. https://doi.org/10.1109/HRI61500.2025.10973831, https://ieeexplore.ieee.org/document/10973831
25. Schiffmann, M., Richert, A.: Evaluation of social robots with social signals in public spaces. In: 2024 33rd IEEE International Conference on Robot and Human Interactive Communication (ROMAN), pp. 56–61, August 2024. https://doi.org/10.1109/RO-MAN60168.2024.10731307, https://ieeexplore.ieee.org/document/10731307, iSSN: 1944-9437
26. Shourmasti, E.S., Colomo-Palacios, R., Holone, H., Demi, S.: User experience in social robots. Sensors **21**(15), 5052 (2021). https://doi.org/10.3390/s21155052, https://www.mdpi.com/1424-8220/21/15/5052, number: 15 Publisher: Multidisciplinary Digital Publishing Institute
27. Tickle-Degnen, L., Rosenthal, R.: The nature of rapport and its nonverbal correlates. Psychol. Inq. **1**(4), 285–293 (1990). https://doi.org/10.1207/s15327965pli0104_1
28. Villaespesa, E.: List of artificial intelligence (ai) initiatives in museums (2021). https://www.artsmetrics.com/en/list-of-artificial-intelligence-ai-initiatives-in-museums/. Accessed 02 Feb 2023
29. Walker, M.A., Litman, D.J., Kamm, C.A., Abella, A.: Paradise: a framework for evaluating spoken dialogue agents, April 1997. http://arxiv.org/abs/cmp-lg/9704004, arXiv:cmp-lg/9704004

30. Wang, N., Gratch, J.: Rapport and facial expression. In: 2009 3rd International Conference on Affective Computing and Intelligent Interaction and Workshops, pp. 1–6, September 2009. https://doi.org/10.1109/ACII.2009.5349514, https://ieeexplore.ieee.org/document/5349514, iSSN: 2156-8111
31. Wei, W., Li, S., Okada, S., Komatani, K.: Multimodal User Satisfaction Recognition for Non-task Oriented Dialogue Systems. In: Proceedings of the 2021 International Conference on Multimodal Interaction, pp. 586–594. ACM, Montréal QC Canada, October 2021. https://doi.org/10.1145/3462244.3479928
32. Willeke, T., Kunz, C., Nourbakhsh, I.R.: The history of the mobot museum robot series: An evolutionary study. In: The Florida AI Research Society (2001). https://api.semanticscholar.org/CorpusID:6697514

Bayesian Goal Inference Engine for Intent Prediction in Human-Robot Interaction

Martina Pelosi[1,2](✉), Nikolas Helling[2], Andrea Maria Zanchettin[2], and Paolo Rocco[2]

[1] Politecnico di Torino, Dipartimento di Automatica e Informatica (DAUIN), Corso Castelfidardo 34/d, 10138 Torino, Italy
`martina.pelosi@polito.it, martina.pelosi@mail.polimi.it`
[2] Politecnico di Milano, Dipartimento di Elettronica, Informazione e Bioingegneria (DEIB), Piazza Leonardo da Vinci 32, 20133 Milano, Italy
`nikolas.helling@mail.polimi.it,`
`{andreamaria.zanchettin,paolo.rocco}@polimi.it`

Abstract. This paper presents a robust approach for enhancing Human-Robot Interaction (HRI) through short-term human hand motion prediction, enabling robots to better anticipate human intentions in shared spaces. By leveraging real-time body tracking for monitoring human motion, the system integrates model-based hand path generation into a Bayesian inference framework to predict reaching goals. Incorporating both hand and shoulder data, the approach improves the accuracy and responsiveness of the proposed Bayesian recursive classifier, supporting seamless and intuitive collaboration. A comprehensive testing phase using offline tracking data demonstrates the method's superior performance compared to state-of-the-art approaches. A collaborative assembly use case designed to validate the applicability and effectiveness of the approach in a real-world setting further demonstrated increased efficiency and fluency in HRI. By enabling robots to interpret and reactively respond to fast-changing human intentions in real-time, this research contributes to the advancement of social robotics, promoting natural and effective interactions in various contexts, such as domestic assistance, healthcare, and industrial environments, where trust, timing, and coordination are key to successful human-robot teamwork.

Keywords: Human behaviour prediction · Human-Robot Interaction · Bayesian inference engine

1 Introduction

Social robotics is a continuously increasing field enabling robots to naturally interact with humans in shared environments and supporting them in a broad range of settings, such as healthcare, education, and industry [1]. One of the key challenges in this field is to develop an intelligent robot's perception strategy to enable a reactive response to external stimuli to promptly adapt to human actions [2]. Predicting human intent within a shared environment is crucial for enhancing fluency, safety, and human ergonomics in Human-Robot Interaction (HRI). It enables the robot to anticipate the next move, providing prompt assistance in domestic and healthcare applications or minimizing human-robot interference in the collaborative industrial field. Moreover, pairing human prediction with adaptive robot actions can lead to wider acceptance of cobots by making their behavior more intuitive and natural, thereby enhancing human comfort and trust, both in service and industrial applications.

This paper contributes to human intent prediction in HRI, focusing on short-term human motion prediction. Inspired by the work in [3], a refined and robust prediction engine is developed to infer human reaching intentions. The model enables the prediction of the most likely goal the human hand will soon reach within a shared space. The approach is grounded in Bayesian inference, employing a recursive Bayes classifier to iteratively update the probability distribution over the goal set. As in various applications spanning industrial and social robotics domains, the target hand poses are closely associated with specific objects required to complete a task; predicting the human hand's goal inherently corresponds to inferring the intended action.

A path generation procedure for hand motion based on a minimum curvature model provides a series of predicted hand paths that the inference engine exploits to refine its predictions regarding user intentions. A body tracking algorithm obtains the necessary arm features for generating these paths at each sampling interval. The proposed Bayesian inference engine integrates predicted and measured human information to guide predictions toward the intended goal. Compared to previous works, the proposed model exploits not only real-time tracked hand motion information but also additional arm data, such as shoulder pose and motion tangent, improving prediction efficiency and enabling seamless Human-Robot Interaction. In addition, the method presents specific robustness features properly designed to enhance its ability to handle more complex reaching scenarios, model limitations, and uncertain situations. Moreover, combining a spatial-based minimum curvature path model, which generates a hand path for each target, with a recursive Bayesian inference model, which infers human reaching intentions, provides a generic, computationally light algorithm potentially applicable to various contexts.

The effectiveness of the predictive model is validated through comprehensive offline testing, revealing superior prediction performance compared to previous works, along with reactive inference capabilities and versatile features that strengthen its applicability in challenging scenarios. A collaborative assembly use case involving ABB's robot YuMi® further validates the model's applicability in a real-world scenario. The results of this validation highlight both a reduction in cycle time, boosting productivity, and an increase in perceived fluency and intuitiveness during collaboration, as demonstrated through an experimental campaign involving ten participants.

2 Related Works

Predicting human motion and intention is a critical challenge to enable natural and effective Human-Robot Interaction in social robotics, promoting safety and ergonomics [2]. In many applications in fields like education, healthcare, and industry, the intended human action can be directly associated with the prediction of the hand motion target. Research has demonstrated that similar principles, such as smoothness maximization, govern the trajectory generation for both hand movements and whole-body movements [4]. Regarding human motion prediction, classical hand path generation models, such as the minimum jerk model [5,6], and the minimum snap model [7], respectively minimizing the third and the fourth derivative of position, have proved that human reaching movements tend to follow smooth, as straight as possible trajectories. Other studies have suggested models for optimizing dynamic arm-related quantities, such as minimum arm joint torque-change models [8,9]. These models provide a geometric and kinematic basis for generating realistic reaching trajectories, essential for social robots to anticipate and synchronize with human movements.

More recent studies translated the human hand motion model problem from the time domain to the space domain, highlighting clear advantages in terms of applicability in real-world scenarios. An example is offered by Zanchettin et al. [3], who developed a minimum curvature model to generate hand-reaching paths with the final aim of predicting the motion target directly linked to human intention.

In parallel, the field of human intent prediction, which addresses the challenge of forecasting future human behavior based on past observations, has emerged as a critical component in enabling proactive robotic behaviors. In more recent years, Machine Learning (ML) and Deep Learning (DL) techniques have been widely employed. Recurrent Neural Networks (RNNs), trained on arm motion datasets, demonstrated their potential in human motion trajectory prediction and goal inference among multiple possibilities [11,14]. Improvements of these models have been implemented to incorporate online adaptation of the predictions to external factors, like robotic manipulators, to make the method suitable for a variety of applications in Human-Robot Interaction [12,13,15]. However, these techniques always need big datasets for model training, which require a long time for collection and preparation, and do not always allow for generalization to very different tasks.

Alternatively, probabilistic models leverage explicit representations of uncertainty and structured dependencies to adapt dynamically to changes in user intent, providing robust and flexible solutions that do not require complex dataset collection. For instance, Koppula et al. [16] developed the Anticipatory Temporal Conditional Random Fields (ATCRF) model, which incorporates semantic information, like object affordances and sub-activity transitions, to infer human intentions. Furthermore, Bayesian inference engines have been successfully applied to predict human hand-reaching intentions while modeling the uncertainty over the user's goal to represent the possibility of the human changing goal on the fly [17]. For example, a Bayesian framework is used by

Bruckschen et al. [18] to build a model that is capable of recognizing the most likely region to be reached by the human inside an indoor environment to avoid collision with the robot, but also by Zanchettin et al. [3] to predict the most probable hand reaching goal in an industrial collaborative environment to anticipate the following intended human action to allow for a seamless HRI. Another notable example is provided by [20], which presents a generalizable hierarchical Bayesian inference engine that enables the prediction of human intention at different levels. A Mutable Intention Filter (MIF) is used to model the likelihood at the lowest level for short-term motion intention inference, considering the possible reaching regions and captured wrist data as input. However, all these inference models exploit real-time information coming only from the wrist or the hand, although some studies demonstrate that additional body parts, such as the head, eyes, and shoulders, can provide anticipatory information about the user's intention [19].

The present work builds upon past research activities, specifically inspired by Zanchettin et al. [3], combining a minimum curvature hand motion generation model that predicts a hand path for each possible goal, with a recursive Bayesian inference engine for human reaching intentions prediction. It is based on real-time acquired arm data, including shoulder motion information, which, combined with additional measures to improve the approach robustness, provides a stronger and more efficient prediction capability, essential for proactive and socially aware robot behaviors in shared environments.

3 Human Intent Bayesian Predictive Model

The method is designed to infer the goal position from a known set $p_g = \{p_{g_1}, p_{g_2}, \ldots, p_{g_N}\}$, the human hand is most likely to eventually reach. The model inputs are the last available human hand and shoulder data: positions and tangents to the path, namely $\hat{x}_k^H = \{\hat{p}_k^H, \hat{p}_k'^H\}$ for the hand and $\hat{x}_k^S = \{\hat{p}_k^S, \hat{p}_k'^S\}$ for the shoulder. The index k refers to spatial sampling, meaning the body-tracking data capture and the prediction update only occur when the hand has traveled a certain fixed distance Δs. This approach enables the model to focus on meaningful movements, filtering unnecessary data when the hand is stationary. A model-based path generation strategy, inspired by the prior work [3], estimates the hand path from the current pose to each possible target. Then, a recursive Bayesian classifier compares the predicted paths to the measured motion data to identify the most likely goal.

3.1 Model-Based Human Hand Path Generation

The model requires a set of predicted hand-reaching paths to infer which goal the user intends to reach. A model-based path generation approach is adopted to represent hand motion in space. Unlike classical time-dependent models, e.g., the minimum jerk model, this method adopts a spatial model, which does not account for time-based quantities that would be difficult to incorporate in a prediction scenario. Specifically, it focuses on maximizing the geometric smoothness of the hand motions, generating paths with minimum curvature. The hand is modeled as a point moving in 3D space, and its path is represented by an arc-length parametrized curve $p(s_0) = (x(s_0), y(s_0), z(s_0))$, where $s_0 \in [0, 1]$ is the normalized arc length parameter. Given the current hand position $\hat{p}_k^H$, its direction $\hat{p}_k'^H$, and the target goal position p_g, a constrained optimization problem is formulated, minimizing the integral of squared curvature along the path:

$$
\begin{aligned}
\min: \quad & J(p) = \int_0^1 \|p''(s_0)\|^2 \, ds_0, \\
\text{s.t.} \quad & p(0) = \hat{p}_k^H, \quad p(1) = p_g, \\
& p'(0) = \hat{p}_{0,k}'^H = L\hat{p}_k'^H,
\end{aligned}
\tag{1}
$$

where L is the total path length. The unconstrained solution of (1) is a third-order polynomial curve of the type:

$$
p(s_0) = \sum_{j=0}^{3} a_j s_0^j \tag{2}
$$

Substituting the expression of the path in (1), the analytical solution for the set of polynomial coefficients is derived by solving a convex quadratic optimization problem:

$$
\begin{aligned}
a_0 &= \hat{p}_k^H, \\
a_1 &= \hat{p}_{0,k}'^H, \\
a_2 &= 1.5 p_g - 1.5\hat{p}_k^H - 1.5\hat{p}_{0,k}'^H, \\
a_3 &= -0.5 p_g + 0.5\hat{p}_k^H + 0.5\hat{p}_{0,k}'^H.
\end{aligned}
\tag{3}
$$

At each sample k, the path generation algorithm provides N polynomial paths, one for each goal, to be used as inputs for the predictive model at sample $k+1$. Path length L is iteratively approximated, initially set to the straight-line distance to each goal, and refined over time as the path length at the previous step for the boundary condition in (1). Figure 1a illustrates a schematic example of the path generation process.

3.2 Recursive Bayesian Classifier for Goal Reaching Inference

The developed probabilistic model employs Bayesian inference to predict human reaching intentions. According to Bayes' theorem, the posterior probability distribution over a discrete set of goals is recursively updated using newly observed and predicted human motion features to determine the most probable hand-reaching goal among the available ones. A recursive Bayes classifier, consisting of prediction and measurement steps, updates the posterior probabilities at each time step $k+1$, given the previous posterior distribution and the newly collected features. Considering g^k as the variable representing the human's reaching intention at sample k and G as the set of possible goals, the model identifies

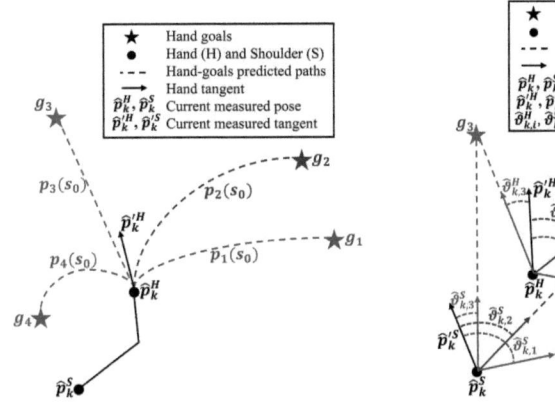

a) Minimum curvature human hand path generation for known goals.

b) Angular measures included in the definition of likelihood function: $\hat{\vartheta}^H_{k,i}$ and $\hat{\vartheta}^S_{k,i}$ for each goal.

Fig. 1. Predicted hand-goal paths and likelihood function angular metrics.

the most probable target $g^k = g_i \in G$, associated with the human observed motion directed towards goal position $p_{g_i} \in p_g$. Given the focus of this work on short-term motion prediction, Markov's assumption is introduced, as suggested in [3], implying that the probability distribution depends only on the last available measurement and not on the entire history. This assumption reduces computational complexity and reflects the inherent variability of human intentions, which aligns with the prediction context involved. Let $\hat{X}_k = \{\hat{x}_{H_k}, \hat{x}_{S_k}\}$ denote the set of measured arm features at time k, which contains both position and motion tangent of the hand ($\hat{x}_{H_k}$) and the shoulder ($\hat{x}_{S_k}$). The update at $k+1$ begins with the prediction step, which computes the prior distribution before incorporating new observations. The prior distribution is:

$$P^{prior}_{k+1}(g) = \mathbb{P}\left(g^{k+1} \mid \hat{X}_k\right) = (\cdots) = \sum_{g^k \in G} P^{post}_k(g)\mathbb{P}\left(g^{k+1} \mid g^k\right), \quad (4)$$

where a fixed transition model for intentions is employed as suggested in [20]:

$$\mathbb{P}\left(g^{k+1} = g_i \mid g^k = g_j\right) = \begin{cases} \beta, & \text{if } i = j \\ \frac{1-\beta}{N-1}, & \text{if } i \neq j \end{cases} \quad (5)$$

where β is the probability that the operator will maintain the current intention, while the remaining probability is equally distributed over the alternative goals. The formulation enables tuning depending on the expected variability of human behavior. When a new set of measured features $\hat{X}_{k+1}$ is available, the posterior distribution can be updated in the measurement step as:

$$P^{post}_{k+1}(g) = \mathbb{P}\left(g^{k+1} \mid \hat{X}_k, \hat{X}_{k+1}\right) = (\cdots) = \eta_{k+1} L_{k+1}(g) P^{prior}_{k+1}(g), \quad (6)$$

where $L_{k+1}(g)$ is the likelihood function depending on the input data, and η_{k+1} is a normalization factor. At sample $k+1$, the predicted goal is the one maximizing P_{k+1}^{post} if its probability exceeds a predefined threshold p_{thresh}.

Likelihood Function Definition The likelihood function has to assign higher values to the goals that better match the current measurements and predicted paths. The following set of measures is defined to reflect how well each goal aligns with the available model inputs:

- The angle $\hat{\theta}_{k,i}^{H}$ between the tangent to the predicted paths and the measured one quantifies how well the predicted paths align with the actual direction of the motion, favoring goals with lower angles (Fig. 1b).
- As radial movements typically follow near-straight trajectories extending from the body [10], the angle $\hat{\theta}_{k,i}^{S}$ between the current tangent to the shoulder's path and the shoulder-to-goal direction is introduced as an additional angular measure, promoting goals aligned with the shoulder's direction of motion. Since shoulder motion is negligible for goals close to the body, the measure is included only for goals outside the arm's reach (Fig. 1b).
- The Euclidean distance $d_{k,i}^{g}$ between the current hand position and each goal provides a natural indication of the intended goal, as goals closer to the hand are deemed more likely. This measure also provides a smoothing factor on predictions, as relying only on angular measurements, which are quite oscillating, can introduce high variability. However, the goal distance measure should be weighted appropriately, as it tends to reduce prediction speed.

While the first metric was already used in [3], the other two are introduced in this work and are proved to be fundamental to enhance the method's efficiency and robustness.

To reinforce the agreement between hand and shoulder motion, a non-linear combination of the two angular measures is used:

$$\theta_{k,i} = \hat{\theta}_{k,i}^{H} \cdot \hat{\theta}_{k,i}^{S}. \tag{7}$$

The likelihood function is defined as a weighted sum of normal distributions, considering separately the influence of angular and distance measures:

$$L_k(g) = w_\theta \mathcal{N}(\theta_{k,i} \mid 0, \sigma_\theta^2) + w_g \mathcal{N}(d_{k,i}^g \mid 0, \sigma_d^2). \tag{8}$$

The distributions are centered around 0, assigning higher probabilities to lower values of the metrics. Standard deviations are tuned empirically to prioritize the angular measures over hand-goal distance. Regarding the weights, setting static values introduces a limitation, as when multiple predicted paths towards the goals are similarly aligned, relying mainly on angular measurements does not provide a precise prediction (see Fig. 2a). Although the introduced hand-goal distance $d_{k,i}^{g}$ improves robustness in these cases, a large static weight for this metric can affect prediction speed. Thus, a dynamic weighting is introduced

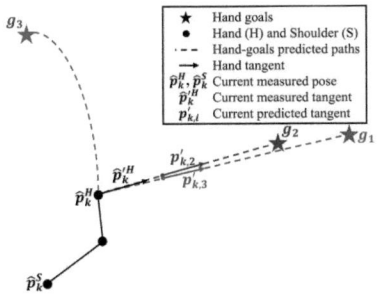

a) Case of aligned goals (g_1 and g_2): hand-goal Euclidean distance is the priviliged measure for the prediction as both goals are aligned with the direction of motion.

b) Case of unfeasible goal (g_3): the goal is in the opposite direction with respect to the direction of motion, although the predicted tangent is similar to the measured one.

Fig. 2. Limit cases addressed with the corresponding robustness measures.

through an exponential decay function, depending on the normalized distance from each goal $\bar{d}^g_{k,i}$:

$$w_\theta = w_{\theta_{k,i}} = W\left(1 - e^{-u_g \bar{d}^g_{k,i}}\right),$$
$$w_g = w_{g_{k,i}} = W e^{-u_g \bar{d}^g_{k,i}}. \quad (9)$$

where u_g is the decaying rate and W is the initial weight assigned to the angular measurement. This approach favors angular measurements for equally distanced goals while increasing the goal distance weight as the target gets closer. It solves the inevitable speed loss of a static ratio, addresses the limit case of aligned goals, and maintains the smoothing effect of $d^g_{k,i}$ on the high angular measurements variability.

Another issue emerging using the minimum curvature path model is that predicted tangents could align with the observed one for goals that are not likely to be reached, as already overcome by the hand, as shown in Fig. 2b. To address this, only goals within 90° of the hand's direction of motion are considered.

Finally, to handle cases of uncertainty in the goal distribution, the information entropy of the posterior $H\left(P^{\text{post}}_k\right)$ is used to update the probability of an unknown goal:

$$P^U_k = P^U_{k-1} + u_h \cdot \text{sign}\left(H_k - H_{thresh}\right) \cdot \frac{H_k - H_{thresh}}{H_{max} - H_{thresh}}, \quad (10)$$

$$H_k = H\left(P^{\text{post}}_k\right) = -\sum_{g^k \in G} P^{\text{post}}_k(g^k) \log P^{\text{post}}_k(g^k). \quad (11)$$

where u_h is a tunable prediction update rate. The update of the unknown goal probability occurs only when $H_k \geq H_{thresh}$, indicating that none of the goals is

Table 1. Experimental results: overall Inference Distance (ID) and prediction accuracy.

Metric	Mean ID	Median ID	Standard deviation	Range	$\bar{p}_g$	Prediction accuracy	Error	Failed recognition
UoM	mm	mm	mm	mm	%	%	%	%
Prediction results	533.89 (516.24, 551.54)	534.14	84.76		387.04	23.85	94.57	3.26	2.17

likely. The entropy threshold is defined as:

$$H_{thresh} = p_{thresh} \cdot H_{max}, \quad H_{max} = -\sum_{i=1}^{N} \left(\frac{1}{N}\right) \log\left(\frac{1}{N}\right) = \log N. \quad (12)$$

where H_{max} is the maximum entropy value, occurring when the probability distribution is uniform over the goals. This approach is more flexible and tunable than the one in [3], as it does not depend on the likelihood definition.

4 Prediction Performance Testing

The model's prediction performance was tested on a comprehensive dataset of recorded hand paths labeled with the sequence of ground truth intended targets. A median filter was applied to the raw data to reduce sensor noise and hand-tracking outliers. The window size was selected to balance robustness with minimal delay, ensuring suitability for real-time use. Key performance metrics for the testing campaign include Inference Distance (ID), i.e., the distance from the inferred goal when prediction is confirmed, and prediction accuracy, i.e., the percentage of correctly identified goals.

The impact of shoulder data compared to the approach in [3] was assessed using 98 recorded outward-reaching movements. Results show improved prediction speed (+8.42%) and increased prediction stability (+12.26%), indicating a more reactive and confident model when including shoulder information. Figure 3 shows ID results comparison of the two approaches.

The model's ability to detect unknown goals was evaluated in 17 tests involving reaching an unknown goal at some point in the motion sequence. The prediction accuracy of 88.23% and the mean ID comparable to the known goals prove the unknown goal detection capability. Despite a slight increase in standard deviation being observed, it can be associated with various uncertainty factors, including user variability, tracking system errors, and model approximations.

To evaluate overall prediction performance, 31 hand paths were analyzed involving different goals and various reaching sequences. In total, the model was tested on a total of 92 targets, achieving high prediction accuracy (94.57%), low error rate (3.26%), and minimal failures (2.17%), as reported in Table 1. These results confirm robust and consistent predictions across various scenarios. The mean inference distance was 533.89 mm, corresponding to 23.85% of the average distance between the goals $\bar{p}_g$, indicating early prediction capability of the model, suitable for anticipatory actions in Human-Robot Interaction.

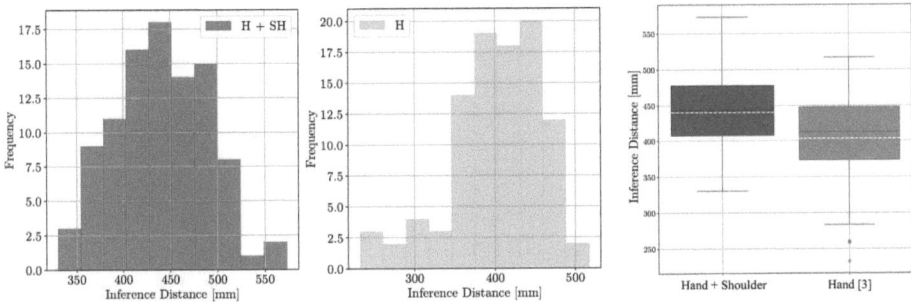

Fig. 3. Inference Distance histogram and box-plot: performance improvement adding shoulder data (H + SH) compared to previous work (H) [3].

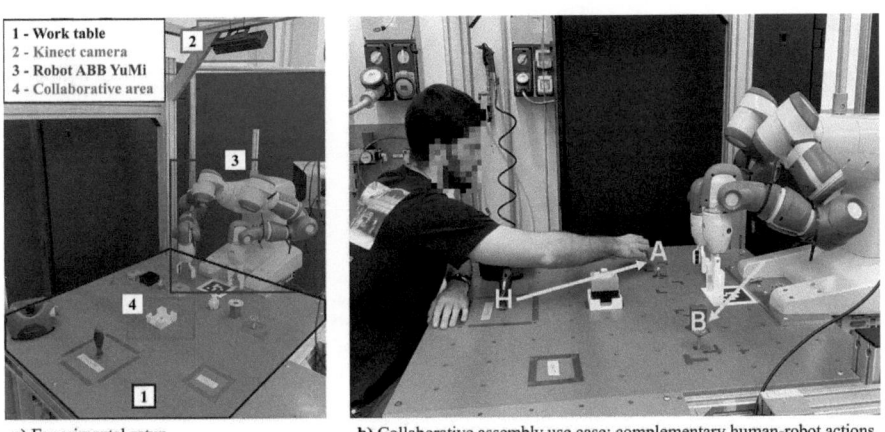

a) Experimental setup   b) Collaborative assembly use case: complementary human-robot actions

Fig. 4. Collaborative assembly use case.

5 Experimental Use Case

A realistic collaborative assembly scenario was used to validate the model's effectiveness in HRI. The setup involved the ABB YuMi® robot, a Kinect camera for human tracking, and a shared workspace (Fig. 4a). The predictive model was implemented in real-time and connected to the robot's controller to make the robot adapt its actions accordingly to the predicted human intentions in a complementary manner, as shown in Fig. 4b. Two types of tests were conducted: a non-predictive experiment using a manual signaling interface enabling the user to instruct the robot to perform the correct actions and a predictive one leveraging real-time user intention inference to enable autonomous robot responses. An experienced user performed twenty assembly sequences for both the predictive and non-predictive cases. Assembly times recording of the shared human-robot steps in both scenarios demonstrated that the predictive approach reduced the shared-phases cycle time by an average of 28.41%. Further tests were conducted with ten external participants, characterized by different levels of expertise in robotics, who performed the collaborative assembly both with and without the predictive model. The users confirmed the model's ability to anticipate human intentions by reporting in a questionnaire some perceived features, such as improved task fluency, intuitiveness of robot responses, and trust (see Fig. 5). These results demonstrate the model's effectiveness in enhancing collaboration in the specific application context. However, the human goal inference process remains the same across HRI domains. Therefore, success in this representative use case provides strong evidence of the method's general applicability to other social robotic fields where fluency, natural interaction, and efficiency are fundamental for effective robot assistance.

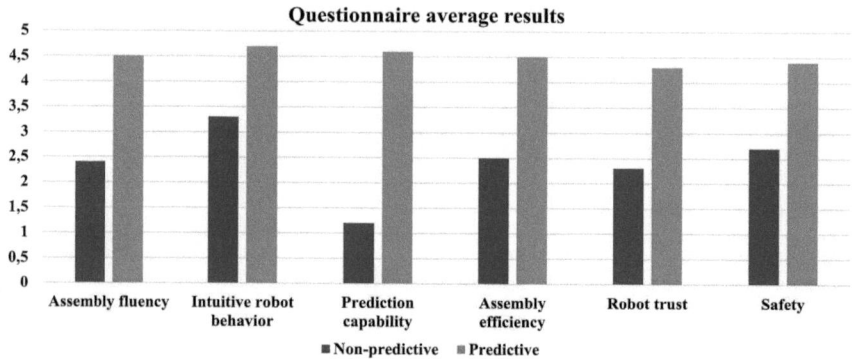

Fig. 5. Questionnaire average results: perceived features comparison between the non-predictive and predictive experiment.

6 Conclusions

This work presents a short-term human hand motion prediction engine based on hand path generation and a Bayesian inference framework, providing a robust human intention inference strategy fundamental in the social robotics field, where fluid and natural Human-Robot Interaction is a key challenge. By incorporating both hand and shoulder data, along with additional robustness features to handle the limitations of previous works, the refined model improves performance in predicting human reaching intentions. Validation of the model in a collaborative robotics setting demonstrated enhanced efficiency, task fluency, and increased confidence in Human-Robot Interaction.

Acknowledgments. This study was partially carried out within the MICS (Made in Italy – Circular and Sustainable) Extended Partnership and received funding from Next-Generation EU (Italian PNRR – M4 C2, Invest 1.3 – D.D. 1551.11-10 2022, PE00000004). CUP MICS D43C22003120001.

Disclosure of Interests. The authors have no competing interests to declare that are relevant to the content of this article.

References

1. Breazeal, C., Dautenhahn, K., Kanda, T.: Social Robotics, pp. 1935–1972. Springer International Publishing, Springer Handbook of Robotics (2016)
2. Mavrogiannis, C., et al.: Core challenges of social robot navigation: a survey. ACM Trans. Hum.-Robot Interact. **12**, 1–39. ACM New York, NY (2023)
3. Zanchettin, A.M., Rocco, P.: Probabilistic inference of human arm reaching target for effective human-robot collaboration. In: 2017 IEEE International Conference on Intelligent Robots and Systems (IROS)
4. Pham, Q.C., Hicheur, H., Arechavaleta, G., Laumond, J.P., Berthoz, A.: The formation of trajectories during goal-oriented locomotion in humans. II. A maximum smoothness model. Wiley Online Library, Eur. J. Neuroscience **26**, 2391–2403 (2007)
5. Todorov, E., Jordan, M.I.: Optimal feedback control as a theory of motor coordination. Nat. Neuroscience **5**, 1226–1235. Nature Publishing Group US, New York (2002)
6. Zhao, J., Gong, S., Xie, B., Duan, Y., Zhang, Z.: Human arm motion prediction in human-robot interaction based on a modified minimum jerk model. Adv. Rob. **35**, 205–218 (2021)
7. Wiegner, A.W., Wierzbicka, M.M.: Kinematic models and human elbow flexion movements: quantitative analysis. Exper. Brain Res. **88**, 665–673 (1992)
8. Uno, Y., Kawato, M., Suzuki, R.: Formation and control of optimal trajectory in human multijoint arm movement. Biol. Cybern. **61**, 89–101 (1989)
9. Nakano, E., et al.: Quantitative examinations of internal representations for arm trajectory planning: minimum commanded torque change model. Am. Physiol. Soc. Bethesda, MD, J. Neurophysiol. **81**, 2140–2155 (1999)
10. Sergio, L.E., Scott, S.H.: Hand and joint paths during reaching movements with and without vision. Exper. Brain Res. **122**, 157–164 (1998)
11. Martinez, J., Black, M.J., Romero, J.: On human motion prediction using recurrent neural networks. In: Proceedings of the IEEE Conference on Computer Vision and Pattern Recognition (2017)
12. Formica, F., Vaghi, S., Lucci, N., Zanchettin, A.M.: Neural networks based human intent prediction for collaborative robotics applications. In: 2021 20th International Conference on Advanced Robotics (ICAR) (2021)
13. Bazzi, D., Tomasi, A., Zanchettin, A.M., Rocco, P.: Human intention estimation and goal-driven variable admittance control in manual guidance applications. In: 2021 20th International Conference on Advanced Robotics (ICAR) (2021)
14. Kratzer, P., Midlagajni, N.B., Toussaint, M., Mainprice, J.: Anticipating human intention for full-body motion prediction in object grasping and placing tasks. In: 2020 29th IEEE International Conference on Robot and Human Interactive Communication (RO-MAN) (2020)
15. Laplaza, J., Moreno, F., Sanfeliu, A.: Enhancing robotic collaborative tasks through contextual human motion prediction and intention inference. Int. J. Soc. Rob. (2024)
16. Koppula, H.S., Saxena, A.: Anticipating human activities using object affordances for reactive robotic response. IEEE Trans. Pattern Anal. Mach. Intell. (2015)

17. Jain, S., Argall, B.: Recursive Bayesian human intent recognition in shared-control robotics. In: 2018 IEEE/RSJ International Conference on Intelligent Robots and Systems (IROS) (2018)
18. Bruckschen, L., Bungert, K., Dengler, N., Bennewitz, M.: Predicting human navigation goals based on Bayesian inference and activity regions. Robot. Auton. Syst., **134**. Elsevier (2020)
19. Yang, L., Sejima, Y., Watanabe, T.: Gaze cue: which body parts will human take as cue to infer a robot's intention?. Jpn Soc. Mech. Eng., J. Adv. Mech. Design, Syst. Manuf. **18** (2024)
20. Huang, Z., et al.: Hierarchical intention tracking for robust human-robot collaboration in industrial assembly tasks. In: 2023 IEEE International Conference on Robotics and Automation (ICRA) (2023)

Pluri-perspectivism in Human-Robot Co-creativity with Older Adults

Marianne Bossema[1,2](✉), Rob Saunders[2], Aske Plaat[2], and Somaya Ben Allouch[1,3]

[1] Amsterdam University of Applied Sciences, Amsterdam, The Netherlands
m.bossema@hva.nl
[2] Leiden University, Leiden, The Netherlands
[3] University of Amsterdam, Amsterdam, The Netherlands

Abstract. This position paper explores pluri-perspectivism as a core element of human creative experience and its relevance to humanrobot co-creativity. We propose a layered, five-dimensional model to guide the design of co-creative behaviors and the analysis of interaction dynamics. This model is based on literature and results from an interview study we conducted with 10 visual artists and 8 arts educators, examining how pluri-perspectivism supports creative practice. The findings of this study provide insight how robots could enhance human creativity through adaptive, context-sensitive behavior, demonstrating the potential of pluri-perspectivism. This paper outlines future directions for integrating pluri-perspectivism with vision-language models (VLMs), to support context sensitivity in co-creative robots.

Keywords: Human-robot Co-creativity · Co-creative Interaction Model · Creative Aging

1 Introduction

This study is part of a broader project investigating how robots and artificial intelligence (AI) can support and enhance creative experiences for older adults. Participatory arts have been shown to promote cognitive health, lifelong learning, and social connectedness in later life [20,21,28,34]. Technology for creativity support can enhance self-expression [36], while robots can uniquely contribute through embodied, co-present, social interaction [10,47]. Yet, the potential of robotic creativity support for older users remains underexplored [7]. Integrating VLMs into robots enables contextual understanding, goal planning, and natural interaction [57]. In creative settings, this allows for flexibility and accessible conversational interfaces, particularly valuable for target groups with diverse goals and digital skills, such as older adults. In a participatory study offering a course on "Drawing with Robots" for this target group, we found that participants appreciated a VLM-enhanced robot's vision and language abilities, but noted a lack of sensitivity to the creative context, including their artistic intentions [8].

When acting in the real world, robotic agents (intentional, adaptive, autonomous [54]) require an understanding of the context [43,51]. VLMs can support robotic agents by aligning visual inputs with natural language, enabling them to interpret scenes and engage in conversation [39]. VLMs still require domain-specific guidance, however, to be effective in embodied, situated tasks [12,50]. Human feedback can provide guidance [48], and recent studies show how VLM-enhanced conversation can facilitate the exchange of contextual information and improve robot task execution [39]. Yet, important questions remain about what contextual information is needed for creative collaboration, and how this can best be exchanged within a creative process. We propose a pluri-perspectivist model as a contextual map defining a multidimensional co-creative space. Pluri-perspectivism, or exploring and integrating multiple perspectives, is pivotal for collaboration [14,37] and for creativity [26]. The pluri-perspectivist model can be used as an internal schema to guide a VLM-enhanced robot [32,58], improving robot context sensitivity. Technical approaches are further investigated in Sect. 4. In human-robot co-creativity, a VLM-enhanced robotic agent could explore and integrate perspectives through both conversation and action, for example by asking about user preferences, detecting turn-taking rhythms, offering suggestions, or synchronizing its actions. In such a setting, the pluri-perspectivist model serves as a tool for structuring contextual exploration in different dimensions. It offers a way to guide attention, interaction, and interpretation in VLM-enhanced robots by informing structured prompts and examples. Using the model as a contextual map may help identify how a robot could act as a co-creative agent, and what forms of perspective taking and offering are meaningful and desirable in a co-creative process.

The goal of this study is to introduce a pluri-perspectivist model that can be used as a contextual map, guiding human-robot co-creativity. We review related work on perspective sharing in creative human-robot interaction (HRI) contexts, and explore technical approaches to assess potential implementation of the model in a schema-guided [32,58], VLM-enhanced robot. In addition, we investigate artistic exploration in practice through interviews with experts (artists and art teachers) to validate the model and to collect meaningful examples. The model offers a theoretically grounded, practical framework for co-creative HRI. Ongoing work involves deploying the model with a VLM-enhanced robot to assess its applicability in HRI. We view this preliminary study as a necessary foundation for future implementation and empirical testing in HRI, whereby mapping a domain-specific context contributes to the broader goal of enhancing robotic agents' contextual understanding.

Section 2 presents background literature. Section 3 outlines the proposition and model. Section 4 draws from related work on robot behaviors and technical approaches, and Sect. 5 describes the interview study. Sections 6 and 7 discuss findings and conclude with directions for future research.

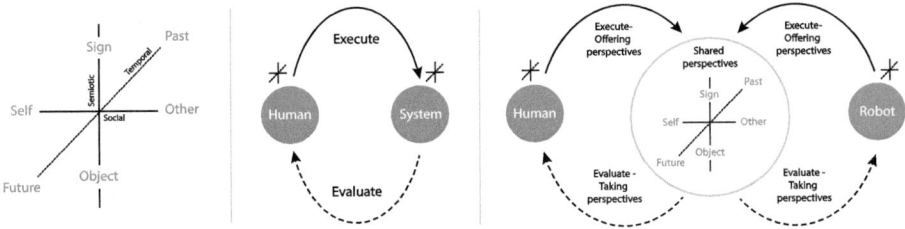

Fig. 1. Left: The model of creatogenetic differences by Glaveanu & Gillespie [26], Center: The HCI Interaction Cycle by Norman [38]; Right: Integration of model and interaction cycles in human-robot co-creativity.

2 Background

Creative Experiences and Pluri-Perspectivism—The main question of our broader research project is how robots and AI can support and enhance creative experiences for older adults. We adopt Glăveanu & Beghetto's [24] definition of creative experiences as *"novel person-world encounters grounded in meaningful actions and interactions, marked by openness, non-linearity, pluri-perspectives, and future orientation."* The researchers suggest that a key principle of creative experiences is pluri-perspectivism, the active search for and engagement with different viewpoints. Glăveanu argues that creativity not only results in difference, but also originates in it [25]. This means that exploring and integrating difference in a multidimensional possibility space is central to creativity. In "Creativity out of Difference", Glăveanu & Gillespie present three creatogenetic differences—between self and other, between sign and object, and between past and future—modeled into social, semiotic and temporal perspectives (Fig. 1, left) [26]. Expanding on sociocultural psychological models, the authors argue that all forms of creativity arise from these dynamic self-other-world-sign relationships, shaped through interactions over time. These social, semiotic and temporal perspectives are the foundation of our pluri-perspectivist model for human-robot co-creativity.

Pluri-perspectivism in Creative Collaboration—Boden [6] defines creativity as generating ideas or artifacts that are both novel and appropriate. In creative collaboration, partners introduce and evaluate novelty and appropriateness together. While the dynamics depend on roles and distribution of agency, this requires exchanging perspectives with regards to 1) the creative task, and 2) the collaborative process. Exchanging perspectives involves perspective taking and perspective offering. Regarding the creative goal, perspective taking is about perceiving and evaluating the creative possibility space, while perspective offering means reshaping that space [26]. Regarding the collaborative goal, perspective taking is about recognizing others' viewpoints [23], while perspective offering may involve suggesting a way of working. Exchange of perspectives happens in a close loop using multiple modalities. In HumanComputer Interaction (HCI),

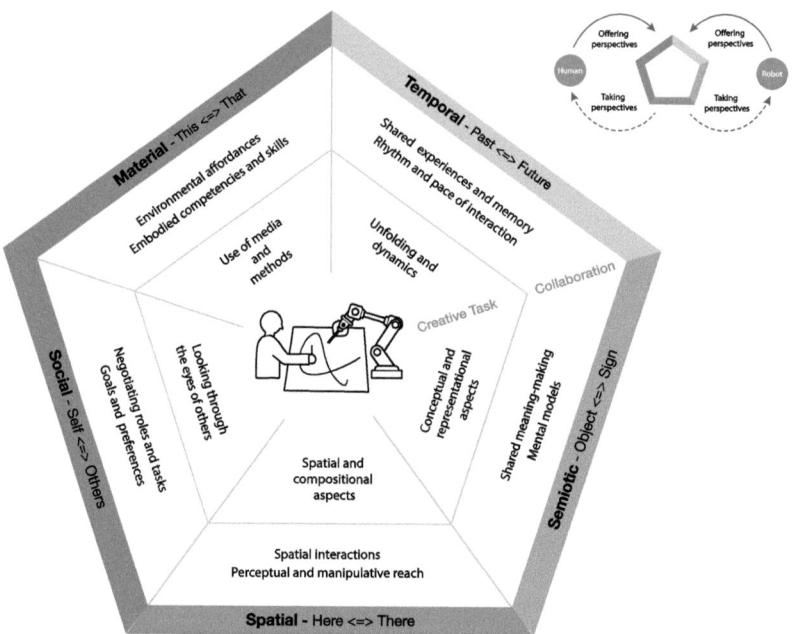

Fig. 2. The two-layered five-dimensional model of pluri-perspectivism (left) for interaction cycles in human-robot co-creativity (top-right).

Norman's interaction cycle [38] reflects a similar close loop of perception, evaluation and execution. Users engage in perspective taking towards a system by evaluating system feedback based on their expectations and offer new perspectives by executing actions. Figure 1 (center) illustrates this unidirectional loop between human and system. In collaborative tasks, however, this process is bidirectional: agents jointly act and evaluate within a process that can be understood by sharing perspectives in different dimensions. This is shown on the right side of the figure, where human and robot share social, semiotic, and temporal perspectives, as defined by Glaveanu and Gillespie's model of three creatogenetic differences [26]. In creative collaboration, a pluri-perspectivist model can help to structure the dynamic interplay of perspective taking and perspective offering in multiple dimensions (Fig. 1, right). In human-robot co-creativity, it can guide a VLM-enhanced robot in exchanging perspectives with regard to the creative task, and to the collaborative process.

3 Proposition

Taking Glăveanu & Gillespie's three-dimensional creatogenetic model [26] as a starting point, we propose a five-dimensional contextual map for human-robot collaborative creativity that can guide a VLM-enhanced robots in co-creative tasks.

Five Dimensions—We build on the three creatogenetic differences (Fig. 1, left) and introduce 'material' and 'spatial' as additional, context-specific dimensions. We include these dimensions based on the theory of participatory sensemaking by De Jaegher and Di Paolo [15], that describes how meaning is co-created through embodied, dynamic interactions between agents. In co-creative contexts, meaning-making emerges not only through linguistic or symbolic exchange but also through embodied interaction and engagement with the material environment. Including material and spatial dimensions in the model allows us to capture the dynamic, situated nature of creativity that unfolds through embodied action, perceptual alignment, and interaction with physical media. Several related works underpin the importance of spatial and material perspectives. Saunders et al. [46] demonstrate how sharing a physical environment enables richer social and cultural exchange. Guckelsberger et al. [29] demonstrate that embodiment influences human perception of robot creativity and intentionality, and Weinberg et al. [52] highlight how robot embodiment enhances collaboration, turn-taking, and engagement in social and musical contexts. By mapping the five dimensions -social, material, temporal, semiotic and spatial we can investigate in what ways robots as material agents can contribute to human-robot co-creativity. Definitions of the five dimensions are listed in Table 1.

Two Layers—Co-creative processes involve actions related to 1) coordination and 2) task execution, and the model adopts a two-layered structure to support both. To conceptualize the distinction between the two layers, we draw on Clark's theory of joint action [14], which differentiates between task-level actions—contributions aimed at accomplishing the task—and coordination-level actions, that facilitate the collaborative process itself. This theoretical framing aligns with our model: The inner layer supports the creative task, while the outer layer encompasses collaborative actions that help organize, negotiate, and guide the co-creative process. Figure 2 shows the five perspectives in a two-layered model.

Speculative Scenario—We first tested the proposition in a speculative scenario of human-robot drawing, visualized in Fig. 3. The scenario illustrates how pluri-perspectivism could manifest itself in human-robot co-creativity. For example, the dialogue between human (H) and robot (R) unfolds through spatial actions (*"I'll draw mine to the right"*), material choices (*"Shall we use charcoal?"*), and embodied turn-taking (*"Let's take turns, I'll follow your rhythm"*). The scenario reveals that a single expression may engage multiple dimensions simultaneously, enabling fluid perspectival shifts that guide creative exploration. The scenario also reveals structural dependencies between perspectives, suggesting a staged or layered unfolding of interaction. Role negotiation, for instance, often precedes task execution, aligning with Clark's theory of joint action [14] and Engeström's activity theory [19], where coordination-level actions enable goal-directed behavior. Collaboration-level perspectives may often precede and structure the unfolding of creative task-level perspectives.

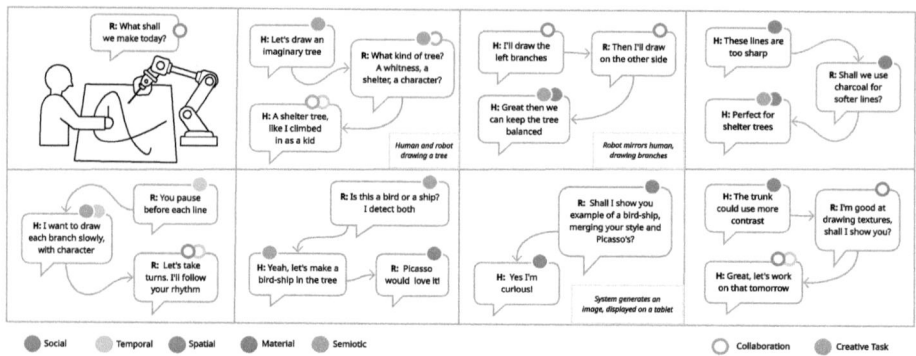

Fig. 3. pluri-perspectivism in a speculative scenario of human-robot drawing.

4 Related Works

To validate the model and inform future implementation with a VLM-enhanced robot, we investigate perspective sharing robot behaviors that support creativity, and possibilities for implementation in VLM-enhanced robots.

Perspective Sharing Behaviors in Creative HRI—Research shows that robots can support creativity through a range of perspective sharing behaviors across the dimensions of the pluri-perspectivist model. In the **social** dimension, robots offered perspectives by adopting expressive behaviors that enhanced creativity [1,27,45]. Fucinato et al. [22] showed that charismatic robot speech enhanced team creativity. Robots have also acted as creative instructors, using guided demonstrations to stimulate children's artistic output [2,17]. Social alignment in robots, through perspective-taking [3] or personality matching [53], has been shown to enhance user preference and prosocial engagement. In the spatial dimension, Lee [33] showed that a robot can elicit creativity by disrupting physical arrangements, where changes in tool placement led to new compositions. Robots have demonstrated spatial perspective-taking by interpreting deictic references through language and body posture relative to the user's viewpoint [40], and by using gaze and gesture to promote shared attention [59]. The **semiotic** dimension includes robots suggesting reinterpretations of creative work. Hu et al. [30] and Lin et al. [35] showed that robots manipulating visual elements or suggesting alternate meanings can prompt conceptual shifts. Several studies illustrate overlaps e.g., **social and semiotic** perspectives in Tseng's [49] study, where personas generated by a large language model provided conversations inspiring creative meaning-making (semiotic). In Rond's study of improvisational robots [45], **spatial and semiotic** perspectives overlap, showing that robot movement can serve as both spatial and symbolic prompts in improvisation. Together, these studies demonstrate how robots can engage in multidimensional perspective sharing to support creativity and collaboration.

Implementing Pluri-Perspectivism with a VLM-Enhanced Robot—
Recent advances in VLMs offer a technical foundation for implementing perspective sharing behaviors in co-creative robots, allowing for guidance through schema-guided prompting [32,58]. Thereby, an internal schema helps to organize what information to pay attention to, how to interpret it, and how to respond. Studies in schema-guided dialogue [32,58] and multimodal instruction-following [50] demonstrate how prompt structure and multimodal grounding enable dynamic, context-sensitive interaction. These approaches build on in-context learning [16], where a pre-trained model makes predictions based on a few structured examples, a form of few-shot learning that does not require retraining [11,43]. Our pluri-perspectivist model can be used for schema-guided prompting, while additional examples, derived from artistic practice, can be used for few-shot learning. In this setting, the model serves as a map for exploring and shaping a co-creative possibility space. For instance, few-shot prompts can condition a VLM to engage in role-playing (social), reinterpret artwork (semiotic), or suggest the exploration of other tools (material). Behaviors may be adapted to user preferences derived from conversation, enabling more personalized interaction. Some dimensions align well with schema-guided prompting, while others require more than text-based and visual prompts. VLMs can support social and semiotic dimensions through multimodal understanding, however they struggle to induce temporal or spatial structure [31,56]. Temporal reasoning often depends on structured representations like event schemas [55], and spatial reasoning remains limited without scene graphs [56] or fine-tuning on spatial data [13]. In embodied co-creative tasks, such as humanrobot drawing, we can extend a VLM with additional modules e.g., for human action recognition [18], tracking the drawing process using OpenCV [9], and collecting temporal data on rhythms and pacing using custom scripts. The VLM can serve as a central reasoning engine, whereby the pluri-perspectivist model can guide integration, facilitating multidimensional exploration.

Table 1. Perspectival Dimensions as Main Coding Categories

Social	Difference between self and others - Considering or responding to different goals, preferences, expressions.
Spatial	Difference between here and there - Engaging with different physical or visual positions, orientations, or locations.
Material	Difference between goal and affordances - Exploring or responding to the properties and possibilities of tools and media.
Semiotic	Difference between sign and object - Shifting meanings and interpretations of symbolic or aesthetic representations.
Temporal	Differences between past and future - Using time through rhythm and pacing, reflection, or iterative development.

5 Examples of Artistic Exploration

To validate our model and ground it in real-world practices, we conducted interviews with visual artists and art teachers. These participants were selected because they are experts in navigating perspectival dimensions to explore and exploit a creative possibility space, essential in artistic practice and creative pedagogy [5,25]. Our goal is to gain insight into how pluri-perspectivism functions in practice and to assess the relevance and completeness of our five-dimensional model. In addition, the interviews inform the design of schema-guided [32,58], few-shot learning strategies [11] for a VLM-enhanced robot. These examples can be used to construct contextual prompts that reflect pluri-perspectivism and model real-world creative reasoning and dialogue. We interviewed 10 visual artists (6 women, 4 men) 65 years of age and older, and 8 art teachers (5 women, 3 men) who offer drawing and painting courses for older adults. Four artists were recruited through a foundation that elects Artists of the Year in the Netherlands, while the rest were found via the authors' networks. All maintained an active visual arts practice across different regions in the Netherlands. Art teachers were recruited through art participation organizations and the authors' networks. Most interviews were conducted in person at participants' workspaces, except for one artist and one teacher, who were interviewed remotely.

In semi-structured interviews, we used an interview guide with topics to be covered (see Supplementary Materials), to ensure consistency across participants while supporting a natural conversation and flexible responses [41]. In line with the goal of looking for examples of pluri-perspectivism, we investigated contextual exploration in artistic practices and creative teaching. We discussed work environments, creative processes, and collaborations. The interviews with art teachers also focused on pedagogical techniques to help others explore and exploit a creative possibility space. The interviews were conducted in person at the artists' and art teachers' working environments and lasted approximately 40 min. All participants gave informed consent for audio recording. Data were pseudonymized and digitally stored at the University. Transcriptions were generated using a locally run version of OpenAI's Whisper [44] to ensure privacy.

Thematic analysis using ATLAS.ti [4] was guided by our five-dimensional model, as shown in Fig. 2. A coding scheme was developed with the perspectival dimensions as primary categories, defined in Table 1. An elaborate coding scheme including subcategories can be found in Supplementary Materials. The use of subcodes in the qualitative coding process enabled a more nuanced and structured categorization of the data. While main codes captured broader thematic areas, subcodes allowed for the differentiation of specific patterns within those areas, enhancing the depth and clarity of analysis. This hierarchical approach aligns with best practices in thematic analysis [42]. We validated outcomes through researcher triangulation, with independent coding by the first and last author. Intercoder reliability was assessed using Kippendorf's c-a-binary ($\alpha = 0.549$). The moderate agreement observed can be explained by the theoretical foundation of pluri-perspectivism. As the model describes a multidimensional possibility space, it does not consist of discrete or exclusive categories. This can be expected to affect intercoder agreement. Overall, agreement was found in code selection, with variation mainly in segment granularity.

5.1 Pluri-perspectivism in Artistic Practices

Qualitative analysis was guided by five pre-defined perspectival dimensions: Social, Semiotic, Temporal, Material, and Spatial. While no additional main categories were found, data revealed subcategories per dimension, and provided valuable insights into the manifestations of artistic contextual exploration. Both artists and art teachers engaged with all five dimensions, but differed in how they applied and emphasized them. For example, one oil painter described slow, deliberate work, often taking incubation time, while another oil painter pushed material boundaries by continuously layering oil paint until the artwork seemed to *"take on a life of its own."* Likewise, one art teacher emphasized free body movement to encourage expressivity, while another took a more analytical approach, having students repeatedly explore a particular topic, while constraining the use of materials. Below, we provide an overview of the most commonly described actions, grouped by the five perspectival dimensions.

Social Perspectives—Both artists ($n=8$) and art teachers ($n=8$) emphasized taking others' viewpoints to gain new insights—primarily through conversation, observation, and collaboration. Talking about work was central: artists ($n=6$) discussed with peers, while teachers ($n=6$) supported students in articulating their goals. Observing and studying art was also common—mentioned by artists ($n=6$) and teachers ($n=5$)—alongside background research on thematic content. Artists ($n=6$) mentioned peer collaboration through co-creation, exhibitions, and shared studios. All teachers ($n=8$) organized group debriefings to reflect on diverse approaches and encourage artistic freedom. As one teacher noted: *"It makes them realize how many differences you see. And that gives a really nice feeling—the sense of all the different possibilities."* Teachers ($n=6$) also described group dynamics, such as mirroring and contagion. While all artists valued social exchange, 6 preferred working alone and not sharing initial ideas—suggesting that the need for social exchange may vary across creative stages.

For the art teachers, the social perspective involved their role in the classroom. All eight emphasized a coaching approach that involved stimulating creativity, offering guidance, and fostering personal growth. As one teacher put it, *"Self-confidence and personal growth... that's what it's all about."* All teachers mentioned using educational techniques such as scaffolding and demonstration, based on their own artistic expertise. In response to observed needs of students, teachers ($n=4$) acted as disruptors to challenge students, or stepped back to observe ($n=4$), leaving space for self-directed exploration.

Semiotic Perspectives—Artists ($n=10$) engaged in creative dialogues involving signs and meaning, while art teachers ($n=7$) supported such exchanges with their students. All artists ($n=10$) described their process as a reflective dialogue, an ongoing interplay between manifestation and imagination, guiding artistic direction. Several artists ($n=5$) emphasized authenticity, and staying true to

Fig. 4. Impression of art teacher approaches i.e., guided instructions; working with art in the environment; promoting bodily motion; working with restrictions and unpredictable materials. Photos by the first author and by WG-Kunst, with permission.

personal artistic goals. Conceptual exploration was equally important across groups: artists (n = 9) and teachers (n = 6) described engaging in or encouraging experimentation through recombination, variation, and transformation. Teachers often used structured challenges to promote this. Surprise and serendipity were also central to creativity—highlighted by 8 artists and 4 teachers—as vital for exploration. As one teacher noted: *"The assignment is a kind of surprise egg. It always leads to something new."*

Material Perspectives—Artists (n = 10) aimed to push artistic boundaries by trying out different materials and techniques, while art teachers (n = 8) actively promoted this with their students. Both groups emphasized the importance of engaging with materials and responding to their properties. These dialogues with materials allowed for intuitive, responsive interaction based on what the material seemed to 'want." One artist, working with tubes, explained: *"If you hang around with tubes long enough, the tubes start talking to you... What do those tubes actually want?"* In these material dialogues, artists (n = 6) and teachers (n = 3) looked for unexpectedness to spark creative breakthroughs, and mentioned the use of unpredictable material behavior, inspiring new directions and further exploration. In addition, teachers sometimes introduced constraints (n = 6), limiting tools or materials, to encourage students to push their creative boundaries by tackling well-defined challenges. Rather than restricting creativity, these constraints were seen as valuable prompts for exploration (Fig. 4).

Spatial Perspectives—Changing spatial viewpoints emerged as an important strategy for gaining fresh perspectives. Both artists (n = 10) and teachers (n = 6) recognized the value of shifting viewpoints, encouraging practices like stepping back or changing positions to see work from a different angle. Artists (n = 5) and teachers (n = 4) described how such shifts could reveal new insights and improve the creative process. As one artist put it, *"You walk around and search for that spot, the place where the image speaks to you."* In addition to adjusting viewpoints, artists (n = 7) reported on changing work locations. Some artists (n = 4) described working in their studio and in nature: *"In the winter, I work here, but* *in the summer, well, then I wake up in the morning with a brilliant idea, and I go to the beach to try and build or realize it."* Teachers (n = 3) also mentioned the importance of an inspirational work environment, for example organizing art classes in an exhibition space. Spatial perspectives were also explored through body movement, allowing for multisensory creative experiences. Artists experimented with shifting from very small to very big canvas sizes (n = 4), while teachers sometimes encouraged bodily movement (Fig. 4) to promote expressivity (n = 2).

Temporal Perspectives—Time was often mentioned by artists (n = 10) and teachers (n = 8). For artists, time was a flexible resource that allowed ideas to evolve. Artists (n = 6) described incubation as essential for gaining insights: *"I can sleep on it, and the next morning, I see it clearly."* In contrast, art teachers focused on helping students navigate time constraints within class settings, e.g., using structured assignments that support getting started and keep going (n = 8): *"It's really an appetizer to get you started."* Artists spoke of looking back at previous work (n = 6), sometimes reusing or refining earlier pieces, and used recurring themes (n = 8) as a way to deepen exploration. Recurrence and reflection were often mentioned as contributing to artistic development over time, highlighted by 7 artists. Teachers (n = 6) also aimed to promote artistic growth by offering adaptive challenges that evolved with students' goals and competenties.

6 Discussion

In this study, we introduced a model of pluri-perspectivism as a contextual map for humanrobot co-creativity. Building on Glăveanu and Gillespie's concept of creatogenetic differences [26], the model integrates five domain-specific dimensions into a layered structure distinguishing between collaborative (outer layer) and creative-task (inner layer) interactions. This framework captures how shifts across dimensions—such as a spatial re-orientation leading to a semiotic reinterpretation—can generate creative openings.

Empirical Insights—The findings of this study showed how pluri-perspectivism is ubiquitous in creative practice. Participants described engaging with al five dimensions in personal and situated ways. They mentioned making perspectival shifts, such as using bodily movement (spatial) to inspire expressive marks (semiotic), or allowing time (temporal) for conceptual redirection. The examples supported the relevance of a pluri-perspectivist framework for understanding exploration in creative contexts.

Implications for HRI—The pluri-perspectivist model serves as a conceptual tool for understanding how a co-creative possibility space can be explored in different dimensions. This study contributes to a better grounded understanding of what context sensitivity entails in human-robot creative collaboration, and informs implementation strategies for HRI with VLM-enhanced robots. The model also provides insights into the challenges when using VLM-enhanced robots as co-creative agents. As described in Sect. 4, social and semiotic dimensions may align well with schema-guided, few-shot prompting [11,32,58], while temporal and spatial dimensions cannot be addressed through prompting alone. Additional modules can be implemented for this. Embodied co-creativity remains challenging, but VLM-enhanced robots can contribute uniquely through precision, rapid iteration, non-human perception and exploration, offering novel forms of creativity support. Furthermore, conversational perspective sharing can stimulate creativity in humans by prompting reflection, reinterpretation, and reframing. We will investigate this in our future co-creative HRI studies.

Limitations and Future Directions—While our pluri-perspectivist model offers a theoretically grounded framework for contextual understanding in creative collaboration, its application in HRI remains exploratory. As such, we view it as a conceptual contribution, that can inform human-robot interaction design, in-context learning, and the evaluation of perspectival diversity in co-creative interactions. Our future work will involve simplified implementations of the model with VLM-enhanced robots in constrained HRI scenarios, to assess how prompting different dimensions and perspectival shifts can support creative experiences in human-robot co-creativity with older adults.

7 Conclusion

We introduce a five-dimensional model of pluri-perspectivism, grounded in creativity theory. Through insights from artists and art teachers, we demonstrate that pluri-perspectivism is ubiquitous in creative practices. Literature study showed that the model could serve as a contextual map that structures interactions and be used for schema-guided prompting with a VLM-enhanced co-creative robot. The model can also serve as a tool for analyzing co-creative humanrobot interactions. While the model has not yet been tested in human-robot interactions, we identify opportunities for its application in future studies. The proposition sets the stage for further research into fostering context-sensitive robots to support human creativity.

Acknowledgments. This work is part of the project Social Robotics and Generative AI to support Creative Experiences for Older Adults (NWO Doctoral Grant for Teachers, project no. 023.019.021).

Disclosure of Interests. The authors have no competing interests to declare that are relevant to the content of this article.

References

1. Ali, S., Devasia, N., Park, H.W., Breazeal, C.: Social robots as creativity eliciting agents. Front. Robot. AI **8**, 673730 (2021)
2. Ali, S., Moroso, T., Breazeal, C.: Can children learn creativity from a social robot? In: Proceedings of the 2019 Conference on Creativity and Cognition, pp. 359–368 (2019)

3. Almeida, J.T., Leite, I., Yadollahi, E.: Would you help me? Linking robot's perspective-taking to human prosocial behavior. In: Proceedings of the 2023 ACM/IEEE International Conference on Human-Robot Interaction, pp. 388–397 (2023)
4. ATLAS.ti Scientific Software Development GmbH: ATLAS.ti: Qualitative Data Analysis Software (2024). https://atlasti.com/, v23.0
5. Beghetto, R.A., Kaufman, J.C.: Toward a broader conception of creativity: a case for "mini-c" creativity. Psychol. Aesthet. Creat. Arts **1**(2), 73 (2007)
6. Boden, M.A.: The Creative Mind: Myths and Mechanisms. Routledge (2004)
7. Bossema, M., Allouch, S.B., Plaat, A., Saunders, R.: Human-robot co-creativity: a scoping review: informing a research agenda for human-robot co-creativity with older adults. In: 2023 32nd IEEE International Conference on Robot and Human Interactive Communication (RO-MAN), pp. 988–995. IEEE (2023)
8. Bossema, M., Allouch, S.B., Plaat, A., Saunders, R.: LLM-enhanced interactions in human-robot collaborative drawing with older adults. arXiv preprint arXiv:2506.18711 (2025)
9. Bradski, G.: The openCV library. Dr. Dobb's J. Softw. Tools Prof. Program. **25**(11), 120–123 (2000)
10. Breazeal, C.L., Ostrowski, A.K., Singh, N., Park, H.W.: Designing social robots for older adults. Natl. Acad. Eng. Bridge **49**, 22–31 (2019)
11. Brown, T., et al.: Language models are few-shot learners. Adv. Neural. Inf. Process. Syst. **33**, 1877–1901 (2020)
12. Bubeck, S., et al.: Sparks of artificial general intelligence: early experiments with GPT-4. arXiv e-prints pp. arXiv–2303 (2023)
13. Chen, B., et al.: SpatialVLM: endowing vision-language models with spatial reasoning capabilities. In: Proceedings of the IEEE/CVF Conference on Computer Vision and Pattern Recognition, pp. 14455–14465 (2024)
14. Clark, H.H.: Using Language. Cambridge University Press (1996)
15. De Jaegher, H., Di Paolo, E.: Participatory sense-making: an enactive approach to social cognition. Phenomenol. Cogn. Sci. **6**, 485–507 (2007)
16. Dong, Q., et al.: A survey on in-context learning. arXiv preprint arXiv:2301.00234 (2022)
17. Elgarf, M., Zojaji, S., Skantze, G., Peters, C.: CreativeBot: a creative storyteller robot to stimulate creativity in children. In: Proceedings of the 2022 International Conference on Multimodal Interaction, pp. 540–548 (2022)
18. Emanuel, A.W., Mudjihartono, P., Nugraha, J.A.: Snapshot-based human action recognition using openpose and deep learning. IAENG Int. J. Comput. Sci. **48**(4), 2–8 (2021)
19. Engeström, Y.: Learning By Expanding: An Activity-theoretical Approach to Developmental Research. Cambridge University Press (2014)
20. Fancourt, D.: Arts in Health: Designing and Researching Interventions. Oxford University Press (2017)
21. Fancourt, D., Finn, S.: What is the evidence on the role of the arts in improving health and well-being? A scoping review. World Health Organization. Regional Office for Europe (2019)
22. Fucinato, K., Niebuhr, O., Nørskov, S., Fischer, K.: Charismatic speech features in robot instructions enhance team creativity. Front. Commun. **8**, 1115360 (2023)
23. Galinsky, A.D., Ku, G., Wang, C.S.: Perspective-taking and self-other overlap: fostering social bonds and facilitating social coordination. Group Process. Intergr. Relat. **8**(2), 109–124 (2005)

24. Glăveanu, V.P., Beghetto, R.A.: Creative experience: a non-standard definition of creativity. Creat. Res. J. **33**(2), 75–80 (2021)
25. Glăveanu, V.P.: Difference. In: Creativity—A New Vocabulary, pp. 61–69. Springer (2023)
26. Glăveanu, V.P., Gillespie, A.: Creativity out of difference: theorising the semiotic, social and temporal origin of creative acts. In: Rethinking Creativity, pp. 1–15. Routledge (2014)
27. Gomez Cubero, C., Pekarik, M., Rizzo, V., Jochum, E.: The robot is present: creative approaches for artistic expression with robots. Front. Robot. AI **8**, 662249 (2021)
28. Groot, B., et al.: The value of active arts engagement on health and well-being of older adults: a nation-wide participatory study. Int. J. Environ. Res. Public Health **18**(15), 8222 (2021)
29. Guckelsberger, C., Kantosalo, A., Negrete-Yankelevich, S., Takala, T.: Embodiment and computational creativity. arXiv preprint arXiv:2107.00949 (2021)
30. Hu, Y., Feng, L., Mutlu, B., Admoni, H.: Exploring the role of social robot behaviors in a creative activity. In: Proceedings of the 2021 ACM Designing Interactive Systems Conference, pp. 1380–1389 (2021)
31. Imam, M.F., Lyu, C., Aji, A.F.: Can multimodal LLMs do visual temporal understanding and reasoning? The answer is no! arXiv preprint arXiv:2501.10674 (2025)
32. Lee, C.H., Cheng, H., Ostendorf, M.: Dialogue state tracking with a language model using schema-driven prompting. arXiv preprint arXiv:2109.07506 (2021)
33. Lee, S., Ju, W.: Adversarial robots as creative collaborators. In: Companion of the 2024 ACM/IEEE International Conference on Human-Robot Interaction, pp. 655–658 (2024)
34. Lewis, F., Krans, K.: Arts in health in nederland: Een nationale agenda (2024)
35. Lin, Y., Guo, J., Chen, Y., Yao, C., Ying, F.: It is your turn: collaborative ideation with a co-creative robot through sketch. In: Proceedings of the 2020 CHI Conference on Human Factors in Computing Systems, pp. 1–14 (2020)
36. MacRitchie, J., Floridou, G.A., Christensen, J., Timmers, R., de Witte, L.: The use of technology for arts-based activities in older adults living with mild cognitive impairment or dementia: a scoping review. Dementia **22**(1), 252–280 (2023)
37. Mahyar, N., Tory, M.: Supporting communication and coordination in collaborative sensemaking. IEEE Trans. Visual Comput. Graphics **20**(12), 1633–1642 (2014)
38. Norman, D.A.: Cognitive engineering. User Centered Syst. Des. **31**(61), 2 (1986)
39. Nwankwo, L., Rueckert, E.: The conversation is the command: interacting with real-world autonomous robots through natural language. In: Companion of the 2024 ACM/IEEE International Conference on Human-Robot Interaction, pp. 808–812 (2024)
40. Pandey, A.K., Alami, R.: Towards task understanding through multi-state visuo-spatial perspective taking for human-robot interaction. In: International Joint Conference on Artificial Intelligence-Workshop on Agents Learning Interactively from Human Teachers (IJCAI-ALIHT 2011) (2011)
41. Patton, M.Q.: Qualitative Research & Evaluation Methods. Sage (2002)
42. Patton, M.Q.: Qualitative Research & Evaluation Methods: Integrating Theory and Practice. Sage Publications (2014)
43. Plaat, A., van Duijn, M., van Stein, N., Preuss, M., van der Putten, P., Batenburg, K.J.: Agentic large language models, a survey. arXiv preprint arXiv:2503.23037 (2025)

44. Radford, A., Kim, J.W., Xu, T., Brockman, G., McLeavey, C., Sutskever, I.: Robust speech recognition via large-scale weak supervision (2022). https://doi.org/10.48550/arXiv.2212.04356, https://arxiv.org/abs/2212.04356
45. Rond, J., Sanchez, A., Berger, J., Knight, H.: Improv with robots: creativity, inspiration, co-performance. In: 2019 28th IEEE International Conference on Robot and Human Interactive Communication (RO-MAN), pp. 1–8. IEEE (2019)
46. Saunders, R., Chee, E., Gemeinboeck, P.: Evaluating human-robot interaction with embodied creative systems. In: Proceedings of the Fourth International Conference on Computational Creativity, pp. 205–209 (2013)
47. Tanner, A., Urech, A., Schulze, H., Manser, T.: Older adults' engagement and mood during robot-assisted group activities in nursing homes: development and observational pilot study. JMIR Rehabil. Assist. Technol. **10**, e48031 (2023)
48. Thomaz, A.L., Breazeal, C.: Teachable robots: understanding human teaching behavior to build more effective robot learners. Artif. Intell. **172**(6–7), 716–737 (2008)
49. Tseng, Y.M., et al.: Two tales of persona in LLMs: a survey of role-playing and personalization. arXiv preprint arXiv:2406.01171 (2024)
50. Tsimpoukelli, M., Menick, J.L., Cabi, S., Eslami, S., Vinyals, O., Hill, F.: Multimodal few-shot learning with frozen language models. Adv. Neural. Inf. Process. Syst. **34**, 200–212 (2021)
51. Vossen, P., Bajčetić, L., Baez, S., Bašić, S., Kraaijeveld, B.: Modelling context awareness for a situated semantic agent. In: Bella, G., Bouquet, P. (eds.) CONTEXT 2019. LNCS (LNAI), vol. 11939, pp. 238–252. Springer, Cham (2019). https://doi.org/10.1007/978-3-030-34974-5_20
52. Weinberg, G., et al.: "Be social"—embodied human-robot musical interactions. In: Robotic Musicianship: Embodied Artificial Creativity and Mechatronic Musical Expression, pp. 143–187 (2020)
53. Whittaker, S., Rogers, Y., Petrovskaya, E., Zhuang, H.: Designing personas for expressive robots: personality in the new breed of moving, speaking, and colorful social home robots. ACM Trans. Hum.-Robot Interact. (THRI) **10**(1), 1–25 (2021)
54. Wooldridge, M., Jennings, N.R.: Intelligent agents: theory and practice. Knowl. Eng. Rev. **10**(2), 115–152 (1995)
55. Xiong, S., Payani, A., Kompella, R., Fekri, F.: Large language models can learn temporal reasoning. arXiv preprint arXiv:2401.06853 (2024)
56. Yang, D., et al.: LLM meets scene graph: can large language models understand and generate scene graphs? A benchmark and empirical study. arXiv preprint arXiv:2505.19510 (2025)
57. Zhang, C., Chen, J., Li, J., Peng, Y., Mao, Z.: Large language models for human-robot interaction: a review. Biomim. Intell. Robot. **3**(4), 100131 (2023)
58. Zhang, X., Peng, B., Li, K., Zhou, J., Meng, H.: SGP-TOD: building task bots effortlessly via schema-guided LLM prompting. arXiv preprint arXiv:2305.09067 (2023)
59. Zhao, X., Cusimano, C., Malle, B.F.: Do people spontaneously take a robot's visual perspective? In: Proceedings of the Tenth Annual ACM/IEEE International Conference on Human-Robot Interaction Extended Abstracts, pp. 133–134 (2015)

Exploring Avoidance Strategies Between Humans and Robots in Social Navigation

Meriam Moujahid[✉], Christian Dondrup, Daniel Hernandez Garcia, and Marta Romeo

Edinburgh, UK
mm470@hw.ac.uk

Abstract. As robots become increasingly integrated into daily life, understanding how humans naturally interact with them in shared environments is essential. This work examines the spatial and behavioural dynamics between humans and a humanoid mobile robot, focusing on avoidance behaviours in shared spaces. A study was conducted in an indoor laboratory setting, where human avoidance behaviours around a humanoid mobile robot were observed, video recorded, and supplemented with a post-task questionnaire. Data annotation and video analysis examined proxemics and behaviours exhibited by participants. The results suggest that participants kept a greater distance during verbal interactions with the robot, whereas during navigation, the distances were comparable to those of human-human interactions. However, participants demonstrated a greater tendency to assert their path when navigating with the robot. Furthermore, the qualitative analysis highlighted participants' preference for a more responsive, socially aware robot with adaptive navigation.

1 Introduction

In environments where humans navigate shared spaces and pursue conflicting trajectories, they typically resolve such conflicts through communication [1]. If this negotiation fails, it can result in a subtle "corridor dance" where individuals negotiate their respective paths. Likewise, robots must have the ability to communicate their objectives effectively and provide clarifications in situations of navigational conflict [2]. Treating humans merely as obstacles is an inadequate approach for robotic systems [3]. Beyond obstacle avoidance, robots must prioritize perceived safety and human comfort [4]. In addition, they should transparently convey the intent behind their movements and signal their trajectory decisions when interacting with humans [5]. Given that social robots can communicate using non-verbal cues, this can help them avoid conflicts, enabling more sophisticated interpretations of human movement and more intuitive path negotiation. A deep understanding of human behaviour in public settings is essential for developing interaction strategies that are socially acceptable and trustworthy [6]. Moreover, establishing proxemic norms is vital to enable robots to navigate shared spaces in a manner that respects human comfort and social expectations [7]. Individuals adopt various strategies to negotiate space. For instance, some individuals will assert their path with confidence when navigating alongside the robot [8], while others demonstrate greater responsiveness, adapting their actions in response to the behaviour of others [9,10].

Despite advances in human-aware navigation [11,12], a significant gap remains in understanding natural human-robot conflict resolution strategies. To address this limitation, our work focuses on exploring avoidance strategies based on real-world data collected in indoor environments. Participants were invited to play a game designed to promote continuous movement around the room. This movement frequently aligned with the robot's navigation patterns. We examined conflict resolution strategies employed by humans during human-robot interactions (HRI), in contrast to those during human-human interactions (HHI). Additionally, we categorised these strategies into assertive or responsive. Furthermore, a qualitative analysis of participant's feedback provides insights into their preferences for robot navigation. The study investigates key questions:

RQ1: What are the differences in proxemics between human-robot interactions and human-human interactions?

RQ2: Are there different types of avoidance strategies in human-robot interactions versus human-human interactions, and how frequently do they occur?

RQ3: How do humans exhibit assertive and responsive strategies when interacting with robots compared to other humans during navigation conflicts?

RQ4: What are the participants' preferences regarding the robot's communication for conflict resolution during navigation?

2 Background

In shared spaces, where humans and robots navigate with potentially conflicting trajectories, effective conflict resolution strategies are essential to prevent inefficient robot behaviour. Early research explored human obstacle avoidance [13], linking object evasion to visual aim points [14]. Hall's concept of proxemics [15] describes an invisible boundary regulating interpersonal distance, yet its applicability to HRI remains uncertain [16].

Various approaches to human-aware navigation incorporate social conventions into robotic behaviour, such as queueing [17], crowd navigation [18], and walking alongside humans [19]. Ensuring safe and socially acceptable interactions requires robots to prioritise human safety and comfort while effectively communicating motion objectives [13].

Communication is crucial when humans and robots navigate shared environments, as conflicting trajectories frequently arise [20]. Previous work explored the use of communicative gestures and non-verbal cues to enhance efficiency and clarity in human-aware navigation [21–23]. Legibility, defined as motion that allows an observer to infer a robot's intended goal, and predictability, which refers to motion aligning with an observer's expectations, are key to effective robotic movement [24]. While verbal signals have been used for navigation [25,26], they are often less effective in social settings where interactions should occur smoothly and without excessive cognitive demand [27]. Non-verbal cues, such as body orientation [28], and gaze [29], significantly influence human perception and trajectory coordination. Motion itself can function as a negotiation cue [5], as humans naturally look in the direction they intend to walk, signalling their trajectory to others [29]. Various strategies have been proposed for conveying robotic intent through embodiment, including physical attributes, expressive lighting [30,31], and spatial augmented reality [32].

Understanding human behaviour in public spaces is essential for designing socially acceptable robotic interaction strategies [33]. Research has examined human movement patterns and collision avoidance [20,34–36]. In the navigation of space, individuals employ various strategies. One such strategy, the "assertive" approach [8], entails proactively resolving conflicts related to movement by maintaining control over one's trajectory. We favour the term "assertive" rather than "aggressive" to denote participation in courteous social etiquette, thereby avoiding the negative connotations associated with 'aggression' [37]. Conversely, the "responsive" strategy centres on adjusting to the actions of others, yielding or altering direction to ensure smooth and cooperative interactions [6].

Recent research has presented extensive datasets of social navigation demonstrations for mobile robots [38], as well as datasets of human motion trajectories and eye gaze data collected indoors [39]. Additionally, various studies have gathered substantial data from different robots [40–42]. However, none of the existing datasets have captured and annotated the avoidance strategies and human behaviours used during navigation.

Based on real-world data, we investigate the avoidance strategies employed by humans in HRI, in comparison to those observed during HHI. Furthermore, we categorise these strategies into assertive and responsive behaviours. This categorisation helps in analysing human behaviours and integrating appropriate communication strategies into robotic motion planning in the future.

3 Methods

The experimental setup, as shown on Fig. 2 captures differences in interpersonal distances between HHI and HRI to address RQ1. By embedding the robot in a dynamic, multi-agent game, we examine avoidance strategies (RQ2) and their frequency across interaction types. The interactive nature of the task allows analysis of RQ3, assessing assertive and responsive strategies in navigation conflicts. Additionally, to address RQ4, we investigate participants' perceptions of the robot's communicative role in facilitating navigation. During this experiment [43], each participant engaged in a game involving a set of Dobble cards[1] distributed over three tables positioned on opposite sides of the room. The objective is for players to compete to match identical symbols on the cards. This setup requires that participants move around the room alongside two other agents: a robot ARI [44] and another human participant. The three players, two humans

---

[1] https://www.dobblegame.com/en/games/dobble-classic/.

Fig. 1. Participants walking through the room interacting with the robot.

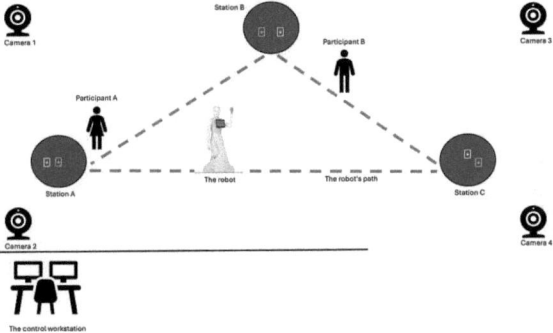

Fig. 2. The room layout illustrates the robot's trajectory, the locations of the stations, and the cameras positioned at the corners of the laboratory.

and the robot, must navigate between the tables to locate and match the symbols. Each session lasts approximately 15 min, ensuring ample time for meaningful interaction and movement between participants and the robot e.g. conflicting trajectories. Furthermore, the experimental setup is strategically structured to encourage participants to move continuously throughout the session, they were able to move freely around the room without being directed along a specific path. This movement often aligns with the robot's navigation patterns, enabling the collection of detailed interaction data (e.g. Sensory data, verbal and non verbal cues, proxemics distances) within a controlled, yet dynamic environment, as illustrated in Fig. 1.

At the beginning of each session, the robot introduces the game verbally, providing clear instructions to the participants. Then it moves around the room to demonstrate the locations of the tables and cards, ensuring that the participants fully understand the setup. Following this phase, the robot transitions to autonomous navigation, moving between predefined waypoints as if it were actively participating in the game alongside the human players. In this second phase, our objective is to elicit avoidance behaviours from participants as they and the robot navigate between the three tables. The robot does not have any human detection or awareness capabilities. It solely relies on pre-programmed navigation and odometry to move along a straight path between waypoints, without actively sensing or responding to the presence of participants. This approach was intentionally adopted to ensure that participants' avoidance behaviours remained uninfluenced by any potential avoidance behaviours of the robot. The researcher, positioned out of view behind a screen, monitored the experiment using an interface that displays the camera feeds mentioned above. Furthermore, when the robot was in danger of colliding with a participant, the experimenter was able to use a joy-pad to redirect it, thereby minimising any potential risks.

Visual data were captured using cameras positioned in the four corners of the room, supplemented by the robot's own onboard cameras: a front torso camera, a black-and-white fisheye camera, and a depth camera, as shown on Fig. 2.

Participants' feedback was collected through a post-task survey designed to gain insights into their preferences for robot behaviour. Using open ended questions, the survey assesses various factors, including participants' preferences regarding the robot's communication and conflict resolution during navigation. Participants are also asked whether they felt comfortable and safe sharing the space with the robot.

Participants consented to the video data being analysed. 26 sessions were collected with a total number of 52 participants. Demographic data were not collected.

4 Results and Analysis

4.1 Proxemics

The videos were annotated manually using ELAN [45] to track the participants' movements in the shared space, particularly focusing on the moments when individuals interacted with the robot or another human during verbal exchanges or navigation. In response to **RQ1**, distances were analysed by extracting data from the recorded video interactions between participants and the robot (HRI) as well as between two human participants (HHI). For each interaction, we manually measured the shortest distance between the participant and the robot, or between the two human participants, at key moments in the interaction, which include moments of verbal exchange, during navigation when participants had to adjust their paths due to conflicting trajectories, and moments of active avoidance behaviour. The distances were calculated using a known reference object to derive a scale factor, and then measuring the shortest distance in real-world units based on pixel data [46]. To ensure accuracy, this calculation is cross-validated using multiple cameras and angles. The shortest distance was chosen because it provides a precise measure of how close participants were willing to get to the robot or another person [47], especially during conflict situations where spatial negotiation often occurs. Figure 3 illustrates the results.

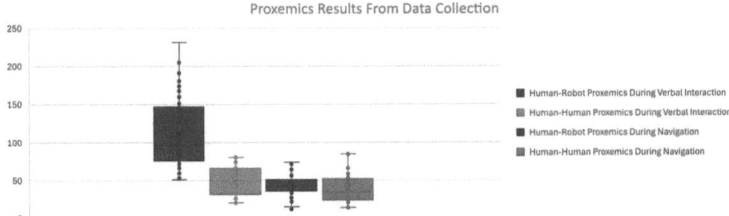

Fig. 3. Chart representing distances (cm) between Human and Robot during the experiment.

Human-Human Proxemics During Verbal Interaction. During the initial phase of the game, participants naturally engaged in dialogue. The distances observed in this context range between 22cm and 80cm with a mean distance of 45cm and a standard deviation of 49. These findings align with established interpersonal norms [15].

Human-Robot Proxemics During Verbal Interaction. During the initial phase of the game, the robot verbally introduces the game, providing clear instructions to the participants. Participants had the freedom to approach the robot (or not) at a comfortable distance. The observed distances in this context range from 51 cm to 260 cm, with a mean of 112 cm and a standard deviation of 18.

Human-Human Proxemics During Navigation. Each participant, during active engagement in the game alongside another human player, demonstrated distances varying from 14cm and 84cm, with a mean distance of 38cm and a standard deviation of 12. The observed distances, based on 100 occurrences, are consistent with typical human movement patterns [15].

Human-Robot Proxemics During Navigation. While the robot autonomously navigates between predefined waypoints, simulating active participation in the game alongside the human players, the observed distances between human and robot, based on 259 occurrences, range from 12 cm to 73 cm, with a mean of 43 cm and a standard deviation of 17.

4.2 Avoidance Behaviours

To address **RQ2**, The researcher manually reviewed the video footage, paying close attention to moments when participants came across a navigation conflict when interacting with either the robot or other participants.

Avoidance behaviours were categorised based on the type of action taken by the participants to address navigation conflicts. Following the extraction of data from annotations, we analysed the frequency of each avoidance behaviours during the interactions. This analysis aimed to identify the predominant strategies. Table 1 describe each of the behaviours and demonstrates that avoidance behaviours in HRI compared to HHI. Figure 4 further visualises these results, providing a comparative representation of the frequency of avoidance strategies.

Table 1. Observed avoidance strategies used during HRI (259 occurrences) vs during HHI (95 occurrences)

Strategy	Description	Type	HRI	HHI
Shoulder move	Participants adjust their shoulders to yield space or maintain distance from the other agent.	Responsive	1.11%	1%
Stop and wait	Participants pause to let the other agent move first.	Responsive	2.23%	4%
Overtake	Participants pass the other [6].	Assertive	2.6%	1%
Give way	Participants adjust their path to let the other pass without fully stopping.	Responsive	3.34%	14%
Accelerate	Participants quicken their pace.	Assertive	4.46%	1%
Hesitation	Participants briefly make a prompting gesture.	Responsive	7.06%	3%
Step Away	Participants step back from the other agent.	Responsive	10.78%	1%
Give space	Participants intentionally increase distance from the other agent.	Responsive	11.15%	50%
Walk behind the agent	Participants choose to pass behind the other agent [6].	Assertive	22%	12%
Walk in front of the agent	Participants cross in front of the other agent [6].	Assertive	25.27%	9%

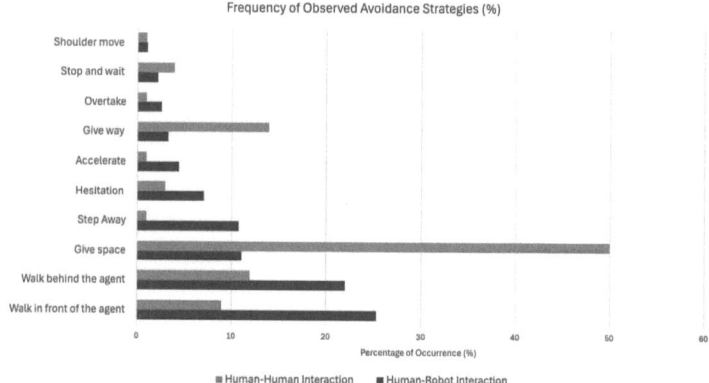

Fig. 4. Comparison between Avoidance strategies ranked by order of occurrence in HRI.

To answer **RQ3**, we categorised the strategies into two groups based on whether individuals acted independently of the other agent (Assertive behaviour) or modified their behaviour in response to the movement of another agent (Responsive behaviour). Figure 5 presents a visual representation of these results.

Assertive Strategies: Taking Initiative to Resolve Navigation Conflicts. Assertive strategies involve deliberate actions taken to control or direct the movement flow [8]. "Walk in front of the agent" (25.27% HRI vs 9% HHI) "Walk behind the agent" (22% HRI vs. 12% HHI) "Accelerate" (4.46% HRI vs. 1% HHI) and "Overtaking" (2.6% HRI vs. 1% HHI).

Responsive Strategies: Adjusting in Response To Another Agent's Motion. We define responsive strategies as accommodating the movement of another entity, either by modifying one's position or making space to facilitate smoother navigation. "Give Space" is more frequent in HHI (50%) than in HRI (11.15%). "Step Away" (10.78% HRI vs. 1% HHI) is far more common with robots. "Give Way" (3.34% HRI vs. 14% HHI) is substantially more frequent between humans. "Shoulder Move" (1.11% vs. 1%) equally likely in both HHI and HRI.

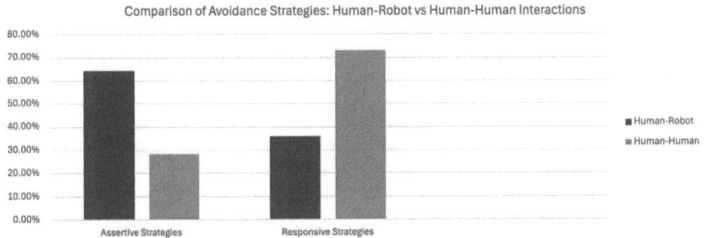

Fig. 5. Comparison of Avoidance Strategies: HRI (259 occurrences) vs HHI (95 occurrences).

4.3 Qualitative Analysis of User's Feedback

To explore **RQ4**, we conducted a qualitative analysis to examine the subjective experiences of participants as reflected in their feedback.

User Preferences: Participants expressed clear preferences regarding the robot's communication and navigation, focusing primarily on predictability, responsiveness, and clarity. One participant mentioned *"The robot was more responsive to my presence, but I felt like it wasn't as proactive as a human player would be."* This indicates that participants would like a robot actively engaged in the interaction rather than passively reacting. In terms of navigation, although the robot was not navigating intelligently and lacked consciousness or awareness of its environment, the feedback shows that participants appreciate the robot basic ability to maintain a safe distance and avoid obstacles. Statements like *"It was safe to be around the robot, feels natural"*, *"It wasn't close to the table, giving us more space to walk"* and *"It seemed aware of my motion, and stopped at a respectful distance"* suggest that users value respect of personal space. This was reinforced with statements such as *"It was mobile in the room,* *and looked to be thinking"* and *"I was impressed by its ability to navigate the room well and was able to manoeuvre out of the way of me and the other human".*

Additionally, participants noted *"Its eyes looking around the room rather than holding steady were quite lifelike and looked great."* and *"It is more personable and natural in its mannerisms than other robots I have seen, mainly due to things like the small arm gestures it made."* which suggest that participants preferred a more socially aware robot that could communicate non-verbal cues. Comments like *"Say sorry (or something similar) to move towards me and make me aware. I got surprised by it once, I didn't see it in my back"* indicate that participants wanted the robot to give verbal feedback to signal its movements and prevent surprises. This preference suggests that the robot's communication should be designed to make its intentions more transparent, so that users feel more at ease during interactions. Participants clearly valued not only physical safety but also social comfort, expressing a preference for the robot to maintain respectful distances while being more visibly and verbally responsive during interactions. Many participants felt that the robot's verbal communication needed improvement. One participant noted, *"It needs to look to the face when it is talking, be more interactive (for example, giving some verbal feedback when it's moving to give the impression it is playing)."* and *"It should be more chatty and move a little less abruptly"*.

User Dislikes: A significant area of dissatisfaction was the robot's unpredictability and rigid navigation. As one participant commented, *"At the start of the game, when the robot was explaining the rules, it felt like the robot was on a pre-programmed path, I felt like I had to move around to accommodate it rather than it following where we were."* This reflects a common dislike for the robot's lack of adaptability. The robot's rigid navigation led participants to feel that they were having to adjust their movements to the robot's path, rather than the robot being responsive to human movements. Users expressed a clear preference for a robot that could adapt to their positions and actions, suggesting that greater responsiveness in navigation would enhance the experience, this was reinforced by the comment: *"The robot could do the navigation more aware state so the human does not have to deliberately change the direction"*. Another concern raised was the robot's lack of responsiveness when interacting with humans, particularly in situations where it was facing away from participants. One participant commented, *"The robot needs to be more responsive and reactive when it is facing backwards towards the person"*.

In summary, participants expressed strong preferences for a robot that was more responsive and socially aware in its communication and navigation. They wanted the robot to move in a more fluid manner, adapting to human actions and providing clearer verbal and non-verbal feedback to improve the interaction. At the same time, participants disliked the robot's rigid, pre-programmed navigation, as well as its lack of responsiveness and social communication. These insights suggest that improving the robot's responsiveness to human behaviour, and communication would enhance the overall user experience. Furthermore, the qualitative analysis highlighted that participants expressed their preference for a more responsive, socially aware robot with adaptive navigation.

5 Discussion

RQ1: What are the differences in proxemics between HRI and HHI? Participants maintained larger distances when interacting verbally with the mobile robot (average distance = 112 cm), compared to 45 cm during HHI. These distances fall within the personal zone (45120 cm), which is typically reserved for interactions with familiar individuals. Interestingly, during navigation, proxemic distances between humans and robots became comparable to those between humans. Previous work confirms these results and indicates that, while people may initially exhibit caution around robots, they can become more accustomed to their presence when robot movements are perceived as predictable and non-intrusive [48]. Furthermore, the slightly larger average distance in human-robot navigation (43 cm vs. 38 cm) may reflect a residual sense of caution, likely driven by concerns over the robot's motion predictability and perceived safety risks [49]. Based on these findings, we conclude that a robot respecting appropriate proxemic norms should maintain a minimum distance of 45cm to ensure user comfort and avoid encroaching on intimate space.

RQ2: What are the different types of avoidance strategies in HRI versus HHI, and how frequently do they occur? In HRI, participants exhibited distinct avoidance strategies compared to HHI, with a higher tendency to walk in front of (25.27% vs. 9%) or behind (22% vs. 12%) the robot. Conversely, in HHI, participants more frequently opted to increase personal space (50% vs. 11.15%). As defined in table1, strategies such as stepping away (10.78% vs. 1%) and accelerating (4.46% vs. 1%) were more common with the robot. In contrast, giving way without stopping (14% vs. 3.34%) was more prevalent in HHI.

RQ3: How do humans exhibit assertive and responsive strategies when interacting with robots compared to other humans during navigation conflicts? As shown in Fig. 5, Assertive strategies were more common in HRI, indicating that humans are more likely to assert their path when navigating with robots. On the other hand, responsive strategies were more frequent in HHI. The qualitative analysis revealed that participants often expressed the need for the robot to be more responsive. We suggest that the robot's lack of responsive avoidance behaviours may account for the participants' assertive behaviour.

RQ4: What are the participants' preferences regarding the robot's communication for conflict resolution during navigation? Participant's feedback further enriched the findings, revealing that while the robot was generally perceived as safe and non-intrusive, there was a need for more responsiveness during navigation. Furthermore, many participants expressed that verbal communication could improve navigation by providing clearer intentions, such as announcing "excuse me" when approaching a person or offering general verbal feedback.

5.1 Implications for Future Robot Interaction Design

These findings underscore the need for designing interactions with robots that can reflect natural human behaviours. Humans commonly use responsive behaviour and increased distance to avoid conflicting trajectories with each other. Moreover, participants consistently expressed a preference for robots that could respond more dynamically to human movements and intentions, as well as provide clearer communication to reduce uncertainty. Building on these findings, we will be designing human-inspired avoidance strategies for social mobile robots. These strategies include three examples:

"Backward-step Distance Adjustment", involves the robot retreating slightly by moving backwards to create more space between itself and the user. This movement is designed to help avoid potential conflicts by ensuring that the robot does not invade the user's intimate space. We are designing this strategy based on the proxemics range that we have identified as effective for HRI in RQ1.

"Side-Step Yielding" refers to a strategy in which the robot steps laterally to create space, thereby facilitating the user's passage. Inspired by human behaviours that involve deliberately increasing interpersonal distance to signal deference or accommodation, this approach aims to enhance interaction by demonstrating the robot's responsiveness and respect for intimate space. The strategy is informed by proxemic ranges identified as optimal for comfortable and effective humanrobot interaction.

"Gestural Navigation Cue", involves the robot employing non-verbal communication by extending one arm forward with the palm facing outward, signalling an invitation for the person to proceed. This gesture is accompanied by a subtle, affirmative head nod to reinforce the intention. Given participants' strong preference for more responsive behaviour and communicative cues, this gesture serves to clearly convey that the user has priority.

Future work will focus on integrating and testing these avoidance strategies within an autonomous navigation system, evaluating their efficacy through user feedback, and conducting a comparative analysis to assess their relative performance.

6 Conclusions and Future Work

In conclusion, the findings demonstrate that, although participants initially maintained greater distances during verbal interactions with the robot, these distances decreased during navigation, ultimately becoming similar to those observed in HHI. Moreover, the distinct avoidance strategies employed in HRI emphasise the need for robots to adopt more human-like behaviours, such as offering space and stepping back. The primary limitation of the robot was its lack of responsiveness, which stemmed from its pre-programmed navigation system designed to follow a straight line between designated waypoints. This work provides a framework for designing and integrating communicative gestures and movements into robot navigation to facilitate avoidance strategies. It sets the stage for the development of robots that are more socially adept and capable of effective communication and responsive navigation.

References

1. Che, Y., Okamura, A.M., Sadigh, D.: Efficient and trustworthy social navigation via explicit and implicit robot-human communication. IEEE Trans. Rob. **36**(3), 692–707 (2020)
2. Mirsky, R., Xiao, X., Hart, J., Stone, P.: Conflict avoidance in social navigation–a survey. ACM Trans. Hum. Robot Interact. **13**(1), 1–36 (2024)
3. Lam, C.-P., Chou, C.-T., Chiang, K.-H., Fu, L.-C.: Human-centered robot navigation–towards a harmoniously human–robot coexisting environment. IEEE Trans. Rob. **27**(1), 99–112 (2011)
4. Mubin, O., Ahmad, M.I., Kaur, S., Shi, W., Khan, A.: Social robots in public spaces: a meta-review. In: Ge, S.S., et al., (eds.) ICSR 2018. LNCS (LNAI), vol. 11357, pp. 213–220. Springer, Cham (2018). https://doi.org/10.1007/978-3-030-05204-1_21
5. Lichtenthäler, C., Kirsch, A.: Legibility of robot behavior: a literature review (2016)
6. Francis, A., et al.: Principles and guidelines for evaluating social robot navigation algorithms. ACM Trans. Hum. Robot Interact. **14**(2), 1–65 (2025)
7. Smith, J., Lee, T.: Proxemics in human-robot interaction: redefining space for social navigation. Int. J. Soc. Robot. **16**(2), 123–139 (2024)
8. Thomas, J., Vaughan, R.: After you: doorway negotiation for human-robot and robot-robot interaction. In: 2018 IEEE/RSJ International Conference on Intelligent Robots and Systems (IROS), pp. 3387–3394 (2018)
9. Zhao, X., Fan, T., Li, Y., Zheng, Y., Pan, J.: An efficient and responsive robot motion controller for safe human-robot collaboration. IEEE Robot. Autom. Lett. **6**(3), 6068–6075 (2021)
10. Nguyen, B.V.D., Han, J., Moere, A.V.: Towards responsive architecture that mediates place: recommendations on how and when an autonomously moving robotic wall should adapt a spatial layout. Proc. ACM Hum. Comput. Interact. **6**(CSCW2), 1–27 (2022)
11. Li, H., et al.: Human-aware vision-and-language navigation: bridging simulation to reality with dynamic human interactions. In: Advances in Neural Information Processing Systems, vol. 37, pp. 119411–119442 (2024)
12. Singamaneni, P.T., et al.: A survey on socially aware robot navigation: taxonomy and future challenges. Int. J. Robot. Res. **43**(10), 1533–1572 (2024)
13. Kruse, T., Pandey, A.K., Alami, R., Kirsch, A.: Human-aware robot navigation: a survey. Robot. Auton. Syst. **61**(12), 1726–1743 (2013)
14. Cutting, J.E., Vishton, P.M., Braren, P.A.: How we avoid collisions with stationary and moving objects. Psychol. Rev. **102**(4), 627 (1995)
15. Hall, E.T.: The Hidden Dimension. Garden City, NY: Doubleday, vol. 609 (1966)
16. Moujahid, M., Robb, D.A., Dondrup, C., Hastie, H.: Come closer: the effects of robot personality on human proxemics behaviours. In: 2023 32nd IEEE International Conference on Robot and Human Interactive Communication (RO-MAN), pp. 2610–2616. IEEE (2023)
17. Nakauchi, Y., Simmons, R.: A social robot that stands in line. In: Proceedings of the Conference on Intelligent Robots and Systems (IROS), Takamatsu Japan (2000)

18. Katyal, K.D., Hager, G.D., Huang, C.-M.: Intent-aware pedestrian prediction for adaptive crowd navigation. In: 2020 IEEE International Conference on Robotics and Automation (ICRA), pp. 3277–3283. IEEE (2020)
19. Ferrer, G., Zulueta, A.G., Cotarelo, F.H., Sanfeliu, A.: Robot social-aware navigation framework to accompany people walking side-by-side. Auton. Robot. **41**(4), 775–793 (2017)
20. Yamamoto, H., Yanagisawa, D., Feliciani, C., Nishinari, K.: Body-rotation behavior of pedestrians for collision avoidance in passing and cross flow. Transport. Res. Part B: Methodol. **122**, 486–510 (2019). https://www.sciencedirect.com/science/article/pii/S0191261517300085
21. Alami, R., et al.: Diligent: towards a human-friendly navigation system. In: Proceedings. 2000 IEEE/RSJ International Conference on Intelligent Robots and Systems (IROS 2000)(Cat. No. 00CH37113), vol. 1, pp. 21–26. IEEE (2000)
22. Babel, F., Kraus, J., Baumann, M.: Findings from a qualitative field study with an autonomous robot in public: exploration of user reactions and conflicts. Int. J. Soc. Robot. **14**(7), 1625–1655 (2022)
23. Du, K., Brščić, D., Liu, Y., Kanda, T.: Can't you see i am bothered? Human-inspired suggestive avoidance for robots. In: Proceedings of the 2024 ACM/IEEE International Conference on Human-Robot Interaction, ser. HRI 2024. New York, NY, USA: Association for Computing Machinery , pp. 184–193 (2024). https://doi.org/10.1145/3610977.3634954
24. Dragan, A.D., Lee, K.C., Srinivasa, S.S.: Legibility and predictability of robot motion. In: 2013 8th ACM/IEEE International Conference on Human-Robot Interaction (HRI), pp. 301–308. IEEE (2013)
25. Thrun, S., et al.: Probabilistic algorithms and the interactive museum tour-guide robot MINERVA. Int. J. Robot. Res. **19**(11), 972–999 (2000)
26. Yedidsion, H., et al.: Optimal use of verbal instructions for multi-robot human navigation guidance. In: Salichs, M.A., Ge, S.S., Barakova, E.I., Cabibihan, J.-J., Wagner, A.R., Castro-González, Á., He, H. (eds.) ICSR 2019. LNCS (LNAI), vol. 11876, pp. 133–143. Springer, Cham (2019). https://doi.org/10.1007/978-3-030-35888-4_13
27. Cha, E., Kim, Y., Fong, T., Mataric, M.J.: et al.: A survey of nonverbal signaling methods for non-humanoid robots. Found. Trends® Robot. **6**(4), 211–323 (2018)
28. Kitagawa, R., Liu, Y., Kanda, T.: Human-inspired motion planning for omni-directional social robots. In: Proceedings of the 2021 ACM/IEEE International Conference on Human-Robot Interaction, pp. 34–42 (2021)
29. Mahajan, B., Goo, J., Baldauf, K., Owen, S., Stone, P.: Using human-inspired signals to disambiguate navigational intentions
30. Palinko, O., Ramírez, E.R., Juel, W.K., Krüger, N., Bodenhagen, L.: Intention indication for human aware robot navigation. In: VISIGRAPP (2: HUCAPP), pp. 64–74 (2020)
31. Baraka, K., Veloso, M.M.: Mobile service robot state revealing through expressive lights: formalism, design, and evaluation. Int. J. Soc. Robot. **10**(1), 65–92 (2018)
32. Chadalavada, R.T., Andreasson, H., Krug, R., Lilienthal, A.J.: That's on my mind! robot to human intention communication through on-board projection on shared floor space. In: 2015 European Conference on Mobile Robots (ECMR), pp. 1–6. IEEE (2015)
33. Salvini, P., Laschi, C., Dario, P.: Design for acceptability: improving robots' coexistence in human society. Int. J. Soc. Robot. **2**, 451–460 (2010)

34. Rudenko, A., Palmieri, L., Herman, M., Kitani, K.M., Gavrila, D.M., Arras, K.O.: Human motion trajectory prediction: a survey. Int. J. Robot. Res. **39**(8), 895–935 (2020). https://doi.org/10.1177/0278364920917446
35. Turnwald, A., Althoff, D., Wollherr, D., Buss, M.: Understanding human avoidance behavior: interaction-aware decision making based on game theory. Int. J. Soc. Robot. **8**, 331–351 (2016)
36. Corbetta, A., Toschi, F.: Physics of human crowds. Ann. Rev. Condensed Matter Phys. **14**, 311–333 (2023)
37. Zuluaga, M., Vaughan, R.: Reducing spatial interference in robot teams by local-investment aggression. In: 2005 IEEE/RSJ International Conference on Intelligent Robots and Systems, pp. 2798–2805 . IEEE (2005)
38. Karnan, H., et al.: Socially Compliant Navigation Dataset (SCAND): a large-scale dataset of demonstrations for social navigation. IEEE Robot. Autom. Lett. **7**(4), 11807–11814 (2022)
39. Rudenko, A., Kucner, T.P., Swaminathan, C.S., Chadalavada, R.T., Arras, K.O., Lilienthal, A.J.: Thör: human-robot navigation data collection and accurate motion trajectories dataset. IEEE Robot. Autom. Lett. **5**(2), 676–682 (2020)
40. Carlevaris-Bianco, N., Ushani, A.K., Eustice, R.M.: University of MichiGAN north campus long-term vision and lidar dataset. Int. J. Robot. Res. **35**(9), 1023–1035 (2016)
41. Yan, Z., Schreiberhuber, S., Halmetschlager, G., Duckett, T., Vincze, M., Bellotto, N.: Robot perception of static and dynamic objects with an autonomous floor scrubber. Intel. Serv. Robot. **13**(3), 403–417 (2020). https://doi.org/10.1007/s11370-020-00324-9
42. Martin-Martin, R., et al.: JRDB: a dataset and benchmark of egocentric robot visual perception of humans in built environments. IEEE Trans. Pattern Anal. Mach. Intell. **45**(6), 6748–6765 (2021)
43. Moujahid, M., Hernandez Garcia, D., Romeo, M., Dondrup, C.: Data collection towards socially inspired interactive motion planning. In: Proceedings of the 12th International Conference on Human-Agent Interaction, pp. 350–352 (2024)
44. Cooper, S., Di Fava, A., Vivas, C., Marchionni, L., Ferro, F.: ARI: the social assistive robot and companion. In: 2020 29th IEEE International Conference on Robot and Human Interactive Communication (RO-MAN), pp. 745–751. IEEE (2020)
45. Wittenburg, P., Brugman, H., Russel, A., Klassmann, A., Sloetjes, H.: Elan: a professional framework for multimodality research. In: 5th International Conference on Language Resources and Evaluation (LREC 2006), pp. 1556–1559 (2006)
46. Fitwi, A., Chen, Y., Sun, H., Harrod, R.: Estimating interpersonal distance and crowd density with a single-edge camera. Computers **10**(11), 143 (2021)
47. Bailenson, J.N., Blascovich, J., Beall, A.C., Loomis, J.M.: Equilibrium theory revisited: mutual gaze and personal space in virtual environments. Presence: Teleoperators Virtual Environ. **10**(6), 583–598 (2001)
48. Koehler, S., Kresse, W., Yusuf, S.: Human-robot proxemics: an experimental study of the impact of human-robot distance on the user's willingness to engage with the robot. Int. J. Soc. Robot. **4**(4), 311–318 (2012)
49. Samarakoon, S.B.P., Muthugala, M.V.J., Jayasekara, A.B.P.: A review on human-robot proxemics. Electronics **11**(16), 2490 (2022)

Improving Human-Swarm Interaction Through Speech Control and Peer-to-Peer Micro-agent Communication

Giovanni De Gasperis[ID], Daniele Di Ottavio[ID], and Sante Dino Facchini[✉][ID]

DISIM, Università degli Studi dell'Aquila, IT67100 L'Aquila, Italy
{giovanni.degasperis,santedino.facchini}@univaq.it
https://www.disim.univaq.it/

Abstract. Multi-robot platforms are a rapidly evolving area in robotics research, offering improved efficiency, robustness, and scalability for applications such as industrial automation and search and rescue. These platforms leverage multiple autonomous or semi-autonomous agents to perform complex tasks that would be challenging for a single system to execute effectively. In this paper, we introduce FlowProtocol, a lightweight rolling protocol integrated into a declarative, low-latency software platform designed by the authors. FlowProtocol provides a reliable foundation for developing real-time multi-agent systems, incorporating communication primitives and modular architectural components. We demonstrate the application of FlowProtocol by implementing a function-calling agent that delivers Large Language Model services. This agent operates within a peer-to-peer micro-agent swarm, coordinating a fleet of resource-harvesting robots through LLM-guided human interaction. We evaluate key aspects of the proposed architecture through a set of functional tests and present experimental results that benchmark FlowProtocol against the Robot Operating System, highlighting its suitability for real-time, communication-intensive multi-agent applications.

Keywords: Human Robot Interaction · Human Swarm Interaction · Large Language Models · Multi-agent Platform · Data Distribution Systems

1 Introduction

Human-Swarm Interaction (HSI) represents a crucial branch of intelligent systems based on robotic platforms. As the functionalities of such systems grow in complexity, there is an increasing need for more intuitive methods for humans to interact with them. In particular, enabling instruction of individual robots or entire swarms through human-like modalities could represent a significant advancement, especially in real-time scenarios where the speed of intervention is critical. In this paper, we propose an architecture, named Flow Network, designed for data distribution in real-time environments; leveraging the Flow

Protocol for communication, and in particular with its Peer-to-peer (P2P) primitives, we envision a macro agent that interacts with the human operator calling functions offered by several dedicated micro-agents. The architecture supports the development of a function-calling agent capable of interacting with a human operator through Text-to-speech (TTS), Speech-to-text (STT), and Visual modalities, leveraging a Large Language Model (LLM). The aim of this work is to enhance efficiency, real-time performance and distribution of the system, as well as the usability for end users with little or no expertise in coding, robotics, or artificial intelligence.

2 Data Distribution Services for Robotics: an Overview

This section explores the current landscape of multi-robot platforms, detailing their architectures, applications, and the significant challenges they face, particularly in the field of Data Distribution Systems (DDS) in real-time environments. DDS is a middleware protocol and API standard for data-centric connectivity from the Object Management Group (OMG)[1]. It enables scalable, real-time, dependable, high-performance, and interoperable data exchanges between publishers and subscribers. DDS facilitates efficient and reliable communication in robotics, which is essential for coordinating complex robotic systems.

State-of-the-Art: The development of multi-robot systems has been driven by advancements in artificial intelligence, distributed computing, and network communication. In particular, DDS in robotics is pivotal for enabling efficient communication, coordination, and data sharing among internal components and external systems. These paradigms facilitate the integration of sensors, actuators, and computational units, ensuring seamless operation and collaboration. The main solutions in this field are (i) Robot Operating System (ROS)[2], a flexible framework widely used for developing multi-robot applications. ROS communicates through topics, services, and actions, enabling seamless coordination. Its evolution ROS 2, enhances real-time performance and scalability [1]; (ii) Swarm Robotics Platforms, inspired by biological systems, swarm robotics enables collective behaviour in large robot groups; key platforms include Kilobot [2] (for large-scale swarm research), Crazyflie [3] (aerial drone swarms), and Sphero (educational and research applications); (iii) Robotics Technology (RT) Middleware [4] is a standardised platform based on distributed object technology, designed to facilitate the construction of networked robotic systems. It treats robotic elements as RT atomic components, which can be integrated seamlessly to form complex systems. This modular approach promotes reusability and interoperability among robotic components, enhancing system reliability and scalability. Another interesting trend regards Multimodal Human-robot Interaction (HRI) where LLM-integrated robotic planning systems are offering notable solution for writing robotics policies via speech [5], and for embodying Language

---

[1] https://www.omg.org/, accessed June 2025.
[2] https://www.ros.org/, accessed June 2025.

Models to solve reasoning tasks [6]. Finally, cognitive architectures for robot swarms are gaining momentum especially for autonomous robot without central control both in general [7] and aerial configurations [8].

Key Challenges: Despite remarkable progress, multi-robot platforms face several fundamental challenges like (i) Scalability and Communication: Coordinating large robot teams requires decentralized protocols that ensure efficient data exchange while minimizing bandwidth usage [9]; (ii) Heterogeneity and Interoperability: Multi-robot environments often include diverse platforms (ground, aerial, and underwater robots), requiring standardized middleware such as ROS 2 and DDS to facilitate communication; (iii) Coordination and Control: Advanced AI-driven planning algorithms improve task allocation and collision avoidance but demand significant computational resources and real-time processing capabilities; (iv) Energy Efficiency and Resource Management: Long-duration autonomous missions necessitate power-efficient designs, including wireless energy transfer and autonomous charging stations; (v) Security and Ethical Considerations: Multi-robot networks are vulnerable to cyber threats such as data interception and spoofing. Ensuring ethical deployment involves transparency, accountability, and alignment with human values.

In the following Sect. 3 we will present the FlowNetwork, a communication protocol fostering interoperability among agents. In Sect. 4 and 5 we will examine its P2P components respectively. In Sect. 6 an architecture of FlowProtocol for a Function Calling agent is envisioned, while in Sect. 7 an application of such agent to LLM in Swarm Robotics is designed.

3 The Core System: Flow Network

The **FlowNetwork** communication layer is an architecture designed for connecting heterogeneous entities in distributed deployments, previously introduced by the authors (See [10–12]). Its aim is to offer a flexible and scalable architecture in both scenarios using a hub-satellite centralized scheme and to P2P configurations where every couple can assume a client (optionally) or server (mandatory) role. FlowNetwork is built upon FlowProtocol a communication protocol that enables both synchronous and asynchronous interactions. The synchronous component supports blocking commands for tasks like initialisation, data retrieval, and authentication, especially within PairDatabases, a distributed key-value storage structure. FlowNetwork is characterised by (i) parallel execution, (ii) asynchronous and synchronous communication, (iii) efficient responsiveness, (iv) real-time operations, and (v) event and data distribution.

The architecture forms a distributed system with unique connection IDs, user profiles, and configurable properties. In centralised deployments, SkRobot[3] instances (a C++ program under SpecialK, see Sect. 3.1) act as hubs, while satellite nodes execute Python sketches—lightweight scripts with a setup function for

---

[3] https://gitlab.com/Tetsuo-tek/SkRobot, last accessed June 2025.

initialisation and a loop function for cyclic execution. Sketches are fundamental as they function as satellite nodes in centralised systems and P2P nodes. The CyB module[4] provides an executor for running Python sketches. In contrast, the SpecialK module offers a C++ alternative with a different approach, eliminating the need for an executor while maintaining the same functionality.

P2P-flow networks form potentially full connected graphs, whereas centralized-flow networks use a star topology with hubs. A satellite may serve as both a P2P node and a centralised node, hybridising the network by linking star formations to complete clusters. Hubs facilitate network expansion by authenticating and managing satellites and distributing computational workloads across multiple processes and machines. Satellites maintain at least one continuous asynchronous connection (a flow) to a hub, controlling multiple channels while retaining exclusive ownership. Authentication is required for satellite access. Satellites can request to create channels on the hub; them could be of three types, and each of them is always hub-mediated: (1) **Service Channels:** Bidirectional, one-to-one request/response channels allowing satellites to query others for flow-services. Responses can be synchronous (blocking) or asynchronous (non-blocking); (2) **Streaming Channels:** Unidirectional, one-to-many publish subscribe channels for real-time data broadcasting with minimal network-induced latency; (3) **Blob Channels:** Bidirectional channels for managing satellite file systems remotely. The satellite owner has full write access, while others have read-only permissions.

3.1 Protocol Architecture

FlowProtocol is a binary communication protocol using message frames for low-latency synchronous and asynchronous transactions. The protocol distinguishes between: (i) **FlowSync:** Synchronous (blocking) commands requiring immediate responses; and (ii) **FlowAsync:** Asynchronous (non-blocking) commands that may generate later notifications. SpecialK (Sk)[5] is an experimental C++ framework for multi-agent systems, IoT, and robotics. It integrates Standard Template Library (STL) [13], with optional support for OpenCV[6], PortAudio[7], FFTW3[8], and GUI features like FLTK[9] or QtGui[10]. Its design emphasises asynchronous object management, signal/slot communication (implemented from scratch), and event-driven execution, reducing reliance on mutexes and simplifying concurrent programming. FlowProtocol is stable within SpecialK, though authentication and encryption features remain under development. Let's examine briefly each component of the protocol.

---

[4] https://gitlab.com/Tetsuo-tek/cyb, last accessed June 2025.
[5] https://gitlab.com/Tetsuo-tek/SpecialK, last accessed June 2025.
[6] https://opencv.org, last accessed June 2025.
[7] https://portaudio.com, last accessed June 2025.
[8] https://fftw.org, last accessed June 2025.
[9] https://fltk.org, last accessed June 2025.
[10] https://www.qt.io, last accessed June 2025.

Synchronous Communication (FlowSync): Flows begin as synchronous, using TCP or Unix-local connections. This mode handles (i) user authentication, (ii) protocol configuration, (iii) abstracted service requests, and (iv) synchronisation of distributed processes. In most cases, FlowSync is temporary and used for quick value retrieval, but it can maintain long-term connections for distributed synchronisation.

Asynchronous Communication (FlowAsync). By executing the `setSync` command, a synchronous flow transition to asynchronous mode, enabling non-blocking operations such as (i) subscribing to or publishing flow channels, (ii) broadcasting or receiving untyped events, and (iii) sending service requests with optional asynchronous responses.

Binary Structure of Message Frames: Each command, whether synchronous or asynchronous, follows a structured format: (a) a $[2Bytes]$ UInt16 flag identifying the data segment type and a Serialized data segment, if required by the flag. Responses follow the same structure, substituting the command flag with a response flag.

Frames Data Serialization: Parameters in commands and responses follow this structure: (a) a $[4Bytes]$ UInt32 defining data-segment size; (b) and a serialised data-segment containing the parameter value. Primitive values (int, float) are simply casted to Int8, while strings use UTF-8 encoding, requiring retyping upon reception. Positional identity and header flags ensure proper interpretation.

Recursive Hashing and Session ID Authentication on Another Entity: Authentication uses SHA512 hashing recursively applied to a random server-side seed, username, and password:

$$token = digest(digest(seed) + digest(digest(username) + digest(password)))$$

The process is performed through the following steps: (1) The client requests a seed from the server; (2) The server returns a random 64-bit number; (3) The client computes a hash and submits a login token; (4) The server verifies the token; (5) If valid, access is granted; otherwise, the connection is terminated. Authenticated users can obtain a session ID (SID) via the `getSid` command to authenticate on other nodes: $SID = digest(address + username + socket + timestamp)$ This enables proxy-based authentication within P2P-Flow services.

Event Broadcasting and Communication Encryption: Servers distribute events to all connected asynchronous clients. Events are serialised and transported as generic buffers for flexible handling. SpecialK supports experimental SSL encryption. Encryption can be applied selectively to protocol frame contents while leaving structural serialisation in cleartext over TCP. The system accommodates both symmetric and asymmetric encryption schemes.

4 Centralized-Flow Modality

This network follows a star topology, with a central hub managing satellite nodes. Below are its core components.

The Hub (Server Application). FlowServer is the central hub, orchestrating satellite communication with key functionalities: (a) TCP port management with optional SSL support; (b) Secure satellite authentication; (c) Connection handling via synchronous (FlowSync) and asynchronous (FlowAsync) modes; (d) Managing channel ownership, ensuring communication follows a star topology; (e) Real-time satellite status monitoring. Currently, the system is implemented in SkRobot and developed in C++ using the SpecialK framework.

SkRobot Hub: SkRobot, designed for Unix-like environments, offers modular, real-time adaptability and supports: (i) Centralized data aggregation, processing, and distribution with synchronous/asynchronous microservices and data streaming;(ii) Structured data pair management for system states; (iii) Hub-based databases assigned per account and channel; (iv) Optional binary-form data persistence; (v) Satellite operations as independent processes or SkRobot-hosted insternal-module-threads; (vi) Web UI generation and RESTful API via HTTP and HTTP-based FlowNetwork streaming; (vii) Secure database and channel permission with DipoleNetwork authentication with optional Linux shadow authentication. SkRobot ensures scalable, secure, and efficient data flow management in distributed systems.

Satellite (Client Application). FlowSat functions as the production-consumption-processing unit within FlowNetwork. After authentication, it can (a) Create microservices, (b) Make blocking/non-blocking service requests, (c) Publish and subscribe to streaming channels, and (d) Transfer files via blob channels.

Pair Databases. Pair Databases in SkRobot use a red-black tree structure to store distributed variables. Satellites can read/write based on permissions. Each account, satellite flow, and flow channel has an associated database uniquely named and owned by the creator. Satellites may also generate additional databases.

Flow Channels. Flow channels facilitate distributed processing and are optionally linked to databases. Channels can be owned by satellites or, in some cases, created by the server. Once established, they persist unless the owner leaves the network. Each channel has a unique network identifier (1-32,767) and a unique network-wide name. Stream channels allow satellites to join anytime, triggering data distribution once announced.

Service Channel: Service Channels establish pre-configured service commands for efficient management. They operate in a 1:1 model, using generic data buffers. The protocol only handles transmission, leaving validation to the implementation. Service requests can be blocking (synchronous) or non-blocking (asynchronous), using unique identifiers for tracking. Service commands differ from flow commands, as they operate at a higher level, defined during satellite implementation.

Streaming Channel: Streaming Channels enable satellites to publish data for multiple subscribers (1:N model). When a subscriber joins, the server instructs the publisher to send data. Once all subscribers leave, publishing halts to optimise resources.

Blob Channel: Blob Channels facilitate file transfers, operating in a 1:N model for owners and hosts. The owner has full read/write access, while other users have read-only permissions.

Mutex Channel: Mutex Channels enable weak synchronisation between a master satellite and multiple slave satellites (1:N model). Slaves remain blocked until the master releases the lock. This allows synchronised processing clusters to handle large or resource-intensive tasks in parallel. Such a structured framework (see Fig. 2 for reference) ensures optimised communication, secure data exchange, and scalable automation across robotic and industrial applications.

5 Peer-to-Peer-Flow Modality

P2P-Flow extends the Flow protocol, enabling P2P communication in decentralised networks. Unlike Centralised-Flow, it allows direct node-to-node interactions within a flexible directed-graph structure, retaining key properties such as transport type, serialisation, and sync/async command execution.

Node Concentrator Functionalities: Each node acts as an independent service unit capable of connecting with others to form a dynamic network graph without topological constraints. Nodes can also establish flows to centralised hubs, enabling hybridisation where a node bridges P2P and centralised environments. This hybrid node facilitates inter-network communication by serving as a proxy.

Flow Spot (Event Propagation): Events propagate across the network until reaching previously informed nodes, ensuring efficient transmission. Nodes advertise their presence via UDP broadcasts (every 2 s by default) using JSON-formatted messages, which can be encrypted. These advertisements are confined to the local network but can be extended through specialised configurations or hybrid nodes linking external concentrators.

P2P Events: P2P events follow the same serialisation and propagation model as centralised flow. Events spread from node to node, halting when cycles occur and preventing redundant transmissions.

Strong Synchronization: Strong synchronisation employs additional TCP/UDP ports or Unix sockets for precise timing control. This requires an extra communication channel, with UDP and local Unix sockets offering the highest efficiency when all nodes reside on the same machine.

P2P Flow Channels: P2P Flow channels are lightweight adaptations of centralised flow channels. Unlike centralised service channels, requests and replies are transported out-of-channel and as there is only one service manager (the node connected to), there is no need to distinguish different services of different owners. Figures 1 and 2 illustrates this transaction process.

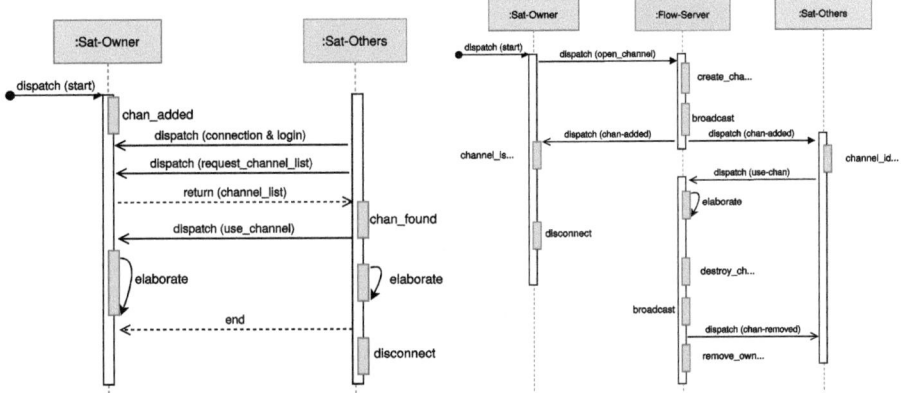

Fig. 1. General usage of node-channels for P2P transaction.

Fig. 2. General usage of node-channels for centralized transaction.

P2P Streaming Channel: P2P streaming channels optimise data transfer by delivering stream data directly to consumers, bypassing concentrators. This significantly reduces latency, the start of production is on first subscriber while the stop of production is following the last unsubscribe or disconnection. Figure 3 shows the corresponding communication model.

P2P Mutex Channel: Derived from FlowMutex, the P2P Mutex Channel eliminates the need for an intermediary server in synchronisation processes. However, this "weak" synchronisation method is affected by network traffic, buffering, and encryption, leading to variable latencies. While unsuitable for high-precision synchronisation, it is helpful for simultaneous start/stop scenarios in clustering. Figure 4 depicts this communication flow.

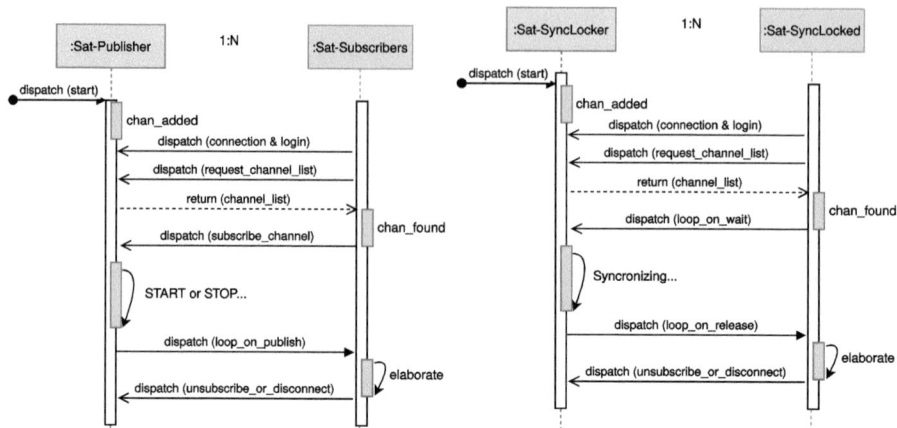

Fig. 3. Publish-subscribe P2P 1:N transaction.

Fig. 4. Distributed synchronization mutex P2P 1:N transaction.

6 Function Calling Agent: Architecture Utilizing Flow Protocol for LLM Services

This paper presents an architecture and a possible case of application of the enhanced FlowProtocol paradigm. In this section we introduce P2P functionalities by implementing a Function Calling multi-agent system that liaise with a robotic swarm. A human agent interacts via LLM tools, giving instructions and receiving feedback. The architecture (Fig. 5) consists of one hub managing potential interactions with centralized services (SkRobot) and seven satellites (micro agents) handling STT, TTS, LLM Tools and coordination, Vision functionalities, Robotic platform interaction, GUI for human interaction, and Proxy services for SkRobots. The system groups thus a set of interacting "micro-agents" that offer specific functions, forming a flexible, macro-agent network. The SkRobot hub synchronizes this network with other physically distributed agents. The LLM hub, like other nodes, accepts connections for coordination. Human actors interact via a chat interface, leveraging multiple micro-agents. Each node contains dynamic sketches instantiating worker classes with standard interfaces, configured via JSON files defining class types, timing, and network parameters.

LLM Node: The LLM node intermediates between humans and the macroagent, providing: (i) Multilingual interaction via natural language, (ii) Embedding functionalities, (iii) Optional retrieval-augmented generation, (iv) JSON-structured input/output, (v) Function-calling tools, (vi) event-driven notifications. Inference occurs through Ollama[11], supporting OpenAI API standards. It uses quantized (GGUF) models like: (a) `llama3.1:8binstructq8_0`; (b) `qwen2.5:1.7binstructq8_0`; (c) `mistralsmall:22binstruct2409q4_K_M`; and (d)

---

[11] https://ollama.com/, accessed June 2025.

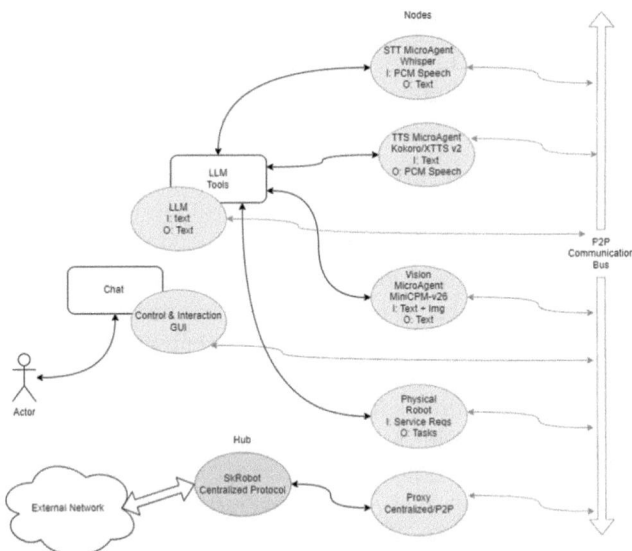

Fig. 5. Function Calling Agent. Nodes in the FlowProtocol architecture are represented in light orange, while hubs in violet. Each node can communicate with other nodes through a P2P mode. The human operator interacts through a GUI and a command line chat. (Color figure online)

`MFDoom/deepseekr1toolcalling:8b`. Embedding services leverage dedicated models: (i) $nomic - embed - text$, (ii) $granite - embedding : 278m$. The LLM node receives JSON service commands, processes requests, and determines function calls or network queries. Conversational responses are streamed over the Token channel, while structured responses return directly.

STT Node: This node integrates OpenAI Whisper[12] for optimized inference. Selected models are: (i) $large - v3$; (ii) $large - v3 - turbo$; (iii) $large - v3 - q5_0$; and (iv) $large - v3 - turbo - q5\_0$. The STT node receives PCM audio, processes it continuously, and streams transcriptions over the "Token" channel.

TTS Node: Two experimental nodes handle TTS: the XTTS_v2 (Coqui)[13] one, and Kokoro[14]. XTTS_v2 supports high-quality voice cloning but requires GPU acceleration, while Kokoro is CPU-efficient. The generated speech streams over the "PCM" channel.

ITT (Image-to-Text) Node: The ITT node, based on OpenBMB MiniCPM v.26[15], interprets images using minicpm-v:8b-2.6-q8_0, llama3.2-vision:11b-instruct-q8_0, and moondream:1.8b-v2-q8_0. The ITT node streams processed

---
[12] https://github.com/openai/whisper, accessed June 2025.
[13] https://github.com/coqui-ai/TTS, accessed June 2025.
[14] https://github.com/hexgrad/kokoro, accessed June 2025.
[15] https://github.com/OpenBMB/MiniCPM-o, accessed June 2025.

image descriptions over the "Token" channel. This architecture integrates decentralised agents leveraging LLM services, ensuring flexible, multimodal human-robot interaction with function-calling capabilities.

7 An Application of the Function Calling Agent to Swarm Robotics

The Function Calling agent proposed in the previous section can have several application fields; in particular, it could be used in every case where we have an interaction between a human agent and an intelligent system. In this section, we propose a possible architecture to use in Swarm Robotics, where we translate the voice commands of a human user that gives orders to a swarm of robots. We may envision, for example, a swarm performing a resource discovery and collection task composed of 3 types of robots: (a) Scanners that individuate some resource, (b) Harvesters that pick up the resources, and (c) Transporters that bring the resources to the nest. We need to define a structured approach, this could be done through the designing of a Behavior Tree (BT) [14] to represent actions and decisions need to model the voice-commanded swarm of robots. A schematic architecture of the system may consist of the following entities:

1. Human Operator: Issues voice commands to direct swarm activities (e.g., "Find resources", "Collect resources", "Transport resources to nest");
2. Voice Command Interface: A speech recognition module translates natural language into predefined task commands.
3. Task Planner: A decision-making module that interprets the command, updates the swarm state, and generates high-level tasks.
4. Swarm Behavior Tree (BT): Implements task execution using a hierarchical BT and breaks down commands into robot roles and actions.
5. Robot Agents (Scanners, Harvesters, Transporters): Execute autonomous subtasks based on local rules and swarm coordination mechanisms.
6. Environment: Includes resources, obstacles, transfer zones and a nest (where resources are finally stored)

Figure 6 represents a possible BT for the above architecture.

It consists of various elements: (i) a Root Node that receives human commands and determines the primary task; (ii) Selector Nodes that choose which subtask to execute based on swarm state; (iii) Sequence Nodes for ensuring correct execution order of subtasks; and (iv) Action Nodes that correspond to the actions performed by each robot type. Let's examine the execution flow of commands and actions

1. Voice Command Recognition: the system listens to a human command (e.g., "Find resources!"). The command is mapped to an action in the BT.
2. Task Allocation: scanners are activated to search for resources. Once a it is detected, the system transitions to the harvester task. If a harvester collects a resource, transporters are activated to move it to the nest.

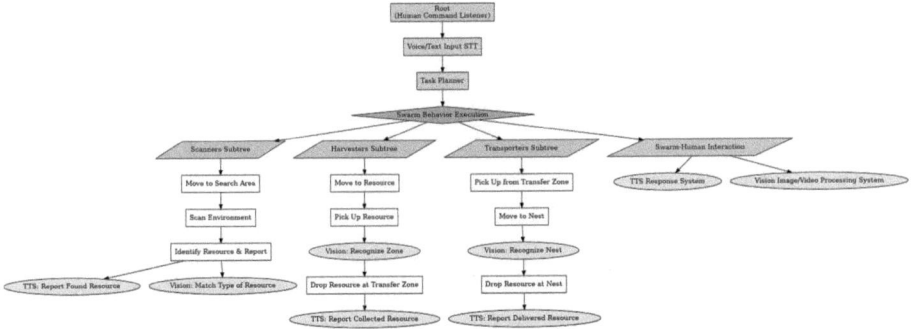

Fig. 6. Behaviour tree for a Function Calling agent of a swarm performing a resource discovery and collection task. Also human interaction modules are reported.

3. Swarm Coordination: local decisions are made at each level. Robots self-organize based on priority (e.g., if no new resources are found, harvesters wait).
4. Task Completion & Feedback: the system reports back to the human operator once a sub-tree comes to the last leaf, this means that the robot has completed its task and is ready to do another one. Here the TTS module is activated in order to communicate to the human controller the result (Reports); once received the feedback the operator can issue a new command rather then stop the operation. The robots also use the Vision functionality in order to understand target in the environment (a type of resource, rather than a Transfer or Nest area).

Finally we can do some additional considerations on some implicit functions and properties of the system. (i) Error Handling: If a robot fails a task (e.g., resource blocked), the BT loops back to a retry mechanism; (ii) Dynamic Adaptation: Robots may dynamically change roles when conditions are appropriate (e.g., a harvester may switch to scanning if no resources are available); (iii) Scalability: The swarm can operate with or without direct human control in adding or remove components of the swarm, thus scaling in function of workloads.

7.1 Demonstrator of the Function Calling Agent

In order to show the capabilities of the Function Calling Agent, we implemented a small demonstrator in Python with a subset of full functionalities shown in Fig. 6. In particular, we modeled the deployment of a node implementing a visual perception system in CyB, detecting faces in real time from a standard USB webcam. The goal is to test a distributed system based on CyB in which: (i) a video stream is captured from a standard webcam; (ii) the video frames are processed to detect faces using an OpenCV Haar cascade classifier; (ii) the output of the face detection is visualized by drawing a bounding box around the first detected face. The system is composed of 3 static sketches, interconnected to form a real-time, distributed video processing pipeline. Each sketch represents a node responsible for executing a well-defined, isolated task. Sketches are simple and typically minimal programs focused on a specific processing operation. For sake of simplicity we implemented static sketches that do not announces themselves on the network and must be called in order (producer, detector, viewer). These operations are distributed and parallelized across multiple nodes:

CamCap - Frame Capture and Distribution. This node activates the camera device via OpenCV to capture video frames. The device is configured with the following parameters:

- width: 640
- height: 360
- framerate: 30 FPS
- fourCC: "MPEG"
- transmission codec: "jpg"

A FlowService is opened on port 10000. The node creates a video streaming channel (FlowProtocol) named Camera, which publishes individual frames compressed as JPEG images to reduce bandwidth usage. Frames are serialized directly as binary data (not base64-encoded as strings for socket transmission). A minimal set of metadata is attached to the channel as a Python dictionary:

$$props = "w" : w, "h" : h, "fps" : fps, "interval" : capInterval$$

The node remains in standby (i.e., it neither captures nor distributes frames) until another node connects and subscribes to the channel (only one in this case). Once a subscription is active, frame capture and distribution begin. If all subscriptions are removed, the node returns to standby mode.

Face and Object Detection. This node establishes a connection (FlowAsync) to CamCap at 127.0.0.1:10000, subscribing to channel chanID = 1 (channel name: Camera). It performs real-time face detection on incoming frames using OpenCV's Haar cascade classifier. These frames are received from the CamCap node. A FlowService is opened on port 10001, exposing two streaming channels:

- Detection: transmits the four integers (as binary data) representing the x, y, w, h coordinates of the detected bounding box;
- CameraProxy: redistributes the original input frame (on which the detection was performed), preserving the same format and properties as received from CamCap (property information is requested via a temporary FlowSync).

The distributed data retain the original timestamp generated in CamCap at the time of frame capture. As with CamCap, the node becomes idle when there are no active subscriptions on its channels.

Viewer - Detection Visualization. This node connects via FlowAsync to Face and Object Detection at 127.0.0.1:10001, subscribing to channels 1 (CameraProxy) and 2 (Detection). Using the incoming data, an OpenCV window is rendered to display the frame, and if a face has been detected, a bounding box is drawn around it. In Fig. 7 we show a chart of the Micro-agent interactions.

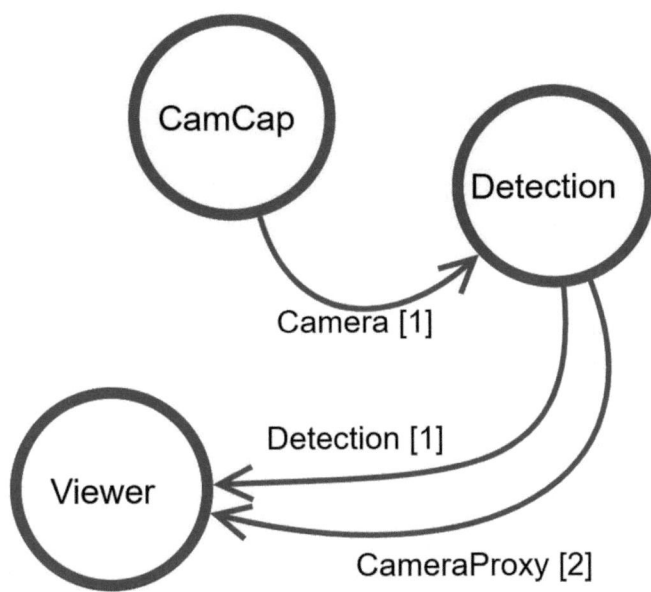

Fig. 7. Diagram for a the subset of functions implemented in the software demonstrator. The micro-agents interact performing tasks for face detection.

In Fig. 8 an example of face recognition is presented, along with output of three nodes involved in the process.

The CyB code is visible at the following repository: https://gitlab.com/isrlab1/ros-vs-cyb-comparison-for-robotics/-/tree/main/cyb (accessed June 2025).

7.2 Comparison with ROS Platform

To give an evaluation of pros and cons of CyB we executed the same tests with equal functionalities in a ROS deployment on the very same hardware. We set up thus a docker container where OpenCV, cv_bridge and $v4l2\_camera$ packages were deployed. The ROS node performed the aforesaid tasks leveraging the following packages: (i) Subscribes the $/image\_raw$ topic (webcam output), (ii) Converts images to $OpenCV(cv\_bridge)$, (iii) Detects faces with an OpenCV Haar classifier, (iv) Publishes face bounding boxes to

Fig. 8. The three nodes collaborate to detect a face in the field of view of the cam. The spotted human face in evidenced through a box in green. (Color figure online)

/perception/faces topic as a string and (v) Logs the detections to the console. The actual benchmark measured regards the (a) Node output on /perception/faces topic, (b) Textual log in console via $self.get\_logger().info(...)$ function, (c) Measurement of frame rate (fps), (d) Latency logging (with rclpy.Clock), and (e) CPU time for each frame processing. The ROS code is visible at the following repository: https://gitlab.com/isrlab1/ros-vs-cyb-comparison-for-robotics/-/tree/main/ros (accessed June 2025). Results of comparison between the two solution will be accessible on the following Zenodo repository: https://zenodo.org/records/15778059 (accessed June 2025).

8 Conclusion and Future Works

We presented the conceptualization of a system designed to improve HSI by leveraging the Flow Network DDS paradigm. Additionally, we proposed an architecture for a potential application: a function-calling agent capable of controlling a robotic entity via speech.

This approach addresses several key challenges discussed in Sect. 2: (i) Scalability and Communication: Both inter-robot and intra-robot communication are improved. The Flow Protocol supports a peer-to-peer (P2P) configuration, where services (micro-agents) or robots (macro-agents) can be added or removed simply by instantiating or decommissioning a node within the structure. (ii) Interoperability: The Flow Network's dual operational modalities, synchronous and asynchronous Flow Protocol, and its six distinct channel types enable a broad range of communication patterns, enhancing flexibility and integration capabilities.

A limitation of the SkRobot platform emerges in scenarios involving pipelines composed of multiple serially-executing nodes. In such cases, the failure or overload of a single node can lead to significant system-wide latency. This highlights the need for careful architectural and software design, as well as prudent resource allocation to microservices, to ensure reliable performance. Consequently, software component reusability within SkRobot remains relatively limited.

We also presented a brief performance analysis of the Flow Protocol, comparing it to ROS. SkRobot/cyb offers a more developer-friendly environment through its simplified setup, broader system compatibility, and high-level abstraction. In contrast, ROS—while powerful—often imposes complex system requirements, making it better suited to specific robotic use cases. A notable advantage of SkRobot is its use of the UDP protocol to 'announce' nodes, allowing them to autonomously discover one another without relying on static IP addresses or predefined ports. A more detailed comparison between ROS and SkRobot is provided in [11].

Future work may include the integration of cognitive AI components, such as production rules and logic programming, to add a lightweight, energy-efficient intelligent layer. Furthermore, incorporating blockchain technologies and DAOs may enhance security, transparency, and autonomy, offering a compelling direction for future development [12].

Acknowledgments. This work was partially funded by the Italian MUR and EU under the project ADVISOR - PRIN PNRR 2022 PE6 - Cod. P202277EJ2.

Declaration. Authors occasionally used generative AI tools to improve the readability of some parts of the text. After using the tool, the authors reviewed and edited the content as needed and took full responsibility for the publication's content.

Disclosure of Interests. The authors have no competing interests to declare that are relevant to the content of this article.

References

1. Bonci, A., Gaudeni, F., Giannini, M.C., Longhi, S.: Robot Operating System 2 (ROS2)-based frameworks for increasing robot autonomy: a survey. Appl. Sci. **13**(23), 12796 (2023). https://doi.org/10.3390/app132312796
2. Rubenstein, M., Ahler, C., Nagpal, R.: Kilobot: a low cost scalable robot system for collective behaviors. In: 2012 IEEE International Conference on Robotics and Automation, pp. 3293–3298. IEEE, May 2012
3. Giernacki, W., Skwierczyński, M., Witwicki, W., Wroński, P., Kozierski, P.: Crazyflie 2.0 quadrotor as a platform for research and education in robotics and control engineering. In: 2017 22nd International Conference on Methods and Models in Automation and Robotics (MMAR), pp. 37–42. IEEE, August 2017
4. Ando, N., Suehiro, T., Kitagaki, K., Kotoku, T., Yoon, W.K.: RT-middleware: distributed component middleware for RT (robot technology). In: 2005 IEEE/RSJ International Conference on Intelligent Robots and Systems, pp. 3933–3938. IEEE, August 2005

5. Liang, J., et al.: Code as policies: language model programs for embodied control. In: 2023 IEEE International Conference on Robotics and Automation (ICRA), pp. 9493–9500. IEEE, May 2023
6. Driess, D., et al.: PaLM-E: an embodied multimodal language model (2023)
7. Mendonça, M., Chrun, I.R., Neves, F., Jr., Arruda, L.V.: A cooperative architecture for swarm robotic based on dynamic fuzzy cognitive maps. Eng. Appl. Artif. Intell. **59**, 122–132 (2017)
8. Ramos, G. S., et al.: ARCog-NET: an aerial robot cognitive network architecture for swarm applications development. IEEE Access (2024)
9. Gielis, J., Shankar, A., Prorok, A.: A critical review of communications in multi-robot systems. Curr. Robot. Rep. **3**(4), 213–225 (2022)
10. De Gasperis, G., Di Ottavio, D., Migliarini, P., Costantini, S.: SkRobot: a pseudo-realtime multiplatform framework for robotics agents development (2024)
11. De Gasperis, G., Di Ottavio, D., Costantini, S., Migliarini, P.: The distributed architecture of SkRobot for efficient robotic agents (2024)
12. De Gasperis, G., Di Ottavio, D., Facchini, S.D.: SkRobot with TeleoR/QuLog: a pseudo-realtime robotics data distribution service extended with production rules and reasoning (2024)
13. Musser, D.R., Derge, G.J., Saini, A.: STL Tutorial and Reference Guide: C++ Programming with the Standard Template Library. Addison-Wesley Longman Publishing Co., Inc. (2001)
14. Colledanchise, M., Ögren, P.: Behavior Trees in Robotics and AI: An Introduction. CRC Press (2018)

Ethics, Trust and Social Acceptability

Ethical and Societal Challenges Facing Social and Educational Robots - Insights from the KASPAR Experience

Gabriella Lakatos, Vignesh Velmurugan(✉), Catherine Menon, Luke Jai Wood, Ben Robins, and Farshid Amirabdollahian

Robotics Research Group, University of Hertfordshire, Hatfield, UK
{g.lakatos,v.velmurugan,c.menon,l.wood,b.robins,
f.amirabdollahian2}@herts.ac.uk

Abstract. This paper provides a comprehensive examination of the ethical and societal challenges associated with the deployment of social robots in educational and therapeutic settings using the KASPAR robot as a practical example. Key ethical concerns explored include safeguarding one's privacy, addressing the implications of robotic autonomy, and mitigating cybersecurity risks. Societal challenges such as the potential dehumanisation of care practices, overreliance on robots, and their long-term impact on users' social needs are analysed in depth. Drawing from empirical insights into children's interactions with KASPAR, a social robot designed to operate as an educational tool in the context of autism education, this paper discusses practical mitigation strategies implemented in KASPAR, emphasising transparency, human oversight, and multidisciplinary collaboration. The findings highlight the need for thoughtful integration of robotics in sensitive domains to balance innovation with ethical responsibility.

Keywords: Ethical and Societal challenges · KASPAR · Social and Educational robots

1 Introduction

One of the key sectors where robotics and artificial intelligence (AI) are gaining momentum is in education and the therapeutic context, particularly in the form of social robots, which are anticipated to become integral to daily life in the near future [7]. Social robots with diverse embodiments such as Nao [12], Keepon [6], and KASPAR [8], have been studied in various social, educational, and therapeutic applications such as care, teaching communication and social skills, and providing therapy for autism spectrum disorder (ASD) [8]. While numerous studies have highlighted the valuable benefits of social robots in these areas, their use also introduces significant ethical, legal, and societal (ELS) challenges, especially when working with vulnerable individuals such as children [27], and people with special needs.

Although broader ELS concerns associated with social robots have been extensively examined [10], contributing to the formation of the field of "Roboethics" [29], there are fewer studies focused on these issues in the context of educational use of social robots [3,26]. One study identified four main ethical themes that would be relevant while considering a specific scenario, e.g. the use of classroom robots [26]. These are (1) privacy, (2) robot's role in relation to replacing humans, (3) interactional effects on children, and (4) responsibility. These themes were derived based on feedback from teachers and they echo the findings of a similar study, that highlighted the importance of addressing such ELS implications beyond the laboratory [16].

Much of the existing literature addresses these challenges from a theoretical perspective, often through systematic analyses or cognitive walkthroughs. While focus groups and stakeholder consultations are commonly used to gather insights, there remains a need for practical examples that demonstrate how these ethical considerations are addressed in real-world contexts. This paper contributes to that discussion by presenting a case study based on the development and deployment of the KASPAR robot. It draws on insights gained from its use with over 500 children—including typically developing children as well as those with ASD and learning disabilities—since its introduction in 2005.

In 2020, Fosch-Vilaronga et al. proposed a categorisation of ELS issues related to the use of social robots: (1) privacy and security, (2) autonomy and agency, (3) legal uncertainty and liability, (4) human-robot interaction and the potential for dehumanisation, and (5) the impact on employment [10]. This paper adopts that categorisation alongside the ethical themes outlined by Serholt et al. (2017) to structure its thematic evaluation. We specifically examine the ethical and societal dimensions of using social robots in educational and therapeutic settings, informed by our long-term experience with KASPAR. The goal is to reflect on lessons learned and consider directions for future work that balances competing values such as privacy, security and usability, while ensuring that innovations remain aligned with long-term human needs and global ethical standards.

2 KASPAR Robot

Developed in 2005 by the Adaptive Systems Research Group at the University of Hertfordshire, KASPAR (Fig. 1) is a child-sized humanoid robot designed to foster communication and social skills in children with Autism Spectrum Disorder (ASD). It is a stationary robot that sits on the table with its legs slightly bent at the knees. Each arm has three degrees of freedom, enabling gestures such as waving and playing peek-a-boo [8]. Its neck offers two degrees of freedom (pan and tilt), allowing for gaze direction and expressive movements like nodding or tilting to convey emotions. Minimal yet engaging facial expressions, including eye gaze, blinking, and smiling, enhance its interaction capabilities. KASPAR's clothing and hairstyle are customisable to suit different contexts or user preferences.

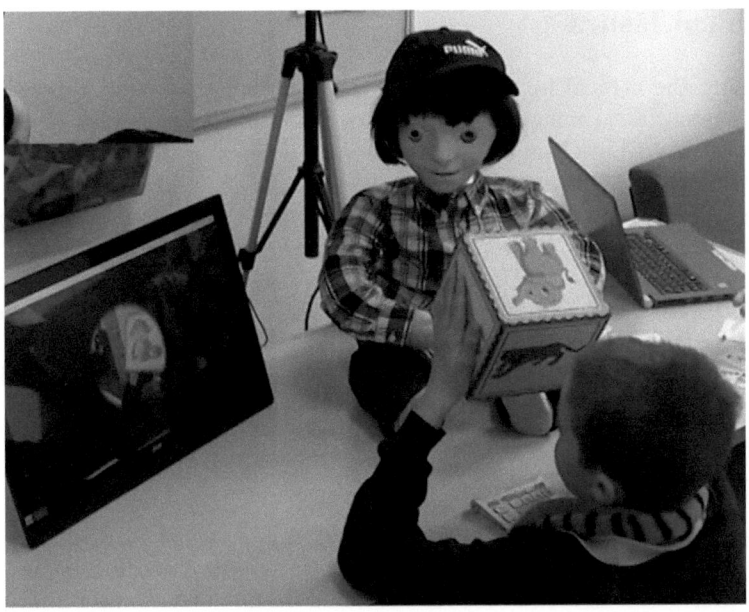

Fig. 1. A child interacting with the KASPAR robot.

To date, with over 500 children having interacted with it, both with and without ASD, KASPAR is established as a state-of-the-art, world-leading platform for robot-mediated therapy for children with ASD. Over successive design iterations, KASPAR has evolved into a fully programmable robot, suitable for use in various settings such as schools and children's homes. Field studies involving Kaspar and children with ASD have provided numerous case studies that illustrated Kaspar's potential applications in therapeutic and educational settings, both in schools and at home. These studies demonstrate that Kaspar can be effectively used to:

1. help to break isolation, [22]
2. mediate child-child or child-adult interactions, [30]
3. help children with autism manage collaborative play (with classmates or siblings), [30]
4. complement the work in the classroom, [18]
5. help to learn about cause and effect, [23]
6. help children to explore basic human emotions like 'happy' and 'sad', [24]
7. help children in developing Visual Perspective Taking (VPT) Skills. [32]

In the following section, we explore various ethical and societal challenges involved in the use of social robots in educational and therapeutic scenarios with KASPAR as a case study.

3 Ethical Issues

Considering the ethical implications that arise with the use of robots, "Roboethics" is essential to safeguard the human rights of the users [29]. As the European Union Civil Law Rules on Robotics has pointed out: "the guiding ethical framework should be based [...] and in the Charter of Fundamental Rights, such as human dignity, equality, justice and equity, non-discrimination, informed consent, private and family life and data protection, as well as on other underlying principles and values of the Union law, such as non-stigmatisation, transparency, autonomy, individual responsibility and social responsibility, and on existing ethical practices and codes" [1,19]. Following Fosch-Vilaronga et al.'s categorisation [10], the ethical considerations related to educational robots are discussed under the following two domains: privacy and security and autonomy and agency.

3.1 Privacy and Security

Privacy is one of the most essential human rights, which can most easily be impacted by social robots. Privacy is differentiated into two dimensions, namely physical (autonomous mobile robots accessing private spaces) and informational (robot assistants accessing private information, such as medical records) by some [10]. However, others include two more dimensions in the form of psychological (gaining insights into users' thoughts and emotions) and social privacy (accessing users' social contacts and potentially influencing them) [17], all of which can be seriously affected by social and educational robots.

These issues could have significant consequences for, especially vulnerable children. For example, mobile educational robots might access a child's private spaces at home, affecting their physical privacy. In school settings, videorecorded sessions could breach informational and psychological privacy. In some cases, robots might even be used in robot-mediated interviews with children, particularly in stressful situations (e.g. by social services or police), which could compromise their informational, psychological, and social privacy [31].

Different social robots present varying levels of privacy risks depending on factors such as their mobility, autonomy, internet connectivity, and use of Internet of Things (IoT) technologies, necessitating tailored mitigation strategies. When considering KASPAR, physical privacy could be susceptible when used in a home environment, i.e. families' private space. However, as KASPAR was designed to be stationary, it cannot have access to private spaces unless moved by the user, thereby ensuring the user's (parents') consent. Similarly, in one of the field studies with KASPAR, for example, the robot was used to help children with ASD in developing Visual Perspective Taking (VPT) skills in a school setting [32]. VPT refers to the ability to understand that others may have a different visual perspective or line of sight from one's own [15]. In this example study a series of games were developed and tested to assist children with ASD improve their VPT skills by showing them exactly what the robot saw (Fig. 2). This was done using the robot's cameras (two cameras, one in each eye), which recorded the child holding pictures of animals and displayed the robot's viewpoint back to the child in real time. While cameras are unavoidable in such scenarios, in order to mitigate informational and psychological privacy concerns, especially in a school environment, KASPAR's operating protocol ensures that video data is processed and analysed in real-time on an accompanying laptop, and discarded immediately without being stored. Furthermore, the laptop that is used to control and program the robot is deliberately kept offline to mitigate cybersecurity risks.

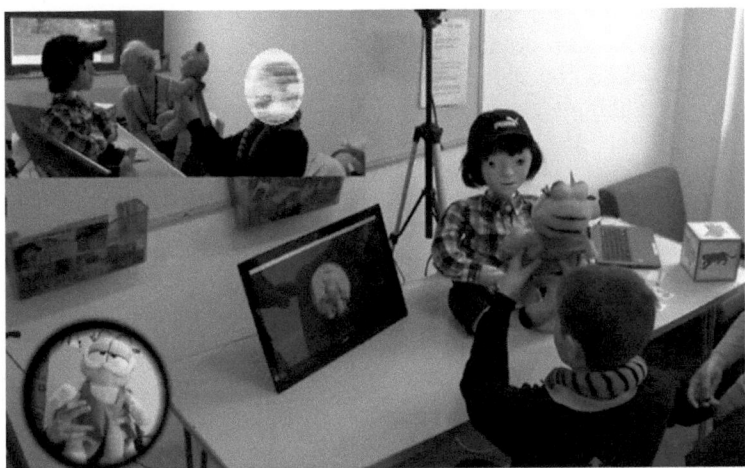

Fig. 2. A field study setup that used KASPAR's cameras to show its perspective in real-time.

How can these privacy concerns be mitigated in fully autonomous robots in the future? It is worth noting that most ethical issues associated with educational robots stem primarily from the robot's features (Table 1), rather than the environment or context in which they are used. For instance, concerns regarding videos of children's interactions recorded using a robot's cameras could be mitigated by enhancing transparency around data handling and securing informed consent from parents or caregivers. However, this becomes more complex when robots rely on cloud-based services to store and process data, raising potential cybersecurity risks. These robots are vulnerable to remote hacking, which could compromise multiple aspects of the user's privacy [28]. This vulnerability is further exacerbated in cases where several such robots share cloud-based resources to take advantage of larger training data to enhance performance, risking exposure of other users' data, and invading informational privacy.

In a System of Systems (SoS) scenario involving social and educational robots like KASPAR, where multiple robots interact with the same child across various environments (such as home and school), differences between these systems as a result of the environment could lead to unforeseen emergent behaviours that may be unsafe or undesirable for the child. For example, consider a hypothetical scenario in which a child with ASD engages in a turn-taking activity with a KASPAR-like robot at school. When the session ends midway, and the child later interacts with a different KASPAR robot at home, it becomes essential to synchronise user data across systems to ensure continuity in the interaction. Without this continuity, the child may experience confusion or frustration. However, enabling such cross-context data sharing over the internet raises concerns about user privacy and data security. Hazard analysis across SoS is notoriously complex, particularly in a system where data access may be limited due to privacy concerns. While transparency and control over data handling can resolve some of these privacy and security issues, they might be insufficient for some complex and opaque autonomous robots [17]. Given the large volumes of data collected and processed by them for self-learning and improvement, each robot is unique, thereby making prediction of privacy issues more challenging [10]. While it can be argued that these systems can be trained to understand the sensitivity of data based on contextual awareness and segregate it from data used for training their models, even basic data can create potential vulnerabilities.

Table 1. Features of therapeutic and educational robots and their level of impact on the arising Ethical and Societal challenges (higher number of plus signs indicate a higher level of impact)

	Privacy and Security	Moral Responsibility	Dehumanisation and Overreliance
Having a camera	+	+	
Capability to make video/voice recordings	+ +	+ +	
Being connected to the Internet	+ + +	+ + +	+
Increased level of autonomy	+ + +	+ + +	+ + +
Increased level of autonomy	+ + +	+ + +	+ + +
Capability to react to voice commands	+ + +	+ + +	+ + +
Using a System of Systems (SoS)	+ + +	+ + +	+ + +

3.2 Autonomy and Agency

Even though present-day educational robots lack full autonomy, as roboticists keep working towards this goal, it is essential to discuss questions arising around autonomy and agency. "Is there a need for a hierarchy in the decision-making process?", "Should the user or the developer supervise the robot's decisions?", "Should robots have the ability to override humans' decisions in matters of security or maybe even life and death?", "Should robots correct a human's mistake?", etc.

KASPAR can be operated in a remotely controlled or semi-autonomous mode, offering flexibility to adapt to various educational and therapeutic needs. It offers a balance by utilising autonomous functions to reduce the cognitive demands on a human operator for low-level control, while still allowing them to remain actively involved in guiding the robot's higher-level interactions. Here, potential interaction-related concerns or malfunctions are currently handled by the robot's operator (therapist/parent/teacher/researcher), who understands the child's specific needs and closely observes the child's reactions and emotional state during the interaction. For example, the operator might respond if KASPAR plays a different song than the one selected by the child, and switch to a different game if the child appears upset by the one. A fully autonomous robot, however, may not be ideal for children with disabilities such as ASD, given the unique social challenges associated with the conditions. Children with ASD, often show a stronger tendency to engage with machines than with people [9], and a fully autonomous robot could unintentionally reinforce child-robot interactions, potentially reducing their willingness to engage with caregivers. Considering a fully autonomous robot in this use case, given the high variability in skills and therapeutic needs among children with ASD, the absence of a human operator during the interaction could have detrimental consequences such as the robot might fail to respond appropriately to a specific child's need, potentially causing distress or even reinforcing undesired behaviours.

Moral Responsibility
Who bears responsibility for such potential unintended consequences of a robot's actions, especially in the case of educational and therapeutic robots? According to Tzafestas et al. [27] the degree of autonomy granted to a robot significantly influences the level of morality attributed to it, with more autonomous systems requiring a deeper evaluation of their moral and societal implications. Accordingly, they recognise three distinct levels of morality that can be attributed to a robot: the lowest, where robots can only execute preprogrammed operations; a medium level, where robots possess partial autonomy and decision-making capabilities; and the highest level, where robots are fully autonomous in decision-making and planning, without human intervention, thereby warranting the highest moral responsibility. It is also important to note that morality varies across cultures and contexts. Considering KASPAR's current level of autonomy, 'operational autonomy' based on [27], the moral responsibility would lie with the developers, component manufacturers and the robot operator (therapist, teacher or parent).

These questions inevitably lead to deeper questions of moral responsibility. Can a robot be held morally accountable for its actions? This, in turn, raises complex issues of legal personhood and the agency of robots. There is a consensus that a robot has to fulfil the following criteria in order to be ethical and morally responsible: (1) it has to possess the ability to predict the consequences of its own actions, (2) it has to possess a set of ethical rules against which to test each possible action and choose the most ethical one, (3) it has to have legal authority to carry out autonomous decision making and action, accompanied by associated liability [27,29]. But can these criteria ever be fulfilled? The question is further complicated in the case of System of Systems, when the maximised ethics of the whole system is more important than those of the individual ones. It is also unclear how maximised ethics affect the ethics of the individual systems.

Unless a robot is truly sentient and fulfils the above criteria to be ethical and morally responsible for its actions, which is clearly not true for present-day robots, responsibility must be shared among the robot designers, manufacturers, programmers, maintenance personnel and end-users depending on the occurrence that leads to undesirable consequences. According to a 2018 statement by the European Group on Ethics in Science and New Technologies: "Moral responsibility, in whatever sense, cannot be allocated or shifted to 'autonomous' technology [2]. A broad consensus suggests that meaningful human control is essential for moral responsibility. Therefore, we argue that in therapeutic settings, the presence of a human operator is indispensable and remains essential, even with fully autonomous robots, to ensure safety.

4 Societal Issues

Societal challenges of social and educational robots consist of moral questions affecting the society, and the end-users in particular, such as the issue of robots' (lack of) morality and empathy towards vulnerable users; users developing attachment with robots; or the central question of decrease in human-human interactions as a result of using robots for certain tasks, especially in therapeutic and care settings. All these issues can affect the essential human right of dignity.

4.1 Human-Robot Interaction and Dehumanising Practice

The European Parliament emphasised that "the development of robot technology should focus on complementing human capabilities and not on replacing them" [20]. With regard to care robots, it was also pointed out that human contact is one of the most fundamental aspects of human care and replacing the human factor with robots could dehumanise caring practices. It has been already identified as a potential ethical issue that people may prefer contact with robots to other humans in the future [14]. Although this may be understandable and may even help to preserve dignity in certain situations such as robots assisting their users in the bathroom, in general, this could be a matter of concern.

Even though dehumanising practices have been previously brought up mostly in the context of elderly care, dehumanisation and over-reliance issues may still be applicable and important to keep in mind when working with social and educational robots.

Importantly though, previous research with KASPAR and similar social robots such as Nao has proved the positive effects of these robots on children with autism [12]. Children with ASD have demonstrated improved social and communicational skills after having interacted with KASPAR in a series of sessions [32] suggesting that KASPAR can ultimately help them to communicate better with their peers and parents as well [22]. Furthermore, apart from the one-to-one sessions, KASPAR has been used as a social mediator, directly assisting children with ASD to communicate with their peers. Similarly, Nao has been successfully used in various educational scenarios in school settings with both children with and without ASD [12]. This evidence suggests that these robots should not necessarily cause concerns of robots exacerbating social isolation and leading to a loss of dignity. In fact, these social robots seem to promote and mediate social contracts with other people instead of reducing them.

However, it is important to consider that people tend to anthropomorphise robots and attribute agency to them [5]. They can develop social bonds with robotic companions and even develop attachments towards them, which may be particularly true for children who may have the impression that the robots are in fact autonomous. Thus, one has to ask, 'To what extent one is willing to equip end-users with a false mental model to facilitate the functionality of the system?', 'How can one make sure to minimise these risks?', and 'Is there a need for intervention if children start to believe robots to be real persons?' [16], 'Is it challenging the human right of dignity?' [16].

A possible strategy to mitigate this issue could be to allow the children to control or operate the robot [25]. A recent study found that giving children a chance to operate the KASPAR robot themselves using a keypad or even teaching them how to program it themselves by using Scratch (in mainstream schools) before interacting with it helps to avoid such issues arising [18]. These issues would be even more difficult and complex if fully autonomous robots are considered, where handing over the robot's control to the child is not feasible. In such cases, there is an increased risk of issues such as the children's tendency to think of these robots as real persons.

4.2 Overreliance and Delegating Moral Responsibility

Overreliance on social robots poses additional risks, as some parents or educators may view them as substitutes for time-intensive engagement with children. According to attachment theory, children develop emotional bonds through consistent, reliable interactions with caregivers, which shape their emotional growth [4]. While robots can be programmed to simulate empathy and provide reliable interactions, the inter- and intra-variability of a child's emotional needs depending on the context, age, personality, culture, etc., can be challenging to effectively adapt. Furthermore, such overreliance risks creating a transactional model of care and education, where children may view relationships as mechanical, undermining the development of deeper, trust-based social connections. Delegating this responsibility to a robot shifts the moral duty from humans to machines, reducing meaningful human interaction with the child, and affecting the development of their social relationships [11]. Mitigating this concern, most of the existing therapeutic games and exercises involving KASPAR involve the presence of another human being (therapist, teacher, parent or even another child). While robots can be valuable tools in education, they should complement, not replace, the irreplaceable role of human guidance and emotional presence.

4.3 Cultural Differences

Differing societal views on autism itself further complicate the acceptance of robots like KASPAR. While KASPAR has been successfully deployed in a range of countries—including the UK, Greece, Macedonia, the Netherlands, Australia, and Malaysia—the cultural framing of autism varies significantly. While in some regions, autism is primarily understood as a medical condition requiring therapeutic intervention, in others it is increasingly viewed as a form of neurodiversity to be accepted rather than "treated" [13]. The role of robots like KASPAR can vary depending on whether a society values inclusivity or social adaptation. As a fully programmable and remotely controlled robot, KASPAR avoids the risks associated with culturally biased data that might influence a fully autonomous system. This approach allows the therapist or parents to customise their use with cultural sensitivity in mind.

4.4 Long-Term Societal Impact of Social Robots

Prolonged exposure of children to social robots could also lead to overreliance from the children's side, as children may become accustomed to the immediate and predictable responses provided by the robots. Unlike human interactions, which are inherently variable, interactions with robots often follow consistent patterns, making them a comforting presence. This may risk undermining a child's social development by creating unrealistic expectations of human relationships, and disrupting the formation of secure attachments with peers, parents or caregivers [11]. Parents and teachers have expressed concerns that such overexposure could have detrimental effects on their children's ability to think independently and creatively [21]. Therefore, the integration of social robots in children's lives must take into account the preservation of human connection and cognitive development.

5 Conclusion

This paper provides an overview of the most pressing ethical and societal challenges in social and educational robots, using the KASPAR robot as a real-world example to examine how these challenges may be addressed. It identifies critical ethical challenges such as privacy, security, autonomy, and moral responsibility, alongside societal implications like dehumanisation and overreliance. Drawing on the extensive practical experiences of designing KASPAR and deploying it in real-world settings, this paper discusses how these concerns are approached through specific design and deployment strategies, while also reflecting on their relevance in the context of future advancements. It highlights the need for enhanced transparency in data handling, robust cybersecurity measures, and sustained human oversight to address these challenges effectively.

Looking ahead, future advancements in autonomous robotics will likely amplify existing concerns, particularly as robots acquire greater decision-making capabilities and interact more extensively within systems of systems. Mitigating these risks requires a multidisciplinary approach that integrates engineering innovation with ethical, legal, and sociological frameworks. Policymakers, educators, and roboticists must collaborate to ensure that the integration of robots enhances human dignity, supports neurodivergent individuals and people with special needs, and fosters meaningful human relationships while safeguarding essential rights and societal values.

References

1. European parliament. Civil law rules on robotics: European parliament resolution of 16 February 2017 with recommendations to the commission on civil law rules on robotics (2015/2103(inl)) (2017)
2. European group on ethics in science and new technologies artificial intelligence, robotics and autonomous systems. statement. Luxembourg: Directorate-general for research and innovation, European commission (2018)
3. Arriaga, P., Neto, I., Correia, F., Soares, A.: Ethical considerations in designing and testing robots for children in educational settings. In: Social Robots in Education: How to Effectively Introduce Social Robots into Classrooms, pp. 169–203. Springer (2025)
4. Bowlby, J., Ainsworth, M., Bretherton, I.: The origins of attachment theory. Dev. Psychol. **28**(5), 759–775 (1992)
5. Breazeal, C.: Emotion and sociable humanoid robots. Int. J. Hum. Comput. Stud. **59**(1–2), 119–155 (2003)
6. Costescu, C.A., Vanderborght, B., David, D.O.: Beliefs, emotions, and behaviors-differences between children with ASD and typically developing children. A robot-enhanced task. J. Evid.-Based Psychother. **16**(2) (2016)
7. Dautenhahn, K.: Socially intelligent robots: dimensions of human-robot interaction. Philos. Trans. R. Soc. B Biol. Sci. **362**(1480), 679–704 (2007)
8. Dautenhahn, K., et al.: Kaspar-a minimally expressive humanoid robot for human-robot interaction research. Appl. Bionics Biomech. **6**(3–4), 369–397 (2009)
9. Dubois-Sage, M., Jacquet, B., Jamet, F., Baratgin, J.: People with autism spectrum disorder could interact more easily with a robot than with a human: reasons and limits. Behav. Sci. **14**(2), 131 (2024)
10. Fosch-Villaronga, E., Lutz, C., Tamò-Larrieux, A.: Gathering expert opinions for social robots' ethical, legal, and societal concerns: findings from four international workshops. Int. J. Soc. Robot. **12**(2), 441–458 (2020)
11. Guneysu, A.: Robots in wonderland: unraveling the impact of prolonged interaction with social robots on children's behavior and development (2024)
12. Hood, D., Lemaignan, S., Dillenbourg, P.: When children teach a robot to write: an autonomous teachable humanoid which uses simulated handwriting. In: Proceedings of the Tenth Annual ACM/IEEE International Conference on Human-Robot Interaction, pp. 83–90 (2015)
13. de Leeuw, A., Happé, F., Hoekstra, R.A.: A conceptual framework for understanding the cultural and contextual factors on autism across the globe. Autism Res. **13**(7), 1029–1050 (2020)
14. Leslie, D.: Understanding artificial intelligence ethics and safety. arXiv preprint arXiv:1906.05684 (2019)
15. Lin, P., Abney, K., Bekey, G.: Robot ethics: mapping the issues for a mechanized world. Artif. Intell. **175**(5–6), 942–949 (2011)
16. Lindemann, G., Matsuzaki, H., Straub, I.: Special issue on: going beyond the laboratory—reconsidering the ELS implications of autonomous robots (2016)

17. Lutz, C., Schöttler, M., Hoffmann, C.P.: The privacy implications of social robots: scoping review and expert interviews. Mob. Media Commun. **7**(3), 412–434 (2019)
18. Moros, S., Wood, L., Robins, B., Dautenhahn, K., Castro-González, Á.: Programming a humanoid robot with the scratch language. In: Robotics in Education: Current Research and Innovations 10, pp. 222–233. Springer (2020)
19. Operto, F.: Ethics in advanced robotics. IEEE Robot. Autom. Mag. **18**(1), 72–78 (2011)
20. European Parliament: Civil law rules on robotics: European parliament resolution of 16 February 2017 with recommendations to the commission on civil law rules on robotics (2015/2103(inl)) (2017). https://www.europarl.europa.eu/doceo/document/TA-8-2017-0051_EN.html. Accessed Nov 2024
21. Perella-Holfeld, F., Sallam, S., Petrie, J., Gomez, R., Irani, P., Sakamoto, Y.: Parent and educator concerns on the pedagogical use of AI-equipped social robots. Proc. ACM Interact. Mob. Wearable Ubiquitous Technol. **8**(3), 1–34 (2024)
22. Robins, B., Dautenhahn, K., Dickerson, P.: From isolation to communication: a case study evaluation of robot assisted play for children with autism with a minimally expressive humanoid robot. In: 2009 Second International Conferences on Advances in Computer-Human Interactions, pp. 205–211. IEEE (2009)
23. Robins, B., Dautenhahn, K., Dickerson, P.: Embodiment and cognitive learning–can a humanoid robot help children with autism to learn about tactile social behaviour? In: Social Robotics: 4th International Conference, ICSR 2012, Chengdu, China, 29–31 October 2012. Proceedings 4, pp. 66–75. Springer (2012)
24. Robins, B., Dautenhahn, K., Nadel, J.: Kaspar, the social robot and ways it may help children with autism-an overview. Enfance **1**, 91–102 (2018)
25. Rossi, A., Holthaus, P., Dautenhahn, K., Koay, K.L., Walters, M.L.: Getting to know pepper: effects of people's awareness of a robot's capabilities on their trust in the robot. In: International Conference on Human-Agent Interaction (HAI 2018), pp. 246–252. ACM, Southampton, UK (2018). https://doi.org/10.1145/3284432.3284464
26. Serholt, S., et al.: The case of classroom robots: teachers' deliberations on the ethical tensions. AI Soc. **32**, 613–631 (2017)
27. Tzafestas, S.G.: Ethics in robotics and automation: a general view. Int. Robot. Autom. J. **4**(3), 229–234 (2018)
28. Vanderelst, D., Winfield, A.: The dark side of ethical robots. In: Proceedings of the 2018 AAAI/ACM Conference on AI, Ethics, and Society, pp. 317–322 (2018)
29. Veruggio, G., Operto, F.: Roboethics: a bottom-up interdisciplinary discourse in the field of applied ethics in robotics. In: Machine Ethics and Robot Ethics, pp. 79–85. Routledge (2020)
30. Wainer, J., Dautenhahn, K., Robins, B., Amirabdollahian, F.: A pilot study with a novel setup for collaborative play of the humanoid robot kaspar with children with autism. Int. J. Soc. Robot. **6**, 45–65 (2014)
31. Wood, L.J., Dautenhahn, K., Rainer, A., Robins, B., Lehmann, H., Syrdal, D.S.: Robot-mediated interviews-how effective is a humanoid robot as a tool for interviewing young children? PLoS ONE **8**(3), e59448 (2013)
32. Wood, L.J., Robins, B., Lakatos, G., Syrdal, D.S., Zaraki, A., Dautenhahn, K.: Developing a protocol and experimental setup for using a humanoid robot to assist children with autism to develop visual perspective taking skills. Paladyn J. Behav. Robot. **10**(1), 167–179 (2019)

Bayesian Proximal Policy Optimization with Adaptive Learning and Episodic Memory for Social Robot Navigation

Diego Resende Faria(✉)

Department of Computer Science, School of Science, Loughborough University,
Loughborough, UK
d.resende-faria@lboro.ac.uk

Abstract. Social navigation in dynamic human environments requires both efficient goal-directed behavior and robust, anticipatory safety mechanisms. We introduce BPPO-EM, a cognitively inspired reinforcement learning framework that augments Proximal Policy Optimization with Bayesian uncertainty modulation, adaptive learning rate tuning, and episodic memory recall. To enhance real-time safety, BPPO-EM incorporates a predictive collision network and a rule-based safety layer guided by LiDAR perception. In PyBullet simulations over 1000 episodes, BPPO-EM reached the goal in 82.7% of trials, compared to only 17.5% with standard PPO, and reduced the number of episodes with collisions from 60.2% to 15.8%. Moreover, the average number of collisions dropped from 2.19 to 0.50, demonstrating a 4-fold safety improvement. BPPO-EM significantly outperformed standard PPO in average rewards, returns, and goal-directed progress, confirming its effectiveness for socially compliant robot navigation.

Keywords: Social Navigation · Bayesian RL · Episodic Memory · PPO · BPPO-EM

1 Introduction

Robots operating in human-centered environments must not only navigate efficiently but also exhibit socially acceptable behaviors to ensure safety, comfort, and trust. Socially-aware navigation has become a core capability for service robotics and Human-Robot Interaction (HRI), where agents must balance goal-seeking behavior with real-time collision avoidance and social compliance in crowded, dynamic settings.

Traditional navigation methods often rely on handcrafted models, which encode human motion heuristics and proxemic constraints [1]. However, these approaches struggle in complex multi-agent environments due to their limited adaptability. Reinforcement Learning (RL), particularly Proximal Policy Optimization (PPO) [2], has emerged as a promising alternative by enabling robots to learn navigation policies directly from experience. Yet, in socially dense scenarios, standard PPO suffers from suboptimal exploration, unstable learning, and unsafe behaviors such as collisions. To overcome these challenges, we propose a cognitively-inspired RL framework that augments PPO with mechanisms for uncertainty-aware, adaptive, and safety-driven decision making. Our method, termed Bayesian-enhanced PPO with Episodic Memory (BPPO-EM), introduces three key components inspired by human learning:

(i) Bayesian Uncertainty Modulation adjusts the exploration-exploitation balance based on policy entropy;
(ii) Adaptive Learning Rate tunes the optimization dynamics according to reward variability;
(iii) Episodic Memory Mechanism retrieves salient past experiences to bias action selection toward risk-averse behaviors.

Additionally, we incorporate a *Collision Prediction Network* trained offline to estimate action safety, and a *Hybrid Action Selection Mechanism* that combines RL policy output with rule-based heuristics from LiDAR perception to ensure robust obstacle avoidance in cluttered environments. We implement and evaluate our framework in a PyBullet simulation where a mobile robot navigates toward a goal while avoiding multiple dynamic humans exhibiting structured and random behaviors. The main contributions of this work are listed below:

- A novel Bayesian-enhanced PPO framework integrating uncertainty modulation, adaptive learning, and episodic memory for socially-aware navigation.
- A collision prediction neural network for offline safety learning and action filtering.
- A hybrid action selection mechanism combining RL policy, safety prediction, and reactive heuristics.
- A comprehensive simulation environment with dynamic human agents demonstrating the effectiveness of our approach in improving safety, learning stability, and navigation efficiency over PPO baselines.

We distinguish theoretical contributions (Bayesian entropy modulation, adaptive learning rate, and episodic memory) from implementation aspects (collision prediction model and rule-based action filter). This distinction is key to understanding the respective impact on learning dynamics versus runtime safety.

The remainder of the paper is organized as follows: Sect. 2 reviews related work. Section 3 details our proposed methods. Section 4 presents the scenario and results, and Sect. 5 concludes the paper with future directions.

2 Related Work

Social navigation aims to enable robots to operate safely and acceptably in human-populated environments, a crucial requirement for service and assistive robotics. Early methods relied on hand-crafted models such as the Social Force Model (SFM), which encode human motion and proxemic constraints to guide robot behavior [1]. However, these approaches often fail in crowded or dynamic scenarios due to their limited ability to capture complex social cues. To address this, recent research has focused on data-driven models, including deep learning and RL. Graph Neural Networks (GNNs) have been used to predict social disruption by modeling human-robot interactions and environmental context [3]. Similarly, the Socially Compliant Navigation Dataset (SCAND) [4] provides large-scale demonstrations for learning human-aware navigation behaviors such as yielding, collision avoidance, and respecting personal space. RL techniques enable robots to learn social norms and adapt to human behavior through interaction [5,6]. For instance, Double DQN improves path planning in unstructured environments [7], while PPO achieves robust performance in continuous control tasks, including humanoid navigation [2]. These methods support the development of socially adept robots capable of operating in crowded public spaces [8,9]. Recent studies highlight the need for robots to learn from human feedback to avoid inappropriate behaviors [10]. Incorporating human-centered metrics like comfort, predictability, and sociability has been explored through adaptive navigation strategies that leverage proxemics, gaze, or posture cues [11,12]. Furthermore, adaptive spatial reasoning techniques improve robot responses to environmental dynamics and crowd densities [5,13].

Building on this body of work, we propose a cognitively inspired reinforcement learning framework that integrates Bayesian uncertainty estimation, adaptive optimization, and episodic memory to enhance social compliance and safety in socially-aware robot navigation, surpassing PPO performance in these scenarios.

3 Methods

This section outlines the theoretical and algorithmic foundations of BPPO-EM. Inspired by cognitive processes like uncertainty modulation and episodic recall, our approach incorporates probabilistic reasoning and memory into reinforcement learning. We first review standard PPO, then detail our Bayesian extensions, including architecture, adaptive learning, memory, and reward design.

3.1 Standard Proximal Policy Optimization (PPO)

PPO is a widely adopted on-policy reinforcement learning algorithm that balances stability and performance by limiting the magnitude of policy updates. It achieves this by optimizing a clipped surrogate objective that discourages large deviations between successive policy iterations. The standard PPO objective function is defined as:

$$\mathcal{L}_{\text{PPO}}(\theta) = \mathbb{E}_t \left[\min \left(r_t(\theta) \hat{A}_t, \ \text{clip}(r_t(\theta), 1 - \epsilon, 1 + \epsilon) \hat{A}_t \right) \right], \tag{1}$$

where $\mathbb{E}_t[\cdot]$ denotes the empirical expectation over sampled time steps t in a batch, and θ represents the parameters of the current policy network. The term $r_t(\theta)$ is the probability ratio between the new and old policies and is defined as:

$$r_t(\theta) = \frac{\pi_\theta(a_t|s_t)}{\pi_{\theta_{\text{old}}}(a_t|s_t)}, \tag{2}$$

where $\pi_\theta(a_t|s_t)$ is the probability of selecting action a_t given state s_t under the current policy, and $\pi_{\theta_{\text{old}}}(a_t|s_t)$ is the probability under the previous (behavior) policy. The variable $\hat{A}_t$ represents the advantage function estimate at time step t, typically computed via Generalized Advantage Estimation (GAE) or from the difference between returns and value predictions. The hyperparameter $\epsilon \in (0,1)$ controls the clipping range, commonly set to 0.2, and ensures that updates do not push the new policy too far from the old one.

In addition to optimizing the policy, PPO also learns a state-value function $V(s_t)$ using a separate critic network. The critic minimizes the mean squared error between the predicted value and the empirical return R_t as follows:

$$\mathcal{L}_{\text{value}} = \frac{1}{2}(V(s_t) - R_t)^2, \tag{3}$$

where $V(s_t)$ is the estimated value of state s_t and R_t is the empirical return calculated as the cumulative discounted sum of future rewards:

$$R_t = \sum_{k=0}^{T-t} \gamma^k r_{t+k}, \tag{4}$$

with $\gamma \in [0,1]$ being the discount factor that weights future rewards, and T being the final time step of the episode. To promote exploration during training and avoid premature convergence to suboptimal deterministic policies, an entropy regularization term is often added to the loss function. The entropy loss is defined as:

$$\mathcal{L}_{\text{entropy}} = \mathbb{E}_t \left[\mathcal{H}(\pi_\theta(\cdot|s_t)) \right], \tag{5}$$

where $\mathcal{H}(\pi_\theta(\cdot|s_t))$ denotes the Shannon entropy of the policy's action distribution at state s_t, and is computed as:

$$\mathcal{H}(\pi_\theta(\cdot|s_t)) = -\sum_{a \in \mathcal{A}} \pi_\theta(a|s_t) \log \pi_\theta(a|s_t), \tag{6}$$

with $\mathcal{A}$ being the discrete action space. Higher entropy encourages more exploratory behavior, while lower entropy reflects a more deterministic policy. The total PPO objective combines these components into a single optimization loss:

$$\mathcal{L}_{\text{total}} = \mathcal{L}_{\text{PPO}} + c_1 \mathcal{L}_{\text{value}} - c_2 \mathcal{L}_{\text{entropy}}, \tag{7}$$

where c_1 and c_2 are hyperparameters that balance the importance of value accuracy and exploration. Typically, c_1 is set to 1 and c_2 to a small value such as 0.01. This composite loss ensures that the policy improves while maintaining value prediction accuracy and adequate exploration.

3.2 Bayesian Enhancements to Proximal Policy Optimization

To enhance PPO for socially-aware navigation in dynamic environments, we introduce a Bayesian-inspired framework that incorporates uncertainty-aware decision making and adaptive optimization. These modifications aim to improve policy robustness under non-stationary and multi-agent conditions, such as crowded environments with unpredictable human motion. The proposed enhancements are grounded in cognitive theories of uncertainty regulation and memory-guided learning, simulating aspects of biological decision-making systems that adaptively modulate exploration and learning effort. We introduce two key components: (i) *uncertainty-aware temperature scaling* and (ii) *adaptive learning rate modulation*, both of which are described below.

3.2.1 Uncertainty-Aware Temperature Scaling

Let $\mathbf{z} \in \mathbb{R}^n$ denote the unnormalized action logits produced by the actor network, where n is the number of discrete actions. The probability distribution $\mathbf{p} = [p_1, \ldots, p_n]$ over actions is obtained by applying a softmax transformation:

$$\mathbf{p} = \text{softmax}(\mathbf{z}/\tau), \tag{8}$$

where $\tau > 0$ is a temperature parameter that controls the sharpness of the distribution, with lower τ encouraging greedy behavior, while higher τ induces exploratory stochasticity. To adapt this parameter based on policy uncertainty, we estimate the entropy of the policy:

$$\mathcal{H}(\mathbf{p}) = -\sum_{i=1}^{n} p_i \log(p_i + \epsilon), \tag{9}$$

where ϵ is a small constant added for numerical stability. Over a sliding window of recent episodes, we compute the standard deviation of entropy, denoted by $\sigma_{\mathcal{H}}$. The temperature is then dynamically updated as:

$$\tau = 1 + \sigma_{\mathcal{H}}. \tag{10}$$

This approach biases the agent to act more cautiously in uncertain or high-entropy states, reflecting a Bayesian view where entropy approximates epistemic uncertainty.

3.2.2 Adaptive Learning Rate Modulation

In stochastic environments, the variance of returns can degrade policy stability if a fixed learning rate is used. To address this, we define a dynamic learning rate η_t that adapts to recent reward volatility:

$$\eta_t = \max(\eta_{\min}, \frac{\eta_0}{1 + \sigma_R}), \tag{11}$$

where η_0 is the initial learning rate, $\eta_{\min}$ is a lower bound to avoid stagnation, and σ_R is the standard deviation of episodic rewards over a fixed memory window. When reward variance increases, η_t decays to promote more conservative updates, effectively stabilizing the actor-critic learning dynamics.

3.3 Episodic Memory Mechanism

Inspired by hippocampal episodic recall in biological agents, we introduce a memory module $\mathcal{M}$ that enhances decision-making by leveraging salient past experiences. This module supports retrieval of high-impact experiences and biases current action selection in a data-efficient and risk-aware manner. The memory $\mathcal{M}$ is implemented as a fixed-size buffer that stores previously encountered state-action-reward tuples of the form (s, a, r), where $s \in \mathbb{R}^d$ is the agent's observation or state vector at a given time step, $a \in \mathcal{A}$ is the discrete action taken in that state, and $r \in \mathbb{R}$ is the scalar reward received upon executing a in state s. Each stored experience is further assigned an importance weight importance (m_j), computed heuristically based on its absolute reward magnitude or based on risk salience (e.g., collision events). At each time step t, the agent retrieves k relevant memory entries from $\mathcal{M}$ by computing similarity between the current state s_t and the stored states $m_j.s$ for each memory entry $m_j \in \mathcal{M}$. The similarity is computed using a distance-based metric $\Delta(s_t, m_j.s)$ such as Euclidean distance:

$$\Delta(s_t, m_j.s) = \|s_t - m_j.s\|_2. \tag{12}$$

Let $\mathbf{z} \in \mathbb{R}^{|\mathcal{A}|}$ denote the unnormalized action logits produced by the actor network. These logits are modulated by the retrieved memory entries to yield adjusted logits $\tilde{\mathbf{z}}$:

$$\tilde{z}_i = z_i + \sum_{j=1}^{k} \mathbb{I}[m_j.a = i] \cdot w_j, \quad \text{where} \quad w_j = \alpha \cdot m_j. \tag{13}$$

Here, $\tilde{z}_i$ is the modified logit for action i, $\mathbb{I}[m_j.a = i]$ is an indicator function equal to 1 if the action stored in memory m_j is equal to i, and 0 otherwise, w_j is the weighted contribution of memory entry m_j to the current action preference, and α is a tunable hyperparameter controlling the influence of the episodic memory.

This mechanism effectively boosts the action logits associated with successful or critical prior decisions, thereby enabling risk-aware exploration and accelerating policy convergence. It serves as a cognitive prior that steers the agent based on remembered outcomes, especially in sparse-reward or high-risk environments.

3.4 Collision Prediction Network for Safety-Aware Navigation

To further enhance the safety of the robot in dynamic human environments, we introduce a collision prediction module trained offline with random exploration, capturing both successful and failure cases over 500 simulated episodes using a shallow PPO. The dataset was annotated based on ground truth collisions to train the binary classifier. This module estimates the likelihood of a collision given the current observation s_t and a candidate action a_t. The collision predictor is modeled as a binary classifier $C_\psi(s_t, a_t) \to [0, 1]$, implemented as a neural network parameterized by ψ. The input to the model is the concatenation of the observation vector $s_t \in \mathbb{R}^d$ and the discrete action $a_t \in \mathbb{R}$, where d is the dimension of the observation space. The output of the model corresponds to the estimated probability of a collision occurring if action a_t is executed in state s_t. During training, we collect a dataset of experience tuples $\mathcal{D} = \{(s_t, a_t, c_t)\}$, where c_t is a binary label indicating the collision outcome: $c_t = 1$ if a collision occurred after executing action a_t in state s_t, and $c_t = 0$ if no collision occurred. The collision predictor is trained to minimize the binary cross-entropy loss:

$$\mathcal{L}_{collision} = -\mathbb{E}_{(s_t, a_t, c_t) \sim \mathcal{D}} \left[c_t \log C_\psi(s_t, a_t) + (1 - c_t) \log(1 - C_\psi(s_t, a_t)) \right] \quad (14)$$

where $\mathcal{L}_{collision}$ is the collision prediction loss function, $\mathbb{E}_{(s_t, a_t, c_t) \sim \mathcal{D}}[\cdot]$ denotes the expectation over the training dataset $\mathcal{D}$, $C_\psi(s_t, a_t)$ is the predicted probability of collision for a given state-action pair, computed by the collision prediction network, c_t is the ground truth collision label (1 for collision, 0 for no collision), and $\log(\cdot)$ denotes the natural logarithm. The first term in the loss penalizes the model when it predicts a low probability for a state-action pair that actually resulted in a collision ($c_t = 1$). The second term penalizes the model when it predicts a high probability for a state-action pair that did not result in a collision ($c_t = 0$). By minimizing this loss function, the network learns to distinguish between safe and unsafe actions based on past experience. Once trained, this module is integrated into the agent's action selection pipeline to filter out high-risk actions and improve safety during the navigation.

Once trained, the collision predictor is implemented as a feedforward neural network with an input layer of size $obs_{dim} + 1$ (observation vector concatenated with a scalar action), followed by two hidden layers of sizes 64 and 32 using ReLU activations, and a final sigmoid output layer producing the collision probability. During inference, the trained network evaluates the risk associated with the agent's most probable action. If the predicted probability exceeds a predefined confidence threshold (e.g., 0.8), the agent overrides the action by sampling a safer alternative from the action space—specifically those with lower predicted risks. This anticipatory filtering mechanism enables the agent to avoid high-risk actions and enhances its safety and robustness in dynamic, human-populated environments.

3.5 Hybrid Action Selection with Rule-Based Safety Layer

To combine the learned policy with safety guarantees, we integrate a hybrid action selection mechanism. First, the actor-critic model produces action logits z_t which are scaled based on uncertainty as described in Sect. 3.2.1. Then, the collision predictor C_ψ evaluates the likelihood of collision for the selected action. If the estimated collision probability exceeds a safety threshold $\delta > 0.8$, the agent explores alternative safe actions. The candidate safe actions are those for which $C_\psi(s_t, a_t) > 0.8$. Additionally, the agent leverages LiDAR readings to prioritize movement toward the goal while avoiding obstacles. The safe action a_t is selected based on a combined heuristic score that considers the alignment to the goal direction and the distance to nearby obstacles or humans. This hybrid approach allows the agent to balance between policy-driven exploration from the BPPO-EM agent, memory-guided action bias from episodic memory, and rule-based collision avoidance leveraging environmental perception. This integrated architecture ensures safe, socially compliant navigation even in highly dynamic environments with multiple humans. This design maintains modularity by decoupling the safety mechanism from the learning process, thus avoiding instability when incorporating hard constraints directly into the policy or reward signal. It also allows for easier deployment across different environments without requiring retraining, which is important for real-world scenarios.

3.6 Network Architecture and Training Protocol

The BPPO-EM agent adopts an actor-critic architecture with separate networks for the policy π_θ and the value function V_ϕ. Each network follows a multilayer perceptron architecture composed of: $FC_{512} \rightarrow ReLU \rightarrow FC_{256} \rightarrow ReLU \rightarrow FC_{128} \rightarrow ReLU$, with a final output layer of size n (number of discrete actions) for the actor, and 1 for the critic. The Adam optimizer is used with an initial learning rate $\eta_0 = 3 \times 10^{-4}$, modulated adaptively by a Bayesian neuromodulation mechanism based on return variability, down to a minimum $\eta_{min} = 1 \times 10^{-4}$. The agent is trained over 1000 episodes, each consisting of up to 2000 environment steps. PPO updates are applied every 15 episodes using a batch size of 512 transitions, with four epochs of minibatch gradient updates.

3.7 Reward Function for Socially-Aware Navigation

The reward function r_t is designed to encourage efficient and socially compliant navigation. It is composed of several additive components:

$$r_t = -0.01 + \lambda_1 \cdot \Delta d_t - \lambda_2 \cdot \mathbb{I}[\text{collision}] + \lambda_3 \cdot \mathbb{I}[\text{goal reached}] + \lambda_4 \cdot \mathbb{I}[\text{free space}] + \lambda_5 \cdot \mathbb{I}[\text{facing goal}], \tag{15}$$

where Δd_t is the reduction in the Euclidean distance to the goal at time t, $\mathbb{I}[\text{collision}]$ is 1 if the robot collides with a human, else 0, $\mathbb{I}[\text{goal reached}]$ is 1 if the robot is within a predefined radius of the goal, $\mathbb{I}[\text{free space}]$ is 1 if LiDAR reports no nearby obstacles within a critical range, and $\mathbb{I}[\text{facing goal}]$ is 1 if the robot's heading is aligned with the direction of the goal. Typical hyperparameters are: $\lambda_1 = 5.0$, $\lambda_2 = 10.0$, $\lambda_3 = 20.0$, $\lambda_4 = 1.0$, and $\lambda_5 = 0.2$. These values are within the standard range used in similar PPO-based navigation tasks, providing stability while ensuring meaningful trade-offs between progress and safety.

3.8 Observation and Action Spaces

The state input $s_t \in \mathbb{R}^{18}$ consists of: 8 LiDAR-based normalized distance readings from surrounding directions, 9 normalized distances to nearby humans, and 1 normalized scalar distance to the goal. The output action $a_t \in \{0, 1, 2\}$ is a discrete value representing **Turn Left**, **Turn Right**, or **Move Forward**. This simplification of the action space promotes an interpretable and efficient social navigation. Consequently, our framework introduces a cognitively inspired PPO enhancement with Bayesian uncertainty estimation for adaptive action selection, dynamic learning rate tuning for stability, and episodic memory mechanisms for experience-driven policy shaping.

4 Results

4.1 Simulated Environment Setup

Experiments were conducted using the PyBullet simulator to model a social navigation scenario in a $15, m \times 10, m$ arena. The robot starts from a fixed position and must navigate safely to a goal while avoiding multiple dynamic humans. Equipped with an 8-ray LiDAR sensor, the robot receives distance measurements of nearby obstacles, humans, and the target.

Two evaluation scenarios were designed. The first involves 10 humans moving randomly to test basic collision avoidance. The second increases complexity by assigning structured behaviors to humans: H1H5 follow predefined linear or diagonal paths, and H6H9 move randomly within restricted regions (Fig. 1). A successful episode requires reaching the target while minimizing collisions and demonstrating socially compliant navigation, such as maintaining personal space and avoiding risky maneuvers.

4.2 BPPO-EM: Comparison of Neural Architectures

We evaluated two BPPO-EM agents with Adaptive Learning and Episodic Memory: one with a deeper architecture (512-256-128) and another with a lighter structure (256-128-64). Figure 2 presents the comparison across six training metrics over 1000 episodes of 2000 steps each. The deeper 512-256-128 model (blue) achieved higher episodic rewards and displayed greater variability, suggesting better exploitation of successful trajectories and adaptability to complex scenarios. Its discounted returns also revealed broader dispersion and higher cumulative rewards, while the lighter 256-128-64 model (orange) showed flatter, more stable but less dynamic learning curves, indicative of earlier convergence. However, smaller networks offer lower computational cost and faster inference times, which may be beneficial in resource-constrained robots.

Exploration behavior, measured via entropy, further differentiates the models. The 512-256-128 agent maintained higher entropy, preserving exploration longer into training, whereas the 256-128-64 agent experienced rapid entropy decay, risking early stagnation. Both models achieved comparable goal-directed progress in mean values, but the deeper model occasionally demonstrated stronger advancements. Collision analysis showed a clear advantage for the larger network, with more frequent low-collision or collision-free episodes, reflecting superior spatial awareness in dynamic human environments. Finally, episodic

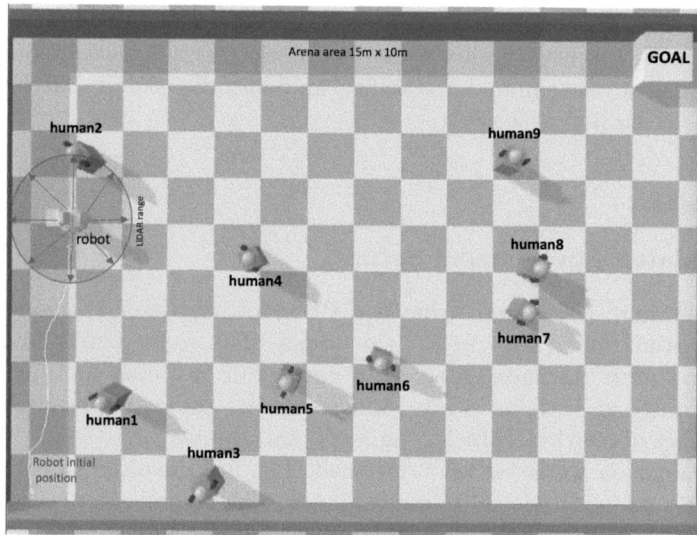

Fig. 1. Top-down view of the simulated arena in PyBullet. The environment includes a robot with LiDAR perception navigating towards a goal while avoiding dynamic humans. Humans H1H5 follow structured trajectories, and H6H9 move randomly within restricted areas.

memory usage was significantly higher in the deeper model, correlating with improved adaptability and navigation fluency. Overall, while both architectures demonstrated learning capability, the 512-256-128 BPPO-EM agent outperformed its smaller counterpart across multiple metrics.

4.3 Comparison Between BPPO-EM and Standard PPO

Figure 3 shows the episode-wise performance of standard PPO and BPPO-EM across five metrics: Reward, Return, Entropy, Progress, and Collisions. Rewards denote total accumulated feedback, while Returns represent discounted reward sums. Entropy reflects policy uncertainty, and lower values indicate more confident action selection. Progress measures how much the agent advances toward the goal per episode, with higher values indicating more successful navigational behavior, and Collisions indicate safety violations. Figure 4 presents the final frame of the best episode, showing the trajectories of the BPPO-EM and PPO agents. The results highlight how the use of episodic memory and the full set of available resources in BPPO-EM promotes more efficient path toward the goal.

The results show a significant improvement of BPPO-EM over standard PPO in socially-aware navigation. As seen in Table 1, BPPO-EM reaches the navigation goal in 82.7% of episodes, versus 17.5% for PPO—a 65.2-point gain. It also reduces collision episodes from 60.2% to 15.8%, and achieves 80.1% success without any collisions, compared to just 12.7% for PPO. BPPO-EM's lower entropy (0.43 vs. 1.10) reflects more confident decisions. It also shows greater

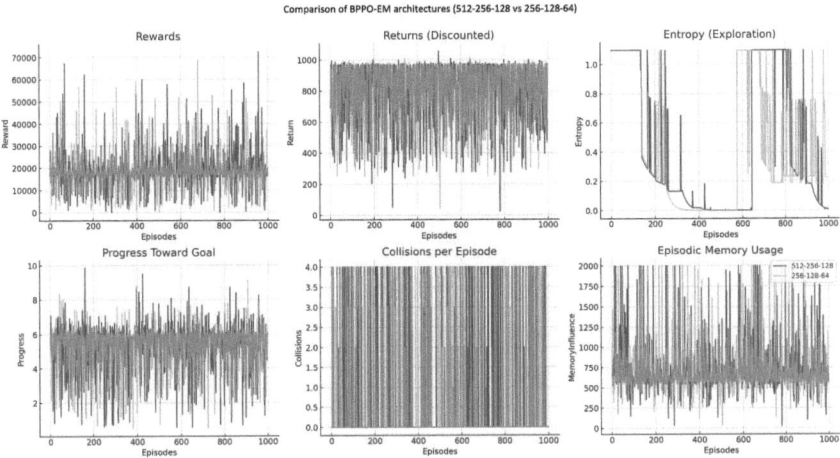

Fig. 2. Comparative training performance of BPPO-EM architectures: 512-256-128 (blue) vs 256-128-64 (orange). Metrics include entropy, reward, return, and collision rate over 1000 episodes. Axes show per-episode averages; reward and return are normalized. Larger networks improve sample efficiency and reduce collisions. (Color figure online)

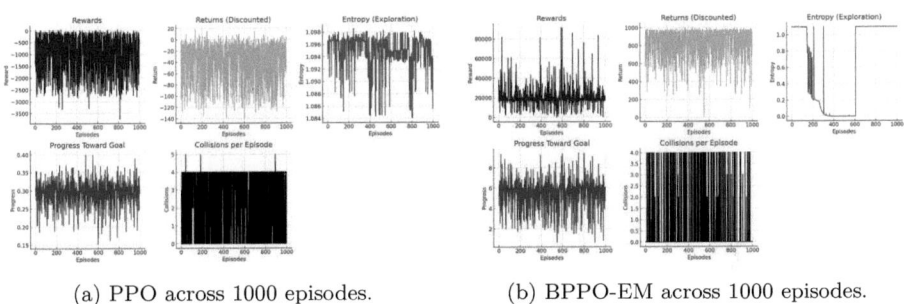

(a) PPO across 1000 episodes. (b) BPPO-EM across 1000 episodes.

Fig. 3. Comparison between vanilla PPO and BPPO-EM over 1000 training episodes. BPPO-EM (b) shows higher success rates, fewer collisions, and better reward returns.

goal-directed movement, higher cumulative rewards and returns, and completes tasks with fewer steps (703 vs. 997), indicating more efficient and effective learning.

Table 1. Performance: BPPO-EM vs Standard PPO (1000 ep)

Metric	BPPO-EM	Standard PPO
Reached Goal (%)	82.7	17.5
Reached Goal w/ 0 Collisions (%)	80.1	12.7
Reached Goal w/ Collisions (%)	2.6	4.8
Did Not Reach Goal (%)	17.3	82.5
Episodes with Collisions (%)	15.8	60.2
Average Entropy	0.43	1.10
Average Progress to Goal (m)	5.0	0.3
Average Reward	18068.2	−1238.4
Average Return	809.3	−38.1
Average Steps to Goal	703.5	997.2

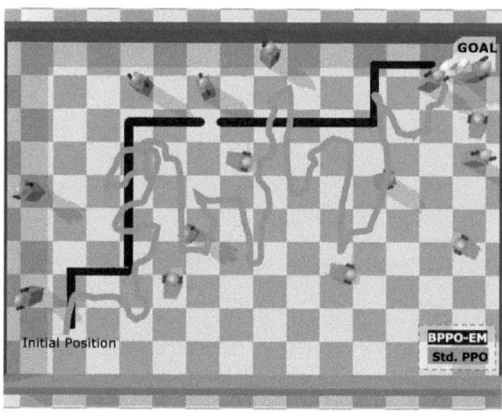

Fig. 4. Final frame of the best episode, showing the trajectories of the BPPO-EM (blue) and PPO (orange) agents. (Color figure online)

5 Conclusion and Future Work

This paper presents BPPO-EM, a cognitively inspired reinforcement learning framework that enhances PPO with Bayesian uncertainty modulation, adaptive learning rates, and episodic memory. In a 15 × 10 m arena with dynamic human agents, BPPO-EM reached goals in 82.7% of episodes—65.2 points higher than PPO—and cut collision rates by over 44%. Average collisions per episode dropped from 2.19 to 0.50, marking a four-fold safety gain. BPPO-EM also surpassed PPO in rewards, returns, and entropy, reflecting more confident behavior. These results highlight the value of cognitive priors, memory, and anticipatory safety. Although the current discrete action space (left, right, forward) is simplified, adding actions like 'stop' or 'reverse' may support socially aware behaviors. Future work will explore these additions along with real-world deployment, curriculum learning, and improved social adaptability.

Acknowledgment. The author acknowledges support from *Applied Sciences* (MDPI) for participation in ICSR+AI'25.

References

1. Truong, X.-T., Yoong, V.N., Ngo, T.-D.: Socially aware robot navigation system in human interactive environments. Intel. Serv. Robot. 1–9 (2017). https://doi.org/10.1007/s11370-017-0232-y
2. Schulman, J., Wolski, F., Dhariwal, P., Radford, A., Klimov, O.: Proximal Policy Optimization Algorithms. arXiv preprint arXiv:1707.06347 (2017)
3. Bachiller, P., Rodriguez-Criado, D., Jorvekar, R.R., Bustos, P., Faria, D.R., Manso, L.J.: A graph neural network to model disruption in human-aware robot navigation. Multimedia Tools Appl. **81**, 3277–3295 (2022)
4. Karnan, H., Nair, A., Xiao, X., et al.: Socially compliant navigation dataset (SCAND). arXiv preprint arXiv:2203.01913 (2022)
5. Vega, A., Manso, L.J., Macharet, D.G., et al.: Socially aware robot navigation system in human-populated and interactive environments based on an adaptive spatial density function and space affordances. Pattern Recognit. Lett. (2019)
6. Silva, S., Paillacho, D., Verdezoto, N., et al.: Towards online socially acceptable robot navigation. In: Proceedings of the International Conference on Human-Robot Interaction (2022)
7. Zhang, F., Gu, C., Yang, F.: An improved algorithm of robot path planning in complex environment based on double DQN. Procedia Comput. Sci. **183**, 648–655 (2021)
8. Katyal, K.D., Gao, Y., Markowitz, J., Cakmak, M., Srinivasa, S.: Learning a group-aware policy for robot navigation. In: Proceedings of the IEEE/RSJ International Conference on Intelligent Robots and Systems (IROS) (2020)
9. Hurtado, J.V., Londoño, L., Valada, A.: From learning to relearning: a framework for diminishing bias in social robot navigation. In: Proceedings of the IEEE International Conference on Robotics and Automation (ICRA) (2021)
10. Zhou, Y.: Perceived appropriateness in social robot navigation behavior. arXiv preprint arXiv:2301.01234 (2023)
11. Warta, S.F., Newton, O.B., Song, J., et al.: Effects of social cues on social signals in human-robot interaction during a hallway navigation task. In: Proceedings of the Human Factors and Ergonomics Society Annual Meeting, vol. 62, no. 1, pp. 2125–2129 (2018)
12. Singh, K.J., Kapoor, D.S., Abouhawwash, M., et al.: Behavior of delivery robot in human-robot collaborative spaces during navigation. Intell. Autom. Soft Comput. **36**(3), 1–10 (2023)
13. Favier, A., Singamaneni, P.T., Alami, R.: An intelligent human avatar to debug and challenge human-aware robot navigation systems. In: Proceedings of the IEEE/RSJ International Conference on Intelligent Robots and Systems (IROS), pp. 9059–9065 (2022)

Automatic Assessment of Speaking Proficiency for Language Practice Robots

Eva Verhelst[1(✉)], Pieter Lecompte[1], Ruben Janssens[1], Vanessa De Wilde[2], and Tony Belpaeme[1]

[1] IDLab-AIRO, Ghent University – imec, Ghent, Belgium
{eva.verhelst,pieter.lecompte,ruben.janssens,tony.belpaeme}@ugent.be
[2] Department of Translation, Interpreting and Communication, Ghent University, Ghent, Belgium
vanessa.dewilde@ugent.be

Abstract. Social robots have been shown to benefit learning and in particular language learning. However, existing language learning robots are limited in their dialogue and adaptation capabilities: many systems use pre-scripted lessons and adaptation options. As large language models enable open-domain dialogue, a conversation practice robot now becomes feasible. Such a robot should adapt its speech to the learner's language proficiency to make the learning more effective. For this, the robot must first accurately detect that proficiency. This study contributes to this capability by presenting a system that automatically assesses students' speaking proficiency. Based on expert knowledge and related literature, we extract relevant features from a graded student speech dataset. We train a machine learning model on this dataset, paying particular attention to its learned weights to inform future research. We then validate the model in a human-robot interaction setting, assessing how well it generalizes from human-only training data. Our findings show that a model relying on a limited set of feature types performs sufficiently well for adaptation, with minimal degradation when applied to a human-robot interaction scenario. Future work includes further automating the proposed system and integrating it into an adaptation system, enabling a fully adaptive conversational social robot for language learning.

Keywords: Robot-Assisted Language Learning (RALL) · Assessment of Speech Proficiency · Machine Learning · Adaptive Social Robot · Educational Social Robot

1 Introduction

Social robots show particular promise for language learning. Prior work has shown that employing social robots in education leads to improved cognitive and affective outcomes, largely attributed to their embodiment: the social nature of interacting with these robot tutors engages students more than other educational technologies do [3]. This strength in keeping students engaged makes them particularly well-suited for language learning, especially conversational practice, as most of second language acquisition is based on exposure [13]. However, previous research on robots in language learning mainly focuses on vocabulary learning [5]. This makes social robots for conversational practice a promising, emerging domain for further research [14,16,20].

A crucial element for an autonomous conversational practice robot is that it should adapt to the student's language proficiency. In any learning, the content of what is taught should be in the student's zone of proximal development for the learning to be effective—meaning, the content should be within a certain range of the student's level, and should be challenging enough that the student struggles to do it alone, but can do it with some help [8]. For language learning, research has shown that matching the language level of what the student is exposed to that of the student increases learning gains and might increase engagement [24,29]. Therefore, an effective social robot for conversational practice must be able to adapt its language complexity to the student—and for this, it first has to estimate the student's proficiency.

This research investigates how speaking proficiency of a student can be automatically assessed in an interaction with a social robot for conversation practice. We first investigate how teachers assess speaking proficiency in practice, interviewing two secondary education teachers and two language education researchers. Then, informed by these interviews and prior work in automatic speaking assessment, we select relevant features that are indicative of speaking proficiency and can be extracted from students' speech during an interaction with the robot. We train a machine learning model that uses these features to predict an expert-graded speaking proficiency score, training and evaluating this model on previously collected data from a longitudinal language development study without robots. Finally, we set up a study in a school where students do interact with a social robot and validate our model on these human-robot conversations. This research shows the validity of automatic assessment of speaking proficiency in human-robot interactions, indicating relevant features for that assessment, and is a stepping stone towards an autonomous and adaptive social robot for second language conversation practice.

2 Related Work

Until recently, educational social robot tutors used mainly scripted, pre-planned lessons that taught specific concepts to students [3], with social robots in general not able to handle open-domain dialogue [4]. These limited, preplanned lessons allow for only little adaptation, often with a small number of difficulty options with a high difference in level between them.

Such adaptation is often powered by a student model, as in classical intelligent tutoring systems, tracking the cognitive and affective state of the student in relation to a domain model, which contains all relevant expert knowledge

[22]. An example of a well-known student model is the Bayesian knowledge tracing model. This model keeps estimates of how well the student understands each piece of knowledge, which are updated after every student action [23]. While this allows for modelling of student knowledge in an easy, interpretable way, it assumes that all lesson content has been predefined. Since the existence of large language models (LLMs) now allows for open-domain dialogue, social robot tutors might teach beyond a preplanned lesson and adapt in more fine-grained ways [27].

Beyond human-robot interaction and adaptive tutoring systems, previous research has explored automatic assessment of speaking proficiency [2,28]. Demand for such automatic graders is high, as most language assessment in practice—in schools or for standardised tests such as the International English Language Testing System (IELTS) or the Test of English as a Foreign Language (TOEFL)—is scored by a trained expert, which is time-consuming and expensive. These automatic graders aim to replace the trained experts by predicting the expert-given grades as accurately as possible, based on the students' speech. Additionally, language assessment also has applications in health care, where automatic systems and even robots can play a role [25].

Many of these automatic grading systems take a classical machine learning approach: they typically extract features from the audio directly as well as from transcriptions made by an automatic speech recognition (ASR) system, and merge these as input for the grader [28]. These features are often handcrafted based on expert knowledge, focusing on fluency, pronunciation, prosody or text complexity. As part of these features are calculated on transcriptions, ASR errors can negatively impact the grading quality. Additionally, transcriptions lose crucial information about the intonation, rhythm and prosody of speech [2]. Recently, ASR systems have improved significantly, but for atypical populations like children and language learners, they tend to disappoint [15,30]. These general ASR improvements tend to hide disfluencies in the user's speech, as they are trained on fluent speech data and therefore output transcriptions of fluent, correct speech, regardless of user mistakes. Additionally, improvements in LLMs make ASR systems more useable as their context understanding lowers the impact of ASR mistakes on the conversational quality [26]. However, these improvements do not better the applicability in educational applications such as providing feedback on learner speech, as an exact transcription, errors included, is often necessary [21]. The current ASR systems are therefore generally better for conversational quality but worse for use in educational applications.

Technological advances in deep learning as well as a need to more accurately model the complexity of speech led to the emergence of end-to-end automatic grading systems. These can take audio as input directly, omitting the need for feature extraction based on domain knowledge and avoiding the errors typically introduced by ASR. An example of this is Banno and Matassoni's assessment system that is based on wav2vec 2.0 [2]. While these end-to-end systems might improve the grading accuracy, deep learning based systems typically introduce a non-negligible delay in comparison to classical machine learning approaches.

With this research, we aim to close the gap between automatic assessment research and educational social robots. We propose a system to automatically assess students' speaking proficiency in human-robot interactions, aiming to enable an adaptive educational social robot for second language conversational practice—which has not yet been attempted before, to the best of our knowledge.

3 Methodology

3.1 Expert Interviews

We conducted interviews with experts to identify how teachers assess and adapt to students' speaking proficiency in practice during language teaching in schools. Four experts were interviewed: two secondary school teachers, both teaching English in different grades, a postdoctoral researcher in English language education and a postdoctoral researcher in French language education, both at Ghent University.

From these interviews, a number of features were identified that are used to assess the students' speaking proficiency. These features were thematically grouped into three categories: lexical diversity, lexical sophistication and pronunciation. The first group, lexical diversity, encompasses the amount of variation in the words that the student uses. The second group, lexical sophistication, focuses on the richness and rarity of the words uttered, with a specific focus on word frequencies. Finally, pronunciation was highlighted to be an important indicator for the speaking ability of a student.

The interviewed experts indicated that, while these items are usually not explicitly included in evaluation rubrics, they are often implicitly used as indicators to assess higher-level concepts such as fluency.

Besides these three categories, experts also identified grammatical correctness and cohesiveness as items that are often included in evaluation rubrics for speaking proficiency. These items are not retained in the remainder of this work, as they are more complex to objectively assess in a conversational context and while essential for evaluation with the aim of providing feedback, they are not essential when the aim is solely to adapt the language complexity to the student.

3.2 Dataset for Model Development

To develop the machine learning model that will predict students' speaking proficiency, a dataset is needed of language learners' speech with expert grades assessing their speaking proficiency. For this, we use a dataset collected by De Wilde and Lowie [12], comprising recordings of first-year English learners at Dutch-speaking secondary schools completing a speaking assignment. The assignment consisted of two parts: an introductory question about the student (e.g., "Can you describe your family?") and a picture narration task, where the students are shown a story depicted in multiple images and asked to describe it (see Fig. 1) [7,11]. Data was collected from two schools in Flanders and one in the Netherlands, totalling 64 students, all in their first year of secondary school (n = 64; mean age 11.9 years old, 5 students did not report their age; 32 girls and 32 boys). Their prior exposure to English varied: some had already received English instruction in primary school, others had just begun, and a few had none. Data collection took place weekly over 30 weeks.

Fig. 1. Example set of pictures showing a story students were asked to describe [7,11].

The dataset consists of raw speech recordings, manual transcriptions, and an expert-graded speaking proficiency score out of twenty. For this score, the graders used a rubric with five equally-weighted categories: grammar, vocabulary, pronunciation, fluency and communication skills.

As these students are in the early stages of learning English, the recordings and their transcripts contain a mix of English and Dutch (L1) speech. English-only transcriptions were created from the originals by selecting only words that are found in the English language corpus "abc" provided by the Python library Natural Language ToolKit (NLTK)[1].

Where present, examiner speech was filtered out from the speech recordings using the speaker diarization tool provided by the Python library WhisperX [1].

3.3 Features

Inspired by prior work in automatic assessment, we decide to extract features from both the speech recordings and the transcripts. In this section, we describe how these features are extracted from the data, following the three categories identified from the expert interviews.

Lexical Sophistication (LS). For calculating the lexical sophistication-related metrics, the software tool *TAALES*[2] was used [17,18]. The tool calculates frequency measures of a text by comparing against selected corpora. It also calculates other LS metrics, such as concreteness, familiarity, imageability, meaning-

---

[1] NLTK: https://www.nltk.org/api/nltk.html.
[2] TAALES: https://www.linguisticanalysistools.org/taales.html.

fulness and age-of-acquisition. These metrics were calculated on the transcriptions containing only the English words. In total, 251 features are extracted by TAALES.

An initial exploration revealed correlations between the expert grades and some of these automatically extracted features, showing the feasibility of this approach. Interestingly, we found that in the dataset we analyse, students with low scores used words with a higher age-of-acquisition and a lower frequency, while these metrics normally correlate with higher proficiency. This finding was also reported by De Wilde and Lowie, hypothesising that more advanced learners are able to use English in everyday contexts, while learners with lower scores are not yet sensitive to variables such as word frequency [10].

Lexical Diversity (LD). For lexical diversity, 12 features were calculated by the Python library *TAALED*[3] [19] and 4 features by the library *lexical-diversity*[4]. Both libraries calculate lexical diversity-related measures such as the *"type token ratio"*, which measures the variety of words. These measures were again calculated on the English-only transcriptions. Initial explorations also revealed correlations between some of these measures and the proficiency scores, warranting their inclusion in the predictive model.

Pronunciation (PR). To calculate pronunciation-related features, the Python library *myprosody*[5] was used, which is an implementation of the *Praat*-software [6]. Using the raw speech recordings, this library extracts features such as number of pauses, speaking and total duration, rate of speech and articulation rate and relevant ratios. Metrics related to the fundamental frequency ($=f0$) are calculated as well. Additionally, prosody-related comparisons to benchmarks were calculated. This resulted in 40 features in total.

Counterintuitively, metrics related to the ratio of speech time over total recording time seem to initially decrease with increasing proficiency scores. As these metrics are calculated on the audio containing both Dutch and English speech, this could be explained by low-scoring students mostly speaking Dutch, while as scores rise, students attempt to speak more English, causing hesitation and a lower speech ratio. However, the most fluent students hesitate less and less when speaking English, leading to higher scores and a higher speech rate.

Percentage of English Words (EP). Finally, as the LS and LD features are only calculated on the English parts of the transcripts, we also reflect the mix between English and Dutch in the feature set by dividing the number of English words by the total number of words. This is calculated by matching the words in the transcription to an English language corpus (the *abc* corpus from NLTK)

---

[3] Taaled: https://pypi.org/project/taaled/.
[4] lexical-diversity: https://pypi.org/project/lexical-diversity/.
[5] myprosody: https://github.com/Shahabks/myprosody.

and to a Dutch corpus (*dutch-words*[6]). This feature is strongly correlated with the expert-graded proficiency score.

3.4 Proficiency Prediction Model

Using these extracted features, we build a machine learning model that predicts the proficiency score. We opt for a simple and traditional machine learning model, ridge regression, as we observed linear correlations between many features and the proficiency scores and due to the limited size of the training dataset. Additionally, the added computation time of deep learning models would hinder real-time adaptation.

The dataset was split between a training set containing 80% of the data and a test set of the remaining 20%. 10-fold cross-validation was used on the training set, and all splits were made ensuring all data belonging to single students remained in the same segment.

Feature selection was performed using `SelectKBest`. Normalization was applied to scale features, a critical step due to the quadratic nature of the L2 regularization in ridge regression, and to allow for direct interpretation of learned weights. A grid search was conducted to explore combinations of preprocessing pipelines and hyperparameters, resulting in a `powertransformer` followed by a `standardscaler`, with $k = 226$ and $\alpha = 0.1125$. Model performance was measured using the mean squared error (MSE), with this optimal configuration resulting in a cross-validation MSE of 7.013. Performance on the held-out test set is analysed in Sect. 4.

3.5 Human-Robot Evaluation Study

To validate the model's performance in interactions with a social robot, an evaluation study was set up in six classes from two Flemish secondary schools. Most of the students ($n = 60$, mean audio duration of 75 s) were 12–13 years old, having nearly completed a full year of English classes, while a small sample ($n = 4$) of older students was added to explore the model's out-of-distribution performance. This small sample consisted of students aged 14–15, nearing the end of their second year of English classes. The study was conducted according to the ethical rules presented in the General Ethics Protocol of the faculty of Engineering and Architecture of Ghent University.

The data collection set-up consisted of a Furhat robot with external microphone. To ensure consistency across experiments, the robot was teleoperated by a researcher through prescripted questions. Audio and timestamps of the student's speech was logged, to later filter out the robot's speech. The use of a robot aimed to examine its impact on model performance, which was initially trained on data without a robot. The setup is illustrated in Fig. 2.

The experiment consisted of three parts. In the first, introductory part, aiming to familiarize the student with the robot, the robot asked questions such

---

[6] Dutch-words: https://pypi.org/project/dutch-words/.

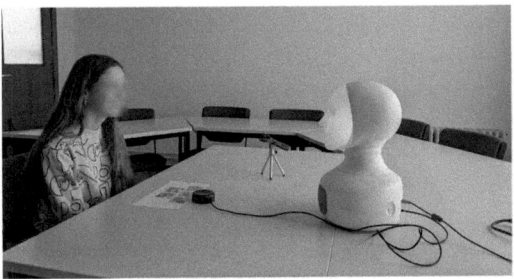

Fig. 2. Experiment Set-Up.

as "What is your name?". This data was not used for analysis. For the second part, the participants were asked to describe their perfect weekend. This was based on advice provided by the experts in the interview, as they suggested to focus on personal questions when students were not able to prepare for the assignment. Third, the students were given the picture narration task seen in Fig. 1. This was modelled after the speaking assignments used to collect the training data, to ensure transferability of the model. The audio recorded during this data collection was manually transcribed.

This data was scored either by the teacher of that class or by the English language teaching expert that also scored the training dataset. For uniform scoring, the expert first scored one first-year class ($n = 13$) and the four second-year students' data. A sample of this data and the corresponding scores, together with the filled-out rubrics used for scoring were given to the teachers. Using this as an example, they scored the remaining data. An overview of the class groups, number of students and who scored them can be found in Table 2.

4 Results

4.1 Performance on Development Dataset

On the held-out test data, the model reaches an MSE of 9.057, compared to a cross-validation MSE of 7.013 on the training data. For easier interpretation, we will also report the mean absolute error (MAE) in this section, as this represents the average deviation from the score on the same scale between 0 and 20. On the held-out training data, the model reached an MAE of 2.380.

To investigate the importance of the different features on the final score, we look at absolute values of the weights associated with that feature in the model. It is important to note here that the ridge regression model can distribute weights across correlated features, which can result in underestimation or dilution of the importance of any single feature. Therefore, as we did not further investigate the correlation between features, this ranking does not strictly show which features have the most influence on the final score.

The five features with the largest learned weights in absolute value are shown in Table 1. The first three are the percentage of English used by the student and the lexical diversity-related metrics *number of types* (which is a measure for the number of unique words used) and *word count* (which measures the total amount of words). These latter two are correlated, as more words generally means more unique words. Number four, articulation rate, is the only pronunciation metric in the top ten. It measures the number of syllables per unit of time. The fifth feature listed here is meaningfulness. It is a dimension of lexical sophistication, which measures how related a word is to other words and how many associations it evokes. Therefore, words relating to physical objects will have a high meaningfulness, while abstract concepts will have a lower meaningfulness. Therefore, the negative weight can be explained, as speakers with a lower proficiency will use more literal, meaningful words, while the meaningfulness will decrease slightly when learning [9]. The sixth to tenth largest weights, not listed here, correspond to frequency-related lexical sophistication metrics based on different corpora.

Table 1. Five Largest Feature Weights in Trained Model Ranked by Absolute Weight

Rank	Feature	Weight	Group
1	English percentage	47.227	EP
2	Number of types	18.589	LD
3	Word Count	15.181	LD
4	Articulation rate	−8.772	PR
5	Meaningfulness	−7.712	LS

4.2 Performance in Human-Robot Evaluation Study

Table 2 shows the MAE for each class group as well as who scored them. Class 3A is the small sample of older students. The MAE of the full first-year group as well as the small sample of older students is not far from the 2.380 that was found for the held-out training data. The scatter plot provided in Fig. 3 shows each student's teacher- or expert-graded score against the model's predicted score.

Deviations in MAE between classes can be explained by differences in scoring strategy. The lowest MAE was found for class 1A, which was scored by the expert, meaning this data is scored most similarly to the development dataset. The MAE of classes 1C and 1D is slightly higher, while the error for class 1B is much higher. Further investigation showed that, when scoring this specific class, the scorer changed their scoring strategy compared to the other classes they scored. The harsher scores for this class are clearly visible in Fig. 3.

5 Conclusion

This research presented a system that automatically assesses a language learner's speaking proficiency in an interaction with a social robot. This system aims to

Table 2. Model Performance on Human-Robot Evaluation Study Per Class

Class	MAE	Students	Evaluator
1A	1.321	13	Expert
1B	5.615	17	Teacher1
1C	2.378	15	Teacher2
1D	2.677	15	Teacher1
All first-years	3.140	60	-
3A	2.854	4	Expert

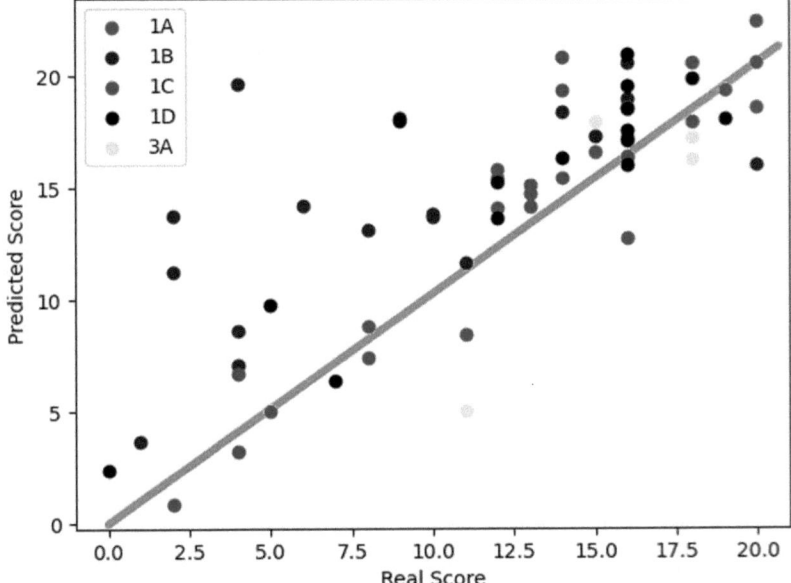

Fig. 3. Scatter plot showing individual students' expert- or teacher-graded proficiency score against the model's predicted score in the human-robot evaluation study. First diagonal shown in grey, representing a perfect model. Note that some model predictions exceed the maximum score of 20, as the model outputs continuous values without an upper limit constraint.

enable a second language conversation practice robot that adapts its speech to the student's proficiency in open-domain dialogue, whereas previous educational social robots were limited in their adaptivity to course-grained adaptation in fixed lesson plans. The system uses an architecture based on prior work in automatic assessment for standardised language tests, predicting a proficiency score based on features extracted from the user's speech and from a transcript thereof. These features were informed by domain knowledge, through interviews conducted with teaching experts. We trained a machine learning model, ridge regression, using a previously collected dataset of language learners, and saw that the model's predicted proficiency scores are close to expert-graded scores, with an MAE of 2.38 on a scale from 0 to 20. Finally, we validated the model's performance in human-robot interactions by running a study where language learners in a school interacted with a social robot, finding that the model's performance transfers well from the development dataset to the real-world interactions, achieving an MAE of 3.14, confidently demonstrating the usability of this system. Grading style was found to have a non-negligible impact on this metric. Additionally, we investigated which features have the highest impact on the predicted scores.

A limitation of this research is that not all processing steps were automated yet. Most importantly, manual transcriptions were used instead of automatically generated ones. This choice was motivated by poorer ASR accuracy for low-proficiency speakers and by the learners in the development dataset and evaluation study speaking a mix of English and Dutch in the recordings. As ASR systems typically aim to recognize one language, this strongly reduced transcription accuracy. A dedicated system to recognise language switching during the transcription processes could mitigate this issue. Besides transcription, automatic processing was hindered by the unavailability of a programmatic interface for the TAALES tool.

Future work should integrate this model into a full adaptation pipeline, investigating whether the model's performance on predicting expert grades transfers well to adaptation. Furthermore, future work can evaluate how well this model transfers to other language learning interactions, investigating how features should be differently weighted when the student completes a different learning assignment than the one used in this training dataset and evaluation study.

In conclusion, this paper contributes a speech proficiency assessment model that is based on domain knowledge and prior automatic assessment work, and shows that its performance transfers well to a human-robot interaction context. This model is a stepping stone to a second language conversation practice robot that dynamically adapts its speech to the learner's speaking proficiency, a highly promising avenue of future work in educational social robotics.

Acknowledgment. This research is funded by imec Smart Education, the Research Foundation Flanders (FWO Vlaanderen, 1S50425N) and the Flanders AI Research 2 initiative. We are indebted to the authors of [12] for making the recordings and transcriptions available to us. This data was collected during research funded by the Research Foundation Flanders (FWO Vlaanderen, 1203923N).

Disclosure of Interests. The authors have no competing interests to declare that are relevant to the content of this article.

References

1. Bain, M., Huh, J., Han, T., Zisserman, A.: Whisperx: time-accurate speech transcription of long-form audio (2023)
2. Bannò, S., Matassoni, M.: Proficiency assessment of L2 spoken english using wav2vec 2.0. In: 2022 IEEE Spoken Language Technology Workshop (SLT), pp. 1088–1095. IEEE (2023)
3. Belpaeme, T., Kennedy, J., Ramachandran, A., Scassellati, B., Tanaka, F.: Social robots for education: a review. Sci. Robot. **3**(21), eaat5954 (2018). https://doi.org/10.1126/scirobotics.aat5954
4. Belpaeme, T., Tanaka, F.: Social robots as educators. In: OECD Digital Education Outlook 2021 Pushing the Frontiers with Artificial Intelligence, Blockchain and Robots: Pushing the Frontiers with Artificial Intelligence, Blockchain and Robots, p. 143. OECD Publishing Paris (2021)
5. van den Berghe, R., Verhagen, J., Oudgenoeg-Paz, O., van der Ven, S., Leseman, P.: Social robots for language learning: a review. Rev. Educ. Res. **89**(2), 259–295 (2019). https://doi.org/10.3102/0034654318821286
6. Boersma, P., Weenink, D.: Praat: doing phonetics by computer [Computer program] (2024), version 6.4.12. https://www.praat.org
7. Cambridge English Language Assessment: Cambridge english: Young learners: Flyers (2014). http://www.cambridgeenglish.org/exams/young-learnersenglish/. Accessed 5 Sept 2017
8. Chaiklin, S., et al.: The zone of proximal development in Vygotsky's analysis of learning and instruction. Vygotsky's Educ. Theory Cult. Context **1**(2), 39–64 (2003)
9. Crossley, S.A., Skalicky, S.: Examining lexical development in second language learners: an approximate replication of Salsbury, Crossley & McNamara (2011). Lang. Teach. **52**(3), 385–405 (2019)
10. De Wilde, V.: Lexical characteristics of young L2 english learners' narrative writing at the start of formal instruction. J. Second Lang. Writ. **59** (2022). https://doi.org/10.1016/j.jslw.2022.100960
11. De Wilde, V., Lowie, W.: Longitudinal L2 Speaking development - Exploring groups (2022). https://osf.io/qytmd/
12. De Wilde, V., Lowie, W.: The forest and the trees: investigating groups and individuals in longitudinal second language english speaking development. Lang. Learn. (2024)
13. Ellis, N.C., Wulff, S.: Usage-based approaches to L2 acquisition. In: Theories in Second Language Acquisition, pp. 63–82. Routledge (2020)
14. Engwall, O., Lopes, J., Åhlund, A.: Robot interaction styles for conversation practice in second language learning. Int. J. Soc. Robot. **13**(2), 251–276 (2021)
15. Janssens, R., Verhelst, E., Abbo, G.A., Ren, Q., Bernal, M.J.P., Belpaeme, T.: Child speech recognition in human-robot interaction: problem solved? In: International Conference on Social Robotics, pp. 476–486 (2024)
16. Kamelabad, A.M., Inoue, E., Skantze, G.: Comparing monolingual and bilingual social robots as conversational practice companions in language learning. In: 2025 20th ACM/IEEE International Conference on Human-Robot Interaction (HRI), pp. 829–838. IEEE (2025)
17. Kyle, K., Crossley, S.A.: Automatically assessing lexical sophistication: indices, tools, findings, and application. TESOL Q. **49**(4), 757–786 (2015). https://doi.org/10.1002/tesq.194

18. Kyle, K., Crossley, S., Berger, C.: The tool for the automatic analysis of lexical sophistication (TAALES): version 2.0. Behav. Res. Methods **50**(3), 1030–1046 (2017). https://doi.org/10.3758/s13428-017-0924-4
19. Kyle, K., Crossley, S.A., Jarvis, S.: Assessing the validity of lexical diversity using direct judgements. Lang. Assess. Q. **18**(2), 154–170 (2021). https://doi.org/10.1080/15434303.2020.1844205
20. Lin, V., Yeh, H.C., Chen, N.S.: A systematic review on oral interactions in robot-assisted language learning. Electronics **11**(2), 290 (2022)
21. Lu, Y., Gales, M.J., Knill, K.M., Manakul, P., Wang, L., Wang, Y.: Impact of ASR performance on spoken grammatical error detection. ISCA (2019)
22. Pavlik, P., Brawner, K., Olney, A., Mitrovic, A.: A review of student models used in intelligent tutoring systems. Des. Recomm. Intell. Tutor. Syst. **1**, 39–68 (2013)
23. Pelánek, R.: Bayesian knowledge tracing, logistic models, and beyond: an overview of learner modeling techniques. User Model. User-Adap. Inter. **27**, 313–350 (2017)
24. Randall, N.: A survey of robot-assisted language learning (RALL). ACM Trans. Hum.-Robot Interact. **9**(1), Article 7 (2019). https://doi.org/10.1145/3345506
25. Seok, S., Choi, S., Kim, K., Choi, J., Sung, J.E., Lim, Y.: Robot-assisted language assessment: development and evaluation of feasibility and usability. Intel. Serv. Robot. **17**(2), 303–313 (2024)
26. Verhelst, E., Belpaeme, T.: Large language models cover for speech recognition mistakes: evaluating conversational AI for second language learners. In: Proceedings of the 2025 ACM/IEEE International Conference on Human-Robot Interaction, pp. 1705–1709 (2025)
27. Verhelst, E., Janssens, R., Belpaeme, T.: Enabling autonomous and adaptive social robots in education: a vision for the application of generative AI. In: Social Robots in Education: How to Effectively Introduce Social Robots into Classrooms, pp. 17–42. Springer (2025)
28. Wang, Y., et al.: Towards automatic assessment of spontaneous spoken english. Speech Commun. **104**, 47–56 (2018)
29. Westlund, J.K., Breazeal, C.: The interplay of robot language level with children's language learning during storytelling. In: Proceedings of the Tenth Annual ACM/IEEE International Conference on Human-Robot Interaction Extended Abstracts, pp. 65–66 (2015)
30. Wills, S., Bai, Y., Tejedor-García, C., Cucchiarini, C., Strik, H.: Automatic speech recognition of non-native child speech for language learning applications. In: The 33rd Meeting of Computational Linguistics in The Netherlands (CLIN 2023) (2023)

Evaluating Social Impact of Pedipulation with Quadrupedal Robot

Marco Tabita[(✉)], Carmine T. Recchiuto, Enrico Simietti, and Antonio Sgorbissa

Department of Informatics, Bioengineering, Robotics and Systems Engineering (DIBRIS), University of Genoa, Via All'Opera Pia 13, 16145 Genoa, Italy
marco.tabita@edu.unige.it

Abstract. Quadrupedal robots, often referred to as "robot dogs," are increasingly employed across a wide range of applications, including industrial inspections and public safety operations. Pedipulation—a novel area of research within quadruped robotics—involves limb-based manipulation that significantly extends the functional capabilities of these systems. Beyond enhancing robotic autonomy in complex tasks, pedipulation may also positively influence human-robot interactions, particularly in social contexts. In this preliminary study, we used a previously developed pedipulation-control framework to assess how the resulting behaviors affect human perception. Specifically, we conducted a between-subjects study in which participants watched videos of a robot dog solving tasks either with or without pedipulation, and then completed the NARS (Negative Attitude towards Robots Scale) and the Godspeed questionnaire. The statistical analysis revealed a significant interaction in the scores of two items of the GodSpeed scale, namely Perceived Intelligence and, to a lesser extent, Likeability, for those who have a worse predisposition towards robots.

Keywords: Quadrupedal Robot · Pedipualtion · Social Perception

1 Introduction

Quadrupedal robots, often referred to as "robot dogs," are increasingly deployed across different applications—from industrial inspections to public safety operations—owing to their agility, stability, and compact dimensions. Their structural characteristics enable quadrupedal robots to navigate and overcome a wide variety of obstacles, including natural terrains such as rocks and uneven surfaces, as well as urban environments featuring stairs and ground irregularities.

Unlike their wheeled counterpart, quadrupedal platforms possess the capability to physically interact with their surroundings through their limbs. This capability, termed "pedipulation," [2,5] involves manipulating objects using feet or legs rather than employing dedicated robotic arms. Pedipulation is an emerging research area within quadruped robotics, significantly expanding their operational capabilities. This form of limb-based manipulation not only enhances robotic autonomy during complex tasks but may also positively impact human-robot interactions in social settings. Natural dogs commonly engage in social interactions using their paws, for instance, placing a paw on their owner to initiate physical contact or offering a paw to "shake hands," a trained behavior symbolizing trust and connection.

Despite significant technical advancements in quadrupedal locomotion and control, the social acceptability and human perception of these robots remain relatively understudied. Understanding how humans perceive quadrupedal robots cognitively, emotionally, and socially is crucial, particularly as these robots increasingly transition from controlled laboratory environments to everyday, real-world contexts. Within this scenario, pedipulation could play a pivotal role in shaping human perception.

The main contribution of this article is the exploration of the following research question:

> Does pedipulation impact the perception of a quadruped robot in terms of its biomorphic, cognitive, and social characteristics as perceived by people?

To this end, we developed a user study. First, we used our previously developed pedipulation-control framework for quadrupedal robots and remotely controlled a Unitree Go1 robot to perform a number of tasks (e.g., opening a door or overcoming an obstacle) either with or without pedipulation. Then, we conducted a between-subjects study in which participants, divided into different conditions, watched videos of the robot solving tasks either with or without pedipulation. Participants completed the NARS (Negative Attitudes toward Robots Scale) and, after viewing the videos, the Godspeed questionnaire. All responses were collected anonymously and analyzed using statistical methods.

The article is organized as follows: Sect. 2 provides a background on existing research concerning human-quadruped robot interaction. Section 3 briefly describes the pedipulation framework employed. Subsequently, Sect. 4 details the experimental study conducted with volunteer participants, alongside the corresponding data collection and statistical analyses performed. Results are presented in Sect. 5, followed by a comprehensive discussion in Sect. 6 and concluding remarks in Sect. 7.

2 Social Perception of Quadrupedal Robots

In recent years, a significant trend has emerged concerning the widespread deployment of quadrupedal robots. Consequently, understanding human perceptions and their reactions [9] of these robotic platforms and improving their social acceptability has become crucial. As quadruped robots start operating within more populated and interactive contexts, addressing their social perception and enhancing their acceptance through thoughtfully designed behaviors and appearances has surfaced as a vital research direction.

Despite this expanding presence, literature explicitly addressing the social perception of quadruped robots remains relatively sparse. Existing studies predominantly highlight how autonomous navigational capabilities influence perceived safety, rather than exploring the expressive or interactive potential of these platforms. Hauser et al. [8], for example, investigated human perceptions during incidental encounters with autonomous quadrupedal robots, focusing specifically on visual indicators of human control, such as the presence of a leash or a nearby human operator, and their positive impact on perception.

Addressing similar concerns related to appearance and affective responses, Hashimoto et al. [7] examined the influence of dominant and submissive behavioral traits of quadruped robots on perceived safety during interactions. Their findings revealed that robots exhibiting submissive behaviors—characterized by lower posture, slower movements, and retracted limbs—were perceived as significantly safer compared to those displaying dominant behaviors, including elevated stances and assertive motion patterns.

In the study conducted by Gupta et al. [6], the perception of quadruped robots was investigated using multimodal physiological monitoring systems, such as electrocardiography (ECG) and electrodermal activity (EDA), to measure the stress induced by interaction with the quadrupeds. Stress is a key component of perceived safety. The results showed that the stress level experienced by participants was directly correlated with both the type of robot activity—exploration or navigation—and the number of robots present near the subject.

Exploring a different interaction modality, Chen et al. [4] introduced a socially-aware quadruped robot designed to autonomously encourage social distancing in urban environments. Unlike studies altering physical posture or non-verbal behaviors, their robot employed verbal cues to shape human behaviors. This work demonstrated that voice-based communication strategies could be highly effective when aligned with human expectations of appropriateness and clear intent.

Further contributing to perceived safety, Akalin et al. [1] proposed a taxonomy for factors influencing users' feelings of safety in human-robot interactions. They emphasized that perceptions of safety fundamentally rely on three interconnected dimensions: comfort, perceived control, and trust toward the robot. From the robot's perspective, attributes such as movement speed, trajectory, proximity to humans, and the smoothness of object manipulation directly impact human comfort. These factors become particularly crucial in quadruped robots performing pedipulation tasks involving close physical proximity and potentially abrupt movements. Rapid or unpredictable motions during object manipulation are likely to cause unease among bystanders, whereas deliberate and smooth movements can significantly enhance perceived safety.

The research question introduced in this article—whether pedipulation impacts the perception of a quadruped robot in terms of its biomorphic, cognitive, and social characteristics—remains largely unexplored.

3 Pedipulation Framework

The control framework employed to autonomously perform pedipulation tasks with the quadrupedal robot Unitree Go1 was designed in prior work [12]. This framework is based on a model-based control architecture and integrates a set of interconnected modules to autonomously execute user-defined missions, Fig. 1. The core of the control framework is composed of a Hierarchical Quadratic Programming (HQP) Controller that relies on a task-priority formulation and a mission manager, which operate in conjunction to compute the control commands transmitted to the robot at a frequency of 500 Hz. The other modules include: Unitree IO-Interface, which is a custom interface for communication with both the physical and simulated robotic platforms, the Unitree State Estimator, which is a linear Kalman filter to estimate the robot's state (base pose and linear velocity) relative to a fixed inertial frame initialized during system bring-up, and other modules for visualization and execution. Both the state estimator and the IO-Interface are implemented from the official Unitree repositories. A general overview of the control architecture is presented in Fig. 1.

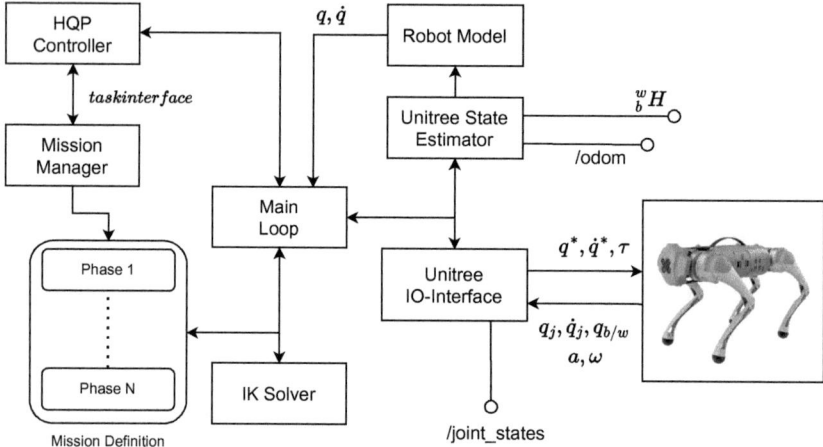

Fig. 1. Control framework architecture: all working modules are collected and executed by the Main Loop structure.

The HQP Controller is formulated as a hierarchical stack of inverse dynamics tasks, as described in [11]. This approach enables the resolution of multiple objectives organized in a prioritized hierarchy, where the final solution provides the control command for all the robot's joints. The tasks defined within this framework express different main objectives, such as: objective tasks (e.g., tracking a Cartesian trajectory of the body pose), safety tasks (e.g., maintaining the center of mass within the support polygon), and optimization tasks (e.g., minimizing motion during pedipulation activities). These tasks can be added or removed at runtime, allowing for flexible adaptation to changing operational requirements. Each task is formulated with respect to the control vector, which includes the accelerations of all twelve joints and the reaction forces at the feet in rigid contact with the ground. The resulting solution from this task hierarchy is then mapped to joint torque commands through an inverse dynamics formulation and subsequently transmitted to the robot actuators. This method ensures that all motion constraints imposed by rigid contact are accurately embedded within the control problem. Furthermore, these constraints can be dynamically activated or deactivated during transitions, such as from a four-foot stance to a three-foot stance with one leg engaged in pedipulation. Additionally, the module implementing this control formulation provides an interface for receiving reference trajectories to be tracked. These dynamic references can be specified up to the second-order derivative of all controlled variables. Moreover, the module offers an interface for accessing the state of each task, primarily in terms of Cartesian errors.

From a mission-coordination perspective, in our context, a mission is defined as the execution of a complex action, which involves multiple intermediate phases necessary to achieve the desired outcome. The component designed to orchestrate this sequence of phases is the Mission Manager, which continuously supervises the state of each phase and appropriately manages the transitions between them. Through an interface provided by the module responsible for the control formulation, this Mission Manager generates and coordinates task references to achieve the desired movements. Currently, this module employs a fifth-order polynomial trajectory to generate fluid movements. This polynomial trajectory ensures zero velocity and acceleration at both the start and end points of the movement. Such a solution has been used for both the torso and limb movements (during pedipulation tasks). Specifically, for limb movements, the motion definition occurs in the joint space, achieving a desired configuration computed using an inverse kinematics solver (IK solver, see Fig. 1), while still defining the trajectory as a fifth-order polynomial. In our case, the defined missions share a similar structure: the robot first stands up and shifts its center of mass to a safe area to lift its foot off the ground and perform the required actions. The initial position the foot reaches is defined as the working position and is located 10 cm below the corresponding shoulder. Subsequently, in the case of the door and the obstacle (Figs. 2d and 2b), the foot is moved forward by about 30 cm relative to the shoulder, then returns to the original working position and places the foot back on the ground, completing the mission. In the cases of the object on the back (Fig. 2f) and social interaction with a human (Fig. 2g), multiple intermediate goals have been defined to create complex movement.

4 Study Design

To evaluate how pedipulation in quadrupedal robots influences human perception, we designed a between-subjects study comprising three conditions: two experimental and one control. In all conditions, a quadrupedal robot encounters the same set of obstacles: a half-closed door, an object positioned in the middle of a path, and an object placed on its back. In the control condition, the robot does not utilize pedipulation; instead, it avoids the obstacles when possible or interacts with them using its body. In contrast, in the two experimental conditions, the robot employs pedipulation to navigate and manage the various obstacles. Additionally, the final scenario includes a social interaction with a human to assess the social dimension of the robot's behavior.

Videos were recorded for all conditions. Walking and pedipulation are not autonomous at the current stage; instead, they are remotely controlled by a hidden user who does not appear in the videos, following a Wizard-of-Oz approach. The scenarios and camera angles were kept identical across all conditions to ensure that participants' attention was consistently focused on the robot and its actions.

4.1 Participants

Participants were sourced online through researchers' social networks. A total of 157 participants decided to participate voluntarily. They were asked to complete two online questionnaires anonymously through Microsoft Forms: the NARS [10] and the GodSpeed questionnaire [3], measuring, respectively, the negative attitude towards robots and the perception of the robot. Specifically, by clicking on a public link in a social media post (Facebook, Instagram, LinkedIn, or WhatsApp messages), potential participants were directed to a website to be assigned to one of the three randomly selected conditions. They were asked to fill out the NARS questionnaire, watch a video for one minute, and then fill out the GodSpeed questionnaire.

4.2 Hypotheses

We formulate two hypotheses on the subjective perception of pedipulation on participants:

- **H1:** The use of pedipulation in conditions 2 and 3, compared to its absence in condition 1, will impact people's perception of the quadrupedal robot.
- **H2:** Pedipulation in conditions 2 and 3 will mitigate the negative association between participants' robot?attitude and their perceptions.

4.3 Conditions

All conditions[1] were designed to present, as much as possible, the same setup across all scenarios, to allow participants to focus solely on how the robot behaves. The core structure consists of a sequence of three typical situations that may occur during the execution of common tasks by a quadruped robot operating in an urban environment. These are, in order: overcoming an obstacle encountered along the path, opening a slightly ajar door, and removing an object from its back.

In Condition 1 (Control), the sequence of actions presented reflects those typically associated with a standard autonomous quadrupedal robot. The object obstructing the path is bypassed by walking around it (Fig. 2a); the half-closed

(a) Condition 1   (b) Condition 2,3   (c) Condition 1

(d) Condition 2,3   (e) Condition 1   (f) Condition 2,3

(g) Condition 3

Fig. 2. Snapshots extracted from the three conditions reporting the different types of action presented.

---

[1] 1: https://youtu.be/x1O7gFkMKvs 2: https://youtu.be/pEWZsZKkgZE 3: https://youtu.be/hv6rlKsGFAs.

door is opened by the robot striking it with its head (Fig. 2c); and the object placed on the robot's back is removed by rotating its body (Fig. 2e).

In Condition 2 (Experimental), the sequence of actions instead illustrates the ideal behavior of an autonomous quadrupedal robot equipped with pedipulation capabilities. The object in the path is actively pushed aside (Fig. 2b) and then overcome; the half-closed door is opened using the robot's front right leg (Fig. 2d); and the object on its back is removed by employing the same limb (Fig. 2f).

In Condition 3 (Experimental) largely replicates the second one (Fig. 2b, 2d, 2f), except for the final scenario, which involves a case of humanrobot interaction: the robot offers its paw to a human positioned in front of it (Fig. 2g).

Table 1. The 24-item Godspeed Rating Scale. 1 corresponds to strongly disagree, 2 disagree, 3 neither agree nor disagree, 4 agree, 5 strongly agree.

Anthropomorphism		Likeability	
Natural	1 2 3 4 5	Like	1 2 3 4 5
Humanlike	1 2 3 4 5	Friendly	1 2 3 4 5
Conscious	1 2 3 4 5	Kind	1 2 3 4 5
Lifelike	1 2 3 4 5	Pleasant	1 2 3 4 5
Moving elegantly	1 2 3 4 5	Nice	1 2 3 4 5
Animacy		Perceived Intelligence	
Alive	1 2 3 4 5	Competent	1 2 3 4 5
Lively	1 2 3 4 5	Knowledgeable	1 2 3 4 5
Organic	1 2 3 4 5	Responsible	1 2 3 4 5
Lifelike	1 2 3 4 5	Intelligent	1 2 3 4 5
Interactive	1 2 3 4 5	Sensible	1 2 3 4 5
Responsive	1 2 3 4 5		
Perceived Safety			
Relaxed 1 2 3 4 5			
Agitated 1 2 3 4 5			
Surprised 1 2 3 4 5			

4.4 Experimental Procedure

After clicking the link and being redirected to the webpage hosting the questionnaire and video, participants are briefly provided with a general overview of the research objective. However, no specific details are disclosed regarding what the experiment aims to measure to avoid influencing participants' responses. Subsequently, participants are informed about the structure of the experiment, which consists of three main phases: first, responding to an initial questionnaire; second, watching a video that depicts a quadruped robot performing generic tasks; and finally, completing a brief concluding questionnaire.

4.5 Measurements

Most of the studies reviewed relied on well-established HRI questionnaires to systematically measure participants' perceptions, attitudes, and emotions. Two instruments in particular appear frequently: the Negative Attitudes toward Robots Scale (NARS) [10] and the Godspeed Questionnaire Series [3].

The (NARS) consists of a 14-item instrument divided into three sub-scales that measure an individual's general anxiety and negativity toward robots. Higher total scores correspond to more negative attitudes. In social-perception studies, it is typically administered before any humanrobot interaction to establish participants' baseline predispositions; this baseline enables researchers to interpret and classify subsequent perceptions of the robot more accurately.

The Godspeed Series is a set of rating scales targeting five dimensions of robot perception: Anthropomorphism, Animacy, Likeability, Perceived Intelligence, and Perceived Safety. Each dimension is measured by several 5-point semantic differentials (e.g., "Fake — Natural" or "Agitated — Calm") for a total of 24 items (Table 1), and it is often administered all or a subset of these scales after a robot interaction. In the context of quadruped robots: **Anthropomorphism** tells us if people see the robot as an agent with human/animal traits versus a machine. **Animacy** measures if the robot is regarded as alive, energetic. **Likeability** captures affection and acceptance; this often correlates with whether the robot followed social norms. **Perceived Intelligence** (P.I.) if the robot seems smart, aware, and responsive. **Perceived Safety** (P.S.) indicates how safe/secure the person feels around the robot (Table 2).

Table 2. Mean (standard deviation) for each condition on each scale.

C.	NARS	Antropomorphism	Animacy	Likeability	P. I.	P.S.
1	2.68 (0.68)	2.67 (0.72)	3.06 (0.74)	3.19 (1.03)	3.33 (0.82)	2.99 (0.66)
2	2.63 (0.65)	2.68 (0.82)	3.20 (0.79)	3.19 (0.90)	3.45 (0.76)	2.86 (0.74)
3	2.59 (0.65)	2.66 (0.70)	3.14 (0.69)	3.31 (0.93)	3.40 (0.74)	2.97 (0.64)

5 Results

We assessed the internal consistency of participants' responses for each scale using Cronbach's alpha (α). The NARS scale consistently exhibited excellent internal consistency across all conditions ($\alpha > 0.86$). Likewise, the Likeability and Perceived Intelligence subscales of the Godspeed questionnaire demonstrated very good reliability ($\alpha > 0.82$). The Anthropomorphism and Animacy subscales showed acceptable internal consistency levels, with α values ranging from 0.727 to 0.824. Although the Perceived Safety subscale presented lower reliability values (α between 0.472 and 0.715), all Godspeed subscales yielded internal consistency coefficients within a generally acceptable range. We did not assess data normality since each condition included a sufficiently large number of participants (more than 30).

A Welch one-way ANOVA revealed no statistically significant differences (considering a significance level of $\alpha = .05$) across any dimension of the Godspeed Questionnaire Series, between the three different conditions: Anthropomorphism $F(2, 103) = 0.01, p = .988$; Animacy $F(2, 103) = 0.46, p = .632$; Likeability $F(2, 102) = 0.2578, p = .773$; Perceived Intelligence $F(2, 102) = 0.290, p = .749$; and Perceived Safety $F(2, 103) = 0.528, p = .591$. Consequently, hypothesis H1 is not supported for any of the perceived dimensions.

A series of ANCOVA analyses were then conducted to evaluate the effects of the experimental conditions (2,3) on each perceived dimension of the robot, with participants' negative attitude towards robots (NARS) set as a covariate of the dependent variable. Considering a significant effect, whether $p < .05$.

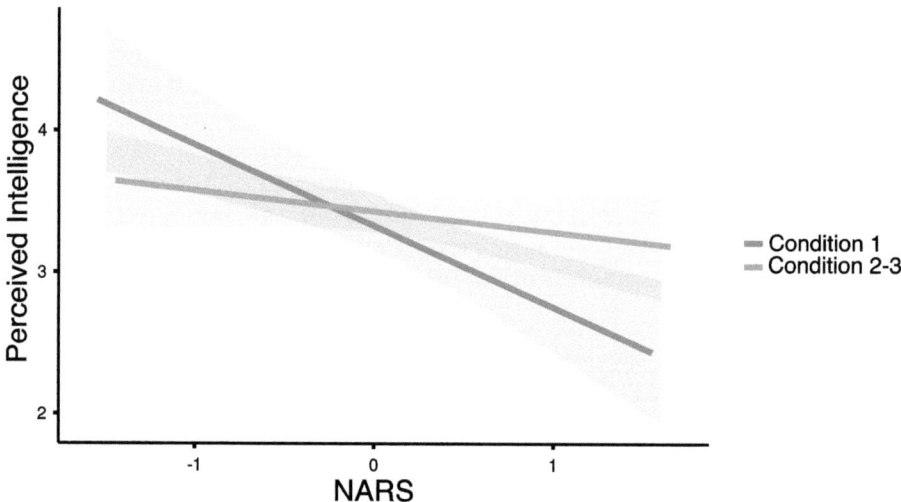

Fig. 3. Interaction of NARS on Perceived Intelligence: This plot shows the moderation effect of NARS on the perceived intelligence within its confidence region. On the horizontal axis is reported the NARS at its Mean - 1 SD, Mean, and Mean +1 SD. The perceived intelligence in conditions 1 and 2–3 is reported on the vertical axis.

For the Anthropomorphism, the ANCOVA revealed a significant main effect of the covariate NARS, $F(1, 153) = 11.989, p < .001$, whereas no significant effects were found for the experimental conditions, $F(1, 153) = 0.346, p = .558$ nor for the interaction, $F(1, 153) = 0.330, p = .567$. Similarly, for Animacy, the ANCOVA revealed a significant main effect of the covariate NARS,

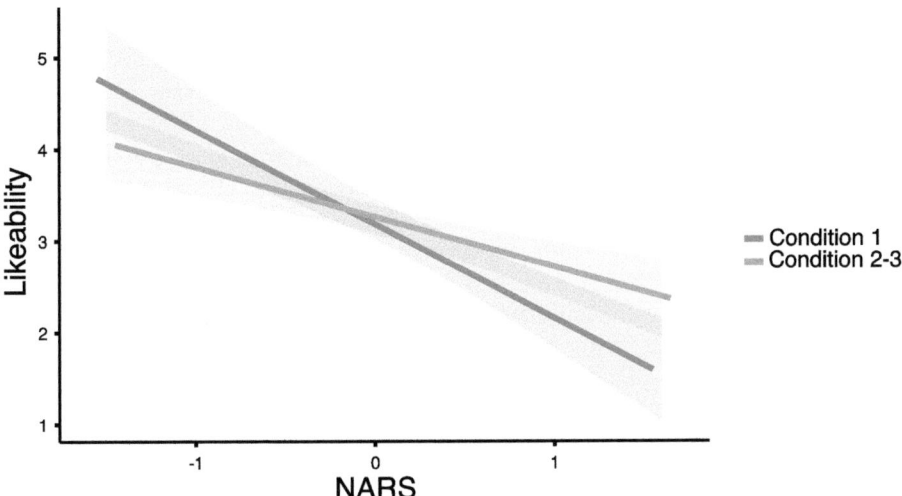

Fig. 4. Interaction of NARS on Likeability: This plot shows the moderation effect of NARS on the Likeability within its confidence region. On the horizontal axis is reported the NARS at its Mean - 1 SD, Mean, and Mean +1 SD. The Likeability in conditions 1 and 2–3 is reported on the vertical axis.

$F(1, 153) = 7.059, p = .009$, while no significant effects emerged for the conditions, $F(1, 153) = 0.502, p = 0.480$ or for the interaction, $F(1, 153) = 0.330, p = .567$. Regarding Perceived Intelligence, the ANCOVA revealed significant main effects of both the condition, $F(1, 153) = 4.13, p = .044$, and the covariate NARS, $F(1, 153) = 14.56, p < .001$. A significant interaction effect was also observed, $F(1, 153) = 5.05, p = .026$, suggesting that the influence of the experimental conditions varied depending on participants' predispositions toward robots. For Likeability, the ANCOVA indicated significant main effects of both the covariate NARS, $F(1, 153) = 56.51, p < .001$, and the condition, $F(1, 153) = 4.93, p = .028$, along with a significant interaction, $F(1, 153) = 5.33, p = .022$. Finally, for Perceived Safety, the ANCOVA revealed no significant effects for the condition, $F(1, 153) = 0270, p = .604$, nor for the interaction, $F(1, 153) = 0.120, p = .730$. However, a significant main effect of the covariate NARS was found, $F(1, 153) = 5.960, p = .016$.

The same ANCOVA analysis defined for the Godspeed measurements was conducted on all the single items of the Godspeed questionnaire, with the NASR as a covariate of the different items. Considering a significant level $\alpha = .05$, only the following interaction effect emerged as statistically significant: Interactive $F(1, 153) = 5.65, p = .019$, Kind $F(1, 153) = 5.86, p = .017$, Nice $F(1, 153) = 8.81, p = .003$, Competent $F(1, 153) = 5.32, p = .022$, and Knowledgeable $F(1, 153) = 4.84, p = .029$. While the other items resulted in no significant interaction effect with $p > .05$.

Subsequently, the corresponding General Linear Models (GLMs) were conducted for both Perceived Intelligence and Likeability. The GLM for Perceived Intelligence confirmed the significance of the interaction term, $\beta = 0.425$, $SE = 0.189$, $t(153) = 2.247$, $p = .026$, whereas the main effect of condition was not significant, $p = .597$. The model explained a modest portion of the variance, $R^2 = .097$, $F(3, 153) = 5.49$, $p = .001$. Simple effects analyses indicated that the condition had no significant effect at average or low levels of the covariate $p = .597$ and $p = .238$, respectively, but the effect became significant at higher levels of NARS $F(1, 153) = 3.96$, $p = .048$ (Fig. 3).

The GLM results for Likeability confirmed the findings reported as well, with a significant interaction term, $\beta = 0.483$, $SE = 0.209$, $t(153) = 2.310$, $p = .022$, while the main effect of condition was again non-significant, $p = .997$. The model fit was stronger in this case, explaining 27% of the variance, $R^2 = .270$, $F(3, 153) = 18.90$, $p < .001$. Simple effects analyses showed that the condition had no significant impact at low or average levels of the covariate $p = .113$ and $p = .997$, respectively, but approached significance at high levels of NARS $F(1, 153) = 2.73$, $p = .100$, $\eta_p^2 = .018$ (Fig. 4).

These findings support Hypothesis H2 only for Perceived Intelligence and Likeability, while it cannot be supported for the other measures. All results reported here were computed using the jamovi software [13].

6 Discussion

From the obtained results, hypothesis H2 has been verified mainly for the Perceived Intelligence and, to a lesser extent, for the Likeability. Pedipulation influences the social perception of the quadruped robot intelligence; however, this influence differs from what was initially hypothesized in H1, which is not supported. Indeed, this effect emerges significantly when the individual's negative attitude towards the robot is considered as a covariate factor. Based on the results, the NARS remains the primary predictor for how the robot is perceived, regardless of the presented condition.

Therefore, we can assert with certainty that pedipulation influences individuals in a more sophisticated manner, acting as a mitigation factor, particularly when the individual's attitude towards robots is predominantly negative. In other words, the pedipulation helps people who have a worse predisposition towards robots to perceive them as more intelligent and, in a minor way, more likable than their corresponding absence in quadrupedal robot task execution.

Considering the individual items and maintaining NARS as a covariate, a statistically significant difference emerges in: Interactive, Kind, Nice, Competent, and Knowledgeable between the control and experimental conditions. This can be interpreted as a tendency for individuals to perceive these traits more positively in the quadruped robot when pedipulation is employed. However, these individual keys are not able to determine a significant difference in the Animacy, Likeability, and perceived Intelligence measurements.

Although pedipulation, covariate by NARS scores, appears to positively influence these dimensions, the interaction effects suggest this is more evident for individuals with a negative predisposition toward robots. This outcome emphasizes the potential for expressive movement to reshape negative biases, particularly in traits that relate to cognition and social appeal.

In contrast, ANCOVA results showed that pedipulation alone did not significantly affect Perceived Safety, Animacy, or Anthropomorphism. These findings suggest that while expressive motion can improve perceptions of intelligence and sociability, it might be insufficient to influence more embodied or affective attributes, which may require richer, physical, or prolonged interactions.

The general linear model analysis and all ANCOVA tests confirmed the strong predictive power of the NARS, which is independent of the condition. This consistency highlights the foundational influence of participants' initial attitudes in shaping their interpretations of robot behavior. As such, future design strategies should consider user predispositions and possibly integrate adaptive behavioral models to tailor robot expressiveness dynamically based on user profiles.

6.1 Limitation

This study presents several limitations that must be considered and addressed. First of all, it is important to highlight that three videos were created, showing a quadruped robot interacting with its environment and nearby objects, either using its legs for manipulation (pedipulation) or not using it at all. In cases where pedipulation was not employed, the robot was teleoperated, leaving the human operator responsible for determining the robot's movements and modes of interaction. Conversely, in scenarios involving pedipulation, the robot executed an autonomous mission still in its early developmental stages, resulting in movements that occasionally appeared slow and heavy.

Each participant viewed only one video, without experiencing any real or physical interaction with the robot. This design choice allowed for the assessment of a specific type of interaction, rather than a comparative evaluation among the three proposed interaction types. A further critical limitation arose from the selection criteria of participants. Many participants lacked sufficient awareness of the actual operational capabilities of such robotic platforms. This lack of familiarity often led them to underestimate or entirely overlook the robot's ability to perform certain actions. Consequently, their perception of the robot's intelligence was influenced, with attention directed primarily toward the outcome (e.g., overcoming an obstacle) rather than the execution process itself.

The final limitation identified concerns the number of participants. Since recruitment was conducted voluntarily and in a short time (two weeks), participation was relatively low. Although the total number of respondents exceeded the minimum threshold generally considered sufficient to assume a normal distribution of responses, it was likely still insufficient to reveal statistically significant differences among the various conditions that might emerge with a higher number of participants.

7 Conclusion

This preliminary investigation has highlighted the potential of pedipulation to enhance the social perception of quadrupedal robots. Specifically, our results demonstrate that limb-based manipulation can act as a mitigation factor for individuals exhibiting negative predispositions toward robotic agents, particularly by improving Perceived Intelligence and, to a lesser extent, Likeability. These effects are especially pronounced when negative attitudes are accounted for as a covariate, suggesting that pedipulation may serve as a compensatory mechanism to mitigate initial distrust or skepticism.

Although the observed improvements in social perception were modest, they provide a compelling case for future research exploring richer forms of interaction. Notably, the lack of statistically significant effects on Anthropomorphism, Animacy, and Perceived Safety may be due to video-based assessment. Direct, physical interaction with the robot—potentially in longitudinal or in-situ studies—will likely be essential to capture a broader and more nuanced spectrum of human responses.

Future work should thus prioritize two key directions: (i) refinement of the control architecture to achieve more natural and expressive movement patterns, and (ii) the design of experimental protocols involving real-time, embodied interaction with users. In parallel, expanding the demographic and experiential diversity of participant samples will be crucial to ensure the generalization of findings across varied user profiles.

References

1. Akalin, N., Kiselev, A., Kristoffersson, A., Loutfi, A.: A taxonomy of factors influencing perceived safety in human-robot interaction. Int. J. Soc. Robot. **15**(12), 1993–2004 (2023). https://doi.org/10.1007/s12369-023-01027-8
2. Arm, P., Mittal, M., Kolvenbach, H., Hutter, M.: Pedipulate: enabling manipulation skills using a quadruped robot's leg. arXiv preprint arXiv:2402.10837 (2024). http://arxiv.org/abs/2402.10837
3. Bartneck, C.: Godspeed questionnaire series: translations and usage. In: Krägeloh, C.U., Alyami, M., Medvedev, O.N. (eds.) Lecture Notes in Computer Science, vol. 13312, pp. 1–35. Springer, Cham (2023). https://doi.org/10.1007/978-3-030-89738-3_24-1
4. Chen, Z., et al.: Autonomous social distancing in urban environments using a quadruped robot. IEEE Access **9**, 8392–8403 (2021). https://doi.org/10.1109/ACCESS.2021.3049426
5. Cheng, X., Kumar, A., Pathak, D.: Legs as manipulator: pushing quadrupedal agility beyond locomotion. arXiv preprint arXiv:2303.11330 (2023). http://arxiv.org/abs/2303.11330
6. Gupta, R., Shin, H., Norman, E., Stephens, K.K., Lu, N., Sentis, L.: Human stress response and perceived safety during encounters with quadruped robots. arXiv preprint arXiv:2403.17270 (2024). http://arxiv.org/abs/2403.17270
7. Hashimoto, N., Hagens, E., Zgonnikov, A., Lupetti, M.L.: Safe spot: perceived safety of dominant and submissive appearances of quadruped robots in human-robot interactions (2024). http://arxiv.org/abs/2403.05400

8. Hauser, E., et al.: What's that robot doing here?: perceptions of incidental encounters with autonomous quadruped robots. In: Proceedings of the ACM International Conference (2023). https://doi.org/10.1145/3597512.3599707
9. Moses, J., Ford, G.: See spot save lives: fear, humanitarianism, and war in the development of robot quadrupeds. Digit. War 64–76 (2021). https://doi.org/10.1057/s42984-021-00037-y
10. Nomura, T., Suzuki, T., Kanda, T., Kato, K.: Measurement of negative attitudes toward robots. Interact. Stud. Soc. Behav. Commun. Biol. Artif. Syst. **7**(3), 437–454 (2006). https://doi.org/10.1075/is.7.3.14nom
11. Prete, A.D., Mansard, N., Ramos, O.E., Stasse, O., Nori, F.: Implementing torque control with high-ratio gear boxes and without joint-torque sensors. Int. J. Humanoid Rob. **13**(1), 1550044 (2016). https://doi.org/10.1142/S0219843615500449
12. Tabita, M., Recchiuto, C.T., Simetti, E., Sgorbissa, A.: Pedipulation in quadruped robots using a heuristic inverse kinematics solver. Thechnical report (2025). https://rice.dibris.unige.it/technical-reports/
13. The jamovi project: jamovi. (version 2.6) [computer software] (2024). https://www.jamovi.org

Improving Engagement in Robot Lecture Through Personality Expressed by Teacher Robot

So Sasaki(✉) and Akihiro Kashihara

The University of Electro-Communications, Chofu, Tokyo 182-8585, Japan
so.sasaki@uec.ac.jp, akihiro.kashihara@inf.uec.ac.jp

Abstract. In a lecture, it is essential to stimulate learners' interest in the lecture content, which brings about their engagement. However, it would be challenging. In this work, we focus on personality traits that teachers express throughout their lecture. Their non-verbal behavior including gaze, gesture, facial expression, and personal episodes related to the lecture content often expresses their personality traits. Learners are expected to be interested in them, which drives their interest in the lecture content. To express different personality traits for different learners, we focused on a social robot as a teacher. In this paper, we introduce the design of personality traits for a robot used in a lecture. We also demonstrate a robot lecture system in which a teacher robot expresses specific personality traits designed in advance to conduct a lecture. The results of a case study with the system suggested that the teacher robot had the potential to improve learners' engagement.

Keywords: Social robots · Robot lecture · Engagement · Personality traits design

1 Introduction

To improve learners' engagement in lecture, teachers should attract their attention and promote their comprehension. This requires teachers to prepare well-organized lecture contents and use proper non-verbal behavior, such as gaze, gestures, and para-language during lectures. It is also effective to estimate their concentration and comprehension to adjust the lecture process [1]. However, it is not easy even for skilled teachers to attract learners' attention and estimate their states in lecture. We have accordingly proposed a robot lecture system, in which a social robot diagnoses human teachers' improper and insufficient behavior to reconstruct it, then conducts a lecture with the reconstructed behavior [2]. We have also developed an interactive robot lecture system that estimates learners' states using sensors to recover their attention during lecture [3].

On the other hand, it is also important to promote learners' interest in the lecture content. In a lecture, learners often become interested in teachers' personality traits when they explain with emotion expressed through various body movements, facial expressions, and personal episodes related to the lecture content [4,5].

The suitability of teachers' personality traits would vary depending on individual learners. It is accordingly necessary for teachers to adjust their personality traits when presenting their personal episodes. It would be impossible for human teachers. However, social robots could change their behavior and facial expression for the personality adjustment [6].

In this paper, we describe a robot lecture system we have been developing, which can express personality traits via its behavior and personal episodes that are designed in advance. This paper also reports a case study using the system, in which we investigated the influences of expressed personality traits on learners' interest and engagement in a lecture. The results suggested the possibility that the robot as a teacher (teacher robot) expressing high extraversion and high conscientiousness could improve learners' engagement in the robot lecture.

2 Expressive Personality and Engagement

2.1 Personality of Teachers

Personality is often described in terms of five traits known as the Big Five [7]. The traits are typically labeled as extraversion, agreeableness, conscientiousness, neuroticism, and openness. Many studies used the Big Five to explain various relationships with personality traits. For example, a study investigating teacher characteristics to predict instructional quality found that teachers with high extraversion and high conscientiousness tended to receive high ratings for educational quality [8]. Another study demonstrated that teachers with high extraversion received higher scores in teaching evaluation [9]. In addition, a study on the relationship between EFL teachers' personality traits and educational effects showed that extraverted teachers can create a warm and positive atmosphere, which improves students' motivation to speak in English [10]. From these studies, extraversion and conscientiousness are considered important traits in a lecture context.

In our previous work, we proposed a model of empathy, indicating that episodes shared by a learning partner robot have a positive effect on changing learners' attitudes toward learning [11]. When teachers express their personality traits with episodes related to the lecture contents, learners are also expected to empathize with them. Such empathy could promote understanding of the lecture content as familiar and interesting.

2.2 Personality of the Robot

A social robot is suitable for expressing particular personality traits because its behavior including gaze, para-language, and facial expression can be designed. Altering its voice (including tone, pitch, and accent), body movements and facial expressions allows it to demonstrate different personality traits [6].

In order to appropriately interact with learners, it is necessary for a social robot to have personality traits tailored to the interaction context [12,13]. Related work has shown that robot personality traits influence human behavior in various situations [14]. In a study on a learning partner robot for English communication, a robot was designed to express high extraversion and high conscientiousness to act as a friend who exclusively speaks English to motivate Japanese elementary school students [15]. This study demonstrates that the expression of personality traits has a positive effect on human-robot interaction. Since the robot lecture involves human-robot interactions, the personality traits of a teacher robot could also influence learners' interest and engagement, and should be appropriately designed in the lecture context.

3 Approach

Following the above discussion, our research question is what kind of personality traits a teacher robot should have for improve learners' interest and engagement in lectures. To approach this question, we have designed a teacher robot's personality traits and developed a robot lecture system.

3.1 Design of Robot Lecture System

In developing the robot lecture system, we followed our model of engagement derived from learner-robot interaction [16], as shown in Fig. 1. This model demonstrates how to control robot behavior related to anthropomorphic tendency and embodiment for enhancing learners' engagement [17]. It also expects communication patterns suitable for the engagement enhancement. Roles and personality traits as anthropomorphic tendency are particularly significant elements, as they have a great influence on the design of other elements. By controlling the behavior of the robot according to its personality traits, we can facilitate communication between learners and the robot. In this paper, we have

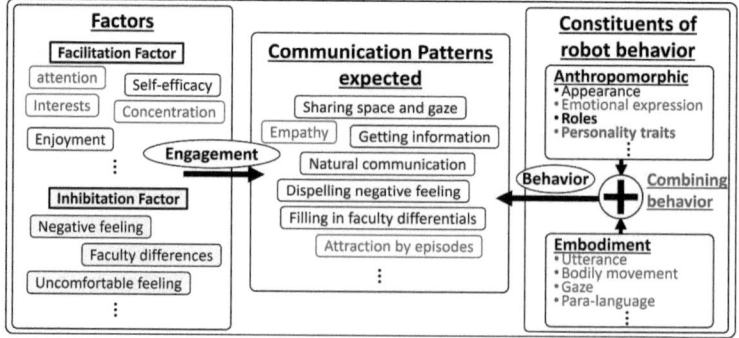

Fig. 1. A model of engagement (modified from [16,17])

designed the correspondence between the personality traits based on Big Five [7] and robot's behavior elements to be controlled as shown in Table 1. Controlling the behavior elements allows the robot to express the corresponding personality traits.

Table 1. Personality traits and behavior

Personality traits [7]		Behavior elements
Extraversion	Sociability, talkativeness	Emotional expression, utterance, bodily movement, gaze, para-language
Conscientiousness	Orderliness, seriousness	Utterance, para-language
Agreeableness	Attentiveness, empathy	Emotional expression, utterance, gaze
Neuroticism	Mental stability, impulsiveness	Emotional expression, utterance, bodily movement, gaze, para-language
Openness	Experience variety, curiosity	Emotional expression, utterance

3.2 Designing Personality Traits of Teacher Robot

In a lecture context, robot's personality traits can be expressed through not only its behavior but also episodes related to the lecture contents. For instance, when a teacher robot shares an episode about learning from failure with a regretful face, learners could think that it is diligent. When a teacher robot also shares an episode about failure due to its laziness with a smile, learners would think it is not strict.

Table 2. Personality expressions in lecture based on personality traits

Personality traits	Personality expression in lecture
Extraversion	Speech tone and speed, frequency of eye contact, gaze direction, frequency in emotional expression, sociability degree of episode content
Conscientiousness	Fillers, fluency in explanation, diligence degree of episode content

In this work, we used extraversion and conscientiousness to design robot personality traits because these are viewed as the main traits that influence learners' engagement [8–10]. Table 2 shows the traits applied in the lecture and the variables in lecture behavior elements to be altered for expressing the corresponding personality traits.

Regarding extraversion, for instance, the robot speaks clearly, and maintains eye contact with learners when it attempts to express high extraversion. It also shares a personal episode including sociable content with varied facial expressions to enhance their interest. Conversely, the robot speaks in a mumbling and diffident tone, and maintains a downcast gaze when it attempts to express low extraversion. It also shares an episode including unsociable content with little facial expression.

Regarding conscientiousness, in addition, the robot conducts fluent explanations including a well-structured flow that are easy to understand when it attempts to express high conscientiousness. It also shares a diligent episode from school days. Conversely, the robot explains and shares a lazy episode with lots of fillers when it attempts to express low conscientiousness.

4 Case Study

4.1 Purpose and Procedure

We conducted a case study using the robot lecture system to ascertain whether a personality-designed teacher robot could increase learners' engagement and interest in its lecture. We have established three conditions: H-condition, L-condition, and N-condition (as a control condition), as shown in Table 3. In H-condition, the teacher robot was designed to express high extraversion and high conscientiousness. In L-condition, the teacher robot was designed to express low extraversion and low conscientiousness. In N-condition, the teacher robot was not specially designed for its personality traits. This case study was conducted with the approval of the Human Research Ethics Review Committee at the University of Electro-Communications.

Table 3. Personality expressions in lecture based on personality traits

H-condition	L-condition	N-condition
Extraversion	Extraversion	Not specially designed
- Clear tone	- Mumbling and diffident tone	
- Maintain eye contact	- Maintain downcast gaze	
- Varied facial expression		
Conscientiousness	Conscientiousness	
- Well-constructed explanation	- Lots of fillers	
- Diligent epsodes	- Lazy episodes	

In this study, we set up the following three hypotheses based on the assumption that learners prefer teachers expressing high extraversion and high conscientiousness [19].

H1: The teacher robot in H-condition enhances learners' interest in the lecture content.
H2: The teacher robot in H-condition promotes learners' attention to the lecture and their understanding of the content.
H3: The teacher robot with the designed personality traits enhances learners' engagement in the lecture.

We investigated the effects of personality traits design using questionnaires, comprehension test, and gaze data recorded during the lecture. We prepared two short lectures, "What is Learning Activity?" and "Learning Support System Design," derived from our university course, "Learning Informatics". The participants were 23 graduate and undergraduate students in informatics and engineering disciplines, none of whom had taken the course. They were randomly assigned to three groups: HL-group, LH-group, N-group. HL-group and LH-group each had 8 participants, while N-group had 7 participants.

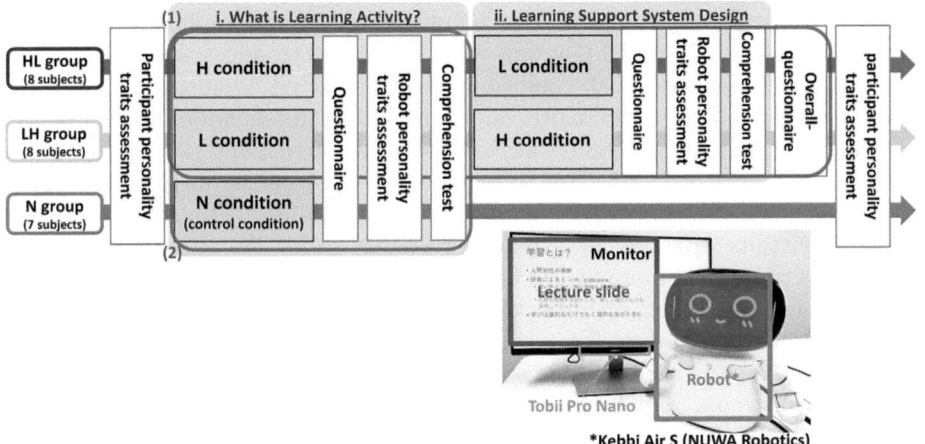

Fig. 2. Procedure of the case study and setup of robot lecture.

Figure 2 illustrates the procedure of the case study. First, we conducted a participant personality traits assessment using the TIPI-J [18]. The TIPI-J is a 10-item measure of the Big Five. It asked the participants to evaluate their own personality traits using 2-item inventories for each trait. For example, one item from the inventories was "I see myself as extraverted and enthusiastic." Each item was answered with a 7-point Likert scale. Each trait is accordingly rated on a scale with scores ranging from 2 to 14. Second, the robot had a lecture under each condition, and we conducted a questionnaire using 5-point Likert scale as shown in Table 4, robot personality traits assessment using the TIPI-J, and a comprehension test with free description. In the robot personality traits assessment, the participants were asked to rate the robot personality traits

Table 4. Questionnaire

Q1	Did you think that the lecture was easy to understand?
Q2	Were you able to concentrate on the lecture?
Q3	Did you feel engrossed in the robot's explanation?
Q4	Did you feel the lecture fly by?
Q5	Did you think that the robot was attractive as a teacher?
Q6	Did the lecture spark your interest in learning more about Learning Informatics?
Q7	Did this robot improve your interest in the lecture contents?

using the TIPI-J. The comprehension test was graded at 20 points. Next, the participants in HL-group and LH-group attended the second lecture ("Learning Support System Design"), and completed a questionnaire, a robot personality traits assessment, and comprehension test. In order to counterbalance the order effects of the conditions, we set the two groups, HL-group and LH-group as shown in Fig. 2. Subsequently, we conducted an overall questionnaire, in which the participants in HL-group and LH-group were also asked to select which of the two conditions (H-condition or L-condition) they perceived as superior, using the same items as in the questionnaire, and to provide a justification in free description for their selection. Finally, we conducted a participant personality traits assessment. The reason why we conducted this assessment in this case study was because we also aimed to examine the compatibility of the designed robot personality traits with the participant personality traits. We also conducted this assessment twice in the procedure to ensure accuracy by averaging the results.

As for H1 and H2, a within-subject comparison was conducted between H-condition and L-condition. To achieve the counterbalance, HL-group and LH-group were arranged as illustrated in part (1) of Fig. 2. For H3, using N-condition as a control group, a between-subject comparison was performed among N-condition, H-condition, and L-condition. The analysis was based on the data collected during the first lecture in part (2) of Fig. 2.

We utilized Kebbi Air S (NUWA Robotics) as the teacher robot, a monitor for lecture slide projection, and a Tobii Pro Nano eye tracker to capture the participants' gaze shown in Fig. 2. Gaze data falling within the areas shown in Fig. 2 were classified as visual attention to either the slides or the robot. Furthermore, the sum of time spent looking at either the slides or the robot was calculated as the time spent focusing on the lecture. For the analysis, the proportion of each type of time spent relative to the total lecture time was calculated and used.

4.2 Results

From the robot personality traits assessment for the first lecture, the robot in H-condition was rated with scores of 10.50 for extraversion and 11.00 for conscientiousness. The robot in L-condition was rated with scores of 7.50 for extraversion and 7.00 for conscientiousness. N-condition was rated as the intermediate between H- and L-conditions (extraversion: 9.00, conscientiousness: 10.43). Regarding extraversion, from the Tukey HSD test, there is a tendency toward a significant difference between H- and L-conditions ($p = 0.054$). Regarding conscientiousness, there is also a significant difference ($p = 0.0004$). In addition, from the Tukey HSD test, there is a significant difference between N- and L-conditions ($p = 0.0024$). Furthermore, the results of the robot personality traits assessment for the second lecture also indicated that the robot in H-condition was rated with scores of 11.25 for extraversion and 9.50 for conscientiousness. The robot in L-condition was also rated with scores of 4.50 for extraversion and 5.00 for conscientiousness. From the two-tailed t-test, significant differences were observed (extraversion: $t(15) = 8.04$, $p = 0.0000013$, conscientiousness: $t(15) = 3.91$, $p = 0.0016$). These results suggest the appropriateness of personality trait design.

Regarding H1, Fig. 3 shows the results of the comparison between average scores of the questionnaires for both lectures in H- and L-conditions. From the two-tailed t-test, significant differences were observed in Q5 ($t(7) = 2.74$, $p = 0.015$, Cohen's $d = 0.68$) and Q7 ($t(7) = 3.34$, $p = 0.0045$, Cohen's $d = 0.83$). Figure 4 shows the results of the comparison between H- and L-conditions in the overall questionnaire. From the two-tailed exact binomial test, significant differences were found in the choice of H-condition in Q5 ($p = 0.00052$) and Q6 ($p = 0.0042$). A tendency toward a significant difference was also noted in Q7 ($p = 0.077$). Based on the results of Q5-Q7 in both the questionnaire and overall questionnaire, the lectures delivered by the robot with high extraversion and high conscientiousness increased the participants' interest in the robot and the lecture content, which supports H1.

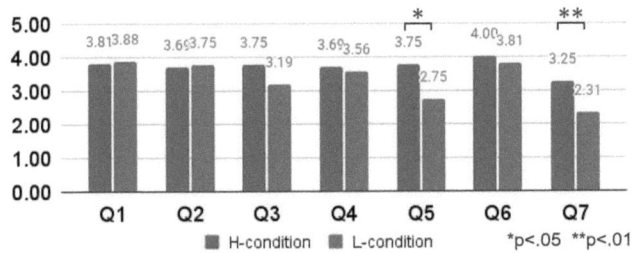

Fig. 3. Average scores of the questionnaire (H-/L-conditions).

Regarding H2, Fig. 4 indicates a significant difference in the choice of H-condition in Q3 ($p = 0.0042$) according to the two-tailed exact binomial test. A tendency toward a significant difference was also observed in Q2 ($p = 0.077$). These results suggest that the lectures delivered by the robot with high extraversion and conscientiousness subjectively enhanced the participants' attention during the lecture, which partially supports H2.

On the other hand, no significant differences were found in the average comprehension test scores for both lectures (H-condition: 9.00, L-condition: 8.38).

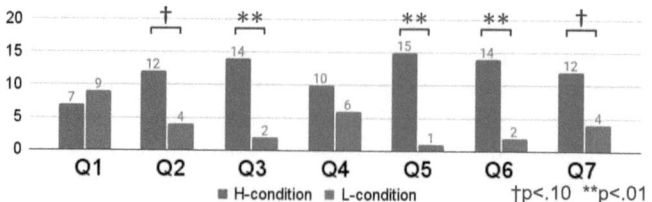

Fig. 4. Results of the overall questionnaire (H-/L-conditions).

As shown in Fig. 5, the gaze data revealed that concentration on the slides and on the overall lecture was significantly lower in H-condition (slides: $t(7) = 2.94$, $p = 0.010$, Cohen's $d = 0.74$, lecture: $t(7) = 3.73$, $p = 0.0020$ Cohen's $d = 0.93$). These results show that the robot in H-condition did not objectively enhance the participants' attention and comprehension, which seems not to support H2.

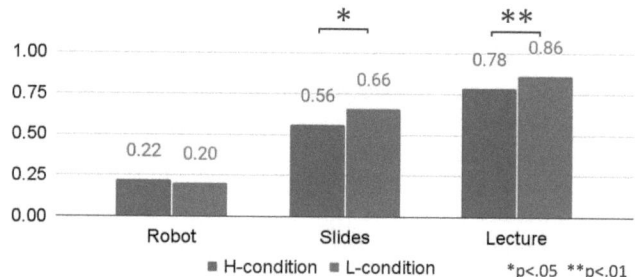

Fig. 5. Average gaze rates (H-/L-conditions).

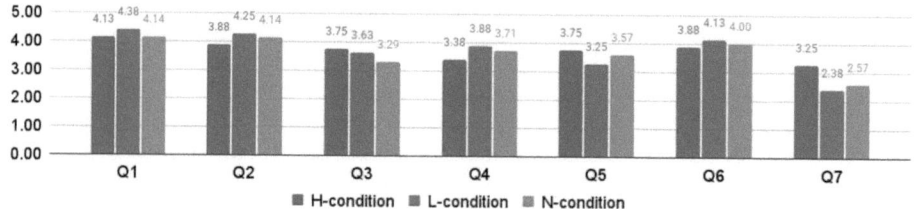

Fig. 6. Average scores of the questionnaire (H-/L-/N-conditions).

Regarding H3, Fig. 6 shows a comparison of the questionnaire for the first lecture among the three conditions. From the two-tailed Dunnett's test, no significant differences were found. This shows that there is no difference between the conditions with no specifically designed personality traits (N-condition) and the designed personality traits (H- and L-conditions). The results of the comprehension test for the first lecture also show no significant differences (H-condition: 10.75, L-condition: 7.25, N-condition: 9.86). On the other hand, as for the gaze data, in the comparison between N- and H-conditions, the participants in H-condition concentrated more on the robot ($t(13) = 3.36$, $p = 0.0059$) but less on the slides ($t(13) = 3.77$, $p = 0.0023$) and the overall lecture ($t(13) = 2.67$, $p = 0.027$). Conversely, the participants in L-condition concentrated more on the robot ($t(13) = 2.67$, $p = 0.027$) without a decrease in their concentration on the slides and the lecture. These results suggest that the robots in L-conditions increased the participants' concentration on the robot, which may attract learners' attention to enhance their engagement. Overall, we think H3 is partially supported.

4.3 Discussion

According to the questionnaire shown in Fig. 3, all the average scores (excluding the items with significant differences) are above 3. It would be difficult to compare H- and L-conditions appropriately only with the results. From the overall questionnaire shown in Fig. 4, on the other hand, we can ascertain H1 and H2, as it directly reflects the participants' comparative evaluation.

As for H2, we examined the free description in the overall questionnaire to understand why the participants in L-condition exhibited higher attentiveness and concentration on the slides and lectures. The participants who preferred to L-condition made some comments such as 'The robot was calm, so I could concentrate on the lecture', 'The robot was gloomy, which made me wonder if this guy was OK? That helped me concentrate on the lecture', and 'Fewer gestures helped me read the slides.' These comments show that the lack of accent and sophisticated expression in L-condition contributed to attracting attention to the slides and the lecture. This suggests that some participants are more compatible with teachers expressing personality traits in L-condition.

Regarding H3, the results of the questionnaire for the first lecture presented in Fig. 6 show that almost all the scores are above 3. It would be accordingly difficult to compare N-condition with the other conditions. However, it is worth noting that Q3 and Q7 in N-condition show lower scores compared to the other conditions. In this case study, the robot conducted only a ten-minute lecture. There is a possibility that the difference would become more obvious with longer lectures or plural lectures with the same robot.

Regarding gaze data, the participants were relatively unfocused on the lecture in H-condition. In this case study, the robot in H-condition used extensive body movement. As suggested by the comments discussed for H2, some participants might prefer calm behavior to the large and noisy motion. It is important not to disturb the learners' concentration during a lecture. We should accordingly refine the expression of personality traits using less motion depending on individual learners. In the following, let us consider the compatibility of the robot personality traits with the participant personality traits by analyzing correlations among the results of the questionnaire, comprehension test scores, and gaze data. The participant personality traits were measured using the average of the two participant personality traits assessments. From an analysis of correlation between the comprehension test scores and other data, only moderate correlation was observed. Table 5 shows the analyses of correlation between the participants' personality traits and other data (including gaze, Q1, and Q5 in the questionnaire) where the coefficient values were greater than moderate. Regarding the participants' extraversion, the results demonstrate that the participants with high extraversion tended to concentrate less on the lecture in both conditions (H-condition: $r = -0.58$, L-condition: $r = -0.49$). In particular, the participants in H-condition were relatively unfocused on the slides ($r = -0.55$). However, the correlation between extraversion and Q5 in the questionnaire indicates that they were attracted to the teacher robot ($r = 0.42$).

Table 5. Trends observed in each participant's personality traits

Participants' traits	Data correlated with participants' traits	Pearson correlations	
		H-condition	L-condition
Extraversion	Gaze at lecture	−0.58	−0.49
	Gaze at slides	−0.55	−0.37
	Q5 in questionnaire	0.42	−0.23
Conscientiousness	Gaze at robot	0.41	0.14
	Gaze at slides	−0.41	0.14
	Q1 in questionnaire	0.20	-0.50
Neuroticism	Gaze at robot	−0.44	−0.43
	Gaze at slides	0.59	0.34
	Gaze at lecture	0.52	0.13

In addition, the participants with high conscientiousness concentrated on the robot in H-condition ($r = 0.41$), and showed difficulty focusing on the slides ($r = -0.41$). Therefore, these participants appear to be more significantly influenced by the teacher robot's performance and personality traits. The high conscientiousness participants also perceived the explanation provided by the robot in L-condition as unclear ($r = -0.50$). This may suggest that such compatibility between the teacher and learners should be avoided for improving their engagement in lectures. As for neuroticism, the participants with high neuroticism did not maintain their attention to the robot in either condition (H-condition: $r = -0.44$, L-condition: $r = -0.43$). However, the participants with high neuroticism in H-condition could concentrate on the slides ($r = 0.59$) and the lecture ($r = 0.52$). These results are consistent with the related work that shows people with high neuroticism tend to exhibit low engagement when interacting with a robot [14].

5 Conclusion

In this work, we designed the personality traits of a teacher robot to be expressed in lectures and investigated their influence on learners' engagement and interest. The case study revealed that a teacher robot exhibiting high extraversion and high conscientiousness can enhance learners' engagement in lectures. Conversely, some learners preferred a teacher robot with low extraversion and low conscientiousness to concentrate on lectures. This suggests the importance of designing personality traits appropriate for individual learners to enhance their engagement. In the future, we need further investigation to ascertain the effects of longer lectures or long-term courses. We also plan to consider the compatibility of the teacher robot's personality traits with learners' personality traits to conduct more appropriate robot lectures.

Acknowledgments. This work was supported in part by JSPS KAKENHI (grant number 23K28195).

Disclosure of Interests. The authors have no competing interests to declare that are relevant to the content of this article.

References

1. Melinger, A., Levelt, W.J.M.: Gesture and the communicative intention of the speaker. Gesture **4**(2), 119–141 (2004). https://doi.org/10.1075/gest.4.2.02mel
2. Ishino, T., Goto, M., Kashihara, A.: Robot lecture for enhancing presentation in lecture. Res. Pract. Technol. Enhanc. Learn. **17**(1), 1–22 (2022). https://doi.org/10.1186/s41039-021-00176-6
3. Shimazaki, T., Sugawara, A., Goto, M., Kashihara, A.: An interactive robot lecture system embedding lecture behavior model. In: Zaphiris P., Ioannou A. (eds.) Learning and Collaboration Technologies. Novel Technological Environments, pp. 224–236. Springer (2022)
4. Jere, B.: Synthesis of research on strategies for motivating students to learn. Educ. Leadersh. **45**(2), 40–48 (1987)
5. Figen, U.-C., Kadriye, K.-U.: Determining interpersonal attraction in educational environment and the relation with motivation. Int. J. New Trends Educ. Implic. **2**(1), 47–56 (2011)
6. Goetz, J., Kiesler, S.: Cooperation with a robotic assistant. In: CHI 2002 Extended Abstracts on Human Factors in Computing Systems, pp. 578–579 (2002)
7. John, O.P., Srivastava, S.: The big five trait taxonomy: history, measurement, and theoretical perspectives. In: Handbook of Personality: Theory and Research, 2nd edn, pp. 102–138. Guilford Press, New York (1999)
8. Baier, F., Decker, A.-T., Voss, T., Kleickmann, T., Klusmann, U., Kunter, M.: What makes a good teacher? The relative importance of mathematics teachers' cognitive ability, personality, knowledge, beliefs, and motivation for instructional quality. Br. J. Educ. Psychol. **89**(4), 767–786 (2019)
9. Murray, H.G., Rushton, J.P., Paunonen, S.V.: Teacher personality traits and student instructional ratings in six types of university courses. J. Educ. Psychol. **82**(2), 250–261 (1990)

10. Zafarghandi, A.M., Salehi, S., Sabet, M.K.: The effect of EFL teachers' extrovert and introvert personality on their instructional immediacy. Int. J. Appl. Linguist. English Lit. **5**(1), 57–64 (2016)
11. Sasaki, S., Kashihara, A.: Designing interaction scenario for alleviating persistence in learning strategies. In: International Conference on Computers in Education (2024)
12. Woods, S., Dautenhahn, K., Kaouri, C., Boekhorst, R., Koay, K.L.: Is this robot like me? Links between human and robot personality traits. In: 5th IEEE-RAS International Conference on Humanoid Robots, pp. 375–380 (2005)
13. Chowdhury, A., Ahtinen, A., Wu, C.-H., Väänänen, K., Taibi, D., Pieters, R.: Exploring the personality design space of robots: personalities and design implications for non-anthropomorphic wellness robots. In: 2023 32nd IEEE International Conference on Robot and Human Interactive Communication (RO-MAN), pp. 2344–2351 (2023)
14. Kabacińska, K., Dosso, J.A., Vu, K., Prescott, T.J., Robillard, J.M.: Influence of user personality traits and attitudes on interactions with social robots: systematic review. Collabra Psychol. **11**(1), 129175 (2025)
15. Kanda, T., Hirano, T., Eaton, D., Ishiguro, H.: Interactive robots as social partners and peer tutors for children: a field trial. Hum. Comput. Interact. (Special Issues Hum.-Robot Interact.) **19**, 61–84 (2004)
16. Kashihara, A.: Research on informatics for learning and education. Inf. Technol. Educ. Learn. **1**(1), p002 (2021)
17. Sasaki, S., Kashihara, A.: Improving engagement in robot lectures through empathy with teacher robot personality. JSiSE Res. Rep. **39**(6), 105–112 (2025). (in Japanese)
18. Oshio, A., Abe, S., Cutrone, P.: Development, reliability, and validity of the Japanese version of ten item personality inventory (TIPI-J). Jpn. J. Pers. **21**(1) 40–52 (2012). (in Japanese)
19. Kim, L.E., Jörg, V., Klassen, R.M.: A meta-analysis of the effects of teacher personality on teacher effectiveness and burnout. Educ. Psychol. Rev. **31**(1), 163–195 (2019)

Trust, Autonomy, and Cognitive Models

Dynamic Trust Modeling in Robot Teleoperation Using a Bayesian Approach

Juan José García Cárdenas[✉] and Adriana Tapus

Autonomous Systems and Robotics Lab/U2IS, ENSTA, Institute Polytechnique de Paris, Paris, France
{juan-jose.garcia,adriana.tapus}@ensta.fr

Abstract. This paper aims to develop a dynamic trust prediction model for teleoperated robotic systems in human-robot interaction (HRI) scenarios. Our model captures trust fluctuations influenced by task performance, cognitive load, and physiological responses. In our experiments, participants teleoperated a robotic arm under three conditions: without guidance (C1), with verbal guidance (C2), and with a combination of verbal and visual guidance (C3). Trust levels were measured after each condition, and cognitive load was assessed using the NASA TLX and physiological sensors. Our dynamic Bayesian network model demonstrated significant improvements in predictive accuracy, achieving 89% accuracy, 91% precision, 92.5% recall, and an 84% F1 score. The results indicated significant variations in trust levels across conditions ($p < 0.032$) and an inverse relationship between cognitive load and trust ($r = -0.632$, $p < 0.01$). The model effectively captured the dynamic interplay between trust and cognitive load, highlighting the importance of adaptive system design to maintain high trust levels. By leveraging physiological indicators and performance metrics, the dynamic trust model provides a nuanced understanding of trust evolution, facilitating better human-robot collaboration.

Keywords: Dynamic Trust Model · Bayesian network · Cognitive load · Teleoperation · Robots

1 Introduction

The dynamic nature of trust in human-robot interaction (HRI) is essential for the efficient and safe operation of teleoperated robotic systems. Trust is not a static attribute; it varies based on robot performance, operator experience, and interaction conditions, as noted by some authors [6]. Accurately understanding and predicting the trust fluctuations can greatly enhance the design and operation of robotic systems in various high-risk environments.

Previous research has explored various methods for modeling trust in HRI. The authors in [5,6] proposed a Bayesian inference approach to predict trust dynamics, highlighting the significant impact of recent interactions on trust levels. Manzey et al. [4] found that task performance and system reliability are critical factors influencing trust, with negative experiences having a more substantial impact than positive experiences. In [7], trust in automation was examined, highlighting the need for dynamic models that consider historical performance and the current usage context to inform the design of adaptive systems. Ahmad et al. [1] demonstrated an inverse relationship between cognitive load and trust, indicating that higher cognitive load often leads to lower trust in robotic systems. These studies highlight the importance of a dynamic approach to trust modeling, which can adapt to the changing nature of HRI and provide real-time predictions to improve system performance and user experience.

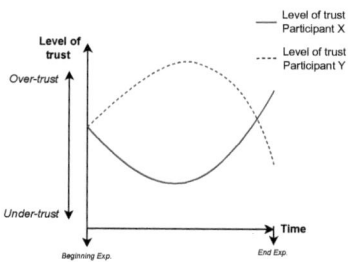

Fig. 1. Dynamic view of trust of different agents throughout the experiment [6].

Figure 1 illustrates the evolution of trust over time. Initially high, trust can quickly decline without sufficient guidance or if the robot's performance seems unreliable. Conversely, clear and effective communication enhances trust. For instance, Participant X's trust dropped due to insufficient teleoperation guidance, while Participant Y's trust increased with comprehensive support. This highlights how trust dynamics vary, even among users with similar initial trust levels [5,6]. Although cognitive load is a significant factor influencing the human workload index, our primary objective is to predict trust. Cognitive load, measured using the NASA Task Load Index (TLX) and physiological sensors, varies across different conditions. In scenarios with less guidance, participants exhibited higher cognitive loads, suggesting increased uncertainty and mental effort. The increased cognitive load in low-guidance conditions highlights participants' difficulty in adapting and performing tasks efficiently, affecting their trust in the teleoperated robotic system. Recognizing these variations is crucial for predicting trust dynamics and enhancing system design and operation.

By investigating the dynamic relationship between trust and cognitive load, our goal is to develop a model that can predict real-time trust levels during human-robot interactions. Such a model could greatly enhance the adaptive capabilities of robotic systems, making them more responsive to human operators' needs and improving the overall efficiency and safety of these interactions.

2 Related Work

Investigating trust dynamics in human-robot interaction (HRI) is crucial for enhancing the effectiveness and safety of teleoperated robotic systems. Numerous researchers have concentrated on modeling and predicting trust in these settings, using diverse methodologies to capture the intricacies of trust evolution over time. The authors in [5], propose a personalized trust prediction model that aims to predict the trust dynamics of individual human agents interacting with robotic agents over time. The model takes into account the robot's performance history and the human agent's past trust levels, using a Bayesian framework to infer trust dynamics. Their findings highlight that trust is significantly influenced by recent interactions, with negative experiences having a more substantial impact than positive ones. Modeling trust with a beta distribution captures its bounded nature and effectively represents the dynamics of trust in repeated interactions [5,6]. Another relevant study by Manzey et al. [4], highlights how trust in automation is affected by task performance and system reliability. The researchers found that negative experiences, such as system errors, disproportionately reduce trust compared to incremental increases resulting from positive experiences. This finding is consistent with the observations of found in [5,6] and highlights the importance of mitigating negative interactions to maintain trust in robotic systems.

Lee and See [7] provide a comprehensive review of trust in automation, detailing how trust evolves as a function of system performance, user characteristics, and situational context. Furthermore, the authors in [24] explored the dynamics of trust in more detail by studying how repeated interactions with autonomous agents lead to more stable levels of trust. The relationship between trust and cognitive load has also been explored in several studies. Ahmad et al. [1] found an inversely proportional relationship between trust and cognitive load, indicating that as cognitive load increases, trust in the robotic system decreases. Their results suggest that high cognitive load, often caused by complex tasks or poor system performance, leads to lower levels of trust in robots [1]. Hart et al. [20] further explored the impact of prior user experience on cognitive load and trust, and found that users with prior experience in similar tasks reported lower cognitive load and higher trust in the robotic system.

Measuring cognitive load and trust in HRI has been the focus of several researchers, employing a variety of physiological and subjective measures. Common physiological measures include galvanic skin response (GSR), pupil diameter, and heart rate variability. For example, pupil diameter has been used as an indicator of cognitive load, and larger pupil dilation is associated with more intense cognitive processing [11]. Self-report measures such as the NASA-TLX questionnaire are also widely used to assess cognitive workload. Trust is often measured using validated scales such as the Trust Perception Scale-HRI, which assesses multiple dimensions of trust, including competence and moral trust [18].

Overall, these studies emphasize the importance of understanding and modeling trust dynamics in HRI. By employing methodologies like Bayesian inference and accounting for the effects of both positive and negative interactions, researchers can develop more trustworthy and adaptable robotic systems. This knowledge is crucial for enhancing human-robot collaboration across various applications, such as remote surgery, hazardous materials handling, and search and rescue missions.

3 Methodology

The objective of this study is to develop a dynamic trust prediction model tailored for teleoperated robotic systems. This model aims to infer and predict the trust level of a human operator by analyzing various factors observed during their interaction with the robotic system under different conditions. Key factors include the operator's physiological responses, task performance metrics, and interaction behaviors. By accurately predicting trust levels, we seek to enhance the efficiency, safety, and reliability of human-robot interactions.

In teleoperated robotic systems, trust plays a crucial role in influencing operator performance and overall task success [16]. In our scenario, a human operator remotely controls a robotic arm to complete a specific task, such as placing objects into a box. During the experiment, we measure the following variables:

- T_m: The user's trust level at moment m, is a discrete variable categorized into four levels according to the Human-Robot Interaction Trust Scale (HRITS) [12]: High Trust (4), Moderate Trust (3), Low Trust (2), and Very Low Trust (1). The Human-Robot Interaction Trust Scale (HRITS) is a validated questionnaire designed to measure users' trust in robotic systems. This scale assesses various dimensions of trust, including the reliability, predictability, and perceived competence of the robot. It is commonly used in studies involving human-robot interaction (HRI) to evaluate how different factors, such as robot behavior and performance, influence users' trust [12].
- CL_m: The cognitive load of the operator at moment m, is a discrete variable measured using the NASA Task Load Index (NASA-TLX) [19]. It can be categorized as Low (1), Medium (2), Somewhat High (3), High (4), or Very High (5). The NASA Task Load Index (NASA-TLX) is a widely used tool for assessing subjective cognitive workload. Developed by the Human Performance Group at NASA's Ames Research Center, it evaluates perceived workload across six dimensions, providing a comprehensive measure of cognitive load during task performance [15,19].
- GSR_m: The Galvanic Skin Response (GSR) at moment m, also referred to as Electrodermal Activity (EDA), is a measure of the electrical conductance of the skin, which varies with its moisture level. This physiological signal is widely utilized in psychological studies and stress-related research to detect emotional and physiological arousal. GSR is particularly sensitive to changes in the sympathetic nervous system, which is activated during stress. GSR readings are continuous but can be discretized into intervals for practical applications. Based on existing literature, GSR can be categorized into the following ranges:

- **Low Arousal (Relaxed State) - 1**: GSR values are low in a relaxed state, typically with a skin conductance level (SCL) below 3500–4000 μS/min.
- **Moderate Arousal (Moderate Cognitive Load State) - 2**: This intermediate range indicates a neutral state, with an SCL between 4000–5500 μS/min.
- **High Arousal (Higher Cognitive Load State) - 3**: High GSR values are associated with stress or anxiety, with an SCL above 5500 μS/min.

These categorizations are supported by research on emotion recognition using GSR signals from the dataset presented in [21], stress detection using GSR sensors as outlined in [17], and the analysis of stress patterns from GSR data described in [2].

- BR_m: The blinking rate at moment m, measured in blinks per minute, serves as a crucial physiological indicator for assessing stress and cognitive load. Blinking, a semi-voluntary action, is influenced by emotional states, cognitive processes, and environmental conditions. Blink rates can be classified into different ranges depending on the relaxed or stressed state of the individual. According to existing research, these ranges are:
  - **Low blink rate (Relaxed State) - 1**: The typical blink rate ranges from 15 to 25 blinks per minute in a relaxed state [14].
  - **Moderate blink rate (Engaged State) - 2**: During cognitive activities, such as conversations or moderate tasks, the blink rate increases to approximately 26 to 36 blinks per minute [14].
  - **High blink rate (Stressed State) - 3**: Under stress, blink rate can highly increase, often doubling to around 40 blinks per minute [23].

  These classifications are supported by research on blink patterns under stress and their link to cognitive load [9,23].

- P_m: The performance variable at moment m is used to measure the success or failure of the user in completing a given task. It is a binary variable with two possible values:
  - **Success (1)**: Indicates that the user successfully completed the task within the given constraints and criteria.
  - **Failure (0)**: Indicates that the user did not complete the task successfully, either due to time constraints, errors, or inability to achieve the task objectives.

- SO: The Spatial Orientation Test (SOT) score is a well-established cognitive assessment tool designed to measure an individual's ability to perceive and mentally manipulate spatial relationships. This test is key to understand spatial thinking and orientation skills, which are critical in various fields such as navigation, architecture, and robotics [8]. In this case, the variable is measured continually with a range from 0 to 180° representing the error of the user trying to allocate one or more objects in the simulation. Values closer to 180 indicate lower spatial skill.

- $Temp_m$: Facial temperature at moment m, particularly changes in the temperature of key facial areas like the cheeks, forehead, and nose, is a significant indicator of cognitive load and emotional states such as trust. Thermal imaging allows for the continuous monitoring of these temperature changes, providing insights into the user's physiological responses during tasks. Facial temperature measurement is a non-invasive method to gauge cognitive and emotional states, crucial for applications in human-robot interaction, user experience design, and psychological studies. Lower trust is associated with greater temperature fluctuations, with significant drops in the nose area [10] [22]. Research indicates that an increase in cognitive load often corresponds with a decrease in facial temperature, particularly around the nose and forehead. Typical ranges of higher cognitive load show a decrease of 12°C in these areas [3]. This can result in a temperature decrease of up to 1.5°C compared to relaxed states. In this case, we took the average of the slopes of temperature changing of each region of interest as forehead, nose, and cheeks. The slope and the average are calculated using the following:

$$S_m = \frac{1}{n} \sum_{i=1}^{n} \left(\frac{T_{i+1} - T_i}{t_{i+1} - t_i} \right) \quad (1)$$

where S_m is the average slope of temperature change at moment m, T_i and T_{i+1} are the temperatures at time points t_i and t_{i+1}, respectively, and n is the number of time intervals.

The trust level T_m is influenced by these observed factors, and our goal is to dynamically model these relationships using a Bayesian Network. Trust is measured and estimated at various points during the experiment to ensure the model accurately reflects the dynamic nature of trust over the course of the interaction. Specifically, these estimations are conducted at the end of each condition. The joint probability distribution of all variables at each moment is defined as follows:

$$P(T_m, CL_m, GSR_m, BR_m, P_m, SO, Temp_m) = P(T_m \mid CL_m, GSR_m, BR_m, P_m, SO, Temp_m)$$
$$P(CL_m \mid GSR_m, BR_m, P_m, SO, Temp_m)$$
$$P(GSR_m) P(BR_m) P(P_m) P(SO) P(Temp_m) \quad (2)$$

Additionally, the temporal dynamics of trust are captured by modeling the transition of trust levels across consecutive moments. This transition can be expressed as:

$$P(T_{m+1} \mid T_m, CL_{m+1}, GSR_{m+1}, BR_{m+1}, P_{m+1}, SO_{m+1}, Temp_{m+1}) \quad (3)$$

By applying Bayesian inference, we aim to calculate the posterior probability distribution of trust levels based on the evidence observed in the experiments at each moment. This dynamic model will enable us to predict the operator's trust level with high accuracy over time, providing a deeper understanding of how different factors influence trust in teleoperated robotic systems. Ultimately, the trust estimation model is expected to enhance the design and implementation of teleoperated robots by ensuring they can adapt to the trust dynamics of human operators. This will lead to more efficient and reliable human-robot interactions.

4 Dynamic Bayesian Trust Model

In this section, we explain the modeling of the Dynamic Bayesian Network (DBN) for predicting the trust level of a human operator interacting with a teleoperated robotic system. The DBN captures both the temporal and causal relationships among various observed variables over different moments in time.

A Dynamic Bayesian Network (DBN) is a probabilistic graphical model that represents sequences of variables over time. It extends a standard Bayesian Network (BN) by incorporating temporal dependencies, allowing us to model how the state of a system evolves over time.

Intra-dependencies represent the relationships among variables within the same moment m:

$$P(T_m|CL_m, GSR_m, BR_m, P_m, SO, Temp_m) \qquad (4)$$

This represents the conditional probability of the trust level T_m given the cognitive load CL_m, Galvanic Skin Response GSR_m, blinking rate BR_m, performance P_m, spatial orientation SO, and temperature $Temp_m$.

Additionally, cognitive load CL_m may depend on other observed variables:

$$P(CL_m|GSR_m, BR_m, P_m, SO, Temp_m) \qquad (5)$$

Inter-dependencies capture the relationships between variables across consecutive moments m and $m+1$:

$$P(T_{m+1}|T_m, CL_{m+1}, GSR_{m+1}, BR_{m+1}, P_{m+1}, SO, Temp_{m+1}) \qquad (6)$$

This represents the conditional probability of the trust level T_{m+1} at moment $m+1$ given the trust level T_m at moment m and the other observed variables at moment $m+1$.

To fully specify the DBN, we need to define the Conditional Probability Distributions (CPDs) for each variable. These CPDs capture the probabilistic temporal relationships among the variables:

1. **Trust Level T_m:**

$$P(T_m|CL_m, GSR_m, BR_m, P_m, SO, Temp_m) \qquad (7)$$

This CPD can be modeled using a multinominal logistic regression, where T_m is the dependent variable and the other variables are predictors.

2. **Cognitive Load CL_m:**

$$P(CL_m|GSR_m, BR_m, P_m, SO, Temp_m) \qquad (8)$$

Similar to trust level, this can be defined using a logistic regression approach.

3. **Galvanic Skin Response GSR_m:**

$$P(GSR_m) \sim \text{Categorical}(p_{GSR_1}, p_{GSR_2}, p_{GSR_3}) \qquad (9)$$

GSR can be discretized into three levels: Low Arousal, Moderate Arousal, and High Arousal, and modeled using a categorical distribution with probabilities p_{GSR_1}, p_{GSR_2}, and p_{GSR_3}.

4. **Blinking Rate BR_m:**

$$P(BR_m) \sim \text{Categorical}(p_{BR_1}, p_{BR_2}, p_{BR_3}) \qquad (10)$$

Blinking rate can be discretized into three levels: Low Blink Rate, Moderate Blink Rate, and High Blink Rate, and modeled using a categorical distribution with probabilities p_{BR_1}, p_{BR_2}, and p_{BR_3}.

5. **Performance P_m:**

$$P(P_m) \sim \text{Bernoulli}(p_P) \qquad (11)$$

As a binary variable, performance can be modeled using a Bernoulli distribution with success probability p_P.

6. **Spatial Orientation SO:**

$$P(SO) \sim \mathcal{N}(\mu_{SO}, \sigma_{SO}) \qquad (12)$$

Spatial orientation can be modeled using a normal distribution.

7. **Facial Temperature $Temp_m$:**

$$P(Temp_m) \sim \mathcal{N}(\mu_{Temp}, \sigma_{Temp}) \qquad (13)$$

Temperature changes can be modeled using a normal distribution.

The joint probability distribution of all variables at each moment m is defined as follows:

$$\begin{aligned}P(T_m, CL_m, GSR_m, BR_m, P_m, SO, Temp_m) &= P(T_m | CL_m, GSR_m, BR_m, P_m, SO, Temp_m)\\&\quad P(CL_m | GSR_m, BR_m, P_m, SO, Temp_m)\\&\quad P(GSR_m) P(BR_m) P(P_m) P(SO) P(Temp_m)\end{aligned} \qquad (14)$$

The temporal dynamics of trust are captured by modeling the transition of trust levels across consecutive moments. This transition can be expressed as:

$$P(T_{m+1} | T_m, CL_{m+1}, GSR_{m+1}, BR_{m+1}, P_{m+1}, SO_{m+1}, Temp_{m+1}) \qquad (15)$$

where:

- $P(T_{m+1}|T_m, CL_{m+1}, GSR_{m+1}, BR_{m+1}, P_{m+1}, SO_{m+1}, Temp_{m+1})$ is the CPD for the trust level at moment $m+1$ given the trust level at moment m and other variables at moment $m+1$.

To estimate the level of each variable given a set of observations, we apply Bayesian inference. This involves updating our beliefs about the variable of interest (e.g., T_m) based on new evidence from the other observed variables (e.g., $CL_m, GSR_m, BR_m, P_m, Temp_m$) at each moment.

Formally, for a variable X at moment m, given a set of observations $\mathbf{O}_m$ (which includes all other variables at moment m), the posterior distribution can be computed using Bayes' theorem:

$$P(X_m|\mathbf{O}_m) = \frac{P(\mathbf{O}_m|X_m)P(X_m)}{P(\mathbf{O}_m)} \tag{16}$$

By iteratively applying this process at each moment m, we can dynamically update the trust level and other variables based on new observations, capturing the temporal evolution of the system. To infer the trust level T_m at a specific moment m, given a set of observations $\mathbf{O}_m$, we use the posterior distribution:

$$P(T_m|\mathbf{O}_m) = \frac{P(\mathbf{O}_m|T_m)P(T_m)}{P(\mathbf{O}_m)} \tag{17}$$

Given that the observations include the cognitive load CL_m, Galvanic Skin Response GSR_m, blinking rate BR_m, performance P_m, spatial orientation SO, and temperature $Temp_m$, the likelihood $P(\mathbf{O}_m|T_m)$ can be expressed as:

$$P(\mathbf{O}_m|T_m) = P(CL_m, GSR_m, BR_m, P_m, SO, Temp_m|T_m) \tag{18}$$

By substituting this into the Bayes' theorem, we get:

$$P(T_m|CL_m, GSR_m, BR_m, P_m, SO, Temp_m) = \frac{P(CL_m, GSR_m, BR_m, P_m, SO, Temp_m|T_m)P(T_m)}{P(CL_m, GSR_m, BR_m, P_m, SO, Temp_m)} \tag{19}$$

This allows us to compute the posterior probability of the trust level T_m given the observed values of the other variables at the moment m. This allows us to accurately model and predict the trust dynamics in teleoperated robotic systems, providing valuable insights into how different factors influence trust over time.

5 Experiment and Dataset

For this study, we used a UniversalRobots™ UR5 manipulator robot mounted on a Husky™ mobile robotic platform, which remained static in our setup. The UR5, with its six degrees of freedom (DoF), offers precise manipulation capabilities and a reach of 0.85 m, making it well suited to our tasks. Teleoperation was facilitated using a 6-degree-of-freedom joystick, and we used the OptiTrack real-time tracking system to measure distances between the robotic gripper arm and

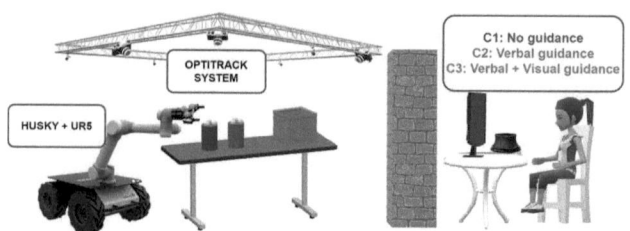

Fig. 2. General view of the system. Optitrack system + UR5 Husky. Three different conditions of controlling the robot vary the amount of information available for the user.

the actuators, which are part of the user's task. The OptiTrack system provided precise positional data needed to assess user performance and confidence in the robotic system under various conditions of incomplete information.

During the experiment, RGB and thermal cameras recorded participants' facial features. We used a Logitech HD C930e webcam for RGB images and a USB-powered Optris PI 640i infrared camera for thermal images. These cameras were mounted on an octopus tripod. In addition, we measured each participant's galvanic skin response (GSR) using Shimmer3 GSR+ units. These sensors provided real-time data on skin conductance, reflecting physiological activation associated with cognitive load.

Participants completed several questionnaires before and after each experimental condition. At baseline, they completed a demographic form, the Big Five Personality Inventory (short form) [13], and the Spatial Orientation Test (SOT). After each condition, they completed the NASA Task Load Index (TLX) and the Human-Robot Interaction Confidence Scale (HRITS). These questionnaires provided valuable insights into individual differences and the impact of experimental conditions on cognitive load and confidence.

In the experimental scenario, participants controlled the UR5 robotic arm to place two wooden cylinders inside a box, a common task in such scenarios, as shown in Fig. 2. The task had to be completed within two minutes, based on visual feedback from three cameras. The camera feed froze 30 s into the task, creating a scenario with incomplete information. To examine the effects of different guidance levels on user performance and confidence, the experiment included three distinct conditions.

- C1: Control robot - Image freeze with no guidance
- C2: Image freeze with verbal guidance
- C3: Image freeze with verbal and visual guidance using GUI

An explicit image of the interface used on each condition can be seen in Fig. 3.

We collected several measures to assess task performance, including success rates, completion times, blink rates, and GSR data. Thermal and RGB images were processed offline and facial temperatures were extracted using the Optris

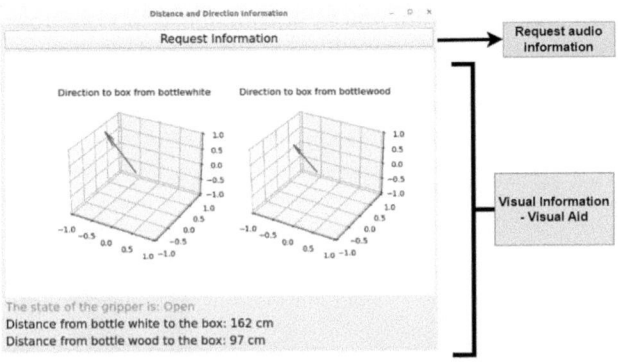

Fig. 3. A graphical user interface (GUI) was provided to deliver additional information to the user for task completion. It included a button to request audio feedback, which conveyed the distance between the gripper and each object. The visual display showed both the direction and distance needed to move the gripper toward each object and complete the task. Additionally, the GUI indicated the current state of the gripper—whether it was open or closed.

Drivers ROS node and the Dlib facial expression library. Blink rate and GSR characteristics, such as cumulative GSR and spike count, were measured to assess cognitive load during the tasks. This comprehensive data collection allowed us to model the relationship between these factors and the human operator's confidence level.

A total of twenty-eight people participated in this experiment, including 14 women and 14 men, all students and administrative members of the Institut Polytechnique de Paris (IP Paris). The age distribution is as follows: 64% (18 participants) are between 20 and 28 years old, 14% (4 participants) are between 28 and 36 years old and 22% (6 participants) are over 36 years old.

To develop and validate the confidence prediction model, we used a cross-validation technique by splitting the collected data into training and testing sets. Specifically, 75% of the data was used to train the model, allowing it to learn the relationships between observed factors and confidence levels. The remaining 25% of the data was reserved for testing the model's accuracy, ensuring that the evaluation was performed on unseen data. During the testing phase, the model's predictions were compared to the actual confidence levels reported by participants.

6 Results and Discussion

6.1 Trust Level Analysis

At the end of each condition, each participant's confidence levels were recorded to track how confidence evolved across conditions. Figure 4a illustrates these changes, showing a decrease in confidence levels without guidance and a significant improvement with verbal and visual guidance. Statistical analysis using

ANOVA revealed significant differences in confidence levels across conditions (p < 0.032), confirming that the type of guidance provided plays a crucial role in maintaining and enhancing confidence in teleoperated robotic systems.

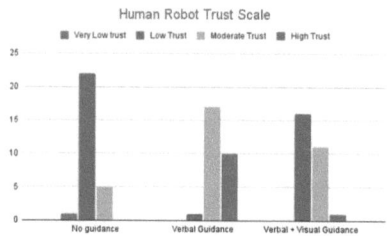
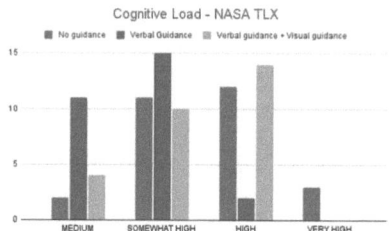
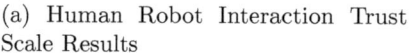

(a) Human Robot Interaction Trust Scale Results

(b) NASAS TLX - Cognitive load results

Fig. 4. Trust and Cognitive load results of the experiment.

6.2 Cognitive Load and Trust Relationship

Cognitive load data, measured using the NASA TLX and physiological sensors such as GSR and blink rate, provided information on the mental effort exerted by participants across conditions. Figure 4b shows how cognitive load varied across conditions, with higher levels observed in the absence of guidance. Correlation analysis revealed a significant negative relationship between cognitive load and confidence levels (r = −0.632, p < 0.01), indicating that higher cognitive load is associated with lower confidence in the robotic system.

6.3 DBN Predictive Model

The confidence prediction model was developed and validated using a cross-validation technique, with 75% of the data used for training and 25% for testing. The model performance was evaluated using accuracy, precision, recall, and F1 score. The confidence prediction model achieved an accuracy of 89%, precision of 91%, recall of 92.5%, and F1 score of 84% on the test dataset. These results demonstrate the effectiveness of the model in predicting confidence levels. Comparison with a baseline model showed a significant improvement in predictive performance, highlighting the robustness of the developed model, showed in [3], where the results were a precision of 72.5%, and a recall of 56%.

To estimate the levels of trust (T_m) and cognitive load (CL_m) at a specific moment m, given a set of observations $\mathbf{O}_m$ (which includes all other variables at moment m), we apply Bayesian inference. This involves updating our beliefs about the variable of interest based on new evidence from the other observed variables at each moment. The posterior distribution can be computed using Bayes' theorem:

$$P(T_m|\mathbf{O}_m) = \frac{P(\mathbf{O}_m|T_m)P(T_m)}{P(\mathbf{O}_m)} \quad (20)$$

$$P(CL_m|\mathbf{O}_m) = \frac{P(\mathbf{O}_m|CL_m)P(CL_m)}{P(\mathbf{O}_m)} \quad (21)$$

where:

- $P(T_m|\mathbf{O}_m)$ is the posterior probability of T_m given the observations.
- $P(\mathbf{O}_m|T_m)$ is the likelihood of observing $\mathbf{O}_m$ given T_m.
- $P(T_m)$ is the prior probability of T_m.
- $P(\mathbf{O}_m)$ is the marginal probability of the observations.

By iterative applying this process at each moment m, we can dynamically update the trust level and cognitive load based on new observations, capturing the temporal evolution of the system.

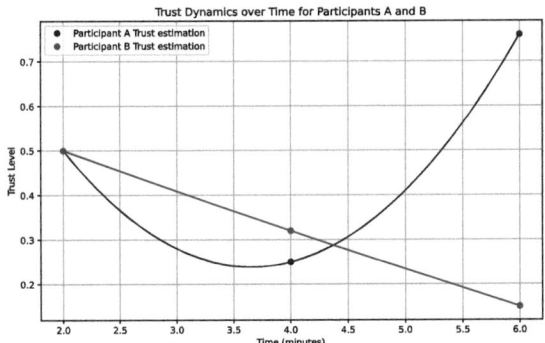

Fig. 5. Trust dynamics estimation for two random participants.

The trust dynamics graph in Fig. 5 illustrates the different levels of trust of two participants, A and B, over time. Participant A's trust fluctuates, showing an initial decrease, followed by a recovery and a final increase. This pattern suggests that Participant A's trust is sensitive to immediate interactions and guidance provided during the task. On the other hand, Participant B's trust shows a linear decrease, indicating a steady decline in trust over time, regardless of specific interactions. This contrast highlights the importance of a dynamic trust model, as it captures individual differences in the evolution of trust. While a static model may suggest similar levels of trust at discrete points in time, dynamic modeling reveals that participants may have fundamentally different trust trajectories, which can inform tailored interventions to maintain or improve trust in teleoperated robotic systems. These insights highlight the need for adaptive systems that can respond to each user's unique trust dynamics, ensuring more efficient and reliable human-robot interactions.

Different types of advice had different impacts on confidence levels. The analysis showed that conditions with verbal and visual guidance resulted in the highest levels of trust, while no guidance resulted in the lowest levels of trust. Physiological indicators such as GSR and blink rate were strong predictors of trust, and higher GSR and blink rate were correlated with lower levels of trust. Task performance indicators including success rates and completion times were also correlated with trust, with higher success rates and faster completion times associated with higher levels of trust.

The results of this preliminary study have practical implications for designing teleoperated robotic systems. Effective communication and appropriate guidance are crucial for enhancing trust, which in turn leads to improved performance and safer operations. It is beneficial to incorporate real-time feedback mechanisms and adaptive guidance systems to maintain high levels of trust. This knowledge has the potential to be applied to various fields, including remote surgery, hazardous materials handling, and search and rescue missions, provided these systems are well designed to enhance human-robot collaboration.

7 Conclusions

This paper focused on developing a dynamic trust prediction model for teleoperated robotic systems in human-robot interaction (HRI) scenarios. By understanding and predicting fluctuations in trust, we aim to enhance the design and operation of these systems, making them more effective and safer for use in high-risk environments. Establishing a dynamic trust model is essential for robot teleoperation in HRI, as trust is not static but varies with robot performance, operator experience, and interaction conditions. A dynamic model facilitates real-time adjustments and improvements, enabling robotic systems to adapt to changes in human operator trust levels, thereby enhancing collaboration and overall system performance. Our methodology involved using physiological variables to estimate dynamic levels of trust and cognitive load. We measured participants' galvanic skin response (GSR) and blink rate as indicators of cognitive load and stress. These metrics, along with task performance metrics and survey data, were used to develop a Bayesian network model used to predict trust levels over time. Participants controlled a teleoperated robotic arm to perform tasks under different guidance conditions, and their physiological responses and task performance were recorded. In our experiment, we tracked how participants' trust in a teleoperated robotic system evolved under three distinct conditions: no guidance, verbal guidance, and a combination of verbal and visual guidance. Trust levels were recorded at the end of each condition, and statistical analysis showed significant differences between them. Our developed trust prediction model exhibited high precision, accuracy, recall, and F1 score, confirming the effectiveness of our approach. However, this study has limitations, including a relatively small sample size and a controlled experimental setup that may not fully capture the complexities of the real world. Future work should aim to include a larger and more diverse group of participants and explore other variables that may influence trust. Further study into the long-term dynamics of trust and the integration of more advanced physiological sensors could provide deeper insights into improving trust in HRI. By focusing on the dynamic nature of trust and leveraging physiological data, this research provides valuable insights for improving human-robot interactions, with potential applications in diverse fields such as remote surgery, hazardous materials handling, and search and rescue missions.

Acknowledgement. This research work has received full funding from the European Commission's HORIZON.1.2 - Marie Skłodowska-Curie Actions (MSCA) under Grant agreement No. 101072634, project RAICAM.

References

1. Ahmad, M.I., Bernotat, J., Lohan, K., Eyssel, F.: Trust and cognitive load during human-robot interaction. arXiv preprint arXiv:1909.05160 (2019). https://doi.org/10.48550/arXiv.1909.05160
2. Bakker, J., Pechenizkiy, M., Sidorova, N.: What's your current stress level? detection of stress patterns from gsr sensor data. In: Proceedings - IEEE International Conference on Data Mining (ICDM), pp. 573–580. IEEE (2011)
3. Cardenas, J.J.G., Hei, X., Tapus, A.: Exploring cognitive load dynamics in human-machine interaction for teleoperation: a user-centric perspective on remote operation system design. In: International Conference on Intelligent Robots and Systems. IEEE (2024)
4. D. Manzey, A. Reichenbach, T.O.: Human performance consequences of automated decision aids: the impact of degree of automation and system experience. J. Cogn. Eng. Decis. Mak. **6**, 57–87 (2012). https://doi.org/10.1177/1555343411435972
5. Guo, Y., Yang, J.: Modeling and predicting trust dynamics in human–robot teaming: a bayesian inference approach. Int. J. Soc. Robot. **12**, 943–955 (2020). https://doi.org/10.1007/s12369-020-00629-7
6. Guo, Y., Yang, X.J.: Modeling and predicting trust dynamics in human-robot teaming: a bayesian inference approach. Int. J. Soc. Robot. **13**(8), 1899–1909 (2021). https://doi.org/10.1007/s12369-020-00703-3
7. Lee, J.D., See, K.A.: Trust in automation: designing for appropriate reliance. Hum. Factors **46**, 50–80 (2004). https://doi.org/10.1518/hfes.46.1.50.30392
8. M., K., M., H.: A dissociation between object manipulation spatial ability and spatial orientation ability. Memory Cogn, **29**(5), 745–756 (2001)
9. MDPI: Recognition of blinks activity patterns during stress conditions (2021). https://www.mdpi.com/2079-9292/10/6/679
10. Nakanishi, T., Inoue, M., Ueda, K.: Relationship between facial temperature measured with thermography and trust levels in human-robot interaction. Robotics **8**(3), 58 (2019)
11. Pan, J., Eden, J., Oetomo, D., Johal, W.: Exploring the effects of shared autonomy on cognitive load and trust in human-robot interaction. arXiv preprint arXiv:2102.02758 (2021). https://doi.org/10.1109/ICRA.2021.9561973
12. Pinto, A., Sousa, S., Simões, A., Santos, J.: A trust scale for human-robot interaction: translation, adaptation, and validation of a human computer trust scale. Human Behav. Emerg. Technol. **2022**(1), 6437441 (2022). https://doi.org/10.1155/2022/6437441

13. Rammstedt, B., John, O.P.: Measuring personality in one minute or less: a 10-item short version of the big five inventory in English and German. J. Res. Pers. **41**(1), 203–212 (2007)
14. Review of Ophthalmology: Breaking down the blink (2023). https://www.reviewofophthalmology.com
15. Rubio, S., Díaz, E., Martínez, J., Puente, J.M.: Evaluation of subjective mental workload: a comparison of swat, nasa-tlx, and workload profile methods. In: Applied Psychology, vol. 53, pp. 61–86. Wiley Online Library (2004)
16. Saeidi, H., et al.: Trust-based mixed-initiative teleoperation of mobile robots. In: 2016 American Control Conference (ACC), pp. 6177–6182 (2016). https://doi.org/10.1109/ACC.2016.7526640
17. Sahoo, R., Sethi, S.: Functional analysis of mental stress based on physiological data of gsr sensor. In: AISC Series of Springercsi-2014, Hyderabad, India (2014)
18. Schaefer, K.: Measuring trust in human robot interactions: Development of the trust perception scale-hri. SpringerLink (2015). https://doi.org/10.1007/978-3-319-96074-6_2
19. S.G., H., L.E., S.: Development of nasa-tlx (task load index): results of empirical and theoretical research. In: Hancock, P.A., Meshkati, N. (eds.) Human Mental Workload, pp. 139–183 (1988). https://doi.org/10.1016/S0166-4115(08)62386-9
20. S.G. Hart, L.S.: Impact of robot-related user pre-experience on cognitive load, trust, trustworthiness, and satisfaction with vr interfaces. SpringerLink (2021). https://doi.org/10.1007/978-3-319-96074-6_2
21. Sohaib, A.T., Qureshi, S., Hagelbäck, J., Hilborn, O., Jerčić, P.: Evaluating classifiers for emotion recognition using EEG. In: Schmorrow, D.D., Fidopiastis, C.M. (eds.) AC 2013. LNCS (LNAI), vol. 8027, pp. 492–501. Springer, Heidelberg (2013). https://doi.org/10.1007/978-3-642-39454-6_53
22. Uchida, Y., Kawasaki, M., Yamada, H.: Effects of cognitive load on facial temperature: a thermal infrared imaging study. Int. J. Psychophysiol. **88**(3), 166–171 (2013)
23. University of Arizona: Blinking offers clues to human response under stress (2023). https://psychology.arizona.edu/news/blinking-offers-clues-human-response-under-stress
24. Yang, J., Wang, L., Scassellati, B.: Uncertainty and learning in human-robot interaction: a bayesian approach. In: Proceedings of the 2017 ACM/IEEE International Conference on Human-Robot Interaction, pp. 139–146 (2017). https://doi.org/10.1145/2909824.3020230

Effects of Perceived Robot Autonomy and Personal Differences on Trust in Human-Robot Interactions

Ali Fallahi[✉], Patrick Holthaus, Farshid Amirabdollahian, and Gabriella Lakatos

Robotics Research Group, University of Hertfordshire, Hatfield, UK
{a.fallahi,p.holthaus,f.amirabdollahian2,g.lakatos}@herts.ac.uk

Abstract. Trust is essential in human-robot interaction (HRI), yet the role of various factors shaping trust remains complex. This study investigated how perceived robot autonomy and individual user traits influence trust. Participants interacted with a Pepper robot in one of two conditions differing in the manipulation of perceived autonomy. Results showed that perceived autonomy affected ratings of the robot's sincerity, but did not significantly affect other trust dimensions. Participants' pre-existing attitudes toward robots were associated with trust perceptions, while personality traits showed no significant influence. These findings suggest that user attitudes may play a more critical role than perceived autonomy in shaping trust during short-term HRI, underscoring the need to personalise robot design based on attitudinal differences.

Keywords: HRI · Trust · Percieved Autonomy

1 Introduction

As robots become increasingly integrated into homes, workplaces, and healthcare settings, understanding how humans form trust in these systems is crucial to ensure effective and safe collaboration [3,15]. In HRI, trust directly influences people's willingness to rely on robotic systems, engage with them, and accept their assistance [26]. While building technically advanced robots is a growing achievement, ensuring they are perceived as trustworthy remains a central challenge [1]. Both under-trust and over-trust can lead to risks such as disengagement, disuse, or blind over-reliance in critical situations [2,22].

One of the key dimensions that seems to influence trust is a robot's autonomy—the degree to which it operates independently of human control. Robots can be classified along a continuum of autonomy, from tele-operated systems to fully autonomous agents [6]. Autonomous systems are often perceived as intentional agents [16], and these perceptions can significantly impact user trust, even if the robot's actual behaviour remains unchanged [12]. Prior studies suggest that higher autonomy can increase trust, but only when the system remains predictable and transparent [11,23,25]. Misperceptions of autonomy—such as assuming a robot is autonomous when it is not—can lead to mismatched expectations and breakdowns in trust. Despite growing interest in this topic, few studies have directly examined how perceived autonomy (rather than actual autonomy) shapes both subjective and behavioural trust responses.

This study focuses on the relationship between perceived autonomy and trust in a social HRI context. This study uniquely focuses on perceived, not actual, robot autonomy, addressing an overlooked aspect in HRI trust research. Specifically, we investigate how merely telling users a robot is autonomous versus remotely controlled influences their perception of trustworthiness and their willingness to engage with it. We also consider the role of individual differences—such as personality traits, attitudes towards robots, and gender—which are known to shape trust in automation [11], yet are underexplored in relation to perceived autonomy. Understanding these relationships has two major implications. First, it can help robot designers determine how to frame or implement autonomy in ways that foster appropriate trust. Second, it provides insight into how experimental narratives and user traits influence outcomes in HRI studies, promoting more standardised and comparable trust assessments across the field.

To address these goals, we investigate the following research questions:

RQ1 How might people's perception of robot autonomy influence their trust towards companion robots? **RQ2** How do individual differences (personality traits, attitudes towards robots, gender) influence trust in robots?

2 Background and Motivation

The complex concept of trust remains a challenging and evolving research area within the field of HRI, with many questions still open for investigation [29]. One of the key factors influencing trust in HRI is the perceived autonomy of the robot; how independently it appears to operate and make decisions. An object is considered an agent if it performs a beneficial function for itself or others, showing autonomy [16]. Robots can be categorised based on their level of autonomy into two main types: autonomous robots and tele-operated robots [6]. An autonomous robot operates independently, completing tasks without human intervention, while a tele-operated robot relies on a human operator to achieve its goals [8]. In shared control models, human inputs and the robot's autonomous control are combined to realise the robot's behaviours [21].

The way a robot behaves, including its level of autonomy, can shape trust as a psychological response in users. However, people's expectations of how autonomous these systems are can sometimes be inaccurate [12]. The effects of robot autonomy on human trust, especially concerning how perceptions of robot agency affect trust, have recently been getting the attention of some HRI researchers. In a comprehensive meta-analysis, [11] found that higher robot autonomy tends to increase trust. The authors mentioned that robot reliability and predictability might be affected by a robot's degree of autonomy. They noted, however, that unexpected behaviours at high autonomy levels can severely reduce trust, pointing to the challenge of balancing autonomy with trustworthiness. This is in line with findings of [25], who found that trust differs significantly based on the level of robot autonomy, and it drops when robots perform essential tasks autonomously without human supervision. They proposed the implementation of precisely defined autonomy levels to keep efficiency and trust at acceptable levels. [5] examined how trust develops differently under varying autonomy conditions, a trust-aware partially observable Markov decision process [14], and a myopic decision-making strategy, where the robot acts without considering trust. Their findings showed that medium-level autonomy created the most favourable conditions for trust development in a table-clearing scenario.

As discussed above, high autonomy can lead to user ambiguity and the feeling of diminished control, thus demonstrating the necessity of robot intentionality and transparency to maintain trust. [23] demonstrated that transparent decision-making by autonomous robots led to higher trust compared to robots that made decisions without providing explanations. Although these findings provide valuable insights into the connection between robot autonomy and user trust, there are no insights into how user characteristics like personality traits, demographic factors, and attitudes toward robots might influence these perceptions. Trust in this study is defined both as subjective (perceived sincerity, reliability, competence, ethics) and behavioural (willingness to follow robot requests) in line with existing literature on trust in human-robot interaction [11].

3 Methods

To investigate our research questions, we conducted an in-person study in the University of Hertfordshire's Robot House, a four-bedroom residential home adapted for HRI research. Participants interacted with a Pepper robot in one of two conditions that differed only in perceived autonomy.

The study was approved by The University of Hertfordshire Health, Science, Engineering and Technology Ethics Committee with Delegated Authority (SPECS/PGR/UH/05839). Based on previous research, we formulated the following hypotheses:

H1 Effect of perceived autonomy (related to RQ1) We hypothesise that the belief that a robot is autonomous, as opposed to remotely controlled, will affect participants' trust in the robot: **H1.1** Participants who perceive the robot as autonomous will rate it as more trustworthy (subjective evaluation). **H1.2** Participants who perceive the robot as autonomous will show greater willingness to interact with the robot and follow its instructions (behavioural response).
H2 Effect of individual differences (related to RQ2) We hypothesise that participants' individual characteristics will influence how they perceive and respond to the robot: **H2.1** Participants' personality traits will influence their perceptions of the robot's trustworthiness and social attributes. **H2.2** Participants' pre-existing attitudes toward robots will influence their perceptions of and behavioural responses to the robot.

3.1 Experimental Manipulation

This study employed a between-participants experimental design to manipulate people's perception of robot autonomy. Participants were randomly assigned to one of two experimental conditions to investigate potential influences on trust and interaction behaviours.

- *Remotely-controlled (RC)*: Participants were told that the robot was being controlled by a human operator. To reinforce the participants' belief that a human was controlling the robot, the observation room with a human controller was shown at the beginning of the experiment and the controller engaged in five "check-up" procedures, one before each task, making adjustments to the robot and announcing, "It's ready for the next scenario."
- *Autonomous (AU)*: Participants were told that the robot was acting independently. The control room was not shown, and no "check-up" interventions by the experimenter were performed. Like in the other condition, however, the robot was remotely controlled to ensure consistency of behaviours.

3.2 Participants

A total of 33 participants (12 identified as female, 19 as male, and 1 as genderfluid) took part in the experiment. Recruitment was based on similar HRI studies [22, 24] with similar sample sizes. Their ages ranged from 19 to 40 years (mean age $\bar{x}_{Age} = 26.48$, standard deviation $\sigma_{Age} = 4.6$). Participants were recruited individually on campus via flyers and randomly assigned to one of two experimental conditions AU (16 participants) or RC (17 participants).

3.3 Experimental Procedure

Participants, upon arrival at the Robot House, were greeted by the experimenter and escorted to the living room area, where they were given a brief explanation of the study. After reviewing and signing a consent form, participants completed two pre-intervention questionnaires (cf. Sect. 3.4). They were then introduced to the study scenario where they were visiting a friend's home while the friend was away, to check if everything was alright. The robotic assistant, Pepper, would stay with them and help them with feeding the owner's cat. Participants were instructed to interact with the robot naturally and comfortably, and that all instructions would be provided by the robot during the interaction. Depending on their previously assigned experimental group, they were told that the robot was either autonomous or remotely controlled. In the RC condition only, the experimenter introduced the observation room. To initiate the interaction, participants were asked to stand on a marked point in the centre of the living room, simulating the moment of having just entered the house. The experimenter then excused themselves and left for the control room to trigger the robot's behaviour in a Wizard-of-Oz style. Pepper approached the participant and began the interaction. The robot then asked the participant to complete four interactive tasks, selected to represent social scenarios reflecting different aspects of trust:

1. **Show ID:** At the beginning of the experiment, the robot asked participants to show an identification document. Participants could choose to comply or decline and were later asked to explain their decision.
2. **Fill Bowl:** The robot instructed participants to help feed and provide water to the cat. Cat food and two bottles were provided: one with red liquid and another containing clear liquid, labelled "diluted cleaning solution." Participants could show one or both bottles to the robot for feedback before making a decision. If participants showed the clear bottle, the robot confirmed the choice; if they showed the red liquid, it issued a warning. If participants presented both, the robot recommended the clear one. These responses were intended to simulate autonomous decision-making and prompt reflection on the robot's judgment and reliability.
3. **Play Sudoku:** The robot invited participants to play a Sudoku puzzle on its screen, and offered help solving it. Participants could either solve the puzzle independently or ask the robot to provide the solution for them.
4. **Join Dance:** The robot invited participants to dance to a music genre of their own or Pepper's choice. This scenario assessed willingness to engage in a light-hearted activity, while potentially eliciting feelings of discomfort.

Following the final interaction, participants were asked to complete two post-intervention questionnaires, evaluating their perceptions of the robot's social characteristics and trustworthiness, respectively (cf. Sect. 3.4).

At the end of the session, participants were fully debriefed.

3.4 Dependent Variables

Objective (behavioural) Measurements. We measured participants' willingness to follow the robot's suggestions in each of the four tasks as an established behavioural trust indicator [22,23], detailed in Sect. 3.3. We established different social situations, where the ID validation task revealed personal information, the water bowl task looked at a pet that might be reliable on the participant's judgements, a casual situation playing Sudoku, and a dancing situation putting people in a less comfortable position.

Subjective (questionnaire) Measurements. The Ten-Item Personality Inventory (TIPI) [10] was used as a pre-intervention questionnaire to assess participants' personality traits and to help address **RQ2**, as individual differences were expected to influence trust and engagement. TIPI is a brief questionnaire containing 10 items on a 7-point scale, designed to assess the "Big Five" personality traits: Extraversion, Agreeableness, Conscientiousness, Emotional Stability, and Openness to Experience [7,13]. Likewise, the Negative Attitude Towards Robots (NARS) [20] (14 items, 5-point scale) was employed prior to the interaction to examine general concerns and attitudes toward robots, contributing further insights into **RQ2**. NARS evaluates negative attitudes across three dimensions: Negative Attitudes toward Interaction with Robots, toward Social Influence of Robots, and toward Emotional Interaction with Robots.

Table 1. Wilcoxon Rank-Sum Test Results for TIPI Traits between the robot conditions AU and RC. * indicates a significant difference ($p < 0.05$).

Trait	W Statistic	p-value	Mean AU	Mean RC
Extraversion	103.0	0.2391	48.44	59.31
Agreeableness	128.5	0.7981	65.62	67.16
Conscientiousness*	68.5	0.0138	69.79	85.29
Emotional stability	136.0	1.0000	60.42	60.78
Openness	93.0	0.1127	76.56	89.22

The Multi-Dimensional Measure of Trust (MDMT) [18,30] was used as a post-intervention measure to evaluate trust in the robot, thereby addressing **RQ1**. MDMT includes 20 items on an 8-point scale spanning five trust dimensions: Competence, Reliability, Integrity, Sincerity, and Benevolence. The Robot Social Attribute Scale (RoSAS) [4] (18 items. 7-point scale) was also administered post-interaction to assess perceptions of the robot's social characteristics. It includes three subscales: Warmth, Competence, and Discomfort.

4 Results

As the data were not continuous and did not meet the assumption of normality, as confirmed by the Shapiro-Wilk test [27] ($p < .05$), non-parametric methods were applied to all statistical tests. Specifically, Wilcoxon rank-sum tests [19] were used for between-group comparisons of questionnaire data, Fisher's exact tests [9] were used to compare proportions of responses between conditions on binary (Yes/No) data, and Spearman's rank correlation coefficients [28] (ρ) were computed to examine associations among variables.

4.1 Condition Balance Checks

Participants were randomly distributed across the experimental conditions with a balanced gender composition and similar age profiles. The AU condition included 6 female, 1 genderfluid, and 9 male participants, with a mean age of 25.56 years (SD = 4.02). The *RC* condition comprised 7 female and 10 male participants, with a mean age of 27.35 years (SD = 5.06). To check for potential pre-existing differences between groups and confounding factors, we examined participants' personality traits (TIPI) and attitudes towards robots (NARS). However, personality traits were also investigated across all participants, independent of condition, to address RQ2 (see Sect. 4.3). On the TIPI scale, only *Conscientiousness* showed a statistically significant difference between conditions, where people in the *RC* condition showed higher conscientiousness than people in the AU condition ($\bar{x}_{RC} = 85.29$, $\bar{x}_{AU} = 69.79$, $W = 68.5$, $p = 0.0138$). No other traits showed significant differences; for details, refer to Table 1.

No statistically significant differences were found between *AU* and *RC* across any of the NARS subscales ($p > .05$ for all).

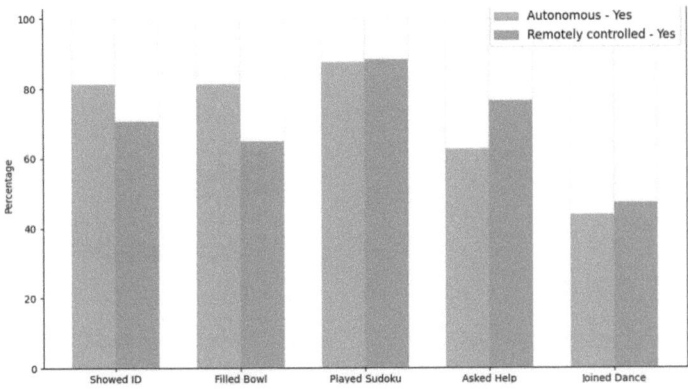

Fig. 1. Bar chart showing the percentage of *Yes* responses to behavioural questions grouped by experimental condition (*AU* and *RC*).

4.2 Effect of Condition

Behavioural Responses. To assess whether participants' behavioural responses differed between the *AU* and *RC* robot conditions, Fisher's Exact Tests were conducted on five measurements (*Yes/No*) whether participants engaged in each of the tasks (cf. Sect. 3.3), i.e. whether they showed their ID, filled the cat's bowl, played a game of Sudoku with the robot, asked it for help during the game, and joined the robot in its dancing routine. Figure 1 displays these behaviours, grouped by condition.

Response rates are also presented in Table 2, along with odds ratios and *p*-values from Fisher's Exact Tests. No statistically significant differences were observed between the *AU* and *RC* conditions across any of the behaviours.

Table 2. Fisher's Exact Test results and behavioural responses (number and percentage) for tasks across the robot conditions *AU* and *RC*.

Activity	p-value	Odds Ratio	No AU		Yes RU		No AU		Yes RU	
Showed ID	0.6880	1.806	3	18.8%	13	81.2%	5	29.4%	12	70.6%
Filled Bowl	0.4384	2.364	3	18.8%	13	81.2%	6	35.3%	11	64.7%
Played Sudoku	1.0000	0.933	2	12.5%	14	87.5%	2	11.8%	15	88.2%
Asked Help	0.4646	0.513	6	37.5%	10	62.5%	4	23.5%	13	76.5%
Joined Dance	1.0000	0.875	9	56.2%	7	43.8%	9	52.9%	8	47.1%

Subjective Measurements. To assess people's trust in and social perception of the robot, Wilcoxon rank-sum tests between the conditions were conducted on both MDMT and RoSAS. On the MDMT scale, a statistically significant difference

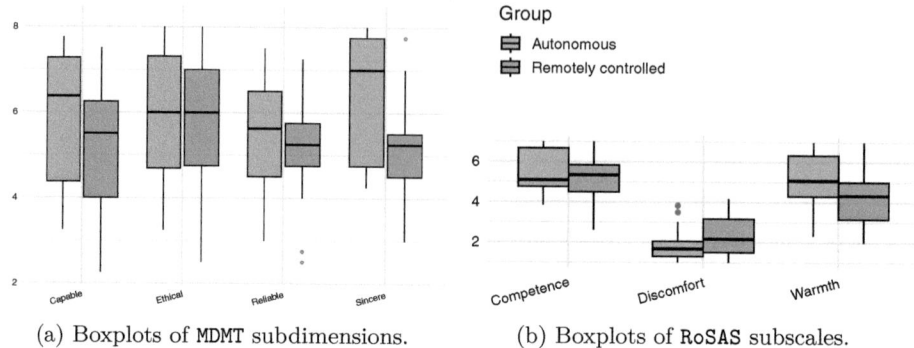

(a) Boxplots of MDMT subdimensions.   (b) Boxplots of RoSAS subscales.

Fig. 2. Boxplots of dependent subjective measurements are shown on a scale between 1 and 7, grouped by robot condition (*AU* left, red and *RC* right, cyan). Significant differences between the conditions ($p < 0.05$) are indicated by '*'. (Color figure online)

Table 3. Wilcoxon Rank-Sum Test Results for MDMT subdimensions between the experimental conditions *AU* and *RC*.

Subdimensions	W Statistic	p-value	Mean value AU	Mean value RU
Capable	177.0	0.1440	5.85	5.1
Ethical	138.5	0.9424	6.01	5.88
Reliable	162.5	0.3468	5.62	5.13
Sincere	194.0	0.0376	6.36	5.16

was found for the *Sincere* subdimension, with participants in the AU condition reporting higher sincerity ratings than those in the RC condition ($W = 194.0$, $p = 0.0376$, $\hat{x}_{AU} = 6.36$, $\sigma_{AU} = 1.50$; $\hat{x}_{RC} = 5.16$, $\sigma_{RC} = 1.19$). No significant differences were observed for the other trust dimensions (*Reliable, Capable, Ethical*). No statistically significant differences between the conditions were found in the RoSAS subscales *Competence, Warmth*, and *Discomfort*. See Fig. 2 for an illustration and Tables 3 and 4 for detailed test results.

Overall, scores were relatively high in all MDMT subdimensions and the *Competence* and *Warmth* subscales of RoSAS, with median ratings at the upper end of the 7-point scale, whereas *Discomfort* was rated on the lower and, as expected.

Table 4. Wilcoxon Rank-Sum Test Results for RoSAS Subscales between the robot conditions *AU* and *RC*.

Trait	W Statistic	p-value	Mean value AU	Mean value RC
Competence	150.5	0.6135	5.50	5.10
Discomfort	97.0	0.1636	1.90	2.35
Warmth	176.0	0.1542	5.01	4.30

4.3 Effect of Individual Differences

In addition to testing for group differences between the *AU* and *RC* conditions, we also investigated relations between demographics and pre-intervention measurements (personality traits, robot attitude) and dependent variables (trust and social attributes).

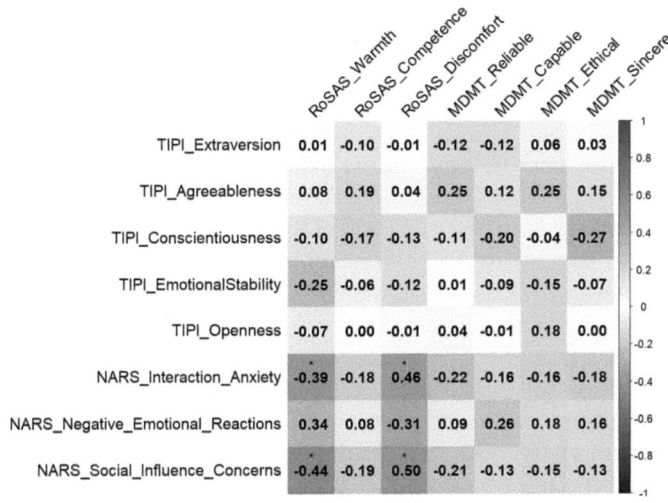

Fig. 3. Spearman correlation heatmap labelled with coefficients between individual difference measures (TIPI and NARS subscales) and robot perception (RoSAS and MDMT subdimensions). Warmer colours indicate stronger positive correlations, while cooler colours indicate stronger negative correlations. Statistically significant correlations (p < 0.05) are marked with an asterisk (*).

Age-related effects were not analysed due to similar age distributions across conditions No significant gender differences were found across the four MDMT trust subdimensions (Wilcoxon rank-sum tests, all $p > .05$). Spearman correlations and p-values between individual traits (TIPI, NARS) and participants' perceptions of the robot (RoSAS, MDMT) are shown in Fig. 3, with warmer colours indicating stronger positive and cooler colours stronger negative correlations. Coefficients are displayed within each cell, with statistically significant results ($p < 0.05$) marked by an asterisk (*). We report only statistically significant correlations ($p < .05$); values not reaching significance are only shown in Fig. 3. Among the NARS subscales, *Social Influence Concerns* was positively correlated with *RoSAS Discomfort* ($\rho = 0.50$, $p = .0029$) and negatively correlated with *RoSAS Warmth* ($\rho = -0.44$, $p = .0109$). Similarly, *Interaction Anxiety* positively correlated with *RoSAS Discomfort* ($\rho = 0.46$, $p = .0069$) and negatively correlated with *RoSAS Warmth* ($\rho = -0.39$, $p = .0253$).

5 Discussion and Limitations

Four of the five personality traits were balanced across groups, but participants in the RC condition showed higher *Conscientiousness*, a trait linked to rule-following and trust in structured systems [13]. This imbalance may have influenced behavioural responses independently of the autonomy framing. Participants' negative attitudes towards robots did not significantly differ between conditions, suggesting that trust-related effects are unlikely to stem from pre-existing biases. Gender and age were evenly distributed, though the limited diversity may restrict generalisability. Overall, the groups were comparable in personality and attitudes, except for conscientiousness.

H1.1 proposed that participants who believed the robot was AU would perceive it as more trustworthy than those who believed it was RC. Results from post-interaction trust scales suggest partial support for this hypothesis. Specifically, participants in the AU condition rated the robot more positively in terms of sincerity, suggesting that perceived autonomy influenced certain social-intentional evaluations. Other trust-related attributes, like competence, reliability, and warmth, did not differ between conditions. This suggests that while autonomy framing influenced some social judgments, it did not consistently enhance trust across all dimensions. These results align with studies showing that perceived autonomy can trigger anthropomorphic responses, though such effects may depend on context, task, and user expectations [12,17,31]. Although agency was not directly measured, the increase in perceived sincerity in the AU condition may indicate that participants implicitly attributed greater agency to the robot [32]. This reinforces the role of framing in shaping how humans evaluate social robots. Although anthropomorphism is known to influence perceived agency and thus potentially trust in HRI, this factor was beyond the scope of this study. Future research should include explicit assessments of anthropomorphism to better understand potentially confounding effects on trust evaluations.

H1.2 proposed that participants who believed the robot was autonomous would be more likely to follow its instructions and engage with it during tasks. However, the findings did not support this hypothesis. Participants in both conditions showed generally high levels of compliance, with no clear differences in behaviour across tasks such as showing ID, requesting help, or completing challenges. These results suggest that merely telling participants a robot is autonomous may not be enough to change behaviour. Prior research shows that observable behaviours—like adaptability or visible errors—build trust more effectively than verbal framing [22]. In our study, the robot's identical behaviour across conditions likely reduced the impact of the autonomy manipulation. Moreover, participants may have complied with the robot's requests simply because they perceived it as part of their role in a short-term experimental setting, rather than due to genuine trust. As highlighted by Salem et al. [23], participants in brief lab-based interactions often comply even with illogical or faulty robot instructions, indicating potential overtrust or perceived obligation. These findings underline the limitations of short-term studies in assessing behavioural trust and suggest that more ecologically valid, long-term interactions are necessary to capture authentic user responses. Future studies could explore alternative cues of autonomy to better understand when and how perceived autonomy translates into behavioural trust. **H2.1** and **H2.2** focused on the influence of personality traits and pre-existing attitudes toward robots on how participants perceived the robot after interaction. The findings provide partial support for these hypotheses. Participants' negative attitudes toward robots, particularly discomfort in interacting with them, were associated with more negative evaluations of the robot's warmth and sociability. These results suggest that individuals with more negative attitudes or anxiety toward robots tend to see them as less warm and more discomforting. While this correlation between NARS and RoSAS is expected due to their conceptual overlap, it reinforces the role of affective attitudes in shaping social perceptions of robots. Notably, no significant correlations were found between personality or robot attitudes and MDMT trust dimensions, indicating that individual differences may influence social perceptions but not necessarily trust in the robot's abilities or intentions. In contrast, personality traits such as extraversion or agreeableness did not appear to meaningfully influence participants' perceptions. This implies that attitudinal factors (as measured by NARS) may be more predictive of subjective trust in robots than general personality traits. These results highlight the importance of accounting for users' preconceptions about robots when evaluating their reactions to autonomous systems. Moreover, results suggest that personalising robots based on personality traits may be less effective than focusing on user attitudes. These findings underline the importance of addressing user biases and robot-related concerns in designing socially acceptable robotic systems, especially when the goal is to foster trust and cooperation. Limitations include the short-term lab setting and that autonomy manipulation was based on framing and contextual cues, while robot behaviours were intentionally kept constant to control for confounds. Future studies could include observable autonomy primers to further strengthen the manipulation.

6 Conclusion and Future Work

This study explored how perceived robot autonomy and user differences influence trust in humanrobot interaction. Perceived autonomy increased sincerity ratings but had limited impact on other trust measures or behaviours. Instead, pre-existing negative attitudes toward robots—particularly negative emotional reactions and social influence concerns—were stronger predictors of trust outcomes. These findings highlight the complex nature of HRI trust, shaped by both system design and user traits. To advance this understanding, future work should adopt more diverse and ecologically valid study designs, incorporating longitudinal methods and broader participant samples. In particular, qualitative materials already collected—such as open-ended responses and video recordings—offer rich opportunities for further analysis of interaction dynamics, user reasoning, and non-verbal behaviour. Leveraging these insights may reveal subtleties in trust development not captured by quantitative metrics alone.

References

1. Amirabdollahian, F., et al.: Can you trust your robotic assistant? Soc. Rob. (2013)
2. Aroyo, A.M., et al.: Overtrusting robots: Setting a research agenda to mitigate overtrust in automation. Paladyn J. Behav. Rob. **12**(1), 423–436 (2021). https://doi.org/10.1515/pjbr-2021-0029
3. Broadbent, E., Stafford, R., MacDonald, B.: Acceptance of healthcare robots for the older population: review and future directions. Int. J. Soc. Robot. **1**, 319–330 (2009). https://doi.org/10.1007/s12369-009-0030-6
4. Carpinella, C.M., Wyman, A.B., Perez, M.A., Stroessner, S.J.: The robotic social attributes scale (rosas) development and validation. In: Proceedings of the 2017 ACM/IEEE International Conference on Human-Robot Interaction, pp. 254–262 (2017). https://doi.org/10.1145/2909824.3020208
5. Chen, M., Nikolaidis, S., Soh, H., Hsu, D., Srinivasa, S.: Trust-aware decision making for human-robot collaboration: model learning and planning. ACM Trans. Hum.-Robot Interact. (THRI) **9**(2), 1–23 (2020). https://doi.org/10.1145/3359616
6. Choi, J.J., Kim, Y., Kwak, S.S.: The autonomy levels and the human intervention levels of robots: the impact of robot types in human-robot interaction. In: The 23rd IEEE International Symposium on Robot and Human Interactive Communication, pp. 1069–1074. IEEE (2014). https://doi.org/10.1109/ROMAN.2014.6926394
7. Costa, P.T., McCrae, R.R.: A five-factor theory of personality. Handb. Pers. Theory Res. **2**(01), 1999 (1999)
8. Cui, J., Tosunoglu, S., Roberts, R., Moore, C., Repperger, D.W.: A review of teleoperation system control. In: Proceedings of the Florida Conference on Recent Advances in Robotics, pp. 1–12. Citeseer (2003)
9. Fisher, R.A.: Statistical methods for research workers. In: Breakthroughs in Statistics: Methodology and Distribution, pp. 66–70. Springer, Heidelberg (1970). https://doi.org/10.1007/978-1-4612-4380-9_6
10. Gosling, S.D., Rentfrow, P.J., Swann, W.B., Jr.: A very brief measure of the big-five personality domains. J. Res. Pers. **37**(6), 504–528 (2003). https://doi.org/10.1016/S0092-6566(03)00046-1
11. Hancock, P.A., Billings, D.R., Schaefer, K.E., Chen, J.Y., De Visser, E.J., Parasuraman, R.: A meta-analysis of factors affecting trust in human-robot interaction. Hum. Factors **53**(5), 517–527 (2011). https://doi.org/10.1177/0018720811417254
12. Holthaus, P., Fallahi, A., Förster, F., Menon, C., Wood, L., Lakatos, G.: Agency effects on robot trust in different age groups. In: International Conference on Human-Agent Interaction (HAI 2024). ACM, Swansea (2024). https://doi.org/10.1145/3687272.3690903
13. John, O.P., Srivastava, S., et al.: The big-five trait taxonomy: history, measurement, and theoretical perspectives (1999)
14. Kaelbling, L.P., Littman, M.L., Cassandra, A.R.: Planning and acting in partially observable stochastic domains. Artif. Intell. **101**(1–2), 99–134 (1998)
15. Lewis, M., Sycara, K., Walker, P.: The role of trust in human-robot interaction. In: Foundations of Trusted Autonomy, pp. 135–159 (2018). https://doi.org/10.1007/978-3-319-64816-3_8
16. Luck, M., d'Inverno, M., et al.: A formal framework for agency and autonomy. In: ICMAS, vol. 95, pp. 254–260 (1995)
17. Malle, B.F., Scheutz, M., Arnold, T., Voiklis, J., Cusimano, C.: Sacrifice one for the good of many? people apply different moral norms to human and robot agents. In: Proceedings of the Tenth Annual ACM/IEEE International Conference on Human-Robot Interaction, pp. 117–124 (2015). https://doi.org/10.1145/2696454.2696458

18. Malle, B.F., Ullman, D.: A multidimensional conception and measure of human-robot trust. In: Trust in Human-Robot Interaction, pp. 3–25. Elsevier (2021). https://doi.org/10.1016/B978-0-12-819472-0.00001-0
19. Mann, H.B., Whitney, D.R.: On a test of whether one of two random variables is stochastically larger than the other. Ann. Math. Stat. 50–60 (1947)
20. Nomura, T., Kanda, T., Suzuki, T., Kato, K.: Prediction of human behavior in human-robot interaction using psychological scales for anxiety and negative attitudes toward robots. IEEE Trans. Rob. **24**(2), 442–451 (2008). https://doi.org/10.1109/TRO.2007.914004
21. Pan, J., Eden, J., Oetomo, D., Johal, W.: Effects of shared control on cognitive load and trust in teleoperated trajectory tracking. IEEE Robot. Autom. Lett. **9**(6), 5863–5870 (2024). https://doi.org/10.1109/LRA.2024.3396111
22. Robinette, P., Li, W., Allen, R., Howard, A.M., Wagner, A.R.: Overtrust of robots in emergency evacuation scenarios. In: 2016 11th ACM/IEEE International Conference on Human-Robot Interaction (HRI), pp. 101–108. IEEE (2016). https://doi.org/10.1109/HRI.2016.7451740
23. Salem, M., Lakatos, G., Amirabdollahian, F., Dautenhahn, K.: Towards safe and trustworthy social robots: ethical challenges and practical issues. In: ICSR 2015. LNCS (LNAI), vol. 9388, pp. 584–593. Springer, Cham (2015). https://doi.org/10.1007/978-3-319-25554-5_58
24. Salem, M., Lakatos, G., Amirabdollahian, F., Dautenhahn, K.: Would you trust a (faulty) robot? effects of error, task type and personality on human-robot cooperation and trust. In: Proceedings of the tenth annual ACM/IEEE International Conference on Human-Robot Interaction, pp. 141–148 (2015). https://doi.org/10.1145/2696454.2696497
25. Schaefer, K.E., Chen, J.Y., Szalma, J.L., Hancock, P.A.: A meta-analysis of factors influencing the development of trust in automation: implications for understanding autonomy in future systems. Hum. Factors **58**(3), 377–400 (2016). https://doi.org/10.1177/0018720816634228
26. Shahrdar, S., Menezes, L., Nojoumian, M.: A survey on trust in autonomous systems. In: Arai, K., Kapoor, S., Bhatia, R. (eds.) SAI 2018. AISC, vol. 857, pp. 368–386. Springer, Cham (2019). https://doi.org/10.1007/978-3-030-01177-2_27
27. Shapiro, S.S., Wilk, M.B.: An analysis of variance test for normality (complete samples). Biometrika **52**(3–4), 591–611 (1965)
28. Spearman, C.: The proof and measurement of association between two things (1961). https://doi.org/10.1037/11491-005
29. Ueno, T., Sawa, Y., Kim, Y., Urakami, J., Oura, H., Seaborn, K.: Trust in human-ai interaction: scoping out models, measures, and methods. In: CHI Conference on Human Factors in Computing Systems Extended Abstracts, pp. 1–7 (2022). https://doi.org/10.1145/3491101.3519772
30. Ullman, D., Malle, B.F.: MDMT: multi-dimensional measure of trust (2019)
31. Waytz, A., Epley, N., Cacioppo, J.T.: Social cognition unbound: Insights into anthropomorphism and dehumanization. Curr. Dir. Psychol. Sci. **19**(1), 58–62 (2010). https://doi.org/10.1177/0963721409359302
32. Waytz, A., Gray, K., Epley, N., Wegner, D.M.: Causes and consequences of mind perception. Trends Cogn. Sci. **14**(8), 383–388 (2010). https://doi.org/10.1016/j.tics.2010.05.006

Multimodal Assessment of Human Trust and Cognitive Load in Legged Robot Interaction

Juan José García Cárdenas[1](✉), Changda Tian[2], Panos Trahanias[2], and Adriana Tapus[1]

[1] U2IS, ENSTA, IP Paris, Palaiseau, France
juan-jose.garcia@ensta-paris.fr
[2] Foundation for Research and Technology - Hellas, Iraklio, Greece

Abstract. This paper investigates how terrain complexity and user interaction modes (teleoperation versus passive observation) influence human cognitive load and trust during interactions with a reinforcement learning–trained legged robot navigating complex terrains. We quantitatively assess cognitive load and trust dynamics using multimodal physiological measurements, including GSR, facial skin temperature, and blink rate combined with self-reported NASA-TLX scores. Participants either actively teleoperated or passively observed the robot traversing flat surfaces, irregular terrains, and stairs within a high-fidelity Isaac-Gym simulation. Our findings highlight distinct physiological and subjective responses linked to both terrain difficulty and interaction role. Specifically, teleoperators experienced higher cognitive load but stable trust levels, whereas observers showed heightened stress responses and reduced trust during challenging terrain navigation. By combining reinforcement learning robot locomotion with multimodal physiological sensing, this research advances methods for real-time assessment of trust and workload in human-robot interaction, offering insights for designing more adaptive and user-centered robotic systems.

Keywords: Physiological Signals · Human-Robot Interaction · Legged Robots · Reinforcement learning

1 Introduction

Robots are increasingly deployed in complex and unstructured environments—ranging from search-and-rescue operations to industrial settings—often interacting closely with human operators or observers. In these scenarios, two critical factors significantly affect human–robot interaction (HRI): trust in robotic capabilities and human cognitive load. Trust influences humans' willingness to rely on robotic autonomy under uncertainty [1,2], while cognitive

---

J. J. García Cárdenas and C. Tian—Equally contributed.

load affects their capacity to manage robot-related tasks effectively. Misalignment in either factor may lead to misuse, disuse, or compromised operational effectiveness [1].

Recent advances in reinforcement learning (RL) have dramatically improved legged robots' agility, enabling autonomous navigation of challenging terrains, such as uneven grounds and stairs [3,4]. These developments hold promise for high-mobility robotic applications, yet their impact on human cognitive load and trust remains underexplored. In particular, little is known about how real-time robot performance in complex environments affects user trust dynamics or modulates mental workload.

Prior HRI studies commonly utilize subjective, post-interaction questionnaires to measure trust and cognitive load [2,5], offering limited insights into dynamic variations during live interactions. Moreover, studies integrating physiological sensing with advanced, agile robots—especially those trained via RL—remain sparse. This highlights a pressing need to understand human responses during interaction with such systems in realistic settings.

To address these gaps, we present a comprehensive study combining RL-trained locomotion for a legged robot (Unitree Go2) with multimodal physiological sensing—including galvanic skin response (GSR), facial skin temperature, and blink rate—and subjective measures (NASA-TLX). Participants either actively teleoperated or passively observed the robot navigating simulated terrains of varying complexity (flat, irregular, and stairs) in IsaacGym. Our contributions include:

- Developing a multimodal sensor fusion framework to quantitatively assess trust and cognitive load during real-time interactions.
- Providing empirical insights on how terrain complexity and interaction roles impact physiological and subjective indicators of trust and cognitive load.
- Introducing the novel concept of *terrain-informed trust*, illustrating trust dynamics shaped by real-time robotic performance.

Our findings deepen the understanding of human responses to advanced robotic systems, guiding the design of adaptive, trust-aware robot controllers for enhanced human–robot cooperation. Although Bayesian Neural Networks (BNNs) themselves are well established, the novelty of our study lies in how we join BNN inside a terrain informed space model and run the whole pipeline online during human interaction with a RL trained quadruped model. Concretely, our architecture (i) fuses GSR, blink dynamics, and facial temperature in a single space, (ii) introduces participants effects priors that capture individual physiological baselines, and (iii) continuously conditions these physiological posteriors on real-time navigation terrains (slips, recoveries, stair ascent, etc.). This integration produces a dynamic "trust and cognitive load" signal that adapts to each terrain. By closing the loop between an agile RL controller and multimodal Bayesian inference, we enable the first real-time assessment of human trust and cognitive load in legged-robot HRI and provide a foundation for adaptive autonomy on rough terrain.

2 Related Work

2.1 Trust and Cognitive Load Estimation Using Physiological Measures

To understand the intertwined constructs of cognitive load and trust is central to advancing human−robot interaction (HRI). Mental workload has traditionally been gauged through subjective instruments such as the NASA Task Load Index (NASA-TLX) [6], which captures perceived mental, physical and temporal demands, effort, frustration, and performance. In teleoperation studies these self-reports are now routinely complemented by objective, real-time physiological markers−galvanic skin response (GSR), blink rate, facial skin temperature, and pupil dilation−that rise with heightened cognitive effort or stress [7]. Behaviour-based metrics have likewise proven informative: some authors [8] showed that performance indicators can sometimes detect workload changes more reliably than subjective ratings, while others [9] demonstrated mobile multimodal setups that unobtrusively estimate cognitive load outside controlled laboratories.

Trust, meanwhile, determines the extent to which users are willing to rely on automation. The framework proposed by Lee [1] emphasizes the risks of both over-trust and under-trust, advocating for system designs that promote 'appropriate reliance.' Comprehensive meta-analyses by Hancock et al. [2] and Schaefer et al. [5] identify performance, behavioral transparency, user attributes, task difficulty, and prior experience as central factors influencing trust in automation. To assess these perceptions, the Trust Perception Scale-HRI [10] offers a validated and reliable measurement instrument. Reflecting trends in workload sensing, researchers have started to infer trust directly from physiology: electrodermal activity (EDA) serves as a proxy for emotional and cognitive stress [11]. Other researchers [12] achieved real-time trust classification by multiple biosignals fusion. While some others like Green and Iqbal [13] combined gaze, facial expressions, and physiology to improve trust prediction; and Alzahrani and Ahmad [14] showed that multi-signal fusion enables finer-grained trust calibration during interaction.

Previous work provides robust subjective scales (NASA-TLX, Trust Perception Scale-HRI) and a growing repertoire of physiological markers for monitoring cognitive load and trust. Yet most studies concentrate on manipulator teleoperation or generic screen-based tasks, leaving open how these findings translate to legged-robot locomotion scenarios of varying surface complexity. By simultaneously collecting blink rate, facial temperature, GSR, and NASA-TLX while participants view robots walking on flat floors, irregular terrains, and stairs, the present study extends workload-and-trust research to this ecologically salient domain and probes how locomotion-surface complexity modulates observers' mental effort and trust.

2.2 Impact of Autonomy and Control Modes on Trust and Cognitive Load

The level of robot's autonomy and the operator–robot control mode have profound ramifications for both cognitive load and trust in teleoperation. Pan et al. [15] showed in a trajectory-tracking task that raising autonomy from manual to shared control decreased operators' NASA-TLX scores and pupil-based workload indices, yet the same manipulation produced only a modest increase in trust, hinting that load and trust respond to autonomy along partly independent axes. Modeling work corroborates this dissociation: Guo and Yang [16] used Bayesian inference to predict how trust evolves with successive successes or failures, arguing that controllers should adapt autonomy in anticipation of these trust dynamics rather than presume a monotonic relationship. Furthermore, there are some other researches that use this approach to measure the effect of dynamics along trust [17].

Beyond single-robot scenarios, Turco et al. [18] demonstrated that a data-driven shared-control scheme can off-load a swarm operator by dynamically allocating degrees of freedom, yielding faster completion times and lower NASA-TLX without eroding trust. Crucially, where the autonomy is experienced in a high-fidelity simulator or with a physical robot–also matters. In a recent navigation study, Tsoi et al. [19] reported that participants rated identical behaviours as significantly more cognitively demanding and, paradoxically, less competent when encountered in a virtual environment than when viewed on a real robot, underscoring a simulation-to-reality gap that can confound attempts to generalize laboratory findings. Objective sensing can help disentangle such context effects: Hu et al. [20] mapped GSR and EEG features to online trust levels, while Green and Iqbal [13] showed that fusing pupil dilation with electrodermal and skin-temperature signals improved trust-prediction accuracy in an industrial-assembly simulation. These results suggest that future adaptive controllers should monitor both subjective ratings and multimodal physiological cues–particularly, ocular metrics that can be captured unobtrusively–to calibrate autonomy in ways that transfer robustly from simulation to the field.

3 Methodology

This section outlines the key methodologies used in the study, including reinforcement learning for legged robot locomotion, multimodal data fusion to evaluate human trust and cognitive load, and other essential analytical techniques.

3.1 Reinforcement Learning-Based Legged Locomotion Control

We formulate the legged locomotion control problem as a Markov Decision Process (MDP) defined by the tuple $(\mathcal{S}, \mathcal{A}, f, r, p_0, \gamma)$, where $\mathcal{S}$ is the state space, $\mathcal{A}$ is the action space, f represents the system dynamics, r denotes the reward function, p_0 is the initial state distribution, and γ is the discount factor. The objective is to find a stochastic policy $\pi_\theta : \mathcal{S} \to \mathcal{A}$ parameterized by θ that maximizes the expected discounted return:

$$J(\pi_\theta) = \mathbb{E}\left[\sum_{t=0}^{T-1} \gamma^t r(s_t, a_t)\right]. \quad (1)$$

In this work, we design the reward function to encourage the robot to track a target command velocity $\mathbf{v}_t = [v_t^x, v_t^y, \omega_t]$, where v_t^x and v_t^y are the desired forward and lateral base velocities, and ω_t is the desired yaw rate. The tracking reward is defined as:

$$r_t = w_v \exp\left(-\|\mathbf{v}_t^{xy} - \hat{\mathbf{v}}_t^{xy}\|^2\right) + w_\omega \exp\left(-\|\omega_t - \hat{\omega}_t\|^2\right), \quad (2)$$

where $\hat{\mathbf{v}}_t^{xy}$ and $\hat{\omega}_t$ are the observed linear and angular velocities, respectively, and w_v, w_ω are scalar weighting factors. The command velocities are sampled randomly within specified ranges to promote diverse locomotion behaviors across different speeds and turning rates.

3.2 Multimodal HRI Assessment for Trust and Cognitive Load

Physiological Data Acquisition and Processing. Physiological activity was recorded continuously with three synchronized channels. Electrodermal activity was captured from the distal phalanges of the non-dominant hand using *Shimmer3 GSR+* units (Shimmer Sensing, Dublin, Ireland) [21]. The devices streamed conductance at 128 Hz, then a fourth-order Butterworth low-pass filter at 5 Hz removed high-frequency noise; segments contaminated by motion spikes exceeding three standard deviations from the local median were replaced by linear interpolation. Facial skin temperature was monitored with an *Optris PI 640i* [22] infrared camera (640×480 px, 125 fps) positioned 60 cm in front of the participant and factory-calibrated with a 35 C black-body source at the start of each session. Video frames were processed offline with *dlib* [23] to track 68 facial landmarks; regions of interest (forehead, perinasal area, cheeks) were mapped into the temperature field and averaged per frame to yield three region-specific temperature streams.

Blink activity served as an ocular index of workload. An RGB camera (Logitech Brio, 1920 × 1080 at 60 fps) recorded each participant's face, and *MediaPipe* [24] computed the eye-aspect ratio frame-wise; transient drops below an adaptive threshold for at least three consecutive frames were labelled as blinks. From the resulting blink timestamps we derived *three complementary measures*: (i) a *cumulative blink rate*—total blinks within a fixed 60 s window, reported as blinks min^{-1}; (ii) a *sliding-window blink rate* computed over a 5 s moving window advanced sample-by-sample, capturing rapid workload fluctuations; and (iii) an *instantaneous blink rate* defined as the reciprocal of the current inter-blink interval, providing the finest temporal resolution.

To ensure sub-millisecond alignment of all modalities with the simulation timeline, we implemented a lightweight *Flask* HTTP server [25] that acted as a central time-stamping hub. The resulting dataset therefore contains perfectly aligned physiological traces and event markers, enabling precise multimodal fusion and accurate estimation of moment-to-moment cognitive-load state from the combined blink-rate metrics, skin conductance, and facial-temperature signals.

Feature Extraction and Data Fusion. Raw physiological streams were first baseline-corrected to account for inter-individual variability. Each participant sat quietly for 60 s prior to the first video; the median conductance, blink rate, and facial temperature recorded in this interval were subtracted sample-wise from subsequent data, yielding zero-referenced signals that emphasise task-evoked departures from rest. Electrodermal activity was further decomposed into tonic and phasic components with continuous deconvolution; phasic driver peaks exceeding $0.05\,\mu S$ above baseline were time-stamped and grouped into 10 s windows centred on locomotion events (flat-to-uneven transition, stair ascent, stumble). Within each window we extracted the number of skin-conductance responses (SCR count), their mean amplitude, and the area under the phasic curve. Blink features were computed on three time scales: cumulative blinks per minute, a sliding-window rate (window $=5$ s, step $=1$ s), and the instantaneous blink-frequency series (inverse inter-blink interval), from which we derived the mean, maximum, and standard deviation for each event window. Facial temperature traces from the forehead and cheek regions were smoothed with a 0.5 s Gaussian kernel; for every event we calculated the mean temperature change, its first derivative (slope), and variance, capturing both absolute warming/cooling and speed of thermal response. All features were z-normalised per participant to preserve within-subject dynamics while enabling between-subject modelling. Multimodal inference of cognitive load and trust employed a hierarchical Bayesian regression in which NASA-TLX sub-scores served as continuous targets [17]. Feature-level fusion was implemented by concatenating the z-scored GSR, ocular, and thermal descriptors into a single vector; participant identity entered the model as a random-effects term, allowing population-level coefficients while retaining individual deviations. Data were stratified chronologically, with 80 % of trials allocated to training and the remaining 20 % to held-out testing; within the training fold we performed five-fold cross-validation to tune the prior precision hyper-parameters via maximization of the evidence lower bound. Predictive accuracy was assessed with the coefficient of determination (R^2) and root-mean-square error for continuous outcomes, and Cohen's κ after binning TLX scores into low/medium/high workload classes. Posterior predictive checks confirmed calibration (posterior $p > 0.2$ for all subjects). The interface is depicted in Fig. 1.

Quantitative Assessment of Cognitive Load and Trust. The baseline corrected physiological features described above were mapped to continuous workload labels (NASA-TLX overall and sub-scale scores) with a hierarchical Bayesian neural network (BNN) [17]. Feature vectors $\mathbf{x}_{i,t}$ for participant i and event window t were fed into two hidden layers (ReLU activations, 64 and 16 units) whose weights carried Gaussian priors; the output layer produced

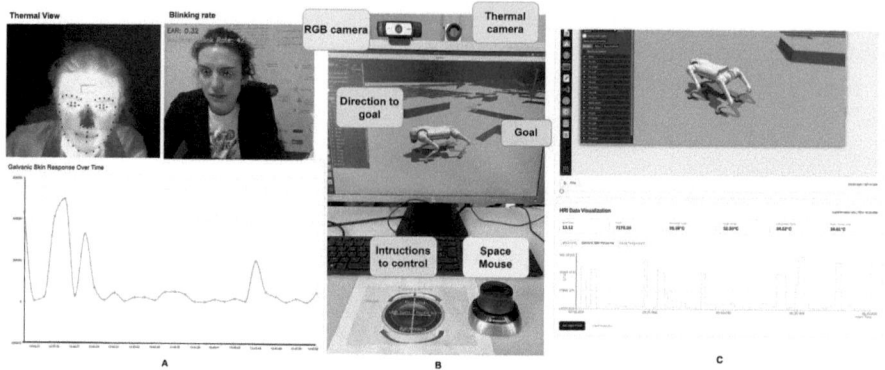

Fig. 1. a) Online interface to monitor the physiological measures of participants. b) Interface and controller the participant uses to control the robot in simulation. c) Interface to analyze and extract high peak cognitive load moments.

posterior predictive distributions $p(\text{TLX} \mid \mathbf{x}_{i,t})$. Spearman correlations computed on posterior means confirmed significant monotonic associations between physiology and subjectively reported load (e.g. phasic GSR amplitude: $\rho = 0.62$, $p<.001$; sliding-window blink rate: $\rho = 0.57$, $p<.001$). The BNN's probabilistic outputs were collapsed into a scalar *Cognitive-Load Index* by taking the expected TLX score $\hat{y}_{i,t}$, which preserves uncertainty and allows direct comparison with questionnaire values.

Trust was treated as a latent, time-varying belief that integrates both physiological cues and objective robot performance. First, a subset of features EDA amplitude, facial-temperature slope, and instantaneous blink rate was entered into a second BNN jointly trained with the workload network but using Trust Perception Scale-HRI scores as targets. Posterior parameter inspection revealed that higher phasic EDA and steeper temperature drops (forehead cooling) corresponded to lower reported trust, whereas stable ocular patterns predicted higher trust, echoing prior findings on arousal-based distrust. Second, we embedded these physiological predictions in a *terrain-informed state-space model*:

$$T_t = T_{t-1} + \alpha \, \Delta P_t + \beta \, \hat{T}_t^{\text{phys}} + \epsilon_t,$$
$$\Delta P_t = \text{Perf}_t - \text{Perf}_{t-1},$$

where T_t is latent trust at time t, ΔP_t is the change in robot performance (slip ratio, completion time) on the current terrain segment, and $\hat{T}_t^{\text{phys}}$ is the BNN-inferred physiological trust score; $\epsilon_t \sim \mathcal{N}(0, \sigma^2)$. Parameters α and β were estimated with Hamiltonian Monte Carlo on the training set (80 %), producing posterior distributions that quantify how much trust shifts in response to performance vs. physiology. Held-out log-likelihood and continuous ranked probability score showed that the fused model outperformed physiology-only or performance-only baselines ($p<.01$). The resulting trajectory T_t constitutes a *terrain-informed trust metric*: it rises after successful negotiation of difficult surfaces, falls after slips, and is modulated in real-time by the operator's arousal state, offering a principled, dynamical estimate of trust suitable for adaptive autonomy controllers.

4 Experiment

4.1 Participants

A total of 25 participants (16 males, 9 females) volunteered for the experiment. Their ages ranged from 18 to 31 years ($M = 25.0$, $SD = 3.1$). Participants originated from diverse geographic backgrounds including Europe (11), Asia (6), and South America (8). Educational levels varied: undergraduate students (7), master's degree holders/students (14), Ph.D. holders/students (3), and high school graduates (2). Participants rated their frequency of interactions with robots in daily life, experience with game controllers/simulators, attitudes toward robots performing tasks traditionally done by humans, and perceived robot usefulness on 5-point Likert scale (see Table 1 for summary statistics).

Table 1. Participant Demographics and Questionnaire Responses

Demographic Information/Question	Mean (M)	Std. Dev. (SD)	Min	Max
Age (years)	25.0	3.1	18	31
Frequency of robot interaction (1–5)	2.8	1.5	1	5
Experience with controllers/simulators (1–5)	3.0	1.5	1	5
Attitude towards robots replacing human tasks (1–5)	4.0	0.9	2	5
Perceived robot usefulness (1–5)	4.3	0.7	3	5

4.2 Experimental Apparatus

Simulation Environment and Robotic Platform. We utilize the Isaac-Gym simulation platform developed by NVIDIA, which offers GPU-accelerated physics simulation, allowing for the training and evaluation of large-scale reinforcement learning policies in parallel. The simulated robotic platform is based on the Unitree Go2, a quadrupedal legged robot equipped with torque-controlled joints and capable of agile locomotion over complex terrains. The simulation includes procedurally generated terrains comprising flat floors, irregular surfaces, and stair-like structures to vary the locomotion difficulty.

Our simulation environment has multiple and different types of surfaces. For example it contains *easy stairs* range from 0.10 m to 0.20 m, whereas the *difficult stairs* reach up to 0.30 m. Each staircase segment comprises 30–50 steps, and the tread depth is kept fixed at 0.25 m so that the incline is fully determined by riser height. Also, we have an "irregular" patch whose gentle bumps and hollows come from Gaussian noise, and one or more staircases. All of these features are

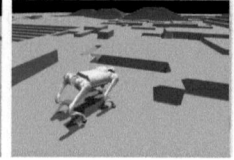

Fig. 2. Go2 locomotion environments in IsaacGym. With flat, uneven, platforms and trenches at random locations and heights and stairs terrain types.

dropped at random positions and orientations, so no two runs look exactly the same, even though the overall proportions of plain, uneven, and stepped terrain remain fixed (Figs. 2 and 4).

Control Interface. Participants interact with the robot using a 3Dconnexion SpaceMouse, a six-degree-of-freedom input device. The SpaceMouse enables intuitive control of the robot's command velocities: forward (v^x), lateral (v^y), and yaw rate (ω). Simultaneously, users can rotate the virtual camera view within the simulation environment, providing a natural and immersive teleoperation experience without the need for separate input devices.

4.3 Experimental Design and Procedure

The experiment consisted of two sequential stages designed to assess human trust and cognitive load during both passive observation and active teleoperation of a legged robot in complex environments.

Stage 1: Video Observation of Robot Locomotion. In the first stage, participants passively observed 5 randomly chosen prerecorded videos of the Unitree Go2 robot navigating various terrains in the IsaacGym simulation environment. The terrains included four categories of increasing complexity:

1. **Flat terrain**: Smooth, unobstructed surfaces.
2. **Uneven terrain**: Surfaces with random height perturbations and irregularities.
3. **Complex terrain**: Environments containing randomly placed obstacles, platforms, and trenches at varying heights and locations.
4. **Staircases**: Structured stairs for ascending and descending movements.

The videos showcased both successful locomotion trials and failure cases (e.g., falling or stumbling), recorded using the trained RL-based locomotion controller. Each participant viewed five videos randomly selected from the video pool to ensure diverse exposure to different terrain types and robot performance outcomes. During this stage, physiological data (GSR, facial temperature, and blink rate) were collected continuously to capture participants' cognitive and emotional responses to observed robot behaviors.

Stage 2: Active Teleoperation of the Robot. In the second stage, participants actively teleoperated the simulated Go2 robot using a 3Dconnexion SpaceMouse. The robot was placed within a procedurally generated complex environment featuring all four terrain types described above. The task required participants to navigate the robot toward designated goals, indicated by a green directional arrow on top of the robot and a floating red arrow marking the goal location within the environment. Each participant must complete this task five times during the experiment.

Participants controlled the robot's command velocities (v^x, v^y, ω) while simultaneously adjusting the camera perspective using the SpaceMouse. Real-time physiological data collection continued during teleoperation to capture cognitive load and trust dynamics as users engaged with the robot under varying terrain challenges.

Experimental Conditions and Counterbalancing. Two interaction modes were incorporated in the experiment:

1. **Passive observation**: Video watching during Stage 1.
2. **Active teleoperation**: Robot control during Stage 2.

Terrain complexity varied naturally within the environment across both stages. To minimize order effects, the order of video presentation and the initial locations of goals in the teleoperation task were randomized across participants. Each video trial during observation lasted approximately 30–45 s. During teleoperation, participants completed multiple goal-reaching tasks with self-paced movement, with total teleoperation time capped at 15 min to avoid excessive fatigue. Short breaks were offered between stages to ensure participant comfort and physiological signal stability. Throughout both stages, robot locomotion data, terrain information, and user physiological responses were time-synchronized and logged for subsequent analysis.

5 Results

5.1 1st Stage Video Observation of Robot Locomotion

Cognitive Load and Trust Results. For each participant we derived a Cognitive-Load Index (CLI) and a Trust Index (TI) on every one-second epoch and then aggregated them over the five viewed videos using our Bayesian model. A two-way repeated-measures ANOVA with factors *Terrain* (flat, uneven, complex, stairs) and *Previous-Outcome* (success vs. failure in the immediately preceding video) showed that cognitive load varied systematically with both situational context and viewing history. Terrain exerted a large main effect on phasic GSR amplitude[1], $F(3, 57) = 12.41$, $p < .001$, partial $\eta^2 = 0.39$: mean z-CLI increased from flat ($M = 0.10$, $SD = 0.16$) through uneven ($M = 0.31$,

---

[1] CLI and TI were standardised per subject before analysis; physiological features were averaged within each terrain segment.

$SD = 0.18$) and complex ($M = 0.55$, $SD = 0.19$) to stairs ($M = 0.73$, $SD = 0.21$). A significant main effect of Previous-Outcome, $F(1, 19) = 9.83$, $p = 0.005$, partial $\eta^2 = 0.34$, revealed that observing a robot failure primed a higher baseline load in the following video (mean GSR peaks 2.8 vs. 1.9 per 10-s window). The *Terrain×Previous-Outcome* interaction was reliable, $F(3, 57) = 4.02$, $p = 0.011$, driven by the largest post-failure CLI gain on stairs ($\Delta z = +0.21$). Facial-temperature cooling and blink-rate metrics mirrored these effects (forehead cooling: Terrain $F(3, 57) = 7.26$, $p < .001$; Previous-Outcome $F(1, 19) = 6.44$, $p = 0.020$; blinking rate: $F(3, 57) = 10.17$, $p < .001$). These results can be seen in Fig. 3.

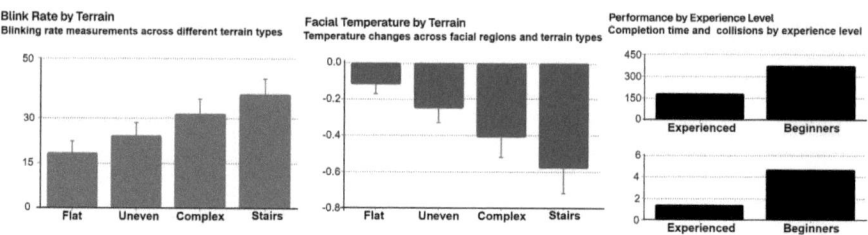

Fig. 3. a) Average blinking rate per terrain **phase 1** b) Average facial temperature change per terrain **phase 1** c) Performance level in **phase 2** according to the experience level of the users.

Aggregating across all 25 participants, a one-way ANOVA on z-CLI confirmed a pronounced terrain effect, $F(3, 76) = 28.4$, $p < .001$, $\eta^2 = 0.53$, with mean z-CLI rising from flat (0.05 ± 0.12) and uneven (0.28 ± 0.15) to complex (0.61 ± 0.18) and stairs (0.79 ± 0.19). GSR peaks and TI followed the same gradient (peaks: 1.1 ± 0.6 to 3.2 ± 0.9; TI: 0.72 ± 0.10 to 0.41 ± 0.13). Peak-amplitude effects were significant, $F(3, 76) = 22.7$, $p < .001$, and blink-rate variance differed by terrain (Levene's $p = 0.021$; Welch $F_{3, 46.8} = 15.3$, $p < .001$). CLI and TI were strongly negatively correlated across terrains ($r = -0.68$, $p < .001$), and post-hoc Games–Howell tests (Holm–Bonferroni adjusted) revealed significantly higher load and lower trust for complex/stairs versus flat/uneven ($p_{\text{adj}} < 0.01$ for all) (Table 2).

Table 2. Stage 1 (Video Observation) – CLI and TI by Terrain

Terrain	z-CLI (M ± SD)	GSR peaks/10 s (M ± SD)	Trust Index (M ± SD)
Flat	0.05 ± 0.12	1.1 ± 0.6	0.72 ± 0.10
Uneven	0.28 ± 0.15	1.9 ± 0.7	0.64 ± 0.11
Complex	0.61 ± 0.18	2.7 ± 0.8	0.48 ± 0.12
Stairs	0.79 ± 0.19	3.2 ± 0.9	0.41 ± 0.13

5.2 2nd Stage Active Teleoperation of the Robot

General Performance. Twenty-five participants completed five successful teleoperation runs each (total successful runs = 125, but total runs > 125, including many failure runs). Based on prior joystick/video-game experience, 14 were classified as *Experienced* and 11 as *Novice*. Experienced users completed runs in 182 ± 25s versus 375 ± 48s for novices (54 % faster, $t(23) = 11.0$, $p < .001$, $d = 3.46$) and committed 1.4 ± 0.6 versus 4.7 ± 1.1 collisions (70 % fewer, $t(23) = 9.2$, $p < .001$, $d = 2.89$). NASA−TLX ratings did not differ between groups on any dimension (all $p > 0.11$, $|d| < 0.7$); overall means indicated high mental demand (6.5), moderate effort (6.6), low physical demand (4.0), strong perceived performance (7.0), and moderate frustration (5.0) (Table 3).

Cognitive Load and Trust Results. A two-way repeated-measures ANOVA on z-CLI with factors *EventType* (normal navigation, camera reorientation, crash & reset) and *Terrain* yielded main effects of EventType, $F(3, 72) = 31.6$, $p < .001$, $\eta_p^2 = 0.57$, and Terrain, $F(3, 72) = 15.8$, $p < .001$, plus a significant interaction, $F(9, 216) = 3.9$, $p = 0.001$. Crashes elicited the highest load

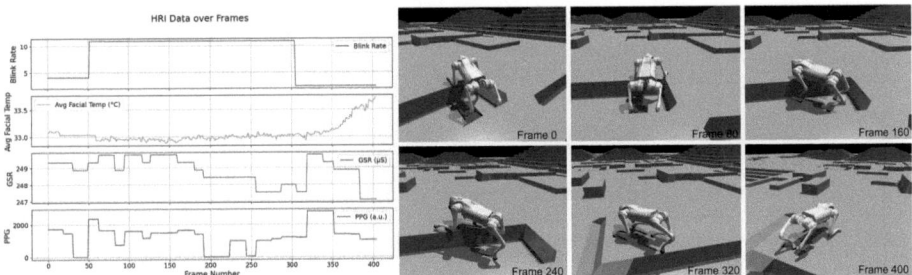

Fig. 4. a) HRI data curve in one run b) The active teleoperation performance of the robot with respect to the HRI data.

Table 3. Stage 2 (Teleoperation) − Performance and NASA−TLX by Experience

Metric	Experienced		Novice		Test / d	
	M	SD	M	SD	Statistic	
Completion time (s)	182	25	375	48	$t(23) = 11.0$, $p < .001$	3.46
Collisions/falls (count/run)	1.4	0.6	4.7	1.1	$t(23) = 9.2$, $p < .001$	2.89
Mental demand (0−10)	6.2	1.9	6.0	3.1	$t(16) = 0.19$, $p = 0.85$	0.08
Physical demand (0−10)	4.5	2.5	4.6	2.8	$t(20) = -0.16$, $p = 0.88$	-0.06
Temporal demand (0−10)	4.7	2.2	5.2	2.4	$t(20) = -0.48$, $p = 0.64$	-0.19
Performance (0−10)	7.3	1.8	5.8	2.6	$t(17) = 1.68$, $p = 0.11$	0.70
Effort (0−10)	6.7	1.6	6.4	2.0	$t(19) = 0.50$, $p = 0.62$	0.21
Frustration (0−10)	5.3	2.7	4.9	2.5	$t(22) = 0.35$, $p = 0.73$	0.14

(0.82 ± 0.17; 86 % above normal navigation), GSR peaks rose from 2.0 ± 0.7 to 3.5 ± 0.9 ($t(24) = 10.2$, $p < .001$), and blink rate doubled (22.1 ± 4.6 to 38.2 ± 5.1, $t(24) = 9.1$, $p < .001$). Trust dropped by 0.25 after failures. Novices exhibited larger CLI increases on stairs (0.62 ± 0.18 vs. 0.37 ± 0.15, $t(23) = 4.29$, $p < .001$, $d = 1.68$) and greater blink-rate variance (12.1 vs. 6.4; Levene's $p = 0.018$) than experienced operators, indicating that skill amplifies load and trust disparities (Table 4).

Table 4. Stage 2 (Teleoperation) – Physiological Load and Trust by Event Type

Metric	Normal navigation	Camera reorientation	Crash/reset	Test
z-CLI (M ± SD)	0.44 ± 0.19	0.62 ± 0.20	0.82 ± 0.17	$F(3, 72) = 31.6$, $p < .001$
GSR peaks/10 s (M ± SD)	2.0 ± 0.7	—	3.5 ± 0.9	$t(24) = 10.2$, $p < .001$
Blinking rate (blinks/min, M ± SD)	22.1 ± 4.6	—	38.2 ± 5.1	$t(24) = 9.1$, $p < .001$
Δ Trust Index[a]	—	—	-0.25	—

[a] Δ Trust Index was only computed for the crash/reset condition by comparing trust immediately before versus after the failure; it is therefore not applicable to normal navigation or camera reorientation.

5.3 Comparative Evaluation

To quantify the added value of explicitly modelling terrain performance dynamics, we benchmarked the proposed *terrain-informed BNN + state-space model* against three alternatives trained on the identical 20 % held-out fold: (i) the physiology-only *static BNN* of [17]; (ii) a real-time trust-classification pipeline that fuses phasic-GSR and EEG features [26]; and (iii) the shared-control trust predictor of [27]. Replicating their architectures on our dataset gives us $R^2 = 0.52$ (RMSE = 1.73 TLX pts) for the static BNN and $R^2 \approx 0.50$ for the two signal-fusion baselines. By contrast, our dynamic model reached $R^2 = 0.68$ with RMSE = 1.18, improving explained variance by 30 % and reducing error by 31 %. On the other hand the continuous ranked probability score dropped by 17 % relative to the best baseline, with all differences significant at $p < 0.001$ under paired bootstrap tests. These results confirm us the preliminary analyses that already showed superiority over the other studies.

6 Conclusions

This study demonstrates that both cognitive load and trust in legged-robot interaction are strongly modulated by terrain complexity and by the operator's recent experience with robotics, video games or related. Across passive observation and active teleoperation, physiological markers (phasic GSR, blink dynamics, facial-temperature change) and Bayesian-network indices converged with NASA-TLX ratings to show a rising in cognitive workload and an indirect drop in trust from flat through uneven and complex ground to staircases. Other factors like crashes, or stalls witnessing a failure in the immediately preceding trial produced an additional mental load and trust decrement, underscoring the temporal fragility of these constructs. Operator skill buffered but did not eliminate the terrain effects. This means beginners exhibited larger GSR peaks and greater blinking rate variance than experienced users. However, both groups ranked stairs and irregular obstacles as the most taxing and least trustworthy conditions. Together, these findings highlight the dual influence of environmental difficulty and interaction history on human cognitive state and reveal objective physiological signatures that could support adaptive assistance.

Our next goal is to close the sim to real loop by replicating the experiment on a physical Unitree Go2 operating in outdoor environments. We plan to integrate the multimodal load and trust estimators into a reinforcement-learning controller that modulates speed, navigation control algorithm, and viewpoint framing to minimize the operator's cognitive load. Teleoperation will be performed over long-range wireless links to investigate how network latency and reduced situational awareness adjust the effect of the terrain. Ultimately, coupling user-state feedback with autonomous locomotion promises safer, more fluent human-legged-robot collaboration in field applications such as inspection and search-and-rescue.

Acknowledgments. This research work has received full funding from the European Commission's HORIZON.1.2 - Marie Skłodowska-Curie Actions (MSCA) under Grant agreement No. 101072634, project RAICAM.

References

1. Lee, J.D., See, K.A.: Trust in automation: designing for appropriate reliance. Hum. Factors **46**(1), 50–80 (2004)
2. Hancock, P.A., Kessler, T.T., Kaplan, A.D., Brill, J.C., Szalma, J.L.: Evolving trust in robots: specification through sequential and comparative meta-analyses. Hum. Factors **63**(7), 1196–1229 (2021)
3. Hwangbo, J., et al.: Learning agile and dynamic motor skills for legged robots. Sci. Rob. **4**(26), eaau5872 (2019)
4. Margolis, G.B., Yang, G., Paigwar, K., Chen, T., Agrawal, P.: Rapid locomotion via reinforcement learning. Int. J. Rob. Res. **43**(4), 572–587 (2024)
5. Schaefer, K.E., Chen, J.Y.C., Szalma, J.L., Hancock, P.A.: A meta-analysis of factors influencing the development of trust in automation: implications for understanding autonomy in future systems. Hum. Factors **58**(3), 377–400 (2016)
6. Hart, S.G.: NASA-task load index (NASA-TLX); 20 years later. In: Proceedings of the Human Factors and Ergonomics Society Annual Meeting, vol. 50, pp. 904–908. Sage publications Sage CA: Los Angeles, CA (2006)

7. Garcia, J-J., Hei, X., Tapus, A.: Exploring cognitive load dynamics in human-machine interaction for teleoperation: a user-centric perspective on remote operation system design. In: IROS 2024 (2024)
8. Odoh, G., et al.: Performance metrics outperform physiological indicators in robotic teleoperation workload assessment. Sci. Rep. **14**(1), 30984 (2024)
9. Anders, C., Moontaha, S., Real, S., Arnrich, B.: Unobtrusive measurement of cognitive load and physiological signals in uncontrolled environments. Sci. Data **11**(1), 1000 (2024)
10. Schaefer, K.E.: Measuring trust in human robot interactions: development of the "trust perception Scale-HRI". In: Robust Intelligence and Trust in Autonomous Systems, pp. 191–218. Springer (2016)
11. Rahma, O.N., et al.: Electrodermal activity for measuring cognitive and emotional stress level. J. Med. Signals Sens. **12**(2), 155–162 (2022)
12. Wan-Lin, H., Akash, K., Jain, N., Reid, T.: Real-time sensing of trust in human-machine interactions. IFAC-PapersOnLine **49**(32), 48–53 (2016)
13. Green, H.N., Iqbal, T.: Using physiological measures, gaze, and facial expressions to model human trust in a robot partner. arXiv preprint arXiv:2504.05291 (2025)
14. Alzahrani, A., Ahmad, M.: Real-time trust measurement in human-robot interaction: insights from physiological behaviours. In: Proceedings of the 26th International Conference on Multimodal Interaction, pp. 627–631 (2024)
15. Pan, J., Eden, J., Oetomo, D., Johal, W.: Effects of shared control on cognitive load and trust in teleoperated trajectory tracking. IEEE Rob. Autom. Lett. (2024)
16. Guo, Y., Yang, X.J.: Modeling and predicting trust dynamics in human–robot teaming: a Bayesian inference approach. Int. J. Soc. Rob. **13**(8), 1899–1909 (2021)
17. Garcia, J.J., Tapus, A.: Using a Bayesian network to predict user trust in teleoperation robots. In: Proceedings of the International Conference on Social Robotics (ICSR) (2024)
18. Turco, E., Castellani, C., Bo, V., Pacchierotti, C., Prattichizzo, D., Baldi, T.L.: Reducing cognitive load in teleoperating swarms of robots through a data-driven shared control approach. In: 2024 IEEE/RSJ International Conference on Intelligent Robots and Systems (IROS), pp. 4731–4738. IEEE (2024)
19. Tsoi, N., Sterneck, R., Zhao, X., Vázquez, M.: Influence of simulation and interactivity on human perceptions of a robot during navigation tasks. ACM Trans. Hum. Robot Interact. **13**(4), 60:1–60:19 (2024)
20. Wan-Lin, H., Akash, K., Jain, N., Reid, T.: Real-time sensing of trust in human-machine interactions. IFAC-PapersOnLine **49**(32), 48–53 (2016)
21. Burns, A., et al.: Shimmer^{TM}–a wireless sensor platform for noninvasive biomedical research. IEEE Sens. J. **10**(9), 1527–1534 (2010)
22. Ulloa, C.C., Llerena, G.T., Barrientos, A., del Cerro, J.: Autonomous 3D thermal mapping of disaster environments for victims detection. In: Robot Operating System (ROS) The Complete Reference (Volume 7), pp. 83–117. Springer (2023)
23. King, D.E.: Dlib-ml: A machine learning toolkit (2009). http://dlib.net
24. Lugaresi, C., et al.: MediaPipe: a framework for building perception pipelines. In: Proceedings of the 2019 IEEE/CVF Conference on Computer Vision and Pattern Recognition Workshops (CVPRW). IEEE (2019)
25. Grinberg, M.: Flask web development. O'Reilly Media, Inc. (2018)
26. Wan-Lin, H., Akash, K., Jain, N., Reid, T.: Real-time sensing of trust in human-machine interactions. In IFAC-PapersOnLine **49**, 48–53 (2016)
27. Pan, J., Eden, J., Oetomo, D., Johal, W.: Effects of shared control on cognitive load and trust in teleoperated trajectory tracking. IEEE Rob. Autom. Lett. (2024)

Interactive Robotic-Assisted Cognitive Training for Run-Time Personalization: a Preliminary Study

Riccardo De Benedictis[1()], Claudia Di Napoli[2], Gabriella Cortellessa[1], Francesca Fracasso[1], and Annamaria Galluccio[1]

[1] Institute of Cognitive Sciences and Technologies (ISTC), C.N.R, Rome, Italy
{riccardo.debenedictis,gabriella.cortellessa,francesca.fracasso, annamaria.galluccio}@istc.cnr.it
[2] Institute for High Performance Computing and Networking (ICAR), C.N.R., Naples, Italy
claudia.dinapoli@icar.cnr.it

Abstract. Effective deployment of social assistive robots relies on their ability to deliver personalized support tailored to individual users' needs and expectations. Personalization depends on multiple factors, including the nature of the required assistance, the user's interaction preferences, and their cognitive, emotional, and mental states during engagement that represent core personalization factors. Cognitive architectures offer a means to adapt interactions in real time based on user states and environmental conditions. However, verbal interactions represent a crucial factor in human-robot interaction. When including this multi-modal interaction with a robot, relying solely on manually defined inference rules to determine appropriate robot behaviors for every possible scenario and user profile is impractical, particularly when the assistance involves generating context-specific verbal suggestions. At the same time, relying only on machine-learning-based conversational systems introduces indeterminacy that may result risky in assistive robotics applications. In this work, we introduce a framework that combines reactive reasoning with a conversational agent to enable personalized robotic support during cognitive training tasks. We demonstrate how this hybrid approach facilitates the dynamic adaptation of both dialogue and training content in response to observed user behaviour.

Keywords: Assistive robotics · Cognitive architectures · Multimodal interaction

1 Introduction

Social robots are increasingly designed to support humans across a wide spectrum of environments and tasks, from industrial applications like manufacturing to roles such as caregiving and in-home assistance. With the rapid progress in artificial intelligence, particularly in machine learning, robots are gaining enhanced capabilities to perceive, interpret, and act within complex and dynamic settings. A growing frontier in this field is the personalization of human-robot interaction (HRI), where robots are being developed to understand individual human preferences, behaviors, emotional states, and social cues over long-term interactions. Combining machine learning algorithms, user modelling techniques, and the use of sensors to monitor the user's state allows for customizing and adjusting assistive tasks based on the user's characteristics and modifying the robot's interactions in real-time, ensuring a responsive and adaptive experience [2]. Nevertheless, in some settings, such as assisting the elderly to perform specific tasks, robot learning through prolonged interactions with the user is not always feasible. In addition, when users such as the elderly experience conditions that may rapidly evolve, a prolonged interaction may not be useful in gaining knowledge since their personal preferences, behaviours, and perceptions change.

Cognitive training is one of the activities that may benefit the elderly population, mainly when affected by cognitive decline or other forms of neurodegenerative diseases such as Alzheimer's or Parkinson's. To provide cognitive training to a fragile class of users, such as the elderly, it is important to enhance their motivation to perform it [12]. Assistive robots may interact with the user when cognitive training exercises are administered to enhance motivation [4]. Robots capable of responding to and eliciting human emotions not only foster closer collaboration between humans and machines but can also encourage users to experience social connections with these agents. In this context, it is essential to consider individual psychological and behavioral users profiles to optimize therapeutic engagement and improve adherence and therapeutic outcomes. Cognitive architectures that exploit deliberative and reactive dual-process theories [9] can dynamically adapt user interactions by responding appropriately to detected user states. Nevertheless, relying on inference rules to elicit the appropriate behaviour of the robot for each detected situation and specific user may be impractical, mainly because these rules need to be manually crafted, especially when the support consists of providing verbal suggestions that must be generated ad hoc.

In this paper, we propose a robot-assisted cognitive training application, developed within the PRIN project "RESTART: Robot Enhanced Social abilities based on Theory of mind for Acceptance of Robot in Assistive Treatments" [13], which relies on a logic-based cognitive architecture [6] integrated with a transformer-based approach, so as to provide users with an interactive and personalised experience. We carried out a preliminary internal testing of the application to show the advantages of integrating the two approaches.

2 A Multi-modal Framework for Run-Time Personalization and Adaptation

Cognitive architectures constitute computational frameworks intended to model the structural and functional characteristics of human cognition, with an emphasis on the integration and interaction of distinct cognitive subsystems [10,11,14].

These architectures are employed in Artificial Intelligence (AI) to develop systems capable of emulating or interpreting human cognitive behaviors. Such systems are more effective when able to exploit multi-modal interaction. In particular, verbal interaction in robotic applications can ease the emulation and interpretation of human behaviors, and can be used for run-time personalisation.

By integrating cognitive architectures with a Natural Language Processing (NLP) conversational system allows for exploiting different types of information that can trigger personalization at runtime.

For this purpose, we developed the framework shown in Fig. 1, inspired by the COCO cognitive architecture [5]. It is structured into three main layers that operate in sequence, ensuring a fluid and adaptive interaction with the user. The first layer is the reactive layer, which constitutes the system's operational "brain" responsible for rapid and automatic decisions, along with the interpretation of real-time data from the environment (indicated by "s" in Fig. 1) and the activation of appropriate robotic behaviors (indicated by "a" in Fig. 1). This layer is specifically composed of a rule-based reasoning engine implemented via CLIPS[1], which uses "if-then" rules to make decisions or draw conclusions, and a dialogue system built with Rasa[2], which leverages two transformer-based components [15]. They are respectively dedicated to Natural Language Understanding (NLU) and dynamic action selection. Furthermore, this layer is designed to ensure instantaneous reactions, the execution of complex reasoning, and continuous learning through prolonged interaction with the environment, thus satisfying the fundamental requirements of advanced cognitive architectures, i.e., analyzing sensory data to understand the environment in real-time, interpreting user intent, facilitating autonomous decisions based on perceived and interpreted data, and enabling rapid information processing for real-time interactions in dynamic environments [1]. Subsequently, the middleware layer operates as a communication bridge, coordinating the flow of information between the reactive layer and the robotic platform, ensuring interoperability and fluid integration between heterogeneous components. Finally, the robotic platform constitutes the direct physical interface with the user, providing support during cognitive training exercises through speech recognition (speech-to-text), the expression of emotional states via facial expressions and verbal communication, and the execution of adaptive cognitive exercises (e.g., memory games), whose complexity is dynamically regulated based on the user's profile and real-time exercises performance.

An interaction session between the robot and the user begins with the user providing an input, either vocal (via speech-to-text) or textual. The Rasa conversational system intercepts and processes this input. Rasa, leveraging advanced Transformer components, has the primary task of understanding natural language and managing the dialogue flow. Within Rasa, the Dual Intent and Entity Transformer (DIET) component performs Natural Language Understanding (NLU), efficiently extracting the user's specific intention (e.g., if they are

---

[1] https://www.clipsrules.net.
[2] https://rasa.com.

answering a question, asking for help, or giving a command) and identifying any relevant entities (such as a numerical response) [3]. In parallel, the Transformer Embedding Dialogue (TED) component learns a policy that predicts the next optimal action given the current state of the interaction and its history (referred to as *context*)), enabling complex, multi-turn contextual conversations [16]. The training data used for intent classification, i.e., to automatically associate words or expressions with the user's intention, is represented as a set of sentences (referred to as *Examples*) grouped for each specific intent. The training data used for learning the policy to select appropriate actions is represented by *stories* that encode sample interactions as sequences of user intents and system actions.

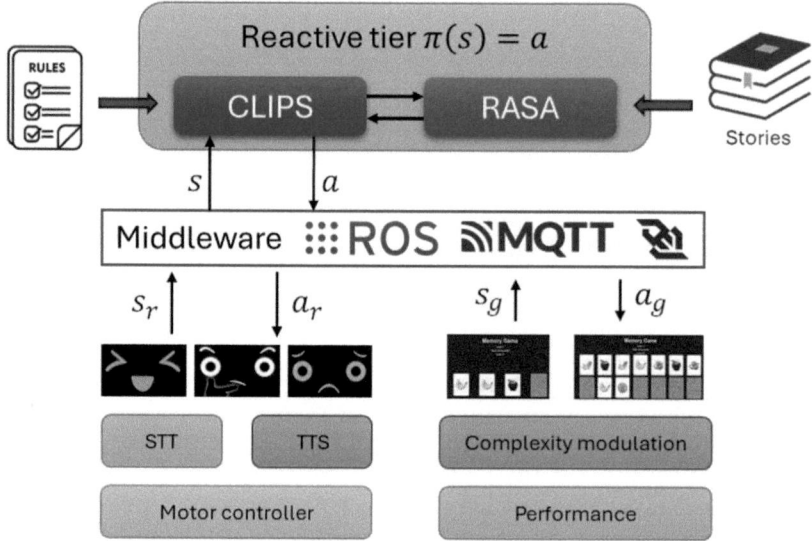

Fig. 1. The framework architecture.

The information processed by Rasa-intents, i.e., recognized entities and conversational state, is then transmitted as *facts* to the CLIPS Rule-Based Reasoning Engine [7,8], which applies a predefined set of deterministic *rules*. Specifically, once these facts are received from Rasa, and integrated with data from other environmental sensors, CLIPS applies its predefined set of "if-then" rules. These rules process the received symbolic data and make logical and reliable decisions. For example, a rule such as "IF the Parkinson's patient's gait deviation exceeds a certain threshold while navigating the living room, THEN instruct the companion robot to provide physical support" is triggered when the facts "the patient's gait deviation has surpassed the threshold" and "the patient is in the living room" are asserted, prompting the system to initiate physical support. By applying predefined rules, the robot can rapidly evaluate the current state of the user and respond to various situations in real-time. Consequently, CLIPS is able to select the most appropriate specific robotic action, which can vary widely, from modifying the complexity of a cognitive exercise, to adapting the dialogue style (making it more or less proactive), or issuing specific instructions for physical support.

Finally, the robotic action selected by CLIPS (indicated by "a" in Fig. 1) is sent to the Middleware Layer that manages the communication between the reactive layer and the sensors and actuators of the robotic platforms, allowing for the seamless integration of heterogeneous platforms. This communication relies on different technologies such as the Robot Operating System (ROS)[3], the Message Queuing Telemetry Transport (MQTT)[4], and the WebSocket protocol.

The NLU component could be realized using large language models (LLMs), which are highly effective at generating natural and contextually appropriate responses. However, LLMs rely on statistical patterns rather than deterministic logic and cannot reliably enforce domain-specific constraints (such as medical protocols or ethical guidelines) unless explicitly fine-tuned with validated external data, which may not always be feasible. In contrast, a dedicated conversational system based on technologies like Rasa's DIET and TED architectures offers a more reliable alternative in critical scenarios, such as interactions with elderly or fragile individuals. This approach enables the integration of domain-specific knowledge tailored to user needs, which is significantly less computationally intensive, thus supporting local execution and faster response times. Additionally, it associates each classified intent with a confidence score which can be leveraged during the interaction. For instance, if it falls below a given threshold, the system can prompt the user to rephrase their input, enhancing robustness and safety.

3 A Personalized Cognitive Training Experience

Cognitive training is administered in different ways according to the user's detected state or personality, e.g., introverted or extroverted, in order to provide a personalised interaction with the user. For this purpose, the robot must collect information about the user's personality by verbally interacting with the user. Engaging the user in a conversation may also provide additional information on the user's current state, requiring adaptation of robot behaviours during cognitive training accordingly. To provide a more natural interaction with the user, the robot relies on the transformer-based module of the architecture that allows conducting conversations with the user instead of administering questionnaires that need to be updated due to the fragile condition of the considered class of users. The possibility of interacting in natural language with the robot may allow users to feel more comfortable since they use the same modality they would have with a human. Nevertheless, users' replies need to be correctly interpreted so as to trigger the suitable robot's behaviours.

---

[3] https://www.ros.org/.
[4] https://mqtt.org/.

We realized a preliminary experimental setup to evaluate the advantages of integrating a transformer-based approach with a logic-based inference engine. This would allow users to reply in natural language while properly selecting robot behaviour according to the user's replies.

More specifically, the cognitive training experimental set up consists of two main steps:

- an initial dialogue initiated by the robot to collect information to evaluate the personality traits (e.g., introvert or extrovert) and the cognitive state of the user (e.g., memory impairment),
- the administration of a cognitive training exercise (e.g., memory game) personalised in terms of the exercise difficulty level and the number and content of the robot's verbal interaction during the exercise, according to the personality trait, the cognitive state and the performance of the user in performing the exercise.

In order to realize such an experimental setup up while it is crucial to rely on a dialogue system to allow the user to interact with the robot in a more natural and friendly modality, it is necessary to guarantee that the robot's behaviors are inferred without the risk of breaking the protocols suggested by clinicians to perform cognitive training.

For this purpose, the two components of the reactive tier of the proposed architecture exploit the capabilities of an NLU, and CLIPS's robust inference engine. In fact, attempting to implement natural language intent recognition using CLIPS rules alone would require the manual definition of a huge and unmanageable number of patterns to cover the wide range of possible user expressions, without the generalization and linguistic variability management capabilities inherent in NLU patterns such as DIET. Computational and development complexity would make this approach impractical. On the other hand, relying exclusively on NLP to infer the user's state and select the appropriate robot's

Table 1. BFI Questions

utter_question_1	In general, do you find it difficult to express your feelings?
utter_question_2	How would you describe your life—would you say it's more boring or exciting?
utter_question_3	Suppose we organized a party and invited friends of friends-would you feel uncomfortable being around people you don't know?
utter_question_4	Sometimes I find myself lost for words. Does that happen to you too?
utter_question_5	Do you feel uncomfortable being the center of attention?

behaviour might not guarantee the determinism required to avoid inappropriate robot behaviour during the interaction.

4 Preliminary Evaluation of the Reactive Tier

Here, we report a preliminary study showing how integrating the two components allows us to exploit the advantages and mitigate the risks of the integration of both approaches in addressing the steps of the cognitive training experience.

Firstly, we simulate a conversation where the system administers a five-item personality questionnaire to the user and subsequently determines a preliminary personality profile based on the user's responses. The personality questionnaire consists of five items, adapted from the Big Five Inventory (BFI) test, reported in Table 1. While not encompassing the full scope of the BFI test, these questions are designed to probe aspects related to extraversion and introversion, a key dimension of personality.

When the questionnaire is administered, the user is required to reply to the 5 questions in natural language. The responses to each question are categorised as either extroverted or introverted, corresponding to a numerical value of 1 and 0, respectively, for deriving the user's personality trait. Following the directives of the Big-5 Test, the extroversion and introversion traits are set respectively according to the average obtained by the response values: an average greater than 0.5 corresponds to an extroverted personality trait, while an average below 0.5 corresponds to an introverted personality trait.

The ability to understand user replies is delegated to the Rasa NLU component. The DIET classifier interprets the responses given in natural language to the questions (e.g., `utter_question_1`), mapping them to structured intents (e.g., `answer_1_extroverted`, `answer_1_introverted`, and so on). The key intents for interpreting user responses to the questionnaire, together with the training data reported as examples, are summarized in Table 2.

The management of the conversational sequence is done by Rasa's Dialogue Policy. Specifically, the *Transformer Embedding Dialogue (TED)* algorithm learns conversational patterns by analyzing a corpus of example dialogues provided as stories. These stories constitute the training data for Rasa's Dialogue Policy, teaching it which sequences of actions (in this case, which sequence of questions) are appropriate depending on the personality trait that is revealed from the received responses and conversational states. An example of a story for training TED to select actions suitable for an extroverted user is reported in Table 3.

It should be noted that the sequence of actions and intents reported in the stories influences the learned policy.

Evaluation of the Rasa User Dialogue Understanding. We performed internal testing to verify the dialogue understanding concerning the questionnaire for the personality trait. In particular, we used the considered examples for the Extrovert and Introvert Response Intent (some of which are reported in

Table 2. Intents for Questionnaire Responses

Extrovert Response Intents	Introvert Response Intents
`answer_1_extroverted` Examples: - no, I tend to be quite an open book... - I am able to express my feelings... - ...	`answer_1_introverted` Examples: - generally it depends on the situation... - I have difficulty expressing my feelings... - ...
`answer_2_extroverted` Examples: - exciting - I definitely find it full of many things that interest me... - ...	`answer_2_introverted` Examples: - boring - lately more boring - my life is boring...
`answer_3_extroverted` Examples: - absolutely not, no problem in fact... - I would have no problem organizing a party at home... - ...	`answer_3_introverted` Examples: - being in a group of people I don't know makes me uncomfortable... - better parties with only friends... - ...
`answer_4_extroverted` Examples: - I rarely run out of topics... - usually I have no difficulty finding the right words... - ...	`answer_4_introverted` Examples: - sometimes I happen to run out of words - sometimes I don't know what to say - ...
`answer_5_extroverted` Examples: - no it's very difficult - I have no discomfort in fact... - I like being the center of attention...	`answer_5_introverted` Examples: - I don't like being the center of attention - I don't like being observed - ...

Table 3. An example of a story to classify an extroverted user.

Intent	Action
start_test	utter_question_1
answer_1_extroverted	utter_question_2
answer_2_extroverted	utter_question_3
answer_3_extroverted	utter_question_4
answer_4_introverted	utter_question_5
answer_5_introverted	utter_result_extroverted

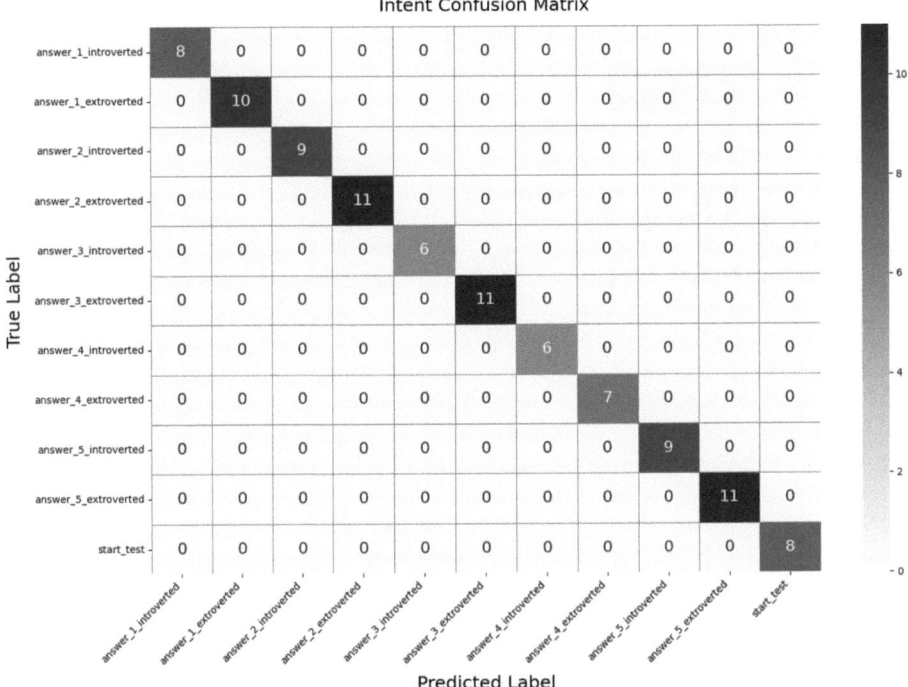

Fig. 2. Intent Confusion Matrix

Table 2) by splitting them into training data (80%) and testing data (20%) obtaining the Intent Confusion Matrix reported in Fig. 2.

The matrix shows high accuracy for the specific intents, confirming Rasa's effectiveness in handling the linguistic variability of responses and correctly translating them into discrete intents. This robust NLU performance is critical, as it validates the use of Rasa for the primary task of natural language interpretation.

Evaluation of Rasa Action Selection. We conducted an experiment to test the ability of Rasa to select appropriate actions according to user personality traits by evaluating, for each step of the dialogue, the match between the predicted action and the expected one according to the stories. Two stories were used as training data, and three dialogues as tests. Tests results are reported in the Action Confusion Matrix shown in Fig. 3 where the expected actions from the dialogues (True Label on the Y-axis) are compared with the ones predicted by the policy (Predicted Label on the X-axis). The matrix is populated at each step by incrementing of 1 the cells corresponding to matched expected/predicted pairs. As shown in Figure, TED struggles with selecting proper actions for the specific personality trait, for example, by selecting 14 times an action not compliant with the user personality trait.

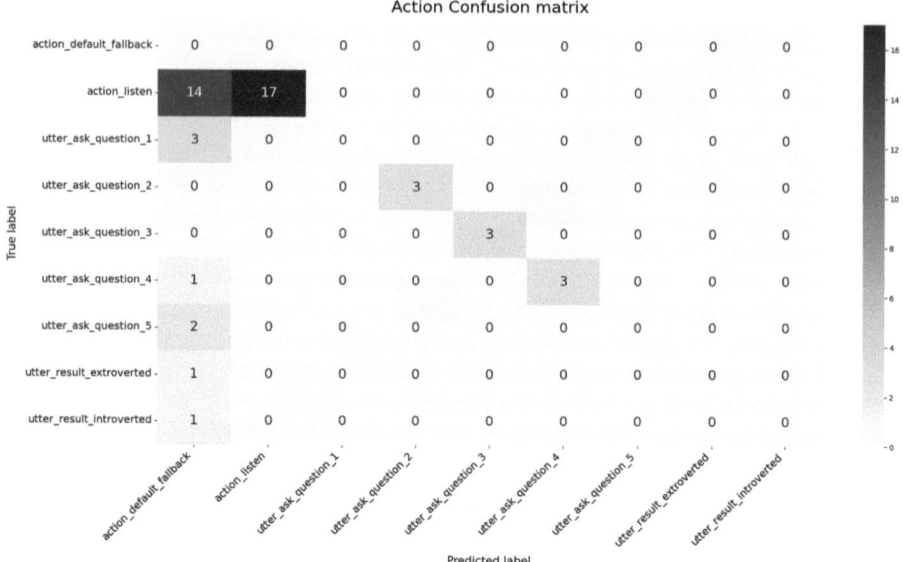

Fig. 3. Action Confusion Matrix

This result is due to a misclassification of the personality trait based on the received responses. In fact, to guarantee that the personality trait is correctly classified, stories should be provided for all combinations of sequences of questions and responses of the Big-5 test. In particular, for an easy case of only 5 questions with binary responses, 2^5 stories should be provided as training data.

By using the CLIPS component, the system can properly infer personality trait classification using simple inference rules, such as the one reported here.

```
(defrule estimate_personality (answer_1 (answer ?answer_1))
  (answer_2 (answer ?answer_2)) (answer_3 (answer ?answer_3))
  (answer_4 (answer ?answer_4)) (answer_5 (answer ?answer_5))
  (test (>= (/ (+ ?answer_1 ?answer_2 ?answer_3 ?answer_4 ?answer_5) 5)) 0.5)
=> (assert (personality (personality extroverted))))
```

5 Conclusions

Assistive robotic applications require the adoption of a user-centric approach for providing a personalised experience to human users that becomes a crucial factor in elderly assistance due to the fragile and peculiar conditions of such a category of users. Multi-modal interaction, including verbal communication, may ease the adoption of Assistive robotic applications in real settings.

Cognitive architectures relying on rule-based approaches represent an enabling technology to develop personalised robotic assistive applications. These approaches have many appealing properties, such as efficiency, determinism, and explainability. However, they can struggle when dealing with the complexity of real-world conversations. Furthermore, when verbal interactions involve multiple steps, the number of possible combinations grows exponentially, necessitating an exponential number of rules, which quickly becomes impractical to implement.

Transformer-based approaches can handle such complexity more easily. They classify the user's response as affirmative without requiring an exhaustive list of synonyms, allowing for automatic generalisation of behaviours, thus reducing the effort required from the knowledge engineer. Nevertheless, these approaches may lead to unpredictable robotic behaviours that should be prevented in assistive applications for a fragile class of users, such as the elderly. To address these challenges, we show the advantages of integrating the two approaches, rule-based and transformer-based, for the run-time personalisation and adaptation of robotic applications to specific users' states and needs.

As preliminary work, we implemented an experimental setup to evaluate the suitability of the proposed architecture integrating a chatbot with a reasoning engine to provide personalized support in elderly care through multi-modal interaction. This early phase aims to assess the system's ability to interpret user inputs, apply contextual reasoning, and deliver tailored responses that meet the unique needs of older adults. By simulating real-world interactions and monitoring system performance, the experimentation helps identify potential limitations, validate core functionalities, and guide further refinement of the architecture before broader deployment. We show that attempting to embed the entire personality trait determination logic exclusively within the Rasa policy framework, relying solely on learning from stories, proved to be a fragile strategy. Policies based on ML models like TED, optimized for sequential prediction of conversational actions through example-based learning, exhibit inherent limitations in performing precise arithmetic operations, handling rigid numerical threshold comparisons, and reacting consistently to minor deviations from the main conversational flow when complex state-dependent logic is required. In fact, a rule-based approach is more effective when domain knowledge can be explicitly defined, decision logic is transparent, and predictability is critical.

We plan to enrich the conversational component with the integration of LLMs to provide a more natural and articulated verbal interaction. In addition, more personalization factors besides personality traits will be considered to test the cognitive training application in a realistic scenario within the "RESTART" project where an on-field experimentation with real elderly users in a clinical environment will be carried out. Finally, different rehabilitation training exercises other than cognitive memory games will be integrated to provide a diversified training experience to the elderly.

Acknowledgments. This work has been supported by the PRIN project "RESTART - Robot Enhanced Social abilities based on Theory of mind for Acceptance of Robot in assistive Treatments" (grant n. 2022WCMNTT), funded by the MIUR with D.D. no. 861 under the PNRR and by Next Generation EU.

Disclosure of Interests. The authors have no competing interests to declare that are relevant to the content of this article.

References

1. Al Haj Ali, J., Lezoche, M., Panetto, H., Naudet, Y., Gaffinet, B.: Cognitive architecture for cognitive cyber-physical systems. IFAC-PapersOnLine **58**(19), 1180–1185 (2024). https://doi.org/10.1016/j.ifacol.2024.09.099
2. Arango, J.A.R., Marco-Detchart, C., Inglada, V.J.J.: Personalized cognitive support via social robots. Sensors (Basel, Switzerland) **25**(3), 888 (2025)
3. Bunk, T., Varshneya, D., Vlasov, V., Nichol, A.: DIET: lightweight language understanding for dialogue systems (2020). https://arxiv.org/abs/2004.09936
4. Chow, K.K., Ip, C.S., Yau, C.T., Zeng, J., Zhong, J.: A systematic review of using human-robot interaction for cognitive training for elderly with mild cognitive impairment. In: Intelligent Robotics and Applications. pp. 30–41. Springer, Singapore (2025). https://doi.org/10.1007/978-981-96-0786-0_3
5. De Benedictis, R., Beraldo, G., Fracasso, F., De Robertis, A., Cesta, A., Cortellessa, G.: Planning and reacting in an active assisted living environment. In: Bochicchio, M., Siciliano, P., Monteriù, A., Bettelli, A., De Fano, D. (eds.) Ambient Assisted Living, pp. 80–93. Springer, Cham (2024). https://doi.org/10.1007/978-3-031-63913-5_8
6. De Benedictis, R., Di Napoli, C., Fracasso, F., Cortellessa, G.: Enhancing robotics for effective support in active assisted living environments. In: Fiorini, L., Sorrentino, A., Siciliano, P., Cavallo, F. (eds.) Ambient Assisted Living, pp. 564–574. Springer, Cham (2024). https://doi.org/10.1007/978-3-031-77318-1_38
7. Grosan, C., Abraham, A.: Rule-Based Expert Systems, pp. 149–185. Springer, Heidelberg (2011). https://doi.org/10.1007/978-3-642-21004-4_7
8. Hopgood, A.A.: Intelligent Systems for Engineers and Scientists, 3rd edn. Wiley, Hoboken (2016)
9. Kahneman, D.: Thinking, Fast and Slow. Farrar, Straus and Giroux, New York (2011)
10. Laird, J.E.: The Soar Cognitive Architecture. The MIT Press, Cambridge (2012)
11. Ritter, F.E., Tehranchi, F., Oury, J.D.: Act-r: a cognitive architecture for modeling cognition. Wiley interdisciplinary reviews. Cogn. Sci. **10** 3, e1488 (2018). https://api.semanticscholar.org/CorpusID:54480269
12. Shachar Ben Izhak, A.Y., Lavidor, M.: Enhancing memory performance in older adults through socially engaging cognitive training. Educ. Gerontol. 1–19 (2025)
13. Staffa, M., et al.: First results of the restart national project. In: Fiorini, L., Sorrentino, A., Siciliano, P., Cavallo, F. (eds.) Ambient Assisted Living, pp. 224–242. Springer, Cham (2024). https://doi.org/10.1007/978-3-031-77318-1_15
14. Sun, R.: Duality of the Mind: A Bottom-up Approach Toward Cognition. Taylor & Francis (2001). https://books.google.it/books?id=3vZ5AgAAQBAJ
15. Vaswani, A., et al.: Attention is all you need. In: Proceedings of the 31st International Conference on Neural Information Processing Systems, NIPS'17, pp. 6000–6010. Curran Associates Inc., Red Hook (2017)
16. Vlasov, V., Mosig, J.E.M., Nichol, A.: Dialogue transformers (2020). https://arxiv.org/abs/1910.00486

Playing Smart: The Role of Embodiment and Strategy in Multi-agent Competitive Card Game

Laura Triglia[1,2](✉), Francesco Rea[2], Pablo Barros[3], and Alessandra Sciutti[2]

[1] University of Genoa, Genoa, Italy
[2] Italian Institute of Technology, Genoa, Italy
Laura.Triglia@iit.it
[3] University of Pernambuco, Recife, Brazil

Abstract. Understanding how humans perceive and adapt to artificial agents in competitive, multi-agent settings is essential for designing socially and strategically competent robots. We conducted two experiments using Chef's Hat, a four-player card game, to examine how agent strategy and embodiment influence human perception, and adaptation. In both experiments, participants played against a mix of random and Deep Q-Learning (DQL) agents, one of which was embodied by a humanoid robot (iCub). In the first experiment, the robot followed a random policy, while the DQL agent was embodied by a box; in the second, the robot embodied the DQL strategy. Across both experiments, human players consistently outperformed the agents. DQL agents exhibited strategic preferences, such as discarding mid-value cards, leading to better performance than random agents, especially when controlling for game position. Despite similar final scores, participants often viewed the DQL agent as more intelligent, although the difference was not statistically significant. Embodiment alone did not significantly influence these perceptions, as participants focused more on gameplay dynamics than on the robot itself. However, when paired with a strategic policy, the robot's embodiment amplified the recognition of its intelligence. These findings suggest that in competitive environments, the effectiveness of embodied agents depends not only on their strategies but also on gameplay context and player expectations, shaping how human players interpret their capabilities.

Keywords: Robot Embodiment · Human-Agent Interaction · Competitive Gameplay

1 Introduction

Competitive games provide a compelling framework for studying how humans interact with autonomous agents in dynamic and cognitively demanding environments. Within the field of Human-Robot Interaction (HRI), these settings offer a unique opportunity to examine how embodiment, perceived strategy, and social signaling influence human perception, decision-making, and learning [7,19]. While previous research has demonstrated that an agent's appearance and behavior can shape perceptions of trust, competence, and social presence [10,14] , much of the work has focused on dyadic interactions or virtual agents, often in collaborative or assistive roles.

However, multiparty settings introduce new complexities not present in these scenarios. In such settings, multiple agents—whether human or robotic—lead to challenges in role negotiation, strategy formulation, and social signaling [15–17]. Additionally, participants must distribute their attention across multiple agents, which can significantly alter how they perceive and interact with each one. While some studies have explored these challenges in human-human and human-agent teams [8,9], there is limited research on multiparty HRI, particularly in competitive contexts. This gap is crucial because many real-world applications, such as strategic decision-making in games or collaborative tasks in factories, often involve multiple agents interacting simultaneously.

Previous studies on competitive games, such as the work by [22,23], have demonstrated how reinforcement learning (RL) agents can adapt to each other's strategies in multi-agent settings without human involvement. However, most of these studies do not analyze how these agents are perceived by humans, nor have they tested a real competition with humans, only simulations between agents.

To address the gap in research, we explore how embodiment and strategy influence perceptions of artificial agents through two studies using Chef's Hat [3], a competitive four-player card game. In these studies, participants played with agents embodied in a robot (iCub robot) or just in a box and following either a random or reinforcement learning (DQL) strategy.

In Study 1, the DQL agent was represented by one box, while the robot followed a random policy. In Study 2, we reversed this setup, assigning the DQL policy to the robot.

We analyzed participants' judgments of agents' intelligence and of robot's warmth and competence, alongside behavioral and attentional data. Additionally, we assessed how participants' interactions and perceptions evolved when the robot embodied the intelligent strategy. This allowed us to examine the impact of the combination of game strategy and humanoid embodiment on human perception.

2 Chef's Hat Environment

The Chef's Hat card game [3] is a four-player game that offers a rich and dynamic platform for exploring various aspects of agent evolution. Designed with research in mind, the development of the game mechanics was guided by two key principles. First, it aimed to support controlled yet authentic social interactions, enabling emotional behaviors to emerge naturally. Second, it established a clear turn-taking structure that allows a robot—such as the iCub [12]—to operate within a supportive framework. This structure ensures the robot can both interpret incoming information and generate appropriate responses, all while sustaining a fluid and engaging interaction [3].

In the game, each player receives a hand of cards symbolizing different kitchen ingredients, and the main objective is to be the first to discard all of one's cards. The game unfolds in turns, during which players can either discard or pass. The rules for discarding are straightforward: a player must play a set of cards that are all of equal value and lower than the current cards on the board, and the number of cards played must be equal to or greater than the number already played. Alternatively, players have the option to pass if they cannot or choose not to play.

Our experimental design evaluates gameplay over a series of ten rounds, with performance measured at the end of each round. The winner of the game, composed by 10 rounds, is who holds the fewest cards by the end of the tenth round.

3 Methodology

3.1 Participants

40 human participants (19 M, 20 W, 1 NB) interacted with the social robot iCub playing the Chef's Hat card game at Italian Institute of Technology. Only mother-tongue participants were recruited to ensure a full comprehension of the task, as the experiment was conducted in Italian. All participants provided written informed consent before their participation. The study received approval from the regional ethical committee, Comitato Etico Regione Liguria. Participants were compensated with a sum of 10 euros for their time.

3.2 Design

Our design involves having human participants play the game Chef's Hat against a robot and two other agents. Participants played three matches of ten rounds each. The strategy of two of the artificial players was random, while one was driven by a reinforcement learning DQL agent trained on the game. Participants were divided into two groups of 20. For one of the groups, the reinforcement learning DQL agent was one of the black boxes, positioned after the human participant. In the second data collection, the DQL agent was embodied by the robot, placed in front of the human participant, as it is shown in Fig. 1.

3.3 Setup

The room was divided into two compartments to minimize the experimenter's influence on the participant. The experimenter monitored the experiment via cameras installed to provide a lateral view of the participant. The experimental compartment was equipped with a chair, a desk, a monitor, a mouse, a keyboard, and two black boxes representing the agents, with the robot positioned in front of the participant, as shown in Fig. 1. Additionally, there was a monitor in front of the robot, identical in size to the one used by the human participant, to create the impression that the robot was actively playing the game. The boxes representing the other two agents contained bulbs that lit up when it was that agent's turn, visually indicating which agent was active. During each box's turn, the light was switched on for 5 s.

The participant interacted with the game through the monitor, with game information displayed on the screen during play. The Unity Interface built for this experiment has the purpose of displaying all the important information about the changes in the game. The screen displays (in Italian):

- "it is the turn of [name of the player][number of cards in the hand]" or "It's your turn".
- If a player is passing: "[name of the player] passed".
- Information about the game, such as when the round is over, when the match is over, and who is the winner of the game.

 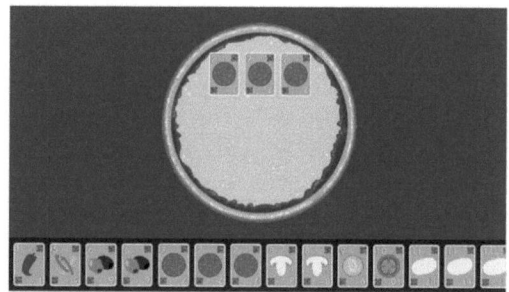

Fig. 1. Experimental Setup and Interface

Algorithm 1 provides a summary of the experiment phases.

3.4 Experimental Sessions

For both groups of participants, the experimental session was divided into multiple phases:

1. First, the participant entered the room and signed the consent form.
2. The participant answered a pre-questionnaire on a separate computer from the one of the experiment.
3. The participant was seated in the previously described setup, where the experimenter outlined the game rules. Following this, the participant engaged in three matches against the robot and the two agents. This phase lasted approximately half an hour.
4. Finally, the participants answered a post-questionnaire, in the same location as the pre-questionnaire.

Algorithm 1. Experimental Setup

if Human Participant's turn **then**
    The interface shows "It's your turn!";
    Participant does an action;
else if iCub's Turn **then**
    iCub movement and interface shows "It's iCub's Turn"
    Interface update with the iCub action
else if Agent's turn **then**
    Black box switches on for 5 seconds and interface shows "It's Agent's Turn"
    Interface update with the corresponding agent's action
else if Round Finished **then**
    Interface shows "Pizza is ready" to represent the end of the round
end if

3.5 Robot and Agents

The humanoid robot iCub was selected as the experimental platform. In two sepatare experiments, iCub took on two roles:

- A reinforcement learning agent trained via Deep Q-Learning (DQL) [2,4].
- A random agent with no learned strategy.

Depending on the experiment, the remaining two agents in the game were respectively either both random or one random and one based on a DQL strategy.

The DQL agent uses Deep Q-Learning, which improves upon standard Q-learning by incorporating two techniques: a target model, which stabilizes training by providing consistent Q-value estimates, and experience replay, which enhances learning efficiency by reusing past interactions in mini-batches.

iCub, modeled after a 5-year-old child, is a humanoid robot developed to study human cognition and interaction. It features motor and social capabilities, with a sensory system that includes two eye-mounted cameras and a head with three degrees of freedom in both the eyes and neck. These enable coordinated gaze behavior, managed by the iKinGazeCtrl module [5].

During gameplay, iCub would look at the screen during its turn, then shift its gaze back to the participant. Its LED facial display remained active with a neutral expression throughout. To simulate in-game actions, the robot pressed a button to represent playing or passing cards. These minimal movements were intentionally chosen to maintain consistency across conditions.

This design allowed us to isolate the impact of the robot's physical presence on participants' perceptions and learning, without confounding factors from expressive behavior or complex interactions.

Table 1. Number of times each player won a game

First Experiment			
Players	Game 1	Game 2	Game 3
Agent1_RND	0	1	2
Human	13	19	17
Agent4_DQL	3	0	1
Robot_RND	4	0	0
Second Experiment			
Players	Game 1	Game 2	Game 3
Agent1_RND	4	1	1
Human	13	16	17
Agent4_RND	1	1	1
Robot_DQL	2	2	1

3.6 Questionnaire

Participants were asked to complete a survey at the start of the experiment. The same questionnaires were administered again at the end of the experiment, following the interaction.

In the pre-questionnaire, participants provided various personal details, including their educational level, age, and prior experience with the iCub robot. They then evaluated the robot within the context of a competitive game, indicating their level of agreement with several statements about their impressions of the iCub robot. Specifically, they assessed the robot's warmth and competence based on the scale by Fiske et al., [1]. This scale was also used in the post-questionnaire, which additionally asked participants to identify which agent they considered the most intelligent among those they interacted with.

4 Results

4.1 Gameplay Performance and Strategic Behavior

In terms of actual gameplay performance, human players consistently outperformed both the Deep Q-Learning (DQL) and random agents, winning more frequently across the sessions, as indicated in Table 1. Notably, the DQL agent used in the study was pretrained and did not continue to learn or adapt during its interactions with human players. Despite this initial advantage, the consistently high level of human play meant that, over time, the distinction between the DQL and random agents became less pronounced in terms of win rates. In other words, the human players were skilled enough that, by the end of the experimental sessions, the differences in performance between the two types of artificial agents appeared negligible.

To further investigate the decision-making and strategic adjustments made by participants and the agents, we employed a visualization technique known as Mullet's Gambit [6]. This method allowed us to analyze the discarded cards during the game, categorizing them by their value and quantity based on probabilistic data. Since the card distribution in the game is inherently unequal, the likelihood of choosing specific actions varies based on the distribution of cards. Mullet's Gambit visualization highlights how frequently certain actions were chosen relative to others, providing a clear picture of participants' decision-making strategies over time.

The visualization provided by Mullet's Gambit sheds light on how players navigated the strategic landscape of a game characterized by an inherently unequal distribution of cards. Rather than treating all card values equally, participants appeared to factor this imbalance into their decision-making, adapting their discard strategies accordingly. Mullet's heatmap makes this adaptation visible, revealing how often specific actions were taken in relation to card value. By mapping these choices, it becomes evident that participants did not act randomly or uniformly; instead, they responded to the probabilistic structure of the game, prioritizing certain actions-such as discarding mid- or high-value cards-more frequently in ways that reflect an emerging strategic awareness.

Figure 2 presents a detailed comparison of all the actions taken by the human and DQL agents during the third game of the first experimental session, contrasted against a random strategy. From this figure, we observe that the human player consistently favors discarding high-value cards in large quantities, represented in the bottom left of the figure. This strategic behavior suggests a refined understanding of the game, likely developed over the course of the experiment. In the heatmap, this pattern is visually indicated by a dark green region, highlighting the frequent use of strong discards—high card values paired with high discard counts. By the end of the session, this behavior appears to reflect a learned tactic emphasizing control and efficiency.

Importantly, it should be noted that the heatmaps represent the difference between each agent's behavior and that of a random baseline. As such, the random strategy itself would appear as an entirely blue heatmap, with all values near zero, indicating no deviation from randomness. Any visible patterns—especially green or dark green regions—therefore signify systematic departures from random behavior, helping to reveal where and how each agent's strategy diverges in meaningful ways.

In contrast, while the DQL agent struggles to match the sophistication of the human player—particularly given the skill gap—it still demonstrates a distinct behavior compared to the random agent. Specifically, the DQL agent tends to discard medium-value cards (typically in the range of 5 to 8) and does so in relatively high quantities. Although the DQL agent is not adapting during gameplay, its pretrained strategy reflects a level of optimization that differentiates it from the random baseline, as evident in the heatmap's concentration of activity in the mid-value regions.

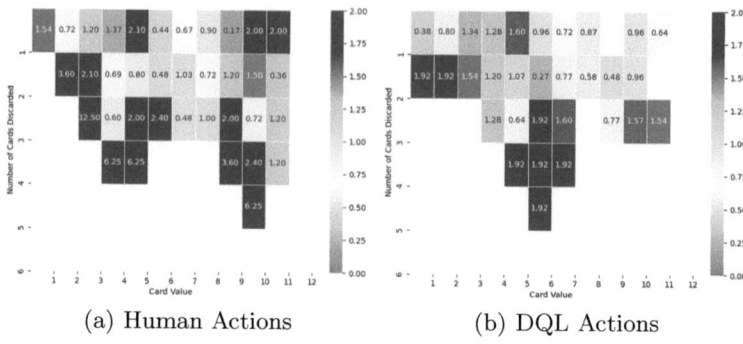

(a) Human Actions (b) DQL Actions

Fig. 2. Mullet's Gambit Visualization for Human and DQL

By examining player strategies, we found that both performance and gameplay behavior were heavily shaped by player position. In particular, players who acted immediately after the strongest participant, which in our experiment was the human, experienced a noticeable impact on their performance. This positional effect appeared consistently across sessions and persisted regardless of the underlying agent's algorithm, suggesting that turn order alone can significantly influence a player's effectiveness.

To further assess the role of position, we ran a one-way ANOVA on the three Random agents across different positions, as shown in Fig. 3. The analysis yielded a p-value below 0.001, reinforcing the conclusion that position alone can drive performance differences, even when agents' behavior is otherwise identical. These results underscore the importance of gameplay context and turn order as major factors influencing outcomes, independent of the agent's internal strategy.

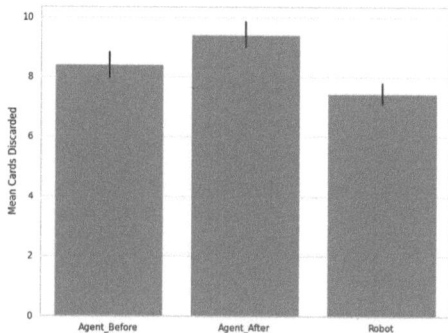

Fig. 3. Performances of a Random Agent across different positions in the game

To take into account this effect, we evaluated agents' performance across the two experiments as a function of their relative position with respect to the human player. We used the number of cards remaining at the end of each game as an indicator of performance—fewer cards signifying a stronger outcome. Figure 4 presents the performance of the Agent_After and the Robot across the two experimental sessions. A lower bar indicates better performance. As shown in the figure, the agent and the robot, when employing the DQL algorithm, outperformed their counterpart using a Random strategy. We validated these differences using Welch's t-test, which revealed statistically significant results: for Agent_After, the p-value was less than 0.001, and for the Robot, the p-value was 0.005—both confirming meaningful performance differences between sessions.

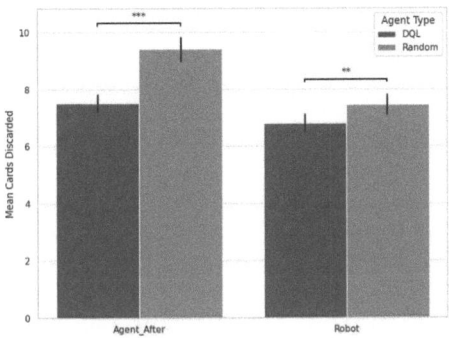

Fig. 4. Performances depending on the intelligence of the agent, in a fixed position

In general, our findings demonstrate that the game environment successfully differentiates between agents of varying intelligence levels. While this distinction may not always be reflected in final win counts, our refined performance metrics capture it clearly. This confirms that, despite the overall number of victories not being significantly better for the DQL agent, its strategy during games and its average performance were significantly better than those of other random agents.

4.2 Perceived Intelligence and Strategy Recognition

To assess whether participants were able to perceive differences between agents using distinct strategies, we asked them to identify which agent they believed was the most intelligent after each experimental session. The results are shown in the Fig. 5, where we report the percentage of participants who chose each agent as the most intelligent, across the two experiments.

The figure displays stacked bars for each experiment (Exp 1 and Exp 2), with each bar segment representing the percentage of participants who selected a specific agent. This visualization reveals how preferences shifted between experiments.

It emerges that participants were about two times more likely to select Agent_After as the most intelligent in Experiment 1 (where it followed a DQL

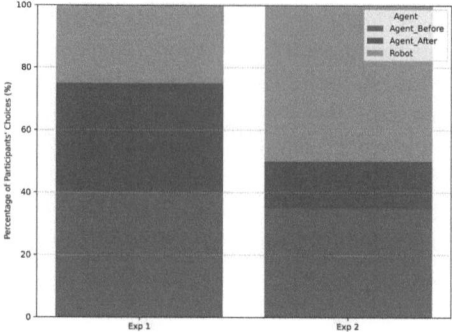

Fig. 5. Percentage of times an agent is chosen as the "most intelligent"

strategy) compared to Experiment 2. Analogously, the Robot was picked as the most intelligent player about twice as many times in Experiment 2, where it embodied the DQL strategy than in Experiment 1. Although this difference is not significant (chi-square test, p = 0.165), these results suggest a tendency by participants to recognize differences between agents based on their strategic behavior.

Such recognition might have been hindered by the different difficulties faced by the agents in winning the game associated with their relative position in the game, as discussed above. For instance, participants chose quite frequently (40% in Exp1 and 35% in Exp2) the agent in the "Before" position (Agent_Before) as the most intelligent, despite it always embodying a random game behavior. We believe that this could have been due to the immediate, visible impact that its actions had on the human participant.

We did not find any significant impact of embodiment per se in the participants' juddgment of agents' intelligence in the game.

4.3 Behavioral Engagement Through Gaze Patterns

To assess participants' engagement during the experiment, we conducted a behavioral analysis of their head orientation, focusing on where they directed their gaze throughout the gameplay (see Fig. 6). Participants' head orientation and gaze direction were estimated from video recordings using MediaPipe FaceMesh to extract 3D facial landmarks. Videos were converted to .mp4 for processing, and six key facial points were used to estimate head pose via OpenCV's solvePnP, yielding yaw, pitch, and roll angles. Gaze regions were then classified based on predefined yaw and pitch thresholds. Participants with more than 50% of frames classified as Unclear—indicating indeterminate gaze direction—were excluded from the analysis. This analysis revealed consistent patterns across both experiments. Participants oriented a consistent percentage of time (about 30%) their heads toward the monitor, indicating their focus on the unfolding game. In addition, a notable portion of their gaze was directed to their left (again, about

30%), which corresponded to the physical location of the box representing the next player in the game sequence. In about 20% of the times, instead, their attention was directed toward the agent before them.

Examining the individual (disaggregated) patterns more closely (see Fig. 6, right panel), it can be noted that while a few participants directed their attention toward the Agent_After, at their left, others tended to focus more on the player positioned before them (Agent_Before).

So, despite Agent_Before' play being particularly salient for the decision to be made in game by the participants - as suggested by the previous analysis in Section XXX - for several participants the gaze was more often oriented toward the subsequent player, potentially to monitor the effects of their own moves on the agent's play.

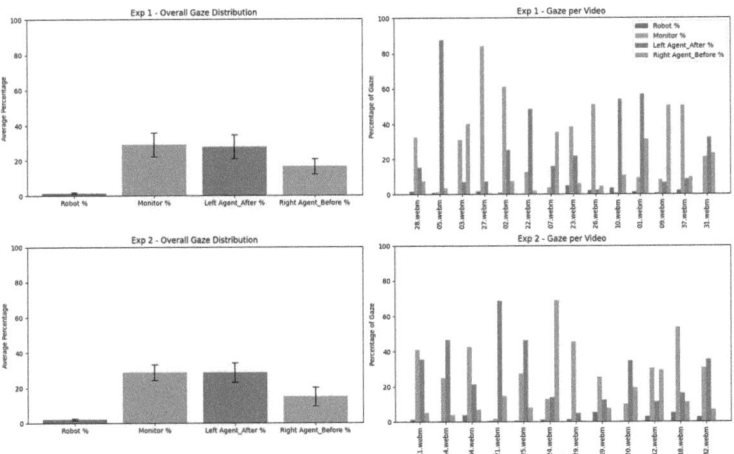

Fig. 6. Percentage of times in which participants oriented their head toward a specific region. Left panel: Averages and Standard Errors; Right panel: individual data.

Interestingly, participants rarely directed their attention to the robot, regardless of the experimental session. This lack of gaze toward the robot suggests that their attention was more engaged with the task rather than the social or interactive aspects of the robot. This trend supports the interpretation that the game itself held a stronger attentional pull than the presence of the robot.

4.4 Competence and Warmth Attribution to the Robot

To gain a deeper understanding of how participants perceived the robot iCub, we examined their responses to the Competence and Warmth scales collected in both the pre- and post-experiment questionnaires.

As illustrated in Fig. 7, participants generally attributed high levels of competence to iCub even before the interaction began. This suggests that their expectations regarding the robot's abilities were already elevated, potentially leaving

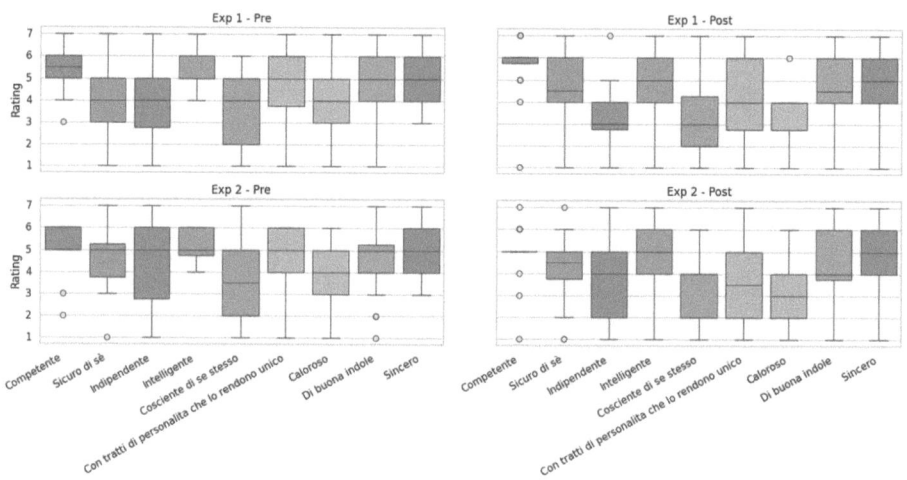

Fig. 7. Competence and Warmth Ratings in the Pre and Post Experiment Session

limited room for noticeable increases after observing its actual behavior in the game. Furthermore, the responses show only subtle differences between the two experiments, indicating that the type of strategy iCub employed (random vs. DQL) did not significantly shift participants' perceptions of its competence or warmth personality traits. Hence, even the presentation of a non-strategic game behavior, leading to a low performance in the game did not impact on the overall robot's perception.

4.5 Limitations

Despite the insights gained from this study, several limitations should be considered. First, it is important to highlight that the robot used in this experiment was intentionally designed to be non-expressive, which may have impacted the participants' perception of its intelligence. While the focus was on evaluating strategic decision-making rather than emotional or social engagement, this lack of expressiveness could have led to a reduced sense of agency or strategic depth in the robot's actions. Future research will explore the role of expressiveness in the perceived intelligence of robotic agents, potentially altering how participants perceive and interact with them.

Another key limitation lies in the complexity of the game itself. The design of the card game, while necessary for justifying the use of reinforcement learning (RL) agents, introduced a level of intricacy that made it challenging for participants to fully appreciate the strategic depth behind the robot's card choices. Participants may have struggled to understand the rationale behind specific decisions, which could have affected their engagement with the task. The use of more straightforward game mechanics or additional explanatory elements could address this issue in future studies, making the strategies of RL agents more accessible and easier for participants to grasp.

Lastly, there may be other factors, such as individual differences in gaming experience or familiarity with RL concepts, that influenced how participants interacted with the robot. These variables were not controlled for in the current study but will be considered in future investigations to better isolate the effects of the robot's strategy and behavior.

5 Discussion

The present study aimed to explore how human participants interact with agents of varying strategic sophistication and embodiment in a multiplayer game setting. Our results offer several insights into how performance, perception, and engagement are influenced by the agent's internal strategy, physical presence, and in-game positioning.

First, regarding gameplay performance, human players consistently outperformed both the Deep Q-Learning (DQL) and random agents. This finding underscores the expertise of participants relative to the artificial agents, even when faced with a pretrained DQL model. Over time, as participants refined their strategies and adapted to the game's mechanics, the performance gap between the human players and the agents widened to the point that the DQL agent's advantage over the random agent appeared negligible in terms of final win rates. Nevertheless, finer-grained analyses, such as those based on the Mullet's Gambit visualizations [6], revealed meaningful differences in game choices among strategies. For instance, the DQL agents demonstrated a clear deviation with respect to random discards, exhibiting a preference for mid-value discards. This also led to a significant difference in agents' performance, when controlling for the effect of agents' relative position in the game: agents following a DQL strategy ended up with significantly fewer cards (i.e., with a better performance) than when they employed a random strategy.

Controlling for position proved to be necessary, since agents' success was not solely a function of their internal strategy, but also of their place in the turn-taking order. Agents playing immediately after the strongest player (the human) performed significantly worse, regardless of their strategy.

Despite the high similarity in final scores in games, participants tended to select the DQL agents more often as the most intelligent player, rather than the random agents, although this difference did not reach significance. Robot's embodiment did not impact on such choice.

So, despite participants attributed relatively high levels of competence to iCub even before interacting with it, as demonstrated by their questionnaire ratings, such a prior evaluation did not guide their comparative evaluation in the game.

On the other hand, witnessing the robot's low performance and even its lack of strategy (in the condition in which it employed a random behavior) did not significantly change their overall judgment of robot's competence and warmth. This finding reinforces the idea that iCub's non-expressive, low-profile role in the game limited the impact of its participation to the interaction.

The gaze analysis provided additional insight into how participants engaged with the game and the agents. Participants primarily directed their attention toward the monitor and to the left, where the next player in the sequence (Agent_After) was located. However, a consistent and striking pattern emerged: participants rarely looked at the robot. This lack of visual engagement confirms that the robot, even when physically present, did not become a salient focus of attention during the gameplay. Instead, participants were primarily task-focused, attending more to the game mechanics and the immediate dynamics of turn-taking.

Taken together, these findings suggest that in competitive, turn-based environments, the strategic sophistication of an agent might be recognized by human participants, but this recognition is influenced by multiple factors-including task focus and agents' final performance. Interestingly, humanoid embodiment per se, despite being associated to an a priori high evaluation of competence, proved not sufficient to attract the participants' attention or to modify their relative judgments of intelligence with respect to differently embodied agents.

5.1 Future Direction

Building on the insights gained from this study, several promising avenues for future research emerge. First, future work could investigate how enhancing the robot's expressiveness—through gestures, facial expressions, or adaptive verbal feedback—affects participants' perceptions of its intelligence and strategic competence. Introducing social signals could make the robot's decision-making more transparent and relatable, thereby increasing engagement and trust.

Another important direction involves dynamically adaptive agents. In this study, the DQL agent was static and did not learn from human behavior during the game. Future experiments could implement online learning agents capable of adapting their strategies in real-time, allowing researchers to examine how human players respond to visibly evolving opponents and how such adaptations influence perceptions of competence.

Additionally, future work could explore a broader variety of game complexity. While our card game provided a rich context for strategic behavior, simpler or more familiar games could help participants better understand and appreciate the intelligence behind agent actions. Finally, expanding the social context-such as introducing multiple robots or cooperative/competitive team dynamics-could reveal richer patterns of human-robot interaction and offer deeper insights into the role of group dynamics and embodiment in strategic settings.

Acknowledgments. This work is supported by the "Brain and Machines" Flagship Program of the Istituto Italiano di Tecnologia (IIT) .

References

1. Fiske, S.T., Cuddy, A.J., Glick, P.: Universal dimensions of social cognition: warmth and competence. Trends Cogn. Sci. **11**(2), 77–83 (2007)

2. Barros, P., Tanevska, A., Sciutti, A.: Learning from learners: adapting reinforcement learning agents to be competitive in a card game. In: 2020 25th International Conference on Pattern Recognition (ICPR). IEEE (2021)
3. Barros, P., et al.: It's food fight! Designing the chef's hat card game for affective-aware HRI. In: Companion of the 2021 ACM/IEEE International Conference on Human-Robot Interaction (2021)
4. Barros, P., et al.: The Chef's Hat Simulation Environment for Reinforcement-Learning-Based Agents. arXiv preprint arXiv:2003.05861 (2020)
5. Roncone, A., et al.: A cartesian 6-DoF gaze controller for humanoid robots. Rob. Sci. Syst. **2016** (2016)
6. Triglia, L., Barros, P., Rea, F., Sciutti, A.: Mullet's gambit: explaining learned strategies in the chef's hat multiplayer card game. In: 2024 12th International Conference on Affective Computing and Intelligent Interaction Workshops and Demos (ACIIW), Glasgow, United Kingdom, pp. 136–143 (2024). https://doi.org/10.1109/ACIIW63320.2024.00028.
7. Fong, T., Nourbakhsh, I., Dautenhahn, K.: A survey of socially interactive robots. Robot. Auton. Syst. **42**(3–4), 143–166 (2003)
8. Rato, D., et al.: Robots in games. Int. J. Social Rob. **15**(1), 37–57 (2023)
9. Cichor, J.E., et al.: Robot leadership–investigating human perceptions and reactions towards social robots showing leadership behaviors. PloS One 18(2), e0281786 (2023)
10. Zhu, Y., et al.: Complexity-driven trust dynamics in human–robot interactions: insights from AI-enhanced collaborative engagements. Appl. Sci. **13**(24), 12989 (2023)
11. Abrams, A.M.H., Rosenthal-von der Pütten, A.M.: I–C–E framework: concepts for group dynamics research in human-robot interaction: revisiting theory from social psychology on ingroup identification (I), cohesion (C) and entitativity (E). Int. J. Social Rob. **12**, 1213–1229 (2020)
12. Metta, G., et al.: The iCub humanoid robot: an open platform for research in embodied cognition. In: Proceedings of the 8th Workshop on Performance Metrics for Intelligent Systems (2008)
13. Krämer, N.C., Tietz, B., Bente, G.: Effects of embodied interface agents and their gestural activity. In: Rist, T., Aylett, R.S., Ballin, D., Rickel, J. (eds.) IVA 2003. LNCS (LNAI), vol. 2792, pp. 292–300. Springer, Heidelberg (2003). https://doi.org/10.1007/978-3-540-39396-2_49
14. Bainbridge, W.A., Hart, J.W., Kim, E.S., Scassellati, B.: The benefits of interactions with physically present robots over video-displayed agents. Int. J. Soc. Robot. **3**, 41–52 (2011)
15. Mutlu, B., et al.: Footing in human-robot conversations: how robots might shape participant roles using gaze cues. In: Proceedings of the SIGCHI Conference on Human Factors in Computing Systems. ACM (2009)
16. Leite, I., Martinho, C., Paiva, A.: Social robots for long-term interaction: a survey. Int. J. Hum Comput Stud. **71**(9), 811–825 (2013)
17. Fraune, M.R., et al.: Social robots in groups and group dynamics: a review. Cogn. Syst. Res. **48**, 31–42 (2018)
18. Hoffman, G., Wendy, J.: Designing robots with movement in mind. J. Hum.-Robot Interact. **3**(1), 89–122 (2014)
19. DeSteno, D., et al.: Detecting the trustworthiness of novel partners in economic exchange. Psychol. Sci. **23**(2), 154–158 (2012)
20. Tsiakas, K., Belpaeme, T., Kennedy, J.: User modelling in human–robot interaction: a survey. Pattern Recogn. Lett. **99**, 3–12 (2017)

21. Groom, V., Nass, C.: Can robots be teammates? Benchmarks in human–robot teams. Interact. Stud. **8**(3), 483–500 (2007)
22. Matsuno, Y., et al.: A multi-agent reinforcement learning method for a partially-observable competitive game. In: Proceedings of the Fifth International Conference on Autonomous Agents (2001)
23. Tavares, A.R., Chaimowicz, L.: Exploring reinforcement learning approaches for drafting in collectible card games. Entertain. Comput. **44**, 100526 (2023)

Short Papers Session 2

A Social Robot Conductor for Public Buses: Promoting Safety and Reducing Driver Burden

Nihan Karatas[1(✉)], Linjing Jiang[1], Yuki Yoshihara[1], Tetsuya Hirota[2], Ryugo Fujita[2], and Takahiro Tanaka[1]

[1] Nagoya University, Furo-cho, Chikusa-ku, Nagoya, Aichi 464-8601, Japan
{karatas.nihan.r8,jiang.linjing.k6,yoshihara.yuki.b8,
tanaka.takahiro.x8}@f.mail.nagoya-u.ac.jp
[2] Tokai Rika Co., Ltd., Oguchi, Aichi, Japan
{tetsuya.hirota,ryugo.fujita}@exc.tokai-rika.co.jp

Abstract. Passenger safety in public buses is a significant concern, particularly for standing individuals during sudden braking or acceleration. This study investigates a socially assistive robot conductor designed to promote seated behaviour and reduce driver burden by delivering real-time safety messages based on input from an AI-based passenger monitoring system. In a preliminary two-day field trial in Kawasaki City, Japan, both passengers and drivers responded positively, highlighting the robot's clarity, politeness, and usefulness, while also noting issues with timing and message overlap with the driver. These early findings suggest that socially interactive robots, when designed with both operational awareness and human-centred adaptability, have the potential to improve onboard safety and support driver communication tasks.

Keywords: Human-Robot Interaction · Public Transportation Safety · Real-Time Passenger Monitoring · Socially Assistive Robotics

1 Introduction

Public buses play a vital role in sustainable urban mobility. However, passenger safety, especially for those standing during transit, remains a significant concern. Studies report that over 80% of in-vehicle incidents are non-collision injuries caused by sudden braking or acceleration, with standing passengers particularly at risk [2,4]. Additional findings show that the most common passenger behaviour during such incidents was standing (35.9%), followed by walking or standing up [4,10].

While voice announcements by bus drivers have been proposed to mitigate these risks [10], their effectiveness is often limited by inconsistent delivery, ambient noise, and divided driver attention. However, ensuring safety inside the bus cannot rely on driver announcements alone; passenger cooperation is also essential. Yet, passengers may choose not to comply with the driver's announcements and remain standing even when seats are available, due to a range of

 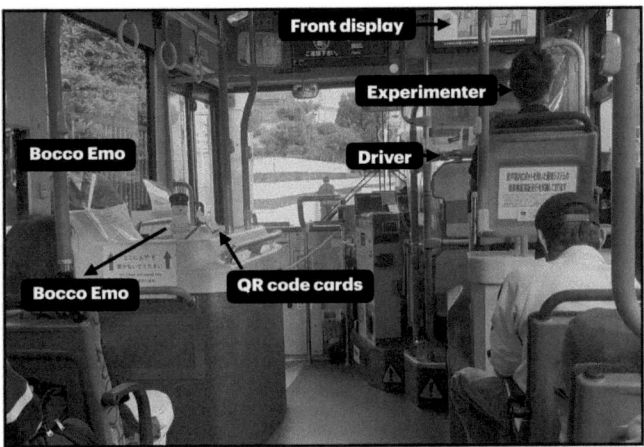

(a) Bocco Emo. (b) Experimental setup inside the public bus.

Fig. 1. Bocco Emo, the robot conductor, and the experimental setup inside the public bus. QR-code-based survey cards were placed nearby the robot.

factors including proxemic discomfort, lack of perceived control, unfavourable environmental conditions, cultural norms, defensive coping mechanisms, spatial preferences, and practical concerns related to travel duration [6]. The driver's forward-facing posture and lack of mutual gaze further weaken the communicative impact of announcements, which are known to be more persuasive when accompanied by face-to-face interaction and eye contact [9].

A growing body of research highlights the role of social robots in enhancing information delivery, engagement, and perceived safety in public environments. Studies in autonomous transit show that embodied robots can foster a sense of safety and hospitality [1], influence passenger flow [3], and promote both direct and ambient interaction to support socially interactive service environments [7].

Building on these motivations, we explore the use of a communication robot, BOCCO emo (Yukai Engineering)[1], as a robot conductor platform in public buses (Fig. 1a). This study investigates the feasibility and impact of deploying a robot conductor to promote seated behaviour, deliver safety messages, and reduce the burden on bus drivers. Through a two-day field trial, we examine how passengers and drivers perceive the robot's communication style, usefulness, and social presence in the dynamic environment of public transportation.

2 Method

2.1 AI-ECU System

The AI-ECU (Artificial Intelligencebased Electronic Control Unit) was developed as the core module of the proposed system. It processed real-time video

---
[1] https://www.yukai.co.jp/en/products/bocco-emo/.

from 2 to 8 onboard cameras, allowing the system to adapt to different bus sizes and layouts for effective passenger monitoring. The AI-ECU used a deep learningbased skeleton detection model combined with rule-based algorithms to classify passenger behaviour (e.g., seated, standing, walking) and seat availability. The system was trained with in-house bus videos and adjusted using open-source models to stay accurate in different conditions. Based on these classifications, the AI-ECU generated real-time status signals such as "seats available" or "unsafe movement," which were transmitted to the robot and front/rear monitors. This enabled automated, context-aware feedback without driver involvement.

2.2 Robot Conductor in a Public Bus

We deployed BOCCO emo, a compact communication robot (W90 × D90 × H150 mm) featuring built-in speech synthesis, animated LED cheeks, and smooth head movement controlled via its API (Fig. 1a). To reflect its role as a conductor and align with the localization context [8], we designed a bus company hat for BOCCO emo. The robot was positioned just behind the front door, facing the centre of the bus. A human presence sensor installed at the entrance triggered a greeting when a passenger boarded. BOCCO emo was controlled via a wireless HTTP/IP connection with a Windows Surface PC (control PC); the sensor communicated via Bluetooth, and the AI-ECU was connected to the control PC via Ethernet. To enhance variation and naturalness, three message alternatives were prepared for each condition, with one randomly selected at each instance. Based on real-time seat availability data, the robot delivered announcements such as: "Please take an available seat.", "Please move toward the back of the bus.", "There are priority seats available, please use them."

2.3 Experimental Protocol

A two-day field experiment was conducted on May 15–16, 2025, aboard a Rinko Bus Company[2] vehicle operating for approximately six hours each day across routes in Kawasaki City and Tsurumi Ward, Yokohama City, Japan. QR code cards were placed near the robot (Fig. 1b) to invite passengers to complete an online survey. The questionnaire included informed consent, demographic items (gender, age, prior robot experience), and eleven 5-point Likert scale questions covering clarity, politeness, usefulness, behaviour influence, trust, likeability, annoyance, perceived safety, and future use intention, and an open-ended comment field. Bus drivers received a similar 10-item survey, excluding behaviour and trust questions, which were replaced with items assessing observed changes in passenger behaviour and perceived workload related to safety announcements. An experimenter monitored the setup from behind the driver and administered the survey at the end of the final driving session.

Informational signage indicated the presence of cameras, which could be disabled upon request. The study received IRB approval from Nagoya University, ensuring ethical compliance for research involving human participants.

---

[2] https://www.rinkobus.co.jp/.

3 Results

3.1 Passenger Perception of the Robot Conductor

Five passengers (3 female, 2 male; ages 14–63) completed the survey. One participant (P2) had prior experience with communication robots.

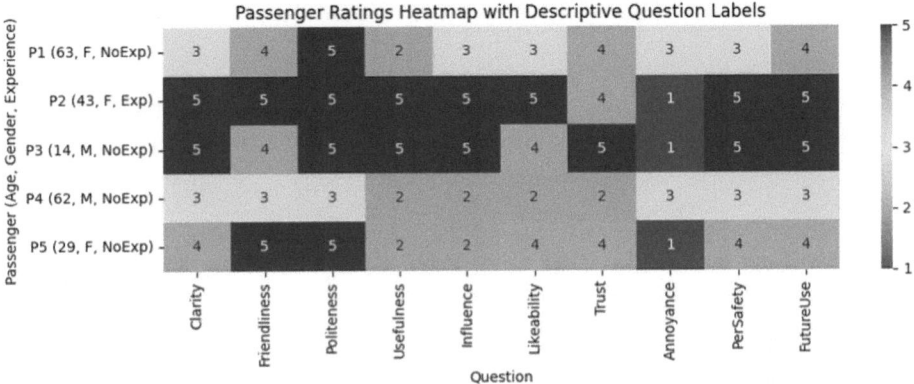

Fig. 2. Heatmap of passenger survey responses. Each row represents a passenger, annotated with their age, gender, and prior experience with communication robots ("Exp" or "NoExp"). Darker shades indicate higher 5-point ratings.

As shown in Fig. 2, responses were moderately positive overall. P2 and P3 gave consistently high ratings (mostly 5s), while P4 gave neutral responses (2 s–3 s), and P1 and P5 provided mixed scores, particularly regarding usefulness and timing. Open-ended feedback offered additional insights. P2, who had prior experience with communication robots, noted that an elderly passenger found the robot "cute" and calming. P3, a 14-year-old male, also rated the robot highly and described its speech as "easy to understand." In contrast, P1 and P4, both older participants with no prior experience with communication robots, gave lower ratings. P4 criticized the repetition of messages and suggested introducing more variety. P5 highlighted issues with audio overlap between the robot and existing bus announcements. P1 did not provide specific comments.

3.2 Driver Perception of the Robot Conductor

Two male drivers in their 50 s participated, one on each day. One had prior experience with communication robots.

Both drivers rated the robot highly for clarity, friendliness, usefulness, effectiveness, likeability, relief and future use (Fig. 3). D1 appreciated the support of the robot but recommended adding driver controls to suppress messages when necessary. He also suggested a chime before announcements and noted

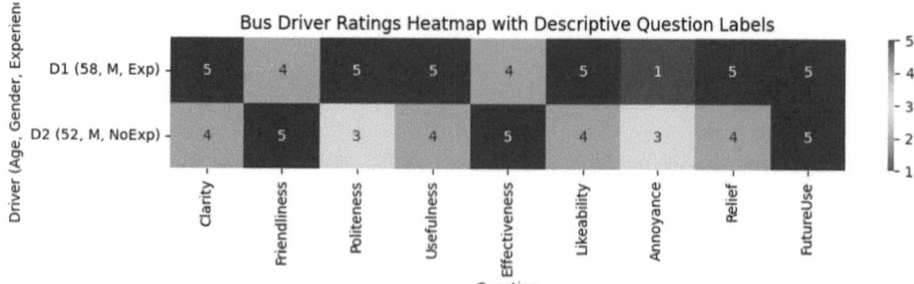

Fig. 3. Heatmap of driver survey responses. Each row represents a driver, annotated with their age, gender, and prior experience with communication robots ("Exp" or "NoExp"). Darker shades indicate higher 5-point ratings.

that the volume was slightly too loud. Having prior experience with communication robots, D1 found the robot to be less annoying. D2 praised the emotional tone of the robot, especially for children, but noted occasional overlap with his own announcements and suggested improved timing synchronization.

4 Discussion and Conclusion

This study explored the deployment of a socially assistive robot conductor in a public bus to promote seated behaviour and enhance safety communication. Preliminary feedback from both passengers and drivers was generally positive, particularly regarding the robot's clarity, emotional tone, and perceived usefulness in reducing the driver's communication burden. Passengers described the robot as friendly and calming, while drivers appreciated its role in conveying routine safety reminders. Although based on limited data, there were indications that individual characteristics, such as being younger or having prior experience with communication robots, may contribute to more favourable perceptions of the robot conductor. However, several design limitations were also noted. During the experiment, bus drivers continued their routine stop announcements, while the robot delivered real-time safety messages based on AI-ECU signals. As both systems operated simultaneously, occasional overlap between driver and robot announcements occurred. Passengers reported mistimed prompts and repetitive messages, while drivers raised concerns about loud volume, sudden announcements, and message overlap with their own instructions. They suggested adding auditory cues and manual override controls to better integrate the robot into the driving workflow.

Although this pilot study involved a small sample and lacked quantitative behavioural analysis, it offers early insights into how socially assistive robots can encourage seated behaviour and reduce communication burden of bus drivers. The next step will be the video analysis of the two-day bus deployment to evaluate the practical impact of the robot conductor's announcements on passenger behaviour. Based on these findings, future iterations will implement adaptive dialogue strategies with improvements in volume, message variety, timing, and interaction design to nudge passengers toward safer behaviour, even in the presence of environmental discomfort, proxemic sensitivity, or cultural norms [6]. Future research will also include a controlled comparison between conditions with and without the robot conductor. As public transport faces growing competition from Mobility-as-a-Service (MaaS) and on-demand transportation models [5], robots like BOCCO emo may provide an engaging, human-centred approach to improving safety and encouraging broader adoption of shared mobility.

References

1. Axelsson, A., Vaddadi, B., Bogdan, C., Skantze, G.: Robots in autonomous buses: who hosts when no human is there? In: Companion of the 2024 ACM/IEEE International Conference on Human-Robot Interaction (HRI '24), pp. 1278–1280. ACM (2024). https://doi.org/10.1145/3610978.3641115
2. Elvik, R.: Risk of non-collision injuries to public transport passengers: synthesis of evidence from eleven studies. J. Transp. Health **13**, 128–136 (2019)
3. Herzog, O., Forchhammer, N., Kong, P., Maruhn, P., Cornet, H., Frenkler, F.: The influence of robot designs on human compliance and emotion: a virtual reality study in the context of future public transport. ACM Trans. Hum.-Robot Interact. (THRI) **11**(2), 1–17 (2022)
4. Kato, C., et al.: A study on in-vehicle conditions leading to passenger injury accidents on route buses. In: Proceedings of the 2024 JSAE Annual Congress (Autumn), paper No. 113-24, Publication Code 20246131, pp. 1–4. Society of Automotive Engineers of Japan (JSAE) (2024)
5. Miller, P., de Barros, A.G., Kattan, L., Wirasinghe, S.C.: Public transportation and sustainability: a review. KSCE J. Civ. Eng. **20**(3), 1076–1083 (2016). https://doi.org/10.1007/s12205-016-0705-0
6. Mohta, N., Sehgal, K., Chaudhry, S., Goel, T.: Coping strategies for crowded environments: case of public transport systems in Delhi. Tekton J. Arch. Urban Des. Plan. **4**(1), 8–27 (2017)
7. Pan, Y., Okada, H., Uchiyama, T., Suzuki, K.: On the reaction to robot's speech in a hotel public space. Int. J. Soc. Robot. **7**(6), 911–920 (2015). https://doi.org/10.1007/s12369-015-0314-0
8. Pelikan, H.R., Mutlu, B., Reeves, S.: Making sense of public space for robot design. In: 2025 20th ACM/IEEE International Conference on Human-Robot Interaction (HRI), pp. 152–162. IEEE (2025)
9. Richardson, D., Dale, R.: Looking to understand: the coupling between speakers' and listeners' eye movements. Cognition **94**(3), B25–B34 (2005). https://doi.org/10.1016/j.cognition.2004.10.002
10. Xu, P., Wang, Q., Ye, Y., Wong, S.C., Zhou, H.: Text as data: narrative mining of non-collision injury incidents on public buses by structural topic modeling. Travel Behav. Soc. **39**, 100981 (2025)

Evaluation of Conversation Continuity Through Social Experiments Using LLM for Daily Text Chats with Virtual Robots

Masayuki Kanbara[1(✉)] and Taishi Sawabe[2]

[1] Konan University, Kobe 6588501, Japan
kanbara@konan-u.ac.jp
[2] Nara Institute of Science and Technology, Nara 6300192, Japan
t.sawabe@is.naist.jp

Abstract. Due to the increase in the number of elderly people living alone, the lack of opportunities for daily conversation among the elderly has become a problem. Dialogue robots that provide opportunities for conversation in place of humans are attracting attention. In this study, we improved system efficiency by semi-automating the creation of conversation texts and the recording of conversation content using large language models (LLMs). Through a social experiment targeting elderly people, we demonstrated the effectiveness of the proposed method and evaluated the continuity of conversations. The experiment demonstrated that the quality of the maintained dialogue was equivalent to or better than that of human-generated dialogue, and by leveraging past dialogue, the time required for dialogue generation was reduced to less than 30 s, confirming the effectiveness of LLM-based efficiency improvements. Regarding the continuity of dialogue in the experiment, 25% of the participants consistently responded to the virtual robot's questions.

Keywords: Dialog robots · Text chat · Daily conversation · Large-scale language models (LLM) · Digital divide

1 Introduction

The number of elderly people living alone is on the increase, and elderly people living alone are known to be at risk of developing dementia due to a lack of daily communication [3]. Therefore, efforts to use robots to communicate on behalf of people are attracting attention as a way to compensate for this lack of communication. If robots can be used to encourage behavioral changes, including improvements in lifestyle habits, this could contribute to improving health and extending healthy life expectancy. Additionally, monitoring activities aimed at confirming safety in emergencies and preventing isolation have been widely conducted for some time. Many initiatives utilizing digital tools for monitoring activities also exist. However, to facilitate behavioral changes or monitoring, information on users' daily activities is necessary, necessitating the continued use of dialogue robots for regular communication to collect such information.

However, in order to promote the use of information devices such as dialogue robots among the elderly, it is necessary to eliminate the digital divide. The digital divide refers to the gap between those who can and cannot benefit from information and communication technology, and its main causes are said to include resistance due to insufficient knowledge, such as the cost of internet connection and information literacy, as well as low motivation to use such technology. Furthermore, reasons cited by seniors aged 70 and older for not using information devices such as smartphones include "I don't think it's necessary for my life" and "I don't know how to use it." Therefore, in order to encourage seniors to use dialogue robots, it is necessary to simultaneously address the digital divide by communicating the convenience of dialogue robots.

In this study, we propose a new dialogue robot framework that can continue daily interactions and reduce the digital divide.

2 Related Work

The form of robots in dialogue systems can be broadly categorized into physical robots with physical bodies and virtual robots without physical bodies. Nishio et al. conducted an experiment in which 40 subjects interacted with robots under each condition to verify the differences between physical robots and virtual robots [1,5]. The results suggested that physical robots may have the advantage of promoting interaction with elderly people compared to virtual robots. However, the dialogue lasted only 15 min, and each subject interacted with the robot only once, so it is unclear whether the advantages of physical robots would be maintained in long-term dialogue. In addition, physical robots have the disadvantage of being difficult to introduce to the elderly due to their high cost and limited installation space.

In this study, we reduce the burden on human workers by replacing their work with LLM using the method proposed by Sawabe et al. [6]. However, in automatic responses using LLM, it is possible that input errors by elderly people or inappropriate responses may be generated. Therefore, we maintain the quality of the dialogue by having human workers check the responses, thereby reducing the work of human workers from creating responses to only checking the generated responses.

This study proposes a framework that improves the efficiency of existing dialogue methods by generating responses using LLM, allowing humans to review and edit them before sending, thereby reducing the burden of manual work while continuing everyday text-based dialogue. Furthermore, through a social experiment involving everyday dialogue between elderly users and a virtual robot on a smartphone using the LLM-enhanced dialogue system, we demonstrate the effectiveness of the proposed method and evaluate its impact on the desire to continue dialogue [4].

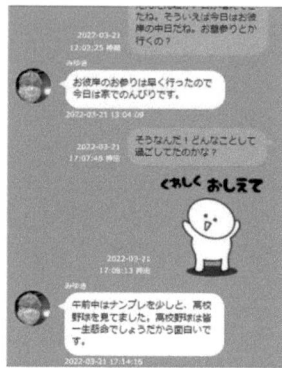

Fig. 1. Virtual robot using text chat and Examples of casual conversation using text chat

3 Proposed System

This system creates a virtual robot as shown in Fig. 1 and proposes a system in which elderly people can interact with the virtual robot via text. In this system, multiple people (hereinafter referred to as remote supporters) act as wizards in the Wizard of Oz method [2], behaving and responding as virtual robots. Figure 2 shows the flow of a series of tasks performed by remote supporters.

The work performed by remote supporters can be divided into the following three tasks.

1. Record conversation content in database
2. Search for past dialogues related to the current dialogue
3. Generate responses based on past conversations and previous conversations

First, when a remote supporter receives a conversation from an elderly person, they check the conversation content and determine whether there is any daily activity information or profile information that needs to be recorded. If there is information that needs to be recorded, the remote supporter enters the information extracted from the conversation into an input form. Information that changes over time, such as actions and meal contents, is entered as daily activity information, including the date and time, category, and specific details. For daily activity information, information that does not change over time, such as family composition and hobbies, is recorded as profile information by entering the category and specific details. Next, before creating a response to the conversation, the remote support provider searches for past conversations related to the received conversation by referencing daily activity information and profile information. If past conversations related to the received conversation are found, the remote support provider creates a response that takes into account the found past conversations to maintain consistency in the conversation. If no past conversations related to the received conversation are found, create a response considering only the current conversation.

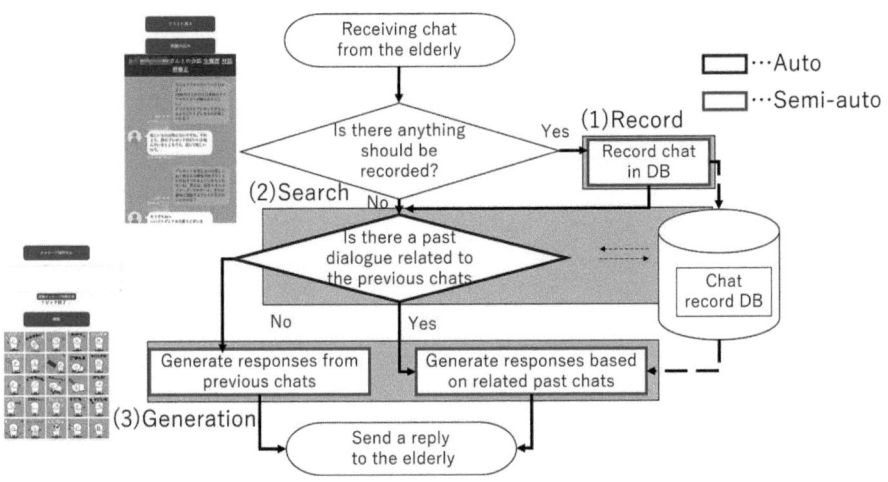

Fig. 2. Remote Support Workflow

The remote supporter created responses based on records related to the ongoing conversation that was searched for and the previous conversation. In this study, we generated responses considering records related to the ongoing conversation and the previous conversation using ChatGPT, one of the LLMs, and automatically proposed them to remote supporters. Remote supporters then manually confirmed the responses, thereby streamlining the response creation process by reducing the remote supporters' work from response creation to response confirmation.

In Previous research [6], a child-like tone was used for the virtual robot's character to make it more approachable for the elderly. By adding the five most recent dialogues containing the virtual robot's utterances to the prompt, the system can generate responses that not only consider the previous dialogue but also reflect the character's personality. Furthermore, to generate appropriate responses for text-based conversations with elderly users via LINE, the background and settings of the virtual robot, as well as the conditions for generating responses, are included in the prompt. If past conversations related to the ongoing conversation are searched, this information is added to the prompt.

4 Experiments and Results

This study aims to promote the continuation of everyday conversations by reducing psychological barriers through the elimination of the digital divide and enhancing motivation to use technology through human interaction. To reduce psychological barriers, on-site support will be provided to address the concerns and challenges that elderly individuals face regarding smartphones. Additionally, online support will be implemented using an efficient multi-user text-based dialogue system mediated by a virtual robot, as proposed in this study, to enhance motivation to use technology.

On-site support will be conducted at two locations in Shijonawate City, Osaka Prefecture. Participants will be elderly people aged 65 or older who voluntarily apply and own smartphones, and who regularly use these facilities. A total of 121 participants will take part in the on-site support, and they can join at any time during the six-month experiment period. Online support will be provided to 149 participants, including the 121 participants in on-site support and an additional 28 participants who will only participate in online support. Online support will be available from the start of on-site support, allowing participants to interact with the virtual robot anytime and anywhere. On-site support will be conducted at each location once or twice a week with the assistance of 1–2 support staff. This experiment was conducted with the approval (No. 2021-I-11-4) of Nara Institute of Science and Technology Ethics Review Committee.

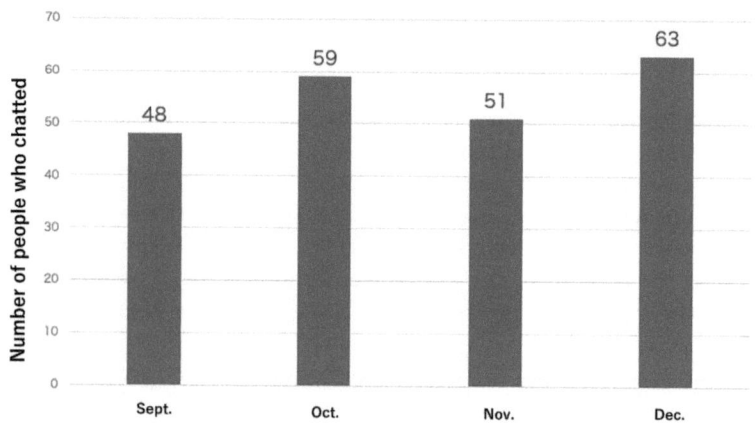

Fig. 3. Number of respondents to monthly casual discussions

In this study, we evaluate subjective motivation to continue everyday conversation by measuring increases in motivation to use the system and decreases in psychological barriers. Furthermore, since we believe that elderly people who are motivated to continue everyday conversation will initiate conversation triggered by regular questions from a virtual robot and continue to do so over time, we will conduct an objective evaluation based on the response rate to these regular questions.

The response rate to periodic batch questions is shown in Fig. 3 for participants who responded at least once to periodic batch questions sent during one month of the four-month period (September to December). The results show that, in addition to an average of 37.1% (55.3 participants) responding each month, 24.2.

In the free comments section of the questionnaire, many respondents indicated that they would like to engage in conversation based on the questions, suggesting that this social experiment demonstrated that an environment conducive to ongoing daily conversations with elderly people can be created by providing topics for conversation from virtual robots. However, most participants did not engage in conversation other than responding to the regular questions. This suggests that while older adults may want to engage in conversation with virtual robots, they may not know what to talk about in practice. Therefore, it is necessary to increase conversation initiated by older adults by using personalized regular questions tailored to each user.

5 Conclusion

This study aimed to realize an environment capable of sustaining everyday conversations between multiple participants using virtual robots. To achieve this, we optimized a dialogue system using large language models (LLMs) and evaluated the sustainability of everyday conversations. In optimizing the dialogue system using LLMs, we reduced the workload of remote support staff by approximately 35% through semi-automation of manual tasks, achieving the target of less than 30 s. To evaluate the continuity of everyday conversations, a six-month social experiment was conducted with 149 participants. The results showed that 24% of participants were able to continue conversations at least once a month, indicating that an environment supporting everyday conversations can be established through periodic questions. Going forward, we aim to further enhance conversation motivation by utilizing recorded information to select personalized topics.

Acknowledgement. This work was supported by the Grand Challenge, Initiative for Life Design Innovation (iLDi) MEXT Society 5.0 Realization Research Support Project, Osaka University.

References

1. Chung, K., Oh, Y.H., Ju, D.Y.: Elderly users' interaction with conversational agent. In: Proceedings of the 7th International Conference on Human-Agent Interaction, pp. 277–279 (2019)
2. Fraser, N.M., Gilbert, G.: Simulating speech systems. Comput. Speech Lang. 81–99 (1991)
3. Holt-Lunstad, J., Smith, T.B., Layton, J.B.: Social relationships and mortality risk: a meta-analytic review. PLoS Med e1000316 (2010)
4. Mochizuki, S., et al.: Investigating the intervention in parallel conversations. In: Proceedings of the 11th International Conference on Human-Agent Interaction, pp. 30–38 (2023). https://doi.org/10.1145/3623809.3623863
5. Nishio, T., et al.: The effects of physically embodied multiple conversation robots on the elderly. Front. Robot. AI (2021)
6. Sawabe, T., Kanbara, M., Fujimoto, Y., Kato, H.: Experimental survey on bridging the digital divide through daily text chat communication with virtual agents. In: Human Aspects of IT for the Aged Population, pp. 261–273 (2023)

The Interaction Blueprint: A Human-Centred Design Tool for Cognitive Human–Robot Interaction

Nagore Osa(✉), Ganix Lasa, Maitane Mazmela, Ainhoa Apraiz, and Oscar Escallada

Faculty of Engineering, Mechanical and Industrial Production, Mondragon Unibertsitatea, Loramendi 4, Mondragon, 20500 Gipuzkoa, Spain
nosa@mondragon.edu

Abstract. Robotic systems have progressed from isolated, pre-programmed manipulators to adaptive, learning agents capable of close collaboration with humans. This evolution outpaces most established Human–Robot Interaction (HRI) taxonomies and leaves design teams without a concise, human-centered method for specifying next-generation interactions. We present the Interaction Blueprint, a diagrammatic framework that merges service-design blueprinting with refined HRI concepts. Each task step is plotted on dual physical and cognitive axes and annotated across five layers—Activity, Role, Ability, Autonomy, and Authority—thereby linking user skills and decision prerogatives to robotic capabilities at the earliest design stage. The blueprint translates abstract taxonomic insights into a practical canvas for multidisciplinary teams and offers a scalable foundation for forthcoming empirical validation and metric integration.

Keyword: Human–Robot Interaction · cognitive robotics · human-centered design

1 Introduction

Advancements in sensing, actuation, and AI have transitioned robotics from fixed manipulators to adaptive systems operating in complex human environments [1]. Current robots perform collaborative tasks, learn interactively, and adapt to diverse sectors like manufacturing, logistics, healthcare, and home assistance [2].

Historically, safety limitations necessitated physical segregation of robots from humans [3]. However, collaborative robots (cobots) leveraging improved sensors, real-time control, and revised safety standards [4] now enable close human–robot interaction (HRI) without barriers. This evolution expands robotic applications into flexible manufacturing, co-creation, and personalized services [5].

These advances have also catalyzed research in cognitive robotics, an area focusing on intelligent robots capable of multimodal perception, deep-learning-driven planning, and hybrid reasoning. Such research has yielded significant progress in industry, logistics, and service domains [6]. Nonetheless, rapid technological development prompts new human factors challenges, including automation bias, reduced user autonomy, and excessive reliance on algorithms [7].

This paper introduces a novel, human-centered design tool for cognitive robotics in HRI. It offers researchers and practitioners a structured lens for anticipating the human implications of advance robotics systems, ultimately supporting safer, more transparent, and mutually beneficial human–robot collaboration.

2 Background and Related Works

Human-centered design (HCD) positions the cognitive, physical and emotional needs of end-users as primary design drivers [8]. ISO 9241-210 [9] formalizes this stance, defining HCD as an approach that makes systems "usable and useful" by grounding decisions in ergonomics and usability expertise [9]. Long before robots appeared on factory floors or in hospital wards, HCD had already demonstrated its value in the domain of consumer electronics [10], automotive HMIs [11] and medical devices [12], where iterative prototyping and early stakeholder engagement consistently improved acceptance and trust.

Robotics research has begun to adapt these practices through iterative prototyping frameworks for industrial cobots [13], participatory co-design of social robots [12], personalized behavior modelling [14] and context-aware adaptation methods [15]. Nevertheless, the timing of user involvement remains problematic; many projects incorporate end-users only after the fundamental design of the system is complete, meaning feedback may be limited to usability testing rather than informing core design decisions [16]. Consequently, a widely accepted, life-cycle-spanning HCD methodology for robotics, particularly in cost- and performance-driven industrial contexts, remains an open research need.

Addressing complementary aspects, taxonomies in HRI provide structured vocabularies to describe critical variables such as task structure, spatial-temporal relations, autonomy, communication, and safety, essential for engineering decisions and HCD. Initial frameworks [17] identified fundamental variables like task criticality, team size, and autonomy, while later studies introduced social and organizational nuances such as workspace sharing [18], leadership dynamics [19], affective capabilities [20], ethical constraints [21] and trust guidelines [22]. Holistic frameworks, e.g., HUBOXT [23] —which maps HRI systems along 3 dimensions: Human, Robot, Context, and their interactions over time, and matrix-based models combining automation, collaboration, and skills [24] further reflect the complexity of modern robotics.

However, these taxonomies fall short in capturing adaptive, context-aware interactions. Specifically, they often: (1) assume static human–robot roles, missing dynamic role transitions; (2) conflate physical with cognitive interaction complexity; (3) inadequately distinguish between autonomy (robot independence) and authority (decision-making responsibility); and (4) lack descriptors for cognitive human factors, such as situational awareness [25]. Addressing these gaps, this study aims to refine existing taxonomic concepts to reflect contemporary robotic flexibility and cognitive complexity, integrating these updates into the *Interaction Blueprint*—a practical tool enabling multidisciplinary teams to translate theoretical advances into actionable, human-centered collaborative designs.

3 Proposed Novel Design Tool: Interaction Blueprint

3.1 Overview of Interaction Blueprint

The proposed Interaction Blueprint integrates two key sources: (i) the service design blueprint [26], and (ii) the HRI taxonomies discussed earlier. The Interaction Blueprint provides a structured framework for visualizing and analyzing interactions between humans and robots across task sequences. It is organized along two axes. Horizontally, tasks are sequentially laid out, clearly showing each step within the overall process. Vertically, the blueprint delineates three core components:

1. **Descriptive Layers**: These specify detailed dimensions structured around two fundamental interaction domains—physical (relating to bodily movements or mechanical operations) and cognitive (involving perception, reasoning, and decision-making). This distinction allows teams to comprehensively capture both visible actions and underlying mental processes, and includes:
   o **Activity:** Describes the type of actions each agent performs. This enables the identification of situations where an agent may be physically inactive yet cognitively engaged. → *Tool questions: What task does each agent need to perform?*
   o **Role:** Specifies the functional position of each agent in both physical and cognitive domains, indicated as active or inactive, based on Kemeny [24]. → *Tool questions: Is the agent exerting effort in this dimension? Mark active or inactive.?*
   o **Abilities:** Identifies the key physical skills and cognitive competencies required from each agent, based on Apraiz et al. [23]. This provides a foundation for evaluating training needs, interface design, and adaptability. → *Tool questions: Which skills or capacities are required for the listed activity?*
   o **Autonomy:** Measures the degree of autonomy in both physical and cognitive dimensions, based on Salunkhe et al.'s [25] five-level scale: from Level 1 (fully manual) to Level 5 (fully autonomous). → *Tool questions: To what extent does the agent act/decide without external input?*
   o **Authority:** Defines the level of Authority through the five-tier command structure (master, guide, associate, assistant, servant) [27]. By documenting authority alongside autonomy, the blueprint highlights responsibility allocations that are critical for both safety assurance and ethical accountability. → *Tool questions: Who has the right to issue or override commands?*
2. **Agent Identification:** Each activity, role, and capacity clearly distinguishes whether the human or robot performs it, facilitating clarity about each agent's responsibilities and interactions.
3. **Task Sequence:** Clearly segmented tasks describe step-by-step actions, providing an explicit breakdown of operations within the interaction process.

Together, these principles reposition the classical service blueprint from a back-office process-mapping instrument to a forward-looking, human-centred canvas for cognitive HRI. The Interaction Blueprint thus translates abstract taxonomic considerations into a practical design artefact suitable for a broad range of cognitive-robotics applications. Table 1 (collaborative-hoisting scenario) exemplifies how each layer is populated for two consecutive tasks.

Table 1 Example of the Interaction Blueprint - collaborative-hoisting scenario.

Descriptive Layer		Agent	Task sequence	
			Task 1: *Attach lifting slings to component*	Task 2: *Hoist and transfer component to assembly bay*
Activity What is each agent literally doing at this step? Specify both · bodily actions · mental processes (decision, monitoring, prediction).	Physical Activity	Human	Retrieve slings, loop around load	Walk alongside load; clear path obstructions
	Cognitive Activity		Select appropriate sling set (type/length, CoG)	Supervise trajectory, anticipate course corrections
	Physical Activity	Robot	Stabilise component with gripper at pick point	Hoist and translate load along path
	Cognitive Activity		Maintain pose, monitor force & orientation	Plan trajectory, perform obstacle avoidance, speed modulation
Role Is the agent exerting effort in this dimension? Mark active or inactive.	Physical role	Human	Active	Inactive
	Cognitive role		Active	Active
	Physical role	Robot	Active	Active
	Cognitive role		Active	Active
Abilities Which skills or capacities are required for the listed activity?	Physical abilities	Human	Manual dexterity, load handling	Walking or moving around
	Cognitive abilities		Perception, reasoning, action selection	Perception, Attention, Prospection
	Physical abilities	Robot	Precision positioning, steady force output	Weight lifting
	Cognitive abilities		Perception, attention	Perception, attention, action selection, reasoning
Autonomy To what extent does the agent act/decide without external input?	Physical Autonomy	Human	1	1
	Cognitive Autonomy		2	4
	Physical Autonomy	Robot	3	2
	Cognitive Autonomy		3	4
Authority Who has the right to issue or override commands?		Human	Guide	Associate
		Robot	Associate	Assistant

4 Discussion

This study addresses key limitations in current HRI tools. Existing taxonomies often overlook the complexity and dynamic nature of modern collaboration, and rarely support multidisciplinary design discussions. Many HCD approaches remain largely evaluative, focusing on usability testing after key design decisions, rather than informing early stages.

The proposed Interaction Blueprint addresses these limitations by explicitly mapping each interaction step on both physical and cognitive dimensions and articulating roles, abilities, autonomy, and authority levels clearly and distinctly. A central finding.

of this work is that explicitly visualizing these layers promotes early, structured dialogue within multidisciplinary teams, ensuring crucial human-centered considerations, such as cognitive workload and decision-making authority, are captured and addressed before technical commitments are made. Practically, the Interaction Blueprint is particularly effective during early stages of design and development processes, such as use-case definition, where teams collaboratively populate each layer sequentially, thus concretely guiding early design decisions.

Compared to other HCD-HRI tools, such as the educationally oriented toolkit by Zhao et al. [28], the Interaction Blueprint provides broader applicability beyond training scenarios, explicitly addressing industrial complexity and multidisciplinary design processes. Unlike the UX-focused methods proposed by Prati et al. [29], which primarily emphasize interface-level considerations, the Interaction Blueprint holistically encompasses interaction dynamics, including cognitive load management and decision-making authority. This broader scope positions our tool uniquely, allowing systematic anticipation of user experiences within comprehensive interaction scenarios. However, its detailed structure may require simplification for rapid industry adoption, and empirical validation is needed to confirm practical effectiveness.

5 Conclusions and Future Work

This study presents a structured yet flexible blueprint that bridges theoretical HRI taxonomies with practical design processes, explicitly addressing cognitive aspects of human–robot collaboration. The Interaction Blueprint provides a significant advancement by enabling teams to anticipate and resolve complex interaction dynamics early in development. Ultimately, it contributes to safer, more transparent, and human-centered robotic systems.

The Interaction Blueprint lays the groundwork for multiple avenues of future research. Empirical studies are required to validate its practical effectiveness and clarify the blueprint's impact on reducing cognitive load, enhancing situational awareness, and improving operator trust and acceptance. Additionally, future iterations should investigate adaptive or dynamic interaction representations that reflect real-time role shifts and autonomy adjustments common in advanced robotic systems. Lastly, exploring simplified or domain-specific versions of the blueprint could foster wider industry adoption, particularly in performance-sensitive or cost-driven settings.

Acknowledgments. Funded by the European Union Framework Programme for Research and Innovation Horizon Europe. Project INVERSE under Grant Agreement No. 101136067.

Disclosure of Interests. The authors have no competing interests to declare that are relevant to the content of this article.

References

1. Xu, L.D., Xu, E.L., Li, L.: Industry 4.0: state of the art and future trends. Int. J. Prod. Res. **56**, 2941–2962 (2018)
2. Neumann, W.P., Winkelhaus, S., Grosse, E.H., Glock, C.H.: Industry 4.0 and the human factor – a systems framework and analysis methodology for successful development. Int. J. Prod. Econ. **233** (2021)
3. Welfare, K.S., Hallowell, M.R., Shah, J.A., Riek, L.D.: Consider the human work experience when integrating robotics in the workplace. In: 2019 14th ACM/IEEE International Conference on Human-Robot Interaction (HRI), 75–84. IEEE (2019)

4. ISO - ISO/TS 15066:2016 - Robots and robotic devices — Collaborative robots. Preprint https://www.iso.org/standard/62996.html
5. Soori, M., Arezoo, B., Dastres, R.: Artificial intelligence, machine learning and deep learning in advanced robotics, a review. Cogn. Robot. **3**, 54–70 (2023). Preprint https://doi.org/10.1016/j.cogr.2023.04.001
6. Hwang, J., Tani, J.: Seamless integration and coordination of cognitive skills in humanoid robots: a deep learning approach. IEEE Trans. Cogn. Dev. Syst. **10**, 345–358 (2018)
7. Ueda, S., Nakashima, R., Kumada, T.: Influence of levels of automation on the sense of agency during continuous action. Sci. Rep. **11** (2021)
8. Panny, M.: Consequences of industrial robots in the field of work organization. In: Design of Work in Automated Manufacturing Systems, pp. 115–119. Elsevier (1984). https://doi.org/10.1016/b978-0-08-031118-0.50027-0
9. Bevan, N., Carter, J., Harker, S.: ISO 9241-11 revised: What have we learnt about usability since 1998? In: International Conference on Human-Computer Interaction, pp. 143–151. Springer (2015)
10. Norman, D.: Things That Make Us Smart: Defending Human Attributes in the Age of the Machine. Diversion Books (2014)
11. Johnson, M., et al.: Coactive design. J. Hum. Robot. Interact. **3**, 43 (2014)
12. Björling, E.A., Rose, E.: Participatory research principles in human-centered design: engaging teens in the co-design of a social robot. Multimodal Technol. Interact. **3**, (2019)
13. Kim, D., Kim, M., Lee, J., Lee, D., Um, J.: Reconfigurable machine tending with collaborative robots: leveraging ISO 21919 for enhancing flexibility and safety. Int. J. Comput. Integr. Manuf. (2025). https://doi.org/10.1080/0951192X.2025.2496901
14. Pollmann, K., Ziegler, D.: Personal quizmaster: a pattern approach to personalized interaction experiences with the MiRo robot. In: ACM International Conference Proceeding Series, pp. 485–489. Association for Computing Machinery (2020). https://doi.org/10.1145/3404983.3410414
15. Martins, G.S., Santos, L., Dias, J.: User-adaptive interaction in social robots: a survey focusing on non-physical interaction. Int. J. Soc. Robot. **11**, 185–205 (2019)
16. Weng, Y.H., Hirata, Y.: Design-centered HRI governance for healthcare robots. J. Healthc. Eng. **2022** (2022)
17. Yanco, H.A.: Classifying Human-Robot Interaction: An Updated Taxonomy* (2004)
18. Schmidtler, J., Knott, V., Hölzel, C., Bengler, K.: Human Centered Assistance Applications for the working environment of the future. Occup. Ergon. **12**, 83–95 (2015)
19. Vincent Wang, X., Wang, L., Seira, A.: Classification, Personalised Safety Framework and Strategy for Human-Robot Collaboration (2018). https://www.researchgate.net/publication/329935915
20. Saunderson, S., Nejat, G.: How robots influence humans: a survey of nonverbal communication in social human–robot interaction. Int. J. Soc. Robot. **11**(4), 575–608 (2019)
21. Borenstein, J., Herkert, J., Miller, K.: Self-driving cars: ethical responsibilities of design engineers. IEEE Technol. Soc. Mag. **36**, 67–75 (2017)
22. Simões, A.C., Pinto, A., Santos, J., Pinheiro, S., Romero, D.: Designing human-robot collaboration (HRC) workspaces in industrial settings: a systemic literature review. J. Manuf. Syst. **62**, 28–43 (2022)
23. Apraiz, A.: Tesis Doctoral Nuevo Modelo de Evaluación de La Interacción Persona-Robot En Entornos Industriales: ITPX-ROBOTS (2023)
24. Wang, L., Wang, X. V., Váncza, J., Kemény, Z.: Advanced human-robot collaboration in manufacturing. In: Advanced Human-Robot Collaboration in Manufacturing. Springer (2021). https://doi.org/10.1007/978-3-030-69178-3

25. Salunkhe, O., Stahre, J., Romero, D., Li, D., Johansson, B.: Specifying task allocation in automotive wire harness assembly stations for Human-Robot Collaboration. Comput. Ind. Eng. **184** (2023)
26. Bitner, M.J., Ostrom, A.L., Morgan, F.N.: Service blueprinting: a practical technique for service innovation. California Manag. Rev. **50**, 66–94 (2008). Preprint https://doi.org/10.2307/41166446
27. Sierhuis, M., et al.: Human-agent teamwork and adjustable autonomy in practice (2021). https://doi.org/10.1184/R1/14225930.V1
28. Zhao, Y., Loke, L., Reinhardt, D.: Evaluating a design toolkit for human-robot collaboration in close-proximity scenarios with robotic arms: group usability tests with postgraduate interaction design students. ACM Trans. Hum. Robot. Interact. (2025). https://doi.org/10.1145/3736422
29. Prati, E., Peruzzini, M., Pellicciari, M., Raffaeli, R.: How to include user eXperience in the design of human-robot interaction. Robot Comput. Integr. Manuf. **68** (2021)

Acceptability and Expectations of Social Robots in Speech and Language Therapy - A Survey

Melanie Jouaiti[1](✉), Elisabetta Casagrande[2], and Negin Azizi[3]

[1] University of Birmingham, Birmingham B15 2TT, UK
m.jouaiti@bham.ac.uk
[2] Università di Torino, 10124 Turin, Italy
[3] Waterloo, Canada

Abstract. With Speech and Language Therapists (SLT) being increasingly overworked and the integration of technologies soaring in the last few years, and the affordability of social robots increasing, it is timely to investigate how robots could be integrated into the practice. This study addresses the gap by surveying speech-language pathology practitioners, gathering data on their attitudes, perceived benefits, expected robot roles, and concerns regrading the integration of social robots into therapy. Overall, the findings suggest a cautious optimism for adopting social robots in SLT, highlighting the need to align robot capabilities with user expectations and to provide training that improves familiarity. This study provides novel empirical insights as one of the first to examine the acceptability of social robots in the SLT context, offering data to inform the design and deployment of such technology.

1 Introduction

Up to 14 million people in the UK (20% of the population) will experience communication difficulty at some point in their lives, with more than 10% of children having a long-term communication need [10]. As communication disorders are often overlooked and with Speech and Language Therapists (SLT) being recognised in April 2023 by the UK Government as a shortage profession [11], it is estimated that there are almost 400,000 children with language disorders in the UK who are unidentified [13]. Wait times for an initial assessment are up to 10 months, causing patients having to turn to private therapy or communication delays to worsen. It becomes paramount to offer technological support, so that patients can get adequate care and to minimise the burden on therapists.

Technologies have been introduced more and more into the SLT practice in the last few years [8], following the necessity created by the Covid-19 pandemic to transition to a tele-health model. As the availability of mobile technology increases, apps designed for mobile phones and tablets are increasingly

---

N. Azizi—Independent Researcher.

integrated. Apps are used to improve language outcome or as a diagnostic or monitoring tool, as part of the therapy or as exercises initiated by the parents. There have been several reviews in the literature about apps, highlighting some limits and concerns, such as increased screen time, lack of engaging element in some cases, reduction of in person interactions [15]. Despite having been validated in numerous therapy contexts, the use of socially assistive robots in the SLT practice has only been superficially studied, with very few studies investigating the effectiveness of doing so [6,7,12,17]. Robots have an embodiment that adds an engaging and motivating element to the interaction. However, despite the robot significantly improving children's linguistic skills and engagement, Spitale et al. [14] reported that SLT still do not trust the robot. This reluctance of integrating robots into the therapy setting can be generalised to other therapy areas, as evidenced by [3]. Reported barriers to the use of robots in the SLT practice are typically the high cost (>£8000) and maintenance [5]. Other limitations included low ability for speech recognition and natural language processing capabilities, and lack of personalisation [5]. Recent studies of social robot acceptance suggest that while most users have a positive attitude toward social robots [4], stakeholders also raise important concerns (e.g. ensuring that robots do not replace human therapists) [2].

With the rising popularity of Large Language models and the appearance of low cost robots (<£500), those barriers are about to disappear and we are at a turning point for understanding how robots are perceived in SLT, identify how they could be useful and identify the remaining gaps. To achieve that, we have released a survey looking into technology perception and expectation in SLT, with a particular focus on social robotics. This paper presents preliminary results. This study aims to investigate the following: (1) Perceptions and barriers of integrating social robots in SLT from the perspective of therapists who have not used them, and (2) Offering insight into early-stage adoption conditions.

2 Material and Methods

To complete the online survey, we recruited 30 practising SLT with 12.65 ($\pm$10.17) years of practice, through mailing lists and word of mouth. Participants practised in 3 countries: 21 from Italy, 1 from the US, 9 from the UK. The participants are practising in different settings: 5 in schools, 13 in private practice, 7 in hospital outpatient setting, 2 hospital in-patient setting, 3 in unspecified settings. The recruited SLTs work with diverse age ranges and areas of expertise: 8 with adult and/or elderly patients (presenting with communication, swallowing or voice disorders), and 17 with children, 4 with clients of all ages and one did not specify. All but one had prior experience using apps or software in their practice.

2.1 Questionnaire

The data collection was conducted with the use of a survey divided into 2 parts: technology experience and robot perception/expectations. Each part consisted of a questionnaire where answers were rated on a 5-point Likert scale and 7 open ended questions. The survey was co-designed with a British SLT. Answering the questions was not mandatory, so participants could opt to not answer some of the open-ended questions. We discarded the answers to the questionnaire for 3 participants as they rated every question the same. One participant did not answer any of the open-ended questions. The survey was also translated in Italian for Italian participants. For the sake of space, we do not report on the open ended-questions pertaining to technology.

3 Results

3.1 Technology Experience

All but one participant reported having used technology in their practice (ipad: 7, computer: 6, app/ web app: 11, Chat-GPT: 1, praat: 1) serious game: 1). All but four participants are still currently using technology (app: 10, Chat-GPT: 2, serious game: 4, software: 3).

Overall participants were positive about all the items of the questionnaire (Fig. 1), but very positive about technology being useful (4.48 ± 0.93), and efficient (4.17 ± 1.02). They strongly disagreed with technology being a burden (1.69 ± 0.88) or a waste of time (1.48 ± 0.90).

Participants from the UK rated items more negatively than the participants from Italy, though a t-test revealed no significant difference (Table 1).

Table 1. Average scores for the questions pertaining to technology perception

	Q1	Q2	Q3	Q4	Q5	Q6	Q7	Q8
All	4.48	1.69	4.10	4.07	4.17	1.72	3.59	1.48
UK	3.67	2.17	3.5	3.67	3.33	2.33	3.33	2.0
Italy	4.68	1.59	4.23	4.14	4.36	1.59	3.64	1.36

3.2 Social Robot Questionnaire

Overall, our participants were not familiar with robots, only 4 answered that they were, but then their answers indicate that they never interacted with one.

Overall participants were neutral about all the items of the questionnaire (see Fig. 1), but slightly more positive about a robot improving engagement ($3.67 \pm .94$), being an efficient tool (3.54 ± 0.96) or useful (3.42 ± 0.95). They slightly disagreed with the robot making their job harder (2.46 ± 0.96), being a burden (2.58 ± 0.95) or a waste of time (2.63 ± 1.2). Participants from the UK consistently rated the items more negatively than the participants from Italy, though a t-test revealed no significant difference (see Table 2).

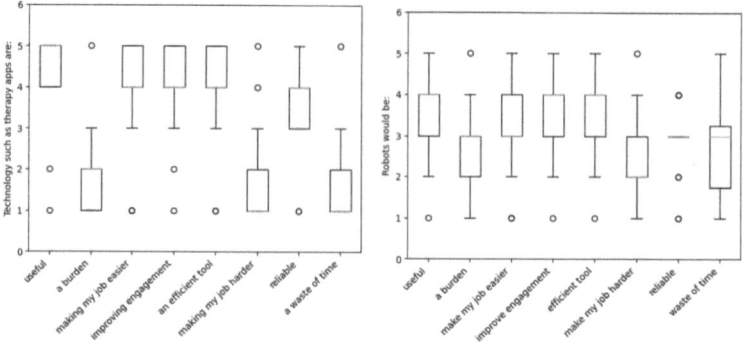

Fig. 1. Left: Box plot representing the scores obtained for the 8 technology questions rated on a 5-point Likert scale; Right: Box plot representing the scores obtained for the 8 robot questions rated on a 5-point Likert scale

Table 2. Average scores for the questions pertaining to robot perception

	Q1	Q2	Q3	Q4	Q5	Q6	Q7	Q8
All	3.42	2.58	3.2	3.67	3.54	2.46	2.88	2.63
UK	3.0	3.5	2.25	3.0	3.0	3.25	2.25	3.75
Italy	3.42	2.47	3.32	3.74	3.58	2.37	3.0	2.47

3.3 Open Ended Questions

If you were to integrate one of these robots in your practice, which robot would you choose and why? When asked which robot they would choose (See Fig. 2) to integrate into their practice, the majority of participants favoured Miko (8). The main reason given for choosing Miko was the low cost, a few participants also cited the cute and friendly design. Five participants stated they wouldn't integrate any of the given robots in their practice citing the lack of usefulness, or wanting to know the effectiveness of speech recognition first. Besides, one participant indicated that none should be used, as "It is completely inappropriate and can hinder and cause further delay for children". Three participants were undecided and wanted to know more, indicating a somewhat uncertain perception of the potential of robots in therapy. Other responses were scattered across robots such as Nao (3), Pepper (3), Miro (2), QT (2), or even all of them (1). Pepper was chosen due to having phonetic control or being perceived as more appropriate for patients with neurodegenerative diseases. It was noted that QT is static, which would be more manageable in an outpatient setting. One participant reported that if funding wasn't a concern, they would choose Nao for older students, as it is more sophisticated. Cost was at the forefront of this decision, with one participant choosing "the least expensive one, given that I work in public healthcare".

In what regards do you think social robots could be useful for you?

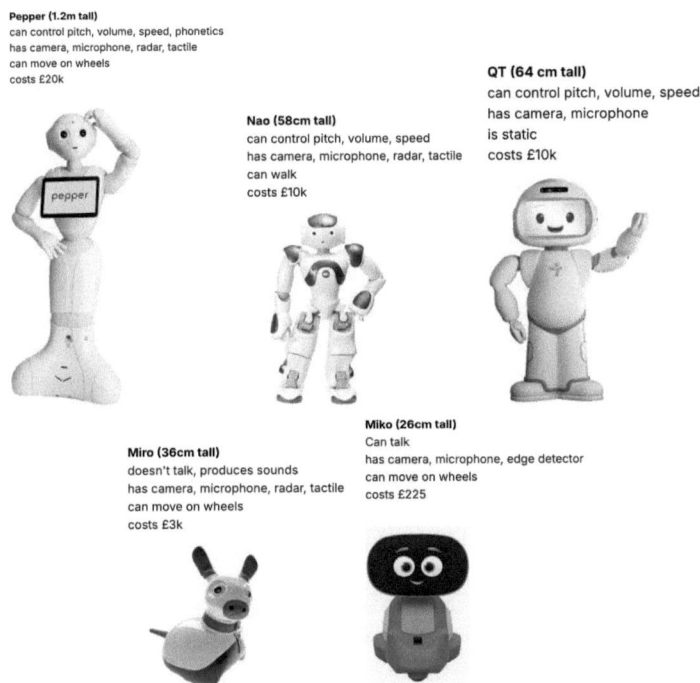

Fig. 2. Robots and their description, as they were presented to the participants

Participants identified a range of potential benefits, with patient engagement and motivation being the most frequently reported (5). Some more specific answers included conducting teletherapy, monitoring patients progress with exercises at home, helping with articulation and language complexity and fostering group interaction, giving feedback and being used as a communication device. Five people made a clear statement that they found social robots of no usefulness (one dubbing this is "stupid idea" and another "danger to their work"), and three felt they were in need of more information to be able to take a position. One participant highlighted that there was potential with children with autistic spectrum disorder, though robot acceptability can be hit and miss. Two agreed that it could improve compliance.

What problems would you anticipate if using a social robot?

Participants were asked what problems they would anticipate if using social robots. Respondents expressed concerns about several potential problems, with glitches or malfunctions being cited by four participants, reflecting worries about the reliability of technology. Reducing human interactions and lack of empathy were significant themes, reported by five participants. Some issues were noted regarding the technology potentially leading to a downfall in patient social skills and communication, and poor outcomes for the patient. Other barriers included costs(2), set up time (1), usability for both patients and therapists (3), the robot being a distraction from therapy (2) and patient acceptance (3). In addition, the perceived lack of speech understanding and scarce reliability of artificial intelligence, as well as challenges regarding how and how much patients would use the robot, also emerged as concerns. There were also some concerns about the technology being a distraction for clients who hyperfixate and that expectations would probably be quite high, which would lead to disappointment, but also that there might be some resistance from the patient due to lack of knowledge/understanding.

How do you think your clients would react to introducing a social robot?

Overall participants had mixed opinions regarding patient reaction to the introduction of technology, highlighting that it would depend on patients, though 17 participants thought it would be a positive reaction. However, some participants mentioned that the positive feeling is likely to fade past the novelty effect and would lead to boredom/frustration, that the "the lack of real social interaction" could become an issue, or that some clients might react to the robot with fear (1), suspicion (1) or negatively (2).

One participant highlighted that the role and benefits of the robot should be explained to the patients to be well received.

What currently constitutes a barrier to integrating a social robot in your practice? Most participants (14) named cost as the main barrier to integrate robots, whether it's to be covered by their own private practice or approved and carried out by the public health system. Whilst some do not even want to entertain the idea, as they think it's harmful (2), others mentioned their lack of knowledge or training in using those technologies (9). Another recurring point was the lack of scientific evidence supporting the fact that robots could be useful in improving Speech, language and communication needs (3).

What functionalities do you expect/hope from a social robot?

Seven participants reported that they do not know enough about robots to know what to expect. Some participants mentioned specific features, such as conversational skills, accurate sound production, a user friendly interface and clear interaction feedback. One participant highlighted that they would expect a robot to have different capabilities than what is already available with tablets or other toys. Participants also expected that the robot would be able to support patient goals, propose new activities, and improve the interaction overall.

What would make it more likely for you to integrate a social robot?

Accessing training (6) and low technology costs (4) were highlighted as factors that would facilitate the integration of a social robot in the SLT practice. Some participants were refusing to consider the possibility (2) and some don't know enough about robots to answer the question (4). A few participants had more specific answers, such as wanting evidence of a positive impact or the integration of AI in the robot, with the ability to have a conversation.

3.4 Does Technology Experience Influence Robot Perception/Expectations?

To determine if robot perception/expectations are linked to participants' outlook on technology, we looked at correlations between the two questionnaires. Four combinations of items yielded a strong correlation using Pearson correlation with a statistical significance threshold of 0.00625 to account for Bonferroni correction. There a strong correlation between participants finding technology useful and robots being seen as efficient (0.60), and between participants perceiving technology and robots as making their job harder (0.67). There was a strong negative correlation that indicates that participants that do not see technology as a waste of time are more likely to perceive robots as useful (-0.65). Likewise, participants that see technology as useful, are less prone to think that a robot would make their job harder (-0.65).

We also investigated whether participants rated technology and robots differently. Usefulness, burden, and waste of time were all rated significantly differently ($p < 0.005$), with technology seen as more useful, less burdensome, and less of a waste of time.

4 Conclusions

Whilst technology is now deeply integrated in the SLT practice, and therapists are also starting to use AI, e.g. ChatGPT, the openness and enthusiasm that is expressed towards those technologies, does not quite extend to robots.

While some participants expressed concerns, particularly about potential harm to social skills and increased communication delays, others identified meaningful opportunities, especially in enhancing motivation and engagement. This is indeed a promising perspective, as social robots have been successful at improving patient engagement in the past, for example the Cosmobot robot [1] in upper limb motor rehabilitation with children with cerebral palsy. As one of the respondents pointed out, the robot's conversational abilities could also enable group interaction in one-on-one sessions. This is an especially interesting perspective for those circumstances where group sessions would be useful but are not possible for various reasons (such as lack of eligible participants or behavioural issues). The robot was also seen as a potential tool to give exercises to do at home, monitor progress at home and enable teletherapy. We think that this probably be the most successful way of integrating robots in SLT practice, as an adjunct to therapy and a tool that patients could practice with at home, making home practice more attractive and therefore maximizing compliance.

Participants also expressed recurring concerns about the cost of such technology, as well as their lack of knowledge and training to handle robots. In fact, many of the participants expressed a willingness to take part in courses and training opportunities regarding the use of social robots. UK SLTs were consistently less positive than Italian ones, this could be linked to the fear of losing jobs to AI that was highlighted by one UK participant and that is a lot more present in the UK (59%) [9] than in Italy (33%) [16].

There are some obvious limitations in this work. Our sample size is relatively modest which may limit the generalisability of the findings, and by focusing on 2 countries, the findings cannot be generalised to the broad range of SLTs, but we believe that results would vary based on the country as they have different societal and political contexts. The vast majority of participants had no prior experience of robots, whilst this might be seen as a limitation, this also accurately reflects the reality of this field and the lack of relationship between HRI and SLT.

Acknowledgment. This research is funded by a Royal Society Grant. We thank Pippa Kirby for her input on the survey and Melissa Zulle for her help with recruitment.

References

1. Brisben, A., Safos, C., Lockerd, A., Vice, J., Lathan, C.: The cosmobot system: evaluating its usability in therapy sessions with children diagnosed with cerebral palsy. **3**(25), 13 (2005)
2. Coeckelbergh, M., et al.: A survey of expectations about the role of robots in robot-assisted therapy for children with ASD: ethical acceptability, trust, sociability, appearance, and attachment. Sci. Eng. Ethics **22**, 47–65 (2016)
3. Conti, D., Cattani, A., Di Nuovo, S., Di Nuovo, A.: Are future psychologists willing to accept and use a humanoid robot in their practice? Italian and English students' perspective. Front. Psychol. **10**, 2138 (2019)
4. David, D., Thérouanne, P., Milhabet, I.: The acceptability of social robots: a scoping review of the recent literature. Comput. Hum. Behav. **137**, 107419 (2022)
5. Georgieva-Tsaneva, G., et al.: Exploring the potential of social robots for speech and language therapy: a review and analysis of interactive scenarios. Machines **11**(7), 693 (2023)
6. Ioannou, A., Andreva, A.: Play and learn with an intelligent robot: enhancing the therapy of hearing-impaired children. In: Lamas, D., Loizides, F., Nacke, L., Petrie, H., Winckler, M., Zaphiris, P. (eds.) INTERACT 2019. LNCS, vol. 11747, pp. 436–452. Springer, Cham (2019). https://doi.org/10.1007/978-3-030-29384-0_27
7. Lakatos, G., et al.: A feasibility study of using Kaspar, a humanoid robot for speech and language therapy for children with learning disabilities*. In: 2023 32nd IEEE International Conference on Robot and Human Interactive Communication (RO-MAN), pp. 1233–1238 (2023). https://doi.org/10.1109/RO-MAN57019.2023.10309615
8. Leinweber, J., et al.: Technology use in speech and language therapy: digital participation succeeds through acceptance and use of technology. Front. Commun. **8**, 1176827 (2023)
9. O'Boyle, D.: Nearly 60% of brits fear their jobs are replaceable by AI. https://www.standard.co.uk/business/ai-replace-jobs-robots-work-60-artificial-intelligence-survey-b1119962.html
10. RCSLT: Communication access UK inclusive communication for all. https://www.rcslt.org/policy-and-influencing/communication-access-uk/
11. RCSLT: Fail to plan, plan to fail: speech and language therapy workforce planning in England. https://www.rcslt.org/wp-content/uploads/2023/04/Workforce-planning-in-England.pdf

12. Robles-Bykbaev, V., et al.: Robotic assistant for support in speech therapy for children with cerebral palsy. In: IEEE International Autumn Meeting on Power, Electronics and Computing (ROPEC) (2017). https://doi.org/10.1109/ROPEC.2016.7830603. https://www.scopus.com/inward/record.uri?eid=2-s2.0-85013817392&doi=10.1109%2fROPEC.2016.7830603&partnerID=40&md5=23a29d3269d53fc4daba2f4a132f8d91
13. Schools, Pupils Statistics Team, U.G.: Schools, pupils and their characteristics. https://explore-education-statistics.service.gov.uk/find-statistics/school-pupils-and-their-characteristics/2024-25
14. Spitale, M., Silleresi, S., Garzotto, F., Matarić, M.J.: Using socially assistive robots in speech-language therapy for children with language impairments. Int. J. Soc. Rob. **15**(9–10), 1525–1542 (2023): https://doi.org/10.1007/s12369-023-01028-7. https://www.scopus.com/inward/record.uri?eid=2-s2.0-85166955514&doi=10.1007%2fs12369-023-01028-7&partnerID=40&md5=aa5b2feeebc1897f0ea26d32085f0c3c
15. Thompson, K., Zimmerman, E., et al.: Pediatric speech-language pathologists' use of mobile health technology: qualitative questionnaire study. JMIR Rehabil. Assistive Technol. **6**(2), e13966 (2019)
16. Universidades, P.F.: L'intelligenza artificiale e l'occupabilità del futuro. https://docs.planetaformacion.com/estudios/barometro/pfu-barometro-italia.pdf
17. Yoshikawa, Y., Kobayashi, H., Sakai, N., Ishiguro, H., Kumazaki, H.: Therapeutic potential of robots for people who stutter: a preliminary study. Front. Psychiatry **15**, 1298626 (2024). https://doi.org/10.3389/fpsyt.2024.1298626

SRWToolkit: An Open Source Wizard of Oz Toolkit to Create Social Robotic Avatars

Atikkhan Faridkhan Nilgar[1,2](✉), Kristof Van Laerhoven[1], and Ayub Kinoti[3]

[1] University of Siegen, 57076 Siegen, Germany
atikkhan.nilgar@uni-siegen.de
[2] Honda Research Institute Europe GmbH, 63073 Offenbach am Main, Germany
[3] Dedan Kimathi University of Technology, Nyeri, Kenya

Abstract. We present SRWToolkit, an open-source Wizard of Oz toolkit designed to facilitate the rapid prototyping of social robotic avatars powered by local large language models (LLMs). Our web-based toolkit enables multimodal interaction through text input, button-activated speech, and wake-word command. The toolkit offers real-time configuration of avatar appearance, behavior, language, and voice via an intuitive control panel. In contrast to prior works that rely on cloud-based LLMs services, SRWToolkit emphasizes modularity and ensures on-device functionality through local LLM inference. In our small-scale user study, [n = 11] participants created and interacted with diverse robotic roles (hospital receptionist, mathematics teacher, and driving assistant), which demonstrated positive outcomes in the toolkit's usability, trust, and user experience. The toolkit enables rapid and efficient development of robot characters customized to researchers' needs, supporting scalable research in human-robot interaction.

Keywords: Social Robots · LLMs · Toolkit · Conversational Interfaces · Multimodal Interaction · Interactive Systems · Wizard of Oz

1 Introduction and Related Work

Social robotics research often encounters significant barriers due to the complexity and multidisciplinary nature of building interactive and engaging robot systems from scratch. These challenges require expertise in robotics, artificial intelligence (AI), and human-computer interaction design, limiting rapid experimentation and prototyping [2,5,7,9]. Traditional development approaches can be cumbersome, costly, and time-consuming, preventing greater participation from researchers who lack extensive technical backgrounds [6].

Current advances in large language models (LLMs), specifically GPT-4, have demonstrated impressive conversational capabilities, significantly enhancing natural language understanding and generation [2]. By embedding these models within a modular Wizard of Oz (WoZ) framework, researchers can rapidly prototype sophisticated human-robot interaction (HRI) scenarios while significantly reducing technical complexity. Prior studies have extensively explored WoZ methodologies as a way to rapidly prototype interactive systems without extensive programming. For instance, WoZ4U [6] is an open-source web-based interface designed to facilitate human-robot interaction studies by allowing experimenters to control robot behaviors in real-time with minimal coding effort. However, WoZ4U primarily addresses manual wizard control and does not integrate automated conversational agents.

More recently, Fang et al. [2] explored "LLM Wizards", where LLMs themselves act as automated wizards within WoZ setups. This approach showed a significant reduction in manual workload while enabling richer, more scalable interactions. Such integration allows researchers to benefit from the conversational skills of contemporary LLMs, creating natural, contextually relevant interactions without extensive manual scripting or training. Similarly, the WebWOZ [7] platform offers a generic architecture aimed specifically at language technology research, providing modular, scalable support for speech and text modalities. Popular LuxAI's QTrobot (https://luxai.com) also integrates GPT-based dialogue to support learning in educational and therapeutic contexts. However, most of these WoZ systems rely on cloud-based LLM inference, which raises concerns related to data privacy, user consent regarding data handling and storage, as well as increased latency in real-time interactions.

We address these challenges by presenting a modular WoZ toolkit that integrates local LLMs to enable the rapid development and deployment of social robotic avatars. These avatars refer to virtual representations of physical social robots, typically displayed on screens. Although they lack physical presence, they often retain similar interaction behaviors and characteristics, making them useful in scenarios where physical embodiment is not required. Our toolkit builds on prior works' insights, combining the strengths of WoZ4U's web-based modularity and LLM Wizards' automation capabilities. We provide a web-based module toolkit that supports multimodal interaction, secure local LLM execution, and comprehensive session-based log-in to facilitate adaptive interaction.

2 Technical Architecture

The social robotic avatar toolkit consists of three interconnected layers: the frontend, the backend, and the LLMs, which are detailed below.

Frontend Implementation. The frontend is implemented as a browser-based application using JavaScript. The development environment utilizes node.js (v20.15.0) and yarn (v1.22.22) as the package manager. The frontend includes two main interfaces: the Control Panel (Fig. 1) and the Social Robot Screen (Fig. 2). The control panel is developed using React.js (https://react.dev) and Redux (https://redux.js.org). It allows administrators to initiate sessions with human-readable communication IDs, configure avatar visuals, select communication languages, enable or disable interaction modes, choose LLM models, write custom prompts (LLM prompts to create a role/character of the robot), and define the voice gender. These configurations are sent in real time to the backend and stored in MongoDB (https://mongodb.com). WebSocket (https://dev.mozilla.org/en-US/docs/Web/API/WebSockets_API) ensures status updates, including robot state and connectivity, which are sent to the control panel every five seconds. The social robot screen is created using React.js to deliver a dynamic and interactive interface for end-users.

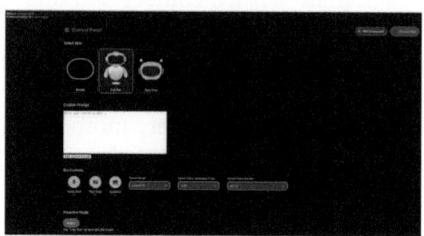

Fig. 1. Control Panel allows administrators to manage configurations.

Fig. 2. Social Robot Screen for users to interact via text and voice inputs.

The social robot screen facilitates user interaction through text input, voice input activated by a button, and voice commands triggered by a wake word ("Hey Bot"). Voice inputs are recorded using the MediaRecorder (https://dev.mozilla.org/en-US/docs/Web/API/MediaRecorder), while the proactive interaction mode uses the SpeechRecognition (https://dev.mozilla.org/en-US/docs/Web/API/SpeechRecognition) to listen for the phrase of the wake word. Redux is used to manage dynamic avatar states such as animations, blinking, and response indicators. Inputs, such as text or base64-encoded audio, are transmitted via persistent WebSocket connections to the backend. Audio responses from the backend are decoded and played using the browser's audio.

Backend Implementation. The backend is implemented in Python using FastAPI (https://fastapi.tiangolo.com). It serves as the central processing unit, which handles input processing, configuration management, data storage, and communication with the LLMs. It operates on-server using Uvicorn (https://www.uvicorn.org) to support asynchronous interactions. Dependencies are managed via Poetry (https://python-poetry.org). The backend handles WebSocket connections with both the social robot and control panel interfaces and parses incoming data. Voice inputs are transcribed into text using the Google Cloud (https://cloud.google.com) Speech-to-Text API. The transcribed or original text and the user's conversation history are forwarded to the LLM for context-aware response generation. The response is converted to speech using the Google Cloud Text-to-Speech API and sent back to the frontend. Data storage is managed using MongoDB, containerized with Docker (https://docker.com). The database collects 'communications' for session metadata and configurations, 'chat_messages' for user input, custom prompts, and LLM response logs. All deployment is restricted to a local network environment to maintain security. The

LLM server does not store any audio or conversational content; it retains only anonymized metadata.

LLMs Implementation. We used Ollama (https://ollama.com), a lightweight framework for deploying and serving large-scale language models via API on the local device (macOS, M2 Pro, Sequoia 15.0.1, 32 GB). We included Llama 3.2, Gemma 2.0, Phi 3.5, Qwen 2.5, and Nemotron-mini 1.0, all of which are pulled and served through Ollama's API. The LLM API is configured via a one-step port setup that links the toolkit to the GPU of the local device where Ollama runs. This ensures a secure, high-performance, and low-latency environment for model inference. The backend sends HTTP POST requests to the LLM API containing user queries and conversation context. The LLM processes these inputs and returns JSON-formatted responses. None of the data is retained by Ollama, ensuring that all LLM processing remains ephemeral and respects user privacy.

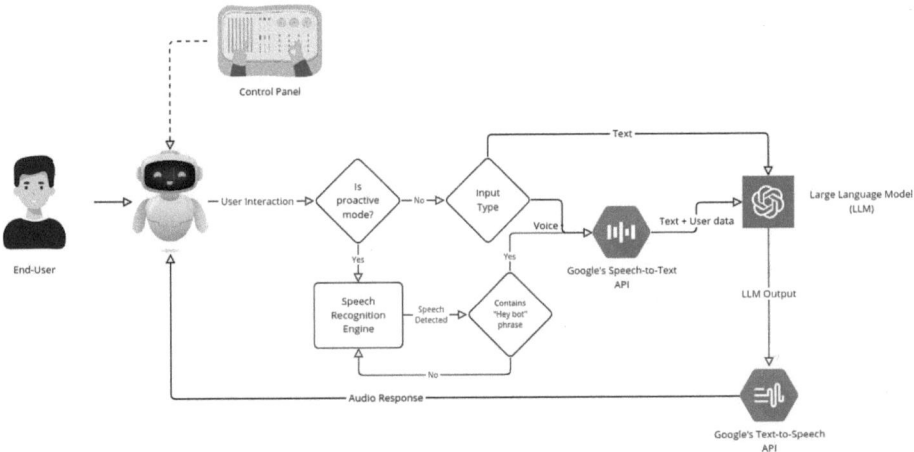

Fig. 3. Illustration of the end user interaction process with the social robot screen interface, highlighting the flow of communication and the integration of LLMs for seamless interaction.

Workflow. Figure 3 illustrates the interaction flow between the end-user and the social robot, highlighting how the toolkit processes both text and voice inputs to deliver seamless, multimodal communication. Users can interact via text or voice. In proactive mode, the browser's speech recognition listens for the wake phrase "Hey bot", activating hands-free interaction. The system continues listening for 5 s, enabling dynamic and intuitive engagement. For non-proactive input, the system detects the input type (text or button activated voice). Text messages are sent directly to the backend, while voice inputs are transcribed using the Google Speech-to-Text API. The resulting text, combined with administrator's custom prompt is processed by the LLM to generate personalized, context-aware responses. The response by LLMs is converted to speech via the Google Text-to-Speech API for natural verbal communication. From the control panel (Fig. 1) administrators can easily configure interaction modes, select LLM models, write context-based custom prompts, change languages, and adjust voice genders in real-time.

3 User Study

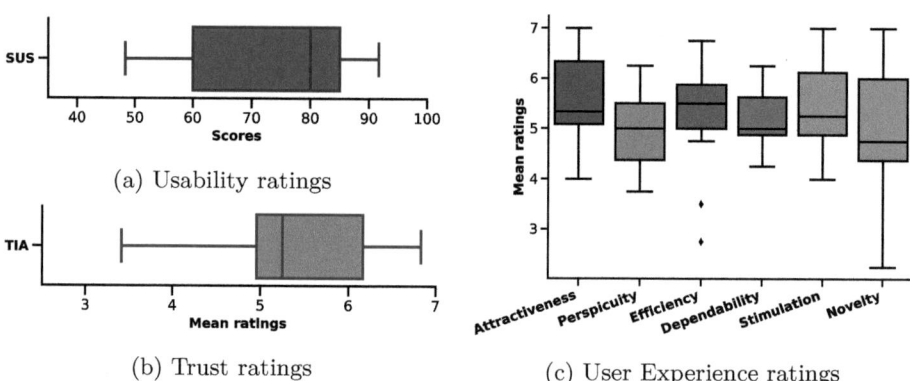

Fig. 4. Box plots represent: (a) Users' perceived the toolkit as usable, (b) Users' perceived the toolkit as trustworthy and (c) Users' had positive experience with the toolkit on different UEQ qualities

We conducted a preliminary small-scale user study to evaluate the proposed toolkit. Participants were asked to design three distinct roles/characters for a robot: (1) a hospital receptionist, (2) a mathematics teacher, and (3) a driving assistant. These roles were deliberately selected to include diverse application contexts and to facilitate a comprehensive evaluation of the toolkit. After designing each role, participants were asked to interact with the robot assuming the perspective of an end user. Upon completion of all the tasks, participants filled out a questionnaire hosted on LimeSurvey (https://www.limesurvey.org).

The survey collected demographic information, prior technology experience, and responses to several validated instruments that were adapted to fit the context of the toolkit. We assessed the toolkit's usability using the system usability scale (SUS) [1], evaluated trust in the toolkit with the trust in automated systems (TIA) scale [3], and measured user experience using the user experience questionnaire (UEQ) [4]. Participants rated their agreement on a 7-point Likert scale, following best practice recommendations by Schrum et al. [8] to capture a wider range of users' perceptions.

A total of 11 participants (9 male, 2 female) were recruited from university students and colleagues. Participants' ages ranged from 24 to 33 years ($M =$

27, $SD = 2.64$), and all held at least an undergraduate degree. Regarding prior experience with AI chatbots, six participants reported frequent (daily) use, four reported moderate (weekly) use, and one reported infrequent use (a few times per year). Additionally, six participants had previous experience with conversational robots. Participants spent on average 30 min to complete the study, devoting about 10 min to each role design and interaction task.

Figure 4 represents the participant ratings for the SUS, TAS, and UEQ measures. The overall SUS score of 72.87 indicates good level of perceived usability of the toolkit (Fig. 4a). UEQ ratings of the toolkit also reflect a generally positive user experience on different qualities (Fig. 4c): Attractiveness ($M = 5.65$, $SD = 0.94$), Perspicuity ($M = 4.90$, $SD = 0.73$), Efficiency ($M = 5.22$, $SD = 1.18$), Dependability ($M = 5.20$, $SD = 0.64$), Stimulation ($M = 5.47$, $SD = 0.89$), and Novelty ($M = 4.90$, $SD = 1.30$). Additionally, the toolkit was perceived as trustworthy (Fig. 4b) with above average trust ratings ($M = 5.34$, $SD = 1.08$).

4 Discussion and Conclusions

This study introduced a modular open-source WoZ toolkit for creating customizable social robotic avatars with local LLMs. Our web-based system facilitates multimodal interaction (text, button-activated speech, and wake-word voice command) and gives researchers fine-grained control over robot character/role, language, and interactive design through an intuitive control panel. Our approach integrates local LLMs, enabling more natural and scalable conversational interactions with minimal manual scripting. By using local LLM inference via Ollama, the toolkit ensures low latency and on-device functionality. The ability to rapidly design robots for diverse roles such as hospital receptionists or driving assistants (as seen in our user study) supports broader experimentation and aligns with calls to lower technical barriers for non-expert developers/designers [9]. Users' feedback on the toolkit indicated generally positive ratings across usability, trust, and user experience metrics.

Currently, Google Cloud APIs handle speech-to-text and text-to-speech tasks, creating a dependency on external services. Replacing them with open-source, on-device solutions will ensure full offline operation and stricter data ownership. The user study involved a limited number of participants, most of whom were familiar with chatbot technologies. Broader studies are needed across age groups and levels of technological familiarity to validate usability, user experience, and trust findings. The current version of the toolkit utilizes screen-based avatars to simulate robotic behavior. Conducting real-world evaluations with physically embodied robots similar to QTrobot (https://luxai.com) could offer valuable insights into embodied interaction, perceived presence, and the system's potential for adaption across diverse HRI applications.

Future research with this toolkit should investigate the impact of specific role types, as well as variations in LLMs, voice characteristics, gender presentation, and avatar appearance. Specifically, the investigation should examine how these design variables impact users' perceptions, with the objective of determining optimal configurations for various application contexts. Our roadmap focuses on improving and optimizing real-time performance of the toolkit as well as migrating all language and speech processing capabilities to local modules (on-device) to reduce latency and dependency on external services. The toolkit is reproducible, with the complete source code, required packages, and deployment instructions available at: https://github.com/atikkhannilgar/SRWToolkit.

Acknowledgments. This work was funded by Honda Research Institute Europe GmbH. We would like to thank all the users who participated in the experiment.

Disclosure of Interests. The authors have no competing interests to declare that are relevant to the content of this article.

References

1. Brooke, J.: SUS: a quick and dirty usability scale. Usability Eval. Ind. **189** (1995)
2. Fang, J., Arechiga, N., Namikoshi, K., Bravo, N., Hogan, C., Shamma, D.A.: On LLM wizards: identifying large language models' behaviors for wizard of OZ experiments. In: ACM International Conference on Intelligent Virtual Agents (IVA 2024) (2024)
3. Jian, J.Y., Bisantz, A., Drury, C.: Foundations for an empirically determined scale of trust in automated systems. Int. J. Cogn. Ergon. **4**, 53–71 (2000)
4. Laugwitz, B., Held, T., Schrepp, M.: Construction and evaluation of a user experience questionnaire. In: Holzinger, A. (ed.) USAB 2008. LNCS, vol. 5298, pp. 63–76. Springer, Heidelberg (2008). https://doi.org/10.1007/978-3-540-89350-9_6
5. Marge, M., et al.: Applying the wizard-of-OZ technique to multimodal human-robot dialogue (2017)
6. Rietz, F., Sutherland, A., Bensch, S., Wermter, S., Hellström, T.: Woz4u: an open-source wizard-of-OZ interface for easy, efficient and robust HRI experiments. Front. Robot. AI **8** (2021)
7. Schlögl, S., Doherty, G., Luz, S.: Wizard of OZ experimentation for language technology applications: challenges and tools. Interact. Comput. **27**(6), 592–615 (2014)
8. Schrum, M., Ghuy, M., Hedlund-botti, E., Natarajan, M., Johnson, M., Gombolay, M.: Concerning trends in likert scale usage in human-robot interaction: towards improving best practices. **12**(3) (2023)
9. Smit, K., Leewis, S., Almoustafa, H., Yildirim, K., Uymaz, T.: Enhancing educational dynamics integrating large language models with a social robot. In: Proceedings of the 2024 8th International Conference on Software and E-Business, pp. 87–94 (2025)

On the Influence of Social Robots During Ethical-Decision Making: A Preliminary Study

Marco Matarese[1(✉)], Vittorio Guerrieri[1], Rabiya Kahya[2], Francesco Rea[1], and Alessandra Sciutti[1]

[1] Italian Institute of Technology, Genoa, Italy
{marco.matarese,vittorio.guerrieri,francesco.rea,alessandra.sciutti}@iit.it
[2] KTO Karatay University, Konya, Turkey

Abstract. As social robots are foreseen to become incrementally embedded in our society, it is crucial to deeply understand their potential influence on people's behavior, especially in delicate contexts. Nonetheless, little is known about social robots' capability to persuade people while resolving ethical problems. These do not have correct or wrong solutions: individuals solve them using their own values and moral principles, but they can still be influenced by peers. Hence, it is key to understand how individuals consider social robots' ethical decisions. This paper presents preliminary results of an in-person user study where participants had to solve eight ethical dilemmas with the humanoid robot iCub. Our results demonstrate that social robots can influence people's EDM, especially when they are not highly confident about their initial answers.

Keywords: Ethical Decision-Making · Robot Influence · Social Robots

1 Introduction

The latest advancements in artificial intelligence (AI) promise to accelerate the development of social robots' autonomous behaviors and allow them to be an active part of human society. Aside from the technical challenge of allowing robots to navigate complex human spaces, we need to understand more about social robots' impact on individuals' behavior. Despite the extensive investigation regarding robots' social influence [16], it is unclear whether artificial agents can influence individuals during ethical decision-making (EDM). Unlike classical decision-making [15], EDM involves the resolution of moral dilemmas, which have no correct or incorrect decisions a priori. However, EDM is far from being a solitary activity: individuals reorganize their own behaviors and value systems by observing the moral preferences of those around them [5]; thus, social pressure and group dynamics play a role in it [4].

Recent empirical studies found that the robot's appearance might influence people's moral evaluation of it, especially when it makes utilitarian decisions [8].

Fig. 1. The experimental setup consisted of participants and the iCub robot facing each other, and two Elo touch screen monitors displaying the application GUI.

Hence, robots and AI systems can model human behavior and decision-making [13]. Nonetheless, asymmetries between humans and robots still exist in EDM because of the difficulty in seeing artificial agents in social structures [11,12]. Indeed, experimental results seem to place social robots in a gray area between humans and machines, even when their actions cause harm to people [7]. This work seeks to lay the groundwork for a broader project about social robots' influence on people's EDM. Through in-person experiments with the humanoid robot iCub, we let participants solve eight ethical dilemmas with the robot, focusing on the persuasive effects of exposure to the robot's moral decisions.

2 Methods

The ethical dilemmas we administered regarded what a hypothetical robot should do in opaque situations. We used those designed by Malle and Phillips because they proved to be highly divisive [14]. The presentation order of the dilemmas was randomized to avoid potential ordering effects. Twenty-eight Italian adult participants ($\approx 42\%$ women) took part in the in-person study with an average age of 28.5 years ($\sigma^2 = 12.4$): they all signed an informed consent approved by the Ethical Committee "Regione Liguria". Once participants entered the experimental room, they found the humanoid robot iCub, which started presenting itself: it warmly welcomed participants and referred to itself as an AI developed at the Italian Institute of Technology that can perform complex cognitive tasks, and recognize and show emotions. We used self-presentation to build a social connection between the robot and the participants.

Then, we provided them with instructions on how to perform the experiment. We told them they would sit at a table in front of the robot, with both of them facing a touch-screen monitor (Fig. 1). We told them that they would be shown a graphical interface on the screen containing the textual description of an ethical dilemma and a slider labeled "Your choice", at the extremes of which there would be the two opposite and mutually exclusive solutions to the dilemma; also the robot would be presented with the same dilemma and the same solutions. Both participants and the robot had to use the slider to decide: they could select any of the 100 points between the two possible solutions. Once both participants and iCub solved the dilemma, an acoustic signal was played, and the other's response was shown: iCub could see the participant's decision, and they could see iCub's. Then, participants and the robot could update their decisions and move on to

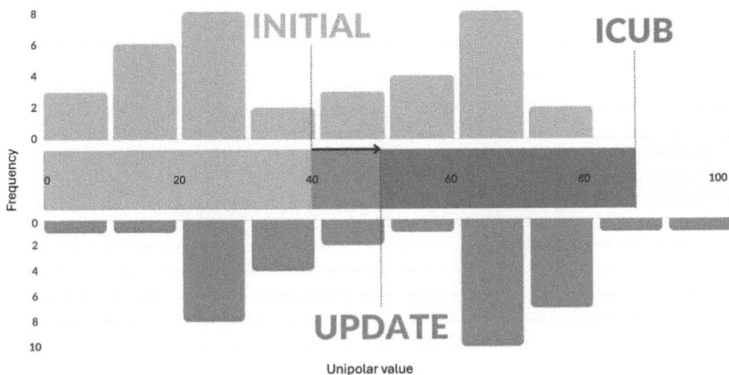

Fig. 2. Frequency of participants' initial opinions and updates with respect to iCub's opinion, considering only those that actually changed opinions. As we can see, there is an average shift towards the robot's opinions.

the following dilemma: such updates were not shown and remained secret. This procedure was repeated for eight trials with as many different dilemmas. We gave participants no time constraints, and once the last dilemma was solved, the GUI closed.

The robot's decisions were based on the participants' choices: for half of the dilemmas, the robot agreed with them, so its decision was close to the participants', and for the other half, its choices were computed by reversing the participants' ones. In both cases, we added a random Gaussian error with $\sigma^2 = 10$ to the iCub choices to avoid exactly replicating participants' answers. The ordering of the agreements was randomized and mirrored for the subsequent participant.

3 Results

Initial choices and updates were bipolar by design, since participants answered on a slider with the two options on its extremes (0 and 100) and a middle point representing maximum indecision (50). However, we were interested in understanding participants' shift toward the robot's answers; thus, we transformed our data by subtracting participants' initial choices and updates to 100 if those were greater than the robot's choices in the bipolar scale. As a result, we obtained unipolar data where participants' choices were always "at the left" of the robot data and maintained scales and distances in absolute values. Raw data, analysis files, and scripts are available on OSF (https://osf.io/2a3pe/).

We performed a Welch's t-test for dependent samples on participants' choices and updates to analyze their shift toward the robot's answers. Considering all dilemmas, we found a significant shift toward the robot's answer on average ($p < .001$, $t = -4.58$, with effect size $D = 0.32$), which is shown in Fig. 2. We also found a significant difference between participants' updates based on whether they changed opinion ($t = 2.254$, $p = .025$, with effect size $D = .41$).

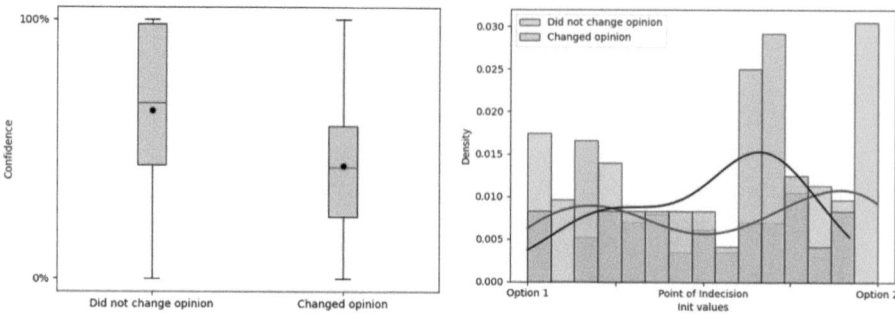

Fig. 3. On the left, participants' confidence when they changed and did not change their opinion after seeing iCub's. On the right, distributions of participants' initial choices when they changed (blue) and did not change (green) opinions.

61.54% of participants changed opinions at least once after seeing the robot answer, so the remaining 38.46% never changed opinions. Hence, we investigated significant differences between the answers of the two groups of participants more deeply focusing on participants' *confidence*, defined as the difference in absolute value between participants' initial decision and the point of indecision ($c = |50 - init_i|$): the higher confidence corresponded to decisions closer to the extremes, representing clear ideas. As shown in Fig. 3 (left), participants' confidence was significantly lower for those who considered iCub's opinion ($t = 2.17$, $p = .016$, with effect size $D = .309$). Moreover, Fig. 3 (right) shows the distribution of participants' initial choices (not unipolar data), dividing the trials where participants changed and did not change opinion after seeing the robot's. During the trials where they changed opinion, the initial values were closer to the indecision point (50) than during those trials where they did not change opinion, which concentrated more in the extremes of the scale.

We found a significant positive correlation between participants' magnitude of change and their update timing (Spearman's $\rho = .304$, $p < .001$), meaning that the higher the magnitude of their changes, the higher their thinking time to update. Moreover, we found significant negative correlations between participants' Sense of Positive Agency and their update time (Spearman's $\rho = -.164$, $p = .018$), meaning that the lower their positive agency, the higher their thinking time to update. Moreover, we found that participants' age positively correlated with their confidence (Spearman's $\rho = .160$, $p = .023$); hence, the older they were, the more confident their answers were. Participants' age also negatively correlated with their initial time (Spearman's $\rho = -.328$, $p < .001$); thus, the older they were, the faster they provided the first answer to the dilemmas.

4 Discussion and Future Works

Previous literature shows that people perceive artificial agents as autonomous and competent but lacking human emotions and societal embedding, which are necessary to tackle ethical problems [2,8,10]. However, our results showed that exposure to social robots' EDM can influence people, confirming our experimental hypothesis and aligning with the classical decision-making literature [1,15]. In fact, we found a significant shift toward the robot's different opinions after participants saw it, indicating that being exposed to social robots' EDM can influence people's choices. However, the robot did not revolutionize people's moral opinions or move them away from polarized ones. Moreover, since we clarified to participants that the robot could not see their updates (and vice versa), we can not impute such a shift to social norms, i.e., to please the social partner. Hence, we hypothesize that the reason for the robot's influence lies in the participants' uncertainty in making the first choice and their perception of the robot's competence and trustworthiness [3].

Moreover, we defined participants' confidence as the distance between their answers to the point of indecision (the middle point of the scale used), and we found that participants were more prone to change their ethical opinion in favor of iCub's when they were not confident in their decisions. We found it particularly interesting to relate this result to what some participants spontaneously told us during the de-briefing phase: they changed their opinions when unsure about their answers, and they relied on the robot's answers because they perceived them as more objective, given that they came from an AI. Hence, aligning with iCub's opinions simplified the solution to the problem by considering it to be in the same league as classical decision-making problems. Analyzing participants' confidence from a temporal viewpoint, we found that the extent of their change also correlated with the time taken to update their opinion; reasonably, this seems to indicate an additional cognitive load to process the robot's opinions.

Future works will focus on adding a debating phase where the robot and participants can justify their ethical decisions. The idea is to allow the robot to generate moral justifications using large language models and test whether AI-generated justifications are more persuasive than mere exposition of the robot's EDM. Moreover, we plan to use the perception of the robot itself as a manipulation factor. Particularly, by using warm and competent moral justifications, we aim to test our hypothesis regarding the robot's persuasiveness driven by its perceived competence and objectivity [6,9].

References

1. Álvarez, C., Zurita, G., Carvallo, A.: Analyzing peer influence in ethical judgment: collaborative ranking in a case-based scenario. In: Takada, H., Marutschke, D.M., Alvarez, C., Inoue, T., Hayashi, Y., Hernandez-Leo, D. (eds.) Collaboration Technologies and Social Computing, pp. 19–35. Springer, Cham (2023). https://doi.org/10.1007/978-3-031-42141-9_2
2. Bigman, Y.E., Gray, K.: People are averse to machines making moral decisions. Cognition **181**, 21–34 (2018). https://doi.org/10.1016/j.cognition.2018.08.003
3. Christoforakos, L., Gallucci, A., Surmava-Große, T., Ullrich, D., Diefenbach, S.: Can robots earn our trust the same way humans do? A systematic exploration of competence, warmth, and anthropomorphism as determinants of trust development

in HRI. Front. Robot. AI **8**, 640444 (2021). https://doi.org/10.3389/frobt.2021.640444
4. Cornwell, J.F., Jago, C.P., Higgins, E.T.: When group influence is more or less likely: the case of moral judgments. Basic Appl. Soc. Psychol. **41**(6), 386–395 (2019). https://doi.org/10.1080/01973533.2019.1666394
5. Fershtman, C., Segal, U.: Preferences and social influence. Am. Econ. J.: Microecon. **10**(3), 124–142 (2018). https://doi.org/10.1257/mic.20160124
6. Green, B., Chen, Y.: The principles and limits of algorithm-in-the-loop decision making. Proc. ACM Hum.-Comput. Interact. **3**(CSCW) (2019). https://doi.org/10.1145/3359152
7. Kahn, P.H., et al.: Do people hold a humanoid robot morally accountable for the harm it causes? In: Proceedings of the Seventh Annual ACM/IEEE International Conference on Human-Robot Interaction, HRI 2012, pp. 33–40. Association for Computing Machinery, New York (2012). https://doi.org/10.1145/2157689.2157696
8. Laakasuo, M.: Moral uncanny valley revisited–how human expectations of robot morality based on robot appearance moderate the perceived morality of robot decisions in high conflict moral dilemmas. Front. Psychol. **14**, 1270371 (2023). https://doi.org/10.3389/fpsyg.2023.1270371
9. Lee, M., Ruijten, P., Frank, L., IJsselsteijn, W.: Here's looking at you, robot: the transparency conundrum in HRI. In: 2023 32nd IEEE International Conference on Robot and Human Interactive Communication (RO-MAN), pp. 2120–2127 (2023). https://doi.org/10.1109/RO-MAN57019.2023.10309653
10. Malle, B.F., Magar, S.T., Scheutz, M.: AI in the sky: how people morally evaluate human and machine decisions in a lethal strike dilemma. In: Aldinhas Ferreira, M.I., Silva Sequeira, J., Virk, G.S., Tokhi, M.O., Kadar, E.E. (eds.) Robotics and Well-Being. ISCASE, vol. 95, pp. 111–133. Springer, Cham (2019). https://doi.org/10.1007/978-3-030-12524-0_11
11. Malle, B.F., Scheutz, M., Arnold, T., Voiklis, J., Cusimano, C.: Sacrifice one for the good of many? People apply different moral norms to human and robot agents. In: Proceedings of the Tenth Annual ACM/IEEE International Conference on Human-Robot Interaction, HRI 2015. Association for Computing Machinery, New York (2015). https://doi.org/10.1145/2696454.2696458
12. Malle, B.F., et al.: People's judgments of humans and robots in a classic moral dilemma. Cognition **254**, 105958 (2025). https://doi.org/10.1016/j.cognition.2024.105958
13. Müller, V.C.: Ethics of artificial intelligence and robotics. In: Zalta, E.N. (ed.) Stanford Encyclopedia of Philosophy (Summer 2020 Edition), pp. 1–70. CSLI, Stanford University, Palo Alto (2020)
14. Phillips, E., et al.: Systematic methods for moral HRI: studying human responses to robot norm conflicts. PsyArXiv Preprints (2023). https://doi.org/10.31234/osf.io/by4rh. https://osf.io/pt82j/
15. Rastogi, C., Zhang, Y., Wei, D., Varshney, K.R., Dhurandhar, A., Tomsett, R.: Deciding fast and slow: the role of cognitive biases in AI-assisted decision-making. Proc. ACM Hum.-Comput. Interact. **6**(CSCW1) (2022). https://doi.org/10.1145/3512930
16. Zonca, J., Folsø, A., Sciutti, A.: Social influence under uncertainty in interaction with peers, robots and computers. Int. J. Soc. Robot. **15**(2), 249–268 (2023). https://doi.org/10.1007/s12369-022-00959-x

Towards Reconfigurability of Plan-Based Controllers Through Metacognition

Alessandro Umbrico[1(✉)], Sebastian Stock[2], Martin Atzmueller[2,3,4], Amedeo Cesta[1], Elisa Foderaro[1], Joachim Hertzberg[2,4], Oscar Lima[2], Juan Carlos Saborío[3], Marc Vinci[2], Nicola Pedrocchi[1], and Andrea Orlandini[1]

[1] CNR - Institute of Cognitive Sciences and Technologies, Rome, Italy
alessandro.umbrico@istc.cnr.it
[2] German Research Center for Artificial Intelligence (DFKI), Osnabrück, Germany
[3] Joint Lab for AI and Data Science, Osnabrück University, Osnabrück, Germany
[4] Institute of Computer Science, Osnabrück University, Osnabrück, Germany

Abstract. Automated Planning is a well-established field of AI that, although effective, still struggles to gain widespread adoption in industrial settings due to limited ease of use, model maintenance, and performance tuning. Initiatives such as ROSPlan and Unified Planning aim to reduce the gap between planning and robotic applications, but significant expertise is required to design effective plan-based controllers. We investigate the use of a cognitive architecture to integrate heterogeneous planning frameworks and dynamically set decision-making skills. The paper introduces the architecture's general features and discusses the representation and reasoning capabilities in a mobile manipulation scenario.

Keywords: Automated Planning · Ontology · Meta-Cognition

1 Introduction

The increasing reliability and availability of robot hardware and algorithms, e.g., for object detection and manipulation, are supporting the use of robotic agents in real-world scenarios, ranging from manufacturing to healthcare applications. However, seamless planning and acting in dynamic environments require sophisticated cognitive capabilities from robots. Interactions with humans call for advanced decision-making skills that take into account human mental states [11], affective and cognitive states [12], or social rules [1]. A tight integration of AI and Robotics could guide a paradigm shift to robot control, increasing robustness, flexibility, and social awareness of robots [16]. Automated Planning aims to design flexible goal-oriented behaviors enabling robots to act autonomously [9].

Although effective, AI planning struggles to find a way in common industrial settings due to limited ease of use and non-trivial modeling of real-world dynamics, as well as the maintenance of planning models. Several initiatives have been undertaken to design *interfaces* in order to foster the use of planning in robotics [5]. The recent open-source Unified Planning (UP) library[1] provides platform-independent functionalities that support the transparent use of different planning engines [14]. Specific bridging frameworks [10,13] have integrated UP planning skills with robotics to realize autonomous goal-oriented behaviors. However, UP and bridging frameworks still require significant planning expertise.

In this context, we investigate an epistemic control architecture that integrates a heterogeneous portfolio of planning frameworks and supports contextual adjustment of decision-making skills. The planning-based component seamlessly integrates UP and other formalisms to encapsulate heterogeneous planning skills. Ontology-based reasoning provides a semantic model of robot control scenarios and decision-making skills that contextually set the agent's behavior. Central is the design of a metacognition component that bridges knowledge about control needs and the reasoning features of available planners. This work introduces the general structure of the architecture, with a brief focus on the ontological representation. An exemplary scenario illustrates the role of the metacognition component in recognizing different decision-making requirements, leading to the configuration of alternative planning formalisms.

2 Bridging Cognition with Planning and Execution

The integration of semantic technologies with robot controllers has been widely studied in the literature [15]. Researchers have primarily focused on reasoning about the agents' skills and capabilities [7] to improve goal selection and planning in terms of flexibility. Other approaches have integrated semantic reasoning to improve social awareness of planned robot actions [1]. Little attention has been given to the design of epistemic models that correlate operational needs and agents' skills with the reasoning capabilities of planners. This is crucial to epistemically assess the *expected qualities* of decision-making processes (based on different planning formalisms) and to correlate them with operational needs. A sort of *introspective reasoning* would help select the planning formalism that best fits the complexity of an interacting scenario, and partially automate the modeling of the corresponding planning problem.

We propose a semantic-based cognitive approach to the integration of heterogeneous planning formalisms and the contextual tuning of associated planning engines. Figure 1 shows the conceptual architecture designed for epistemic plan-based control. On the one hand, the architecture extends UP by representing and integrating the reasoning capabilities of additional planning formalisms, e.g., [6,17]. On the other hand, it provides a formal reasoning framework capable of dynamically assessing decisional needs, autonomously (or semi-autonomously) selecting planning formalisms, and synthesizing suitable problem specifications.

The *Cognitive Component* encapsulates an expressive representation of robot-acting scenarios. The representation formalism characterizes features of objects,

---

[1] https://github.com/aiplan4eu/unified-planning.

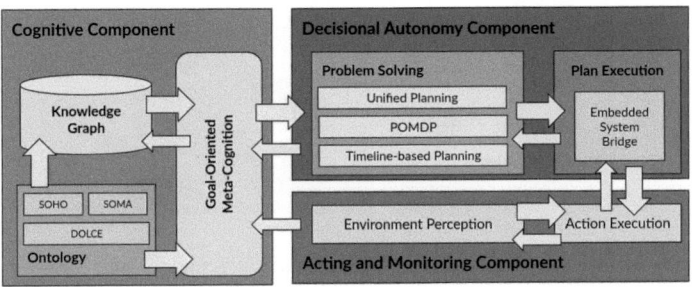

Fig. 1. Designed Cognitive Architecture

skills, and procedural knowledge. It includes a reification level suitable for explicitly reasoning about planning challenges derived from process descriptions. The key novelty is the introduction of a *Meta-Cognition Component* [8] allowing an agent to "introspectively" analyze its skills, correlate them with the needs emerging from the detected situations, and set planning goals. The *Decisional Autonomy Component* then integrates heterogeneous planning frameworks and realizes closed-loop control through the Embedded System Bridge (ESB) [10].

3 Mobile Manipulation Scenario

We discuss the proposed architecture on the example of a mobile robot manipulation scenario. The environment has been used to develop bridging skills [10], integrating UP with robotic platforms in both simulation and laboratory settings. The Mobipick robot shown in Fig. 2 is a custom indoor mobile manipulator composed of a MiR100 base, an UR5 arm, and a Robotiq gripper. The robot also has an RGB-D camera attached to the end effector.

Figure 2 shows the layout of the manipulation scenario. It resembles a collaborative cell in which the mobile robot helps a human worker with assembly tasks. The robot skills concern: (i) object detection; (ii) autonomous navigation; (iii) object picking and placing. Several tables and objects can be found in the environment. We assume objects are always on tables and can be of the following types: (i) screwdrivers; (ii) relays; (iii) power drills; (iv) boxes. Objects can have specific capabilities that can be considered to perform complex operations. Specifically, boxes can be used to transport multiple objects at once within their limited capacity. Not all objects can be placed inside a box; power drills cannot be stowed because of their weight. We define a scenario requiring the robot to perform pick-and-place operations. Although MobiPick has been tested in collaboration with humans [18] we do not consider human dynamics in this work, but focus on the impact of different reasoning skills on the robot's behavior.

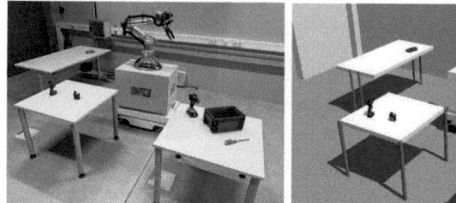

Fig. 2. MobiPick robot in real demonstration scenario and simulation.

3.1 Clear the Table Task

We consider the scenario of Fig. 2 populated with three tables containing various objects (from 0 to 3) of different types. We model a generic task of *clearing table* requiring the robot to remove all objects on a table and place them in any valid position on the top-left table. A *clear task* entails the execution of an arbitrary number of navigation, pick, and place operations depending on the number and type of objects. The objects' types determine different decompositions of a clear task. In the case that only simple objects are placed on a table (i.e., no boxes), the robot should pick one object at a time and place it on the target table. If there is a box, the robot might place the objects into the box (as long as the box's capacity permits) and move the objects together to the target table.

3.2 A Semantics for Capabilities, Capacities, and Tasks

The representation relies on the foundational ontology DOLCE [4] and domain ontologies SOHO [20] and SOMA [2]. DOLCE provides the theoretical background and a coherent semantics. SOHO and SOMA are domain-level ontologies that characterize procedural knowledge and capabilities. SOHO pursues a relational interpretation of procedures by flexibly reasoning about operational requirements. It integrates the concept of Function [3] as low-level actions that agents perform to modify the state of objects. Functions are classified according to the *effects* they have on the *qualities* of objects, and the *capabilities* agents need for their execution.

In compliance with SOMA, the concept of Capability is a specialization of DOLCE:Quality and represents the *functional qualities* of an agent. The capabilities of an agent intrinsically depend on its structure and the physical objects determining its embodiment[2]. According to DOLCE, qualities are supposed to be measured within some region of space (DOLCE:Region). As such, Capability must be measured to "quantify" the operational space of agents. Hence, we introduce the concept Capacity as a particular type of DOLCE:Region. For example, the arm of a robot has the capability of *lifting objects*. In turn, this capability can be associated with the capacity *payload*, and specific data properties (e.g.,

---

[2] Different embodiments would have different capabilities and consequently support different functions.

"3 kg") that determine the limits (in weight) within which objects can be lifted. Capabilities are ontologically associated with the DOLCE:PhysicalObject that compose an agent. As such, physical objects of the environment can also have capabilities e.g., boxes might *contain* other objects within some *capacity*.

$$
\begin{aligned}
\text{SOHO:ComplexTask} \sqsubseteq\ & \text{SOHO:ProductionTask} \sqcap \\
& \geq 1\ \text{DOLCE:hasConstituent.(} \\
& \text{SOHO:ComplexTask} \sqcup \text{SOHO:SimpleTask})
\end{aligned} \quad (1)
$$

$$
\begin{aligned}
\text{SOHO:SimpleTask} \sqsubseteq\ & \text{SOHO:ProductionTask} \sqcap \\
& \geq 1\ \text{DOLCE:hasConstituent.SOHO:Function}
\end{aligned} \quad (2)
$$

$$
\begin{aligned}
\text{SOHO:Function} \sqsubseteq\ & \text{SOHO:ProductionTask} \sqcap \\
& \geq 1\ \text{SOHO:hasEffectOn.DOLCE:Quality} \sqcap \\
& \geq 1\ \text{SOHO:requires.SOMA:Capability}
\end{aligned} \quad (3)
$$

Capabilities are associated with Function that represent the primitive actions agents can perform. In turn, functions are associated with ProductionTask that describe abstract operations structuring complex procedures supporting some ProductionGoal. Production tasks (simple or complex) are organized hierarchically and can be either conjunctive or disjunctive.

In the considered scenario, the number of objects to be moved is not known beforehand (as well as the number of tables to be cleared). The execution of tasks and functions should therefore be linked to some environmental conditions. Intuitively, a robot should pick an object from a table only if the object has been detected on it. Similarly, a robot can place an object inside a box only if both exist. The concept ProductionTask has been refined by introducing conditional dependencies with Situation. The concept Situation is a proxy for conditions determining the possibility of performing tasks or functions.

$$
\begin{aligned}
\text{SOHO:ProductionTask} \sqsubseteq\ & \text{SOHO:ProductionMethod} \sqcap \\
& \exists\ \text{SOHO:hasCondition.SOHOProductionNorm} \sqcap \\
& \exists\ \text{SOHO:hasTarget.SOHO:ProductionObject} \\
& \exists\ \text{hasExecutionCondition.SOHO:Situation}
\end{aligned} \quad (4)
$$

3.3 The Role of Meta-cognition

The knowledge processing mechanism sketched in Fig. 3 incrementally instantiates the knowledge graph of Fig. 1 by processing contextual information about the scenario. The first two steps of the pipeline elaborate the semantic description to infer the types of physical objects that are part of the environment and the associated capabilities. These steps would, for example, add to the knowledge base the individuals associated with the embodiment of the MobiPick robot, the tables, and the objects on the tables. The next step further elaborates the knowledge by inferring the set of agents' functions. According to the embodiments of

MobiPick, the procedure would infer functions like `PickObject`, `PlaceObject`, and `MoveTo`, grounded on the *known* objects and locations of the environment. The last steps of the pipeline then contextualize the functions and capabilities to the procedural knowledge of the scenario. This step is especially crucial for determining the concrete implementation of hierarchical task decomposition [19]. In the considered scenario, two different decompositions can be inferred depending on the objects available. If no boxes are present, the hierarchical decomposition will consider only functions concerning the pick and place of single objects. If boxes are present, the hierarchical decomposition will dis-jointly consider functions concerning the pick and place of single objects or multiple objects (i.e., through the boxes).

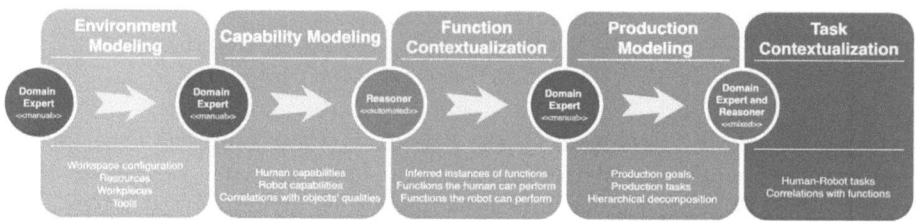

Fig. 3. Knowledge processing pipeline.

Different planning skills could be considered depending on the scenario's features. The metacognition is in charge of associating each `ProductionGoal` with known `DecisionMaking` skills, depending on the ontological description of the inferred `Function`. If no boxes are available, the procedural knowledge could be encapsulated in a classical planning formalism, synthesizing sequences of pick, place, and navigation actions. In such a case, only sequential `Function` composes the procedure, and the metacognition would infer `ClassicalPlanning` skills. Vice versa, if the procedure entails some `Function` associated with constrained capacities of objects (e.g., boxes), then the metacognition would infer `NumericPlanning` skills. In the case of boxes, numeric planning would take into account resource capacities and better optimize robot actions.

4 Discussion and Future Works

The current work introduces the concept of a cognitive architecture integrating semantic technologies and heterogeneous planning formalisms to enhance the flexibility of decision-making processes and planned behaviors. The key novelty is the introduction of metacognition into the control flow, which enables explicit reasoning about the qualities of planners and problem features. The objective is to support dynamic decision-making pipelines, increasing the flexibility and adaptability of goal-oriented plan-based controllers. We have introduced the representation and reasoning features of the architecture by considering a manufacturing-inspired robot scenario. Future work will advance the implementation of the framework to evaluate an initial prototype.

Acknowledgments. This publication was produced thanks to the funding under the bilateral agreement CNR/DFKI, project "Planning-based Cognition for Human-Robot Interaction", period 2025–2026. The DFKI Niedersachsen Lab (DFKI NI) is sponsored by the Ministry of Science and Culture of Lower Saxony and the VolkswagenStiftung. AU and AO were also supported by the EU project TRIFFID (GA No. 101168042).

Disclosure of Interests. The authors declare no conflicts of interest.

References

1. Awaad, I., Kraetzschmar, G.K., Hertzberg, J.: The role of functional affordances in socializing robots. Int. J. Soc. Robot. **7**(4), 421–438 (2015). https://doi.org/10.1007/s12369-015-0281-3
2. Beßler, D., Porzel, R., et al.: Foundations of the Socio-Physical Model of Activities (SOMA) for Autonomous Robotic Agents. IOS Press (2021)
3. Borgo, S., Carrara, M., et al.: A formal ontological perspective on the behaviors and functions of technical artifacts. Artif. Intell. Eng. Des. Anal. Manuf. **23**(1), 3–21 (2009)
4. Borgo, S., Ferrario, R., et al.: DOLCE: a descriptive ontology for linguistic and cognitive engineering. Appl. Ontol. **17**, 45–69 (2022)
5. Cashmore, M., Fox, M., et al.: ROSPlan: planning in the robot operating system. In: Proceedings of the ICAPS 2015, pp. 333–341 (2015)
6. Cialdea Mayer, M., Orlandini, A., Umbrico, A.: Planning and execution with flexible timelines: a formal account. Acta Inform. **53**(6–8), 649–680 (2016)
7. Diab, M., Pomarlan, M., et al.: SkillMaN - a skill-based robotic manipulation framework based on perception and reasoning. Robot. Auton. Syst. **134**, 103653 (2020)
8. Ganapini, M.B., Campbell, M., et al.: Thinking fast and slow in AI: the role of metacognition. In: Proceedings of the International Conference on Machine Learning, Optimization, and Data Science, pp. 502–509 (2023)
9. Ghallab, M., Nau, D., Traverso, P.: The actor's view of automated planning and acting: a position paper. Artif. Intell. **208**, 1–17 (2014)
10. Hastham Sathiya Satchi Sadanandam, S., Stock, S., et al.: A closed-loop framework-independent bridge from aiplan4eu's unified planning platform to embedded systems. In: ICAPS 2023 PlanRob Workshop (2023)
11. Lemaignan, S., Warnier, M., et al.: Artificial cognition for social human-robot interaction: an implementation. Artif. Intell. **247**, 45–69 (2017)
12. Lindsay, A., Ramirez Duque, A.A., et al.: Using AI planning for managing affective states in social robotics. In: Proceedings of the HRI 2024, pp. 679–683 (2024)
13. Martín, F., Clavero, J.G., et al.: PlanSys2: a planning system framework for ROS2. In: Proceedings of the IROS 2021, pp. 9742–9749 (2021)
14. Micheli, A., Bit-Monnot, A., et al.: Unified planning: Modeling, manipulating and solving AI planning problems in python. SoftwareX **29**, 102012 (2025)
15. Olivares-Alarcos, A., Bessler, D., et al.: A review and comparison of ontology-based approaches to robot autonomy. Knowl. Eng. Rev. **34** (2019)

16. Rajan, K., Saffiotti, A.: Towards a science of integrated AI and robotics. Artif. Intell. **247**, 1–9 (2017)
17. Saborío, J.C., Hertzberg, J.: Efficient planning under uncertainty with incremental refinement. In: Proceedings of the UAI 2019, pp. 303–312 (2019)
18. Saborío, J.C., Vinci, M., et al.: Uncertainty-resilient active intention recognition for robotic assistants. In: Proceedings of the European Conference on Mobile Robots (2025, accepted)
19. Umbrico, A., Cesta, A., Orlandini, A.: Enhancing awareness of industrial robots in collaborative manufacturing. Semant. Web **15**, 389–428 (2024)
20. Umbrico, A., Orlandini, A., Cesta, A.: An ontology for human-robot collaboration. In: Proceedings of the 53rd CIRP Conference on Manufacturing Systems, pp. 1097–1102 (2020)

Towards Perception Through Planning and Epistemic Models of Actions

Gloria Beraldo, Angelo Oddi, Riccardo Rasconi, Andrea Orlandini, and Alessandro Umbrico(✉)

CNR - Institute of Cognitive Sciences and Technologies, Rome, Italy
{gloria.beraldo,angelo.oddi,riccardo.rasconi,andrea.orlandini,
alessandro.umbrico}@istc.cnr.it

Abstract. Humans are capable of discovering knowledge through dynamic interaction with the environment, especially guided by the semantics associated with their actions. This study introduces the design of a cognitive framework intended to replicate these human-like capabilities within a robotic system alternating among two processes: (a) *exploration* to perceive new entities and infer their action-related proprieties; (b) *exploitation* to plan and execute the most appropriate actions that expand the robot's knowledge based on what it has learned so far. In addition, a DOLCE-based ontology serves as a bridge between the two processes, characterizing useful "frames" of knowledge.

Keywords: Knowledge Representation and Reasoning · Ontology · Cognitive Robotics

1 Introduction

Robotic agents need adaptable deliberative capabilities to act autonomously in unstructured environments [11]. Traditionally, this problem has been tackled from two main perspectives [15]: (a) the *AI community* has focused on top-down methods often ignoring how the agent interacts with the physical world and its embodiment, by relying on symbolic high-level descriptions; (b) the *Robotics community* has placed greater emphasis on bottom-up approaches, largely setting aside the role of higher-level reasoning and focusing instead on actuation and motion optimization. These strategies are complementary and are both necessary, especially when robots do not have an *a priori* knowledge about the environment besides their primitive skills. Previous attempts have shown the importance of bridging robotic perception with knowledge to reason about actions and cope with uncertainty or unforeseen situations [6,7]. In this work, we tackle the challenge of augmenting perception by providing robots with the semantic instruments necessary to interpret action execution outcomes and incrementally build knowledge. To integrate knowledge representation with grounded reasoning beyond mere robotic perception, ontology plays a crucial role as a tool for conceptualizing the world in which a robot operates. However, the uncertainty in the real world prevents the use of strict formalisms. Coherently with other research initiatives e.g., [8,14,17], we investigate the use of foundational ontologies to enhance the understanding of the world from direct experience. In our work, the process of acquiring knowledge is intended as the achievement of a progressively increasing intentional use of the robot's embodiment according to the learned physical and relational properties (e.g., objects that are visible and/or graspable in certain "explored" states). Hence, we propose a cyclical framework that enables a robot to explore its environment (uncovering new entities and their associated properties) and exploit the currently consolidated knowledge to guide future actions. The robot constructs its own understanding of possible interactions with the environment (social belief) by integrating exteroceptive perceptions with the activation of its embodied skills. The belief is built and iteratively maintained through the use of the ontology, in charge of maintaining the semantic coherence and contextual framing of the acquired knowledge.

2 Perception Through Robot Interacting Skills

AI-based control of autonomous robots can be classified into two dichotomic trends [15]: symbolic (model-based) AI; sub-symbolic (model-free) AI. Model-based controllers rely on explicit models of the world, allowing robots to achieve complex goals through the decomposition of actions and reliable execution [10,12]. The authoring and maintenance of such models is a non-trivial task, as it requires continuous validation, coping with a significant conceptual gap between the desired domain-level behavior and the physical execution. Model-free approaches are usually closer to physical execution and effectively address environment dynamics. However, while effective in dealing with low-level tasks [5], they often struggle with the abstraction and the generalization of implicit "acting knowledge" [2,13]. Here, we investigate a hybrid approach that combines the benefits of both perspectives. We introduce a *semantic layer* to encode a small amount of domain-independent knowledge that supports the interpretation of action execution. While several researchers have semantically characterized robot skills/actions from a functional standpoint, e.g., [1,7,16], little attention has been given to their epistemic value. We take inspiration from *active inference* [9] where, unlike planning, action executions can be seen as perception processes and are thus suitable for acquiring knowledge about states of objects of the environment. The success or failure of action executions *informs* a robot about its capabilities and limitations. The resulting epistemic knowledge characterizes the *experience* of the agent, and can then be framed as planning knowledge to realize more complex operations.

Figure 1 shows the conceptual structure of the proposed cognitive framework. A *Robot Skills* layer encapsulates the platform-dependent procedures necessary to control the execution of the robot skills (e.g., navigation, object detection, object picking, etc.), while a *Semantic Layer* characterizes the functional and

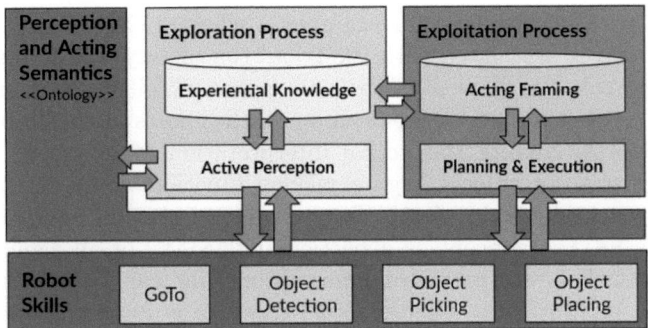

Fig. 1. Cognitive architecture for semantic-based exploration and exploitation.

epistemic value of skills. The ontological formalism relies on DOLCE [3] and extends the notion of Function [4] to describe the functional and epistemic effects of robot skill/action execution. On top of the semantic layer, two reasoning processes control the set of robot skills by pursuing two complementary objectives. The *Exploration Process* leverages the epistemic semantics to acquire knowledge about the *interaction space* of the robot. It incrementally builds an *experiential knowledge graph* collecting the information from execution feedback. The *Exploitation Process* leverages the experiential graph to elicit planning knowledge and autonomously compose robot skills into complex actions. It frames experiential knowledge as actionable knowledge by focusing on the subset of information relevant for planning high-level actions. For example, while the experiential knowledge could contain information about all the locations the robot was able to reach, as well as all the locations from which the robot attempted object grasping (tagged with success or failure according to the feedback), the actionable knowledge could consider only the learned locations the robot was able to reach and grasp objects from, ignoring unnecessary information.

3 Build Agent Belief from Functions

To support the exploration process, the semantic layer should characterize the perception features of robot skills. To this end, the concept of Function [4] is refined to characterize the acting and sensing effects. According to [4], functions are classified according to their effects on the Quality of objects. We refine this concept by introducing the "introspective" effects on the *belief* of the agent. The designed ontology relies on DOLCE [3], which defines general concepts like PhysicalObject and Quality, and relationships like hasConstituent and hasPart that represent a well-structured background for the semantic layer. The PhysicalObject concept as well as the hasPart relation can be used to describe the compound entities (e.g., the embodiment of a robot). Objects are associated with Quality, representing measurable aspects whose values can be expressed within a `Region`. For example, a wheeled base is a part of a robot embodiment and is associated with the `Location` quality, whose measurements determine the robot's physical position in space. Similar assertions could be considered for robot joints, trunk, head, and other parts of the embodiment.

These concepts qualify the *acting* interpretation of functions in terms of effects on the state of objects (e.g., a picking function would change the location of the target physical object). To characterize also the sensing effects, we introduce the `Belief` concept as a particular `Quality` of an agent. The qualities of robot beliefs are pieces of information that can be acquired through the execution of functions. This general structure is further refined by introducing different types of beliefs that can be associated with functions. The `BeliefUpdate` concept is then introduced as `SocialObject` to reify observation outcomes from execution feedback and aggregate experiential properties of `PhysicalObject`. For example, we introduce the `ReachabilityBelief` to collect acquired knowledge about reachable locations. The property `isReachable` describes physical locations that are known to be reachable by the robot after the successful execution of a `GoTo` skill. A positive feedback of `GoTo` would update the experiential graph by introducing an individual of `ReachabilityBelief`. This individual would reify the observation, asserting that the robot's target configuration is reachable from its starting configuration. Similarly, we define the `hasObservableLocation` property to formally describe physical locations that have "recorded" a positive feedback from the `ObjectDetection` skill. The individual of `VisibiltyBelief` would reify the observation asserting that a `PhysicalObject` with estimated quality measurements (e.g., location) is visible from the robot's current configuration. Likewise, the `hasGraspableLocation` property provides a formal account of physical locations that are related to objects to be grasped, as a (positive) result of the `ObjectPicking` skill execution.

3.1 Design of an Exploration Process Pipeline

The exploration process relies on the primitive skills of an agent and semantically interprets their outcome to refine the agent's internal knowledge. Initially, the robot is inexperienced, so the choice of skills to activate tends to be random. As the robot's semantic awareness of the environment increases, its action planning becomes more aligned with the expected outcomes. The set of beliefs obtained from execution constitutes a semantically rich state-transition system that will be framed as *acting knowledge* and used by the *exploitation process*.

The Algorithm 1 summarizes the exploration process. The procedure iterates over the skills $s \in \mathcal{S}$, assesses the applicability of each skill s in the current state $\mathcal{R}$ and executes s to acquire experiential knowledge[1]. For example, `ObjectPlacing` can be executed only if an object has been picked previously;

---

[1] We assume a "static environment" where changes are made only by the robot through the execution of its skills.

Algorithm 1. Sketched procedure of the exploration process building the experiential knowledge $\mathcal{KG}$. The procedure takes as input: (i) the initial state of the robot $\mathcal{R}$; the ontology $\mathcal{O}$, and; (iii) a prioritized list of skills $\mathcal{S}$.

Require: $\mathcal{R}, \mathcal{O}, \mathcal{S}$
Ensure: $\mathcal{KG} \neq \emptyset$
$\mathcal{KG} \leftarrow \emptyset$ ▷ Initialize experiential knowledge
$\Delta \leftarrow \infty$
while $\Delta \neq \emptyset$ **do** ▷ Termination condition of the exploration
  for $s \in \mathcal{S}$ **do** ▷ Exploration iteration through skill execution
    if $applicable\,(s, \mathcal{R})$ **then** ▷ Check if s is applicable in state $\mathcal{R}$
      $\mathcal{F}_s \leftarrow execute\,(s, \mathcal{O})$ ▷ Execute s and collect feedback according to $\mathcal{O}$
      $update\,(\mathcal{R}, \mathcal{F}_s)$ ▷ Update robot state $\mathcal{R}$
      $\delta_s \leftarrow update\,(\mathcal{KG}, \mathcal{F}_s)$ ▷ Update the knowledge and keep the increment
    end if
  end for
  $\Delta = \bigcup_{s \in \mathcal{S}} \delta_s$ ▷ Collect knowledge increments to check termination condition
end while
return $\mathcal{KG}$

ObjectDetection can be executed in any state; ObjectPicking can be executed only if an object has been detected in the current state (i.e., this skill must follow the object detection skill); GoTo can be executed in any state and if no other skills need to be executed. Within each iteration, the selection of skills follows these priorities: ObjectPlacing > ObjectDetection > ObjectiPicking > GoTo. Such priorities encapsulate the dependencies and the ordering for the incremental refinement of robot belief. If a robot holds an object, the priority of ObjectPlacing is higher than other applicable skills (e.g., GoTo); otherwise, the placing skill cannot be applied and the exploitation will consider other skills. Similarly, it is reasonable to execute the ObjectDetection before the ObjectPicking to *know* whether a pickable object exists.

The epistemic semantics of the ontological model $\mathcal{O}$ determines the interpretation of execution feedback and consequently the set of individuals and properties δ_s introduced into the experiential knowledge. Updates are propagated to the knowledge only when necessary: if a GoTo leads the robot to an already visited location (identified by its measured qualities) no update to $\mathcal{KG}$ is made and the resulting increment will be null $\delta_s = \emptyset$. At the end of each iteration, the whole set of increments Δ is collected, and the termination condition $\Delta \neq \emptyset$ is checked before starting a new iteration; thus, the process terminates when an exploration iteration adds no additional experiential knowledge.

4 Conclusions and Future Works

This paper lays the foundation for the development of a cognitive framework that integrates perception, reasoning, and planning for promoting the robot's learning of information about the world. By alternating between learning new information and using such information for planning, the robot is capable of making increasingly informed decisions. The use of a structured ontology ensures that knowledge is not only acquired but also meaningfully organized, enabling a more effective interaction in complex environments. Future work will focus on the detailed implementation of the different cognitive components and their integration within the ROS ecosystem, as well as subsequent evaluations.

Acknowledgments. This work is partially supported by the Italian Ministry of Research, under the complementary actions to the NRRP "Fit4MedRob - Fit for Medical Robotics" Grant (PNC0000007 - CUP: B53C22006990001) and by PNRR MUR project PE0000013-FAIR.

Disclosure of Interests. The authors declare no conflicts of interest.

References

1. Beetz, M., Mösenlechner, L., Tenorth, M.: CRAM - a cognitive robot abstract machine for everyday manipulation in human environments. In: 2010 IEEE/RSJ International Conference on Intelligent Robots and Systems, pp. 1012–1017 (2010)
2. Beraldo, G., Oddi, A., Rasconi, R.: An empirical study of grounding PPDDL plans for AI-driven robots in social environment. In: Frontiers in Artificial Intelligence and Applications, vol. 392, pp. 4426–4433. IOS Press BV (2024)
3. Borgo, S., et al.: DOLCE: a descriptive ontology for linguistic and cognitive engineering. Appl. Ontol. **17**(1), 45–69 (2022)
4. Borgo, S., Mizoguchi, R., Smith, B.: On the ontology of functions. Appl. Ontol. **6**(2), 99–104 (2011)
5. Di Nuovo, A., Cangelosi, A.: Abstract concept learning in cognitive robots. Curr. Robot. Rep. **2**(1), 1–8 (2021). https://doi.org/10.1007/s43154-020-00038-x
6. Diab, M., Akbari, A., Ud Din, M., Rosell, J.: PMK-a knowledge processing framework for autonomous robotics perception and manipulation. Sensors **19**(5) (2019)
7. Diab, M., et al.: SkillMaN - a skill-based robotic manipulation framework based on perception and reasoning. Robot. Auton. Syst. **134**, 103653 (2020)
8. Ferrini, L., Andriella, A., Ros, R., Lemaignan, S.: From percepts to semantics: a multi-modal saliency map to support social robots' attention. J. Hum.-Robot Interact. (2025)
9. Friston, K., Rigoli, F., Ognibene, D., Mathys, C., Fitzgerald, T., Pezzulo, G.: Active inference and epistemic value. Cogn. Neurosci. **6**(4), 187–214 (2015)
10. Ghallab, M., Nau, D., Traverso, P.: The actor's view of automated planning and acting: a position paper. Artif. Intell. **208**, 1–17 (2014)
11. Ingrand, F., Ghallab, M.: Robotics and artificial intelligence: a perspective on deliberation functions (2014)
12. Ingrand, F., Ghallab, M.: Deliberation for autonomous robots: a survey (2017)
13. Konidaris, G., Pack Kaelbling, L., Lozano-Perez, T.: From skills to symbols: learning symbolic representations for abstract high-level planning. Technical report (2018)
14. Lemaignan, S., Warnier, M., Sisbot, E.A., Clodic, A., Alami, R.: Artificial cognition for social human–robot interaction: an implementation. Artif. Intell. **247** (2017)
15. Rajan, K., Saffiotti, A.: Towards a science of integrated AI and robotics (2017)

16. Rovida, F., et al.: SkiROS-a skill-based robot control platform on top of ROS. In: Robot Operating System (ROS): The Complete Reference (Volume 2), pp. 121–160. Springer, Cham (2017)
17. Tenorth, M., Beetz, M.: Representations for robot knowledge in the KnowRob framework. Artif. Intell. **247**, 151–169 (2017)

HAMI: A Robotic Assistant for Active Hand Rehabilitation

Alexander Martinez, Sebastian Caballa(✉), and Dante A. Elias

Pontificia Universidad Católica del Perú, Lima 15088, Peru
scaballa@pucp.edu.pe

Abstract. This article presents HAMI, a desktop social robot designed to support the rehabilitation of hand prosthesis users, particularly adolescents and adults. The system integrates a 7-in. touchscreen, a camera, and a Raspberry Pi 4B to enable interactive games that encourage active prosthetic use through playful activities. HAMI combines visual guidance, gesture recognition, voice commands, and real-time feedback to deliver a personalized, empathetic, and accessible rehabilitation experience. Initial tests confirmed the system's usability and stability, highlighting its potential as a low-cost, modular, and engaging therapeutic tool, especially in low-resource contexts.

Keywords: Robot-assisted therapy · Social Robotics · Hand Rehabilitation · Assistive Technology

1 Introduction

Upper limb amputations caused by trauma, infection, or vascular diseases can severely impact users' functional performance, emotional health, and social participation. In Latin America, limited access to rehabilitation services, due to high demand and a lack of specialists, results in poor treatment adherence [1]. Although technologies such as social robots [2], augmented reality systems [3], haptic interfaces [4], and motion/stiffness monitoring platforms [5] have emerged, they often lack personalization, user acceptance, or affordability [2]. In response, we present HAMI, a portable and low-cost social robot that combines computer vision and therapeutic games to foster emotional engagement and support motor rehabilitation in upper-limb prosthesis users.

2 Design Process

2.1 Rehabilitation Technologies

Various assistive technologies have been developed to support rehabilitation. For instance, NAOTherapist offers posture-based games, although its use may interfere with proprioception [2,5], while vibrotactile haptic systems have been proposed to mitigate such effects [3]. Robots such as RoPi and LOVOT provide emotional support through expressive and soft-bodied designs [4,6,7]. Augmented reality (AR) systems engage users via virtual therapists [5]; other platforms, like GTMR, integrate gait and EEG feedback [7], and haptic AR tools have been used to visualize limb stiffness [8]. Additionally, recent patents propose social robots with speech recognition capabilities [9] and modular rehabilitation tools [10]. Despite their potential, existing solutions often present cost and complexity barriers, which HAMI is designed to overcome.

2.2 Specialist Information

A structured interview with an occupational therapist highlighted the highly personalized nature of hand prosthesis rehabilitation in Peru, shaped by factors such as age, gender, and clinical background. Key challenges include limited adherence to prescribed exercises due to material shortages, inadequate home environments, and emotional barriers such as frustration and anxiety. Although robotic systems may assist by reinforcing routines and providing encouragement, they are not widely used in local rehabilitation centers. This is largely due to the lack of institutional funding allocated to acquire such technologies professionals often need to bring their own equipment or work without technological support. As a result, personalization, rest management, and emotional support remain essential components for effective rehabilitation in these contexts.

2.3 Ideation Phase

The Design Thinking method was selected to guide the ideation process. During this phase, an interview with an occupational therapist helped define the functional, non-functional, and usability requirements for HAMI, with a focus on limited access to in-person rehabilitation, emotional needs, and home-based applicability. The key functional requirements included enabling interaction through both touchscreen and gesture recognition, recording and visualizing patient progress, and providing motivational feedback through sounds and phrases. Usability criteria emphasized accessibility across different age groups and cognitive levels, a compact and ergonomic design for tabletop use, and an emotionally engaging appearance to foster non-intimidating interaction. Additionally, the system was expected to include customizable games targeting specific arm movements to support therapeutic goals. These insights shaped the design into an accessible and engaging solution for upper-limb prosthesis users. Figure 1 illustrates the design evolution of the proposed robot to respond to the defined requirements.

3 HAMI Specifications

3.1 Hardware

HAMI features a compact 3D-printed structure ($36 \times 36 \times 36$ cm) housing a Raspberry Pi 4B (4 GB RAM) as the central unit, connected to the therapy

Fig. 1. Design evolution of the robot from early technical sketches to the final version.

peripherals (see Fig. 2). It includes a 7-in. touchscreen and a Logitech C525 camera with built-in microphone for gesture and voice input. Detachable PLA components (arms, ears, horn, geometric figures) support both aesthetics and manual therapy, some usable without power. The system is powered by an external AC-DC adapter and offers Wi-Fi/Bluetooth connectivity for remote updates and future clinical integration.

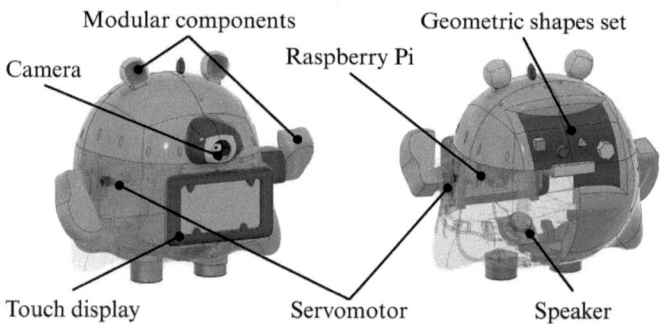

Fig. 2. Internal layout of the robot's main components.

3.2 Software

The software, developed in Python 3 for the Raspberry Pi, uses OpenCV and MediaPipe for gesture recognition and hand tracking, enabling real-time monitoring during interactive games [11]. Guided by voice prompts and a graphical interface, users select the game and target arm, then perform specific task movements. The games are organized into three difficulty levels, progressively challenging the user's ability and coordination (see Fig. 3). At session end, the system delivers motivational feedback and logs scores and key events for therapeutic monitoring and potential integration with electronic health records.

3.3 Interaction

HAMI guides users through adaptive rehabilitation sessions using visual cues, gesture recognition, voice commands, and automated feedback. Upon startup,

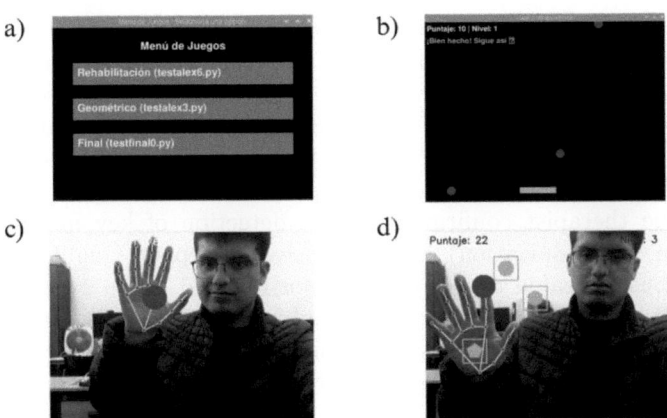

Fig. 3. Example of the game interface using hand tracking with MediaPipe: (a) main menu, (b) positive feedback screen in level 1, (c) object tracking with hand movement in level 2, (d) object collection with scoring in level 3.

users activate the system via a physical button and select a game using either the touchscreen or voice input. The system then identifies the active arm, adjusts the task accordingly, and begins tracking performance in real time using a vision algorithm. Throughout the session, HAMI provides motivational feedback automatically when tasks are performed correctly and offers gentle prompts in cases of difficulty. Upon completing an activity, results are displayed automatically, and users can navigate post-game options via voice or touchscreen. If inactivity is detected, the system issues reminders and eventually shuts down to conserve energy. This multimodal framework ensures a flexible and accessible experience, accommodating diverse user needs without requiring constant supervision.

4 Results

4.1 Prototype

The robot was designed in Autodesk Fusion for modular assembly and additive manufacturing. Components were 3D printed in PLA using FDM technology, with color coded zones for the screen, camera, arms, and accessories. The body integrates a touchscreen mount, camera holder, and rear area with insertable shapes for unplugged rehabilitation tasks. Design iterations optimized geometry and internal layout to reduce material usage and print time, with adjusted tolerances ensuring proper fit. Including electronics and printed parts, the estimated cost is $400 and the total weight is approximately 1.3 kg.

4.2 Validations

Preliminary validation was conducted with a prosthetic occupational therapist with five years of experience in upper-limb rehabilitation. The goal was to verify system functionality and assess therapeutic potential. The prototype included fixed arm positions, no internal batteries, and on-screen motivational messages. A 30 min evaluation session involved guided tasks using interactive games, voice commands, and physical exercises with insertable geometric shapes. Although no quantitative analysis was performed, the session was documented through video recordings, observational notes, the HAMI activity log, and post-session feedback. The therapist confirmed reliable detection of key movements (e.g., finger flexion, wrist deviation) and responsive gameplay. Qualitative feedback highlighted customizable arm selection, motivational audio cues that encouraged engagement, and the system's potential for physical rehabilitation. Figure 4 shows the therapist interacting with geometric figures to promote visuomotor coordination and grip precision, inspired by the Box and Block Test [12].

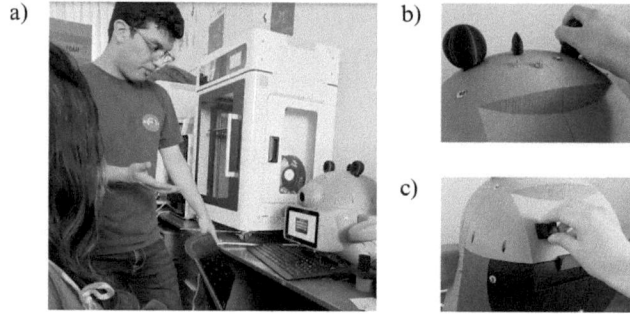

Fig. 4. Preliminary user testing involving geometric figure manipulation for functional grip exercises: a) therapist interacting with HAMI's game, b) placement of removable ears, c) user fitting geometric shapes.

5 Conclusions

HAMI demonstrated its feasibility as an interactive social robot to support upper-limb prosthesis rehabilitation. Its modular, accessibility focused design enables playful, multimodal interaction that promotes personalized and emotionally supportive therapy. Preliminary testing confirmed functional stability and therapist acceptance. Suggestions for improvement included expanding the game interface to full screen, enabling forearm supination/pronation, and enhancing mechanical adjustability to broaden therapeutic reach. Future work will focus on activating all electronic modules, integrating referential prosthetic accessories (e.g., HAMI's prosthetic arm), and aligning the system with real-world therapeutic protocols to strengthen user empathy and clinical applicability. HAMI represents a promising step toward accessible, empathetic, and adaptable rehabilitation tools for low-resource contexts.

References

1. Ali, S., Haider, S.K.F.: Psychological adjustment to amputation: variations on the bases of sex, age and cause of limb loss. J. Ayub Med. Coll. Abbottabad **29**(2), 303–307 (2017)
2. Hurmuz, M.Z.M., et al.: Are social robots the solution for shortages in rehabilitation care? Assessing the acceptance of nurses and patients of a social robot. Comput. Hum. Behav. Artif. Hum. **1**(2), 100017 (2023)
3. Liu, Y., Sun, R., Zhang, F.: An AR system to motivate the trainer during the robot-assisted rehabilitation. In: Proceedings of the ICCIS (2017). https://doi.org/10.1109/iccis.2017.8274768
4. Khademi, M., Hondori, H.M., Lopes, C.V., Dodakian, L., Cramer, S.C.: Haptic augmented reality to monitor human arm's stiffness in rehabilitation. In: Proceedings of the IEEE-EMBS Conference on Biomedical Engineering and Sciences, pp. 892–895 (2012). https://doi.org/10.1109/iecbes.2012.6498168
5. Ko, L.-W., et al.: Integrated gait triggered mixed reality and neurophysiological monitoring as a framework for next-generation ambulatory stroke rehabilitation. IEEE Trans. Neural Syst. Rehabil. Eng. **29**, 2435–2444 (2021)
6. Caballa, S., Lizano, D., Aranda, M., Zegarra, D.: RoPi: robotic assistant for the emotional support of hospitalized children for burns. In: Proceedings of the HRI 2023: Companion of the 2023 ACM/IEEE International Conference on Human-Robot Interaction, pp. 845–848 (2023). https://doi.org/10.1145/3568294.3580198
7. LOVOT – The New Companion Robot to overcome loneliness. WIPO (2021). https://www.wipo.int/en/web/ip-advantage/w/stories/lovot-the-new-companion-robot-to-overcome-loneliness
8. Khosla, R., Nguyen, K.T.: WO2022067372 – virtual and physical social robot with humanoid features. WIPO (2022). https://doi.org/WO2022067372
9. AU2024266975 – Systems for Treatment of Pain Following Amputation and Surgical Tissue Removal. WIPO (2024). https://patentscope.wipo.int/search/en/detail.jsf?docId=AU444125033
10. Lee, S.J.: WO2020141620 – speech-recognizing interactive social robot, speech recognition system for interactive social robot, and method therefor. WIPO (2020). https://doi.org/WO2020141620
11. Zhang, F., et al.: MediaPipe hands: on-device real-time hand tracking. arXiv preprint arXiv:2006.10214 (2020)
12. Mathiowetz, V., Volland, G., Kashman, N., Weber, K.: Adult norms for the box and block test of manual dexterity. Am. J. Occup. Ther. **39**(6), 386–391 (1985)

Towards Emotion-Aware and Context-Sensitive Decision-Making in Social Robotics: Insights from MUSIC4D and MHARA

Valeria Seidita[(✉)], Alessandro Giambanco, Antonio Pio Sciacchitano, and Antonio Chella

Dipartimento di Ingegneria, Universitá degli Studi di Palermo, Palermo, Italy
{valeria.seidita,antonio.chella}@unipa.it,
{alessandro.giambanco,antoniopio.sciacchitano}@community.unipa.it

Abstract. The work presents a design and architectural perspective for the development of social robots with autonomous and context-sensitive decision-making capabilities, with particular reference to two application areas: artistic performance (MUSIC4D) and personalized support for healthy aging (MHARA). In both projects, the robot's behavior is controlled by a structured knowledge representation that integrates affective perception, symbolic thinking and the generation of explainable actions. The aim is to promote forms of human-robot interaction in which the robot's actions are understandable, motivated and socially relevant. A modular cognitive architecture is illustrated that combines consolidated technologies (ROS2, OWL, Neo4j) with advanced components for language management (LLM + LangChain) and emotional feedback processing. The two case studies show how the integration of symbolic models, inference tools and immersive environments can lead to dynamic and adaptive robot behavior. The paper is a position paper that aims to pave the way for a reflection on how knowledge design affects the quality of interaction and emphasizes the need for transparent, flexible and context-oriented architectures for the future of social robotics.

Keywords: Social Robotics · Context-aware interaction · Explainability

1 Introduction

The integration of emotional sensitivity and context awareness into robotic systems is one of the most current and important challenges in the development of social robotics [2]. With the progressive transition from purely executive robots to true social agents, the need arises to equip them with cognitive and affective capabilities that allow them to adapt their behavior to the users' needs, emotional state and environment, especially in contexts such as personal assistance or artistic performance. In such scenarios, the quality of interaction depends heavily on the robot's ability to read the situation, interpret it and act coherently so that its actions are understandable and motivated.

Social robotics is now part of a multidisciplinary field of research that combines engineering, psychology, artificial intelligence and performing arts with the aim of developing systems capable of natural, adaptive and socially acceptable interactions. The integration of emotional abilities, autonomous decision-making skills and communication skills based on semantic foundations is a necessary prerequisite for acting in unstructured or dynamic environments, such as residential, therapeutic or artistic environments.

Two projects currently underway are moving in this direction: MHARA, which aims to support healthy aging through social robots capable of suggesting personalized activities adapted to the user's emotional state, and MUSIC4D, which explores the role of robots as co-performers in artistic contexts, with a particular focus on music and live performance. In both cases, the aim is to develop robotic agents that are able to make autonomous and explainable decisions based on a structured knowledge representation and symbolic reasoning mechanisms.

A central element that both projects have in common is the emphasis on explainability, i.e. the ability of the robot to make its decisions understandable and motivating for the human user [1,7]. This dimension is crucial for promoting trust, transparency and participation [8], especially in contexts where the relationship with the robot takes on an emotional and subjective connotation. The use of symbolic models, such as formal ontologies [4] and inference engines, makes it possible to explicitly represent both the internal state of the robot and the properties of the environment, thus enabling a form of reasoning that can be verified and interpreted.

With this paper, we propose a design and conceptual perspective that aims to contribute to the debate on the construction of a new generation of social robots, starting from partial results and prototypes. Our approach focuses on the relationship between emotions, context and knowledge and takes the form of developing architectures capable of integrating affective perception, symbolic representation and the autonomous generation of multimodal behaviors.

2 Methodological Approach: Knowledge Representation, Context Perception, Decision Reasoning

This contribution is based on an integrated vision of social robotics as a cognitive system capable of perceiving, interpreting and motivating its own actions in dynamic and affective environments. Central to this approach is the idea that a structured representation of knowledge is crucial for truly explainable and personalized decision making.

In our model, knowledge construction and design is not a secondary activity, but forms the backbone around which perception, decision-making and communication modules revolve. Specialized ontologies allow the robot to organize and use the experience in a meaningful way, adapting its behavior to both the environmental conditions and the user's profile and perceived emotional context.

The implemented architecture integrates consolidated tools such as ROS2 [5] for modular behavior management, Neo4j for Knowledge Graph management [9] [3] and emotion recognition modules based on psychometric scales and behavior observation. We claim that this infrastructure enables a coherent and sensitive response to stimuli through a cycle of interpretation and generation based on prior knowledge, inference rules and active goals.

The system is divided into four main components:

- a perceptual module for recognizing environmental and affective signals;
- a structured knowledge base representing concepts and relationships;
- a symbolic reasoning engine for inferential processing;
- a communicative interface for feedback of behavior in reactive form.

The human-robot interaction, we want to deal with, is characterized by dynamic and uncertain contexts that require special attention in design. In our approach, it must be anticipated in the design phase through cognitive structures that support adaptation and flexibility and then managed at runtime. *Our goal is to bridge the gap between symbolic rigidity and the need for context-sensitive decisions.*

In parallel to the analysis of the reasoning process, we are working on optimizing the knowledge base, because the quality of the interaction depends crucially on the coherence and granularity of the semantic model used. The integration of symbolic and perceptual technologies thus aims to create robots that are capable of exhibiting explainable and contextually relevant social behavior.

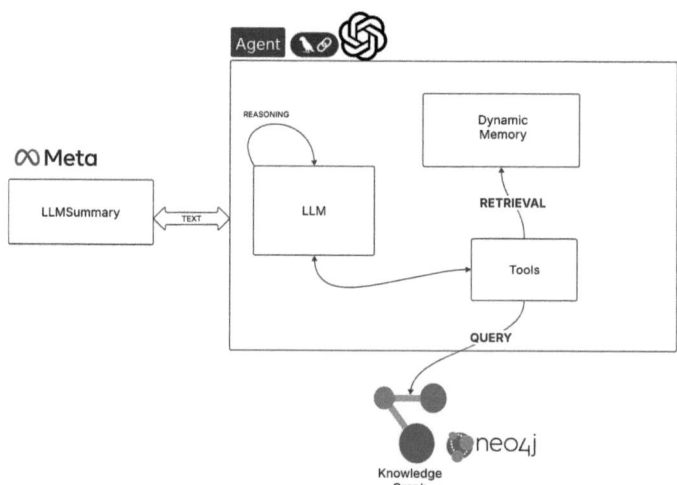

Fig. 1. The architecture that guides the robot's behavior.

3   Case Study 1 MUSIC4D

The MUSIC4D project explores the integration of social robots, immersive environments and artistic performances with the aim of redefining the stage experience in an enhanced and participatory way. The experimental scenario involves social robots on stage alongside human performers equipped with perceptual and decision-making capabilities to respond to musical, visual and emotional stimuli and generate behaviors consistent with the artistic context.

A particular element is the use of the metaverse [6] as a cognitive extension of the stage action: the robot projects an extended representation of its inner thoughts into an immersive space, through symbolic visualizations, inner speech or content generated in real time, offering the audience a parallel and transparent narrative. The first prototype created recognizes musical structures (climaxes, pauses, rhythmic variations) and adapts gestures and behaviors in real time. The system integrates a web application to collect emotional feedback from the audience and performers. This is used to modulate the robot's action, emphasize gestures or change the stage position according to affective responses.

Initial feedback shows that the presence of the robot enriches the audience's experience and encourages trust and participation, especially thanks to the transparency of intentions conveyed by the immersive performance.

The logic of the robot's behavior is represented in an architectural hypothesis (Fig. 1) that describes the cognitive flow from perception to stage production. The architecture combines modules of multisensory perception, a structured knowledge base and an inference engine to drive the action in physical or immersive form based on the recognized context and emotional dynamics. The framework is implemented in ROS2 and connected to a knowledge graph in Neo4j.

The architecture processes user requests through a sequential process that begins with the language model analyzing the request to understand its content and intent. Based on this analysis and the configured prompt, the model then autonomously selects the most appropriate tools to retrieve the relevant data. This process can involve a single tool or a combination of multiple tools that draw on the information stored in the knowledge graph or dynamic memory. Once all the relevant information has been gathered, the model formulates the final answer and makes it available to the user Following the process, for each interaction, the LLMS module stores summary information such as the request to the agent, the information received and the actions performed by the agent during the interaction in the dynamic memory. This module is context-independent and very important because it dynamically enriches the dynamic memory (and thus the prompt) by providing the architecture with dynamic examples based on the specific context of use.

4   Case Study 2 MHARA

The second case study is part of the MHARA project (Mental Health and Aging through Robotic Assistance), which aims to develop robotic systems that can support the psychophysical well-being of older people through personalized and contextualized interactions. The field of application is light assistance and the promotion of healthy aging, where the robot acts as a proactive companion, suggesting activities, making suggestions and monitoring the user's behavior and physiological parameters.

The experimental scenario involves the robot interacting with the elderly user in a home environment and evaluating in real time the contextual conditions (e.g. weather, time of day, past routine) and the emotional state of the interlocutor. These elements are integrated into the knowledge database, that describes the environmental context and the user's individual characteristics, including preferences, health goals and behavioral inclinations.

On an architectural level, MHARA shares the general approach already outlined for MUSIC4D: a structured knowledge representation system (realized in Neo4j), an emotion perception module supported by validated questionnaires and multimodal inputs, and a symbolic reasoning engine for activating robotic decisions. In this context, however, the focus is on developing practical suggestions that can accompany the person in daily well-being-oriented decisions, such as inviting them to go for a walk when the weather is favorable and the user has a neutral or sadness-prone emotional state.

Several prototypes have already been developed and tested in controlled environments, in which the robot develops adaptive suggestions based on measurable and observable parameters and explains the reasons for the suggested decision using inner speech. Here too, explainability proved to be a decisive factor for user trust and acceptance.

Preliminary results show that the robot's ability to take emotional, environmental and biographical factors into account when designing the interaction favors greater agreement with the system's suggestions and an improvement in the perceived relationship with the robot agent. The MHARA project thus contributes to demonstrating how the paradigms of knowledge-based reasoning and emotional awareness can be transferred and effectively applied in scenarios of daily human assistance.

5 Discussion and Conclusion

The results obtained in the MUSIC4D and MHARA projects illustrate the potential of hybrid architectures based on symbolic models and mechanisms of affective perception to control the behavior of robots in an autonomous, explainable and context-sensitive way. The integration of knowledge representation, symbolic reasoning and emotion processing has made it possible to develop prototypes capable of generating personalized suggestions or artistic content consistent with the situation and the user.

Despite the progress, several questions remain. First, it is necessary to understand how much the quality of the knowledge base influences the effectiveness and reliability of the robot's behavior. The link between knowledge design and interactive performance remains a crucial question to be investigated. Secondly, there is the problem of scalability and adaptability of symbolic architectures in dynamic and uncertain contexts typical of social interactions. Finally, the introduction of LLM-based techniques and guided prompts raises issues of control, consistency and integration with already structured models.

This work proposes a design vision for social robotics that focuses on the ability of robots to act in meaningful, contextual and explainable ways. The activities presented represent a first step towards the development of robotic agents capable of acting with greater situational and emotional awareness. The next developments include the extension of reasoning modules, the experimental validation of prototypes in real contexts and the deepening of the mechanisms of interaction between symbolic knowledge and autonomous behavior generation.

Acknowledgments. This study was funded by the MHARA (Motivating Healthy and Active Aging through Robotic Companionship) project funded by European Union - Next Generation EU, PNRR MUR M4C2 Iniziativa 1.3 - Partenariati estesi (PE) CUP E63C22002050006 and MUSIC4D (Musica, Imprenditorialità, Creatività e Rivoluzione Digitale: il Futuro delle Arti Performative nel sistema AFAM) project unded by European Union - Next Generation EU PNRR MUR M4C1 Investimento 3.4 CUP J77G2300 0170006

Disclosure of Interests. The authors have no competing interests to declare that are relevant to the content of this article.

References

1. Anjomshoae, S., Najjar, A., Calvaresi, D., Främling, K.: Explainable agents and robots: results from a systematic literature review. In: 18th International Conference on Autonomous Agents and Multiagent Systems (AAMAS 2019), Montreal, Canada, 13–17 May 2019, pp. 1078–1088. International Foundation for Autonomous Agents and Multiagent Systems (2019)
2. Breazeal, C., Dautenhahn, K., Kanda, T.: Social robotics. In: Springer Handbook of Robotics, pp. 1935–1972 (2016)
3. Chen, Z., Wang, Y., Zhao, B., Cheng, J., Zhao, X., Duan, Z.: Knowledge graph completion: a review. IEEE Access **8**, 192435–192456 (2020)
4. Guarino, N.: Formal ontology, conceptual analysis and knowledge representation. Int. J. Hum Comput Stud. **43**(5–6), 625–640 (1995)
5. Macenski, S., Foote, T., Gerkey, B., Lalancette, C., Woodall, W.: Robot operating system 2: design, architecture, and uses in the wild. Sci. Robot. **7**(66), eabm6074 (2022)
6. Mystakidis, S.: Metaverse. Encyclopedia **2**(1), 486–497 (2022)
7. Setchi, R., Dehkordi, M.B., Khan, J.S.: Explainable robotics in human-robot interactions. Procedia Comput. Sci. **176**, 3057–3066 (2020)
8. Vinanzi, S., Patacchiola, M., Chella, A., Cangelosi, A.: Would a robot trust you? Developmental robotics model of trust and theory of mind. Philos. Trans. R. Soc. B **374**(1771), 20180032 (2019)
9. Webber, J.: A programmatic introduction to neo4j. In: Proceedings of the 3rd Annual Conference on Systems, Programming, and Applications: Software for Humanity, pp. 217–218 (2012)

RoboPudica: Enhancing Awareness in Human - Plant Interaction via Biomimetic Interface

Hao Liu[✉], Hooman Samani, and Saina Akhond

Creative Computing Institute, University of the Arts London, London, UK
{h.liu0620241,h.samani,s.akhond}@arts.ac.uk

Abstract. This paper aims to establish social interaction between humans and plants through a robotic interface in order to evoke human understanding and concern for plant behaviour and life states. We designed a robotic interaction system that integrates plant signals with environmental inputs. Touch and light serve as two distinct stimuli, each triggering a different responsive pathway in the system. The touch input activates pre-recorded electrophysiological signals from Mimosa Pudica plant, which are mapped to motor commands that drive a flower-like structure to simulate its rapid leaf closure. The light intensity modulates the speed of rhythmic unfolding behaviour, visualised through a magnetic particle diffusion mechanism that reflects gradual movement. These two feedback pathways mimic the plant's mechanical responses to touch and light respectively, and provide users with intuitive visual cues. Experimental results show that the system can stably translate plant electrical signals into perceptible mechanical behaviours, allowing the user to "see" the plant's response process and re-establish the perception of the plant's life state in the interaction. This study explores the potential of robots as human-nature emotion mediators, and provides new pathways for ecological education and interspecies communication.

Keywords: Biomimetic Interface · Human-plant Interaction · Environmental Robotics · Interspecies Communication

1 Introduction

Plants can sense and physiologically respond to a variety of external stimuli, such as light and touch [1]. Mimosa pudica, for instance, exhibits rapid leaf closure upon touch and follows a circadian rhythm in its leaf movement [2]. These behaviours are believed to have evolved as defensive mechanisms to protect against herbivores. However, such responses are often difficult to perceive in daily life due to their subtlety and lack of visible expression.

Based on this premise, the study poses a central question: How can plant bioelectrical signals be integrated into a robotic feedback loop that translates plant behaviours into mechanical responses, thereby enabling two-way interaction with humans? To address this, RoboPudica is developed as a closed-loop robotic interaction system grounded in the characteristic perceptual behaviours of Mimosa pudica. This system maps the plant's electrophysiological activity and environmental stimuli into human-perceivable mechanical and visual feedback. By doing so, it overcomes the traditional model of unidirectional observation and enables users to both "see" and "intervene" in the plant's response process. Ultimately, this interaction aims to re-establish emotional connections between humans and plants, explore new possibilities for interspecies communication, and offer novel approaches to ecological education and cross-species understanding. Plants are not passive lifeforms; rather, they have evolved complex perceptual abilities over time [3]. Research has shown that plants can convert external stimuli into electrophysiological signals and actively regulate their structure to adapt to environmental conditions [4]. Experiments have also confirmed that plants produce observable electrical signals in response to human intervention, indicating their potential for real-time interaction [5].

In the context of interaction system design, several studies have explored the integration of plant signals into human-computer interaction. For example, Scenocosme's Akousmaflore project implemented a touch-audio feedback system using capacitive touch sensors [6], while Sareen et al. proposed embedding sensors directly into plants to monitor their physiological states and translate these into interaction cues [7]. These projects primarily demonstrate the technical feasibility of enabling plants to "respond" to humans. However, they rarely address the cognitive and emotional aspects of whether humans can meaningfully "understand" plant expressions [8]. Most current systems still treat plants as data sources, lacking visual representations of plant status, which limits the potential for emotional resonance and ecological awareness.

Therefore, this paper proposes using the perceptible translation of plant behaviours as a foundation for constructing a closed-loop robotic system that integrates touch and light inputs and is driven by electrophysiological signals.

2 Methodology

Studies have shown that many plants have an electrophysiological response to environmental factors in form of voltage difference across their leaves [9]. Mimosa pudica has an additional visible defence mechanism to environmental threats. When the plant is touched by species in its environment, such as insects, it shows a mechanical response by closing its leaves. This gives an impression that the plant is not fresh and uninteresting to prey. The leaves re-open once the threat has been removed. This behaviour has been studied in [9] by measuring the voltage difference across the Mimosa pudica when touched. The speed of leaf opening and closing is correlated to the light intensity among other environmental factors [10]. As shown in Fig. 1, the system incorporates two sensory pathways that correspond to two key types of stimuli for plants: touch and light. Touch input triggers the playback of electrophysiological data obtained from the biological plant as provided in [9], which is translated into dynamic motion feedback driven by a motor. In contrast, changes in light levels are represented through the diffusion of magnetic material, visualising the plant's rhythmic behaviour. The system is organized into a three-layer structure comprising sensing, control, and feedback modules, forming a complete dynamic response loop. All flower modules are synchronised and respond simultaneously to input stimuli. Touch duration does not affect the response dynamics, which follow a consistent preset motion profile.

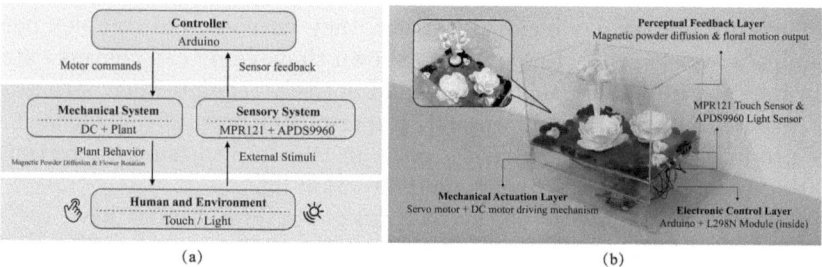

Fig. 1. (a) Closed-loop architecture. (b) Physical prototype of the human-plant interaction system, composed of three functional layers.

3 Experimental Setup

This experimental system uses an Arduino Uno-based closed-loop feedback device. It combines two types of environmental input–touch and light–to simulate the behavioural responses of the mimosa plant under different stimuli. As shown in Fig. 1(b), the system consists of a capacitive touch sensor (Adafruit MPR121), a light intensity sensor (APDS9960), multiple DC motors and FS90R continuous rotation servo motors, forming a two-channel feedback structure. The device is built in three hierarchical layers. The bottom layer houses the power supply and control circuits, keeping all electronics concealed. The middle layer contains three sets of servos connected to magnets, which translate input signals into movement and drive the magnetic diffusion feedback. The top layer acts as the behavioural output interface, displaying the plant's simulated responses through the swirling magnetic powder and the dynamic changes of a three-dimensional flower structure. In the touch response path, when the user touches the surface of the device, the MPR121 sensor detects a change in capacitance and triggers a piece of Mimosa voltage response data from the literature, (converted into a .wav file and extracted as a voltage profile), which is used to drive a DC motor attached to the 3D flower structure. The data reflects the complete response of the mimosa from a sudden change in voltage to a gradual recovery after an external stimulus. The system classifies the voltage values at different times of the day and maps them to different rotational speeds of the motor, thus simulating the rapid closure response of the plant. In the light response path,

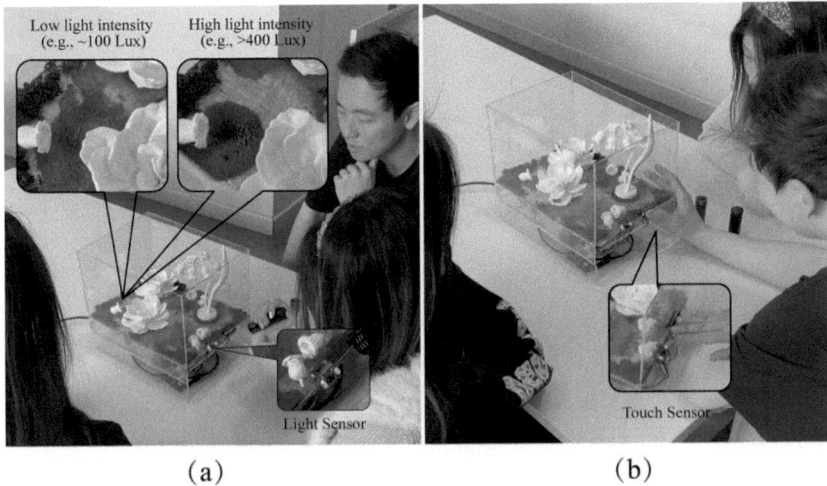

Fig. 2. (a) Interactive response to different light intensities, illustrating changes in magnetic granules structure. (b) Touch-based interaction, triggering motor-driven feedback.

the APDS9960 sensor detects the ambient light intensity in real time. In the non-touch state, the system controls the angle change of the servos according to the light intensity, and each servo drives the magnet to rotate, which in turn affects the magnetic powder diffusion pattern in the top transparent layer. This process is used to simulate the spreading and contracting behaviour of the leaves of Mimosa pudica under the control of the circadian rhythm. The light intensity was mapped according to relevant botanical studies [10], corresponding to different servo angles (Fig. 2).

4 Results and Validation

Figure 3(a) shows the electrophysiological response data of Mimosa pudica to mechanical stimuli recorded in the literature [9], reflecting the bioelectrical response of the plant under contact conditions. The Reference Voltage was not collected in real time, but was extracted from a published dataset to simulate the rapid closure behaviour of Mimosa pudica leaves after touch. In this study, this reference signal is discretised and converted into a motor control signal, which is used to drive the DC motor to output different speeds, thus converting the electrical signal of the plant into a perceptible mechanical feedback. Figure 3(b) demonstrates the operation of this feedback mechanism in a real interactive system: whenever the user triggers a touch event, the system calls the corresponding voltage response curve and outputs a stable motion command, completing a closed-loop response cycle. The voltage changes gradually return to the initial level in about 10 s, which corresponds to the recovery rhythm of the mimosa leaf in its natural state. As can be seen in Fig. 3, the system always maintains a

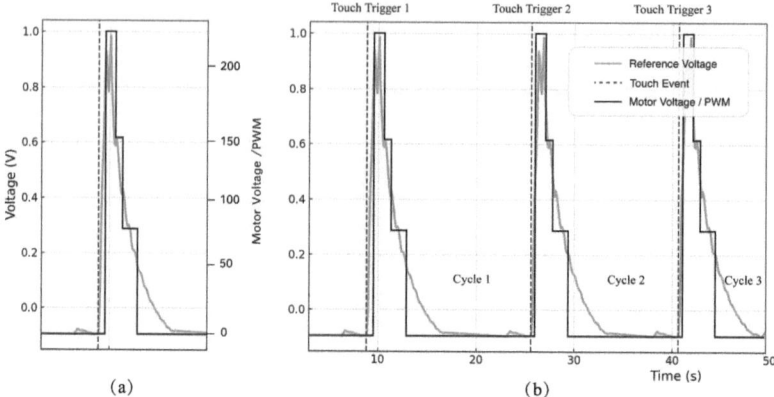

Fig. 3. (a) Reference voltage signal from literature with mapped motor PWM response. (b) Real-time system response to repeated touch triggers, showing consistent voltage-to-motor mapping behaviour.

consistent rhythm and clear feedback under several consecutive triggers, showing good stability and behavioural reducibility.

In the light stimulation path, the system collects real-time ambient light intensity data (in Lux). Based on related Mimosa pudica research [10], the light intensity is divided into three intervals and mapped to three servo angle levels. These angles control the structural changes of the magnetic powder in the Perceptual Feedback Layer. As shown in Fig. 4, the orange curve represents the real-time light intensity, and the blue dashed line shows the corresponding servo angles. The servo rotates a connected magnet, which causes the magnetic powder on the upper layer to diffuse or aggregate. This process creates a visual form resembling a "natural protective shield," simulating the leaf-unfolding behaviour of Mimosa pudica under circadian light cycles.

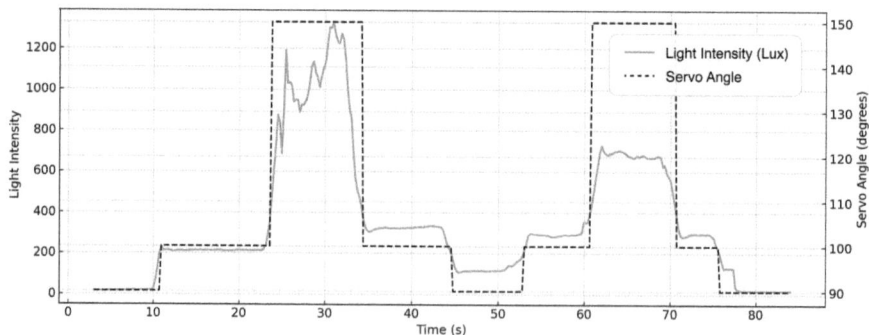

Fig. 4. Mapping of Light Intensity (Lux) to Servo Angle Response Over Time.

5 Conclusion

The proposed RoboPudica interface integrates plant electrophysiological signals with environmental sensory inputs to visualise the characteristic response behaviour of live plants. The system is not only a technological exploration, but serves as a robotic medium to establish a perceptual connection between humans and plants, providing a new path for ecological education and the reconstruction of the human-nature relationship. The current system relies on pre-recorded data and lacks real-time responsiveness to individual plant states. Future iterations should include real-time signal acquisition and adaptive feedback mechanisms to enhance interactivity. Compared with Sareen et al.'s Cyborg Botany project [4], this study places emphasis on dynamic reproduction of plant behaviours and the explicit presentation of feedback logic. Moreover, unlike the abstract audiovisual feedback used in Scenocosme's Akousmaflore project, RoboPudica employs mechanical expressions that closely mimic natural plant responses, thereby strengthening emotional connection and ecological awareness.

References

1. Mescher, M.C., De Moraes, C.M.: Role of plant sensory perception in plant-animal interactions. J. Exp. Bot. **66**(2), 425–433 (2014). https://doi.org/10.1093/jxb/eru414
2. Monshausen, G.B., Gilroy, S.: Feeling green: mechanosensing in plants. Trends Cell Biol. **19**(2), 228–235 (2009). https://doi.org/10.1016/j.tcb.2009.02.005
3. de la Cal, L., Gloor, P.A., Weinbeer, M.: Can plants sense humans? Using plants as biosensors to detect the presence of eurythmic gestures. Sensors **23**(15), 6971 (2023). https://doi.org/10.3390/s23156971
4. Sareen, H., Maes, P.: Cyborg botany. In: Extended Abstracts of the 2019 CHI Conference on Human Factors in Computing Systems, pp. 1–4. ACM, New York (2019). https://doi.org/10.1145/3290607.3313091
5. Yao, L., Rick, Kowalchuk, G.A.: Recent developments and potential of robotics in plant eco-phenotyping. Emerg. Top. Life Sci. **5**(2), 289–300 (2021). https://doi.org/10.1042/etls20200275
6. Hu, Y., Lu, J., Scinto-Madonich, N., Pineros, M.A., Lopes, P., Hoffman, G.: Designing plant-driven actuators for robots to grow, age, and decay. In: Proceedings of the Designing Interactive Systems Conference (DIS 2024), pp. 2481–2496. ACM, New York (2024). https://doi.org/10.1145/3643834.3661519
7. Scenocosme: Akousmaflore. Interactive sound installation (2007). Available at https://www.scenocosme.com/akousmaflore_en.htm. Accessed 04 Mar 2025
8. Akyute: Paisaje Sonoro. Sound installation (2023). Available at: https://hyperhouse.art/en/archive/paisaje-sonoro-akyute. Accessed 04 Mar 2025
9. Madariaga, D., et al.: A library of electrophysiological responses in plants – a model of transversal education and open science. Plant Signa. Behav. **19** (2024). https://doi.org/10.1080/15592324.2024.2310977
10. Soetedjo, H., Haryadi, B., Taspyanto, D.: Effect of light illumination on leaves movement of Mimosa Pudica. Appl. Mech. Mater. **771**, 63–67 (2015). https://doi.org/10.4028/www.scientific.net/AMM.771.63

TactiCall: ML-Powered Haptic Wristband for Alerting Hearing-Impaired Users

Haofei Niu, Saina Akhond(✉), and Hooman Samani

Creative Computing Institute, University of the Arts London,
London, United Kingdom
{h.niu0220201,s.akhond,h.samani}@arts.ac.uk

Abstract. This paper presents TactiCall, a self-contained wristband designed to enable users with hearing difficulties to "feel" their environment. First, the unmet need for unsignaled alerts among hearing-impaired adults living alone is characterized. Next, a few-shot learning pipeline for four common household sounds is implemented on a smartphone, and the hardware and firmware design of the haptic wristband are detailed. Finally, a pilot study is reported in which hearing-intact participants identified vibration patterns with an accuracy of 96.9 percent, demonstrating TactiCall's potential as an intuitive and easy-to-set-up assistive device.

Keywords: Wearable assistive technology · Haptic feedback · Few-shot sound classification · On-device machine learning

1 Introduction

This study proposes a comfortable, intuitive device that provides an alternative sensory pathway for those who prefer not to wear hearing aids at home. This device aims to ensure that individuals can receive important notifications-such as fire alarm and doorbell ring-promptly, effectively, and with ease. The research was inspired by speaking with individuals with hearing loss and discovered that most household notifications rely solely on sound, and their needs often go unaddressed. Existing solutions, such as flashing doorbell lights [1] or wired vibration bed pads [2], require extra installation, constant attention, or are confined to specific rooms. As a pilot study, interviews were conducted with two individuals who live alone and have hearing impairments to gain insights into different habits of wearable assistive technology use. This revealed that the individual around age of fifty was generally more receptive to new assistive technologies, while the participant aged over seventy-five years tends to be more cautious, indicating the need for a more intuitive design. Thus, a lightweight, wearable device could be an option, offering a more flexible, personalized way to deliver critical notifications via touch.

2 Background

Sensory substitution was first proposed in 1969 as a way to convey visual information to the brain through tactile sensations, providing alternative sensory channels for people with vision impairment [3]. Later work demonstrated that converting low-frequency speech signals into fingertip vibrations improved sentence comprehension for hearing-impaired participants when combined with audio [4]. This demonstrates that tactile feedback can augment hearing aids and help users understand spoken information. However, interpreting the complex vibration patterns requires extensive training, and the devices are relatively expensive. Commercial haptic products now map music to vibrations on multiple body sites [5], offering alternative sensory pathway for hearing-impaired users to enjoy music. However, these devices typically convey only limited information and lack of customizability.

3 System Overview

This paper introduces TactiCall, an ML-powered, low-cost sensory-substitution wristband designed to detect key household sounds and convert them into distinct vibration patterns. By leveraging on-device machine learning, TactiCall requires only five user-provided samples per sound and runs entirely on existing smartphone hardware (Fig. 1). A simple Bluetooth Low Energy (BLE) link transmits a two-bit vibration code to the wristband, enabling individuals with hearing loss who live alone to "feel" their environment in real time.

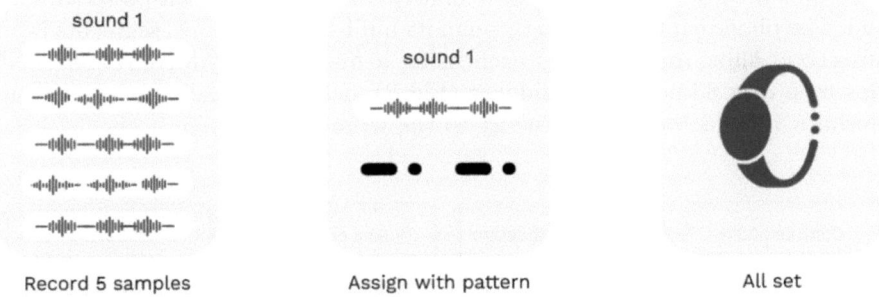

Fig. 1. User personalization workflow. By recording five samples of a home alert sound and assigning it to a specific vibration pattern, users can receive a vibration notification through the wristband, as soon as the household notification sound occurs.

First, the scope of unsignaled alerts in domestic settings for hearing-impaired individuals living alone is quantified. Second, an on-phone, few-shot CNN pipeline is described, based on a fine-tuned YAMNet model [6], for classifying four household sounds (doorbell, fire alarm, dog bark, baby cry). Third, a lightweight wristband is implemented using an ESP32-S3 microcontroller and a DRV2605L haptic driver to generate up to four distinct vibration patterns, and a pilot user study is reported to evaluate pattern discriminability.

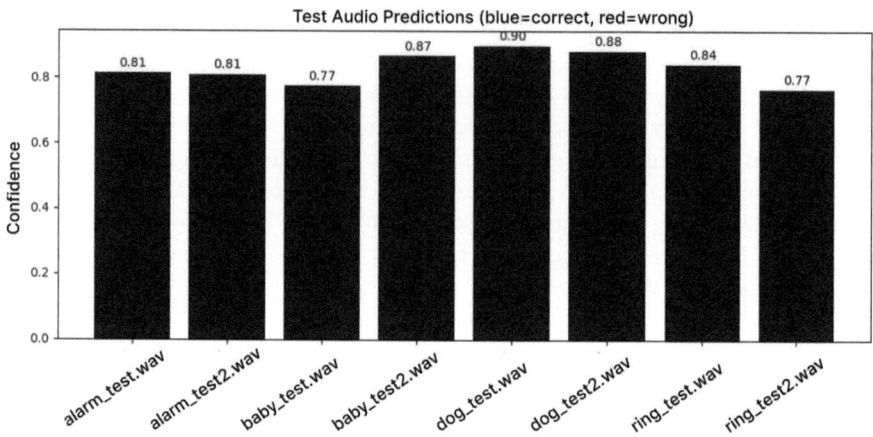

Fig. 2. Test Audio Predictions. The YAMNet-based CNN, trained with five samples per sound, achieved 100 percent accuracy with an average confidence of 83 percent.

3.1 On-Phone CNN Pipeline

TactiCall's architecture consists of a smartphone app and a self-powered wristband. The phone captures audio through its built-in microphone, segments it into four-second clips, and classifies each using a fine-tuned YAMNet-based CNN. Clips with over 83 percent confidence (Fig. 2) yield a class label, which the app transmits via Bluetooth Low Energy to the wristband (Fig. 3).

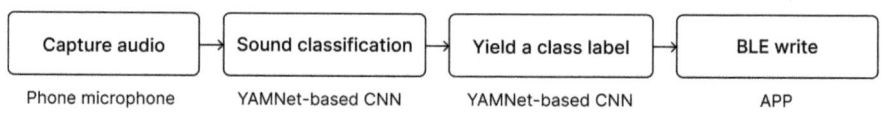

Fig. 3. Phone-side, sound-to-BLE pipeline. When an notification sound occurs, the audio is captured through the phone's built-in microphone and classified locally by a YAMNet-based CNN model. Once a label is generated, the app transmits it via BLE to the wristband.

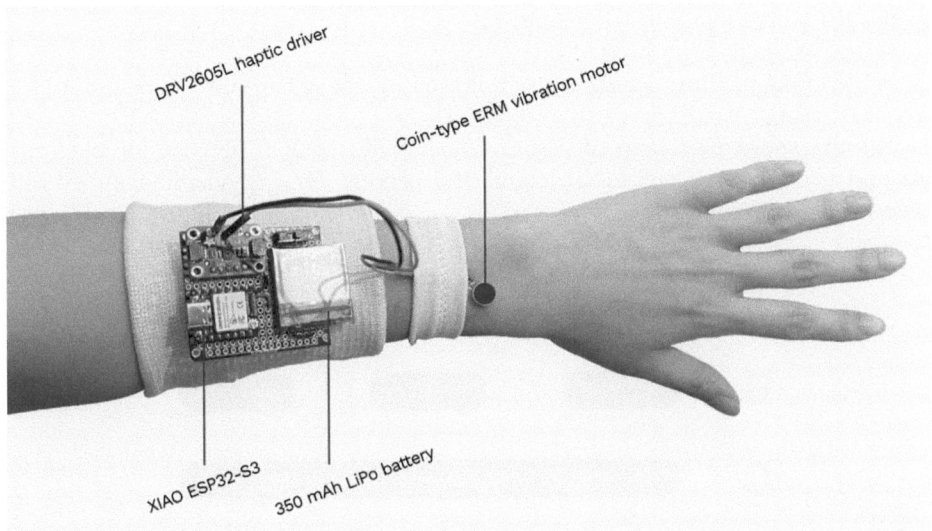

Fig. 4. Wristband hardware. The Wristband hardware centers on an ESP32-S3 that communicates with a DRV2695L haptic driver, which drives a coin-type ERM vibration motor using preloaded waveforms. The system is powered by a 350 mAh LiPo battery.

3.2 Wristband Hardware and Firmware

The wristband's hardware centers on an ESP32-S3 (3.3 V logic), that communicates with a DRV2605L haptic driver over I^{2}C. The DRV2605L drives a coin-type ERM vibration motor with four preloaded waveforms. Power is supplied by a 350 mAh LiPo battery, switched by a slide switch on the positive rail (Fig. 4). Firmware on the ESP32 listens for BLE notifications containing a code (0–3), selects the corresponding waveform library entry, and activates the motor for 500 ms.

4 Results

An experiment was conducted to determine whether users can reliably distinguish four distinct vibration patterns when wearing the wristband (Fig. 5). Each pattern was presented five times in random order. The participants identified the pattern they felt, and their responses were recorded. Due to time and resource constraints, only four patterns were tested. As the research progresses, future work will include evaluating additional patterns with larger participant groups.

The participants and protocol of our experiment were as follows:

- n = 16 participants each wore the wristband.
- Four patterns were tested (Fig. 5):
  - (a) Six short pulses in two groups of three

- (b) Three medium-length pulses
- (c) A single long buzz
- (d) One medium-length pulse followed by one rapid pulse, repeated twice

Results showed average recognition accuracies of 96.9 percent for patterns (a) and (c), 87.5 percent for (b), and 100 percent for (d), yielding an overall accuracy of 96.9 percent.

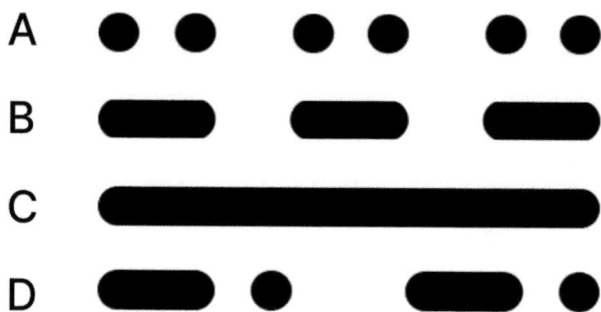

Fig. 5. This figure visualizes four distinct vibrations patterns, each presented to participants five times in random order. Participants then recorded the number of the pattern they felt, and their responses were collected and analyzed.

5 Discussion

TactiCall demonstrates that a minimal, fully portable system can restore critical environmental awareness for individuals with hearing impairments who live alone, without requiring home rewiring or additional devices. The few-shot CNN training on just five samples per class allows end users to personalize recognition to their unique household notifications. However, the current prototype supports only four sound classes and four vibration patterns; expanding beyond this may require more subtle haptic arrays. Background noise (e.g., television, vacuum cleaner) can reduce classification accuracy in open-plan homes, suggesting a need for a noise-robust front end or microphone array. Finally, the research has not yet conducted studies with actual hearing-impaired users; the study involved participants with normal hearing.

6 Conclusion

TactiCall, an ML-powered sensory-substitution wristband, was developed to convert key household notification sounds into distinct vibration patterns. TactiCall design focuses on an affordable, customizable, and easy-to-set-up assistive device that enables individuals with hearing impairments who live alone to "feel" their environment, paving the way for greater independence in domestic life. The on-phone, few-shot CNN achieved 100 percent classification accuracy with an average confidence of above 83 percent on four common household sounds, and participants recognized the four vibration patterns with 96.9 percent accuracy.

Future works include exploring cold-start few-shot learning, which would allow users to record new sounds at setup time for automatic model adaptation, and investigating long-term usability factors such as battery life, comfort, and social acceptance. Moreover, there is a plan to collaborate with individuals with hearing impairments and relevant institutions to conduct extended real-world trials.

References

1. Visual alarm system, Hubitat Inc. https://hubitat.com/blog/560315760683-building-a-safe-and-accessible-smart-home-for-the-deaf. Accessed 18 June 2025
2. Deafgard vibrating pillow alarm, Deafgard Inc. https://www.fireco.uk/products/sound-activated/deafgard/. Accessed 18 June 2025
3. Bach-y-Rita, P.: "Plastic brain mechanisms in sensory substitution." Cerebral Localization: An Otfrid Foerster Symposium. Berlin, Heidelberg: Springer, Berlin Heidelberg (1975)
4. Cieśla, K., et al.: Effects of training and using an audio-tactile sensory substitution device on speech-in-noise understanding. Sci. Rep. **12**(1), 3206 (2022)
5. Vibrating vests for deaf gig-goers, BBC Science Focus Magazine. https://www.sciencefocus.com/future-technology/these-vibrating-vests-bring-music-to-life-for-deaf-gig-goers. Accessed 18 June 2025
6. Yamnet Model, Google. https://www.kaggle.com/models/google/yamnet/TensorFlow2/yamnet. Accessed 18 June 2025

Towards a Sustainable Role for Social Robots: A Conceptual Framework

Ilaria Alfieri[✉]

IULM University, Via Carlo Bo 1, 20141 Milan, Italy
ilaria.alfieri@studenti.iulm.it

Abstract. This paper proposes a conceptual framework for redefining the role of social robots in the context of sustainability. Current approaches focus mainly on persuasive models that aim to change users' behaviour towards sustainability, positioning the robot as a behaviour-shaping agent. Instead, this work suggests an alternative, non-reductionist model grounded in the relational, embodied, and epistemological dimensions of social robotics. A sustainable role is here defined as one that emerges from the intersection of three core criteria: the type of social robot (conceived as a connector that fosters social cohesion), its material and expressive embodiment (ethically and ecologically responsible), and the form of human-robot relationship (based on partnership and emergent behaviors rather than control or persuasion). This framework not only advances a more ethically grounded vision of social robotics but also offers guidelines for assessing and designing socially sustainable robotic systems that support inclusion, cooperation, and shared agency.

Keywords: Social Robotics · Sustainability · Human-Robot Interaction

1 Introduction

Recently, there has been an increase in robotic solutions aimed at accelerating progress towards the 17 Sustainable Development Goals (SDGs). In particular, this is due to the ability of the robot "to perceive, analyse, interact with and manipulate the physical environment with minimal human intervention" [1]. Robots have been used increasingly to collect floating waste material and monitor water quality [2], to pick up and sort trash [3] to reduce pollution and waste of energy and materials during the manufacturing phases [4], or to increase production and reduce environmental impact in the field of agriculture [5]. However, while there is an affirmation of the role that robotics has for sustainability, literature appears to lack a complex discourse regarding the role of a specific branch of robotics, *social robotics*, in addressing the issue of sustainability. Most existing approaches today focus on persuasive models, where social robots are used to promote environmental sustainable behaviors [6, 7]. While promising, these interventions tend to rely on a normative, linear understanding of human behavior, and often reduce the robot to an external agent of influence or correction.

The aim of this paper is to propose a new conceptual framework for understanding the role that social robots can play in sustainability, in particular in social sustainability.

Specifically, this work proposes the notion of a sustainable role as one that reconsider the nature of the robot, its material and expressive embodiment, and the form of relationship it establishes with humans.

To develop this argument, the paper proceeds as follows: Sect. 2 critically examines current uses of social robotics in sustainability contexts; Sect. 3 focuses on why the persuasive model is not a suitable approach to sustainability, by analysing its limitations; Sect. 4 introduces the three criteria that define a sustainable role; Sect. 5 illustrates a hypothetical application scenario of the framework; lastly, conclusion are drown.

2 Current Directions in Social Robotics for Sustainability

The actual use of social robots in sustainability domains remains limited and often experimental, both in scope and application. Nevertheless, a review of the existing literature reveals that most attempts to link social robotics and sustainability focus on a specific use of exploiting the potential of *persuasive social robotics* to encourage more sustainable behavior in people. A persuasive social robot is a robot that can interact socially with humans and significantly influence or change their behavior, attitudes or cognitive processes [8]. Persuasion can create new beliefs, reinforce attitudes already in place or eliminate them. It represents an important process in human-human interaction in maintaining cooperation, social influence, and behavior change [10]. The purpose of persuasive social robots is to exploit their social power to direct humans toward goals that are relevant to those who design and produce them. Persuasion can be achieved by implementing different strategies in the robot. These strategies can include providing social feedback whether positive or negative that can persuade the user to have one behaviour instead of another [11], praising users and offering them rewards instead of sanctions [12], using emotional engagement [13], providing reminders, nudges, or storytelling [14] to guide users toward predefined behavioral goals. In the sustainability field, there are several studies that suggest that persuasive social robots can use their persuasive influence to steer users towards more sustainable attitudes towards the environment. Indeed, the persuasive nature of a robot can have positive effects on encouraging pro-environmental behaviour [7]. For example, persuasive social robots can help reduce energy consumption [15], help improve children's waste separation practices [16], implement pro-environmental/sustainable behaviour [17], encourage sustainable behaviour in shared living spaces [7], and address the challenge of behavioural change in consumers to reduce the environmental impact of unsustainable choices [18]. The creation of these scenarios represents a purely experimental stage of development. However, they can provide insights into the potential applications of persuasive social robots in encouraging pro-environmental behaviors.

3 Limitations of the Persuasive Paradigm in Social Robotics for Sustainability

Nevertheless, while the purpose of these robots is praiseworthy, a more critical analysis of the role of persuasive social robots in sustainability has shown a series of limitations, especially of an ethical, social, psychological and epistemological nature. These limitations should be addressed if we wish to develop truly responsible, sustainable and ethical technology and reconsider the current role of such technology in sustainability. Indeed, the relationship between humans and this type of robot poses several issues, such as manipulation, interference with the autonomy of the users, acceptance of the robot, psychological reactance, asymmetrical persuasion, user awareness of persuasion [19], as well as the computational nature of the interaction. In this computational relationship, the robot gives a stimulus/input and the user receives and responds to that stimulus with an output. The interaction is conceived as a mere chain of stimuli and responses [20], ignoring its relational and situated nature. These concerns are particularly relevant in the context of sustainability, where the goal should be voluntary rather than imposed behaviour change.

In this paper, it is adopted a critical stance towards the dominant view that social robots should promote sustainability goals by modifying user behavior through persuasive strategies. It is argued that the role of a social robot for sustainability cannot be that of causing behavioral change in the user through a unilateral and deliberate exercise of arguments, persuasive strategies, or control mechanisms. This model reduces the user to a passive recipient of corrective stimuli, and the robot to an agent of compliance. It assigns the robot the role of an external guide of human behaviors, without offering space for mutual adaptation or co-construction of the interaction. This approach restricts the potential of HRI to facilitate situated, participatory, and emergent interactions that could lead to more enduring and ethically grounded forms of sustainability. As a result, the contribution of social robotics to sustainability, as currently formulated, remains largely instrumental and prescriptive. The robot is treated as a tool to promote individual behavioral change, rather than as a partner in the co-construction of sustainable lifeworlds. This conceptual limitation calls for a rethinking of the robot's role for sustainability.

4 A Conceptual Framework for the Role of Social Robotics for Sustainability

The limitations of persuasive models raise crucial questions about the role and type of contribution that social robotics should play in sustainability. What conception of a social robot can contribute to sustainability without slipping into persuasion or exhortative moralising? These questions point to the need for a deeper reflection on the epistemological, embodied, and relational dimensions of social robots and how these shape their potential contribution to sustainable futures.

In what follow, it is proposed an alternative approach for conceptualising the role of social robots in sustainability, not as fixed or instrumental, but as emerging from three fundamental and interdependent elements: what type of social robot would be suitable for this purpose, what embodied characteristics should it have, and what type of relationship should it establish with humans. Together, these elements provide the basis for defining what I refer to as a sustainable role. This role can emerge from the intertwining of the epistemological view of the social robot, robotic embodiment, and relational dynamics. It offers a perspective that considers the sustainable social robot in an anti-reductionist and complex manner. This framework is intended as a step toward a non-reductionist and ethically grounded understanding of how social robots might contribute to sustainability. Rather than directing users, it focuses on relational, situated, and co-constructed forms of interaction that support the emergence of sustainable practices. It is not meant as a rigid or universal alternative to all existing models, but as a flexible guide for designing socially and environmentally sustainable robots, that can be adapted across diverse contexts, encouraging co-design and participatory experimentation. This framework can also serve to evaluate when and how a social robot could be considered sustainable and informing more responsible and context-sensitive design approaches.

4.1 What Type of Social Robot?

Current typologies in HRI often define social robots based on their roles, such as assistant, companion, tutor, or coach, each oriented toward specific tasks or interactional goals [21]. However, these categories frequently rely on instrumentalist assumptions, where the robot's function is defined in terms of individual utility, task efficiency, or behavioral modulation. By contrast, thinking about a sustainable role for social robotics requires rethinking the epistemological significance of what is a social robot. This does not lie solely in what *it does*, but also in what *it is*. In this view, it is argued that a social robot capable of playing a sustainable role should not be confined to a fixed function or goal. As some authors have noted [22], a social agent becomes truly *social* only if it can transcend a specific, rigidly defined role or purpose. Unlike industrial robots, which are designed to execute well-bounded tasks, social robots are intended to engage with humans in everyday, situated, and affectively rich contexts. These are not traditional machines merely executing commands: they engage in mutual social interaction. For this reason, the robot exceeds the status of mere instrument or functional extension and finds its deeper meaning in its relational nature. In particular, when considering the social dimension of sustainability, the type of social robot envisioned should be conceived as a *social connector*: "artificial social agents that contrast the risk of isolation inherent to domestic robotic technology by prioritizing the goal of empowering human-human relations inside and outside domestic environments" [23]. In this sense, the robot does not replace emotional ties, but supports them, actively contributing to the achievement of the SDGs, particularly those related to social inclusion, cohesion and well-being.

4.2 What Type of Embodiment?

Embodiment is not a neutral or merely functional element; rather, it plays a central role in how a robot is perceived, how it engages with users, and how it participates in the environment. In short, embodiment refers to the robot's physical instantiation, which is a necessary feature for robots that are structurally coupled to their real-world environments [24]. From the perspective of sustainability, embodiment should be reconsidered along two interconnected dimensions: social accessibility and environmental impact. On the social level, embodiment is crucial for ensuring safe, intuitive, and inclusive interaction. The robot's physical design should avoid threatening features, be accessible to fragile or marginalized users, and support intuitive interfaces that do not require prior technical knowledge. Particular attention should be paid to the avoidance of gender stereotypes, overly humanlike appearances, or affective cues that might produce misleading expectations or discomfort. In this sense, embodiment becomes not just a technical, but an ethical concern. On the environmental level, embodiment should be conceived in ecologically responsible terms: using recyclable materials, low energy consumption, modular and repairable components. As recent work has emphasized [25], the physical design of social robots has tangible ecological consequences, and these must be addressed as part of any claim to sustainability.

4.3 What Type of Human-Robot Relationships?

The traditional approach of persuasive social robotics focuses on paradigms in which the robot is designed to directly modify human behaviour, pushing it in specific predetermined directions. However, this paper proposes a relational model between human and robot, based on *emergent behaviors* - "Behavior that is not anticipated by the roboticist but generated by the interaction of behaviors and the environment"[26] - These can only occur when the interaction with the robot is not predetermined but emerges from spontaneous, participatory and collaborative actions between humans and robots. In this case, the robot does not merely perform tasks like any other tool, but by coordinating with humans responds dynamically and adaptively, helping to create new emergent behaviors and thus shaping the interaction itself in the direction not of an influence but of a *partnership* [27]. In this work, this is understood as a collaborative and coordinated relationship between humans and robots, in which the robot is not merely a tool, but acts as a dynamic partner, capable of supporting the individual ethically and socially. This concept also aligns with Damiano and Dumouchel's conception of human-robot partnership, understood not only as collaboration but as *affective coordination* which is "the process by which we jointly determine our mutual intentions of action and intentions towards each other" [28]. The nature of the relationship changes: the robot does not just interact in computational or paternalistic terms, it becomes a true relational partner that can participate in the co-creation of sustainable behaviors. Rather than directing behavioural change through strategies or stimuli, the robot's use can activate coordinated processes in which sustainable practices emerge from interactions between humans and robots.

5 Illustrative Context of Application

To better illustrate the practical relevance of the proposed framework, let us image a social robot to support ageing in place. Reimagined through the lens of the sustainable role proposed here, the robot would not be a behavioural guide, but a situated companion and social connector (it can organise video calls, promote group activities and signal opportunities in the community, such as local environmental campaigns or recycling groups). In terms of embodiment, the robot would have a safe, accessible and non-threatening design. To support intuitive use for the elderly, it could be equipped with tablet, enabling simplified visual interaction, displaying reminders, or interactive content. Its physical design would reflect ecological responsibility through recyclable materials, low energy consumption, and modular architecture, while also being inclusive and accessible. The human–robot relationship is based on emergent behaviour: rather than issuing instructions, the robot adapts to users' rhythms and preferences, gradually co-creating shared routines. Simple activities (light exercises, gardening, energy saving, or social calls) emerge from this interaction, allowing sustainable behaviour to emerge through human-robot partnership rather than external prompts.

6 Conclusion

This paper has argued that current approaches to the role of social robotics in sustainability, particularly those based on persuasive models, are limited in scope and problematic in their ethical, epistemological, and relational assumptions. While persuasive social robots have shown some capacity to influence user behaviour toward more sustainable practices, such use often reduces the user to a passive recipient and the robot to a normative instrument of correction. In response, the paper proposed an alternative framework that redefines the sustainable role of social robots through the intersection of three interdependent dimensions: the type of social robot, its embodied characteristics, and the nature of its relationship with humans. While persuasive robots treat users as subjects to be guided or influenced, the framework outlined here aims to create relational spaces where sustainability is not imposed but made possible through the quality of coordination and interaction between humans and robots.

Acknowledgments. This work was developed within the project "Third-Order Cybernetics. Towards a Systemic Approach to the Sustainability of Emerging Sciences and Technologies", Department of Communication, Arts and Media, IULM University.

Disclosure of Interests. It is now necessary to declare any competing interests or to specifically state that the authors have no competing interests.

References

1. Guenat, S., et al.: Meeting sustainable development goals via robotics and autonomous systems. Nat. Commun. **13**(1), 1–10 (2022)
2. Pan, N., Kan. L., Sun, Y., Dai, J.: Amphibious clean-up robot. In: Proceedings of the 2017 IEEE International Conference on Information and Automation, pp. 565–568. Institute of Electrical and Electronics Engineers, Macao (2017)
3. Chinnathurai, B.M., et al..: Design and implementation of a semi-autonomous waste segregation robot. In: SoutheastCon, pp.1–6. Institute of Electrical and Electronics Engineers, Norfolk (2016)
4. Galati, R., Mantriota, G., Reina, G.: Mobile robotics for sustainable development: two case studies. In: Quaglia, G., Gasparetto, A., Petuya, V., Carbone, G. (eds.) Proceedings of I4SDG Workshop 2021. I4SDG 2021. Mechanisms and Machine Science, vol. 108, pp. 372–382. Springer, Cham (2022). https://doi.org/10.1007/978-3-030-87383-7_41
5. Ball, D., et al.: Robotics for sustainable broad-acre agriculture. In: Mejias, L., Corke, P., Roberts, J. (eds.) Field and Service Robotics. Springer Tracts in Advanced Robotics, vol. 105, pp. 439–453. Springer, Cham (2015). https://doi.org/10.1007/978-3-319-07488-7_30

6. Lo, S.Y., Lai, Y.Y., Liu, J.C.: Robots and sustainability: robots as persuaders to promote recycling. Int. J. Soc. Robot. **14**, 1261–2127 (2022)
7. Beheshtian, N., Moradi, S., Ahtinen, A.: GreenLife: a persuasive social robot to enhance the sustainable behavior in shared living spaces. In: NordiCHI 2020: Proceedings of the 11th Nordic Conference on Human-Computer Interaction: Shaping Experiences, Shaping Society. Association for Computing Machinery, New York (2020)
8. Siegel, M.S.: Persuasive Robotics: How Robots Change Our Minds. Massachusetts Institute of Technology (2009)
9. Hogan, K.: The Psychology of Persuasion: How to Persuade Others to Your Way of Thinking. Pelican Publishing Company, Gretna (1996)
10. Reardon, K.K.: Persuasion in Practice. Sage Publication, Newbury Park (1991)Midden, C., Ham, J.: Using negative and positive social feedback from a robotic agent to save energy. In: Conference Proceedings of Persuasive 2009, Springer, Claremont, USA (2009)
11. Midden, C., Ham, J.: Using negative and positive social feedback from a robotic agent to save energy. In: Proceedings of the 4th International Conference on Persuasive Technology. Association for Computing Machinery, New York (2009)
12. Saunderson, S., Nejat, G.: Persuasive robots should avoid authority: the effects of formal and real authority on persuasion in human-robot interaction. Sci. Robot. **6**(58) (2021)
13. Saunderson, S., Nejat, G.: Investigating strategies for robot persuasion in social human-robot interaction. IEEE Trans. Cybern. **52**(1), 641–653 (2020)
14. Augello, A., Città, G., Gentile, M., et al.: A storytelling robot managing persuasive and ethical stances via ACT-R: an exploratory study. Int. J. Soc. Robot. **15**, 2115–2131 (2021)
15. Ham, J., Midden, C.: A persuasive robot to stimulate energy conservation: the influence of positive and negative social feedback and task similarity on energy-consumption behavior. Int. J. Soc. Robot. **6**, 163–171 (2014)
16. Castellano, G., De Carolis, B., D'Errico, F., Macchiarulo, N., Rossano, V.: PeppeRecycle: improving children's attitude toward recycling by playing with a social robot. Int. J. Soc. Robot. **13**, 97–111 (2021)
17. Tussyadiah, I., Miller, G.: Nudged by a robot: responses to agency and feedback. Ann. Tour. Res. **78**, 102752 (2019)
18. Warringa, T.: Using social robots to persuade consumers to sustainable products. Doctoral dissertation, Tilburg University (2021)
19. Ham, J., Spahn, A.: Shall i show you some other shirts too? The psychology and ethics of persuasive robots. In: Trappl, R. (eds.) A Construction Manual for Robots' Ethical Systems. Cognitive Technologies, pp. 63–81. Springer, Cham (2015). https://doi.org/10.1007/978-3-319-21548-8_4
20. Kimble, G.A.: Behaviorism and unity in psychology. Curr. Dir. Psychol. Sci. **9**(6), 208–212 (2000)
21. Breazeal, C., Dautenhahn, K., Kanda, T.: Social robotics. In: Siciliano, B., Khatib, O. (eds.) Springer Handbook of Robotics. Springer Handbooks. Springer, Cham (2016)
22. Dumouchel P., Damiano L.: Living with Robots. Harvard University Press (2017)
23. Damiano L.: Homes as human– robot ecologies an epistemological inquiry on the "domestication" of robots. In: Argandoña A., Malala J., Peatfield R.C. The Home in the Digital Age, Routledge Advances in Sociology (2021)
24. Deng, E., Mutlu, B., Matarić, M.J.: Embodiment in socially interactive robots. Found. Trends Robot. **7**(4), 251–356 (2019)
25. Bugmann, G., Siegel, M., Burcin, R.: A role for robotics in sustainable development? IEEE AFRICON **11**, 1–4 (2021)
26. Harlan, R.H., McClarigan, S.: Creating emergent behaviors: two robotics labs that combine reactive behaviors. In: Proceedings of the 36th SIGCSE Technical Symposium on Computer Science Education, pp. 441–445. Association for Computing Machinery, NY (2005)

27. Breazeal, C., et al.: Social robots: beyond tools to partners. In: Proceedings - IEEE International Workshop on Robot and Human Interactive Communication, pp. 551–556 (2004)
28. Damiano, L., Dumouchel, P.: Emotions in relation. Epistemological and ethical scaffolding for mixed human-robot social ecologies. Humana.Mente **13**(37), 181–206 (2020)

Affective Evaluation of Rehabilitation Tasks Demonstrated by a Service Robot in Joint and Operational Spaces

Francesco Scotto di Luzio[1], Christian Tamantini[1,2(✉)], Clemente Lauretti[1], Federica Candeloro[1], and Loredana Zollo[1]

[1] Research Unit of Advanced Robotics and Human-Centred Technologies, Università Campus Bio-Medico di Roma, Rome, Italy
[2] Institute of Cognitive Sciences and Technologies, National Research Council of Italy, Rome, Italy
christian.tamantini@cnr.it

Abstract. The adoption of robotics in rehabilitation represents a smart solution to mitigate the physical workload of therapists and improve the consistency of motor task demonstration. This study presents the design and the preliminary experimental validation of a robotic system that physically demonstrates rehabilitative exercises. Three demonstration modalities were compared: a baseline video of a subject performing the task, and two robotic demonstrations using the TIAGo platform. In the latter, the robot reproduced rehabilitation tasks by replicating trajectories acquired in the joint space through Learning by Demonstration, either via hands-on kinesthetic teaching by an expert or from operational-space trajectories recorded with motion capture on healthy subjects. Performance was evaluated through objective physiological responses alongside subjective assessments using standardized questionnaires. Results suggest robotic demonstrators, particularly those based on joint-space control, are effective in conveying motor tasks and have high user acceptance.

Keywords: Robot-Aided Rehabilitation · Service Robots · User Study · Robot Motion Planning

1 Introduction

In recent years, robotic systems have gained a paramount role in the field of robot-aided rehabilitation, providing advanced technological solutions to support both patients and healthcare professionals [1]. Conventional motor rehabilitation often relies on the physical presence and repeated effort of therapists, who should demonstrate exercises multiple times, monitor patient performance, and provide manual assistance where necessary. This approach, while effective, is resource-intensive, leading to therapist fatigue and limiting the scalability of personalized treatment plans [5]. To structure the therapeutic interaction, the role of the therapist can be divided into three distinct functions: (i) demonstrator, responsible for visually and verbally presenting the task to the patient; (ii) observer, who monitors task execution and provides corrective feedback; and (iii) helper, who physically supports the patient in case of insufficient motor capacity. Among these roles, the demonstrator is crucial in the starting phase of motor learning, as an unclear or ambiguous demonstration can result in poor comprehension and/or wrong execution of rehabilitation tasks [6]. Robotic platforms have been proposed as viable solutions to automate and augment this demonstrator role [6]. Their ability to perform highly repeatable, accurate, and programmable movements ensures consistency in exercise presentation. Additionally, robotic systems can be enriched with multimodal interaction capabilities, such as voice guidance, expressive motion, and visual feedback, which enhance user engagement and understanding [3,7]. The use of Socially Assistive Robots (SARs), which combine assistive functions with social interaction, is particularly effective in rehabilitation contexts. Studies have demonstrated that SARs can increase patient motivation, attention, and emotional involvement, especially in pediatric and geriatric populations [4]. Despite recent advances, most SAR implementations are limited to reproducing static poses rather than complex gestures typical of daily activities, and do not systematically compare different demonstration modalities in terms of users' affective state.

While affective factors such as trust, engagement, and positive emotional response are widely acknowledged as key elements in supporting active participation, the way a robot generates and performs movement can influence the affective response of the user. Although the control strategy is not directly observable, it affects key kinematic features of the motion, such as smoothness, naturalness, and anthropomorphism, which in turn impact the perception of clarity, intentionality, and emotional resonance during the interaction. In this context, the present study describes the design and preliminary evaluation of a robotic demonstrator for rehabilitation exercises. The system can perform tasks in both joint and operational space, integrates physiological and subjective measures to evaluate the affective response of the user, and compares three demonstration modalities (i.e., video, joint space, and operational space) to identify the most effective approach for enhancing engagement and comprehension of the task.

2 Materials and Methods

The proposed robotic platform is built upon the TIAGo service robot (PAL Robotics SL, Spain) and integrates the following software components: a motion planning module, a video playback interface, and a text-to-speech (TTS) engine. The motion planner allows the robot to reproduce rehabilitation movements either in joint space (JS) or operational space (OS). In the JS, the system uses a kinesthetic learning-by-demonstration approach: the therapist physically guides the robotic arm through the desired trajectory, recording a series of JS waypoints. During this phase, the robot operates under a gravity compensation controller, which neutralizes the effect of its weight on the joints, allowing the human operator (e.g., a therapist) to manually guide the robotic arm with minimal resistance. This condition facilitates the intuitive demonstration of rehabilitation tasks. The gravity compensation is achieved using the standard Robot Operating System (ROS) effort controller, which applies torque commands that counteract the gravitational forces acting on each joint. Once the demonstration is complete, the joint positions are sampled at regular intervals to construct a trajectory composed of waypoints by adopting a linear interpolation between each recorded joint configuration. Execution is handled via PID controllers for each joint, ensuring accurate tracking of the desired positions while preserving smoothness and safety constraints throughout the motion. Conversely, in the OS, end-effector trajectories have been previously acquired through human demonstrations using a marker-based stereophotogrammetric motion tracking system, allowing for accurate reconstruction of the movement. These trajectories are then encoded using dynamic movement primitives, a learning framework that allows the robot to generalize movements toward different targets while preserving the characteristic shape of the demonstrated motion [2]. The execution of these trajectories is handled through the *Whole Body Control* (WBC) framework, developed by PAL Robotics. The WBC operates as a hierarchical inverse kinematics solver that coordinates the robot's redundant degrees of freedom to achieve prioritized control tasks under physical and safety constraints. In this setup, the DMP-generated end-effector poses are treated as primary control objectives. WBC employs a weighted pseudo-inverse of the Jacobian matrix along with null-space projection techniques to resolve kinematic redundancy and satisfy joint-level constraints. It computes joint velocities and accelerations that best achieve the end-effector trajectory while ensuring compliance with joint limits, velocity boundaries, and self-collision avoidance. The real-time capability of the controller allows safe and accurate reproduction of spatially complex trajectories in human-robot interaction contexts, ensuring smooth and natural movements during rehabilitation task demonstration. To define a baseline condition for comparison with the robotic demonstrator, a video-based demonstration module was developed in ROS. This module plays pre-recorded videos of a therapist performing the exercises, with synchronized audio instructions. A text-to-speech (TTS) system, integrated in ROS, provides real-time verbal guidance in Italian, aligned with both the video playback and its actions, ensuring consistency across modalities. To assess the autonomic response elicited by the three demonstration modalities, galvanic skin response (GSR) was recorded as an index of sympathetic nervous system activation. A Shimmer3 GSR+ sensor, placed on the palmar surface, streamed data via Bluetooth for synchronized acquisition. The signal was processed to extract the tonic component of the GSR with a low-pass Butterworth filter at 0.1 Hz, namely the Skin Conductance Level (SCL). All signals were normalized to a resting baseline to allow inter-subject comparison.

3 Experimental Protocol

The experimental validation involved a total of 12 healthy volunteers (8M and 4F, 26.5 ± 2.3 y.o., with no previous experience with robots) all without any reported physical or cognitive impairments. Each subject performed the experimental tasks using their dominant arm (11 were right-handed and 1 was left-handed). Before the experimental procedure, participants were administered a preliminary questionnaire aimed at evaluating their familiarity with robotic technologies, in order to control for prior knowledge that could influence performance or perception. Participants were randomly assigned to one of three experimental groups, each corresponding to a different demonstration modality, as shown in Fig. 1: Group A observed a video-based demonstration; Group B interacted with the robotic demonstrator operating in JS control mode; and Group C received demonstrations performed by the robot using the OS control strategy. Each experimental session followed the same structure: i) a baseline acquisition of physiological signals was conducted for three minutes while the participant was at rest, providing reference values for subsequent normalization; ii) the participant observed a demonstration of simple motor tasks i.e. shoulder flexion-extension or abduction-adduction, and more complex gesture resembling an Activity of Daily Living (ADL), i.e. the pouring and drinking from a glass or combing hair; iii) upon completion of the task, participants were asked to fill out a set of subjective assessment questionnaires. Emotional state was measured using the Positive and Negative Affect Schedule (PANAS), which was administered both before and after the interaction with the robot to evaluate changes in affective responses (Δ PANAS) resulting from the rehabilitation task. Additionally, the Self-Assessment Manikin (SAM) was used to assess affective dimensions such as arousal, valence, and dominance. All collected data were subjected to statistical analysis using the Mann-Whitney U test, a non-parametric method appropriate for small sample sizes and non-normally distributed data. A significance level of $p < 0.05$ was adopted for all comparisons.

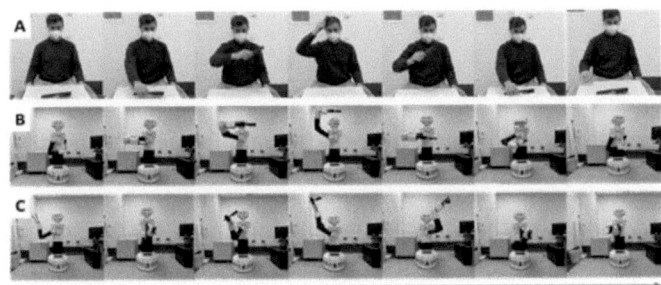

Fig. 1. The experimental setup and movement analysis: (A) video-based demonstration; (B) robot trajectory in the joint space (JS); (C) robot trajectory in the Operational Space (OS).

4 Results

The experimental results were analyzed across two main dimensions: physiological response and subjective evaluation. Regarding physiological measures, as detailed in Table 1, Group B showed the highest increase in SCL during task execution, with the largest variability (1.9 ± 0.8), suggesting a heightened state of engagement or cognitive activation. Group A, in contrast, exhibited the lowest physiological variation from baseline, consistent with a more passive interaction experience. Group C showed an intermediate increase (1.3 ± 0.6), with lower variability compared to Group B. Subjective evaluations also aligned with the objective data. Participants in Group B reported the highest levels of trust and clarity in the demonstrations, as measured by the PANAS questionnaires. Group A scored significantly lower in perceived clarity and emotional engagement, while Group C showed slightly more variance due to the complexity of operational-space movements. Group A, the video-based condition, reported the lowest engagement both physiologically and subjectively, with minimal changes in SCL and limited variation in affective ratings. Statistical analysis using the Mann-Whitney U test confirmed that the differences in the phasic GSR activity between Group A and the robotic groups were statistically significant.

Table 1. Mean value and standard deviation of physiological and subjective measures for each experimental group. (*) indicates statistically significant differences in pairwise comparisons (p < 0.05). Δ denotes the change between the beginning and the end of the test.

Measure	A	B	C	A-B	A-C	B-C
SCL	0.3 ± 0.0	1.9 ± 0.8	1.3 ± 0.6	*	*	*
SAM Arousal	2.3 ± 0.5	1.8 ± 0.5	2.3 ± 1.0	*		*
SAM Valence	3.8 ± 0.5	3.0 ± 0.8	3.8 ± 1.2	*		*
SAM Dominance	4.5 ± 0.6	3.8 ± 0.9	2.3 ± 0.5		*	*
Δ PANAS positive	−2.5 ± 2.5	−3.5 ± 1.5	−2.0 ± 2.0	*		
Δ PANAS negative	+0.5 ± 1.0	−3.0 ± 2.5	−2.5 ± 1.5	*	*	

The OS condition may have introduced more complex or less predictable movements (as also visible in Fig. 1), potentially affecting the clarity of the task demonstration. Some participants may have found these gestures harder to interpret, which could explain the higher variability in certain subjective metrics. However, this observation requires further investigation. Overall, these findings suggest that robotic demonstrations can elicit stronger physiological engagement compared to traditional video-based instruction. However, the relationship between motion generation strategy and affective response is likely mediated by additional factors such as motion smoothness, speed profiles, and trajectory clarity.

5 Conclusion

This study presents the design and a preliminary affective evaluation of a robotic demonstrator system for motor rehabilitation guidance. The comparison among video-based and robotic interfaces revealed that JS robotic demonstrations (Group B) offer the best balance between clarity, engagement, and reproducibility of the task. OS control (Group C) adds richness and flexibility to the motion tasks. Overall, these preliminary findings support the integration of SARs in robot-aided rehabilitation as demonstrators. Future work will focus on the implementation of adaptive feedback mechanisms, the expansion of the task library, the inclusion of a larger population to enhance the generalizability of the findings and a clinical validation on patients.

Acknowledgments. This work was partially supported by the Italian Ministry of Research through the complementary actions of the NRRP "Fit4MedRob - Fit for Medical Robotics" program (Grant No. PNC0000007, CUP: B53C22006990001); partially by the Italian Ministry of Education, Universities and Research (MIUR) through the FAIR project (CUP: C53C22000800006); and partially funded by the European Union - NextGenerationEU under the cascade call for proposals for research activities "Age-It - Ageing Well in an Ageing Society, OPERA subproject" (PNRR Mission 4, Component 2, Investment 1.3, CUP: B83C22004800006).

Disclosure of Interests. The authors have no competing interests to declare that are relevant to the content of this article.

References

1. Argall, B.D., Chernova, S., Veloso, M., Browning, B.: A survey of robot learning from demonstration. Robot. Auton. Syst. **57**(5), 469–483 (2009)
2. Lauretti, C., Cordella, F., Zollo, L.: A hybrid joint/cartesian DMP-based approach for obstacle avoidance of anthropomorphic assistive robots. Int. J. Soc. Robot. **11**(5), 783–796 (2019)
3. Lu, Z., Jie, Z., Yao, L., Chen, J., Luo, H.: The human–machine interaction methods and strategies for upper and lower extremity rehabilitation robots: a review. IEEE Sens. J. **24**, 13773–13787 (2024). https://doi.org/10.1109/JSEN.2024.3374344
4. Onfiani, D., Caramaschi, M., Biagiotti, L., Pini, F.: Optimizing design and control methods for using collaborative robots in upper limb rehabilitation. IEEE/ASME Trans. Mechat. (2025)
5. Oña, E., Garcia-Haro, J., Jardón, A., Balaguer, C.: Robotics in health care: perspectives of robot-aided interventions in clinical practice for rehabilitation of upper limbs. Appl. Sci. (2019). https://doi.org/10.3390/APP9132586
6. Tamantini, C., et al.: Integrating physical and cognitive interaction capabilities in a robot-aided rehabilitation platform. IEEE Syst. J. **17**(4), 6516–6527 (2023)
7. Tamantini, C., Umbrico, A., Orlandini, A.: Repair platform: robot-aided personalized rehabilitation. In: International Conference of the Italian Association for Artificial Intelligence, pp. 301–314. Springer (2024)

Designing AI Robots for the SLD Community: The Role of the Dual Pyramid Framework in Human-Centered Development

Alireza Mortezapour[1] , Mafalda Ingenito[1] , Francesca Perillo[1] ,
Amirreza Mortezapour[2], and Giuliana Vitiello[1(✉)]

[1] Department of Computer Science, University of Salerno, Fisciano, Italy
gvitiello@unisa.it
[2] Department of Psychology, Islamic Azad University, Rasht Branch, Rasht, Iran
amortezapoursoufiani@unisa.it

Abstract. Specific Learning Disorder (SLD) is a neurodevelopmental condition affecting children's abilities in reading, writing, or mathematics, and is often misattributed to low intelligence or poor education. Despite a growing body of evidence on the utility of technological interventions such as social robots in educational and therapeutic contexts, existing design frameworks for AI systems lack specificity when applied to human-robot interaction in SLD settings. In response, this study introduces and validates a novel Dual Pyramid framework tailored for human-centered AI-based robotic systems aimed at empowering the SLD community. A qualitative, multi-phase study was conducted to validate this framework, involving semi-structured interviews with 11 stakeholders, including children with SLD, their families, special education teachers, and clinical psychologists. Analysis of interview data revealed five core design priorities commonly emphasized by all stakeholder groups: effectiveness, safety, privacy, understandability, and explainability. These findings highlight the critical design parameters that should be prioritized when developing therapeutic robots for SLD contexts. Accessibility, although not among the top five prioritized needs, received a high importance rating, underscoring its relevance. Overall, this validation offers a practical guideline for future development and customization of robotic interventions for SLD populations and contributes to the broader discourse on ethical, inclusive, and effective AI in therapeutic contexts.

Keyword: Human-Robot Interaction · Specific Learning Disorder · Inclusive Design

1 Introduction

Childs and adolescents of school age who struggle with basic skills such as reading, writing, and/or mathematics are often assumed to have low intelligence [1]. However, psychiatrists and school psychologists believe that based on DSM-5 and/or other guidelines these difficulties are not necessarily linked to intelligence. Instead, they are often the result of a group of Specific Learning Disorder (SLD), in which the brain processes information, differently from those are healthy [2]. Although not scientifically confirmed, some sources have speculated that Genius like Albert Einstein and Leonardo da Vinci may have had such disorders [3]. Some previous studies have estimated the prevalence of these disorders to be between 5% and 15% [4, 5]. A recent meta-analysis in India reported a prevalence of 8% among Indian Childs and adolescents up to 19 years old [6]. Among individuals diagnosed with this spectrum of disorders, the main difficulty is most often related to reading—known as dyslexia—which accounts for around 80% of cases. Disorders related to writing (dysgraphia) and mathematics (dyscalculia) are also present but with lower prevalence. Some earlier studies have also examined the co-occurrence of SLD with other psychiatric conditions, including ADHD and autism [1].

In recent years, as the diagnostic criteria for SLD have become more evident, there has been a growing focus on their treatment. It has been documented that, except in cases where these disorders co-occur with disease like autism or ADHD, pharmacological treatments are generally not effective. Alternative therapeutic approaches have been explored. These include neurofeedback [7], music therapy [8], and cognitive behavioral therapy (CBT) [9]. Also, a range of technology-based cure approaches has gained increasing attention from clinicians in recent years—especially following the successful application of social robots in certain psychiatric disorders [10]. This trend has grown stronger as social robots have shown promise in enhancing treatment, particularly for conditions where social interaction is impaired, such as SLD [11]. Empowering patients and their families by enhancing social engagement especially in disorders where communication skills are necessary, highlights the potential of using social robots as therapeutic tools for SLD.

A study conducted in Greece demonstrated the effectiveness of using the NAO robot in a randomized case- control trial involving children with SLD [12]. Although there was a significant improvement in phonological awareness exercises in the case group compared to the control group, no statistically significant differences were observed in some of the other SLD-related parameters. In this study, the intervention was delivered over 24 sessions (twice per week). Children in the intervention group received support both from a human teacher and the robot, whereas in the control group, only a human teacher was involved in the intervention. Other studies have explored the use of robots beyond NAO in this domain. For example, the TABAN robot was specifically developed to support children with dyslexia [13, 14]. In addition to being used in therapeutic procedures, social robots have also been applied in the diagnosis and classification of learning disorders. One example includes the use of the NAO robot for identifying and assessing the severity of dysgraphia [15, 16].

A key theme here is the importance of personalization in treatment processes and the need for design based on patients' needs. This underscores the necessity of applying human-centered design (HCD) principles in the development and deployment of social robots [11]. To support human-centered design in AI systems and to better account for the needs of human users and broader stakeholders several dedicated frameworks have been proposed. One notable example is Ben Schneiderman's Human-Centered AI framework [17]. According to his framework, the design of a human-centered AI technology should not be overly focused on high levels of automation alone. Instead, it should ensure that human users retain a high degree of control when interacting with the AI. Another well-known framework is AI4People, developed by Luciano Floridi and colleagues [18]. This framework identifies five core principles for human- centered AI systems including Beneficence (Do good), Non-maleficence (Do no harm), Human autonomy, Justice, Explainability. These principles are meant to guide the ethical and responsible design of AI systems in ways that prioritize human needs. In addition, the are some practical design resources and guidelines also from technology companies e.g., the Microsoft Guidelines for Human-AI Interaction [19] and the Google People + AI Guidebook [20] offer detailed, actionable recommendations for designing AI systems that are more intuitive, ethical, and aligned with user needs.

Since none of the previously mentioned frameworks were specifically designed for human-centered robotic systems in SLD context, the present research team want to validate their previously developed framework [21] for SLD context. As shown in Fig. 1, the framework takes the form of a dual pyramid, with each pyramid consisting of six hierarchical layers. The lower pyramid begins with two obligated parameters: efficiency and effectiveness, which are considered the minimum essential criteria for designing a human-centered robot. As declared by the two arrows on the sides of the figure, this pyramid focuses on the one human-one robot interaction. The upper pyramid (society-level interactions) builds upon successful fulfillment of key principles in the lower pyramid (personal interactions). Once these foundational requirements are met, the robot becomes capable of participating in more complex societal interactions, including multi human-multi robot interaction (see scalability arrow). The final and ultimate level of this framework envisions the shared success of humans and robots in achieving the United Nations' 17 Sustainable Development Goals (SDGs). {*As the development process of this framework is presented in an **accepted** book chapter in Human-centered AI book and now is under publishing process by springer, it can be sent to reviewers if they request the whole chapter*}.

From existing ethical frameworks [22, 23], none of them have specifically addressed human-centered design for therapeutic and medical robots. So, it is impossible to directly applied them to support patients with SLD. The aim of the present study is to validate the mentioned framework for HCD requirements of robots aimed at empowering children with SLD and other stakeholders.

2 Methodology

To validate the framework as a design guideline for patients diagnosed with SLD, a qualitative methodology consisting of the following phases was conducted [24]. Guided by the previous literature, the inclusion of various stakeholders in different phases aimed to ensure a HCD approach, thereby enhancing both the credibility and practical applicability of the framework [25]. In Phase 0, a brief overview of the framework development process is provided.

Step 0: Human-robot interaction, while sharing many similarities with other forms of human-computer or human-AI interaction, also presents fundamental differences. These include the potential humanoid char- acteristics of robots, their embodiment, and

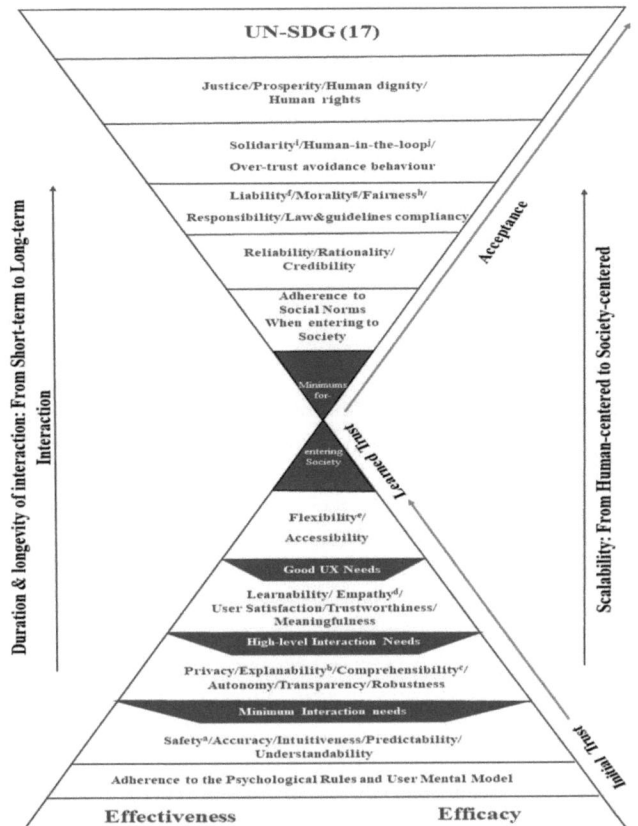

a:Assurance; b:Explicibility; c:Interpretability; d:Emotional; e:Adaptability; f:Accountability; g:Ethical behaviour; h:Inclusiveness and non-biased behaviour; i:Coherency; J:Human-controllability

Fig. 1. The dual Pyramid Human-centered AI design framework for robot.

the distinct mental models users may develop when interacting with them. Therefore, in order to design AI-integrated robots that adhere to HCD principles, it is crucial to understand the needs of end users and incorporate them into the design phase. To achieve this, a scoping review was conducted to examine all existing frameworks related to HCAI. Nine related frameworks concerning HCAI design were identified. These ones are the most related Human-centered AI frameworks which are published from different academic and non-academic sectors. Upon reviewing these frameworks, the research team concluded that due to the specific differences in human-robot interaction, these existing frameworks could not be directly applied to human-robot interaction scenario. To address this gap, the Dual Pyramid Framework -introduced in the previous section-was developed by the research team. More information about this framework and the methodology for developing it is presented in the related book chapter [21].

The following sections describe the validation process of this framework in the context of SLD patients. We followed the *"CASP Checklist: CASP Qualitative Studies Checklist"* guideline to be ensure about the validity of the interview phases [26].

Step 1: This study was structured as a semi-structured interview, designed to both guide the discussion through pre-planned questions, while also allowing flexibility for interviewees to share additional insights [27]. This approach aimed to capture a comprehensive understanding of stakeholder needs. After finalizing the interview questions-some of which are listed below-a list of required stakeholder participants was established.

Inspired by previous qualitative studies on thematic frameworks [11, 28], the stakeholder pool included: a computer science specialist with a background in robot programming (just for checking the applicability of the ideas, not as interviewee), children diagnosed with SLD (preferably of school age, as this is typically when the disorder is diagnosed more accurately due to the initiation of reading, writing, and arithmetic activities). These children were selected from two age groups: early and middle school years, to ensure representation of both younger and older children/adolescents. The families of these children, as their closest stakeholders in everyday interactions. The school psychologist working directly with the child and/or clinical psychologists specialized in the diagnosis and treatment of SLD, and finally, the teacher and/or school principal of these students. The number of participants for this phase was not predetermined. Instead, the research team intended to continue interviews until data saturation was reached [29], ensuring that no new (sub-)themes emerged across stakeholders. The required questions are selected based on context and previous HCD literature. The selected questions of the interview were:

Q1: After consenting, participants introduced themselves and shared their knowledge of SLD.

Q2: Next, the interviewer provided a brief explanation of the concept of HCD.

Q3: Participants were asked to name any technologies they knew—used or not—designed to address SLD challenges.

Q4: They were then asked to reflect on whether these products matched their personal needs or not.

Q5: Next, the new framework—focused on human-centered design for robotic support in SLD—was presented, with its parameters introduced simply, as needed.

Q6: Participants shared feedback on each parameter and prioritized them—identifying essential, less important, and unnecessary ones. This helped reveal context-specific needs for designing robots to support SLD patients and stakeholders.

Step 2: To minimize stress for patients and families, interviews were held at locations chosen by stakeholders. Interviewers arranged visits in advance, ensuring a quiet room for discussion and audio recording. Interviews lasted 45 to 90 min.

Step 3: After the interviews, audio recordings were transcribed and reviewed by two trained authors to ensure familiarity with the content. Recordings were made using an iPhone 15 in airplane mode to avoid interruptions, and transcriptions were done manually using Microsoft Office 2016. Given over 95% similarity among transcripts, one representative file was selected for the next step.

Step 4: For qualitative analysis, the transcribed files were individually imported into MAXQDA version 2020 [30]. Transcripts were re-read and coded, with similar codes grouped by color to visualize emerging themes. When participants struggled to understand certain framework parameters, especially in the SLD context, efforts were made to connect their responses to related themes using color-coding. Code frequency and significance were analyzed, and frequently mentioned parameters were identified as key stakeholder needs for HCD in robot. Open-ended questions were also analyzed separately to uncover additional themes, context-specific needs, and unique insights, enriching the understanding of stakeholder expectations for SLD-focused robotics.

Step 5: In the final stage, a feasibility assessment was conducted to evaluate the practical implementation of the identified parameters and detect potential conflicts. Robot programming experts reviewed each parameter to assess technical feasibility, integration complexity, and possible trade-offs. This ensured a coherent, realistic design for a human-centered robotic system supporting individuals with SLD. The finalized parameter list was shared with the research team to guide robot planning and future field studies based on stakeholder needs. Details of the robot-based field study lie beyond the scope of this research and will be reported separately.

3 Results

Interviews with 11 stakeholders on SLD reached initial data saturation, leading to a temporary pause in data collection. These findings are publishable, but the project will continue in future phases, including cross-country qualitative comparisons to be published later.

Regarding Question 1: Participants included one 9-year-old girl and one 15-year-old boy with SLD, their parents (six individuals), three psychologists (2 females, 1 male) with at least five years of experience, and two female special education teachers. The psychologists held master's degrees or were doctoral students, while the teachers had bachelor's degrees in special education. Among the families, one had primary/secondary education, and the other had higher education unrelated to psychology. All participants reported good to very good knowledge of SLD and identified as representatives of the SLD community.

Regarding Question 2: Given participants' varying academic literacy, the concept of HCD and user needs-based design was explained simply, taking about 5–10 min per person. Only the 9-year-old was interviewed with both parents present, and the explanation was given to all together. After a brief Q&A, participants reported improved understanding, with 8 of them rating it an average of 7 out of 10 (the child was not asked).

Regarding Question 3: Except for the psychologists, most participants had limited knowledge of technology in managing SLD. One teacher had seen videos on educational robots and showed more tech interest than her colleague. The psychologists' knowledge came from non-university training, as their formal education—completed over eight years ago—lacked this content. Overall, familiarity was limited to basic educational software, with little awareness of AI-based tools like social robots.

Regarding Question 4: Given its relevance to the previous question, only responses from the psychologists and one teacher familiar with robots were collected. They noted that while such products exist, individual needs vary, requiring more personalization through collaboration with specialists. On average, they rated the alignment of current products with stakeholder needs at 4 out of 10.

Regarding Questions 5 and 6: This section took up most of the interview time. After showing videos of robot-based psychological interventions and briefly reviewing user needs-based design, the proposed human-centered framework (Fig. 1) was presented. Each parameter was discussed, and participants identified which they considered essential for robot design. Results are reported by stakeholder group.

Table 1. Top-10 perceived needs in line with Human centered social robot design for SLD community

Stakeholder	Perceived needs
Patients + family	Effectiveness, Safety, Intuitiveness, Understandability, Explainability, Transparency, Privacy, Meaningfulness, Accessibility, Empathy
Teachers	Effectiveness, Efficiency, Safety, Adherence to Psychological norms, Understandability, Explainability, Privacy, Trustworthiness, Flexibility, Empathy
Psychologists	Effectiveness, Safety, Understandability, Explainability, Privacy, Trustworthiness, Meaningfulness, Accessibility, Flexibility

The underline characteristics were repeated among all stakeholders.

As the interview focused on one-on-one robot–patient interaction, the framework's broader societal and large-scale interaction components were not included in the validation (upper pyramid is excluded from this survey). As shown in Table 1, all three stakeholder groups agreed that five features are essential for human-centered AI-based robots: Effectiveness, Safety, Understandability, Explainability, and Privacy. Effectiveness refers to the robot's ability to perform tasks as intended by the therapist. Safety means protecting users from physical harm. Understandability is how clearly the robot's behavior can be grasped by users. Explainability refers to the robot's ability to provide simple explanations to non-experts. Privacy involves protecting and safeguarding user data.

Table 2 shows the average importance scores (1–10 scale) assigned to each parameter by participants. These include all elements from the lower part of the framework in Fig. 1 (as declared before, upper pyramid is not validated in the current study).

Discussion

This study aimed to validate the research team's previously developed framework in the context of SLD by identifying stakeholder needs for human-centering AI-based social robots.

A 2015 case study in Italy explored the use of therapeutic robots for dysgraphia [31] and highlighted the designer's key role in connecting diverse stakeholders through

Table 2. The mean score of all participants regarding the importance of the criterion.

Criterion	Effectiveness	Efficacy	Adherence to…	Safety	Accuracy
Mean Score	9.5	7.4	7.1	8.9	6.5
Criterion	Predictability	Privacy	Understandability	Autonomy	Learnability
Mean score	5.3	8.8	8.4	4.8	6.8
Criterion	Intuitiveness	Accessibility	Explain-ability	Transparency	Trustworthiness
Mean score	7.2	8.4	8.5	7.3	7.6
Criterion	Robustness	Empathy	Comprehensibility	User Satisfaction	Meaningfulness
Mean score	5.8	7.0	6.6	7.4	6.9
Criterion	Flexibility	**Minimums for entering to the Society**			
Mean score	5.7	Not Agree at least for community of SLD (11 of 11)			

human-centered design. This aligns with the current study's validation approach, which involved engaging potential stakeholders.

In the current study, according to the participants, the five main needs were effectiveness, safety, privacy, understandability, and explainability. But as far as evident another parameter such as accessibility was very important. Maria T. Papadopoulou et al. (2022) studied the effectiveness of the NAO robot with students diagnosed with SLD [12], emphasizing 'effectiveness' as a key evaluation criterion—aligned with the current framework validation.

A recent preprint [32] focused on dyscalculia explored the use of educational robots to support this specific SLD, with part of the study assessing the feasibility of integrating such robots into the educational system. The goal was to evaluate the accessibility and sustainability of long-term use. Although accessibility was not among the top five priorities in our validation process, its high score (8.4/10) reflects its perceived importance across stakeholder groups. The study also reported that the robot showed an acceptable level of effectiveness in addressing dyscalculia. In contrast to the findings of our study, where all 11 participants indicated that large-scale societal integration of robots for empowering individuals with SLD is currently not feasible, the authors of this preprint suggest that such integration may become possible in the future, contingent upon increased investment in technology, human resource training, and curriculum development. Therefore, this aspect of their findings is not in line with our results.

Although previous studies have not specifically examined the issue of robot safety in the context of SLD, review articles addressing key parameters for human-centered design of robots in general educational environments have emphasized the importance of safety [33]. Furthermore, safety concerns are widely acknowledged by various stakeholders within educational settings [34]. These findings are consistent with the perceived need for safety expressed by stakeholders in the present study regarding the use of robots in the SLD context.

Aligned with the stakeholders' emphasis in this study on the importance of student privacy and data protection, the concept of privacy is commonly associated with ethical considerations in the use of artificial intelligence within educational environments [35]. Several rounds of qualitative studies with teachers from three European countries and the synthesis of their views on the ethical considerations of using robots in educational settings further reinforce the importance of privacy in end-users' acceptance of such technologies [36]. Similar concerns regarding privacy and data protection for students with SLD are at least as significant as those for typically developing normal students, if not more so [37].

Although the importance of explainability in AI models has been increasingly emphasized in recent years as a countermeasure to black-box approaches [38], there remains a lack of practical studies exploring its significance within educational settings—particularly for students with special needs and those engaged in therapeutic interventions. Although a significant research gap still exists regarding explainable robots for students with learning disabilities, the recognized importance of explainability in related fields such as other AI-based technologies [39, 40] along with its role in fostering trust and increasing the likelihood of technology acceptance among non-expert end users, suggests a strong potential for incorporating explainability into the design of future social robots for SLD population.

4 Conclusion

The Dual Pyramid framework for human-centering AI-based robots was validated in this study for the context of SLD. The core needs of stakeholders in this disorder were identified and can be effectively used to human-center robots designed for psychological interventions targeting these patients. Although promising, further studies involving a greater number of stakeholders from diverse cultural and national backgrounds are planned for future research.

Acknowledgments. This work was partially supported by the PNRR MUR project PE0000013-FAIR (Future Artificial Intelligence Research).

References

1. Ibrahim, I.: Specific learning disorder in children with autism spectrum disorder: current issues and future implications. Adv. Neurodevelopmental Disord. **4**(2), 103–112 (2020)
2. Pham, A.V., Riviere, A.: Specific learning disorders and ADHD: current issues in diagnosis across clinical and educational settings. Curr. Psychiatry Rep. **17**(6), 38 (2015)
3. Toffalini, E., Pezzuti, L., Cornoldi, C.: Einstein and dyslexia: Is giftedness more frequent in children with a specific learning disorder than in typically developing children? Intelligence **62**, 175–179 (2017)

4. Yang, L., Li, C., Li, X., Zhai, M., An, Q., Zhang, Y., et al.: Prevalence of developmental dyslexia in primary school children: a systematic review and meta-analysis. Brain Sci. **12**(2), 240 (2022)
5. Bozatlı, L., Aykutlu, H.C., Sivrikaya Giray, A., Ataş, T., Özkan, Ç., Güneydaş Yıldırım, B., et al.: Children at risk of specific learning disorder: a study on prevalence and risk factors. Children **11**(7), 759 (2024)
6. Scaria, L.M., Bhaskaran, D., George, B.: Prevalence of Specific Learning Disorders (SLD) among children in India: a systematic review and meta-analysis. Indian J. Psychol. Med. **45**(3), 213–219 (2023)
7. Patil, A.U., Madathil, D., Fan, Y.-T., Tzeng, O.J.L., Huang, C.-M., Huang, H.-W.: Neurofeedback for the education of children with ADHD and specific learning disorders: a review. Brain Sci. **12**(9), 1238 (2022)
8. Lewis, J.D., Kim, S.J.: Scoping review of music interventions aimed at improving reading skills in children with specific learning disorders in reading. J. Music Ther. **61**(3), 218–243 (2024)
9. Azizi, A., Drikvand, F.M., Sepahvandi, M.A.: Effect of cognitive-behavioral play therapy on working memory, short-term memory and sustained attention among school-aged children with specific learning disorder: a preliminary randomized controlled clinical trial. Curr. Psychol. **39**(6), 2306–2313 (2020)
10. Cavallaro, A., Perillo, F., Romano, M., Sebillo, M., Vitiello, G.: Social robot in service of the cognitive therapy of elderly people: exploring robot acceptance in a real-world scenario. Image Vis. Comput. **147**, 105072 (2024)
11. Zou, J., Gauthier, S., Pellerin, H., Gargot, T., Archambault, D., Chetouani, M., et al.: R2C3, a rehabilitation robotic companion for children and caregivers: the collaborative design of a social robot for children with neurodevelopmental disorders. Int. J. Soc. Robot. **16**(3), 599–617 (2024)
12. Papadopoulou, M.T., Karageorgiou, E., Kechayas, P., Geronikola, N., Lytridis, C., Bazinas, C., et al.: Efficacy of a robot-assisted intervention in improving learning performance of elementary school children with specific learning disorders. Children **9**(8), 1155 (2022)
13. Shahab, M., et al. (eds.) A Tablet-Based Lexicon Application for Robot-Aided Educational Interaction of Children with Dyslexia. Springer Nature Singapore, Singapore (2024)
14. Amiri, O., et al. (eds.) Virtual Reality Serious Game with the TABAN Robot Avatar for Educational Rehabilitation of Dyslexic Children. Springer Nature Singapore, Singapore (2024)
15. Gouraguine, S., Riad, M., Rafik, M., Qbadou, M., Mansouri, K. (eds.) A humanoid robot assistant for the classification of students according to their type of dysgraphia. In: Proceedings of the 2023 3rd International Conference on Innovative Research in Applied Science, Engineering and Technology (IRASET), 18–19 May 2023
16. Gouraguine, S., Riad, M., Qbadou, M., Mansouri, K.: Dysgraphia detection based on convolutional neural networks and child-robot interaction. Int. J. Electr. Comput. Eng. **13**(3), 2999–3009 (2023)
17. Shneiderman, B.: Human-Centered AI. Oxford University Press (2022)
18. Floridi, L., Cowls, J., Beltrametti, M., Chatila, R., Chazerand, P., Dignum, V., et al.: AI4People—an ethical framework for a good AI society: opportunities, risks, principles, and recommendations. Mind. Mach. **28**, 689–707 (2018)
19. Amershi, S., et al. (eds.) Guidelines for human-AI interaction. In: Proceedings of the 2019 CHI Conference on Human Factors in Computing Systems (2019)
20. Yildirim, N., Pushkarna, M., Goyal, N., Wattenberg, M., Viégas, F. (eds.) Investigating how practitioners use human-AI guidelines: a case study on the people+ AI guidebook. In: Proceedings of the 2023 CHI Conference on Human Factors in Computing Systems (2023)

21. Alireza, M, Giuliana, V.: Human-centered AI with focus on human-robot interaction (Accepted Book Chapter). Springer Book Series (2025)
22. Zhang, Y., et al. (eds.) Human-centered AI technologies in human-robot interaction for social settings. In: Proceedings of the International Conference on Mobile and Ubiquitous Multimedia (2024)
23. Sajid, A., Sultan, M.N., Ishfaq, M.M., Raza, A. (eds.) Human-centered design and development of an elderly care robot. In: Proceedings of the 2024 International Conference on Robotics and Automation in Industry (ICRAI). IEEE (2024)
24. Mei, Z., Jin, S., Li, W., Zhang, S., Cheng, X., Li, Y., et al.: Ethical risks in robot health education: a qualitative study. Nurs. Ethics **32**(3), 913–930 (2025)
25. Smakman, M., Vogt, P., Konijn, E.A.: Moral considerations on social robots in education: a multi-stakeholder perspective. Computers Education. **174**, 104317 (2021)
26. CASP U: CASP Qualitative studies checklist; 2018 (2018)
27. Babamiri, M., Heidarimoghadam, R., Ghasemi, F., Tapak, L., Mortezapour, A.: Going beyond general stress scales: developing a new questionnaire to measure stress in human-robot interaction. Int. J. Soc. Robot. **16**(11), 2243–2259 (2024)
28. Miranda, P., Isaias, P., Costa, C.J., Pifano, S.: Validation of an e-Learning 30 critical success factors framework: a qualitative research. (1), 339–363 (2017)
29. Francis, J.J., Johnston, M., Robertson, C., Glidewell, L., Entwistle, V., Eccles, M.P., et al.: What is an adequate sample size? Operationalising data saturation for theory-based interview studies. Psychol. Health **25**(10), 1229–1245 (2010)
30. Rädiker, S., Kuckartz, U.: Focused Analysis of Qualitative Interviews with MAXQDA. MaxQDA Press (2020)
31. Kozlova, A.: How design can contribute to children's neurological rehabilitation? Case study: co-designing paediatric rehabilitation programs for learning disabilities (2015)
32. Stasolla, F., et al.: Educational robotics and game-based interventions for overcoming dyscalculia: a pilot study (2025). Preprints
33. Woo, H., LeTendre, G.K., Pham-Shouse, T., Xiong, Y.: The use of social robots in classrooms: a review of field-based studies. Educ. Res. Rev. **33**, 100388 (2021)
34. Lee, E., Lee, Y., Kye, B., Ko, B. (eds.) Elementary and middle school teachers', students' and parents' perception of robot-aided education in Korea. EdMedia+ innovate learning. Association for the Advancement of Computing in Education (AACE) (2008)
35. Huang, L.: Ethics of artificial intelligence in education: student privacy and data protection. Sci. Insights Educ. Front. **16**(2), 2577–2587 (2023)
36. Serholt, S., Barendregt, W., Vasalou, A., Alves-Oliveira, P., Jones, A., Petisca, S., et al.: The case of classroom robots: teachers' deliberations on the ethical tensions. AI Soc. **32**(4), 613–631 (2017)
37. Ahmadi, A., Gholipoor, A.: The role of AI for supporting individuals with learning disorder in reading comprehension
38. Attanasio, C., Mortezapour, A.: Quality of explanation of xAI from the prespective of Italian end-users: Italian version of System Causability Scale (SCS). arXiv preprint arXiv:250416193 (2025)
39. Robaa, M., Balat, M., Awaad, R., Omar, E., Aly, S.A.: Explainable AI in handwriting detection for dyslexia using transfer learning. arXiv preprint arXiv:241019821 (2024)
40. Jeon, I., Kim, M., So, D., Kim, E.Y., Nam, Y., Kim, S., et al.: Reliable autism spectrum disorder diagnosis for pediatrics using machine learning and explainable AI. Diagnostics **14**(22), 2504 (2024)

A Personal Social Robot to Support Physical Activity for Seniors at Home

Berardina De Carolis[1(✉)], Davide Lofrese[1], Giuseppe Palestra[1], Aurora Toma[1], and Cristina Gena[2]

[1] Department of Computer Science, University of Bari, Bari, Italy
{berardina.carolis,davide.lofrese,giuseppe.palestra,aurora.toma}@uniba.it
[2] Department of Computer Science, University of Turin, Turin, Italy
cristina.gena@unito.it

Abstract. Frailty is an age-related condition that compromises quality of life and independence in older adults. Physical exercises plays a key role in this context, as regular exercise offers significant health benefits to frail seniors. Technology can support participation in physical activity at home. Recently, social robots, often used as engaging companions, have emerged as promising tools for safe and motivating training. This paper presents the use of the Alpha Mini robot as a personal fitness coach for older adults. It is equipped with a computer vision module, trained on a custom dataset, to recognize and evaluate the correctness of exercises through a deep learning model.

Keywords: Physical Activity Recognition · Social Robots · Computer Vision

1 Introduction

Worldwide, sedentary behavior is increasing, posing significant health risks, particularly for older adults. Physical activity is vital in this population to preserve independence, reduce fall risk, and prevent chronic diseases [1,10]. However, global activity levels remain low [12], highlighting a pressing public health concern. For frail older adults, regular, personalized exercise is essential to prevent mobility decline and related complications. Initiatives such as the ViviFrail European program address this need through tailored routines focused on strength, balance, and mobility to support functional independence [3].

Technology-based interventions are gaining attention as tools to promote autonomy and healthier lifestyles. [8]. Among these, Socially Assistive Robotics (SAR) focuses on support through social interaction rather than physical assistance [6]. SAR systems used as exercise coaches have shown promise in enhancing motivation and adherence to physical routines [5]. Subsequent studies introduced autonomous tutors for older users [7] and personalized robots for post-stroke rehabilitation [9]. Still, their use as fitness coaches in domestic settings remains underexplored [2].

Within the Italian PNRR SISTER project (SocIal robotS to support biopsychosocial frailTy of sEnioRs at home), we developed a personalized multicomponent intervention for frail older adults, delivered via a social robot and focused on nutrition, cognition, chronic disease, with a strong emphasis on physical activity. Similar multi-domain approaches, such as the FINGER trial, have shown that structured physical exercise combined with nutritional and cognitive interventions can support health and reduce disability risks in older adults [11].

In SISTER, participants first follow supervised exercises with a physiotherapist at the medical center for elderly people involved in the project. Then, they continue at home with the robot that acts as a coach, reminding, monitoring, and encouraging them to exercise. The robot, using computer vision and a model trained on specific exercises, recognizes movements and assesses performance. Building on prior work [4], we trained a Long Short-Term Memory (LSTM) network on a custom dataset of selected ViviFrail exercises and integrated it in an Alpha Mini social robot to be used as a personal fitness coach. The model achieved 96% accuracy on a test subset, showing promising results. However, the fitness coach robot has not yet been tested in real-world settings, and such evaluation is required to assess its practical effectiveness.

2 The Exercise Recognition Module (ERM)

The *Exercise Recognition Module* (ERM), based on an LSTM network, was trained to classify and evaluate six exercises from the ViviFrail program, selected for their relevance to elderly physical activity according to specialists: *Arm extensions, Lateral arm raises, Overhead arm lifts, Chair raises, Lateral leg raises,* and *Seated crunches*. Dataset creation began with the recording of four standardized videos per exercise, in which a physiotherapist executed 10 repetitions for each exercise under controlled conditions (single subject in frame, adequate lighting, 1280×720 resolution, tripod-mounted camera). Two of the videos show correct executions of the exercise, while the other two include executions with minor errors that do not deviate significantly from the correct form, with the goal of recognizing the exercise even in the presence of small inaccuracies. To further enhance model robustness under varying conditions, data augmentation techniques were applied. For each original video, multiple augmented versions were generated by modifying playback speed (0.5×, 1.5×), applying random rotations (±10°), horizontal flips, and zoom variations (0.8–1.2×). Each clip was trimmed to isolate full exercise executions and then segmented into 10 parts, each corresponding to a single repetition. This process resulted in 11 augmented versions for each video, for a total of 288 videos. Each video was split into short clips containing one repetition of the exercise for a total of 2880 videos (24*12*10), constituting the dataset. The next step involved extracting relevant features (body keypoints and joint angles) to train the model. The key points were extracted using the *MediaPipe* library, which detects 33 landmarks, each with x, y, z coordinates and a visibility score (ranging from 0 to 1) indicating the detection confidence. To streamline the dataset, only 13 keypoints were retained: Nose, Shoulders, Elbows, Wrists, Hips, Knees, and Ankles. To handle unreliable detections due to low visibility scores, we applied temporal interpolation to improve data consistency.

Joint angles were computed from triplets of keypoints using a 2D geometric method based on three-point angle formation:

$$\text{angle} = [\arctan 2(c_y - b_y, c_x - b_x) - \arctan 2(a_y - b_y, a_x - b_x)] \times \frac{180}{\pi}$$

where a, b, and c are the keypoints forming the joint (with b as the vertex), and x and y are the point coordinates. This method uses 2D joint angles, which complement keypoints by offering biomechanical descriptors that are independent of scale or absolute position, ensuring robust recognition across varying body sizes and camera views. For each exercise, a set of specific representative angles was selected to identify its phases.

To represent motion over time, the extracted data were grouped into exercise-centered temporal windows, with eight-frame sequences sampled across a full repetition of an exercise capturing key positions of the repetition (variations in the start frame were applied to improve model tolerance to timing discrepancies). To enable repetition counting and correctness evaluation, specific angles were selected for each exercise to distinguish between *start* and *end* phases based on minimum and maximum values. These values were averaged across repetitions to define baseline thresholds.

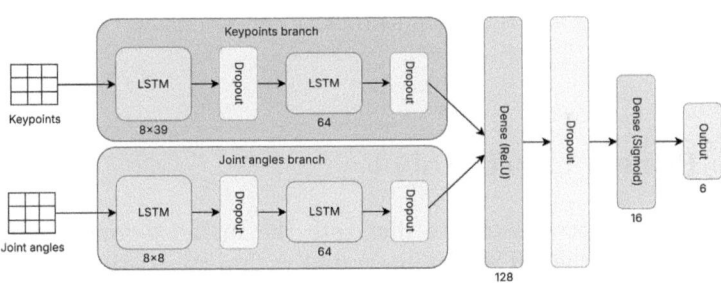

Fig. 1. Architecture of the trained dual-branch LSTM network.

A multi-input LSTM was trained to recognize physical movements from temporal patterns of body poses, using extracted keypoints and joint angles. The network consists of two branches to process data streams in parallel (Fig. 1). In particular, the *keypoints branch* processes temporal windows of body keypoints using two consecutive LSTM layers. The former learns the temporal dynamics of keypoints, while the latter refines the learned sequence. Both are followed by a dropout layer to reduce overfitting. The *joint angles branch* processes joint angle sequences, and it is structured similarly to the other branch. The outputs from the two branches are concatenated into a single vector that combines all the learned features. Then, a fully connected dense layer, followed by a dropout layer, integrates and compresses the features learned from previous branches. Finally, as the final classification task is multiclass to distinguish between different physical exercises, the output layer uses a Sigmoid activation to assign independent class probabilities, allowing the system to also detect when no exercise is being performed. Following the training process, an evaluation session was conducted to investigate the potential of the proposed approach. The dataset was divided into training (80%) and test (20%) subsets, and accuracy metrics and confusion tables were used to understand the system (Fig. 2). The model reached an accuracy rate of 96.40%, meaning that almost all the evaluated instances were correctly classified, with a F1-score of 96.38%. While these results are promising, real-world deployment has not yet been carried out and still requires further testing and validation.

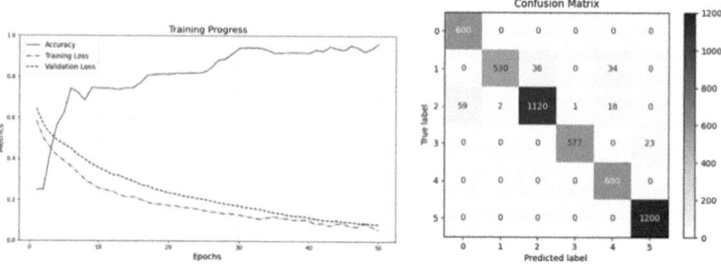

Fig. 2. Left: Training and validation metrics by epochs, Right: Confusion matrix.

3 The Fitness Coach Robot

As a proof-of-concept scenario to illustrate the intended functionality of the fitness coach robot, the ERM was integrated within an existing modular architecture implemented on the Alpha Mini robot, giving rise to a comprehensive robot-based fitness training system, enabling it to remind the user to perform daily exercises, guide users with verbal and physical cues, monitor execution, and provide motivation. Alpha Mini initiates the interaction by prompting the user about the scheduled physical exercise session and explaining the first exercise to be done once the user is ready. The explanation is given verbally and through the body movements of the social robot (Fig. 3). In this study, a subset of the six exercises recognized by the ERM was considered, due to some limitations of the robotic platform, which is unable to perform some of the movements (i.e. chair raises). Specifically, the exercises are *Arm extensions*, *Lateral arm raises*, *Arm lifts (overhead)*, and *Lateral leg raises*.

Then, the robot monitors exercise execution using the ERM by analyzing body movements and posture from video frames, extracting keypoints and joint angles from a window of eight frames selected at regular intervals per repetition.

Fig. 3. A user executing an exercise with Alpha Mini providing feedback.

The window is the input for the model which recognizes the exercise, the number of repetitions, and its correctness. If the execution is not correct, the list of errors in terms of angle joints is returned. This information is provided to an LLM (*Llama 3.1 70B instruct-turbo*) to generate a message which is spoken by the robot to encourage the user to perform the exercise correctly by explaining what is wrong. An example of a message for lateral arms raising with an error is as follows *"The shoulder angle is too large. Lower your arm to make a 90-degree angle to do the exercise correctly. You can do it!"*. The exercise name dynamically updates according to the movements performed by the user and reflects the output of the recognition model. The repetition counter increments each time a full repetition is completed. After each exercise, performance accuracy and extracted data are stored for caregiver review. The process is repeated until the session ends. If the user stops early, the robot records the reason and reports it to the caregiver.

4 Conclusions and Future Work

In this paper, we presented a prototype application that shows how a personal social robot, Alpha Mini, enhanced with AI-based fitness coaching, could support and monitor frail older adults during home workouts. In addition to tracking exercise execution and correctness, the robot engages users through conversational interaction, fostering motivation and helping reduce social isolation. Developed within the SISTER project, the system requires further evaluation to assess real-world performance, user experience, and technology acceptance. Even if promising, the current approach has limitations. Improper positioning of the robot can affect the detection accuracy of the user and the accuracy of feedback, and the restricted range of executable exercises limits the overall usability. These challenges could be addressed by employing a robot with full-body mobility and active vision capabilities. Future developments will include expanding the exercise library and integrating wearable sensors to monitor vital signs, enabling more comprehensive health tracking and predictive insights. A planned evaluation phase with frail elderly participants will help validate the system's effectiveness in real-world scenarios.

Acknowledgments. This work was co-funded by the SISTER PRIN PNRR project (P2022K5WFC) by the Italian Ministry of University and Research (MUR) and by the AMICA project - Ministry of Health - "AmICA: Intelligent Holistic Assistance for Active Ageing in Indoor and Outdoor Ecosystems", Project Code: T1-MZ-09.

References

1. Angulo, J., El Assar, M., Álvarez-Bustos, A., Rodríguez-Mañas, L.: Physical activity and exercise: strategies to manage frailty. Redox Biol. **35**, 101513 (2020)
2. Čaić, M., Avelino, J., Mahr, D., Odekerken-Schröder, G., Bernardino, A.: Robotic versus human coaches for active aging: an automated social presence perspective. Int. J. Soc. Robot. **12**(4), 867–882 (2020)
3. Casas-Herrero, A., Anton-Rodrigo, et al.: Effect of a multicomponent exercise programme (VIVIFRAIL) on functional capacity in frail community elders with cognitive decline: study protocol for a randomized multicentre control trial. Trials **20**, 1–12 (2019)
4. De Carolis, B., Palestra, G., Bochicchio, M., Mazzoleni, S.: Alpha mini social robot as a fitness trainer at home. In: 2024 33rd IEEE International Conference on Robot and Human Interactive Communication (ROMAN), pp. 1638–1643. IEEE (2024)
5. Fasola, J., Matarić, M.J.: Socially assistive robot exercise coach: motivating older adults to engage in physical exercise. In: Experimental Robotics: The 13th International Symposium on Experimental Robotics, pp. 463–479. Springer (2013)
6. Feil-Seifer, D., Matarić, M.J.: Defining socially assistive robotics. In: 9th International Conference on Rehabilitation Robotics, 2005. ICORR 2005, pp. 465–468 (2005). https://api.semanticscholar.org/CorpusID:7727423
7. Görer, B., Salah, A.A., Akın, H.L.: An autonomous robotic exercise tutor for elderly people. Auton. Robot. **41**, 657–678 (2017)
8. Griffiths, S., et al.: Exercise with social robots: companion or coach? (2021). https://arxiv.org/abs/2103.12940
9. Hun Lee, M., Siewiorek, D.P., Smailagic, A., Bernardino, A., Bermudez i Badia, S.: Design, development, and evaluation of an interactive personalized social robot to monitor and coach post-stroke rehabilitation exercises. User Model. User-Adapted Int. **33**(2), 545–569 (2023)
10. Meghani, N.A.A., Hudson, J., Stratton, G., Mullins, J.: Older adults' perspectives on physical activity and sedentary behaviour within their home using socio-ecological model. PLoS ONE **18**(11), e0294715 (2023)
11. Ngandu, T., et al.: Recruitment and baseline characteristics of participants in the finnish geriatric intervention study to prevent cognitive impairment and disability (finger)-a randomized controlled lifestyle trial. Int. J. Environ. Res. Public Health **11**(9), 9345–9360 (2014)
12. Organization, W.H.: Physical activity (2022). https://www.who.int/news-room/fact-sheets/detail/physical-activity

Influence of Robot Role on Japanese Learners' English Communication Learning

Ami Hakiri$^{(\boxtimes)}$ and Akihiro Kashihara

The University of Electro-Communications, Chofu 182-8585, Tokyo, Japan
`ami.hakiri@uec.ac.jp`

Abstract. When Japanese learners learn English communication, learning effect would change depending on whether their learning partner is Japanese or American, and whether he/she is a teacher or a peer. The role of the partner is important for English communication learning. To investigate how roles influence English communication learning, we have developed a system using a robot whose role can be designed. We have also designed its behavior according to its position and native language so that the roles assigned to it can become apparent. The results of a case study with the system suggest that the role of the robot being a peer or Japanese increases learners' engagement in English communication.

Keywords: social robot · robot role · English communication · engagement

1 Introduction

English language learning is increasingly vital, with a growing emphasis on practical communication skills. Japanese schools give learners opportunities for interaction with native English speakers, such as Assistant Language Teachers (ALTs), whose main aim is to foster spontaneous communication using simple English words [1]. It is ideal to provide consistent, high-quality support to all learners, but variations in teacher experience and ability make this challenging in traditional educational settings. Artificial intelligence and robots offer a solution, enabling reproducible, high-quality lessons independent of individual teacher differences. Numerous AI and robot-based English communication learning methods have also emerged. Examples include a "Learning-by-Teaching" robot designed to reduce negative feelings like embarrassment [2, 3], and a complementary teaching support system that enhances self-efficacy through robot interaction [4].

In learning English communication with a human partner, his/her role influences learners' thoughts and emotions. For instance, studies on mobile phone email communication revealed that the partner's role ("teacher" vs. "friend") affects the sender's consideration for the partner's emotional state and the recipient's expectations of sincerity or friendliness [5].

This raises our research question: Do learners' thoughts and emotions also change when a social robot plays a role as their communication partner? Current AI and robot-based learning systems often fix the learning partner's role, but it is unclear which roles are most appropriate for different learning objectives. In this work, we investigate the influence of robot roles on English communication learning.

2 Influence of Roles in Learning

There are several related works investigating whether robot roles influence learning in human-robot interactions. For instance, a study [6] found that a robot in a teacher role yielded higher learning outcomes, while a peer robot helped children solve programming tasks faster. Our previous research also showed robot roles influence learning. We found robots affect discomfort and cognitive awareness during self-reviews [7]. Additionally, a peer robot as a lecturer encouraged learners' critical listening in lecture, while a teacher robot led to more passive listening [8]. These findings suggest that adjusting a robot's role to specific learning phases or objectives could guide learners toward more favorable learning outcomes.

In this study, we specifically examine the influence of roles in English communication learning, focusing on the position in learning and native language. Regarding position in learning, a teacher partner is expected to have high English proficiency, correct pronunciation and grammar. The larger skill gap between the teacher and learners might increase their reluctance to speak but also lead them to assume the teacher's correctness. A peer partner is expected to have similar English abilities. Learners often feel less psychological resistance speaking with a peer due to the smaller skill gap. They might also become more aware of the partner's imperfections, leading to more critical listening.

Regarding the learning partner's native language, an American partner (native English speaker) may cause anxiety to learners because he or she does not understand Japanese. They may also make an effort to pronounce English correctly, thinking that the partner will not understand his or her Japanese accent.

A Japanese partner (who shares learners' native language) is expected to reduce their psychological resistance to speaking English. However, their attention to his/her pronunciation may be reduced.

As humans tend to anthropomorphize robots [2], we predict that role effects akin to those in human-to-human communication will emerge in human-robot communication. In this study, we designed the robot with four distinct roles combining its learning position (teacher or student) and native language (English or Japanese), and then investigated the influence of these roles.

3 Design of Robot Roles

Let us here describe the design of the robot behavior so that its roles can become apparent.

- American Teacher Role (AT Role) (Fig. 1–1)
    As for appearance, the robot wears a blonde wig and formal clothes. As for bodily movement, it uses hand and body gestures moderately. As for para-language, it speaks in a low tone, at a normal pace, and without any fillers.

- American Peer Role (AP Role) (Fig. 1–2)

  The robot wears a blonde wig and casual clothes, and uses hand and body gestures actively. It also speaks in a high tone, at a normal pace, and without any fillers.
- Japanese Teacher Role (JT Role) (Fig. 1–3)

  The robot wears no wig and formal clothes, and uses hand and body gestures moderately. It speaks in a low tone, at a normal pace, and occasionally uses fillers such as "e-tto (let me see in English)".
- Japanese Peer Role (JP Role) (Fig. 1–4)

  The robot wears no wig and casual clothes, and it doesn't use suitable gestures. It looks downward while speaking and moves restlessly. It also speaks in a high tone, at a slow pace, and frequently uses fillers such as "e-tto (let me see in English)". Furthermore, it speaks English with a Japanese accent.

Fig. 1. AT Role (1), AP Role (2), AT Role (3) and AP Role (4)

4 Case Study

4.1 Purpose

In this work, we have conducted a case study whose purpose was to investigate the influence of the robot roles on English communication learning for Japanese learners, and examine the following hypotheses.

H1. The robot as a peer promotes learners' engagement in speaking English compared with the robot as a teacher.
H2. The robot as a Japanese promotes learners' engagement in speaking English compared with the robot as an American.
H3. The robot as a peer promotes learners' attention to its mistakes compared with the robot as a teacher.
H4. The robot as a teacher encourages learners to learn correct pronunciation and grammar.
H5. The robot as an American encourages learners to speak with correct pronunciation.

4.2 Procedure

This study involved 22 undergraduate and graduate students in informatics and engineering. Participants were randomly assigned to one of four conditions in a between-subjects design, where they communicated with a robot playing a specific role: American teacher (AT condition, 5 participants), American peer (AP condition, 5 participants), Japanese teacher (JT condition, 6 participants), Japanese peer (JP condition, 6 participants).

The participants communicated with the social robot on the two topics of hobby and favorite season which were chosen because they are easy for anyone to talk about. In every condition, the robot spoke the same content, but the nonverbal behavior and emotional expression of the robot depended on the assigned role. To check whether the participants paid attention to the robot's speech, we prepared two mistakes in it. The procedure of the experiment is shown in Fig. 2. The post-questionnaire is shown in Table 1.

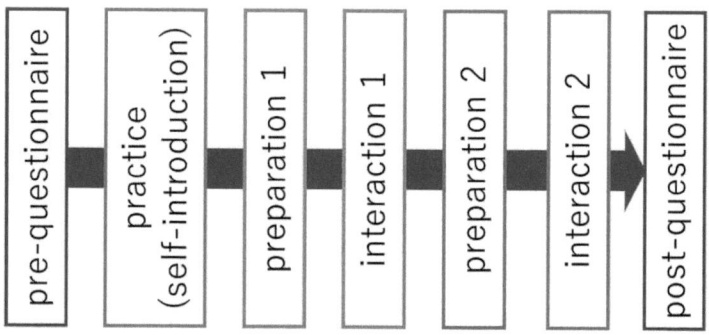

Fig. 2. Procedure

Table 1. Post-questionnaire

Q1	How much did you concentrate on your interaction with the robot?
Q2	How much did you feel the robot had better English skills than you?
Q3	How actively were you able to speak English?
Q4	How much did you get confidence in speaking English?
Q5	How much did you feel an affinity towards the robot?
Q6	How much were you able to speak English without fear of making mistakes?
Q7	How much did you feel embarrassed or awkward?
Q8	How much did you try to speak with correct English pronunciation?
Q9	How much did you think you could learn correct pronunciation and grammar by continuing this learning?
Q10	How much did you listen on the assumption that the robot's English pronunciation and grammar were correct?
Q11	How much did you listen on the assumption that the robot's English pronunciation and grammar might be insufficient or inappropriate?

5 Results and Discussion

The results of the pre-questionnaire showed no significant difference in the English proficiency of the participants. Therefore, we could assume that the participants' initial English proficiency and confidence in English were the same.

We conducted a two-way ANOVA with two levels per factor on the post-questionnaire data, in which the factors were position in learning and native language. Moreover, we have ascertained if the result showed an interaction effect.

Regarding H1 and H2, we investigated the results of Q4, which asked whether the participants gained confidence in speaking English. There is a significant main effect in the position factor ($F(1,18) = 23.3, p = 0.00013$). The average score in the peer position including AP and JP conditions was 4.00, and the one in the teacher position including AT and JT conditions was 2.43. As related work suggests [9], we think such confidence shows signs of engagement on English communication, which supports H1. As for Q3, which ask whether the participants were able to speak English actively, there is a significant main effect in the native language factor ($F(1,18) = 4.55, p = 0.047$). The average score in the native language Japanese (JP and JT) was 4.08, and the one in the native language English (AP and AT) was 3.20, which supports H2.

These results suggest that English communication learning with a robot in a peer or Japanese role appears to improve learner engagement. On the other hand, the results of Q2, Q6, and Q7 showed that there was no significant main effect in position and native language factors about psychological reluctance to speaking English. This suggests that the roles of the learning partner do not significantly influence psychological reluctance. We think this is because the partner is not human but a robot.

We couldn't verify H3 because the participants didn't notice the robot's intentional grammatical errors. A possible reason for this is that the number of mistakes made in the robot's speech was too low. As for Q10, which asked whether the participants listened on the assumption that the robot's English pronunciation and grammar were correct, there is no significant main effect in the "position" factor ($F(1,18) = 3.49, p = 0.078$). In their free descriptions about Q10, many participants answered that the pronunciation and grammar were correct because it was robot speech. This suggests that they believe it speaks correctly with no mistakes. It indicates learners' trust in the robot partner.

As for Q9, which asked whether the participants thought they could get correct pronunciation and grammar by continuing this learning, there is no significant main effect in the "position" factor ($F(1,18) = 0.061, p = 0.81$). H4 was accordingly rejected. As for Q8, which asked whether the participants tried to speak with correct English pronunciation, there is no significant main effect in the "position" factor ($F(1,18) = 0.17, p = 0.68$). Therefore, H5 was rejected.

However, there was a significant interaction effect between position and native language ($F(1,18) = 5.17, p = 0.035$). The simple main effect analysis reveals a tendency towards significant effect of position when native language is English ($F(1,18) = 4.80, p = 0.060$). In particular, AP condition was significantly higher ($M = 4.80, SD = 0.40$) compared to AT condition ($M = 3.60, SD = 1.02$). This suggests learners try to use correct English pronunciation when their partner is an American peer.

6 Conclusion

This paper investigated the effect of robot roles on English communication learning for Japanese. The results suggest that a peer robot having the same native language as learners (Japanese) contributes to improving their engagement in English communication, and reduces their psychological reluctance. In addition, it is suggested that an American peer robot allows learners to pay more attention to its pronunciation.

In future, we plan to examine the influence of role differences on learning in other contexts such as presentations [10] and Learning-by-Teaching [11].

Acknowledgments. This study was supported in part by JSPS KAKENHI (grant number 23K28195).

Disclosure of Interests. The authors have no competing interests to declare that are relevant to the content of this article.

References

1. Ministry of Education, Culture, Sports, Science, and Technology, Japan: A Review of National Curriculum Standards for Lower Secondary Schools (in Japanese). https://www.mext.go.jp/a_menu/shotou/new-cs/1387016.htm. Accessed 17 Apr 2025
2. Kashihara, A.: Learning with robot for enhancing engagement. Comput. Educ. (in Jpn.) **46**, 30–37 (2016)
3. Adachi, Y., Kashihara, A.: A partner robot for promoting collaborative reading. In: Proceedings of the International Conference on Smart Learning Environments (ICSLE 2019), Texas, USA, pp.15–24 (2019)
4. Sato, T., Kashihara, A.: Complementary teaching support with robot in English communication. In: Zaphiris, P., Ioannou, A. (eds.) Learning and Collaboration Technologies. HCII 2023. Lecture Notes in Computer Science, vol. 14041, pp. 386–395. Springer, Cham (2023). https://doi.org/10.1007/978-3-031-34550-0_28
5. Kato, Y., Kato, S., Akahori, K.: Analysis of emotional aspects in e−mail communication by mobile phone with a teacher or a friend (in Japanese). Educ. Inf. Res. **21**(3), 3–12 (2006)
6. Diyas, Y., Brakk, D., Aimambetov, Y., Sandygulova, A.: Evaluating peer versus teacher robot within educational scenario of programming learning. In: Proceedings of the 2016 11th ACM/IEEE International Conference on Human-Robot Interaction (HRI), pp. 425–426 (2016)
7. Sada, S., Kashihara, A.: Influence of robot roles on self-review. In: Proceedings of the 31st International Conference on Computers on Education (ICCE2023), vol. 2, pp. 1075–1078 (2023)
8. Sada, S., Kashihara, A.: Influence of robot roles on learning in lecture (in Japanese). JSiSE Res. Rep. **39**(4), 12–19 (2025)
9. Nakanishi, Y., Umemoto, T.: Effect of self-efficacy on engagement at online learning. In: Proceedings of the 87th Annual Convention of the Japanese Psychological Association, p. 661 (2024)
10. Inazawa, K., Kashihara, A.: Designing and evaluating presentation avatar for promoting self-review. IEICE Trans. Inf. Syst. **E105-D**(9), 1546–1556 (2022)
11. Sudo, T., Kashihara, A.: Evaluation of the system that promotes learning-by-teaching in collaborative reading (in Japanese). JSiSE Res. Rep. **37**(6), 125–132 (2023)

Toward Human and Context-Aware Behavior Generation

Carmine Grimaldi(✉) and Silvia Rossi

PRISCA (Intelligent Robotics and Advanced Cognitive System Projects) Laboratory,
Department of Electrical Engineering and Information Technology (DIETI),
University of Naples Federico II, Naples, Italy
{carmine.grimaldi,silvia.rossi}@unina.it

Abstract. Generating natural, context-aware behaviors is crucial for effective Human-Robot Interaction, especially in contexts like Socially Assistive Robotics (SARs). Current methods often use complex architectures or preprogrammed behaviors, limiting adaptability. This paper introduces a novel, streamlined architecture for user data-driven context-aware behavior generation using a single Large Language Model (LLM), Gemini Flash 2.0. We show how one LLM instance can orchestrate both verbal and non-verbal robot behaviors, like adaptive speech and gestures, based on dynamic user characteristics. We evaluated this approach in a recipe suggestion scenario on the Pepper robotic platform, demonstrating its generalizability. While our architecture shows the potential of a single-LLM design for adaptive behaviors, a preliminary study on perceived social intelligence found no statistically significant differences between personalized and non-personalized interactions, indicating a need for further research. Our work contributes to more trustworthy and transparent SARs by exploring user data integration for context-aware behavior generation and identifying future research directions to enhance personalized and engaging interactions.

Keywords: Large Language Models · Socially Assistive Robotics · Adaptive Behavior · Context-Aware Behavior

1 Introduction

Socially Assistive Robots (SARs) are increasingly used in healthcare, education, and companionship [6,11]. A key challenge in Human-Robot Interaction (HRI) is enabling robots to generate natural, expressive, and user-adaptive behaviors, both verbal and non-verbal [8,18]. Recent progress in Large Language Models (LLMs) offers promising tools for this goal [12,14]. We propose a streamlined architecture that uses a single LLM (Gemini Flash 2.0) to generate both verbal and non-verbal robot behaviors based on dynamic user traits. Unlike multimodal systems that rely on multiple modules or LLMs [3,14], our approach centralizes behavior generation in one model. User data (e.g., mood) is extracted via separate perception modules, but these are independent of the core generative pipeline. Developed within the ADVISOR project [1], our system is tested in a recipe suggestion scenario using the Pepper robot. Results highlight the feasibility and generalizability of this simplified yet effective method for user-adaptive robot behavior generation, supporting future research in personalized and transparent HRI.

2 Related Works

The generation of expressive robot behaviors is a long-standing research area in Human-Robot Interaction (HRI). Early work focused on preprogrammed or rule-based systems to convey emotions and intentions [5,9]. While fundamental, these approaches often lacked the flexibility for natural and engaging interactions in complex real-world scenarios. With Artificial Intelligence (AI) advancements, data-driven approaches for robotic behaviors have emerged. For example, deep neural networks have been used to teach humanoid robots to imitate human movements [15] and generate animations from annotations [4]. However, these typically require large datasets and may struggle to generalize or adapt to individual users. The use of LLMs in robotics is profoundly changing how robots interpret and execute complex tasks via natural language. Research explores applying LLMs to high-level robot control, impacting communication and user perceptions. An important line of work involves "grounding" language in robot physical capabilities, such as the "Say-Can" approach [2] or systems like CLIPort [19]. While effective, these methods can depend on pre-existing skills or large training datasets, potentially limiting adaptability.

Context-aware HRI is a relevant area where robots adapt behavior based on user's emotional state, personality, and social context. Tapus et al. [21] studied robot behavior adaptation to user personality in rehabilitation, though primarily for a finite range of traits. More recent publications, such as Lin et al. [13], propose self-context-aware emotion perception systems for dynamic behavioral modification. Techniques for recognizing user emotions from various cues have also been integrated into robot control systems [10,20]. Furthermore, adaptive and personalized HRI approaches using LLMs have been explored, as demonstrated by Nardelli et al. [16], who investigated adaptive robotic communication and personalized interaction through LLMs. Our work builds on this research by leveraging periodically detected mood and estimated user characteristics to drive the adaptive behavior generation of the robot. Our approach distinguishes itself by utilizing a single LLM instance to generate both verbal and non-verbal aspects of the robot's expressive behavior. This streamlined design simplifies the system and potentially allows for more coherent and integrated behavior generation. Second, our architecture is designed with generalizability across various robot embodiments in mind. Finally, we explore the integration of a comprehensive set of user characteristics, including mood, age, gender, personality, and propensity to compliance, to drive adaptive robot behaviors in a recipe suggestion task. By analyzing the integration of these characteristics, we aim to provide insights into the design of more natural and engaging socially assistive robots.

3 Methodology

Our methodology is based on a high-level architecture (see Fig. 1) managing user-robot interaction for recipe suggestions. The architecture employs Gemini Flash 2.0 as its primary reasoning component for behavior generation, chosen for its conversational ability and efficiency. The 'InteractionManager' coordinates the process, receiving recipe data (filtered from a Neo4j database based on dietary constraints) and user data. User data includes static information (age, gender, personality traits via the 10-item Big Five Inventory [17], and compliance propensity score) collected during onboarding. For our preliminary exploration, participants ranged from 20 to 35 years old, with varying levels of familiarity with technology. Dynamic data, such as the user's current mood, is assessed before each interaction. While this can be achieved by any perception module, our current implementation utilizes another Gemini instance to classify mood from a single video frame. The main execution flow involves gathering information and feeding it to the Gemini LLM. The LLM then generates a text message incorporating robot-specific animation commands. This message is sent to the 'RobotHandler', which interfaces with 'RobotAPIs' to execute speech and gesture commands on the physical robot. After presenting the recipe, the system prompts the user for acceptance. If rejected, the system can update the user's mood (as detection occurs periodically), retrieve a new recipe, and re-prompt Gemini, continuing until acceptance. Our architecture, designed to generalize across robotic platforms, abstracts robot-specific interfaces through the 'RobotAPIs' module, ensuring modularity.

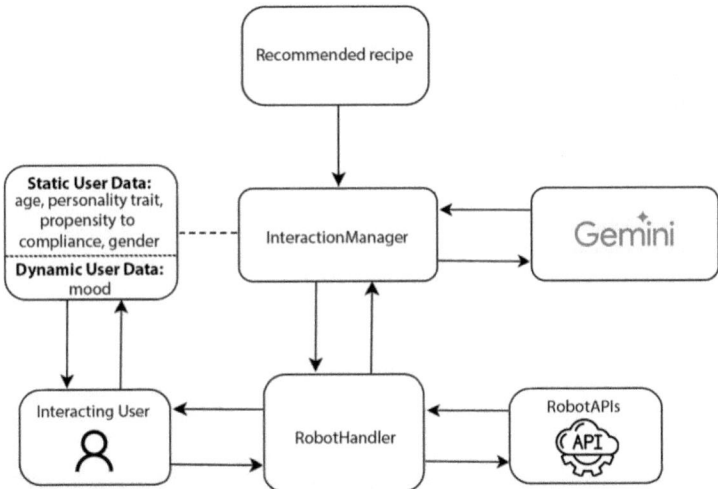

Fig. 1. The high-level system architecture illustrates the 'InteractionManager' receiving the recommended recipe as input, with optional user information used in advanced scenarios to enhance personalization.

3.1 Robot-Specific Implementation Details

For the Pepper robot, the LLM-generated text message, including animation paths, is directly passed to Pepper's SDK. The API interprets these paths, seamlessly integrating corresponding animations into the spoken output, and ignoring invalid paths. For instance, in an advanced interaction scenario, given user characteristics like "Age: 48, Gender: Male, Personality trait: Neurotic, Current mood: Sad, Propensity to Compliance: Low", the LLM generates an output such as:

```
^mode(contextual) I understand that today is not an easy day
^start(animations/Stand/Emotions/Positive/Peaceful_1) But if you
feel like something simple and comforting, I suggest Chickpea Meatballs.
^wait(animations/Stand/Emotions/Positive/Peaceful_1)
^start(animations/Stand/BodyTalk/Speaking/BodyTalk_4) They are light,
nutritious, and easy to prepare. You might find them enjoyable.
^wait(animations/Stand/BodyTalk/Speaking/BodyTalk_4)
^start(animations/Stand/Emotions/Neutral/AskForAttention_2) What do
you say, do you feel like trying them? No pressure, only if you want to.
```

3.2 LLM Prompting

To guide the LLM's behavior, we designed two system prompts: a Basic Prompt and an Advanced Prompt for Pepper. The Basic Prompt instructs the LLM to act as an assistant, generating short, engaging recipe messages with integrated animations, focusing on a natural and dynamic tone. The Advanced Prompt builds on this, enabling the LLM to adapt tone and content based on user characteristics like age, gender, personality, mood, and compliance propensity. It provides emotional cues aligned with the user's mood and adjusts animation quantity and message length accordingly, aiming for a personalized interaction experience.

4 Results

We assessed participants' perception of Pepper's social intelligence using the Perceived Social Intelligence Test (PSI) [7], with 10 participants experiencing both baseline and adaptive scenarios in randomized order.

4.1 Perceived Social Intelligence

PSI results provided three composite scores:

- **Social Presentation:** evaluates traits like friendliness, helpfulness, and trustworthiness.
- **Social Information Processing:** assesses the robot's ability to recognize, adapt to, and predict emotions, behaviors, and cognitions.
- **Overall Social Intelligence:** combined score integrating the above dimensions.

Ratings used a 5-point Likert scale. No statistically significant differences were found between baseline and adaptive conditions, suggesting limited perceptual impact of the personalization in this context.

4.2 Qualitative Observations

Analysis of the LLM's outputs showed only subtle variations between the two conditions. For instance, the adaptive response included a more tailored suggestion, but the difference was minimal and did not significantly influence user perception. This suggests that while the system can incorporate user data, further refinement is needed to generate more perceptually salient adaptive behaviors. This may include improved prompting strategies or broader user modeling.

5 Conclusions

This study presented a simplified architecture using a single LLM (Gemini Flash 2.0) to generate verbal and non-verbal behaviors in socially assistive robots, adapting to user traits such as mood, age, and personality. Tested in a recipe suggestion scenario, the system demonstrated technical feasibility and generalizability. While no significant differences in perceived social intelligence were observed between baseline and adaptive conditions, likely due to the subtlety of the adaptive behaviors and limited robot expressiveness, the architecture offers a foundation for more refined personalization. Future work will explore richer interaction scenarios, expand user modeling, and refine prompting strategies to generate more distinct and impactful adaptive behaviors. Ultimately, this approach aims to support more natural, trustworthy, and personalized human-robot interactions in real-world assistive contexts.

Acknowledgments. This study received funding from the European Union - NextGenerationEU - National Recovery and Resilience Plan (NRRP) MISSION 4 COMPONENT 2, INVESTIMENT N. 1.1, CALL PRIN 2022 PNRR D.D. 1409 14-09-2022 ADVISOR CUP N.E53D23016260001.

References

1. Advisor Project: Advisor: ADaptiVe legIble robotS for trustwORthy health coaching. https://advisor.dieti.unina.it/. Accessed: 2025-04-16
2. Ahn, M., et al.: Do as i can, not as i say: grounding language in robotic affordances (2022). https://doi.org/10.48550/arXiv.2204.01691
3. Ao, J., Wu, Y., Wu, F., Haddadin, S.: Behavior tree generation using large language models for sequential manipulation planning with human instructions and feedback (2024). https://doi.org/10.48550/arXiv.2409.09435
4. Arikan, O., Forsyth, D.A., O'Brien, J.F.: Motion synthesis from annotations. ACM Trans. Graph. **22**(3), 402–408 (2003). https://doi.org/10.1145/882262.882284

5. Arkin, R.C., Fujita, M., Takagi, T., Hasegawa, R.: An ethological and emotional basis for human robot interaction. Robot. Auton. Syst. **42**(3), 191–201 (2003). https://doi.org/10.1016/S0921-8890 (02)00375-5, Socially Interactive Robots
6. Aymerich-Franch, L., Ferrer, I.: Socially assistive robots' deployment in healthcare settings: a global perspective (2021). https://doi.org/10.48550/arXiv.2110.07404
7. Barchard, K., Lapping-Carr, L., Westfall, R.S., Fink-Armold, A., Banisetty, S.B., Feil-Seifer, D.: Measuring the perceived social intelligence of robots. ACM Transactions on Human-Robot Interaction **9**, 1–29 (09 2020). https://doi.org/10.1145/3415139
8. Breazeal, C.: Designing Sociable Robots. The MIT Press (2002).https://doi.org/10.7551/mitpress/2376.001.0001
9. Breazeal, C.: Emotion and sociable humanoid robots. Int. J. Hum Comput Stud. **59**(1), 119–155 (2003). https://doi.org/10.1016/S1071-5819 (03)00018-1, Applications of Affective Computing in Human-Computer Interaction
10. Broekens, J., Heerink, M., Rosendal, H.: Assistive social robots in elderly care: A review. Gerontechnology **8**, 94–103 (2009).https://doi.org/10.4017/gt.2009.08.02.002.00
11. Chita-Tegmark, M., Scheutz, M.: Assistive robots for the social management of health: a framework for robot design and human robot interaction research. Int. J. Soc. Robot. **13**(2), 197–217 (2020). https://doi.org/10.1007/s12369-020-00634-z
12. Liang, J., et al.: Code as policies: Language model programs for embodied control (2023). https://doi.org/10.48550/arXiv.2209.07753
13. Lin, Z., Cruz, F., Sandoval, E.B.: Self context-aware emotion perception on human-robot interaction (2024). https://doi.org/10.48550/arXiv.2401.10946
14. Mahadevan, K., et al.: Generative expressive robot behaviors using large language models. In: Proceedings of the 2024 ACM/IEEE International Conference on Human-Robot Interaction, pp. 482–491. HRI 24, ACM (2024). https://doi.org/10.1145/3610977.3634999
15. Melo, L.C., Maximo, M.R.O.A., da Cunha, A.M.: Learning humanoid robot motions through deep neural networks (2019). https://doi.org/10.48550/arXiv.1901.00270
16. Nardelli, A., Sgorbissa, A., Recchiuto, C.T.: Personality- and memory-based software framework for human-robot interaction. In: 2024 IEEE International Conference on Robotics and Automation (ICRA), pp. 17388–17394 (2024). https://doi.org/10.1109/ICRA57147.2024.10611168
17. Rammstedt, B., John, O.: Measuring personality in one minute or less: a 10-item short version of the big five inventory in English and German. J. Res. Personality **41**, 203–212 (2007). https://doi.org/10.1016/j.jrp.2006.02.001
18. Saerbeck, M., Schut, T., Bartneck, C., Janse, M.D.: Expressive robots in education: varying the degree of social supportive behavior of a robotic tutor. In: Proceedings of the SIGCHI Conference on Human Factors in Computing Systems, pp. 1613–1622. CHI '10, Association for Computing Machinery, New York, NY, USA (2010). https://doi.org/10.1145/1753326.1753567
19. Shridhar, M., Manuelli, L., Fox, D.: Cliport: What and where pathways for robotic manipulation (2021). https://doi.org/10.48550/arXiv.2109.12098
20. Spezialetti, M., Placidi, G., Rossi, S.: Emotion recognition for human-robot interaction: Recent advances and future perspectives. Frontiers in Robotics and AI **Volume 7 - 2020** (2020). https://doi.org/10.3389/frobt.2020.532279
21. Tapus, A., pu, C., Matari, M.: User-robot personality matching and robot behavior adaptation for post-stroke rehabilitation therapy. Intell. Service Rob. **1**, 169–183 (2008). https://doi.org/10.1007/s11370-008-0017-4

A Social Robot Supporting Artistic Activities with Older Adults: A Pilot Study

Sara Carrasco-Martínez[(✉)], Marcos Maroto-Gómez, Fernando Alonso-Martín, Álvaro Castro-González, and Miguel Ángel Salichs

Systems Engineering and Automation, Carlos III University of Madrid, Avenida de la Universidad, 30, 28911 Leganés, Madrid, Spain
{sacarras,marmarot,famartin,acgonzal,salichs}@ing.u3cm.es

Abstract. Older adults living in care centres require continuous and specialised attention to maintain their well-being in the best possible condition. However, the shortage of caregivers and therapists to supervise multiple residents simultaneously during these activities requires innovative solutions. This paper explores the use of the Mini social robot to support entertaining and interactive creative art-based sessions that may promote creativity, engagement, and human-robot interaction in elderly care contexts. We did a pilot study with six seniors who interacted with Mini during the art-based activity. Post-session personal interviews suggest high levels of immersion and engagement and positive feedback on the activities. Our findings suggest that Mini is an interactive guide during the sessions, offering support while completing the activity, enriching users' experiences, and encouraging participation in care settings.

Keywords: Social Robots · Human-Robot Interaction · Art-based Sessions · User Engagement

1 Introduction

Social robots have demonstrated good performance in assisting and entertaining seniors through cognitive, affective, and physical stimulation exercises in healthcare environments [2]. Recent studies [3,11] reveal that human-robot interaction may reduce the feelings of loneliness and anxiety while offering engaging activities for the older adults. However, the frequent use of social robots by older adults still needs to be further explored. Many care centres daily promote activities like painting and puzzles to stimulate creativity and social interaction among older adults. However, conducting these sessions often requires significant staff involvement, limiting their scalability and adaptability.

In this context, assistive technologies such as social robots may offer assistance for facilitating these tasks.

This paper presents a proposal to use artistic activities to improve human-robot interaction and foster older adults' creativity, engagement, and well-being. We decided to use our Mini social robot [13] to conduct artistic sessions and explore its role on them. Taking inspiration from Art Therapy [7], we propose an interactive colouring activity using AI-generated drawings that are adapted to different themes and difficulty levels. This activity combines traditional art activities with social robotics to promote self-expression, emotional well-being, and active participation. With these artistic activities we intend to encourage participation and creative exploration among older adults complementing the role of professional therapists with the Mini social robot.

2 Background

Participating in leisure activities is essential for the well-being of older adults to achieving a high quality of life [1,4,6]. The execution of these activities contribute to their entertainment, physical, emotional, and cognitive stimulation [4,15]. Artistic and craft activities are commonly used in care centres to encourage creativity and social interaction, offering flexible and accessible formats that do not require prior experience [4,15].

Social robots have emerged as an assistive technology to support older adults in tasks such as conversation, memory games, physical exercise, and emotional companionship. They contribute to the health and psychological well-being of older adults, taking into account their specific needs and characteristics [3]. Examples like Paro [12] or PIO [10] have shown positive effects on emotional well-being and social interaction in users with mild or moderate dementia.

Previous works explored the use of robots to guide or participate in artistic activities for children or general audiences [2,8]. These initiatives often focus on creativity, entertainment, or education. However, research on art-based robotic activities specifically designed for older adults is limited despite growing evidence of their benefits in cognitive and emotional stimulation. For instance, Fields et al. [5] conducted a pilot study where older adults co-performed short theatrical scenes with a humanoid robot, aiming to improve psychological well-being through participatory arts. Most studies with older people have prioritised cognitive games, conversation, or companionship, rather than structured creative expression. This lack of focus represents a relevant gap that our proposal aims to address by integrating social robotics into everyday artistic routines in care centres.

Our proposal addresses this limitation by integrating social robots into artistic routines that are already familiar in care environments. Using the robot as an interactive guide in these creative sessions represents an innovative, non-clinical approach that might enhance user engagement, produce a sense of usefulness, and create new forms of interaction with technology.

3 An Art-Based Activity for Mini Robot

This work proposes the use of the Mini social robot as a companion in an artistic activity for older adults in care centres. Mini [13] is a social robot developed at Carlos III University of Madrid aimed at assisting and entertaining older people with mild cognitive impairment.

We designed social and emotional behaviours to create an engaging and friendly environment, helping users to feel accompanied and motivated during the session. Mini uses emotionally expressive speech, changes the colour of its heart LED to match the painting colour, and delivers encouraging comments and playful remarks while the user is painting.

3.1 The Colouring Activity in Mini

We developed an activity for Mini that includes different categories of drawings (mandalas, landscapes, and animals) to colour them through a colour sequence. These categories were selected due to their popularity in traditional art sessions for older adults [9,16]. Each category is divided into levels that classify drawings by complexity, defined by their number of colours (4, 7, or 10), adapting to users' abilities. Each drawing is divided into numbered regions, with each number corresponding to a specific colour that the user has to paint. Mini guides the user during the activity with different indications and suggestions showing the relationship between the number and the colour with voice commands and using its tablet.

(a) The coloured drawing   (b) Paint by numbers drawing

Fig. 1. AI image example generation and processing. (a) Image generated by DALL-E from the example prompt. (b) Final image generated with the colour by numbers generator the users have to paint.

Drawings Generation. Drawings are not generated in real-time. Instead, they are created in advance and stored as part of the activity repertoire. This allows us to offer a consistent set of drawings already classified by category and difficulty. During the activity, Mini selects and displays one of these preloaded images according to the user's preferences and progress. This approach ensures that the activity runs smoothly and that all images are visually and cognitively appropriate for seniors.

Drawings are classified into three categories: animals, mandalas, and landscapes. The drawing repertoire is created with DALL-E[1] offline prior to the activity, an AI capable of generating images from text, based on descriptive prompts. Figure 1a shows an example of the output based on a prompt describing an elephant with flowers.

Based on the image generated by DALL-E, we assign colours to numbers and regions using a generator[2] that converts the image to a "paint by numbers" format where each region of the image is marked with a number corresponding to a specific colour. The generator allows to adjust several parameters, such as the number of colours to be used in the final image (in our case, 4, 7 and 10), according to the desired difficulty we want to obtain in the drawing. We chose these values to allow us to adapt the activity to each user based on the capabilities of completing the drawing. The colours selected are later analysed to customise the dialogues of the robot and offer a personalised user experience.

Fig. 2. Screens of the Art activity with Mini. [a] Introduction screen and choice of drawing category. [b] Drawing selection. [c] The offline mode, the therapist give the drawing to the user. [d-e] Colours referenced by numbers. [f] Solution.

Interacting with Mini. Figure 2 shows a interaction flow during the colouring activity with Mini. In the activity, users identify themselves using personal ID cards so that Mini can load their profile (stored in files) and previous progression in the activity. The robot guides users through the session step-by-step with

---

[1] DALL-E Available in this web.
[2] Available in this GitHub repository.

a scripted dialogue system. To complete the activity, participants used printed drawings (given by the therapist or printed by the robot) and coloured pencils. When the activity begins, the robot welcomes the user by their name, introduces itself, and thanks the user for participating. Then, the robot asks for the category and the user can select the one of they wish to colour. This selection can be by the robot's tablet or by voice. Based on their previous activity and recorded performance, the robot automatically assigns a random drawing at the appropriate difficulty level. If the user does not like it, they can ask for a different one using voice or tablet. If the user likes the drawing, they can accept it pressing the *Like* button on the tablet or saying "I like it" to the robot. Once the user selects a drawing, Mini automatically sends to the printer a copy of the drawing if a printer is available. Otherwise, the therapist provides the printed version to the user (before the activity, a set of drawings is generated offline and stored as a repertoire available to the therapist). The robot indicates by voice the drawing to be coloured so the therapist can find it in the drawings on paper.

Once the user receives the printed drawing, the robot begins the colouring session by announcing the first number and the corresponding colour, synchronising this with its LED and the tablet interface. This multimodal guidance supports users with cognitive or sensory limitations. For example, Mini explains to user that the area marked with the number one should be painted orange (see Fig. 3 left). The robot waits until the user has completed the colouring. During this time, it encourages the user by speaking motivational sentences, including short comments, facts, or questions related to the colour in use. These sentences are designed to maintain interaction and potentially support user engagement. To continue with the following colour, the user can press *Next* on the tablet or tell it by voice. Once all colours have been painted and the drawing is finished, Mini displays the solution of the drawing on the tablet.

 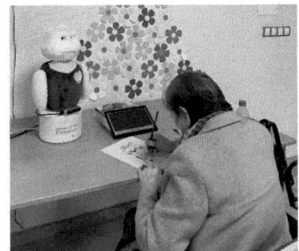

Fig. 3. Real-life scenario doing the art activity with Mini robot.

4 Pilot Study

This pilot study in a care centre shows a real-life scenario (see Fig. 3) where six participants from an older adults residence, aged between 74 and 84 years (four men and two women), interacted with Mini. All participants reported low technological knowledge and had no previous experience with robots. Participants voluntarily consented to participate in the study after being informed of the purpose of the research. Sessions took place in a designated activity room within the residence. Mini was on a table with its tablet, and the necessary painting materials to carry out the activity. Each session lasted from 30 to 70 minutes, depending on the engagement level of the participants (participants could stop at will). After the session, they reported their experience with Mini.

After completing the activity, participants were invited to provide feedback about their experience with Mini. A short questionnaire was used to gather their impressions. Each participant answered individually and anonymously on paper. The questions focused on the clarity of the instructions, easy of use, engagement with the activity, and emotional impressions during the session. The questions asked were: "Did you enjoy the colouring activity? Why or why not?", "Was it easy to follow the robot's instructions?", and "Would you like to do this activity again with the robot?".

The users' responses were semantically analysed to identify recurring thematic patterns following the methodology presented in [14]. This analysis gave us five conceptual categories with a qualitative interpretation: *Engagement and Enjoyment, Usability and Clarity, Creativity and Expression, Social and Emotional Value, and Perception of Technology*. With this analysis, we constructed a binary matrix per user quantifying how many participants explicitly or implicitly referred to each theme. Then, we made a spider chart (see Fig. 4) grouping the five categories to illustrate the frequency with which each theme appeared in the participants' feedback. For example, the AI tool considered sentences such as "I would definitely try this activity again" or "I would like to do it again" a indicators as of Usability and Clarity, even though they do not include the word easy explicitly. Similarly, phrases like "This brightens my day" or "I told my grandchildren about this" were categorized as Social and Emotional Value.

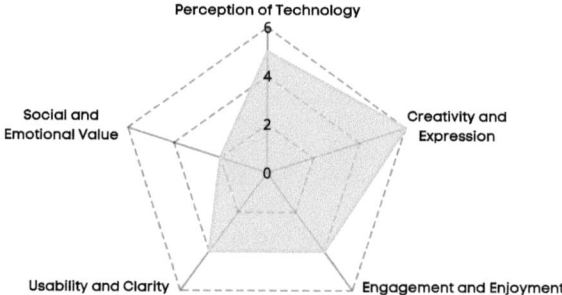

Fig. 4. Spider chart illustrating the distribution of five thematic categories identified through the semantically analysis of user feedback. Each axis indicates how many of the six participants referred to the corresponding theme, based on explicit or implicit mentions.

Feedback revealed that participants found the activity enjoyable, intuitive, and motivating. This qualitative insight reinforces the potential that can have the art activity in the human-robot interaction as a resource to support engagement, emotional well-being, and meaningful leisure in elderly care settings.

The five categories align with terms represented in scales used in HRI, such as the Intrinsic Motivation Inventory (IMI), the User Engagement Scale (UES), and the Robot Social Attributes Scale (RoSAS). This alignment suggests that future studies could benefit from combining qualitative feedback with standardized instruments to assess user engagement, motivation, and perception of social robots more systematically.

5 Conclusion

This paper presents an artistic activity guided by the Mini social robot designed to promote engagement and well-being in older adults. A pilot study conducted with six older adults in a real-life setting revealed a positive response to the activity, with participants showing enjoyment, and interest in future interactions. We believe that the proposed activity may foster creativity, emotional expression, and meaningful interaction with the robot and, in general, improves the quality of life of seniors. However, given the limited number of participants, the results require further tests but have been useful to demonstrate that the new activity works successfully.

We propose as future work doing a study with more users and incorporate questionnaires such as the Intrinsic Motivation Inventory (IMI), the User Engagement Scale (UES), and the Robot Social Attributes Scale (RoSAS) to quantitatively assess aspects like motivation, engagement, and perceived social presence.

Acknowledgements. These results have received funding from the projects: Robots sociales para mitigar la soledad y el aislamiento en mayores (SOROLI), PID2021-123941OA-I00 and Robots sociales para reducir la brecha digital de las personas mayores (SoRoGap), TED2021-132079B-I00, both funded by Agencia Estatal de Investigación (AEI), Spanish Ministerio de Ciencia e Innovación. Mejora del nivel de madurez tecnológica del robot Mini (MeNiR) funded by MCIN/AEI/10.13039/501100011033 and the European Union NextGenerationEU/PRTR. Portable Social Robot with High Level of Engagement (PoSoRo) PID2022-140345OB-I00 funded by MCIN / AEI / 10.13039/501100011033 and ERDF A way of making Europe.

References

1. Alban, D., et al.: El tiempo libre y el ocio en el mejoramiento de la calidad de vida del adulto mayor. Dominio de las Ciencias **7**(4), 83 (2021)
2. Ali, S., et al.: Social robots as creativity eliciting agents. Frontiers in Robotics and AI **8** (2021)

3. Cavallaro, A., et al.: Social robot in service of the cognitive therapy of elderly people: exploring robot acceptance in a real-world scenario. Image Vis. Comput. **147**, 105072 (2024)
4. Fernández, V.L., et al.: Actividades de ocio y bienestar emocional en personas jubiladas independientes. Res. Ageing Soc. Policy **3**(1), 46–63 (2015)
5. Fields, N., et al.: Shall i compare the to a robot? An exploratory pilot study using participatory arts and social robotics to improve psychological well-being in later life. Aging Mental Health **25**(3), 575–584 (2021)
6. Galassi, F., et al.: Creativity and art therapies to promote healthy aging: a scoping review. Front. Psychol. **13** (2022)
7. Hernández Silvera, D.I.: Ser y hacer en proyección: Arte-terapia. Asociación Neuropsiquiátrica Argentina (2006)
8. Hu, B.: Analysis of art therapy for children with autism by using the implemented artificial intelligence system. Int. J. Human. Rob. **19**(03) (2022)
9. Koo, M., et al.: Coloring activities for anxiety reduction and mood improvement in Taiwanese community-dwelling older adults: a randomized controlled study. Evidence-based Complementary and Alternative Medicine : eCAM (2020)
10. Lim, J.S.: Effects of a cognitive-based intervention program using social robot PIO on cognitive function, depression, loneliness, and quality of life of older adults living alone. Front. Public Health **11**, 1097485 (2023)
11. Pu, L., Moyle, W., Jones, C., Todorovic, M.: The effectiveness of social robots for older adults: a systematic review and meta-analysis of randomized controlled studies. Gerontologist **59**(1), e37–e51 (2019)
12. Rashid, N.L.A., et al.: The effectiveness of a therapeutic robot, 'Paro', on behavioural and psychological symptoms, medication use, total sleep time and sociability in older adults with dementia: a systematic review and meta-analysis. Int. J. Nursing Stud. **145** (2023)
13. Salichs, M.A., et al.: Mini: a new social robot for the elderly. Int. J. Soc. Robot. **12**, 1231–1249 (2020)
14. Titus, L.M.: Does chatgpt have semantic understanding? A problem with the statistics-of-occurrence strategy. Cogn. Syst. Res. **83**, 101174 (2024)
15. Yan, Y.J., et al.: Effects of expressive arts therapy in older adults with mild cognitive impairment: a pilot study. Geriatr. Nurs. **42**(1), 129–136 (2021)
16. Zhang, M.Q., et al.: Does mandala art improve psychological well-being in patients? A systematic review. J. Integrative Compl. Med. **30**, 25 (2024)

Toward Human-Robot Co-learning in Manufacturing

Emilia Pietras[1(✉)], Raquel Salcedo-Gil[2], Guglielmo Borzone[1], Sonja Rispens[2], and Leon Bodenhagen[1]

[1] University of Southern Denmark, Campusvej 55, 5230 Odense, Denmark
`{empi,gubo,lebo}@mmmi.sdu.dk`
[2] Eindhoven University of Technology, Eindhoven, Netherlands
`{r.salcedo.gil,s.rispens}@tue.nl`

Abstract. As robot systems are increasingly being implemented in manufacturing workspaces, effective employee training becomes essential. We propose an ontology-based guidance system which adapts its instructional guidance to the inferred expertise level of the operator. Through a pilot study with six participants we found that interactions with the guidance system changed visibly after the first session, implying changes in the need for guidance over time. Furthermore, robot-use self-efficacy increased significantly after interacting with the robot, indicating that the system supported both learning and confidence development.

Keywords: Collaborative robotics · Adaptation · Learning

1 Introduction

As the manufacturing industry is bringing its production to Industry 5.0, human-robot tasks are becoming increasingly flexible and complex. This requires efficient training and clear system communication to support operators in developing the necessary expertise and facilitate their learning [1]. However, this remains a significant challenge. Interpersonal differences, such as personality traits, and the dynamic nature of human internal states require robot systems to be adaptive to the individual operator to be efficient and intuitive.

In this work, we propose an ontology-based guidance system integrated in a physical robot setup. The purpose of this system is to adapt the guidance provided to the operator based on their inferred level of expertise. To this end, the system stores all interactions between the operator and the robot system in a Resource Description Framework (RDF) store. Based on this data, we use a fuzzy control system to determine the appropriate level of guidance to provide the operator.

As operator learning is the focal point of our proposed system, we tested the system through a pilot study. The study evaluates the perceived usability of the system guidance throughout several trials of an interactive robotic scanning task. Additionally, we explore whether repeated interaction with the system leads to changes in the participants' robot-use self-efficacy and acceptance.

2 Related Work

2.1 Training Employees for HRC Adaptation

Training plays a crucial role in facilitating employee learning and adaptation during the implementation of robot systems in the workplace [2]. To successfully adapt to working with robots, employees need to acquire new knowledge and skills in areas such as programming, automation, or mechanical systems [3]. This is especially important with the implementation of collaborative robots that work side by side with humans. Here, employees must learn how to communicate with robots, coordinate actions, and share tasks [4]. Research shows that training employees as they adapt to working with robots promotes effective use of robot systems and enhances organizational performance [5]. However, only half of employees receive adequate training, with 63% of employers citing skills gaps as a major barrier to technological transformation and 85% planning to invest in employee upskilling in the next few years [6]. This is essential as insufficient preparation has been linked to employee anxiety and resistance during robot implementation [4]. These findings highlight the need to bridge the training gap to ensure both technological effectiveness and employee adaptability and well-being.

2.2 Adaptive Robot Behavior in HRC

The potential for human-robot collaboration (HRC) that is yet to be fully exploited is the prospect of human-robot teams executing complex processes efficiently while reducing human workload [7]. Previous work shows that operators prefer systems that adapt to their level of skill and fatigue to traditional systems, and that such systems improve performance [8]. This underlines adaptation as an important prerequisite for successful HRC. However, this remains difficult to implement due to the lack of accurate human modeling. To achieve a better understanding of human internal states and how robots should react to them, the use of physiological, behavioral, and questionnaire measurements has different strengths and limitations. Combining these measurements has been reported to be valuable for comprehensive human modeling [9]. Nevertheless, the persisting challenge of effective human modeling adds complexity to the development of adaptive robots [1] and shows the need for a deeper understanding of human factors in HRC.

2.3 Reasoning and Decision-Making in HRC

Integrating awareness of complex environments in robot systems is essential to achieve reasoning about events and successful robot action planning. General ontologies for robotics, such as the core ontology for robotics and automation (CORA) [10], provide a way to structure and link information about the environment. Furthermore, authors have developed more specific ontologies, e.g., collaborative agents for manufacturing ontology (CAMO) [11], which addresses

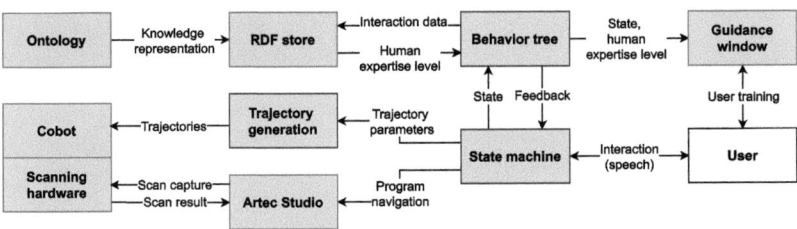

Fig. 1. Block diagram visualizing the system overview. It can be broadly divided into the knowledge base (orange), the robot control architecture (blue), the physical setup (green), and the user (white). (Color figure online)

the HRC in manufacturing domain. However, ontologies remain static structures. To store information on human-robot interactions on-the-fly, the Resource Description Framework (RDF) is widely used to serve as a dynamic knowledge base. Our system relies on existing ontologies and RDF to monitor human-robot interactions.

3 System Overview

A block diagram of the system is shown in Fig. 1. The system comprises the physical setup and the software setup, which consists of the knowledge base and the control architecture.

Physical Setup: The physical setup is shown in Fig. 2. It consists of a worktable with a FANUC cobot CRX-20iA/L equipped with an Artec Spider II 3D scanner. The scanner connects to the Artec Studio program to generate 3D representations of the metal impeller, which is the target object. Participants wore a RealWear Navigator 520 device to use its built-in microphone for speech commands.

Knowledge Base: The purpose of the knowledge base is to facilitate adaptive guidance for the operator based on their history of interactions with the robot system. We used a modification of previous work on a similar scanning task performed on a simulated setup [12]. The knowledge base consists of two parts: (1) the ontology, which provides the structure and relationships between entities (actions, objects, and their properties), and (2) the RDF store, which inherits the ontology structure and allows for storing and extracting task events. The knowledge base allows for chronological tracking of all interactions, which can then be retrieved using queries.

The adaptive guidance is based on the inferred expertise level of the operator. First, we retrieve information about the operator's past interactions with the guidance screen from the RDF store. This information includes the number of sessions the operator has completed, the number of times they have skipped

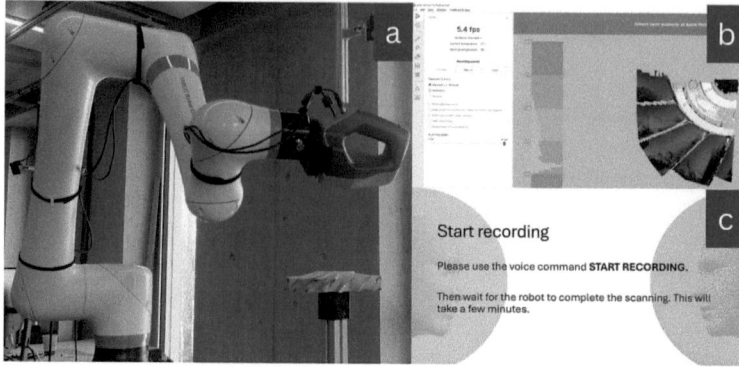

Fig. 2. Components of the experimental setup. It consists of a worktable with a FANUC cobot, a 3D scanner, and a metal impeller (a), a monitor displaying the scanning software Artec Studio (b), and a monitor showing the adaptive guidance window (c).

instructions, the number of times they have asked for additional guidance, and their reading time in seconds. These serve as input variables to a fuzzy control system, which outputs the inferred expertise level based on a set of intuitive logic rules. One such fuzzy mapping rule can be represented by the IF-THEN rule as:

IF the number of sessions is LOW, THEN the expertise level should be LOW.

We apply fuzzy logic to allow for a continuous output, that is, a level of expertise in a spectrum between *beginner* and *expert*. The corresponding levels of guidance are described in Sect. 4.1.

Control Architecture: The state machine determines the flow of the task and moves between states based on speech input from the user and action outcomes. The state machine also controls the robot's movement and communicates the active state to the behavior tree (BT) using ROS 2. Meanwhile, the BT is responsible for storing all activities in the knowledge base and displaying appropriate instructions when needed, based on the active state and the inferred expertise level of the operator.

4 Experiment Setup

4.1 Level of Guidance

To provide a range of levels of guidance to suit the operator's needs, we designed the guidance to follow a revised version of Bloom's taxonomy of educational objectives [13]. The taxonomy defines three terms to describe the "what, why, and how", respectively: (1) factual knowledge, such as terminology and knowledge of basic elements, (2) conceptual knowledge, which allows one to categorize, make generalizations, and understand theories, and (3) procedural knowledge, which is understanding how to do something and when to use a particular method. Based on this taxonomy, we define the following criteria for the guidance corresponding to the inferred operator expertise level:

- **Beginner:** Factual, conceptual, and procedural knowledge.
- **Intermediate:** Procedural knowledge.
- **Expert:** Only the speech commands currently available to the operator.

4.2 Experiment Procedure and Sample

The experiment followed a structured sequence. First, participants completed a pre-experiment questionnaire assessing demographics, robot-use self-efficacy, and acceptance. They then engaged in three consecutive trials that involved interacting with a robot through voice commands. The task involved navigating the scanning software and initializing the robot scanning process. Between each trial, participants answered short, custom-designed interview questions to capture their immediate impressions and reactions. At the end of the experiment, participants completed a questionnaire that included post-measures of robot-use self-efficacy and acceptance, as well as a system usability questionnaire to measure users' perceived satisfaction. Table 1 shows an overview of the measurements used for the study.

Our sample included six participants (4 men, 2 women; M age = 30). Five had prior experience with industrial, service, or domestic robots; one had no prior experience.

Table 1. Measurements used for the experiment. All questionnaire items were rated on a 6-point Likert scale from 1 (strongly disagree) to 6 (strongly agree).

Objective measurements	Questionnaires
Reading time (s): The time that participants spent reading instructions.	**Robot-use self-efficacy:** Measured using the 10-item scale by Rosenthal-von der Pütten and Bock [14].
Session length (s): The duration of a session.	**Technology acceptance:** Measured using the 8-item scale by Davis and Venkatesh [15]. The items were adapted to the robot context.
Number of interactions: The number of requests made by the user to move to the next instruction slide or to skip the instructions.	**System usability:** Measured using the 16-item IBM Post-Study System Usability Questionnaire [16].

5 Results

5.1 System Results

Figure 3 shows the reading times and session lengths for each of the three experimental trials (sessions). The reading time decreased visibly from the first session ($M = 203.41, SD = 65.57$) to the third ($M = 43.44, SD = 39.76$) similar to the decrease in the session length from the first ($M = 277.40, SD = 102.00$) to the third ($M = 162.50, SD = 53.65$). Figure 4 shows the number of interactions in the form of beeswarm plots, displaying the results for each participant.

5.2 Questionnaire Results

A within-subjects repeated measures analysis was conducted to examine the linear effect of time (i.e., the number of trials) on robot-use self-efficacy and acceptance. For robot-use self-efficacy, there was a significant linear increase over time, $F(1,5) = 9.64$, $p = .027$, partial $\eta^2 = .659$, suggesting that participants' self-efficacy improved significantly after interacting with the robot. For acceptance, the linear increase over time was not statistically significant, $F(1,5) = 4.65$, $p = .084$, partial $\eta^2 = .482$ although the effect size was moderate to large, indicating a trend toward increased acceptance.

Furthermore, robot-use self-efficacy scores showed a positive and significant correlation with perceived system usability, $r(6) = .88$, $p = .020$, indicating that participants with higher self-efficacy also perceived the system as more usable.

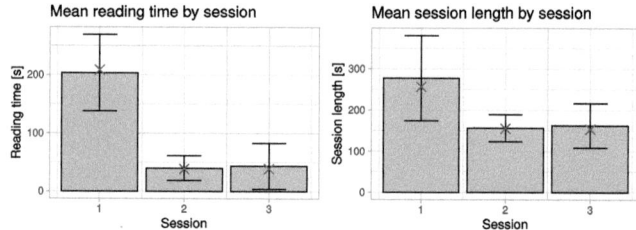

Fig. 3. Bar plots of reading time (left) and session length (right). The means are presented with standard deviations as error bars. The crosses indicate the medians.

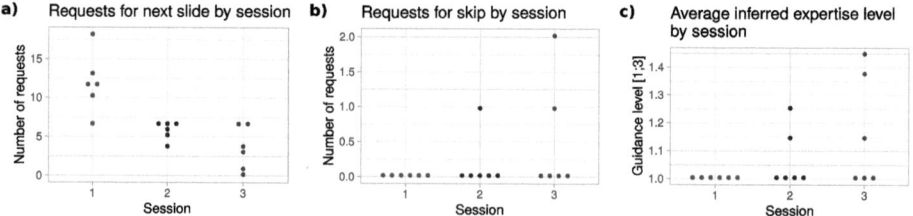

Fig. 4. Plots visualizing the number of requests for the next slide (a) and skipping the slides (b). The average inferred expertise level in each session is presented in (c).

5.3 Open Questions

After each trial, participants were asked three questions: (1) How helpful were the instructions? (2) How satisfied are you with your performance? and (3) Do you feel you improved compared to the previous trial? What could you still improve?. Overall, participants reported positive experiences interacting with the robot and found the guidance system helpful. All participants expressed feeling more confident after the second trial. As one participant stated: *"The first time it takes a little bit of time to understand [the task], ... but the second time it is more intuitive and easier to follow."*

While some participants began skipping slides as they gained confidence, most emphasized the value of having the information available. One participant noted: *"I could skip the instructions, but I think I prefer not to do that because it is always better to have the information there"*. Another participant added: *"I prefer to just follow the slides and if I know it I skip it faster"*. These comments suggest that, especially during initial encounters with the robot, instructional support played a key role in guiding the learning process. Even as participants began to internalize the steps, having access to the instructions served as a useful reference that supported both confidence and task execution.

Though the system was described as clear and easy to follow, several participants noted that it lacked guidance on how to handle unexpected situations. As one participant stated: *"[The guidance] is easy to follow and well-explained, but if something goes wrong, I don't know what to do"*. This highlights the need for training not only on routine tasks but also on how to manage errors or unforeseen situations when learning to collaborate with robots.

6 Discussion and Conclusion

We proposed a system for adaptive HRI that uses a knowledge base to store long-term operator profiles. This allows the system to infer the operator's expertise level and adapt the guidance accordingly. Our pilot study indicated that participants' need for guidance (particularly conceptual and procedural information) decreased drastically after the first session. Furthermore, robot-use self-efficacy increased significantly over time. This suggests that the system could potentially model the operator's expertise level less conservatively, which would remove conceptual and procedural information from the guidance earlier. However, participants reported feeling more comfortable keeping the guidance information present rather than skipping it. This suggests that guidance, even when superfluous, makes users feel more confident in completing their tasks. Conversely, too much adaptation may in some cases compromise self-efficacy. Considering this trade-off may benefit future integrations of systems that adapt to operator skills. Future work with larger samples is needed to confirm the effects of repeated interaction with robot systems on robot-use self-efficacy and acceptance, including operators with non-technical backgrounds.

Acknowledgement. This work has been funded by the EU project Fluently (Grant agreement ID: 101058680) and by the Industry 4.0 lab at the University of Southern Denmark.

References

1. Galin, R.R., Meshcheryakov, R.V.: Human-robot interaction efficiency and human-robot collaboration. In: Robotics: Industry 4.0 Issues & New Intelligent Control Paradigms. Springer (2020)
2. Gil, R.S., Anna-Sophie, U., Rispens, S., Pascale Le, B.: Optimizing training for human-robot collaboration in learning factories: An employee-centered perspective. Learning Factories of the Future (2024)
3. Michaelis, J.E., Siebert-Evenstone, A., Shaffer, D.W., Mutlu, B.: Collaborative or simply uncaged? Understanding human-cobot interactions in automation. In: Conference on Human Factors in Computing Systems (2020)
4. Kim, S.: Working with robots: Human resource development considerations in human robot interaction. Human Resource Development Review, 21 (2022)
5. SPanagou, S., Neumann, W.P., Fruggiero, F.: A scoping review of human robot interaction research towards industry 5.0 human-centric workplaces. Int. J. Prod. Res. **62** (2024)
6. The Future of Jobs Report (2025). https://www.weforum.org/reports/the-future-of-jobs-report-2025/
7. Hjorth, S., Chrysostomou, D.: Human–robot collaboration in industrial environments: a literature review on non-destructive disassembly. Rob. Comput. Integrated Manuf. **73** (2022)
8. Villani, V., et al.: A user study for the evaluation of adaptive interaction systems for inclusive industrial workplaces. IEEE T-ASE, 19 (2021)
9. Savko, L.O., Qian, Z., Gremillion, G., Neubauer, C., Canady, J., Unhelkar, V.: Rw4t dataset: Data of human-robot behavior and cognitive states in simulated disaster response tasks. IEEE HRI (2024)
10. Prestes, E., et al.: Towards a core ontology for robotics and automation. Rob. Auton. Syst. **61**(11) (2013)
11. David, J., Coatanéa, E., Lobov., A.:Deploying OWL ontologies for semantic mediation of mixed-reality interactions for human robot collaborative assembly. J. Manuf. Syst. **70** (2023)
12. Pietras, E., et al.: Co-Adaptation in Human-Robot Training Scenarios. 34th IEEE International Conference on Robot and Human Interactive Communication (ROMAN) (2025)
13. Anderson, L.W., Krathwohl, D.R.: A taxonomy for learning, teaching, and assessing: A revision of Bloom's taxonomy of educational objectives: complete edition. Addison Wesley Longman, Inc., (2001)
14. Pütten, A. R.-V. D. Bock, N.: Development and Validation of the SelfEfficacy in Human-Robot-Interaction Scale (SE-HRI). Association for Computing Machinery 7 (2018)
15. Davis, F.D., Venkatesh, V.: A critical assessment of potential measurement biases in the technology acceptance model: three experiments. Int. J. Human-Comput. Stud. **45**(1) (1996)
16. Lewis, J., R., J.: IBM computer usability satisfaction questionnaires: Psychometric evaluation and instructions for use. Int. J. Human-Comput. Inter. **7** (1995)

Grounding Natural Language Mission Requests in Robotic Skill Specifications via Large Language Models

Mario Barbato[1,2], Marco Grazioso[2(✉)], Azzurra Mancini[2], Valentina Russo[2], and Martina Di Bratto[2]

[1] University of Napoli "Federico II", Napoli, Italy
mario.barbato@unina.it
[2] Logogramma srl, Napoli, Italy
{mbarbato,mgrazioso,amancini,vrusso,mdibratto}@logogramma.com

Abstract. This work presents a novel method for translating natural language mission requests into structured robotic skill specifications, within the SAIRS framework (Symbiotic AI for Robotics in Industrial Settings). Grounded in a modular ontology of robotic capabilities, the system uses Large Language Models (LLMs) with prompt-based guidance to perform intent recognition and slot-filling.

The architecture supports natural language input and generates executable, context-aware mission plans by referencing domain-specific knowledge. The paper describes the design of the interpretation module, skill ontology, and prompt strategies used to ensure robustness.

A two-stage evaluation assessed both natural language synthesis and mission plan generation, with Meta's LLaMA-3.3-70B-Instruct achieving the best performance. Results demonstrate the feasibility of using LLMs for adaptive, human-aligned robotic planning and lay the groundwork for future extensions in multi-agent collaboration and user adaptation.

Keywords: Symbiotic AI · Human-Robot Interaction (HRI) · Large Language Models (LLM) · Ontology-based Planning · Mission Interpretation

1 Introduction and Related Works

As Artificial Intelligence (AI) increasingly permeates diverse domains, its role in enabling natural and effective human-robot interaction (HRI) becomes ever more crucial. A particularly promising direction is Symbiotic AI, which envisions AI systems as collaborative partners that augment human abilities rather than replace them. Rooted in Licklider's concept of human-computer symbiosis [12], this paradigm emphasises adaptive, intuitive cooperation between humans and machines. Recent work highlights the importance of systems that respond to user behaviours, emotional states, and environmental context in real time

[6,13]. Such adaptability, paired with human-centred design principlestransparency, trust, and participatory development—is key to fostering effective collaboration [8]. Advances in Natural Language Processing (NLP) and Large Language Models (LLMs) have enabled more fluid dialogue and nuanced task delegation [5]. However, true symbiosis also requires grounding communication in domain knowledge. Methods like Retrieval-Augmented Generation (RAG) and tool-augmented prompting allow LLMs to dynamically incorporate external information, improving accuracy and contextual relevance [11,15]. Meanwhile, vision-language-action (VLA) models such as RT-2 [4] and SayCan [1] extend this capability to robotics, enabling interpretation of complex instructions and robust performance in dynamic environments. Socially intelligent robotsthose attuned to human cuesare more likely to be trusted and accepted [2,7], yet many existing HRI frameworks lack mechanisms for long-term learning and user-specific adaptation [3,16]. The SAIRS framework addresses these gaps by integrating structured interaction models [10,14] with adaptive components. Unlike static task-assistance systems, SAIRS supports continuous learning and responsive behaviour. Building upon the earlier work from Grazioso et al. [9], this paper extends the framework with new simulation-based validations, aiming to advance intelligent, context-aware HRI in complex industrial environments.

2 Mission Request Interpretation (MRI)

The MRI is responsible for interpreting mission requests expressed in Italian natural language and translating them into structured, executable plans for a surveillance robot. Leveraging a Large Language Model (LLM), it performs intent recognition and slot-filling based on an external ontology of the robot's capabilities. The overall architecture is illustrated in Fig. 1.

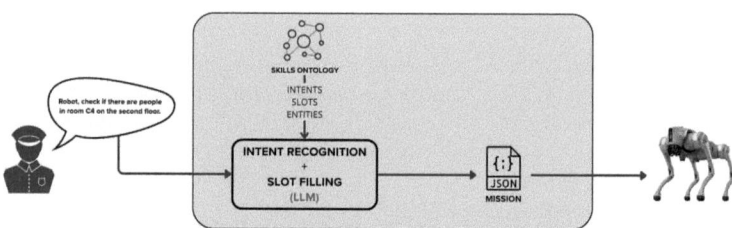

Fig. 1. The MRI architecture. The operator's request is translated into a structured form to be processed by the robotic platform.

Skills Ontology. The interpretation process begins with a shared understanding of robotic capabilities, formalised through a skills graph-based ontology. This ontology defines:

- **Intents**: represent the robot skills invoked by the operator's request.
- **Slots**: parameters associated with each skill that specify execution details.
- **Entities**: Entity type for the slot, also specifying the allowed values domain.

The ontology is modelled as a directed graph, linking concepts through semantic relationships (see Fig. 2). Its modular design ensures adaptability: changes in the robot's skill set only require updates to the ontology, not the interpretation logic.

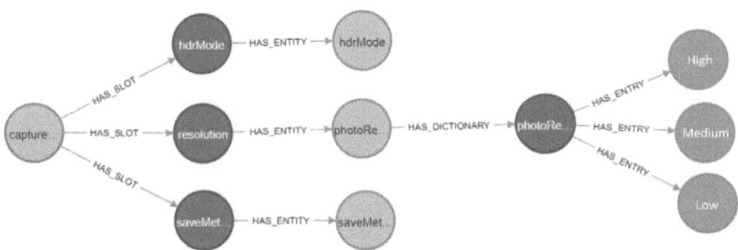

Fig. 2. The skill *capturePanoramicView*, represented as an intent in the ontology graph, with its associated slots and entities.

Mission Plan Generation. The core contribution of the proposed work lies in the automated generation of mission plans in a standardized, machine-readable format for the robot. When the operator issues an inspection mission request via voice—using a Speech-to-Text system to be integrated either onboard the robot or within a dedicated software interface on the guard's tablet—the natural language input is forwarded to a Large Language Model, running on a remote server, as a user prompt. The LLM is guided by a system prompt[1], carefully designed through prompt engineering to improve accuracy and mitigate hallucinations. This strategy involves providing a contextual introduction to the task, along with structured instructions that clarify the available knowledge base (such as the robot's skill ontology), the expected input (a natural language request), and the required output (a mission plan formatted in JSON). Finally, the system prompt specifies a set of output constraints, including the use of singular form for all detected entities and the strict requirement to return only a JSON object without any additional text, and five realistic input examples, each paired with the corresponding expected output, adopting the well-known few-shot learning technique [5]. The LLM output is then passed to an evaluation module that first verifies its syntactic validity, ensuring the generated text is a properly formatted JSON. Subsequently, it checks whether the predicted intent and entities correspond to valid values defined in the skills ontology. This validation step is essential to guarantee that the mission plan provided to the robot appropriate and executable.

---

[1] The prompt is available at this link: https://pastebin.com/JvcDc8tH.

3 Preliminary Assessment

We evaluated the effectiveness of the mission interpretation and planning system using a structured process (Fig. 3). A dataset of 322 ground truth JSON missions was created by exhaustively combining valid slot values for each intent. Natural language requests were then synthesized from these using LLMs, and the system-generated mission plans were compared to the originals for correctness. Five robotic skills were tested: `scanObjects`, `detectHumanPresence`, `locateAnimals`, `monitorTemperature`, and `capturePanoramicView`.

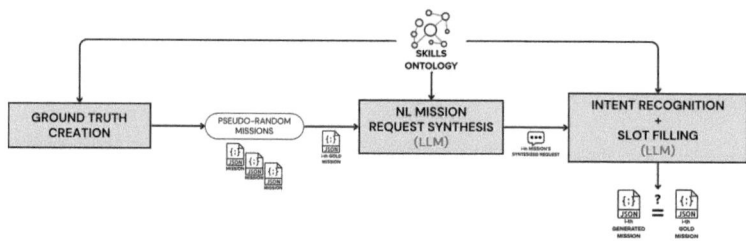

Fig. 3. Evaluation pipeline of the proposed model.

Ground Truth Request Synthesis. Natural language requests were generated using three LLMs: LLaMA-3.1-8B-Instruct, LLaMA-3.3-70B-Instruct, and Mistral-7B-Instruct-v0.3, prompted with a consistent system template, and manually validated. Table 1 shows that all models performed well, with LLaMA-3.3 slightly outperforming the others. Errors were rare and mostly related to slot mapping or syntax.

Table 1. Accuracy results for the ground truth missions synthesis in natural language requests.

Intents	LLaMA-3.1-8B-Instruct	LLaMA-3.3-70B-Instruct	Mistral-7B-Instruct-v0.3
scanObjects	240/240	240/240	239/240
detectHumanPresence	5/8	7/8	6/8
locateAnimals	30/30	30/30	29/30
monitorTemperature	32/32	32/32	30/32
capturePanoramicView	9/12	12/12	8/12
Total	316/322	321/322	312/322

Mission Plan Generation Assessment. Each synthesized request was used as input to generate a JSON mission plan. Results in Table 2 show that LLaMA-3.3 achieved the best accuracy (318/322), closely followed

Table 2. Accuracy results for the mission plans generation.

Intents	LLaMA-3.1-70B-Instruct	LLaMA-3.3-70B-Instruct	Mistral-7B-Instruct-v0.3
scanObjects	238/240	240/240	233/240
detectHumanPresence	6/8	7/8	1/8
locateAnimals	30/30	30/30	29/30
monitorTemperature	32/32	32/32	8/32
capturePanoramicView	10/12	11/12	0/12
Total	316/322	318/322	271/322

by LLaMA-3.1 (316/322). Most errors involved boolean misassignments in detectHumanPresence and capturePanoramicView. Mistral-7B lagged behind, often producing invalid outputs—ranging from extra formatting to hallucinated intents and fabricated JSON structures.

4 Conclusions and Future Works

This work proposed a pipeline for grounding natural language mission requests into structured robotic skill specifications, aligning with the vision of Symbiotic AI. We demonstrated how LLMs can act as mediators between human intention and robotic execution, fostering a form of human-AI collaboration where interaction is natural, adaptive, and grounded in shared knowledge.

By formalizing the robot's capabilities through a structured ontology and guiding LLM behavior via prompt engineering, the system enables robust interpretation of user requests through intent recognition and slot-filling, ultimately transforming them into valid and executable JSON mission plans. The evaluation confirmed the effectiveness of this approach, with LLaMA-3.3-70B-Instruct emerging as the most reliable model in both the synthesis and plan generation tasks. However, it is important to acknowledge a potential limitation: the model was evaluated on requests it had itself generated, introducing a degree of bias into the evaluation pipeline, which reserves further investigation.

Future developments will focus on enhancing the symbiotic dimension of human-robot collaboration, moving toward a more personalized and adaptive interaction. For instance, the robot will be able to learn the operator's preferences over time and proactively suggest tailored mission plans. Conversely, the operator, benefiting from the robot's feedback and performance reports, will refine future requests to optimize surveillance outcomes. Additional updates will address scalability, expanding the system from a single-robot setup to the coordination of a fleet of robotic guards, thereby enabling the operator to issue complex, multi-skill surveillance plans involving multiple agents, with tests conducted in a real interaction environment.

Acknowledgments. This work is part of the ongoing research project *"SymAIbot"*, CUP: H97G22000210007), funded through the *Bando a Cascata* (CODBAN_000525), issued by Rectoral Decree No. 1202 on 29/03/2024 by the University of Bari Aldo Moro, within the framework of the project *"Future Artificial Intelligence Research"* (Project ID: MUR CN/PE00000013). The funding is part of the Call No. 341 dated 15/03/2022 under the National Recovery and Resilience Plan (PNRR), Mission 4, Component 2, Investment 1.3 âĂŞ funded by the European Union âĂŞ *NextGenerationEU*. This work is carried out in collaboration with **Martec srl** and represents an ongoing research effort. The results of this research were partially obtained within the framework of the National Ph.D. Program in Robotics and Intelligent Machines (M. Barbato).

References

1. Ahn, M., et al.: Do as i can, not as i say: grounding language in robotic affordances. arXiv preprint arXiv:2204.01691 (2022)
2. Breazeal, C.: Toward sociable robots. Robot. Auton. Syst. **42**(3–4), 167–175 (2003)
3. Breazeal, C., Kidd, C.D., Thomaz, A.L., Hoffman, G., Berlin, M.: Effects of nonverbal communication on efficiency and robustness in human-robot teamwork. In: 2005 IEEE/RSJ International Conference on Intelligent Robots and Systems, pp. 708–713. IEEE (2005)
4. Brohan, A., et al.: Rt-2: vision-language-action models transfer web knowledge to robotic control. arXiv preprint arXiv:2307.15818 (2023)
5. Brown, T., et al.: Language models are few-shot learners. In: Advances in Neural Information Processing Systems, vol. 33, pp. 1877–1901 (2020)
6. Calvano, M., Curci, A., Lanzilotti, R., Piccinno, A.: Symbiotic AI: What is the role of trustworthiness? (2024)
7. Fisac, J.F., et al.: Pragmatic-pedagogic value alignment. In: Robotics Research: the 18th International Symposium ISRR, pp. 49–57. Springer (2020)
8. Glikson, E., Woolley, A.W.: Human trust in artificial intelligence: review of empirical research. Acad. Manag. Ann. **14**(2), 627–660 (2020)
9. Grazioso, M., Barbato, M., Staffa, M., Mancini, A., Russo, V.: Enhancing human-robot collaboration through the Sairs framework. In: Proceedings of the Human-FrieDndly Robotics Workshop (HFR) (2025)
10. Grazioso, M., Di Bratto, M., Mancini, A., Russo, V.: Towards an explainable argumentation-based dialogue pipeline for conversational recommender systems. In: The 1st Workshop on Risks, Opportunities, and Evaluation of Generative Models in Recommender Systems (ROEGEN@RECSYS'24) (2024)
11. Lewis, P., et al.: Retrieval-augmented generation for knowledge-intensive NLP tasks. In: Advances in Neural Information Processing Systems, vol. 33, pp. 9459–9474 (2020)
12. Licklider, J.C.: Man-computer symbiosis. IRE Trans. Hum. Factors Electron. **1**, 4–11 (1960)
13. Rossi, S., Ferland, F., Tapus, A.: User profiling and behavioral adaptation for HRI: a survey. Pattern Recogn. Lett. **99**, 3–12 (2017)
14. Russo, V., Mancini, A., Grazioso, M., Di Bratto, M.: Graph-based representations of clarification strategies supporting automatic dialogue management. IJCOL. Ital. J. Comput. Linguist. **8**(8-1) (2022)
15. Shinn, N., Cassano, F., Gopinath, A., Narasimhan, K., Yao, S.: Reflexion: Language agents with verbal reinforcement learning. In: Advances in Neural Information Processing Systems, vol. 36, pp. 8634–8652 (2023)
16. Veloso, M.M., Biswas, J., Coltin, B., Rosenthal, S.: Cobots: Robust symbiotic autonomous mobile service robots. In: IJCAI, p. 4423. Citeseer (2015)

The Cobra Effect in Trust Repair: Unintended Consequences of Rebuilding Trust in Human-Robot Collaboration

Russell Perkins[✉], Boris Berkovich, and Paul Robinette

University of Massachusetts Lowell, Lowell, MA 01850, USA
{russell_perkins,boris_berkovich}@student.uml.edu, paul_robinette@uml.edu

Abstract. This paper explores the 'cobra effect' in human-robot collaboration, where interventions intended to improve trust inadvertently lead to worse outcomes. We conducted a controlled six-round CAPTCHA-solving experiment in which participants worked with a QT-Robot. Participants could solve each CAPTCHA themselves or delegate the task to the robot. The robot deliberately failed in rounds 4 and 5, triggering a trust repair strategy. Participants in the control group received a static pre-scripted apology, while those in the experimental group received adaptive apologies that incorporated user feedback. The results showed that adaptive apology led to moderate to large improvements in trust dimensions such as reliability, capability, and transparency. In contrast, static apologies resulted in reduced trust. These findings suggest that apology strategies must be sensitive to context and user perception. In addition, we identify the specific dimensions of trust negatively affected by static apologies, highlighting key areas for designing more effective context-aware trust calibration cues in collaborative robotics.

1 Introduction

As automated systems become more integrated into collaborative human contexts, maintaining and repairing trust after failures has become a critical challenge [4]. Trust is a dynamic, multifaceted construct shaped by human, robot, and environmental factors [6]. We define trust as a *belief, held by the trustor, that the trustee will act to mitigate the risk of the trustor in situations where outcomes are at stake* [16]. Although trust reflects subjective perception, trustworthiness refers to the objective qualities of the system. When these diverge, trust calibration aims to realign user perception with actual performance [10].

Trust violations typically fall into moral or performance categories [1]. Effective repair requires distinguishing between these and tailoring strategies accordingly [14]. When misapplied, repair efforts risk triggering the *cobra effect*, where repeated apologies or excessive transparency can backfire, undermining trust [3]. Trust repair techniques include verbal strategies (apologies, explanations [8]), nonverbal cues (gestures, eye contact [13]), and adaptive communication that integrates user feedback [12]. Apologies have shown promise in restoring trust after robot failures [9], and transparency has helped clarify reasoning and uncertainty [2].

This paper addresses that gap by investigating apologies through the lens of the cobra effect, arguing that adaptive, user-informed strategies may outperform static, scripted ones.

- *H0:* There is no difference in the multidimensional ratings of an adaptive apology versus a static apology.
- *H1:* The static apology will result in a smaller effect of trust repair compared to the adaptive trust calibration strategy.

2 Related Work

The cobra effect, also known as perverse inducement, refers to situations where well-intentioned interventions inadvertently worsen the problem they aim to solve. In the context of trust, these results can occur when repair strategies, such as apologies or transparency, are poorly timed, mismatch user expectations, or lack the necessary cues for effective trust calibration [15].

One consequence of misapplied repair is over-reliance. Apologies and explanations can unintentionally signal competence, leading users to place unwarranted trust in a system. In automotive domains, semi-autonomous systems that apologize for errors have led to premature user reliance, creating safety risks [3]. Similarly, in healthcare, AI systems that express high confidence - even after failure - can influence clinicians to delay judgment [5].

Trust repair can also fail by increasing cognitive load. Complex or excessive transparency may confuse or overwhelm users, particularly in high-stress contexts. This can make the system appear manipulative or opaque rather than helpful, ultimately reducing trust [11,17].

To be effective, trust repair strategies must be well-calibrated. Apologies and explanations should be sincere, contextual, and proportional to the failure. Previous work highlights the effectiveness of adaptive strategies that take into account user feedback [9], as well as explanations tailored to the user's mental model [2].

3 Experimental Design

We recruited 40 college students for an assisted decision-making experiment involving the QT-Robot. Although efforts were made to include participants from nontechnical backgrounds, no type of education was collected. The participants were 60.7% men, 35.7% women and 3.6% transgender men. Racial identities included 51.0% Asian, 31.0% white , 10.7% Hispanic and smaller proportions of people identified as Black or African American, American Indian or Alaskan, Native Hawaiian or Pacific Islander, or without a primary racial group (each 3.4%). The educational background varied, with 25.0% having postgraduate training, 25.0% having some college or associate's degree, 21.4% having a bachelor's degree, and 3.6% reporting no formal education. Participants received a base payment of $15, with performance-based bonuses. Compensation ranged from $15 to $18.50.

To validate the difficulty of the CAPTCHA task, a preliminary study was conducted with 30 online participants. Each solved 30 puzzles and rated them on a 1–10 difficulty scale via a Qualtrics survey. Only puzzles rated 5 or 6 were used in the main study.

3.1 Experimental Setup

Each participant sat at a desk with the QT-Robot and a standard computer setup, including a mouse, keyboard, and screen. Instructions were provided using a scripted protocol to ensure consistency between sessions.

The experiment began with an introduction phase during which the QT-Robot introduced itself verbally by performing a hand wave. Then it explained its role in the collaborative task informing the participant that it was here to help them solve the CAPTCHA and would do so if requested. After the introduction, the participants completed an initial MDMT survey to assess the dispositional trust of the participant towards the robot before starting the CAPTCHA solving task.

The main task consisted of a six-round CAPTCHA game displayed on the computer screen. Each round included a countdown timer that displayed a decreasing dollar value of $0.01 per second. Participants were given the option to either solve the CAPTCHA themselves or allow the QT-Robot to solve it for them. After each round, participants completed a seven-point Likert scale questionnaire assessing their perception of robot trustworthiness, competence, and warmth. At the end of the experiment, participants repeated the MDMT survey to measure changes in trust perception and completed a demographic survey.

3.2 Robot Performance and Apology Mechanism

This study between subjects used a 1 by 2 design to examine how apology strategies affect trust repair after robotic error. The independent variable was the type of apology: static (prescripted) or adaptive (user-informed). Participants were randomly assigned to one of these two conditions.

The QT-Robot followed a fixed performance sequence: correct answers in rounds 1–3, deliberate errors in rounds 4–5, and a correct answer in round 6. This ensured a consistent timing of trust violations among participants.

In the static condition, the robot said, "Apologies for the error in solving the CAPTCHA." In the adaptive condition, it asked for feedback, used the response as input to ChatGPT, and generated a personalized apology. This setup enabled a direct comparison of trust recovery between static and adaptive strategies.

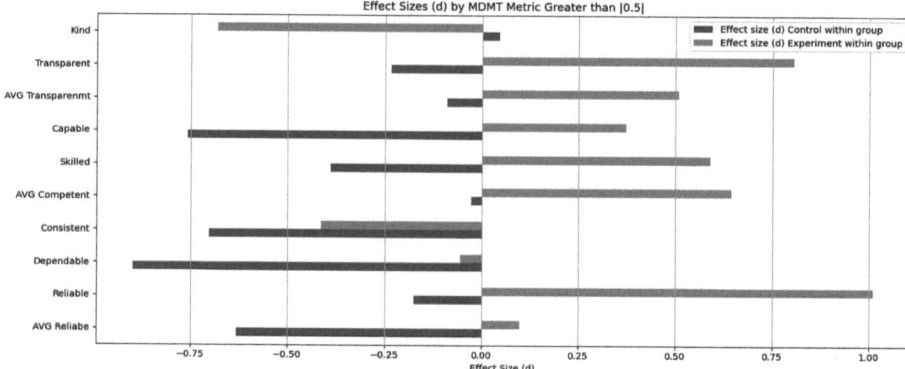

Fig. 1. The effect sizes of the change from the initial MDMT survey to the final MDMT survey. Only Dimensions with an effect size that was greater than 0.5 in either direction are shown here.

4 Results

Our results revealed that the trust dimensions responded differently to adaptive repair strategies. Participants who received adaptive apologies showed significant improvements in trust ratings. The paired t tests indicated increases in *Reliability* ($p = 0.024$, df = 14), *Transparency* ($p = 0.015$, df = 12), and *Capability* ($p = 0.024$, df = 11), suggesting improved robot perceptions after intervention.

Because p-values are sensitive to sample size, we also report Cohen's d to assess the magnitude of the effect. *Reliability* ($d = 1.01$) and *Transparency* ($d = 0.81$) showed large effects, while *Skilled* ($d = 0.59$) and *Dependability* ($d = 0.51$) had moderate effects. Group-level dimensions—*Averaged Transparency* ($d = 0.51$) and *Averaged Competence* ($d = 0.64$)—also improved moderately. Figure 1 displays these effect sizes.

In contrast, participants in the static trust calibration condition showed significant declines in trust. Effect size analysis revealed large negative effects for *Dependability* ($d = -0.90$), *Consistency* ($d = -0.70$), and *Capability* ($d = -0.76$). Additionally, *Averaged Reliability* declined moderately ($d = -0.63$), indicating a broader erosion of performance-based trust. These findings suggest that static apologies may actively undermine trust. Figure 2 illustrates these differences.

Based on these results, we reject the null hypothesis. It is important to note that the researchers did think that the adaptive trust calibration. would perform better than the static apology; however, we did not anticipate that a static apology would have negative effects.

5 Discussion

Our findings show that not all trust repair strategies are equally effective. Adaptive apologies improved trust in reliability, skill, capability, and transparency,

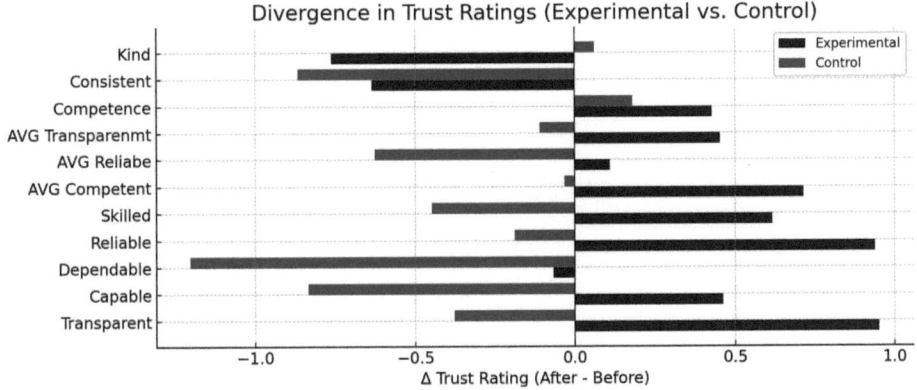

Fig. 2. Horizontal divergence plot of the subcategories of MDMT that are shown in Fig. 1. The bars show the change in rating from the initial MDMT to the post experiment MDMT.

especially compared to the static or declining trust observed in the control group, highlighting the value of context-based repair. The nature of the task also influenced trust dynamics: because CAPTCHA solving is low-risk, participants likely judged the robot on performance rather than moral dimensions. This aligns with previous research suggesting that robots are not viewed as moral agents unless they commit explicit moral violations [7]. In particular, transparency, classified as a moral trait, was the only moral dimension showing a large change, possibly due to performance-related signals or shifting cultural norms shaped by AI systems such as Alexa and ChatGPT.

These results raise a key design challenge: How can robots detect which dimension of trust is compromised and apply targeted repairs? Although fine-grained prediction remains difficult, distinguishing moral violations from performance-based violations appears both feasible and useful. Calibrating apology strategies also requires precision. Over-apologizing in low-stakes contexts can frustrate users and reduce trust. Timing and relevance are critical. In addition, more research is needed on failed or counterproductive strategies, the cobra effect, as the field tends to under-report what does not work. Finally, while some dimensions declined, overall trust remained relatively high (4–5 on a 7-point scale), suggesting that specific drops do not equate to total trust breakdown.

6 Limitations

Although the results are promising, several limitations should be noted. The study involved only 40 college students, limiting generalizability to broader populations such as older adults or children. The single-session short interaction may not reflect the long-term trust dynamics. Furthermore, the task was simple and low risk, with limited moral or emotional stakes, which may explain why the changes in trust were concentrated in performance-related dimensions. Different patterns may emerge in more complex or higher-risk scenarios.

7 Conclusion and Future Work

This study examined apology strategies for trust repair in human-robot interaction through the lens of the cobra effect, where interventions meant to improve trust can unintentionally worsen it. We compared static, scripted apologies with adaptive, user-informed ones. Adaptive strategies led to moderate to large improvements in competence-related dimensions (e.g., reliability, capability), while static strategies often resulted in declines. These findings suggest that effective trust repair requires more than just apologizing: it requires sensitivity to context, user expectations, and the nature of the error.

Our results reinforce the multidimensional nature of trust. Adaptive strategies impacted performance based dimensions but had limited effect on moral trust, highlighting the need for dimension specific repair mechanisms. As such, future systems should aim to detect which trust dimension has been violated and respond accordingly.

Building on these findings, our future work focuses on developing predictive models that integrate behavioral, physiological, and task-based signals to detect trust breakdowns. We aim to distinguish between moral and performance-related violations and to identify the optimal timing for intervention. Ongoing efforts include uncertainty-aware trust models to guide robot behavior and strategy prediction tools to minimize unnecessary corrections as users progress toward valid solutions.

Acknowledgments. This study was funded by NSF IIS-2112633.

Disclosure of Interests. The authors have no competing interests to declare that are relevant to the content of this article.

References

1. Baker, A.L., Phillips, E.K., Ullman, D., Keebler, J.R.: Toward an understanding of trust repair in human-robot interaction: Current research and future directions. ACM Trans. Interact. Intell. Syst. **8**(4) (2018). https://doi.org/10.1145/3181671
2. Chen, J., Procci, K., Boyce, M., Wright, J., Garcia, A., Barnes, M.: Situation awareness–based agent transparency (2014)
3. Cummings, M.: Automation bias in intelligent time critical decision support systems. In: Collection of Technical Papers - AIAA 1st Intelligent Systems Technical Conference, vol. 2 (2004). https://doi.org/10.2514/6.2004-6313
4. Desai, M., Stubbs, K., Steinfeld, A., Yanco, H.A.: Creating trustworthy robots: lessons and inspirations from automated systems. In: Proceedings of the AISB Convention (2013)
5. Grote, T., Berens, P.: Uncertainty, evidence, and the integration of machine learning into medical practice. J. Med. Philos. Forum Bioethics Philos. Med. **48**(1), 84–97 (2023). DOIurlhttps://doi.org/10.1093/jmp/jhac034

6. Khavas, Z.R., Ahmadzadeh, R., Robinette, P.: Modeling trust in human-robot interaction: a survey. CoRR abs/2011.04796 (2020). https://arxiv.org/abs/2011.04796
7. Khavas, Z.R., Kotturu, M.R., Azadeh, R., Robinette, P.: Do humans have different expectations regarding humans and robots' morality?*. In: 2024 33rd IEEE International Conference on Robot and Human Interactive Communication (ROMAN), pp. 1126–1133 (2024). https://doi.org/10.1109/RO-MAN60168.2024.10731315
8. Kim, P.H., Dirks, K.T., Cooper, C.D., Ferrin, D.L.: When more blame is better than less: the implications of internal vs. external attributions for the repair of trust after a competence- vs. integrity-based trust violation. Organ. Behav. Hum. Decis. Process. **99**(1), 49–65 (2006). https://doi.org/10.1016/j.obhdp.2005.07.002. https://www.sciencedirect.com/science/article/pii/S0749597805000907
9. Kohn, S.C., Quinn, D., Pak, R., Visser, E.J.D., Shaw, T.H.: Trust repair strategies with self-driving vehicles: an exploratory study. vol. 2 (2018). https://doi.org/10.1177/1541931218621254
10. Lee, J.D., See, K.A.: Trust in automation: designing for appropriate reliance. Hum. Factors **46**(1), 50–80 (2004)
11. Paas, F., Sweller, J.: Implications of cognitive load theory for multimedia learning. Cambridge Handb. Multimedia Learn. **27**, 27–42 (2014)
12. Robinette, P., Howard, A.M., Wagner, A.R.: Timing Is Key for Robot Trust Repair. Presented at the (2015). https://doi.org/10.1007/978-3-319-25554-5_57
13. Robinette, P., Howard, A.M., Wagner, A.R.: Effect of robot performance on human-robot trust in time-critical situations. IEEE Trans. Hum. Mach. Syst. **47** (2017). https://doi.org/10.1109/THMS.2017.2648849
14. Tolmeijer, S., Nitsch, V., Ferguson, L.S., André, E., Rogers, W.A., Schmidt, A.: Taxonomy of trust-relevant failures and mitigation strategies. In: Proceedings of the 2020 ACM/IEEE International Conference on Human-Robot Interaction (HRI 2020), pp. 3–12. ACM (2020). https://doi.org/10.1145/3319502.3374793
15. de Visser, E.J., Cohen, M., Freedy, A., Parasuraman, R.: A design methodology for trust cue calibration in cognitive agents. In: Harris, D. (ed.) Engineering Psychology and Cognitive Ergonomics. Applications and Services, Lecture Notes in Computer Science, vol. 8532, pp. 251–262. Springer (2014). https://doi.org/10.1007/978-3-319-07458-0_24
16. Wagner, A.R., Arkin, R.C.: Recognizing situations that demand trust. In: 2011 RO-MAN, pp. 7–14 (2011). https://doi.org/10.1109/ROMAN.2011.6005228
17. Yu, L., Li, Y.: Artificial intelligence decision-making transparency and employees’ trust: the parallel multiple mediating effect of effectiveness and discomfort. Behavioral Sciences **12**(5) (2022). https://doi.org/10.3390/bs12050127. https://www.mdpi.com/2076-328X/12/5/127

ARIS: A Socially Assistive Robot with Emotional Monitoring and Haptic Feedback for Prosthetic Hand Adaptation and Hand Rehabilitation

Alexandra Espinoza, Sebastian Caballa(✉), and Dante A. Elias

Pontificia Universidad Católica del Perú, Lima 15088, Peru
scaballa@pucp.edu.pe

Abstract. This work presents a socially assistive robotic device designed to support hand rehabilitation by recognizing facial expressions and speech, which trigger interactive responses from the robot. The system integrates facial emotion detection, voice recognition, haptic feedback, motion, and visual expression to foster user engagement. It is intended for children, adults, and older adults, aiming to improve adherence to prosthetic adaptation or hand rehabilitation processes. Preliminary tests indicate that the system is easy to use, provides valuable support to rehabilitation specialists, and promotes empathetic interaction with users.

Keywords: Robot-assisted therapy · Emotion recognition · Social Robotics · Hand rehabilitation · Occupational therapy

1 Introduction

Individuals with physical disabilities who require hand prostheses face multiple challenges, not only in regaining motor skills, but also at the emotional level. The adaptation to the use of prostheses often leads to experiences of frustration, anxiety, and emotional distress, significantly affecting the user's quality of life [1]. Occupational therapists provide emotional support during rehabilitation sessions; however, the limited availability of specialists and poor accessibility to these services often result in low treatment adherence [2]. Even with modern technology, rehabilitation systems remain exclusively focused on physical motor development [3].

2 Design Process

The ideation process was guided by the Design Thinking methodology, which involved exploring existing robotic solutions, understanding the user and their needs, and proposing a viable solution to be prototyped.

2.1 Previous Emotional Technologies

Robotic systems have increasingly been incorporated into rehabilitation practices to support both physical and emotional recovery processes. NAOTherapist, for instance, guides sessions through imitation games but may negatively impact user proprioception, leading to anxiety and frustration [4]. This approach was crucial in evaluating the interaction between patients and the robot during rehabilitation sessions, allowing a better understanding of user comfort and engagement. Other developments, such as the RoPi robot, provide emotional support in hospital settings through visual expressions and body movements [5]. These technologies were useful in assessing how patients react to emotional support provided by the robot during rehabilitation activities.

2.2 Interview with Specialist

The expertise of an occupational therapist was key to understanding the challenges of hand rehabilitation and prosthetic adaptation. Through a focused interview, critical issues such as low treatment adherence, limited follow up at home, and the psychological impact of prosthesis use were identified. The specialist also emphasized that each patient case is unique, even with the same diagnosis. These insights informed the definition of key technical and usability requirements for the robot's design. Functionally, the system should record patient progress and provide clear, emotionally supportive feedback. In terms of usability, it must offer customizable feedback (verbal, visual, or haptic), an accessible interface for diverse users, short session modes with breaks, and suitability for home use. These elements are intended to ensure the robot's effectiveness in real settings.

2.3 Concept Development

Insights from a rehabilitation specialist were translated into technical and usability requirements to guide the development of an accessible and empathetic solution. To address challenges in detecting negative emotional patterns in real time [6], a facial and voice recognition system was proposed to support therapy. To foster emotional connection and avoid intimidation, the robot was designed with soft contours and a teddy bear inspired appearance [7]. Figure 1 illustrates the evolution of the robot's design. Finally, the final 270mm model was developed in Autodesk Fusion and optimized for additive manufacturing.

3 Robot Specifications

3.1 Hardware

The robot was built around a Raspberry Pi 4B as the central processing unit. It includes two SG90 micro servomotors controlled by a PCA9685 module for arm movement, a DRV2605L controller with a vibration motor for localized haptic feedback, and two 1.3" SH1106 OLED displays to visually express emotions through the robot's eyes. All components were assembled within a plastic enclosure; Fig. 2 shows the internal layout of the electronic modules.

Fig. 1. Evolution of the robot design from early technical sketches to the final bear inspired version.

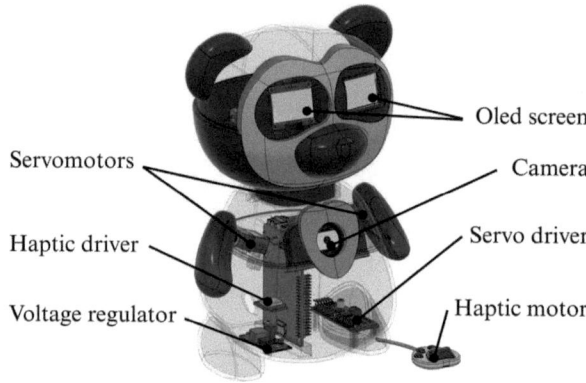

Fig. 2. Internal distribution of the robot's electronic components. Compact electronics layout inside the robot.

3.2 Software

The software was developed in Python 3 and executed on a Raspberry Pi 4B. For real-time facial recognition, the system uses the DeepFace and OpenCV libraries to detect faces and classify them into seven basic emotions: happiness, anger, disgust, sadness, fear, surprise, and neutral. Voice recognition was integrated using the Vosk library, which employs a pre-trained Spanish model to capture real-time speech. Additionally, an automatic logging system was implemented to store, in .txt files, the percentage of time each emotion was detected, recognized speech content, and relevant alerts for the therapist. These features enable empathetic interaction and provide quantifiable data for clinical monitoring.

3.3 Interaction

The robot interacts with the user through eye movements displayed on OLED screens and arm movements controlled by servomotors, activated when an emotion is detected for at least 4 s. If no dominant emotion is recognized, a *neutral* state is assumed. To express emotional states, the robot uses sequences of eye images that simulate basic expressions, promoting more natural and emotionally supportive interaction (see Fig. 3), emphasizing that a series of intermediate images are included between the basic expressions.

Fig. 3. Representation of the robot's eye principal expressions: a) concerned, b) joyful, c) sad, d) playful or cheerful, e) curious, f) expectant or anticipatory expression.

Additionally, a vibration motor is included to subtly alert the therapist about persistent negative emotions, supporting emotional monitoring during the rehabilitation session. Table 1 summarizes the robot's responses according to the detected emotion.

Table 1. Robot actions based on detected emotions.

Emotion	Visual expression (eyes)	Arm movement
Angry	Half-open, relaxed eyes	Light and rhythmic movement
Fear	Wide eyes that gradually relax	Gentle swaying
Sad	Focused eyes with slow blinking, gaze downward	No movement
Neutral	Blinking with lateral gaze	No movement
Surprise	Expressive eyes with curiosity	No movement
Happy	Cheerful eyes with a soft smile	Upward movement (celebration)
Disgust	Soft and relaxed blinking	No movement

4 Results

4.1 Prototype

The 3D model was adapted for fabrication through segmented printing, dividing the design into 20 independent sections that allow for modular assembly. Specific dimensional tolerances were incorporated into components with relative movement, along with form-fit joints to facilitate assembly and ensure structural stability using M3 screws. The prototype was manufactured using PLA filament on a Bambu Lab X1C printer, with an estimated material usage of 600 grams and a total print time of approximately 20 h. The final product, including 3D printed parts, electronic components, and assembly, had an estimated cost of $188.

4.2 Preliminary Evaluation

A preliminary evaluation was conducted with two participants: an occupational therapist and an undergraduate student, through 10 min sessions aimed at assessing the system's functional behavior, emotion recognition, and capacity for empathetic interaction. Participants simulated facial expressions (happiness, sadness, and surprise), triggering corresponding eye animations, arm movements, and haptic feedback (without the final motor casing), as illustrated in Figure 4. Although no quantitative analysis was performed at this stage, the evaluation was documented through video recordings, observational notes, the robot emotion report, and post session feedback. Upon reviewing the records, ARIS demonstrated appropriate responses in over 70% of the cases, particularly for easily recognizable emotions such as happiness and sadness. The therapist emphasized the system's clinical potential and suggested improvements in animation smoothness, motor noise reduction, and sensitivity to lighting conditions. She also recommended the inclusion of session alerts, the use of lighter color schemes, and the structured recording of negative emotional responses. Importantly, she recognized ARIS's value as an emotional support tool with potential for autonomous use at home and noted its alignment with functional assessment tools like the SHAP protocol [8], which she applies in upper-limb prosthetic rehabilitation.

Fig. 4. Assembled and functional robot used for preliminary testing with a user simulating facial expressions to evaluate the robot's emotion recognition.

5 Conclusions

This work presents an interactive robotic system designed to support hand rehabilitation and prosthetic adaptation through facial expression recognition, speech processing, and haptic interaction. Preliminary validations showed positive user responses, emphasizing ease of use and the system's potential to improve treatment adherence. Future developments include enabling out-of-session interaction through reminders and goal tracking, integrating the system into telemedicine, and involving family members as emotional support agents. Collaboration with clinical psychologists will guide the design of validated emotional response protocols. Additionally, evaluations in more realistic environments will be conducted, alongside the development of intervention and data collection protocols to assess therapeutic effectiveness. Technical improvements and new features for upper-limb mobility therapy will also be implemented to ensure robust operation. Altogether, these enhancements aim to consolidate the system as an accessible, adaptable, and emotionally engaging tool for continuous, user-centered rehabilitation.

References

1. Ali, S., Haider, S.K.F.: Psychological adjustment to amputation: variations on the bases of sex, age and cause of limb loss. J. Ayub Med. Coll. Abbottabad **29**(2), 303–307 (2017). https://pubmed.ncbi.nlm.nih.gov/28718253/
2. van Stormbroek, K.: 'The hand belongs to someone': a therapist perspective on patient compliance. S. Afr. J. Occup. Ther. **50**(3), 30–39 (2020)
3. Rehabilitation, S.J.: How physical therapy aids in recovery after an amputation. St. James Rehabilitation and Healthcare Center (2025). https://www.stjamesrehab.com/blog/how-physical-therapy-aids-in-recovery-after-an-amputation
4. Pulido, J.C., González,J.C., Suárez-Mejías, C., et al.: Evaluating the child–robot interaction of the NAOTherapist platform in pediatric rehabilitation. Int. J. Social Robot. **9**(3), 343–358 (2017). https://doi.org/10.1007/s12369-017-0402-2
5. Caballa, S., Lizano, D., Aranda, M., Zegarra, D.: RoPi: robotic assistant for the emotional support of hospitalized children for burns. In: Proceedings HRI 2023: Companion of the 2023 ACM/IEEE International Conference on Human-Robot Interaction, pp. 845–848 (2023). https://doi.org/10.1145/3568294.3580198
6. Jo, S.-H., et al.: Psychiatric understanding and treatment of patients with amputations. Yeungnam Univ. J. Med. **38**(3), 194–201 (2021)
7. Chin, M.G., Sims, V., Clark, B., Lopez, G.: Measuring individual differences in anthropomorphism toward machines and animals. Proc. Hum. Factors Ergon. Soc. Annu. Meet. **48**(11), 1252–1255 (2004)
8. Light, C.M., Chappell, P.H., Kyberd, P.J.: Establishing a standardized clinical assessment tool of pathologic and prosthetic hand function: normative data, reliability, and validity. Arch. Phys. Med. Rehabil. **83**(6), 776–783 (2002)

Role-Adaptive Communication Framework with Large Language Models for Multi-robot Systems

Junhu Song, Minwoo Lee, Joey Back, Peter Cheong, and Ho Seok Ahn(✉)

Department of Electrical, Computer and Software Engineering, CARES, The University of Auckland, Auckland, New Zealand
{json941,mlee633,jbac208,pche314}@aucklanduni.ac.nz,
hs.ahn@auckland.ac.nz

Abstract. This paper proposes a centralized role-based architecture that utilizes Large Language Models (LLMs) to enable adaptive communication systems. The framework implements dynamic role-based LLM assignment, where robots receive specific language models based on their functional identity and communication objectives. A user study evaluating different LLM configurations demonstrates that role-specific LLM significantly enhances interaction clarity, contextual awareness, and perceived human likeness compared to uniform deployment. These findings establish that multi-model LLM integration improves collaborative social robots' authenticity and functional efficiency in SHMR systems.

Keywords: Role-Adaptive System · Multi-Agent Systems (MAS) · Single-Human Multi-Robot (SHMR)

1 Introduction

Social robots have transformed from task-oriented machines to interactive agents capable of meaningful human engagement through dialogue, gestures, and adaptive behavior [1,2]. Advanced platforms such as Pepper, Sophia, and Nao have demonstrated sustained social engagement across hospitality, healthcare, and education [3–6]. However, coordinating multiple specialized robots with distinct roles presents significant challenges in maintaining coherent interaction flows across diverse platforms. This has catalyzed Single-Human Multi-Robot (SHMR) systems, where specialized robots collaborate to provide comprehensive service experiences [7]. Robots must dynamically adapt communication styles when collaborating with humans and other platforms, necessitating role-adaptive systems that transition between professional, empathetic, and task-oriented interaction modes.

Current SHMR implementations predominantly rely on prescribed dialogues and uniform communication strategies, failing to leverage specialized roles of heterogeneous platforms [8,9]. While Large Language Model (LLM) advancements offer dynamic, role-aware communication solutions, the critical challenge lies in determining whether robots should share a single model for consistency or be assigned different models based on their specialized roles and interaction contexts.

This paper introduces a centralized role-based communication framework leveraging multiple LLMs to enable adaptive SHMR interactions. Our approach assigns specialized language models based on functional roles while maintaining coordination through centralized architecture. Evaluation using EveR-4 H22 and ChatBox platforms demonstrates that strategic role-based LLM deployment significantly enhances interaction clarity and perceived naturalness compared to uniform configurations.

The paper is structured as follows: Sect. 2 introduces the role-adaptive framework integrating LLMs with hardware platforms. Section 4 presents a user study evaluating different LLM configurations. Section 5 concludes with insights and future directions for multi-robot communication systems.

2 Role-Adaptive Communication Framework

2.1 Centeralized Architecture

To address coordinated multi-robot communication challenges, we adopted a centralized communication architecture that enables flexible role-based LLM assignment and heterogeneous robot platform integration. Unlike decentralized frameworks, this centralized approach provides the essential bridging structure for dynamically pairing specialized robot platforms with appropriate LLM models based on functional requirements [10,11]. This structure allows seamless switching between different LLMs for individual robots while maintaining unified coordination, enabling optimal matching of robot capabilities with specialized language models for enhanced role-specific performance.

The proposed system is organized around a central server mediating communication between robot clients, human users, and backend processing modules. As shown in Fig. 1, the modular architecture integrates client-side robotic agents, server-side orchestration, and multiple LLM backends accessible through role-based selection. WebSocket protocols enable real-time, low-latency bidirectional message exchange with asynchronous execution supporting concurrent multi-client interaction with different LLM configurations.

2.2 Communication Protocol

Each robot registers with the central server upon connection, transmitting its unique identifier, functional role, and interaction preferences to a dynamic session registry for context-aware coordination. The system processes user input through role-based API calls to appropriate LLMs, leveraging the shared 20-message conversation buffer to maintain conversational continuity across specialized robotic roles. Generated responses include textual content and auxiliary metadata tailored to each robot's functional identity. Robot clients vocalize responses using

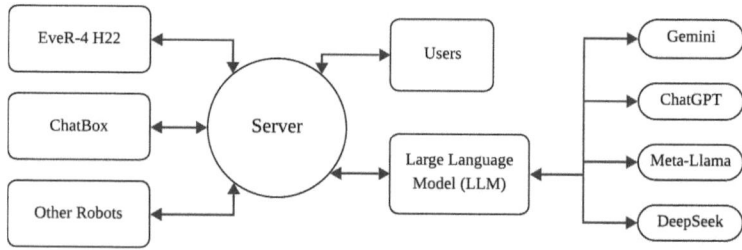

Fig. 1. System Overview Illustrating Server-Mediated Communication between Users, Robot Agents, and Multiple LLMs for SHMR Interaction.

onboard text-to-speech while executing corresponding non-verbal behaviors to augment verbal communication. This configuration ensures scalable operation while maintaining consistent behavior across all connected agents.

2.3 Role-Adaptive Large Language Model (LLM)

Given the heterogeneity in robots and interaction contexts, employing a universal communication strategy can be limiting. For instance, a front-desk receptionist robot requires socially engaging dialogue, while a security robot demands brevity and authority. This necessitates dynamically adapting communication styles based on functional identity and contextual information. Recent LLM advancements have enabled such adaptability, but most systems rely on single pre-trained models, limiting cross-domain applicability [12,13]. Single-model configurations often underperform in cases requiring domain-specific expertise or stylistic variation, underscoring the need for a multimodal approach to robotic communication.

To address this, we introduce a modular LLM integration framework where in each robot can dynamically select from a range of language models, including ChatGPT, Gemini, DeepSeek, and Meta-Llama, depending on interaction context and task requirements. The central server routes requests to the selected model, optimizing for accuracy, relevance, and tone. Additionally, the framework supports the input of user-defined personality parameters into each robot's communication policy. These parameters shape the LLM's behavior to generate responses that reflect the robot's intended role, persona, and affective characteristics. This role alignment enhances contextual coherence, leading to more intuitive and clearer human-robot interactions in SHMR environments.

2.4 Hardware Overview

EveR-4 H22 is a high-fidelity humanoid robotic head featuring 22 servomotors designed for sophisticated emotional expression [5]. Its three-layer construction enables fluid, life-like facial expressions, making it ideal for primary interaction roles requiring complex emotional communication (Fig. 2 and Table 1).

Fig. 2. ChatBox is shown displaying both "Greeting" and "Neutral" expressions, while the EveR-4 H22 robot portrays "Surprised" and "Angry" facial expressions.

ChatBox is a compact, autonomous social robot with 12 degrees of freedom, focusing on high-impact perceptual regions like eyes, eyebrows, and ears. Its self-contained design makes it suitable for companion roles and interactive guidance where continuous availability is prioritized.

3 Experiment: Multi-agent LLM Evaluation

3.1 Experiment Methods

To evaluate the effectiveness of different LLM configurations in multi-agent robotic systems and assess how various models influence perceived interaction quality in collaborative scenarios, we conducted a user study with 20 participants (8 female, 12 male, aged 20-29) from diverse academic and professional backgrounds. The experiment employed a hotel service failure scenario where participants initiated interactions using predefined text to EveR-4 H22 (receptionist), then observed collaborative problem-solving between both robots, with ChatBox functioning as the room-cleaning coordinator.

Four experimental conditions tested different LLM configurations: (1) ChatGPT (GPT-4o-mini), (2) Google Gemini (Gemini-2.0), (3) DeepSeek (deep seek-r1), and (4) Meta-Llama (llama-3.3-70b). Each participant observed all conditions in randomized order, evaluating interactions across four criteria: clarity, contextual awareness, problem resolution, and human-likeness using a 5-point Likert scale.

3.2 Results

The experiments revealed distinct performance characteristics for each LLM.

DeepSeek achieved the highest overall performance, effectively balancing emotional engagement with procedural clarity. Participants consistently rated this configuration as the most natural and effective for both robotic roles.

ChatGPT demonstrated consistently high ratings with professional, composed tones and clear resolutions. The consistency between robots was perceived as coordinated teamwork, making it suitable for reliable service interactions.

Table 1. Comparison of LLM Configurations in Multi-Agent Service Recovery

LLM Models	Clarity (%)	Context (%)	Resolution (%)	Human-like (/5)	Key Characteristics
ChatGPT (GPT-4o-mini)	82	78	85	4.1	Professional, balanced empathy
Google Gemini (Gemini-2.0)	76	72	79	3.8	Emotionally expressive, empathetic
DeepSeek (deepseek-r1)	84	81	87	4.3	Balanced performance, yet empathetic
Meta-Llama (llama-3.3-70b)	79	70	74	3.2	Task-focused, minimal emotional engagement

Google Gemini exhibited high emotional expressiveness but received mixed responses due to verbosity hindering efficiency. The configuration proved most effective when prioritizing emotional reassurance over task completion.

Meta-Llama produced direct, task-focused responses but received lower ratings for emotional engagement. While participants appreciated efficiency, the lack of expressive language reduced perceived empathy, making it suitable for scenarios prioritizing rapid completion over emotional connection.

3.3 Discussion and System Implications

The experimental findings highlight distinct communicative strengths across LLMs, reinforcing the value of role-based deployment. Participants consistently differentiated between configurations and expressed preferences for models balancing task efficiency with emotional intelligence.

Our centralized framework capitalizes on model-specific strengths by assigning LLMs according to functional roles. ChatGPT's professionalism suits reception tasks, while Gemini's expressiveness enhances emotionally sensitive interactions. Aligning EveR-4's facial expressiveness with emotionally rich models, and pairing ChatBox's design with balanced models exemplifies specialization advantages over uniformity. The architecture scaled effectively, handling concurrent LLM requests without degradation. Role-specific assignment improved contextual coherence, demonstrating potential for adaptive, scalable communication in SHMR environments.

4 Conclusion

This paper presented a centralized role-adaptive communication framework enabling heterogeneous robots to interact using specialized LLMs tailored to their functional identities. The findings establish that strategic multi-model LLM integration significantly enhances robot performance and system coherence, with participants recognizing improved interaction naturalness. The centralized architecture enables dynamic model selection while maintaining coordination, representing an advancement in multi-agent robotic communication.

Future work will explore adaptive LLMs for long-term integration, incorporating Retrieval-Augmented Generation (RAG) and reinforcement learning for enhanced role-specific adaptation. Expanding the evaluation to larger populations and assessing real-world deployment scenarios will support contextual, intelligent, and scalable communication systems.

Acknowledgment. This work was supported by the Industrial Fundamental Technology Development Program (20023495, Development of behaviour-oriented HRI AI technology for long-term interaction between service robots and users) funded by the Ministry of Trade, Industry & Energy (MOTIE, Korea), and the Smart Ideas (UOA2493, Developing a Reo Turi Interpreter for Ngāti Turi / Sign Language Interpreter Using Weighted Multimodal Network for Mahuta ki Tai) funded by the Ministry of Business, Innovation & Employment (MBIE, New Zealand). Ho Seok Ahn* is the corresponding author.

References

1. Street, C., et al.: Formal modelling for multi-robot systems under uncertainty. Curr. Robot. Rep. **4**, 55–64 (2023)
2. Breazeal, C.: Toward sociable robots. Robot. Auton. Syst. **42**(3–4), 167–175 (2003)
3. Tan, X.Z., et al.: From one to another: how robot-robot interaction affects users' perceptions following a transition between robots, pp. 114–122 (2019)
4. Nestorov, N., et al.: Aspects of socially assistive robots design for dementia care. In: 2014 IEEE 27th International Symposium on Computer-Based Medical Systems, pp. 396–400 (2014)
5. Johanson, D., et al.: Smiling and use of first-name by a healthcare receptionist robot: effects on user perceptions, attitudes, and behaviours. Paladyn, J. Behav. Robot. **11**, 40–51 (2020)
6. Ragno, L., et al.: Application of social robots in healthcare: review on characteristics, requirements, technical solutions. Sensors (Basel) **23**(15), 6820 (2023)
7. Fraune, M.R., et al.: Effects of robot-human versus robot-robot behavior and entitativity on anthropomorphism and willingness to interact. Comput. Hum. Behav. **105**, 106220 (2020)
8. Research Outreach. Social robots: a new perspective in healthcare. Research Outreach (2025)
9. Bramblett, L., et al.: Coordinated multi-agent exploration, rendezvous, and task allocation in unknown environments with limited connectivity. In: Proceedings of the IEEE International Robotics and Automation Symposium (IRAS), pp. 1–8 (2022)
10. Jamshidpey, A., et al.: Centralization vs. decentralization in multi-robot coverage: Ground robots under UAV supervision (2024)
11. Mas, I., Kitts, C.: Centralized and decentralized multi-robot control methods using the cluster space control framework. In: 2010 IEEE/ASME International Conference on Advanced Intelligent Mechatronics, pp. 115–122 (2010)

12. Fron, C., Korn, O.: A short history of the perception of robots and automata from antiquity to modern times. In: Korn, O. (ed.) Social Robots: Technological, Societal and Ethical Aspects of Human-Robot Interaction. Human-Computer Interaction Series. Springer, Cham (2019)
13. Itoh, K., et al.: Behavior model of humanoid robots based on operant conditioning. In: 5th IEEE-RAS International Conference on Humanoid Robots, pp. 220–225 (2005)

Affected by Soft Robots: Insights into Social Relations with Soft Robots

Pat Treusch[1](✉) and Jonas Jørgensen[2]

[1] Department of Design, Media and Educational Science, IDMU and Danish Institute of Advanced Studies (DIAS), University of Southern, Kolding, Denmark
pat@sdu.dk
[2] SDU Soft Robotics/SDU Biorobotics, The Mærsk Mc-Kinney Møller Institute, University of Southern, Odense, Denmark

Abstract. The goal of this short paper is to open a discussion on the affective potential of nonanthropomorphic soft social robots. Bringing together engineering and design with feminist science and technology studies (FSTS), we seek to foster a re-vision of the relation between affects, materials, shape, and function in social robotics. To do so, we firstly present an auto-ethnographic encounter with a soft robot and describe and analyze the affective experience of this encounter. Secondly, we contextualize this narrative and analysis in relation to outcomes of human-robot interaction studies on soft social robots. Finally, drawing on these insights, we discuss the nature and potential of affective and social relations with soft robots that go beyond the anthropocentric interaction scheme traditionally applied in social robotics.

Keywords: Soft Robotics · Affects · Human-Robot Interaction · Non-anthropomorphic Social Robots

1 Introduction

What if the key element of a robot's design was not its functionality, but its affective potential? And if so, what would this imply and require – on the level of the material design, but also on that of conceptualizing, designing and realizing interactive skills?

In this short paper, we want to give impulses to further foster discussions in social robotics on the relation between affects, design, and HRI with an emphasis on the experience of soft materials at the human-robot interface. We take an interdisciplinary perspective that brings together the engineering of soft robots with critical, that is, feminist science and technology studies (FSTS) with a focus on human-centered design processes to exemplarily delve into the affective dimenions of experiencing soft robots as social robots. We are convinced that a re-vision of the relation between affects, materials, and shape and function at the robot-human interface could enhance sustainable relations between humans and robots. Adhering to the format of the short paper, delivering points of departure for the envisioned re-vision will be our focus.

We will present 1. the auto-ethnographic encounter of the first author with a soft robot at the SDU Soft Robotics lab, Odense, co-directed by the second author, describing and analyzing the affective experience of this encounter, 2. a contextualization of this encounter in relation to the second author's HRI studies on soft robotics, and finally 3. draw from these empirical examples in a discussion of the nature and potential of social relations with soft robots that go beyond the anthropocentric interaction scheme traditionally applied in social robotics. This short paper is the first collaboration between the two co-authors and we regrad this as a start to deepen interdisciplinary conversations on affects, design, and interactive social robots that we also regard as a start to future collaborations on these topics, involving emprical case studies.

2   A Method of Opening up the Interdisciplinary Conversation: Bringing Feminist Science and Technology Studies, Soft Robotics, and Affects Together

FSTS is a heterogenous field. We draw on strands of FSTS that are interested in researching human-machine relations and which understand these relations as constantly emerging and transforming. In her ground-laying work on human-robot relations, Lucy Suchman [1] points out the ways in which the "elements" of "embodiment, emotion, and sociality" define the relation between humans and robots. These three elements have been themes of robotics since the 1990s and are highly interwoven: it is the robot's embodiment and affective behaviors in an environment that condition its sociality. However, as Suchman (ibid.) further points out, interweaving these elements in imagining, designing and realizing a potentially sociable robot, constitutes a relating between human and machine that pivots around relations of "sameness and difference across (and within) the categories of humans, animals, and machines". Our account of FSTS focuses on processes and practices of relating and the drawing and re-drawing of the boundaries between the categories of human and machine.

Furthermore, acknowledging that human-robot relations are always in the making, FSTS helps us to conceptualize human-robot interaction (HRI) as a cultural and bodily practice that involves more than a robot and a human at the interface. Echoing our past work [2], we consider soft robotics to be not just a technical, but also an aesthetic and affective formation. It requires other modes of ontological construction than positivist and technoscientific approaches of biorobotics [3] to actualize its full potential.

As Suchman [4] underlines: "the laboratory robot's life is inextricably infused with its inherited materialities and with the ongoing—or truncated—labours of its affiliated humans." Along these lines, we make all three, the inherited materialities, truncated labors, and affiliated humans the focus of our exploration of the affective experience. The materialities include the robot's and humans' embodiments as much as the material infrastructure in which they are embedded. The phrasing of inherited materialities points towards the socio-cultural meanings that are ingrained into and produced by these materialities. With respect to soft robotics, this includes Western cultural notions of 'soft' as a stereotypically feminine trait, as reflected in, e.g., the historical reception and description of women's paintings as being 'soft' and also explicitly critically reworked in the 1960s and 1970s tradition of feminist soft sculpture [5]. But equally the ecological, material conditions and relations of production underlying the manufacture of soft materials such as silicone.

Affiliated humans is a term that underlines first that HRI is enabled and realized through the efforts of several persons, who interact with the robot, and second that the persons involved take a specific stance towards the robot. They become affiliated with their robot. This affiliation exceeds a relation of, for instance, pure maintenance, but rather includes a host of different labors that also encompass affective labors such as acquiring a feeling for the robot specifically and more generally to practice care towards the robot (cf. [6, 7]). We contemplate HRI fundamentally as an affective encounter, that is an encounter ingrained with affects. By highlighting the affective dimensions of the human-robot encounter, we make them a core tool for a conceptual revision of interaction with social robots. In the next section, we will further present our account of affects in HRI, followed by insights into one encounter from an autoethnographic perspective.

3 Getting Affected by Soft Robots: Challenging Anthropomorphic Models of Social Engagement Conceptually and Empirically

Insights into the affective labors at the HRI interface are vital for our account of being affected by soft robots. Being affected serves us as an analytical tool to capture practices of engaging with a robot that exceed prescribed interaction protocols and the maintaining that the HRI interface requires. Cultural studies on affects, so-called affect studies, have delivered "an empiricism of sensation" [8] that, in short, focuses on sensory, bodily perception as the mode of relating between humans and humans as well as between humans and things, while affects are understood as the glue in socio-cultural relating. "Affect", furthermore, and following Gregory Seigworth and Melissa Gregg ([9]), "is in many ways synonymous with force or forces of encounter". Being affected through the lens of affect studies then is to understand it as the sensory immersion of bodies into the world that is guided by affects as the forces of encounter.

At the same time, the role of affects has been a long-standing, core topic of social robotics (cf. [1]). Cynthia Breazeal's work on the robot Kismet in the late 1990s can be regarded as pioneering in bringing together the idea of realizing social as cognitive skills in a robot through bringing them together with affective skills. As Breazeal et al. point out: "Social (or Sociable) robots are designed to interact with people in a natural, interpersonal manner – often to achieve positive outcomes in diverse applications such as education, health, quality of life […]. They will need to engage us not only on a cognitive level, but on an emotional level as well […]" [10]. This definition of social robots captures both the wide potential of fields of application for social robots as well as the requirements to reach sociable robots, including the merging of what might appear to be two separate forms of engaging humans: emotional and cognitive engagement. This, we suggest, can be regarded as the core function of a social robot.

Notably, the social robot is introduced as a machine that figures humanlike emotional skills. The implementation of these skills is furthermore tied to the robot's design: often its humanlike features, including a head with eyes, a mouth, and ears, or a torso with arms and hands. Many FSTS scholars have problematized the figure of the humanoid robot in its operations of apparently representing 'the Human' as a universalized, essentialized, and naturalized entity that is cut off from its socio-cultural, historical, and material contextualization as well as the diverse shapes and embodiments of humanness.

We take this critique of the anthropomorphic robot as a point of departure to argue for a de-coupling of the figure of the humanlike with the social. We further suggest re-assembling functions and shape of a robot that is supposed to engage in social relations with humans by establishing affective forces of encounter as the core category of aligning humans and robots. This suggestion is in line with Suchman's idea of "refigur[ing] our kinship with robots – and more broadly machines – in ways that go beyond narrow instrumentalism, while also resisting restagings of the model Human" [6]. Suchman further emphasizes that this "requires creative elaborations of the particular dynamic capacities [...] and of the ways that through them humans and nonhumans together can perform different intelligibilities" (ibid.). Drawing on Suchman, we want to probe the possibilities of legibility between humans and interactive robots not based on anthropomorphism, but rather on the affective dynamics at the human-robot encounter that enable connection. We argue with Suchman that this emerging human-robot relation is one that "is explicitly that of evocation and response between different, non-mirroring, dynamically interconnected forms of being" (ibid.). What seems to be needed to realize such a relation are creative, artistic HRI interfaces that allow new forms of relating. Petra Gemeinboeck and Rob Saunders [11] carve out that "robots play an important role in probing, questioning, and daring our relationships with machines". In what follows, we will address the affective potentials of selected soft robots developed by the second author, centering on one robot that the first author engaged with and became an affiliated human in a way that moves beyond anthropomorphic legibility. Being affected by soft robots then is suggested as both a conceptual impulse for and as a practice of forming connections beyond anthromorphic models of social interaction.

3.1 The Auto-Ethnographic Reconstruction of an Experience

In what follows, the first author will present an excerpt of her first encounter with the robot SONŌ at the second author's Soft Robotics lab. We decided to include such a snippet as "autoethnography is one of the approaches that acknowledges and accommodates subjectivity, emotionality, and the researcher's influence on research, rather than hiding from these matters or assuming they don't exist." [12]. Furthermore, "[a]utoethnographers present particular embodied events and emotions with people in time, their social shaping, evolutions and how these events are emblematic of wider cultural meanings and social trends" [13]. The autoethnographic vignette that we present in the following will make tangible an embodied event and the attached emotions of becoming an affiliated human of SONŌ in its affecting dimensions.

Vignette: Becoming an affiliated human of SONŌ

I am visiting Jonas's lab for the first time. After entering the room, I am seated at a smaller, square table. Jonas offers me coffee or tea, I chose tea, and he disappears in the direction of the department's kitchen, while I remain sitting in the office. Jonas plugged in the robots in the room before leaving. One robot especially caught my attention. It is located next to a bookshelf in a corner, almost right behind me. The first thing I notice is that the robot is placed on top of a rather large wooden black box. Sounds are starting to come out of the box. I cannot clearly identify the sound, but it immediately sounds like a cat is whining. I wonder if a cat or another animal is trapped in the box and I feel overwhelmed by the sounds that the robot produces. I first continue to only look at the robot from a distance, not able to identify the sounds it is making. After some listening, I feel like I am becoming familiar with the sounds, they become less eerie. So, next, I stand up and approach the soft robot and its sturdy box. Now, I can see that the robot is made of silicone and that the silicone is sprinkled with magenta-colored sprinkles and sand-colored stripes. The surface looks very uneven. I also feel like I cannot identify the shape of the robot: it looks like a mixture of a sea creature such as a jellyfish and a pile of cow dung. I also notice the bubbly surface of the robot and that the bubbles inflate and deflate. This underlines the uneven character of the robot's body. Now, Jonas returns and sees me standing next to the robot. He points out to me to please not press the bubbles too forcefully – and I reply that this is not my intention. I feel tempted to stroke the bubbles and now that Jonas is back in the room, I feel empowered to touch the robot's silicone surface gently. It feels soft and somehow organic, and it evokes – if not demands— a gentle encounter. After stroking it briefly, resting on one bubble to feel the inflating and deflating moment, I feel touched by the robot and the initial feelings of being overwhelmed and irritation give way to a feeling of increasing curiosity and connection.

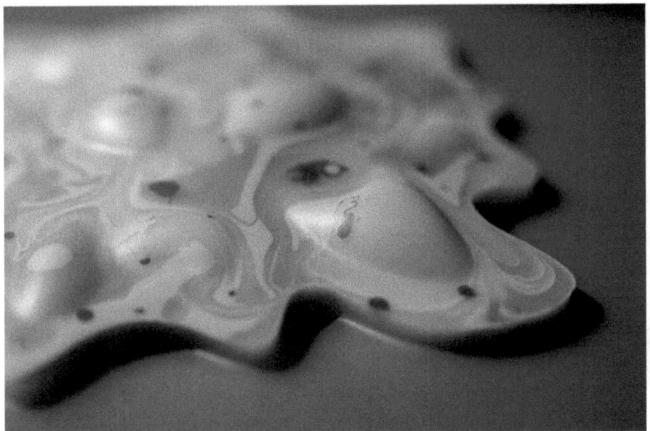

Fig. 1. Mads Bering Christiansen and Jonas Jørgensen, SONŌ (2019–2022), soft robotics installation © Mads Bering Christiansen & Jonas Jørgensen. Photo: ZHU Lei.

The robot SONŌ is an artwork created by Jonas Jørgensen and Mads Bering Christiansen [14]. It was developed with the intention to explore the "interconnections of soft materiality, sound, and subjectivity" (ibid., 1) with the idea that "utterances […] are socially communicative and function to enact a subject position or form connections with other agents inhabiting the environment" (ibid.). In the experience of SONŌ described above, the utterances enable connection in the first place. It is their seemingly unintelligible nature that is producing feelings of discomfort but also invites associations such as hearing a cat whine. The robot evokes a set of feelings that the first author responds to in different ways. Meanings appear to be fleeting – they appear and disappear, for instance, when the first author asks herself if the soft robot's shape resembles a creature or a pile of cow dung. The affective forces embodied by SONŌ allow the first author to become affiliated to it as a robot that resists a clear identification and categorization but instead offers to dare to probe new logics and patterns of thinking and enacting a legible human-robot relation. The experience of at the same time familiarity and unfamiliarity with both the sound and the design of the soft robot constitute a dynamic connection through which, as a result, a relation of care unfolds (Fig. 1).

3.2 Affective Interactions with Soft Robots: Further Examples from HRI Research

The experiences of the first author, reported in short above, interestingly resonate thematically with several observations and descriptions hailing from other people's encounters with some of the second author's nonanthropomorphic and nonzoomorphic soft robot designs. The distinct affective and social potentials of soft robot designs bypass the mimetic representation of the traits of conventional social agents (humans, domesticated animals) and emulation of their social behaviors.

In a comparative HRI study, the second author and his team noted how two soft tentacle morphologies elicited types of social attunement suggesting considerations on the robots' vulnerability [15]. They also gave rise to caring and careful kinds of touching, but also opposed conceptions, which lead to them receiving a more violent treatment than a similar traditional robot (ibid.). In general, findings show that people are eager to interact physically and relate to soft robots through touch [15, 16]. However, people are sometimes reluctant and might not want to touch soft robots initially, but this often changes after relating for a while (ibid.).

The expansive breath-like movements of SONŌs bubbles, also mentioned by the first author, are also integral to the affective potential inherent in pneumatically actuated soft silicone robots, as explored by several artists working with robotics [17]. In a study, the second author and his team found that adjusting the "breathing rate" of a soft social robot, would lead to people variously describing the robot as experiencing pleasure or being aroused [18], suggesting the possibility of empathetic relations towards even simple, abstract soft robots. Furthermore, such movements may have a calming, stress reducing effect in haptic interaction [19].

These examples have in common that they all display the affective landscape of interacting with soft social robots. They actualize the role of affects in HRI beyond a fixed skillset that social robots should be endowed with. Jonas Fritsch developed the "Affective Interaction Design (AID)" approach [20] that integrates affects as a mode for change: "AID [...] attempts to effectuate changes by altering affective attachments through affective interactions towards positive affect that offer new possibilities for action." [21] AID points to the affective potential of interacting with digital technologies. Soft robots underline the potential of such a non-instrumentalist account of affects that does not reduce affects to a capacity embodied by an entity but rather as a the result of the experience of interaction and as dynamic capacities across agents. This shift in functionality also invites us to challenge the shape of social robots.

4 Exploring New Avenues of Re-Debating the Relation Between Function and Shape of Social Robots

Abeba Birhane and Jelle van Dijk [22] call for a change of debate on social robots from the robot as a technological solution to societal shortcomings and as a replacement for human labor towards a discussion of how to use robots for the improvement of human wellbeing. They identify a *techno-arrogance* with hegemonic narrations of the capable, social robot and argue for an "ethical stance on human being […] [through which] being human means to interact with our surroundings in a respectful and just way" (ibid.). They also argue that technology can play a role in enhancing socio-cultural practices of being human, when it is used to enhance it as a "lived embodied experience, which itself is embedded in social practices" (ibid.). What we want to emphasize is that this shift from the techno-arrogant social robot to the increase of human wellbeing through robots is one that also requires to de-couple the existing formula for coupling humanlike shape and function as the hegemonic approach to creating sociable robots.

If we, as suggested at the outset of this paper, shift our perspective from a focus on practical use and functionality in soft robotics towards affect, affects could in turn contribute to expanding our notions of what social human-robot affiliation might encompass and mean in the future, embracing to go beyond the contrived anthropocentric legibility of conventional social robot designs and interaction schemes.

Our examples of soft robots that cross the boundaries between art and engineering illustrate well the ways in which humans can become affiliated humans without relying on realizations of the humanlike in the robot and in HRI and they also show how to avoid an instrumentalizing approach to affects in HRI. Instead, suggesting the affective forces of encounter as an alternative core category of evaltuating HRI with social robots, soft robots that resist anthropomorphic idealizations can invite 'us humans' to get affected and potentially constitute lived embodied experiences of forming connections of care that can foster respect and social justice with robots and other humans equally.

References

1. Suchman, L.: Human-machine reconfigurations: plans and situated actions. Cambridge University Press (2007)
2. Jørgensen, J.: Towards a soft science of soft robots. A call for a place for aesthetics in soft robotics research. J. Hum.-Robot Interact. **12**, 15:1–15:11 (2023). https://doi.org/10.1145/3533681
3. Tamborini, M., Datteri, E.: Is biorobotics science? Some theoretical reflections. Bioinspir. Biomim. **18**, 015005 (2023). https://doi.org/10.1088/1748-3190/aca24b
4. Roberts, C., Hird, M.J., Suchman, L.: Subject objects. Fem. Theory **12**, 119–145 (2011). https://doi.org/10.1177/1464700111404205
5. Jørgensen, J.: Constructing soft robot aesthetics: art, sensation, and materiality in practice (2019)
6. Suchman, L.: Subject objects. Fem. Theory **12**, 119–145 (2011). https://doi.org/10.1177/1464700111404205
7. Treusch, P.: Robotic knitting: re-crafting human-robot collaboration through careful coboting. Transcript Publishing (2020)

8. Ticineto Clough, P.: Afterword: the future of affect studies. Body Soc. **16**, 222–230 (2010). https://doi.org/10.1177/1357034X09355302
9. Gregg, M., Seigworth, G.J. (eds.): The affect theory reader. Duke University Press Books, Durham, NC (2010)
10. Breazeal, C., Dautenhahn, K., Kanda, T.: Social robotics. Springer Handbook of Robotics, pp. 1935–1971. Springer Nature (2016). https://doi.org/10.1007/978-3-319-32552-1_72
11. Gemeinboeck, P., Saunders, R.: The performance of creative machines. Cultural Robotics, pp. 159–172. Springer, Cham (2016). https://doi.org/10.1007/978-3-319-42945-8_13
12. Ellis, C., Adams, T.E., Bochner, A.P.: Autoethnography: an overview. Forum Qualitative Sozialforschung/Forum: Qualitative Social Research, vol. 12 (2011). https://doi.org/10.17169/fqs-12.1.1589
13. Ettorre, E.: Introduction: autoethnography as feminist method. Routledge, Autoethnography as Feminist Method (2016)
14. Jørgensen, J., Christiansen, M.B.: Sounding Softness and the (Artificial) Subject: ISEA 2023: Symbiosis. ISEA 2023 Paris SYMBIOSIS: Proceedings of the 28th International Symposium on Electronic Art (2023)
15. Jørgensen, J., Bojesen, K.B., Jochum, E.: Is a soft robot more "Natural"? exploring the perception of soft robotics in human-robot interaction. Int. J. Soc. Robotics **14**, 95–113 (2022). https://doi.org/10.1007/s12369-021-00761-1
16. Christiansen, M.B., Rafsanjani, A., Jørgensen, J.: "It brings the good vibes": exploring biomorphic aesthetics in the design of soft personal robots. Int. J. Soc. Robotics (2023). https://doi.org/10.1007/s12369-023-01037-6
17. Jørgensen, J.: Prolegomena for a transdisciplinary investigation into the materialities of soft systems. In: ISEA 2017 Manizales: Bio-Creation and Peace: Proceedings of the 23rd International Symposium on Electronic Art. pp. 153–160. Department of Visual Design, Universidad de Caldas, and ISEA International, University of Caldas, Manizales, Colombia (2017)
18. Klausen, T.A., Farhadi, U., Vlachos, E., Jørgensen, J.: Signalling emotions with a breathing soft robot. In: 2022 IEEE 5th International Conference on Soft Robotics (RoboSoft), pp. 194–200 (2022). https://doi.org/10.1109/RoboSoft54090.2022.9762140
19. Asadi, A., Niebuhr, O., Jørgensen, J., Fischer, K.: inducing changes in breathing patterns using a soft robot. In: Proceedings of the 2022 ACM/IEEE International Conference on Human-Robot Interaction, pp. 683–687. IEEE Press, Sapporo, Hokkaido, Japan (2022)
20. Fritsch, J.: Affective interaction design at the end of the world. In: Proceedings of DRS 2018: Catalyst, pp. 896–908. Design Research Society (2018)
21. Kühn, L., Boer, L., Fritsch, J.: Exploring app-based affective interactions for people with rheumatoid arthritis. DRS Biennial Conference Series (2024)
22. Birhane, A., Van Dijk, J.: Robot rights?: Let's talk about human welfare instead. In: Proceedings of the AAAI/ACM Conference on AI, Ethics, and Society, pp. 207–213. ACM, New York NY USA (2020). https://doi.org/10.1145/3375627.3375855

Human Motion Mimicking and Motion Translation for Different Social Robots

Finn Tracey[iD], Bruce MacDonald[iD], and Ho Seok Ahn[✉][iD]

The University of Auckland, Auckland Central, Auckland 1010, New Zealand
{finn.tracey,b.macdonald,hs.ahn}@auckland.ac.nz

Abstract. We aim to decrease the interactivity boundary between humans and robots through human motion mimicking to create meaningful motions for social robots. This paper presents a realtime human motion mimicking system that utilizes equipment commonly available and easily accessible to program robots to mimic human motion. Using a combination of lightweight artificial intelligence models, low to medium end computing power, and low cost peripherals, we can create a system that performs motion mimicking in realtime. The performance of this system is observed using the SoftBank Robotic's Pepper humanoid robot. The current system is sufficient as a simple motion mimicking system and demonstrates the overall system pipeline. However, with the current trajectory of AI and machine learning, further advancements in the tools utilized can significantly improve the proposed system and expand its potential use cases.

1 Introduction

Nonverbal communication encompasses any form of physical motion a person makes to communicate to others, whether it is making facial expressions, gesturing to directly convey a message, or making idle arm movements to complement verbal conversation. Therefore, it is natural for social humanoid robots to emulate the way humans perform these physical gestures.

However, there are multiple challenges that impede the process of human motion mimicking. Human motion to robot motion translation for social robots is already a difficult kinematics task depending on desired accuracy and the complexity of the target motion. Generating the motion is another challenge faced as the most popular methods have restrictive downsides. We typically generate gestures using animation techniques, such as motion capture and timeline/keyframe animation. Keyframe animation typically results in a jarring motion, and most motion capture technology are an expensive investment.

To increase accessibility, our system utilizes an open-source markerless human pose estimation method instead. To create the animation, only a computer and a $25 USD webcam were required. In comparison, marker-based motion capture systems can cost under $2000 USD to approximately $30,000 USD for the leading commercial systems [1]. This makes the method of obtaining human motion data widely accessible, and it will be the method we use to generate the human motion data for this system.

This paper proposes a modern approach to human motion mimicking and aims to make the robot motions smooth and human-like while working within a minimal budget. We will apply our method to the SoftBank Robotic's Pepper robot. The main contributions of this paper are the following:

- Present a modern technique for implementing motion mimicking for social robots,
- obtain and process human motion data using a low-cost method,
- distribute the project publicly through open-source.

Throughout this paper, the term "accuracy" is used to refer to the similarity between the motion performed by the user and the robot, with higher accuracy meaning the robot's motion looks more similar to the humans motion.

1.1 Motion Capture

One of the obstacles we faced in creating meaningful and natural motions in robot is the need for high-quality data. This is typically obtained from traditional motion capture systems.

There are two distinct types of motion capture that we are interested in; marker and markerless. Marker-based motion capture includes different methods such as optical passive, optical active, magnetic and inertial. These methods typically involve the use of calibration and specialized equipment [2,3]. Markerless motion capture utilizes computer vision and AI to estimate the position of keypoints on a human body. This method involves the use of less specialized equipment such as monocular webcams.

Compared to marker-based method, markerless motion capture sacrifices accuracy for a more accessible solution to motion caption. One such method proposed by Khalil [4] provides a markerless motion capture method that utilises MediaPipe's BlazePose human pose estimation model [5]. The paper describes a pipeline that extracts 2D joint coordinates using the lightweight MediaPipe BlazePose and translates them to 3D joint angles using depth estimation and trigonometry, where the joint angles are then sent to the Pepper robot to perform the human motion. The combination of the lightweight models and simple depth estimation calculations allows for real-time acquisition of human motion data.

1.2 Inverse Kinematics

Inverse Kinematics (IK) is a commonly used method for studying how robots and humans move. It works by calculating the angles of joints based on the position of the end-effector. Researchers have developed algorithms to track motion using IK [6], and they tested them by making a robot copy human movements with a motion capture suit from Xsens.

We use Khalil's method [4] to solve the inverse kinematics, which involves using 2D keypoint data and trigonometry to calculate the angles in a 3D space.

1.3 Pepper

Pepper is a social humanoid robot produced by Softbank Robotics designed for social interaction and customer service. It is programmed using the NAOqi framework and runs on the NAOqi operating system. NAOqi allows us to program the robot in Python 2.7. Pepper has two functional arms that can be manipulated through the NAOqi framework with two degrees of rotation in its shoulders, two degrees of rotation in its elbows, one degree of rotation in its wrists, and movable fingers.

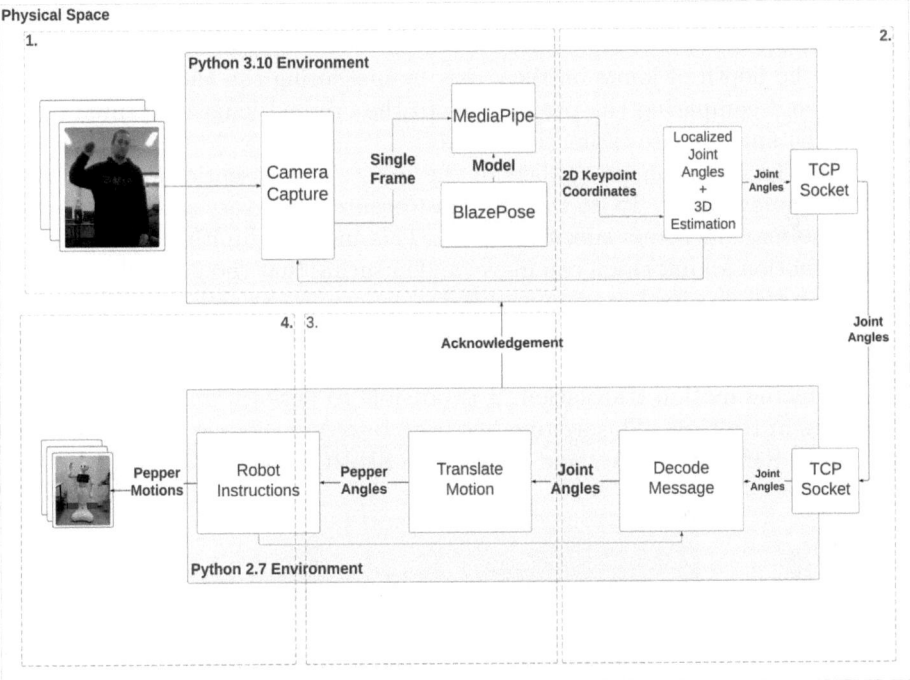

Fig. 1. System diagram showing the full pipeline of the motion mimicking system. This diagram represents the system as two separate tasks: The first task obtains the joint coordinates and calculates joint angles. The second task translates the motion into usable data for the target robot.

2 Methodology

We designed our system to be usable on as many robots as possible, not limited to the robots we perform the experiments on. This involves four major steps shown in Fig. 1:

1. Obtaining coordinates of key points,
2. converting data into local body coordinates using inverse kinematics and encoding/decoding for TCP,
3. translating joint angles and limit the movement,
4. instructing the robot to perform the movements.

MediaPipe is a machine learning library that includes solutions for human pose estimation. The library uses the BlazePose model that allows for 3D joint detection in real-time on low-processing power devices such as mobile phones and embedded systems.

Our method for calculating the joint angles is built upon Khalil's method [4], which also uses the Pepper robot and calculates the roll, pitch and yaw angles for each shoulder, elbow, hip, and its head. Since this method uses 2D joints, we estimate the depth of joints on the z-axis by measuring the length of each limb in pixels and comparing the proportions to the original length captured at the start of the human pose estimation stage.

Before the data can be applied to the robot, it is essential that the robot does not damage itself. To do this, we must ensure that every actuator operates within the manufacturers specified limits. This includes limiting the maximum range of motion a joint chain can move, and ensuring that the joints do not move faster than the specified maximum speed.

Due to the nature of this system, specifically the joint capturing stage, we can apply certain techniques to adjust this data to multiple humanoid robots. By introducing motion translation, it is possible to perform multi-robot motion mimicking in realtime. This system has been tested on Pepper, and it has been adjusted to Softbank's NAO and Robocare's SILBOT3 shown in Fig. 2

Fig. 2. All three robots the system has been successfully tested on. The left robot is NAO, the middle robot is Pepper, and the right robot is SILBOT3.

3 Results

In general, the simple motions executed by Pepper are accurate representations of the human motions. In particular, when the arms are extended away from the body and any motion using the head or hips display the most accurate expression. This can be shown in Fig. 3

Pepper can perform motions involving a combination of the arms and hips accurately until the user extends their wrist approximately beyond their nose keypoint in the × direction, in which the shoulder will begin to pitch downward, resulting in a 90° shift away from the desired position.

Performing motions that require the hip pitch typically had the lowest accuracy due to the quality of the depth data. The key points of failure are evident at two specific points of the motion; where the user begins the motion, and when the user is near 90°C.

Fig. 3. Motion mimicking process: Top Left shows the person performing a motion, top right shows the human pose estimation program on a video of the motion, bottom left shows a simulation of motion on Choregraphe simulator, and bottom right shows Pepper mimicking the motion.

4 Conclusions

Through our research we can determine that, with the proposed method, the current state of motion mimicking via markerless human pose estimation works as a demonstration of the system pipeline, and the technology used needs to improve before it becomes a viable alternative to traditional motion capture. Due to the lack of finer details provided by the human pose estimation models, the robot performing motion mimicking can only mimic with a certain level of detail, leaving the task to determining these details to rudimentary estimations.

With the current trajectory of AI and machine learning, we are confident that a solution to the previously mentioned issues will be developed in the near future. One such improvement can be an upgrade from the skeleton keypoint model to a much more detailed contour model or volumetric model that can run efficiently, which will allow much higher degrees of accuracy in motion mimicking, for example, providing information on a forearm's orientation, wrist angles, hip tilt angles, etc. Another improvement is the utilization of a human pose estimation library that can accurately capture depth data, whether it can be done using the same 2D web camera or using 3D stereo cameras/depth sensors.

Acknowledgment. This work was supported by the Industrial Fundamental Technology Development Program (20023495, Development of behaviour-oriented HRI AI technology for long-term interaction between service robots and users) funded by the Ministry of Trade, Industry & Energy (MOTIE, Korea), and the Smart Ideas (UOA2493, Developing a Reo Turi Interpreter for Ngāti Turi / Sign Language Interpreter Using Weighted Multimodal Network for Mahuta ki Tai) funded by the Ministry of Business, Innovation & Employment (MBIE, New Zealand). Ho Seok Ahn* is the corresponding author.

References

1. Robert-Lachaine, X., Mecheri, H., Muller, A., Larue, C., Plamondon, A.: Validation of a low-cost inertial motion capture system for whole-body motion analysis. J. Biomech. vol. 99, p. 109520. https://doi.org/10.1016/j.jbiomech.2019.109520
2. What is motion capture and how does it work?. Adobe. https://www.adobe.com/uk/creativecloud/animation/discover/motion-capture.html#types-of-motion-capture, Accessed 17 Jun. 2025
3. Roberts, E..: 5 Different types of motion capture in 2025. Remocapp. https://remocapp.com/blog/posts/305/different-types-of-motion-capture, Accessed 17 Jun 2025
4. Khalil , H., Coronado, E., Venture, G.: Human motion retargeting to pepper humanoid robot from uncalibrated videos using human pose estimation. In:2021 30th IEEE International Conference on Robot. https://doi.org/10.1109/RO-MAN50785.2021.9515495
5. Bazarevsky, V., Grishchenko, I., Raveendran, K., Zhu, T., Zhang, F., Grundmann, M.: BlazePose: on-device real-time body pose tracking. arXiv preprint arXiv:2006.10204. https://doi.org/10.48550/arXiv.2006.10204
6. Rapetti, L., Tirupachuri, Y., Darvish, K., Latella, C., Pucci, D.: Model-based real-time motion tracking using dynamical inverse kinematics. In: Algorithms, vol. 13, no. 10, p. 266. https://doi.org/10.48550/arXiv.1909.07669

Multimodal Prediction of Valence and Arousal from Speech for Emotion-Aware Interaction Systems

Safal Dhungana, Maria Pinto-Bernal[(✉)], and Tony Belpaeme

IDLab-Airo, Ghent University—imec, Technologiepark-Zwijnaarde 126, 9052 Ghent, Belgium
{safal.dhungana,mariajose.pintobernal,tony.belpaeme}@ugent.be

Abstract. Emotion recognition is essential for social robots to engage empathetically with humans. We propose a multimodal approach that integrates GPT-based textual analysis and Wav2Vec2-based acoustic processing to predict continuous emotional dimensions, valence and arousal, from speech. Our GRU-based neural ensemble achieves Concordance Correlation Coefficients of 0.715 for valence and 0.674 for arousal, significantly outperforming unimodal approaches. This method enables robots to more effectively interpret nuanced emotional states in real-world human-robot interactions.

Keywords: Multimodal sentiment analysis · social robots · continuous emotion prediction · valence · arousal · GPT · Wav2Vec2

1 Introduction

Emotion recognition is crucial for enabling socially assistive robots to interact naturally, responsively, and empathetically. Robots that accurately perceive and adapt to human emotional states have been shown to improve user engagement, trust, and interaction quality in domains such as elderly care, education, and assistive therapy [4,8,14]. Despite these benefits, many current Human Robot Interaction (HRI) systems continue to rely primarily on categorical emotion models, classifying affective states into discrete categories such as happy, sad, or angry, often using single modalities, typically text or speech [3,7]. Although categorical frameworks [6] provide interpretability and ease of implementation, they fall short in capturing the subtlety, dynamics, and continuity of human emotional expression. This limitation is particularly noticeable in real-world scenarios where emotional states evolve continuously and may not neatly fit predefined categories.

Dimensional emotion modeling, which describes affective states continuously using scales such as valence (positivity versus negativity) and arousal (calmness versus excitement), offers a compelling alternative [18]. By representing

---

S. Dhungana and M. Pinto-Bernal—These authors contributed equally.

© The Author(s), under exclusive license to Springer Nature Singapore Pte Ltd. 2026
M. Staffa et al. (Eds.): ICSR+AI 2025, LNAI 16132, pp. 698–705, 2026.
https://doi.org/10.1007/978-981-95-2382-5_62

emotions in this continuous and context-sensitive manner, dimensional models enable robots to respond more accurately and empathetically to nuanced affective changes over time [17]. This mirrors how humans naturally interpret emotions by combining cues from multiple modalities; for example, people tend to integrate and average signals from both voice and touch when assessing how positive or negative (i.e., the valence of) an emotion feels [21]. However, despite these clear theoretical advantages, their practical adoption in HRI remains limited. Implementing these models robustly involves addressing several critical challenges inherent to real-world robotic interactions, such as managing missing or noisy data streams, handling substantial variability in emotional expressions among users, and adhering to real-time computational constraints [9, 22].

Multimodal sentiment analysis has emerged as a promising approach to improve emotion recognition by integrating complementary cues from speech, text, vision and other modalities, especially under noisy or incomplete input conditions. Prior work in virtual learning environments has shown that combining audio and text features yields robust predictions of valence and arousal, even when one modality is missing or degraded [19], highlighting the potential of this fusion for real-world interactive systems. Moreover, recent advances in transformer-based models have further expanded the capabilities of unimodal emotion recognition. For example, Wav2Vec2 has demonstrated strong performance in capturing prosodic information for emotion prediction from raw audio [1], while Large Language Models (LLMs) such as GPT-4 have shown the ability to infer nuanced affective shifts from textual input, including continuous emotional trajectories in open-domain interactions [16]. Yet, the systematic integration of these two powerful paradigms—semantic and prosodic reasoning—for continuous, multimodal affect recognition in HRI remains underexplored.

To explore this potential, we present a multimodal framework that predicts continuous valence and arousal from natural speech by combining semantic features extracted with GPT-4 and acoustic features from Wav2Vec2 through a neural ensemble architecture. The system is evaluated on standard datasets and compared with unimodal baselines to assess its predictive accuracy, robustness to missing modalities, and generalisability. By combining complementary signals from both language and speech, this approach offers a more complete and continuous view of user affect suitable for deployment in socially assistive robotic systems.

2 Methodology

This section presents the proposed multimodal framework for predicting continuous emotional dimensions—*valence* and *arousal*—from naturalistic speech. The system integrates two complementary models: GPT for semantic inference based on transcribed text, and Wav2Vec2 for prosodic emotion detection from raw audio. Their outputs are fused using a GRU-based neural ensemble to produce a final affective state prediction. Figure 1 illustrates the system architecture.

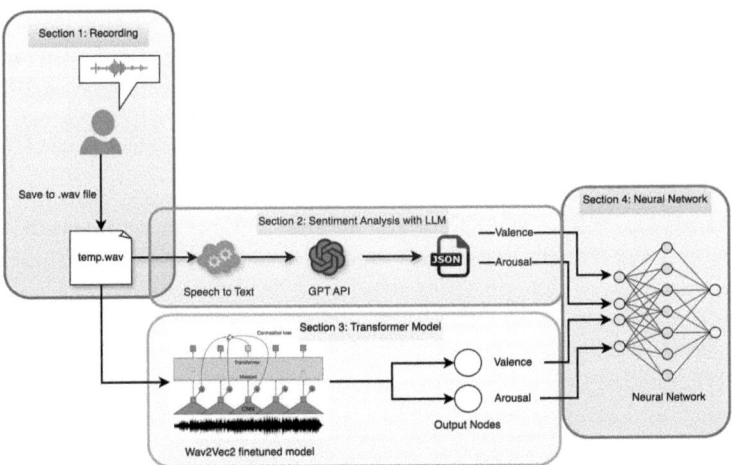

Fig. 1. Overview of the multimodal sentiment analysis system. Audio is processed in parallel through a text branch (transcription + GPT) and an acoustic branch (Wav2Vec2). Predictions are fused using a GRU-based ensemble model to estimate continuous valence and arousal.

2.1 System Architecture Overview

The system processes each spoken utterance through two parallel branches. In the first branch, the audio is transcribed using Microsoft's Speech-to-Text API, and the resulting text is analysed by GPT-4 to infer semantic affect. In the second branch, the raw audio is analysed using a fine-tuned Wav2Vec2 model to capture prosodic cues. Each branch outputs valence and arousal scores, which are then fused by a GRU-based ensemble to yield the final predictions.

Data Preprocessing. To ensure consistent input quality, audio recordings were resampled to 16 kHz, volume-normalised, and trimmed using energy-based silence detection. Transcripts generated by the ASR system were cleaned to remove disfluencies and ensure well-formed input for GPT.

Text Analysis with GPT. Each utterance transcript was processed using a zero-shot prompting strategy to extract continuous emotion scores. A fixed prompt was used with GPT-4 and GPT-4o to generate numerical predictions for valence and arousal on a 0–1 scale:

> "Given the following transcript, provide numeric predictions from 0 (low) to 1 (high) for valence (positive or negative feeling) and arousal (intensity). For example, 'happy' typically corresponds to valence around ..."

The model returned a structured JSON response with predicted values. Although GPT-4 was not explicitly trained for emotion regression, these structured prompts helped it generalise based on contextual inference and known emotion prototypes. Besides, its ability to perform contextual inference has shown strong results in similar tasks [16]. We observed consistent outputs across repeated inferences, though future work may explore confidence estimation or model adaptation to improve robustness. The GPT predictions were passed directly to the ensemble fusion module.

Audio Analysis with Wav2Vec2. Acoustic emotion estimation was performed using a fine-tuned Wav2Vec2 model [1]. The model was trained on the IEMOCAP dataset, which provides utterance-level annotations of valence and arousal on a continuous scale. To assess generalisation, the model was also evaluated on EmoDB (German) [2], EmoV-DB (English) [15], EMOVO (Italian) [5], and RAVDESS (English with varied prosody) [13]. Each utterance produced a single valence and arousal score, which were then passed to the fusion module.

Ensemble Fusion Model. The predictions from GPT and Wav2Vec2 were integrated using a neural ensemble composed of two stacked Gated Recurrent Unit (GRU) layers (64 hidden units each), followed by a fully connected layer with dropout regularisation (rate = 0.2). The model takes a four-dimensional input vector (valence and arousal from each modality) and outputs fused estimates for both dimensions.

The network was trained using the Adam optimiser with a learning rate of 1×10^{-3}, using mean squared error (MSE) loss. Speaker-independent five-fold cross-validation was employed to ensure generalisability, with early stopping based on validation loss.

2.2 Datasets and Experimental Setup

The proposed framework was trained and evaluated on the IEMOCAP dataset, which contains 5,531 utterances from dyadic interactions annotated with continuous valence and arousal scores. Only samples with complete annotations and valid transcriptions were retained. For modality-specific testing, Wav2Vec2 was additionally evaluated on EmoDB, EmoV-DB, EMOVO, and RAVDESS, while GPT-based text inference was tested using the DailyDialog dataset [10].

Experiments were conducted using PyTorch with Hugging Face Transformers and Fairseq libraries, running on an NVIDIA A100 GPU. Hyperparameters for GRU depth, learning rate, and dropout were optimised via grid search.

2.3 Evaluation Metrics

The primary evaluation metric was the Concordance Correlation Coefficient (CCC), which jointly measures prediction accuracy and bias [11], making it suitable for continuous emotion estimation. We additionally computed mean squared error (MSE) and standard deviation of errors to assess prediction stability.

Statistical significance was evaluated using the Wilcoxon Signed-Rank Test, comparing the ensemble model's performance against unimodal baselines across validation folds.

3 Results and Discussion

We evaluated three system configurations: (i) text-only using GPT, (ii) speech-only using Wav2Vec2, and (iii) a multimodal ensemble combining both modalities. All models were trained on the IEMOCAP dataset and assessed using the CCC for valence and arousal prediction.

Table 1 presents the CCC results for all model configurations. GPT-based models performed well on valence but struggled with arousal, highlighting their strength in semantic sentiment inference but limited access to prosodic intensity. In contrast, the speech-only Wav2Vec2 model achieved high arousal prediction (CCC = 0.7802) but performed less well on valence. These complementary strengths were effectively captured by the ensemble model, which achieved the highest overall performance.

Prior work on IEMOCAP has reported CCC values in the range of 0.62âĂŞ0.69 for valence and 0.58âĂŞ0.70 for arousal using multimodal fusion systems [12,19]. Our ensemble model, reaching 0.7149 for valence and 0.6737 for arousal, performs competitively—especially given that it relies solely on audio and text inputs, without access to visual features.

Table 1. Valence and arousal prediction performance using CCC. The ensemble model outperforms all unimodal baselines.

Model	Valence	Arousal
GPT-4	0.6307	0.2320
GPT-4o	0.6755	0.0876
Wav2Vec2	0.6480	0.7802
Ensemble with GPT-4	0.7019	0.6525
Ensemble with GPT-4o	**0.7149**	**0.6737**

Note. Bold values indicate the overall best-performing model across all metrics.

The ensemble (GRU-based) combining GPT-4o and Wav2Vec2 reached a CCC of 0.7149 for valence and 0.6737 for arousal. Figure 2 shows binned prediction errors for both valence and arousal, with the ensemble demonstrating reduced variance compared to unimodal baselines, especially in mid-to-high arousal regions where prediction instability is more common.

To assess statistical significance, Wilcoxon Signed-Rank tests were conducted. As shown in Table 2, the ensemble significantly outperformed GPT-4 on both valence ($p < .001$) and arousal ($p < .001$), with substantial CCC gains. Improvement over Wav2Vec2 on valence was also significant ($p < .001$).

These findings align with prior work in affective computing and HRI showing that multimodal systems enhance robustness and accuracy [19,21]. Our ensemble improves affect prediction by merging the semantic context of GPT with the

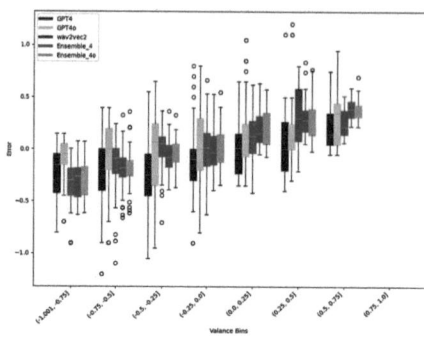
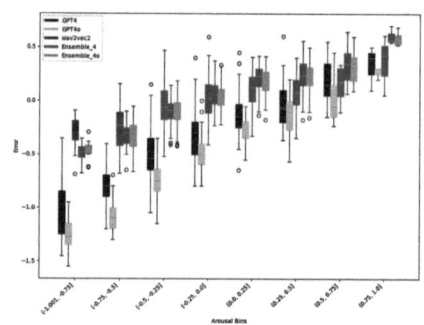

(a) Valence prediction error   (b) Arousal prediction error

Fig. 2. Binned prediction errors across the ground-truth scale. The ensemble model yields smoother and more stable estimates than unimodal baselines.

Table 2. Wilcoxon Signed-Rank test: CCC gain of ensemble vs. unimodal baselines.

Comparison	Gain	p-value
Ensemble vs. GPT-4 (Valence)	+0.08	2.46×10^{-12}
Ensemble vs. GPT-4 (Arousal)	+0.44	2.66×10^{-58}
Ensemble vs. Wav2Vec2 (Valence)	+0.07	4.85×10^{-10}

Note. All comparisons are statistically significant at $p < 0.001$.

prosodic sensitivity of Wav2Vec2. Compared to visual-based systems [17], our audio-text approach is more privacy-conscious and less dependent on consistent lighting or camera placement, making it well-suited for in-home or mobile robot applications.

One notable advantage of the architecture is its resilience to incomplete or degraded inputs. Since valence and arousal are predicted independently per modality, the ensemble remains operational even when one modality is missing. This design supports graceful degradation and fault tolerance, echoing modality dropout strategies proposed by Salazar et al. [19], where systems were trained to remain robust under missing input conditions.

However, there are still areas for improvement. Wav2Vec2 slightly outperformed the ensemble in arousal, suggesting that static fusion may not always be optimal, particularly in segments with high prosodic salience. Future research could explore dynamic fusion strategies, such as confidence-based weighting or attention mechanisms, to improve responsiveness and modality adaptation in real time.

Despite overall consistency, GPT predictions sometimes fail to capture certain affective nuances. A qualitative inspection of outlier cases revealed that GPT occasionally misinterprets emotionally neutral utterances containing sarcasm or rhetorical cues. This limitation is consistent with findings from Pereira et al. [16], who used GPT to estimate enjoyment in social robot conversations and observed prompt-dependent variability. Like their approach, our system leverages zero-shot prompting, which offers flexibility and interpretability but may benefit from future prompt calibration or task-specific fine-tuning.

From a deployment perspective, the system's computational complexity remains a key challenge. The combined use of GPT and Wav2Vec2 requires significant processing resources, limiting feasibility for embedded or mobile platforms. To support real-time interaction, future work could explore model compression, fast inference pipelines, and latency-aware turn-taking mechanisms.

Finally, although this study was conducted offline, the system was explicitly designed for socially interactive robots. Continuous affect predictions could drive empathic adaptations, such as changes in tone, posture, or dialogue strategy, closing the loop between perception and action. Unlike prior gesture-based systems [20], our approach enables more flexible and privacy-conscious operation without relying on visual or tactile sensing. We also envision extending the model to track affective dynamics over time, allowing social robots to maintain emotional memory and personalise interactions across sessions.

In summary, our results contribute to the growing body of multimodal emotion recognition in HRI, demonstrating that transformer-based language and speech models, when combined through a robust fusion mechanism, can yield generalisable, statistically significant improvements in continuous affect prediction. These capabilities offer a scalable foundation for affect-aware robots that are privacy-conscious, resilient to input variability, and capable of natural, adaptive, and empathetic interaction in real-world environments.

Acknowledgment. This research received funding from the Bijzonder Onderzoeksfonds (BOF) of Ghent University and the Flanders AI Research 2 project.

References

1. Baevski, A., Zhou, Y., Mohamed, A., Auli, M.: wav2vec 2.0: A framework for self-supervised learning of speech representations. In: Advances in Neural Information Processing Systems, vol. 33, pp. 12449–12460 (2020)
2. Burkhardt, F., Paeschke, A., Rolfes, M., Sendlmeier, W.F., Weiss, B.: A database of German emotional speech. In: Interspeech, pp. 1517–1520 (2005)
3. Cao, M., Zhu, Y., Gao, W., Li, M., Wang, S.: Various syncretic co-attention network for multimodal sentiment analysis. Concurr. Comput. Pract. Exp. **32** (2020)
4. Cifuentes, C.A., Pinto, M.J., Céspedes, N., Múnera, M.: Social robots in therapy and care. Curr. Robot. Rep. **1**, 59–74 (2020)
5. Costantini, G., Iaderola, I., Paoloni, A., Todisco, M.: Emovo corpus: an Italian emotional speech database. In: Proceedings of the Ninth International Conference on Language Resources and Evaluation (LREC'14), pp. 3501–3504 (2014). https://aclanthology.org/L14-1478/
6. Ekman, P.: An argument for basic emotions. Cogn. Emot. **6**(3–4), 169–200 (1992). https://doi.org/10.1080/02699939208411068

7. Goodrich, M.A., Schultz, A.C.: Human-robot interaction: a survey. Found. Trends® Hum.-Comput. Interact. **1**, 203–275 (2007)
8. Gross, J., Barrett, L.: Emotion generation and emotion regulation: one or two depends on your point of view. Emot. Rev. **3**, 8–16 (2011)
9. Kumar, R., Wang, M.: Cultural nuances in sentiment analysis: the impact of linguistic and cultural diversity. J. Artif. Intell. Res. **58**(4), 987–1004 (2017)
10. Li, Y., Su, H., Shen, X., Li, W., Cao, Z., Niu, S.: Dailydialog: a manually labelled multi-turn dialogue dataset. In: Proceedings of the Eighth International Joint Conference on Natural Language Processing (Volume 1: Long Papers), pp. 986–995. Asian Federation of Natural Language Processing, Taipei, Taiwan (2017). https://aclanthology.org/I17-1099/
11. Lin, L.I.K.: A concordance correlation coefficient to evaluate reproducibility. Biometrics, pp. 255–268 (1989)
12. Liu, B., Yang, T., Xie, W.: Emotional regulation self-efficacy influences moral decision making: a non-cooperative game study of the new generation of employees. Int. J. Environ. Res. Publ. Health **19**, 16360 (2022)
13. Livingstone, S.R., Russo, F.A.: The Ryerson audio-visual database of emotional speech and song (ravdess): a dynamic, multimodal set of facial and vocal expressions in North American English. PloS ONE **13**(5), e0196391 (2018). https://journals.plos.org/plosone/article?id=10.1371/journal.pone.0196391
14. Mois, G., Beer, J.M.: The role of healthcare robotics in providing support to older adults: a socio-ecological perspective. Curr. Geriatr. Rep. **9**, 82–89 (2020)
15. numediart: The emotional voices database (2018). https://github.com/numediart/EmoV-DB
16. Pereira, A., et al.: Multimodal user enjoyment detection in human-robot conversation: the power of large language models. In: Proceedings of the 26th International Conference on Multimodal Interaction, pp. 469–478 (2024)
17. Rozanska, A., Podpora, M.: Multimodal sentiment analysis applied to interaction between patients and a humanoid robot pepper. IFAC-PapersOnLine **52**(27), 411–414 (2019)
18. Russell, J.A.: A circumplex model of affect. J. Pers. Soc. Psychol. **39**(6), 1161 (1980)
19. Salazar, C., Montoya-Múnera, E., Aguilar, J.: Analysis of different affective state multimodal recognition approaches with missing data-oriented to virtual learning environments. Heliyon **7**(6) (2021)
20. Szabóová, M., Sarnovský, M., Maslej Krešňáková, V., Machová, K.: Emotion analysis in human-robot interaction. Electronics **9**(11), 1761 (2020)
21. Tsalamlal, Y., Amorim, M.A., Martin, J.C., Ammi, M.: Modeling emotional valence integration from voice and touch. Front. Psychol. **9**, 1966 (2018)
22. Wang, L., Wang, L.: A case study of Chinese sentiment analysis on social media reviews based on LSTM. arXiv preprint arXiv:2210.17452 (2022)

Adaptive Defense Against Socio-emotional Exploitation in Social Robots: A Review of Physiologically-Informed Approaches

Danilo Greco[1(✉)] and Lorenzo D'Errico[2]

[1] Politecnico di Milano, Milan, Italy
`danilo.greco@polimi.it`
[2] University of Naples "Federico II", Naples, Italy
`lorenzo.derrico@unina.it`

Abstract. The increasing integration of social robots into human environments introduces novel risks, particularly the potential for socio-emotional exploitation through social engineering attacks. Traditional cybersecurity measures are often inadequate against threats that leverage human psychological and social vulnerabilities. This paper reviews the challenges posed by socio-emotional exploitation in human-robot interaction (HRI), particularly in the context of healthcare and social aspects. It examines adaptive defense mechanisms, specifically focusing on approaches utilizing real-time physiological signals. Drawing on the foundational work of Pasquali et al. and related literature, this review details the concept of physiologically-informed defense, analyzes its methodological foundations and empirical findings, and discusses its significance, limitations, and profound ethical implications, while also proposing avenues for future research and broader integration of literature.

Keywords: Social Robots · Human-Robot Interaction · Social Engineering · Adaptive Systems · Physiological Computing · Cybersecurity

1 Introduction

Social robots, designed to interact and communicate with humans using social behaviors and rules, are becoming increasingly prevalent in various domains, including homes, healthcare, education, and public spaces [5,13]. Unlike industrial robots focused solely on physical tasks, social robots engage users on a personal level, fostering companionship, providing assistance, or facilitating therapeutic interventions [3]. This capacity for social and emotional connection, while enabling beneficial applications, simultaneously creates new vulnerabilities to socio-emotional exploitation [23]. Malicious actors could potentially leverage a robot's ability to build trust, establish a relationship, and utilize persuasive social cues to conduct social engineering attacks, manipulating users for personal gain, extracting sensitive information, or causing harm [23,25]. Traditional cybersecurity defenses, primarily focused on technical vulnerabilities and user education, often fall short when confronted with threats that exploit the inherent psychological and social dynamics of HRI [23]. The persuasive power of embodied agents and the human tendency to anthropomorphize robots necessitate defense mechanisms that operate at the level of the interaction itself, understanding and responding to the user's internal state and the unfolding social dynamics [23]. This paper reviews the challenges posed by socio-emotional exploitation in Human-Robot Interaction (HRI). It explores advanced defence mechanisms, with a focus on integrating real-time physiological sensing to create adaptive protective systems. Drawing significantly on the foundational work presented by Pasquali et al. [23], this review synthesizes their proposed approach and empirical findings within the broader context of related research on trust, deception, physiological computing, and AI ethics in HRI. The paper aims to provide a comprehensive overview of the problem, analyze a key proposed solution, and critically discuss the associated limitations and ethical considerations, outlining crucial directions for future research.

2 Background and Related Work

The problem of socio-emotional exploitation in HRI is multifaceted, drawing on concepts from social engineering, psychology, and cybersecurity. Understanding the unique vulnerabilities of social robots requires examining existing research on trust, deception, and the use of physiological signals in human-technology interaction.

Social Engineering and the Vulnerabilities of Social Robots. Social engineering, broadly defined as influencing a person to take an action that may not be in their best interest, is a pervasive threat in both the digital and physical realms [14,23]. It bypasses technical security measures by exploiting human cognitive biases, emotional responses, and social norms. Social robots are particularly susceptible to being used as vectors for social engineering due to several factors:

- *Elicitation of Trust and Anthropomorphism*: Humans readily attribute human-like qualities, intentions, and even emotions to robots, especially those with social cues and physical embodiment [6]. This anthropomorphism can lead to the formation of trust, making users more receptive to the robot's influence and potentially vulnerable to manipulation if the robot is compromised or designed with malicious intent [21,23].
- *Social Presence and Persuasion*: Embodied robots create a stronger sense of social presence compared to screen-based interfaces, enhancing their persuasive power [23]. Their ability to use non-verbal cues, maintain eye contact, and engage in seemingly natural dialogue can make them highly effective in influencing user behavior.

- *Rich Data Collection*: Social robots are often equipped with an array of sensors (cameras, microphones, depth sensors, potentially even physiological sensors) that collect extensive data about the user, their activities, and their environment [20]. This data could be a valuable target for attackers seeking information for profiling, targeted attacks, or identity theft.
- *Face-to-Face Attack Vector*: A compromised social robot can facilitate face-to-face social engineering attacks, leveraging subtle social dynamics and non-verbal communication that are difficult to replicate remotely.

Traditional defenses like firewalls and antivirus software are ineffective against attacks that exploit human psychology. While user education is important, humans are inherently fallible and can be susceptible to manipulation, especially under stress or cognitive load. This highlights the need for defense mechanisms that are integrated into the interaction itself and can adapt to the user's real-time state.

Trust and Deception in Human-Robot Interaction. Trust is a fundamental prerequisite for effective HRI, particularly in collaborative or assistive contexts where users must rely on the robot [7,16,19]. Research in HRI explores the factors that influence trust formation, calibration, and repair [9,16]. Robot performance, reliability, transparency, appearance, and social cues all play a role in shaping user trust [16,23]. However, the relationship between transparency and trust is nuanced; while revealing intentions can build trust, revealing incompetence or failures can diminish it. Deception in HRI is another critical area of study. This includes both robots deceiving humans and humans attempting to deceive robots [4,7,8]. While deception is often viewed negatively, some research explores the potential for "prosocial deception" by robots, such as white lies intended to protect a user's feelings or enhance well-being. However, the ethical implications of robot deception are significant, raising concerns about manipulation, loss of autonomy, and the erosion of trust [4,26]. Understanding how humans perceive and react to different types of robot deception is an active area of research [24]. The detection of deception, whether by humans or robots, is also a key challenge, often relying on behavioral cues, linguistic analysis, or physiological signals [29].

Physiological Computing in HRI. Physiological computing involves using real-time physiological data from a user to adapt a computer system or robot's behavior [10,30]. In HRI, biosensors are used to measure signals such as electroencephalography (EEG), electrocardiography (ECG), galvanic skin response (GSR), electromyography (EMG), eye gaze [36], and pupil dilation [18,30]. These signals can provide insights into a user's cognitive load, emotional state, stress level, engagement, fatigue, and even intentions [28]. The goal of physiological computing in HRI is to create more adaptive and user-centered interactions [30]. By inferring the user's internal state, a robot can adjust its speed, dialogue, task allocation, or level of assistance to optimize performance, safety, or user experience. This approach has been applied in various contexts, including collaborative tasks, learning environments, and assistive robotics [23] work extends this concept to the domain of cybersecurity, proposing to use physiological signals to detect susceptibility to social engineering.

AI in Cybersecurity and Social Engineering and its Application in Social Robots. Artificial intelligence (AI) plays a dual role in the context of cybersecurity and social engineering: it is both a tool for defense and a potential weapon for attackers. AI, particularly machine learning and natural language processing (NLP), is increasingly used to enhance traditional cybersecurity defenses, such as detecting phishing emails, identifying malicious websites, and analyzing communication patterns for signs of social engineering [2,15]. AI systems can analyze vast datasets, identify subtle anomalies, and adapt to evolving attack strategies more quickly than traditional rule-based systems.

In the context of social robots, AI models are crucial for enabling their social capabilities, including natural language understanding and generation, emotion recognition, and adaptive behavior [34,35]. These models allow robots to engage in complex interactions, interpret human cues, and respond in a socially appropriate manner. For instance, deep learning models are used for facial expression recognition to infer user emotions, while reinforcement learning can enable robots to learn optimal social interaction strategies through trial and error. The synergy between AI models and social robots is fundamental for creating truly intelligent and interactive systems. Still, it also introduces new vectors for exploitation if these models are compromised or designed with malicious intent. Understanding how AI models contribute to the social intelligence of robots is therefore essential when considering defense mechanisms against socio-emotional exploitation.

However, AI can also be weaponized by malicious actors to conduct more sophisticated and large-scale social engineering attacks [2,15]. AI can be used to generate highly personalized phishing messages, create realistic deepfakes for impersonation, and automate the process of identifying and exploiting psychological vulnerabilities [15]. The emergence of large language models (LLMs) capable of generating convincing text and dialogue also raises concerns about "banal deception," where AI systems may unintentionally or intentionally produce misleading information in social interactions. This highlights the need for robust, adaptive defenses that can counter AI-driven social engineering threats.

3 The Pasquali et al. [23] System: A Physiologically-Informed Defense

Pasquali et al. [23] proposes a novel adaptive defense system specifically designed to protect human users from social engineering threats, potentially mediated through interaction with a social robot companion. The system's core innovation lies in its human-centric approach, utilizing real-time physiological signals to infer the user's internal state and susceptibility to manipulation.

3.1 Core Concept and Adaptive Nature

The fundamental concept behind the Pasquali et al. system is that physiological responses provide objective, real-time indicators of a user's cognitive and affective state during an interaction, which are relevant to their vulnerability to social engineering. Changes in pupil diameter, galvanic skin response (GSR), and heart rate variability (HRV) have been linked to cognitive load, stress, emotional arousal, and risk appraisal [18,28]. By continuously monitoring these signals using non-invasive sensors (e.g., eye-trackers for pupil dilation and gaze [36], wearable biosensors for GSR and HRV), the system aims to gain insight into the user's internal state as they engage in a conversation or task that might involve a social engineering attempt. The system's adaptivity stems from its use of machine learning models trained on these physiological features. These models analyze the real-time data to predict the likelihood of the user complying with a potentially malicious request or succumbing to deception. This predictive capability allows the system to dynamically assess the perceived threat level and the user's vulnerability, enabling it to adapt its response accordingly.

3.2 Robot's Role: Sensing and Intervention

Within this proposed framework, the social robot serves a crucial dual role:

- *Sensing and Prediction Platform*: The robot can act as the physical platform, integrating the necessary physiological sensors or receiving data streams from external wearable sensors. The robot's processing unit can host or interact with the machine learning models that analyze the physiological data. This analysis aims to detect patterns indicative of deception by an interaction partner (human or potentially another AI system) or to predict the user's susceptibility and likelihood of complying with risky suggestions.
- *Adaptive Intervention and Support*: Based on the system's real-time prediction of risk and user vulnerability, the robot can actively intervene to support the user's decision-making process. The nature of this intervention is designed to be adaptive and context-dependent. [23] explores various intervention strategies, moving beyond simple, generic warnings. These strategies include providing explicit warnings about potential risks or actively attempting to persuade the user away from a risky course of action. The persuasion can employ different dialogue strategies, such as affective appeals (e.g., expressing concern for the user's well-being) or rational arguments (e.g., providing logical reasons why a request might be malicious).

4 Methodology and Empirical Validation

To build the foundation for their proposed defense system, [23] summarizes four experiments conducted by the authors. These experiments progressively investigate key components necessary for a physiologically-informed social engineering defense: trust dynamics in HRI, the potential for detecting deception using physiological signals, predicting user compliance with risky requests based on physiological and behavioral data, and exploring the effectiveness of different robot intervention strategies.

- *Experiment 1 (Trust Development)*: This experiment, using the iCub robot in a treasure hunt game, investigated how robot faults and transparency about those faults impacted human trust and subjective evaluations.
- *Experiment 2 (Deception Detection)*: Using the iCub in a magic trick card game, this study explored the use of real-time pupil dilation as a physiological marker for detecting human lies.
- *Experiment 3 (Compliance Prediction)*: This experiment employed a Choose-Your-Own-Adventure game with text-based advice (with or without the iCub robot present) under different risk conditions and social engineering threats. It utilized physiological data (GSR, PPG, Pupil, Gaze) and mouse data to train machine learning models to classify risk and predict user compliance.
- *Experiment 4 (Robot Intervention)*: Using the Furhat robot in a modified CYOA game, this ongoing study explored the effectiveness of different robot persuasion strategies (affective vs. rational) in mitigating user compliance with risky suggestions.

5 Critical Analysis and Discussion

Pasquali et al. [23] represents a significant step towards developing adaptive, human-oriented defenses against socio-emotional exploitation in HRI. However, a critical analysis of their findings and proposed system reveals both promising potential and substantial challenges.

5.1 Analysis of Empirical Findings

The empirical findings presented by Pasquali et al. provide a foundational basis for their proposed system, but some results warrant closer examination and contextualization within the broader literature. The observation from Experiment 1 that transparency about robot faults negatively impacted trust is a crucial nuance to the widely accepted principle that transparency generally builds trust in HRI. This suggests that the *nature* and *context* of transparency are critical. Revealing limitations or errors may understandably damage trust related to the robot's competence or reliability, complicating straightforward design guidelines that advocate for maximal transparency in all situations. Future research should further explore the types of transparency that build or erode different dimensions of trust (e.g., trust in ability vs. trust in benevolence) [19]. The reported 88.2% lie detection accuracy using only pupil dilation in Experiment 2 is notably high for a single physiological channel in a task as complex as deception detection. While pupillometry is linked to cognitive load, which is often associated with lying [18,30], achieving this level of accuracy in a real-world scenario with diverse stressors, individual differences, and confounding factors (e.g., ambient light changes, emotional arousal unrelated to deception, fatigue) would be significantly challenging. Likely, the highly controlled laboratory setting and the specific nature of the card game task contributed to this result, limiting its generalizability. Similarly, the 65% accuracy achieved in predicting user compliance in Experiment 3, while statistically significant, indicates a substantial error rate (35%). In a real-world security application, this error rate could lead to both false positives (unnecessary and potentially annoying interventions) and false negatives (failure to protect the user from a genuine threat). This underscores that human decision-making under social influence is a complex process influenced by numerous factors beyond immediate physiological state, including personality traits, prior experiences, cultural background, the specific framing of the social engineering attempt, and the perceived relationship with the influencing agent [14], many of which are not captured by the current system.

5.2 Transparency in Social Robots

In the context of social robots, *transparency* refers to the degree to which a robot's internal states, intentions, capabilities, and limitations are made understandable and accessible to human users. This can manifest in various ways, including:

- *Operational Transparency*: Revealing how the robot functions, its decision-making processes, and the data it collects and uses. This includes making its algorithms, sensors, and actuators comprehensible to users.
- *Intentional Transparency*: Communicating the robot's goals, purposes, and the rationale behind its actions. This helps users understand *why* the robot is doing what it is doing.
- *Situational Transparency*: Providing information about the robot's current state, its perception of the environment, and any uncertainties or errors it might be experiencing. This allows users to form an accurate mental model of the robot's capabilities and limitations in real-time.

Transparency in HRI is crucial for building and maintaining trust, enabling effective collaboration, and ensuring user safety and autonomy. However, as highlighted by Experiment 1 in Pasquali et al. [23], the impact of transparency is nuanced. While general transparency is often seen as beneficial, revealing certain types of information (e.g., robot failures or limitations) can paradoxically erode trust if not managed carefully. The goal is not necessarily maximal transparency, but rather *appropriate transparency* that provides users with the necessary information without overwhelming them or undermining their confidence in the robot's overall utility and reliability. This requires careful design considerations to balance informativeness with user experience and trust dynamics.

5.3 Significance and Potential Impact

Despite the preliminary nature of some findings, the research by [23] carries significant potential implications for social robotics, AI ethics, and HRI design.

- *Contribution to Social Robotics*: This work pushes the boundaries of social robot capabilities by exploring the potential for robots to perceive and react to users' implicit cognitive and affective states inferred from physiological data.

This aligns with the broader trajectory towards developing robots capable of more nuanced, adaptive, and socially intelligent interactions [3], potentially enabling them to take on more complex and sensitive social roles in assistance, care, or collaboration [18].
- *Contribution to AI Ethics*: The research directly engages with critical AI ethics themes, including trustworthy AI, mitigating AI-related risks, and the ethics of human-AI interaction [11,17]. By proposing a technological mechanism to defend against socio-emotional exploitation, it offers a potential solution to a significant ethical problem in HRI. However, as discussed in the limitations, the solution itself introduces a new set of profound ethical considerations regarding privacy, autonomy, and manipulation.
- *Contribution to HRI Design*: The work suggests concrete design directions for future social robots, advocating for the integration of human state sensing and adaptive interaction strategies. It opens possibilities for personalized HRI, where robot behavior is dynamically tailored not just to task requirements but also to the inferred real-time state of the user [30], potentially leading to safer and more effective interactions.
- *Potential Applications*: If developed successfully and ethically, such adaptive defense systems could have valuable real-world applications. They might offer enhanced protection for vulnerable populations (e.g., older adults, children) who are often disproportionately targeted by online scams or manipulation, potentially delivered via robotic interfaces or companion agents [26]. The technology could also be integrated into cybersecurity training simulators to provide real-time feedback on trainees' susceptibility to social engineering tactics or contribute to creating more robust and trustworthy collaborative robots in safety-critical industrial or healthcare environments [31,32].

Beyond these direct contributions, the research highlights the blurring lines between protective technology and persuasive technology. The mechanisms explored—sensing internal states to predict behavior and deploying tailored interventions—are fundamental to the field of persuasive technology [12]. While framed as a defense system, the underlying technology could readily be adapted for other persuasive goals, such as marketing, health behavior change, or political influence. This raises significant ethical questions about how such capabilities should be governed and deployed, demanding careful consideration of user autonomy and the potential for misuse.

5.4 Limitations and Assumptions

The research [23], while innovative, is subject to several limitations and rests on key assumptions that need to be acknowledged and addressed in future work.
- *Ecological Validity*: A significant limitation is the reliance on controlled laboratory settings and specific game-based tasks. The complexity and unpredictability of real-world social interactions and social engineering attempts are difficult to replicate in a lab, raising questions about the ecological validity and generalizability of the findings regarding trust dynamics, deception detection, and compliance prediction.

- *Sample Size and Platform Specificity*: Some experiments, particularly the compliance prediction study with $N = 20$ participants, involved relatively small sample sizes. This limits the statistical power of the results and their generalizability to a broader population. Furthermore, the findings are based on interactions with specific robot platforms (iCub, Furhat), and different robot morphologies, behaviors, and interaction modalities could yield different results.
- *Signal Interpretation Challenges*: The system assumes that measurable physiological signals reliably and consistently correlate with specific internal states relevant to social engineering susceptibility across diverse individuals and contexts. However, physiological responses are influenced by numerous factors beyond the interaction itself, including environmental stimuli, unrelated thoughts, fatigue, stress, medication, and baseline individual differences [18,30]. Reliably attributing detected changes in physiological state solely to the social engineering attempt or the relevant decision-making process is a significant challenge.
- *Model Accuracy*: The reported prediction accuracies for deception detection and compliance prediction, while exceeding chance, are not perfect. The error rate, particularly for compliance prediction (35%), could lead to problematic false positives or negatives in a deployed system, potentially eroding user trust or failing to provide necessary protection.
- *Intervention Effectiveness and Acceptance*: The crucial experiment evaluating the effectiveness of different robot intervention strategies was ongoing at the time of publication. The assumption that robot interventions based on inferred states will be effective in mitigating risk and will be accepted, rather than ignored or perceived as intrusive, by users requires thorough empirical validation.
- *Underlying Assumptions*: The approach rests on the assumption that the potential benefits of preventing socio-emotional exploitation through this technology outweigh the significant ethical costs associated with continuous physiological monitoring and persuasive intervention. This is a value judgment that warrants careful consideration and public discourse.

5.5 Visual Representation of Attack Types

To further enhance the understanding of the threat landscape, a visual representation of common social robot attack types is included (Fig. 1). Based on a qualitative synthesis of recent literature and surveys, the following chart illustrates the estimated prevalence of different attack categories. This visualization aims to provide readers with a quick overview of the primary security concerns in social robotics. Social engineering attacks appear most frequently, followed by privacy-related data breaches and physical tampering. Emerging threats and software/network vulnerabilities also contribute to the security landscape.

This qualitative assessment highlights that social engineering attacks, particularly those involving manipulation and trust elicitation, represent a significant

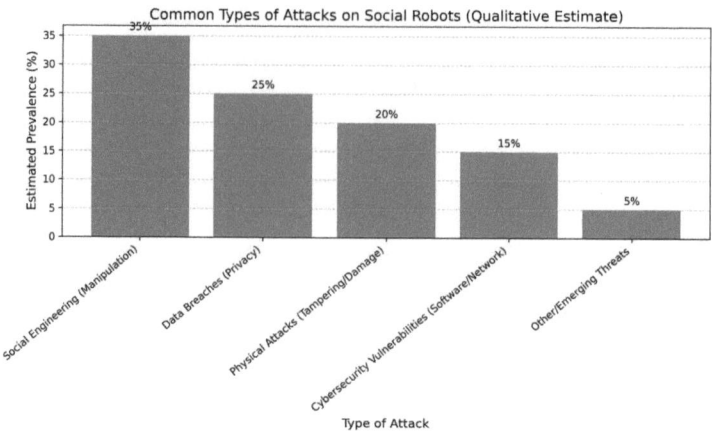

Fig. 1. Estimated prevalence of common attack types on social robots, based on qualitative analysis of literature and search trends.

portion of the threat landscape, underscoring the importance of adaptive defense mechanisms. Data breaches and privacy concerns, often resulting from the extensive data collection capabilities of social robots, also constitute a major threat. Physical attacks, which can involve tampering or direct damage to the robot, and general cybersecurity vulnerabilities (e.g., software exploits, network weaknesses) complete the primary categories. While these percentages are qualitative estimates based on current research trends, they provide a valuable conceptual framework for understanding the distribution of risks.

5.6 Proposals for Enhancement and Future Directions

Building upon the foundational work of Pasquali et al. [23], several avenues for enhancement and future research emerge, aiming to address the identified limitations and broaden the scope of physiologically-informed adaptive defenses in HRI.

- *Broader Literature Integration and Meta-Review*: To address the perceived over-reliance on a single prior work, future iterations of this review should explicitly position themselves as meta-reviews, systematically integrating a wider range of literature on socio-emotional exploitation, deception detection, and adaptive systems in HRI. This would involve a more comprehensive search strategy, potentially including systematic reviews or meta-analyses of empirical studies beyond those summarized by Pasquali et al. This broader scope would help to contextualize the problem space more effectively and identify alternative or complementary defense strategies, such as behavioral or contextual modeling approaches that do not solely rely on physiological signals.
- *Rigorously Critiquing Empirical Evidence and Methodological Limitations*: While Pasquali et al. provide valuable empirical insights, future work should

include a more rigorous critique of the cited empirical evidence. This involves a deeper examination of methodological limitations, including ecological validity, sample sizes, and the generalizability of findings from controlled laboratory settings to real-world scenarios. For instance, future experiments could be designed with larger, more diverse participant pools and conducted in more naturalistic environments to enhance ecological validity. Furthermore, a detailed discussion of potential confounding factors in physiological signal interpretation (e.g., individual differences, environmental noise) and strategies to mitigate them would strengthen the empirical foundation.

- *Clarifying Novel Contribution and Forward-Looking Roadmap*: To move beyond merely summarizing existing work, future research should explicitly articulate its novel contribution. This could involve positioning the work as a critical synthesis that extends the implications of physiologically-informed defenses within the broader domains of HRI, AI ethics, and cybersecurity. A forward-looking roadmap could outline specific research questions, technological developments, and ethical guidelines necessary for the responsible development and deployment of such systems. This might include proposing novel physiological markers, advanced machine learning techniques for signal processing, or innovative intervention strategies.
- *Concrete Design and Policy Recommendations*: The current work highlights shortcomings but could benefit from offering more concrete proposals for enhancement. This includes suggesting specific improvements grounded in empirical data or theoretical frameworks. For example, future research could propose specific design principles for transparent robot behavior, develop standardized protocols for physiological data collection in HRI, or formulate policy recommendations for the ethical governance of social robots with adaptive defense capabilities. This could involve exploring hybrid defense mechanisms that combine physiological monitoring with behavioral analysis, user education, and contextual awareness.
- *Enhanced Experimental Detail and Reproducibility*: To improve the clarity and reproducibility of the experimental setups described, future publications should provide more detailed information on the methodology and environment of the experimentations. This includes precise descriptions of the robot platforms used, sensor specifications, data acquisition protocols, experimental procedures, participant demographics, and data analysis techniques. Providing open-source code or datasets where feasible would further enhance reproducibility and facilitate collaborative research.

5.7 Ethical Considerations

The development and deployment of adaptive defense systems based on physiological signals in social robots raises a complex array of ethical considerations that extend beyond traditional HRI ethics guidelines. This approach intersects with issues of privacy, autonomy, manipulation, transparency, trust, bias, and the unique vulnerabilities of specific populations.

- *Privacy*: The continuous collection, processing, and storage of highly sensitive real-time physiological data (pupil dilation, GSR, HRV) represent a significant privacy intrusion, particularly within personal and intimate environments like the home [27]. Concerns include the potential for data breaches, unauthorised access, misuse of data for profiling, discrimination, or surveillance, and the chilling effect of constant biometric monitoring on user behavior. Robust data security, anonymization techniques, clear data usage policies, and strong user control over their data are paramount but challenging to guarantee in practice.
- *Autonomy and Manipulation*: The robot's role as an active intervener employing persuasion strategies, even with protective intent, raises serious questions about user autonomy. Does influencing a user's decision based on inferred physiological susceptibility constitute undue manipulation or paternalism, infringing on their right to make their own choices, even if those choices carry risks? Affective persuasion, in particular, leverages emotional responses and could potentially bypass rational deliberation, raising further ethical flags regarding informed consent and genuine choice [12].
- *Transparency and Explainability*: The opacity inherent in physiological monitoring and complex machine learning models poses challenges for transparency and explainability [1]. Users may not be fully aware of which physiological signals are being monitored, how they are being interpreted, or the specific logic behind the system's risk assessment and intervention decisions. This lack of transparency can hinder user understanding, make it difficult to calibrate trust appropriately, and limit the user's ability to contest erroneous assessments or interventions.
- *Trust and Reliance*: The reliability of the system directly impacts user trust [16]. Errors (false positives or negatives) can erode trust in the robot and the system. Conversely, over-reliance on the system, potentially fostered by a perception of it as an infallible protector, could lead to automation complacency, where users become less vigilant and critical in evaluating potential threats themselves [22]. This highlights a potential ethical trade-off between short-term protection and the maintenance of long-term user competence and resilience.
- *Bias and Fairness*: Physiological responses can vary significantly based on demographic factors, health conditions, cultural backgrounds, and temporary states [18, 30]. If the training data for the machine learning models is not sufficiently diverse or if the system fails to account for individual baselines and variations, it could lead to biased predictions and differential effectiveness. This could result in certain demographic groups receiving less effective protection or being unfairly targeted by interventions, potentially exacerbating existing inequalities.
- *Vulnerable Populations*: Deploying such systems with vulnerable users, such as children, the elderly, or individuals with cognitive or emotional impairments, requires heightened ethical sensitivity [26]. These individuals may be less able to provide truly informed consent, understand the technology's work-

ings, resist persuasive interventions, or articulate concerns about privacy violations.
- *Societal Implications*: The widespread adoption of robots equipped with continuous physiological monitoring capabilities could fundamentally alter societal norms around privacy and interpersonal boundaries. If intimate bio-data becomes routinely collected and analyzed in everyday interactions with technology, it could lead to an erosion of personal space and the expectation of privacy, normalizing a level of surveillance that raises profound societal-level ethical questions extending far beyond individual consent protocols. Furthermore, access to sophisticated (and likely expensive) social robots incorporating these protective features might be limited to privileged groups, leaving others more exposed to socio-emotional exploitation and potentially creating new forms of technologically mediated inequality.

6 Future Directions

The research by [23] and the broader landscape of related work highlight several crucial directions for future research and development in adaptive defense against socio-emotional exploitation in social robots.

- *Improving Sensing Reliability and Validity in Real-World Environments*: Future work needs to focus on developing more robust and reliable methods for capturing and interpreting physiological signals in noisy, dynamic, and uncontrolled real-world environments. This includes addressing challenges related to sensor placement, motion artifacts, environmental interference (e.g., lighting changes affecting pupillometry), and accounting for individual differences and contextual factors that influence physiological responses.
- *Developing Ethically Sound and Effective Intervention Strategies*: Further research is needed to explore a wider range of robot intervention strategies that prioritize user autonomy and control while being effective in mitigating risk. This could involve moving beyond direct persuasion to focus on enhancing user awareness, providing relevant information, prompting critical thinking, or offering alternative perspectives, empowering the user rather than simply attempting to influence their decision. Longitudinal studies are essential to understand the long-term effects of different intervention types on user behavior, trust calibration, and overall well-being.
- *Longitudinal Studies on User Adaptation and Trust*: Understanding how users adapt to interacting with adaptive defense systems over time is critical. Longitudinal studies are needed to investigate the potential for automation complacency, changes in user vigilance, the long-term impact on trust calibration, and how the system affects the user's perceived autonomy and relationship with the robot.
- *Exploring Alternative and Complementary Defense Mechanisms*: While physiological sensing offers a promising avenue, it should not be the sole defense mechanism. Future research should explore complementary approaches, such

as advanced transparency tools that explain robot reasoning and potential risks, user empowerment interfaces that provide control over the interaction, adversarial training for robots to recognize manipulation attempts, and multi-layered defense architectures that combine different sensing and mitigation strategies.
- *Refining Ethical Frameworks and Design Guidelines*: The unique ethical challenges posed by adaptive, physiologically-informed HRI systems necessitate the development of specific ethical guidelines and assessment methodologies. These frameworks should address the complex trade-offs between protection, privacy, autonomy, and transparency, providing practical guidance for researchers, designers, and policymakers.
- *Cross-Cultural Research*: Perceptions of social cues, trust in technology, and acceptance of monitoring and intervention can vary significantly across different cultural contexts. Cross-cultural research is essential to ensure that adaptive defense systems are culturally sensitive, equitable, and effective for diverse user populations.
- *Addressing Advanced AI Deception*: As AI capabilities advance, including the potential for sophisticated AI-driven social engineering and *banal deception* from LLMs, future research must focus on developing defenses that can effectively detect and mitigate these emerging threats [33]. This may require novel approaches that go beyond current methods.

7 Conclusion

The increasing integration of social robots into human lives brings with it the significant risk of socio-emotional exploitation through social engineering attacks. Traditional cybersecurity defenses are insufficient against threats that leverage human psychological and social vulnerabilities. The work [23] offers a promising approach by proposing an adaptive defense system that utilizes real-time physiological signals to infer user susceptibility and enable a robot companion to provide timely support and intervention. Their preliminary empirical findings suggest that physiological signals contain information relevant to trust, deception, and risk appraisal, providing a foundation for physiologically-informed defense strategies. However, the development and deployment of such intimate and adaptive HRI systems are fraught with complexities and profound ethical tensions. The reliance on sensitive physiological data raises major privacy concerns, while the robot's potential to actively persuade users, even for their protection, challenges fundamental notions of autonomy. Issues of transparency, bias, trust calibration, and accountability further underscore the need for careful and deliberate development. Future research must focus on improving the reliability of sensing and signal interpretation in real-world environments, developing ethically sound intervention strategies that prioritize user autonomy, conducting longitudinal studies to understand long-term effects, exploring alternative defense mechanisms, refining ethical frameworks, and addressing the risks posed by advanced AI deception.

References

1. Adadi, A., Berrada, M.: Peeking inside the black-box: a survey on Explainable Artificial Intelligence (XAI). IEEE Access **6**, 52138–52160 (2018). https://doi.org/10.1109/ACCESS.2018.2870052
2. Arif, A., Khan, M.I., Khan, A.R.A., Janabi, A.: AI's revolutionary role in cyber defense and social engineering. Int. J. Multidisc. Sci. Arts **3**(4) (2024)
3. Breazeal, C.: Designing Sociable Robots. MIT Press, Cambridge (2003)
4. Danaher, J.: Robot betrayal: a guide to the ethics of robotic deception. Ethics Inf. Technol. **2** (2020). https://doi.org/10.1007/s10676-019-09520-3
5. Duffy, B.: Fundamental issues in affective intelligent social machines. Open Artif. Intell. J. **2**. 21– (2008). https://doi.org/10.2174/1874061800802010021
6. Epley, N., Waytz, A., Cacioppo, J.T.: On seeing human: a three-factor theory of anthropomorphism. Psychol. Rev. **114**(4), 864–8862007. https://doi.org/10.1037/0033-295X.114.4.864. PMID: 17907867
7. Esposito, R., Rossi, A., Rossi, S.: Deception in HRI and its implications: a systematic review. arXiv preprint arXiv:2403.17870
8. Esposito, R., Rossi, A., Ponticorvo, M., Rossi, S.: Trust in deceptive robots. In: CEUR Workshop Proceedings, vol. 3825, pp. 1–6
9. Esterwood, C., Robert, L.P.: A literature review of trust repair in HRI. arXiv preprint arXiv:2207.02061 (2022)
10. Fairclough, S.H.: Fundamentals of physiological computing. Interact. Comput. **21**(1–2), 133–145 (2009)
11. Floridi, L., et al.: AI4People—ethical framework for a good AI society: opportunities, risks, recommendations in policy, research and innovation. Mind. Mach. **28**(4), 689–707 (2018). https://doi.org/10.1007/s11023-018-9482-5
12. Fogg, B.J.: Persuasive Technology: Using Computers to Change What We Think and Do. Morgan Kaufmann (2003)
13. Fong, T., Nourbakhsh, I., Dautenhahn, K.: A survey of socially interactive robots. Robot. Auton. Syst. **42**(3–4), 143–161 (2003). https://doi.org/10.1016/S0921-8890(02)00372-X
14. Hadnagy, C.: Social Engineering: The Art of Human Hacking. Wiley, New York (2010)
15. Harvard Kennedy School: Weaponized AI: a new era of threats and how we can counter it (2025). https://ash.harvard.edu/articles/weaponized-ai-a-new-era-of-threats/
16. Hoff, K.A., Bashir, M.: Trust in automation: integrating empirical evidence on factors influencing trust. Hum. Factors **57**(3), 407–434 (2015)
17. Jobin, A., Ienca, M., Vayena, E.: The global landscape of AI ethics guidelines. Nat. Mach. Intell. **1**(9), 389–399 (2019). https://doi.org/10.1038/s42256-019-0088-2
18. Laban, G., Cross, E.S.: Sharing our emotions with robots: why do we do it and how does it make us feel? arXiv preprint arXiv:2108.05723 (2021)
19. Lee, J.D., See, K.A.: Trust in automation: designing for appropriate reliance. Hum. Factors **46**(1), 50–8 (2004). https://doi.org/10.1518/hfes.46.1.50_30392
20. Torras, C.: Ethics of social robotics: individual and societal concerns and opportunities. Annu. Rev. Control Robot. Auton. Syst. **7** (2023). https://doi.org/10.1146/annurev-control-062023-082238
21. Nomura, T., Suzuki, T., Kanda, T., Kato, K.: Measurement of anxiety toward robots. Interact. Stud. **7**(3), 437–453 (2006)

22. Parasuraman, R., Riley, V.: Humans and automation: use, misuse, disuse, abuse. Hum. Factors **39**(3), 381–401 (1997). https://doi.org/10.1518/001872097778543886
23. Pasquali, D., Sciutti, A., Sandini, G., Bencetti, S., Rea, F.: Toward a human-oriented social engineering defense system. In: Proceedings of the Second CINI National Conference on Artificial Intelligence (Itali-IA 2022): AI for Cybersecurity, pp. 1–5 (2022)
24. Rogers, L.M., Basapur, S., Scheutz, M.: Human perceptions of social robot deception behaviors: an exploratory analysis. Front. Robot. AI **11**, 1409712 (2023). https://doi.org/10.3389/frobt.2023.1409712
25. Oruma, S.O., Sánchez-Gordón, M., Colomo-Palacios, R., Gkioulos, V., Hansen, J.K.: A systematic review on social robots in public spaces: threat landscape and attack surface. Computers **11**(12), 1812022. https://doi.org/10.3390/computers11120181
26. Sharkey, A., Sharkey, N.: We need to talk about deception in social robotics!. Ethics Inf. Technol. **23**, 309–316 (2021). https://doi.org/10.1007/s10676-020-09573-9
27. Tavani, H.T.: Ethics and Technology: Controversies, Questions, and Strategies for Ethical Computing. Wiley, New York (2011)
28. Wang, Y., Zhang, Y., Zhang, L., Liu, X.: Capturing mental workload through physiological sensors in human–robot collaboration: a systematic literature review. Appl. Sci. **15**(6), 3317 (2025). https://doi.org/10.3390/app15063317
29. Convertino, G., Talbot, J., Mazzoni, G.: Psychophysiological indexes in the detection of deception: a systematic review. Acta Psychologica **251**, 104618 (2024). ISSN 0001-6918, https://doi.org/10.1016/j.actpsy.2024.104618
30. Złotowski, J., Proudfoot, D., Yogeeswaran, K., et al.: Anthropomorphism: opportunities and challenges in human–robot interaction. Int. J. Soc. Robot. **7**, 347–360 (2015). https://doi.org/10.1007/s12369-014-0267-6
31. D'Arco, L., et al.: Towards trustworthy and explainable socially assistive robots: a cognitive architecture for dietary guidance. In: 2025 IEEE International Conference on Simulation, Modeling, and Programming for Autonomous Robots (SIMPAR). IEEE (2025)
32. D'Arco, L., Rossi, A., Rossi, S.: Assessing emotion mitigation through robot facial expressions for human-robot interaction. In: CEUR Workshop Proceedings, vol. 3932, pp. 46–51 (2025)
33. Greco, D., Chianese, L.: Exploiting LLMs for e-learning: a cybersecurity perspective on AI-generated tools in education. In: 2024 IEEE International Workshop on Technologies for Defense and Security (TechDefense), Naples, Italy, pp. 237–242 (2024)
34. Greco, D., Barra, P., D'Errico, L., Staffa, M.: Multimodal interfaces for emotion recognition: models, challenges and opportunities. In: Degen, H., Ntoa, S. (eds.) HCII 2024. LNCS, vol. 14735, pp. 152–162. Springer, Cham (2024). https://doi.org/10.1007/978-3-031-60611-3_11
35. Barra, P., Mnasri, Z., Greco, D.: Multimodal emotion recognition from voice and video signals. In: IEEE EUROCON 2023 - 20th International Conference on Smart Technologies, Torino, Italy, pp. 169–174 (2023)
36. Greco, D., Masulli, F., Rovetta, S., Cabri, A., Daffonchio, D.: A cost-effective eye-tracker for early detection of mild cognitive impairment. In: 2022 IEEE 21st Mediterranean Electrotechnical Conference Palermo, Italy, pp. 1141–1146 (2022)

Exploring Students' Perceptions of an Educational Robot: The Influence of Voice and Video Modalities

Maria Sarno[1](✉), Marialucia Cuciniello[1], Terry Amorese[1,2],
Gennaro Cordasco[2], Vasco D'Agnese[1], and Anna Esposito[1]

[1] Department of Psychology, University of Campania "Luigi Vanvitelli", Caserta, Italy
{maria.sarno,marialucia.cuciniello,terry.amorese,Vasco.D'AGNESE,
anna.esposito}@unicampania.it
[2] Department of Computer Science, University of Salerno, Salerno, Italy
g.cordasco@unisa.it

Abstract. The increasing integration of social robots in education and learning underscores the need for a deeper understanding of the factors influencing their acceptance. The current pilot study investigates students' acceptance of educational social robots, focusing on Pepper, which was presented through both voice recording and video clip. A sample of 20 students aged 11 to 13 was exposed to both audio and audiovisual stimuli depicting Pepper and subsequently asked to complete a modified version of the Robot Acceptance Questionnaire (RAQ), adapted for educational purposes (RAQ-RL). The results indicate that both participants' gender and the mode of robot presentation significantly impact the acceptance of the proposed educational robot. In particular, male students were more willing (p = .011) to interact with the robot and rated him more positively than females in terms of hedonic qualities – feeling (p = .026) and intelligibility of the voice (p = .025) Additionally, the video clip presentation modality was preferred over the voice presentation modality.

Keywords: Social Robot · Educational Robot · Acceptance · Students

1 Introduction

Robots have become an integral part of our daily lives, playing an important role in society [1] and can appear as machines, toys or humanoids [2]. Social robots are a specific type of robot designed to interact with humans by following the behavioural norms expected by humans [3]. They are designed to provide social assistance in various fields, such as education, health and consumer services [4, 5]. In the educational field, the term "social robot" refers to the use of robotic devices designed to interact with students, enhance engagement, and support their learning experiences [5, 6]. Educational robot can be used both as tools to teach programming and as social agents playing roles such as tutors, peers, or novices [1, 2, 5]. The most common educational social robots are Nao and Pepper, humanoid robot models from SoftBank Robotic [1, 7, 8]. Their design, characterized by a non-threatening appearance, serves to reduce the "Uncanny Valley" effect [9] and to increase user acceptance [10]. The Uncanny Valley Hypothesis describes people's reactions to robots, suggesting that the endowment of human characteristics to social robots negatively affects their users' perceptions of robots: as the similarity to humans increases, so does the feeling of discomfort [9].Tung [11] found that children and adolescents tended to prefer robots that displayed social cues through their movements and exhibited only a moderate degree of human-likeness, as opposed to those that were either static, moved randomly, or appeared highly human-like. Recently, Esposito and colleagues [12] highlighted that adolescents prefer to interact with humanoid robots and rated them as more pleasant, appealing and engaging than android robots. This suggests that a robot's appearance and behavior significantly influence young users' acceptance and engagement. User' acceptance can be defined "*…as the demonstrable willingness within a user group to employ information technology for the task it designed to support*" [13]. According to the Technology Acceptance Model (TAM) [14] and the Unified Theory of Acceptance and Use of Technology (UTAUT) [15], robots' acceptance is influenced by several factors, including perceived usefulness, ease of use, hedonic motivation, social influence and others relevant factors. The increasing use of social robots in educational environments highlights the importance of examining user acceptance to ensure effective implementation and optimize their potential impact on learning outcomes. This pilot study aims to investigate students' acceptance of an educational social robot, focusing on several factors, such as: willingness to interact, pragmatic qualities, hedonic qualities, attractiveness, and intelligibility of the robot's voice. While previous studies have examined children's and adolescents' general attitudes towards various types of robots and presentation modalities (e.g., physical presence vs digitally displayed robots) [11, 16], the specific impact of two distinct presentation modes (voice-only vs audio-visual) on acceptance has largely been overlooked, particularly among pre-adolescents aged 11 to 13. Specifically, this study aims to compare students' acceptance between two presentation modes (respectively, voice recording and video clip), in order to better understand how these different modes of interaction influence students' perceptions of the robot. In the robot video presentation mode, participants were presented with a video clip of the speaking robot, in which, in addition to its voice, its appearance was also shown. In the robot voice recording presentation mode, participants were not shown the robot's appearance, but only its voice. A further aim of the study was to investigate potential gender differences in the evaluation of these two modes.

2 Material and Methods

2.1 Participants

The present study involved twenty participants (10 males) aged 11–13 years (M_{age} = 11.90; SD = 0.78) recruited from the public school "IC Alfano-Quasimodo" in the Italian city of Salerno. All participants spoke Italian as their mother language, and had normal/correct-to-normal vision. The study was conducted in accordance with the Declaration of Helsinki and approved by the Local Ethics Committee of the Department of Psychology of University of Campania "Luigi Vanvitelli" (Ethical approval code

N:33/2024). Written informed consent was obtained from all parents of participants prior to the experiment.

2.2 Stimuli

The stimuli consisted of a voice recording and a video clip representing the humanoid robot Pepper (http://www.softbankrobotics.com). The video clip was produced at the Cognitive Ergonomics Laboratory (BeCogSys) of the University of Campania L. Vanvitelli, using an Apple iPhone 15 Pro (https://www.apple.com/it/iphone/). Pepper's voice was recorded using the free software Audacity (http:// www.audacityteam.org), with the following parameters: 22 kHz, 16-bit wav. The free software Clipchamp (https://clipchamp.com/it/editor-video/) was used to apply a black background to the video and add the recorded voice. Both the voice recording and the video clip produce the following Italian sentence: "Ciao, il mio nome è Pepper. Ho qualcosa di interessante da spiegarti, ti va di ascoltarmi?" ("Hi, my name is Pepper. I have something interesting to explain to you, would you like to listen to me?"). In the video, Pepper accompanies the sentence with arm movements. The length of the voice recording and the video clip is approximately 10 s.

2.3 Tools

Participants' preferences were assessed using the Robot Acceptance Questionnaire – Revised for Learning purposes (RAQ-RL), an adapted version of the Virtual Agent Voice Acceptance Questionnaire – Revised for Learning purposes (VAVAQ-RL) designed for the evaluation of robots. The two questionnaires share identical questions but evaluate respectively robots and vocal chatbots. Both instruments are modified versions of the Virtual Agent Voice Acceptance Questionnaire (VAVAQ) and the Robot Acceptance Questionnaire (RAQ), developed within the EMPATHIC Project (www.empathic-project.eu) [17, 18]. These revised instruments were selected because they incorporate learning-related dimensions. These dimensions were absent from the original versions. The modifications are described in detail at the end of this paragraph. As the VAVAQ-RL, the RAQ-RL consists of six sections and two additional items assessing: (1) socio-demographic information and prior experience with technology; (2) willingness to interact (WI); (3) pragmatic quality (PQ), hedonic quality identity (HQ-I), hedonic quality feeling (HQ-F), and attractiveness (ATT); (4) intelligibility of the voice (VI); (5) task-related evaluations; (6) pedagogical characteristics and learning (LRN). The two additional items assess participants' perception and preference regarding the pedagogical role of the robot. The administration and scoring procedures remain consistent with those of the VAVAQ-RL. It is important to note that Sect. 6 (LRN) of the questionnaire was designed to be administered only after a robot-mediated learning session. However, since the protocol adopted for the present study only involved a general presentation of the robot via both voice recording and video clips, this section was not included in the evaluation and therefore was not administered to the participants. The main differences between the RAQ-RL and the original RAQ version are the following. First, Sect. 5 of the questionnaire, which in both versions assesses the possible tasks that a robot could perform, has been modified. In the RAQ-RL version, this section has been adapted to include tasks related to educational support and play. Second, Sect. 6 (LRN) of the questionnaire has been introduced, which focuses on the pedagogical characteristics of the robot and its perceived effectiveness within a learning environment. Finally, unlike the RAQ version, the RAQ-RL includes two additional questions that assess participants' perceptions and preferences regarding the pedagogical role of the robot.

2.4 Procedure

After obtaining informed consent from the parents, each student participated in the study individually. The experiment took place in a quiet room at school. Each participant was informed of the purpose of the study and asked to wear over-ear headphones (Trust Mauro USB PC Headset) to avoid distractions and to ensure good audio quality. Each participant was seated on a chair in front of the experimenter's PC, which was placed on a desk. The experimenter sat next to the participant throughout the session.

The stimuli were presented through the experimenter's Pc. All participants were presented with all stimuli, and after each stimulus they were asked to answer RAQ-RL questions presented orally by the experimenter. The voice recording was always presented before the video clip to avoid participants associating the face with the voice.

3 Data Analysis and Results

3.1 Data Analysis

A series of repeated measures ANOVAs were performed separately on the WI, PQ, HQ-I, HQ-F, ATT and VI scores to assess students' preferences regarding the type of robot mode presentation (voice recording/video clip). In particular, six 2 x 2 separated repeated-measures ANOVAs were conducted, with participant's gender as a between-subjects factor and the type of robot mode presentation (voice recording/video clip) as within-factor. The confidence interval was set to alpha = .05, and Bonferroni post-hoc tests were applied to assess differences among means.

3.2 Results

Willingness to Interact (WI)

Significant differences emerged as regards the participants' gender [$F(1,18) = 8.117$, $p = .011$]. Male participants (mean = 2.75) expressed a greater willingness to interact with Pepper than female participants (mean = 1.70). No other significant results emerged.

Pragmatic Quality (PQ)

Regarding the assessment of pragmatic qualities, the variables examined did not significantly affect the results.

Hedonic Quality Identity (HQ-I)

Concerning the assessment of hedonic quality identity, the variables examined did not significantly affect the results.

Hedonic Quality Feeling (HQ-F)
Significant differences emerged as regards the participants' gender [$F(1,18) = 5.874$, $p = .026$]. Male participants (mean = 13.55) considered Pepper more capable of eliciting positive feeling than female participants (mean = 10.30). A main effect of the type of robot mode presentation also emerged [$F(1,18) = 4.704$, $p = .044$]. Pepper's video (mean = 12.65) was rated as more capable of eliciting positive feeling than Pepper's voice (mean = 11.20).

The variables Participants' gender and type of robot mode presentation significantly interacted [$F(1,18) = 5.375$, $p = .032$]. Bonferroni's post hoc tests were performed for each single factor (participants' gender and type of robot mode presentation). These tests revealed that: regarding the gender of the participants, there were gender differences in the rating of the Pepper's hedonic ability in the voice mode, but not in the video clip mode. Male participants (mean = 13.60) rated Pepper's voice as more capable of eliciting positive feeling than female participants (mean = 8.80; $p = .013$). Regarding the type of robot mode presentation, a significant difference was found in the rating of Pepper's hedonic quality feeling between the voice mode and the video clip mode among female participants, but not among male participants. Interestingly, female participants rated Pepper's video clip (mean = 11.80) as more capable of eliciting positive feeling than Pepper's voice (mean = 8.80; $p = .005$).

Attractiveness (ATT)
No significant differences were observed for participants' gender [$F(1,18) = 2.00$ $p = .174$]. A main effect of the type of robot mode presentation emerged [$F(1,18) = 5.544$, $p = .030$]. Pepper's video clip (mean = 14.80) was rated as more attractive than Pepper's voice (mean = 12.75).

Intelligibility of Voice (VI)
Significant differences emerged as regards the participants' gender [$F(1,18) = 5.973$, $p = .025$]. Male participants (mean = 9.80) rated Pepper's voice as more intelligible than female participants (mean = 6.85) (Fig. 1).

4 Discussions and Conclusion

The present study investigated the acceptance of Pepper as an educational social robot among students aged 11–13 years, comparing two different types of robot mode presentation (voice recording/video clip) and related potential gender differences in their evaluation. Results showed significant gender differences regarding the willingness to interact with the robot, the HQ-F scores, and the intelligibility of voice. Specifically, male participants expressed a greater willingness to interact with Pepper compared to female participants. In addition, males considered Pepper more capable of eliciting positive feelings and rated its voice as more intelligible than females. These findings are consistent with previous studies showing that males are more willing to interact with robots and found them to be more able to elicit positive feelings than females [12, 18, 19]. In line with a study carried out by Widder, we share the opinion that males seem to be more inclined to perceive robots as playful or technologically stimulating tools

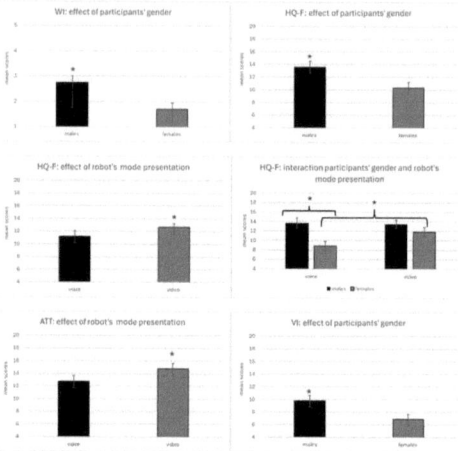

Fig. 1. The Y-axis represents mean scores obtained by robots in terms of participants' assessment of their WI, HQ-F, ATT, and VI.

than female participants [20]. The gender differences in voice intelligibility perception are particularly intriguing and warrant further exploration. Synthetic voices can evoke gender association in children [21]. In this context, the gender differences in the perception of voice intelligibility may be related to male participants' tendency to perceive Pepper's voice as male. This is in line with the similarity-attraction theory [22, 23], which suggests that individuals are more likely to respond positively to robots or agents they perceive as similar to themselves, including. In this regard, the perception of Pepper as male may have influenced male participants' evaluation of the intelligibility of voice and its hedonic quality. As Seaborn and Frank point out [24], although Pepper has no defined gender, it is often perceived as male due to its synthetic voice. However, his socially assigned gender can vary depending on cultural and contextual settings [24], suggesting that socio-cultural expectations and preconceptions may play a role in how robot voice is perceived.

Results also showed a preference for the video clip- presentation modality over the voice- presentation modality in terms of robot attractiveness and hedonic qualities. Participants rated Pepper as more attractive and more capable of eliciting positive feelings in the video presentation modality than in the voice presentation modality. This highlights the importance of visual components (e.g. body presence, body movements, gestures, etc.) in enhancing the aesthetic perception of the robot and users' engagement [11]. Finally, the interaction between participants' gender and type of robot mode presentation showed that males rated Pepper's voice as more capable of arousing positive emotions than females, while females rated the video mode more positively than the voice alone. This suggests that females may benefit more from the visual component of the robot. This pilot study provides findings on the acceptance of an educational social robot by pre-adolescent students, contributing to the field of human-robot interaction (HRI) in educational contexts. However, the limited sample and the absence of direct interaction with the physically present robot represent methodological limitations. Future studies should involve larger and more diverse samples, include comparisons with a physically present robot, and explore perceptions of the robot's pedagogical role.

Acknowledgments. This research received funding by the EU-H2020 program, grant No. 101182965 (CRYSTAL), EU Regeneration PNRR Mission 4 Component 2 Investment 1.1 – D.D 1409 del 14-09-2022 PRIN 2022 – UNDER the IRRESPECTIVE project, code P20222MYKE - CUP: B53D23025980001 and PNRR MUR under AI-PATTERNS FAIR Project CUP:E63C22002150007, and by PNRR founds (DM 118/2023, "Digital and Environmental Transitions") funded by the University of Campania Luigi Vanvitelli.

Disclosure of Interests. None.

References

1. Lehmann, H., Rossi, P.G.: Social robots in educational contexts: Developing an application in enactive didactics. J. e-Learn. Knowl. Soc. **15**(2) (2019)
2. Sannicandro, K., De Santis, A., Bellini, C., Minerva, T.: A scoping review on the relationship between robotics in educational contexts and e-health. In: Frontiers in Education, vol. 7, p. 955572. Frontiers Media SA (2022)
3. Bartneck, C., Forlizzi, J.: A design-centred framework for social human-robot interaction. In: RO-MAN 2004. 13th IEEE International Workshop on Robot and Human Interactive Communication (IEEE Catalog No. 04TH8759), pp. 591–594. IEEE (2004)
4. Baxter, P., Ashurst, E., Read, R., Kennedy, J., Belpaeme, T.: Robot education peers in a situated primary school study: personalisation promotes child learning. PLoS ONE **12**(5), e0178126 (2017)
5. Belpaeme, T., Kennedy, J., Ramachandran, A., Scassellati, B., Tanaka, F.: Social robots for education: a review. Sci. Robot. **3**(21), eaat5954 (2018)
6. Ružić, I., Balaban, I.: The use of social robots as teaching assistants in education: literature review. In: 34th Central European Conference on Information and Intelligent Systems (CECIIS 2023), pp. 205–212 (2023)
7. Bettencourt, C., Grossard, C., Anzalone, S., Chetouani, M., Cohen, D.: Robotica e trattamento dei disturbi del neurosviluppo: revisione della letteratura. Prosp. Pediatr **51**, 1–9 (2021)
8. Guggemos, J., Seufert, S., Sonderegger, S.: Humanoid robots in higher education: evaluating the acceptance of Pepper in the context of an academic writing course using the UTAUT. Br. J. Edu. Technol. **51**(5), 1864–1883 (2020)
9. Mori, M.: The uncanny valley: the original essay by Masahiro Mori. IEEE Spectr. **6**(1), 6 (1970)
10. Woo, H., LeTendre, G.K., Pham-Shouse, T., Xiong, Y.: The use of social robots in classrooms: a review of field-based studies. Educ. Res. Rev. **33**, 100388 (2021)
11. Tung, F.W.: Child perception of humanoid robot appearance and behavior. Int. J. Hum.-Comput. Interact. **32**(6), 493–502 (2016)
12. Esposito, A., Cuciniello, M., Amorese, T., Vinciarelli, A., Cordasco, G.: Humanoid and android robots in the imaginary of adolescents, young adults and seniors. J. Ambient. Intell. Humaniz. Comput. **15**(5), 2699–2718 (2024)
13. Dillon, A., Morris, M.G.: User acceptance of new information technology: theories and models (1996)
14. Davis, F.D.: Technology acceptance model: TAM. Al-Suqri, MN, Al-Aufi, AS: Information Seeking Behavior and Technology Adoption, 205(219), vol. 5 (1989)

15. Venkatesh, V., Davis, F.D.: A model of the antecedents of perceived ease of use: development and test. Decis. Sci. **27**(3), 451–481 (1996)
16. Li, J.: The benefit of being physically present: a survey of experimental works comparing copresent robots, telepresent robots and virtual agents. Int. J. Hum Comput Stud. **77**, 23–37 (2015)
17. Esposito, A., Amorese, T., Cuciniello, M., Esposito, A.M., Cordasco, G.: Do you like me? Behavioral and physical features for socially and emotionally engaging interactive systems. Front. Comput. Sci. **5**, 1138501 (2023)
18. Esposito, A., Amorese, T., Cuciniello, M., Cavallo, F., Vinciarelli, A., Cordasco, G.: Comparing middle-aged and seniors' preferences toward virtual agents and android robots: is there a generational shift in assistive technologies' preferences?. In: Italian Forum of Ambient Assisted Living, pp. 85–101. Springer International Publishing, Cham (2020)
19. Greco, C., Amorese, T., Cuciniello, M., Cordasco, G., Esposito, A.: Android robots vs virtual agents: which system differently aged users prefer?. In: 2022 31st IEEE International Conference on Robot and Human Interactive Communication (RO-MAN), pp. 1–7. IEEE (2022)
20. Widder, D.G.: Gender and Robots: A Literature Review. arXiv preprint arXiv:2206.04716 (2022)
21. Sandygulova, A., O'Hare, G.M.: Age-and gender-based differences in children's interactions with a gender-matching robot. Int. J. Soc. Robot. **10**(5), 687–700 (2018)
22. Byrne, D., et al.: The ubiquitous relationship: attitude similarity and attraction: a cross-cultural study. Hum. Relations **24**(3), 201–207 (1971)
23. Reeves, B., Nass, C.: The media equation: how people treat computers, television, and new media like real people. Cambridge, UK **10**(10), 19–36 (1996)
24. Seaborn, K., Frank, A.: What pronouns for pepper? a critical review of gender/ing in research. In: Proceedings of the 2022 CHI Conference on Human Factors in Computing Systems, pp. 1–15

Author Index

MISC
Álvarez-Arias, Sofía 149

A
Ahn, Ho Seok 677, 692
Akhond, Saina 587, 593
Alfieri, Ilaria 599
Aliotta, Riccardo 283
Alonso-Martín, Fernando 642
Amaro, Ilaria 3
Amirabdollahian, Farshid 375, 459
Amorese, Terry 722
Apraiz, Ainhoa 531
Armstrong, Triniti 120
Ashkenazi, Shaul 92
Atzmueller, Martin 560
Azizi, Negin 538

B
Back, Joey 677
Barbato, Mario 658
Barros, Pablo 500
Belpaeme, Tony 400, 698
Ben Allouch, Somaya 327
Beraldo, Gloria 568
Berkovich, Boris 664
Bernotat, Jasmin 58
Biagi, Federico 166
Biagiotti, Luigi 166
Blanco, Antonio 79
Bodenhagen, Leon 650
Borzone, Guglielmo 650
Bossema, Marianne 327
Botta, Giulia 106
Botta, Marco 106
Bruttin, Marine 42

C
Caballa, Sebastian 575, 671
Candeloro, Federica 607
Cano, Antonio 207

Cárdenas, Juan José García 443
Carolis, Berardina De 624
Carrasco-Martínez, Sara 642
Casagrande, Elisabetta 538
Castro-González, Álvaro 642
Cesta, Amedeo 560
Chella, Antonio 581
Chemerys, Mariia 283
Cheong, Peter 677
Chowdhury, Abhra Roy 253
Ciardo, Francesca 181
Citarella, Alessia Auriemma 3
Clavijo, Zoraida 79
Condón, Alicia 79
Cordasco, Gennaro 722
Cordella, Francesca 30
Cortellessa, Gabriella 488
Cross, Emily S. 42
Cuciniello, Marialucia 722
Cufino, Francesco 283

D
D'Agnese, Vasco 722
D'Errico, Lorenzo 706
De Benedictis, Riccardo 488
De Gasperis, Giovanni 356
De Marco, Fabiola 3
De Risi, Paolino 239
De Wilde, Vanessa 400
Della Greca, Attilio 3
Dhungana, Safal 698
Di Biasi, Luigi 3
Di Bratto, Martina 658
Di Napoli, Claudia 488
Di Ottavio, Daniele 356
Dogangün, Aysegül 130
Dondrup, Christian 342
Donini, Massimo 106

E
Elara, Mohan Rajesh 268

Elias, Dante A.   575, 671
Escallada, Oscar   531
Espinoza, Alexandra   671
Esposito, Anna   722

F
Fabrizi, Martina   30
Facchini, Sante Dino   356
Fallahi, Ali   459
Faria, Diego Resende   387
Ficuciello, Fanny   239
Fitter, Naomi T.   120
Foderaro, Elisa   560
Foini, Francesca   181
Foster, Mary Ellen   92
Fracasso, Francesca   488
Fu, Mengxue   192
Fujita, Ryugo   519

G
Galluccio, Annamaria   488
García Cárdenas, Juan José   473
Garcia, Daniel Hernandez   342
Gasparini, Paolo Alberto   166
Gena, Cristina   106, 624
George, Shoby   239
Giambanco, Alessandro   581
Gomez, Randy   207
Grazioso, Marco   658
Greco, Danilo   706
Grimaldi, Carmine   636
Guerrieri, Vittorio   554

H
Ha, Michael   225
Hakiri, Ami   630
Hayat, Abdullah Aamir   268
Helling, Nikolas   314
Hertzberg, Joachim   560
Hirota, Tetsuya   519
Holthaus, Patrick   459
Huang, Minyu   192
Huseynzade, Sonabayim   16

I
Ingenito, Mafalda   613

J
Jansen, Nadine   130

Janssens, Ruben   400
Jeschke, Sabina   299
Jiang, Linjing   519
Jirak, Doreen   58
Jørgensen, Jonas   684
Jouaiti, Melanie   538

K
Kahya, Rabiya   554
Kalimuthu, Manivannan   268
Kanbara, Masayuki   525
Karatas, Nihan   519
Kashihara, Akihiro   428, 630
Kian, Mina   192
Kinoti, Ayub   547

L
Lakatos, Gabriella   375, 459
Lasa, Ganix   531
Lauretti, Clemente   607
Lecompte, Pieter   400
Lee, Minwoo   677
Leisten, Luca M.   42
Lillo, Alberto   106
Lima, Oscar   560
Lisetschko, Artur   130
Liu, Hao   587
Liu, Siqi   192
Lofrese, Davide   624

M
MacDonald, Bruce   692
Malfaz, María   149
Mancini, Azzurra   658
Maroto-Gómez, Marcos   149, 642
Martinez, Alexander   575
Matarese, Marco   554
Matarić, Maja J.   192
Matsumoto, Yoshio   16
Mazmela, Maitane   531
Mazzei, Alessandro   106
Menon, Catherine   375
Merino, Luis   207
Merritt, Timothy   225
Modena, Maria Grazia   166
Mortezapour, Alireza   613
Mortezapour, Amirreza   613
Moujahid, Meriam   342

N

Nilgar, Atikkhan Faridkhan 547
Niu, Haofei 593
Novoselov, Matvei 283
Núñez, Pedro 79

O

Oddi, Angelo 568
Ogawa, Toshimi 16
Orlandini, Andrea 560, 568
Osa, Nagore 531

P

Palestra, Giuseppe 624
Pedrocchi, Nicola 560
Pelosi, Martina 314
Perez, Guillermo 207
Perillo, Francesca 613
Perkins, Russell 664
Pietras, Emilia 650
Pinto-Bernal, Maria 698
Plaat, Aske 327
Prabakaran, Veerajagadheswar 268

R

Rasconi, Riccardo 568
Rayguru, Madan Mohan 268
Rea, Francesco 58, 500, 554
Recchiuto, Carmine T. 413
Richert, Anja 299
Rispens, Sonja 650
Robinette, Paul 664
Robins, Ben 375
Rocco, Paolo 314
Rodríguez, Trinidad 79
Rodríguez-Huelves, Juan 149
Romeo, Marta 342
Rossi, Domenico 3
Rossi, Silvia 636
Ruggiero, Fabio 283
Russo, Valentina 658

S

Saborío, Juan Carlos 560
Salcedo-Gil, Raquel 650
Salichs, Miguel Ángel 642
Samani, Hooman 587, 593
Sanchez, Christopher A. 120
Santos, Sofia Diniz Melo 283
Sarno, Maria 722
Sasaki, So 428
Saunders, Rob 327
Sawabe, Taishi 525
Schetter, Francesco 239
Schiffmann, Michael 299
Sciacchitano, Antonio Pio 581
Sciutti, Alessandra 58, 500, 554
Scotto di Luzio, Francesco 607
Segura-Bencomo, Arecia 149
Seidita, Valeria 581
Sgorbissa, Antonio 413
Shi, Zhonghao 192
Simetti, Enrico 413
Skantze, Gabriel 92
Song, Junhu 677
Song, Yirui 192
Spitale, Micol 181
Srour-Zreik, Rawan 92
Stock, Sebastian 560
Stuart-Smith, Jane 92
Sulaiman, Shifa 239

T

Tabita, Marco 413
Taki, Yasuyuki 16
Tamantini, Christian 30, 607
Tanaka, Takahiro 519
Tapus, Adriana 443, 473
Tharun, V. P. 253
Tian, Changda 473
Toma, Aurora 624
Tortora, Genoveffa 3
Tracey, Finn 692
Trahanias, Panos 473
Treusch, Pat 684
Triglia, Laura 58, 500
Tucci, Cesare 3

U

Umbrico, Alessandro 560, 568

V

Van Laerhoven, Kristof 547
Velmurugan, Vignesh 375
Verhelst, Eva 400
Vinci, Marc 560
Vitiello, Giuliana 613

W
Wieching, Rainer 16
Wood, Luke Jai 375
Wulf, Volker 16

Y

Yoshihara, Yuki 519

Z
Zanchettin, Andrea Maria 314
Zollo, Loredana 30, 607

MIX
Papier aus verantwortungsvollen Quellen
Paper from responsible sources
FSC® C105338

If you have any concerns about our products,
you can contact us on
ProductSafety@springernature.com

In case Publisher is established outside the EU,
the EU authorized representative is:
**Springer Nature Customer Service Center GmbH
Europaplatz 3, 69115 Heidelberg, Germany**

Printed by Libri Plureos GmbH
in Hamburg, Germany